Countries with the Most Companies on *Fortune's* Global 500 List

United States	161
Japan	128
Great Britain	40
Germany	32
France	30
Sweden	14
South Korea	12
Australia	9
Switzerland	9
Canada	8

10 Largest Companies on *Fortune's* Global 500 List

Company	Headquarters
General Motors	United States
Exxon	United States
Ford Motor	United States
Royal Dutch/ Shell Group	Great Britain/ Netherlands
Toyota Motor	Japan
IRI	Italy
IBM	United States
Daimler-Benz	Germany
General Electric	United States
Hitachi	Japan

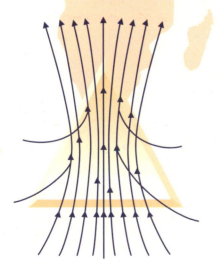

Traditional Career Flow Pattern

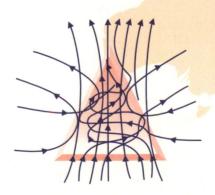

Today's Career Flow Pattern

FIFTH EDITION

MANAGING HUMAN RESOURCES

FIFTH EDITION

MANAGING HUMAN RESOURCES

RANDALL S. SCHULER

New York University

West Publishing Company

Minneapolis/St. Paul • New York
Los Angeles • San Francisco

WEST'S COMMITMENT TO THE ENVIRONMENT

In 1906, West Publishing Company began recycling materials left over from the production of books. This began a tradition of efficient and responsible use of resources. Today, up to 95 percent of our legal books and 70 percent of our college and school texts are printed on recycled, acid-free stock. West also recycles nearly 22 million pounds of scrap paper annually—the equivalent of 181,717 trees. Since the 1960s, West has devised ways to capture and recycle waste inks, solvents, oils, and vapors created in the printing process. We also recycle plastics of all kinds, wood, glass, corrugated cardboard, and batteries, and have eliminated the use of Styrofoam book packaging. We at West are proud of the longevity and the scope of our commitment to the environment.

Copyediting:	Luana Richards
Illustration:	Patti Isaacs/Parrot Graphics
Interior Design:	Geri Davis/Quadrata, Inc.
Composition:	Parkwood Composition Services, Inc.
Index:	Evergreen Valley Indexing Service

Production, Prepress, Printing and Binding by West Publishing Company.

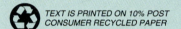 TEXT IS PRINTED ON 10% POST CONSUMER RECYCLED PAPER

 PRINTED WITH SOY INK™

COPYRIGHT ©1983,
1986, 1989, 1992
COPYRIGHT ©1995

By WEST PUBLISHING COMPANY
By WEST PUBLISHING COMPANY
610 Opperman Drive
P.O. Box 64526
St. Paul, MN 55164-0526

02 01 00 99 98 97 96 95   8 7 6 5 4 3 2 1

Library of Congress Cataloging-in-Publication Data

Schuler, Randall S.
    Managing human resources / Randall S. Schuler.—5th ed.
        p.   cm.
    Includes index.
    ISBN 0–314–03908–2 (hard)
    1. Personnel management.   2. Personnel management—Case studies.
I. Title.
HF5549.S24895   1994   94-5533
658.3—dc20   CIP

To Wilson and Mary Schuler, who by their own actions have instilled in me the belief that working hard, doing one's best and continuous improvement are satisfying and rewarding.

BRIEF CONTENTS

CONTENTS

SECTION 2   UNDERSTANDING THE ENVIRONMENT AND PLANNING FOR
HUMAN RESOURCE NEEDS   **59**

SECTION 5   COMPENSATING   381

PREFACE

The business environment that frames this Fifth Edition of *Managing Human Resources* has radically changed since 1983 when the First Edition was published, and it is likely to change even more by the year 2000. Currently, there are slightly more than 5 billion people, and by the year 2000, this number will reach 6 billion or so! At current growth rates, the work force in the Third World *alone* will expand by about 700 million over the next 20 years. Between 1990 and 2000, Asia's work force is projected to grow by 244 million, while Europe's is projected to grow by only 6 million. The U.S. population will reach 275 million by the year 2000, an increase of 15 percent from that in 1985. All this means that *huge* labor and consumer markets exist worldwide, and this has tremendous implications for us as individuals, for the firms we will work for, and for our society in general.

Not only do worldwide labor surpluses exist and will continue to exist, but the world's educational profile is shifting dramatically. No longer will the industrialized nations be able to count themselves as the only educated work forces. The distribution of students worldwide is changing. Since 1970 the percentage of high school students in the industrialized nations has gone from 44 percent of the world's high school students to 25 percent. For college students, this share has gone from 77 to 45 percent! These trends—labor surpluses and shifting educational profiles—certainly point to the globalization of business; it is now possible for companies to open up shop in literally any part of the world, all of which will keep a downward pressure on wages for some time.

The world market is becoming more and more strategic for American business. Just 15 years ago, exports accounted for only 15 percent of U.S. gross domestic product (GDP). Today, exports account for 30 percent. Some U.S. firms such as General Motors, Ford, Quaker Oats, Coca Cola, and Dow Chemical generate substantial earnings in the global marketplace. Of the top ten pharmaceutical companies in the world, a majority are based in America. Of the top 25 industrial sectors in the world, the largest firms in half of them are American. In the service sector alone, U.S. firms dominate the top 500. This is particularly important given that the worldwide service economy accounts for more than 60 percent of the world's gross domestic product and for most of the newly created jobs in industrial economies. Clearly, then, the global environment can only become more important in this decade.

Even as the global environment becomes more important to the United States, our dominance of it has been slipping. For example, the share of the U.S. automobile market held by the three U.S. automakers has dropped from 71 percent to 62 percent in the past twenty years, although it is now coming back strongly. American manufacturers accounted for 94 percent of the computers sold in the U.S. in 1980 and for only 66 percent ten years later. Their share of the worldwide semiconductor market slipped from 57 to 36 percent during that same time. Even in the service sector, U.S. firms today lead in only one category—retailing. Japan, by contrast, is tops in three: diversified services, insurance, and banking; the majority of the largest 50 banks in the world are Japanese. When the 1980s began, the two largest banks were American; today only three in the top 50 are American, and all top five are Japanese.

There is some evidence, however, that U.S. firms are staged for a resurgence. American business is more productive because of the downsizing and restructuring that occurred as a result of events in the 1980s. Data on export growth indicate American firms are making greater inroads into overseas markets; they have more productive capacity abroad and are entering into more alliances than ever. For example, U.S. automakers today build small cars for Mexico's rapidly expanding economy from a sprawling network of mostly new factories built in Mexico.

To some observers, however, much of this resurgence and revival in competitive position has been bought with borrowed funds—by selling off assets, laying off employees, and reducing wages relative to the country's major competitors. To the extent these strategies have peaked in use, the 1990s could be the decade in which firms prevail in the global marketplace by more effectively managing their human resources. It has been noted that practically any type of international problem, in the final analysis, is either created by people or must be solved by people.

> Floris Maljers, Chief Executive Officer of Unilever, a top ten company in *Fortune's* Global 500, expands on this by saying, "Limited human resources— not unreliable capital—are the biggest constraint when companies globalize.

Yes, the world around us is changing, and we are too. No longer can American workers and American business consider their share of the "good life" a given. If we are to maintain some semblance of it, we as individuals, as organizations, and as a society will have to actively "fight" for it on the "battlefield" of an increasingly competitive global economy. So, the implications for individuals, for organizations, and for our society can be summed up as: *Challenges and Opportunities For Everyone!* And here's where the management of human resources comes in:

> The fact is, the only thing that differentiates us from our competition is our people. The equipment, the building—they're all the same. It's the people who make the difference. Effective management of HR becomes an issue for everyone.

> CHUCK NIELSON,
> VICE PRESIDENT OF HUMAN RESOURCES,
> TEXAS INSTRUMENTS

Thus, our focus in this textbook will be on managing human resources as effectively as possible.

PURPOSES OF THE BOOK

Managing Human Resources, Fifth Edition, attempts to make you comfortable in identifying and dealing with the opportunities and challenges facing human resource management. A careful reading of this book will give you an understanding of the fundamental ways that organizations and their human resource departments go about managing their people, their human resources. Just as people are different, so are organizations and their human resource departments. Some are more effective than others and thereby serve as better examples from which to learn. Thus we discuss the ways the following firms manage their human resources: Wal-Mart, Texas Instruments, General Electric, Avon, Saturn, Levi Strauss, Swiss Bank Corporation, Chrysler, Coca-Cola, Dow Chemical, Disney, Lincoln Electric, Avon, Aetna, Waste Management, Weyerhaeuser, Federal Express, UPS, PepsiCo, Grand Union, and Aid Association to Lutherans. These firms are typically effective year after year and are considered to be innovators in the management of their human resources.

To further familiarize you with the major issues facing human resource management today, you will encounter five themes running through this book: partnership, ethics, globalization, diversity, and total quality management. It is important that you devote some energy and thought to these issues, for you will encounter them in one form or another throughout your working life, no matter what path your career takes because they have become societal issues and strategies as well. Even governments find themselves embracing and implementing many of these strategies as they strive to become more cost effective; to deal with our ever more diverse workforce; and, of course, to assist in the process of making and keeping America competitive.

This Fifth Edition also provides you with opportunities to increase your skills in managing human resources. Analyzing the end-of-chapter cases can increase your problem-solving, writing, and oral presentation skills. The field projects can increase your analytical skills and your abilities to relate human resource activities to the needs of the business. The various questionnaires, such as that found in Chapter 4 on Career Management, are meant to increase your self-diagnostic skills. Being aware of your career goals, desires, strengths, and weaknesses can help you choose a career in which you will be satisfied and productive. Specific Career Management Exercises are found at the end of most chapters. These ask you to apply the chapter material to the job/career you would like to have.

Because the international arena has and will become so much more important to business and human resource management, it is crucial to know as much about it as possible. This text will acquaint you with various aspects of this issue and thereby expand your international awareness. Accordingly, comparisons of how other countries manage their human resources, and human resource issues related to U.S. firms operating in other nations, are discussed throughout the chapters.

This text will enable you to view the issues and challenges of this field from the viewpoints of the employee, employer, and society, and your own viewpoint will be better informed. Each of these groups can have different viewpoints and agendas, and HR professionals must know everyone's viewpoint to accomplish their organization's goals.

This edition also conveys the importance of managing human resources with an awareness of the needs of the business and of the legal and regulatory environment. Human resource managers must work with, and understand the needs of, the business if their organization is to be effective. Remember, managing human resources effectively in organizations today is the responsibility of everyone in the organization. The 1990s will witness greater and greater cooperation among top management HR managers, line managers, and employees as teams strive to make their organizations more capable of being successful. *Thus this book is written for everyone who is or will one day work in an organization!*

ORGANIZATION OF THIS BOOK

Our guiding principle in presenting this exciting material has been that of a flow model. That is, we begin by describing the human resource activities that apply to individuals before they come to the organization and then as they move from newly hired job applicant to seasoned veteran. Thus, before seeking job candidates, organizations should understand the environment in which they operate and then plan for the number and types of employees they need. This includes comparing present and future employee needs in light of information about such concerns as labor market demand, competition, and strategy of the organization. Information about job requirements is necessary to further specify types of skills, knowledge, and abilities. Once this information is gathered, recruitment and selection activities begin. Decisions are made about where and how to seek job applicants. The HR department may need to develop tests to screen and select those job applicants most likely to succeed.

Once on the job, employees need performance standards. Their performance should be evaluated, and any performance deficiencies identified and corrected. A system of direct and indirect pay for the employees must also be established. Conditions may change, requiring new skills, so employees need training and development opportunities. Beyond this, organizational conditions may need to be altered to improve organizational effectiveness. Consideration should be given to the rights of employees. Because employees may belong to unions, organizations may need to engage in collective bargaining and contract negotiations. Issues of employee health and safety must be addressed.

The chapters reflect this flow model and are organized to describe the human resource activities of understanding the environment, planning, staffing, appraising, compensating, training and developing, establishing work relationships with employees, and improving and assessing. The first two chapters provide you with an understanding of what managing human resources is about and the role of the human resource department. The remaining chapters then discuss the other human resource activities, beginning with a brief description of purposes and importance. Consequently, the flow of the other chapters is

- Understanding the environment and planning for human resource needs
- Staffing the organization's human resource needs
- Appraising employee performance
- Compensating employee performance
- Training and organization development
- Establishing and maintaining effective work relationships
- Monitoring and assessing the work environment

There are many terms and expressions in human resource management. Some get used in a consistent manner, but others get used in various ways. Recognizing and appreciating the value and reality of this diversity, a short glossary of the terms used frequently in this book is included in Chapter 1.

FEATURES

Many of features from the Fourth Edition are found in this edition. They include margin notes, although in a much expanded form; key concepts; end-of-text glossary; review and discussion questions; and appendixes summarizing the relevant laws, court decisions and regulations. A listing of human resource journals and magazines is provided, as are suggestions for validating selection tests and sample résumés. The endnotes have been updated and serve as further sources of information that you can use to pursue a favorite topic in more detail. Also retained are the features "Managing Human Resources. . . ." These provide examples of what many excellent companies are doing today in this field.

NEW TO THIS EDITION

Every chapter has been extensively rewritten and reorganized to incorporate the most current ideas, research results, and real, organizational examples of human resource practices in action. There is more emphasis on providing you with opportunities to build your human resource management skills. Thus an additional case has been added to some chapters. Some also have role plays and exercises, and many

Ethics

Partnership

Diversity

*Total Quality
Management*

Globalization

have field projects. To further support your skill building and awareness of what companies, large and small, are doing, a new feature has been added: "HR Advice and Application."

This edition uses five major themes throughout the chapters: ethics, partnership, diversity, total quality management and globalization. These themes seem to be receiving the most attention in managing human resources today and are likely to continue through the end of the century. To highlight these themes, small icons are found throughout the book in the chapter margins.

Ethics   This edition has many examples of how firms deal with ethical issues. For example, there is a "Managing Human Resources at Waste Management: Building an Ethical Culture" feature in Chapter 3 and a follow-up to this on Waste Management's training program in ethics in Chapter 14. Practically all chapters have discussions on ethics and human resource management.

Partnership   Placed near the beginning of each chapter is the feature entitled "Partnership . . ." This feature reflects the important theme in HR today: managing human resources effectively requires the involvement of everyone.

Diversity   Management of diversity is another theme that is highlighted much more in this edition. For example, Jim Preston, CEO of Avon in New York, offers his advice on managing diversity in the "HR Advice and Application" feature in Chapter 3. The implications of the *Americans with Disabilities Act* are described extensively in several chapters, as are many legal considerations.

Total Quality Management   Total quality management (TQM) and its implications for managing human resources are also presented extensively in several chapters. Chapter 15 is now dedicated to it with discussions of the Baldrige Award, TQM at Xerox, and the famous fourteen principles of total quality by W. Edwards Deming. As part of this, many examples of teamwork are also included throughout the chapters.

Globalization   Because we live in an increasingly global environment, this edition has more descriptions of human resource practices in other countries. For example, in Chapter 11, Total Compensation, Exhibit 11.8 compares hourly costs for production workers in 25 countries. Exhibit 18.7 in the Collective Bargaining chapter compares wages and working conditions in the United States, Mexico, and Canada. By the way, more comparative information is provided throughout this edition on these three countries. This edition also has more discussion of human resource management practices of U.S. firms that operate abroad, the multinationals (MNCs). For example, Chapter 13, Training and Development, has a "Managing Human Resources" feature that describes how the Gillette Company in Boston develops global managers.

SUPPLEMENTS AVAILABLE

Supplementary materials for MANAGING HUMAN RESOURCES, Fifth Edition, prepared by Paul Buller and Randall Schuler, include:

- An Instructor's Resource Manual that contains:
  - Chapter outlines
  - Lecture enhancements including experiential and skill building exercises, end of chapter case notes, and additional cases related to the major themes of the text
- A Test Bank including Multiple Choice, True-False, and short essay questions with answers page-referenced to the text
- WesTest—a computerized version of the Test Bank
- Transparency Masters
- Acetate Transparencies of the key transparency masters

- Videos including short segments of companies illustrating topics discussed in various chapters and additional videos in West's Personnel and Human Resource Management Video Library are available to qualified adopters

To further enhance human resource management skills, there are *Case Problems in Human Resource Management*, by R. S. Schuler and S. A. Youngblood; and *Personal Computer Projects for Human Resource Management*, by N. J. Beutell.

All these materials are available from West Publishing Company.

ACKNOWLEDGMENTS

As with the previous editions, many fine individuals were of critical importance in the completion of the final product. They include Paul Buller at Gonzaga University; Peter Dowling at the University of Tasmania in Australia; Hugh Scullion at the University of Newcastle in England; Paul Sparrow at Manchester Business School in England; Shimon Dolan at the University of Montreal; Susan Jackson at New York University; Stuart Youngblood at Texas Christian University; Gary Florkowski at the University of Pittsburgh; Bill Todor at the Ohio State University; Nancy Napier at Idaho State University; Vandra Huber at the University of Washington; John Slocum at Southern Methodist University; Lynn Shore at Georgia State University; Mary Ahmed at Grand Forks; Ed Lawler at the Center for Effective Organizations, University of Southern California; Hrach Bedrosian at New York University; Lynda Gratton and Nigel Nicholson at the London Business School; Chris Brewster and Shaun Tyson at the Cranfield Management School; Michael Poole at the Cardiff Business School; Paul Stonham at the European School of Management, Oxford; Jan Krulis-Randa and Bruno Staffelbach at the University of Zurich; Albert Stahli and Cornel Wietlisbach at the GSBA in Zurich; Per Jenster and Jean Marie Hiltrop at IMD; Susan Schneider and Paul Evans at INSEAD; Jason Sedine at ISA/HEC; Stewart Black and David Ricks at Thunderbird; Mark Mendenhall at the University of Tennessee, Chattanooga; Helen De Cieri and Denise Welch of Monash University; Yoram Zeira of Tel-Aviv University; Dan Ondrack, the University of Toronto; Cal Reynolds, ORC; Vladimir Pucik, Cornell University; Moshe Banai, Baruch College; Steve Kobrin, Wharton School; Steve Barnett, York University; Carol Somers, Lowell University; Christian Scholz, University of Saarlandes; Pat Joynt, Henley Management College; Reijo Luostarinen, Helsinki School of Economics & Business Administration; Mickey Kavanagh, SUNY, Albany; Wayne Cascio, University of Colorado, Denver; Ricky Griffin, Texas A&M University; Ed van Sluijs, University of Limberg; and Mark Huselid, Rutgers.

The following individuals provided many good ideas and suggestions for changes and alterations in their roles of reviewers and evaluators of the Fourth Edition. They include James W. Dick, Jamestown College; Janice M. Feldbauer, Austin Community College; David M. Leuser, Plymouth State University; Barbara McIntosh, University of Vermont; Oliver J. Mulford, Mankato State University; Jane Pettinger, North Dakota State University; John T. Samaras, University of Central Oklahoma; Christina Shalley, University of Arizona; Mark R. Sherman, University of Houston-Clear Lake; P. C. Smith, University of Tulsa; Frederick F. Tesch, Western Connecticut State University; and Deborah L. Wells, Creighton University.

Several human resource managers, practicing line managers and publishers also contributed in many important ways to this edition, particularly with their examples and insights from their work experiences. They include Mike Mitchell, Judith Springberg, Tom Kroeger, Patricia Ryan, Margaret Magnus, Betty Hartzell, Don Bohl, Bob Kenny, Jack Berry, Steve Marcus, Paul Beddia, Mark Saxer, John Fulkerson, Cal Reynolds, Joan Kelly, Michael Losey, Jo Mattern, Larry Alexander,

Lyle Steele, Rowland Stichweh, Bill Maki, Rick Sabo, Bruce Cable, Gil Fry, Bill Reffett, Jerry Laubenstein, Richard Hagan, and Horace Parker.

The following individuals graciously provided case and exercise materials: George Cooley, Bruce Evans, Mitchell W. Fields, Hugh L. French, Jr., Susan E. Jackson, Stuart Youngblood, Ed Lawler, John Slocum, Jeff Lenn, Hrach Bedrosian, Kay Stratton, Bruce Kiene, Martin R. Moser, James W. Thacker, and Arthur Sharplin.

The support, encouragement, and assistance of many individuals was absolutely critical in the completion of the total project. They include Paul Buller, who not only discussed early drafts of the chapter, but also prepared the *Resource Manual* and other ancillaries; Lou DeCaro and Christine Diaz who worked extensively and carefully in the preparation of the final chapter drafts; and Dave Rogers and George Daly, chair of the management department and Dean of the Stern School of Business, respectively. Also, several people at West Publishing deserve our special thanks for their help and support: Esther Craig, developmental editor, Dick Fenton and Sharon Adams, acquisitions editors, Cliff Kallemeyn, production editor, and Erin Ryan, promotion manager. Without their professional dedication and competence, this book would not have been possible.

RANDALL S. SCHULER
New York

TO BE EFFECTIVE in the highly competitive environments of today, American business needs to devote a significant amount of skill, knowledge, and attention to managing human resources. Chief executive officers, managers, and people at all levels of an organization need to be involved in this process: all the people in an organization need to see themselves as actually sharing the human resource function, in partnership with each other. At the same time, the department leader needs to be seen as part of the senior management team making decisions vital to the business.

Chapter 1 describes the reasons why effective management of this resource is growing in importance. Managing people well influences many business outcomes, and we will look into exactly how effective management can be attained. Many people now see themselves as responsible for this activity. This new vision has created a sense of joint responsibility, of partnership. There is, however, a profession for human resource management, and we will discuss in some detail what the human resource professional has to offer this emerging partnership.

We will then explore some major trends, including linking with the environment, being systematic, and the "greening" of this profession. In the summary, we list five themes that you will see throughout the remainder of this text. These five themes—partnership in managing human resources, ethics and ethical issues, diversity in the work force, globalization, and total quality management—are impacting just about every human resource management activity today and will likely do so for the foreseeable future.

SECTION 1

MANAGING HUMAN RESOURCES

Chapter 2 details the roles and activities of the formal human resource (HR) department. These roles include performing activities that assist an organization in improving its bottom-line results; being more creative and adaptive to change; and continuously evaluating and improving HR activities.

The various roles of the HR leader and staff are described. You will see that there are many roles to be played and many jobs to be done—in short, there are many opportunities to find a niche that suits your mix of skills and abilities.

Chapter 2 also discusses how HR departments organize and "customerize" themselves to better serve the needs of line managers, employees, and the business. Here we dwell again on the theme of partnership.

The first of several discussions on the impacts of globalization takes place in Chapter 2 as we begin to look at the HR issues facing American firms doing business abroad and at how cultural differences can impact the way a firm manages its human resources in a foreign country. Of vital importance to businesses today, we will return to this issue in future chapters.

Chapter 2 concludes with the discussion of a major trend within HR departments—the development of mission statements. Such statements tell everyone what the HR department is doing, what its values are, and how important it is to the rest of the organization. Mission statements have become an important avenue for change and a way to focus direction and implement strategies.

CHAPTER 1

HUMAN RESOURCE MANAGEMENT

LEARNING OBJECTIVES

When you have finished studying this chapter, you should be able to:

1. Explain why managing human resources effectively is becoming so important.
2. State the goals of human resource management.
3. Describe major activities of human resource management.
4. Describe who is responsible for managing human resources.
5. Describe professionalism in human resource management.
6. Discuss the current trends in human resource management.

CHAPTER OUTLINE

"Managing Human Resources at Wal-Mart"

HUMAN RESOURCE MANAGEMENT
WHY IS HUMAN RESOURCE MANAGEMENT IMPORTANT?

"Managing Human Resources at General Electric"

THE GOALS OF HUMAN RESOURCE MANAGEMENT

"HR Advice and Application
GETTING EVERYONE INVOLVED: PRINCIPLES FOR EFFECTIVE
ORGANIZATIONS"

ACTIVITIES IN HUMAN RESOURCE MANAGEMENT
WHO IS RESPONSIBLE FOR MANAGING HUMAN RESOURCES?
PROFESSIONALISM IN HUMAN RESOURCE MANAGEMENT

"HR Advice and Application
ETHICAL BEHAVIOR"

HISTORICAL NOTES ON HUMAN RESOURCE MANAGEMENT
CURRENT TRENDS

"Managing Human Resources
HOW HR MANAGERS HELP COMPANIES BECOME GREEN"

Case: People-Related Business Issues at the Barden Corporation:
Solutions through Partnership

MANAGING HUMAN RESOURCES
at Wal-Mart

WHAT do people have to do with the success of the world's largest retailer? The answer is, EVERYTHING!

The founder of Wal-Mart, Sam Walton, believed that the essence of successful retailing lies in giving the customers what they want. Yes, customers want a great selection at the lowest possible prices. But they also want friendly and knowledgeable service that is accessible. In today's highly competitive environment, most customers can easily get great selection at low prices. What they can't get as easily is the friendly and knowledgeable service!

Yes, people—associates—are an integral part of Wal-Mart's success. Sam Walton knew that people are important—his motto (and the company's motto today):

> It takes a team, and we're a team and we are together!

In his golden rules of retail competition, the majority are about people—for example: share your profits; motivate your associates; communicate everything to your associates; appreciate everything your associates do for the company; celebrate your successes; and listen to everyone. By the way, the other rules are commit and be passionate about the business; control costs; exceed customers' expectations; and ignore conventional wisdom (Sam Walton was always told that a town of 50,000 couldn't support a discount store for very long—about the typical size town where Wal-Mart stores have been located).

But just how much has this attention to people paid off for Sam Walton and Wal-Mart? The first Wal-Mart store opened in Bentonville, Arkansas, in 1962. About fifteen years later, the market value of Wal-Mart stock was $135 million. Today, it is over $60 billion! If you had bought 100 shares of the company in 1962 at a cost of $1,650, you would have (because of 2-for-1 splits) more than 60,000 shares today valued at more than $3 million! The number of associates has gone from fewer than 50 to more than 520,000! Only General Motors has more employees in the United States. Wal-Mart's profits and revenues have seen double-digit growth every year, and there are now about 2,000 stores.

Sam Walton created a great deal of wealth—not only for himself and his family, but also for many others. Typical of the people who have worked for the company for more than 20 years is Joyce McMurray:

> One Arkansas worker, Joyce McMurray, said that since she joined the company as a high-school graduate in 1969, her profit-sharing account had grown to $492,230, including an increase of $175,000 in the last year.

Joyce's good fortune is due to one of Sam's golden rules of retailing: share the profits with your associates.

With results like these, you would think everyone would be doing the same thing, right? Yes, but then why aren't they? Is it really that hard to manage people? This is the key, isn't it?

Well, let's see what Wal-Mart does. First, Wal-Mart's philosophy is that it is easier to take care of the associates you have than to replace them and train someone else. The company therefore automatically makes a commitment to do a great job in selection and recruitment, and also in motivating associates. Wal-Mart's generous profit-sharing plan, which is tied directly to performance outcomes, has a way of motivating associates, and it has attracted many others who want to make a good living.

The company believes in giving customers friendly and knowledgeable service. It follows then that the associates need to be trained and retrained, extensively and often. But what makes them friendly? Ah, here is the part that is difficult for competitors to duplicate! This is where the company culture comes in. Sam Walton believed in management by walking around, by visiting the stores and talking to associates and customers, and his legacy remains strong. Typical is Andy Wilson, one of 15 regional vice presidents, who continually takes Sam Walton's message to associates in stores around the country:

> My job isn't important. *You're* the people who make it happen.

Continued on the next page

For a vice president to say this is one thing, for associates to truly believe it is another. The associates at Wal-Mart believe it. They have heard the same thing for years, and they have seen the behavior: the managers at Wal-Mart "walk the talk." Related to this humble profile assumed by managers is the role they play to support the importance and value of the associates. Managers constantly ask the associates, "Is there anything we can do for you?"

The team spirit of Wal-Mart is apparent throughout the company. They remember: "it takes a team, and we're a team." The team at Wal-Mart believes that it is important to have fun; team rallies and other spirit-building activities are common. Combining this team spirit with the profit sharing and the down-to-earth management style sustains a company in which the associates truly care about the customer. Needless to say, these qualities have contributed no small amount to Wal-Mart's astonishing success. And because many of these qualities are seemingly so hard for others to do, the firm has a formula that is hard to beat.

One more thing, remember that one of Sam's golden rules was doing things not usually done by others? Well, the human resources department at Wal-Mart is called the "people division." All these people components add up to a real success story in which human resource management really makes a big contribution![1]

In Wal-Mart, human resource management is

- **Effective**
- **Linked to business decisions**
- **Done in partnership with everyone**

The preceding discussion illustrates three important themes in human resource (HR) management. One is the link that exists between the success of a firm and the quality of its people. At Wal-Mart, current chief executive officer (CEO), David Glass, believes and acts (as Sam Walton did before him), in ways that demonstrate the company's belief in the importance of people (associates) to the business. This gives associates reason to believe and trust in the company. In return, the associates deliver high-quality, friendly, and knowledgeable service—the essence of retailing according to Sam Walton.

Another theme is the conscious attempt to actively link the employees to the success of the business. Wal-Mart joins its business and people management philosophies through great recruitment and selection, performance appraisal and compensation, extensive training, and excellent leadership. Leadership is critical in making the other HR activities work so effectively. Wal-Mart's leadership is basically humble leadership: it is the manager catering to the associates and putting them first and not putting management first. Then there is the team spirit, the hearty enthusiasm and willingness to celebrate and have fun. Together these practices contribute to the success of the firm and make it very difficult for other firms to do the same thing. And HR management is central to this unbeatable combination.

The third theme is related to the first two. It involves sharing the responsibility for this important activity—people management. The golden rules of retailing that Sam Walton articulated announce loud and clear that top management is responsible for managing human resources. And, of course, the people division under the leadership of Suzanne Allford and Michael Bergdahl is responsible as well. This kind of partnership, a recent development in American business, is gaining widespread acceptance. Some organizations are taking this idea even further: they are actively encouraging the involvement of the employees themselves in HR management! This certainly has been happening at Wal-Mart since 1962, but it wasn't nearly so prevalent then. It is becoming so today! And it is happening in many other companies—to name a few, Chrysler, Lincoln Electric, Coca-Cola, Harley-Davidson, Disney, L.L. Bean, Deere & Co., Levi Strauss, General Electric, Campbell Soup Company, U.S. West, Microsoft, Texas Instruments, First Chicago, AT&T, Apple Computer, Ben and Jerry's Homemade Inc., Johnson and Johnson and Merck. Many corporations giant and small, are joining the ranks.

Because these developments are so important and so pervasive in organizations today and are likely to be important for the foreseeable future, they influence everything we will discuss in this book, beginning here with the definition of the central topic of this book.

HUMAN RESOURCE MANAGEMENT

Human resource management *is about managing people in organizations as effectively as possible for the good of the employees, the company, and society.*

Human resource management is about managing people in organizations for the good of the employees, the company and society.

WHY IS HUMAN RESOURCE MANAGEMENT IMPORTANT?

Today, organizations large and small face an environment characterized by:

- Extremely high levels of competition
- Hundreds of thousands of small, new entrepreneurial firms
- A vast number of nations with low wages and highly skilled workers
- Rapid technological advances
- Dynamic legal, political, and social realities
- Changing values and educational qualifications
- Consumers demanding high quality at low prices[2]

The result is that organizations are having to do things much differently! Successful firms now resemble the profile given in Exhibit 1.1. The implications for HR management are enormous. At home and around the world, CEOs are attesting to just how important this activity is.

LEARNING OBJECTIVE 1
Explain why managing human resources effectively is becoming so important.

EXHIBIT 1.1
CHARACTERISTICS OF SUCCESSFUL ORGANIZATIONS

TODAY'S ORGANIZATIONS ARE

- Global
- Flatter
- Populated by cross-functional teams
- Oriented toward differentiation, producing high value-added goods and services, creating niche markets
- Total quality conscious
- Cost conscious
- More responsive, concerned about speed
- Faster to innovate
- Reliant on highly trained and flexible people
- Networks of competencies and partnerships
- Continually evolving strategies, structures, and practices
- Customer-focused
- Concerned about ethics and environment
- Concerned about managing diversity

Unilever is the large Dutch-British company that is a major competitor of Procter & Gamble.

I am the ultimate believer in people first, strategies second. To me, strategy starts with the person you hire. If a business lacks a good strategy, then put in charge of the business someone who will develop one.

JACK WELCH, CEO
GENERAL ELECTRIC[3]

Limited human resources—not unreliable capital—are the biggest constraint when companies globalize.

FLORIS MALJERS, CEO
UNILEVER[4]

Jack Welch's belief in the value of managing human resources effectively goes far beyond just hiring the right person. For a great discussion of just how far, see the feature "Managing Human Resources at General Electric."

While these statements are substantial in themselves, there is more. According to the international consulting firm of Korn Ferry, who conducted a worldwide survey of 1,500 CEOs on what expertise they need to run their businesses, the response was

> Management of people is an indispensable component of sustained corporate performance and competitive advantage. Accordingly, human resource management as an area of CEO expertise rises from the third most important ranking in 1988 to the number two position in 2000.[8]

Thus while we have in the past thought of this activity as "personnel" and something to be done by those in the HR department, it is a different story today and will continue to be so for the forseeable future. Management is more interested than ever before and more willing to participate in this activity.

> There is a saying at Merck that goes like this, "Human resources are too important to be left to the HR department." Fully one-third of the performance evaluation of the managers is related to people management.[9]

We must have people who use facts and knowledge to add something . . . to add value to our customers' businesses. In an age where everyone has basically the same information at the same time, the advantage goes to people who can take information and quickly put it to effective and profitable use. It means having people with what can be called the "mind of the strategist" . . . people who can create a competitive advantage . . . out of common knowledge.

Roberto C. Goizueta
CEO, Coca-Cola Company

In the best companies, human resource management is a concern of everyone!

Line managers are those directly responsible for producing products or services through and with employees.

All of this interest and involvement in HR management by CEOs and other managers stems from their recognition that to be competitive in the world today, they need their people to be as effective as possible. And effective people means people who are

- Adaptable
- Committed
- Motivated
- Skilled/reskilled
- Possessing high energy levels
- Good performers in diverse employee groups
- Good team players

With the recognition by management of the importance of this endeavor comes the recognition that the HR department cannot do it alone. Managers are now embracing this responsibility—people management—more than ever before. But because a large body of expertise and knowledge is required, line managers are looking for the HR department to help them out. Of course, in small businesses, the owner is usually the one with this expertise. In either case, for line managers to succeed today, they need some knowledge of the activities described here. We begin with an understanding of the goals of human resource management.

MANAGING HUMAN RESOURCES
at General Electric

GENERAL Electric Company's dramatic changes during the 1980s and early 1990s reflect a company adjusting to an increasingly competitive environment in innovative and successful ways. The firm's management of human resources during the period offers an example of how the firm successfully meshed its human resource policies and the needs and strategy of the business.

During the 1970s, GE's chief executive, the highly regarded "financial wizard" Reginald H. Jones, built the firm into one of the strongest financial performers in the United States. He also led a diversification effort that put the company into about 100 different businesses, ranging from appliances and light bulbs to coal mines, TV sets, and computer chips. Company earnings per share rose an average of 4.9 percent yearly. In the process of building a profitable and diverse conglomerate, however, Jones also built a massive organization that became mired in bureaucracy. Reporting requirements, for example, were legendary. One manager finally had to stop computers from generating seven daily reports on sales of hundreds of thousands of products; the paper from just one of those reports stood 12 feet high!

In 1981, at age 45, Jack Welch assumed the post of GE's chief executive officer. In picking Welch as his successor, Jones supported Welch's objectives of making the $27-billion GE a "world class competitor," able to thrive in an increasingly global marketplace. In taking the helm of a strong yet somewhat complacent firm, one of Welch's key challenges was to "instill in . . . managers a sense of urgency when there is no emergency."[5] When Welch took over the top job at GE in 1981, his first goal was to prepare the company to meet the challenges of the 1980s and 1990s. Welch saw the world marketplace as a tough and increasingly competitive playing field that would eventually be dominated by a few large firms. To compete in such a world, Welch believed GE had to identify and operate only in markets in which it could be the first or second player worldwide. Such a move led to major restructuring: GE

exited all but about 14 businesses, reducing its labor force by 25 percent. During the 1980s, about 100,000 employees left GE through layoff, attrition, or divestiture of businesses.

In addition to the external competitive forces driving change, GE's increasingly diverse work force has also posed a challenge. Like other American firms, GE faces a situation in which employees with "different career objectives, different family aspirations, [and] different financial goals" operate in one firm. Welch wants them to "share directly in [GE's] vision, the information, the decision-making process, and the rewards."[6] In practical terms, this means Welch and his 200 highest ranking managers must build a commitment to the changes resulting from restructuring among the other 99 percent of the company's 300,000 employees.

Welch views effective human resource management as part of the solution to making GE a firm well-positioned for the next century. He argues that the company needs new ways of doing business, and that includes human resource management. In planning and staffing business units for the future, for example, Welch says the company must seek managers who are "business leaders," able to "create a vision, articulate the vision, passionately own the vision, and . . . relentlessly drive it to completion."[7] Also extremely important is for business leaders to be open and willing to change. Welch considers the process of identifying and preparing future leaders to be so important that he regularly reviews files of selected employees from the time they join the firm, to get a sense of their potential for future positions.

To increase productivity and reward performance, GE is increasingly shifting responsibility for decision making down the line. The firm uses several methods to enhance that effort. First, to expose weaknesses in the company and reduce changes for mediocrity, Welch reduced the layers of line management, increasing managers' span of control from an average of six to

Continued on the next page

seven subordinates to ten to fifteen. His reasoning is that "overstretched" managers perform better on important tasks because they have no time for trivia or to interfere with subordinates' tasks. This increased span of control also allows people down the line to take on more responsibility, again enabling people to show their ability to perform.

Another change reduced corporate staff and forced those remaining units to ask how they could help people on the line "be more effective and competitive." In addition, the company seeks to communicate information more quickly throughout the firm: to transfer "with lightning speed" the best practices, such as a new pay plan, a drug testing program, or a program for stock options.

Training and communication are also among Welch's top priorities for the firm. He takes his message directly to employees during training sessions at GE's in-house university in Crotonville, New York, which trains 5,000 employees annually. To improve the work environment and further reduce bureaucracy, GE initiated a program called "Work-Out" in late 1989. The heads of the fourteen business units meet regularly with subordinates to identify and eliminate unnecessary activities—meetings, reports, any unproductive work. The process also seeks to identify better ways to evaluate and reward managers.

Finally, Welch has tried to bring GE's labor unions into the new way of thinking and managing as well. He wants labor, as well as white-collar managers, to gain a sense of "ownership" of the company and its direction.

During the 1980s and early 1990s, GE overhauled its strategy, streamlined business lines to compete for the future, and used human resource management to achieve its massive change. As the company moves toward the year 2000, managing human resources effectively will play an important role in the success of the firm's strategy.

Specific goals:

- attracting
- retaining
- motivating
- retraining

Overall goals:

- productivity
- quality of working life
- legal compliance
- competitive advantage
- work force adaptability

THE GOALS OF HUMAN RESOURCE MANAGEMENT

The specific goals traditionally associated with human resource management are attracting applicants, retaining desirable employees, and motivating employees:

> The quality of work from motivated people is light-years ahead of what you get from people not well motivated.
>
> FRANK POPOFF, PRESIDENT[10]
> DOW CHEMICAL COMPANY

Increasingly, another goal is being added—that of retraining employees.

How a firm manages its human resources has an impact, positive or negative, on the firm's overall direction and, ultimately, on its bottom line. The term **bottom line** refers to the organization's survival, growth, profitability, competitiveness, and flexibility in adapting to changing conditions.

Focusing on the bottom line is a key way in which HR departments can gain recognition and respect in organizations. The feature on General Electric describes specific ways in which the HR department can influence the bottom line. Improving productivity, improving the quality of working life, increasing the firm's legal compliance, gaining competitive advantage, and assuring work force adaptability—these are the overall goals of managing human resources. These relationships are illustrated in Exhibit 1.2.

PRODUCTIVITY

Without a doubt, productivity is a goal of every organization. Human resource management can do many things to improve productivity. The most productive organizations in the United States know this and treat their HR departments in ways that are different from less productive organizations.

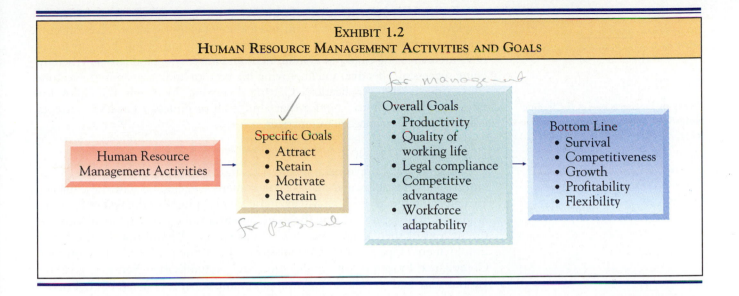

EXHIBIT 1.2
HUMAN RESOURCE MANAGEMENT ACTIVITIES AND GOALS

for management

Human Resource Management Activities → Specific Goals
- Attract
- Retain
- Motivate
- Retrain

for personnel

→ Overall Goals
- Productivity
- Quality of working life
- Legal compliance
- Competitive advantage
- Workforce adaptability

→ Bottom Line
- Survival
- Competitiveness
- Growth
- Profitability
- Flexibility

- They ensure that the department participates in strategic decisions affecting the successful implementation of business strategies.
- They focus on important current problems before they add new programs.
- Their HR staffs initiate programs and communicate with line managers, and vice versa.
- The corporate staffs share responsibility for policy formation and program administration across organizational levels.[11]

Today, HR management has a unique opportunity to improve productivity, and this does not mean merely increasing output. It means increasing output with higher quality than ever before and at a lower cost! Fortunately, all of this is possible:

> [S]ometimes, to their surprise, companies are discovering that boosting quality saves money. Reducing the cost of fixing mistakes, both before and after a product is sold, can cut production costs as much as 30%. It also increases sales.[12]

This is particularly possible in organizations where the employees experience a high quality of working life.

QUALITY OF WORKING LIFE

To get employees to improve productivity and product quality, and at the same time look for ways to reduce costs, takes a special type of organization. It takes an organization that is willing to recognize and respond to the needs of its employees. Those companies that do provide a higher quality of working life to their employees are more successful than those that do not.

Organizations are doing many things to accomplish this goal. For example, they are making it possible for employees to contribute in meaningful ways. They give employees greater opportunities to participate and a larger say in decision making. They encourage employees to develop and improve their work skills through extensive training and skill-based pay systems. Additionally, many companies organize their work around teams and reduce the number of layers of management hierarchy.

9

Professor Lawler is one of the leading authorities in human resource management.

Because legal compliance is so important, it is discussed in all chapters of this text.

Gaining competitive advantage means using HR practices to gain lasting advantage over the competition.

"In business, there is only one true long-term competitive advantage and key to stakeholder satisfaction: People. Our ongoing challenge at Harley-Davidson is to ensure that we have the most talented employees in our industries addressing the many issues of our markets and keeping us ahead of our competitors."

Harley-Davidson
Annual Report

Work force adaptability means that workers are ready *and* able to change.

The result of providing a high quality working environment is increased employee commitment, satisfaction, and feeling of empowerment. These in turn lead to improved productivity. An excellent description of just how organizations are increasing employee commitment and improving productivity (thereby being successful, effective, and improving the bottom line) is given in the feature "HR Advice and Application: Getting Everyone Involved: Principles for Effective Organizations." Notice that almost all of Professor Lawler's concepts are standard HR management practices.

LEGAL COMPLIANCE

In managing their employees, organizations must comply with many laws, regulations, court decisions, and edicts of government agencies. Because these impact virtually all HR activities, we will examine them throughout the text. Appendix A gives a brief listing. Among the more important ones to be familiar with are the actions of the Occupational Safety and Health Administration, the Equal Employment Opportunity Commission, the Office of Federal Contract Compliance Programs, the Immigration and Naturalization Services, and the various state and city equal employment commissions and human or civil rights commissions.[14] Multinational corporations in the United States also have to be aware of employment laws outside this country.

If HR departments fail to maintain an awareness of current laws and regulations both domestically and worldwide, their companies may find themselves faced with costly lawsuits and large fines. Fortunately, these costs can be avoided by constantly monitoring the legal environment, by complying with changes, and by careful management of personnel.

GAINING COMPETITIVE ADVANTAGE

Although there are many ways by which companies can gain a competitive edge—that is a lasting advantage over the competition—one way often overlooked is through their HR management practices. Using HR practices in this manner is called gaining competitive advantage.[15] Such practices are particularly potent weapons because it is often difficult for competitors to formulate an effective response quickly. Consequently, it is likely that firms in highly competitive environments will continue to seek ways to gain competitive advantage through human resources.

WORK FORCE ADAPTABILITY

Firms in highly competitive environments need to be flexible. This means having the capability to shift and adjust to new technologies, skills, strategies, and HR practices. One way to attain this adaptability is to train people in many skills, and many companies are doing this. Such employees are ready for change and comfortable with continuous learning.[16]

Cautious outlooks in forecasting long-term and short-term HR needs is another trend. Companies are finding that it is better not to overhire—that is, to have more people than they really need. People are important for organizational effectiveness, but they are also expensive, particularly in smaller firms. Furthermore, firms prefer not to hire and then have to terminate employees in only a year or so. And for those employees that they do hire, companies prefer them to be adaptable and also capable of doing several jobs.

Organizations need to value *work force* adaptability and *worker* adaptability. This depends on doing several HR management activities well. Although these activities usually begin in the HR department, they are increasingly done in close cooperation with line managers and employees. Thus it pays for everyone in an organization to be knowledgeable about these activities.

GETTING EVERYONE INVOLVED: PRINCIPLES FOR EFFECTIVE ORGANIZATIONS

"The enormous changes in corporate structures and needs over the past decade have necessitated a refocusing of management approaches," according to Ed Lawler, Director of the Center for Organizational Effectiveness at the University of Southern California. Professor Lawler's research has focused on exactly what it means when organizations adapt new management approaches. Recently he summarized and updated this research, and while he has been focused mainly on modern manufacturing plants, he concludes now that the following principles of management apply to any product or service organization, large or small, wanting to be highly effective and successful. He generally defines *effectiveness* in terms of *high-quality, customer-driven organizations* that survive and flourish by staying ahead of their competitors with new and better products and services.

Based on extensive research that he and his colleagues have done over the years, Professor Lawler suggests that there are several governing ideas that effective organizations share today. One is an organization design that makes extensive use of *self-managing teams* and a relatively *limited number of hierarchical levels of management*. This enables employees to feel a sense of ownership in what they are doing and therefore a heightened sense of responsibility and accountability. Teams in effective organizations have direct contact with suppliers. For example, at the Digital Equipment plant at Enfield, Connecticut, the teams producing electronic boards deal directly with both suppliers and customers.

Today's effective organizations do not restrict the use of teams to the production floor only, but *extend the team concept to all areas of the company*. This broader use of self-managed teams further "flattens" the organization by reducing the number of supervisors and managers.

Teamwork can be extended to allow cross-functional teams to work together. This *cross-functional integration* might combine manufacturing, product engineering and product design. Not only can a better product be produced, but the employees involved will have a better understanding of the needs of the business. The extensive use of information technology can enhance this understanding; such technology allows workers in the manufacturing area to have *direct access to marketing and sales* and even to answer questions from customers.

In today's effective organizations, *reward systems compensate* individuals for successful teamwork, for gaining more skill-based competencies, for continuous improvement, and for business and organizational performance. Of course, the teams themselves have a significant input in compensation decisions, such as deciding when employees have attained mastery of needed skills. Some of these skills relate to the use of information and data technology. The effective organization today is networked with computers and relies extensively upon videos for training and on television screens to link employees in various parts of the firm.

No less important than the above aspects of effective organizations are the following: a) [the use of total quality management tools and principles in problem-solving approaches and in] a continuous commitment to process and product improvement; b) continuous and widely available training for all employees on topics ranging from technical job details to business strategy; and c) employee commitment to participation, continuous learning, and constant improvement.[13]

ACTIVITIES IN HUMAN RESOURCE MANAGEMENT

The activities include (1) understanding the environment and meeting its demands; (2) staffing the organization; (3) appraising employee behavior; (4) compensating employee performance; (5) training and development; (6) establishing and maintaining effective work relationships; and (7) monitoring and assessing the work environment.

> **LEARNING OBJECTIVE 3**
>
> Describe major activities of human resource management.

Partnership is the cooperation of everyone in the organization in managing human resources.

It is important to understand the:
- external environment
- internal environment

Human resource planning entails:
- planning and forecasting
- career management
- designing jobs
- analyzing jobs

The staffing activity includes:
- recruiting job applicants
- selecting job applicants

Enabling an organization to do these activities effectively is a primary objective of the HR department, which must be willing to work closely with managers and employees. Again, the idea of **partnership**—HR professionals working together with line managers and employers—is critical to the success of this endeavor. (This idea and exactly what needs to be done is discussed in Chapter 2.)

UNDERSTANDING THE ENVIRONMENT AND MEETING ITS DEMANDS

Increasingly, successful HR management depends on understanding the environment, both internally and externally. A particularly important aspect of the external environment is the ever-increasing set of legal considerations. Legal considerations affect virtually all HR activities. Consequently, we will examine them throughout the text. Other important aspects of the external environment include levels of domestic and international competition, work force and demographic changes, and general economic and organizational trends.

Important aspects of the internal environment include the business strategy of the firm, its technology, the goals and values of top management, the size of the firm, its culture, and its structure. These aspects of the internal environment are discussed in Chapter 3. Understanding the external and internal environments and scanning them constantly ensures that the needs of the business are being served.

Central to meeting the demands of the business environment is effective HR planning. This activity involves (1) planning and forecasting short- and long-term requirements; (2) career management programs; (3) analyzing jobs; and (4) designing the jobs in the organization. In fact, planning and all that it involves can be viewed as essential for the other HR activities to be performed effectively. It must indicate (1) what types of employees and how many of them are needed both today and in the future, (2) how employees will be obtained (for example, from outside recruiting or by internal transfers and promotions), and (3) any training programs the organization may need. In fact, HR planning can be viewed as the major factor influencing the staffing and development functions of the entire organization. It enables the organization to accommodate an increasingly diverse work force.

STAFFING THE ORGANIZATION

Once the organization's personnel needs have been determined, staffing can take place. This includes (1) recruiting job candidates and (2) selecting the most appropriate job applicants for the available jobs. Both activities must be done in accordance with legally mandated fair employment practices and with attention to the effect they will have on the overall direction of the firm. Doubtless, they will have a significant impact on the firm's success:

> Ask Bill Gates, Chairman of Microsoft, what the most important thing he did last year was and he will answer: "I hired a lot of smart people."[17]

The organization must cast a wide net in their recruitment of employees to ensure a full and fair search for job candidates. After the candidates have been identified, final selections must be made. Common selection procedures include obtaining completed application forms or resumes; interviewing the candidates; checking education, background, experience, and references; and administering various forms of tests.

APPRAISING EMPLOYEE BEHAVIOR

Once on the job, employees' performances must be evaluated. If they are not doing well, it is necessary to find out why. Employee training may be necessary, or some type of motivation such as more rewards, feedback, or a redesigned job may be in order. All of this is often accomplished by the HR department cooperating with line managers in (1) gathering performance appraisal information and then (2) utilizing the information.

Although conducting performance appraisals can be painful to both manager and employee, it is a critical activity. Legal considerations necessitate that employee decisions be made on the basis of performance. This is a sound employment practice, with or without legal requirements. Improving the performance appraisal process entails involving the employees themselves, a process called self-management. Because this is likely to affect your life in organizations, several self-management career exercises and a questionnaire on career planning are included in this book. Self-management is discussed in Chapter 4.

COMPENSATING PERFORMANCE

Employees are generally rewarded on the basis of the value of the job, their personal contributions, and their performance. Although rewarding performance can increase motivation, rewards are often given only according to the value of the job. Other rewards (namely, indirect benefits) are provided just for being a member of the organization. The compensating activity includes administering (1) direct compensation, (2) performance-based pay, and (3) indirect compensation benefits.

Because of the rising medical costs over the past decade, cost containment in the benefits area has become a major concern for many firms. It has resulted in more cost-sharing with employees and even the reduction of some benefits. The challenge here is to manage costs and at the same time keep employee commitment high. Managing health care costs is likely to be an important topic for some time.

TRAINING AND DEVELOPMENT

Activities related to training and development include (1) determining, designing, and implementing programs to increase ability and employee performance, and (2) creating and implementing the organizational practices and HR activities to improve total quality management efforts within organizations.

ESTABLISHING AND MAINTAINING EFFECTIVE WORK RELATIONSHIPS

This activity is composed of the following sets of activities: (1) respecting employee rights, (2) understanding the reasons and methods used by employees in organizing, and (3) bargaining and settling grievances with employees and the groups representing them.

Employees are increasingly gaining more rights. Consequently, employment decisions such as terminations, layoffs, and demotions must be made with care and evidence. It is important that the company managers be aware of all employee rights. The HR manager is in an excellent position to inform line managers of these rights.

The work relationship is particularly important for organizations that have unionized employees. Unions can be instrumental in developing new programs for the improvement of human resources.

MONITORING AND ASSESSING THE WORK ENVIRONMENT

The crucial activity here is monitoring and improving the physical and sociopsychological workplace to maximize employee safety and health. The federal regulations specified in the *Occupational Safety and Health Act of 1970* have had a

Appraising employees involves:
- gathering performance appraisal information
- utilizing performance appraisal information

Three compensating activities are
- administering direct compensation
- providing performance-based pay
- administering indirect benefits

Training and development involve:
- Increasing ability and performance
- Increasing total quality management

Total quality management is a systematic and coordinated effort to continuously improve the quality of the firm's products and services.

Effective work relationships involve:
- employee rights
- understanding employee organizations
- bargaining and grievance settlements

Monitoring and assessing the work environment involves:
- safety and health
- HR data and information systems and assessment systems

direct influence on the physical safety and security of employees and their well-being. Failure to improve work conditions for health and safety is illegal and can be very costly.

Another crucial activity involves assessing and improving. Management data and information systems must be created and then used to ensure that decisions are made with timely and accurate information. This requires conducting organizational surveys, developing valid tests for selection, and in general, assessing all the HR activities.

WHO IS RESPONSIBLE FOR MANAGING HUMAN RESOURCES?

Everyone should be responsible for managing human resources, and, as organizations demonstrate more openness and mutuality in their policies and practices, everyone will be.

THE HUMAN RESOURCE PROFESSIONAL

Effective HR management is the task of individuals who have specialized in this field—that is, HR professionals. These professionals have acquired the special knowledge and skills necessary for managing human resources.

PARTNERSHIP: WORKING TOGETHER IN MANAGING HUMAN RESOURCES

LINE MANAGERS	HR PROFESSIONALS	EMPLOYEES*
Work closely with HR professionals and employees to develop and implement HR activities.	Work closely with line managers and employees to develop and implement HR activities.	Work closely with line managers and HR professionals to develop and implement HR activities.
Share responsibility for managing the human resources of the company.	Work with line managers to link human resource activities to the business.	Accept responsibility for managing their own behavior and careers in organizations.
Set policy that is supportive of ethical behavior.	Prepare practices for ethical conduct.	Recognize the need for flexibility and adaptability.

*While line managers and HR professionals are employees, the term employees as used here refers to all other personnel in the company—the nonmanagers.

THE LINE MANAGER

While HR professionals have the special knowledge and skills, it is the line manager who must ultimately manage the employees. Because line managers want to be effective in this endeavor, they need to work hand in hand with HR professionals. This is happening with all managers today, from the CEO on down.

Thus CEOs, HR managers, and all levels of senior management need to be involved in managing this resource. While this *is* happening, both CEOs and senior HR managers in the recent IBM/Towers Perrin survey agreed that co-involvement should become much more prevalent by the year 2000. Exhibit 1.3 indicates the type of involvement most favored. In this scenario, the HR department's leader will be counted among senior executives and will play significant roles in attracting, retaining and motivating the firm's most vital resources.

The HR leader will be indistinguishable from other senior executives in the concern for, and understanding of, the needs of the business. Likewise, the HR staff will appear indistinguishable from their counterparts in the firm. Sharing this function together, line managers, HR staff, and nonmanagerial employees will forge and implement all of the activities entailed in the human resources discipline.

> **DID YOU KNOW?**
>
> Jack Welch, CEO of GE, believes that CEOs are in essence personnel directors because "If we get the right people in the jobs, we've won the game."

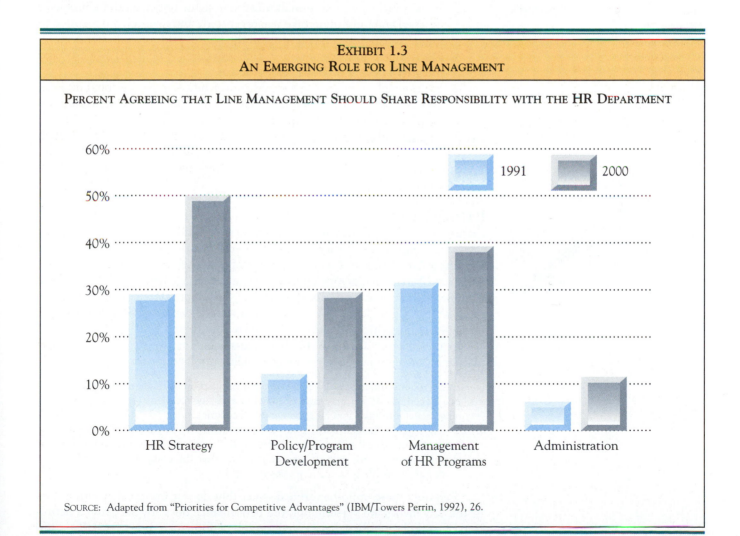

EXHIBIT 1.3
AN EMERGING ROLE FOR LINE MANAGEMENT

PERCENT AGREEING THAT LINE MANAGEMENT SHOULD SHARE RESPONSIBILITY WITH THE HR DEPARTMENT

SOURCE: Adapted from "Priorities for Competitive Advantages" (IBM/Towers Perrin, 1992), 26.

Human resource professionalism entails maintaining:

- public interest
- competence
- integrity
- humanity
- responsibility

THE EMPLOYEE

Employees are taking an ever more active role in HR management. For example, employees are now often asked to appraise their own performance or that of their colleagues. It is no longer uncommon for employees to write their own job descriptions. Perhaps most significantly, employees are actively managing their careers and assessing their own needs and values. Nonetheless, the HR department is often asked to assist in this process. To these ends, the HR department must be staffed with qualified individuals; staffing is discussed in Chapter 2.

PROFESSIONALISM IN HUMAN RESOURCE MANAGEMENT

Like any profession, HR management follows a code of professional ethics and has an accreditation institute and certification procedures. All professions share the code of ethics that human resource management follows.

1. Practitioners must regard the obligation to implement public objectives and protect the public interest as more important than blind loyalty to an employer's preferences.
2. In daily practice, professionals must thoroughly understand the problems assigned and must undertake whatever study and research are required to assure continuing competence and the best of professional attention.
3. Practitioners must maintain a high standard of personal honesty and integrity in every phase of daily practice.
4. Professionals must give thoughtful consideration to the personal interest, welfare, and dignity of all employees who are affected by their prescriptions, recommendations, and actions.
5. Professionals must make sure that the organizations that represent them maintain a high regard and respect for the public interest and that they never overlook the importance of the personal interests and dignity of employees.[19]

ETHICAL ISSUES

Increasingly, HR professionals are becoming involved in ethical issues. Some of the most serious issues center around differences in the way people are treated because of favoritism or a relationship to top management. In a recent survey, conducted by the Society for Human Resource Management (SHRM) and the Commerce Case Clearing House (CCCH), HR professionals identified more than 40 ethical incidents, events, and situations relevant to HR activities. The ten most serious ethical situations are shown in Exhibit 1.4.

In the SHRM/CCCH study, the professionals surveyed agreed that workplace ethics require people to be judged solely on job performance.

> Ethics requires managers to eliminate such things as favoritism, friendship, sex bias, race bias, or age bias from promotion and pay decisions (it is, of course, also *unlawful* to take sex, race, or age into account).
>
> Is ethics a "bottom line" issue? It becomes one when we consider that by acting in an ethical manner, companies will, in fact, hire, reward and retain the best people. This will, in turn, help assure that the company has the best work force possible to achieve its business goals.

Certainly there are other ethical issues that do not impact the bottom line in the way favoritism versus employee performance does. By adopting a definition of workplace ethics that centers on job performance, however, HR profes-

---

EXHIBIT 1.4
THE TEN "MOST SERIOUS" ETHICAL SITUATIONS REPORTED BY HR MANAGERS IN THE 1991 SHRM/CCH SURVEY

SITUATION	PERCENT
Hiring, training, or promotion based on favoritism (friendships or relatives)	30.7
Allowing differences in pay, discipline, promotion, etc., due to friendships with top management	30.7
Sex harrassment	28.4
Sex discrimination in promotion	26.9
Using discipline for managerial and nonmanagerial personnel inconsistently	26.9
Not maintaining confidentiality	26.4
Sex discrimination in compensation	25.8
Nonperformance factors used in appraisals	23.5
Arrangements with vendors or consulting agencies leading to personal gain	23.1
Sex discrimination in recruitment or hiring	22.6

"Percent" is the percent responding with 4 or 5 on 5-point scale measuring "degree of seriousness" (5 = "very great").

SOURCE: *1991 SHRM/CCH Survey* (Chicago: Commerce Case Clearinghouse, June 26, 1991), 1.

---

sionals will be in a better position to persuade others in the organization that making ethical behavior a priority will produce beneficial results.[20]

ENCOURAGING ETHICAL BEHAVIOR

To assume however, that a single policy can be devised to ensure that everyone in an organization behaves ethically and legally all the time is unrealistic. Nevertheless, there are a number of ways in which business ethics can be improved. A good starting point is for top management to examine such management practices as reward systems, managerial style, and decision-making processes. In some organizations, the reward system promotes unethical behavior by encouraging the achievement of organizational goals at almost any cost. Clearly then, HR professionals can play a major role in influencing ethical behavior in organizations. Accordingly, in the following chapters we present relevant ethical issues. For more discussion on what ethical behavior is and how it differs from illegal behavior, see the feature "HR Advice and Application: Ethical Behavior."

PROFESSIONAL CERTIFICATION

The Society for Human Resource Management (SHRM) has established the Human Resource Certification Institute to certify human resource professionals.[22] The institute has the following purposes:

1. To recognize individuals who have demonstrated expertise in particular fields
2. To raise and maintain professional standards

How to encourage ethical behavior:
- **Ensure that the reward system and other management policies do not create pressure for unethical behavior**
- **Have top management set a good example**
- **Establish a code of ethics**
- **Conduct internal audits**
- **Enforce laws more thoroughly**

DID YOU KNOW?

Approximately 50,000 HR professionals are members of SHRM.

3. To identify a body of knowledge as a guide to practitioners, consultants, educators, and researchers
4. To aid employers in identifying qualified applicants
5. To provide an overview of the field as a guide to self-development

The certification institute has two levels of accreditation: basic and senior. The basic accreditation is the Professional in Human Resources. This designation requires an examination covering the general body of knowledge and four years of professional experience. A bachelor's degree in HR management or social sciences counts for two years of professional experience.

The senior level accreditation is the Senior Professional in Human Resources. This accreditation requires a minimum of eight years of experience, with the three most recent years including policy-development responsibilities. All professionals receiving accreditation will be listed in the *Register of Accredited Personnel and Human Resource Professionals*.[23]

CAREERS IN HUMAN RESOURCE MANAGEMENT

There are many opportunities in the HR profession.

Numerous career possibilities in human resources exist. Human resource specialists can pursue their fields of specialization within a company and still sell some of their time to external organizations as consultants. Generalists in this field can remain in human resources and also occasionally serve on companywide task forces for special issues such as downsizing or capital improvement projects.

HR ADVICE AND APPLICATION

ETHICAL BEHAVIOR

What is ethical and unethical behavior? How does it differ from legal or illegal behavior? Many instances of ethical as well as unethical behavior do not make headlines. Consider the purchasing agent who repeatedly refuses gifts of any kind from suppliers and the manager who always charges personal calls made from the office to his home number. A large number of managers turn in scrupulously honest expense accounts. And many managers believe that acting only in the interest of shareholders, without considering employees and consumers, is unethical behavior.

The term ethics is a slippery one. For example, an early study on ethics found that all the people surveyed believed they were behaving ethically, according to their own standards. Furthermore, society's ideas about laws and ethics keep changing. Almost everyone would agree that child labor in factories is not only illegal but unethical. Yet when the U.S. Congress passed the *Fair Labor Standards Act* in 1938 in which child labor provisions were established, the act was bitterly contested.

Laws and ethics are related but not identical. **Illegal behavior** is behavior that violates a law in a particular jurisdiction or area. Ethical behavior stems from values and gives rise to laws. Thus behavior can be legal but unethical. Lavish entertainment of, and gifts to, customers is an accepted business practice in the United States. At what point, however, does the practice remain legal but become unethical?

While values influence a person's beliefs and behavior, **ethics** is concerned with moral rights and wrongs and with the individual's moral obligations to society. From the viewpoint of the manager, ethics is "the rules or standards governing the moral conduct of the organization management profession." In simple terms, **ethical behavior** is behavior that society considers right. But determining specific rights and wrongs is complicated since moral concepts, like other ideas, change over time and differ from individual to individual. Thus ethics is also a set of guiding principles that helps individuals retain their self-respect while behaving justly toward others. Ethics, then, is a personal responsibility for each individual.[21]

Generalists are likely to be from three ranks: career HR professionals with degrees in business or psychology, former line managers who have switched fields, and line managers on a required tour of duty. As human resources becomes an activity more heavily valued by organizations, required tours of duty by line managers will become more frequent. Finally, as U.S. organizations become more global, there will be increased opportunities for careers in international HR management. Career issues are discussed further in Chapter 4.

HISTORICAL NOTES ON HUMAN RESOURCE MANAGEMENT

THE BEGINNINGS OF PERSONNEL MANAGEMENT

As with many disciplines, procedures for managing people have changed rather dramatically during this century. In 1911, under the influence of the works of Fredrick W. Taylor, personnel management in industry focused on developing precise analytical schemes to select and reward individuals, typically for the purposes of motivating, controlling, and improving the productivity of entry-level employees. During the 1920s, work on these analytical schemes expanded to encompass issues of appraising and training individuals, essentially for the same purposes.

While the focus during the first quarter century was on the individual employee, the second quarter was to see it shift to the group. Elton Mayo and his work at the Hawthorne plant (the "Hawthorne Studies") focused on improving productivity of individuals through group experimentation. His efforts included changing the group's composition and incentive schemes. He also looked into changing environmental conditions—namely, lighting and physical arrangements. Knowledge of groups and the impact of the group on individuals advanced with the work of Kurt Lewin during the 1930s and 1940s. Yet with few notable exceptions (Chester Barnard's work on CEOs), this work was primarily focused on the employees doing the work.[24]

During the 1950s and 1960s, much of the work concerned with managing employees highlighted individual needs and motivation. Advances made in selection and development in the military during World War II expanded to the private sector. The development of tests for selection and placement and work in performance appraisal and training continued. Yet, again, most of the work focused, explicitly or implicitly, on improving the performance of the individuals doing the work. At this time, however, a new applied methodology focusing on management and motivational techniques became the domain of researchers working in personnel psychology and industrial and organizational psychology. The more theoretical work came under the domain of organizational behavioralists.

ENTER HUMAN RESOURCE MANAGEMENT

During the 1970s, a new discipline evolved under the name of human resource management. Encompassing the methodological tradition of the personnel management and industrial and organizational psychologists and the theoretical frameworks of the organizational behaviorists, HR management took on a broader focus than the earlier work. Besides the traditional focus, concerns for the safe-

DID YOU KNOW?

Most U.S. firms see growth coming from abroad, thereby, having overseas assignments is a typical part of any manager's career.

LEARNING OBJECTIVE 5

Describe professionalism in human resource management.

History gives us a useful perspective on managing human resources today.

ty and health of the worker were explored, as were individual satisfaction and performance. A changing society and workplace required that industrial relations and planning for personnel needs be examined under the domain of human resource management. Yet through all the work on these topics, the primary attention centered on the entry-level employee.

In the late 1970s and 1980s, the discipline of organizational strategy started to have an impact on HR management. The environment—namely, more intense international and domestic competition for companies—began to impact the discipline. The result of this dual influence was the recognition that a number of organizational characteristics not generally addressed have a substantial impact on managing human resources. Thus, such organizational characteristics as structure, strategy, size, culture, and product and organizational life cycle began to be incorporated into the work of this profession.[25]

Today, forces of global competition, worldwide labor availability, business ethics and the ecological environment are winning the attention of HR professionals everywhere. Of course, this does not mean that the issues of the 1970s and 1980s can be forgotten. To the contrary, these are all carried forward, making the job of the HR professional challenging, rewarding, and exciting. For more details on the historical development of HR, see Exhibit 1.5.

LEARNING OBJECTIVE 6

Discuss the current trends in human resource management.

Trends in human resource management:
- linking with the environment
- being systematic
- the greening of HR

As managers deal with global competitiveness, they will see that human resources are the core of a company's strategic competence and organizational capabilities.

Christopher Bartlett,
Professor, Harvard Business School

Being systematic means determining the HR needs of the organization and then putting together HR activities and practices that send the same message to employees consistently.

CURRENT TRENDS

What is happening today in the field of HR management is nothing short of revolutionary. This organizational function is more important than ever. Line managers are getting involved in the process and HR managers are becoming members of the management team. Also, because this endeavor is seen as critical to the success of organizations, it is recognized that virtually everyone in an organization can make a contribution to the management of people and the success of the organization at the same time. Three trends accompany this excitement and challenge.

LINKING WITH THE ENVIRONMENT

In comparison with the past, today's and tomorrow's characterizations of HR management reflect the more intense levels of national, regional, and global competition, dramatic demographic and work force changes, anticipated legal and regulatory changes, and significant technological developments. Requiring major changes in organizational strategy, structure, and technology, these environmental forces demand speed, quality, innovation, and globalization on the part of firms wishing to survive the "battlefield" of international competition. The characterization of effective firms in highly competitive environments—the firms in which the most exciting things in HR management are happening—reflects the corporate consensus that the requirements for successful "combat" will require the most effective human resource management possible. Chapter 2 is devoted to what's happening in world class HR departments.

BEING SYSTEMATIC

Companies that seek to gain the maximum benefit from their personnel management activities must take a **systematic approach**. While this trend will be elaborated on throughout the remainder of the book, it is important to introduce it here. Basically, in the evolution of this discipline, HR professionals have come to realize that, to be effective, they need to know what the business is, what the

EXHIBIT 1.5
CHANGING CONCERNS OF HUMAN RESOURCE MANAGEMENT

TIME PERIOD	PRIMARY CONCERN	EMPLOYEE PERCEPTIONS	TECHNIQUES OF INTEREST
Before 1900	Production technologies	Indifference to needs	Discipline systems
1900–1910	Employee welfare	Employees need safe conditions and opportunity	Safety programs, English language classes, inspirational programs
1910–1920	Task efficiency	Need high earnings made possible with higher productivity	Motion and time study
1920–1930	Individual differences	Employees' individual differences considered	Psychological testing, employee counseling
1930–1940	Unionization	Employees as adversaries	Employee communication programs, anti-unionization techniques
	Productivity	Group performance	Improving conditions for groups
1940–1950	Economic security	Employees need economic protection	Employee pension plans, health plans, fringe benefits (pensions, etc.)
1950–1960	Human relations	Employees need considerate supervision	Foremen training (role playing, sensitivity training)
1960–1970	Participation	Employees need involvement in task decisions	Participative management techniques
	Employment laws	Need to widen employee involvement	Affirmative Action, Equal Opportunity
1970–1980	Task challenge and Quality of working life	Employees need work that is challenging and congruent with abilities	Job enrichment, integrated task teams
1980–1990	Employee displacement	Employees need jobs—lost through economic downturns, international competition, and technological changes	Outplacement, retraining, downsizing
1990–2000	Productivity Quality Adaptability	Employees need to balance work and nonwork and make contributions	Linking the needs of the business, training, total quality, ethics, diversity, workplace accommodation, and globalness.

SOURCE: Adapted from S. J. Carroll and R. S. Schuler, "Professional HRM: Changing Functions and Problems," in *Human Resources Management in the 1980s*, edited by S. J. Carroll and R. S. Schuler (Washington D.C.: Bureau of National Affairs, 1983), 8–10.

business needs from its people, and then they need to establish policies and practices that are consistent with this.

Policy and practices that are consistent and coordinated with each other communicate the same message to employees. A performance appraisal system that evaluates employees on the basis of long-term goal attainment and a compensation system that rewards them on the same basis send consistent messages.

On the other hand, a policy that describes employees as the most valuable resource and a practice that results in constant layoffs and little training send conflicting messages.

Consistency across all policies and practices results in a clear understanding of what is expected, what is rewarded, and what is important. Consistency and clarity result in effective use of human resources and therefore in effective organizations. HR departments achieve consistency and clarity when they and their leaders approach HR management in a very systematic and integrated way.

THE GREENING OF THIS DISCIPLINE

Human resources is more concerned than ever with ethics and ethical behavior, about linking the environment to the needs of the company, and in being more systematic and more global in orientation. It is much more externally focused than ever before, and it subscribes to the values of the baby-buster generation:

> The consciousness of the generation right now is that they're very environmentally aware. That's something that's a concern of theirs, and if they can get involved with a company that's environmentally aware, it's more in tune with their own ethics.
>
> TERRI WOLFE,
> DIRECTOR OF PERSONNEL
> PATAGONIA[26]

The baby-buster generation was born between 1965 and 1975. More in Chapter 3.

Thus, issues of the ecological environment are becoming a concern of HR management! While this may seem a bit far-fetched at first, consider the issues raised in the feature, "Managing Human Resources: How HR Managers Help Companies Become Green."

SUMMARY

DID YOU KNOW?

The body of scientific knowledge doubles every seven years.

Human resource management is about managing people in organizations as effectively as possible for the good of the employees, the company, and society. As such, HR management is becoming more and more important to organizations in their efforts to manage people as effectively as possible.

The environment around us is changing rapidly. The challenges and demands facing organizations today is causing a serious reexamination of ways to manage the business. In doing so, companies are discovering that a key way is through the effective management of human resources. Of course, there are differences among companies. You probably know of some companies where being serious about effective people management has never existed. And these companies may have always done alright. A closer look, however, may reveal that these companies may actually owe their success largely to their human resources! They may have had people with the right skills and with the right motivation: people who would have done well even without all the best HR activities. But also realize that the environment until recently was much more predictable and stable than it is today. Worldwide competition was almost nonexistent 30 years ago. So today organizations are saying, "We are in tough times now: competition is fierce; there is constant pressure on prices; it is becoming more costly to bring on more

MANAGING HUMAN RESOURCES

How HR Managers Help Companies Become Green

As interest in the environment has increased in the United States, companies are recognizing and responding to the environmental push from management and employees. Often, an in-house recycling program results.

"Recycling is one activity that allows people to express their environmental commitment in a tangible way," says Ralph Earle, a senior consultant for Arthur D. Little, a Cambridge, Massachusetts-based environmental consulting firm. "If you recycle that aluminum can you're drinking out of—something that you can touch, feel, and see—it helps the environment."

But interest in cleaning the environment hasn't always been so strong. "Three years ago, when I was talking to companies about recycling, it was very much a missionary role," remembers Earle. Organizations looked at recycling simply as extra work, "Now companies are asking, 'How do we do it?'" he says.

Earle also explains that companies are differentiating themselves from their competition through their environmental posture and actions. "One of the things that we preach is that, for an environmental strategy to work, it can't be viewed as a separate issue. It *has* to permeate the corporation," he says. Everybody must be involved.

There are two objectives in starting an in-house recycling program. "The first is to reclaim the material and prevent it from being disposed of," says Earle. "But the second, from an HR standpoint, is to provide programs that enable workers to feel proud about their workplace and to feel that they're making a contribution during working hours. People tend to separate their personal beliefs from what they do at the office—recycling is a way of bringing the two together."

Earle says he's noticed a direct trend linking employee interest and the growth of recycling programs in business. Why? "Recycling is extremely motivational for employees and therefore generates high participation because it's so tangible and it's so personal."

Human resource departments can get involved in communicating the environmental message by setting up payroll deduction programs for workers to donate money to such environmental causes as the National Resources Defense Council or the World Wildlife Fund.

Another way to gather employees' environmental thoughts? Through an employee suggestion box, says Earle. "One of the keys to competitive advantage is pollution prevention, not so much from an environmental or altruistic point of view, but from the point of view of saving money," says Earle. "One company used an employee suggestion to cut its manufacturing generation of waste by 60%." Even if a company doesn't make money selling items to recycling vendors, at least it will save money on trash removal and landfill costs.

What if no one on staff can spare the time to organize the recycling project? "I've seen a number of companies hiring groups of individuals who have disabilities or are learning-disadvantaged to run their in-house recycling programs," says Earle.

Another way to get involved is to become a facilitator between departments. "An objective party, such as HR, can get such groups as office workers and facilities personnel working together to make a recycling project happen," suggests Earle.

Perhaps the most important way to get the environmental message out is through constant communication. In addition to such media as company newsletters, bulletin boards, and posters, employees can learn about recycling through an in-house video on the subject.

The environmental department at Federal Express in Memphis, Tennessee, for example, is producing such a video and is even considering using the company's own television station, called FX/TV, to update employees on current environmental policies and guidelines. "It's a superb method, because it gives us instantaneous access to all of our employees," says Louis Lechleiter, the company's environmental manager.

Continued on the next page

employees; and even when we get them it is a challenge to keep them motivated." Consequently, companies are doing everything possible to become and stay effective and to manage their organizations in order to survive and be profitable. Of course, these are all the things that HR management can do. And this is exactly what some of the most successful firms have learned over the past several years!

In managing their human resources effectively, successful firms in today's highly competitive environments have found that it pays to have everyone involved in the effort. Employees, line managers, and HR professionals have to work together if their firm is to be effective in managing their human resources. Because you are likely to be in one or more of these categories, we want to discuss the activities of HR management from all these viewpoints.

And in our discussions in the next several chapters, you will also see that a particular emphasis is given to certain themes, in particular, ethics and ethical issues, diversity in the work force, globalization, total quality management, and partnership.

Although you may not work in an HR department, or at least think you may not do so in your career, it is important for you to be familiar with these themes because they are impacting how organizations conduct business. And because of the partnership theme in managing human resources, it is very likely that you will be more involved in this endeavor than you might believe right now. Times change. This book is written to help you prepare for a future that is becoming more dependent on its human resources than ever before. The key terms used in this book are defined in Exhibit 1.6.

In the next chapter we will discuss issues associated with the HR department. Again, even if you do not end up working in such a department, it is important to know what the department could be doing and how they can help you in your efforts to manage human resources (including yourself). If you do work in an HR department, you will have a much better idea about the issues and challenges they face. As we discuss these issues and all the others in the following chapters, examples of what some of the best companies are doing will be used. They will show that the job can be done and, in fact, that it must be done if organizations are to be effective in a highly competitive, global environment!

Major themes in this book are

- **ethics and ethical issue**
- **diversity**
- **globalization**
- **total quality management**
- **partnership**

KEY CONCEPTS

bottom line	human resource	illegal behavior
ethics	management	systematic approach
ethical behavior	partnership	

EXHIBIT 1.6
WHAT IS HUMAN RESOURCE MANAGEMENT?

A GLOSSARY OF KEY TERMS

Recognizing that some variations exist within and across organizations in the use of words in HR management, this book uses the following definitions:

Employees All those in the company who are nonmanagers. They work with HR professionals and line managers in managing human resources.

Human resource management Managing people in organizations as effectively as possible for the good of the employees, the company, and society.

HR activities Understanding the business environment and planning; staffing; appraising; compensating; improving; establishing and maintaining effective work relationships; and monitoring and assessing.

HR administration Performing day-to-day operations such as writing job descriptions and preparing recruiting ads.

HR department/leader/staff (HR professionals) A formal unit and individual(s) designated to be in charge of the HR function and, therefore, responsible and accountable for the organization's HR management activities.

HR function A set of activities, practices, roles, responsibilities, and structures in an organization concerned with HR management that may be carried out by any and all employees (managers and nonmanagers).

HR issues/concerns Those topics, areas, and thoughts related to HR management.

HR philosophy A general statement about the value of employees to the firm that in turn shapes the content of HR policies.

HR policies General guidelines, based on the HR philosophy, that are referred to in the development of the HR practices and activities to be used by the firm.

HR practices Specific HR actions used to attract, motivate, retain, and retrain employees.

HR professionals The HR leader and staff, generalists and specialists.

HR programs Action plans that direct and implement a set of HR practices and that are consistent with HR policies and philosophy.

Human resources The people being attracted, motivated, retained, or retrained by an organization.

HR strategy Developing and implementing overall plans that effectively link HR management activities with the business.

Line manager The person responsible for producing a product or service through and with employees.

Partnership The cooperative relationship among the HR department and staff, line managers, and employees in managing human resources.

REVIEW AND DISCUSSION QUESTIONS

1. Why are organizations giving greater importance to managing human resources?
2. What are common characteristics of today's effective organizations?
3. What are the specific and overall goals of human resource management activities?
4. Briefly summarize the major activities of human resource management.
5. Who is responsible for managing human resources?
6. Who are HR professionals and line managers?
7. What are ethical HR issues in organizations?
8. What is the Society of Human Resource Management? If you plan to pursue a career in human resource management, where could you go for more information?
9. Briefly describe the professional certification process for HR managers. Why is professional certification important in human resource management?
10. Name three trends in human resource management.

EXERCISES AND CASES

FIELD PROJECT

Look at the most recent issues (say, the last five issues) of *Fortune, Business Week, The Wall Street Journal, Personnel Journal,* and any other pertinent journals or papers including your local newspaper. Present to the class one story on, or related to, managing human resources.

CASE

PEOPLE-RELATED BUSINESS ISSUES AT THE BARDEN CORPORATION: SOLUTIONS THROUGH PARTNERSHIP

BACKGROUND

The largest segment of the Barden Corporation is the Precision Bearings Division. It manufactures high-precision ball bearings for machine tools, aircraft instruments and accessories, aircraft engines, computer peripherals, textile spindles, and medical and dental equipment. Currently, the division employs about 1,000 people and includes a marketing department and a small corporate staff. It was founded during World War II to manufacture the special bearings needed for the Norden bombsight and has been nonunion since the beginning (which gives you a hint about the culture). Mr. Donald Brush, Vice President and

General manager of the Precision Bearings Division, gives the following description of his division.

Reporting directly to me is a small staff comprising a manufacturing manager, a quality manager, an engineering manager, a director of manufacturing planning, and a manager of human resources (Exhibit 1). We meet several times a week to discuss current problems, as well as short- and long-range opportunities and needs. On alternate weeks, we augment this group by including the supervisory personnel who report to the senior managers listed above. I might interject here that all supervisors meet with hourly employees on either a weekly or biweekly basis to review specific departmental successes and failures, and to otherwise keep employees informed about the business and to encourage ownership of their jobs. The managers themselves meet on call as the Employee Relations Committee to discuss and recommend approval of a wide range of issues that include the evaluation and audit of hourly and salaried positions, as well as the creation and modification of all divisional personnel policies.

A few words about our Human Resource (or Industrial Relations) Department: There are six employees who together provide the basic services of employment, affirmative action, employee activity support, labor relations, interpretation of the plethora of federal and state laws, benefits administration, wage and salary administration, records preparation and maintenance, cafeteria supervision, and so on. There are, in addition, two people who coordinate our rather extensive training activities.

As currently organized, the Medical Department comes under the supervision of the manager of human resources. Its authorized staff includes a medical director, the manager of employee health and safety (who is an occupational health nurse), a staff nurse, a safety specialist, and secretary/clerk.

The development and execution of plans and programs, including those of a strategic nature, almost invariably involve the active participation of HR. And that's how we want it to be. On the other hand, the HR Department doesn't run the business. By this I mean they don't hire or fire, promote or demote. They don't write job descriptions or determine salaries or wages. All these things are done by the line managers with the HR Department providing a framework to ensure consistency and that all actions are appropriate to company goals. You might say that HR is our "Jiminy cricket"—they are there for advice, consent, and, importantly, as a conscience.

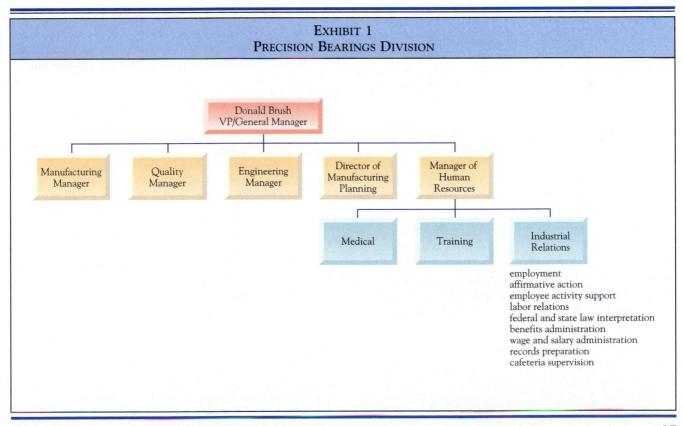

EXHIBIT 1
PRECISION BEARINGS DIVISION

Donald Brush
VP/General Manager

- Manufacturing Manager
- Quality Manager
- Engineering Manager
- Director of Manufacturing Planning
- Manager of Human Resources
  - Medical
  - Training
  - Industrial Relations
    - employment
    - affirmative action
    - employee activity support
    - labor relations
    - federal and state law interpretation
    - benefits administration
    - wage and salary administration
    - records preparation
    - cafeteria supervision

PEOPLE-RELATED BUSINESS ISSUES

During the past several months, we have been running into many issues that are affecting the very essence of our business: growth, profits, survival, and competitiveness. Because the issues involve our human resources, we call them people-related business issues (PRBIs). Would you please give us your experience, expertise, and suggestions as to how we can solve them? Thanks! The following briefly describes the nature of each of the four PRBIs.

ISSUE: RECRUITING AND TRAINING NEW HOURLY EMPLOYEES

The need to recruit and train approximately 125 new hourly workers to respond to a surge in business in a high-cost-of-living area at a time when the unemployment rate is low is very challenging. By mid-1993, it had become evident that we had an opportunity to significantly increase our business. In order to achieve otherwise attainable goals, we have to increase our hourly work force by a net of about 125 employees (that is, in addition to normal turnover, retirements, etc.) in one year. I have asked Personnel to test the waters, recognizing the unemployment in the Danbury labor market for skilled workers has reached an unprecedented low of about 2.5%.

ISSUE: SAFETY AND OCCUPATIONAL HEALTH ISSUES

The need to create a heightened awareness by the work force for safety and occupational health considerations is very important. This is an evolving mission born of a dissatisfaction on our part about "safety as usual." Over the years, Barden employees have assumed that, because we are a metalworking shop, people were just going to get hurt. But we cannot afford to have people get hurt and miss work anymore. Yet, as our work force ages, the employees seem to get out of shape and become more injury and illness prone.

ISSUE: SPIRALING HEALTH COSTS OF AN AGING POPULATION

The spiraling health costs of an aging and sometimes, out-of-shape work force are very costly. All employers face this. Barden's problem is a little unique in that hourly employees tend to stay with the company and retire from the company. For example, we still have several employees whose careers began with us 45 years ago

shortly after the company was founded. Our average age approaches 45 for employees and their dependent spouses. Generally, our jobs do not require much physical effort, and it's easy to become out of shape and overfed. As a consequence, employees get sick, use hospitals, and have accidents.

ISSUE: NEW MACHINES AND THE DEVELOPMENT OF QUALIFIED WORKERS

The technological evolution of increasingly complex machinery and related manufacturing equipment, and the development of trained workers to operate and maintain these machines and equipment, are important facts of life. This process is unceasing and requires a good deal of planning for both the short and the long run. For example, what should we do in the next year, or five years out, in order to remain competitive in terms of cost, quality, and service? Buying and rebuilding machines is part of the story. Running them efficiently is quite another. As you know, modern equipment of this sort requires operational people who are not only knowledgeable about the turning or grinding of metals, but also conversant with computerized numerical controls. The employee who sets up and operates a $500,000 machine must be well trained. Yet finding trained people is getting more difficult.

SUMMARY

Mr. Brush knows that these people-related business issues all reflect the increasing diversity of the work force. Because of this, he knows these issues will be around for a long time. Therefore, he requests that you provide him with your ideas and suggestions.

SOURCE: This case was prepared by Randall S. Schuler who expresses his appreciation for the cooperation of Donald Brush.

CASE QUESTIONS

1. Are these people-related business issues facing Mr. Brush really very important?
2. On which people-related business issues is the HR department able to be most helpful?
3. At Barden, who are the line managers and who are the employees?
4. How can the HR manager, the line managers and the employees work together to solve these people-related business issues?

1. Materials here on Wal-Mart and Sam Walton were compiled from several sources including:

S. Walton, "Sam Walton in His Own Words," *Fortune* (June 29, 1992): 98–106;

B. Saporito, "A Week Aboard the Wal-Mart Express," *Fortune* (Aug. 24, 1993): 77–84;

V. Johnston and H. Moore, "Pride Drives Wal-Mart to Service Excellence," *HR Magazine* (Oct. 1991): 79–82;

J. Huey, "America's Most Successful Merchant," *Fortune* (Sept. 23, 1991): 46–59;

T. C. Hayes, "Wal-Mart's Late Founder Still Stirs Stockholders," *The New York Times* (June 6, 1992): 39.

By no means is Wal-Mart without fault or criticism. For some commentary on this, particularly in their alleged use of low-wage Chinese workers for products made in China (at a time when the firm was known for its "Made in America" campaign), see T. C. Hayes, "Wal-Mart Disputes Report on Labor," *The New York Times* (Dec. 24, 1992): D1, D4. For some discussion on its movements into areas that bring competition to towns, see B. J. Feder, "Message for Mom & Pop: There's Life After Wal-Mart," *The New York Times* (Oct. 24, 1993): F4; J. Steinberg, "One Town's Stores Plot Survival As Wal-Mart Grows in Northeast," *The New York Times* (Nov. 28, 1993): A1; 4.

2. R. S. Schuler (ed.), *Managing Human Resources in the Information Age*, Vol. 6 (Washington, D.C.: SHRM/BNA, 1991).

3. J. Welch, quoted in J. W. Peters, "Strategic Staffing: A Key Link in Business and Human Resource Planning," *Human Resource Planning 11* (No. 2) (1988): 155.

4. C. A. Bartlett and S. Ghosal, "What is a Global Manager?" *Harvard Business Review* (Sept.–Oct. 1992): 131.

5. L. Landro, "GE's Wizards Turning from the Bottom Line to Share of the Market," *The Wall Street Journal* (July 12, 1982): 1.

6. N. Tichy and R. Charan, "Speed, Simplicity, and Self-Confidence: An Interview with Jack Welch," *Harvard Business Review* (Sept.–Oct. 1989): 116.

7. *Ibid.*, p. 113. Also from material in GE Annual Reports 1992 and 1993; and T. Smart, "GE's Money Machine," *Business Week* (March 8, 1993): 62–68; T. S. Fiske, "HR Issues Drive Production Offshore," *Personnel Journal* (Jan. 1991): 84–88; N. Tichy and S. Sherman, *Control Your Destiny or Someone Else Will* (New York: Currency/Doubleday, 1993).

8. *Reinventing the CEO* (New York: Korn/Ferry International and Columbia University, 1989): 1.

9. R. S. Schuler, "World Class HR Departments: Six Critical Issues," *Accounting and Business Review* (Jan. 1994): 43–72.

10. E. Faltermayer, "Is this Layoff Necessary?" *Fortune* (June 1, 1992): 86.

11. R. S. Schuler and J. W. Walker, "Human Resources Strategy: Focusing on Issues and Action," *Organizational Dynamics* (Summer 1990); 5–19; C. A. Lengnick-Hall and M. L. Lengnick-Hall, *Interactive Human Resource Management and Strategic Planning* (New York: Quorum Books, 1990); R. S. Schuler, "Repositioning the Human Resource Function: Transformation or Demise?" *Academy of Management Executive*, Vol. 4, 1990, 49–60.

12. "Improve Quality," *Business Week* (June 8, 1987): 158. See also R. S. Schuler and D. Harris, *Managing Quality* (Reading, Mass.: Addison-Wesley, 1992); O. Port, "Quality," *Business Week* (June 8, 1987): 131–143; A. Bernstein, "Can America Compete?" *Business Week* (April 20, 1987): 45–52. It appears that firms are competing on all fronts—that is, quality, cost, and innovation. Increasingly, speed is becoming important as well. See M. E. Porter, *Competitive Strategy* (New York: Free Press, 1985); M. E. Porter, *Competitive Advantage* (New York: Free Press, 1985): J. Main, "The Winning Corporation," *Fortune* (Sept. 26, 1988): 50–56; B. Dumaine, "How Managers Can Succeed through Speed," *Fortune* (Feb. 13, 1989): 54–59.

13. Adapted from E. Lawler, "The New Plant Approach: A Second Generation Approach," *Organizational Dynamics* (Summer 1991): 5–14.

14. M. G. Miner, "Legal Concerns Facing Human Resource Managers: An Overview," in *Readings in Personnel and Human Management*, 3rd ed., R. S. Schuler, S. A. Youngblood, and V. L. Huber, eds. (St. Paul, Minn.: West, 1988): 40–54.

15. R. S. Schuler and I. C. MacMillan, "Gaining a Competitive Advantage Through Human Resource Management Practices," *Human Resource Management* (Fall 1984): 241–256.

16. N. Alster, "What Flexible Workers Can Do," *Fortune* (Feb. 13, 1989), 62–66.

17. "Microsoft: Bill Gates' Baby is on Top of the World. Can It Stay There?" *Business Week* (Feb. 24, 1992): 60–65.

18. "Priorities for Competitive Advantage," (New York: IBM/Towers Perrin, 1992).

19. S. H. Applebaum, APD, "The Personnel Professional and Organization Development: Conflict and Synthesis," *Personnel Administrator* (July 1980): 57–61; F. R. Edney, "The Greening of the Profession," *Personnel Administrator* (July 1980): 27–30, 42; F. R. Edney, "Playing on the Team," *Personnel Journal* (Aug. 1981): 598–600; L. B. Prewitt, "The Emerging Field of Human Resources Management," *Personnel Administrator* (May 1982): 81–87.

20. F. H. Applebaum, APD, *1991 SHRM/CCH Survey* (June 26, 1991); M. T. Brown, *Working Ethics: Strategies for Decision Making and Organizational Responsibility* (San Francisco: Jossey-Bass, 1990); L. L. Nash, *Good Intentions Aside: A Manager's*

Guide to Resolving Ethical Problems (Boston, Mass.: Harvard Business School Press, 1990); L. Tone Hosmer, *The Ethics of Management* (Homewood, Ill.: Irwin, 1991).

21. Adapted from E. F. Huse, *Management*, 2nd ed (St. Paul, Minn.: West, 1982); and P. F. Buller, J. J. Kohls, and K. S. Anderson, "The Challenge of Global Ethics," *Journal of Business Ethics* Vol. 10(1991): 767–775.

22. *Certification Information Handbook*, (Alexandria, VA: HR Certification Institute, 1994); D. Yoder and H. Heneman, Jr., *PAIR Jobs, Qualifications, and Careers, ASPA Handbook of Personnel and Industrial Relations* (Washington, D.C.: The Bureau of National Affairs, 1978), 18; W. M. Hoffman, R. Frederick, and E. W. Petry, Jr., eds., *The Ethics of Organizational Transformation: Mergers, Takeovers and Corporate Restructuring* (New York: Quorum Books, 1989).

23. W. W. Turnow, "The Codifications Project and Its Importance to Professionalism," *Personnel Administrator* (June 1984): 84–100; C. Haigley, "Professionalism in Personnel," *Personnel Administrator* (June 1984): 103–106. Also contact the Institute directly by calling the Society for Human Resource Management at 1-800-331-2772.

24. B. Rice, "The Hawthorne Defect: Persistence of a Flawed Theory," *Psychology Today* (Feb. 1982): 70–74; F. J. Roethlisberger, *The Elusive Phenomena* (Cambridge, Mass.: Harvard University Press, 1977); F. J. Roethlisberger, W. J. Dickson, and H. A. Wright, *Management and the Worker* (Cambridge, Mass.: Harvard University Press, 1939; E. Mayo, *The Human Problems of an Industrial Civilization* (Cambridge, Mass.: Harvard University Press, 1933); I. C. Barnard, *The Functions of the Executive* (Cambridge, Mass.: Harvard University Press, 1938); A. Bolton, "The Hawthorne Studies: Relay Assembly Participants Remember," unpublished dissertation, NOVA University, 1985; G. Greenwood, A. Bolton, and A. Greenwood, "Hawthorne a Half Century Later: Relay Assembly Participants Remember." *Journal of Management* Vol. 9(2)(1983): 217–231; S. J. Carroll and R. S. Schuler, "Professional HRM: Changing Functions and Problems," in *Human Resource Management in the 1980's*, S. J. Carroll and R. S. Schuler, eds. (Washington, D.C.: Bureau of National Affairs, 1983).

25. S. E. Jackson, R. S. Schuler, and J. C. Rivero, "Organizational Characteristics as Predictors of Personnel Practices," *Personnel Psychology*, 43(1989): 727–786; A. K. Gupta and V. Govindarajan, "Build, Hold, Harvest: Converting Strategic Intentions into Reality," Journal of Business Strategy 4 (1984): 34–47; A. K. Gupta and V. Govindarajan, "Business Unit Strategy, Managerial Characteristics, and Business Unit Effectiveness as Strategy Implementation," *Academy of Management Journal* 9 (1984): 25–41; T. A. Kochan, R. B. McKersie, and P. Cappelli, "Strategic Choice and Industrial Relations Theory," *Industrial Relations* 23 (1984): 16–39; T. A. Kochan and P. Cappelli, "The Transformation of the Industrial Relations/Human Resource Function," in *Internal Labor Markets*, P. Osterman, ed. (Cambridge, Mass.: MIT Press, 1983), 133–162; C. A. Lengnik-Hall and M. L. Lengnik-Hall, "Strategic Human Resource Management: A Review of the Literature," *Academy of Management Review* (July 1988): 454–470.

26. C. M. Solomon, "Managing the Baby-Busters," *Personnel Journal* (March 1992): 56.

27. J. J. Laabs, "The Greening of HR," *Personnel Journal* (Aug. 1992): 68. Used by permission. Also read F. Rice, "Who Scores Best on the Environment," *Fortune* (July 26, 1993): 114–122.

CHAPTER 2

THE HUMAN RESOURCE DEPARTMENT

LEARNING OBJECTIVES

When you have finished studying this chapter, you should be able to:

1. Discuss how the HR department has been changing and is likely to change.
2. Describe the roles that the human resource department plays in organizations.
3. Describe the various HR professionals in the HR department.
4. Tell how an HR department changes when it becomes international.

MANAGING HUMAN RESOURCES at Levi-Strauss & Co.

OVER the past few years, the Levi Strauss organization has linked its HR department and practices closely to the business:

> HR participates in every major business decision, and every HR program directly supports a business goal. The payoff is enormous.
>
> DONNA GOYA, SENIOR VICE PRESIDENT OF HUMAN RESOURCES[1]

Instrumental in this approach has been the chairman and CEO Robert D. Haas. Working with the employees, Haas and Goya have crafted a mission statement for human resources that emphasizes the importance of people and that guides the management of the firm's human resources. As a result, according to Goya:

> I really think that our senior directors do understand now that people can give you the competitive edge.[2]

For the employees at Levi Strauss, this has meant empowerment. It is essential, says Goya, that all employees know where they fit into the organization and how they contribute to the broader vision and goals of the company. Sounds easy, but try doing it with more than 30,000 employees in 78 production, distribution, and finishing facilities throughout the world!

This insistence on linking their people to the business has also made the HR department more aware of the issues that line managers face daily: keeping employees excited about what they are doing and keeping their productivity high—so high that Levi Strauss continues to be one of the most competitive manufacturers in the world. This awareness has resulted in the development of several programs, including:

- Management and awareness training organizationwide, to communicate the company's commitment to creating a comfortable work-and-family environment
- Flexible work hours to accommodate plant employees' needs to address family responsibilities
- A new time-off-with-pay program, to replace separate vacation, sick leave, and floating holiday plans
- Child-care leave, expanded to cover care for other family members, including elders and significant others
- Corporate child-care fund, to enhance the existing community services, ranging from infant day care to after-school programs, based on worker needs
- Child-care voucher system for hourly employees working in field locations
- Elder-care programs
- Expansion of employee assistance program services in the field[3]

Developing and running these programs successfully is the work of a partnership of HR professionals, line managers, and staff. This takes time and energy—and money—and is indicative of the company's level of commitment. At the San Francisco headquarters alone, there are 100 employees in human resources with another 200 in various facilities around the United States and overseas!

This feature highlights several things about HR management: (1) it is very important in making organizations effective; (2) it means developing effective policies and programs, aspiration statements as well as a mission statement and the HR practices that go with them; and (3) it can be very effective in coordination and facilitation.

Of course, Levi Strauss & Co. is doing much more in HR management, and we will discuss other aspects throughout this chapter. In the meantime, what is your impression of Levi Strauss? Do you think it is a good company? Do you think that your opinion is due in part to how well the firm manages its people? It appears that many people think so; Levi Strauss gets *thousands* of student resumes annually. Not a small part of this phenomenon is due to its HR department. But remember, this department is important not only at Levi Strauss, it is very important in many organizations. Let's see what is going on inside HR departments today and whether there is a job in there for you.

The HR department is the group formally established by the firm to assist in managing the organization's people as effectively as possible for the good of the employees, the company, and society.

THE HUMAN RESOURCE DEPARTMENT

The **human resource department** *is the group formally established by an organization to assist in managing the organization's people as effectively as possible for the good of the employees, the company, and society.* As indicated in Chapter 1, the working partnership of HR staff, line managers, and employees is a major trend in business today. At times, this partnership extends outside the organization— for example, as the firm strives to forge better working relationships with its suppliers. It may venture into local education facilities as the HR staff works with schools to prepare students for internships in the firm.

Today there is a lot happening in HR departments, in both small and large organizations. This department is being looked to anew as a key function that can improve the firm's competitiveness, profitability, and thus "survivability"!

There was a time when the HR department was the last to know. "Now, the first thing you do is call human resources and say 'Can you help me do things properly'."

Richard Zimmerman, CEO
Hershey Food Corporation

WHY IS THE HUMAN RESOURCE DEPARTMENT IMPORTANT?

In 1991, IBM and the internationally recognized HR consulting firm of Towers Perrin conducted a study of nearly 3,000 senior HR leaders and CEOs worldwide. Results indicate that about 70 percent of HR managers see the HR department as critical to the success of organizations. By the year 2000, more than 90 percent expect this department to be critical. While the HR respondents were perhaps a bit more positive about this trend, the CEOs were very close behind. These results are illustrated in Exhibit 2.1.

Human resource departments perform a broad variety of activities (described in Chapter 1) and they play a broad variety of roles. We will discuss these here, along with issues associated with staffing and globalization.

By the year 2000, 90% of HR managers think their department will be critical to the success of the business.

THE MANY ROLES OF THE DEPARTMENT

Effective firms in the highly competitive environments of today encourage their HR departments to play many **roles** in the organization. And, the more roles they play well, the more likely they will be effective in improving the organization's productivity, enhancing the quality of work life in the organization, complying with all the necessary laws and regulations related to managing human resources effectively, gaining competitive advantage, and enhancing work force flexibility.

Roles of the HR department:
- business
- enabler
- monitoring
- innovator
- adapter

THE BUSINESS ROLE

Traditionally, HR departments had a relatively limited involvement in the total organization's affairs and goals. Personnel managers were often only concerned with making staffing plans, providing specific job training programs, or running

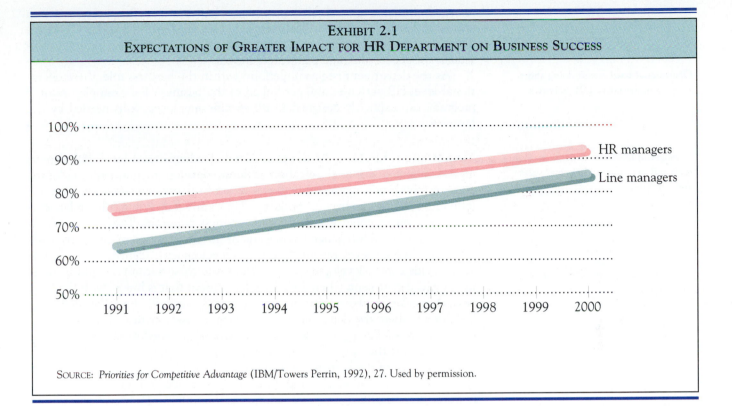

EXHIBIT 2.1
EXPECTATIONS OF GREATER IMPACT FOR HR DEPARTMENT ON BUSINESS SUCCESS

SOURCE: *Priorities for Competitive Advantage* (IBM/Towers Perrin, 1992), 27. Used by permission.

annual performance appraisal programs (the results of which were sometimes put in the files, never to be used). They focused on the short-term—perhaps day-to-day—needs of personnel.

With the growing importance of human resources to the success of the firm (see Exhibit 2.1 again), HR managers and their departments are becoming more involved in the organization. They are getting to know the needs of the business—where it's going, where it should be going—and are helping it to get there.[4] More typical today then is the comment by Jim Alef, Corporate Senior Vice President and Head, Human Resources, First Chicago Corporation:

> "All of our HR programs serve the bank's mission. If they didn't, we wouldn't have them. In the last five years, we've become increasingly a part of the decision-making process at the bank," he says. "We assist with business strategy development by defining the HR implications of those strategies."
>
> "It's much more rewarding," he adds, "to be a thinking participant on the front end of a decision, rather than someone who undoes the damage created by those decisions."[5]

Linking HR to the business is the newest role played by the HR department, and it may be the most important one. One consequence of this role is the increased involvement in the longer-term, strategic directions of the organization. A second consequence is the new emphasis on long-term activities in addition to the more typical medium- and short-term activities. Within these three distinct time horizons, HR departments are really functioning at three levels: strategic, managerial, and operational.

OPERATIONAL LEVEL. At the operational (short-term) level, the HR departments make staffing and recruitment plans, set up day-to-day monitoring sys-

Managing human resources is done on three levels:

- strategic
- managerial
- operational

Operational level means doing short-term, administrative HR activities.

Managerial level means doing medium-term HR activities to help managers and employees.

Strategic level means doing HR activities that focus on long-term needs of the business.

tems, administer wage and salary programs, administer benefits packages, set up annual or less frequent appraisal systems, and set up day-to-day control systems. They also provide for specific job skill training and on-the-job training, fit individuals to specific jobs, and plan career moves.

As the department begins to perform within the business role, these operational-level HR activities also get linked to the business. For example, training programs are explicitly designed to fill specific employee skills needed by the business.

MANAGERIAL LEVEL.   At the managerial (medium-term) level, HR departments validate personnel selection criteria, develop recruitment marketing plans, establish new recruiting markets, set up five-year compensation plans for individuals, and set up benefits packages. They also set up systems that relate current employment conditions and future business potential. They set up assessment centers, establish general management development programs, participate in organizational development, foster self-development, identify career paths, and provide career development services. While these activities could be done in any HR department, when done in a department that is linked with the business, they take on two specific characteristics. For one, the formulating process is different—here the department begins with an assessment of what is needed by the business. The types of leaders and managers needed to successfully drive the business are then identified before the assessment center is set up. For another, the content of the human resource activities begins to represent the views of all employees—the managers and nonmanagers, inside and outside the human resource department.

STRATEGIC LEVEL.   At the strategic (longer-term) level, HR departments get involved in broader decisions—those that provide overall direction and vision for the organization. For example, according to Kathryn Connors, Vice President of HR at Liz Claiborne,

> Human resources is part of the strategic planning process. It's part of policy development, line extension planning, and the merger and acquisition processes. Little is done in the company that doesn't involve us in the planning, policy, or finalization stages of any deal.[6]

This process of linking HR to the broader, longer-term needs of firms is the essence of *strategic* human resource management.[7]

Typically, strategic business needs arise from decisions organizations make, such as what products and services to offer and on what basis to compete—quality, cost, or innovation, or for purposes of survival, growth, adaptability, and profitability. These decisions are associated with the formulation and implementation of the organization's strategy, so they are likely to reflect characteristics of the external and internal environments. The internal environment includes the nature of the business (that is, manufacturing or service), top management's goals and values, organizational size, current and desired levels of profitability, technology, structure, and the life cycle of the business. Characteristics in the external environment that have an impact on organizational strategy include the basis upon which competitive battles are being won in the industry (for example, cost, quality, innovation); the life cycle of the industry; social, legal, political, and cultural factors; economic conditions; scope and degree of competition; labor pool attributes; and customers. These are the focus of Chapter 3.

Together these aspects of the environment influence an organization's broader, longer-term, strategic needs and even its mission statement. In turn, the aspiration statement at Levi Strauss, which indicates how the firm will manage its human resources, is closely linked with the mission statement of the firm. Both of these are shown in Exhibit 2.2.

Thus, as HR departments begin to link their activities to the business, they must become knowledgeable in all these aspects of the environment; they must become strategic players. This not only helps link HR to the strategic level, but it also provides the necessary knowledge and confidence that allows this role to be played in a proactive manner, rather than in a reactive manner. Of course, it also helps HR departments to play the enabler role much more effectively.

Levi Strauss's Aspiration Statement is its HR philosophy showing how important human resources are to the company.

EXHIBIT 2.2
ASPIRATION STATEMENT

We all want a Company that our people are proud of and committed to, where all employees have an opportunity to contribute, learn, grow and advance based on merit, not politics or background. We want our people to feel respected, treated fairly, listened to and involved. Above all, we want satisfaction from accomplishments and friendships, balanced personal and professional lives, and to have fun in our endeavors.

When we describe the kind of LS&CO. we want in the future, what we are talking about is building on the foundation we have inherited: affirming the best of our Company's traditions, closing gaps that may exist between principles and practices, and updating some of our values to reflect contemporary circumstances.

What Type of Leadership Is Necessary To Make Our Aspirations a Reality?

New Behaviors: Leadership that exemplifies directness, openness to influence, commitment to the success of others, willingness to acknowledge our own contributions to problems, personal accountability, teamwork and trust. Not only must we model these behaviors, but we must coach others to adopt them.

Diversity: Leadership that values a diverse work force (age, sex, ethnic group, etc.) at all levels of the organization, diversity in experience, and a diversity in perspectives. We have committed to taking full advantage of the rich backgrounds and abilities of all our people and to promote a greater diversity in positions of influence. Differing points of view will be sought: diversity will be valued and honesty rewarded, not suppressed.

Recognition: Leadership that provides greater recognition—both financial and psychic—for individuals and teams that contribute to our success. Recognition must be given to all who contribute: those who create and innovate and also those who continually support the day-to-day business requirements.

Ethical Management Practices: Leadership that epitomizes the stated standards of ethical behavior. We must provide clarity about our expectations and must enforce these standards through the corporation.

Communications: Leadership that is clear about Company, unit, and individual goals and performance. People must know what is expected of them and receive timely, honest feedback on their performance and career aspirations.

Empowerment: Leadership that increases the authority and responsibility of those closest to our products and customers. By actively pushing responsibility, trust and recognition into the organization, we can harness and release the capabilities of all our people.

Mission Statement

The mission of Levi Strauss & Co. is to sustain profitable and responsible commercial success by marketing jeans and selected casual apparel under the Levi's brand.

We must balance goals of superior profitability and return on investment, leadership market positions, and superior products and service. We will conduct our business ethically and demonstrate leadership in satisfying our responsibilities to our communities and to society. Our work environment will be safe and productive and characterized by fair treatment, teamwork, open communications, personal accountability and opportunities for growth and development.

SOURCE: J. L. Laabs, "HR's Vital Role at Levi Strauss," *Personnel Journal* (Dec. 1992): 38. Used by permission.

In the enabler role, HR helps line managers fulfill their people responsibilities.

Customerization means viewing everybody, whether internal or external to the organization, as a customer and then putting that customer first.

We exist because of customers. They are our *raison d' etre.*

Michael Mitchell, Vice-President of Human Resources, Swiss Bank Corporation

Benchmarking is a structured approach for looking outside an organization and adapting the best practices to complement internal operations with creative, new ideas.

In the monitoring role, HR tries to ensure a fair and consistent management of the firm's people.

DID YOU KNOW?

The HR departments in most firms monitor human resources by establishing policies and writing "Employee Handbooks" that inform everyone about company HR policies, procedures, benefits, and discipline.

THE ENABLER ROLE

In reality, human resource programs succeed because line managers make them succeed. The department's bread-and-butter job, therefore, is to enable line managers to make things happen. Thus, in the more traditional activities—such as selecting, interviewing, training, evaluating, rewarding, counseling, promoting, and firing—the HR department is basically providing a service to line managers. In addition, the department administers direct and indirect compensation programs. It also assists line managers by providing information about, and interpretation of, equal employment opportunity legislation and safety and health standards.

To fulfill these responsibilities, the HR department must be accessible, or it will lose touch with the line managers' needs. The HR staff should be as close as possible to the employees. Being accessible and providing services and products to others (customers) is a trend called *customerization.*

CUSTOMERIZATION.   Adding to the HR department's ability to gain strategic involvement are its knowledge of the business, its creative insights into how the organization can be more effective, and its familiarity with, and acceptance by, top management. More and more, these qualities are being found in departments that practice customerization. **Customerization** means viewing everybody, whether internal or external to the organization, as a customer and then putting that customer first. For human resource departments, customers are typically other line and staff managers but increasingly include other organizations and the nonmanagerial employees.

Essential to this philosophy is the realization that all HR departments produce and deliver products and have "customers."[8] So too is the realization that the products provided to satisfy the customer are determined *with* the customer. Together, in partnership, both the customers and the HR representatives themselves determine what is best for the situation. This is exactly the situation at Levi Strauss & Co. under the leadership of Donna Goya.

Another important part of customerization is benchmarking. **Benchmarking** is a structured approach for looking outside an organization to study and adapt the best outside practices to complement internal operations with creative, new ideas. Learning about the practices used by competitors and other companies is of great value. As such, benchmarking usually challenges "business as usual" methods.[9]

THE MONITORING ROLE

Although the HR department may delegate much of the implementation of its activities to line managers, it is still responsible for seeing them implemented fairly and consistently—that is monitoring the outcomes of its programs. This is especially true today because of fair employment legislation. Various state and federal regulations are making increasingly sophisticated demands on organizations. Responses to these regulations is best made by a central group supplied with accurate information, the needed expertise, and the support of top management.

Expertise is also needed for implementing human resource activities such as employee benefit administration. Since HR management experts are costly, organizations hire as few as possible and centralize them as well. Their expertise then filters to other areas of the organization.

In organizations with several locations and several divisions or units, tension often exists between the need to decentralize—or "flatten"—and the need to centralize expertise. (More on this later.) A major trend in this role of monitoring and coordinating development is the use of computer technology and human resource information systems described in Chapter 20.

The Innovator Role

Important and ever-expanding roles for the HR department include providing up-to-date application of current techniques and developing and exploring innovative approaches to personnel problems and concerns. Benchmarking certainly helps in this role.

Today, organizations are asking their human resource departments for innovative approaches and solutions on how to improve productivity and the quality of work life while complying with the law in an environment of high uncertainty, energy conservation, and intense international competition. They are also demanding approaches and solutions that can be justified in dollars and cents. Past approaches don't always make the cut in this environment; innovation is no longer a luxury—it's a necessity.

The Adapter Role

It is increasingly necessary for organizations to adapt new technologies, structures, processes, cultures, and procedures to meet the demands of stiffer competition. Organizations look to the human resource department for the skills to facilitate organizational change and to maintain organizational flexibility and adaptability. One consequence of this adapter role is the need to be more future oriented. For example, as external environments and organizational strategies change, new skills and competencies are needed. To ensure that the right skills and competencies are available at the appropriate time, HR departments must anticipate change. Having a mind-set of continuous change and continuous education, as Motorola has, fosters a flexible and adaptable work force. The HR department can be the role model of change and adaptability.

Flexible Role Model. Human resource departments face the same demands as their organizations. They must continually streamline their operations. Not waiting for mandated cutbacks, they review and evaluate expenses and implement incremental changes to become, and stay, lean. Flexible HR departments aggressively seek to be perceived as "bureaucracy busters," setting an example for other staff functions and line organizations.[10]

How effective the human resource department is in playing all these roles depends on (1) how effective the leader is, (2) how well the department is staffed, and (3) how the department is organized.

Roles for the Leader

For the HR department to perform all these roles effectively, it needs to have a very special leader. The leader must not only be knowledgeable in HR activities, but must also be familiar with the needs of the business and be able to work side by side with line management as a partner. The leader must be well versed in topics such as mergers and acquisitions, productivity, and total quality efforts. Being part of the management team means the HR leader must assume some new key roles. These roles and their criteria for success are illustrated in Exhibit 2.3.

Roles for the Staff

As the HR leader begins to play many of the roles listed in Exhibit 2.3, staff members must recognize this and adapt accordingly. After all, the leader is playing the roles in Exhibit 2.3 because of the need to better link to the business, to be more effective, and to establish a partnership with the employees and the line managers. Just as the department and its leader must change, so must the staff

DID YOU KNOW?

A recent HR innovation at Hewlett-Packard is a work force balancing plan that helps the company avoid layoffs and achieve its no-layoff goals.

In the innovator role, HR identifies and develops new practices and methods for managing people.

To be competitive, HR departments have to be flexible and adaptable.

Roles for the HR leader include being a

- businessperson
- shaper of change
- consultant
- strategy planner
- talent manager
- people asset manager

Roles for the HR staff include being a

- businessperson
- shaper of change
- consultant
- strategy planner
- talent manager
- people asset manager

EXHIBIT 2.3
KEY ROLES FOR THE HR LEADER

KEY ROLE	WHAT'S EXPECTED ON THE JOB
1. Businessperson	• Shows concern for bottom line • Understands how money gets made, lost, and spent • Knows the market and what the business is • Has long-term vision of where business is headed
2. Shaper of change in accordance with the business	• Can execute change in strategy • Can create sense of urgency • Can think conceptually and articulate thoughts • Has sense of purpose—a steadfast focus, a definite value system
3. Consultant to organization/partner to line management	• Has ability to build commitment into action • Responds to organizational needs • Recognizes importance of teamwork • Is capable of relationship building
4. Strategy/business planner	• Knows plan of top executives • Is involved in strategy formulation of executive committee—is not an afterthought • Develops and sells own plans and ideas—able to get needed resources • Has three- to five-year focus
5. Talent manager	• Sees the movement from an emphasis on strictly numbers or bodies needed to the type of talent and skills needed in the organization • Sees the emphasis on talent needed for executing future strategies as opposed to today's needs • Is capable of educating line managers • Knows high-potential people and anticipates their concerns—for example, who is bright but bored?
6. HR asset manager/ cost controller	• Initiates—does not wait for others to call attention to need for action • Can educate and sell line managers • Can creatively measure effectiveness in own areas of responsibility and other areas of organization • Can use automation effectively

SOURCE: Adapted from "How to Develop HR Professionals for Today's Business Environment," *HR Reporter* (Aug. 1987), 6–7. Used by permission.

members. While they may not play the roles listed in Exhibit 2.3 to the same depth as their leader, the staff members still need to know the business, facilitate change, be conscious of costs and benefits, and work with line managers (though this is probably more true for the generalist than the specialist). The HR staff is active at the operational level and the managerial level while the majority of the leader's time is spent at the strategic level with some spent at the managerial level.

STAFFING THE DEPARTMENT

The top human resource leaders and staff members are often expected to be functional experts, capable administrators, business consultants, and problem solvers with global awareness. Management expects the HR staff "to have it all." Administrative skills are also essential for efficiency. Specialized expertise is also important, but particularly in combination with business knowledge and perspective. In flexible organizations, problem-solving and consulting skills are vital in guiding and supporting new management practices.

In effective organizations, managers like the HR staff to work closely with them in solving people-related business challenges. While line managers may best understand their own people, many desire the more distant perspective of HR staff in handling problems. As the HR staff actively builds working relationships with line management, the managers will find it easier to work with them as partners.

How effectively an organization's human resources are managed depends in large part upon the knowledge, skills, and abilities of the people in the human resource department, particularly the HR leader, the HR generalists, and the HR specialists (collectively referred to as HR professionals).

THE HUMAN RESOURCE LEADER

Of course, the most effective person who can head the department is an outstanding performer in the organization with both HR management expertise and line management experience:

> In essence, to be a true professional in many areas of HR management, individuals virtually have to have an advanced degree in the subject and spend full time in that field. Areas like compensation have become incredibly complicated because of their close connection to strategic, legal, financial, and tax matters . . . [But] with the exception of technical specialists, HR managers need to spend a significant amount of time in line management positions. It is not enough for senior HR managers to have worked in different areas of the HR function; they must have had some line business experience so that they have a first-hand familiarity with the business operations.[11]

Line experience gives the HR leader an understanding of the needs of the business and the needs of the department's customers. To prepare potential leaders for this, the department's staff should rotate through various line positions over the course of several years. Short of actually serving as a line manager, such individuals could serve as special assistants to line managers or head up a special task force for a companywide project.

To be effective in playing the roles described in Exhibit 2.3, the leader needs the following knowledge, skills, and abilities (competencies):[12]

- problem-solving skills
- business knowledge/organization sensitivity
- knowledge of compensation techniques that reinforce business plans
- strategic and conceptual skills
- knowledge of succession planning/career planning systems
- acknowledged leadership skills
- ability to analyze data and plan from it

LEARNING OBJECTIVE 3

Describe the various HR professionals in the HR department.

The HR leader needs the knowledge, skills and abilities (competencies) to perform the roles in Exhibit 2.3.

- computer literacy
- competence in HR functional areas
- awareness of financial impacts, particularly in areas such as pension costs, health care, and compensation

While this list of competencies is rather extensive, these will be the ones that effective HR leaders in firms in highly competitive environments will need. Some firms are now adopting procedures to identify competencies for their HR staff:

> At Weyerhaeuser each major division, led by its human resources director, is responsible for developing a list of specific, required competencies. Of course, overlaps occur among major divisions. The HR directors help generate a slate of competencies based on their interviews with the "customers"—others in the organization—and HR professionals, and on their own requirements. The corporation is also aiming to predict future HR issues as a basis for updating human resources stategies and developing future competency requirements for HR staff.

Some ways companies that train their HR professionals to gain these competencies are described in Chapter 14 (see Exhibit 14.5).

HUMAN RESOURCE GENERALISTS

Line management positions are one important source for **human resource generalists.** A brief tour by a line supervisor in an HR staff position, usually as a generalist, conveys the knowledge, language, needs, and requirements of the line in a particularly relevant way. As a result, the HR department can more effectively fill its roles. Another source of generalist talent is the nonmanagerial employee. Like line managers, these people bring with them information about employee needs and attitudes.

Some companies assign line managers to work in the corporate HR department for two or three years as a part of their career development. Indeed, in the IBM/Towers Perrin survey, having experience in HR is seen as critical for the careers of line managers—at least, this is what the results indicate for the year 2000. Currently the story is a bit different. In 1991, as shown in Exhibit 2.4, only 25 percent of the CEOs and line managers identify the HR experience as critical for a line manager. However, fully 65 percent said it would be critical in the year 2000. This latter result certainly fits the criteria for potential CEOs in the year 2000, also. According to a major worldwide survey conducted by the Korn Ferry consulting firm and the Columbia Business School and referred to in Chapter 1, knowledge and skill in HR management is seen as second in importance for CEOs, right behind skill and knowledge in strategy formulation. These results are shown in Exhibit 2.5. A position as a generalist is a good place to gain such expertise.

Generalists should possess many of the same qualities as human resource specialists, but the generalist's level of expertise in a human resource specialty will usually not be as great. After serving as a nonmanagerial generalist, the next job might be to manage a human resource activity or even one of the firm's field locations. Whereas the former may result in specialization, fieldwork is likely to result in a broadening of one's experience.

HUMAN RESOURCE SPECIALISTS

Human resource specialists should have skills related to a particular specialty, an awareness of the relationship of that specialty to other HR activities, and a knowledge of where the specialized activity fits in the organization. Since specialists may work at almost any human resource activity, qualified applicants can

Generalists are capable of performing several HR activities.

Specialists are capable of performing one HR activity to the last detail.

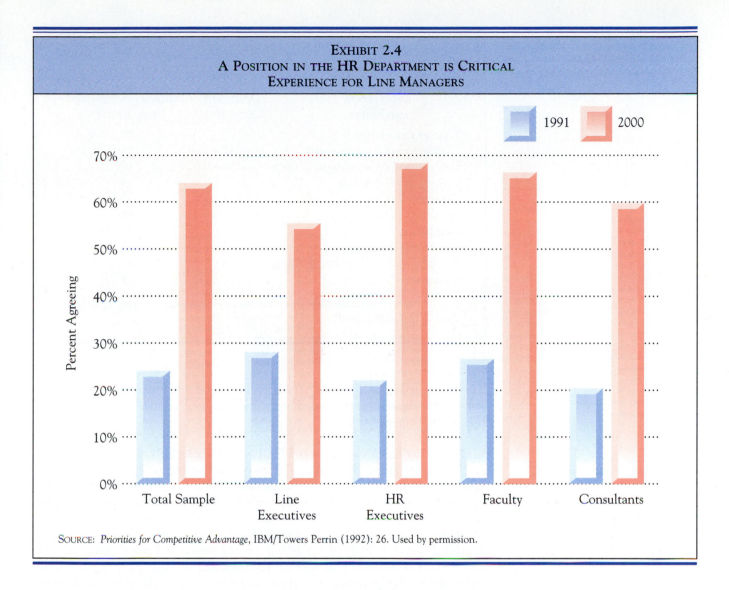

EXHIBIT 2.4
A POSITION IN THE HR DEPARTMENT IS CRITICAL EXPERIENCE FOR LINE MANAGERS

SOURCE: *Priorities for Competitive Advantage*, IBM/Towers Perrin (1992): 26. Used by permission.

come from specialized programs in law, organizational and industrial psychology, labor and industrial relations, HR management, counseling, organizational development, and medical and health science. In addition, specialists are needed in the newer areas of total quality management, service technologies, behavioral performance improvement systems, and organizational change and design.

With the increases in regulatory requirements and the levels of expertise needed to deal with complex HR activities, some organizations have moved away from generalists and now rely more on specialists. However, under pressure to better serve the customer, other organizations are finding they still need generalists. Both are valuable, and both reflect this profession's drive to ever-increasing standards of excellence.

ORGANIZING THE DEPARTMENT

In organizing the HR department, two major questions need to be addressed:

1. Where are the HR decisions made?
2. What alternatives does the company have?

43

EXHIBIT 2.5
WHAT TRAITS CEOS HAVE—AND WILL NEED

KNOWLEDGE AND SKILLS	DOMINANT NOW (%)	IMPORTANT IN THE YEAR 2000 (%)
Strategy formulation	68	78
Human resource management	41	53
International economics and politics	10	19
Science and technology	11	15
Computer literacy	3	7
Marketing and sales	50	48
Negotiation	34	24
Accounting and finance	33	24
Handling media and public speaking	16	13
Production	21	9

SOURCE: "What Traits CEOs Have—and Will Need," *Fortune* (May 22, 1989), 57. © 1989 Time Inc. All rights reserved.

The first question has to do with the advantages and disadvantages of centralized and decentralized organizations. The second question has to do with the issue of budgets and compensation.

CENTRALIZATION VERSUS DECENTRALIZATION

Centralization means that essential decision making and policy formulation are conducted at one location (at headquarters); **decentralization** means that the essential decision making and policy formulation are conducted at several locations (in various divisions or departments of the organization).

Centralization means that essential decision making and policy formulation are organized and done at one location. *Decentralization* means that these activities are organized and done at several locations.

How HR departments are organized differs widely from one company to another not only because of the differing requirements of various industries, but also because of differing philosophies, cultures, and strategic plans of individual organizations. For purposes of illustration, let us compare the centralized structure of Merck with the decentralized structure of TRW.

In the centralized HR structure of Merck, large specialized corporate staffs formulate and design human resource strategies and activities. These are then communicated to the small HR staffs of operating units for implementation. High consistency and congruence with corporate goals are thus attained. In the decentralized model of TRW, small corporate staffs only manage the HR systems for executives and only act as advisors to operating units. Here there tends to be wider divergence in practices and a greater flexibility in addressing local concerns.[14]

Looking at the nature of the businesses of Merck and TRW, it is apparent that the organizational structures they use are very appropriate for their respective types of business. TRW, a high-technology company with a diverse array of businesses, cannot use the consistent, stable approach to HR that Merck, with a more singular product focus, is able to use.[15]

Because of the rapidly changing and highly competitive environment, the trend seems to be toward greater decentralization. This entails a greater delegation of responsibilities to lower HR levels and to the operating units and line managers themselves. Along with this is the trend toward less formalization of policies—that is, fewer rules that are seen as bureaucratic hurdles. Human resource departments and their organizations thus have greater flexibility to cope with the continually changing environment. Diminished bureaucratization can also lead to a greater openness in approaches to problems. Of course, some activities such as fair employment issues and compensation matters may have to be centralized because of legal requirements and for the sake of consistency. Nevertheless, the general trend is for less formalization and less centralization. Thus we see firms such as Levi Strauss & Co. developing broad policy statements. Local units then develop HR practices that are tailored to specific needs and yet consistent with overall company philosophy.

THE BUDGET AS AN ORGANIZATIONAL FORCE

The amount of money that organizations allocate to their HR departments continues to rise yearly. For example, the average per-employee costs allocated to the human resource department rose from $697 in 1990 to $863 in 1991. The median 1991 expenditure for this function was much lower among manufacturing companies ($563,671) than nonmanufacturing companies ($765,842). Not surprisingly, total department expenditures increase steadily with company size. Firms with fewer than 250 employees recorded a median expenditure of $194,173 in 1991, compared with $355,136 in companies with 250 to 499 employees; $532,780 among employers with 500 to 999 employees; $856, 180 in organizations with 1,000 to 2,499 workers; and over $2.4 million among firms with 2,500 or more employees. However, per capita expenditures for HR activities and staffs decline as the size of the work force increases. ($1,348 per employee for the smallest firms and $478 per employee for the largest firms).[16]

For all firms, the median ratio of HR department staff to the work force currently is 1.1 staff member for every 100 workers. Among firms with fewer than 250 employees, the median ratio is 1.7 staff per 100 workers and among companies with 250 to 499 employees it is 1.2 per 100 employees. Ratios of HR staff to total employment are substantially lower in organizations with 500 to 2,499 employees (0.8 per 100), and lowest among employers with 2,500 or more workers (0.6 per 100).[17]

COMPENSATION AS AN ORGANIZATIONAL FORCE

Human resource management is becoming very attractive as a field of employment. The results of a recent compensation survey, along with the types of jobs in a human resource department, are shown in Exhibit 2.6. In that survey, salaries were generally higher for those individuals in larger organizations, for those with more experience, and for those with more education. In addition, salaries were higher in the Northeast. The corporate HR director (sometimes called senior vice-president) was the most highly paid in the survey, of course, earning an average of more than $350,000 (including salary plus cash bonus and profit sharing)![18]

As shown in Exhibit 2.6, there are many jobs in HR departments!

GLOBALIZATION

The globalization of world markets is inevitable. More and more firms are moving operations outside their domestic borders. The last two decades in particular have seen dramatic changes in international trade and business. Once safe markets are now fierce battlegrounds where firms aggressively fight for market share against both foreign and domestic competitors. It is, therefore, not surprising to find that, in an increasing number of firms, a large proportion of the work force is located in other countries. For example,

LEARNING OBJECTIVE 4

Tell how an HR department changes when it becomes international.

EXHIBIT 2.6
AVERAGE EARNINGS* IN HUMAN RESOURCE MANAGEMENT

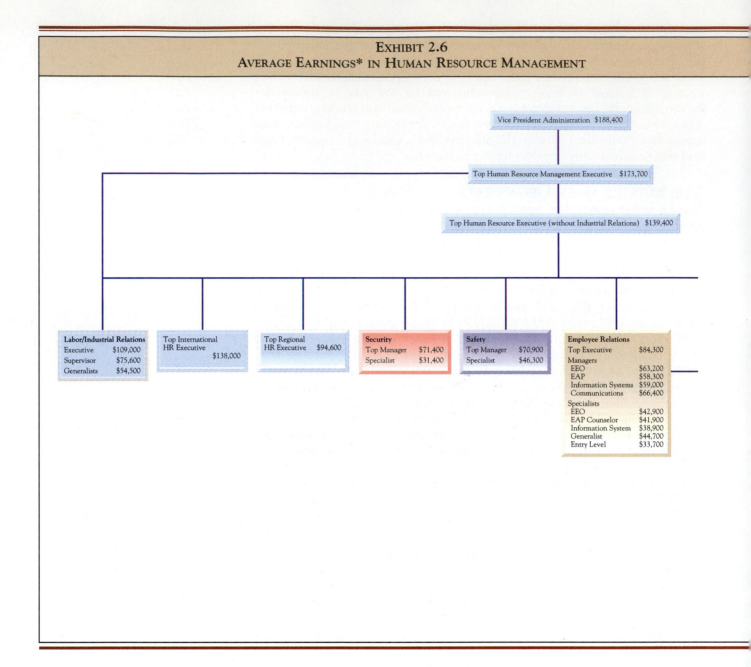

Vice President Administration $188,400

Top Human Resource Management Executive $173,700

Top Human Resource Executive (without Industrial Relations) $139,400

Labor/Industrial Relations
Executive	$109,000
Supervisor	$75,600
Generalists	$54,500

Top International HR Executive $138,000

Top Regional HR Executive $94,600

Security
Top Manager	$71,400
Specialist	$31,400

Safety
Top Manager	$70,900
Specialist	$46,300

Employee Relations
Top Executive	$84,300
Managers	
EEO	$63,200
EAP	$58,300
Information Systems	$59,000
Communications	$66,400
Specialists	
EEO	$42,900
EAP Counselor	$41,900
Information System	$38,900
Generalist	$44,700
Entry Level	$33,700

For all practical purposes, all business today is global. Those individual businesses, firms, and industries, and whole societies that clearly understand the new rules in a world economy will prosper; those that do not will perish.

Ian Mitroff, Professor of Management, University of Southern California

- The Ford Motor Company has half its employees outside the United States.
- Philips has three-fourths of its employees working outside The Netherlands.
- More than half of Matsushita Electric's employees are outside Japan.
- Just over half of Ericsson's staff work outside Sweden.

These trends are likely to continue throughout the 1990s as employers increasingly reach across borders to find the skills they need. The multicultural work force is beginning to slowly percolate to the top echelons of the management of multinationals as well: Unilever headquarters staff includes 30 different nationalities, and Du Pont appointed its first non-American president in 1991.

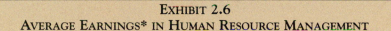

EXHIBIT 2.6
AVERAGE EARNINGS* IN HUMAN RESOURCE MANAGEMENT

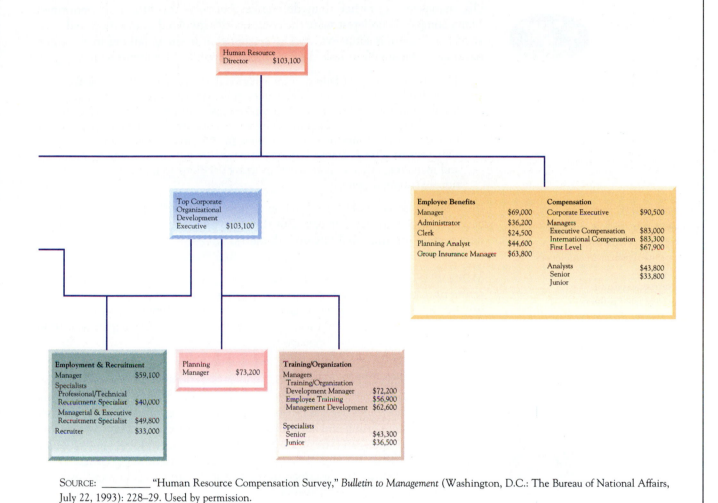

| Human Resource Director | $103,100 |

Top Corporate Organizational Development Executive $103,100

Employee Benefits		Compensation	
Manager	$69,000	Corporate Executive	$90,500
Administrator	$36,200	Managers	
Clerk	$24,500	Executive Compensation	$83,000
Planning Analyst	$44,600	International Compensation	$83,300
Group Insurance Manager	$63,800	First Level	$67,900
		Analysts	
		Senior	$43,800
		Junior	$33,800

Employment & Recruitment
Manager	$59,100
Specialists	
Professional/Technical Recruitment Specialist	$40,000
Managerial & Executive Recruitment Specialist	$49,800
Recruiter	$33,000

| Planning Manager | $73,200 |

Training/Organization
Managers	
Training/Organization Development Manager	$72,200
Employee Training	$56,900
Management Development	$62,600
Specialists	
Senior	$43,300
Junior	$36,500

SOURCE: _____ "Human Resource Compensation Survey," *Bulletin to Management* (Washington, D.C.: The Bureau of National Affairs, July 22, 1993): 228–29. Used by permission.

Globalization is forcing managers to grapple with complex issues as they seek to gain or sustain a competitive advantage. Faced with unprecedented levels of foreign competition at home and abroad, firms are beginning to recognize that not only is international business high on the list of priorities for top management, but finding and nurturing the human resources required to implement an international or global strategy is also of critical importance. Thus effective HR management is essential, especially for small- and medium-sized firms, where international expansion places extra stress on the limited pool of people. As Duerr points out;

> Virtually any type of international problem, in the final analysis, is either created by people or must be solved by people. Hence, having the right people in the right place at the right time emerges as the key to a company's interna-

tional growth. If we are successful in solving that problem, I am confident we can cope with all others.[19]

ACROSS COUNTRIES

The complexities of operating in different countries and of employing different nationalities are the main factors that differentiate domestic and international HR management, rather than differences between the functions performed. Many companies underestimate the complexities involved in international operations, and there is some evidence to suggest that business failures in the international arena are often linked to poor management of human resources.

> The primary causes of failure in multinational ventures stem from a lack of understanding of the essential differences in managing human resources, at all levels, in foreign environments. Certain management philosophies and techniques have proved successful in the domestic environment: their application in a foreign environment too often leads to frustration, failure, and underachievement. These "human" considerations are as important as the financial and marketing criteria upon which so many decisions to undertake multinational ventures depend.[20]

International HR operations have

- **more functions and activities**
- **a broader perspective**
- **more involvement in employees' lives**
- **more risk exposure**
- **more external influences**

Increasingly, domestic HR is taking on an international flavor as the work force becomes more and more diverse. But there *are* differences. The following issues differentiate international HR from domestic HR.

MORE FUNCTIONS AND ACTIVITIES. To operate in an international environment, the HR department must engage in a number of activities that would not be necessary in a domestic environment: international taxation, international relocation and orientation, administrative services for expatriates, host government relations, and language translation services.

BROADER PERSPECTIVE. Domestic managers generally administer programs for a single national group of employees who are covered by a uniform compensation policy and who are taxed by one government. International managers face the problem of designing and administering programs for more than one national group of employees, and they must therefore take a more global view of issues. This is exactly what is being done at Baxter, an international pharmaceutical company. Its activities are described in the feature "Managing Human Resources at Baxter: Managing Global Diversity."

MORE INVOLVEMENT IN EMPLOYEES' LIVES. A greater degree of involvement in employees' personal lives is necessary for the selection, training, and effective management of expatriate employees. The international HR department needs to ensure that the expatriate employee understands housing arrangements, health care, and all aspects of the compensation package provided for the assignment.

RISK EXPOSURE. Frequently, the human and financial consequences of failure in the international arena are more severe than in domestic business. For example, expatriate failure (the premature return of an expatriate from an international assignment) is a persistent, high-cost problem for international companies. Another aspect of risk exposure that is relevant to international HR is terrorism. Major multinational companies must now routinely consider this factor when planning international meetings and assignments.

BAXTER is approaching its growing international business with the same people-awareness that it used to successfully manage its merger with American Hospital Supply Corp. "We do business in 100 countries, and over one-third of our revenue comes from overseas," said Tony Rucci, senior vice president of human resource. "And that percentage is growing. As a result, we've made managing diversity a long range corporate goal.

"We define 'diversity' differently than most companies," said Rucci. "We look at it as 'what does it mean to do business in different countries around the world,' not just as 'how will we work with women and minorities?'

"As global marketers, we need to be sensitive to different cultural values around the world. As an example, we often think of Gemany's culture as not that different from ours. But when we marketed our disposable surgical drapes and gowns in Germany, they just didn't sell. Why? Because in Germany there's a cultural norm against throwing things away. So a concept that made a lot of sense in the U.S. couldn't be translated there. We've learned from these experiences that we can't anticipate everything. To function well globally we are going to have to have a diverse range of opinion within our own company.

"We are approaching this with the same seriousness we used to implement our merger, and with many of the same values and techniques. We have established three corporate task forces to work on the diversity issue. Each addresses one of these issues:

- How should senior management send a visible commitment to this issue?
- Awareness and training: How can we broaden our company's perspective? How extensive and how deep should the training be?
- How do we identify, promote, and develop a more diverse pool of talent globally?

"Each of the top 27 officers of the company serves on one of these task forces—9 staff officers and 18 line officers. I'm on the third one myself. What we're looking for is five or six actionable things to do so that five years from now we really do have a more diverse work force. One of the things we're starting to do now is rotate managers in our foreign subsidiaries more actively with our U.S. people. We're bringing more European managers here, as well as rotating them within Europe. And we're sending more U.S. people overseas. With the European market opening up in 1992, we think this is even more important.

"Aside from the task force activities, we're giving the process an extra push by building diversity goals into our compensation and performance appraisal systems. Like everything else, we've made sure there's commitment from the top. One of the CEO's major objectives (one of four or five) is to promote work force diversity. Each of the top 100 officers, including the CEO, has a major portion of his or her bonus dependent on meeting diversity objectives. These objectives vary depending on the person's job, but every manager has at least one.

"We're not where we want to be yet. But we are making progress. As our people get more experience with diverse cultures, they are gaining more awareness. I think we've progressed to the point where at least people 'know they don't know.' They know that in another culture, they have to challenge everything they think is the right way to get something done. They know they can't rely on their intuition the way they used to be able to do at home."[21]

MORE EXTERNAL INFLUENCES. Other factors that influence the international arena are the type of host government, the state of its economy, and business practices that may differ substantially from those of the originating country. A host government can, for example, dictate hiring procedures, as was the case in the late 1970s in Malaysia. The government required that foreign firms comply with what became known as the "30:30:30 Rule,"—that is, that 30 percent of employees be indigenous Malay, 30 percent Chinese Malays, and 30 percent Indian Malays, at all levels of the organization with monthly statistics required to corroborate this.

ACROSS CULTURES

Another variable that heavily impacts HR activities in the international arena is the widely differing cultural mores of the world—the cultural environment.

Culture here means that members of a group share a distinct way of life with common values, attitudes, and behaviors that are transmitted over time in a gradual, yet dynamic process.

THE CULTURAL ENVIRONMENT.   There are many definitions of **culture,** but they all in some way describe a "shaping" process. That is members of a group or society share a distinct way of life with common values, attitudes, and behaviors that are transmitted over time in a gradual, yet dynamic, process.

> A person is not born with a given culture; rather she or he acquires it through the socialization process that begins at birth. An American is not born with a liking for hot dogs, or a German with a natural preference for beer; these behavioral attributes are culturally transmitted.[22]

Culture is so subtle a process that we are not always conscious of its effect on values, attitudes, and behaviors. We usually have to be confronted with a different culture in order to fully appreciate this effect. Anyone traveling abroad, either as a tourist or businessperson, experiences situations that demonstrate cultural differences in language, food, dress, hygiene, and attitude to time. While the traveler can perceive these differences as novel, even enjoyable, for people required to live and work in a new country, such differences can prove difficult. They experience **culture shock**—a phenomenon experienced by people who move across cultures. The new environment requires many adjustments in a relatively short period of time, challenging the person's frame of reference to such an extent that his or her sense of self, especially in terms of nationality, comes into question. The person, in effect, reacts with shock to new cultural experiences. This causes psychological disorientation because he or she misunderstands or does not recognize the cues. Culture shock can lead to negative feelings about the host country and its people and a longing to return home.[23]

Culture shock is the reaction to new cultural experiences that causes psychological disorientation.

THE IMPORTANCE OF CULTURAL AWARENESS.   It is now generally recognized that culturally insensitive attitudes and behaviors stemming from ignorance or from misguided beliefs ("my way is best," or "what works at home will work here") not only are inappropriate, but often cause international business failure. Therefore, an awareness of cultural differences is essential for the HR manager. Activities such as hiring, promoting, rewarding, and dismissal will be determined by the practices of the host country and are often based on a value system peculiar to that country's culture. A firm may decide to head up a new overseas operation with an expatriate general manager, but appoint a local, a person who is familiar with the host country's HR practices, as the department manager. This practice can cause problems, though, for the expatriate general manager, as happened to an Australian who was in charge of a new mining venture in Indonesia. The local responsible for recruitment could not understand why the Australian was upset to find that he had hired most of his extended family rather than staff with the required technical competence. The Indonesian was simply ensuring that his duty to his family was fulfilled—since he was in a position to employ most of them, he was obligated to do so. The Australian, however, interpreted the Indonesian's actions as nepotism, a negative practice according to his own value system.[24]

Here is an example of the fallacy of assuming "what works at home will work here" when dealing with work situations in another culture.[25] The HR staff of a large organization in Papua New Guinea were concerned over a number of accidents involving operators of very large, expensive, earth-moving vehicles. The expatriate managers investigating the accidents found that local drivers involved in the accidents were chewing betel nut, a common habit for most of the coastal peoples of Papua New Guinea and other Pacific islands. Associating the betel nut with depressants such as alcohol, the expatriate managers banned the chewing of betel nut during work hours. In another move to reduce the number of accidents, free coffee was provided at loading points, and drivers were forced to alight from their vehicles at these locations. What the managers did not realize was that betel nut, like their culturally acceptable coffee, is, in fact a stimulant, though some of the drivers were chewing it to cover up the fact that they had had a few beers before commencing work. Many indigenous workers used betel nut as a pick-me-up in much the same way as the expatriates used coffee!

Adjusting to a new cultural environment can also cause problems not only for the expatriate employee, but also for the accompanying spouse and family members. Coping with cultural differences is a constant challenge for the international manager. Preparing expatriates and their families for the cultural environment they will encounter is now a key activity for HR departments in those international firms that appreciate (or have been forced, through experience, to appreciate) the impact that the cultural environment can have on staff performance and well-being.

CURRENT TRENDS

BECOMING A WORLD-CLASS DEPARTMENT
Human resource departments and professionals alike are striving for world-class competency. Many of the firms mentioned in this book certainly have world-class HR departments, and this basically means that they are

- Relating HR to the needs of the business
- Seen as a business unit within the firm (operating in the same way as other units—having customers, doing benchmarking, etc.)
- Organized in a way that brings maximum service to the customer and maximum motivation to the HR staff
- Making the best HR products available for the customers
- Implementing HR programs that fulfill the agendas of the HR group and the customers
- Actively sharing an HR vision with the entire group
- Being a proactive group
- Involved in key business discussions
- Seen as a great place to work and as a model of a great organization

Because doing all these things is not necessarily easy, many firms choose not to do them; some departments may say their companies are not big enough or global enough. While this may be true, their competitors couldn't care less. The way things are today, the world is the playing field for *all* companies. However, those firms that do strive for world-class competency usually capture the competitive advantage and find that their ability to survive and grow, to be adaptable and

Trends in the HR department include:

- **striving to become world-class**
- **re-engineering**
- **creating HR mission statements**

Re-engineering means taking a look at what the HR department is doing to see whether it can be done better.

An *HR mission statement* is a general statement, developed with the participation of all concerned, that describes the values, objectives and goals of the HR department.

profitable increases. Those HR departments that are choosing to be world-class face many challenging but exciting demands on their talents.

RE-ENGINEERING

Re-engineering the HR department basically means taking a look at what the department is doing to see whether it can be done better and more effectively.[26] Customerization is certainly consistent with re-engineering because it asks, What are we doing for our customers, what do they want, and how can we fill in the gaps between what they get and what they want? Re-engineering, however, while including this, goes much further. It seeks to examine all the parts of the department with these questions in mind: What is the purpose of this group, what and how does it do its jobs, and can it be done better, more effectively? As in customerization, benchmarking can be used to ensure that, in the interest of continual improvement, the best available HR practices and activities are obtained. Partnership, mentioned in Chapter 1, is often a result of re-engineering. The end product of such an endeavor is often a more effective department that better serves and involves the employees. Consequently, re-engineering is likely to grow in significance during the remainder of the 1990s.

CREATING MISSION STATEMENTS

The aspiration statement of Levi Strauss & Co. (Exhibit 2.2) is typical of what is happening in firms that have HR departments dedicated to doing the best job possible. They create an HR philosophy indicating how important people are to the firm (there is more discussion on the HR philosophy in Chapter 3 under Corporate Culture). Then the HR departments take the next step: they create an HR mission statement for the department. An **HR mission statement** is a general statement, developed with the participation of all concerned, that describes the values, objectives, and goals of the HR department. Mission statements can also be made by companies (such as Levi Strauss shown in Exhibit 2.2) that describe the values, objectives and goals of the entire company. While HR mission statements may seem to the outsider to be mere platitudes, they are anything but. Often the significance of the mission statement lies in the process by which it is created. If the HR mission statement is created in a highly participatory process—that is, where all the employees, line managers, and HR staff are involved, and where the public discussion brings clarity, understanding, and commitment—then the end result is not merely a piece of paper, but a new atmosphere of partnership within the company. Everyone has a basis that they have created together upon which they can evaluate the nature and quality of

---

EXHIBIT 2.7
THE SWISS BANK CORPORATION HR MISSION STATEMENT

OUR MISSION IS TO
- Provide quality, innovative, and sensitive human resource products and services that meaningfully support the needs and vitality of our organization and its employees.
- Create a business strategy for our function that challenges the limitations of the HR practice and provides the potential for us to become a successful business enterprise in our own right.
- Be the best at who we are and what we do.

the practices that are developed. These types of HR mission statements become beacons of understanding and cooperation. They enable firms to develop a crucial consistency in HR philosophies, policies, and practices as discussed in Chapter 1. It is this consistency that in turn enables human resource management to positively influence the bottom line of the organization. Another example of an HR mission statement, this one developed by Mike Mitchell and his HR team at the Swiss Bank Corporation, is shown in Exhibit 2.7. This was one product from the HR department described in our end of chapter case: "Bringing the Human Resource Department to the Business."

SUMMARY

Because of the increasing complexity of human resource management, nearly all organizations have established an HR department. Not all of these departments, however, perform all the activities discussed in Chapter 1. A department's activities—and the way it performs them—depend greatly on the roles the department plays in the organization. Organizations that are most concerned with HR management allow their departments to perform the business role as well as the roles of enabler, monitor, innovator, and adapter. When this occurs, the departments are able to link their activities to the business and demonstrate their value to their organizations by showing how their activities influence productivity, quality of working, life, competitive advantage, adaptability, and legal compliance—all goals associated with the organization's bottom line, shown in Exhibit 1.2.

For each of the human resource activities described in Chapter 1, departments can choose from many human resource practices. For example, in performance-based pay, human resource departments may choose to use a merit pay plan or profit-sharing plan. In addition to being familiar with all the human resource practices, human resource departments need to know which ones to use depending upon the needs of the business. Thus, human resource departments need to be staffed with individuals who are aware of all the human resource activities and practices and have a knowledge and appreciation of the business. They should also be knowledgable about the goals and roles of human resource management in organizations.

Human resource professionals also need to be knowledgeable about the issues of globalization. By going global, companies create many additional challenges for the HR department, what with radically differing employment laws in countries around the world to say nothing of subtle and opaque cultural differences that affect HR management. The knowledge needed to deal with these challenges can be gained through understanding the environment in which firms operate today. Thus, this is the focus of Chapter 3.

KEY CONCEPTS

benchmarking	HR mission statements	human resource
centralization	human resource	specialists
culture	department	managerial level
culture shock	human resource	operational level
customerization	generalists	re-engineering
decentralization	human resource roles	strategic level

REVIEW AND DISCUSSION QUESTIONS

1. How does Levi Strauss & Co. link its HR department to the needs of the business?
2. Why is the HR department seen as critical to the success of organizations? Do line managers and HR managers agree on this?
3. What roles can the human resource department play in an organization? How are the basic activities related to these roles?
4. What types of HR issues are faced at the operational, managerial and strategic levels?
5. What can HR departments gain from customerization?
6. Describe the process of benchmarking and how it can be used by HR departments.
7. What are the roles for the HR leader and the staff?
8. Distinguish between generalists and specialists.
9. Why are some human resource management departments centralized while others are decentralized?
10. What is the purpose of HR mission statements?

EXERCISES AND CASES

FIELD PROJECT

Make appointments and visit local companies (even the college) to interview a line manager and the human resource manager about their views of the HR department in the organization. It is best if these interviews are done separately. The human resource manager can probably arrange the interview with a line manager. Interview your working parents to solicit their opinions of HR management and of the role it plays in the companies in which they work.

CASE

BRINGING THE HUMAN RESOURCE DEPARTMENT TO THE BUSINESS

Mike Mitchell left the Bank of Montreal to become vice president of personnel at the North American branch of the Swiss Bank Corporation (SBC) in the autumn of 1986. It was a move up for him in terms of status, responsibility, monetary compensation, and challenge. Of these, it was the challenge that was most intriguing to Mitchell.

In his mid-30s, he saw this as perfect time to take a risk in his career. He realized that if he succeeded he would establish a prototype that could be marketed to other firms. In addition, success could lead to further career opportunities (and challenges). While he had a general idea of what he wanted to do and had gotten verbal support from his superiors, the senior vice president of personnel and the president of SBC, NA, the details of exactly what he was going to do and how he was going to do it, remained for him to decide.

In 1985, the parent company of SBC (a $110 billion universal bank) headquartered in Basel, Switzerland, decided it needed a clearer statement of its intentions to better focus its energies and resources in light of growing international competition. Accordingly, it crafted a vision (mission) statement to the effect that the bank was going to better serve its customers with high-quality products that catered customers' needs rather than just those of the institution. While the North American operation was relatively autonomous, it was still expected to embrace this vision. The details of its implementation, however, were in local hands. For the personnel side, the hands were those of Mike Mitchell.

Although Mitchell had spent some time in personnel at the Bank of Montreal in New York, the bulk of his work experience was as an entrepreneur in Montreal, Canada. It was this experience that impacted his thinking the most. Thus when he came to the SBC, his self-image was that of a business person who happened to be working in personnel. It was in part because of this image that his stay at the Bank of Montreal was brief: personnel was still a bit too conservative for his style. Too many of his ideas "just couldn't be done." In interviewing with the top managers at SBC, however, they warned him of the same general environment. He thus knew he would have to go slow to change the attitudes of almost 1,000 employees including those of his own department of 10 employees, but he really didn't know what this meant.

CASE QUESTIONS

1. Who are the customers of Mitchel and his HR staff?
2. Do you think that the line managers will cooperate with Mitchell and his staff? What will it take to see that they do? What would be their reasons for resisting a partnership with the HR department?
3. Develop a matrix with projects, dates, milestones and people involved (i.e., HR, line managers and employees) for Mitchell and his staff.

SOURCE: This case was prepared by Randall S. Schuler who expresses his appreciation for the cooperation of Michael Mitchell.

CASE

A BROADER VIEW SEIZES MORE OPPORTUNITIES

Don English, corporate vice president in charge of human resources, is now finally able to take a pause from the ongoing stream of "fire fighting" he has been engaged in since he came to Bancroft ten years ago! Like many of his colleagues in other firms, Don's knowledge of human resource management came as much from doing it as from formal education.

Because of his workload, Don tended to keep pretty narrowly focused, and he rarely read HR journals or attended professional conferences. However, recently, things have been easing up. He has been able to recruit and train almost all the division managers in charge of human resources. It is Don's intention that the newly trained division managers will put out most of the company's "fires," and he will be freed to look at the "big picture." And he has been doing more reading than ever before. Of course, Don has not been totally out of touch with the rest of the world or the growing importance of HR management planning. When he started filling the slots for division HR managers, he made sure that it was a learning experience for him. Don always required job candidates to prepare a one-hour talk on the state of research and practice in different areas of personnel—for example, selection, appraisal, compensation, or training. He would even invite MBA candidates who had no course work in HR and ask them to relate their field of interest to human resource management.

Don is planning to become the chief executive officer of Bancroft or some other firm of similar or larger size within the next five to seven years. He thinks he can achieve this if he remains in human resources and does an outstanding job. He will have to be outstanding by all standards, both internal and external to the firm. From his interviews during the past three years, Don knows that it is imperative to move human resources in a strategic direction while at the same time doing the best possible job with the "nuts and bolts" operational activities.

During a moment of reflection, Don begins to scribble some notes on his large white desk pad. In the middle is Bancroft, a well-established clothing manufacturer. To its left are its suppliers and to its right are its customers. In his head are all the human resource practices he is so familiar with. He has a hunch that there must be a way to use the firm's expertise in performance appraisal and training to help Bancroft be more effective. Bancroft has been learning tremendously from its five-year drive to improve quality, but during the past year, quality gains have slowed. Bancroft must continue to improve its quality to gain and sustain competitive advantage, but large internal quality gains are becoming more and more diffi-

cult as Bancroft climbs the learning curve. Don wonders, How can he help Bancroft experience the excitement of seeing large gains in quality improvement again? Don circles the list of suppliers and begins to formulate a plan that will improve his chances of becoming CEO. He now seeks your advice in exactly what to do and how to go about doing it.

CASE QUESTIONS

1. Is it reasonable for Don and the rest of Bancroft management to think about the suppliers of Bancroft as a source of competitive advantage?
2. Should Don go directly to the Bancroft's suppliers and talk to them or should he work with others in his company such as the person in charge of purchasing or even the CEO?
3. Is there really a place here for the corporate vice president of human resources to help his company gain competitive advantage by working with the suppliers?
4. Can Don become a CEO by being effective in human resources?

This is a useful case to discuss other HR issues, such as the trend in total quality management for firms to have close relationships with their suppliers. Thus we will return to Don in Chapter 15.

© Randall S. Schuler, New York University

ROLE PLAY—DON ENGLISH

You are Don English, corporate vice president of human resources at Bancroft. You have decided to visit the CEO of one of your suppliers, Softstyle. While this is definitely not the way things have been done in the garment industry before, you want to do things differently. After all, you do want to improve things, and you want to be the first to do it. Actually, you think that getting better supplies is absolutely critical to your success in moving Bancroft's line of men's spotswear upscale.

You are planning to visit with Paul Schaller, the CEO of Softstyle, who is uncertain about your visit. Yes, you have told him about your ideas over the phone, but all this is very new to him as well as the industry.

Nevertheless, he is one of your five suppliers of cloth pieces to your Men's Sports Division.

You want to improve the quality and timeliness of Softstyle's shipments to you. Because of your experience at Bancroft, you think that by working on Softstyle's human resource practices, you can improve the business. Of course, it would help your rapport with Paul Schaller if you conveyed an understanding of his business, what your ideas would cost, and what benefits (or lack thereof) he could garner from your approach.

You are now being invited by Paul Schaller to sit down in his office. He only has a few minutes to listen to your presentation.

You are Paul Schaller, CEO of Softstyle, a supplier of cloth pieces to the garment industry. Bancroft is a valued, long-term customer, and you know them rather well. You also know that they want to move their men's sportswear upscale. This means, among other things, better quality fabrics, faster response time to customer demands, and a better understanding of the needs of the customer.

Don English, corporate vice president of human resources at Bancroft, arranged for an appointment to dis-cuss some ideas with you about moving Bancroft's business upscale. You are not entirely sure who he is and what he wants to discuss. Nevertheless, Bancroft is a customer and you want to continue having their business. Consequently, you told him you would be more than happy to give him ten minutes.

Please welcome Don into your office.

NOTES

1. J. L. Laabs, "HR's Vital Role at Levi Strauss," *Personnel Journal* (Dec. 1992): 34.

2. *Ibid.*, 35.

3. *Ibid.*, 43. Also read A. Halcrow, "A Day in the Life of Levi Strauss," *Personnel Journal* (Nov. 1988): 14–15.

4. R. S. Schuler, "Strategic Human Resource Management: Linking the People with the Strategic Needs of the Business," *Organizational Dynamics* (Summer 1992): 18–32.

5. S. Caudron, "Strategic HR at First Chicago," *Personnel Journal* (November 1991): 56. Also see P. Stuart, "HR and Operations Work Together at Texas Instruments," *Personnel Journal* (April 1992): 64–68.

6. S. Lawrence, "Voice of HR Experience," *Personnel Journal* (April 1989): 64.

7. *Ibid.*

8. "Customers for Keeps: Training Strategies," *Bulletin to Management* (31 March 1988): 8. See also R. L. Desatnik, *Managing to Keep the Customers* (San Francisco: Jossey-Bass, 1987).

9. P. Hawken, "The Employee as Customer," *INC.* (Nov. 1987): 21–22; A. Halcrow, "Operation Phoenix: The Business of Human Resources," *Personnel Journal* (Sept. 1987): 92–109; R. S. Schuler and S. E. Jackson, "Customerizing the HR Department," *Personnel Journal* (June 1988): 36–44; R. N. Bramson, "The Secret Weapon in the War for Customers," *HR Magazine* (Jan. 1991): 65–68.

10. J. Walker, "Managing Human Resources in Flat, Lean and Flexible Organizations: Trends for the 1990's," *Human Resource Planning* 11 (1988): 129.

11. E. E. Lawler, III, "Human Resources Management: Meeting the Challenge," *Personnel* (Jan. 1988): 25. See also R. E. Walton and P. R. Lawrence (eds.) *HRM Trends & Challenges* (Cambridge, Mass.: Harvard Business School Press, 1985); W. H. Wagel and H. Z. Levine, "HR '90: Challenges and Opportunities," *Personnel* (June 1990): 18–21.

12. "Roundtable Report," *HR Reporter* (Dec. 1988): 3–6.

13. J. Walker, "What's New in HR Development?" *Personnel* (July 1990): 41.

14. J. Walker, "Human Resources Roles for the '90's," *Human Resource Planning,* 12 (1989): 55.

15. S. Carroll, "HRM Roles and Structures in the Information Age," in R. S. Schuler (ed.), *HRM in the Information Age* (Washington, D.C.: SHRM/BNA, 1991).

16. *Human Resource Compensation Survey* (Dearfield, Ill.: William M. Mercer, Inc., 1993); "Human Resource Compensation Survey," *Bulletin to Management* (July 22, 1993): 228–229.

17. *Ibid.*

18. "The $350,000 HR Director," *Personnel Journal* (June 1993): 18.

19. P. J. Dowling, R. S. Schuler, and D. Welch, *International Dimensions of Human Resource Management,* 2nd ed. (Belmont, Calif.: Wadsworth, 1994).

20. *Ibid.*

21. "Giving and Getting Respect at Baxter," *HR Reporter* (April 1992): 7. Used by permission.

22. Dowling, Schuler & Welch, *International Dimensions . . .*; C. M. Solomon, "Transplanting Corporate Cultures Globally," *Personnel Journal* (Oct. 1993): 78–87.

23. P. R. Harris and R. T. Moran, *Managing Cultural Differences* (Houston, Texas: Gulf, 1979); R. S. Bhagat and S. J. McQuaid, "Role of Subjective Culture in Organization: A Review and Directions for Future Research," *Journal of Applied Psychology* 67 (1982): 653–685.

24. P. J. Dowling, D. E. Welch, and H. DeCieri, "International Joint Ventures: A New Challenge for Human Resource Management," in *Proceedings of the 15th Conference of the European International Business Association*, ed. R. Luostarinen (Helsinki, Finland: Dec. 1989).

25. T. Wyatt, "Understanding Unfamiliar Personnel Problems in Cross-Cultural Work Encounters," *Asia Pacific HRM* 27 (1989): 5–18.

26. T. A. Stewart, "Re-engineering: The Hot New Management Tool," *Fortune* (Aug. 23, 1993): 41–48; M. Hammer and J. Champy, *Re-engineering the Corporation* (New York: Harper-Collins, 1993); C. M. Solomon, "Working Smarter: How HR Can Help," *Personnel Journal* (June 1993): 54–64.

INCREASINGLY, successful management of organizations and the human resources therein depends on knowing what is happening in the environment and also on anticipating what is going to happen. How could you possibly plan your career without knowing what types of jobs may be available in the future and what skills and abilities they will require? To do a great job with your career planning, you have to find out more than just what jobs are available. Similarly, organizations need to analyze a great deal of data in order to deal effectively with critical human resource issues. Organizations have to know as much as they possibly can about the environment.

Gathering and analyzing information from a wide range of sources is necessary for organizational survival and success. In the external environment, organizations look at the events and trends in domestic and international competition; the sizes of, and projections for, the global and domestic population and work force; economic and organizational trends; and the legal environment. Organizations must also understand aspects of the organization itself (the internal environment) that have a big impact on HR management. The internal environment includes such things as the organization's strategy, culture, technology, size, and the goals and values of top management.

As we shall see in Chapter 3, both environments have tremendous implications for human resource management. Fortunately, an extensive data-gathering and analysis capability enables HR professionals to develop plans to deal with these environments.

Planning involves two major activities: (1) planning and forecasting short- and long-term HR requirements, and (2) developing and offering career planning and management activities. Both of these activities are important for the organization and the employees. Today many of the largest and smallest organizations are relating human resource planning to corporate goals and strategies. They recognize the importance of people to an organization's survival. (To complement this discussion and bring home the importance of planning to you, a career planning guide is included in Chapter 4.)

In order to make planning activities as effective as possible, organizations must look closely at the jobs they have—that is, at the design of their jobs. They need to see how jobs can be made more interesting and challenging so employees will be motivated and how jobs can accommodate individual needs—for example, in alternative work schedules. They also need to determine the duties and purposes of jobs and the skills, knowledge, and abilities needed to perform them. This is essential in performing many other human resource management activities. For example, a precise knowledge of the organizations jobs can indicate present and future needs regarding numbers and types of employees. It can help determine how the employees will be obtained (from outside recruiting or internal transfers) and what training needs organization will have. We will look at these activities in Chapters 5 and 6. In these chapters you will be asked to describe your desired job/career in more detail.

SECTION 2

UNDERSTANDING THE ENVIRONMENT AND PLANNING FOR HUMAN RESOURCE NEEDS

CHAPTER 3

UNDERSTANDING EXTERNAL AND INTERNAL ENVIRONMENTS

LEARNING OBJECTIVES

When you have finished studying this chapter, you should be able to:

1. Indicate changes in domestic and international competition affecting human resource management.
2. Describe the tremendous work force and demographic changes and their impact on managing human resources.
3. Describe how economic and organizational trends are impacting how firms manage their human resources.
4. Explain how top management's goals and values, organizational strategy, structure, culture, and technology influence human resource management.

CHAPTER OUTLINE

IT has been more than seven years and $3.5 billion since General Motors Corporation (GM) launched the Saturn Corporation, located in Spring Hill, Tennessee. This people-oriented car manufacturer has enjoyed favorable customer reaction despite limited product availability and two partial recalls. With awards for design and engineering, Saturn has been compared to the Honda Accord, Japan's most popular U.S. model.

Although these accomplishments serve as signs to Saturn executives that the company is doing something right, product-wise, the jury is still out on whether the enterprise is a success. Nevertheless, as former HR executives at Saturn and GM, we think that some lessons have been learned from the start-up of Saturn, especially in the area of people.

SITE SELECTION
WAS AN IMPORTANT PROCESS

A site-selection process that focuses on people issues is as crucial as such financial issues as possible tax abatements, logistics, and transportation costs. The process by which Saturn chose Spring Hill may seem obvious from today's business perspective, but it was unprecedented in the history of GM. The human factors most important to this site selection included:

- Attractiveness or livability of the location, in terms of its beauty, terrain, climate, and recreational opportunities

- Business climate, as reflected in the attitudes and interest shown by local communities, the state government, and its congressional delegation
- Proximity to quality higher-education opportunities, including engineering schools
- Availability of well-established employee-training facilities and resources
- An ambience conducive to creating an innovative business venture

AN INTEGRATED AND ACTIVE HR STRATEGY
WAS VITAL

It's important to recognize that the people-focused process by which Saturn located its first plant wasn't formulated in isolation. Instead, the process arose from an emphasis on participative teamwork, enabling Saturn to construct an HR strategy that was directly connected to the new organization's overall approach to business.

During 1985, Saturn's human resources function—established significantly earlier in the organizational cycle than with many of GM's previous green-field ventures—formed a proactive partnership with its peer departments and the United Auto Workers. This was done so that people issues and participative, collaborative team behavior would be considered to be just as important as engineering, manufacturing, and finance.[1]

The preceding feature illustrates how important the environment is in managing human resources and in running the business. Human resource concerns were very important to Saturn first in locating then in operating their plant. The HR professionals were involved right from the beginning both in the process of site selection and in the earliest stages of long-term business planning. Who else would be better prepared to gather environmental information on education and training facilities in the local area?

The attitude at Saturn is an example of a successful link between HR management and the business as described in the first two chapters. The values and goals of top management are actively influencing the HR management philosophy that Saturn has become known for. Thus are the HR practices in the company being shaped today, including the high levels of employee participation, empowerment, teamwork and total quality management. It is obviously very important for HR professionals to know the values and goals of top management and how to translate them into the appropriate HR practices.

By the way, the folks at Saturn learned other things as well from their start-up process, among them the importance of union-management collaboration and cooperation, the importance of high levels of training, how concern for work-family issues pays back, how minimizing status differences such as the elimination of special cafeterias and parking spaces for executives improves attitudes, and how having good community relationships helps to create a good public image that in turn helps attract more job applicants. We will return to these issues throughout the text, especially in the union-management relations chapters.

UNDERSTANDING THE EXTERNAL AND INTERNAL ENVIRONMENTS

Understanding the external and internal environments means know-ing what's going on out there and determining what it means for HR management.

Thus what Saturn's experience brings home to us is that the HR department needs to be attuned to the environment—they need to know what is happening in the environment and then to identify the implications for human resource management. **Understanding the external and internal environments** *means knowing what is going on out there—that is continuously scanning the environment—and then determining what this means for human resource management.*

Because environmental understanding is such a big and important activity, we will examine it thoroughly. As such, let us begin by breaking this activity down into the following steps: gathering current data, forecasting future conditions, identifying and prioritizing major issues that affect HR management, developing plans that anticipate those issues, and preparing the organization for successfully dealing with them.

In this chapter use these steps in examining several critical aspects of the internal and external environments that influence the management of human resources.

WHY IS AN UNDERSTANDING OF ENVIRONMENTS IMPORTANT?

Human resource activities do not exist in a vacuum; HR professionals increase their effectiveness when they scan many aspects of the environment and not merely a few, or worse, one. They can thus link people management to the needs of the business and the demands of the external environment. While input from the scanning is useful for all HR activities, it is particularly critical for planning.

Understanding the environment prevents surprises and aids in planning.

Without understanding these environments, organizations are likely to be blindsided by events that could imperil their long-run success. Meaningful and timely responses to major events take time to develop and implement. Continuous scanning and analysis can give an organization the time it needs. Even in the short run, though, organizations must know about the environment in which they do business; for example, substantial fines and penalties are likely to be levied on firms that violate one or several of the numerous employment laws.

Before continuing, study Exhibit 3.1 carefully. Take a moment to figure out what your responses would be, and note three of them on a separate sheet of paper.

What aspects of the environment do you think are likely to have the greatest impact on human resource management? Now, describe the implications of your responses that have the biggest discrepancies between today and the year 2000.

THE EXTERNAL ENVIRONMENT

While many characteristics of the external environment have an impact on a firm's efforts to manage its human resources effectively, we will consider the following:

EXHIBIT 3.1
IMPLICATIONS OF CHANGES IN THE ENVIRONMENT

Many observers have predicted significant changes in the environment for the twenty-first century. Some of these changes are listed below. Please choose and rank the *five* changes that you think currently have the most impact on HR management, and the *five* that you think will have the most impact in the future: "1" indicates the highest impact, "2" indicates the next highest impact, etc.

TODAY	ENVIRONMENT	2000+
_____	a. Increased national/international competition	_____
_____	b. Increased governmental regulation	_____
_____	c. Globalization of corporate business structure	_____
_____	d. Growth in nontraditional business structure (e.g., business alliances, joint ventures)	_____
_____	e. Globalization of the economy/breakdown of trade barriers	_____
_____	f. Increased energy costs	_____
_____	g. Increased reliance on automation/technology to produce goods and services	_____
_____	h. More sophisticated information/communication technology	✓
_____	i. Changing attitudes of society toward business	_____
_____	j. Heightened concern about pollution and natural resources	_____
_____	k. Heightened focus on total quality/customer satisfaction	_____
_____	l. Changing employee values, goals, and expectations (e.g., less loyalty to current employer)	_____
_____	m. Fewer entrants into the work force	_____
_____	n. Inadequate skills of entrants into the work force	_____
_____	o. Cross-border application of employee rights	_____
_____	p. Changing composition of the work force with respect to gender, age, and/or ethnicity	_____
_____	q. Greater concerns about the confidentiality of personal information	_____

SOURCE: Adapted from *Priorities for Competitive Advantage* (IBM/Towers Perrin, 1992). Used by permission.

HR professionals must constantly ask about the environment and identify the most important HR implications.

LEARNING OBJECTIVE 1

Indicate changes in domestic and international competition affecting human resource management.

We are in a global business world, and we need to know as much about the world as possible.

At Wal-Mart, our philosophy is that the best ideas come from associates—employees—on the firing line.

David Glass, CEO, Wal-Mart Stores

To empower employees means to give them freedom and responsibility to make job related decisions.

Empowered employees make companies more competitive.

- Domestic and international competition
- The emerging work force
- Demographics
- Economic and organizational trends

The impact of these environments is changing, literally, the face of business.

DOMESTIC AND INTERNATIONAL COMPETITION

Given the worldwide business climate, "the most important characteristic of today's business environment—and therefore the yardstick against which managerial techniques must be measured—is the new competition."[2] This competition comes both from abroad and from within the United States. Imports of shoes, textiles, and electronics represent an ever-increasing share of the U.S. market. Fewer than ten years ago, U.S. companies dominated the office copier business here and abroad. Today their domestic share is approximately 50 percent. Similar situations are occurring all through American business because of lower-priced products or inventive marketing techniques, or both. An analysis of U.S. performance between 1970 and 1992 indicates that U.S. share of markets in several other industries declined dramatically.

The dollar has also fluctuated dramatically. Wage disparities and a fluctuating dollar make it challenging for the United States to compete in markets with products requiring a great deal of labor. They also make it harder for U.S. companies to maintain employees abroad. The successes of large U.S. multinationals such as Ford, IBM, and Dow Chemical, however, show it is possible; it simply takes a lot of hard work and a global perspective. For many firms, developing a global perspective is no longer an option. Consequently, organizational structures with global functions are becoming a necessity, and the work force to staff them mandatory. Human resource managers can aid their organization's transition into the arena of worldwide competition.[3]

EMPLOYEE EMPOWERMENT. Intense levels of domestic and international competition are forcing organizations to be more productive, more effective management of human resources is seen as a way to improve productivity. The nature of work force demographics means that efforts to improve productivity must include employees in the decision-making process. Greater employee involvement in workplace decisions is a growing trend: many individuals want a greater say.

Organizations seeking to improve product and service quality go to great lengths to get their employees involved. Many **empower** employees—that is, give them the freedom and responsibility to make job-related decisions. They recognize employee empowerment as one sure way to improve quality. Many firms such as Corning Glass and Ford have found that empowerment is often the best way to reduce costs and improve profitability:

> Officials at Ford Motor Company believe in empowerment. After watching profits and quality drop sharply in the late 1970s, management knew something had to be done. By using employee involvement and participative management programs, Ford not only listened and responded to employee problem-solving ideas, but management also encouraged employees to take the lead. As a result of these efforts, Ford experienced one of the most dramatic turnarounds of the past decade.[4]

THE EMERGING WORK FORCE

Ongoing changes in the work force in the United States contribute to several new and major HR concerns.

WORK FORCE EDUCATIONAL ATTAINMENT. After installing millions of dollars worth of computers in its Burlington, Vermont, factories, the IBM Corporation discovered, much to its dismay, that it had to teach high school algebra to thousands of workers before they could run the computers. David Kearns, Xerox's former chairman and CEO, has said

> . . . [T]he American work force is running out of qualified people. If current demographic and economic trends continue, American business will have to hire a million new workers a year who can't read, write, or count. Teaching them how, and absorbing the lost productivity while they're learning, will cost the industry $25 billion a year for as long as it takes.[5]

David Davis, former chairman of Stanley Works, a firm specializing in power tools, observes:

> . . . [T]he cost of incompetence in U.S. industry is higher than any of us realizes. You can't quantify it, but it shows up in missed opportunities, in bad decisions, and other ways. It's all around us.[6]

In addition to these numbers, approximately 25 percent of U.S. adults are functionally illiterate.[7] In Japan, less than 5 percent of the population is functionally illiterate. And as for the future work force:

> A 1991 report by the Educational Testing Center in Princeton, New Jersey, showed U.S. kids (age 13) finished fourteenth among fifteen countries in a standardized math test. U.S. kids answered 55% of the questions correctly. Korean and Taiwanese students, at the top, answered 73% correctly. And China, whose students also score much higher in math than do U.S. kids, spends just 3.7% of its gross national product (GNP) on education compared to the U.S., which spends 6.8% of its much larger GNP.[8]

Illiteracy is but one symptom of a much larger problem afflicting the U.S. economy. The $100 billion plus yearly trade deficit and a foreign debt of nearly a trillion dollars reflect the inability of a large percentage of the American work force to compete effectively in an integrated world economy. "Much of the success of Japan stems from the fact that its blue collar workers can interpret advanced mathematics, read complex engineering blueprints, and perform sophisticated tasks on the factory floor far better than blue collar workers in the United States," says Merry I. White, professor of comparative sociology at Boston University and author of *The Japanese Education Challenge*.[9] As a consequence, firms

> . . . are energetically training and retraining their work forces. At the same time, more managers and executives are exposed to new and sometimes eccentric methods and styles of training, aimed at shaping their behavior toward more effective leadership and greater productivity. In the name of leaner, meaner, and more efficient management, corporate educators are forging ahead with no evidence beyond the promise that these emerging techniques produce long-term results.
>
> There is, however, a solid base for all the technical training and retraining that needs to be done in factories and offices. In the next five years, four out of five people in the industrial world will be doing jobs differently from the way they have been done in the last 50 years. Most people will have to learn new skills. By the year 2000, 75% of all employees will need to be retrained in new jobs or taught fresh skills for their old ones. Corporate trainers, in the interest of saving time, will explore alternative and faster methods of delivering new skills and learning, including interactive video, audiotapes, take-home video discs, computer-based instruction, and expert systems.[10]

Of U.S. adults, 25% are functionally illiterate—that is, unable to read job manuals or make job-related basic math calculations.

An excellent example of what one business in Ohio is doing to train and educate its work force is detailed in the feature "Managing Human Resources at Will-Burt."

VALUES.   This is a common business complaint: slower increases in productivity rates are occurring at the same time as the work ethic disappears. According to some commentators, however, the work ethic has not disappeared. People today are willing to work hard at "good" jobs, providing they have the freedom to influence the nature of their jobs and to pursue their own life-styles. People value work, but the type of work that interests them has changed. They want challenging jobs that allow them the freedom to make decisions. Increasingly, people may not seek or desire rapid promotions, especially when they involve geographic transfers, but they do seek influence and control.

A recent study compares the work values of persons more than 45 years old with those less than 45 years old.

- Members of the older generation, products of the World War II era, accept authority, while employees from the younger generation, who grew up during the Vietnam War, do not trust authority.
- While members of the older generation see work as a duty and a vehicle for financial support, those of the younger generation think work should be fun and a place to meet other young people.
- Employees who are over 40 believe that experience is the necessary road to promotion and are willing to spend time in an "apprenticeship," with the expectation of reward for that effort. Younger employees, on the other hand, believe people should advance just as quickly as their competence permits.
- "Fairness" to the older generation means treating people with equality; for the younger generation, it means allowing people to be different.[12]

These values tend to reflect the concerns of the **baby boomers** (born between 1946 and 1964) rather than their parents, the **traditionalists** (born between 1925 and 1945), who are still in the work force. The values of these parents and even some of the older baby boomers (remember, this group ranges in age from approximately 30–48) focus on job security, employment security, and income security. Because the traditionalists tend to be less mobile, organizations need to be concerned with targeting training and retraining not just at the entry-level worker but at older workers as well.[13]

As organizations begin to look at the values of their employees in the workplace, however, they realize the need to make room for another age category—those individuals born between 1965 and 1975, the **baby busters**. According to a recent study, this group values recognition and praise; time with their managers; opportunity to learn new things; fun at work; unstructured, flexible time; and small, unexpected rewards for jobs well done. Increasingly, companies recognize that these values are different from the other groups and must be accommodated. For example, at Patagonia, the Ventura, California–based manufacturer of products for outdoor enthusiasts, a full 40 percent of 450 employees are in their twenties. Patagonia has nontraditional open offices, flexible work schedules, and flexible personal leave times for up to four months each year. Specific actions and advice for managing baby busters in firms are offered in the feature, "HR Advice and Application;" it also highlights the trend to reduce classes and descriptions.

Firms are increasingly beginning to recognize that they must pay more attention to the ways they can manage an age-heterogeneous work force. Not only do these employees have different workplace values, they also have different per-

- *Traditionalists:* born between 1925–1945
- *Baby boomers:* born between 1946–1964
- *Baby-busters:* born between 1965–1975

The baby busters are also known as the X generation because they are the tenth generation of Americans.

MANAGING HUMAN RESOURCES at Will-Burt

One Plus One Equals a Thriving Business

DENNIS Donahue, president of Will-Burt, Inc., a $20 million machine-parts manufacturer in Orrville, Ohio, confesses that when the company started a remedial training program for employees in 1985, it wasn't just for the benefit of the employees. "The company had to save itself," he says. "The reasons weren't altruistic, to be honest with you."

With 2,000 hours of rework a month and a 35 percent product-rejection rate, Will-Burt teetered on the brink of bankruptcy. The company hired professors from nearby University of Akron and set up classrooms in the factory. Classes were mandatory and included basic math courses, as well as reading and other subjects.

Now, eight years later, the company has not only saved itself, it is thriving. According to Donahue, Will-Burt spends less than 1 percent of annual sales on remedial training. But as a result, defective products have fallen from 8 percent of sales to 2 percent. Employee tardiness has dropped, as well—from 70 late employees a day to 2 in seven months. Disability costs also have been cut.

Central to the program was math instruction. "If the worker does the math wrong in making a product, the quality is bad," says Donahue. "They have to have a certain level of math skills, especially with the computers we're using now."

But some employees weren't eager to learn the new math, especially when they felt they were being held up for ridicule. "The employees didn't react very well to the program at first," admits Donahue. "When we started getting publicity for it, they thought management was telling people we had dumb employees.

"Now they understand there is a nationwide problem of employees not being able to do calculations on new machinery. It's being received better. Part of that has to do with everyone in the plant—secretaries, purchasing people, as well as lathe operators—taking the courses."

Will-Burt is now held up as a shining example. The Department of Labor endorsed the program, and the National Association of Manufacturers will include it in a remedial training package it plans to offer its 13,000 members.[11]

---

ceptions of each other. Take a look at these perceptions in Exhibit 3.2. Which age group do you fit into? Are these your perceptions? Describe and then discuss three implications of the perceptions presented in the exhibit.

OWNERSHIP.   One value that seems to cut across employee age groups is the desire for ownership:

Ownership can mean either an equity share (stock ownership) or just a worker's sense that (s)he counts.

> The new buzzword in employee motivation is "ownership," which can mean either an equity share or just a worker's sense that [s]he counts. Says Harvard business school professor J. Richard Hackman: "If you want me to care, then I want to be treated like an owner and have some real voice in where we're going." The concept grows out of the "employee involvement" of the 1980s, which got off to a shaky start with quality circles that never amounted to much, then grew stronger as workers were brought into decision making.[15]

Some firms are responding.

> Ownership goes a step further by seeking to put employees in the shoes of entrepreneurs. Xerox, 3M, and Honeywell help finance startups by employees who have promising ideas in return for a minority share. Alfred West, founder

ASK THE EXPERTS—MANAGING "BABY BUSTER" EMPLOYEES

By Mike Bibeau, quality and productivity manager of Neles-Jamesbury, Inc. (Worcester, Massachusetts).

Q-1 Your company recently reduced the number of job descriptions from 120 to 7. Why did you take that step?

A-1 We had too many barriers and bottlenecks that hampered the workflow through our plant where we manufacture valves and accessories. Each new job description was cross-functional, enabling every employee to handle a variety of jobs. Once trained, employees are organized into small groups, working on products from start to finish and taking responsibility for their work.

Q-2 How did employees deal with the changes?

A-2 Some veteran employees made it clear that they were more comfortable in small niches, doing repetitive work and taking orders. We found it was younger employees who most easily made the transition. As a generation, I think they're more cooperative than competitive in the workplace. And they're much more adaptive.

The younger workers are like educated sponges who draw on their formal education and try to apply it constructively to their work situations. They thrive on change. They're comfortable taking action, responsibility, and ownership. They like to think on the job.

Q-3 What have you found to be the key to managing the "baby busters"—that is, workers between the ages of 18 and 30?

A-3 The real key to future productivity improvement is not training these employees to work in old systems, but rather creating new systems to capitalize on their interests and abilities. Suitable new systems don't need to be a complete revamping of a company's entire production process. They can be confined to a single department or even to a single job within a department.

Q-4 What, beyond preparing development plans, can you do to more effectively manage these employees?

A-4 The answers are common to good management everywhere, regardless of employees' ages.

- **Beware of stereotypes.** Don't concentrate so intensely on employees' age, race, or gender that you start "slotting" them. Remember that thinking in terms of stereotypes can be evidence of impermissible bias or discrimination. And it can stop you from fairly evaluating an employee's strengths or weaknesses.
- **Listen to the employees' opinions and ideas.** The baby busters have a powerful interest in professional training and development. They want to lead fuller, more interesting lives, and they want opportunities to set the directions of their lives and their careers.
- **Expose them to as many areas of your organization's operations as possible.** This exposure will maintain their interests, broaden their skill profiles, and show them how their work fits into the company's overall goals. Once our employees began working in their expanded job roles, several complaints and perennial problems were eliminated. The employees are more satisfied because they can identify with the outcome of their work. And, even more significantly, they're now more attuned and sensitive to the needs of the end-use customer.
- **Encourage employees to participate in decisions.** Responsibility without authority is responsibility in name only. The start-to-finish product responsibility that our employee teams now have is a powerful motivator mainly because team members have unprecedented authority to make their own decisions as a product moves through the process. And they're capable of making good decisions because of the cross-functional training and the broad experience that the new system provides.[14]

and chairman of SEI Corp., a $123 million-a-year financial services company in Wayne, Pennsylvania, is planning a more radical experiment with his 1,100 workers. He intends to divide his company into entrepreneurial units, each led by a so-called champion who has been particularly effective in promoting whatever the unit does. West will give each group of employees a 20% inter-

---

EXHIBIT 3.2
HOW EMPLOYEES YOUNG AND OLD VIEW EACH OTHER

Traditionalists
(born 1925–1945) see

Baby boomers as disrespectful, overly blunt, too "warm and fuzzy."
Younger workers as very young, impatient, unethical.

Baby Boomers
(born 1946–1964) see

Traditionalists as caught in the by-the-book syndrome, overly cautious, conservative, inflexible.
Younger workers as selfish, manipulative, aloof.

Baby Busters
(born 1965–1975) see

Traditionalists as old, outdated, rigid.
Baby boomers as workaholics, unrealistic, disgustingly "new age."

SOURCE: *Twentysomething: Managing & Motivating Today's New Work Force*, in C. M. Solomon, "Managing the Baby Busters," *Personnel Journal* (March 1992): 56. Used by permission.

---

est in their unit. After a suitable period, he will invite an investment bank to put a price on the unit. Then West will pay members their 20%. If the unit flops, the members get nothing more than their salaries. Says West: "I'm an entrepreneur, and I want more people like that here."[16]

DEMOGRAPHICS

THE WORLD. Currently there are slightly more than 5 billion people on this planet. By the year 2000 the worldwide population is projected to be around 6 billion. At current growth rates, over the next 20 years the work force in the Third World or industrializing nations alone will expand by about 700 million. Between 1995 and 2000, Asia's work force is projected to grow by 240 million, while Europe's is projected to grow by only 6 million.[17] What this means for many firms is the existence of a huge labor market worldwide. With what almost assuredly amounts to a worldwide labor surplus, a downward pressure on wages is likely to persist for some time.

UNITED STATES. With a population of more than 250 million today, projections indicate that this figure will slowly swell into the twenty-first century. By the year 2000, the U.S. population will reach 275 million, an increase of 15 percent over the 240 million U.S. residents in 1985. Population is expected to hit 383 million by 2050. These figures are significant because they are upward revisions of figures published only two years ago, and because they make the United States even more unusual than Europe and Japan; for a comparison, see the "HR Advice and Application" feature. Study this feature, and discuss three positive trends and their implications resulting from these population projections for the United States, Japan, and Europe.

THE UPSIDE OF AMERICA'S POPULATION UPSURGE

If demography is destiny, then America's economy in the next century may be very different from that of its chief trading rivals. Almost alone among industrial nations, the United States now looks forward to sizable population growth through 2050 and beyond.

This prospect was underscored by new Census Bureau projections released last year. As recently as 1989, the agency had predicted that the population of the United States, about 258 million today, would peak at about 302 million in 2038. But now it anticipates that the population will hit 383 million by 2050 and keep growing.

This picture is in sharp contrast to other industrial nations, where growth is now grinding to a halt. While the world is adding a record 90 million people a year, almost all of that growth is in developing nations. "The only major exception is the U.S.," says Carl Haub of the Population Reference Bureau. (Canada and Australia are also growing, but their populations are only 17 percent of the United States total.)

Why is America the odd man out in the industrial world? Haub notes that the U.S. fertility rate, which had dipped below the population-replacement level of 2.1 children per woman in the 1970s, has moved back close to that level. By contrast, the fertility rate averages only 1.5 to 1.6 in Japan and Europe.

At the same time, U.S. immigration, enhanced by liberalized legislation a few years ago and by a sizable influx of illegal immigrants, is now on a par with the great migrations of the early twentieth century. The United States now absorbs 1 million immigrants a year, which amounts to 1 out of every 100 people added to the world population. Meanwhile, other industrial countries are in the process of closing their doors to both legal and illegal immigrants.

The growing opposition among Europeans—and among more and more Americans—to further immigration reflects tensions spawned by the high unemployment plaguing the industrial world. But the more liberal U.S. policy could turn out to be advantageous in the long run.

For one thing, other industrial nations must cope with static or declining labor forces. By 2025, for example, Japan will lose 12.2 million people aged 15–64, Germany 4.5 million, and Italy 4 million. But the United States will actually add some 38 million.

More important, all advanced nations face rapidly aging populations and a sharp drop in the ratio of working-age people to the elderly early in the next century. Because the U.S. baby boom generation is now entirely in the labor force, there are more than five Americans 15–64 years old for each older person, compared with an average ratio of only 4.3 to 1 in Western Europe.

Although most of America's baby boomers will be age 65 and older by the year 2025, current projections indicate that the U.S. ratio will still be higher than that of most other advanced nations—holding at about 3.3 to 1 in the U.S., compared with 2.9 to 1 in Britain, 2.7 in France, 2.5 in Germany, and just 2.3 in Japan, where 30 percent of the population will be elderly. "America's high fertility and immigration could prove to be a big plus in the decades ahead," says economist Philip Suttle of Morgan Guaranty Trust Co.[18]

WOMEN IN THE WORK FORCE. During the 1990s, women are expected to continue to join the work force in substantial numbers. By the year 2000, approximately 50 percent of the work force will be women, and 61 percent of all U.S. women will be working. Women will have comprised almost three-fifths of the new entrants into the labor force between 1985 and 2000.

For many women, especially those with more than average education and with career prospects, there is an economic and opportunity cost for bearing children that may be limiting their lifetime fertility, as well as encouraging them to postpone childbearing. Demographers now expect the average U.S. woman to bear fewer than two children, although she herself may anticipate having at least two. Many more women will be childless than had planned to be. While the consequences of these trends have yet to be fully estimated, one likely outcome is childbearing that is explicitly planned to coincide with career choices.[19]

By contrast, of new entrants into the labor force in this same period of time, only 15 percent will be native white males. This figure and others illustrating the increasing heterogeneity of the U.S. labor force are shown in Exhibit 3.3.

Currently, the occupational makeup of the civilian labor force reflects much higher percentages of women in clerical positions and higher percentages of men in managerial and administrative jobs and employed as crafts workers.

At present, about 20 percent of women occupy professional and technical positions; most of those are in the nursing and teaching professions. Thus, most working females are in service, clerical (secretarial), nursing, and teaching jobs. The majority of men, on the other hand, are in semiskilled (operative), skilled (crafts workers), managerial and administrative, and professional and technical jobs.

This distribution has, in part, resulted from the notion of **job sex-typing.** That is, a job takes the image of being appropriate only for the sex that dominates the job. Consequently, once a job becomes sex-typed, it attracts only persons of that sex. Job sex-typing, combined with sex-role stereotyping, has traditionally restricted perceived job choices and preferences for both men and women. Whereas job sex-typing refers to the labeling of jobs as either "men's" jobs or "women's" jobs, **sex-role stereotyping** refers to labels, characteristics, or attributes that become attached to men and women solely because they are members of their respective sexes.

Evidence now indicates that the range of perceived job choices and preferences is expanding for both men and women. This trend has been facilitated in part by the gradual reduction of sex-role stereotyping in our society. In addition, some of the job sex-typing has been reduced through sex-neutral job titles (often crafted by HR departments) and because of the increased number of women graduating from professional schools.

Job sex-typing means a job takes on an image of being appropriate for only the gender that dominates the job.

Sex-role stereotyping refers to labels, characteristics, or attributes that become attached to men and women solely because they are members of their respective sexes.

EXHIBIT 3.3
NEW ENTRANTS INTO THE LABOR FORCE

CATEGORY	LABOR FORCE (%), 1985	NET NEW WORKERS (%), 1985–2000
Native white men	47	15
Native white women	36	42
Native nonwhite men	5	7
Native nonwhite women	5	13
Immigrant men	4	13
Immigrant women	3	9
Total workers	115,461,000	25,000,000

SOURCE: *Workforce 2000* (Washington D.C.: U.S. Government Printing Office, Department of Labor, 1987).

The *glass ceiling* is the invisible but
seemingly unbreakable barrier
women and minorities face in climbing the organizational ladder.

DID YOU KNOW?

In 1950 the U.S. population was
150,000,000 and broke down as:

- White 89.5%
- African-American 10.0%
- Asian 0.5%

In 1990, at 248 million, it was:

- White 76%
- African-American 12.1%
- Hispanic 9.0%
- Asian 2.9%

These changes, however, definitely appear to be gradual, as illustrated in Exhibit 3.4. Furthermore, the real choices of women and minorities in the top levels of management still seem to be limited.

In 1978, *Fortune* counted ten women among the 6,400 highest paid officers and directors of major publicly held firms. The comparable figures for 1990 were 19 of 4,012.[20]

This surprisingly slow progress is due in part to the phenomenon called the **glass ceiling**—an invisible but seemingly unbreakable barrier. In today's progressive atmosphere, it may seem hard to believe glass ceilings still exist in corporate America. However, according to "Women and Minorities in Management," a recent study by researchers Mary Ann Von Glinow and Ann Morrison, women and minorities are still prevented from entering top executive ranks.

Clearly, although women have made significant inroads into management, they have fallen short of the top. Furthermore, they often do not find themselves on a path that might take them there.[21]

MINORITY GROUPS IN THE WORK FORCE. In recent years, a minority group that has become increasingly vocal is the group comprised of disabled people. When the *Americans with Disabilities Act* was passed in 1990, supporters argued that (1) there are almost 45 million disabled Americans; and (2) the rest of the Americans might think of themselves as "temporarily abled." According to this way of looking at it then, almost everyone could at some point be disabled. This is a new way of looking at disabilities with some important implications for HR management practices.

Over the next decade, the racial profile of the American work force will change dramatically. African-Americans, Native Americans, Asians, and Hispanics will make up a larger share of the work force than ever before. Between 1990 and 2000, they will contribute 20 percent to the new work force. By the

---

EXHIBIT 3.4
THE WORK THAT WOMEN DO

1890	1940	1990
1. Servant	1. Servant	1. Secretary
2. Agricultural laborer	2. Stenographer, secretary	2. Cashier
3. Dressmaker	3. Teachers	3. Bookkeeper
4. Teacher	4. Clerical worker	4. Registered nurse
5. Farmer, planter	5. Sales worker	5. Nursing aide, orderly
6. Laundress	6. Factory worker (apparel)	6. Elementary school teacher
7. Seamstress	7. Bookkeeper. accountant, cashier	7. Waitress
8. Cotton-mill operative	8. Waitress	8. Sales worker
9. Housekeeper, steward	9. Housekeeper	9. Child-care worker
10. Clerk, cashier	10. Nurse	10. Cook

SOURCE: *Fortune* (23 Sept. 1991), 9. Used by permission.

way, "Hispanic" identifies a group comprised of a number of nationalities and ethnicities of Hispanic origin—including persons from Mexico, Cuba, Puerto Rico, and the countries of Central and South America and the Dominican Republic. By far the largest nationality in this category hails from Mexico, which accounts for 63 percent of all Hispanics in the U.S. labor force.

Thus, while America has always been a land of immigrants, it was also thought to be a "melting pot," where differences in background would disappear. Today, many individual differences are recognized by law and society as being very important. Consequently, we see many employment laws (which we will cover in other chapters) that deal with diversity and a much larger concern in both society and business for understanding and managing it. Thus we discuss diversity as a major human resource theme throughout this book.

IMMIGRANTS IN THE WORK FORCE.   The number of immigrants in the work force is expected to increase dramatically over the next ten years. This is the result of a significant increase in immigrant population. The *Immigration Act of 1990* allocates 750,000 visas annually, up from the previous limit of 500,000. While most of these visas are granted to reunite family members, job-based immigration is now at 150,000, up from 54,000. The Census Bureau predicts that during the 1990s California will add almost 2 million immigrants, followed by New York, Texas, Illinois, and Florida. Once here, two-thirds or more of the immigrants of working age are likely to join the labor force.

IMPLICATIONS FOR MANAGING HUMAN RESOURCES

MANAGING DIVERSITY.   The radical demographic transformation in the work force means organizations must learn to manage a very diverse work force—African-Americans, Hispanics, Asians, males, females, young, old, and much more.[22] **Work force diversity** means having workers with many different characteristics. For companies it can mean many, many groups. For Northern States Power (NSP) in Minneapolis, it means all the groups identified in the "HR Advice and Application: Diversity is Valuing Differences at NSP." NSP sees the emerging work force diversity not only as a reality, but also as an opportunity. To support this philosophy, NSP has many human resource programs that enable it to "capitalize on diversity."

In general, successful organizations react to diversity as the important business issue it is by implementing proactive, strategic human resource planning. Short-term strategies designed to circumvent the situation prevent an organization from effectively positioning itself in tomorrow's world of cultural, gender, and life-style diversity.[23] Top management in corporations, then, needs to emphasize to line managers two goals of "diversity competence": productivity growth and market-share expansion, both domestically and internationally.

Human resource managers typically need to focus on nine key areas in managing diversity.[24]

- *Recruitment:* Mount a concerted effort to find quality minority employees by improved college relations programs.
- *Career development:* Expose those minority employees with high potential to the same key developmental jobs that traditionally have led to senior positions for their white, male counterparts.
- *Diversity training for managers:* Address stereotypes and cultural differences that interfere with the full participation of all employees in the workplace.

Work force diversity means having workers with many different characteristics.

Diversity is Valuing Differences at NSP

Race	Age
Minnesotan	I.Q.
Non-Minnesotan	Smoking Preference
Weight	Differently Abled
Traditional Thinker	Economic Status
Nontraditional Thinker	Marital Status
	Nationality
Nontraditional Job	Appearance
Education	White-Collar
Religion	Blue-Collar
Language	Single Parent
Height	Affectional
Gender	Preference

- *Upward mobility:* Break the "glass ceiling" and increase the number of minorities in upper management through mentors and executive appointment.
- *Diverse input and feedback:* Ask minority employees themselves what they need versus asking managers what they think minorities need.
- *Self-help:* Encourage networking and support groups among minorities.
- *Accountability:* Hold managers accountable for developing their diverse work forces.
- *Systems accommodation:* Develop respect and support for cultural diversity through recognition of different cultural and religious holidays, diet restrictions, and so forth.
- *Outreach:* Support minority organizations and programs, thus developing a reputation as a multicultural leader.

Businesses are taking the diversity issue very seriously. Digital Equipment Corporation now has a manager with the title of Manager of Valuing Differences. Honeywell, Inc., has a Director of Work Force Diversity and Avon Products, Inc., has a Director of Multicultural Planning and Design.[25] Hewlett-Packard conducts training sessions for managers to teach them about different cultures and races and about their own gender biases and training needs,[26] and Procter and Gamble has implemented "valuing diversity" programs throughout the company. A mentor program designed to retain black and female managers was developed at one plant, and one-day workshops on diversity is given to all new employees.

Equitable Life Assurance encourages minorities and women to form support groups that periodically meet with the CEO to discuss problems in the company pertaining to them. At Avon, several councils represent various groups, each having a senior manager present at meetings. These councils inform and advise top management. Specific advice on managing diversity from the CEO of Avon, Jim Preston, is found in the "HR Advice and Application" feature.

REASONS FOR THE GLASS CEILING.   With the number of qualified women entering the work force growing at an astonishing rate, why is it taking so long for them to reach top positions in corporate America? According to several leading business analysts and corporate recruiters, there are many reasons for the impasse, ranging from male managers' discomfort with female executives to women's pressures of balancing work and family concerns. "Mention women in management and the instant association in the minds of most men (and women) is: women have babies. The conclusion follows naturally that women can't be counted on to make a full-time, open-ended commitment to their careers," says Felice Schwartz, founder of Catalyst, a research organization that studies work-family issues.[28] Schwartz contends that it costs companies more to employ women managers than men. "Given a man and a woman of equal abilities and motivation, investing in a woman is undeniably riskier."[29] The implication is that women are more likely to interrupt their careers, or forego them altogether, to pursue motherhood. In fact, one large industrial company estimates that turnover for top managerial women is approximately two and one-half times greater than for their male counterparts.[30] These perspectives can dissuade corporate decision makers from spending the time, money, and effort to groom women for top spots in their corporations and are a major factor contributing to the glass ceiling.

A second, more subtle hurdle for women to overcome is the comfort level (or lack thereof) that male managers and executives have with female executives. According to Linda Jones, president of Women in Management, a professional group of 250 female executives, "Male CEOs accept women as professionals, but they're not ready to accept them as true peers."[31] Margaret Hennig, dean of the Simmons College Graduate School of Management, believes male executives are often disturbed by the thought of a woman taking their place. "Usually, he's threatened because his identity as a male and his job are intermeshed."[32] This feeling by many advocates of women's rights is summed up in a quote by Schwartz.

> . . . [I]t goes against the grain of most senior executives to encourage and welcome the women, so unlike their wives, who put their career before marriage and rearing children. Talent in women is not difficult to recognize, but the very qualities that bespeak motivation—determination, drive, aggressiveness, single-mindedness—still tend to promote discomfort and uncertainty, even among male executives who have decided they should be developing female leaders.[33]

It is also conceivable that some of the barriers facing women who strive to reach positions in management have been somewhat self-imposed. For example, many women have opted for staff jobs, as opposed to line-oriented jobs—the

TALK WITH THE EXPERTS— EFFECTIVELY MANAGING A DIVERSE WORK FORCE

Jim Preston, Chief Executive Officer of Avon Products (New York).

Preston, like many executives, is concerned about shaping the work force at Avon Products to meet a diverse future. "We needed to know our minority and women employees better—how they felt about working at Avon, what they liked and didn't like," says Preston. "So we encouraged (and now sponsor) employee networks to advise management and to work with us on key issues."

RAISING ISSUES

There are three networks at Avon—for African-Americans, Hispanics, and Asians. Each has a senior officer who acts as guide and mentor. The information that comes out of these groups is provided to the Minorities and Women's Participation Council, which then considers changes that might need to be made.

For example, "the Hispanic network raised the issue of presentation skills," Preston recalls. "Being able to give a forceful presentation is a requisite for success at Avon and most companies. People need to make a good appearance, speak well, and be handy with a flip chart or overhead projector.

"The Hispanics pointed out that their accents and syntax often put them at a disadvantage. Our human resource people met with various managers to talk to them in general terms about Hispanics giving presentations."

The typical approach was "We know you don't do this, but some managers seem to give Hispanics poor marks because of the way they talk. As you know, that shouldn't count. In fact, it's a good idea to talk to your Hispanic people and tell them not to worry—that an accent is more than just okay. It's great because we value diversity."

The ethnic networks also arrange for cultural events—art exhibits in the employee lounge area, speakers, and theatrical productions staged by professionals in the company auditorium. The events are well attended by the entire employee population, not just those in the particular ethnic group.

MULTICULTURAL TRAINING

Avon sends its managers to a variety of multicultural training groups, but the most prominent is the Institute for Managing Diversity in Atlanta, Georgia. There, attendees discuss the role and skills of general management and how multiculturalism can pay off on the bottom line—specifically at Avon. The class is broken down into small teams that address specific problems.

"After a while, participants open up and begin to express feelings about one another that they've been holding back," says Preston. "One of our people—a white male manager—said he had no idea that minorities who worked for him thought he was an insensitive stuffed shirt. He was astounded."

Another attendee—a minority manager— had always prided himself on being a hard driver, tough but fair. He was surprised to learn that he had been turning people off. Back on the job, he still insists on the same high standards, but he's toned down the toughness. Now he gets the results he wants.

"Overall, the importance of this training is that participants discover the real power of diversity," says Preston. "Once you make that discovery, you can begin to attract and keep the very best talent, because you know that talent is color-blind and gender-blind."

MAKE DIVERSITY WORK FOR YOU

The dictionary defines diversity as "the condition of being different." So, a diverse work force is merely one that is composed of several different individuals from different backgrounds who are expected to work together. Your goal as an employer is to help your employees build constructive working relationships while valuing each other's differences.[27]

most likely track to senior management posts. In addition, line jobs were more frequently open to them than staff jobs. Women have also had fewer opportunities to share information through professional networks. These conditions, however, seem to be changing.

BREAKING THE GLASS CEILING.   Two main avenues can be taken to "shatter" or at least raise the glass ceiling. Until recently, the dominant approach has been to focus on the individual developing a "winning style" to succeed in a "man's" world. This has worked to some extent to help women advance into upper management, but it is not enough. A long-term approach, and one that might determine whether businesses survive in the future, is the idea that it is management's responsibility to assure that there are no barriers to women's day-to-day activities or advancement. In an ever-enlightened environment, women will offer their individual talents to a company, rather than suppress them to conform to deep-rooted prejudices.

However, until management accepts women solely on their merits and value to a company, it is a practical idea for women to at least be aware of the kinds of behavior that management currently prefers. "To be successful in upper management, women must constantly monitor their behavior, making sure they are neither too masculine nor too feminine."[34] Some women in upper management have achieved success by altering their behavior to what is desirable to the male management hierarchy already in place. This is helping women at lower levels because male managers are becoming more comfortable with the idea of women in upper management as they gain direct experience with it. However, training women to "fit" into the male-dominated upper management ranks is simply not a long-term solution, merely a short-term expedient.

What is management's role in helping women break the glass ceiling? The overall objective is to increase an organization's effectiveness by improving management practices. "Impacting organizational norms and changing those policies and structures which inhibit utilization of females" is the goal, according to Elsie Y. Cross & Associates, Inc., a consulting firm dedicated to training companies to encourage women and other minorities in the workplace.[35] The organizational "norms" above refer to the idea that, in the past, many corporations sought employees who looked, acted, and dressed alike. These ideas must change not only for the employee's benefit, but to ensure that companies will be able to attract qualified employees from the ever-changing applicant pool. Training programs are of value because they provide an outside, hopefully unbiased, view of how a company can improve its practices, and the consultants can evaluate and monitor the program's progress.

Two activities are useful to increase sensitivity in a corporation. First, heighten awareness of discriminatory attitudes and how this has an impact on work relationships. Second, implement strategies that will tie elimination of such barriers into incentive plans.

Several programs can be used to increase awareness of problems concerning discriminatory attitudes and practices:

1. Managers can be trained to work and manage in a diverse work force. For example, women are often characterized as less aggressive than their male counterparts. Managers can be sensitive to this and elicit input from all employees, not just those who speak first and loudest.

2. Goal setting and action plans can be designed to maximize an employee's truly useful qualities. Work can be done with managers and supervisors to identify ways in which traditional performance ranking and rating systems can be improved so they are more objective and do not perpetuate disadvantage. Continuing the example above, employees can be rewarded for quality input rather than slighted for timidity or lack of confidence when presenting their ideas. Task forces made up of managers and supervisors can be formed to plan new programs and make recommendations for change based on problems discovered in the workplace. These task

Glass ceiling programs are efforts to break the barriers up the organizational ladder.

Glass-ceiling programs include:

- training
- goal setting
- accountability
- compensation
- career assistance

forces could also review and monitor such programs on a continuing basis.

3. Management can then be held accountable for improving utilization of females in upper management. Managers' objectives and performance appraisals should include their hiring, development, and advancement of women as well as ensuring minimum turnover of women in key positions.

4. Compensation can be tied to achievement of these objectives. For instance, managers can be rewarded or penalized for their affirmative action plan results in hiring and/or promoting women. These plan goals can be challenging; they should represent significant utilization of women; and

5. In addition to solving problems related to discriminatory practices, other programs can be implemented that will benefit women in indirect ways. Management can provide opportunities for women to gain experience, knowledge, and exposure as well as provide career planning. Mentorship programs can be encouraged. Some of the problems women face in climbing the ranks of management stem from the fact that, because of their growing responsibility with their company, they are forced to make trade-offs between their work and family lives. More and more companies provide initiatives such as pregnancy leave of absence and flexible hours, but fewer provide on-site child care, flexible projects, and opportunities to work at home. More comprehensive programs are necessary to help women balance their work and family responsibilities.[36]

Companies that have acted to remove the glass ceiling are already seeing an impact. For example, Merck reports that 25 percent of its current middle managers are women versus approximately 10 percent in 1980,[37] and the Prudential Insurance Company has 50 percent women managers now versus 30 percent ten years ago.[38]

Thus, important work force and demographic changes are already affecting human resource management and will continue to do so throughout the 1990s. As more minorities and immigrants enter the work force, more and better diversity management training programs will be needed. As more women move to management positions, more and better glass ceiling programs will be needed. These changes present significant challenges and opportunities. To be best understood, they must also be addressed in the context of several major economic and organizational trends.

LEARNING OBJECTIVE 3

Describe how economic and organizational trends are impacting how firms manage their human resources.

ECONOMIC AND ORGANIZATIONAL TRENDS

National, state, and local economies can have a significant impact on managing human resources. So can the international economy, whose recent impact has increased the level of competition and has forced U.S. corporations to become more flexible, competitive, and bottom-line oriented. The impact of these economies on the HR department is described in "Managing Human Resources Around the World: The Environment Is Transforming the HR Management Department."

A strong economy tends to lower the unemployment rate, increase wage rates, make recruitment more necessary and more difficult, and increase the desirability of training current employees. In contrast, a weak economy tends to increase the unemployment rate, diminish demands for wage increases (and even result in wage concessions), make recruitment less necessary and easier, and reduce the need for training and developing current employees.[39] Although a

MANAGING HUMAN RESOURCES
Around the World

The Environment Is Transforming
the HR Department

A STUDY was released in 1992. International Business Machines Corporation and the HR consulting firm of Towers Perrin surveyed almost 3,000 CEOs and human resource managers of firms in twenty countries. The firms were selected because they are effective and operate in highly competitive environments. Translated into eight languages, the survey was based on the premise that characteristics of the environment have been having a major impact on events in personnel management. A major objective of the study was to test this premise and to explore what characteristics are having the most impact today and are predicted to have the most impact in the year 2000. Of course, the researchers were also interested in knowing whether characteristics with the most impact would vary depending on the country of the survey respondents.

The results of the study strongly supported the premise that the environment plays a major role in shaping personnel and human resource management around the world. While several characteristics of the environment impact this role, some are regarded as more significant than others, and significance varies country by country. The results are shown in Exhibit 3.5. (Compare this exhibit against the evaluations you made using Exhibit 3.1.) Certain factors were more important to some countries than others. For example, respondents in the United States and Japan indicated changing work force demographics as

Continued on the next page

EXHIBIT 3.5
GEOGRAPHIC DIFFERENCES FOR THE SIX MOST IMPORTANT ENVIRONMENTAL FACTORS

ENVIRONMENTAL FACTORS FOR HR	RELATIVELY HIGH RATINGS IN . . .	SOMEWHAT LOWER RATINGS IN . . .	ENVIRONMENTAL FACTORS FOR HR	RELATIVELY HIGH RATINGS IN . . .	SOMEWHAT LOWER RATINGS IN . . .
Increased national/ international competition	Mexico, Brazil	Japan, U.S.	Globalization of the economy	Latin America, Italy	Japan, U.S.
Focus on quality/ customer satisfaction	Latin America, Australia	Japan, Korea	Fewer entrants to the work force	Japan	Latin America, Korea, Australia
Changing employee values	Korea, Japan, Germany	Latin America, Italy	Changing work force demographics	Japan, U.S.	Latin America, Korea, Australia

SOURCE: *Priorities for Competitive Advantage* (IBM/Towers Perrin, 1992), 13. Used by permission.

relatively high in importance, while respondents in Korea and Australia indicated them as comparatively low in importance (but still high in the overall results).

Increased levels of national and international competition refer to more commerce and competition from firms in countries all over the world. Globalization of the economy refers to what a firm must do in order to compete on a global basis—for example, to operate in all countries of the world or just in some.

Notice that results are presented with no indication of the present or the year 2000; regarding the impact of the environment, respondents said "the future is today." They said the same thing when it came to identifying the most important goals. Here, worldwide, the two most important goals selected were productivity/quality/customer satisfaction and linkage of human resources to the business.

In addition to indicating the most significant aspects of the environment, respondents were asked how these aspects were specifically affecting HR management. Basically, respondents saw the personnel department literally being transformed from a functional specialist to a business partner. The impact of this transformation on four areas of human resource management is shown in Exhibit 3.6.

EXHIBIT 3.6
A MODEL OF THE HR DEPARTMENT'S TRANSFORMATION

	FUNCTIONAL SPECIALIST	BUSINESS PARTNER
Nature of HR programs and function	Responsive →	Proactive
	Operational →	Strategic
	Internal →	Societal
Creation of HR strategy and policy	HR department has full responsibility. →	HR department and line management share responsibility.
Organization of HR department	Employee advocate →	Business partner
	Functional structure →	Flexible structure
	Reporting to staff →	Reporting to line
Profile of HR professionals	Career in HR →	Rotation
	Specialist →	Generalist
	Limited financial skills →	Financial expertise
	Current focus →	Focus on future
	Monolingual →	Multilingual
	National perspective →	Global perspective

SOURCE: Adapted from *Priorities for Competitive Advantage* (IBM/Towers Perrin, 1992), 6. Used by permission.

---

weak economy may diminish the importance of some HR activities, other events in the external environment act to increase their importance.

American executives feel a sense of vast impending change in the world and for their organizations. Many of the reasons for their feelings result from the rapidly changing demographic conditions just described and the fast-paced, highly competitive international marketplace. Executives look at these and other conditions and realize that the 1990s are tougher than the 1980s. They see companies being forced to make decisions faster. Consequently, they are adopting more fluid structures that can be altered as conditions change. More than before, companies are living by computers, shaping strategy and structure to fit information technology. They are engaging in more mergers, joint ventures, acquisitions, downsizing, and development in order to become and stay competitive, and they are coping with a more demanding work force, increasingly characterized by its overall diversity. This, along with the increasing level of computer usage and automated facilities and techniques, is changing the nature of jobs and requiring more skilled workers at a time when functional illiteracy is twenty-five percent.

CHANGING JOBS AND SKILLS NEEDED.   What will the work force of 2000 be doing? The changes projected for the nation's industries will restructure U.S. occupational patterns. The jobs that will be created between now and 2000 will be substantially different from those in existence today. According to the Bureau of Labor Statistics, 23.4–28.6 million new wage and salary jobs will be created by 1995. Most of the job growth will be in the service-producing and not the goods-producing area. Of these, only between 1.0 and 4.6 million will be in high-technology industries. Thus, a substantial number of new jobs will be in industries other than high technology.[40]

Exhibit 3.7 shows the occupations that will have the greatest number of new jobs by 2005. A number of jobs in the least-skilled job classes will disappear, while high-skilled professions will grow rapidly. Overall, the skill mix of the economy is moving rapidly upscale, with most new jobs demanding more education and higher levels of language, math, and reasoning skills (see Exhibit 3.8).

> Skills critical to the future of the workplace are emerging, but some are or will be in short supply. Several factors are driving the shift toward new skills for work: greater use of information technologies, the move away from craft and assembly manufacture and toward computer-mediated processes, the larger amount of knowledge work in almost every occupation, new requirements for education and the ability to manage complexity, and the redesign of many jobs to include computer-based work. Frequently, several skills will be folded into one job, often with a new title and greater individual responsibility.[41]

These changes are occurring because future jobs require substantially more education than the current jobs. This is why the illiteracy situation is especially critical[42] and why companies

> . . . are reaching into the educational system with a variety of incentives, new ideas, and cooperative agreements. In Minneapolis, for example, corporate contributions underwrote extensive participatory planning, which was used in the successful restructure of the city's school system, particularly its inner-city high schools. In Peking, Illinois, IBM's "Writing to Read" program helped first graders, cutting the number who needed remedial teaching from 11% to 2%.[43]

THE CHANGING ORGANIZATION.   Organizations today are more global, leaner, flatter, more flexible, faster, more customer oriented, more quality focused, and more innovative. Above all, today's organizations are constantly changing. Change has become a constant. Restructuring, retraining, and retooling are the *modus operandi*. There is more employee involvement and skill utilization. At the same time, leaner and flatter organizational structures mean fewer jobs are needed. While organizations are benefiting from these trends, there is opportunity only for persons with the requisite skills, who are willing and able to retrain and retool, and for whom jobs exist.

Eliminating layers of employees continues to be an important aspect in shaping the organization. The typical target is middle management. The elimination of this group facilitates the process of decentralizing, the process so necessary to

Jobs and organizations are changing faster than ever. They are becoming more fluid, adaptable, and high-skilled.

EXHIBIT 3.7
THE JOBS AMERICANS HOLD

	JOBS IN 1990 (THOUSANDS)	PROJECTED GROWTH (%) 1990–2005
Executive, Administrative, and Managerial		
General managers & top executives	3,100	14–24
Accountants & auditors	985	25–34
Financial managers	701	25–34
Other managers	701	N.A.
Restaurant & food service managers	557	25–34
Personnel & labor relations managers	456	25–34
Marketing, advertising, & PR managers	427	35 or more
Wholesale & retail buyers	361	14–24
Education administrators	348	14–24
Engineering & data-processing managers	315	25–34
Purchasing agents & managers	300	14–24
Health services managers	257	35 or more
Property & real estate managers	225	25–34
Administrative services managers	221	14–24
Inspectors & compliance officers	216	25–34
Industrial production managers	210	14–24
Construction contractors & managers	183	25–34
Cost estimators	173	14–24
Loan officers & counselors	172	25–34
Management analysts & consultants	151	35 or more
Marketing and Sales		
Retail sales workers	4,754	25–34
Cashiers	2,633	25–34
Manufacturers' & wholesale sales reps	1,944	14–24
Service sales representatives	588	35 or more
Insurance agents & brokers	439	14–24
Real estate agents, brokers, & appraisers	413	14–24
Counter & retail clerks	215	25–34
Securities & financial services sales reps	191	35 or more

EXHIBIT 3.7 (CONT.)
THE JOBS AMERICANS HOLD

	JOBS IN 1990 (THOUSANDS)	PROJECTED GROWTH (%) 1990–2005
Professional		
Registered nurses	1,727	35 or more
Kindergarten & elementary teachers	1,520	14–24
Engineers	1,519	25–34
Secondary-school teachers	1,280	25–34
Other professionals	865	N.A.
College & university faculty	712	14–24
Lawyers & judges	633	25–34
Social & human services workers	583	25–34
Physicians	580	25–34
Adult-education teachers	517	25–34
Computer systems analysts	463	35 or more
Physical, speech, & other therapists	382	25–34
Musicians and other performing artists	356	14–24
Designers	339	25–34
Ministers, priests, & rabbis	312	14–24
Architects & surveyors	236	14–24
Reporters, announcers, & PR specialists	233	14–24
Writers & editors	232	25–34
Visual artists	230	25–34
Social scientists	224	35 or more
Coaches & sports instructors	221	14–24
Recreation workers	194	14–24
Dentists	174	5–13
Pharmacists	169	14–24
Physical scientists	157	14–24
Transportation and Material Moving		
Truck drivers	2,700	14–24
Other transportation workers	698	5–13
Bus drivers	561	25–34
Industrial truck & tractor operators	431	5–13
Operating engineers	157	25–34
Technical Support		
Engineering technicians	755	25–34
Licensed practical nurses	644	35 or more
Computer programmers	565	35 or more
Other health technicians	522	35 or more
Other technicians	346	24–35

EXHIBIT 3.7 (CONT.)
THE JOBS AMERICANS HOLD

	JOBS IN 1990 (THOUSANDS)	PROJECTED GROWTH (%) 1990–2005
Technical Support *(continued)*		
Drafters	326	5–13
Medical technologists & technicians	258	14–25
Science technicians	246	14–25
Production		
Miscellaneous production workers	1,997	5–13
Supervisors	1,800	5–13
Metal- & plastic-working machine ops.	1,473	−4–4
Apparel workers	1,037	−5 or more
Inspectors, testers, & graders	668	−4–4
Welders, cutters, & welding machine ops.	427	−4–4
Machinists	386	5–13
Butchers & meat cutters	355	−5 or more
Precision assemblers	352	−5 or more
Woodworkers	349	5–13
Textile machinery operators	289	−5 or more
Printing press operators	251	14–24
Electrical & electronic assemblers	232	−5 or more
Prepress workers	186	14–24
Laundry & drycleaning machine ops.	173	14–24
Painting & coating machine ops.	160	−4–4
Repairs and Installation		
General maintenance mechanics	1,128	14–24
Automotive mechanics	757	14–24
Other mechanics	718	5–13
Industrial machinery repairers	474	5–13
Electronic equipment repairers	444	5–13
Diesel mechanics	268	14–24
Line installers & cable splicers	232	−5 or more
Automotive body repairers	219	14–24
Heating, a/c, & refrigeration mechanics	219	14–24

EXHIBIT 3.7 (CONT.)
THE JOBS AMERICANS HOLD

	JOBS IN 1990 (THOUSANDS)	PROJECTED GROWTH (%) 1990–2005
Unskilled Labor		
Miscellaneous unskilled workers	2,082	5–13
Freight, stock, & material movers	881	5–13
Packers & packagers	667	5–13
Construction trades helpers	549	5–13
Machine feeders & loaders	255	5–13
Service station attendants	245	–5 or more
Vehicle & equipment cleaners	240	14–24
Agriculture and Forestry		
Farm operators & managers	1,223	–5 or more
Farm workers	837	–5 or more
Other farm & forestry workers	338	5–13
Construction Trades		
Carpenters	1,077	14–24
Other trades & miners	863	N.A.
Electricians	548	25–34
Painters & paperhangers	453	14–24
Plumbers & pipefitters	379	14–24
Bricklayers & stonemasons	152	14–24
Highway maintenance workers	151	14–24
Administrative Support		
Record clerks	3,761	5–13
Traffic, shipping, & stock clerks	3,755	5–13
Secretaries	3,576	14–24
General office clerks	2,737	14–24
Word processors & data-entry keyers	1,448	–4–4
Information clerks	1,400	35 or more
Clerical supervisors & and managers	1,218	14–24
Adjusters, investigators, & collectors	1,088	14–24
Teacher aides	808	25–34
Postal clerks & mail carriers	607	5–13
Bank tellers	517	–5 or more
Other clerical workers	501	5–13

EXHIBIT 3.7 (CONT.)
THE JOBS AMERICANS HOLD

	JOBS IN 1990 (THOUSANDS)	PROJECTED GROWTH (%) 1990–2005
Administrative Support (*continued*)		
Telephone operators	325	−5 or more
Computer operators	319	5–13
Mail clerks & messengers	280	5–13
Credit clerks & authorizers	240	14–24
Duplicating & office machine operators	169	5–13
Miscellaneous Service		
Food & beverage service workers	4,400	25–34
Chefs, cooks, & kitchen workers	3,100	25–34
Janitors & cleaners	3,000	14–24
Nursing & psychiatric aides	1,374	35 or more
Preschool workers	990	35 or more
Guards	883	25–34
Gardeners & groundskeepers	874	35 or more
Private-household workers	782	−5 or more
Other service workers	727	14–24
Barbers & cosmetologists	713	14–24
Police, detectives, & special agents	665	14–24
Home health & housekeeping aides	391	35 or more
Firefighters	280	14–24
Correction officers	230	35 or more
Amusement & recreation attendants	184	14–24
Dental assistants	176	25–34
Medical assistants	165	35 or more
Armed Forces		
Enlisted personnel	1,742	−5 or more
Officers	295	−5 or more

SOURCE: W. Woods, "The Jobs Americans Hold," *Fortune* (July 12, 1993): 54–55. Used by permission.

Contingent workers are those hired on a limited-time basis.

enhance the speed with which decisions can be made. Along with this trend is the use of more contingent workers. **Contingent workers** are individuals hired on a limited-time basis. They are subject to dismissal on short notice and typically do not receive as many benefits as regular employees. There is also greater use of subcontracting. For example, IBM subcontracts with Pitney Bowes to run its mailrooms, stockrooms, and reproduction operations. Companies are increas-

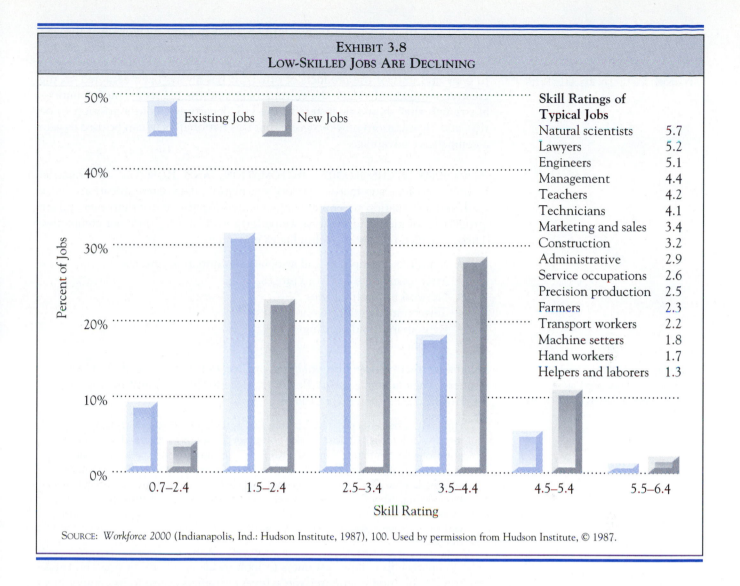

EXHIBIT 3.8
LOW-SKILLED JOBS ARE DECLINING

Existing Jobs   New Jobs

Percent of Jobs

50%

40%

30%

20%

10%

0%

Skill Rating: 0.7–2.4   1.5–2.4   2.5–3.4   3.5–4.4   4.5–5.4   5.5–6.4

Skill Rating

Skill Ratings of Typical Jobs

Natural scientists	5.7
Lawyers	5.2
Engineers	5.1
Management	4.4
Teachers	4.2
Technicians	4.1
Marketing and sales	3.4
Construction	3.2
Administrative	2.9
Service occupations	2.6
Precision production	2.5
Farmers	2.3
Transport workers	2.2
Machine setters	1.8
Hand workers	1.7
Helpers and laborers	1.3

SOURCE: *Workforce 2000* (Indianapolis, Ind.: Hudson Institute, 1987), 100. Used by permission from Hudson Institute, © 1987.

ingly **outsourcing** their payroll activities to payroll processing firms such as ADP (Automatic Data Processing). Again, these activities are occurring in concert as new lean and trim organizations form in the 1990s.

While it is becoming more difficult for U.S. firms to compete on the basis of cost, they can often do so by differentiating their products. Improving quality is one way of differentiating a product or service. Organizations started to focus on total-quality management in the 1980s as they moved to respond to customer preferences for the quality products supplied by Japan and Germany. Companies such as Xerox, L. L. Bean, and Ford became exemplars of the total quality approach to business. Their successes prove it can be done.

Companies are succeeding in their efforts to improve quality in many ways. While automation is often suggested as a way to improve quality (by getting the "unreliable" human element out of the process), examples such as the NUMMI (New United Motor Manufacturing Incorporated) plant in Fremont, California, and L.L. Bean demonstrate that state-of-the-art automation is not mandatory in enhancing quality. In many cases, automation is neither feasible nor desirable. Alternative ways to improve quality are discussed further in Chapter 15.

Outsourcing is the process of transferring to another company work that was previously done inside the company.

87

Perhaps the most likely avenue for U.S. firms to compete globally is through the development of new products. Other nations can copy U.S. products and improve them, but this still takes time. The United States has not been a nation to copy and imitate the products of others; it has always been centered on the creative-minded individual, the entrepreneur, and the pioneer. This is a national strength that should be fostered. The HR department is in a position to do this, and organizations now recognize that this national focus can be used to gain a competitive advantage.

ADVANCED TECHNOLOGIES, AUTOMATION, AND ROBOTS. Information technology, office automation, factory automation, data communications, voice mail, and information systems are implemented together faster than ever and are virtually revolutionizing the ways we perform work and organize our companies. These so-called **telematics technologies** encompass

- Mainframe computers and associated information systems
- Microcomputers and word processors
- Networking technologies
- Telecommunications technologies
- Reprography and printing
- Peripherals[44]

Telematics technologies enables organizations to respond more quickly, operate faster, and be more flexible.

Telematics technologies are enabling organizations to shape themselves into winners. They facilitate speed, flexibility, decentralization, and staying in close touch with the customer. For example:

> How fast is fast enough? The Limited (an upscale retail store with headquarters in Columbus, Ohio), tracks consumer preferences every day through point-of-sale computers. Orders, with facsimile illustrations, are sent by satellite to suppliers around the U.S. and in Hong Kong, South Korea, Singapore, and Sri Lanka. Within days clothing from distant points begins to collect in Hong Kong. About four times a week, a chartered 747 brings it to the company's distribution center in Ohio, where goods are priced and shipped to stores within 48 hours. Says Chairman Leslie Wexner: "That's not fast enough for the 90s."[45]

Computers also allow customers to look inside an organization. The trucking firm Pacific Intermountain Express gives customers access to its computers so they can check the status of their shipments. Banks and brokerage firms use computers to enable customers to conduct business from their homes and offices.

These technologies enhance quality by ensuring better parts and services from suppliers. Already retail chains are linked with their suppliers so that they know the timing and the nature of needed shipments. Telematics will also facilitate R&D capabilities and give managers more free time to get to know their companies better.

Automation, whether in the factory or the office, will continue to change organizational structures and culture. Because information is instantaneously available, there is little need for layers of management between the top and first-line management. Top management can bypass middle managers on their way to the first-line management, and this breaks the chain of command and can lead to ambiguity in reporting relationships.[46]

Thus, as the telematics technologies produce better products and faster and leaner organizations, so will they undermine traditional authority structures. At advanced plants, blue-collar workers will become information managers by becoming computer operators. Traditional managers may no longer be needed.

DID YOU KNOW?

Machines on the assembly line today are built for organizational flexibility. Power is moving away from managers and into the hands of workers. All of this is made possible by information technologies.

A few observers believe the computers in the workplace will lead to far more than better information and better products. Shoshana Zuboff, an associate professor at the Harvard Business School and author of *In the Age of the Smart Machine*, argues that computerization undermines traditional forms of authority and breaks down barriers between job categories and functions. "You have people doing work that is more abstract, more analytical," says Zuboff. "People not considered managerial in the past are managing information." Zuboff concludes that the role of the managers will have to be redefined in the 90s. Says she: "Since managers are no longer the guardians of the knowledge base, we do not need the command-control type of executive."[47]

In summary, more telematics implementation will provide organizations with opportunities to downsize, decentralize, and make their organizations more flexible and responsible. However, organizations must also be prepared to retrain workers, out-place workers (especially managers), and redesign jobs.

THE INTERNAL ENVIRONMENT

Several aspects within organizations influence how effectively a firm manages its human resources. They include top management's goals and values, organizational strategy, corporate culture technology, organizational structure, and organizational size. These aspects often influence each other—for example, top management's values shape organizational strategy, which in turn influences several HR management activities.

TOP MANAGEMENT'S GOALS AND VALUES

Top management determines how critical human resource management will be in organizations. If top management minimizes the importance of people to the organization's overall success, so will the line managers. In turn, those in the HR department will perform only operational-level resource activities. A likely consequence will be minimally effective human resource management in the firm.[48]

GOALS AND GUIDANCE.   The jobs created by an organization are management's most explicit statements of what they believe are the most appropriate means for accomplishing their goals. Stated goals and the subsequent standards of excellence that an organization establishes for job performance also give clear cues to employees about what is important and what behaviors are required. Thus, goals determine the criteria against which workers and their behaviors will be evaluated. The criteria in turn determines the kinds of individuals who will be attracted to the organization and how they will be evaluated and promoted. Thus, organizational goals establish reasons for jobs, the organization's expectations for workers, and even the legitimacy of the job demands.

DEVELOPING PEOPLE.   Top management's goals and values plus the support and commitment of the chief executive officer are important in the development of people.

> Grab any Wall Street analyst by the lapel and he'll tell you PepsiCo is a brilliant marketing company. Well, sure, but then ask CEO Wayne Calloway how it got that way and he'll talk not about those slick ads starring Madonna and Michael Jackson, but about what he calls the three P's. "people, people, people." Ah, touch-feely management? Anything but. Behind Calloway's alluringly alliterative slogan lies the country's most sophisticated and

> **LEARNING OBJECTIVE 4**
>
> Explain how top management's goals and values, organizational strategy, structure, culture, and technology influence human resource management.

At Harley-Davidson, we are committed to a corporate Vision that mandates how we run our businesses. Our Vision says: "Harley-Davidson, Inc. is an action-oriented, international company— a leader in its commitment to continuously improve the quality of profitable relationships with stakeholders (customers, employees, suppliers, shareholders, governments and society). Harley-Davidson believes the key to success is to balance stakeholders' interests through the empowerment of all employees to focus on value-added activities."

comprehensive system for turning bright young people into strong managers. Says he: "We take eagles and teach them to fly in formation."

PepsiCo takes people development more seriously than perhaps any other American corporation. Calloway spends up to two months every year personally reviewing the performance of his top 550 managers, discussing their futures with their bosses and with the personnel department. Calloway, who says he knows most of the 550 managers and spends anywhere from 5 to 30 minutes reviewing each one, states with conviction, "There's nothing I do that's more important." In all, he spends 40% of his time on people issues. He expects the people below him to do the same, so that by the end of each year every one of the company's 20,000 managers knows exactly where he or she stands.[49]

Without top management support for and commitment to developing people, the major focus of an organization is likely to be on other activities. This is particularly true when the focus is on short-term goals and immediate results. The short-term orientation allows too little time for the benefits of training and development to come through. Top management at PepsiCo began to emphasize training and development when they recognized that they had to develop their people and businesses in order to be effective.

RIGHTS AND ETHICS.   Top management shares responsibility in setting the stage for employee rights and ethical conduct because they set policy, with input from the HR department, on the treatment of employees and on the definition of ethical behavior. Top management's policy regarding these rights and what is ethical is important in shaping the way the organization's people are treated and the conduct of employees with respect to each other, customers, and to themselves.

For an excellent description of the role of top management regarding ethics, read the feature, "Managing Human Resources at Waste Management Corporation: Building an Ethical Culture." Note the role the HR department plays in the communication process. Its role in the training process is described in Chapter 14. All of this is influenced by corporate culture.

CORPORATE CULTURE

Corporate culture is an organization's value system.

Organizational or **corporate culture** represents an organization's value system.[51] Strongly influenced by top management, corporate culture typically indicates how an organization regards its customers, suppliers, competitors, the environment, and its employees.

HR philosophy is a statement of how the organization regards its employees.

The aspect of corporate culture that refers to employees can be referred to as a company's HR philosophy. The **HR philosophy** is a statement of how the organization regards it human resources—what role people play in the overall success of the business and how they are to be treated and managed. Such a statement is typically very general, thus allowing interpretation at more specific levels of action within an organization. For example, The Weyerhaeuser Company in Tacoma, Washington, uses its HR philosophy statement to describe what employees mean to the company and how they are to be managed. The following is an excerpt:

- People are mature, responsible individuals who want to contribute.
- People hold themselves to high standards of integrity and business ethics; they are responsible stewards of the land and environment.
- Our work environment is based on mutual respect, personal satisfaction, and growth opportunities for everyone.
- People recognize that teamwork, cooperation, and a clean, safe, well-maintained workplace are essential to fulfilling our customer commitments.

Sherwin-Williams HR Philosophy: To get profitable growth through HR policies and programs to attract and retain highly skilled and productive employees and develop organizational capability to get competitive advantage.

MANAGING HUMAN RESOURCES
at Waste Management Corporation

Building an Ethical Culture

WASTE Management Corporation, or WMX (Oak Brook, Illinois), the largest U.S. waste services company, with over $6 billion in sales, is taking a leading role in building ethics awareness into the company culture for its 60,000 employees. Under the impetus of Chairman and CEO Dean Buntrock and an Executive Environmental Committee, Waste Management is seeking to gain employee commitment and leadership awareness through a number of management systems.

Overall responsibility for the effort belongs to Jodie Bernstein, vice-president of Environmental Policy and Ethical Standards, also general counsel for Chemical Waste Management, and a former general counsel for the Environmental Protection Agency and the Department of Health, Education and Welfare (now Health and Human Services) in Washington, D.C. She believes that explicit and active management of ethical issues is vital to Waste Management because of the nature of its business, but it's also becoming increasingly important to other businesses as well. "Increasingly, we are seeing a breakdown in government's ability to regulate environmental and other ethical issues, and there is a growing public distrust of government interference in these matters. Moreover, on the individual level, we just can't make the assumptions we used to about our shared value systems. The diverse work force and our increased globalization mean we have to recognize that people have different ideas about what is and isn't ethical. Rather than leave things up to chance, we're going to spell it out for people."

RULES VS. CLIMATE
"In some areas, like compliance with EPA regulations, for example, we tell people exactly what the rules and expectations are," says Bernstein. "Falsifying information on a regulatory filing, for example, means immediate dismissal. But we think it has to go beyond that. Ethics is more than following the rules. You can't make enough rules to cover all the things that can come up, so it's important that all employees have a general level of ethical awareness, so that they will at least be asking the right questions. And you have to create a climate in which it's possible—easier, even—for employees to do the right thing. Most of the programs we are developing focus on this latter area: increasing awareness of ethical issues and building an ethical climate throughout the company."

ETHICS COMMUNICATION
To do that, the company is adapting many of its existing human resource and communication systems. Under Jodie Bernstein's direction, explicit business conduct guidelines are being written, and she is considering the establishment of a regular ethics column in the employee publication. Ethics goals are also being developed for the performance appraisal system, which already includes factors related to environmental compliance and health and safety. The company is also trying to rejuvenate an existing employee hotline program to encourage more use. Established in 1984, the hotline may be used by employees who wish to call attention to a situation they find disturbing or to ask questions on ethical, environmental, or safety issues.

The bottom line, according to Bernstein, is ethical leadership: "This is the lifeblood of our company. We are an environmental services company. How we handle these issues is critical to our success."[50]

- Continuing education is an ongoing commitment that involves everyone.[52]

Instead of using the term HR philosophy or HR values to describe how employees are regarded and how they are to be treated and managed, some organizations just use the term culture—that is, "We will create a culture that recognizes how important we feel about people and how we are going to treat them."

Downsizing means reducing the
number of employees.
Decentralizing means moving the
decision making to lower levels of
the organization.

Culture is always reflected in the company's HR activities. For example, companies such as Levi Strauss that have a culture of caring for and respecting the individual are likely to offer employment security and provide for a variety of employee needs. This is reflected in Levi Strauss' Aspiration Statement (Exhibit 2.2). Many employees learn the culture and the HR philosophy of the organization through HR activities—how it selects, what criteria it evaluates, and what it compensates most highly.

Corporate culture is very important for companies doing business worldwide. For example, as Pepsi-Cola (PepsiCo) expands its global business, it still wants to retain a certain image and a certain way of doing business. Having a culture that is shared worldwide helps Pepsi-Cola and its international division, Pepsi-Cola International (PCI) achieve a consistent image, as described in the feature, "Managing Human Resources Around the World: Pepsi-Cola International."

TECHNOLOGY

Technology generally refers to the equipment and knowledge used to produce goods and services. What we are witnessing today in organizations is a virtual discarding of yesterday's technology. For example, old technology such as Henry Ford's mass production are ending up in the junkyard. In their place are new technologies, such as the "lean" production systems of Eiji Toyoda of Toyota and his production genius, Taiichi Ohno:

> Just as the mass-production principles pioneered by Henry Ford and General Motors' Alfred Sloan swept away the age of craft production after World War I, so the ideas of Toyoda and Ohno are today chipping away at the foundations of mass production. We call their system "lean" production because it uses less of everything than a comparable mass-production operation: half the human effort in the factory, half the manufacturing space, half the investment in tools, half the engineering hours to develop a new product. Lean production is built not simply on technical insight but on a precisely defined set of relationships that extends far beyond the factory floor to encompass designers, suppliers, and customers.[54]

In many organizations today, current employee skills are insufficient because of these technological changes. Consequently, retraining employees at organizations such as Xerox, Ford, GM, and General Electric is becoming common. Others are training new hires to meet their needs.

With the pace of technology accelerating, the most likely scenario is one of organizations continually retraining current employees and recruiting new employees with unique skills. Changing technology necessitates continual training program formulation and implementation, and employees who are willing to adapt, to be reassigned to different jobs, and to be retrained. By encouraging and supporting employees in these efforts, employers may provide employment security.[55]

ORGANIZATIONAL STRUCTURE

Organizational structure describes the number of levels of employees in an organization—the number of nonmanagement and management levels, and the distribution of the decision-making process. Companies have tended to restructure themselves to be most effective in terms of quality and cost. They have done this by reducing the number of levels of employees (**downsizing**) and by **decentralizing** the decision-making process (moving decision making to lower levels):

Pepsi-Cola International (PCI) always knew it needed a certain kind of savvy, intelligent manager to succeed in the complex world of international production and marketing. But just to be sure, the international division quantified its values and expectations, says John Fulkerson, personnel director for Pepsi-Cola International (Somers, New York).

"We recently studied 100 successful managers and 100 unsuccessful managers, with the help of the Center for Creative Leadership, and came up with eleven qualities that seem to make a difference in success at Pepsi-Cola International. We looked at very junior to very senior managers over a three-year period.

"We were not surprised by any of the qualities—especially the top three:

- The ability to handle business complexities
- The ability to lead and manage people
- Drive and a results orientation

"All these qualities support our company's success and results orientation, which lies at the heart of our corporate culture. It sounds hard to maintain a workable corporate culture when doing business across cultures. However, Pepsi-Cola International has built a set of values that transcend petty differences and apply to everyone, everywhere.

"What's important is how you treat people. We operate on the principles of telling people what we expect, showing them how to develop, and helping them reach the goals. Those ideas work in any of the 150 countries we do business in.

"People are more similar than we think; they want the same things. They want to be successful. That even applies in the Communist bloc countries. After all, they invited us in. They just want to be successful, too.

"Our 1,200 international employees help us sell 40 billion 8-ounce servings of Pepsi annually in 145 countries through 16 regional offices. Our people need to be mature and savvy. They must be able to handle complex business and understand global issues.

"We need these kinds of people to do business in the complex international arena, and Pepsi-Cola needs people like this to operate in the result-oriented culture that (former Pepsi chairman) Don Kendall pioneered here. We key on results because, especially in international, you quickly learn there are 100 ways to do anything. . . .

"Our culture centers around clear communication of the expected results, and risk taking with no punishment for making mistakes. Along with this expectation that our mature, savvy people will know what to do is another expectation that they'll know when it's time to ask for help. We emphasize the criticality of communication. We make it known that we expect, for example, a manager in Spain to know when it's appropriate to check with New York to see what Australia is doing in a certain circumstance. If you talk to others, you lessen the chance of making a mistake.

"Our culture also tells managers that being defensive will get you nowhere and that you are not viewed as being mature if you just complain. Things are very open and above board here, and that is even reflected in a formalized personnel program we call 'Instant Feedback.' It's a system for reinforcing our desire to have constant quick communication.

"Some cultures don't like this, and we are flexible. For example, in the Far East, you can't give feedback in front of peers, you wait until you're alone. In Latin America, on the other hand, people are much more vocal in discussing performance issues. They throw it out on the table and it's a jump ball.

"Though we try to emphasize similarities in our culture, and hope that most of our values cut across cultures, we are not unmindful of varying customs in different cultures and regions. We're willing to modify our practices to get results, because wanting results is at the heart of our culture.[53]

A shrinking world has meant an expanding clock. Managers have shaped organizations that can respond quickly to developments abroad. As speed and agility become paramount virtues, we will see even more decentralization, with responsibility closer to the operating level.[56]

And as we see the need for continual downsizing and decentralizing, we will continue to see announcement of plant/office closings, layoffs, early retirement programs, and use of contingent and part-time workers. Thus we will discuss these again, particularly in Chapter 16, Employee Rights.

ORGANIZATIONAL SIZE

Organizational size is also an important factor in HR activities. Although exceptions exist, generally the larger the organization, the more developed its internal labor market and the less its reliance on the external labor market. In contrast, the smaller the organization, the less developed its internal labor market and the greater its reliance on the external labor market.

The organization that relies more on an internal labor market is itself the critical factor in deciding how much to pay people and what job evaluation, job classifications, and equity will be used. For the organization that relies mostly on the external labor market, the determining factor in such issues as pay rates and equity will be what other organizations are doing in these areas.

Human resource departments in smaller organizations also tend to be small. As mentioned in Chapter 2, the number of HR professionals per 100 is about 1. Well, if an organization has 50 employees, it may very well not even have an HR department. Yes, there may be an administrative assistant or special outside firm such as ADP that does the payroll; but most things related to managing people will fall to the line managers. In this situation, then, the partnership is between the line managers and the employees. As firms get larger, they take on a staff of HR professionals who share in this partnership. It is important, however, that the line managers stay involved in this relationship.

When the size of firms is discussed, several measures can be used. The federal government typically defines small organizations as having fewer than 500 employees. Others define small to mean fewer than 100 employees. In either case, firms over 500 employees are then labeled as large organizations. The median size of firms in the United States is 20 employees.

Firm size is important not only because it determines the size of the HR department and whether internal or external labor markets take precedence, but also because legal considerations impact large and small firms differently. Federal legislation generally applies to firms with 15 or more employees. State and city employment legislation, however, can apply to firms of all sizes. It is incumbent on firms themselves to know which categories they fall under and which laws apply to them.

COMPETITIVE STRATEGIES

Organizations continually develop strategies to beat their competitors. Harvard's Michael Porter suggested three ways firms can beat their competitors:

- quality improvement
- cost reduction
- innovation

These are significant for HR management because they determine needed employee behaviors. That is, for competitive strategies to be successfully implemented, employees have to behave in certain ways. Keep in mind the general model shown in Exhibit 3.9 as you read the following text.

DID YOU KNOW?

Many firms, such as General Electric and Johnson & Johnson do everything possible to put the "Soul of the Small Company" into their large organizations.

Three key competitive strategies:
- quality improvement
- cost reduction
- innovation

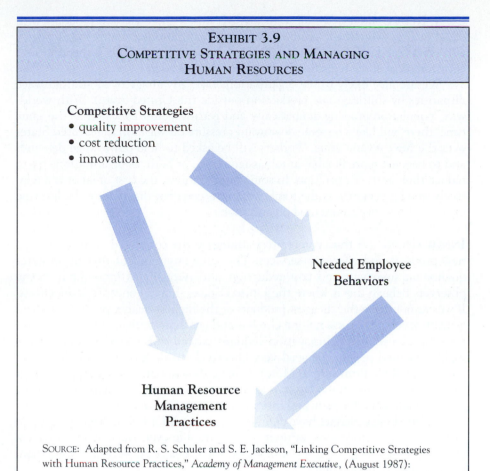

EXHIBIT 3.9
COMPETITIVE STRATEGIES AND MANAGING
HUMAN RESOURCES

Competitive Strategies
- quality improvement
- cost reduction
- innovation

Needed Employee Behaviors

Human Resource Management Practices

SOURCE: Adapted from R. S. Schuler and S. E. Jackson, "Linking Competitive Strategies with Human Resource Practices," *Academy of Management Executive*, (August 1987):

QUALITY IMPROVEMENT. Organizations are continually confronted and challenged with the need to deliver quality goods and services. Domestic and international competition forces this, of course, but so do consumers. As consumers, we continue to demand high-quality products and are willing to buy from whomever offers such products. To keep matters interesting, the ante on playing in this international arena of high quality keeps going up: what was acceptable quality yesterday is unacceptable today. Thus, organizations must continue to pursue quality improvement with a vengeance; HR management is central to quality improvement.

Do you think the quality of service you get from a bank has anything to do with the treatment you get from the bank's tellers? Do you think the quality of the stereo, VCR, CD player, or car you drive has anything to do with level of motivation, dedication, training, and commitment of the individuals making these products? Of course. In both cases, *product quality* depends on the people we are dealing with as well as on the people behind the scenes who make the products. *Total quality* depends on all parts of the organization working together. Consequently, organizations are bound to give increasing attention to their human resources as they seek to enhance their product quality. Further implications of quality improvement are described in detail in Chapter 15, Total Quality Management.

Quality improvement means improving product and service qualities that customers value.

Cost reduction means reducing the cost of the service or product.

Innovation means discovering and developing new products and services.

COST REDUCTION. We all want quality; but, if there are two products with equal quality, which will you buy? Even as organizations enhance quality, they also seek to reduce costs. Consequently, we are likely to see large organizations continue work force reductions throughout this decade.

We are also likely to see organizations take advantage of substantial wage disparities by shifting some production outside the United States. With worldwide population growing dramatically and getting better educated at the same time, there will likely be some downward pressure on wages in the United States over the next several years. Workers will be asked to hold down wage demands and to become more flexible in job assignments, or both, as organizations try to reduce their costs of operation. In some organizations, the cost of labor is a relatively small percentage of the total operations cost, but this tends to be less true in most of our service-oriented organizations.

INNOVATION. A third competitive strategy is the continued need to develop new products and offer new services. The same environment that necessitates quality improvement and cost reduction also necessitates innovation. Some observers believe this is where the United States should concentrate its efforts. If we cannot make the cheapest products or the highest quality products, we can at least develop products no one else has and get them to market faster once we have developed them. Innovation requires careful HR management; it takes highly talented people managed very effectively to develop new products and ideas. Some U.S. firms such as Motorola have shown that they can do this rather well. The challenge in the future is for more firms to do this and for those doing it to stay ahead of domestic and international competitors.

While these strategies have definite implications for HR management, so do other strategies. Since some of them such as the life-cycle stage of a firm have a particularly significant impact on compensation practices, we will discuss them in Chapter 11, Total Compensation.

INTERNATIONAL COMPARISONS

We have selected three important international issues for human resource management to examine here: worldwide population figures, worldwide educational attainment levels, and HR management in Mexico.

WORLDWIDE POPULATION AND EDUCATIONAL ATTAINMENT

Between now and the year 2020, the developing nations are expected to increase their population in an amount equal to the total population of the industrialized nations. As this happens, the average age in the developing nations will decrease, and that in the industrialized nations will increase. Comparing industrialized nations with those in the process of industrializing, the developing nations, we also see substantial differences in educational levels. Exhibit 3.10 shows that the percentage of the total high school and college students in industrialized and developing nations is changing dramatically.[57]

Together, these data suggest an increasing worldwide labor supply with a large component of highly educated individuals. From a human resource point of view, the implications of this will be significant. To say the least, these trends can certainly facilitate the globalization of businesses; it may be feasible for companies to open up shop in literally any part of the world. What other possible implications do *you* see?

EXHIBIT 3.10		
SHARE OF SCHOOL STUDENTS BY INDUSTRIALIZED NATIONS*		
YEAR	AGES 15–18 (HIGH SCHOOL)	AGES 19–22 (COLLEGE)
1970	44% of 160 million	77% of 26 million
1985	30% of 280 million	51% of 58 million
2000	21% of 450 million	40% of 115 million

*Industrialized nations include those in North America, Western Europe, and the Asia–Pacific Region.

SOURCE: Compiled from W. B. Johnston, "Global Work Force 2000: The New World Labor Market," *Harvard Business Review* (Mar.–Apr. 1991), 115–29.

MEXICO

Because of our rapidly developing trade relationship with Mexico—witness the NAFTA agreement—a better understanding of this country is imperative. A significant difference exists between HR practices in the United States and Mexico. Historical as well as cultural differences contribute to this. Mexico's HR practices reflect concerns of both employee and employer and are heavily government regulated. Labor laws are derived from the federal labor law of Mexico; therefore, the Mexican government dictates most of what HR professionals can do in Mexico.

Mexico is an excellent source for the study of governmental influences on HR practices. In 1965, it established the Border Industrialization Program (BIP) to fight high unemployment. Currently, more than 100,000 Mexicans work for U.S. auto companies in border plants called **maquiladoras,** which grew out of the BIP. The work force assembles, processes, and finishes foreign material and components in the maquiladoras, most of which are located along the U.S.–Mexico border, where the bulk of Mexico's economic activity takes place. The program permits duty-free import of all tools (equipment, raw materials) required for production if the final product is to be exported.

Since its inception, BIP goals have remained the same: to increase Mexico's level of industrialization; to create new jobs; to raise the domestic income level; to facilitate the transfer, absorption, and skills of technology; and to attract much-needed foreign exchange. Foreign firms have located here for the low cost of labor, high-quality workmanship, and high productivity.[58]

Maquiladoras **refers to manufacturing plants, typically on the Mexican border.**

SOCIAL AND LEGAL STRUCTURE.   Mexico's social structure is similar to its family structure. One of the biggest issues in Mexico—and also in Japan—is paternalism. In the Mexican mind, all institutions—whether government, business, or church—are like an authoritarian family structure. A plant manager, like the president of Mexico, fills an authoritarian and fatherly role, rather than a mere organizational function.

Mexican law and history reflects this view that the employer has a moral and paternal responsibility for all his employees, even when there is a union. The

Mexican employee is not just working for a paycheck. Workers expect to be treated as the "extended family" of the boss, thereby receiving a wider range of services and benefits than those provided north of the border. Examples include food baskets and medical attention for themselves and their families (apart from social security). The medical benefits are not considered "an extra" or discretionary; in the Mexican worker's mind, they simply fulfill the employer's role and responsibilities.

In return, Mexican workers feel they have a reciprocal obligation to be loyal, to work hard, and to be willing to do whatever is requested of them. American managers who accept the Mexican sense that a job is more than a paycheck and who try to fulfill their part of the "bargain" can reap the benefits of employee loyalty, including employee willingness to come to work every day and to work conscientiously.

To gain a better perspective of Mexican economic conditions and employment concerns as compared to those of other nations, see Exhibit 3.11. Note that this exhibit provides information on only those countries that are our biggest trading partners.

 ## CURRENT TRENDS

RESPONSIVENESS TO THE ENVIRONMENT

Rising concerns about quality, cost, and innovation indicates that business is positioning itself to be more responsive to the environment. This entire chapter, of course, is about the environment. It is filled with facts that suggest the world order is changing and will continue to change. While some trends are predictable, others are increasingly less predictable—even as they have a greater impact on managing human resources. Response speed is now more critical than ever, and to respond rapidly, the HR manager must continually seek to understand the environment. Results of the worldwide IBM/Towers Perrin study support this need. Two significant conclusions of the study are that, for effective firms in highly competitive environments, the HR departments must

- be responsive to a highly competitive marketplace and global business structures
- be closely linked to the business

SUMMARY

The decade of the 1990s will continue to be filled with change, challenge, uncertainty, and intense global competition, all demanding ever higher standards of quality and rates of innovation at the same time as costs are reduced. There is a higher than ever premium on obtaining and utilizing information. This means the HR department must continually scan the external environment to stay abreast of international and national economic activity, social and demographic changes, and technological trends and developments. With this information in hand, the HR department can create scenarios on how these external environmental forces will impact the organization. For example, an environmental scan of work force demographics may indicate coming skilled labor shortages but also

EXHIBIT 3.11
WORK FORCE OF SEVERAL MAJOR COUNTRIES IN EUROPE, ASIA-PACIFIC AND NORTH AMERICA

EUROPE

Great Britain has about 25 million employees—14 million men and 11 million women. Unemployment rate is less than 10%. Major concerns: competitiveness, worker-flexibility, skills and education, and social class distinctions.

Germany has about 56 million employees—30 million men and 26 million women. Unemployment is about 10% (but as much as to 40% in what was East Germany!). Major concerns: high costs of labor, need to reduce worker inputs into products, integrating the eastern part of Germany, a strong labor movement, and an aging population.

France has about 25 million employees—15 million men and 10 million women. Unemployment is 11%. Major concerns: unemployment, privatization, competitiveness, difficulty in firing, extensive benefits, and short work years. Average work year approximately 1,600 hours.

Sweden has about 4.3 million employees—2.2 million men and 2.1 million women. Unemployment is less than 10%. Major concerns: competitiveness, high wage levels, and high tax levels.

ASIA-PACIFIC

Japan has about 60 million employees: 36 million men and 24 million women. Unemployment is less than 3%. Major concerns: increasing consumerism, high tax rates, high wages, and bureaucratic procedures. Average work year approximately 2,400 hours.

South Korea has about 16 million employees—9.5 million men and 6.5 million women. Unemployment is less than 5%. Major concerns: 50-hour work week, low wages, government is anti-union and increasing consumerism. Average work year approximately 2,700 hours.

People's Republic of China has about 400 million workers (of these 275 million are farmers) with 50% men and women. Unemployment is less than 3%. Major concerns: low skill utilization, low mobility, low quality, and planned economy and industry.

Australia has about 7 million employees—4.3 million men and 2.7 million women. Unemployment is about 10%. Major concerns: competitiveness, unionization and wage tribunals, wage inflexibility, and legal integration of the work force.

NORTH AMERICA

Canada has about 12 million employees—6.7 million men and 5.3 million women. Unemployment is about 10%. Major concerns: provincial versus federal strength, competitiveness, high wages, and decentralized labor relations.

United States has about 120 million employees—63 million men and 57 million women. Unemployment is about 6%. Major concerns: competitiveness, skills, downsizing, and medical costs. Average work year approximately 2,100 hours.

Mexico has about 50 million employees, 30 million men and 20 million women. Unemployment is less than 15%, and wages are among the lowest in the industrialized world. Major concerns: maintaining low wages among a highly educated and high-quality work force, keeping labor peace, and maintaining high levels of motivation.

that any shortfalls may be made up by immigrants. Keeping abreast of external environmental changes allows the HR department craft effective organizational responses.

Given the current external environment, organizational success results when organizations are

- Capable of rapid response
- Flexible
- Adaptable
- Focused
- Lean and cost oriented
- Quality oriented
- Customer oriented
- Innovation oriented

For responses to be effective, they must be sufficiently anticipated, discussed, and shared with all employees, and then implemented with full support of the organization.

The decade of the 1990s also means that the HR department must scan the internal environment to stay attuned to changes in organizational strategies and directions, the needs of the work force and line managers as they seek to make their organizations more competitive, flexible, adaptable, and focused. Combining these internal characteristics with the external conditions, HR professionals suggest that successful firms in highly competitive environments are likely to have—indeed, will be required to have—employees who are

- Adaptable
- Committed
- Motivated
- Skilled/reskilled
- Highly energetic
- Good performers in diverse employee groups
- Good team players

Taken together, the changing internal and external environments are having a major impact. They are virtually transforming the operation and staffing of HR departments and their organizations. We will see this impact reflected upon throughout this book.

KEY CONCEPTS

baby boomers	external environment	organizational strategy
baby busters	glass ceiling	organizational structure
contingent workers	HR philosophy	ownership
corporate culture	internal environment	sex-role stereotyping
decentralizing	job sex-typing	telematics technologies
downsizing	maquiladora	traditionalists
empower	organizational size	work force diversity

REVIEW AND DISCUSSION QUESTIONS

1. What is the impact of domestic and international competition on managing human resources?
2. What work force and demographic changes are likely to significantly affect HR management? Describe the nature of the effects.
3. How can organizations increase decision making and power at the lower levels of the organization without upsetting middle managers?
4. Will the trend toward employee ownership make firms more competitive? What is the limit of this trend?
5. What can U.S. firms do to manage diversity in the work force?
6. Do you expect that by the year 2000 jobs will no longer be sex-stereotyped?
7. Should U.S. employers encourage a greater influx of immigrants? What are the HR implications of this issue? See references in Note 58.
8. How are the economic and organizational trends discussed in this chapter impacting HR management?
9. Will employers have to do even more basic education training if they are to have any hope of being competitive?
10. Briefly describe how each of the aspects of the internal environment affects HR management.

EXERCISES AND CASES

FIELD PROJECT

Interview four people, two from each of two different organizations. Ask them to describe their organization's culture, particularly as it relates to managing people (that is, the part we refer to as the HR philosophy). Compare and contrast the responses of the people in the same organization and then the set of responses from both organizations. Report for the class on the differences and your explanation for them.

CASE

WORK FORCE 2000

USA Telecommunications Company (USATC) is faced with a major HR planning problem. The company is currently planning for the year 2000. It is already clear from company trends that the labor force predicted in "Work Force 2000" (WF2000), as USATC management calls the planning effort, will be very different from today's force. Andrea Nelson, manager of Human Resource Planning, is gathering data on this as she and USATC's top managers are very concerned about the availability of qualified personnel. Highly qualified personnel are crucial to meeting the company's strategic objective—to be the number one communications company in the world.

Andrea noted several reasons why the changes predicted in WF2000 are so important to USATC in a memo to Juana Lopez, vice-president of Human Resources. First, strategic business forecasts indicate increased competition for "basic" telecommunications services and dramatic increases for "high-end" features such as videoconferencing. USATC is aggressively pursuing a leading-edge strategy in the market. Second, significant demographic shifts in the population will affect the composition of the work force. Third, the demand for service-sector employees will far exceed the availability of qualified workers. Competition for qualified employees will be fierce.

Using an environmental scan, the WF2000 team has collected various data under Andrea's direction. Environmental scanning uses forecasting techniques and statistical approaches. Experts are asked to forecast or create scenarios for the future. Statistical analyses are used to find trends in historical data. The WF2000 environmental scan revealed the following trends:

- The growth rate of the labor force is declining as the population ages and the "baby boomers" (1946–1964) give way to the "baby busters" (1965–1975). From the employers' perspective, the labor markets will be much tighter, especially for new entrants into the work force.
- The median age of employees will rise from 32 in 1987 to 36 in the year 2000. This has been called the "middle aging" of the work force. The median age of USATC's work force is 41 years.
- An increasing number of USATC employees are becoming eligible to collect pensions. By 2000, approximately 40 percent of employees in all business units will be pension eligible. In the "emerging technologies" unit, 63 percent will be pension eligible.
- Most new entrants into the labor force will be women, minorities, and immigrants. For example,

by 2000, women will comprise almost 50 percent of the work force.
- New jobs requiring new skills will emerge as USATC moves full blown into the "information age."
- The fastest growing occupations are computer service technicians (96 percent growth), legal assistants (94 percent), computer systems analysts (85 percent), and computer programmers (77 percent). The most rapidly declining occupations are railroad conductors (32 percent decline), shoe-making machine operators (30 percent), aircraft structure assemblers (21 percent), and central telephone office operators (20 percent).
- Dual-income and single-parent families are on the rise. Demands for child care and dual-income family support services will increase.
- There will be a strong trend toward globalization as companies look for markets abroad. In 1994, the United States accounted for 20 percent of the gross world product, down from 40 percent in 1960. USATC will need employees with language skills who are sensitive to cultural diversity, are knowledgeable about world markets, and who are seeking employment abroad.

Andrea has just distributed this summary from the environmental scan to the seven-member WF2000 Team. Each member is familiar with sections of the data, but this is the first time they have seen a compilation of each other's work. The group must now use these trends to develop specific human resources planning programs for USATC.

CASE QUESTIONS

1. Are the data Andrea has gathered really useful for USATC? How?
2. What programs should USATC initiate to deal with the changing demographics?
3. Are the programs to be initiated all longer term? Which ones should begin now?
4. Should another environmental scan be conducted to collect other data?

GLASS CEILINGS OR GLASS DOORS?

Southwestern State University prides itself on its rapid growth and expansion of facilities during the decades of the 70s and 80s. Now, in the decade of the 90s, many see Southwestern poised to become, as college presidents are wont to say, a preeminent university. A traditional land grant university with an emphasis on agriculture, Southwestern currently boasts one of the largest schools of business and engineering in the country.

John DeNisi, an employee relations specialist in the personnel department, has witnessed firsthand the rapid growth and transformation of Southwestern during his eleven-year tenure in university administration at Southwestern. John is less sanguine about the future, though. Growth will continue but at a considerably reduced rate given projected population trends for the region. Moreover, John, like others, is worried about Southwestern's stance toward minority recruitment.

Three years ago, John served on a universitywide committee that examined the status of minorities at Southwestern in staff, faculty, and student areas. The final report his committee delivered to the president was not optimistic, to say the least. Southwestern was under-represented in all areas with regard to both blacks and Hispanics. Potentially, Southwestern stands to lose federal funds unless the university undertakes significant moves to attract and retain more minorities in the future. Accordingly, the committee's report recommended renewed efforts to recruit aggressively in all areas, to set aside money for minority recruitment, and to set up minority scholarships to attract more students.

Recently though, John is wondering what impact the current administration policy from Washington would have on Southwestern's steps toward affirmative action. John closely follows reports in the *Chronicle of Higher Education* and the College and University Personnel Association newsletter of the battle in Washington over the status of voluntary affirmative action plans. Although professional groups such as the National Association of Manufacturers and the Society for Human Resource Management support affirmative action as "good business policy," the Department of Justice and the Equal Employment Opportunity Commission (EEOC) seem to have taken a major retreat from earlier administration positions on affirmative action.

The Department of Labor, though, seems to be at odds with the Justice Department and the EEOC because it supports goals and timetables in its enforcement of affirmative action plans for federal contractors. Moreover, the Supreme Court appears to support voluntary affirmative action plans in several recent decisions dealing specifically with such plans. Vocal critics of the new administration stand on affirmative action argue that without affirmative action, minorities will merely bump up against the "invisible ceiling." John wonders what implications these developments could have for Southwestern's stance for the future. If Southwestern initiates such a plan and the Depart-ment of Justice then successfully challenges the constitutionality of affirmative action plans, the university could strap itself with discrimination and reverse discrimination suits well into the twenty-first century.

John's ruminations were abruptly interrupted by a call from the front office informing John that an applicant had requested a meeting. Usually this meant that a disgruntled applicant was unhappy with the impersonal treatment received from the front office. John would then spend a few minutes with the applicant, try to smooth ruffled feathers, and, when necessary, reprimand office staff for rude or discourteous behavior. More often than not, though, John encountered an obnoxious faculty spouse that not only expected immediate employment but also demanded it publicly in a crowded front office.

As John girded himself, he was introduced at the door to Alma Fisher, a well-dressed and attractive black woman. Alma did not beat around the bush. "Mr. DeNisi," Alma blurted out, "this university doesn't want to hire blacks, and I want to know what you're going to do about it!" After a few minutes of discussion, John learned that Alma previously worked at the university as a secretary but had left two years ago on maternity leave. Upon reentering the labor force, Alma visited the university employment office, took the clerical tests, and qualified, based on her performance, for a senior secretary position, the highest paid clerical position at the university.

John's office had matched Alma's qualifications to a position request submitted by the Medical College and referred Alma to the dean of the Medical School for an interview. According to Alma, during the interview the dean asked Alma if she had children and how she supported herself. The straw that broke the camel's back, though, came when the dean asked Alma if she was on welfare. At that point, Alma suggested to the dean that his line of questioning was "inappropriate" and asked the dean to stick to job-related questions concerning her qualifications to do the job. "You know, Mr. DeNisi," asserted Alma, "I did not tell the dean that my previous position with the university was as a secretary to the affirmative action officer. I could sue this university based on his behavior!"

John was struck by the irony of this moment. Why worry about glass ceilings at Southwestern, he thought, when the glass doors aren't open?

CASE QUESTIONS

1. What is the evidence for the existence of glass ceilings or glass doors at Southwestern?
2. As the affirmative action officer for Southwestern, would you be more likely to follow the opinions of the Supreme Court or the current administration?
3. Are the goals and timetables sufficient to achieve racial integration of colleges and universities? (See Chapter 7 for more discussion of affirmative action programs.)
4. Is Alma Fisher a victim of illegal discrimination?

NOTES

1. J. L. Lewandowski and W. P. MacKinnon, "What We Learned at Saturn," *Personnel Journal* (Dec. 1992): 30. For a similar story, see "HR Propels the Launch of a New Production Site," *Personnel Journal* (Jan. 1993): 54; T. S. Fiske, "HR Issues Drive Production Offshore," *Personnel Journal* (Jan. 1991): 84–88.

2. D. Q. Mills, *The New Competitors* (New York: Wiley, 1985): 19; and J. C. Grayson and C. O'Dell, *Two Minute Warning* (New York: The Free Press, 1988).

3. P. J. Dowling, R. S. Schuler, and D. Welch, *International Dimensions of Human Resource Management*, 2nd ed. (Belmont, Calif.: Wadsworth, 1994).

4. K. Matthes, *HR Focus* (March 1992): 1.

5. W. H. Miller, "Employers Wrestle with 'Dumb' Kids," *Industry Week* (July 4, 1988): 47.

6. *Training America: Learning to Work for the 21st Century* (Alexandria, Va.: American Society for Training and Development, 1989).

7. B. Nussbaum, "Needed: Human Capital," *Business Week* (Sept. 19, 1988): 100; A. P. Carnevale, L. J. Gainer, and A. S. Meltzer, *Workplace Basics: The Essential Skills Employers Want* (San Francisco: Jossey-Bass, 1990); A. P. Carnevale, L. J. Gainer, and E. Schulz, *Training the Technical Work Force* (San Francisco: Jossey-Bass, 1990).

8. R. Glier, "The Math Gap," *Profiles* (Aug. 1993): 58.

9. Nussbaum, "Needed: Human Capital," 101.

10. J. F. Coates, J. Jarratt, and J. B. Mahaffie, "Future Work," *The Futurist* (May–June 1991); J. F. Coates, J. Jarratt, and J. B. Mahaffie, *Future Work: Seven Critical Forces Reshaping Work and the Work Force in North America* (San Francisco: Jossey-Bass, 1990).

11. Glier, "The Math Gap," 58.

12. C. M. Solomon, "Managing the Baby Busters."

13. J. Spiers, "The Baby Boomlet is for Real," *Fortune* (Feb. 10, 1992): 101–104; "Downward Mobility," *Business Week* (March 23, 1992): 56–63; N. Hale, *The Older Worker* (San Francisco: Jossey-Bass, 1990); also see S. Ratan, "Why Busters Hate Boomers," *Fortune* (Oct. 4, 1993): 56–70. L. Zinn, "Teens," *Business Week* (April 11, 1994): 76–86.

14. *FEP Guidelines* (August 10, 1993): 8. Used by permission.

15. N. Perry, "Saving the School: How Business Can Help," *Fortune* (Nov. 7, 1988): 45.

16. *Ibid.*

17. W. B. Johnston, *Workforce 2000* (Indianapolis: Hudson Institute, 1987); G. Gallup, *Forecast 2000* (New York: Simon and Schuster, 1988); C. D. Fyock, *America's Work Force Is Coming of Age* (Lexington, Mass.: Heath/Lexington Books, 1990).

18. G. Koretz, "The Upside of America's Population Surge," *Business Week* (August 9, 1993): 20.

19. J. F. Coates, J. Jarratt, and J. B. Mahaffie, "Future Work," *The Futurist* (May–June 1991): 11.

20. *Personnel* (Dec. 1990), p. 17. For a discussion of these data and issues, see Johnston, *Workforce 2000*; W. H. Wagel and H. Z. Levine, "HR '90: Challenges and Opportunities," *Personnel* (June 1990): 18–19; R. R. Thomas, Jr., "From Affirmative Action to Affirming Diversity," *Harvard Business Review* (March–April 1990): 107–117; C. M. Solomon, "Careers Under Glass," *Personnel Journal* (April 1990): 96–105; J. Fierman, "Why Women Still Don't Hit the Top," *Fortune* (July 30, 1990): 41–62; W. Konrad, "Welcome to the Woman-Friendly Company," *Business Week* (Aug. 6, 1990): 48–52; J. Nelson

Horchler, "Derailing the Mommy Track," *Industry Week* (Aug. 6, 1990): 22–26.

21. F. Schwartz, "Don't Write Women Off As Leaders," *Fortune* (June 8, 1987): 185; C. Cockburn, *In the Way of Women: Men's Resistance to Sex Equality in Organizations* (Ithaca, N.Y.: ILR Press, School of Industrial and Labor Relations, Cornell University, 1991); K. A. Matthews and J. Rodin, "Women's Changing Work Roles: Impact on Health, Family, and Public Policy," *American Psychologist* (Nov. 1989): 1389–1393. But also see E. Riley, "More Women Are Executive VPs," *Fortune* (July 12, 1993): 16.

22. J. J. Laabs, "Diversity Training Is a Business Strategy," *Personnel Journal* (Sept. 1993): 25–26; S. E. Jackson and Associates, *Diversity in the Workplace: Human Resource Initiatives* (New York: The Guilford Press, 1992); J. D. Goodchilds (ed.), *Psychological Perspectives on Human Diversity in America: Master Lectures* (Washington, D.C.: American Psychological Association, 1991); J. P. Fernandez, *Managing a Diverse Workforce: Regaining the Competitive Edge* (Lexington, Mass.: Lexington Books, 1991); D. Jamieson and J. O'Mara, *Managing Workforce 2000: Gaining the Diversity Advantage* (San Francisco: Jossey-Bass, 1991); L. I. Kessler, *Managing Diversity in an Equal Opportunity Workplace* (Washington, D.C.: National Foundation for the Study of Employment Policy, 1990); S. B. Thiederman, *Bridging Cultural Barriers for Corporate Success* (Lexington, Mass.: Lexington Books, 1991); R. R. Thomas, Jr., *Beyond Race and Gender: Unleashing the Power of Your Total Workforce by Managing Diversity* (New York: AMACOM, 1991); P. Stuart, "What Does the Glass Ceiling Cost You?" *Personnel Journal* (Nov. 1992): 70–79.

23. B. P. Foster, "Workforce Diversity and Business," *Training and Development Journal* (April 1988): 59; M. Galen and A. Palmer, "White, Male, and Worried," *Business Week* (Jan. 31, 1994): 50–56.

24. L. Copeland, "Valuing Diversity, Part 2: Pioneers and Champions of Change," *Personnel*, (1988): 48; H. Jain, B. M. Pitts, and G. De Santis (eds.), *Equality for All: National Conference on Racial Equality in the Workplace—Restrospect and Prospect* (Hamilton, Ontario, Canada: McMaster University and IRRA, Hamilton and District Chapter, 1991); A. Dastmalchian, P. Blyton, and R. Adamson, *The Climate of Workplace Relations* (New York: Rutledge, a Division of Rutledge, Chapman and Hall, 1991).

25. *Ibid.*

26. J. Nelson-Horchler, "Demographics Deliver a Warning," *Industry Week* (April 18, 1988): 58.

27. *FEP Guidelines* (April 25, 1993): 8. Used with permission.

28. Schwartz, "Don't Write Women Off as Leaders."

29. *Ibid.*

30. B. Brophy, "The Truth About Women Managers," *U.S. News & World Report* (March 13, 1989): 57; and F. Schwartz, "Women as a Business Imperative," *Harvard Business Review*

(March–April 1992): 105–114; R. Sharpe, "Women Make Strides, But Men Stay Firmly in Top Jobs," *Wall Street Journal*, (March 29, 1994): A1, 10.

31. B. Brophy and M. Linnon, "Why Women Execs Stop Before the Top," *U.S. News & World Report* (Dec. 29, 1986).

32. See Note 27.

33. Schwartz, "Don't Write Women Off as Leaders."

34. A. Morrison, R. P. White, and E. Van Velsnor, "Executive Women: Substance Plus Style," *Psychology Today* (Aug. 1987): 18–21; 24–26.

35. See Note 22.

36. K. Myers, "Cracking the Glass Ceiling," *Information Week* (Aug. 27, 1990): 38–41; G. N. Powell, "Upgrading Management Opportunities for Women," *HR Magazine* (Nov. 1990): 67–70; D. T. Hall, "Moving Beyond the 'Mommy Track': An Organization Change Approach," *Personnel* (Dec. 1989): 23–29; E. Ehrlich, "The Mommy Track," *Business Week* (March 20, 1989): 126–34; F. N. Schwartz, "Management Women and the New Facts of Life," *Harvard Business Review* (Jan.–Feb. 1989): 65–76; W. Zellner, "Women Entrepreneurs," *Business Week* (April 18, 1994): 104–110.

37. Information provided by Jennifer Hunt, Merck & Company, as part of an MBA project, Fall 1990, New York University.

38. Information provided by Mike Penso, Prudential Inc.

39. P. B. Doeringer and M. J. Piore, *Internal Labor Markets and Manpower Analysis* (Lexington, Mass.: Heath, 1971); P. Osterman, ed., *Internal Labor Markets* (Cambridge, Mass.: London, 1984).

40. J. E. Ellis and C. Del Valle, "Tall Order for Small Businesses," *Business Week* (April 19, 1993): 114–118; J. Gordon, "Into the Dark," *Training* (July 1993): 21–30; W. Woods, "The Jobs Americans Hold," *Fortune* (July 12, 1993): 33–41; L. S. Richman, "Jobs That Are Growing and Slowing," *Fortune* (July 12, 1993): 52–55.

41. J. F. Coates, J. Jarratt, and J. B. Mahaffie, "Future Work," *The Futurist* (May–June 1991).

42. *Training America: Learning to Work for the 21st Century* (Alexandria, Va.: American Society for Training and Development, 1990).

43. Coates, Jarratt, and Mahaffie, "Future Work."

44. Coates, "An Environmental Scan . . ."

45. A. Kupfer, "Managing Now for the 1990's," *Fortune* (Sept. 26, 1988): 44–47.

46. J. Main, "The Winning Organization," *Fortune* (Sept. 26, 1988): 50–56; J. A. Byrne, "The Horizontal Corporation," *Business Week* (Dec. 20, 1993): 76–81.

47. Kupfer, "Managing Now for the 1990's," p. 47.

48. J. J. Sherwood, "Creating Work Cultures with Competitive Advantage," *Organizational Dynamics* (Winter 1988): 4–27.

49. B. Dumaine, "Those High-flying PepsiCo Managers," *Fortune*, (April 10, 1989): 78–86.

50. "Waste Management: Building an Ethical Culture," *HR Reporter* (April 1991): 1, 3.

51. T. E. Deal and A. A. Kennedy, *Corporate Cultures* (Reading, Mass.: Addison-Wesley, 1982); R. Pascale, "Fitting New Employees into the Company Culture," *Fortune* (May 28, 1984): 28–40.

52. R. S. Schuler, "Strategic Human Resource Management: Linking People with the Strategic Needs of the Business," *Organizational Dynamics*, (Summer 1992): 32.

53. Source: "Pepsi's Expectations," *HR Reporter* (July 1987): 4–5. Used by permission of *HR Reporter*, copyright 1987.49.22

54. J. P. Womack, D. T. Jones, and D. Roos, "How Lean Production Can Change the World," *The New York Times Magazine* (Sept. 23, 1990): 20–24, 34, 38; A. Taylor III, "New Lessons From Japan's Carmakers," *Fortune* (Oct. 22, 1990): 165–166, 168.

55. S. Zuboff, *In the Age of the Smart Machine: The Future of Work and Power* (New York: Basic Books, 1988). Also see B. Garson, *The Electronic Sweatshop* (New York: Simon and Shuster, 1988); P. B. Doeringer, *Turbulence in the American Workplace* (New York: Oxford University Press, 1991); S. E. Forrer and Z. B. Leibowitz, *Using Computers in Human Resources* (San Francisco: Jossey-Bass, 1991); U. E. Gattiker, *Technology Management in Organizations* (Newbury Park, Calif.: Sage, 1990); A. Majchrzak, *The Human Side of Factory Automation: Managerial and Human Resource Strategies for Making Automation Succeed* (San Francisco: Jossey-Bass, 1988); P. S. Goodman, L. S. Sproull and Associates, *Technology and Organization* (San Francisco: Jossey-Bass, 1990).

56. A. Kupfer, "Managing Now for the 1990's," *Fortune* (Sept. 26, 1988): 44–47; A. Ross, "Synergistics: A Strategy For Speed in the '90's," *Business Quarterly* (1990): 70–74; C. A. Bartlett and S. Ghoshal, "Organizing for Worldwide Effectiveness: The Transnational Solution," *California Management Review* (Fall 1988): 54–74; M. S. Scott Morton, *The Corporation of the 1990s: Information, Technology, and Organizational Transformation* (New York: Oxford University Press, 1991).

57. W. B. Johnston, "Global Work Force 2000: The New World Labor Market," *Harvard Business Review* (March–April 1991): 115–129.

58. "Detroit South," *Business Week* (March 16, 1992): 98–103. For a greater discussion of these and related issues, see: D. Harkrecht, W. C. Symonds, and G. Smith, "Why NAFTA Just Might Squeak Through," *Business Week* (Aug. 30, 1993): 36; J. Fierman, "Is Immigration Hurting the U.S.?" *Fortune* (August 9, 1993): 76–79; and T. Morganthau, "America: Still A Melting Pot?" *Newsweek* (Aug. 9, 1993): 16–23.

CHAPTER 4

HUMAN RESOURCE PLANNING AND CAREER PLANNING AND MANAGEMENT

LEARNING OBJECTIVES

When you have finished studying this chapter, you should be able to:

1. Describe the steps in developing and implementing a human resource plan.
2. Explain why companies offer career planning and management programs.
3. Tell what companies are doing for their employees in career planning and management.
4. Discuss the problems and issues that arise during organizational entry, midcareer, and late career.

CHAPTER OUTLINE

PLANNING for an organization's future staffing is fraught with challenges. Worldwide skills shortages in the industrialized nations is forcing countries to examine options they haven't considered before. Japan, which by the year 2025 will have 4.4 retirees per 10 workers (compared with 2.2 in 1990), is considering loosening its immigration requirements. Several European nations are also experiencing declining population growth and may in the future encourage older workers to stay on their jobs longer, rather than retire early. Such demographic issues make even *finding* workers a continuing challenge.

Staffing ranks with the "right" kinds of managers and workers is another issue in planning. Finding and keeping talented senior managers who "fit" the organization has become increasingly difficult, leading firms to take unprecedented steps such as hiring executives from outside their industries.

When firms seek senior management talent, a major question is whether to draw from the existing ranks or go "outside" to hire. The advantages of internal candidates, of course, include such factors as their knowledge of the business and the firm's culture and their established credibility. Having this knowledge can reduce the time managers need to make changes in direction. On the other hand, developing senior managers is time-consuming. If a firm has no clear candidate, external candidates become more attractive.

John Sculley's decision to leave Pepsi-Cola, where he was in line for the top position, and join Apple Computer in 1983 illustrates many issues important in human resource planning, both from the firm's and the individual's perspectives. After the phenomenally successful years under its cofounder, Steve Jobs, Apple found itself fighting for survival. While the company was able to produce innovative computers, it seemed unable to market them successfully, and with IBM entering the personal computer market in force, Apple faced new challenges. Thus, Apple's board of directors, after wrestling with questions of what type of senior leader the firm needed for the future, sought a CEO who could take the firm into "new" territory—marketing and selling computers. Sculley's marketing know-how was a big draw and, for the board, outweighed his lack of knowledge about the computer industry.

For Sculley, joining Apple meant serious risk-taking. The success rate for "outside CEOs" moving to a new industry is usually less than 50 percent; advisors told him that typically only one in five CEOs succeed when joining firms outside their "home industries." Nonetheless, he moved to Apple and, as we know, ultimately confronted Jobs and the board about the future direction of the firm. The fight created controversy both inside and outside the firm and led to Jobs' resignation.

In the summer of 1993, Sculley became chairman of Apple, and Michael Spindler, a long-time Apple employee, replaced Sculley as CEO. Spindler was brought in because the board believed that his operational and technical background would serve Apple's interests better during a time of financial losses and layoffs. In October of that year, Sculley resigned from Apple entirely![1] Because of upheavals within the industry it is too early as of this writing to know how Apple will do.

Human resource planning, and in particular succession planning for senior managers, is an ongoing challenge for firms, in large part because of constantly changing business and external environments. The firms that achieve effective human resource planning will emerge as stronger competitors in the future.

Apple Computer's selection of CEOs highlights several important aspects of human resource planning. One is that HR planning is critical to the success of the organization's strategical planning. Another is that it is tied to the very nature of an organization—its business, its culture, and its health. As the organizations change and become more flexible and adaptable, the planning horizon becomes shorter. A third aspect is that line managers and HR managers share responsibility in this area. A fourth is that the external and internal environments must be analyzed and incorporated into an organization's HR planning.

HUMAN RESOURCE PLANNING

In general terms, planning is the base upon which human resource management is constructed. More specifically, **human resource planning** *means forecasting personnel needs for an organization and deciding on the steps necessary to meet these needs.* Human resource (HR) planning consists of developing and implementing plans and programs that will ensure that the right number and type of individuals are available at the right time and place to fulfill organizational needs.

As such, HR planning is directly tied to business planning.[2] Once the business plans are determined, the HR planner assists in developing workable organizational structures and in determining the numbers and types of employees that will be required.[3] After the structures and employee requirements are identified, the planner develops HR programs to implement the structure and obtain the employees. Line managers, however, are responsible for providing the necessary information for HR planning. They work with the HR manager to ensure that the organization's needs are met and that its people are used as effectively as possible.

Human resource planning means forecasting personnel needs and detailing the steps necessary to meet these needs.

WHY IS HUMAN RESOURCE PLANNING IMPORTANT?

Human resource planning serves many purposes. It enables an organization to use its people effectively. It thus serves the interests of both the individual employee and the organization. Specifically, planning enables an organization to:

- Reduce costs by anticipating and correcting labor shortages and surpluses before they become unmanageable and expensive
- Make optimum use of workers' aptitudes and skills
- Improve the overall business planning process
- Provide more opportunities for women, minority groups, and disabled individuals in future growth plans
- Identify the specific skills available and needed
- Promote sound human resource management throughout all levels of the organization
- Evaluate the effect of alternative HR actions and policies[4]

These purposes are more easily attained now, thanks to the computer. This technology allows vast job-related records to be maintained on each employee, in essence creating a **human resource information system (HRIS)**. An HRIS is a logical and systematic record of human resource information. These records include information on employee job preferences, work experiences, and performance evaluations. They allow a job history to be kept on each employee, and they provide a complete set of information on the jobs and positions within the organization. In turn, HRIS can be used in the interests of the individual as well as the organization.[5] For more details, see Chapter 20.

The changing external and internal environments described in Chapter 3 make HR planning more important than ever. The growing shortage of skilled

HRIS is a logical and systematic record of human resource information.

workers for certain jobs makes planning crucial to an organization. There are shortages in both blue-collar occupations and entry-level white-collar occupations. Tool and die makers, bricklayers, and other skilled crafts workers are in short supply, and so are health care workers, legal secretaries, robotics engineers, machinists, and mechanics.[6] Refer back to Exhibit 3.7 for details.

Yet, while certain shortages exist, there is a growing abundance of another category—middle managers.[7] Outplacing of middle managers, a by-product of heightened global competitiveness and the need to downsize and reduce costs, is a recent addition to the growing list of HR activities.

The increasing potential for both technical and managerial obsolescence is another critical issue. Rapid changes in knowledge make it difficult for professionals, engineers, and managers to remain adept at their jobs. It has been speculated that entrants into the labor force in the 1990s will be retrained more than ten times during their work lives, and half of what today's managers, scientists, and professionals know will be obsolete by the year 2000.[8]

Another recent development is the increasing resistance of employees to relocation. Social changes such as two-income families and single parents means an organization can no longer assume that its employees can be moved anywhere and anytime. Careful planning is essential to address this issue.

These changes in the environment increase the importance of HR management and the need for firms of all sizes to have a good planning process.

THE PLANNING PROCESS

As the story about John Sculley and Apple and the preceding discussion illustrate, the human resource planning process takes place in a dynamic environment and in close relationship to the planning process of the business. Accordingly, the HR planning process, in mirroring the business planning process, must consider both longer-term and the short-term time frames. In fact, firms typically go out five years in their planning and then work back to the present. Similarly, in *your* own career planning, you should go out five, ten, even twenty years and then work back, noting what milestones must be reached along the way in order to achieve the objectives of year twenty. Of course, modifications can and will be made, both in your career planning and in a firm's business and human resource planning. Exhibit 4.1 shows the integration of business and human resource planning across several time horizons. At the core—and common to planning regardless of the time horizon—are four phases.

1. Assess supply and demand.
2. Develop objectives.
3. Design and implement programs.
4. Evaluate outcomes.

Regardless of time horizon, the essential theme of linking back to the business remains, and these phases therefore need to occur in a consistent manner.

THE FOUR PHASES OF HUMAN RESOURCE PLANNING

Determining an organization's personnel needs lies at the base of human resource planning. The two major components of this determination are identifying the *supply* of workers and the *demand* for workers—the first phase in human resource planning. Although these determinations are critical, until recently,

Outplacing occurs when an organization actively assists an employee who is being removed in obtaining employment elsewhere.

LEARNING OBJECTIVE 1

Describe the steps in developing and implementing a human resource plan.

All of our HR programs serve the bank's mission. If they didn't, we wouldn't have them.

Jim Alef, Corporate Senior Vice-President and Head, Human Resources, First Chicago Corporation

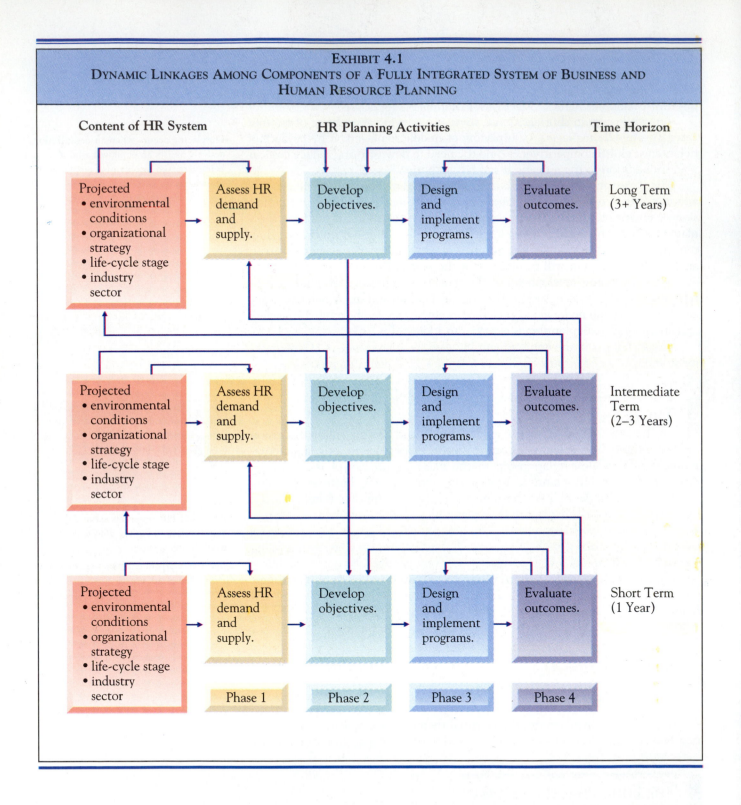

EXHIBIT 4.1
DYNAMIC LINKAGES AMONG COMPONENTS OF A FULLY INTEGRATED SYSTEM OF BUSINESS AND HUMAN RESOURCE PLANNING

Content of HR System — HR Planning Activities — Time Horizon

Long Term (3+ Years)

Projected
• environmental conditions
• organizational strategy
• life-cycle stage
• industry sector

Assess HR demand and supply.

Develop objectives.

Design and implement programs.

Evaluate outcomes.

Intermediate Term (2–3 Years)

Projected
• environmental conditions
• organizational strategy
• life-cycle stage
• industry sector

Assess HR demand and supply.

Develop objectives.

Design and implement programs.

Evaluate outcomes.

Short Term (1 Year)

Projected
• environmental conditions
• organizational strategy
• life-cycle stage
• industry sector

Assess HR demand and supply.

Develop objectives.

Design and implement programs.

Evaluate outcomes.

Phase 1 — Phase 2 — Phase 3 — Phase 4

organizations have strangely avoided making them. Indeed, some organizations avoid, or at least resist, engaging in any of the four phases of planning.[9] We will examine typical roadblocks later in the chapter. Planning is generally accomplished in four phases.[10]

Data is developed in this first phase. It will be used to determine corporate objectives, policies, and plans as well as HR objectives and policies. Information will be retrieved from the past, observed in the present, and forecasted for the future. Obtaining data from the past can be difficult because of inadequate or nonexistent records, and forecasting data with reliability and accuracy involves uncertainty, the more so the farther out the forecast goes. Nevertheless, this data should be developed, however tentatively. The more tentative the data, the more flexible and subject to revision it should be. Contingencies causing uncertainties in the forecasts should be incorporated, perhaps in the form of estimated ranges. Organizations in unstable, complex environments are faced with many more contingencies than are organizations in stable, simple environments.

Exhibit 4.2 shows the four steps in Phase 1. Each is important for successful planning. Step 1 consists of analyzing the personnel situation in an organization;

HRP depends on a thorough scanning of the environments.

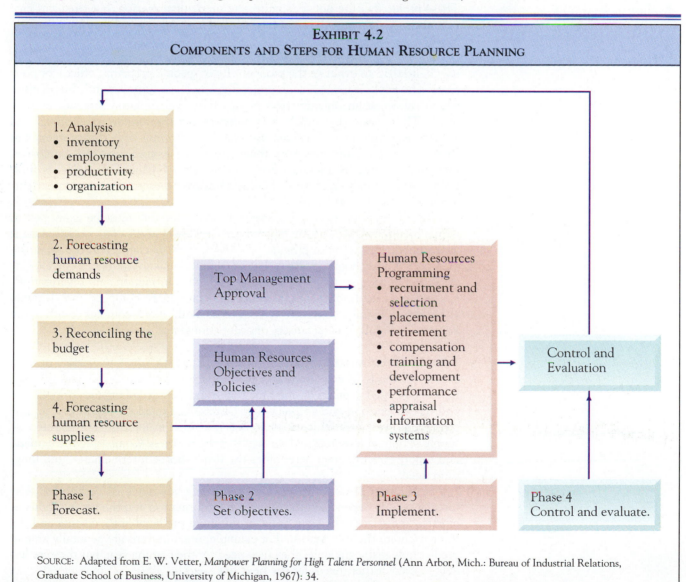

EXHIBIT 4.2
COMPONENTS AND STEPS FOR HUMAN RESOURCE PLANNING

SOURCE: Adapted from E. W. Vetter, *Manpower Planning for High Talent Personnel* (Ann Arbor, Mich.: Bureau of Industrial Relations, Graduate School of Business, University of Michigan, 1967): 34.

Four aspects of analysis include:

- taking inventory
- analyzing the future
- measuring productivity
- examining organizational structure

it has four aspects, all of which are applicable for the three time horizons shown in Exhibit 4.1.

STEP 1. ANALYSIS.   The first aspect of an HR analysis is the inventory of the current work force and the current jobs in the organization. Both tasks must occur if a careful determination of the organization's capability to meet current and future needs is to be made.

Computers make compiling inventories much more efficient, and they enable a program to be dynamic and integrated. Through computers, employees in separate divisions and in different geographic areas find it easier to participate in the organization's network for matching jobs and employees.

A *second* aspect of this analysis is determining the probable future composition of the work force. This determination is often based on wage, occupational, and industrial groups. Historical data on work force composition, along with current demographic and economic data, are used to make employment projections. These projections are not specific to any single organization, but they can provide an organization with useful information for its personnel plans, particularly for the long term.

A *third* aspect is assessing current and future productivity. Organizations can use their HRIS to evaluate the productivity of specific programs, offices, or positions. The HRIS is invaluable in projecting employee turnover and absenteeism, which influence an organization's productivity and its future human resource needs. These projections might also indicate that the reasons for turnover and absenteeism need to be analyzed. Strategies for dealing with this problem can then be formed. Note, however, that at some times and for some employees, increased turnover is desirable. For example, if an organization suddenly finds itself with too many employees, increased turnover—especially among poor performers— might be welcomed.[11]

Finally, a *fourth* aspect, the organizational structure, must be examined in which the probable size of the top, middle, and lower levels of an organization is determined. This exercise provides information about changes in the organization's needs and about specific activities or functional areas that can be expected to experience particularly severe growth or contraction. As organizations become more technologically complex and face more complex and dynamic environments, their structures will become both more complex (with more departments and a greater variety of occupations) and more fluid.[12]

STEP 2. FORECASTING HUMAN RESOURCE DEMANDS.   A variety of forecasting methods—some simple, some complex—are used in this task. Which type will be used depends on the time frame and the type of organization, its size and dispersion, and the accuracy and certainty of available information. The time frame used here frequently parallels that used in forecasting the potential supply of human resources and the needs of the business. Comparing the demand and supply forecasts then determines the firm's short-, intermediate-, and long-term needs.

Forecasting results in approximations—not absolutes or certainties. The forecast quality depends on the accuracy of information and the predictability of events. The shorter the time horizon, the more predictable the events and the more accurate the information. For example, organizations are generally able to predict how many graduates they may need for the coming year, but they are less able to predict their needs for the next five years.

A recent study indicates that 60 percent of major firms conduct some form of employment forecast. More than half of these firms prepare forecasts for both the short term and the long term. The emphasis is generally on predicting demand rather than supply. In fact, more than half of the firms predicted *only* demand, while only one-third formally forecast supply *and* demand.[13]

Two classes of forecasting techniques are frequently used to determine projected demand for human resources. These are **judgmental forecasts** and **conventional statistical projections**.

Judgmental forecasting employs experts who "judge" or estimate what the demand will be. The most common group used in this method is managers.[14] **Managerial estimates** can be made by top managers (top-down). Alternatively, the review process can begin at lower levels (bottom-up) with the results sent to higher levels for refinement. The success of these estimates depends on the quality of the information available to the experts. Useful information can include data on current and projected productivity levels, market demand, and sales forecasts, as well as current staffing levels and mobility information.

Another way to make demand judgments is the **Delphi technique**. At a Delphi meeting, experts take turns at presenting their forecasts and assumptions to the others, who then make revisions in their own forecasts. This combination process continues until a viable composite forecast emerges. The composite may represent specific projections or a range of projections, depending on the experts' positions.

The Delphi technique has been shown to produce better one-year forecasts as compared to linear regression analysis, but it does have some limitations. Difficulties can arise, for example, in integrating the experts' opinions. This technique, however, appears to be particularly useful in generating insights in highly unstructured or undeveloped subject areas such as human resource planning.

A related method is the **nominal group technique**. Several people sit at a conference table and independently list their ideas on a sheet of paper.[15] The ideas presented are recorded on larger sheets of paper so everyone can see all the ideas and refer to them in later parts of the session.

The two techniques are similar, but the Delphi technique is more frequently used to generate predictions, and the nominal group technique is more frequently used to identify current organizational problems and solutions to those problems. Although all these judgmental forecasts are less complex and rely on less data than those based on the statistical methods discussed next, they tend to dominate in practice.[16]

The most common **conventional statistical projections** are simple and multiple linear regression analyses. In **simple linear regression analysis**, the projection of future demand is based on a past relationship between the organization's employment level and a variable related to employment such as sales. If a relationship can be established between the level of sales and the level of employment, predictions of future sales can be used to predict future employment.

Multiple linear regression analysis is an extension of simple linear regression. Instead of relating employment to one variable, several variables are used. For example, instead of using only sales to predict employment demand, productivity data may also be used. Because it incorporates several variables related to employment, multiple regression analysis can produce more accurate demand forecasts. It appears, however, that only relatively large organizations use multiple regression analysis.[17]

STEP 3. RECONCILING THE BUDGET. The third step puts the whole activity into an economic perspective. The forecast must be expressed in terms of dollars, and this figure must be compatible with the organization's profit objectives and budget limitations. Of course, the reconciliation process may indicate that the

Judgmental forecasts:
- managerial estimates
- Delphi technique
- nominal group technique

Conventional statistical projections:
- simple linear regression analysis
- multiple linear regression analysis

budget needs to be adjusted to accommodate the human resource plan. This activity is an opportunity to align the objectives and policies of the organization with those of the HR department.

STEP 4. FORECASTING HUMAN RESOURCE SUPPLY. Although supply forecasts can be derived from both internal and external sources of information, internal information is generally most crucial and more readily available. As in demand forecasting, two kinds of techniques—judgmental and statistical—are used to forecast the internal labor supply. Once made, the supply and demand forecasts can be compared to determine what actions need to be taken to identify talent and balance supply and demand. However, most current forecasting of labor supply and demand is short range and is used for budgeting and controlling costs. Forecasts for longer than a five-year period, when done, are used in outlining corporate strategy, planning facilities, and identifying managerial replacements.[18]

Two judgmental techniques used by organizations to forecast supply are replacement and succession planning. In **replacement planning**, charts are developed that list the current and potential occupants of positions in the firm. Potential promotions and developmental needs are indicated by the performance levels of employees. Incumbents are listed directly under the job title. Those individuals likely to fill potential vacancies are listed next. An example of a replacement chart is shown in Exhibit 4.3.

Succession planning **identifies and grooms candidates for top management jobs.**

Succession planning is similar to replacement planning except that it is usually longer term and more developmental. Organizations are planning successions more than ever. With rapidly changing environments, organizations realize that what makes a good manager today may not be true in the year 2000. Consequently, organizations are engaged in efforts both to identify what will make a good manager in the year 2000 and to design developmental activities that will ensure that the right people are available with the right skills at the right time.

At Allstate Insurance, Frank Berardi of the corporate human resource department sees that line managers perceive preparing management talent for the future as critical. He describes it as a people-related issue of a

> lack of management talent in the near future in the face of the changing world and the need for a new type of manager, one who can deal with diversity of workers and deliver programs, e.g., empowerment, in a variety of ways. While there is some concern for numbers, it is primarily the concern for skills that [line managers] are worried about and they want HR to help them develop management education programs and new succession programs. So this is a business issue that is HR in nature.[19]

Transition matrices model the flow of human resources so supply estimates can be made.

In addition to succession planning and replacement planning, organizations are examining the supply of human resources with sophisticated statistical models. An important component of these statistical models is the **transition matrix**, which models the flow of human resources—that is, the movement of people from one job to another. The public accounting firm of Deloitte and Touche uses a transition matrix similar to the one presented in Exhibit 4.4. The percentages in a transition matrix indicate average rates of historical movement between job categories from one period to the next. For example, a supervisor during year T (the first year) has a 12 percent chance of being promoted to manager, a 60 percent chance of remaining a supervisor, and a 28 percent chance of exiting the firm in the following year.

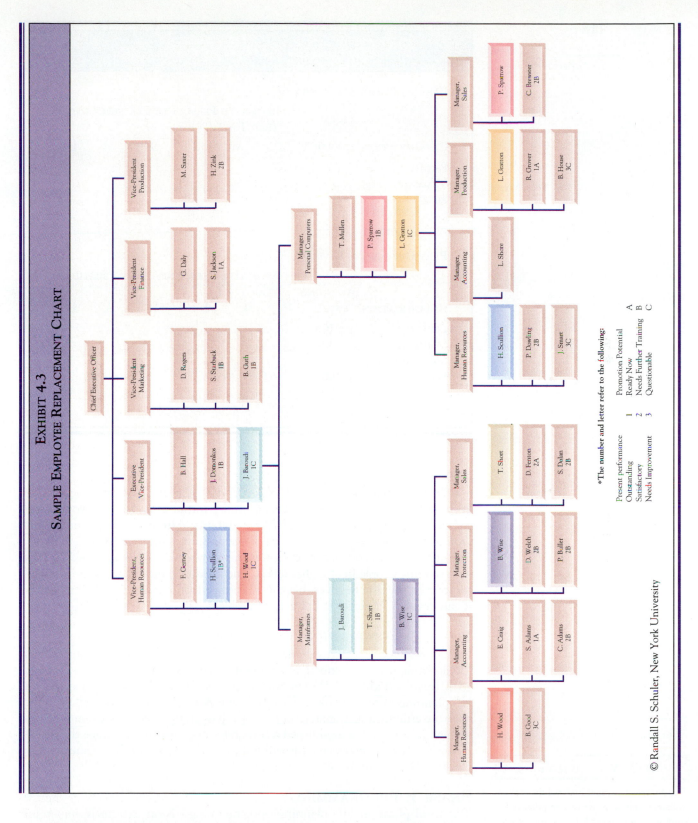

Exhibit 4.3
Sample Employee Replacement Chart

Chief Executive Officer

Vice-President, Human Resources
- F. Gerney
- H. Scullion 1B*
- H. Wood 1C

Executive Vice-President
- B. Hall
- J. Domonkos 1B
- J. Baroudi 1C

Vice-President Marketing
- D. Rogers
- S. Starbuck 1B
- B. Guth 1B

Vice-President Finance
- G. Daly
- S. Jackson 1A

Vice-President Production
- M. Saxer
- H. Zink 2B

Manager, Mainframes
- J. Baroudi
- T. Short 1B
- B. Wise 1C

Manager, Human Resources
- H. Wood
- B. Good 3C

Manager, Accounting
- E. Craig
- S. Adams 1A
- C. Adams 2B

Manager, Protection
- B. Wise
- D. Welch 2B
- P. Buller 2B

Manager, Sales
- T. Short
- D. Fenton 2A
- S. Dolan 2B

Manager, Personal Computers
- T. Mullen
- P. Sparrow 1B
- L. Gratton 1C

Manager, Human Resources
- H. Scullion
- P. Dowling 2B
- J. Smart 3C

Manager, Accounting
- L. Shore

Manager, Production
- L. Gratton
- R. Grover 1A
- B. Hosse 3C

Manager, Sales
- P. Sparrow
- C. Brewster 2B

*The **number** and letter refer to the **following:**

Present performance		Promotion Potential	
Outstanding	1	Ready Now	A
Satisfactory	2	Needs Further Training	B
Needs Improvement	3	Questionable	C

© Randall S. Schuler, New York University

These data can also be used to estimate future supply and demand (see Part B of Exhibit 4.4). This is done by multiplying the staffing levels at the beginning of the planning period by the probabilities of movement. In this example, the

117

EXHIBIT 4.4
A SAMPLE TRANSITION MATRIX

PART A: PERSONNEL SUPPLY

CLASSIFICATION IN YEAR T	ESTIMATED PERSONNEL CLASSIFICATION IN YEAR T + 1 (%)					
	P	M	S	Sr	A	EXIT
Partner	.70					.30
Manager	.10	.80				.10
Supervisor		.12	.60			.28
Senior			.20	.55		.25
Accountant				.15	.65	.20

PART B: STAFFING LEVELS

CLASSIFICATION	BEGINNING LEVELS	ESTIMATED PERSONNEL AVAILABILITIES IN YEAR T + 1					
		P	M	S	Sr	A	EXIT
Partner	10	7					3
Manager	30	3	24				3
Supervisor	50		6	30			14
Senior	100			20	55		25
Accountant	200				30	130	40
		10	30	50	85	130	

anticipated availabilities are 10, 30, 50, 85, and 130 in the five job categories. To keep staffing levels at the same level as in the initial year, the firm would need to hire 15 senior accountants and 70 accountants. Alternatively, the firm could promote 15 more accountants to senior accountant and recruit 85 accountants. This may be more cost-effective. However, if new ideas are needed, the firm may wish to bring people in at higher levels. The transition matrix also shows rates of turnover. If the firm believes that the 30 percent turnover in partners is too high, it can develop strategies to correct the problem. *stop here 1/30/96*

PHASE 2: ESTABLISHING OBJECTIVES

Human resource objectives are developed in Phase 2. They are (or should be, if the planning process is effective) a natural outcome of the established corporate goals (refer to Exhibit 4.2). The importance of an organization's objectives for HR planning seems difficult to deny; thus, it is not surprising that more and more firms are establishing human resource objectives and policies. For example, firms such as Tenneco have established a corporate objective to encourage the development of female managers; this will influence the types of HR programs put in place in their organizations.

PHASE 3: PROGRAMMING

The third phase in HR planning—programming—is an extremely important extension of the previous activities. After an organization's needs are assessed, action programming must be developed to serve those needs. Action programs can be designed to increase the supply of the right employees in the organization

DID YOU KNOW?

The Marriott Company develops great human resource programs so potential employees will regard it as a great place to work, thus helping to ensure a good supply of job applicants.

(for example, if the forecasts in Phase 1 showed that demand exceeded supply) or to decrease the number of current employees (if the forecasts showed that supply exceeded demand). Organizations today use many programs to address these purposes: diversity programs to make organizations more attractive to a broader array of applicants; programs to improve the firm's socialization efforts so that good employees want to remain with the organization; and programs to downsize or "rightsize" the organization such as early retirement incentives and generous severance packages to complement the normal attrition process. Some of these programs are described in the feature, "Managing Human Resources for Greater Opportunities."

Regardless of which program is implemented, it must be monitored and evaluated. This allows for controlling how well the program is being implemented and revising it as appropriate. Thus, control and evaluation comprise the necessary fourth phase in HR planning.

PHASE 4: CONTROL AND EVALUATION

Control and evaluation of HR programs are essential to manage people effectively. Efforts in this area are clearly aimed at *quantifying* the value of human resources. These efforts recognize that people are the main asset an organization has. An HRIS facilitates rapid and frequent collection of data. Data collection is important not only as a means of control, but also as a method for evaluating programs and making adjustments.

Evaluation is an important process not only for determining the effectiveness of HR plans, but also for demonstrating the significance of planning and therefore of the department itself to the organization as a whole.

Possible criteria for evaluating planning include measuring:

- Actual staffing levels against established staffing requirements
- Productivity levels against established goals
- Actual personnel flow rates against desired rates
- Programs implemented against action plans
- Program results against expected outcomes (improved applicant flows, reduced quit rates, improved replacement ratios)
- Labor and program costs against budgets
- Ratios of program results (benefits) to program costs[21]

Cause and effect is an important issue related to evaluation, revision, and adjustment. Human resource management as presented in Chapter 1 is based on the notion of integrated, related activities. For example, if the recruiting program is not working well, the conclusion that the total program needs revision may be invalid. Perhaps the salaries offered to recruits were too low and not competitive with other organizations. It is also possible that, despite the best recruiting efforts, few acceptable applicants applied. The integrated approach makes the evaluation of any single program more comprehensive and thus more accurate.

In reality, evaluation can be so complex that it tends not to get done. Indeed, roadblocks can be erected along the entire process of planning.

ROADBLOCKS TO PLANNING

A key roadblock to initiating HR planning is the lack of top management support. Human resource staff can often remove this roadblock with hard data and bottom-line facts that demonstrate the effectiveness of HR planning.

It can be difficult to integrate planning with other activities—a necessary step if HR planning is to work. A challenge for managers then is to create a system in which all activities discussed in Chapter 1 are integrated with the orga-

Sidebar notes:

Rightsizing means ensuring that in downsizing the right positions are eliminated.

Roadblocks to HRP include lack of:
- top management support
- integration
- line involvement
- career planning

MANAGING HUMAN RESOURCES
for Greater Opportunities

JAMES L. Ketelsen, Tenneco Inc.'s chief executive, was frustrated. For a decade, he had been telling his people to promote more women, with little effect.

So in 1988, Mr. Ketelsen tried the grass-roots approach. He established eight women-only advisory councils—a central one at the Houston headquarters, and satellites at each of the divisions—and charged *them* with helping him help women get ahead.

Since then the advisory councils have suggested—and Tenneco has implemented—bonus plans that penalize male managers who do not promote women; benefits plans aimed at women's needs, and networking conventions attended by Mr. Ketelsen, Tenneco's divisional chiefs and as many as 200 Tenneco women. Today, more than 30 women have moved into Tenneco's upper management ranks; in pre-council days there were only 10.

"What we've done is identify the barriers to women, and help Jim knock them down," says Mary Lou Roaseau, treasurer of Tenneco's Newport News Shipbuilding and Drydock subsidiary, and chairwoman of the central council. That's Mr. Ketelsen's take, too: "It certainly helps when women tell us what impediments they run into."

More and more corporate chiefs are acknowledging that, despite their good intentions, there is still a shortfall of women, as well as minorities, in management. And, since statistics indicate a looming shortage of management-caliber men, that skew scares them. So companies as disparate as Dow Chemical, Ryder Systems, Honeywell, Equitable Life Assurance, and Polaroid are turning to women's groups for help.

"Management finally recognizes that it takes discipline, not just awareness, to help women percolate up the ranks," says Gail M. McDonald, a corporate officer of Ryder Systems Inc., and a member of the Miami transportation company's women's management association. The result, says Tatyana Doughty, a consultant at Catalyst, a New York women's research group, is that "there is definitely more management support for corporate women's groups."

The groups vary in the formality of their links to management. In some—Dow is one—a high-ranking individual, a male, serves as liaison. In others—Ryder is an example—a team of male management advisors regularly meets with the women's group. In still others—most decentralized companies fit here—the women's groups have splinter groups that deal with division heads.

But patterns do run through the groups: they all have rich budgets for meetings and research; they are run by high-level women; and they are treated as business advisors, not political adversaries.

"We approach upward mobility for women as a business issue, as something that shows good returns," says Rita J. Shellenberger, Dow Chemical U.S.A.'s manager of diversity and head of its committee on women's issues. "We provide role models for women, as well as a highly visible reminder to top management that women operate successfully in their midst."

Dow's committee, which meets every two months, has tagged numerous women as promotable, and Shellenberger says some have already been moved up, although she would not provide numbers. Slated for next year: development of strategies to groom more women for promotability.

At Ryder, too, the women's group is educating women as vigorously as it is educating management. Its eight chapters, which meet at least six times a year, often ask Ryder chairman M. Anthony Burns and various Ryder directors to speak to them about the business. They have also asked women from sales and other field jobs—rare spots for women in masculine-dominated fields like trucking and aviation, Ryder's main areas—to speak.

"We feel that Ryder women could best help their careers by understanding the business better," says Ms. McDonald. "We have no desire to have this be a political caucus."

Those sentiments are echoed by Dianne Lathrop, the Polaroid Corporation's director of executive development and a founder of the company's four-year-old women's action team. The group was formed, at management's request, to nominate women to sit on

Continued on the next page

nization's business plan. Line managers sometimes lack involvement in the planning process. Failure to include line management in the design, development, and implementation of a human resource plan is a common oversight for first-time planners. Often tempted to develop or adopt highly quantitative approaches to planning, HR professionals can find themselves with a final product that has little pragmatic value on the line. A plan must be useful, and that means the needs of the line must be met.

The lack of career planning and career management is another roadblock. Human resource planning is essentially about moving people around. To do this effectively requires that both the company and the individual make the right choices. The company's path set out via its objectives is important, and individuals can better fit into this path—and even enable it—if they have an idea of where they as individuals are going. Employee empowerment and self-management are helping organizations and individuals figure this out. Thus, **career planning** *is the process of identifying career goals and establishing activities that must be accomplished to attain those goals.* Thus, **career management** *is the assistance provided by an organization to aid its employees in their careers.* The following section will give you a head start in this important process. Good luck!

> *Career planning* is the process of identifying career goals and establishing activities that must be accomplished to retain these goals.

> *Career management* is the assistance provided by organizations to aid their employees in their careers.

CAREER PLANNING AND CAREER MANAGEMENT

The feature, "Managing Human Resources for Greater Opportunities," illustrates several aspects of career planning and career management. The first is that times are changing and that policies and procedures of the past need updating and, in some cases, overhauling. In particular, organizations need policies and procedures to promote the upward mobility of women and minorities. Key to success is the development of systematic programs of career support, top management involvement, and the leadership of the women and minorities themselves. Issues such as the glass ceiling, diversity, family considerations, and demographic trends require different policies and programs from what has existed previously. Key to the success of these programs will be the commitment of top management and the leadership of the employees [or groups] themselves. While current efforts appear promising, firms will also have to reach out and involve the larger community. The following two discussions showcase efforts being made by two organizations.

DOW CHEMICAL

Another aspect of career planning and career management is that some firms such as Dow Chemical find success by approaching upward mobility for women and minorities as a *business issue*. Indeed, they treat the entire issue of managing diversity as a business issue. This approach results from the realization that fewer than 15 percent of the entrants into the labor force in the 1990s will be white men. As a consequence, the success of firms in the future will increasingly be determined by how effectively they manage women and minorities.

QUAKER OATS COMPANY

Updating policies became especially challenging in view of the fact that organizations need to cut costs, and each issue brings with it different approaches. Reducing corporate layers to cut costs means outplacing middle management. The work-life-cycle bulge of the baby boomers will create problems as they retire and even now as they are followed by a smaller work force. More women in the work force brings a whole other set of issues. Firms and individuals are therefore increasingly forced to rethink notions of career planning and management. As firms "restructure" and cut back on positions, making corporate structures flatter, there are fewer opportunities for upward mobility.

In such an environment, Quaker Oats Company has been a leader in addressing career issues from both organizational and employee perspectives. In the fast-paced world of product brand management, Quaker Oats is experimenting with the idea of a "part-time brand manager." Rather than lose a valuable brand manager after the birth of her son, the company agreed to let her work three days per week, an unprecedented move in such a position. The company is documenting the "pilot program" on a quarterly basis, using the objectives that the manager negotiated with senior managers. Going on two years, the program has been quite successful.

With the full force of baby boomers now in the labor force, Quaker Oats and its employees have come to view careers in new ways. The company's "pyramid" has flattened to the point where one manager, after six promotions in nine years, has remained in the same job for three years. While his initial reaction at staying in one place was one of frustration that he was not being viewed as successful, the advantages of staying in one job have changed his mind. He gets to see the results (both good and bad) of earlier decisions, whereas before he often moved on before the results were in. In addition, he has been able to take the time to create a team and develop his subordinates more thoroughly. Quaker Oats has actually begun to encourage lateral moves as a way to broaden manager experience, allowing people to become knowledgeable about many aspects of the company, which can have benefits when and if those managers do move into senior management positions.[22]

While you may or may not work for Dow Chemical or Quaker Oats, it pays to be aware of what companies are doing for the careers of their employees. It also pays to take charge of your career and assess both you goals and then your strengths and weaknesses in attaining them. To get you started, we will now look at several aspects of career planning and career development that you may find useful.

WHO'S RESPONSIBLE FOR CAREER PLANNING AND MANAGEMENT?

Both individuals and organizations are responsible for career planning and management, each for a different component. Organizations can provide career management programs for employees to help them match their needs, goals, and abilities with organizational job demands and rewards. Such programs include:

- Career pathing
- Career counseling
- Career planning workshops

A successful career depends upon your taking responsibility for it.

- Work-family interface programs
- Outplacement
- Stress
- Retirement
- Glass ceiling

Individuals should undertake career planning activities to ensure their own career success, job security, self-esteem, growth, and comfort. Such activities you can do now include:

- Make résumé
- Plan for job type
- Get interview
- Have interview
- Negotiate salary
- Do well
- Get promoted
- Manage boss

A HISTORICAL PERSPECTIVE. Traditionally, an individual's career was decided by the organization. If the organization needed someone in another location, an individual was transferred. The success of one's career was often measured by the number of moves that were made, since these moves were generally rewarded by promotions to more important and better-paying jobs. The organization was rarely concerned with whether the new job was what the individual wanted, and the individual had limited control over his or her career.[23]

CAREERS TODAY. Now, organizations such as Tenneco, Quaker Oats, and Dow Chemical are concerned with whether an individual's abilities and preferences are really matched to the job. For example, organizations are beginning to accept the fact that not all people want to be promoted. The new attitude is one can have a successful career without climbing to the top. Organizations are also responding to these new issues by offering stress management programs, day-care accommodations, and retirement programs.

Career success does not always mean climbing to the top of the organization.

Most career management programs are based on the premise that both the employee and the organization are responsible for these activities. That is, you, as an individual, must evaluate your personal strengths and weaknesses, preferences, values, interests, and motivations and be responsible for seeking out and taking advantage of opportunities afforded by an organization's career management programs. You must be ready and able to undertake career planning activities.[24]

WHY IS CAREER PLANNING AND MANAGEMENT IMPORTANT?

It is both costly and time-consuming not only for organizations to offer career management programs, but also for individuals to plan their careers. The investments of money and time, however, are worthwhile because career management fulfills many important purposes for both employer and employee.

The general purpose of career management programs is to match employees' needs, abilities, and goals with current and future opportunities and challenges within the organization. In other words, these programs are designed to increase the chances that the organization places the right people in the right place at the right time. Thus, these programs aim at matching skills, knowledge, and ability and job demands with personality, interests, and preferences and job rewards.

LEARNING OBJECTIVE 3

Tell what companies are doing for their employees in career planning and management.

Individuals feel pressure to engage in career management because the current work environment is highly competitive. Indeed, employees today are willing to assert themselves to achieve control over work and nonwork pursuits. In addition, the meaning of success has been broadened to encompass not only salary and status, but also personal contribution and the realization of one's potential. Employees today feel that they are entitled to such things as enriched tasks, participation in decision making, job security, and equitable treatment. Finally, employees are increasingly concerned with balancing the demands of work, family, and leisure activities.[25]

Effective career management means effective utilization of human resources and equal employment opportunity, both of which are important to an organization. If people are an organization's most important asset, then employees whose skills are underutilized or misutilized and who become disillusioned and dissatisfied are wasted assets. Since the image of the "organization man" has eroded, companies can no longer assume blind loyalty and automatic acceptance of promotions and relocations. Thus, active involvement in the career management process is in the best interest of the organization.

Equal employment opportunity concerns initially focused on recruitment and selection. During the next decades, however, equal employment emphasis is likely to shift to individuals who are already employed by the organization. Providing career opportunities for women and ethnic minorities is particularly important. Various protected groups (for example, women, ethnic minorities, disabled workers, older workers) are seeking assistance in career development. Already companies are realizing that in order to help women and minorities advance they must develop programs to break the "glass ceiling" (as discussed in Chapter 3), and some companies are working hard on this issue. Mentoring programs are a promising development. For example, according to Gordon Smyth, senior vice-president of employee relations, at DuPont:

> Mentoring is informal. We urge people who are good at it to do it. We have tried to encourage other people to get good at it. One of the best things you can do is know your people; they'll tell you whether they are getting any help.
>
> One of the most helpful things that we are working on lately in addressing the glass ceiling problem is to define it as a corporate and not a departmental or divisional problem. Most units say they have a management position candidate, but chances are the candidate is a white male. We come in now and say that there may be other candidates somewhere else that are minorities or female. It is in the corporate interest to place those people in that position. It has to be done carefully. You have to have a good person who can do the job.[26]

CAREER DEVELOPMENT: STAGES AND ISSUES

As organizations seek to help employees by establishing specific career management programs, they find that is it useful to think in terms of the stages in a career. Employees have different needs at different stages. Thus, by understanding the stages in a career, firms can more effectively design career management programs.

A career is a dynamic process that spans an individual's life. In this section, we will discuss the stages of career development and some of the major issues during three critical career stages (that is, organizational entry, midcareer, and late career).

Career is a patterned sequence of attitudes and behaviors associated with work experiences that span a person's life.

Most career development models suggest that careers include various stages that are predictable sequences of events that apply to most people independent of the specific type of job they have. A knowledge of career stages can help individuals and organizations understand the "typical" issues and events across a career's life span. We will briefly examine five stages: (1) preparation for work, (2) organizational entry, (3) early career, (4) midcareer, and (5) late career (see Exhibit 4.5). The feature "HR Advice and Application: The Meaning of Career" gives a thought-provoking definition.

STAGE 1: PREPARATION FOR WORK. This stage extends from birth to approximately 25 years of age. The major tasks during this stage are developing an initial occupational choice and following an educational curriculum that will assist in implementing that choice. Overall, an occupational self-image is developed during childhood, adolescence, and early adulthood.

The major stages of career development are

- preparation for work
- organizational entry
- early career
- midcareer
- late career

EXHIBIT 4.5
FIVE STAGES OF CAREER DEVELOPMENT

STAGE 1: PREPARATION FOR WORK

Typical age range:	0–25
Major tasks:	Develop occupational self-image, assess alternative occupations, develop initial occupational choice, pursue necessary education.

STAGE 2: ORGANIZATIONAL ENTRY

Typical age range:	18–25
Major tasks:	Obtain job offer(s) from desired organization(s), select appropriate job based on accurate information.

STAGE 3: EARLY CAREER

Typical age range:	25–40
Major tasks:	Learn job, learn organizational rules and norms, fit into chosen occupation and organization, increase competence, pursue goals.

STAGE 4: MIDCAREER

Typical age range:	40–55
Major tasks:	Reappraise early career and early adulthood, reaffirm or modify goals, make choices appropriate to middle adult years, remain productive in work.

STAGE 5: LATE CAREER

Typical age range:	55–retirement
Major tasks:	Remain productive in work, maintain self-esteem, prepare for effective retirement.

SOURCE: From J. H. Greenhaus, *Career Management* (Hinsdale, Ill.: The Dryden Press, 1987).

THE MEANING OF CAREER

What is a career? The word *career* has many different meanings. A career can be a sequence of related or unrelated jobs. For example, an individual's career may include seventeen different jobs with four organizations. In a different vein, many people think of a career with reference to "the professions" (for example, law or medicine). Perhaps the most common connotation of career is the idea of advancement or "climbing the company ladder." According to this view, career success is measured in promotions and salary. Although all of these views are reasonable, a more formal definition of a career is required. For our purposes, a **career** *is a patterned sequence of attitudes and behaviors associated with work-related experiences that span a person's life*. According to this definition, each of us has a career.

Several things should be noted about this definition. First, the notion of a patterned sequence suggests that there is order in the career planning and management process. Second, neither success nor failure is implied; note that research has attempted to understand the processes involved in career management and to avoid value judgments about what constitutes success. Third, careers span a long period of time from an individual's earliest jobs through retirement. Various career stages have been identified, and we discuss them in this chapter. Fourth, a career includes both attitudes and behaviors. Attitudes include feelings, thoughts, and anticipated actions, whereas behaviors are things that individuals actually do. Thus, a career has both subjective aspects (for example, feelings of success and pride) and objective aspects (a job offer, a promotion). Fifth, virtually any type of work (paid or unpaid) performed over a long period of time constitutes a career. And lastly, there are many things individuals can do to manage their careers and that companies can do to help them.[27]

Reality shock is the gap between one's expectations and the reality of the new job and organization.

STAGE 2: ORGANIZATIONAL ENTRY.   Selecting a job and an organization are the major focus here. A major issue during this stage is **reality shock**. Individuals usually have unrealistically high expectations and find that many entry-level jobs are not particularly challenging, at least initially. This stage usually occurs between the ages of 18 and 25.

STAGE 3: THE EARLY CAREER.   The essential task at this stage is establishing oneself in a career and organization. Two periods are encompassed by this stage: fitting into the adult world and struggling for success in one's chosen field. This usually occurs between 25 and 40 years of age.

STAGE 4: THE MIDCAREER.   The midcareer stage (age 40–55) begins with the midlife transition—the link between early and middle adulthood. Characteristic of the midcareer is the reassessment of the life-style that governed the early career. A new life structure is forged that may or may not be in keeping with the previous structure. Employees typically review the goals that they have attained and consider how many additional goals they can achieve in the future. Possible career stage issues include obsolescence and plateauing.

STAGE 5: THE LATE CAREER.   The final career stage, the late career, involves continued productivity and eventual preparation for disengagement from work life. Although very little research has been directed toward the late career, it is known that a negative bias against older individuals exists.[28]

In addition, successfully disengaging from the work role is a major challenge, and organizations are attempting to assist older workers with this life transition. Retirement can also be an opportunity to pursue activities that could not be enjoyed during employment.

CRITICAL ISSUES

Of the career stages, three raise particularly critical career management issues and problems for organizations and individuals: organizational entry, midcareer, and late career (retirement). In the following sections, we discuss these issues in greater detail.

ORGANIZATIONAL ENTRY ISSUES. Although organizational entry always involves moving inside an organization from outside, it also frequently entails moving from an educational environment to an organizational environment. Newcomers (especially those coming from college) generally have inflated expectations even if they have engaged in self-assessment activities aimed at awareness of self and work environment. Inflated expectations may lead to disappointments (reality shock).

Organizations can use realistic job previews to counteract the effects of reality shock. Unrealistically high expectations can stem from the educational process, the recruitment process, and organizational stereotypes. Realistic previews attempt to present both the positive and negative aspects of the job and organization. Such realistic previews have been shown to reduce voluntary turnover among new employees.[29]

Organizational entry issues include:

- **expectations**
- **disappointments (reality shock)**

MIDCAREER ISSUES. Two critical issues facing employees in the midcareer years are the midlife transition and the career plateau. Many employees experience a crisis between the ages of 40 and 55. This crisis, which has been called the **midlife transition**, entails a reexamination of one's accomplishments relative to one's initial career goals. Feelings of restlessness and insecurity are common. Individuals in this transition become aware of advancing age and death, the signs of aging, a growing sense of obsolescence, and changes in family relationships. All of these factors can create stress.

Organizations can help employees cope with this crisis by encouraging them to develop new skills and to serve as mentors for younger employees. Individuals can also engage in **self-assessment** activities. Self-assessment during the midlife transition should focus on the individual's feelings about middle age and determining the relative priority of work, family, leisure, and self-development.[30]

At some point, nearly every employee reaches a **career plateau**, a situation in which the career slows and the prospects for promotion dramatically decrease. Plateaus can be personal or organizational. Personal plateauing means that the employee has decided not to accept additional promotions in the organization. Organizational plateauing occurs when the employee desires advancement but no opportunities exist, or the organization does not consider the employee promotable. Since fewer opportunities exist at each higher level in companies, plateauing is natural and not indicative of success or failure.[31] Employees, however, may need help in dealing with plateauing because our culture views advancement as a yardstick of success, and many employees feel like failures when they are no longer promotable.

Managers can take a number of steps to help employees cope with career plateauing. These steps include making the facts visible, being realistic about the strengths and weaknesses of others, counseling people, eliminating skill obsolescence, letting people know they are appreciated, creating new rewards, encouraging initiative, discouraging employees from leading a "workoholic" life, giving honest appraisals, and managing by "walking around" and being available when needed.[32]

Midcareer issues include:

- **midlife transition**
- **plateauing**

Self-assessment activities involve stating one's feelings about events and stating their importance.

LATE CAREER ISSUES. Individuals in the late career stage must continue to be productive and eventually prepare for retirement. Retirement is a major

Late career issues include:
- **remaining productive**
- **preparing for retirement**

Career management programs include:
- **career pathing**
- **career ladders**
- **career planning**
- **job progression**
- **glass ceiling**
- **work-family**
- **outplacement**
- **career counseling**
- **stress management**
- **retirement**

career transition for many employees because it represents the culmination of 40 or more years of work involvement. Moreover, older individuals may be viewed as less productive, versatile, less open to new ideas, and less adaptable.[33] Such stereotyping can make continued effective performance even more difficult.

Organizations can help employees in the late career stage in a number of ways by:

- Carefully examining HR policies and procedures affecting older workers
- Surveying the needs of older workers
- Providing realistic retirement previews
- Developing retirement programs
- Implementing flexible work patterns and options[34]

Organizations must also consider the legal issues that affect the treatment of older workers. The *Age Discrimination in Employment Act* forbids discrimination in hiring, placement, compensation, promotion, and termination for individuals aged 40 and over. Treating these workers fairly makes good business sense and also helps to avoid costly litigation.

Late-career individuals should actively manage their careers just as employees do at earlier career stages. Successful late-career management may help to dispel some myths and stereotypes about older workers. Late-career employees can also help themselves by actively planning for their retirement, whether the organization provides retirement programs or not. The retirement transition can raise many fears, but it also contains many opportunities. We will discuss retirement programs later in this chapter.

We have sketched what organizations and individuals can do in these career stages, and we are now ready to go into more detail. First we begin with specific things organizations can do and specific things individuals like you can do in your own career planning.

CAREER MANAGEMENT PROGRAMS IN THE ORGANIZATION

Career management programs are offered by organizations to assist employees in career planning and management. A number of programs will be examined here to illustrate the diversity of needs filled by these programs and the wide range of concerns that organizations consider important in career management.

CAREER PATHING

Career pathing programs consist of three major activities: career ladders, career planning, and job progression. Career ladders address the issues of opportunity. Career planning activities help employees identify their abilities, values and goals, and strengths and weaknesses. **Job progression** provides a set of job experiences that helps employees (1) satisfy some of their values or goals, (2) utilize some of their strengths and abilities, and (3) improve upon some of their weaknesses identified in the career planning activity.

CAREER LADDERS. Providing career ladders involves several decisions on the part of an organization. First, should there be an active policy of promotion from within? Second, should there be a training and development program to provide sufficient candidates for internal promotion? If the answers to these questions are yes, then the organization must identify career ladders consistent with organizational and job requirements and employee skills and preferences. This may result

PARTNERSHIP: WORKING TOGETHER IN HR PLANNING

LINE MANAGERS	HR PROFESSIONALS	EMPLOYEES
Describe their business plans and human resource needs.	Identify human resource implications of business plans.	Assume responsibility for career planning and work with HR professionals and line managers in career development programs.
Work with HR professionals to ensure human resources are used effectively.	Develop programs that match employee supply to demand.	
Support the offering of career management programs.	Identify the supply of human resources that matches the needs of line managers.	

in wide career ladders where employees can move across many areas and functions within the company, or it may result in narrow career ladders where employees only move within a few areas and functions.

An organization may identify several career paths for different groups or types of employees—for example, fast-track or slow-track. Such an approach is based on the premise that an organization cannot afford to place applicants in jobs at the lower rungs of the ladder when they already possess the skills necessary for jobs at the higher rungs. This actually occurs, however, with many people recruited from college. Although new recruits may be essentially overqualified for their first jobs, the organization hires them for more difficult "future" jobs. This approach is partially to blame for the higher turnover rate among new college graduates and also has implications regarding legal compliance. Employers may claim that a college degree is necessary for an entry-level job when they may actually consider the degree necessary only for the second- or third-level job. Such a policy can lead to discriminatory barriers in recruitment and promotion.

One way to reduce potential discriminatory barriers is through career ladders and paths. When career ladders and paths are in place with clearly specified requirements anchored in sound job-content analyses, organizations can present better legal defenses for their recruitment policies. In essence, sound HR planning establishes a case for long-term job relatedness. Organizations with clearly defined career ladders may also have an easier time attracting and recruiting qualified job applicants and a better chance of keeping them.

CAREER PLANNING. The career planning activity aids an individual in his or her personal appraisal or self-assessment. When an organization provides this ser-

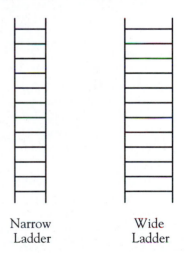

Narrow Ladder   Wide Ladder

vice, however, it is likely to be related as much to the organization's needs as to the individual's. An individual's personal appraisal, however, need not be related to a specific organization. An example of a career planning guide from a large organization appears in Exhibit 4.6.

JOB PROGRESSION. The job progression programs enhance the relationship between career planning and management and serve the practical needs of both

---

EXHIBIT 4.6
ORGANIZATIONAL CAREER PLANNING GUIDE

1. My job satisfaction on my present job is (circle)..
   Very   Very
   Low   Low   Average   High   High
2. I would like to progress in my work by   Yes   No
   A. Developing improved performances and results on my present job...
   B. Qualifying for the next logical higher position above my present one....................................
   C. Qualifying for a different type of work within another department...
   D. Qualifying for several positions above my present one ....
3. I consider myself best suited to
   A. Supervision...
   B. Supporting staff work ....
   C. Production of operation management ....
4. Goals
   A suitable job goal for me is _____
   _____
   _____
5. Qualifications
   Evaluate your own qualifications based on current standing and what is needed for your job goal.*
6. My Development Balance Sheet
   A. My strong points are _____
   B. I like to do work that is _____
   C. My limiting factors are _____
   D. I dislike work that is _____
7. Development
   If I want to develop either on my present job or to qualify for a different job, I need the following:
   A. More job knowledge in _____
   B. I like to do work that is _____
   C. A better attitude or outlook concerning _____
8. Taking Action to Reach Your Job Goal
   List how you can develop greater knowledge, job skills, or personal abilities that will help you reach your career goals.
   A. Formal study of a subject (list seminars, night school, company training program, or correspondence courses that will increase your knowledge of a subject): _____
   _____
   _____
   _____
   _____

*When this form is used within the company, space is provided so an individual is able to write a lengthy response. This is true for items 5–8.

the employees and the organization. To do this, firms focus on the job as the vehicle for career development. Firms base this approach on the following principles:

- The most important influences on career development occur on the job.
- Different jobs demand the development of different skills.
- Development can occur only when a person has not yet developed the skills demanded by a particular job.
- By identifying a rational sequence of job assignments for a person, the time required to develop the necessary skills for a chosen target can be reduced.[35]

The essence of job progression programs is the identification of job demands or dimensions. For example, Sears used the Hay Plan (described in Chapter 11) to analyze jobs in three basic dimensions: know-how, problem solving, and accountability. Because these dimensions require different employee skills, a rational sequence of job assignments for an employee's career development would consist of jobs with different dimensions. Consequently, Sears used its program to identify rational paths to target jobs (those that represent the end of employee's paths), to classify paths according to speed and the level of development attained, to justify and identify lateral moves and even downward moves, and to assess training needs and provide input into an HR planning program.

Used appropriately, a job progression program can be very helpful in aiding an organization's equal employment efforts and in opening up career opportunities. "This kind of system can lift career planning out of informal corporate 'old boy' networks and reduce the employee's dependence upon a well-informed boss."[36] Assisting this objective are glass ceiling and diversity management programs discussed in Chapter 3. Closely related are work-family interface programs.

WORK-FAMILY INTERFACE PROGRAMS

Balancing work and family demands has become an increasingly important organizational issue. The "traditional" family with a husband who is the breadwinner, a wife who is a full-time homemaker, and two children is coming to constitute a minority of U.S. households. With the dramatic influx of women into the work force and the growing number of dual-career and two-wage couples, individuals are finding it difficult to avoid conflict between work and family areas. Since work and family have been treated as "separate worlds" in the past, many people feel that conflict is not supposed to happen, that they are the only people experiencing such problems and that the organization will not be impressed if family problems are causing poor job performance. Perhaps the most significant aspect of work-family programs is the recognition that work and family life are interdependent, that it is important to our society and to business that they be interdependent, and that family issues can affect work performance and career development.

In fact, career development can now be viewed as a family affair. Family-friendly organizations provide a setting for employees to discuss work-family issues and to identify coping strategies that can reduce the conflict.[37] In a more direct way, organizations can provide child-care assistance, flexible work schedules, and career and life-planning activities. Securing new jobs for working spouses of employees being relocated or transferred is a service provided by a growing number of firms, according to The Conference Board in New York:

> More than one-half of American corporations currently offer some sort of reemployment assistance to spouses of transferred employees. Nearly 500,000 employees are transferred annually, with an average cost per transfer of $41,000. Aid to spouses adds $500 to $2,000 to that figure. Much of this

Work-family interface programs are meant to help employees balance the demands of work and family.

largesse is impelled by changes in the U.S. family and emerging trends in the work force, the report says, pointing out that "about 70 percent of all American couples represented in the work force are dual earners."[38]

Typically, companies providing job-information materials to spouses use such materials *in addition* to other approaches; for example:

- US West gives working partners a choice of either a self-guided workbook with audio tapes or up to $2,500 to apply to job search costs such as employment agency fees, interview trips, and job counseling. While the printed information is aimed at satisfying the needs of most spouses, the reimbursement option can be used by those facing more difficult job transitions.
- Compaq Computer Corporation supplements its information package with a "Career Corner" at the company's relocation resource center. The company also participates in a consortium of Houston employees who cooperate in circulating spouse résumés. Compaq provides the materials to all its married transferees, even if not requested.
- Johnson & Johnson offers personal counseling to relocating families to supplement its package of in-depth information on job-search techniques.[39]

CHILD-CARE ASSISTANCE.   Along with society and technology, the percentage of wage-earning women in the United States is rapidly changing. Between 1960 and 1990, for example, the percentage of married women with children under six years of age who work outside the home jumped from 19 percent to 55 percent. Today more than one child in five lives with a single parent. More companies than ever before are providing some kind of child-care services for their employees. Because child-care services is such a critical employee benefit, we will discuss them in detail in Chapter 13, Indirect Compensation.

Small firms as well as large firms are developing innovative family-assistance programs. And employees appreciate their efforts. In a recent *INC.* magazine survey of the "best small companies" to work for, many had highly creative programs for child- and family-care assistance. Some of the programs are described in the feature "Managing Human Resources at the Best Small Companies."

OUTPLACEMENT PROGRAMS

Being terminated for any reason can be a very traumatic career transition. Unfortunately for many individuals, outplacement has become very common in recent years because of cuts in middle management, mergers and acquisitions, shifts in corporate goals, and the general business climate. When it occurs, job loss can threaten self-esteem and confront the individual with various concerns about competency and career direction. **Outplacement programs** assist terminated employees in finding suitable employment or in career exploration. For example, a middle manager may decide that starting his or her own business is a more desirable option than working for another company as a manager. The degree of organizational assistance usually depends on the employee's level in the company with higher-level employees usually receiving more support. Outplacement services are usually provided through outside consulting firms that specialize in this activity.

Outplacement programs assist terminated employees in finding employment elsewhere.

CAREER COUNSELING

Career counseling typically involves a discussion of an individual's work values, career goals, current job activities and performance, and action plans.

Counseling can be formal or informal in nature. Formal career counseling is usually conducted by career counselors and vocational psychologists in individual sessions. On an informal level, discussions with supervisors are very important.

Supervisors are considered a primary source of career information and can do a number of things to facilitate the career counseling process. They can

- develop a knowledge of occupational information and career source material
- develop an understanding of career theories and applications
- subscribe to professional career development journals
- understand the elements of an effective relationship
- develop good listening and questioning skills
- learn to respect the confidentiality of employees[41]

STRESS MANAGEMENT
Although individuals experience stress for many reasons, uncertainty and lack of control seem to be the major causes. Many employees in the process of managing their careers encounter much uncertainty about the future and lack of con-

trol over career direction, especially promotion. Sources of stress can include lack of challenge on the job, job demands that exceed an individual's skills and/or training, inequity, and lack of career opportunities. In addition, many employees find the thought of retirement stressful because they are uncertain what it will be like. Retirement planning programs are successful in part because they help reduce this uncertainty. Stress-management programs help individuals identify sources of stress and develop strategies for coping. It is crucial that organizations offer these programs because the symptoms of stress can result in serious health and safety outcomes. Symptoms may be psychological, such as apathy and dissatisfaction; physiological, such as headaches and backaches; or behavioral, such as absenteeism and accidents. We will discuss these in detail in Chapter 19, Health and Safety.

RETIREMENT PLANNING

Many companies accommodate the career needs of employees who are about to retire. Typically, companies offer seminars that provide information on finances, housing or relocation, family relations, and legal affairs. Since research has shown that retirees also face social and psychological adjustments, many retirement planning programs now include additional components that allow for the sharing of emotional and developmental issues. Some companies have formed **social support groups**, for retirees, which address the special social and emotional needs of this group. Social support groups can be an important part of a person's successful adjustment to retirement.

Social support groups provide unconditional support and acceptance of others.

In addition to retirement planning seminars, companies offer retirement rehearsal arrangements. For example, employees in Polaroid's retirement rehearsal program can leave the program for three months and then decide whether they want to return to work or to continue the retirement; they can also enter a tapering-off program. In this program, the employees gradually work fewer and fewer hours per week.[42]

Both retiring employees and organizations benefit from retirement planning options and seminars. By encouraging more senior employees to retire, companies open up jobs and promotion opportunities for less senior employees. Because of these mutual benefits and the baby-boom bulge in the work force described in Chapter 3, it is likely that companies will continue to offer retirement planning accommodations.

SHARING THE RESPONSIBILITY: YOUR CAREER ACTIVITIES

By actively managing your career, you'll do better than by not managing it. "Better" can be measured by any standard you choose—job security, self-esteem, growth, comfort, success in climbing to the top of the organization, or salary level. By planning and managing, you'll increase your chances of obtaining whatever you realistically identify as most important. Exhibit 4.7 outlines a general strategy for planning and managing your career. Fundamental to this is the personal appraisal. **Personal appraisal** (or career self-appraisal) is really the basis of career planning activities. It consists of identifying the strengths and weaknesses an individual possesses. The following provides space for you to itemize your own strengths and weaknesses as you do your own personal appraisal and complete all the career planning activities shown.

Personal appraisal consists of identifying strengths and weaknesses in relation to career goals.

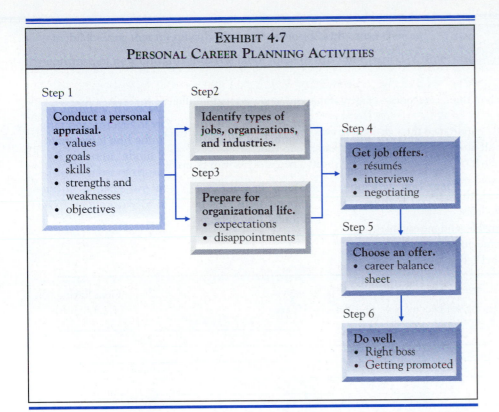

EXHIBIT 4.7
PERSONAL CAREER PLANNING ACTIVITIES

STEP 1: CONDUCTING A PERSONAL APPRAISAL

This step involves taking a personal inventory of the following:

- values
- goals
- skills
- strengths and weaknesses
- objectives

Do this step by completing the career self-appraisal exercise shown in Exhibit 4.8.

STEP 2: IDENTIFYING TYPES OF JOBS, ORGANIZATIONS, AND INDUSTRIES

Because the job or jobs you choose will have such an impact on your life, it is important to carefully analyze what you want from your first job and your first company. You may want to start by first identifying industries in which you may want to work. For example, you may choose to work in an industry with great potential such as the following (see also Exhibit 3.7):

- health care
- computer science, data processing
- communications

Then within these industries or any others, you next need to gather information on a particular company. You can gain direct information through summer work experience, internships, and part-time work; these are valuable ways to gain exposure to new companies. Although some work experiences may be boring,

EXHIBIT 4.8
CAREER SELF-APPRAISAL

Steps

1. List five goals you have for each of three categories—career, affiliations, and personal fulfillment (or create other categories).
2. Go back and rate them (1–little importance through 5–great importance). Which list has the most 4s and 5s?
3. Merge the three lists and rank all fifteen goals in order of importance to you.
4. Select your top goal and describe it on the top of the second sheet. Then, discuss it in terms of:
   a. Personal strengths and weaknesses
   b. Obstacles to prevent achieving the goal
   c. Strategies to circumvent obstacles
   d. Are the goals realistic, attainable, and measurable?
   e. What are the rewards for achieving the goal?
   f. Steps for achieving the goal (Do this for all your goals)

Career Goals, e.g., become president by 45; become vice-president by 35, etc.

Goal Rating (1,2,3,4 or 5)

1. _____ _____
2. _____ _____
3. _____ _____
4. _____ _____
5. _____ _____

Affiliation/Interpersonal, e.g., family, friends, clubs, group members, etc.

1. _____ _____
2. _____ _____
3. _____ _____
4. _____ _____
5. _____ _____

Personal Fulfillment/Achievements, e.g., master the piano, run a marathon, get an MBA degree, etc.

1. _____ _____
2. _____ _____
3. _____ _____
4. _____ _____
5. _____ _____

Goal Ranking

Please list (in order of importance) the fifteen goals from above.

1. _____ _____
2. _____ _____
3. _____ _____
4. _____ _____
5. _____ _____
6. _____ _____
7. _____ _____
8. _____ _____
9. _____ _____
10. _____ _____
11. _____ _____

EXHIBIT 4.8 (CONT.)
CAREER SELF-APPRAISAL

12. _____

13. _____

14. _____

15. (least important) _____

Take one important goal, restate it here, and then continue by dicsussing your personal strengths and weaknesses.

_____

_____

Personal strengths in relation to attaining the goal

1.

2.

3.

4.

5.

Personal weaknesses in relation to attaining the goal

1.

2.

3.

4.

5.

Obstacles in the way to goal attainment	Strategy to overcome obstacles
1.	1.
2.	2.
3.	3.
4.	4.
5.	5.

Rewards for achieving the goal (rank in terms of value)

1.

2.

3.

4.

5.

Indicators that you have achieved the goal (short and long term)

1.

2.

3.

4.

5.

Steps for achieving the goal (starting now)	Time deadline
1.	
2.	
3.	
4.	
5.	

you need to consider them as learning experiences, ways of getting to know yourself better. Other sources of information are newspapers and professional magazines, school placement offices, libraries, direct mail, job-search firms, friends, and family.

In thinking about the types of jobs, organizations, and industries, weigh the relative value to you of such things as more salary and fewer benefits versus less salary and more benefits and more opportunities to learn more skills.[43]

If you are skilled with your hands and you enjoy working with things, consider becoming any of the following: air-conditioning, refrigeration, and heating mechanic; appliance service person; television and radio service technician; business machine, computer, or industrial machinery service person; truck or bus mechanic; or vending machine mechanic. Research by the Department of Labor indicates that if you learn one of these skills, you'll have plenty of job opportunities through the 1990s. Exhibit 3.7 in Chapter 3 illustrates occupations with the largest job growth by 2005.

There are many types of jobs to be considered, including self-employment and the more traditional entry-level jobs in larger organizations that are the first step in a series through promotions to senior management positions. Within larger organizations, these traditional paths are available in many functional areas such as human resource management, marketing, manufacturing, and finance. Whatever functional field you may choose, in a larger organization, there is always the possibility for an international assignment as an expatriate.

An *expatriate* is an employee who works for a domestic company but in its foreign location.

EXPATRIATE CAREERS.   For many U.S. firms, being competitive now means being globally competitive, and this means developing more **expatriates** (Americans who work in other countries for U.S. companies) to run the businesses overseas. While offering clear career paths for expatriates would seem to be necessary to encourage individuals to become expatriates, it appears that as yet few U.S. firms have done this as indicated in this survey of HR managers at 56 U.S.-based multinational companies.

- 56 percent say a foreign assignment is either detrimental to, or immaterial in, one's career.
- 47 percent say their returning expatriates aren't guaranteed jobs with the company upon completion of their foreign assignments.
- 65 percent say their expatriates' foreign assignments are not integrated into their overall career planning.
- 45 percent view returning expatriates as a problem because they are so hard to fit back into the company.
- 20 percent consider their company's repatriation policies adequate to meet the needs of their returning expatriates.[44]

It is entirely possible you will be offered the chance of working abroad as an expatriate.

Despite this, it is likely the development of career paths for expatriates will become a trend.

CAREERS IN INTERNATIONAL HR.   A thorough description of these opportunities is provided in the feature "Managing Human Resources: Careers at the International Level."

A *local-country employee* is one working in the United States but for a foreign-owned firm.

LOCAL-COUNTRY NATIONAL.   You may also wish to consider working as a **local-country national** for a foreign-owned firm. While it may be glamorous to work for a British or Japanese firm and travel abroad, there can be some potential drawbacks. They include possible limited promotion opportunities and limited freedom to manage as you would like. As with any decision, it is important

MANAGING HUMAN RESOURCES

Careers at the International Level

THE globalization of business is occurring at a much faster pace than American economic growth. According to the U.S. Department of Commerce, the gross national product increased by 15 percent between 1985 and 1990. During that same period, U.S. exports grew by 72 percent; nearly five times as fast. Exports now constitute 15 percent of GNP. In the late 1980s, U.S. foreign direct investment climbed by 34 percent. Even much faster at 105 percent was the growth of direct investment by foreigners in the United States. Every indication is that globalization will continue and in all probability accelerate.

All this suggests that from a career perspective, international business is a good place to be. If corporations are to succeed in the global arena, they must manage human resources effectively. International human resource management should be one of the great growth functions of the 1990s and beyond.

How can you break into the field? What is the potential for growth? As many have already discovered, there are few recruiters at colleges and graduate schools clamoring for candidates.

Entry-level positions in international human resources (IHR) are very hard to find, even with the MBA in human resources or international management. The one exception is as an expatriate compensation and benefits specialist. Expatriate compensation and benefits is currently the largest and most time-consuming IHR activity of U.S.-headquartered companies.

From a career perspective, however, there are serious limitations to entering the field through the expatriate compensation door. Most importantly, the skills developed in this area have virtually no applicability in other functions. The subject is incredibly complex, and those who master it are in high demand and under great pressure to remain within the specialty. While many in the field find expatriate compensation and benefits fascinating because of its variety and complexity, experience suggests that it is an area with limited upward mobility.

In a recent survey of 35 major U.S. multinationals, it was found that over 90 percent of senior IHR executives have had experience in other human resource functions. Nearly half have held line positions and managed a business; 60 percent have had overseas assignments.

Those aspiring to upper levels of HR management (global, international, or domestic) will have a much better chance of success if they have a degree in human resources and/or international business and enter the field through one of the domestic functions, such as planning, management development, executive compensation, or industrial relations. Solid experience in two or more domestic HR areas will vastly improve the opportunities for transfer into the international arena at a significant management level.

However, a major problem for those whose experience is limited to human resources is the difficulty of obtaining an overseas assignment. There are very few Americans overseas with a primary responsibility for HR management. It is easier to gain overseas experience in other functions such as marketing, finance, and engineering. Indeed, many senior IHR executives got their overseas experience in other functions.

Is overseas experience necessary for IHR executives? Perhaps not, but it is interesting to note that the 40 percent of senior HR executives who have not worked abroad cited their lack of overseas experience as their greatest weakness.

In all probability, there will be dramatic changes in IHR management over the next decade, including much more emphasis on strategic issues and support for business objectives. IHR will become a more vital management function, and greater emphasis will be placed on staffing the function with executives possessing overseas and line experience, as well as having a solid grounding in general human resources.

In the meantime, it is important to know how to pick your way through the career maze. Those who desire careers as functional specialists may find expatriate compensation and benefits fascinating and challenging. Those who aspire to higher IHR management would be well advised to acquire a solid domestic base and experience in a line function before seeking an

Continued on the next page

overseas assignment. Clearly there are other options; working for a foreign multinational or consulting firm, for example. Regardless, those who will be managing IHR in the major multinationals of the future will find the challenges exciting.

Mr. Reynolds is a senior counselor of Organization Resources Counselors, Inc. (New York) and directs its international HR consulting, publications, meeting groups, and compensation services. Mr. Reynolds is on the board of the Institute for International Human Resources.[45]

to gather as much information as possible before considering this option. However, because of increased foreign ownership in the United States, these jobs will be increasingly available.[46]

STEP 3: PREPARING FOR ORGANIZATIONAL LIFE

It is one thing to know the type of job you might want and the type of industry or organization in which you want to work, but it's an entirely different thing to know the realities of life and work in that organization. Two facets of organizational life that you should be aware of are organizational expectation and disappointment.

ORGANIZATIONAL EXPECTATION.   Most organizations expect new employees to have certain characteristics:

- Competence to get a job done
- Ability to accept organizational realities
- High personal integrity, strength, and ethics
- Capacity to grow[47]

ORGANIZATIONAL DISAPPOINTMENT.   Although an organization has high expectations of you, it may not always live up to its end of the bargain. What it does or doesn't do may bring you disappointments (reality shock).[43] Here are several likely reasons why:

- *Low initial job challenge.* Although some findings have indicated the usefulness of giving new recruits a challenging job initially, many organizations continue to ease the new recruit into the organization. This is consistent with the organization's perception of the new recruit as a novice.
- *Low self-actualization and need satisfaction.* The new recruit may fail to experience the autonomy and challenge necessary to grow and to develop self-esteem and competency.

  Some researchers have suggested that an individual may actually lose competency in the job if not given the opportunity to advance in the direction of the growth and independence characteristic of mature adults.
- *The vanishing performance appraisal, or inability to determine what the real criteria are.* New recruits come on board with the expectation of receiving clear and unambiguous evaluations of their performance. In reality, new recruits report having little feedback on their performance, although their supervisors may claim the opposite.
- *Unrealistically high aspirations.* Most recruits have higher expectations of being able to use their skills and abilities than actually occur. The gap between an individual's skills and the skills actually used on the job is probably increased because of the manager's belief that the new recruit is not capable of assuming responsibility:

- *Source of threat to the boss.* A new recruit's first boss plays a critical role for the recruit's future in the organization. The role tends to be negative, especially if the boss feels threatened—this may be a supervisor who is in a terminal position and can't go any further in the organization. The new recruit may be seen as a "comer" with a great deal more potential than the boss. In addition, the new recruit is probably younger and has different values and styles. As a result, this first relationship may not provide many positive experiences.
- *Amount of conflict and uncertainty in the organization.* New recruits think that rules and procedures, directions, and communications will be clear, crisp, and without conflict. The reality in many situations is just the opposite.[49]

Individuals (you) can do a number of things to facilitate successful organizational entry including the following:

- *Development of self-awareness.* This activity, known also as self-assessment, involves an inventory of values, goals, skills, strengths and weaknesses, and objectives. Individuals must develop an awareness of themselves and their preferred work environment. You can use Exhibit 4.8 for this purpose.
- *Identification of prospective employers.* Because the job or jobs individuals choose have such an impact on their lives, they must analyze carefully what they want from their first job and their first company. Information about companies can be gathered through summer work experience, internships, and part-time work.
- *Effective job interview behavior.* "Selling" oneself to prospective employers requires a high degree of self-awareness. The interview is the individual's chance to create a favorable impression, gather additional information about the company, emphasize past accomplishments, demonstrate initiative and leadership through extracurricular activities, and practice interviewing skills (perhaps through information interviews).
- *Choice of organizations.* Although choosing the best job offer may be more art than science, a **career balance sheet** can help. This involves listing the positive and negative aspects of each offer, making a separate balance sheet for each one. Individuals should consider how each aspect will affect them and others such as their spouse, friends, or family. Balance sheets assist the decision-making process because they organize the information systematically.

A *career balance sheet* lets you list all the good things and bad things about various job choices.

STEP 4: GETTING JOB OFFERS

Now that you've narrowed down (but not too much) the types of jobs, organizations, and industries you are interested in and have prepared yourself for organizational life, the next thing to do is get some job offers. Three aspects of getting job offers are as follows:

- Résumé writing
- Interviewing
- Negotiating

RÉSUMÉ WRITING.   The standard résumé lists work experience from your current job or student status on back to those two years you spent delivering the daily paper (to show youthful vitality, industry, and responsibility for customers and money). Often it's a chronology of dates, titles, and responsibilities (whether they are previous jobs or positions held in school organizations). Some examples are shown in Appendix D. In addition to taking it with you to an interview, the ques-

Start your résumé writing now so you have plenty of time to revise it.

tion becomes, "Is it okay to fax it?" See the "HR Advice and Application: To Fax or Not to Fax" feature for a discussion of accepted etiquette. Whether you mail it or fax it, always include a cover letter tailored to the job and the company.

JOB INTERVIEWING.   Step 1 has great value as preparation for job interviews. If you know yourself inside and out, you will find it easier to "sell" yourself to potential employers. Here are six suggestions for participating in job interviews.

- Sell yourself to the recruiter with the same determination you would use in selling a product or service to a customer. The interview period is brief, yet a favorable impression of your appearance, sense of purpose, and clarity of self-expression will probably weigh more heavily with the recruiter than your transcript, your résumé, or your references.
- Familiarize yourself ahead of time with the employer to be interviewed— know what the company does and what products or services it offers. Ask only pertinent questions during the interview, and suggest how your skills and abilities may benefit the organization.
- Develop your ability to communicate, but do not come on too strong or be overly confident.
- Cite academic achievement, especially if the recruiter appears to relate to the job area you are interested in. Remember that companies often view your college work as a preparatory period. Hence, cite your academic efforts as evidence that you can attain long-range goals and objectives.
- Mention extracurricular activities that demonstrate your leadership or initiative.
- Learn the art of interviewing by accepting as many interview opportunities as you can, even with organizations you think you may not want to join. Interviews can be practiced by role playing.[51]

NEGOTIATING.   An important topic that will surely arise in your interviewing is salary. How you handle this topic could make a substantial difference in how much you get paid. Here are a few tips on how to handle this aspect in your job search:

It's "dumb" for a job candidate to raise the question of salary early in the hiring process, says Pfizer divisional vice-president Max Hughes. And it is. Until

HR ADVICE AND APPLICATION

TO FAX OR NOT TO FAX?

Receiving a résumé through the fax machine apparently isn't as taboo as it once was, according to a recent attitude survey of HR professionals. The survey was conducted by an independent research firm for Office Team, a division of Robert Half International, based in Menlo Park, California.

The survey inquired whether it was acceptable for job candidates to fax their résumés to an organization that has advertised a job opening and stated no specific submittal guidelines. Researchers found that 77 percent of the senior managers polled would accept a résumé by fax if they hadn't specified otherwise. Although 21 percent of the respondents indicated that they would not consider faxed résumés, 2 percent indicated that they weren't sure whether they would consider such applicants or not. Times have changed. As recently as a few years ago, business etiquette prohibited job seekers from sending résumés to prospective employers by way of facsimile technology.[50]

the employer has had time to make up his or her mind to hire you, you aren't worth anything to the employer. To negotiate the highest possible salary, listen and ask questions so that you can identify the other person's needs and communicate how you can help meet them. It's best to delay the subject of salary until later in the interview. Loaded with information about your strengths, the employer should see you as a more valuable asset than when you began to talk. . . .[52]

STEP 5: CHOOSING AN OFFER

In the job market today, you may have to exercise your patience! Jobs may not come immediately and you may have to work a bit harder at getting job offers, but offers will come. Once you start receiving job offers, you must be astute in your choice. Although choosing the best offer is really more of an art than a cast-in-concrete method, the career balance sheet described above is a helpful place to start.[53]

STEP 6: DOING WELL

Doing well involves getting what you want from the organization in which you are working. It means having things go your way. It may mean getting promoted, and it certainly means staying valuable and useful to the organization. As such, it requires that you know about the following:

- dealing with your boss
- getting promoted

THE RIGHT BOSS.   People are more likely to develop strong leadership qualities if they work for a boss who has something to teach, who is on the move, and who is capable of taking others along. The preference for being on a winning team is a survival mechanism. People are less dependent and uncertain if they're allied with bosses who are strong leaders. Consequently, it pays to try to be in a position to select your boss. This is especially true for your first boss. You can enhance your chances of working for the boss of your choice by your own outstanding performance and by being a critical subordinate who is not threatening.[54]

GETTING PROMOTED.   Getting promoted is much easier when you

- *Have credibility with senior managers.* Managers with credibility can take greater risks and make more mistakes because it is known they produce results. You must have credibility with your superiors before you can develop it with subordinates. Take this example: a manager brought in from the outside to run an equipment-design division could barely get the information he needed from headquarters—he had few connections and no clout. Although he had a better idea of what was going on, without the support of top management, his subordinates thought little of him.[55]
- *Have a reputation as being an expert.* When an individual is considered an expert, others tend to defer to that person on issues involving his or her expertise. This is important in large organizations where many people have only secondhand knowledge about one's professional competence.[56]
- *Are the first in a position.* An individual who holds a new position—that is, no one has ever held it before—and who takes risks and succeeds is more likely to be rewarded than one who accomplishes the same thing but who is not the first to hold the position. While excellent performance on routine tasks is usually valued, being innovative is a big plus.[57]

A *network* is a collection of friends and acquaintances inside and outside one's workplace who can be counted on for some kinds of help.

• *Know and use networks.* Knowing about and using networks can be critical to your job success. Essentially a **network** is a collection of friends and acquaintances, both inside and outside one's work place, that can be counted on for some kind of help. Networks can provide many kinds of help including information, services, support, and access.

While getting promoted is certainly still possible, it is becoming more difficult to do it rapidly. The days of the "fast track" appear to be all but over for most employees.[58] Thus you need to prepare yourself for:

• Getting as much out of each job as possible
• Being flexible and open-minded
• Being a team player
• Excelling at your job
• Furthering your own education

CURRENT TRENDS

ALIGNING HUMAN RESOURCES WITH THE NEEDS OF THE BUSINESS

Ensuring that business needs are met by human resources will be a significant issue through the twenty-first century. In particular, human resources must be a strategic partner to the line manager, international needs must be addressed, and sufficient programs must be put in place to ensure cost efficiency. Success in all these areas will depend on the organization's HR planning skills and programs.

Planning at organizational and individual levels will continue to change into the twenty-first century. At the organizational level, there will be a greater focus on shaping and managing change. Planning, as an identifier of needs and mobilizer of human resources, will increasingly be used to identify business needs and the ways in which employees can meet those needs. To deal with the rapidly changing environment, planning will become more tentative and short-term focused. At the same time, long-term needs will still be important because some organizational change efforts—such as quality improvement—take time.

Human resource planning will also be done with demographics in mind. As skilled labor shortages develop, there will be more concern both for retaining *and* retraining good employees. As employee commitment and empowerment are causally linked to quality improvement, there will be even stronger emphasis on this area.

However, there will be a corresponding need to link HR planning and business planning so that excess supply of personnel is not created. As the external environment changes, so may the strategy and business needs of the firm. Therefore, HR planning must cultivate work force flexibility and adaptability. Planning professionals will assume the responsibility for systematically orchestrating all the HR practices to stimulate and reinforce employee flexibility and adaptability. This orchestration will become more important as the need to link business strategies with labor supply grows.

Finally, businesses must ensure that the most effective human resource practices are being used. To that end, continuous and extensive environment scanning will be an important feature of successful firms in highly competitive environments in the twenty-first century as described in Chapter 3.

SELF-MANAGEMENT

Self-management teaches people to exercise control over their own behavior. Self-management begins by having people assess their own aspirations and set specific concrete goals in relation to those aspirations. Once goals are set, the employees can discuss ways in which the environment facilitates or hinders goal attainment. The challenge here is to develop strategies that eliminate blocks to performance success. Put another way, self-management teaches people to observe their own behavior, compare their outputs to their goals, and administer their own reinforcement to sustain goal commitment and performance.

The concept of self-management is important in programs of empowerment. For employees to work effectively in a firm that delegates power and responsibility, they need to have the basic skills of self-management. Also, as organizations move from individual-based systems to group- or team-based systems of management, the concept of self-management extends to self-managed work groups, described in Chapter 5.

Self-management teaches people to exercise control over their own behavior.

SUMMARY

One key idea of this chapter is that planning is a vital function to any successful organization. Human resource planning by definition, however, is a *derived* function. That is, before an organization can plan for its people needs, it must know something about its organizational goals and strategy. Thus, HR planning takes on strategic importance because it requires that human resource objectives be linked to organizational objectives.

Human resource planning is needed because of societal changes: (1) changes in population and labor force characteristics, such as age, gender, and race composition, job preferences, and job openings; (2) changes in general economic conditions and the increased use of automation and robots; (3) changes in social values, especially those regarding work, mobility, and retirement; and (4) changes in legislation and the level of government activity.

These changes mean that HR departments must develop strategic and operational plans for everything related to personnel. By moving planning into a more vital position in total organization management, HR management can begin to play the several roles described in Chapter 2, one of which is the business role, to ensure that the organization's human resources are used as effectively as possible.

Human resource planning is accomplished in four phases: (1) forecasting supply and demand of labor; (2) estimating surpluses or shortages of people based on objectives in organizational expansion or contraction; (3) planning specific human resource activities based on Phase 2 forecasts—for example, recruitment if shortages are expected, layoffs if surpluses are expected; and (4) evaluating both the implementation and administration of programs.

Roadblocks exist that increase the challenge and difficulty of human resource planning. A primary barrier is the lack of top management support. Because HR planning is derived from corporate goals and objectives, this support is necessary as is the involvement of the HR manager in corporate-level planning.

Career planning and management has much to offer individuals and organizations. Because organizations and people are continually changing, career planning and management activities have a dual focus: to help individuals find jobs that are consistent with their personality, interests, and preferences, and to help organizations match available jobs to the skills, knowledge, and abilities of their work force.

Because organizations are dynamic and present a variety of job transitions (staffing at entry levels, promotions and transfers, layoffs, discharges, retirement), career planning and management activities are relevant to all members of an organization. The different stages of career development (that is, preparation for work, organizational entry, early career, midcareer, and late career) present different issues and problems both to the organization and to the employee. One thing is clear, however: career development is a continuous process. From the organizational perspective, career management activities can contribute to other key human resource functions that enable the company to simultaneously attract and retain the best people. From the individual perspective, each person is responsible for his or her career planning. Career planning enables individuals to proactively manage the numerous transitions that occur during the span of their work lives. Throughout the remaining chapters you will have several opportunities to engage in further career planning activities in the end-of-chapter feature entitled "Career Management Exercise." This begins with the next chapter on job design and worker accommodation.

KEY CONCEPTS

career
career balance sheet
career ladders
career management
career pathing
career planning
career plateau
conventional statistical
    projections
Delphi technique
expatriate
human resource
    planning

job progression
human resource
    information system
    (HRIS)
judgmental forecast
local country national
managerial estimate
midlife transition
multiple linear
    regression analysis
network
nominal group
    technique

outplacement programs
personal appraisal
reality shock
replacement planning
self-assessment
self-management
simple linear regression
    analysis
social support group
succession planning
transition matrix

REVIEW AND DISCUSSION QUESTIONS

1. If human resource planning is so difficult, why do companies engage in it?
2. Why does planning become more difficult as the planning horizon increases from one year to five years?
3. Discuss the roadblocks to human resource planning, and explain how each roadblock might be removed.
4. Provide a step-by-step overview of the four phases of human resource planning.

5. What is meant by the term *career*?
6. Responsibility for career planning and management is shouldered by both the individual and the organization. What does each party gain from career planning and management?
7. How might career planning and management from an individual perspective differ today from that of 50 years ago? Is it more difficult today? Why?
8. The organizational entry stage of career development suggests that reality shock is a fact of organizational life. What can human resource managers do to lessen reality shock?
9. What can managers do to motivate employees at each of the five stages of career development? What is your present career development stage?
10. What are some examples of organizational career development programs?

EXERCISES AND CASES

FIELD PROJECT

Interview two working people and discuss career planning and management with them. Ask them what career aids their firms offer. Ask them how much they have planned for their own careers, and what they would do differently. Report back to the class and compare results.

CAREER MANAGEMENT EXERCISE: WHAT DO YOU WANT YOUR FIRST JOB TO BE?

If you have completed the material presented in Exhibits 4.6 and 4.8, you have begun a very important process that should enable you to place yourself in a life and work situation best suited to your needs. But remember, this is an ongoing process. The following is another task in this process.

Your full-time job after graduation may not be your first job, but it will be a very important one, as you know. Describe the type of job you would like to have and the type of organization you would like to work for after graduation. Type of Job:

_____

_____

_____

Type (Name) of Organization:

_____

_____

To provide you with the opportunity to prepare for your career in as much detail as possible, Chapters 5, 6, 8, 12, 13, and 14 will ask you to use the job and organization you have indicated here as a basis for further exercises.

ARE YOU STAYING?

During their traditional reunion on Cape Cod, Bob and Steve are contemplating their futures for the first time. Although only 24 years old, both are already wondering how to better manage their careers. Since graduating together three years ago, they have already attained some success. Both passed the CPA exam the first time through, and both have enjoyed significant pay increases the first two years. Their similarities end here however, for while Bob is contemplating advancement in the same firm he joined two years ago, Steve is contemplating changing firms. They are taking this weekend to reflect on their career experiences thus far.

BOB LEMMON GETS LUCKY

Whether or not it was luck, Bob is mighty pleased about working for one of the more successful offices of the "Big Six" accounting firm he joined three years ago. He was excited even before he was hired. During the holiday break in December of his senior year, he remembers going to a party thrown by the firm for accounting students from schools from which the office typically recruited. The party gave the students an informal opportunity to meet several partners, including the managing partner. It also gave the office an informal chance to look at the new crop of rookies. Bob couldn't help but be impressed by this party and the chance to meet the managing partner. He also got the chance to meet some of the other students who were eventually hired by the office.

Bob's first two years in the office were extremely gratifying. He worked on a variety of assignments, each one exposing him to different challenges, each one requiring slightly different skills. Any problems, personal or professional, were comfortably discussed with the senior "brother" to whom he was assigned. He would have felt as comfortable, however, talking with a manager or even the managing partner. Managers, partners, and even the managing partner felt it was extremely important to have an open door policy with all employees, especially the new assistants. To facilitate this, the managing partner always made sure they hired for "anticipated growth" rather than as a catch-up mechanism. Although this resulted in "excess hiring" until growth caught up, doing so ensured that managers and partners didn't exceed a 70–75 percent

utilization rate. Year-end review time resulted in Bob being told exactly how well he was doing relative to the other assistants. His two pay increases were directly related to the performance appraisal results. As far as the office was concerned, this pay-for-performance policy and candor in telling folks where they stood resulted in enhanced loyalty and a low premature turnover rate. This was reinforced by the "excess hiring" that ensured that assistants were not overutilized, which in turn facilitated good leverage ratios and the manager and partner utilization rate of 70–75 percent. Thus Bob's pressing career question was whether he should stay in audit or transfer to tax in the next year or two.

STEVE LUCK GETS A LEMON

Steve also works in an office of the same "Big Six" firm, but as far as he is concerned, it is on a different planet from Bob's. Because Steve lived on the West Coast, he wasn't able to attend the party that Bob attended. Talk about being in the wrong place at the wrong time! Subsequently, Steve was hired by another office of the same firm in the following spring by someone he never saw again. Steve's first two years in the office were extremely frustrating and dissatisfying. Although he was given a variety of job assignments, his recollection of the experience was one of exhaustion rather than of the desired variety, growth, and challenge. In each of his first two years, he worked approximately 350 hours of overtime. He knew of three assistants who left because of the excessive overtime (excessive for them at least). What he didn't know, however, was that many of the managers and partners were working as much overtime as he was. Manager utilization rates were reaching as high as 85 percent. Consequently, the managers and partners really didn't have time to sit down and listen to the assistants. While Steve realizes that the "Big Six" accounting firms aren't in business to "coddle" people, he also knows he could have used a pat on the back or an occasional word of encouragement. This environment prevented him from knowing anyone very well, and he has yet to meet the managing partner. This of course makes performance review time one filled with uncertainty. The managers and partners seem to be uncomfortable giving negative feedback and the assistants have no idea where they stand. The assistants thus have only job assignments and pay raises to tell them how the firm thinks they are doing. Thus Steve's pressing career question is whether he should leave the firm now or stay through a third year. He can't think of any reason to stay, but he is hoping discussions with Bob might clarify his options.

CASE QUESTIONS
1. Does overutilization of assistants result in high levels of premature turnover?
2. Is overutilization the only cause of premature turnover?
3. From an individual point of view, why is Bob's office so satisfying?
4. What would you advise Steve to do?

© Randall S. Schuler, New York University

CASE

CAREER MANAGEMENT FOR WHOM?

Franklin Hudson (FH), a large regional accounting firm in Atlanta, has experienced a smooth growth curve over the past five years.

Although the favorable funding cycle has enabled FH to grow at a steady rate, the firm is finding it increasingly difficult to keep its really good, young assistants. Based on extensive turnover, analyses conducted by Ned Jackson, the human resources planning partner, FH's problem seems to be its inability to keep young assistants beyond the "critical" two-year point. Ned's conclusion is that FH has been essentially serving as an industry college. Many of the assistants who do leave, move over, go into their own practice, join investment banks, or join a small- to mid-sized corporation. Such turnover is costly and prevents FH from achieving desired leverage ratios. Their staffing strategy has always been to hire the best and brightest accounting students from the best business schools in the United States.

Ned believes that these young assistants often get lost in the shuffle at the time they join the firm. For example, most (if not all) of the new hires work on numerous projects, and they never really develop a camaraderie with any particular group of assistants. Furthermore, they work in an environment where there traditionally is little feedback given to the new assistants on how well they are doing. Consequently, the new assistants often have difficulty learning the organizational culture—such as who to ask when you have a problem, what the general do's and don'ts are, and why the organization does things in a certain way.

After heading a task force to address this issue, Ned is about to present a proposal to the managing partner designed to reduce turnover among young assistants and recruits. The essence of his plan is to create a mentor program, except that in his plan the mentors will not be the seasoned graybeards of FH, but rather those accountants in the critical two- to three-year service window, the period of highest turnover. These accountants will be paired with new recruits before the recruits actually report to FH for work.

According to the task force, the program is twofold: (1) it benefits the newcomer by easing the transition into the firm, and (2) it empowers the two- to five-year senior accountants by having them serve in an important role for the firm. In performing this mentor role, these accountants will become more committed and hence less likely to leave. As Ned prepared his fifteen-minute presentation for the managing partner, he wondered whether he had adequately anticipated the possible objections to the program so that he could defend it intelligently.

CASE QUESTIONS
1. Why is the firm finding it increasingly difficult to keep really good assistants?
2. Should FH change its recruiting strategy?
3. How can FH change its career-related HR practices?
4. What objections is Ned likely to hear from the managing partner?

© Randall S. Schuler, New York University

1. K. Rebello, R. Mitchell, and E. Schwartz, "Apple's Future," *Business Week* (July 5, 1993): 22–28; J. Markhoff, "It's Batter-Down, Button-Down Time at Apple," *New York Times* (July 9, 1993): D1, D4; J. Markhoff, "At Apple, Search for Direction," *New York Times* (Oct. 1, 1993): D1, D4. Information for the case was also drawn from B. Geber, "Should you build top executives . . . or buy them?" E. Lesly, Z. Schiller, S. Baker, and G. Smith, "CEOs with the Outside Edge," *Business Week* (Oct. 11, 1993): 60–67; S. Richman, "The Coming World Labor Shortage," *Fortune* (April 9, 1990): 69–77; R. M. Kanter, *When Giants Learn to Dance* (New York: Simon and Schuster, 1989).

2. W. F. Casico, ed., *Human Resource Planning, Employment and Placement* (Washington, D.C.: Bureau of National Affairs, 1989).

3. J. W. Walker, *Human Resource Planning* (New York: McGraw-Hill, 1980), uses the term *business plan*. It is used here to refer to those plans for the total organization that help drive the long- and short-range planning needs for HR planning; J. W. Walker, "Managing Human Resources in Flat, Lean and Flexible Organizations: Trends for the 1990s," *Human Resource Planning* 11, No. 2 (1988): 125–132.

4. E. W. Vetter, *Manpower Planning for High Talent Personnel*, (Ann Arbor, Mich.: Bureau of Industrial Relations, Graduate School of Business, University of Michigan, 1967), 15; G. Milkovich, L. Dyer, and T. Mahoney, "HRM Planning," in *Personnel Management*, eds., K. M. Rowland and G. R. Ferris (Boston, Mass.: Allyn & Bacon, 1982), 52–77.

5. V. J. Brush and R. Nardoni, "Integrated Data Supports AT&T's Succession Planning," *Personnel Journal* (Sept. 1992): 103–9.

6. A. Etzioni and P. Jargonwsky, "High Tech, Basic Industry, and the Future of the American Economy," *Human Resource Management* (Fall 1984): 220–40; L. Greenhalgh, R. B. McKersie, and R. W. Gilkey, "Rebalancing the Workforce at IBM: A Case Study of Redeployment and Revitalization," *Organizational Dynamics* (Spring 1986): 30–47; P. H. Mirvis, "Formulating and Implementing Human Resource Strategy: A Model of How to Do It, Two Examples of How It's Done," *Human Resource Management* (Winter 1985): 385–412.

7. J. F. Coates, "An Environmental Scan: Projecting Future Human Resource Trends," *Human Resource Planning* 10, no. 4 (1987): 209–19; G. F. Gallup, *Forecast 2000: George Gallup, Jr. Predicts the Future of America* (New York: William Morrow, 1984).

8. D. W. Allen, "We Don't Know What 50% of the Jobs Will Be in the Year 2000," in *The Changing Composition of the Workforce: Implications for Future Research and Its Applications*, ed. A. S. Glickman (New York: Plenum Press, 1982); S. B. Wehrenberg, "Training Megatrends," *Personnel Journal* 62, no. 4 (1981): 279–80.

9. C. Mackey, "Human Resource Planning: A Four-Phased Approach," *Management Review* (May 1981): 17–22.

10. For an extensive description of each of these phases, see J. J. Leach, "Merging the Two Faces of Personnel: A Challenge of the 1980s," *Personnel* (Jan.–Feb. 1980): 52–57: "Manpower Planning and Corporate Objectives: Two Points of View," *Management Review* (Aug. 1981): 55–61.

11. For a discussion, see D. R. Dalton, "Absenteeism and Turnover in Organizations," in *Applied Readings in Personnel and Human Resource Management*, eds. R. S. Schuler, J. M. McFillen, and D. R. Dalton (St. Paul, Minn.: West, 1980).

12. J. A. Byrne, R. Brandt, and O. Port, "The Virtual Corporation," *Business Week* (Feb. 8, 1993): 98–102.

13. M. J. Feuer, R. J. Niehaus, and J. A. Sheridan, "Human Resource Forecasting: A Survey of Practice and Potential," *Human Resource Planning*, 11, no. 2 (1988): 85–97.

14. See description of managerial estimates in J. W. Walker, *Human Resource Planning* (New York: McGraw-Hill, 1980).

15. For a more extensive discussion of group techniques, including the nominal group technique, see A. C. Delbecg, A. H. Van De Ven, and D. H. Gustafson, *Group Technique for Program Planning* (Glenview, Ill.: Scott, Foresman, 1977); J. K. Murnigham, "Group Decision Making: What Strategy Should You Use?" *Management Review* (Feb. 1981): 56–60.

16. H. Kahalas, H. L. Pazer, J. S. Hoagland, and A. Leavitt, "Human Resource Planning Activities in U.S. Firms," *Human Resource Planning* 3 (1980): 53–66.

17. Milkovich, Dyer, and Mahoney, "HRM Planning," 2–9.

18. R. B. Frantzreb, "Human Resource Planning: Forecasting Manpower Needs," *Personnel Journal* (Nov. 1982): 850–57; N. Scoarborough and T. W. Zimmerer, "Human Resource Forecasting: Why and Where to Begin," *Personnel Administrator* (May 1982): 55–61.

19. R. S. Schuler, ``Repositioning the Human Resource Function: Transformation or Demise?'' *Academy of Management Executive*, 4, no. 3 (1990): 49–59.

20. C. H. Deutsch, "Putting Women on the Fast Track," *New York Times* (Dec. 16, 1990): F25.

21. H. L. Dahl and K. S. Morgan, "Return on Investment in Human Resources," unpublished manuscript, Upjohn Company, 1982.

22. From D. Kirkpatrick, "Is Your Career On Track?" *Fortune* (July 2, 1990): 38–48; E. Ehrlich, "The Mommy Track," *Business Week* (March 20, 1990): 126–134.

23. A. Brown, "Career Development 1986," *Personnel Administrator* (March 1986): 45–48; J. Morabito, "Baby Boomers:

The Young and the Restless," *Personnel Administrator* (July 1987): 103–108.

24. T. Jackson and A. Vitberg, "Career Development, Part 3: Challenges for the Individual," *Personnel* (April 1987): 54–57; M. London and S. Stumpf, *Managing Careers* (Reading Mass.: Addison-Wesley, 1982).

25. J. H. Greenhaus, *Career Management* (Hinsdale, Ill.: The Dryden Press, 1987); J. H. Greenhaus and N. J. Beautell, "Sources of Conflict Between Work and Family Roles," *Academy of Management Review* (Jan. 1985): 76–88.

26. A. Halcrow, "Voices of HR Experience," *Personnel Journal* (May 1989): 38.

27. J. H. Greenhaus, *Career Management*; D. C. Feldman, *Managing Careers in Organizations* (Glenview, Ill.: Scott, Foresman, 1988); D. Hellriegel, J. W. Slocum, Jr., and R. W. Woodman, *Organizational Behavior*, 5th ed., (St. Paul, Minn.: West, 1989), see Chapter 18, 500–531.

28. *Business and Older Workers* (Washington, D.C.: AARP, 1989).

29. B. L. Dilla, "Descriptive Versus Prescriptive Information in a Realistic Job Preview," *Journal of Vocational Behavior* (1987): 33–48.

30. J. Fierman, "Beating the Midlife Career Crisis," *Fortune* (Sept. 6, 1993): 52–62; J. Bardwick, *The Plateauing Trap* (New York: AMACOM, 1986); J. Slocum, W. Cron, and L. Yows, "Career Plateauing: Who's Likely to Plateau," *Business Horizons* (1987): 31–38; D. C. Feldman and B. A. Weitz, "Career Plateaus Reconsidered," *Journal of Management* 14 (1988): 69–80; D. T. Hall and M. R. Louis, "When Careers Plateau," *Research-Technology Management* 31, 2 (1989): 41–45.

31. Slocum, Cron, and Yows, "Career Plateauing."

32. J. Bardwick, *The Plateauing Trap*.

33. W. A. Campione, "The Married Woman's Retirement Decision: A Methodological Comparison," *Journal of Gerontology* (1987): 381–86; B. Rosen and T. H. Jerdee, *Older Workers; New Roles for Valued Resources* (Homewood, Ill.: Dow Jones-Irwin. 1985).

34. N. J. Beutell, "Managing the Older Worker," *Personnel Administrator* (Aug. 1983): 31–40; N. J. Beautell and O. C. Brenner, "Employee Retirement Decisions," *Personnel Review* (1987): 31–33; M. Cahill and P. R. Salomone, "Career Counseling and Worklife Extension: Integrating the Older Worker into the Labor Force," *The Career Development Quarterly* (1987): 188–96.

35. R. J. Sahl, "Succession Planning: A Blueprint for Your Company's Future," *Personnel Administrator* (Sept. 1987): 101–108.

36. *Ibid*.

37. N. J. Beutell and J. H. Greenhaus, "Balancing Acts: Work-Family Conflict and the Dual Career Couple," in L. Moore, *Not as Far as You Think: The Realities of Working Women* (Lexington, Mass.: Lexington Books, 1986); M. R. Frone and R. W. Rice, "Work-Family Conflict: The Effect of Job and Family Involvement," *Journal of Occupational Behavior* (1987): 45–53.

38. "Relocating Dual Career Couples," *Bulletin to Management*, October 4, 1990, 320. Also see "Relocating Two-Earner Couples," The Conference Board, 845 Third Avenue, New York, N.Y. 10022; M. Moravec and B. McKee, "Designing Dual-Career Paths and Compensation," *Personnel* (Aug. 1990): 4–9; C. Trost, "How One Bank Is Handling A 'Two Track' Career Plan," *The Wall Street Journal* (March 13, 1989): B1, B8; Z. B. Leibowitz, B. H. Feldman, and S. H. Mosley, "Career Development Works Overtime at Corning, Inc.," *Personnel* (April 1990): 38–46; O. C. Brenner, "Career Reporters To Know Them Could Be to Keep Them," *Personnel* (Nov. 1988): 55–59; J. R. Bratkovich, B. Steele, and T. Rollins, "Develop New Career Management Strategies," *Personnel Journal* (Sept. 1990): 98–107.

39. "Relocating Dual Career Couples," 320.

40. J. Kerr, "The Best Small Companies to Work For in America," *INC.* (July 1993): 57.

41. J. W. Gilley and H. L. Moore, "Managers as Career Enhancers," *Personnel Administrator* (March 1986): 51–59.

42. Cahill and Salomone, "Career Counseling and Worklife Extension."

43. R. Henkoff, "Winning the New Career Game," *Fortune* (July 12, 1993): 46–64; S. Sherman, "A Brave New Darwinian Workplace," *Fortune* (Jan. 25, 1993): 50–56.

44. "Views on the Expatriate," *The Wall Street Journal* (Dec. 11, 1989): B1.

45. C. Reynolds, "Careers in International Human Resources," *The SHRM Student Newsletter* (Jan./Feb. 1992): 1.

46. J. J. Fucini and S. Fucini, *Working for the Japanese* (New York: The Free Press, 1990); S. Moffat, "Should You Work for the Japanese?" *Fortune* (Dec. 3, 1990): 107–108, 112, 116, 120; W. Zellner, "Help Wanted, Room To Advance—Out the Door," *Business Week* (Oct. 30, 1989): 42.

47. E. H. Schein, "How to Break in the College Graduate," *Harvard Business Review* (March–April 1964): 70; D. T. Hall and Associates, *Career Development in Organizations* (San Francisco: Jossey-Bass, 1986).

48. D. E. Berlew and D. T. Hall, "Some Determinants of Early Managerial Success," Working paper 81–64 (Cambridge, Mass.: Sloan School of Management, MIT, 1964); R. A. Webber, "Career Problems of Young Managers," *California Management Review* (1976): 19–33.

49. D. T. Hall, "Careers and Socialization," *Journal of Management* (1987): 301–21; J. L. Pierce and R. B. Dunham, "Organizational Commitment: Pre-Employment Propensity and Initial Work Experiences," *Journal of Management* (1987): 163–74.

50. "Faxed Résumés Now May Be Considered Proper Etiquette," *Personnel Journal* (Aug. 1993): 16.

51. J. H. Conley, J. M. Hueghi, and R. L. Minter, *Perspectives on Administrative Communication* (Dubuque, Iowa: Kendall/Hunt, 1976): 172; W. J. Morin, "The Four Interviewer Breeds: How to Tame Them," *New York Times Recruitment Survey* (Oct. 11, 1981): 59, 62; J. T. Yenckel, "Careers: Facing the Interview," *The Washington Post* (Oct. 20, 1981): D5

52. S. Chastain, "On the Job: The Winning Interview," in *Winning the Salary Game; Negotiations for Women*, eds. D. Littman and C. Stegel (New York: Wiley, 1980).

53. I. Janis and D. Wheeler, "Thinking Clearly about Career Choices," *Psychology Today* (May 1978): 67–76, 121–22.

54. A. L. Ball, "Mentors & Proteges: Portraits of Success," *Working Woman* (Oct. 1989): 134–142; D. Jacoby "Rewards Make the Mentor," *Personnel* (Dec. 1989): 10–14.

55. "Living with the New Guidelines on Sexual Harassment," *People and Business* (July 1981): 3.

56. *Ibid.*

57. *Ibid.*

58. "Farewell, Fast Track" *Business Week* (Dec. 10, 1990): 192–200.

CHAPTER 5

JOB DESIGN

LEARNING OBJECTIVES

When you have finished studying this chapter, you should be able to:

1. Discuss the meaning and importance of reasonable accommodation.
2. Explain the features of the four approaches to job design.
3. Make recommendations concerning different job designs to companies.
4. Describe the process and content models of motivation.
5. Describe the alternative arrangements for employee accommodation.

CHAPTER OUTLINE

"Managing Human Resources at Lincoln Electric"

JOB DESIGN

WHY IS JOB DESIGN IMPORTANT?

LEGAL CONSIDERATIONS

"HR Advice and Application
ALLERGIC TO LATEX"

APPROACHES TO JOB DESIGN

"Managing Human Resources at Small Companies
JOB AUTONOMY"

"Managing Human Resources at Levi Strauss & Co.
WHEN AIDS HITS HOME"

EMPLOYEE MOTIVATION

ALTERNATIVE ARRANGEMENTS FOR EMPLOYEE ACCOMMODATION

Review Questions: *Americans with Disabilities Act of 1990 (ADA)*

Exercise: What Characteristics Do You Want in Your Job?

Career Management Exercise

Case: Job Redesign at Aid Association for Lutherans

Role Play: Jerry Laubenstein

Role Play: Marie Saxer

Case: Redesign or Relocation

MANAGING HUMAN RESOURCES
at Lincoln Electric

IN 1992, the production workers at Lincoln Electric in Cleveland, Ohio, received bonuses averaging between $18,000 and $22,000. Their total pay, including wages, profit sharing, and bonuses, averaged 45,000! According to Paul Beddia, vice-president of human resources for Lincoln, the company's productivity rate is two to three times that of any other manufacturing operation that uses steel as its raw material and that employs more than 1,000 people (Lincoln has about 3,000 employees). While Lincoln is widely cited as an example of a firm with a highly motivated work force, it is important to keep in mind a few unusual things about this company. First, Lincoln has no paid holidays. Sick days are not paid for by the firm. Workers must accept job reassignment, and overtime is mandatory. There is no seniority and no special parking spaces or special cafeterias. Workers take care of their own retirement needs. Yet, the postprobationary turnover is less than 3 percent per year, and the company receives nearly 1,000 unsolicited job applicants or résumés per month!

How does Lincoln do it? This is a question many ask. While its famous piecework system is credited with the high level of employee motivation, it is the company's fundamentally different approach to job design that sets it apart. At Lincoln Electric, the jobs are narrowly and clearly defined and have been so since its inception. Both jobs and the procedures to operate them have been systematically analyzed to gain as much efficiency as possible.

What is seen today at Lincoln reflects its history. Lincoln Electric's famous piecework system was established in 1914, in the heyday of Fredrick W. Taylor and scientific management! Thus the organizational culture is firmly in place. The workers know what to expect, and they are trained to live up to the company's expectations in a broad variety of jobs. Such broad and careful training enables employees to do a variety of jobs at a moment's notice without any loss of quality. With very specific and clear job descriptions, everyone knows what each job is about. Any improvements to the job designs are done through suggestions that are then carefully studied by industrial engineers.

The nature of the jobs further allows Lincoln to motivate employees with *individual* piecework payment systems. Not only are the job designs narrowly defined, they are also defined for the individual, not for a team. Thus at a time when many organizations are implementing job enrichment and team-based job designs, Lincoln Electric remains an example of the scientific approach to job design, and it demonstrates that this approach can still work. Would it work for you?[1]

This feature on Lincoln Electric illustrates some important ideas about job analysis and job design. Perhaps the most critical one is that the scientific management approach to job design can be very effective. While job enrichment programs are popular today, there are still opportunities to use the more narrowly defined jobs from the days of scientific management. The scientific management approach to job design facilitates the writing of clear and understandable job descriptions; here job descriptions detail how to do the job. Training is made easier with the result being that a number of workers can do any given job, and job assignments can be based on need. Such a flexible system can enable a firm to adapt to a rapidly changing environment.

There are times, however, when the jobs themselves need to be changed. Changes may be needed to provide more motivation, thus making workers more productive, satisfied, involved, and committed. Changes may be needed to accommodate physical capabilities of the work force or individuals. Companies may need to change the time and location in which the job is performed. These kinds of changes are called alternative arrangements for employee accommodation. We will discuss all of these in this chapter.

In Chapter 6, we will examine the process of analyzing jobs in detail, but to gain an understanding of job design, we will touch on job analysis briefly in this chapter. It is important to keep in mind that job design and job analysis influence everything else in human resource management: recruitment, selection, appraisal, compensation, and training and development. We return to Lincoln Electric in Chapter 12 to discuss its compensation.

Job design is the process by which the characteristics and qualities of jobs are determined and created.

JOB DESIGN

Job design *is the process by which the characteristics and qualities of jobs are determined and created.* Jobs are created in job design, and they are described in job analysis. There are several approaches to job design. We will consider each in some detail after we address the question of why job design is important and the accompanying legal considerations.

WHY IS JOB DESIGN IMPORTANT?

Since the times of Fredrick W. Taylor and the development of scientific management, jobs have been designed for:

- Efficiency, finding the one best way to produce a product
- Productivity, obtaining maximum use of human and physical resources

Today job design serves as a vital way by which organizations can accommodate a more diverse work force—diverse, as we have discussed previously, in terms of age, gender, life-style, and ability. Thus, to our list of purposes, we can add:

- Accommodation of a diverse work force
- Motivation of a diverse work force

Together, all these purposes are being served by job design in organizations today. In fact, organizations are emphasizing careful job design more than ever because they recognize that total-quality management often depends on enriching jobs and creating self-managed teams. And they know, because of the diverse work force, that they must actually accommodate the needs of this emerging group in order to attract the best people. In doing so, they are also complying with some important legal considerations.

Major legal considerations for job design are:

- *National Labor Relations Act*
- *Americans with Disabilities Act of 1990*

LEGAL CONSIDERATIONS

Organizations today are not only concerned with creating new job designs but also with creating job designs from existing jobs. Particularly in the latter case—redesigning existing jobs, which many firms find themselves doing when they move to total-quality management—employees are heavily involved in the design decisions. The self-managed team, which is itself a job design where employees make many decisions under the guidance of a supervisor, is often created as a result of the design process. As the team begins to function, the company needs to be aware of the *National Labor Relations Act*.

PARTNERSHIP: WORKING TOGETHER IN JOB DESIGN

LINE MANAGERS	HR PROFESSIONALS	EMPLOYEES
Make adjustments and accommodations to employees.	Adjust for workplace accommodations.	Participate in the identification of their preferences for job design and alternative arrangements for accommodation.
Make job design decisions with employees, unions, and HR professionals.	Assist in making job design decisions	
Establish a philosophy of managing people.	Make sure that job design decisions are linked with other HR activities.	

✳ NATIONAL LABOR RELATIONS ACT

The *National Labor Relations Act* (NLRA) is particularly relevant in job design programs. In cases where a union represents the employees, the employer must consider that almost all issues, including the establishment of programs to change job designs, may need to be negotiated with the union. In many cases, however, employers and unions can cooperatively work together. When this is done, the NLRA requires employers to provide information to the union, when requested, for purposes related to the job design program. In cases where the employees are not represented by a union, employers can implement job design programs unilaterally. There are some limitations, however. For example, employers may not be able to create and dominate employee teams for the sake of modifying job and working conditions because this may constitute behavior that undermines the role of union activity according to the National Labor Relations Board in the cases of *Electromation* (1992) and *DuPont* (1993). Because this issue relates to total quality management, it is described again in Chapter 15.

✳ AMERICANS WITH DISABILITIES ACT OF 1990 ✳

The design of a job is an important determinant of who can do the job. In one of the earliest cases in equal opportunity and affirmative action (the mid-1970s), the American Telephone & Telegraph Company (AT&T) entered into an agreement with the Equal Employment Opportunity Commission (the EEOC, to be discussed more extensively in Chapter 7, Recruitment) to change the nature of the job design for telephone pole climbers. If you were to take a look at these poles, you would have seen that the climbers (the telephone repair line workers) had to go up the poles by placing their feet on either side of the pole on horizontal spikes. In the process of trying to employ more women as telephone repair line workers, AT&T realized that most women were physically unable to climb the poles—the placement of the horizontal spikes was too far apart! AT&T

LEARNING OBJECTIVE 1

Discuss the meaning and importance of reasonable accommodation.

Reasonable accommodation is any modification or adjustment that allows qualified applicants or employees with disabilities to participate in the application process or to do the job's essential functions without causing undue hardship to the employer.

accommodated the needs of a specific group of individuals by reducing the distance between the spikes. Although several thousand poles, had to be changed, the accommodation was regarded as "reasonable."

This principle of **reasonable accommodation** is now commonly used because of the *Americans with Disabilities Act of 1990* (ADA). Applying to organizations with 15 or more employees, this act

> prohibits bias against qualified individuals with disabilities in all aspects of employment and requires employers to make reasonable accommodations for such individuals so long as the accommodations do not pose an undue hardship to the employer's business.[2]

Exactly what reasonable accommodation means in practice varies with the nature of the company. AT&T had to change the distance between telephone pole spikes. In another case, reasonable accommodation could mean changing the type of glove worn by employees who perform emergency medical work! Just such an accommodation is described in the feature, "HR Advice and Application: Allergic to Latex."

Legal considerations in job design can thus heavily influence the nature of job activities and the context in which jobs take place. They also influence the process used to design (and redesign) jobs. In both cases, job design is an important technique companies can use to accommodate the needs of workers. By accommodating workers' needs, more jobs can be made available to more types of people; this can in turn be quite motivational to groups formerly excluded. Such a situation is obviously one in which the individual, the company, and society all win. Besides reasonable accommodation, companies are also offering various forms of alternative work schedules; these also have legal considerations. First, however, let us look at alternative approaches to job designs.

LEARNING OBJECTIVE 2
Explain the features of the four approaches to job design.

The *scientific approach* to job design carefully analyzes jobs and breaks them into incremental tasks.

Frederick W. Taylor was the father of the scientific approach to job design.

The ways jobs are designed has a big impact on employees.

APPROACHES TO JOB DESIGN

THE SCIENTIFIC APPROACH

Under the **scientific approach,** job analysts (typically, industrial engineers) take special pains to design jobs so that the tasks performed by employees do not exceed their abilities. The jobs designed this way often result in work being partitioned into small, standardized segments. These tasks lend themselves well to time and motion studies and to incentive pay systems, each for the purpose of obtaining high productivity. The scientific approach to job design is still an important part of many fine organizations.

Through meticulous human engineering, United Parcel Service (UPS) is highly successful despite stiff competition. In a business where "a package is a package," UPS succeeds through its application of scientifically designed work standards. Their approach has been key to their continuing gains in efficiency and productivity since the privately held company was founded in 1907. In the 1920s, UPS engineers cut away the sides of UPS trucks to study how the drivers performed. The engineers then made appropriate changes in techniques to enhance worker efficiency.

Time and motion studies enable the company to closely monitor the performance of the workers. At UPS, more than 1,000 industrial engineers use the time study to set standards for a variety of closely supervised tasks. In return, the UPS drivers, all of whom are represented by the Teamsters, earn wages of approx-

ALLERGIC TO LATEX

"I have a doctor's note that says I can return to my job, but I have to avoid contact with latex," medical technical Dan Coleman explained.

"I'm truly sorry, but we can't accept this," personnel director Pat Kubricki responded. "All medical technicians have to wear rubber gloves in compliance with safety rules, so there's no way you can come back to work and avoid contact with latex."

Was the employer's action justified?

Facts: An employee whose duties included emergency medical work had been employed more than ten years without any problems on the job. Due to increasing concerns over bloodborne pathogens such as AIDS, however, new health guidelines required the employee to wear latex gloves on the job whenever there was a chance of contact with bodily fluids. The employee eventually developed an allergy to both the gloves and a powder in the gloves that made them easier to get on and off.

In time, the employee became so highly sensitized that he had an allergic reaction to powder residue on the steering wheel of a vehicle that previously had been operated by another employee wearing the latex gloves. After suffering a series of allergic reactions requiring emergency medical care, a doctor told the employee that in order to be completely risk free, everyone in his workplace would have to stop using the latex gloves.

The employee eventually missed so much work that he used up all his sick leave. When he attempted to return to work, he brought a doctor's note explaining that he must "avoid all contact with latex and latex products." The employer refused to allow his return, saying it would be impossible for the employee to avoid such contact.

The employee objected to the decision, asserting that it amounted to termination. He charged that the employer was obligated to make reasonable accommodations to facilitate his return to work.

Decision: The employer must reinstate the worker and accommodate his disability.

Discussion: The employee's medical records show that he is fully able to perform his job duties as long as he avoids contact with latex gloves and the powder in the gloves, the arbiter notes. Therefore, the arbiter finds, the "entire department would have to be supplied with vinyl or powderfree, hypoallergenic latex gloves" in order for the employee to return to his job.

Supplying different gloves is an "entirely reasonable accommodation" to protect the job of a ten-year employee, the arbiter says. The cost of the accommodation would be "minimal," at about $150 extra per year, he points out. Moreover, medical journals suggest that the prevalence of latex allergies is increasing, and it is likely that other employees would eventually develop allergies to latex as well. Finding the accommodation an appropriate solution to the problem, the arbiter orders the employer to reinstate the employee with back pay and supply new gloves to all employees.

Pointers: Under the *Americans With Disabilities Act,* an employer must make reasonable accommodations for employees with disabilities. However, determining what is "reasonable" is a fact-specific issue that will vary with the employer and individual in question. Under various circumstances, appropriate accommodations might include such things as making existing facilities readily accessible, job restructuring, modifying work schedules, acquiring or modifying equipment or devices, or providing readers or interpreters.

At the same time, an accommodation is not required if it would impose on the employer's business an "undue hardship"—that is, a significant difficulty or expense. Factors that must be considered to ascertain whether an accommodation would impose an undue hardship include:

- The nature and cost of the accommodation
- The size, type, and financial resources of the specific facility where the accommodation would have to be made
- The size, type, and financial resources of the covered employer
- The covered employer's type of operation, including the composition, structure, and functions of its work force, and the geographic separateness and administrative or fiscal relationship between the specific facility and the covered employer[3]

imately $17 per hour or $28 with benefits.[4] Because of the company's success in these endeavors they are able to offer employees better job security.

UPS's scientific approach to job design is, of course, only part of the picture. The company complements this approach with an employee-oriented HR philosophy and modern technology:

> UPS is the world's largest package distribution company serving a network of more than 185 countries and territories with a daily delivery volume of more than 11.5 million packages.
>
> Quality service has been woven into the company since its beginnings in 1907 as a messenger service in Seattle.
>
> Throughout its existence, UPS has constantly analyzed its procedures, refined its equipment, and devised new systems to enable employees to provide customers with high-quality service.
>
> UPS takes the view there is a direct correlation between quality service and the quality of its people.
>
> To that end, UPS employs the best people it can find, trains them thoroughly and continuously, rewards them generously, and involves them personally in the business through daily prework communication meetings and periodic districtwide service awareness programs.
>
> Succeeding as it does in a highly competitive industry, UPS engineers and fine tunes its service in every way possible. The performance of delivery drivers, for example, is a model of human engineering. Drivers are taught 340 professional, individual methods for delivering and picking up packages.
>
> This "human engineering" approach extends throughout the company . . . from the details of sorting packages in the safest, most efficient way possible to teaching methods that result in the successful handling of customer inquiries on the telephone.
>
> Technology too plays an important part in allowing UPS people to work smarter, not harder. Hand-held computers enable delivery drivers to capture signatures and other vital information essential to the tracing of packages. Automated sorting and scanning equipment complement the ability of inside operations to handle the flow of package volume efficiently.
>
> UPS's overall objective is to achieve worldwide leadership in package distribution. To do this, the company will continue to rely on its people, allowing them to develop their individual capabilities that will provide job satisfaction and the opportunity to advance through UPS's policy of promotion from within.[5]

✳ THE INDIVIDUAL CONTEMPORARY APPROACH

Because the scientific approach is not always effective, organizations began searching for alternative job design approaches. One result is the **individual contemporary design.** As shown in Exhibit 5.1, five positive personal and work outcomes—high motivation, quality work performance, satisfaction, and low absenteeism and turnover—result when people are allowed to function in an environment where work enables the individual to obtain a sense of:

- meaningfulness
- responsibility
- empowerment (not shown in Exhibit 5.1)
- knowing the results

According to researchers, these are critical psychological states that evolve from five core job characteristics: (1) **skill variety** (degree to which tasks are performed that require different abilities and skills); (2) **job significance** (degree to which the job has substantial importance); (3) **job identity** (degree to which a whole and identifiable piece of work with a visible outcome is produced); (4) **autonomy** (degree of freedom and discretion in work scheduling and proce-

---

Through the "Delivering Our Future" program, we are gaining further proof of how valuable our drivers and other employees can be in developing our business. This year should present even more opportunities for our people to contribute to the success of their company.

Kent C. Nelson
Chairman and Chief Executive
Officer, UPS

The *individual contemporary design approach* enlarges the scope of the job.

Individual contemporary design results in feelings of

- meaningfulness
- responsibility
- empowerment
- satisfaction in knowing results

EXHIBIT 5.1
THE CORE JOB CHARACTERISTICS MODEL

CORE JOB CHARACTERISTICS	CRITICAL PSYCHOLOGICAL STATES	OUTCOMES
Skill variety Job identity Job significance	} Meaningfulness of the work	} Less absenteeism Less turnover High satisfaction
Job autonomy	} Responsibility for outcomes of the work	High motivation
Feedback from job	} Knowing the actual results of the work activities	} High-quality work performance

SOURCE: Adapted from J. R. Hackman and G. R. Oldham, *Work Redesign* (Reading, Mass.: Addison-Wesley, 1980): 77, Figure 4.2. Reprinted with permission.

dures); and (5) **feedback** (amount of direct and clear information about performance effectiveness). **Job enrichment** results when jobs are high on these core characteristics. When employees value feelings of meaningfulness, responsibility, empowerment, and knowing the results, job enrichment leads to positive personal and work outcomes.[6]

Several different strategies can be used to stimulate core job characteristics. For example, **job rotation** doesn't change the nature of a specific job, but it does increase the number of duties an employee performs over time. This increases task variety and can also boost job identity and scope of purpose because the employee is performing several jobs.

Job enlargement is the opposite of the scientific approach, which seeks to reduce the number of duties in any given job. Job enlargement seeks to increase skill variety. Task identity can also improve when the employee completes a "whole and identifiable piece of work."

Horizontal loading involves adding more duties with the same types of task characteristics; **vertical loading** means creating a job with duties that have many different characteristics. The former approach may increase skill variety, but it's also likely to foster resentment because the employee is expected to do more of the same. Vertical loading is more promising because it closes the gap between planning, doing, and controlling the work. As a result, it affects job autonomy, skill variety, and possible feedback.

Today, providing job autonomy appears to be a particularly effective way to obtain high worker commitment and quality. This is because many employees value responsibility and empowerment. Yet providing autonomy depends on more than merely changing the job. In fact, companies with a high level of job autonomy usually have these characteristics:

- They invest a lot of time and effort in hiring, to make sure new recruits can handle workplace freedom.
- Their organizational hierarchy is flat.
- They set loose guidelines, so workers know their decision-making parameters.

Job rotation means the individual moves from job to job.

Horizontal loading means adding more of the same. *Vertical loading* means adding more variety.

- Accountability is paramount. Results matter more than process.
- High-quality performance is always expected.
- Openness and strong communication are encouraged.
- Employee satisfaction is a core value.[7]

Many large companies have been moving to provide these workplace conditions. Small companies by nature are already there. Examples of what can come from small companies who are successfully providing job autonomy are detailed in the feature, "Managing Human Resources in the Best Small Companies: Job Autonomy."

✳ THE TEAM CONTEMPORARY APPROACH

Whereas the individual contemporary and scientific approaches design jobs for individuals, the **team contemporary approach** designs jobs for teams of individuals. These designs generally show a concern for the social needs of individuals as well as the constraints of the technology. Here teams of workers often rotate jobs and may follow the product they are working on to the last step in the process. If the product is large—for example, an automobile—teams may be designed around sections of the final car. Each group then completes only a sec-

The team contemporary approach designs jobs around groups of employees.

tion and passes its subproduct to the next team. In the team contemporary design, each worker learns to handle several duties, many requiring different skills. Thus, they can satisfy preferences for achievement and task accomplishment and some preferences for social interaction. When faced with decisions, teams that work well together have **teamwork,** generally try to involve all members. If their decisions and behaviors result in greater output, all team members share the benefits.

Although teamwork may be unusual for some employees, it appears that most employees are able to adapt to it:

> The A. O. Smith Corporation, a 100-year-old auto components company in Milwaukee has proved that work-team systems can be put into operation in an established American factory and office without closing the plant of curtailing production. This company, with seven established unions, implemented an effective union-management planning and problem-solving process at all levels of the organization. Having learned to manage jointly, the company and the union successfully initiated a restructuring of its organizational and production systems. But the experience of A. O. Smith contrasts with new plants that begin without a set corporate culture and therefore have no set way of doing things.[9]

Thus the team approach can be successful when establishing new plants or offices or when converting old plants. This is due in part to the flexibility of the people involved and their adaptability to change, and to the fact that there are different degrees of teamwork. Typically, teams may start out making only a few decisions. After time, training, and familiarity, they begin to make many more decisions. Essentially, the team members pass through stages of greater empowerment. In each new stage, they make more decisions, resulting in **self-managed teams.** The tasks these teams most often make decisions on are shown in Exhibit 5.2. As shown, some decisions are made without the supervisor and some with.

ERGONOMICS AND JOB ACCOMMODATION

Ergonomics is concerned with fitting jobs to the basic physical abilities and characteristics of people so they can perform the jobs without undue effects on their health. Studies have shown that when jobs are designed along ergonomic principles, worker productivity is greater. In a recent study done by the National Institute for Occupational Safety and Health (NIOSH), two groups of employees working under an incentive pay system were compared. The group whose jobs had been designed according to ergonomic principles was 25 percent more productive than the group whose jobs had not.

NIOSH, along with several unions, is also actively involved in using ergonomic principles to design jobs that will reduce the incidence and severity of **carpal tunnel syndrome**. This is a condition characterized by numbness, tingling, soreness, and weakness in the hands and wrists. It is caused or aggravated by jobs requiring repetitive hand motions such as meat cutters and cashiers. Jobs that eliminate these motions are now being performed at companies such as Armco, Inc., and Hanes Corporation.[10]

Ergonomic principles of job design can allow organizations to provide job accommodation to employees with disabilities as described in the *Americans with Disabilities Act of 1990*.[11] Combining ergonomic principles with job sharing and team member involvement can enable firms to even accommodate people with life-threatening illnesses such as AIDS. An example of just how this is being done is described in the feature, "Managing Human Resources at Levi Strauss & Co: When AIDS Hits Home."

Teamwork means working together to solve problems on the job.

DID YOU KNOW?

One survey revealed that most corporations utilize five or six types of teams: functional teams, continuous improvement teams, product teams, project teams, management teams, and problem-solving teams.

Self-managed teams are those making many management decisions for their group.

Ergonomics is about designing the work place so it is more physically accommodating to employees.

THE *Americans with Disabilities* Act may be just an abstract concept for companies and employees that have not yet dealt with a seriously ill employee. When a co-worker contracts a life-threatening disease, however, the business and human ramifications hit home.

San Francisco-based Levi Strauss supports employees and work groups that grapple with these situations. Here's how one person's battle with AIDS was handled at the company.

The employee, whom we will call Bill, worked in a nine-person work group and didn't reveal his AIDS diagnosis until his first hospitalization, according to Yvonne Ellison-Sandler, corporate manager for health promotion.

His first step was to inform his manager, and the two decided how to approach the work group with the news. With Bill's consent, the manager explained Bill's condition to his co-workers.

The company had conducted mandatory AIDS education classes several years earlier, so employees possessed some knowledge about HIV, AIDS, and transmission of the virus in the workplace. After Bill's diagnosis, the training was given again. "For most of these people, this was their second hit," Ellison-Sandler says. This time, of course, there was a difference. Now that a co-worker was ill, this was a real-life situation.

During the session, workers shared their reactions to the news, which ranged from sadness to shock to worry. "One of the women in the group was pregnant, and she was worried about her baby," Ellison-Sandler says. "There was another person who was very, very angry and felt that he was entitled to know as soon as [Bill had become] HIV-positive. They had drunk off the same glass during the Christmas party." The facilitator maintained the ground rule that no one's reaction be censured or criticized, and the session proved cathartic to most of the group members.

The work-group members met eight times to discuss their reactions to Bill's diagnosis. The man who had become angry in the first session continued to be irate and was finally referred for individual counseling and HIV testing, although he continued to meet with the work group.

Once the group accepted Bill's diagnosis, the members began to attack the problem of how to distribute his work load as his disease progressed. "They had a commitment to Bill, because, I think, they were touched that he would share with them what was going on," says Ellison-Sandler. So when Bill was released from the hospital to continue recovering at home, his co-workers instituted a system for getting the work done, volunteering for extra jobs instead of waiting for them to be assigned.

The work group also came up with a way to communicate with Bill that would minimize the number of telephone calls he would have to answer. Each week a designated caller would report to the group on the state of Bill's health.

When Bill was able to return to work, the work load had to be redistributed again. The health-promotion department was asked back to help the work group deal with issues such as what co-workers should say to him. Bill told Ellison-Sandler that he encouraged all questions, and he wanted his colleagues to talk to him and not be afraid.

After only three weeks back on the job, Bill became too sick to come into the office, which meant more work shifting. He decided to work from his home, and group members came up with a plan that allowed him to do so. "They worked with him all the way until the day that he died, and they went to the funeral together as a department," says Ellison-Sandler. "It was such an incredible process to observe, and it spoke to the power of dealing with this stuff up front."[12]

WHICH DESIGN TO USE?

Selection of a job design approach must take into account not only such considerations as the corporate culture, the characteristics of the available work force, and the environment, but also the advantages and disadvantages of each

---

EXHIBIT 5.2
TASK RESPONSIBILITIES OF SELF-MANAGED TEAMS

The most frequently cited tasks for which work teams take responsibility:

- Perform routine equipment maintenance
- Ensure workplace cleanliness
- Stop production for quality problems
- Assign daily tasks
- Make team-member assignments

The most frequently cited tasks for which work teams share responsibility with the supervisor:

- Identify training needs
- Select team members
- Develop work methods/procedures
- Ensure workplace safety
- Monitor and report on unit performance
- Set team production goals
- Provide training
- Coordinate work with suppliers/vendors

The most frequently cited tasks for which supervisors assume prime responsibility:

- Discipline employees
- Prepare unit budgets
- Conduct performance appraisals

SOURCE: Adapted from S. T. Johnson, "Work Teams: What's Ahead in Work Design and Rewards Management," *Compensation and Benefits Review* (March–April 1993): 37.

---

approach. To help in the selection, Exhibit 5.3 lists advantages and disadvantages of each. The final selection will also be influenced by such several factors as cost considerations and the technology and machines available. What's happening in the rest of the company will impact the type of design approach chosen. The HR philosophy of the company is an important factor, too. For example, when organizations such as UPS and Lincoln Electric value their people and continually demonstrate this, the employees give back more, making the business even more successful. When employees are offered the opportunity to grow with the business and when they know the business goals and concerns of the company, the job designs that result from the increased partnership are sure to be more effective. Perhaps these company's approaches to job design would be less effective if their HR philosophy was different, but then they have long recognized the importance of people, and their HR philosophies reflect this.

EMPLOYEE MOTIVATION

This is a good place to pause for a moment and look at employee motivation. An understanding of motivation enables us to see *how* and *why* HR activities such as job design and compensation work. It also enables us to make revisions in HR activities based on the responses and behaviors of employees. Because of

---

LEARNING OBJECTIVE 3

Make recommendations concerning different job designs to companies.

The people we work with deserve the best at all times. We do this by providing opportunities for growth, participation and teamwork. Thus, we strive to create an environment where employees can achieve company goals and personal goals simultaneously.

Paul Beddia, Vice-President,
Human Resources,
Lincoln Electric

EXHIBIT 5.3
ADVANTAGES AND DISADVANTAGES OF THE FOUR JOB DESIGN APPROACHES

APPROACH	ADVANTAGES	DISADVANTAGES
Scientific	Ensures predictability Provides clarity Fits abilities of many people Can be efficient and productive	May be boring May result in absenteeism, sabotage, and turnover
Individual contemporary	Satisfies needs for responsibility, growth, and knowledge of results Provides growth opportunity Reduces boredom Increases quality and morale Lowers turnover	Some people prefer routine predictability May need to pay more, since more skills needed Hard to enrich some jobs Not everyone wants to rotate
Team contemporary	Provides social interaction Provides variety Facilitates social support Reduces absenteeism problem	People may not want interaction Requires training in interpersonal skills Group no better than weakest member
Ergonomics	Accommodates jobs to people Breaks down physical barriers Makes more jobs accessible to more people	May be costly to design some jobs Structural characteristics of the organization may make job change impossible

its importance, we discuss motivation here and in Chapters 9, Performance Appraisal, and 11, Compensation.

Motivation is the process that energizes and directs an individual's behavior toward the fulfillment of the individual's needs and values.[13] Individuals are motivated to behave (perform) in particular ways based on their perception of the situation—namely, the intrinsic and extrinsic rewards being offered and the importance of their needs and values that are likely to be fulfilled. To reiterate, motivation depends on:

Motivation is the process that energizes and directs an individual's behavior toward the fulfillment of the individual's needs and values.

- Needs and values
- Intrinsic rewards
- Extrinsic rewards

The *quality* and *quantity* of the behavior (performance) depends upon ability and motivation. In other words, individuals perform in ways that will help them satisfy their needs, and they avoid activities that do not satisfy their needs or that result in punishment. Performance is based on an individual's perception of the situation, as shown in Exhibit 5.4. The individual's perception of the situation includes what is seen as the degree of probability of reaching objectives set by the manager or organization and also the potential for extrinsic and intrinsic rewards.

Extrinsic rewards such as pay are given by the organization.

Extrinsic rewards are rewards given by the organization such as pay, promotion, praise, tenure, and status symbols. When a person acts to receive an extrinsic reward (say, money or a better job) or to avoid punishment (say, loss of money or criticism), that person is *extrinsically motivated*.

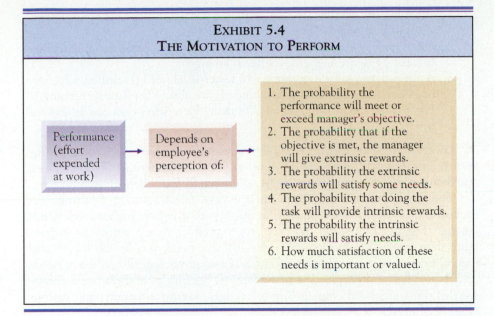

EXHIBIT 5.4
THE MOTIVATION TO PERFORM

Performance (effort expended at work) → Depends on employee's perception of: →

1. The probability the performance will meet or exceed manager's objective.
2. The probability that if the objective is met, the manager will give extrinsic rewards.
3. The probability the extrinsic rewards will satisfy some needs.
4. The probability that doing the task will provide intrinsic rewards.
5. The probability the intrinsic rewards will satisfy needs.
6. How much satisfaction of these needs is important or valued.

✳ **Intrinsic rewards** cannot be given by the organization; they originate within the person. Among them are a sense of meaningfulness, a sense of responsibility, and empowerment and satisfaction in knowing the results. The stronger these intrinsic drives are, the more likely job enrichment programs will result in the outcomes shown in Exhibit 5.1. A person who acts for no externally given reward is *intrinsically motivated:* performing the activity well is a reward in itself.

Extrinsic and intrinsic rewards motivate performance only when the performance appears necessary to obtain them. Organizations can directly control extrinsic rewards such as pay, but their influence on intrinsic rewards is indirect.

Managers cannot change people; they can only change behavior. To do this, they usually must change the *work situation*—the place and the circumstances of work—so it will allow people to satisfy work-related needs through performance. The balance of our discussion looks at some of the *needs* people have and examines how work situations can be changed to satisfy these needs. We will look at several different models of motivation. As used here, the word *model* means a mental representation or idea of why people behave as they do.

We will differentiate between content and process models, although basically they differ only in their relative focus, and they overlap considerably. **Content models** focus on the wants and needs that individuals are trying to satisfy (achieve) within the situation. **Process models** focus on how managers can change the situation to better tie need satisfaction to performance. The manager must consider both areas of focus if performance is to be improved.

CONTENT MODELS OF MOTIVATION

Two content models of motivation are discussed in this section. The first, the **need hierarchy model,** describes a hierarchy of needs existing within people. The second, the **motivation-hygiene model,** describes factors in the workplace that dissatisfy people and factors that motivate them.

THE NEED HIERARCHY MODEL.   This model, developed by psychologist Abraham Maslow and adapted for use in management by psychologist Douglas McGregor, suggests that:

Intrinsic rewards originate within the person.

Content models focus on the wants and needs individuals are trying to satisfy. *Process models* focus on how managers can change the situation to better satisfy employee needs.

Need hierarchy model describes a hierarchy of needs existing within people.

Motivation-hygiene model describes factors in the workplace that dissatisfy people and factors that motivate them.

The five levels of needs are

- self-actualization
- ego
- social
- safety
- physiological

1. *Adult motives are complex.* No single motive determines behavior; rather, a number of motives operate at the same time.
2. *Needs form a hierarchy.* In general, lower-level needs must be at least partly satisfied before higher-level needs emerge.
3. *A satisfied need is not a motivator.* If a lower-level need is satisfied, a higher-level need emerges. In a sense, humans are always wanting something.
4. *Higher-level needs can be satisfied in many more ways than can lower-level needs.*

Levels of need are identified as physiological, safety (security), social (affiliation), ego (esteem), and self-actualization (or developmental). The sequence and relative importance of these levels are shown in Exhibit 5.5.

The *physiological* level includes the universal needs for food, clothing, and shelter. These needs must be met, at least partly, before higher-level needs emerge. The need for *safety* has been interpreted by recent writers to include more than freedom from physical harm—that is, freedom from job layoffs and loss of income. In most Western countries, basic physiological and safety needs are satisfied for most people. The new emerging definitions of these needs can be seen in the widespread emphasis on job tenure, savings accounts, and various types of insurance.

The *social* level includes the need to belong—to be accepted by others and to give and receive friendship and love. The use of teamwork helps to fulfill social needs.

The *ego* level involves the need to have a firm, stable, and reasonably high evaluation of oneself. This level has both internal and external aspects. The

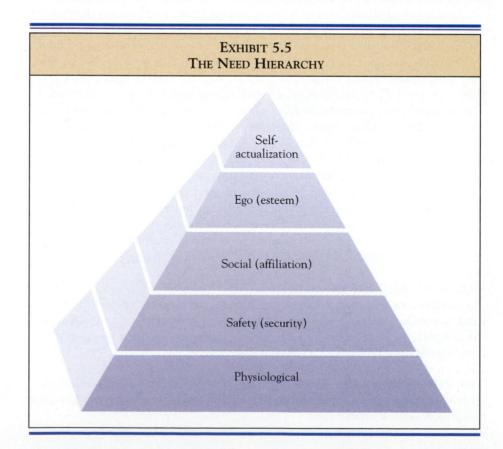

EXHIBIT 5.5
THE NEED HIERARCHY

Self-actualization

Ego (esteem)

Social (affiliation)

Safety (security)

Physiological

internal aspect is a personal feeling of self-worth, an assurance of one's achievement, knowledge, and competence. The external aspect involves receiving appreciation, recognition, and respect from others. At the *social* level of need, a person wants only to be accepted; at the ego level, a person wants to be admired or at least perceived as competent.

At the fifth and highest level, *self-actualization,* individuals are concerned with achieving their full potential through self-development, creativity, and psychological health. The need cannot be completely satisfied by any job. Many people never attempt to satisfy this need, because they remain preoccupied with satisfying the lower-level needs. Maslow estimated some years ago that, in the United States, 85 percent of physiological needs, 70 percent of safety needs, 50 percent of social needs, 40 percent of ego and esteem needs, and only 10 percent of self-actualization needs were being satisfied.[15] Although current estimates may have changed, they probably are very similar.

Care should be taken not to overgeneralize from this model.[16] A number of different needs may be in operation at any one time, and not all of them can be satisfied simultaneously. Some aspects of the job may be more satisfying than others, and although some needs are involved only with job behavior or performance, others may be reserved for behavior off the job. For example, as mentioned earlier, it may be impossible for a job to completely satisfy self-actualization or growth needs.

THE MOTIVATION-HYGIENE MODEL. About 35 years ago, Frederick Herzberg and his associates asked engineers and accountants what they liked and disliked about their work. After analyzing the data, Herzberg concluded that there were two vital kinds of factors in any job: hygiene and motivation. The motivation-hygiene model is based on the idea that one set of job characteristics determines the degree of worker dissatisfaction (hygiene), and another set determines the degree of positive satisfaction (motivation). In other words, the hygiene factors can be changed to reduce worker dissatisfaction, but these changes are not sufficient to create motivation.

The **hygiene factors** involve the context in which the work is performed. They include company policy and administration; job security; interpersonal relations with supervisors, peers, and subordinates; salary; and working conditions. Herzberg's findings suggested that if these conditions were poor, they could lead to physical or psychological withdrawal from the job. The improvement of conditions is a little like vaccination; it can keep someone from getting sick, but it doesn't make the sick person well—hence the term *hygiene*. The conditions surrounding the job (the hygiene factors) must be adequate before a person is motivated to work, but other factors are necessary to produce that motivation.

The **motivation factors** include a sense of achievement, recognition, advancement, enjoyment of the work itself, the possibility of personal growth, and a sense of responsibility. Increasing job satisfaction and motivation and improving mental health, therefore, tend to increase productivity.

To summarize Herzberg's findings, what motivates employees toward effective work is a job that is challenging and that encourages feelings of achievement, growth, responsibility, advancement, earned recognition, and enjoyment of the work itself. What disinclines them are primarily factors that are not directly part of the job itself such as poor working conditions, bad lighting, insufficient coffee breaks, lack of opportunity to socialize, unpleasant work rules, unneeded titles, a rigid seniority system, low wages, and a lack of fringe benefits.[17]

THE RELATIONSHIPS BETWEEN THE CONTENT MODELS. Although the models discussed so far have different sources, they showed marked similarities,

Herzberg's hygiene factors:

- **company policy**
- **salary**
- **job security**
- **co-worker relations**
- **working conditions**

Herzberg's motivation factors:

- **sense of achievement**
- **recognition**
- **advancement**
- **enjoyment of work**
- **personal growth**
- **sense of responsibility**

as Exhibit 5.6 indicates. The hygiene factors are roughly equivalent to the lower-level hierarchy needs, and the motivational factors are roughly equivalent to the higher-level hierarchy needs.

All the models are slanted toward humanistic concerns; that is, they assume that most people want more self-esteem, which is achieved through greater opportunity for achievement, advancement, and responsibility. This assumption is clearly not true for all people. Thus, the manager using the content approaches should analyze the individuals and the circumstances surrounding the job to determine whether they are satisfactory. If they are, the manager should try to provide opportunities for interesting work, earned recognition, and additional responsibility for those willing to accept it.

PROCESS MODELS OF MOTIVATION

The content models of motivation provide some idea of the needs people try to satisfy. However, they do not show how people attempt to satisfy needs at work or how managers can change the work situation to enable people to satisfy needs through improved job performance. The process models of motivation are more explicit in these areas. We will examine one of them, the expectancy model, in this section. The positive reinforcement model, is discussed in Chapter 9, Performance Appraisal, and the equity model, is discussed in Chapter 11, Compensation.

THE EXPECTANCY MODEL.   The expectancy model of motivation, designed by Victor Vroom, has been the subject of a great deal of research and attention since its development. The **expectancy model** suggests that people are motivated at work to choose among different behaviors or intensities of effort if they believe their efforts will be rewarded and if the rewards they expect to get are important to them. The three primary factors in this model are choice, expectancy, and preference.[18] **Choice** is the freedom to select from among different possibilities or alternatives. People choose from among a wide range of behaviors: they choose to come to work or to call in sick and to work hard on the job or to take it easy. A student may decide to study hard to get a good grade in a particular course (positive outcome) but may have to pass up going to a party (negative outcome). Sometimes the choice is relatively simple, as in these examples. Other times it is more difficult, as in choosing a career.

Vroom's expectancy model keys:

- perceptions
- effort-performance relationships
- performance-reward relationships
- performance
- outcomes/preference
- equity
- satisfaction
- choice

EXHIBIT 5.6
A COMPARISON OF THE MASLOW/MCGREGOR AND HERZBERG MODELS

MASLOW/MCGREGOR NEED HIERARCHY	HERZBERG MOTIVATION-HYGIENE MODEL
Physiological needs	Pay; job security; work conditions
Safety needs	Relationships with boss, co-workers
	Company policy; job hazards
Social needs	Recognition from others
Ego needs	Achievement
	Advancement
Self-actualization needs	Growth potential; work itself

Expectancy is the belief, expressed as a subjective estimate or probability (odds), that a particular act will or will not be successful. Individuals who want to attain a particular goal must usually expend some effort to do it. However, people have certain expectations or beliefs about whether their behavior will be successful. If they see the odds as zero, they will not even try.

The expectancy model was once explained in the following manner to a group of managers meeting in a conference room. A thousand dollars was offered to anyone who could, without special help, kick the ceiling with either foot. When no one even tried, it was pointed out that everyone had subjectively estimated that the odds of kicking the ceiling were zero and, on the basis of this expectancy, had made a choice not to attempt it!

As with positive reinforcement, the standards of an expectancy model should be seen by the employees as challenging but attainable. The probability of accomplishing a task must be low enough that a feeling of achievement can be imparted. **Preferences** involve valuing some rewards more highly than others and avoiding punishment.

The expectancy model of behavior suggests that people will work (behave) to accomplish goals that satisfy certain needs. The goals may either be ends in themselves or means to an end. For example, an engineer attempting to solve a technical problem worked on Saturdays and Sundays until the problem was solved. Coming to work on the weekend was her *choice*, based on her *preference* for solving the problem rather than enjoying some other activity. Her *expectation* that she would solve the problem was necessary for this choice and preference to operate.

The process of choice, expectancy, and preference can be expressed in *five propositions:*

1. Behavior is directed toward satisfying needs by means of achieving certain goals. The goals may be valued for themselves or because they lead to still other goals, such as passing a course to get a diploma to get a better job.
2. The behavior must be seen as a way of making the goal possible, or it will not be chosen. Working on weekends helped the engineer solve a difficult problem. Studying harder usually results in higher grades.
3. In most circumstances, individuals choose among a range of different behaviors to reach certain outcomes. For example, a student who wants high grades can study hard, take easy courses, or join a study group.
4. The more an individual perceives a desired outcome as a direct result of personal behavior, the greater the motivation. For example, if everybody has job security for minimum effort, there is little motivation to work hard for that outcome. However, the motivation to work hard may exist for other outcomes such as a pay increase, promotion, or increased recognition and praise from the boss.
5. Most behaviors have both positive and negative outcomes. Working harder, as in the case of the engineer working weekends, may lead to a quicker solution (positive outcome) but may also lead to fatigue (negative outcome) or loss of social life (negative outcome). However, she clearly felt that the positive outcome were greater than the negative outcomes.

Positive outcomes include:
- job security
- praise
- salary
- promotion
- fairness
- freedom
- respect
- job variety
- challenge
- participation

The expectancy model can be summarized as follows: performance at work is a function of the expectation that a desired outcome will be achieved and of a preference for that particular outcome over other desired outcomes. The outcome toward which the performance is directed is also a function of an expectation that it can indeed be achieved.

People are constantly making choices based on the subjective probability that what they do will have a payoff. The situation illustrated in Exhibit 5.7 is that of a married man with two young children who recently graduated from law school. He has an unsatisfied need for status. This need can be satisfied by obtaining the high regard of those with whom he works in the prestigious law firm or by being seen as an attentive, caring husband and father. He can choose to work harder at the law firm, which may result in the desired outcome of increased status but also may bring negative outcomes of fatigue and emotionally impoverished family life. Or he can choose to spend fewer hours at work and devote more time to his family, which may gain him increased appreciation from family and friends but cause him to lose prestige at work.

Consciously or subconsciously, he will probably subjectively work out answers to a series of expectancy questions before making a choice. What is the probability (expectancy) that harder work will lead to greater status on the job? What is the probability (expectancy) of receiving more recognition from the family by spending more time with them? By teaching his daughter to swim? Although he may not be aware of calculating the relative values of these choices, the calculations nevertheless occur.

In making choices, people constantly ask themselves, "What is the payoff for me?" Exhibit 5.7 is, of course, oversimplified. Our complexity as human beings ensures that a number of needs are usually in operation at the same time. This model effectively shows, however, that we will consider our needs in light of the best known subjective probabilities and that we choose particular behaviors to

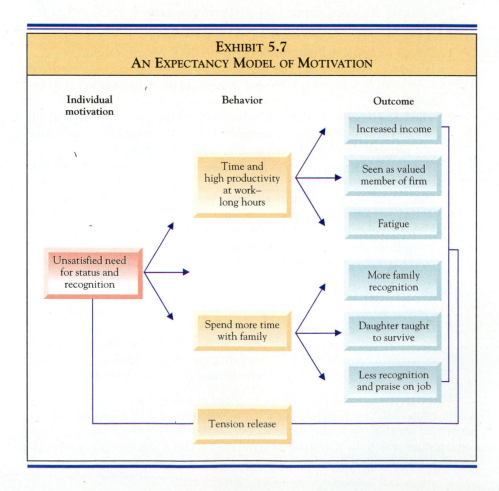

EXHIBIT 5.7
AN EXPECTANCY MODEL OF MOTIVATION

Individual motivation

Behavior

Outcome

Time and high productivity at work— long hours

Spend more time with family

Unsatisfied need for status and recognition

Increased income

Seen as valued member of firm

Fatigue

More family recognition

Daughter taught to survive

Less recognition and praise on job

Tension release

bring about outcomes to satisfy our needs. Our behavior choices depend on what we perceive to be the greatest reward. Obviously, this perception varies from individual to individual. Some of us occasionally skip an 8:00 or 9:00 A.M. class in order to sleep longer; others of us never do.

The expectancy model forces the manager to focus on a fundamental problem. If workers are to be motivated to perform satisfactorily on the job, they must see a clear-cut payoff. If they do not, it is the manager's responsibility to change the work situation in one of two ways: provide a payoff if none exists or clarify the path to an existing payoff.

This model motivation has significantly influenced the thinking of many managers. Effective managers apply and adapt what is most useful in the model to particular situations with particular employees. In so doing, they serve both the needs of the individuals and the needs of the organization by making individuals more productive, involved, and committed employees. Managers also accomplish these objectives when they consider alternative arrangements for employee accommodation.

ALTERNATIVE ARRANGEMENTS FOR EMPLOYEE ACCOMMODATION

The growing number of single-parent families, the high costs of commuting, the desire for larger blocks of personal time, and the desire of older workers to reduce their hours, all suggest that alternative work arrangements can reduce the stresses caused by the conflicts of juggling job demands, family needs, leisure values, and educational needs. Thus organizations can expect to reduce absenteeism and turnover by offering alternatives to their standard work arrangements. Firms can also increase their attractiveness to a more diverse pool of applicants when they are willing to accommodate individuals. As firms seek to comply with the ADA, they may design jobs to accommodate differently abled people. They can also offer more flexibility in time schedules and job sharing as well as telecommuting arrangements.

STANDARD WORK SCHEDULES

In the 1860s, the average workweek was 72 hours—twelve hours a day, six days a week. It was 58 hours in 1900 and remains approximately 40 hours a week today. Standard work schedules include day, evening, and night sessions as well as overtime, part-time, and shift work over a 40-hour week. A shift worker might report from 7:00 A.M. to 4:00 P.M. one week and from 4:00 P.M. to midnight the next. Since the end of World War I, shift work has become more prevalent in industrialized countries. Currently, about 20 percent of all industrial workers in Europe and the United States are on shift work schedules. The percentage of employees on part-time schedules has also increased steadily—from approximately 15 percent in 1954 to more than 25 percent today.

These standard work schedules all have advantages and disadvantages. Initially, employees may select a given schedule, but after that, the days of the week (five) and the hours of the day (eight) are generally fixed. Because employee preferences and interests change over time, what once was an appropriate work schedule may no longer be so. If alternative arrangements are not provided, the employee may leave the organization. Furthermore, the organization may have a difficult time attracting similar types of employees. As a result, it pays to give employees a choice between a nonstandard and standard schedule, as well as a choice of hours, days, and total number of hours to work per week.

Flextime is a nonstandard work schedule giving individuals choices in their
working hours.
Band width is the maximum length of
the workday—the range of hours during which workers must arrange their
schedule.
Core time is the period of time when
everyone needs to be at work.

Compressed workweeks are schedules
where more time is worked in a shorter
time period.

Permanent part-time is the regular
assignment of less than a full week of
work.

Job sharing is a special part-time
arrangement where two people share
one job.

✳FLEXTIME SCHEDULES

Flextime, a nonstandard work schedule, is popular with organizations because it decreases absenteeism, increases employee morale, induces better labor-management relations, and encourages a high level of employee participation in decision making, control over the job, and discretion. Simply stated, flextime is a schedule that gives employees daily choice in the timing of work and nonwork activities. Consideration is given to **band width,** or maximum length of the workday. This band (often ranging between ten and sixteen hours) is divided into core time and flexible time. **Core time** is the period the employee has to work; flexible time allows the employee to choose the remaining work time. Exhibit 5.8 shows how a twelve-hour band width can be divided into blocks of flexible and core times.

Among the advantages of flextime is its ability to increase overall employee productivity. It also enables organizations to accommodate employee preferences, some of which may be legally protected such as reasonable religious obligations. On the other hand, flextime forces the supervisor to do more planning, sometimes makes communications difficult between employees (especially those with different schedules), and complicates record keeping. Furthermore, most flextime schedules still require employees to work five days a week.

COMPRESSED WORKWEEKS

An option for employees who want to work fewer than five days is the **compressed workweek.** By extending the workday beyond the standard eight hours, employees generally need to work only three to four days to equal a standard 40-hour week. For example, at two General Tire and Rubber plants, some employees work only two 12-hour shifts each weekend and yet are considered full-time employees. Compressed workweeks are becoming especially popular for certain occupations such as nursing.

Compressed workweeks permit an organization to make better use of its equipment and to decrease turnover and absenteeism. Scheduling and legal problems may accompany such arrangements, but legal exceptions can be made, and scheduling can become a joint negotiation process between supervisors and employees.

PERMANENT PART-TIME AND JOB SHARING

Traditionally, part-time work has meant filling positions that lasted only for a short time such as those in retail stores during holiday periods. Now some organizations have designated **permanent part-time** positions. A permanent part-time work schedule may be a shortened daily schedule (for example, from 1:00 to 5:00 P.M.) or an odd-hour shift (for example from 5:00 to 9:00 P.M.). Organizations can also use part-time schedules to fill in the remainder of a day composed of two 10-hour shifts (representing a compressed workweek).[19]

Job sharing is a particular type of part-time work. In job sharing, two people divided the responsibility for a regular full-time job. Both may work half the job, or one person may work more hours than the other. Part-time workers generally receive little or no indirect compensation, but workers on permanent part-time and job-sharing schedules often do. The benefits of these workers are not equal to those of full-time workers but are prorated according to the amount of time they work.

Both permanent part-time and job sharing provide the organization and the individual with opportunities that might not otherwise be available. They offer staffing flexibility that can expand or contract to meet actual demands, using employees who are at least as productive, if not more so, than regular full-time

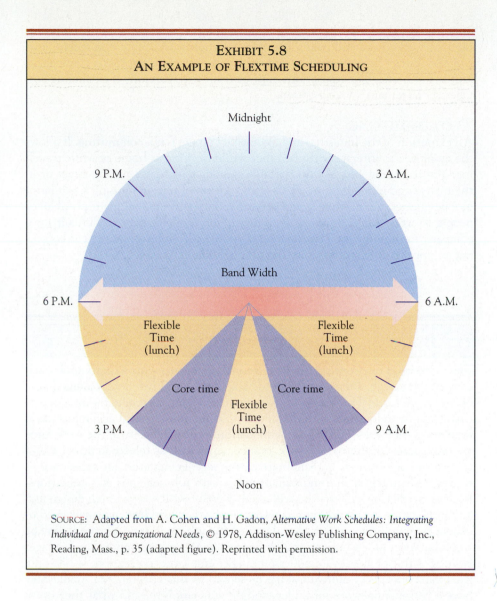

EXHIBIT 5.8
AN EXAMPLE OF FLEXTIME SCHEDULING

SOURCE: Adapted from A. Cohen and H. Gadon, *Alternative Work Schedules: Integrating Individual and Organizational Needs*, © 1978, Addison-Wesley Publishing Company, Inc., Reading, Mass., p. 35 (adapted figure). Reprinted with permission.

employees. Individuals benefit from being able to enjoy permanent work with less than a full-time commitment to the company.

INDUSTRIAL AND ELECTRONIC COTTAGES

To provide individuals with even more choices in how to arrange their work and work schedules, companies are allowing employees to work at home. Work-at-home arrangements can be made for those with a full-time commitment to the company and for those wanting only part-time employment. Increasingly, individuals are working at home by means of computer terminals linked to the computers at their regular office or plant. In essence, the employee's home then becomes an **electronic cottage.** Individuals can also take home work that involves assembly, such as small toys. After a batch is done, the worker takes it to the regular plant and turns it in for more parts. In this example, the home becomes an **industrial cottage.**[20]

The use of industrial and electronic cottages is increasing. These arrangements offer workers yet another choice. One drawback, though, is the difficulty

Electronic and *industrial cottages* are work-at-home arrangements.

of protecting the health and safety of the employee at home. Another is ensuring that workers are still paid a fair wage for their work. State and federal laws can also restrict home work. One federal law, for example, prohibits commercial knitting at home. The restrictions must be dealt with carefully if expanding cottages are to remain a viable option.

TELECOMMUTING

An extension of the industrial and electronic cottage is **telecommuting.** It allows the employee to interact with the office while working at home or while traveling. You see many people with portable cellular telephones on the street or in their cars conducting business. This is also a form of telecommuting. Cellular or mobile phones, fax machines, and personal computers are making it possible for people to work almost anytime and anywhere. While it may be difficult for a company to monitor the performance of people who telecommute, it is becoming an important way companies can accommodate employees.[21]

SUMMARY

The worker-job relationship can be effectively managed with a thorough knowledge of job design. Increasingly, job design is seen as a way to accommodate a diverse work force. This ranges from individuals with preferences for more repetitive tasks to individuals with disabilities that require physical accommodation to perform their jobs. Further accommodations to the diversity of the work force are provisions for alternative work arrangements such as telecommuting. All of these forms of job design and alternative work arrangements enable organizations to more effectively match individuals needs with job demands and conditions. Because predicting exactly who will need or prefer which type of job design and accommodation is critical, human resource managers and line managers need to encourage employee input as they diagnose the job situation. One result may be a combination of job designs and alternative work arrangements. The manager is aided in this process by an understanding of employee motivation. While only the basic concepts of motivation are presented in this chapter, you should now have a better framework for understanding why employees do what they do in organizations. We will discuss motivation and employee behavior again in our chapters on performance appraisal and compensation. First, we turn next to the activity of analyzing the jobs that have been designed.

KEY CONCEPTS

band width	ergonomics	hygiene factors
carpal tunnel syndrome	expectancy	individual contemporary
choice	expectancy model	design
compressed workweek	extrinsic rewards	industrial cottage
core time	feedback	intrinsic rewards
content models	flextime	job autonomy
electronic cottage	horizontal loading	job design

REVIEW AND DISCUSSION QUESTIONS

1. Why does Lincoln Electric have so much success with its operations?
2. How do job enrichment programs differ from job enlargement programs?
3. What are important factors influencing the choice of job design approaches?
4. How can approaches to job design be used to accommodate employees?
5. Describe how the core job characteristics model influences the psychological states of employees.
6. What are process and content models of motivation?
7. Why is it useful to know about various models of motivation?
8. How can alternative work arrangements accommodate employees?
9. How can organizations manage workers who are telecommuters?
10. What impact do telecommuters have on companies' attempts to have teamwork?

REVIEW QUESTIONS

AMERICANS WITH DISABILITIES ACT OF 1990 (ADA)

QUESTIONS AND ANSWERS FOR EMPLOYERS

Q. What does Title I of the *Americans With Disabilities Act* (ADA) do?

A. Title I of the ADA prohibits employers from discriminating against a qualified employee or job applicant with a disability.

Q. Which employers are affected by the ADA, and when does the law take effect?

A. All employers with 15 or more employees are affected; these include private employers, state and local governments, employment agencies, and labor unions. For employers with 25 or more employees, the law took effect on July 26, 1992. For employers with 15–24 employees, the law took effect July 26, 1994.

Q. What employment practices and activities are covered by Title I of the ADA?

A. The ADA prohibits discrimination in all employment practices, including job application procedures, hiring, firing, advancement, compensation, training, and other terms, conditions, and privileges of employment. It applies to recruitment, advertising, tenure, layoff, leave, fringe benefits, and all other employment-related activities.

Q. Who is protected against employment discrimination?

A. Employment discrimination is prohibited against "qualified individuals with disabilities." Persons discriminated against because they have a known association or relationship with a disabled individual are also protected—for example, the wife of a man who is parapelegic would be protected, as would the son of a person with muscular distrophy or the friend of a person with AIDS.

Q. Who is a person with a disability?

A. A person with a disability is a person who

1. Has a physical or mental impairment that substantially limits that person in one or more major life activities—for example, caring for oneself, performing manual tasks, walking, seeing, hearing, speaking, breathing, learning, and working;

2. Has a record of such impairment—for example, a person who has recovered from cancer or a recovering alcoholic; or

3. Is *regarded* as having an impairment—for example, a person who is severely scarred, disfigured, or even obese, but who is not actually disabled.

Q. Who is a "qualified" person with a disability?

A. A qualified person with a disability is a person who meets the skill, experience, education, and other job-related requirements for the job and who, with or without "reasonable accommodation," can perform the "essential functions" of the job.

Q. What are a job's "essential functions"?

A. A job's "essential functions" are job functions that are basic, necessary, or vital.

Q. What is a "reasonable accommodation"?

A. A "reasonable accommodation" is any modification or adjustment that allows qualified applicants or employees with disabilities to participate in the application process or to do the job's essential functions. Reasonable accommodation also includes adjustments to assure that a qualified individual with a disability has the same job rights and privileges as nondisabled employees.

Q. What kinds of actions should an employer take to reasonably accommodate applicants and employees?

A. The actions that an employer should take to reasonably accommodate applicants and employees include:

1. Analyzing and describing the job's essential functions.

2. Talking with the person with a disability to discuss what adjustments need to be made to accommodate the employee. Accommodations may include: making existing facilities readily accessible to, and usable by, persons with disabilities; job restructur-

ing; work schedule restructuring; reassignment; acquisition of equipment or devices; providing readers or interpreters; and appropriate modifications of training materials, policies, and examinations.

Q. Are there limits to an employer's obligation to make "reasonable accommodation"?

A. Yes. The person with a disability requiring the accommodation must be otherwise qualified for the job; an employer does not have to hire a person who poses a direct threat to the health and safety of himself or of others; and it is the responsibility of the individual to make his or her disability known to the employer.

Q. Must an employer modify existing facilities to make them accessible?

A. Depending on the nature of the needed modification and the employer's circumstances, an employer *may* be required to modify facilities to enable an individual to perform essential job functions and to have an equal opportunity to participate in other job-related activities.

Q. Is an employer required to provide a "reasonable accommodation" if it is an undue hardship on the employer?

A. No.

Q. What is an "undue hardship"?

A. An "undue hardship" requires significant difficulty or expense in relation to the size and nature of the business and the type and cost of the accommodation. The employer must prove undue hardship. What may be an undue hardship for one employer may not be an undue hardship for another. Undue hardship will be determined on a case-by-case basis.

Q. May an employer ask if a prospective employee is disabled?

A. An employer may *not* make a pre-employment inquiry on an application form or in an interview as to whether, or to what extent, an individual is disabled. The employer may ask a job applicant whether he or she can perform the essential functions of the job.

Q. Can employers require pre-employment medical examinations of persons with disabilities?

A. No. An employer cannot require a pre-employment medical examination, but post–job-offer medical examinations are allowed under specific circumstances. A job offer may be conditioned on the results of a job-performance–related medical exam *only* if it is required of *every* new employee in the same job category. Medical information obtained from medical exams must be handled according to the ADA's confidentiality requirements.

SOURCE: *Americans with Disabilities Act (ADA) Title 1, Employment* (Washington, D.C.: AARP, 1992). Used by permission.

Q. Are current users of illegal drugs, whether applicants or employees, protected by the ADA?

A. No. However, persons participating in supervised rehabilitation programs (and who are no longer engaging in illegal drug use) are protected.

REVIEW QUESTIONS

Please mark which condition(s), under the *Americans with Disabilities Act* is (are) not considered a disability:

Severe vision problem _____

Wheelchair confinement _____

Severe hearing problem _____

Mental illness _____

Alcoholism _____

Drug usage _____

Cancer _____

AIDS _____

Diabetes _____

Answer: All of the above except drug (i.e., illegal) usage.

EXERCISES AND CASES

FIELD PROJECT

Interview one of the overnight delivery carriers (you might have to interview them as they are walking!) and ask them to describe the nature or characteristics of their jobs (number of skills used, degree of freedom, and so forth). Report your findings to the class in terms of the core job characteristics model.

In Chapter 4, you indicated the type of job you want and organization you would like to work for after graduation. Now indicate the amount of the five job core dimensions (low, medium, high) you would like to have on your job:

	LOW	MEDIUM	HIGH
Skill variety	_____	_____	_____
Significance	_____	_____	_____
Task identity	_____	_____	_____
Task autonomy	_____	_____	_____
Task feedback	_____	_____	_____

In addition to these job dimensions, are there any other workplace accommodations you would request?

_____

_____

_____

_____

What are your preferred hours of work (and/or how many days and hours per week/year are you willing to work?

Preferred weekly schedule: _____

Number of days per week: _____ ;

Weeks per year:_____

We will return to your job requirements again in Chapter 8, Selection and Placement.

JOB OBJECTIVE FOR DATA ENTRY EMPLOYEES

To get information from printed or written media entered into computer data files.

CURRENT SITUATION

There are fifteen employees in this unit reporting to one supervisor. They handle a wide variety of data entry work, which is supplied by various departments and groups. Some jobs are small, while others can involve entering up to 100,000 bits of information. Some work comes with a due date, and the remainder has been prescheduled on a routine basis.

The work is supplied to the Data Entry employees by an assignment clerk. He attempts to see that each employee gets exactly one-fifteenth of the work. The assignment clerk looks at the work before he assigns it to the data entry employee and makes sure that it is legible. If it is not, he gives it to the supervisor who returns it to the originating department. Usually, the Data Entry unit has been able to enter about 65,000 data points per employee per day. Because of the exactness of the work and the cost of data entry, the work is sent to verifiers to review, to keep errors to a minimum. However, some errors are not discovered until after the finished job is returned to the client. Turnover is high, and many due dates are not met.

CASE ASSIGNMENT

Listed below are some proposals that might result in improving work performance. Read through the list, and decide which things you would or would not do.

Put an X on the appropriate line next to each of the items in the list.*

	WOULD	WOULD NOT	RANK ORDER
1. Make sure the forms from which the Data Entry employees get their information are arranged in the best way.	_____	_____	_____
2. Let some Data Entry employees decide whether their work should be verified.	_____	_____	_____
3. Tell the Data Entry employees to do the work that has specific due dates first.	_____	_____	_____
4. Train the assignment clerk so he can help with data entry when the work load is heavy.	_____	_____	_____
5. Split the group so that fewer Data Entry employees report to a supervisor.	_____	_____	_____
6. Have the Data Entry employees inspect the media they receive for legibility.	_____	_____	_____
7. When errors are discovered, feed back the details to the Data Entry employee who made the error.	_____	_____	_____
8. Have the Data Entry employees verify their own work.	_____	_____	_____
9. Assign responsibility for entering all of a particular job to an individual.	_____	_____	_____
10. Arrange for departmental client contacts for certain employees.	_____	_____	_____
11. Let some Data Entry employees schedule their own day.	_____	_____	_____
12. Make sure that jobs for a particular group or account always go to the same employee.	_____	_____	_____

*Next, rank order the action you would take first, and number it #1. Then pick #2, etc., and continue to do the same for as many changes as you feel are necessary.

© Susan E. Jackson, New York University.

CASE

JOB REDESIGN AT AID ASSOCIATION FOR LUTHERANS (AAL)

Jerome (Jerry) H. Laubenstein, new vice-president of the insurance department at AAL, is wondering what the best way is to improve the work conditions and performance of his 500 employees. Currently, his employees are broken down into three major groups: clerks (the majority), technicians, and managers.

AAL is a nonprofit fraternal society (mutual benefit association) with 1.5 million members (customers) throughout the United States. AAL has over $6 billion in assets, putting it in the top 2 percent of life insurers. In the early 1980s, AAL grew dramatically, nearly doubling in size to approximately 2,000 employees. Unfortunately, productivity did not increase at the same rate. It was this latter point that drew the attention of Richard L. Gunderson, the new president and CEO as of 1985. Knowing that AAL, though nonprofit, must still compete with other insurers, Gunderson has established the goals of cutting costs by $50 million over five years and reducing the number of jobs by 250. At the same time, he remains committed to the society's policy of no layoffs or terminations. Thus work force reductions will occur only through attrition.

While Gunderson's main concern is productivity, he knows that customer service is an important objective as well. He is aware of the increase in the number of customer complaints over the past twelve months. He is also aware that the service agents (the sales force) are having trouble getting the information they need to service the customers (the policyholders) property.

Jerry is even more aware than Gunderson of what is going on; after all, it is his department. He also has in his hands the results of a survey done by his five newly appointed regional managers and the 200 employees who volunteered to assist in the efforts to improve the department. They have an interest in improving things, too. In the past few years, as the department has grown, management layers have been added, and the clerks and technicians have been left with less discretion than before. In addition to this, they work on narrowly defined jobs unconnected to other employees' jobs. The work of each employee is passed on to others randomly and very inefficiently. Of course, this situation is compounded by the functional structure of the department. That is, there are three sections, health insurance, life insurance, and support services (shown in Exhibit 1). Typically, if a service agent wants to change a policy, all three sections get involved, but somewhat randomly and very inefficiently. It takes an average of 20 days to get back to the policyholder. This is also due in part to the climate that has been created over the past few years, described by some as

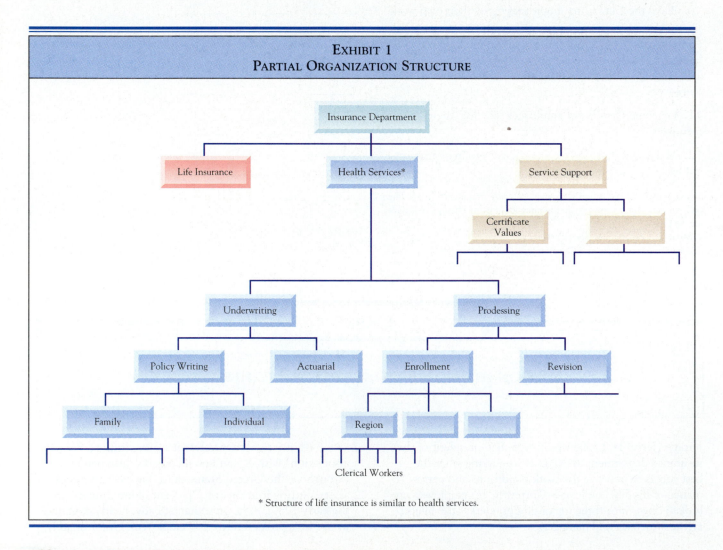

Exhibit 1
Partial Organization Structure

Insurance Department

Life Insurance — Health Services* — Service Support

Service Support: Certificate Values

Health Services*: Underwriting — Prodessing

Underwriting: Policy Writing — Actuarial

Prodessing: Enrollment — Revision

Policy Writing: Family — Individual

Enrollment: Region

Clerical Workers

* Structure of life insurance is similar to health services.

"waiting for marching orders." Jerry is determined to do something. Based on the survey, his basic premises are that the number of separate jobs that exist in the department can be reduced from the current 167 and that the concept of self-directed teams can be put in place. Thus the functional structure is not sacred, and neither are the jobs of the managers.

DISCUSSION QUESTIONS

1. What would you recommend as the final design of the jobs in the insurance department?
2. Who really should decide on the exact number of jobs and their content?
3. Will anyone have to be trained or retrained? Will all employees be able to change?
4. How should the changes be made? Should they be done one section at a time or with all 500 employees at once? Again, who should decide?

© Randall S. Schuler, New York University

ROLE PLAY: JERRY LAUBENSTEIN

You are Jerry Laubenstein, vice-president of the insurance department at AAL. Based on the situation at AAL, you have decided to go ahead and make several changes in the structure and jobs of the insurance department. With information from the survey, you have decided to base many of your changes on the concept of self-directed teams. This concept means that all your employees (most have not been to college) will work in specific teams and learn many tasks (they will become multiskilled). Thus far, most have worked alone (like the typical office of many companies) and have only used a few skills, skills that they learned ten years ago. They have established their routines in life and family situations like everyone else. They are not going any place in life other than where they are now.

You are about to talk with one of the employees, Marie Saxer, about the changes you want made. Ms. Saxer represents the 300 workers who are not part of the survey group. This employee is known to support the current situation and believes that a change is not necessary. You, of course, depend on her cooperation and cannot afford to lose her or any of the other workers.

Your challenge is to explain to this worker the changes you want. You want her to cooperate and explain your changes to the other workers in a way that they can understand and accept.

ROLE PLAY: MARIE SAXER

You are Marie Saxer, one of the 300 employees at AAL who was not involved in the survey conducted by Jerry Laubenstein, the new vice-president of the insurance department. As a consequence, you know nothing about what is going on. This, of course, is typical. The managers have never spoken with the workers in the past, except to tell them what to do and when to do it. Because you are a gifted speaker and full of energy, the other workers elected you to be their representative and find out what is going on. Currently, you and the others (not in the survey group of 200) are not interested in changing. You have gotten used to things the way they are. You know what to do and you have established relationships with the workers around you. You have good social relationships with many of the workers during the weekends.

You are about to see Mr. Laubenstein, the new vice-president of the insurance department (he's your big boss). He wants to convince you to cooperate with him and go along with the changes he has decided on (with suggestions from the other 200 workers and the regional managers). You are not impressed with this person because he doesn't associate with the employees and doesn't seem to care about the workers. You are comfortable with your life now and are looking forward to retirement in 10 more years. You and your co-workers are not interested in changing, and you know that Jerry really needs to keep you around because good workers are impossible to find and because the other workers see you as their leader.

REDESIGN OR RELOCATION

During the past five years, productivity and worker satisfaction at the Jackson Toy Company have been declining. Productivity is now so low that Dr. Jackson, the company's founder and president, is seriously considering closing the plant and moving the business south. She wants, however, to retain the company.

When Dr. Jackson, a mechanical engineer, originally founded the toy company in 1965, she installed an assembly line so that workers could become specialized at their jobs and, hence, very productive. Although the employees were very productive during the first ten years of operation, several of the younger, newly hired employees began complaining about the repetitive, boring nature of the work. It was about that time that Dr. Jackson began to notice a decline in productivity. Her first response was to assume that pay was too low. Whereas many of the original employees were essentially second-income earners, the newly hired employees were sole-income earners. Since pay was only the minimum wage, Jackson assumed that the younger employees were moonlighting in order to earn more money. Then when they came to work, they were too tired to work efficiently. Consequently, she increased everyone's salary by 20 percent. Since there were 75 employees, this represented a substantial increase in payroll expense. Nevertheless, she was concerned about productivity as well as the "plight" of the workers.

About two months after the salary increase, Jackson noted that the level of productivity had not increased. In fact, productivity actually declined slightly. Disappointed, but resolved to do something, Jackson called the local university. Professor Brief, a specialist in job redesign, suggested that Dr. Jackson needed to redesign the jobs for the employees or implement a job rotation program. Although it would be more costly to redesign the jobs than to implement a rotation program, Professor Brief said that it would accomplish her objectives. Dr. Jackson, however, wondered if it would be more trouble than it's worth.

DISCUSSION QUESTIONS:

1. What is more motivating for the employees: intrinsic or extrinsic rewards?
2. On what basis does Professor Brief claim that job redesign would be worth it?
3. What would you recommend to Dr. Jackson?
4. Was Dr. Jackson's salary increase of 20 percent a valid way to test her assumption? What would you have done?

NOTES

1. C. Wiley, "Incentive Plan Pushes Production," *Personnel Journal* (Aug. 1993): 86–91.

2. "Employers' ADA Responses—Concerned But Waiting," *Fair Employment Practices* (July 30, 1992): 87.

3. "Allergic to Latex, *Bulletin to Management* (October 22, 1992): 331. Used by permission.

4. D. Machalaba, "United Parcel Service Gets Deliveries Done by Driving Its Workers," *The Wall Street Journal* (April 22, 1986): 1 and 23; A. Bernstein, "In the Line of Fire at the Teamsters," *Business Week* (August 30, 1993): 39.

5. Personal correspondence with Bob Kenney, UPS, Atlanta.

6. Y. Fried and G. R. Ferris, "The Dimensionality of Job Characteristics: Some Neglected Issues," *Journal of Applied Psychology* 71, no. 3 (Aug. 1988): 419–426; J. Thomas and R. Griffin, "The Social Information Processing Model of Task Design: A Review of the Literature," *Academy of Management Review* (Oct. 1983): 672–82; M. A. Campion and P. W. Thayer, "Development and Field Evaluation of an Interdisciplinary Measure of Job Design," *Journal of Applied Psychology* (Feb. 1985): 29–43.

7. J. Kerr, "The Best Small Companies to Work For in America," *INC.* (July 1993): 63.

8. *Ibid.*

9. S. P. Rubenstein, "Don't Fear Teams, Join Them," *New York Times* (June 11, 1989): 56.

10. "Ergonomics Training Eases Man-Machine Interface," *Management Review* (Oct. 1984): 55; "Ergonomic Makeover Produces Savings," *Bulletin to Management* (May 20, 1993): 160.

11. N. L. Breuer, "Resources Can Relieve ADA Fears," *Personnel Management* (Sept. 1993): 131–142.

12. P. Froiland, "Managing the Walking Wounded," *Training* (Aug. 1993): 39.

13. This discussion is adapted from E. F. Huse, *Management*, 2nd ed. (St.Paul: West, 1982): 383–404; E. Lawler III and J. Rhode, *Information and Control in Organizations* (Pacific Palisades, Calif.: Goodyear, 1976).

14. A. Maslow, *Motivation and Personality* (New York: Harper & Row, 1954); and D. McGregor, *The Human Side of Enterprise* (New York: McGraw-Hill, 1960).

15. Maslow, *Motivation and Personality*.

16. C. Alderfer, Existence, *Relatedness and Growth: Human Needs in Organizational Settings* (New York: Free Press, 1972); L. Waters and D. Roach, "A Factor Analysis of Need Fulfillment Items Designed to Measure Maslow Need Categories," *Personnel Psychology* 26 (Summer 1973): 185–190; and D. Hall and K. Nougaim, "An Examination of Maslow's Need Hierarchy in an Organizational Setting," *Organizational Behavior and Human Performance* 4 (February 1968): 12–35.

17. F. Herzberg, B. Mausner, and B. Snyderman, *The Motivation to Work* (New York: Wiley, 1959); and F. Herzberg, "One More Time: How Do You Motivate Employees?" *Harvard Business Review* 46 (Jan.–Feb. 1968): 53–62.

18. V. Vroom, *Work and Motivation* (New York: Wiley, 1964); and L. Porter and E. Lawler III, *Managerial Attitudes and Performance* (Homewood, Ill.: Dorsey Press, 1968).

19. S. J. Mahlin, "Peak-Time Pay for Part-Time Work," *Personnel Journal* (Nov. 1984): 60–65; S. R. Sacco, "Are In-House Temporaries Really an Option?" *Personnel Administrator* (May 1985): 20–24.

20. D. Kroll, "Telecommuting: A Revealing Peek Inside Some of the Industry's First Electronic Cottages," *Management Review* (Nov. 1984): 18–23.

21. "Drawbacks of Telecommuting," *Bulletin to Management* (May 20, 1993): 153; "Ask the Experts: Managing Telecommuters," *FEP Guidelines* (June 10, 1993): 8.

CHAPTER 6

JOB ANALYSIS

LEARNING OBJECTIVES

When you have finished studying this chapter, you should be able to:

1. Discuss the purposes and importance of doing job analysis.
2. Describe the ways to collect job analysis information.
3. Write job descriptions and job specifications.
4. List the reasons companies develop job families.

CHAPTER OUTLINE

"Managing Human Resources
SENIOR VICE-PRESIDENT, HUMAN RESOURCES"

JOB ANALYSIS
WHY IS JOB ANALYSIS IMPORTANT?
LEGAL CONSIDERATIONS
ASPECTS OF JOB ANALYSIS
TECHNIQUES IN JOB ANALYSIS

"Managing Human Resources at Aetna
MANAGERS MAKE PAY DECISIONS THROUGH JOB FAMILIES"

INTERNATIONAL COMPARISONS
CURRENT TRENDS
Career Management Exercise
Case: Decter Computer Corporation

MANAGING HUMAN RESOURCES

Senior Vice President, Human Resources

POSITION PROFILE

THIS position represents the personnel point of view in the strategic and operational direction of the business. The incumbent is expected to provide, with the support and concurrence of the President, a philosophy and guiding principles for managing the human resources of the company. Authority is limited to the protection of the company's interests in relation to laws and regulations pertaining to personnel. The position directly impacts all functions and areas of the company in matters of morale, management practices, employee well-being, compensation, benefits, structure, and development. The incumbent is expected to positively affect these matters through his/her personal influence and professional credibility rather than vested authority.

This position requires an incumbent with broad managerial and professional knowledge and experience. From the managerial standpoint, the Human Resources group comprises ten interrelated yet disparate functional areas: personnel relations, compensation, benefits, training, organization development, recruiting, personnel administration, field personnel services, communications and home office personnel services. The current staff consists of 75 people, including 42 professionals. The incumbent also has functional responsibility for personnel services to four distribution centers. Budget administration responsibilities approximate $29.7 million.

On the professional side, with the exception of the directors of compensation and staffing and of human resource development and the managers of benefits and of media projects, virtually all staff members have been developed inside the company. Technical and professional direction and training rest with the incumbent. The incumbent is expected to provide the company with systems, programs, and processes that effectively support business goals and organization values. The company's principal executives rely on the incumbent's personal experience, skills, and resources to bring the company to current "State-of-the-Art" status.

Critical competency requirements include preventive labor relations, personnel/labor law, compensation practices, benefit practices, training and organization development practices, and employee involvement processes. The company's widespread training needs are especially important at this time. The incumbent must have highly developed consulting and communication skills.

Although the incumbent is not expected to create or invent systems and programs, he/she is expected to introduce successful practices and adapt them to the company's particular needs. The incumbent must be able to judge when to act and when not to act with patience and persistence. He/she must be able and willing to modify actions to gain agreement and consensus. The incumbent must be able to place the priorities of the company over those of the personnel function. At the same time, the incumbent is expected to be a strong advocate for employee interests and well-being.

CANDIDATE QUALIFICATIONS

Broad experience is required in the following areas:

- Personnel/labor relations in both organized and unorganized situations, including union-free policies and practices, organizing campaigns, unfair labor practice charges, arbitrations, labor contract negotiation and administration
- Personnel policy formulation, communication, and administration
- Corporate culture change, including the facilitation of improved organizational effectiveness
- Human resource development with special emphasis on all facets of training but also including: organization planning, succession and manpower planning, performance standard/expectations, performance review, personal/management development, assessment of management potential, organization development, career pathing, and recruitment/selection process
- Compensation programs, including job evaluations, wage and salary plan design and administration, short- and long-term incentive plan

Continued on the next page

- design and administration, bonus and gain-sharing plans
- Benefit programs, including the design and administration of health care, dental, life and disability insurance and of defined benefit/contribution plans, vacation, sick pay, holiday, and other policies
- Corporate communications, using print, video and other media, including booklets, newspapers and other publication, institutional and informational videos and meetings of management personnel
- Participatory and responsive management, including use of employee and other involvement processes (PCs), project management/

task force/focus group techniques, attitude surveys, and bottom-up (suggestion, coffee hours, "Express Yourself," hotline, etc.) communications
- Human resource information systems, including the development and utilization of cost/time effective reports and analyses
- Departmental direction, management and administration, including staff selection, training/development and deployment; short- and long-term departmental planning, project management, program development and execution, delivery of human resource services, budget development and administration[1]

The preceding feature is, of course, an official job description that could have come from the personnel files of any number of organizations today. It gives an indication of just how complex and significant the job of a senior vice president of human resources can be. As noted in the description, this is a large HR department: 75 individuals in the HR staff and a budget of $29.7 million. The position profile, or what can also be called the job description, states that the position entails responsibility for all the HR activities to be discussed in this book. There is almost no HR activity that is unimportant for this position! The candidate qualifications, or job specifications, needed to adequately perform the duties in this position profile are thus rather extensive. How many years do you think it would take to acquire these qualifications? Perhaps 20–25 years? Probably, but maybe this is something to aim for if you want to have a significant position of HR responsibility and challenge someday! You might want to go back to your career planning activity in Chapter 4 and revise your goals accordingly!

Job descriptions and job specifications convey to others what is expected from a person in a job or position. They help in the recruitment and selection process too! How can recruitment and selection activities successfully occur without job descriptions that are well thought-out and that are approved by the company?

We take a detailed look at job analysis in this chapter. Along with the design of jobs, job analysis is an essential building block for all the other human resource management activities. As we proceed, you will see the various ways of performing job analysis and why it is so important.

JOB ANALYSIS

Job analysis *is the process of describing and recording aspects of jobs and specifying the skills and other requirements necessary to perform the job.* Typically described and recorded are the purposes of a job, its major duties or activities, and the conditions under which the job is performed. These three components form the essential parts of a **job description**. **Job specifications** are based on the job

Job analysis is the process of describing and recording aspects of jobs.

Job descriptions describe the purposes, duties, and conditions of a job.

188

PARTNERSHIP: WORKING TOGETHER IN JOB ANALYSIS

LINE MANAGERS	HR PROFESSIONALS	EMPLOYEES
Work with HR manager and employees to prepare job descriptions and job specifications.	Prepare job descriptions with line managers and employees. Train line managers and employees in job analysis.	May write job descriptions. Assist in the preparation of job specifications.

description. *They detail the skills, knowledge, and abilities that individuals need to perform a job.*[2] They may also detail the personality, interests, and preferences that best fit the job.

Job specifications indicate the skills, knowledge, and abilities needed to do the job.

WHY IS JOB ANALYSIS IMPORTANT?

Job analysis is the basis of job descriptions and specifications. It is necessary for legally validating the methods used in making employment decisions such as selection, promotion, and performance appraisal and also serves several other purposes; job analysis

LEARNING OBJECTIVE 1

Discuss the purposes and importance of doing job analysis.

- Aids the supervisor and employee in defining each employee's duties and related tasks
- Serves as a reference guide to move employees in the correct work-related direction
- Prescribes the importance and time requirements for a worker's effort
- Provides job applicants with realistic job information regarding duties, working conditions, and job requirements
- Identifies reporting relationships for supervisors and subordinates
- Guides change in work design and task management
- Determines a job's relative worth to maintain external and internal pay equity
- Ensures that companies do not violate the *Equal Pay Act of 1963*
- Provides selection information necessary to make employment decisions consistent with the *Civil Rights Act of 1964* and *1991*
- Serves as a basis for establishing career development programs and paths for employees
- Identifies worker redundancies during mergers, acquisitions, and downsizing
- Guides supervisors and incumbents in respectively writing references and preparing résumés for employees leaving and seeking new employment[3]

- Identifies essential job functions that can assist organizations in complying with the *Americans With Disabilities Act of 1990*

These purposes are attained in the process of job analysis that reflects several legal considerations.

LEGAL CONSIDERATIONS

Job analysis is faced with several legal constraints, largely because it serves as the basis for selection decisions, performance appraisals, compensation, and training determinations. These constraints have been articulated in the *1978 Uniform Guidelines on Employee Selection Procedures (Uniform Guidelines)* and several court decisions. For example, Section 14.C.2 of the *Uniform Guidelines* states that "there shall be a job analysis which includes an analysis of the important work behaviors required for successful performance." Any job analysis should thus focus on work behavior(s) and the tasks associated with them.[4]

Where job analysis has not been performed, the validity of selection decisions has been successfully challenged (*Kirkland v. New York Department of Correctional Services*, 1974; *Albemarle Paper Company v. Moody*, 1975). Numerous court decisions regarding job analysis and promotion and performance appraisal also exist. For example, in *Brito v. Zia Company* (1973), the court states that the performance appraisal system of an organization is a selection procedure and therefore must be validated—that is, it must be anchored in job analysis. And in *Rowe v. General Motors* (1972), the court ruled that to prevent discriminatory practices in promotion decisions, a company should have written objective standards for promotion. In *U.S. v. City of Chicago* (1978), the court stated that, in addition to having objective standards for promotion, the standards should describe the job to which the person is being considered for promotion. In both cases, these objective standards can be determined through job analysis.[5]

AMERICANS WITH DISABILITIES ACT OF 1990

The *Americans With Disabilities Act of 1990* (ADA) prohibits bias against qualified individuals with disabilities who can perform the "essential functions" of a job with or without reasonable accommodations. Although the ADA does not require written job descriptions, employers can conduct analyses to identify essential functions and formulate job descriptions to facilitate compliance with the law.

Written job descriptions may also provide evidence, although not conclusive, of the job's "essential functions" and serve as baselines for performance reviews. It is important, therefore, that written job descriptions be accurate and correspond to the current requirements of the job.

Accurate job descriptions should result when job analyses

- Specify minimum educational requirements and training
- Describe what is done
- Eliminate unneeded requirements
- Estimate time spent on each duty
- Determine minimum experiential qualifications
- Describe mental functions
- Outline physical functions
- Describe current manner of doing job
- Specify the required output level
- List environmental factors in the workplace
- Describe equipment used
- Build flexibility into the description
- Specify how the job is supervised[6]

DID YOU KNOW?

In the first case under ADA, a director of a security firm was awarded $572,000 after being fired when he was diagnosed with terminal brain cancer.

DID YOU KNOW?

ADA also requires merchants to accommodate disabled customers by making sure they can enter stores, navigate aisles, make purchases, and do it in an easy manner.

These tasks can be done properly only when all the aspects of job analysis are addressed.

ASPECTS OF JOB ANALYSIS

The renewed interest in job analysis has been spurred in part by organizational efforts to comply with the *Uniform Guidelines* and numerous court decisions, but it is also a result of the fact that job analysis serves so many purposes and has such an extensive set of relationships with other HR activities. As a consequence, organizations are now engaged in all aspects of job analysis, starting with collecting the information for it.

COLLECTING INFORMATION FOR THE ANALYSIS

As defined earlier, job analysis entails both the process of job description and job specification. The attributes of both the job and the person needed to perform the job vary greatly. Possible attributes are listed in Exhibit 6.1. Since the information gathered on these attributes must comply with the *Uniform Guidelines,* it is important to know who collects the information as well as how it is collected.

> **LEARNING OBJECTIVE 2**
>
> Describe the ways to collect job analysis information.

WHO COLLECTS THE INFORMATION?   Typically, someone in the HR department, backed up by a supervisor, collects the job information. The **incumbents**, or the persons performing the job, also provide information. Obtaining information from as many sources as possible leads to a greater understanding of the job's particular duties and the skills, knowledge, and abilities needed to perform those duties. Because of the legal considerations and the importance of careful job design (the result, after all, of this process) to the organization, the data collector should be trained and then allowed to practice the steps in gathering the information so that the data fulfills a number of important requirements. Not only must the information be accurate, detailed, and complete, it must also be collected in a manner that is in legal compliance and that has not "ruffled any feathers" of either the workers or the supervisors. *Remember, job analysis information is some of the most valuable HR information:*

Job analysis information is collected by:

- the HR department
- department supervisor
- job incumbent

> The data generated by job analyses have significant use in nearly every phase of human resource administration: designing jobs and reward systems, staffing and training, performance control and more. Few other processes executed by organizations have the *potential* for being such a powerful aid to management decision making.
>
>   But the word *potential* must be emphasized. The typical manner in which job analyses are conducted leaves much to be desired because the data tend to be incomplete, inaccurate, and inappropriate. Indeed, using job analysis information as it is commonly collected can create as many problems for an organization as it helps resolve.
>
>   One reason the analyses tend to be highly flawed is that the data are often gathered by novices or employees who lack appreciation and understanding of the final use of the facts. Too frequently management delegates the task to a new employee or to someone with little experience, assuming that the procedure is routine and elementary. In reality, data collection for job analyses requires practice and considerable human relations skills.[7]

COMMUNICATION ABOUT JOB ANALYSES.   The launching of a job analysis program can be unpopular. It is not only time-consuming, but also potentially threatening to incumbents who perceive that it can lead to changes in job responsibilities, compensation, and training. To defuse potential resentment and misunderstanding, the HR department needs to convey to all employees the pur-

Exhibit 6.1
Job Analysis Attributes

Job Description

Work Activities
Job-oriented activities (usually expressed in terms of what is accomplished;
sometimes indicating how, why, and when a worker performs the activity)
 Work activities/processes
 Procedures used
 Activity records (films, etc.)
 Personal accountability/responsibility
Worker-oriented activities
 Human behaviors performed in work (sensing, decision making, perform-
 ing physical actions, communicating, etc.)
 Elemental motions (such as those used in methods analysis)
Personal job demands (energy expenditures, etc.)
Machines, Tools, Equipment, and Work Aids Used
Job-Related Tangibles and Intangibles
Materials processed
Products made
Knowledge dealt with or applied (such as law or chemistry)
Services rendered (such as laundering or repairing)
Work Performance
Work measurement (time taken)
Work standards
Error analysis
Other aspects
Job context
Physical working conditions
Work schedule
Organizational context
Social context
Incentives (financial and nonfinancial)

Job Specifications

Personal Requirements
Job-related knowledge/skills (education, training, work experience, etc.)
Personal attributes (aptitudes, physical characteristics, personality, interests,
etc.)

Source: Adapted from E. J. McCormick, "Job and Task Analysis," in M. D. Dunnette, ed.,
Handbook of Industrial and Organizational Psychology, copyright © 1976 by Rand McNally
College Publishing Company, p. 653.

pose of the program, who will be involved, and exactly what will happen as a
result of the program. Involving the incumbent and supervisor increases the perceptions of procedural fairness and reduces resistance to change.

Methods of Gathering Information. Ways of gathering information
are as extensive as the number of possible attributes to be described. Methods of

> **EXHIBIT 6.2**
> **SAMPLE QUESTIONNAIRE (EXEMPT POSITIONS)**
>
> Instructions: This is a preliminary step in the preparation of a position description for your job. Complete the questionnaire carefully and give it to your immediate superior to review. He or she will then pass it on to the analyst responsible for your area. Use the back of the page if there is not sufficient space for your answers, but try to keep them as concise and relevant as possible.
>
> Your Name: _____ Date: _____
> Job Title: _____ Department: _____
> Immediate Superior: _____ His/Her Title: _____
>
> 1. How would you describe the primary purpose of your job? (i.e., why does it exist?)
> 2. What is the position immediately superior to yours?
> 3. List the titles of the jobs you supervise or direct and the number of incumbents in each. Briefly describe the nature of your supervisory activities.
> 4. What kind of supervision or direction do you receive (if any)? (e.g., to whom you report, from whom do you receive assignments)
> 5. What procedural controls are you subject to? (e.g., sales goals, budgets, cost standards)
> 6. What are the positions or departments with which you have close working relationships and frequent contacts? What is the nature of these contacts?
> 7. Describe your major job activities (include planning, scheduling, coordinating, etc.)
>
> SOURCE: *How to Analyze Jobs: A Step-by-Step Approach* (1982), 72–73. Reprinted by permission of the publisher, Bureau of Law & Business, Inc., 64 Wall Street, Madison, Conn. 06443. All rights reserved.

collecting information include (1) observation; (2) interviews with the job incumbents; (3) conferences with job analysts and experts; (4) observations by job analysts, (5) diaries kept by the job incumbents; (6) questionnaires (see Exhibit 6.2 for an example) filled out by the incumbents or observers such as the supervisor or job analyst; (7) critical incidents written by incumbents or others who know the jobs; and (8) mechanical devices such as stopwatches, counters, and films.

> Methods for collecting job analysis information include:
>
> - observations
> - interview (incumbent)
> - conference (with analyst/expert)
> - diaries
> - questionnaires
> - critical incidents
> - mechanical devices

JOB DESCRIPTIONS

Job descriptions and specifications are generated from the data gathered in job analysis. On the basis of job descriptions, performance appraisal forms can be developed and job classification systems established for job evaluation and compensation purposes. Because job specifications identify the education and training needed to perform a job, appropriate recruitment, selection, and training and development programs depend on this process. Typically, a single document is

> **LEARNING OBJECTIVE 3**
>
> Write job descriptions and job specifications.

Position description is a collection of
duties performed by a single person.

The *Dictionary of Occupational Titles*
(DOT) is a valuable source of job
analysis information.

Knowledge is the body of information
related to a job; *skill* or *ability* is a person's observable capability to perform
a job.

written to describe job duties and underlying tasks.[8] The final job analysis document should include:

- *Job Title* refers to a group of positions that are identical in regard to their
  significant duties. In contrast, a **position description** refers to a collection
  of duties performed by a single person. A company with 50 accounting
  assistants has 50 accounting positions but probably fewer than five dis-
  cernable job titles. Differentiating these terms as they apply to particular
  jobs can be deceptive because jobs in different departments or in different organizations can have the same title yet be quite different in their
  duties. Thus, to determine whether jobs are similar for purposes of pay or
  selection procedures, an analyst needs to focus on the degree of overlap
  in job duties rather than the similarity in job titles.
- *Department* or *division* where the job is located.
- *Date* when the job was analyzed. This will cue job analysts as to when the
  description should be updated.
- *DOT Code* is a standard job code published in the **Dictionary of
  Occupational Titles** by the Department of Labor. It provides some desirable but not essential information for validation reports pertaining to
  the job.
- *EEO-1/AAP Categories* are the reporting categories for annual equal
  employment opportunity reporting and affirmative action plans.
- *Job Summary* is an abstract of the job. It can be used for job posting,
  recruitment advertisements, and salary surveys.
- *Supervision Received and Given* identifies reporting relationships. If the job
  is supervised, the duties associated with the supervision should be detailed
  under work performed.
- *Work Performed* identifies the duties and underlying tasks that make up a
  job. A task is something that workers perform or an action they take to
  produce a product or service. Duties are a collection of tasks that recur
  and are not trivial. For maximum information use, duties should be prioritized in terms of the time spent as well as importance. A duty may take
  little time to complete but be critical to job success. Weighted duty statements that prioritize work for incumbents are useful in establishing performance standards and may be important in determining whether job
  accommodations for individuals protected under the *Rehabilitation Act* are
  reasonable. A weighted listing of job duties is also important to determine
  whether jobs are exempt from overtime provisions of the *Fair Labor
  Standards Act* and whether two jobs with different titles are similar in
  skill, effort, responsibility, and working conditions as provided under the
  Equal Pay Act.[9]
- *Job Requirements* (specifications) delineate the experience, education,
  training, licensure and specific knowledge, skills, and abilities needed to
  perform a job. **Knowledge** relates to a body of information in a particular
  subject area that, if applied, makes adequate performance of the job possible (for example, knowledge of Word Perfect or OSHA regulations).
  The terms **skill** and **ability** are often used interchangeably and relate to
  observable capabilities to perform a learned behavior (operate a drill
  press, for example).

  Job requirements should be limited to the **minimum qualifications** that
  a new employee can be expected to bring to the job. Minimum qualifications are likely to be the prime focal point for EEO investigations because
  of potential abuses and the potential for disparate impact are present. For

example, a high school diploma is unnecessary for the position of janitor, but the janitor may need basic reading skills to identify cleaning agents. Thus an appropriate requirement would be the ability to read labels and instructions—not a high school diploma. Similarly, an M.S. degree in social work may be an inappropriate qualification for the position of child-welfare worker if individuals without the degree have been shown to perform the job as well. An M.S. degree *may* be necessary, however, if required by state law.

Job requirements are also controversial when employers impose artificially high minimum standards to reduce the number of applicants to be processed, to justify high salaries, or to enhance the prestige of the job or organization. High minimums may result in disparate impact. Acceptable minimum qualifications should be the least necessary to do the job: if an incumbent has a college degree, yet the job requires only a high school diploma, only the high school diploma should be listed as required.

- *Job Context* deals with the environment in which the job is performed. For example, work may be conducted outdoors (construction worker), in close quarters (film editor), in remote areas (forest ranger), in high temperatures (chef), or low temperatures (meat cutter). The job may involve extensive standing (sales clerk), sitting (data entry clerk), exposure to fumes (fiberglass fabricator), noise (drill press operator), electrical shocks (electrician), exposure to diseases (laboratory technician), or stress (pension fund manager). Such details provide an understanding of the setting in which the job is conducted.

An important aspect not to be forgotten in creating job descriptions is the writing style. The *Handbook for Analyzing Jobs* suggests the following:

- A terse, direct style should be used.
- The present tense should be used throughout.
- Each sentence should begin with an active verb.
- Each sentence must reflect an objective, either specifically stated or implied in such a manner as to be obvious to the reader. A single verb may sometimes reflect both objective and worker action.
- All words should impart necessary information; any others should be omitted. Every precaution should be taken to use words that have only one possible connotation and specifically describe the manner in which the work is accomplished.
- The description of tasks should reflect the assigned work performed and, where possible, worker performance ratings.

Job descriptions should be written in a brief and active style.

Keep in mind that the job should be described in enough detail that the reader can understand (1) what is to be done (the domains, behaviors, results, and duties); (2) what products are to be generated (the job's purposes); (3) what work standards are applied (for example, quality and quantity); (4) under what conditions the job is performed; and (5) the job's design characteristics. Design characteristics are included so that individuals can select and be placed on jobs that match or suit their personalities, interests, and preferences and/or be physically accommodated to the job. Job design characteristics are described in Chapter 5.

Exhibit 6.3 is an example of a job description. It does not specifically provide information on performance standards or design characteristics. Performance standards are not typically specified in job descriptions because organizations prefer to retain flexibility and thus include them in the performance appraisal form.

EXHIBIT 6.3
POSITION DESCRIPTION (EXEMPT)

Functional Title: Corporate Loan Assistant   **Department:** Corporate Banking

Division:

Function Code: **Location:** Head Office

Incumbent: **Date:** June 1994

Note: Statements included in this description are intended to reflect in general the duties and responsibilities of this classification and are not to be interpreted as being all-inclusive.

Relationships

Reports to: Corporate Account Office A or AA; or Sr. Corporate Account Officer B or BB

Subordinate staff: None

Other internal contacts: Various levels of management within the Corporate Banking Department

External contacts: Major bank customers

Summary Statement

Assist in the administration of commercial accounts, to ensure maintenance of profitable Bank relationships.

Domains

A. Credit Analysis (Weekly)

Under the direction of a supervising loan officer: Analyze a customer company's history, industry position, present condition, accounting procedures, and debt requirements. Review credit reports, summarizing analysis and recommending course of action for potential borrowers; review and summarize performance of existing borrowers. Prepare and follow-up on credit communications and reports and Loan Agreement Compliance sheets.

B. Operations (Weekly)

Help customers with banking problems and needs. Give out customer credit information to valid inquirers. Analyze account profitability and compliance with balance arrangements; distribute to customer. Direct Corporate Loan Note Department in receiving and disbursing funds and in booking loans. Correct internal errors.

C. Loan Documentation (Weekly)

Develop required loan documentation. Help customer complete loan documents. Review loan documents immediately after a loan closing for completeness and accuracy.

D. Report/Information System (Weekly)

Prepare credit reports, describing and analyzing customer relationship and loan commitments; prepare for input into Information System. Monitor credit reports for accuracy.

E. Customer/Internal Relations (Weekly)

Build rapport with customers by becoming familiar with their products, facilities, and industry. Communicate with customers and other banks to obtain loan-related information and answer questions. Prepare reports on customer and prospect contacts and follow-up. Write memos on significant events affecting customers and prospects.

F. Assistance to Officers (Monthly)

Assist assigned officers by preparing credit support information, summa-

EXHIBIT 6.3 (CONT.)
POSITION DESCRIPTION (EXEMPT)

rizing customer relationship, and accompanying on calls or making independent calls. Monitor accounts and review and maintain credit files. Coordinate paper flow to banks participating in loans. Respond to customer questions or requests in absence of assigned officer.

G. Assistance to Division (Monthly)
Represent bank at industry activities. Follow industry/area developments. Help Division Manager plan division approach and prospect for new business. Interview loan assistant applicants. Provide divisional back-up in absence of assigned officer.

H. Knowledges and Skills (Any item with an asterisk will be taught on the job)
Oral communications skills, including listening and questioning. Intermediate accounting skills. Writing skills. Researching/reading skills to understand legal financial documents. Organizational/analytical skills. Social skills to represent the Bank and strengthen its image. Sales skills. Knowledge of Bank credit policy and services.* Skill to use Bank computer terminal.* Knowledge of bank-related legal terminology. Independent work skills. Work efficiently under pressure. Courtesy and tactfulness. Interfacing skills. Knowledge of basic business (corporate) finance. Skill to interpret economic/political issues.

I. Physical Characteristics
See to read fine print and numbers. Hear speaker twenty feet away. Speak to address a group of five. Mobility to tour customer facilities (may include climbing stairs). Use of hands and fingers to write, operate a calculator.

J. Other Characteristics
Driver's license. Willing to: work overtime and weekends occasionally; travel out of state every three months/locally weekly; attend activities after work hours; wear clean, neat businesslike attire.

SOURCE: Used by permission of Biddle and Associates.

TECHNIQUES OF JOB ANALYSIS

In this section we will discuss the most common techniques of job analysis. Motion studies focus on job efficiency. Task listings and inventories, the Position Analysis Questionnaire, and Job Element Inventory are structured questionnaires that can be computer analyzed. Three other methods (Functional Job Analysis, Critical Incident Technique, and Guidelines-Oriented Job Analysis) are designed to meet specific HR information needs. Finally, three methods (Hay Plan, Management Position Description Questionnaire, Supervisor Task Description Questionnaire), which focus specifically on managerial work, are examined.

There are several methods by which jobs can be analyzed.

METHODS ANALYSIS

Methods analysis focuses on analyzing **job elements**, the smallest identifiable component of a job. The need for methods analysis often comes from (1) changes in tools and equipment, (2) changes in product design, (3) changes

Methods analysis focuses on analyzing job elements, the smallest component of a job.

in materials, (4) modifications of equipment and procedures to accommodate handicapped workers, and (5) health and safety concerns.

While human resource managers have downplayed the importance of methods analysis in recent years, it is still widely used in manufacturing settings. In fact, the use of new technologies, collectively referred to as programmable automation, has increased the need for methods analysis. These new processes include computer-aided design (CAD), computer-aided manufacturing (CAM), computer-aided engineering (CAE), flexible manufacturing systems (FMS), group technology, robotics, and computer-integrated manufacturing (CIM).

These new manufacturing technologies can create shock waves in an organization because they require a quantum jump in precision and integration. Automated machine tools can produce parts to more exacting specifications than can the most skilled human machinist, but to do so they need explicit, unambiguous instructions in the form of computer programs.

The new hardware provides added freedom, but it also multiplies the ways to succeed or fail. It therefore requires new skills on the part of managers—for example, *an integrative imagination* and *a passion for detail*. To prevent process contamination, for example, it is no longer possible to rely on people who have a "feel" for their machines, or to merely note on a blueprint that operators should "remove iron filings from the part." When using the new automated machine tools, everything must be stated with mathematical precision: "where is the blower is that removes the filings, and what's the orientation of the part during operation of the blower?"[10]

Thus it is increasingly important to study and document work processes. A variety of techniques is available for conducting methods analysis.

FLOW PROCESS CHARTS. These are used to examine the overall sequence of an operation by focusing on either the movement of an operator or the flow of materials. For example, flow charts have been used in hospitals to track patient movements, in grocery stores to analyze the checkout process, in small-batch manufacturing facilities to track material flows from machine to machine, in banks to examine the sequence associated with document processing, and in supervisor-incumbent interactions during performance appraisal interviews.

WORKER-MACHINE CHARTS. These are useful for envisioning the segments of a work cycle in which equipment and operator are busy or idle. The analyst can easily see when the operator and machine are working jointly or independently. One use of this type of chart is to determine how many machines or how much equipment an operator can manage. A team process chart is an extension of worker-machine charts. Rather than focusing on the operations of a single operator and machine, this chart simultaneously plots the worker-machine interfaces for a team of workers. Such charts are particularly useful for identifying equipment utilization as well as for pinpointing bottlenecks in interdependent tasks.

TIME AND MOTION STUDY. Also called motion study, this technique has its origins in industrial engineering and the work of Frederick W. Taylor and Frank and Lillian Gilbreth. In essence, **work measurement** determines times for all units of work activity in a given task or job. Combining these times gives a standard time for the entire job. **Observed time** is simply the average of recorded times. **Normal time** is the observed time adjusted for worker performance. This is accomplished by determining a performance rating for observed performance. The performance rating is an estimation of the difference between the normal rate at which a worker can be expected to perform and the observed rate. The adjustment is necessary because workers may deliberately slow down or speed up

Because of the advanced technologies, used by such companies as Saturn, Nissan, Corning, Eaton, and Honda, industrial engineers play an important role in job design and methods analysis.

DID YOU KNOW?

Taylor's ideas took root in our nation's factories and are still alive and well today in both factories and offices.

Time and motion study measures times for units of work.

the processes when observed. For instance, a performance rating of 1.20 indicates that an observed pace is much faster than normal. By comparison, a performance rating of 0.80 assumes that observed performance is slower than normal (a possible occurrence if the job is being studied to set rates of pay).

Standard time is the normal time adjusted for routine work interruptions. These delays may include personal delays (getting a drink of water, going to the washroom) as well as variable allowances specific to the job (mental or physical effort, lighting, atmospheric conditions, monotony, and detail). Industrial engineers have developed tables listing the allowances for different work delays.

These standard times can be used as a basis for wage incentive plans (incentives are generally given for work performance that takes less than the standard time), cost determination, cost estimates for new products, and balancing production lines and work crews.[11] Establishing standard times is a challenge of some consequence since the time it takes to do a job can be influenced as much by the individual doing the job as by the nature of the job itself. Consequently, determining standard times often requires measurement of the "actual effort" the individual is exerting and the "real effort" required. This process may involve trying to outguess someone else.

Work sampling is not only a technique for determining standard times, but also a form of methods analysis. **Work sampling** is the process of taking instantaneous samples of the work activities of individuals or group of individuals.[12] The activities are timed and classified into predetermined categories. The result is an activity description by classification and the percentage of time required.

Work sampling can be done in several ways: (1) the job analyst can observe the incumbent at predetermined times; (2) a camera can be set to take photographs at predetermined times; or (3) at a given signal, all incumbents can record their activity at that moment.

Work sampling was utilized in a recent study to examine the differences between successful managers and effective managers. **Successful managers** are those who move up formal hierarchies quickly, while **effective managers** are those who have achieved high levels of quality and quantity of work performance and satisfaction. Managers in general were found to spend their time in the following activities: traditional management (32 percent), routine communication (29 percent), human resource management (20 percent), and networking (19 percent). Successful managers spent more time on networking activities and less on HR management activities than did effective managers. The latter spent additional time on routine communication and management.[13]

STRUCTURED QUESTIONNAIRES

In addition to the various methods analyses used for gathering data for job analysis, any of several paper-and-pencil questionnaire methods may also be used.

TASK INVENTORIES. In contrast to the multiple methods used in work sampling to gather data, the task inventories method of job analysis is based solely on a structured questionnaire. As such, **task inventories** are a listing of tasks for the job being analyzed, with a provision for some type of response scale for each task. The incumbent, supervisor, or analyst performs the job analysis by checking the appropriate responses.

Suppose an analyst wanted to study three tasks of a specific secretarial job using a task inventory. Part of the questionnaire might look like Exhibit 6.4. Because the development of task inventories requires large samples of employees and complex statistical analysis, their use is usually limited to organizations that employ many people in the same occupation (police, fire fighter, data entry). As a consequence, the use of task inventories is fairly widespread in city and state

As conditions change, jobs have to be reanalyzed.

Work sampling is the process of taking samples from work activities to measure and analyze them.

Successful managers climb the hierarchy fast, and *effective managers* are great performers.

Task inventories are a job analysis method done by questionnaire.

EXHIBIT 6.4
SAMPLE OF A TASK INVENTORY QUESTIONNAIRE

	IS TASK DONE?	IMPORTANCE	TIME SPENT
	1. Yes	1. Extremely unimportant	1. Very much below average
	2. No	2. Very unimportant	2. Below average
		3. Unimportant	3. Slightly below average
		4. About medium importance	4. About average
		5. Important	5. Slightly above average
		6. Very important	6. Above average
		7. Extremely important	7. Very much above average
Prioritize typing requirements	①②	①②③④⑤⑥⑦	①②③④⑤⑥⑦
Type address labels	①②	①②③④⑤⑥⑦	①②③④⑤⑥⑦
Type business correspondence	①②	①②③④⑤⑥⑦	①②③④⑤⑥⑦

governments and the military, which typically have many people performing the same job.[14]

POSITION ANALYSIS QUESTIONNAIRE (PAQ). This is a structured questionnaire used for research purposes that contains 187 job elements and 7 additional items relating to amount of pay. The **Position Analysis Questionnaire (PAQ)** is organized into six divisions; each division contains some of the job elements. The divisions and a sample of elements include the following:

1. *Information input:* Where and how does the worker get the information used in performing the job? Examples are the use of written materials and near-visual differentiation.
2. *Mental processes (information processing activities):* What reasoning, decision-making, planning, and information-processing activities are involved in performing the job? Examples are the level of reasoning in problem solving and coding/decoding (see in Exhibit 6.5).
3. *Work output:* What physical activities does the worker perform, and what tools or devices are used? Examples are the use of keyboard devices and assembling/disassembling.
4. *Relationships with other people:* What relationships with other people are required in performing the job? Examples are instructing and contacts with the public or with customers.

The PAQ is a structured questionnaire.

EXHIBIT 6.5
SAMPLE PAQ ITEM MENTAL PROCESSES

INFORMATION PROCESSING ACTIVITIES

In this section are various human operations involving the "processing" of information or data. Rate each of the following items in terms of how *important* the activity is to the completion of the job.

CODE	IMPORTANCE TO THIS JOB (l)
N	Does not apply
1	Very minor
2	Low
3	Average
4	High
5	Extreme

39. l_____ Combining information (*combining*, synthesizing, or integrating information or data from two or more sources to establish new facts, hypotheses, theories, or a more complete body of *related* information, for example, an economist using information from various sources to predict future economic conditions, a pilot flying aircraft, a judge trying a case, etc.)

40. l_____ Analyzing information or data (for the purpose of identifying *underlying* principles or facts by *breaking down* information into component parts, for example, interpreting financial reports, diagnosing mechanical disorders or medical symptoms, etc.)

41. l_____ Compiling (gathering, grouping, classifying, or in some other way arranging information or data in some meaningful order or form, for example, preparing reports of various kinds, filing correspondence on the basis of content, selecting particular data to be gathered, etc.)

42. l_____ Coding/decoding (coding information or converting coded information back to its original form, for example, "reading" Morse code, translating foreign languages, or using other coding systems such as shorthand, mathematical symbols, computer languages, drafting symbols, replacement part numbers, etc.)

43. l_____ Transcribing (copying or posting data of information for later use, for example, copying meter readings in a record book, entering transactions in a ledger, etc.)

44. l_____ Other information processing activities (specify) _____

SOURCE: E. J. McCormick, P. R. Jeanneret, and R. C. Mecham, *Position Analysis Questionnaire*, Occupational Research Center, Dept. of Psychological Sciences, Purdue University, West Lafayette, IN 47907. Copyright 1969 by Purdue Research Foundation.

5. *Job context:* In what physical or social contexts is the work performed? Examples are high temperature and interpersonal conflict situations.

6. *Other job characteristics:* What other activities, conditions, or characteristics are relevant to the job?[15]

Each job element is also rated on one of six rating scales: (1) extent of use, (2) importance of the job, (3) amount of time, (4) possibility of occurrence, (5) applicability, and (6) other.

Using these job elements and rating scales, the nature of the job is essentially determined in terms of communication, decision making and social responsibilities, performance of skilled activities, physical activity and related environmental conditions, operation of vehicles and equipment, and processing of information. With these six dimensions determined, jobs with similar specifications can be compared and placed into families.

While task inventories limit comparisons of jobs within occupations, the PAQ is more general and can be applied to a variety of jobs and organizations without modification. Responses to the items are computer analyzed to produce a job profile that indicates how a particular job compares with other jobs in regard to the six job elements detailed above. The PAQ data base also contains information about the relationship between PAQ responses, job aptitudes, and labor market pay rates. These scores can then be used to set qualification or compensation levels for jobs. Thus, the PAQ is a potential selection and job evaluation tool as well as a job analysis tool.

Using the PAQ to set qualification levels is less subjective than a supervisor's opinion. However, there is no direct evidence that obtaining a given test score makes an applicant more likely to perform well on the job. Care is also needed in using the PAQ to set compensation rates since the worth of jobs is not determined independently of the labor market. Thus, jobs highly valued by an organization but less valued in a labor market would be paid the lower market rate. Another concern with the PAQ is that it must be bought from a consulting firm. Consequently, direct costs appear to be high. Finally, it requires a postcollege reading comprehension level to respond to the items. Thus, the PAQ is not well suited to job analysis situations in which job incumbents or supervisors serve as raters.[16]

Job Element Inventory is a more basic form of a structured questionnaire.

JOB ELEMENT INVENTORY. Closely modeled after the PAQ, the 153-item **Job Element Inventory** has a readability index estimated to be at the tenth grade level and is explicitly designed for completion by incumbents. The dimensional structure of the Job Element Inventory is similar to that of the PAQ. The advantage of this instrument lies in the cost savings associated with the fact that incumbents rather than trained analysts can complete the instrument.[17]

Functional Job Analysis of the federal government describes job concerns about people, data, and things.

FUNCTIONAL JOB ANALYSIS. The U.S. Training and Employment Service developed functional job analysis to describe concerns (people, data, and things) and to develop job summaries, job descriptions, and employee specifications. **Functional Job Analysis** was designed to improve job placement and counseling for workers registering at local state employment offices.[18]

The Functional Job Analysis is both a conceptual system for defining worker activities and a method of measuring activity levels. Its fundamental premises are as follows:

- A fundamental distinction must be made between what gets done and what workers do to get things done. Bus drivers do not carry passengers; they drive vehicles and collect fares.
- Jobs are concerned with data, people, and things.
- In relation to things, workers draw on physical resources; in relation to data, on mental resources; and in relation to people, on interpersonal resources.
- All jobs require workers to relate to data, people, and things to some degree.
- Although workers' behavior or the tasks they perform can apparently be described in an infinite number of ways, only a few definitive functions are involved. Thus, in interacting with machines, workers feed, tend, operate, and set up; in the case of vehicles, functions vary in difficulty and content. Each behavior draws on a relatively narrow and specific range of worker characteristics and qualifications for effective performance.
- The functions appropriate to dealing with data, people, or things are hierarchical and ordinal, proceeding from the complex to the simple. Thus, to indicate that a particular function—say, compiling data—reflects the job requirements is to say that it also includes lower-function requirements, such as comparing, and excludes higher-function requirements, such as analyzing.[19]

Exhibit 6.6 lists the worker functions associated with data, people, and things. These worker functions have been used as a basis for describing over 30,000 job

---

EXHIBIT 6.6

FUNCTIONS ASSOCIATED WITH DATA, PEOPLE, AND THINGS

DATA	PEOPLE	THINGS
0 synthesizing	0 mentoring	0 setting up
1 coordinating	1 negotiating	1 precision working
2 analyzing	2 instructing	2 operating/controlling
3 compiling	3 supervising	3 driving/operating
4 computing	4 diverting	4 manipulating
5 copying	5 persuading	5 tending
6 comparing	6 speaking/signaling	6 feeding/offbearing
	7 serving	7 handling
	8 taking instructions/helping	

SOURCE: U.S. Department of Labor, *Dictionary of Occupational Titles*, 4th ed. (Washington, D.C.: Government Printing Office, 1977): xviii.

---

titles in the *Dictionary of Occupational Titles* (DOT) and for creating job families (groupings of jobs) based on similar data, people, and things.

It even provides a simple job description for most job titles. Thus, the human resource manager who has to prepare job descriptions and specifications might start with the *Dictionary of Occupational Titles* to determine general job analysis information. See, for example, the DOT descriptions in Exhibit 6.7 for three jobs in the HR department.

USE OF THE DOT. In Exhibit 6.7, the identification code for Manager, Personnel (166.117-018), can be used to give a brief description of how the DOT is used. The first three digits (166) indicate the occupational code, title, and industry designations. The next three digits (117) represent the degree to which a personnel manager *typically* has responsibility and judgment over *data*, *people*, and *things*. The final three digits (018) are used to indicate the alphabetical order of titles within the occupational group having the same degree of responsibility and judgment.

The DOT can be very helpful to those companies just starting up or to existing companies expanding and creating jobs they have never had before. Because each company is different, the DOT is usually a starting point—the descriptions often need to be reworded and revised for specific conditions.

CRITICAL INCIDENTS TECHNIQUE. A frequently used technique for developing behavioral criteria is the **Critical Incidents Technique.** This technique requires that those knowledgeable about a job describe it to a job analyst. What they describe are called the critical job incidents (that is, those incidents observed over the past six to twelve months that represent effective and ineffective performance). Sometimes the job analyst needs to prompt the person describing the incidents by asking them to write down key things the incumbent must be good at or to identify the most effective job incumbent and then describe that person's behaviors.[20]

Those describing the incidents are also asked to describe what led up to the incidents, what the consequences of the behavior were, and whether the behavior was under the incumbent's control. After the critical incidents (often several hundred for each job) have been gathered and described, they are rated by

Critical Incidents Technique develops a list of effective and ineffective job performance behaviors.

EXHIBIT 6.7
DOT DESCRIPTIONS FOR THREE HUMAN RESOURCE JOBS

166.117-018 MANAGER, PERSONNEL (profess. & kin.) alternate titles: manager, human resources

Plans and carries out policies relating to all phases of personnel activity: Recruits, interviews, and selects employees to fill vacant positions. Plans and conducts new employee orientation to foster positive attitude toward company goals. Keeps record of insurance coverage, pension plan, and personnel transactions, such as hires, promotions, transfers, and terminations. Investigates accidents and prepares reports for insurance carrier. Conducts wage survey within labor market to determine competitive wage rate. Prepares budget of personnel operations. Meets with shop stewards and supervisors to resolve grievances. Writes separation notices for employees separating with cause and conducts exit interviews to determine reasons behind separations. Prepares reports and recommends procedures to reduce absenteeism and turnover. Represents company at personnel-related hearings and investigations. Contracts with outside suppliers to provide employee services, such as canteen, transportation, or relocation service. May prepare budget of personnel operations, using computer terminal. May administer manual and dexterity tests to applicants. May supervise clerical workers. May keep records of hired employee characteristics for governmental reporting purposes. May negotiate collective bargaining agreement with business representative, labor union.

166.167-018 MANAGER, BENEFITS (profess. & kin.) alternate titles: manager, employee benefits; manager, employee services; manager, personnel services; personnel administrator

Manages employee benefits program for organization: Plans and directs implementation and administration of benefits programs designed to insure employees against loss of income due to illness, injury, layoff, or retirement. Directs preparation and distribution of written and verbal information to inform employees of benefits programs, such as insurance and pension plans, paid time off, bonus pay, and special employer sponsored activities. Analyzes existing benefits policies of organization, and prevailing practices among similar organizations, to establish competitive benefits programs. Evaluates services, coverage, and options available through insurance and investment companies, to determine programs best meeting needs of organization. Plans modification of existing benefits programs, utilizing knowledge of laws concerning employee insurance coverage, and agreements with labor unions, to ensure compliance with legal requirements. Recommends benefits plan changes to management. Notifies employees and labor union representatives of changes in benefits programs. Directs performance of clerical functions, such as updating records and processing insurance claims. May interview, select, hire, and train employees.

166.267-018 JOB ANALYST (profess. & kin.) alternate titles: personnel analyst

Collects, analyzes, and prepares occupational information to facilitate personnel, administration, and management functions of organization: Consults with management to determine type, scope, and purpose of study. Studies current organizational occupational data and compiles distribution reports, organization and flow charts, and other background information required for frequency of occurrence, importance, and the extent of ability required to perform them. The critical incidents and their characteristics can be clustered into job dimensions. These dimensions, which may often use only a subset of all the critical incidents obtained, can then be used to describe the job.

They can also be used to develop performance appraisal forms, particularly Behavioral Anchored Rating Scales and Behavioral Observation Scales (described in Chapter 9). Additionally, critical incidents can be used to develop job-specific situational questions for selection purposes (described in Chapter 8).

As with this technique and those that follow, the major disadvantages are the time required to gather the incidents and the difficulty of identifying average performance. The latter disadvantage, however, can be overcome by obtaining examples of multiple levels of performance.

GUIDELINES-ORIENTED JOB ANALYSIS. This was developed in response to the *Uniform Guidelines*—hence its name. The steps in the **Guidelines-Oriented Job Analysis** each involve the job incumbents. Before any of these steps begin, the incumbents indicate their names, length of time on the job, experience, and the location of the current job.

In the first step, incumbents list their **job domain**, which is a category with related duties. Related duties in a job often fall into broad categories. For example, a secretary may type letters, contracts, and memos. Since these duties are related, they are put into the same domain—in this instance, typing. Jobs typically have several domains.

Second, after the domains are identified, the incumbents list the critical duties typically performed in each domain. **Duties** are observable work behaviors and something that incumbents are expected to perform. Often each domain contains several duties. Third, once the critical duties are identified, the incumbents indicate how frequently the duties are performed. Then each duty's degree of importance is determined. The fourth step is the incumbents' determination of the skills and knowledge required to perform each duty. Only those skills and knowledge that cannot be learned or acquired in eight hours or less are included. This is consistent with the *Uniform Guidelines*. Failure to select an applicant who could have learned the necessary skills in less than eight hours is not a defensible (job-related) practice.

Guidelines-oriented job analysis is an approach to job analysis based upon the *Uniform Guidelines*.

Job domain is a category of related duties.

Duties are observable work behaviors to be performed as part of the job.

The fifth step is determining the physical characteristics that incumbents need to perform their job duties. Here the incumbents respond to five open-ended statements, each related to a physical characteristic.

The results of these steps are a job description, similar to the one in Exhibit 6.3 for the Corporate Loan Assistant; a set of individual skills, knowledge, and abilities needed to perform the job; and a basis for developing job-related selection procedures and performance appraisal forms.

Both the Critical Incidents Technique and the Guideline-Oriented Job Analysis, because they focus on behaviors, are useful for developing performance appraisal forms and spotting training needs. In addition, since skills (physical and mental) and knowledge are identified, selection procedures can also be developed, as described in Chapter 8. Both techniques also enhance employee understanding and validity of job analysis since job incumbents are involved in the process. This involvement, however, takes time.[21]

MANAGERIAL JOBS

There are a number of special concerns in the analysis of managerial jobs. One is that managers adjust job duties to fit their work style rather than adjust their work style to fit the job. Another concern is that it is difficult to identify what a manager does over time because activities vary from hour to hour or day to day. As immediate situations or exceptions arise, the content of a manager's job changes. Despite these complications, several methods have been developed to analyze managerial jobs.

Methods to analyze managerial jobs include:

- **Managerial Position Description Questionnaire**
- **Supervisor Task Description Questionnaire**
- **Hay Plan**

MANAGEMENT POSITION DESCRIPTION QUESTIONNAIRE. Although the Functional Job Analysis approach is thorough, using it well requires considerable training, and its nature is quite narrative. The narrative portions tend to be less reliable than more quantitative techniques such as the **Management Position Description Questionnaire.**[22] This questionnaire relies on the checklist method to analyze jobs. It contains 197 items related to managers' concerns, responsibilities, demands, restrictions, and miscellaneous characteristics. The items have been condensed into the following thirteen job factors:

- Product, market, and financial planning
- Coordination of other organizational units and personnel
- Internal business control
- Products and services responsibility
- Public and customer relations
- Advanced consulting
- Autonomous consulting
- Approval of financial commitments
- Staff service
- Supervision
- Complexity and stress
- Advanced financial responsibility
- Broad human resource responsibility

Responses to the items vary by managerial level in any organization and also in different organizations. It is appropriate for determining the training needs of employees moving into managerial jobs, evaluating managerial jobs, creating job families and placing new managerial jobs into the right job family, compensating managerial jobs, and developing selection procedures and performance appraisal forms.

SUPERVISOR TASK DESCRIPTION QUESTIONNAIRE. While the Management Position Description Questionnaire can be used to describe, compare, classify, and evaluate management jobs at all levels, the **Supervisor Task Description Questionnaire** is limited to the work of first-line supervisors. The questionnaire describes 100 work activities of first-line supervisors in these areas:

- Working with subordinates
- Planning subordinates' work
- Maintaining efficient production and quality
- Maintaining safe and clean work areas
- Maintaining equipment and machinery
- Compiling records and reports

A study of more than 250 first-line supervisors in 40 plants showed that job responsibilities are universal regardless of technology or product type.[23]

THE HAY PLAN. Another method for analyzing managerial jobs is the **Hay Plan**, which is used by a large number of organizations. Although less structured than the two previous questionnaires, it is systematically tied into a job evaluation and compensation system. Thus use of the Hay Plan allows an organization to maintain consistency not only in how it describes managerial jobs, but also in how it rewards them. The Hay Plan is intended to develop, place, and recruit management; evaluate jobs; measure the execution of a job against specific standards of accountability; and analyze the organization. The information gathered relates to four aspects of the incumbent's job: objectives, dimensions, nature and scope of the position, and accountability objectives.

Because the Hay Plan is based on information gathered in an interview, the plan's success depends on the interviewer's skills. Interviewers can be trained, however, enabling the information to be used for job descriptions, job evaluation, and compensation. The Hay Plan results from one organization can be compared with those from other organizations to ensure external pay comparability. This plan is discussed further in Chapter 11.

✳ DEVELOPMENT OF JOB FAMILIES

The initial results of job analyses are typically many separate and unique job descriptions and employee specifications—as many descriptions as there are jobs. Often, however, these jobs are not greatly different from each other. That is, employees who perform one job can most likely easily perform several others. Those jobs are also likely to be of similar value to the organization. This is why organizations group jobs into **job families** or classes. Jobs are placed in the same family to the extent that they require similar job specifications or have similar tasks and are of similar value to the organization (as determined by a job evaluation study as described in Chapter 11).[24]

There is no one best way to construct job families. A recently developed method is through the job competency framework, which is based on identifying the **competencies** (knowledge, skills, abilities, attitudes, and personality) that individuals need to perform jobs such as the Senior Vice President, Human Resources at the beginning of this chapter. Jobs requiring similar competencies for excellent performance can be grouped into the same job family. The methods of job analysis described in this chapter can also be used to construct families. The use of job families gives companies a lot more flexibility in dealing with changes in job conditions and even in making pay decisions. An excellent description of this is in the feature, "Managing Human Resources at Aetna: Managers Make Pay Decisions Through Job Families."

DID YOU KNOW?

At the plants of the Eaton Corporation, many of these supervisory activities are now done by the workers? This results from their empowerment and total quality management philosophies.

LEARNING OBJECTIVE 4

Know the reasons companies develop job families.

Job families are groups of related jobs.

Competencies are more than knowledge, skills, and abilities.

DID YOU KNOW?

Key competencies for entrepreneurs include:

- achievement orientation
- moderate risk taking
- information seeking
- confidence
- proactivity
- stamina

MANAGING HUMAN RESOURCES
at Aetna

Managers Make Pay Decisions Through Job Families

LIKE many large companies, Aetna Life and Casualty Co. in Hartford, Connecticut, always has relied on a highly stratified job-classification system. Everything is connected to job class, from salary levels and promotional opportunities to job descriptions and supervisory responsibility. "You know your job class, you know everything," explains Mary Fitzer, Aetna's director of base-salary development.

But this system no longer is working. As a diversified financial services company, Aetna operates in a fast-moving and increasingly competitive environment. The existing job-classification and compensation system, however, doesn't encourage employees to work any harder or respond any faster to market changes. Why not? Because if a task isn't written into a job description, what incentive is there for an employee to take on added responsibility?

"There's too much work to be done to spend our time continually rewriting 7,000 detailed job descriptions," explains Fitzer. "We need to look at work in a much broader sense."

For this reason, Aetna is in the process of identifying the major skills and competencies that are needed by employees and grouping those skills into a broad job-family structure. "The entire point is to define work, not by what class it's in, but by the actual functions performed," Fitzer says. "Then, we will look at how the market prices that work, give that information to managers, and let them make pay decisions based on an individual's performance." When Aetna completes this process, the company expects to have just 200 job families representing all of the company's 42,000 employees.

Managers always have made the pay decisions at Aetna, but through this new structure, the compensation department will be able to provide them with more specific information about what the market is paying for certain jobs. "Instead of saying to them, 'Here's a salary minimum and maximum and you shouldn't pay above or below that,'" says Fitzer, "we'll be able to give them some market guidelines that they can interpret in light of their own budgets and performance levels." This effort in turn will force managers to clearly define employee performance expectations at the start of each business cycle.

With fewer promotional levels, the primary way for employees to get ahead at Aetna will be to earn bonuses by performing better. The company isn't eliminating promotions altogether—there will still be layers, such as entry-level underwriter, underwriter, senior underwriter, and underwriting manager, for example—but compensation decisions will be based on performance and market pricing, not job title.

Aetna realizes that not all employees will do well under the new system. Fitzer explains, "If employees have high security needs and are focusing on the old ways of doing things, it will be difficult for them in the new environment."

Not only will the job-family structure change the ways in which employees are evaluated and managers set salaries, but it also will change the relationship between the HR department and line managers.

"With the job families, we're trying to get rid of all the extraneous details and allow managers and their employees to do what is needed to serve their customers extremely well," says Fitzer.[25]

INTERNATIONAL COMPARISONS

Not all countries practice job analysis in precisely the same manner described in this chapter. In more than 40 countries, including Korea, Japan, Germany, England, Australia, and the former Soviet Union, a type of time and motion study called MODAPTS is utilized to assess the elements that make up manufacturing, government, banking, and dental jobs. Little known in the United States, MODAPTS is fundamentally simple. It is based on the assumption that the time taken for any body movement can be expressed in terms of a multiple of the time taken for a simple finger move. The time for a finger move is called a MOD (set at 129 milliseconds). The code of a MODAPTS move consists of a mnemonic character (G = Grasp) and a number, which is the MOD value of that movement. Thus, a hand move becomes M2 (0.129 second × 2).

The MODAPTS system answers four questions:

- What is a reasonable time for a "normal" (nondisabled for the task) person to carry out a defined task?
- What is a reasonable output for a "normal" person in a given time period?
- What are the relative efficiencies of two or more ways of performing the task?
- When a particular person takes longer than "normal" to perform a specific task, what is the degree of deficiency?

An advantage of MODAPTS is that a series of 21 "workability" tests have been developed to assess the functional capabilities of workers against the performance standard of a "nondisabled" individual. The results of the test can be used to place people on tasks that maximize their strengths, to train workers in areas of identified deficiencies, to redesign jobs to minimize worker deficiencies, and to determine if a performance loss is due to injury or handicap.

GERMANY

In Germany, workers perform in "work islands" where they avoid boredom by rotating jobs, socializing, and working in cycles of up to 20 minutes rather than a few seconds. In assembling electronics products, automobiles, and appliances, the Germans appear to be well ahead of other countries in modifying or reducing the conventional assembly line and its simple, repetitive jobs. This enlightened position in alternative job design is a product of the work humanization movement in Germany, initially funded by the German government in 1974 and maintained by the cooperative relationship between labor and management. Many companies also furnish their own funds for work design innovation projects.

Although each company's project may result in different types of job design, emphasis is commonly placed on enlarging assembly jobs by adding more complex tasks. One goal is to ensure that the job cycle is more than 1.5 minutes, the point below which employees have been found to become dissatisfied with the job. As a consequence of the experiments in various companies, three major ways are being used to modify the traditional assembly line and its jobs. In group assembly, workers rotate jobs as they follow the product from the first to the last step in the assembly process. This is the notion of the work island, where workers have the opportunity to socialize and are tied together by a group incentive pay plan. With individual work stations, work is done by the individual in a cycle time of ten to fifteen minutes. During this time, the worker assembles a major subcomponent of the total product (for example, an electric motor for a washing machine). Finally, assembly lines are being modified to make work easier and lighter. Where the assembly line cannot be easily replaced, as in automotive assembly, the line has been altered so that the worker stands on platforms moving at the same speed as the car.

Putting job descriptions on each *job* enables organizations to move workers from job to job more easily.

Broadbanding clusters jobs in broad tiers.

CURRENT TRENDS

JOB ANALYSIS AND EMPLOYEE FLEXIBILITY

Today's environment requires that organizations be adaptable and that individuals be flexible. At the same time, organizations also need highly repetitive and reliable behavior on jobs to produce and deliver high-quality goods and services, and individuals typically need to know what's expected and to have some degree of certainty and predictability in their life—that is they need a comfort level.

Job analysis methods were developed in a time when everything was more stable and predictable. People could be hired to do a particular job. This arrangement was convenient for management and workers, except when management wanted the workers to change or do something "not in their job descriptions."

Today, organizations focus on how they can get flexibility without worker resistance, yet at the same time satisfy workers' needs for comfort. Organizations such as Nissan Motor Manufacturing and Honda hire applicants to work for the company rather than to do a specific job. These companies, of course, have specific jobs: *consequently, it is the job rather than the individual that gets the job description.* As the worker moves form job to job, the description stays with the job. In this way, the worker knows what is expected, and management gets not only flexibility to move workers around as needed, but also high-quality performance.

Increased employee flexibility is also coming about through the growing use of skill-based pay, which is described in Chapter 11, and broadbanding. **Broadbanding**, or the clustering of jobs (even job families) into wide tiers for the purposes of managing employee career growth and administering pay, has become an attractive alternative to traditional pay structures.

Companies favor broadbanding because it reflects their flatter organizational structures. Multiple salary grades with narrowly defined pay ranges are collapsed into fewer salary grades with more pay potential. Broadbanding has the impact of clustering more job descriptions into broader job family categories. Job descriptions are still used here, but the focus is on a broad class of jobs rather than on specific jobs. This approach is typical of Japanese companies. This not only serves the needs of the organization, but also those of the individual. The same can be said for offering alternative arrangements for employee accommodation described in Chapter 5.

SUMMARY

The creation and maintenance of effective organizations today requires that the worker-job relationship be understood and managed. The belief that the way jobs are organized and perceived by job incumbents affects job attitudes and behaviors is a compelling reason for understanding job analysis. Job analysis provides information about what jobs are about and what individuals need to perform them. Job analysis information can be collected by several different individuals using several different methods. Together, they provide the information for job descriptions and job specifications. These go a long way in linking the individual to the organization and the job analysis activity to all the other human resource activities.

The choice of a job analysis method should be a result of the intended purpose, as defined by the type of human resource issue to be served by the analysis, as well as practical concerns.

Regardless of the approach, it is important to bear in mind that job analysis serves as the backbone for nearly all the human resource activities described in the chapters ahead. The value of job analysis will become even more apparent in the following two chapters on recruiting and selecting.

KEY CONCEPTS

ability
broadbanding
Critical Incident
    Technique
competencies
conditions
*Dictionary of
    Occupational Titles*
duties
effective managers
Functional Job Analysis
Guidelines-Oriented Job
    Analysis
Hay Plan
incumbent

job analysis
job descriptions
job domain
Job Element Inventory
job elements
job families
job specifications
knowledge
Management Position
    Description
    Questionnaire
methods analysis
minimum qualifications
normal time
observed time

Position Analysis
    Questionnaire
    (PAQ)
position description
purposes
standard time
skill
successful managers
Supervisor Task
    Description
    Questionnaire
task inventories
time and motion study
work measurement
work sampling

REVIEW AND DISCUSSION QUESTIONS

1. List several purposes of job analysis.
2. Are jobs static? That is, will a job change over time? If so, what might cause a job to change? What implications does this have for job analysis?
3. How do job descriptions differ from job specifications?
4. Do you think that the existence of job analysis might make a human resource function (such as recruitment, performance appraisal, or compensation) less legally vulnerable? Explain.
5. How does the use of job families give companies more flexibility with their employees?
6. What are the advantages and disadvantages of time and motion studies?
7. What are the important legal considerations in job analysis? Refer also to Chapter 5.
8. How can job descriptions give clarity to workers and also flexibility to the organization?

CAREER MANAGEMENT EXERCISE

This exercise will give you experience in conducting a job analysis as well as in writing a job description. To complete this project:

1. Select a job that you are interested in knowing more about or might like to perform during some stage of your career, or better yet, your first one indicated in Chapters 4 and 5.

2. Select a method to conduct your job analysis.

3. Select a person or persons to interview and observe. Identify and give the telephone number of the individual(s) you interview.

4. Conduct your job analysis.

5. Type up a complete job description for the position. Rank the job duties in order of their importance. Indicate the percent of time spent on each duty. Also, indicate the criticality of error if this duty is performed incorrectly.

6. On a separate typed sheet, explain the method of job analysis you used, why you chose it, and its strengths and weaknesses.

7. Respond to this question: from the perspective of (a) an employee and (b) a manager, why it is important to have an accurate, up-to-date, job description for the position being analyzed?

We will return to your job in Chapter 8 (selection) and then again in several of the remaining chapters.

CASE

DECTER COMPUTER CORPORATION

Cynthia Lee has just been hired as an HR assistant at Decter Computer Corporation (DCC). Cynthia recently finished her bachelor's degree at Northeast University in human resource administration, and she is excited about her first HR job. She is eager to apply the skills that she acquired in her undergraduate major. Angela Richards, Cynthia's immediate supervisor, is the HR director at DCC. Cynthia's first major task is to formalize DCC's job descriptions and job specifications based on a job analysis of each position.

DCC is a mid-sized company located in an industrial park in Parsippany, New Jersey. A leading producer of electronic equipment and a major contender in microcomputers and calculators, DCC is one of the leading distributors of microcomputers to large corporations. The company's business has been growing rapidly in recent years despite increased competition. The primary reasons for this are technological advancements DCC has put in place that have increased production capacity, an aggressive marketing strategy, and a reputation for excellent products and service. But the rapid growth has also placed some strain on the human resource department and created pressures to formalize work activities and compensation strategies.

Cynthia, who joined DCC two months earlier, has been assigned to create job descriptions for positions at DCC, a project that Angela has estimated will take eight weeks to complete. Angela told Cynthia that she would be responsible for the entire project and made it clear that she would be given autonomy to interview both supervisors and employees. Although Angela stressed the significance of the project, Cynthia sensed that Angela had a number of other responsibilities and deadlines to meet and that she did not have much time to spend on job analysis activities. Cynthia viewed the project as a challenge—a chance to prove herself.

Angela sent a memo to all supervisors explaining that Cynthia was responsible for completing a job analysis of each of the positions they supervised. Angela asked for their full cooperation and requested that they call her if they had any questions. After the memo was circulated, Cynthia began lining up interviews with the supervisors. She decided that the supervisors would be the best source of data for job descriptions and specifications, and planned to develop a narrative format similar to a sample job description in one of her personnel texts. As a final step in collecting job information, Cynthia decided to interview at least one employee in each of the positions being studied.

After three weeks, Cynthia became discouraged over the progress she was making on what she believed was a straightforward project. She had managed to interview only 7 of the 20 supervisors. The supervisors seemed unwilling to cooperate with Cynthia. They often missed interview meetings and dragged their feet in rescheduling them. Although Cynthia had originally planned to talk to all of the supervisors first, the delays prompted her to begin interviewing job incumbents.

After only a few interviews with employees, Cynthia became concerned about the quality of information that she was obtaining. The employees appeared to be giving her conflicting information on both their job duties and the skills required to perform their jobs. In general, the employees saw their jobs as more demanding, requiring more duties, and utilizing more skills than the supervisors had indicated. Despite these conflicts, Cynthia decided to push ahead so that she could submit the completed descriptions and specifications to Angela by the agreed-upon deadline.

At the end of the eight weeks and several long nights, Cynthia proudly presented a packet of job descriptions and specifications to Angela. Despite the obstacles, Cynthia believed that she had achieved the major objectives of the project. Angela assigned Cynthia another project. Several weeks later when Cynthia had all but forgotten about the job descriptions and specifications, Angela met with Cynthia to discuss a problem that had developed. It seems that several of the supervisors were annoyed about the difference in opinion with their subordinates over job duties.

CASE QUESTIONS
1. Was Cynthia's strategy of interviewing one employee in each position a good one?
2. Why were the supervisors unwilling to cooperate with Cynthia?
3. On becoming concerned about the quality of the data, should Cynthia have changed her methods?
4. Do the job descriptions and specifications need to be rewritten? How?

NOTES

1. Material used by the search firm, Kenny, Kindler, Hunt and Howe, New York City, from *The Changing Human Resources Function* (New York: The Conference Board, 1990): 15. Used by permission.

2. R. Page and D. Van De Voort, "Job Analysis and HR Planning," in *Human Resource Planning, Employment and Placement*, ed. W. F. Cascio (Washington, D.C.: Bureau of National Affairs, 1989): 2/34–2/72; More traditional definitions of job analyses are found in C. P. Sparks, "Job Analysis," in *Readings in Personnel and Human Resource Management* 3rd ed., eds. R. S. Schuler, S. A. Youngblood, and V. Huber (St. Paul, Minn.: West, 1988); E. J. McCormick, "Job and Task Analysis,"

in *Handbook of Industrial and Organizational Psychology*, M. D. Dunnette, ed. (Chicago: Rand McNally, 1979), 651–96; E. J. McCormick, *Job Analysis: Methods and Applications* (New York: AMACOM, 1979).

3. For more discussion on the purpose of job analysis, see R. J. Plachy, "Writing Job Descriptions That Get Results," *Personnel* (Oct. 1987): 56–63.

4. The essence of the *Civil Rights Act of 1964* and *1991*, the *Equal Opportunity in Employment Act of 1972*, and various court decisions is that employment decisions be made on the basis of whether the individual will be able to perform the job. To deter-

mine this, organizations should conduct job analyses to determine what skills, knowledge, and abilities individuals need to perform the jobs. Once this is known, selection procedures can be developed. Chapter 8 expands on the job relatedness of selection procedures. For more legal review, see D. E. Thompson and T. A. Thompson, "Court Standards for Job Analysis in Test Validation," *Personnel Psychology* 35 (1982): 865–74.

5. "Objective Employee Appraisals and Discrimination Cases," *Fair Employment Practices* (Dec. 6, 1990): 145–146; R. J. Nobile, "The Law of Performance Appraisals," *Personnel* (January 1991): 7.

6. "Job Analyses and Job Descriptions Under ADA," *Fair Employment Practices* (April 22, 1993): 45.

7. P. C. Grant, "What Use is a Job Description?" *Personnel Journal* (Feb. 1988): 45–49; M. A. Jones, Levine, *Everything You Always Wanted to Know About Job Analysis* (Tampa, Fla.: Mariner, 1983); R. J. Plachy, "Writing Job Descriptions That Get Results," *Personnel* (Oct. 1987): 56–63.

8. See McCormick, *Job Analysis*, and M. A. Jones, "Job Descriptions Made Easy," *Personnel Journal* (May 1984): 31–34.

9. Equal Employment Opportunity Commission. "Uniform Guidelines of Employee Selection Procedures," *Federal Register* 43 (1978): 38290–38315; J. Ledvinka and V. Scarpello, *Federal Regulation of Personnel and Human Resource Management*, 2nd ed. (Boston, Mass.: Kent, 1990).

10. R. H. Hayes and R. Jailkumar, "Manufacturing's Crisis: New Technologies, Obsolete Organizations," *Harvard Business Review* (Sept.–Oct. 1988): 77–85.

11. E. E. Adam Jr. and R. J. Ebert, *Production and Operations Management* (Englewood Cliff, N.J.: Prentice Hall, 1986); H. T. Amrine, V. L. Huber, and N. L. Hyer, "The Human Factor in Cellular Manufacturing," *Journal of Operations Management* 5 (1985): 213–28.

12. McCormick, *Job Analysis* (1979).

13. F. Luthans, R. M. Hodgetts, and S. A. Rosenkrantz, *Real Managers* (Cambridge, Mass.: Ballinger, 1988).

14. McCormick, *Job Analysis* (1979).

15. E. McCormick and J. Tiffin, *Industrial Psychology*, 6th ed. (Englewood Cliffs, N.J.: Prentice-Hall, 1974). Reprinted by permission of Prentice-Hall, Inc. The Position Analysis Questionnaire (PAQ) is copyrighted by the Purdue Research Foundation. The PAQ and related materials are available through the University Book Store, 360 West State Street, West Lafayette, Ind. 47906. Further information regarding the PAQ is available through PAQ Services, Inc., P.O. Box 3337, Logan, Utah 84321. Computer processing of PAQ data is available through PAQ Data Processing Division at that address.

16. For a discussion of the PAQ, see E. T. Cornelius III, A. S. DeNisi, and A. G. Blencoe, "Expert and Naive Raters Using the PAQ: Does It Matter?" *Personnel Psychology* (Autumn 1984): 453–464; J. B. Shaw and J. H. Riskind, "Predicting Job Stress Using Data from the Position Analysis Questionnaire," *Journal of Applied Psychology* (May 1983): 253–261.

17. R. J. Harvery, F. Friedman, M. D. Hakel, and E. T. Cornelius, "Dimensionality of the Job Element Inventory, a Simplified Worker-Oriented Job Analysis Questionnaire," *Journal of Applied Psychology* 73 (1988): 639–646.

18. McCormick, *Job Analysis* (1979). See Chapter 30, "Job and Task Analysis."

19. S. A. Fine, "Functional Job Analysis: An Approach to a Technology for Manpower Planning," *Personnel Journal*, 3rd ed. (Washington, D.C.: Government Printing Office, 1965); *Dictionary of Occupational Titles,* 4th ed. (Washington, D.C.: Government Printing Office, 1991); Department of Labor, Manpower Administration, *Handbook for Analyzing Jobs* (Washington, D.C.: Government Printing Office, 1965); Department of Labor, *Task Analysis Inventories: A Method of Collecting Job Information* (Washington, D.C.: Government Printing Office, 1973); J. Markowitz, "Four Methods of Job Analysis," *Training and Development Journal* (Sept. 1981): 112–121.

20. J. C. Flanagan, "The Critical Incident Technique," *Psychology Bulletin* 51 (1954): 327–358; G. P. Latham and K. N. Wexley, *Increasing Productivity Through Performance Appraisal* (Reading, Mass.: Addison-Wesley, 1981).

21. Guidelines-Oriented Job Analysis is a specific technique developed by Biddle and Associates, Sacramento, California, and is described here with their permission.

22. W. W. Tornow and P. R. Pinto, "The Development of Managerial Job Taxonomy: A System for Describing, Classifying, and Evaluating Executive Positions," *Journal of Applied Psychology* 61 (1976): 410–418. See also W. F. Cascio, *Applied Psychology in Personnel Management*, 2nd ed., (Reston, Va.: Reston, 1982).

23. B. C. Dowell and K. N. Wexley, "Development of a Work Behavior Taxonomy for First Line Supervisors," *Journal of Applied Psychology* 63 (1978): 563–572.

24. For an excellent description of issues related to job family or classes, see K. Pearlman, "Job Families: A Review and Discussion of Their Implications for Personnel Selection," *Psychological Bulletin* 87 (1980): 1–28.

25. S. Caudron, "Master the Compensation Maze," *Personnel Journal* (June 1993): 64D. Used by permission.

ONCE the environment has been scanned and understood and jobs designed and analyzed, human resource activities that are center stage at this point have to do with staffing. Of course, getting the people we need in order to run the company as effectively as possible is a key task of HR management. The competition for qualified people is so stiff that companies find they must market themselves as top notch career opportunities. If a company has a great reputation in this area, more and better qualified people will apply at the company, and this increases the chances that selected applicants will perform well once hired.

Getting people interested in working for a company is the essence of recruitment. Effective recruitment results from knowing both the work force's and the organization's views on recruitment. As always, knowing the needs of the applicants and of the business is important here. Which gets priority depends on the situation. When labor supply is high and demand is low, a buyer's market exists, and the needs of the business tend to prevail. When demand for labor is high and supply is low, a seller's market exists, and the needs of applicants tend to prevail.

Because conditions vary, effective firms find that it pays to be consistent—to develop a great set of recruitment procedures and use them consistently. While this may result in more worker accommodation than from some firms might initially desire, such approaches can pay off in the long run since reputations take time to establish, and good reputations result in a company being more attractive to candidates in good and bad employment and economic conditions. Once decisions about the company's recruitment philosophy have been made, the appropriate recruiting procedures can be put in place. We will discuss these issues and ideas associated with recruitment in Chapter 8, Staffing.

After recruitment has taken place, the organization must decide whether to offer the job, and the applicant must decide whether to accept the offer. The HR department is key in developing and utilizing procedures for selecting the best recruits. Organizations have found that it pays to develop selection procedures that are as job-related as possible. There are also legal considerations in the process of selection. Of course, the recruit has a say in this process as well. There are important questions to be answered: Is this the right organization? Will I be happy with the job and the opportunities to work here? Will my career be advanced if I accept the job offer? Because *you* the individual are the only one who can answer these questions, it helps to have many aids available to you as you make your selection. That is why we included Career Management Exercises for your use in Chapters 4 and 6. At the end of Chapter 8 there is another Career Management Exercise for your use.

Throughout Chapters 7 and 8 you will see once again how many opportunities there are for partnership among line managers, HR professionals, and employees. You will also see how the themes of diversity, globalization, ethics, and total quality management impact recruitment, and selection and placement.

SECTION 3

STAFFING

CHAPTER 7

RECRUITMENT

LEARNING OBJECTIVES

When you have finished studying this chapter, you should be able to:

1. Describe the details of affirmative action programs.
2. Discuss sources and methods for obtaining job applicants.
3. Indicate how organizations can increase their pools of potentially qualified job applicants by methods other than the traditional ones.
4. Describe the impact of work force diversity on a firm's recruitment policies.

CHAPTER OUTLINE

"Managing Human Resources at McDonald's"

RECRUITMENT

WHY IS RECRUITMENT IMPORTANT?

LEGAL CONSIDERATIONS

SOURCES AND METHODS FOR OBTAINING JOB APPLICANTS

"Managing Human Resources
GENIUS FOR HIRE—THE SOVIETS' BEST, AT BARGAIN RATES"

"HR Advice and Application
WINNING HELP-WANTED ADS"

MULTIPLE AND NEW SOURCES AND METHODS

INCREASING THE POOL OF POTENTIALLY QUALIFIED APPLICANTS

ADDRESSING THE NEEDS OF APPLICANTS: SOCIALIZATION

INTERNATIONAL COMPARISONS

CURRENT TRENDS

"Managing Human Resources at Burger King"
Case: Downsizing: Anathema to Corporate Loyalty?
Case: The New Recruit

As do many service-oriented firms, McDonald's faces problems finding the variety of employees it needs—those who staff its restaurants as well as those intended for management positions, either as restaurant managers or franchise owners.

For its restaurant staff positions, McDonald's has used a variety of recruiting approaches. First, rather than rely on its traditional labor pool, McDonald's has looked to new groups to hire such as retirees and mothers with young children. To attract these groups, the firm offers flexible working hours. With young people, particularly from inner-city locations, the firm has in the past been able to recruit and hire them but unable to retain them. The company found that inner-city teenagers would often work for a few months and then quit. The teenagers worked just long enough to earn money to buy specific items such as new clothes or a boom box. To retain such employees, McDonald's sought ways to make the jobs more fun. In some parts of the country, for example, the young people are allowed to choose the music played in the restaurant or to wear favorite clothes on particular days, rather than the standard McDonald's uniforms. Such flexibility in company practices has made it a more attractive employer for different groups in the work force. Finally, to attract employees with potential for restaurant management, McDonald's sponsors summer internships and management training programs for minority students.

Its recruitment of franchise operators, particularly those for overseas restaurants, has been easier because of the opportunities the company offers. For overseas franchisees, in particular, the opportunity to be an entrepreneur is uncommon in many countries. Thus, "recruitment" varies greatly depending on the area and type of employee the firm needs.[1]

This feature illustrates several aspects of recruitment today. One is the impact of the declining skilled labor pool. Another is the increasing efforts by organizations to attract and retain workers they have not previously employed. A third aspect is the need for organizations to be systematic in their identification of human resource needs and development of recruitment strategies to ensure that their business needs are filled. Another is the impact of the local economy, particularly on the ability of employers to attract sufficient numbers of job applicants. These issues, some ongoing and some recent developments, form the subject of this chapter.

RECRUITMENT

Recruitment involves searching for and obtaining qualified job candidates in such numbers that the organization can select the most appropriate person to fill its job needs. In addition to filling job needs, the recruitment activity should be concerned with satisfying the needs of the job candidates.[2] Consequently, recruitment not only attracts individuals to an organization, but also increases the chance of retaining them once they are hired. Of course, the recruitment activity must be done in compliance with legal regulations. Thus **recruitment** is *the set of activities used to obtain a pool of qualified job applicants*. In other words,

Recruitment is concerned with searching for and obtaining a pool of qualified job candidates.

217

recruitment finds the organization its most important asset—its human resources.

Recruitment is comprised of several key activities; these include (1) determining the organization's long- and short-range needs by job title and level in the organization; (2) staying informed of job market conditions; (3) developing effective recruiting materials; (4) developing a systematic and integrated program of recruitment in conjunction with other HR activities and with the cooperation of line managers; (5) obtaining a pool of qualified job applicants; (6) recording the number and quality of job applicants produced by the various sources and methods of recruiting; and (7) following up on applicants, those hired and not hired, in order to evaluate the effectiveness of the recruiting effort. All of these activities must be accomplished within the proper legal context.

WHY IS RECRUITMENT IMPORTANT?

The general purpose of recruitment is that of providing a pool of potentially qualified job candidates. More specifically, the purposes of recruitment includes the following:

- Determine the present and future recruitment needs of the organization in conjunction with HR planning and job analysis activities
- Increase the pool of qualified job applicants with minimum cost
- Increase the success rate of the selection process by reducing the number of obviously underqualified job applicants
- Reduce the probability that job applicants, once recruited and selected, will leave the organization after only a short period of time
- Increase organizational and individual effectiveness in the short and long term
- Evaluate the effectiveness of various recruiting techniques and sources for all types of job applicants
- Meet the organization's responsibility for affirmative action programs and other legal and social considerations regarding the composition of its work force[3]

LEGAL CONSIDERATIONS

Legal considerations play a critical role in the recruitment process of most companies in the United States. Although much of the legal framework facing human resource management is directed at employment decisions concerning hiring, firing, health and safety, and compensation, it really begins with the organization's search for job applicants, whether inside or outside the organization. Although the fair employment laws in regard to staffing decisions (hiring, firing, demoting, transferring, and training) specifically apply only to selection, they directly affect recruitment. (Some of the laws and acts applicable to selection are discussed in Chapter 8.) Because they essentially identify who will be *selected*, they also identify who should be *recruited*. Fair employment or equal employment laws most directly relevant to recruitment are those that set out the affirmative action programs. While the *Family and Medical Leave Act of 1993* can influence recruitment, its major provisions impact benefits so we will discuss it in Chapter 13.

AFFIRMATIVE ACTION PROGRAMS

Affirmative action programs (AAPs) are intended to ensure proportional and fair representation of qualified individuals on the basis of race, color, ethnic ori-

Affirmative action programs (AAPs) are intended to ensure proportional and fair representation of all qualified individuals.

PARTNERSHIP: WORKING TOGETHER IN RECRUITMENT

LINE MANAGERS	HR PROFESSIONALS	EMPLOYEES
Prepare a list of job duties and skills needed to fill jobs.	Take information from line managers to prepare recruitment activities.	Participate in recruitment efforts such as referring the company to potential employees.
Prepare for interviews with job applicants.	Develop sources and methods of recruiting to ensure a sufficient number of qualified applicants.	Work with HR professionals and line managers in the organization's efforts to effectively manage work force diversity.
Work with HR professionals on equal employment and work force diversity.	Ensure that equal employment considerations are met and work force diversity is effectively managed.	
Identify critical job assignments		

gin, sex, and disability.[4] As shown in Exhibit 7.1, many firms have AAPs; they generally arise from three different conditions.

FEDERAL CONTRACTS. If a company has a federal contract greater than $50,000 and has 50 or more employees (thereby referred to as a federal contractor), it is required to file, with the Office of Federal Contract Compliance Programs, a written plan outlining steps to be taken for correcting underutilization in places where underutilization has been identified.

Affirmative action programs are designed to facilitate an organization's commitment to provide and achieve proportional representation or parity (or to correct underutilization) in its work force with the relevant labor market of protected group members. Title VII of the *Civil Rights Act of 1964* includes women and Americans of African, Hispanic, Native-American, and Asian/Pacific Islands descent.

The components of AAPs for federal contractors are specified by the Department of Labor in the Office of Federal Contract Compliance Programs (OFCCP). The programs are currently enforced by the OFCCP and the Equal Employment Opportunity Commission (EEOC) through Executive Order 11246.

The components include utilization and availability analyses, goals, and timetables. A **utilization analysis** determines the number of members of minorities and women employed in different jobs within an organization. An **availability analysis** measures how many members of minorities and women are available to work in the relevant labor market. If an organization is employing fewer members of minorities and women than are available, a state of **underutilization**

Federal Express Corporation is firmly committed to afford Equal Employment Opportunity to all individuals regardless of age, sex, race, color, religion, national origin, citizenship, physical handicap, or status as a Vietnam era or special disabled veteran. We are strongly bound to this commitment because adherence to Equal Employment Opportunity principles is the only acceptable way of life. We adhere to those principles not just because they're the law, but because it's the right thing to do.

Company Policy Statement
Federal Express Annual Report

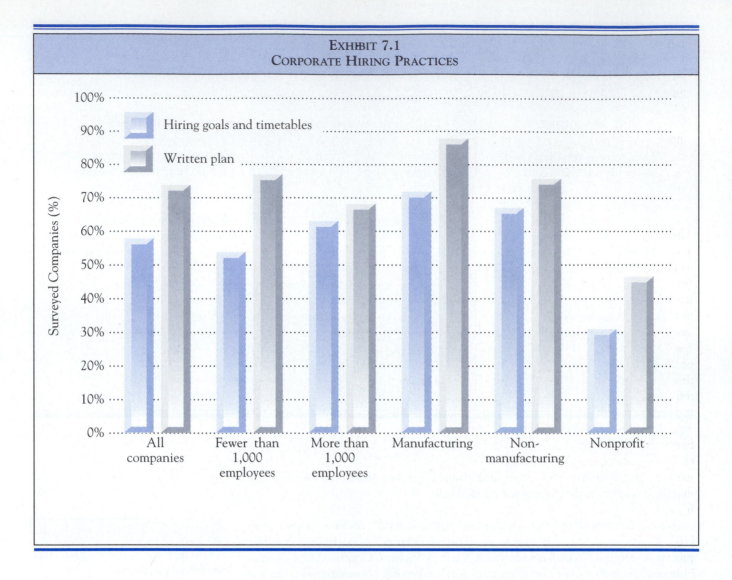

EXHIBIT 7.1
CORPORATE HIRING PRACTICES

Hiring goals and timetables

Written plan

Surveyed Companies (%)

All companies · Fewer than 1,000 employees · More than 1,000 employees · Manufacturing · Non-manufacturing · Nonprofit

---

Underutilization exists when the organization uses fewer women and members of minority groups than are available in the relevant labor market.

Prima facie means on its face or just as it appears.

exists. White men are also covered by most equal employment laws, but most examples, except of reverse discrimination, exclude them because they are usually in the majority.

A **relevant labor market** is generally defined as the geographical area from which come a substantial majority of job applicants and employees. Published population data sources such as the Standard Metropolitan Statistical Analysis can provide initial guidance in determining this defined area. Within a relevant labor market, availability data can be gathered from sources such as the U.S. Census, local and state Chambers of Commerce, and city and state governments. Because organizations may fill certain job openings with applicants in the local area and fill others with applicants from across the nation, organizations may have several relevant labor markets. These markets are important in both AAP development and in defending cases of *prima facie* illegal discrimination. As such, we will discuss them further in the next chapter on selection under "defending against charges of illegal discrimination."

After the utilization and availability analyses are completed, goals and timetables are written to specify how an organization plans to correct any underutilization. Because goals and timetables become the organization's commitment to equal employment, they must be realistic and attainable. An example of a utilization plan for one job group in an organization is shown in Exhibit 7.2.[5]

Federal contractors are also required to "take affirmative action to employ and advance in employment qualified handicapped individuals at all levels of employment" (Section 503 of the *Rehabilitation Act of 1973*). The *Rehabilitation Act*, as amended in 1980 and in 1990 by the *Americans with Disabilities Act of 1990 (ADA)*, names three categories of disabled persons as protected against employment discrimination:

- Any individual who has a physical or mental impairment that greatly limits one or more of life's major functions.
- Any individual who has a history of such an impairment.
- Any individual who is perceived as having such an impairment.

The impairments in the first category are usually evident conditions such as amputations, Down's syndrome, paralysis, hearing or visual problems, and so forth. Impairments in the second category can't be readily discerned. Nevertheless, some employers shy away from applicants whose medical histories include cancer, heart disease, diabetes, and similar health problems, perhaps out of fear that a recurrence or other effects of the disease will result in increased insurance costs, a higher rate of absenteeism, and decreased efficiency. In one case, an employer refused to hire a worker who had leukemia because he was prone to infection from even minor injuries; but a Wisconsin circuit court found that the man was qualified to perform his job; therefore, the company could not refuse employment.

Notice that an employer's misconceptions can bring an individual who isn't actually disabled under the coverage of the act or a similar state law. That's what happened, for instance, when an employee was terminated because his employer thought he had epilepsy. The Washington Court of Appeals awarded the worker two years back pay and ordered him reinstated. Also included are individuals who have suffered from alcoholism and drug abuse and those suffering from AIDS.

Individuals who are well but test positive for the AIDS virus likely will be covered by the third category of the *Rehabilitation Act*. This portion of the act protects any individual who is perceived as having a disability.[6]

According to the ADA, "a qualified individual with a disability" is anyone who has the skill, experience, and education required for the job and can perform the "essential functions" of the job, with or without reasonable accommodation. The act permits medical exams only after the job offer has been made. The offer can be made conditional upon the results of the exam, but the employer must make reasonable accommodation. Before the job offer is made, the employer can describe the essential functions to the individual, but the employer cannot inquire about any disabilities the applicant might have (see Chapter 5).

The rules further state that employers with 50 or more employees who hold federal contracts totaling more than $50,000 must prepare written AAPs for disabled workers in each of their establishments—for example, in each plant or field office. This condition must be met within 120 days after the contractor receives the federal contract. Those who hold contracts or subcontracts of less than $2,500 are not covered by this act. Those with federal contracts that range from $2,500 to $50,000 are required to include an affirmative action clause in their contracts, but they do not need a written AAP.

To aid an organization in its efforts to attain specified goals and timetables, the HR department must make sure its employment policies, practices, and procedures are operating to facilitate this. An assessment of current policies, prac-

A qualified person with a disability is anyone who can perform the essential functions of a job with or without reasonable accommodations.

EXHIBIT 7.2
UTILIZATION, GOALS, AND TIMETABLES

Job Group: ABC
As of: 2/14/94
Availability source: 8-factor analysis

Current Utilization

	MALE	FEMALE	WHITE	BLACK	HISPANIC	ASIAN	NATIVE AMERICAN	MINORITY	TOTAL
Employees (#)	193	7	186	4	3	6	1	14	200
Employees (%)	96.5	3.5	93.0	2.0	1.5	3.0	0.5	7.0	
Availability (%)	88.0	12.0	66.0	15.0	14.0	4.0	1.0	34.0	100.0
Underutilized ?	No	Yes	No	Yes	Yes	Yes	Yes	Yes	

GOALS

Based on expansion of 36

		FEMALE		BLACK	HISPANIC	ASIAN	NATIVE AMERICAN	MINORITY	TOTAL
Long-range goal (%)		15.0		15.5	14.5	4.0	1.0	35.0	100.0
Long-range goal (#)		35		37	34	9	2	82	236
Annual placement (%)		22.5		21.0	19.7	7.2	1.8	49.7	

Timetables

If 12 openings (5.1% turnover)—Employment opportunities 1st yr. = 48

	FEMALE	BLACK	HISPANIC	ASIAN	NATIVE AMERICAN	MINORITY
Year to goal (#)	14	15	15	1	3	15
Hired 1st year	11	10	9	3	<1	24
Hired 2nd year on	3	3	2		<1	6

If 24 openings (10.2% turnover)—Employment opportunities 1st yr. = 60

	FEMALE	BLACK	HISPANIC	ASIAN	NATIVE AMERICAN	MINORITY
Years to goal (#)	7	11	10	1	2	9
Hired 1st year	14	13	12	4	1	30
Hired 2nd year on	5	5	5		<1	12

If 47 openings (19.9% turnover)—Employment opportunities 1st yr. = 83

	FEMALE	BLACK	HISPANIC	ASIAN	NATIVE AMERICAN	MINORITY
Years to goal (#)	4	5	5	1	1	4
Hired 1st year	19	17	16	6	2	41
Hired 2nd year on	11	10	9			23

Projected openings 18 (7.6% turnover)—Employment opportunities 1st yr. = 54

	FEMALE	BLACK	HISPANIC	ASIAN	NATIVE AMERICAN	MINORITY
Years to goal (#)	10	14	14	1	2	11
Hired 1st year	12	11	11	4	<1	27
Hired 2nd year on	4	4	4		<1	9

Utilization Analysis

	MALE	FEMALE	WHITE	BLACK	HISPANIC	ASIAN	NATIVE AMERICAN	TOTAL
Employees (#)	193	7	186	4	3	6	1	200
Employees (%)	96.5	3.5	93.0	2.0	1.5	3.0	0.5	
Availability (%)	88.0	12.0	66.0	15.0	14.0	4.0	1.0	100.0
Should have (#)	176	24	132	30	28	8	2	
Underutilized?	No	Yes	No	Yes	Yes	Yes	Yes	
Calculation type		Z		Z	Z	Z	P	
Statistical value		3.59		5.05	4.99	0.54	0.73	
Z or probability		0.00		0.00	0.00	0.59	0.36	
Significant?	No	Yes	No	Yes	Yes	No	No	
Additional needed		8		16	15			

tices, and procedures is generally required. Should the assessment reveal that goal attainment is not being facilitated, the policies, practices, and procedures will need to be modified.

PAST DISCRIMINATION.   This is the second way an affirmative action program may arise. A federal court may require an AAP if a discrimination suit brought against the organization through the Equal Employment Opportunity Commission has found evidence of past discrimination. An AAP under these conditions is generally part of a **consent decree**, a statement indicating specific affirmative action steps to be taken by the organization.

A famous affirmative action program resulting from a consent decree involved American Telephone and Telegraph (AT&T), which the EEOC found to be discriminating against women. Although AT&T did not admit nor was required to admit any act of discrimination, it entered into a consent decree after the EEOC opposed its application for a rate increase (see Chapter 5). In a more recent settlement,

> State Farm Insurance Co. agreed to set aside for women half of its new sales agent jobs in California over the next 10 years, and to pay damages and back pay to women who were refused sales jobs during a 13-year period, according to a consent decree settling a long-running sex bias case against the company.
>
> Female employees filed a class action suit in 1979, claiming that State Farm in California had discriminated against women in recruitment, hiring, job assignments, training, and termination decisions. A federal district court found the company had discriminated and was liable for damages to all women who unsuccessfully applied for or were deterred from applying for trainee agent jobs since 1974. The settlement covers 1,113 sales jobs that became vacant and were filled by men between 1974 and 1987, and is expected to result in back pay awards totaling between $100 and $300 million.
>
> The agreement provides that State Farm will use its best efforts to give women 50 percent of the trainee agent appointments each year for the next decade. The company is required to nominate one women in each of its three California regions to serve as a recruitment administrator to train agency managers to recruit and retain qualified women. In addition, procedures are specified for the company to follow in publicizing openings for sales agent jobs.
>
> Women affected by the decree who wish to make a claim may file for damages during a four-month period beginning May 1. (*Kraszewski v. State Farm*, 1988).[7]

By the way, State Farm reached a settlement in April 1992 with those women affected by the decree who filed for damages. The settlement was worth $157 million, the largest settlement ever brought under the *Civil Rights Act of 1964*.

Although goals set by consent decrees, or as part of the federal contractor's AAP, only specify percentages, they are often seen as establishing quotas. That is, the goals establish that an organization must hire, for example, a certain number of women or African-Americans to correct underutilization or past discrimination in employment. Setting quotas may result in a violation of the Fourteenth Amendment, as well as against Title VII protection against all employment discrimination; for example, white men might not be hired because an organization has a quota to meet. However, the courts have generally held in favor of goals as the only way to reverse previous practices of discrimination (*Detroit Police Officer's Association v. Coleman Young*, 1979; *Charles L. Maehren v. City of Seattle*, 1979; and *City of St. Louis v. U.S.A.*, 1980).

Nevertheless, the issue of reverse discrimination is being heard. For example, the Supreme Court ruled that federal courts could not ignore a seniority-based layoff policy and modify a consent decree to prevent the layoff of black workers (*Firefighter Local Union 1784 v. Stotts*, 1984). In related cases, the Supreme Court has ruled that there are limits to the use of rigid racial and ethnic criteria to accomplish remedial objectives (*Fullilove v. Klutznick*, 1980; *Richmond v. Croson*, 1989).

We will address this issue in more detail in Chapter 8 on selection. Reverse discrimination as it relates to recruitment is discussed here as an issue in organizations establishing voluntary AAPs.

VOLUNTARY AAPS.   In addition to AAPs related to federal contracts and consent decrees, organizations may voluntarily establish goals for hiring and promoting women, members of minority groups, and individuals with disabilities. The exact content of such AAPs depends on the organization and the extent to which various groups are underrepresented.

Organizations often establish voluntary programs without pressure from the EEOC or OFCCP. In fact, organizations can benefit from voluntary AAPs. The key considerations in an organization's establishment of a legal, voluntary AAP are that it be remedial in purpose, limited in its duration, restricted in its reverse discrimination impact—that is, it does not operate as an absolute ban on non-minorities—and flexible in implementation. When an organization's voluntary AAP has these characteristics, the risk of losing a reverse discrimination suit may be minimized. Nonetheless, there is still some risk of being found liable for reverse discrimination (*Martin v. Wilks*, 1989).

LEARNING OBJECTIVE 2

Discuss sources and methods for obtaining job applicants.

SOURCES AND METHODS FOR OBTAINING JOB APPLICANTS

We now examine the sources where potentially qualified job applicants can be found and the methods used to recruit them. Both sources and methods can be external to the organization as well as internal. A list of both types is shown in Exhibit 7.3.

INTERNAL SOURCES

Internal sources involve present employees; this recruitment occurs through promotions and transfers, job rotation, and rehires and recalls.

PROMOTIONS.   The case for **promotion-from-within** rests on sound arguments. Internal employees can be better qualified. Even jobs that do not seem unique require familiarity with the people, procedures, policies, and special characteristics of the organization in which they are performed. Employees are likely to feel more secure and therefore identify their long-term interests with an organization that provides them the first choice of job opportunities. Availability of promotions within an organization can also motivate employees to perform.

Internal promotion can also be much less expensive to the organization in terms of time and money. By comparison, the outside recruit is often brought in at a higher salary than that earned by people already in similar positions, and the costs to the company of relocating the new recruit and his or her family may range from $50,000 to $500,000. The result, especially if the new recruit fails to contribute as expected, is dissatisfaction among the current employees. In addition, the incentive value of promotions diminishes.

Disadvantages of a promotion-from-within policy are several. One, there is always the possibility the best-qualified person is not to be found internally. Two, if the best person is found, he or she may not take the promotion for personal reasons such as a desire to stay in familiar surroundings. Other disadvantages

---

Internal sources for obtaining job applicants include:

- promotions
- transfers
- job rotation
- rehires and recalls

Disadvantages of promotion-from-within include:

- infighting
- inbreeding
- lack of varied perspectives

EXHIBIT 7.3
RECRUITMENT SOURCES AND METHODS USED BY COMPANIES (%)

| | OCCUPATION | | | | | |
METHOD	ANY JOB CATEGORY*	OFFICE/ CLERICAL	PRODUCTION/ SERVICE	PROFESSIONAL/ TECHNICAL	COMMISSIONED SALES	MANAGERS/ SUPERVISORS
(Number of companies)	(245)	(245)	(221)	(237)	(96)	(243)
Internal Sources						
Promotion from within	99%	94%	86%	89%	75%	95%
Advertising						
Newspapers	97	84	77	94	84	85
Journals/magazines	64	6	7	54	33	50
Direct mail	17	4	3	16	6	8
Radio/television	9	3	6	3	3	2
Outside Referral Sources						
Colleges/ universities	86	24	15	81	38	45
Technical/ vocational institutes	78	48	51	47	5	8
High schools/ trade schools	68	60	54	16	5	2
Professional societies	55	4	1	51	19	37
Community agencies	39	33	32	20	16	9
Unions	10	1	11	1	—	1
Employee referrals	91	87	83	78	76	64
Walk-in applicants	91	86	87	64	52	46
Employment Services						
State employment services	73	66	68	38	30	23
Private employment agencies	72	28	11	58	44	60
Search firms	67	1	**	36	26	63
U.S. Employment Service	22	19	20	11	7	7
Employee leasing firms	20	16	10	6	2	—
Computerized résumé service	4	—	—	4	—	2
Video interviewing service	2	—	—	1	—	1

EXHIBIT 7.3 (CONT.)
RECRUITMENT SOURCES AND METHODS USED BY COMPANIES (%)

Special Events

Career conferences/ job fairs	53	20	17	44	19	19
Open house	22	10	8	17	8	7
Other	9	5	5	7	6	7

*Percentages for each job category are based on the number of organizations that provided data for that category, as shown by the number in parentheses.

SOURCE: Reprinted by permission from *Personnel Policies Forum*, Survey No. 146, Recruiting and Selection Procedures, 4–5 (The Bureau of National Affairs, Inc., Washington, D.C., 1988). Data still accurate as of 1994 according to the Bureau of National Affairs

include infighting, inbreeding, and an ensuing lack of varied perspectives and interests, and an organization with this policy may end up having to pressure candidates for the promotions.

Given the case for and against the internal promotion policy, it is not surprising to find that organizations often combine it with obtaining applicants from external sources. The type of employee sought often determines whether the organization looks inside or outside. For example, many organizations are more likely to hire highly trained professionals and high-level managers from the outside. Occasionally, promotions are made on the basis of personal impressions by the organizations. This is particularly true for middle- and upper-level managerial positions. Because it is difficult to defend under current legal guidelines, many organizations have had to reconsider this method of promotion. The use of test results from managerial assessment centers is one alternative to personal impressions. Since assessment centers are used more as a selection than a recruiting device, they are discussed in Chapter 8. Specific applicant sources are discussed later in this chapter.

TRANSFERS. Another way to recruit internally is by transferring current employees without promotion. Transfers are often important in providing employees with the broad-based view of the organization necessary for future promotions.

Once affirmative action and equal employment requirements are met, the basis used to select the internal candidates for transfer must be decided. The choice is often seniority versus merit. Unions seem to prefer seniority, while some organizations prefer transfers based on ability. Where seniority systems exist, decisions can be made on that basis even if the results appear contrary to affirmative action and equal employment guidelines (*California Brewers Association v. Bryant*, 1980; *International Brotherhood of Teamsters v. U.S.*, 1977).

JOB ROTATION. Whereas a transfer is likely to be permanent, job rotations are usually temporary in nature. Job rotation has been used effectively to expose management trainees to various aspects of organizational life. Job rotation has also been used to relieve job burnout for employees in high-stress occupations. For example, the Utah Department of Social Services has a job rotation program in which human service workers swap jobs with workers in other divisions or with employees in federal agencies for periods of up to one year. At the end of the contracted year of service, employees have the opportunity to return to their original positions or remain in the new position. Such programs give employees different perspectives, as well as an opportunity to try out new positions without fear of failure. Management, on the other hand, gets a chance to preview the employee prior to long-term commitment.

A relatively new disadvantage for both job rotation and transfers is the cost of relocation. For the first time at the Mitre Corporation, a Bedford, Massachusetts, systems engineering firm with 6,000 employees, real estate has become a consideration in selecting a candidate to fill a job.[8] This has been largely due to the housing slump in parts of the United States. With housing actually worth less than before, companies have to pay employees for the housing loss they experience when they sell their homes in order to relocate.

REHIRES AND RECALLS.   Each week, thousands of employees are temporarily laid off from work, and others are recalled to former jobs. The rehire of former employees or employees temporarily laid off is a relatively inexpensive and effective method of internal recruiting. Unlike new job candidates, the organization already has information about the performance, attendance, and safety records of these employees. Because they are already familiar with job responsibilities, rehires may be better performers than recruits from other sources. Additionally, they tend to stay on the job longer and have better attendance records.

In considering rehiring as a recruitment strategy, organizations need to weigh the costs against the benefits. Rehiring and recalls are particularly beneficial to organizations that have seasonal fluctuations in the demand for workers (for example, department stores, canneries, construction jobs, ski resorts). Canneries in eastern Washington recall large numbers of employees—some who have been employed for more than 20 years—each summer and fall during the apple harvest. This reduces employee costs. The down side of this recruitment approach is that employee commitment may be low. By the time of the recall, a qualified recruit may have found alternative employment—possibly with a major competitor. Finally, because turnover is continual, an organization's contribution to unemployment compensation programs is likely to increase.

INTERNAL METHODS

Job vacancies can be located by posting a notice on the bulletin board, word of mouth, company personnel records, promotion lists based on performance, potential ratings obtained from assessment activities, seniority lists, and lists generated by the skills inventory in an organization's HRIS (human resource information system). Frequently used methods include job posting and skills inventories.

JOB POSTING.   **Job posting** prominently displays current job openings, thereby extending an open invitation to all employees in an organization. It serves the following purposes in that it:

- Provides opportunity for employee growth and development
- Provides equal opportunity for advancement to all employees
- Creates a greater openness in the organization by making opportunities known to all employees
- Increases staff awareness of salary grades, job descriptions, general promotion and transfer procedures, and what comprises effective job performance

Job posting displays notice of job openings to all.

Job posting provides:
- **opportunity for growth**
- **equal opportunity**
- **openness**
- **staff awareness**
- **communication**

- Communicates organizational goals and objectives and allows each individual the opportunity to help find a personal fit in the organization's job structure[9]

Although job postings are usually found on bulletin boards, they also appear in company newsletters and are announced at staff meetings. Sometimes specific salary information is included, but job grade and pay range are more typical. Job posting is beneficial for organizations because it improves morale, provides employees opportunity for job variety, facilitates a better matching of employee skills and needs, and fills positions at a low cost.[10]

These benefits, of course, are not always realized. Job posting can create problems such as the following:

- Conflicts are sometimes created if an "heir apparent" in the department is passed over in favor of an outside candidate.
- Conversely, the system may lose credibility if it appears that the successful candidate within the department has been identified in advance and the managers are merely going through the motions in considering outsiders.
- The morale of the unsuccessful candidates may suffer if feedback is not carefully handled.
- Choices can be more difficult for the selecting manager if two or three equally qualified candidates are encountered.

SKILLS INVENTORIES.   Aiding internal job posting and employee recalls are **skills inventories**. Most organizations have skill-related information buried in personnel files. When needed, much time and effort are required to get at it. A formal skills inventory aggregates this information through the use of an HRIS. Any data that can be quantified can be coded and included in a skills inventory.

Common information includes name, employee number, job classification, prior jobs, prior experience, and salary levels. The results of formal assessments, such as those attained in assessment centers, during work sample tests, and with job interest inventories, are usually included. While often overlooked, skill inventories should also include information regarding the employee's job interests, geographical preferences, and career goals. The inclusion of the latter information ensures that potential job assignments will meet individual as well as organizational goals.

Skills inventories are only as good as the data they contain. They are also time-consuming and somewhat costly to maintain. Still, a skills inventory can ensure that *any* individual who has the necessary qualifications for a position is considered.[11]

EXTERNAL SOURCES

Recruiting internally does not always produce enough qualified applicants. This is especially true for rapidly growing organizations or those with a large demand for high-talent professional, skilled, and managerial employees. Organizations therefore need external sources. Recruiting from the outside has a number of advantages, including bringing in people with new ideas. It is often cheaper and easier to hire an already trained professional or skilled employee, particularly when the organization has an immediate demand for scarce labor skills and talents. External sources can also supply temporary employees who provide the organization with flexibility in expanding and contracting.

In general, organizations need to use both internal and external sources of recruitment. A summary of the advantages and disadvantages of each source appears in Exhibit 7.4.

AMP, a 25,000 employee manufacturing firm in Harrisburg, Pennsylvania, instituted a telephone based job posting system in 1992.

Potential problems in job posting include:

- conflict
- credibility loss
- morale issues
- difficult choices

Skills inventories are data files containing information on skills that employees have.

External sources for obtaining job applicants include:

- employee referrals
- walk-ins
- employment agencies
- temporary-help agencies
- trade associations and unions
- schools
- foreign nationals

EXHIBIT 7.4
SOURCES OF JOB APPLICANTS

Internal Sources

ADVANTAGES	DISADVANTAGES
Morale of promotee	Inbreeding
Better assessment of abilities	Possible morale problems of those not
Lower cost for some jobs	promoted
Motivator for good performance	"Political" infighting for promotions
Have to hire only at entry level	Requires strong management
	development program

External Sources

ADVANTAGES	DISADVANTAGES
"New blood," new perspectives	May not select someone who will "fit"
Cheaper than training a	May cause morale problems for those
professional	internal candidates
No group of political supporters in	Longer adjustment or orientation time
organization already	May bring in an attitude of "This is
May bring competitors' secrets, new	the way we used to do it at XYZ
insights	Company."
Helps meet equal employment needs	

SOURCE: Adapted from R. L. Mathis and J. H. Jackson, *Personnel: Contemporary Perspectives and Applications*, 7th ed. (St. Paul, Minn.: West Publishing Co., © 1994). Reproduced by permission. All rights reserved.

EMPLOYEE REFERRAL PROGRAMS. **Employee referral programs** are word-of-mouth advertisements in which current employees refer applicants from outside the organization. Because of the involvement of current employees, this recruiting method blends internal with external recruitment and is a low cost-per-hire means of recruiting.[12] Informal referrals consist of informing current employees about job openings and asking them to encourage qualified friends and associates to apply. Formal referral programs, on the other hand, reward employees for referring skilled applicants to organizations. The financial incentive may be as little as $15 or as much as $2,000 for referring someone with a critical skill such as robotics engineering or specialized nursing care. Financial incentives can be linked to the completion of an application, acceptance of employment, or the completion of work for a specified period of time on the part of the recruit.

Compared to other external recruiting methods, employee referrals for most occupations generally result in the highest one-year survival rates. The findings are less clear regarding performance and attendance by source. One explanation for the success of employee referral programs is that employees provide a balanced view of organizational life. Another explanation is that employees tend to recruit applicants who are similar to them in skills, interests, and abilities. Since the employee is already integrated in the organization culture, this prematching process increases the likelihood that applicants will also fit into the environment. On first blush, referring individuals who are similar in type (age, sex, race, and religion) is beneficial. However, such referrals—particularly if they are

DID YOU KNOW?

Fortune magazine's ranking of the best cities to get knowledge workers is:

1. Raleigh/Durham
2. New York
3. Boston
4. Seattle
5. Austin
6. Chicago
7. Houston
8. San Jose
9. Philadelphia
10. Minneapolis

required for employment—may be detrimental in regards to equal employment opportunity obligations.[13]

WALK-INS.   As illustrated in Exhibit 7.3, recruitment of walk-ins is especially prevalent for clerical and service-job applicants. Individuals become applicants by walking into an organization's employment office—they have not been referred by anyone. This method, like employee referrals, is informal and relatively inexpensive and is almost as effective as employee referrals in retaining applicants once hired.[14] Unlike referrals, walk-ins know less about the specific jobs available and come without the implicit recommendation of a current employee. This may be a disadvantage compared to referrals since current employees are unlikely to refer or recommend unsatisfactory applicants.

Managerial, professional, and sales applicants, however, are seldom walk-ins, and because this method tends to be a passive source of applicants, it may not provide sufficient numbers to fulfill affirmative action and equal employment requirements. These two problems can be addressed by sponsoring open house events to attract all types of applicants from the nearby community.

OPEN HOUSES.   An excellent way to introduce individuals to the organization and also attract individuals who might not otherwise apply, is the use of open houses. These are events where the firm opens its doors so that individuals can come and take a look at what the company is about and what jobs it might have available. In doing so, open houses can give the individual a realistic organizational preview and the firm a chance to look at potential applicants in an informal setting. When done during a weekend, the firm might also attract a wider range of applicants—that is, those who work elsewhere during the week.

Employment agencies are both public and private.

EMPLOYMENT AGENCIES.   Public and private employment agencies are a good source for temporary employees—and an excellent source for permanent ones. American public employment agencies are under the umbrella of the U.S. Training and Employment Service. The Service sets national policies and oversees the operations of state employment services, which have branch offices in many cities. The *Social Security Act* provides that, in general, any worker who has been laid off from a job must register with the state employment agency to be eligible for unemployment benefits. The agencies then have a roster of potential applicants to assist organizations looking for job candidates.

State employment agencies provide a wide range of services, most of which are supported by employer contributions to state unemployment funds. The agencies offer counseling, testing, and placement services to everyone. They provide special services to individuals, military veterans, minority groups, and college, technical, and professional people. The state agencies also make up a nationwide network of job and applicant information in the form of job banks. These job banks have one drawback, however: the Service and its state agencies do not actually recruit people but only passively assist those who come to them. In addition, those who do come in are often untrained or only marginally qualified for most jobs.

Private employment agencies tend to serve two groups of job applicants—professional and managerial, and unskilled. The agencies dealing with unskilled applicants often provide job candidates that employers would have a difficult time finding otherwise. Many of the employers looking for unskilled workers do not have the resources to do their own recruiting or have only temporary or seasonal demands for them.

Private agencies play a major role in recruiting professional and managerial candidates.[15] These agencies supply services for applicants of all ages; most, however, have had some work experience beyond college. During the past ten years, the executive recruiting industry has grown phenomenally. Some estimates suggest that the search firms now generate more than $200 million in billings. The fees charged by these agencies range up to one-third of the first year's total salary and bonus package for the job to be filled.

Even when successful, the cost of using a search firm may be much greater than the fees charged. In the prescreening process, for example, the search firm can err by rejecting a candidate who would do well. These errors pose additional costs to the organization.[16] The organization, however, can minimize these costs by closely monitoring the search firm's activities. Note also that these agencies may prescreen applicants who are already working with other organizations. Consequently, in addition to the expense, this method of dealing with a potential candidate is apt to be secretive and counter to the openness that is desirable in an organization's employment process. Whatever the situation, it is nevertheless still subject to equal employment guidelines.

TEMPORARY-HELP AGENCIES. At the same time that the private recruiting agencies provide applicants for full-time positions, temporary-help agencies annually employ more than 3 million people.[17] There are over 4,500 of these agencies, and they generate more than $25 billion in annual revenues. Their use is growing as skilled and semiskilled individuals find it preferable to work less than a 40-hour week or on a schedule of their own choosing. Temporary employees (or temps) usually work in a variety of organizations; consequently, they can satisfy preferences for schedule flexibility and workplace variety. Furthermore, temps can receive higher pay than the organization's permanent staff, although they also generally forego benefits.

Organizations are using temporary-help agencies more than ever because certain hard-to-get skills are available nowhere else. (This is especially true for small companies that are not highly visible or cannot spend time recruiting.) In addition, many organizations need people for only a short time. Getting them without an extensive search while retaining the flexibility to reduce their work force without costly layoffs and potential unemployment compensation payments is an obvious advantage. We will discuss the use of temporary workers further under contract recruiting in the section on trends.

TRADE ASSOCIATIONS AND UNIONS. Unions for the building trades and maritime workers assume responsibility for supplying employers with skilled labor. This practice takes many labor decisions, such as job assignment, out of company hands. The *Taft-Hartley Act*, however, restricts these "hiring hall" practices to a limited number of industries.

Trade and professional associations are important sources for recruiting. Their newsletters and annual conferences often provide notice of employment opportunities. Annual conferences can give employers and potential job applicants an opportunity to meet. Communities and schools have adopted this idea and now bring together large numbers of employers and job seekers at **job fairs**. Of course, with only a limited time for interviews, such fairs or career conferences are only an initial step in the recruitment process. They are nevertheless, effective for both employers and individuals.

SCHOOLS. Schools can be categorized into three types—high schools, vocational and technical schools, and colleges and universities. All are important

The use of temps or temporary help is growing rapidly. Manpower, Inc., a temp agency, is one of the largest employers in the United States today.

Foreign nationals can serve U.S. firms abroad as either host-country nationals or third-country nationals.

Foreign nationals working for U.S. firms in the United States are also called aliens.

External methods for obtaining job applicants include:

- radio and television
- newspaper and trade journals
- computerized services
- acquisitions and mergers
- open houses

sources of recruits for most organizations, although their importance varies depending on the type of applicant sought. For example, if an organization is recruiting managerial, technical, or professional applicants, then colleges and universities are more important, while high schools and vocational and technical schools become important when an organization is seeking plant/service and clerical employees (see Exhibit 7.2).

Recruiting at colleges and universities is often an expensive process, even if the recruiting visit eventually produces job offers and acceptances. Approximately 30 percent of the applicants hired from college leave the organization within the first five years of their employment. This rate of turnover is even higher for graduate students. Some people attribute this high rate of turnover to the lack of challenge in the initial job assignments. Organizations claim, however, that people just out of college have unrealistic expectations. Partly because of the expense, organizations are now questioning the necessity of hiring college graduates for some of their jobs. Another reason for this reevaluation is the potential legal burden that an organization must assume if adverse impact results. In this event, the organization may have to show that a college degree is related to the performance of the job.

Nevertheless, college placement services are helpful to an organization recruiting in particular fields such as engineering and microelectronics and those seeking highly talented and qualified minorities and women. In addition, organizations make campus visits to recruit college alumni, not just those about to graduate. Outreach programs by college and universities that provide placement services for their alumni enhance the attractiveness of the campus to employers, who benefit by having a broader and more experienced pool of applicants from which to recruit.

FOREIGN NATIONALS.   As indicated in Chapter 3, certain labor shortages exist; these include professionals such as chemical engineers, nurses, and geologists. As a result, employers sometimes recruit foreign nationals—either overseas or in college placement offices.[18] Organizations use foreign nationals for operations both in the United States and abroad. When they work abroad, foreign nationals can serve as **host-country nationals (HCNs)** (persons working in their own country, which is not the country of the parent company) or **third-country nationals (TCNs)** (persons working in a country that is neither their own country nor the country of the parent company). In either capacity, these employees are critical for any company operating internationally. A novel use of host-country nationals is the recent use of Russian scientists by U.S. firms. This practice not only represents a global solution to a domestic skill shortage, but also an economical way to get highly skilled workers. This practice is described in the feature, "Managing Human Resources: Genius for Hire—The Soviet's Best, at Bargain Rates."

Foreign nationals have become so critical that U.S. companies have increased efforts to ensure that their foreign employees either are legal or become legal. Under the 1986 *Immigration Reform and Control Act* and the *Immigration Act of 1990*, it is unlawful for employers to hire foreign nationals who are not authorized to work in the United States.

EXTERNAL METHODS

Many organizations looking for applicants of all types engage in extensive advertising on radio and television, in the local paper, and in national newspapers such as *The Wall Street Journal*.

THE millions of scientists and engineers of the former Soviet Union, once feared and respected throughout the world for their big rockets and thermonuclear bombs, for their mathematical rigor and breakthroughs in fields like nonlinear optics, are now desperate amid a crumbling economy. Many have been thrown out of work. The lucky ones who still have jobs often help support themselves and their families by moonlighting. Inevitably, a growing number who can afford to do so are leaving to work in the West. And those left behind can often be hired for a song.

That point was driven home last week as a top team of more than 100 fusion scientists at the Kurchatov Institute of Atomic Energy in Moscow signed a contract to go to work for Uncle Sam. The cost to American taxpayers for one year's effort was an amazingly low $90,000. So eager was the team to work for the United States that it fired up its world-class apparatus for exploring the feasibility of nuclear fusion even before the contract was signed.

There are some areas of science where the old Soviet Union was a world leader. There were centers of excellence. If those dry up and disappear, it's a loss not just for Russia and former Soviet republics, but for world civilization.

It was the Russian chemist Dmitri Mendeleev who came up with the periodic table of the elements in the 19th century. In the early 20th century, Ivan Pavlov probed the riddle of behavior. Soviet scientists put the first satellite and man into space. Pytor Kapitsa, Nikolai Basov, and Lev Landau won Nobel prizes for physics.

Dr. Mohamed S. El-Genk, a nuclear engineer at the University of New Mexico, recently brought experts from the Kurchatov Institute in Moscow for a semester in Albuquerque, even though he says it is better to fund them at home in Russia. "If you bring them over here, there's a chance they won't want to go back," he said. "You'll be draining the country of its talent."

Scientists left behind are signing Western contracts as fast as they can to supplement dwindling incomes. A Russian computer scientist, Boris A. Babayan, is setting up a laboratory in Moscow for Sun Microsystems, Inc., based in Mountain View, California, that will employ his team of about 50 software and hardware designers. Mr. Babayan created the supercomputers used by the Soviets to design nuclear arms. Sun Microsystems will pay each of his team's members a few hundred dollars a year—ample pay by Moscow standards.[19]

RADIO AND TELEVISION. Of the approximately $3 billion spent annually on recruitment advertising, only a tiny percentage is spent on radio and television. Companies are reluctant to use these media because they fear media advertising will be too expensive or that it will make the company look desperate and damage the firm's conservative image.

Yet, organizations are desperate to reach certain types of job applicants such as skilled workers. In reality, of course, there is nothing inherently desperate about using radio and television. Rather it is the content and delivery that can imply some level of desperation. Recognizing this, organizations are increasing their recruitment expenditures for radio and television advertisements, with favorable results.[20]

NEWSPAPERS AND TRADE JOURNALS. Newspapers have traditionally been the most common method of external recruiting. They reach a large number of potential applicants at a relatively low cost per hire. Newspaper ads are used to recruit for all types of positions, from unskilled to top managerial. The ads range from matter-of-fact to creative.

Trade journals enable organizations to aim at much more specific groups of potential applicants than do the newspapers. Ads in trade journals are often more creative and of a higher quality. Unfortunately, long lead times are required, and the ads can thus become dated.

Whatever the medium, preparing ads requires considerable skill. Many organizations hire advertising firms to do this. Selecting an advertising agency must be done with the same care used to select a private recruiting agency.[21] However, for firms that want to prepare the ads themselves, the feature, "HR Advice and Application," offers several tips.

COMPUTERIZED SERVICES. A recent addition to external methods is the computerized recruiting service and use of the information highway. This works both as a place to list job openings and a place to locate job applicants.

> Personnel officers using a Job/Net terminal "can find people in fifteen minutes that would take eight hours to find going through paper résumés," says Janice Kempf, a vice president and cofounder, M/A Com, a microwave and telecommunications company in Burlington, Massachusetts, recently hired a $30,000 quality-control engineer through Job/Net. "If we paid an agency fee, it would have been $6,500 to $7,000," says Richard L. Bove, the staffing and development manager. He adds that the service lets him see more résumés of qualified people and lets him choose people who don't require expensive relocation.[23]

ACQUISITIONS AND MERGERS. Another method of staffing organizations are mergers and acquisitions. In contrast to the other external methods, this one can facilitate the immediate implementation of an organization's strategic plan by acquiring a company with skilled employees. This ready pool may enable an organization to pursue a business plan, such as entering a new product line, that would otherwise be unfeasible using standard recruiting methods. The need to displace employees and to integrate a large number of them rather quickly into a new organization, however, means that the human resource planning and selection process becomes more critical than ever.[24]

MULTIPLE AND NEW SOURCES AND METHODS

Because of the growing shortage of qualified workers, organizations find themselves using new approaches to recruitment. In addition to combining the previously discussed sources and methods, they are using sources and methods not used before. This includes advertising in movie theaters and enticing retired senior citizens back to work. Days Inn, the national motel chain, is doing exactly this. According to Richard A. Smith, executive vice president for Days Inn:

> Days Inns started actively recruiting older employees in the mid-1980s when, because of a shrinking labor market, we had to look for alternative labor sources to fill jobs. We couldn't find all the individuals needed to fill 65–85 positions a week at our largest reservation center, which at that time was in Atlanta, Georgia. Fast-food restaurants were gobbling up the labor market. The senior market seemed the most likely for us.
>
> Days Inns started with an exhibit at a local job fair for seniors. With assistance from older employees already on the payroll, the company organized its

ASK THE EXPERTS— WINNING HELP-WANTED ADS

Q-1. How do you make sure that your ad meets equal employment opportunity requirements while accurately describing the position available?

A-1. Before you can begin your search, you'll need to go to your job description. If you don't already have one, bring two or three of your top people from the area you're trying to fill, and with their input, write one. The job description should include all essential and marginal job functions as required by the *Americans with Disabilities Act*. Then you can write a newspaper ad that matches the job description. You must include only objective, job-related requirements.

Q-2. What have you done when an ad didn't work?

A-2. I kept going back to my job description, designing my ad around it. Eventually, I came up with an ad that was very effective and brought in just the type of applicant I was looking for.

Q-3. What should be included in the ad?

A-3. Your recruitment ad—whether it's to be placed in a local paper or a trade magazine—needs to include certain basic elements. The ad should

- **Be descriptive and deal with specific needs**. If you're looking for a sales representative, say SALES REPRESENTATIVE in bold type. This will focus attention on the ad by telling the reader exactly what you're looking for.
- **Tell the readers exactly what you're selling**. Don't make the ad generic or misleading. Given applicants the geographic area of the position you're trying to fill. Does the job require traveling? If so, mention how much travel is required.
- **Tell the reader something about your company**—and what qualities and qualifications the successful applicant will need. For instance, if the job requires that the applicant have a roadworthy vehicle, say so. Always ask for references. For example, "Applicant must have a reliable auto, strong sales background, and good references."
- **Include all essential information**. Don't leave

anything to the imagination of the applicant. You'll screen out applicants, but that's better than wasting time interviewing people who will only turn you down, anyway, when they find out that no expenses are paid.

Q-4. How do you deal with responses to the ad?

A-4. I have all applicants call a central location and make an appointment for an interview. See them all. Don't screen any applicants over the phone.

A good ad will have done most of your screening for you. For instance, if I ask for good references, a reader who doesn't have them probably isn't going to apply, because he or she doesn't want to be embarrassed when I check them out. My ads usually bring in 15–20 applicants, and most of them are exactly what I'm looking for.

Q-5. Once you've interviewed the applicants, how do you determine which is the best one?

A-5. First, you have to be sure that the applicant understands the job, the benefits, and what's expected of him or her. Be scrupulously honest about compensation. Don't mislead a candidate for a sales job, for instance, with stories about $100,000 income for hard work when you know your average salesperson makes less than $45,000.

To see if there really is a match, ask a promising candidate to go home and think about the position for a few days. This will give you an additional opportunity to check references—and it will give your prospective hire the opportunity to check references about your company as well.

Check References. A careful reference check is time-consuming, but it's essential. To call an applicant's previous employer and ask him or her to be candid is sometimes difficult, but you have to try. In today's litigious society, some companies may be hesitant about giving out any information at all except to confirm that the person was employed there.

Some companies require all applicants to sign release forms noting that former employers will be contacted for references. When you contact a former employer, you may need to do it in writing, on company letterhead, with a copy of the release form enclosed. Even this procedure isn't a guarantee, but you may have better luck getting a more candid reference than you would without it.[22]

own job fair, which was held on a Saturday and was well publicized. It attracted about 100 older applicants and 75–85 were hired, many of whom still work for the company. Once the company had about 85 older employees, it relied on these employees rather than on additional job fairs to pass the word that the company wanted to hire additional seniors.

People who are 55 years old or older are hired for both part-time and full-time positions at the reservations center at starting wages of $4–$6 an hour. As is true with other Days Inns employees, they are not required to pass a physical examination. In addition, because the reservation system is a 7-day-a-week, 24-hour-a-day operation, new hires can virtually choose their own schedules.[25]

As labor shortages increase, companies are learning to become more skillful and more creative at recruiting. They look at the recruiting process from the applicant's perspective and can thus design better recruiting programs.

LEARNING OBJECTIVE 3
Indicate how organizations can increase their pools of potentially qualified job applicants by methods other than the traditional ones.

Organizations can do many things to attract applicants.

2/20/96

INCREASING THE POOL OF POTENTIALLY QUALIFIED APPLICANTS

Although organizations may use many sources of recruitment, they may not always obtain the desired number of applicants nor retain the most valued employees. This is especially true in competitive labor markets. But an organization can enhance its recruitment by offering inducements such as relocation assistance or through efforts to establish auxiliary programs such as career development or child care. Many ideas that organizations are using to increase their pools of qualified job applicants have the added benefit of increasing the probability that once hired, the applicant-employee will stay.

CONVEYING JOB AND ORGANIZATIONAL INFORMATION

The traditional approach to recruiting matches the applicant's abilities, with the skills required on the job. A more recent approach, although still concerned with matching skills and abilities, is also concerned with matching the applicant's personality, interests, and preferences both with the job and with organizational characteristics. Getting new hires to stay is as important as finding applicants who can do the job. Obtaining both is possible by (1) devoting attention to the job interview, (2) developing policies regarding job offer acceptances, and (3) carefully timing recruitment procedures.

Organizations can become more attractive by conveying job and organizational information realistically.

JOB INTERVIEW.   A vital aspect of the recruitment process is the interview. A good interview provides the applicant with a **realistic preview** of what the job will be like. It can definitely be an enticement to join an organization, just as a bad interview will deter an applicant.

The quality of the interview is, of course, just one aspect of the recruitment process. Other things being equal, however, the chances of a person accepting a job offer increases when interviewers show interest and concern for the applicant. In addition, college students feel most positive toward the recruitment interview when they can use at least half of the interview to ask questions and when they are not embarrassed or put one the spot by the interviewer.

The content of the recruitment interview is important. Organizations often assume that it is in their best interest to tell a job applicant only the positive aspects of the organization. But studies by the life insurance industry have reported that providing realistic (positive and negative) information actually increases the number of eventual recruits. In addition, those who receive realistic job information are less likely to quit once they accept the job.[26]

Assuming that recruits pass the initial screening (discussed in more detail in Chapter 8, Selection), they should be given the opportunity to interview with a potential supervisor and even with co-workers. The interview with the potential supervisor is crucial, for this is the person who often makes the final decision.

POLICIES REGARDING JOB OFFER ACCEPTANCE. Employers can influence applicants' selection decisions through the amount of time they allow individuals to ponder the offer. Given unlimited time to ponder their decision, most job seekers will delay decision making until they have heard from all organizations in the job search net. Thus, setting deadlines is an important detail because the lack of one places the organization at a distinct disadvantage. Unless its job openings are unlimited, it cannot extend an offer to a second-choice candidate until a decision is made by their first choice. Since job markets are dynamic, high-potential candidates may commit elsewhere. Thus, most organizations have recall policies, policies to bring back former employees, and job seekers find themselves in the dilemma of having to decide on a minimally acceptable offer before possibly receiving a preferred offer.

TIMING. In markets where recruiting occurs in well-defined cycles (such as college recruiting), organizations can opt to be early participants. Assuming that most individuals evaluate job options sequentially, organizations enhance their chances of obtaining high-potential candidates by participating early in the cycle. For example, high-technology companies involve high-potential juniors in summer internships or cooperative education programs. Progressive organizations are also bypassing traditional second-semester campus interviews and inviting high-potential candidates directly to corporate headquarters early in their senior years. Most major accounting firms have job offers out and accepted by years end. Such strategies are designed to induce commitment from top graduates before exposure to competing firms. Organizations who rely upon traditional second-semester interviews and long, drawn out selection processes may find themselves in a less competitive position than their proactive recruiting rivals.[27]

Good timing will secure the best applicants.

ADDRESSING THE NEEDS OF APPLICANTS: SOCIALIZATION

Dealing with increased labor shortages of qualified workers can in part be solved by effectively managing the socialization process. **Socialization** is the process that companies use to expose new employees to their culture and ways of doing things. When done successfully, it results in intensely loyal employees who are dedicated to the company. Companies that have perfected the socialization process include Procter & Gamble, Morgan Guaranty Trust, and Corning Glass.

Socialization is a key HR process in organizations.

Often, the socialization process begins before the employee is hired. At Procter & Gamble (P&G), for example, an elite cadre of line managers trained in interviewing skills probe applicants for entry-level positions in brand management for qualities such as the "ability to turn out high volumes of excellent work." Only after successfully completing at least two interviews and a test of general knowledge is the applicant flown to P&G headquarters in Cincinnati, where the applicant confronts a day-long series of interviews. If the applicant passes this extensive screening process, he or she is confronted with a series of rigorous job experiences calculated to induce humility and openness to new ways of doing things. Typically, this phase of socialization involves long hours of work at a pressure cooker pace. Throughout this and other phases of the socialization process, the new employee is constantly made aware of transcendent company values and organizational folklore, including the emphasis on product quality and the dedication and commitment of employees long since past. This intense socialization results in increased commitment to the success of the company, willingness to work long hours, and decreased absenteeism and turnover.[28]

The intensity of the socialization often depends on employee's backgrounds. Organizations usually recruit from familiar sources that have supplied good applicants in the past. They may also recruit individuals who are already socialized but by other organizations. Whatever recruitment and selection methods are used, they are not likely to produce new employees who know corporate culture. Thus, socialization is a cost-effective endeavor. Of the possible formalized methods of socialization, two deserve particular attention: orientation programs and job assignments.

ORIENTATION PROGRAMS

Orientation programs welcome new employees and inform them about the company.

Orientation programs are frequently used to brief new employees on benefit programs and options, to advise them of rules and regulations, and to provide them with a folder or handbook of the policies and practices of the organization.[29]

Orientation programs require more than folders or handbooks, however. The handbooks usually contain information about equal employment opportunity practices, safety regulations, work times, coffee breaks, the structure and history of organization, and perhaps the products or services of the organization. Typically, however, the orientation program does not tell employees about the politics of the organization—for example, that the organization may soon be going out of business, that it may be merging with another company, or even that an extensive layoff may soon occur.[30]

The orientation program conveys some information about the norms, values, attitudes, and behaviors appropriate for new employees, the majority of socialization is left to informal day-to-day interactions among employees.

Orientation programs are almost always coordinated by the HR director. The program itself is usually run by HR staff, with some participation by line managers and other employees, depending on the design of the program.

Once employees are hired, they should immediately begin formal orientation programs.

Arthur Nathan, Vice President,
Human Resources,
Mirage Casino Hotel

In large organizations, orientation programs are often conducted every week. Some programs have two orientation sessions one week apart, which are typically presented to groups of new hires. Although efficient, this approach tends to negate each employee's sense of identity and importance. To counterbalance this, each employee is often assigned to a trainer or "buddy" (sometimes the immediate supervisor) who can answer further questions and introduce the new hire to other employees in the work unit or department.

Orientation programs can last longer than one or two days. The orientation program at Corning Glass Works, for example, lasts 15 months. The critical components of the program at Corning include:

- Pre-arrival period—the supervisor gets the office ready and, based on discussions with the new hire, creates a preliminary management-by-objectives (MBO) list.
- First day—following breakfast with the supervisor, the new hire goes through personnel processing, attends a half-day "Corning and You" seminar, tours the facility, and meets co-workers.
- First week—this time is set aside for getting settled in the department or office and for one-on-one discussions with the supervisor and co-workers. Performance expectations and other general job-related matters are discussed, and details of the MBO plan are formalized.

- Second through fourth weeks—regular assignments begin. The new hire also attends a special employee benefits seminar.
- Second through fifth months—assignments increase and progress is reviewed biweekly with the supervisor. The employee also attends six two-and-one-half-hour seminars on such topics as quality and productivity and reviews these with the supervisor.
- Sixth month—the new employee reviews the MBO list with the supervisor and receives a performance review.
- Seventh through fifteenth months—MBO and performance and salary reviews are conducted.[31]

In contrast to this lengthy process, most orientation programs last only a few hours, though, and are done within the first week or two of employment. Occasionally, an orientation follow-up takes place a year or so later. Because orientation programs do only part of the job of socialization, other methods such as job assignments are also used.

JOB ASSIGNMENTS

The aspects of **job assignments** that impart socialization are the characteristics of the initial job, the nature of the early experiences, and the first supervisor. The initial job often determines the new hires future success. The more challenge and responsibility the job offers, the more likely the person will be successful with the organization.[32] A challenging (but not overwhelming) job assignment implies that the organization believes the employee can do well and that the organization values him or her. Many times, organizations assign a simple job or rotate the new hire through departments to get a feel for different jobs. But employees may interpret these practices to mean that the organization does not yet trust their abilities or loyalties.

Employees' initial experiences can be heavily influenced by supervisors. These experiences assist new employees in acquiring appropriate values, norms, attitudes, and behaviors. Supervisors serve as role models and set expectations. The positive influence that a supervisor's expectations can have on a new employee is referred to as the **Pygmalion effect**. A supervisor who believes that the new employee will do well conveys this belief to the employee, who then tends to live up to those expectations.[33]

The effectiveness of the socialization process is enhanced when the HR department has actively developed skills in managing work force diversity, and an effective socialization process increases the chances that an employee will stay. Because this can also increase an organization's applicant pool, skill in managing work force diversity is an important trend affecting recruitment; it involves many other human resource activities as McDonald's experience (see the feature at the beginning of the chapter) indicates.

■ INTERNATIONAL COMPARISONS

JAPAN
The recruitment of graduates in Japan takes place only once a year, although this is changing somewhat. In a company's direct recruitment, college professors play dominant roles. Company Y asks Professor X to recommend so many students with special qualifications in certain fields. Social sciences, law, and humanities students are considered for administrative jobs such as planning, human

The first job assignment can be one of your most important.

Managers can increase employee retention simply by treating workers as they hope to be treated themselves.

Arthur Nathan, Vice President,
Human Resources,
Mirage Casino Hotel

The *Pygmalion effect* is the impact that the boss's expectations have on the behavior of the worker.

Japanese firms have traditionally had a very organized system for recruitment.

resources, sales, or purchasing while technically oriented students are considered for the technical jobs such as engineering, chemistry, and computer science. An example illustrates the process.

Aspiring administrators are asked to apply directly to employers for jobs. Following the formal application, the candidate is asked to appear for a set of interviews with company employees, managers, and executives. The basic criteria for hiring—besides an employee's potential or ability—are "balanced" personality and moderate views. The evaluation of job candidates is often supplemented by background checks assigned to private investigators who interview the candidate's neighbors and acquaintances, check local police records, and examine the family history. Those who pass the last round of interviews are invited to sit for the company entrance examination. Officially, this exam determines who is best qualified for the job, but in many corporations over 90 percent of candidates are preselected on the basis of earlier interviews. The exam usually asks essay questions on such topics as family background, career/life objectives, or the applicant's strengths and weaknesses. A number of firms use the exam as an assessment tool to determine the career interests of new employees.[34]

The reliance on intermediaries (that is, college professors) for selection decisions serves a number of purposes. First, it is difficult to evaluate a student's technical potential on the basis of a short interview only, when the majority of interviewers have little up-to-date technical background. If a company waited for a written examination, it could not preselect and would risk losing the best candidates to the competition. Second, because of the competition for graduates, recruiters cultivate good relations with college professors, who then recommend individual firms to the students. In this way, the firms get their "fair share" of talent; this prevents a self-defeating bidding war that would not only raise starting salaries, but more critically would disrupt the carefully balanced compensation structures of internal labor markets. And last, college grades are not an important selection tool. Specific seminars (courses taken with a professor's permission) are seen as more selective than others and, thus, develop an "elite" reputation for the students taking them. The educational credentials of the school from which the student is graduating are weighted heavily. Given the intense and rigorous competition to enter first-tier schools, the companies rely on the university entrance examination as an indicator of the employee's "latest ability."

During the 1970s, many factors in Japanese management practice demanded modification. Economic growth rates were declining and automation was broadly implemented. At this point, Japanese companies began hiring significantly fewer workers in entry-level positions. This resulted in the average age of employees increasing as they moved up the seniority ladder. In turn, pressure was added on average wage costs. The most powerful and negative effect of this era was the low morale caused by few opportunities for real advancement.

The Japanese responded to these problems quickly instead of ignoring them. They increased their flexibility in employment. This was accomplished with temporary transfers of surplus employees to other companies that are part of the "extended organization." This form of organization, called *keiretsu*, is a vertical linkage of companies that are mutual suppliers and customers.[35]

MEXICO

Mexican employers in the maquiladoras, (border region companies) recruit personnel as the need arises. There is always an abundance of applicants; this allows companies to intensively screen applicants for assembly work. Mexican workers accept this screening because of the relatively good wages and benefits they can get at maquiladoras compared with other employment.

Since the cost of newspapers makes help-wanted advertisements useless, recruitment is done primarily by approaching people and asking them to apply. Therefore, it is common to find many family members working at the same maquiladora. Not surprisingly, traditional Mexican values and social structure are apparent in many organizational programs since workers feel they are part of the organization in a very different way than do American workers. Employers celebrate numerous holidays, and it is common for companies to throw parties for a variety of events to maintain a family atmosphere.[36]

It is possible, however, that this informal and family-oriented approach to recruitment may begin to change. With the passage of the North American Free Trade Act (NAFTA) in 1993, economic activity has increased significantly in Mexico. With this likely to continue, companies in Mexico will need to hire workers in greater numbers than family referrals will be able to supply. As this occurs, firms will begin to formalize their recruiting procedures. With the economy and wages increasing, individuals will find the cost of newspapers more accessible to them, thus making the formalized recruiting procedures more effective than previously. And as the recruiting activity increases and formalizes, the selection, performance appraisal, compensation and training activities will also. Thus, the next several years should see a substantial increase in concern for human resource management in Mexico.

CURRENT TRENDS

Key trends in recruitment include managing work force diversity, contract recruiting, work flow management, and truth-in-hiring.

MANAGING WORK FORCE DIVERSITY

As we discussed in Chapter 3, the rapidly changing demographics of the U.S. population has created a mosaic of peoples. Consequently, organizations are looking at a labor force that varies by age, gender, nationality, ethnic and cultural background and physical abilities. To facilitate the entry of this broad array of people into work a day world, firms are using many recruitment methods, not just one or two, and they no longer rely solely on their tried-and-true methods. They continually scan the environment, keep themselves well-informed on diversity issues, and look for new ways to recruit populations that may have been overlooked in standard approaches to recruitment. The feature, "Managing Human Resources at Burger King," illustrates a multimethod approach to recruiting in a diverse work force.

CONTRACT RECRUITING

In response to up-and-down employment cycles and cost containment, there is a trend toward **contract recruiting**. Contract recruiting is the hiring of an individual (contract recruitee) to work for only a limited and specified period of time (for example, three to six months) and then leave. These individuals may seek the work themselves (independent contractors) or they work for an agency that specializes in placing individuals in organizations for limited periods of time. While contracting recruiting can be used to find individual's to work in virtually all jobs an organization has, they can be used quite effectively by HR departments who have a temporary need. For example, an organization may win a large contract and it needs to hire a great many new job applicants as fast as possible.

Trends in recruitment include:

- **managing diversity**
- **contract recruiting**
- **work flow management**
- **truth-in-hiring**

LEARNING OBJECTIVE 4

Describe the impact of work force diversity on a firm's recruitment policies.

Contract recruiting is the practice of hiring an individual for a limited period of time as specified in a contract.

MANAGING HUMAN RESOURCES
at Burger King

RECRUITMENT

IN the recruiting area, Burger King managers use many typical tools. They participate in high school job seminars and job fairs, work with local and state agencies to gather referrals, and solicit referrals from politicians who receive work requests from their constituents.

In addition, Burger King has some interesting recruiting programs:

- *Disabilities agencies:* The Florida region is experiencing great success with its "Be Capable" program. More than 100 differently abled young people work in Burger King stores there.

    "Early information indicates that we're experiencing much better retention with this group," said Robert Morrison, director of human resources. "They're more loyal and thankful for the company's efforts in hiring and training them."

- *Senior citizens:* This growing population is being reached through senior citizens centers. "We're hoping that they will have a positive influence on the young people," said Morrison. "They are a great opportunity for the fast food industry."

- *Operations recruiters:* Three regions—Boston, Atlanta, and Detroit—are experiencing the most severe labor shortages, so Burger King is testing a new position in those areas—operations recruiter. In most regions, recruitment is part of the store manager's job. But in these areas, the operations recruiter is now responsible.

- *Theater commercials:* Recruiting commercials are being aired before the main feature in theaters in Detroit and San Francisco.

- *"Ask me …":* Using employees as recruiters is

a proven winner. "Ask me about working for Burger King" buttons, T-shirts, posters, etc., are being used successfully in the Florida region.

- *Crew referral:* Burger King offers cash awards for recruiting. Different regions handle this in different ways. In the areas where young people are exceptionally hard to find, the cash award is simply for bringing in an applicant; in others it is for a new hire.

- *Shift premiums:* Six regions are paying a higher hourly wage for certain, less desirable shifts.

- *Providing transportation:* When a store cannot hire from its own community because it is in an affluent neighborhood where young people don't work or in an industrial area where there are not many young people, Burger King provides transportation or bus fare.

- *Applicant sharing:* Restaurants transfer applications to other stores in the area. "Surprisingly, the restaurant industry hasn't done much of this," said Morrison. "Now we're seeing our managers share their applicants."

- *Ex-employee log:* Some stores call back their good ex-employees to either offer them jobs or ask them to refer their friends.

- *Translates:* Just recently some stores have put recruitment ads in the menu board spot where the pictures of new products are usually placed.

- *TV show:* Burger King is working with an advertising agency to develop a fourteen minute television program that will promote the idea of learning through work. It will not focus on Burger King, but on the fast-food industry and the many advantages for young people found there.[37]

The HR department is then faced with much more work than it can do, but this large volume of work will only last a short period of time. For example, when GTE in Needham, Massachusetts, won a major contract with the government, they needed 1,200 professionals to be on board within 16 months. At the peak of recruiting twelve contract recruiters worked full-time to establish a recruiting and selection system. At the end of the 16 months only two remained.

With the switch to a service economy, banks, financial services, and insurance and health-care organizations are expected to increasingly use contract recruiting. Recently, Fidelity Investments opened up a new consumer division in Salt Lake City. Rather than relying on a permanent staff to recruit applicants, the firm trained personnel graduate students in Fidelity's selection procedures. *En masse*, these contract recruitees were able to secure enough staff for the new office to be operational within two months. Similarly, Kendall Co. used contract recruiters to reduce cost per hire. Then during downsizing, Kendall again used contractors, this time for outplacement counseling.[38]

WORK FLOW MANAGEMENT

As you have been reading this chapter, you have probably said to yourself, "This guy always keeps talking about organizations having to deal with a labor shortage, yet all I see in the paper are stories about layoffs and the difficulties of getting a job!" This is an excellent point and one that identifies the importance of work flow management.

Yes, companies in the United States and now in Japan and Europe, are downsizing—at both managerial and nonmanagerial levels, but this is occurring mainly in large companies. Many smaller companies are expanding faster than they can find workers to fill their needs.

That employees continually come and go is a fact of workplace life. The process of recruitment is continually needed at some level to ensure that the best applicants are attracted to the firm and that the best employees stay. Because of rapid changes in technology, the need for balance is even more important. Companies cannot afford to be without the latest in technological skills, so they must continually look at their recruitment methods and sources to make sure that needed skills are coming in and that skills no longer needed are either being outplaced or retrained. In this respect, the HR planning and recruitment activities work hand-in-hand. Staff involved in these activities need to continually scan the environment and work closely with the business to know what's going on, what technologies are likely to be needed, and when new employees are likely to be required and when others are not. Recruitment is a dynamic activity: to be effective, it must keep on top of the outflow of human resources as much as it must supply the inflow.[39]

TRUTH-IN-HIRING: ETHICS IN RECRUITMENT

Is it ethical, acceptable behavior for firms to promise something to a job candidate in order to make the firm attractive and then not deliver on the promise? The courts are now saying that if firms do make false promises to job candidates they can face costly lawsuits (*Stewart v. Jackson & Nash, 1992*). Such truth-in-hiring lawsuits, in which employers are sued for not keeping recruitment promises, have yielded damage awards as high as $10 million! Thus, truth-in-hiring appears to be a legal as well as an ethical issue that is of importance both to the individual and to the organization.

The HR department is in a crucial position to ensure that line managers and others involved in recruitment are aware of the law, and that they do not make

Contract employees may need to be trained by the firm before they can be fully productive.

The demographic data indicate that baby-busters will be in high demand in a growing economy because there are relatively few of them.

Even in tough times, we have to bring some level of entry-level talent into the organization to keep the business revitalized.

Andy Esparza, Director of Recruitment and College Relations, AT&T Global Information Solutions (formerly NCR)

DID YOU KNOW?

Colorado's highest court upheld a jury's award of $451,600 because a company withheld information about its financial difficulties from a prospective employee. (*Berger v. Security Pacific Information Systems*)

exorbitant promises. Yes, firms are hiring and they do need good people, but they must look at the short-term and the long-term implications of the contract of trust they hold with job applicants—for ethical and legal reasons.

SUMMARY

Organizations are dynamic, and the need to attract the right number of people at the right time and place is perpetual. By now, you have probably recognized that effective recruitment cannot be conducted in a vacuum. Two important human resource activities that guide effective recruitment are (1) human resource planning and (2) job analysis. Planning establishes personnel requirements and permits adequate time to anticipate and carry out recruitment activities. Job analysis enables the organization to convey information accurately (via job descriptions and job specifications) to applicants so that both individuals and organizations are well matched.

Legal compliance plays a large role in recruitment, primarily in requiring organizations to meet federal and state fair employment regulations in their staffing activities. Affirmative action programs, though usually designed explicitly for legal compliance, illustrate how availability and utilization analyses aid organizations in both planning for, and recruitment of, human resources.

Recruitment involves internal and external searches, often as a result of promotion, transfer, and turnover decisions. Although organizations vary considerably in terms of the types of jobs available, both external and internal labor markets exist for the recruitment of suitable applicants. Over time, organizations weigh costs and benefits of internal and external methods in order to choose the most effective one for a given job. Recruitment is fundamentally the search for information, specifically for a given position. Managing people effectively and efficiently means obtaining this information at the lowest cost possible. Selection is closely connected to recruitment because staffing requires not only the recruitment of the right number of qualified people at the lowest cost, but also the matching of the right person to the right job at the right time, this connection is addressed in the next chapter.

KEY CONCEPTS

affirmative action programs	job fairs	recruitment
availability analysis	job profiles	relevant labor market
consent decree	job posting	skills inventories
contract recruiters	orientation programs	socialization
contract recruiting	private employment agencies	state employment agencies
employee referral programs	*prima facie*	third-country nationals (TCNs)
host-country nationals (HCNs)	promotion-from-within	underutilization
job assignments	Pygmalion effect	utilization analysis
	realistic preview	
	recall policy	

REVIEW AND DISCUSSION QUESTIONS

1. What are the purposes of recruitment? How do these purposes affect other organizational activities?
2. Just-in-time inventory is a concept that enables manufacturers to assemble products from parts that are delivered as needed rather than kept in inventory, which is costly. Could this concept be applied to recruitment function and the management of human resources? Explain.
3. How does HR planning contribute to effective recruitment? What are the roles of the line manager and human resource manager in each of these activities?
4. Why do some organizations use external searches, whereas others use internal searches?
5. The search for job applicants involves finding not only the right number, but also the right kind of applicants. Are some recruitment sources "richer" than others—that is, do they yield more information about the kind of applicant needed? Can you give examples?
6. What impact has the legal environment had on recruitment? Has this impact been positive or negative for organizations? Explain.
7. Assessment of recruitment activities requires an estimate of costs as well as benefits. Choose an organization that you are familiar with, and describe how you would measure and compare the costs and benefits of the recruitment methods used in that organization.
8. How can organizations increase their attractiveness to potential job applicants?
9. How can organizations increase the chances that applicants will stay once hired?
10. What is the impact of work force diversity on a firm's recruitment policies?

EXERCISES AND CASES

FIELD PROJECT

Outline the information that would be contained in a realistic job preview for prospective college students, and then prepare the preview. This information would be communicated to students in their job interviews. Choose a specific company on which to base your preview.

DOWNSIZING: ANATHEMA TO CORPORATE LOYALTY?

Jim Daniels suspected things could be worse, but nonetheless he was unprepared for the dilemma facing Defense Systems, Inc. Jim, vice president of human resources for DSI, joined the company one year ago when he was pirated away from one of the company's major competitors. DSI manufactures electronic components used in weapons supplied to the Air Force and many other firms. In addition, DSI makes semiconductors used in many of the weapons systems as well as in personal computers and automotive computers.

When Jim joined DSI, a major drive to build up the staff in engineering was undertaken in anticipation of a major upturn in the semiconductor market. Unfortunately, industry analysts' projections were optimistic, and the semiconductor market failed to pick up. DSI had recently completed an aggressive hiring policy at the major universities around the United States wherein the company had selected 1,000 engineers who were among the cream of the crop with an average GPA of 3.4. Without a pickup in business, however, DSI was confronted with some fairly unpleasant alternatives.

From one point of view, potential cutbacks at DSI were only part of an overall pattern of cutbacks, restructuring, and downsizing of major U.S. companies during the past few years. The motives among firms who have trimmed their work forces vary—some to please Wall Street and the stockholders, others to keep pace with foreign competitors or to shrink an unwieldy organizational structure. To Jim, the DSI layoffs or terminations were poor alternatives to dealing with a turbulent environment.

The major problem, as Jim saw it, was to preserve as many of these jobs as possible until business picked up. To terminate these new hires would irreparably harm DSI's future recruitment efforts. On the other hand, underemploying these talented recruits for very long was bound to lead to major dissatisfaction. Although terminations would improve the balance sheet in the short run, Jim worried about the impact of such a move on corporate loyalty, a fragile and rare commodity at other major firms that have had to cut their white-collar work force by as much as 20 percent.

Jim is scheduled to meet with the executive committee of DSI in three days to discuss the overstaffing problems and to generate alternatives. In preparation for this meeting, Jim is trying to draw on his experience with his past employer to generate some ideas. A number of differences between DSI and Jim's old employer, though, makes comparisons difficult.

For one, DSI does not employ nearly the number of temporaries or student interns as did his old employer. Nor does DSI rely on subcontractors to produce parts needed in its assembly operation. Because of extra capacity, DSI can currently produce 50 percent of the parts it purchases, whereas Jim's ex-employer could produce only 5 percent.

Another major difference is the degree of training provided by DSI. At Jim's old employer, each employee can expect a minimum of 40 hours of additional training a year; at DSI, however, training consists of about 10 hours per year, much of it orientation training.

Jim wondered whether there might be some additional ways to remove slack from the system and at the same time preserve as many jobs as possible. For example, overtime hours are still paid to quite a few technicians. Would the engineers be willing to assume some of these duties in the interim until business picked up? Some older employees have accumulated several weeks of unused vacation. Could employees be encouraged to take unpaid leaves of absence? Perhaps early retirement incentives could be offered to make room for some of the bright young engineers. DSI also has fourteen other geographic locations, some in need of additional workers.

As Jim thought about these options, one thing was clear: he will need to organize and prioritize these ideas concisely if he is to be prepared for his upcoming meeting.

CASE QUESTIONS

1. Why is Jim sensitive to DSI's recruitment efforts?
2. What are some potential problems for the current class of engineers recruited at DSI?
3. How could the use of temporaries, student interns, or subcontractors potentially help DSI?
4. Evaluate Jim's alternatives for reducing DSI's labor surplus.

THE NEW RECRUIT

General Instruments (GI), a defense contractor, employs nearly 1,000 engineers and designs and manufactures a number of electronic systems for nuclear submarines. Recruiting qualified engineers has been difficult for GI because of the competitive market in Palo Alto and the substantial cost-of-living increase for anyone relocating to the area. Stan Fryer, project leader at GI, knew that today would be one of those proverbial Mondays that managers so often fear. Stan's boss and group manager Harry Hoskinsson, had left town on business the previous Friday and would not return until the following week.

Stan's problem this morning concerns a new engineer recruit, June Harrison, a single, 25-year-old systems engineer who was hired three weeks ago upon graduation from San Diego State University. Much to Stan's surprise, June has submitted a letter of resignation, stating personal reasons as the cause of her departure. In addition to the letter of resignation, Stan also has a memo from June's supervisor, Lou Snider, describing the events leading up to June's resignation.

As Stan reconstructed these events, it seemed that June was expecting overtime payment in this week's paycheck because of the extra hours she had put in over the previous three weeks. Lou Snider, however, had neglected to file the proper payroll paperwork so that June could receive her overtime in the current pay period. This did not surprise Stan, given Lou's prior history in other supervisory positions. Apparently, Harry Hoskinsson had spoken to Lou about filing so much overtime for his section. So Lou decided to spread out some of the overtime charges over several pay periods.

What Lou hadn't realized was that June had finally secured an apartment in Palo Alto (she had been renting a room in a nearby hotel) and had committed to making a three-month payment and deposit with her paycheck and the additional overtime payment she was expecting. When June realized what was going to happen, she called Harry Hoskinsson to set up a meeting to discuss how she could cover her housing expense. June remembered that when she was being recruited, Harry had emphatically told her to contact him if she ever needed anything or had any problems settling into her new job at GI. Harry

was in a bit of a rush to make a staff meeting, so he agreed to see June early the following day. When June reported to Harry's office the next morning, she was understandably upset when Harry's secretary told her that Harry had left town on a business trip. With that, she returned to her office and drafted her resignation letter.

As Stan contemplated how to resolve his "Monday morning" problem, he recalled the speech Harry had given him two years ago when he joined GI. Harry had made clear his distaste for young engineers who tended to live beyond their means and to count on bonuses and overtime as if they were regular and assured components of their paycheck. Nonetheless, Stan decided, despite Harry's speech, that GI must try to arrange for a loan covering June's housing expenses and, more importantly, to persuade her to reconsider her hasty decision.

No sooner had Stan decided on a course of action when June appeared in his doorway. She had done some thinking over the weekend after talking with another GI project engineer, a temporary employee hired only for the duration of his project. It seemed that temporary employees earned about 20 percent more than comparable permanent employees at GI, although they received considerably fewer benefits (such as retirement and health insurance). June made a proposal to Stan: she would retract her resignation letter if GI would permit her, in effect, to quit and be rehired as a temporary project engineer. Otherwise she planned to leave GI and accept a standing offer she had received from an engineering firm in her home city of San Diego. As Stan listened, he wondered how Harry would handle this situation. To Stan, June's proposal sounded like blackmail.

CASE QUESTIONS
1. Should June have resigned over the overtime issue?
2. Should GI accept June's proposal of rehiring her as a temporary employee?
3. How could the recruiting process for June have been done better?
4. Was the socialization process for June lacking something? What?

1. Information came from P. Sellers, "Look Who Learned About Value," *Fortune* (October, 18, 1993): 75, 78; B. J. Feder, "McDonald's Finds There's Still Plenty of Room to Grow," *The New York Times* (January 4, 1994): F5; B. J. Feder, "Dining Out at a Discount Store," *The New York Times* (August 16, 1993): D1, D2.

2. "Employer Recruitment Practices," *Personnel* (May 1988): 63–65; B. Schneider and N. Schmitt, *Staffing Organizations*, 2nd ed. (Glenview, Ill.: Foresman, 1986).

3. *Basic Skills in the U.S. Work Force* (New York: Center for Public Resources, 1983); L. S. Fink and M. M. Harris, "A Field Study of Applicants Reactions to Employment Opportunities: Does the Recruiter Make a Difference?" *Personnel Psychology* (Winter 1987): 765–84.

4. R. D. Dickson, "The Business of Equal Opportunity," *Harvard Business Review* (Jan.–Feb. 1992): 46–53; W. Guzzardi, "A Fresh View of Affirmative Action," *Fortune* (23 Sept. 1991): 210–13; R. Turner, *The Past and Future of Affirmative Action: A Guide for Human Resource Professionals and Corporate Counsel* (Westport, Conn.: Quorum Books/Greenwood Press, 1990); S. Carter, *Reflections of an Affirmative Action Baby* (New York: Basic Books, 1991); A. J. Jones, Jr., *Affirmative Talk, Affirmative Action: A Comparative Study of the Politics of Affirmative Action* (Westport, Conn.: Praeger Publishers, 1991); D. P. Twomey, *Equal Employment Opportunity Law* 3rd ed. (Cincinnati, Ohio: Southwestern, 1994).

5. The steps in utilization and availability analysis are based on the eight-factor analysis. For a description, see R. H. Faley and L. S. Kleiman, "Misconceptions and Realities in the Implementation of Equal Employment Opportunity," in *Readings in Personnel and Human Resource Management*, 3rd ed., R. S. Schuler, S. A. Youngblood, and V. L. Huber, (eds.) (St. Paul, Minn.: West, 1988); and Biddle and Associates, 2100 Northrup Ave., Suite 200A, Sacramento, CA 95825).

6. "Hiring the Disabled: A Firm Commitment," *Fair Employment Practices* (Feb. 4, 1988): 16; "Reasonable Job Accommodations for Employers and Employees," *Fair Employment Practices* (April 14, 1988): 45; B. Solomon and W. H. Wagel, "Spreading the Word on New Technologies for People with Disabilities," *Personnel* (July 1988): 14–17; W. H. Wagel, "Project Ace: New Opportunities for People with Disabilities," *Personnel* (Jan. 1988): 9–15; J. M. Williams, "Technology and the Disabled," *Personnel Administrator* (July 1988): 81–83.

7. S. Marshall, "$157 Million Ends Sex Bias Suit," *USA Today* (April 29, 1992): 14.

8. A. Swasy, "Housing Slump Boosts Relocation Costs," *The Wall Street Journal* (August 21, 1990): B1.

9. T. Rendero, "Consensus," *Personnel* (Sept.–Oct. 1980): 5.

10. J. R. Garcia, "Job Posting for Professional Staff," *Personnel Journal* (March 1981): 189–92; G. A. Wallrop, "Job Posting for Nonexempt Employees: A Sample Program," *Personnel Journal* (Oct. 1981): 796–98; L. S. Kleiman and K. J. Clark, "An Effective Job Posting System," *Personnel Journal* (Feb. 1984): 20–25.

11. W. Glueck, *Personnel: A Diagnostic Approach* (Plano, Tex.: Business Publications, Inc., 1982).

12. B. Stoops, "Employee Referral Programs: Part I," *Personnel Journal* (Feb. 1981): 98; Stoops, "Part II," (March 1981): 172–73.

13. Ibid.

14. D. P. Schwab, "Recruiting and Organizational Participation." In *Personnel Management*, K. M. Rowland and G. R. Ferris, eds. (Boston, Mass.: Allyn and Bacon, 1982): 103–28.

15. J. A. Byrne, "Dream Jobs All Over," *Business Week* (April 4, 1994): 34–36; M. S. Taylor and T. J. Bergmann, "Organizational Recruitment Activities and Applicants' Reactions at Different Stages of the Recruitment Process," *Personnel Psychology* (Summer 1987): 265–85.

16. For a detailed discussion of these errors in recruiting decisions, see S. Rubenfeld and M. Crino, "Are Employment Agencies Jeopardizing Your Selection Process?" *Personnel* (Sept.–Oct. 1981): 70–78.

17. S. Deisenhouse, "A Temp Firm with a Difference," *The New York Times* (Dec. 26, 1993): F3.

18. M. A. Camuso, "The Employment Recruitment Trip–6 Stages to Success," *Personnel Journal* (Nov. 1984).

19. *The New York Times* (March 15, 1992): E3. Used by permission. Also see D. Stead and R. D. Hof, "Math Genius with Lab Will Work for Food," *Business Week* (June 14, 1993): 84–86.

20. J. Bredwell, "The Use of Broadcast Advertising for Recruitment," *Personnel Administrator* (Feb. 1981): 45–49; R. Stoops, "Radio Recruitment Advertising: Part II," *Personnel Journal* (July 1981): 532; "Affirmative Action in the 1980's: What Can We Expect?", *Management Review* (May 1981): 4–5; R. Stoops, "Television Advertising," *Personnel Journal* (Nov. 1981): 838; R. Stoops, "Reader Survey Supports Market Approach to Recruitment," *Personnel Journal* (March 1984): 22–24.

21. R. Stoops, "Recruitment Ads that Get Results," *Personnel Journal* (April 1984): 24–26; R. Siedlecki, "Creating A Direct Mail Recruitment Program," *Personnel Journal* (April 1983): 304–307; B. S. Hodes, "Planning for Recruitment Advertising: Part I," *Personnel Journal* (May 1983): 380–384; and J. P. Bucalo, "Good Advertising Can Be More Effective Than Other Tools," *Personnel Administrator* (Nov. 1983): 73–78.

22. *FEP Guidelines*, (July 10, 1993): 8. Copyrighted material reprinted with permission of Fair Employment Practices and Bureau of Business Practice, 24 Rope Ferry Road, Waterford, CT 06386.

23. *The Wall Street Journal* (February 8, 1983): 35. Reprinted by permission of *The Wall Street Journal*. Copyright Dow Jones & Company, Inc., 1983. All rights reserved.

24. D. M. Schweiger, J. M. Ivancevich and F. R. Power, "Executive Actions for Managing Human Resources Before and After Acquisitions," *Academy of Management Executive* (May 1987): 127–38.

25. "Ask the Experts–Recruiting Older Workers," *Fair Employment Practice Guidelines* (May 10, 1993): 8.

26. R. A. Dean and J. P. Wanous, "Effects of Realistic Job Previews on Hiring Bank Tellers," *Journal of Applied Psychology* (Feb. 1984): 61–68; B. M. Meglino and A. S. DeNisi, "Realistic Job Previews: Some Thoughts on Their More Effective Use in Managing the Flow of Human Resources," *Human Resource Planning* (1987) (3): 157–167; and B. M. Meglino, A. S. DeNisi, S. A. Youngblood, and K. J. Williams, "Effects of Realistic Job Previews: A Comparison Using an Enhancement and Reduction Preview," *Journal of Applied Psychology* (May 1988): 259–266.

27. Meglino and DeNisi, "Realistic Job Previews …" See also S. M. Colarelli, "Methods of Communication and Mediating Processes in Realistic Job Previews," *Journal of Applied Psychology* (August, 1984): 633–642.

28. J. Van Ahn, "The Voice of Experience," *Personnel* (Jan. 1991): 17; R. Pascale, "Fitting New Employees into the Company Culture," *Fortune* (May 28, 1984): 28–40.

29. Bureau of National Affairs, "Orientation Goals: Better Learning, Reduced Turnover," *Bulletin to Management*, (May 9, 1985): 1–2.

30. P. Popovich and J. Wanous, "The Realistic Job Preview as a Persuasive Communication," *Academy of Management Review 7* (1982): 570–578; M. R. Louis, "Managing Career Transitions: A Missing Link in Career Development," *Organizational Dynamics* (Spring 1982): 68–78.

31. *Bulletin to Management* (May 9, 1985): 1, 2. Reprinted by permission from *Bulletin to Management* copyright 1985 by The Bureau of National Affairs, Inc., Washington, D.C. 20037.

32. D. Berlew and D. T. Hall, "The Socialization of Managers: Effects of Expectations on Performance," *Administration Science Quarterly* (Sept. 1966): 297–223.

33. J. S. Livingston, "Pygmalion in Management," *Harvard Business Review* (July–Aug. 1969): 81–89.

34. V. Puick, "White-Collar Human Resource Management in Large Japanese Manufacturing Firms," *Human Resource Management 20*, no. 2; (1986) 264; "Learning from Japan," *Business Week* (Jan. 27, 1992): 52–60.

35. Ibid.

36. I. Peritz, "Montreal Firm Found Cheap Labor, Lax Rules in Mexico," *The Gazette* (March 16, 1992): A1, A7.

37. *HR Reporter* (June 1988): 1–2. Reprinted by permission of *HR Reporter*, copyright 1988.

38. J. S. Lord, "Contract Recruiting: Coming of Age," *Personnel Administrator* (Nov. 1987): 49–53; also see L. Carroll, "Strategies to Make Outplacement an INHOUSE Program," *HR Focus* (Sept. 1993): 12–13.

39. D. Gunsch, "Comprehensive College Strategy Strengthens NCR's Recruitment," *Personnel Journal* (Sept. 1993): 58–62; B. Smith, "Pinkerton Keeps Its Eye on Recruitment," *HR Focus* (Sept. 1993): 1, 6.

CHAPTER 8
SELECTION AND PLACEMENT

LEARNING OBJECTIVES

When you have finished studying this chapter, you should be able to:

1. Identify legal considerations in selection and placement.
2. Describe the types of information to gather on job applicants.
3. Discuss several methods of gathering information for selection decisions.
4. Discuss ways the information is used in making selection and placement decisions.
5. Describe how the use of expatriates, third-country nationals, and host-country nationals impacts selection and placement.

CHAPTER OUTLINE

"Managing Human Resources at Walt Disney"

SELECTION AND PLACEMENT
LEGAL CONSIDERATIONS

"Managing Human Resources
THE BURDEN OF PROOF GROWS HEAVIER"

CONSIDERATIONS IN THE CHOICE OF SELECTION TECHNIQUES
TYPES OF JOB APPLICANT INFORMATION

"HR Advice and Application
ASK THE EXPERTS—INVESTIGATING APPLICANT FRAUD"

"Managing Human Resources
PSYCHOLOGICAL TESTING LEADS TO COSTLY LAWSUIT"

"HR Advice and Application
EXPERT OPINION—INTERVIEWING SKILLS: USING PAST PERFORMANCE
TO PREDICT THE FUTURE"

USING INFORMATION IN SELECTION AND PLACEMENT DECISIONS
INTERNATIONAL ASPECTS OF EMPLOYEE SELECTION
CURRENT TRENDS
REVIEW: DO'S AND DON'TS IN JOB INTERVIEWS AND ON JOB
APPLICATION BLANKS
Career Management Exercise
Case: The Apprentice
Case: False Positive or Positive Step?

MANAGING HUMAN RESOURCES
at the Walt Disney Company

THE next time you visit Walt Disney World in Florida or Disneyland in California, consider the complexity of finding more than 25,000 people needed to fill more than 1,000 types of jobs that make the entertainment complexes so effective. With over 50 million visitors to Disney World and Disneyland yearly, the company is a reigning star in the entertainment business. Since the mid-1980s, when it went through a major change in senior management and strategic direction, the Walt Disney Company has developed a reputation for creativity, strong financial management, and unique—and very effective—approaches to managing people. An example of how that management process works is evident in the approach to staffing—or in Disney parlance, "casting for a role."

The managers and employees of the Walt Disney Company view themselves as part of a large show or production. This is reflected in the way they speak of themselves, their activities, and the process of selecting new members. Eager applicants to the firm are "cast for a role," rather than "hired for a job." Rather than being "employees," applicants who join the firm become "cast members" in a major entertainment production. A "cast director" interviews applicants.

The "casting" process for hourly jobs, for example, reveals a number of effective personnel management practices. A "casting director," or interviewer spends at least eight to ten minutes with every applicant for an hourly job. During that interview, the "casting director" evaluates the applicant in terms of his or her ability to adapt to the firm's very strong culture. This includes, for instance, acceptance of grooming require-ments (no facial hair for men, little make up for women) and willingness to work on holidays, since the facilities are open year-round. After the first "screening," the remaining applicants are assessed as they interact with each other and judged as to how well they might fit with the "show."

Once people join the firm, they become "cast members" whose inputs and talents are highly valued by the Walt Disney Company. The company fills 60–80 percent of its managerial positions by promoting existing "cast members." In addition, the firm draws on suggested referrals from current "cast members" for help in hiring the 1,500–2,000 temporary employees required during particularly busy periods—Easter, Christmas, and summers.

Every newly hired "cast member" participates in an orientation and training program at "Disney University." "Cast members" first receive an overview of Walt Disney Company and learn about its traditions, history, achievements, and philosophy. In addition, "cast members" learn about the key Disney "product"—happiness—and their roles in helping to provide it. Next, each "cast member" learns about the benefits (health, social, recreational) of being part of the Disney "family," gains more direct information about his or her "role" in the production, and has a tour of the complex. Tailored to reflect the needs of each type of cast member and group, the initial orientation and subsequent training has a theme of bringing cast members into the "family" and developing a team sense, as well as a focus on courtesy to "guests," safety, and putting on a good "show" (entertainment).[1]

This feature highlights aspects of selection that we will discuss in this chapter, including (1) how to collect information on job applicants, (2) how to make selection and placement decisions, (3) how selection can be used to improve the profitability of the company, and (4) how selection ties into the basic philosophy of a company. In addition, we will also look at issues in the selection process for international employees and compare the selection process in other countries with ours.

Selection is the process of gathering legally defensible information about job applicants.
Placement is concerned with matching people to jobs.

I am the ultimate believer in people first, strategies second. To me, strategy starts with the person you hire.

—Jack Welch, CEO, General Electric

SELECTION AND PLACEMENT

Selection *is the process of gathering legally defensible information about job applicants in order to determine who should be hired for long- or short-term positions.*

Placement *is concerned with matching individual skills, knowledge, abilities, preferences, interests, and personality to a job.*

Effective selection and placement involve finding the match between organizational needs for qualified individuals and individuals' needs for jobs in which they are interested.[2]

Line managers play an important role in the selection and placement activity. They help identify the need for staffing through the organization's HR planning activity, assist with job analysis, and evaluate employee performance.

The human resource department, however, is usually responsible for gathering information and should arrange interviews between job applicants and managers for several reasons:

- Applicants have to go to only one place to apply for a job and have a better chance of being considered for a greater variety of jobs.
- Outside sources of applicants can clear employment issues through one central location.
- Operating managers can concentrate on their operating responsibilities—especially helpful during peak hiring periods.
- Hiring is done by specialists trained in staffing techniques, so selection is often better.
- Costs can be cut because duplication of effort is avoided.
- With increased government regulation of selection, it is important that people who know about these rules handle a major part of the hiring process.

WHY ARE SELECTION AND PLACEMENT IMPORTANT?

Selection and placement are critical to any organization—they provide an organization with its core—its human resources. Employees who perform well is, of course, the objective of these two activities with all the attendant benefits—among them, productivity improvements and cost savings. Serving the organization's needs by providing effective selection and placement means attaining several purposes, which are

- To contribute to the organization's bottom line through efficient and effective production.
- To ensure that an organization's financial investment in employees pays off (for example, hiring an employee with a starting salary of $25,000, annual cost of living adjustments (COLAs) of only 1.5 percent, and no benefits results in an investment of $128,000 in that employee in 5 years and $578,092 in 20 years).
- To evaluate, hire, and place job applicants in the best interests of both the organization and the individual.
- To minimize multimillion-dollar verdicts and settlements in litigation brought by victims of criminal, violent, or negligent acts perpetrated by employees who should not have been hired or kept in their jobs.[3]
- To enable organizations to fulfill their strategies.
- To fulfill hiring goals and timetables specified in affirmative action programs.

LINE MANAGERS	HR PROFESSIONALS	EMPLOYEES
Help HR professionals develop selection test.	Develop selection tests and coordinate their administration.	Interview candidates who may work in their group.
Coordinate interview process with applicant and HR professionals.	Arrange interviews between applicant and line managers.	Work with HR professionals and line managers in orienting new employees to the organization.
Make final selection decisions.	Assemble selection data for line managers.	
	Assure that legal considerations are addressed in all selection steps and decisions.	

To accomplish the above, selection and placement must be congruent with the internal environment and integrated with other HR activities. They must also be done in a manner consistent with the law.

LEGAL CONSIDERATIONS

Legal considerations are extensive for selection and placement. Numerous acts, executive orders, regulations, and agencies have an impact on these activities in all organizations, particularly in cases of illegal discrimination.

ACTS

The historical development of equal employment legislation began with the *Civil Rights Act of 1866*, Section 1981, which prohibits employee discrimination based on race, color, and national origin. The *Civil Rights Act of 1871*, Section 1983, enforces the Fourteenth Amendment to the U.S. Constitution, which has been held to prohibit discrimination based on race, color, national origin, religion, gender, and age.

The *Civil Rights Act of 1964* and, in particular, *Title VII*, prohibits discrimination against individuals on the basis of gender, race, color, national origin, and religion. The *Civil Rights Act of 1991* has redefined discrimination and exposed employers to greater financial liability. Passage of this act was in part triggered by

Relevant federal acts include:
- *Civil Rights Act of 1866/1871*
- *Civil Rights Act of 1964/1991*
- *Age Discrimination in Employment Acts of 1967/1978/1986/1990*
- *Vietnam Era Veterans Readjustment Act of 1974*
- *Equal Employment Opportunity Act of 1972*
- *Equal Pay Act of 1963*
- *Rehabilitation Act of 1973*
- *Americans with Disabilities Act of 1990*

several Supreme Court decisions in the 1980s, including *Wards Cove Packing v. Atonio* (1989). These decisions had, among other things, shifted the burden of proving discrimination to the employee. The *Civil Rights Act of 1991* returned this burden to the employer.[4] Other major provisions and issues of this act are described in the feature, "Managing Human Resources: The Burden of Proof Grows Heavier." Many of the terms in this feature, which outlines the basic framework for proving illegal discrimination, are discussed over the next several pages.

The *Equal Employment Opportunity Act of 1972* amended the *Civil Rights Act of 1964* that had first created the Equal Employment Opportunity Commission. This 1972 amendment expanded the coverage of Title VII to include public and private employers with fifteen or more employees, labor organizations with fifteen or more members, and public and private employment agencies. Elected officials and their appointees are excluded from Title VII coverage but are still covered under the Fourteenth Amendment and the *Civil Rights Acts of 1866 and 1871*. The 1972 amendment also identified exceptions or exemptions to Title VII, including bona fide occupational qualifications, seniority systems, pre-employment inquiries, use of job-related tests for selection, national security interests, and veterans' preference rights. Much of what is discussed under the section below on proving illegal discrimination is based on the *Civil Rights Acts of 1964* and *1991*.

The *Age Discrimination in Employment Act of 1967* (ADEA) as amended in 1978, 1986, and 1990, prohibits discrimination against employees and applicants who are more than 40 years old. While age discrimination (bias) has been a significant legal issue in the United States for some time, it is just now becoming an issue in Europe.

> Rampant job bias against older Europeans is just starting to decline, thanks to a scarcity of young people and the spread of U.S.–style advocacy groups. Unlike America, Europe lacks tough laws broadly barring age discrimination. Employers routinely run advertisements seeking workers under 40, force staffers as young as 55 to retire, and fire people simply for being too old.[6]

> The *Civil Rights Act,* on top of the *Americans with Disabilities Act* (ADA), is the final kick in the pants for managers. Managers have to think differently.
>
> —Attorney Fred Sullivan of the Springfield, Massachusetts, firm Sullivan & Hayes

As already described, the *Americans with Disabilities Act of 1990* substantially extends the coverage of the *Rehabilitation Act* to include the same organizations covered by the *Civil Rights Act of 1991*. Coverage began in 1992, with organizations making accommodations for individuals (employees and customers) with disabilities. As defined by the act, an estimated 45 million Americans are classified as disabled. The impact of the act is regarded as the most significant since Title VII. It is likely to supersede both the *Rehabilitation Act* and the *Vietnam Era Veterans' Readjustment Act of 1974*, which protects disabled veterans and veterans of the Vietnam era.[7]

In addition to these major federal acts pertaining to equal employment opportunity, there are state and local government acts and executive orders that employers must follow.

EXECUTIVE ORDERS

Executive orders are directives issued by the President of the United States.

The equal employment opportunity acts have been supported by a number of executive orders (EOs). *EO 11246* of 1965 prohibits discrimination on the basis of race, color, religion, and national origin by federal agencies, contractors, and subcontractors. In 1966, *EO 11375* was signed to prohibit discrimination in these same organizations on the basis of sex. *EO 11478* of 1969 prescribes that employment policies of the federal government be based on merit and that the

THE *Civil Rights Act of 1991* has redefined discrimination and exposed employers to greater financial liability. The law now in effect reverses several Supreme Court rulings and shifts the burden of proof for cases of intentional discrimination from the employee to the employer. In addition, workers who successfully prove they were discriminated against can now receive compensatory and punitive damages that previously were not allowed. Under the original civil rights legislation (1964), employees could only receive reinstatement, back pay, and attorneys' fees.

The total amount of compensatory and punitive damages allowed by the law is determined by the number of employees at the company and cannot exceed the following limits:

- $50,000 for companies with 15–100 employees
- $100,000 for employers with 101–200 employees
- $200,000 for companies with 201–500 employees
- $300,000 for employers with over 501 employees

These damages would be added on top of attorneys' fees, which can range anywhere between $40,000 and $150,000, according to professionals in the employment law field. Companies also may be responsible for paying the fees of expert witnesses called by the plaintiffs, which often range between $10,000 and $15,000.

Legal experts agree that damages will be awarded more easily now because an employee can have his or her case heard before a jury. Previously, discrimination cases were tried before judges, many of whom were considered more sympathetic to employers. Juries, on the other hand, historically have decided against businesses and awarded plaintiffs huge sums of money for damages.

"The *Civil Rights Act*, on top of the *Americans with Disabilities Act* (ADA), is the final kick in the pants for managers," said attorney Fred Sullivan of the Springfield, Massachusetts, firm Sullivan & Hayes. "Managers have to think differently."

This new way of thinking represents a radical departure for businesses, according to Sullivan. Companies must approach their employment practices from the perspective of a jury, rather than from a managerial viewpoint. The underlying question employers need to consider regarding any potentially liable action is, "How can this be perceived differently than the way we perceive it," Sullivan added.

"The *Civil Rights Act* and the ADA place more limitations on recruiting as well as on discharging employees," said Howard Flaxman, an attorney with the Philadelphia firm Blank, Rome, Comisky & McCauley. "The stakes are very high right now."

THE BURDEN IS SHIFTED

The stakes are high because any employer brought before a court on a "disparate impact" discrimination case today must prove that the challenged employment practice was a result of a business necessity (job-relatedness). In the past, companies only had to submit evidence of a business justification, and the employee was responsible for persuading the court against the employer's evidence.

The act also shifts the burden of proof to employers in dual motive cases—that is, cases in which both lawful and unlawful factors were involved. Before, a company that used an illegal factor, such as race or gender, to make an employment decision could prevail if it proved that the same decision would be made even if that factor were not considered. Now an employer must show that only lawful factors were used to make the employment decision. The employee only has to prove that his or her protected status, such as race, gender, or disability, was a "motivating factor" in the decision regardless of other factors involved.

Flaxman said that such changes in the law, in addition to increased monetary awards, will provoke

Continued on the next page

255

more litigation, particularly for marginal cases that would not have gone to court in the past. Attorneys also may be more likely to use the law as a bargaining tool to negotiate better out-of-court settlements for their clients.

AN EMPLOYER'S DEFENSE

Companies must now review all of their personnel policies to protect themselves against any litigation that could result from the new law. As part of the review process, Flaxman advises employers to make sure they have established a sexual harassment policy. Businesses also need to study their disciplinary policies to ensure that every problem is dealt with through progressive and corrective actions that are thoroughly documented.

"With juries, the issue is more of fairness, not discrimination. That's the issue even though it's not supposed to be," Flaxman said. "Juries are punishing employers who appear to be almost cavalier in their attitude."

"You want to show to the jury that efforts went beyond what was normally expected," Sullivan added. "Go beyond the final warning; issue a second warning."

Hiring practices must also be reviewed to comply with the new law. Employers must make sure that the people conducting the screening process ask the proper questions and conduct the proper investigations.

Although the law encourages both parties to seek an alternative method to resolve disputes, such as arbitration, its effectiveness remains questionable. Unless the employee is legally bound by an arbitration agreement, the matter can still go to court.

Sullivan, however, said the use of a third party can be helpful in settling disputes. Many employers have resisted arbitration, believing they did not need a third party to tell them how to manage their business. "But today there is a third party—the jury."[5]

---

head of each agency establish and maintain a program of equal employment opportunity.

Key equal employment guidelines are

- *FEA Guidelines*
- *Uniform Guidelines*
- sexual harassment
- national origin
- religion

GUIDELINES

While acts and executive orders delineate protected classes, guidelines provide the mechanisms, such as selection tests, by which these acts and orders are implemented. The first set was issued in 1970 by the EEOC and originally intended to provide a workable set of ideal standards for employees, unions, and employment agencies. Those guidelines defined a test as being

> . . . all formal, scored, qualified or standardized techniques of assessing job suitability, including . . . background requirements, educational or work history requirements, interviews, biographical information blanks, interview rating scales and scored application blanks.

Rather than becoming a flexible set of ideal standards (as originally intended), the guidelines became a sort of checklist of *minimum* standards that the courts used for test validation. Concern over this trend prompted the Equal Employment Opportunity Coordinating Council to develop a set of uniform guidelines, to be used by all federal agencies, that were based on sound psychological principles and that were technically feasible. As a result, the *Federal Executive Agency (FEA) Guidelines* were published in 1976 followed by the *Uniform Guidelines on Employee Selection Procedure* in 1978. These *Uniform Guidelines* are a 14,000-word catalog of do's and don'ts and of questions and answers for hiring and promotion (and job analysis as mentioned in Chapter 6). They contain interpretation and guidance not found in earlier EEOC guidelines.

The EEOC has also published other guidelines. On November 10, 1980, the commission issued *Guidelines on Discrimination Because of Sex*. These guidelines are premised on the assumption that sexual harassment is a condition of employment if women are exposed to it more frequently than men (more on this in

Chapter 16). Six weeks later, the EEOC issued its *Guidelines on Discrimination Because of National Origin*. The national origin guidelines extended earlier versions of this protection by defining national origin as a *place* rather than a *country* of origin. It also revised the "speak-English-only rules." This means employers can require that English be spoken only if there is a compelling business–related necessity. On September 29, 1981, the EEOC issued guidelines on age discrimination in essence identifying what the *Age Discrimination in Employment Act* meant to do and what it should mean to employers and employees.[8]

Under the *Guidelines on Discrimination Because of Religion*, an employer is obliged to accommodate the religious preferences of current and prospective employees unless the employer demonstrates undue hardship. It appears, however, that if an employer shows "reasonable attempts to accommodate," the courts may be satisfied that no religious discrimination has occurred (*State Division of Human Rights v. Rochester Housing Authority*, 1980; *Philbrook v. Ansonia Board of Education*, 1986).

PROFESSIONAL STANDARDS

Selection processes are also monitored by the American Psychological Association. In 1966 and again in 1974, the American Psychological Association (APA) released its *Standards for Education and Psychological Tests*. These standards were updated in 1985. In 1975 and again in 1987, the Society for Industrial-Organizational Psychology, a division of the APA, published its *Principles for the Validation and Use of Personnel Selection Procedures*. Drawing from relevant research, these standards and principles help clarify issues regarding test fairness and discrimination.

PROVING ILLEGAL DISCRIMINATION

While the *Civil Rights Act of 1991* explicitly prohibits discrimination, nowhere in the law is discrimination defined. Essentially, a jury must decide whether or not illegal discrimination has occurred. Broadly speaking, however, the act prohibits differences in the treatment of employees who belong to one of the five protected groups (race, color, religion, gender, and national origin). Discrimination based on age, physical and mental handicaps, or against disabled or Vietnam-era veterans is prohibited by other acts. Discrimination on all other bases or qualifications is untouched by federal law, except when discrimination on *nonprohibited* factors is disguised as legal discrimination. For example, using minimum height and weight requirements as substitute measures of physical strength may adversely affect women and certain ethnic groups (Asians, Hispanics). When this occurs, the *Civil Rights Act of 1991* is violated.[9]

PRIMA FACIE CASES. In a typical discrimination suit, a person alleges discrimination due to unlawful employment practices. The person may first go to the Equal Employment Opportunity Commission (EEOC) office. The EEOC may seek out the facts of the case from both sides, attempting a resolution. Failing a resolution, the person may continue the case and file a suit. In the first phase of a discrimination suit, it is the obligation of the plaintiff (the person filing the suit) to establish a *prima facie* case of illegal discrimination by showing disparate impact or disparate treatment.

Disparate treatment means there is an apparent case of illegal discrimination against an *individual* while **disparate impact** is against a *group*. (Occasionally, the term **adverse impact** is used in making references to the **effects** of disparate treatment or disparate impact.) The basic criteria for establishing a *prima facie* case of disparate impact were specified by the Supreme Court in *Griggs v. Duke*

Disparate treatment refers to an apparent case of illegal discrimination against a person.
Disparate impact is an apparent case of illegal discrimination against a group.

Power (1974), and those for a disparate treatment case in *McDonnell Douglas Corp. v. Green* (1973). While a charge of disparate treatment has always required evidence of intent to discriminate, only more recently has the Court required the same of some disparate impact cases (*Wards Cove Packing v. Atonio*, 1989). The *Civil Rights Act of 1991*, however, substantially revises the plaintiff's burden of proof responsibility described in the feature, "Managing Human Resources: The Burden of Proof Grows Heavier."

DISPARATE IMPACT.   Cases of disparate impact rely on three types of statistical evidence.

Three statistics for disparate impact:

• comparative
• demographic
• concentration

One approach relies on **comparative statistics** or comparisons of the rates or ratios of hiring, firing, promoting, transferring, and demoting for protected and nonprotected groups. The *Uniform Guidelines* suggest that disparate impact (adverse impact) has been demonstrated if the selection rate "for any racial, ethnic, or gender subgroup is less than four-fifths or 80 percent of the highest selection rate for any group." This has come to be known as the **four-fifths or 80% rule**. Originally, this bottom-line criterion was aimed at identifying disparate impact only for an entire set of selection procedures, rather than for any single part. This has now been modified to apply to each part of the procedures as well as to the entire set (*Connecticut v. Teal*, 1982). The EEOC can examine an organization's personnel records and determine the existence of this type of illegal discrimination. The personnel records that employers are required to keep and that the EEOC can examine are called EEO-1 reports, shown in Exhibit 8.1.[10]

In contrast, the argument using **demographic statistics**, a second approach, centers on a comparison of an organization's work force to the relevant labor market. This argument is rooted in the *Civil Rights Act of 1964*. For example, an employer's selection procedures can be shown to be discriminatory (*prima facie*) if the employer's work force fails to reflect parity with the race or sex composition of the relevant labor market. Organizations may determine their relevant labor market in several ways. One is by identifying where 85 percent of current employees and job applicants reside. Another is by identifying the labor market from which they generally select applicants. The EEOC, however, may suggest that organizations expand their labor markets; as a consequence, determining relevant labor markets is often an art rather than a science.

Once the relevant labor market has been determined, it is subject to revisions because of changing demographic characteristics in the U.S. labor force. Organizations are witnessing dramatic demographic changes based on comparisons of the 1980 and 1990 national census. As a result of these changes, organizations are having to redetermine their relevant labor markets to defend AAPs and cases of *prima facie* claims of discrimination successfully. *Prima facie* cases of this type are likely to be successfully defended to the extent that parity is attained (that is, the extent to which the proportions of protected group members in an organization's work force mirror the proportions in the relevant labor market).

The third basis for establishing a case of disparate impact is through the use of **concentration statistics**. The argument here is that a *prima facie* case of illegal discrimination exists to the extent that protected group members are located in one particular area or job category in the organization. For example, equal numbers of male and female employees may be hired into entry-level jobs in the organization, but the women may be placed predominantly in secretarial jobs. Such a situation provides a case of disparate impact.

Promotion practices can also create unbalanced demographic concentration. For example, in *Wards Cove Packing v. Atonio*, the Wards Cove Packing Company in Alaska was charged by Atonio and other minority workers (pri-

EXHIBIT 8.1
EQUAL EMPLOYMENT OPPORTUNITY REPORT EEO-1

Joint Reporting Committee

- Equal Employment Opportunity Commission
- Office of Federal Contract Compliance Programs (Labor)

EQUAL EMPLOYMENT OPPORTUNITY
EMPLOYER INFORMATION REPORT EEO-1

Standard Form 100
(Rev. 5–84)
O.M.B. No. 3046–0007

100–211

Section A—TYPE OF REPORT
Refer to instructions for number and types of reports to be filed.

1. Indicate by marking in the appropriate box the type of reporting unit for which this copy of the form is submitted (MARK ONLY ONE BOX).

   (1) ☐ Single-establishment Employer Report

   Multi-establishment Employer:
   (2) ☐ Consolidated Report (Required)
   (3) ☐ Headquarters Unit Report (Required)
   (4) ☐ Individual Establishment Report (submit one for each establishment with 50 or more employees)
   (5) ☐ Special Report

2. Total number of reports being filed by this Company (Answer on Consolidated Report only) _____

Section B—COMPANY IDENTIFICATION (To be answered by all employers)   OFFICE USE ONLY

1. Parent Company

   a. Name of parent company (owns or controls establishment in item 2) omit if same as label   a.

   Name of receiving office   Address (Number and street)   b.

City or town	County	State	ZIP code	b. Employer Identification No.

2. Establishment for which this report is filed. (Omit if same as label)   OFFICE USE ONLY

   a. Name of establishment   c.

Address (Number and street)	City or Town	County	State	ZIP code	d.

   b. Employer Identification No.   (Omit if same as label)   e.

Section C—EMPLOYERS WHO ARE REQUIRED TO FILE (To be answered by all employers)

☐ Yes ☐ No 1. Does the entire company have at least 100 employees in the payroll period for which you are reporting?

☐ Yes ☐ No 2. Is your company affiliated through common ownership and/or centralized management with other entities in an enterprise with a total employment of 100 or more?

☐ Yes ☐ No 3. Does the company or any of its establishments (a) have 50 or more employees AND (b) is not exempt as provided by 41 CFR 60–1.5, AND either (1) is a prime government contractor or first-tier subcontractor, and has a contract, subcontract, or purchase order amounting to $50,000 or more, or (2) serves as a depository of Government funds in any amount or is a financial institution which is an issuing and paying agent for U.S. Savings Bonds and Savings Notes?

   If the response to question C–3 is yes, please enter your Dun and Bradstreet identification number (if you have one):

☐ Yes ☐ No 4. Does the company receive financial assistance from the Small Business Administration (SBA)?

NOTE: If the answer is yes to questions 1, 2, or 3, complete the entire form, otherwise skip to Section G.

NSN 7540–00–180–6384

---

marily Filipinos and Alaska Natives) with illegal discrimination because they were never promoted. Concentration statistics supported this claim. The Court, while not denying the accuracy of the data, stated that Atonio also had the burden of showing intentional discrimination and suggesting alternative procedures that would be equally valid but less discriminatory. This scenario, which was a

EXHIBIT 8.1 (CONT.)
EQUAL EMPLOYMENT OPPORTUNITY REPORT EEO-1

SF 100 Page 2

Section D—EMPLOYMENT DATA

Employment at this establishment—Report all permanent full-time or part-time employees including apprentices and on-the-job trainees unless specifically excluded as set forth in the instructions. Enter the appropriate figures on all lines and in all columns. Blank spaces will be considered as zeros.

JOB CATEGORIES		OVERALL TOTALS (SUM OF COL. B THRU K) A	NUMBER OF EMPLOYEES									
			MALE					FEMALE				
			WHITE (NOT OF HISPANIC ORIGIN) B	BLACK (NOT OF HISPANIC ORIGIN) C	HISPANIC D	ASIAN OR PACIFIC ISLANDER E	AMERICAN INDIAN OR ALASKAN NATIVE F	WHITE (NOT OF HISPANIC ORIGIN) G	BLACK (NOT OF HISPANIC ORIGIN) H	HISPANIC I	ASIAN OR PACIFIC ISLANDER J	AMERICAN INDIAN OR ALASKAN NATIVE K
Officials and Managers	1											
Professionals	2											
Technicians	3											
Sales Workers	4											
Office and Clerical	5											
Craft Workers (Skilled)	6											
Operatives (Semi-Skilled)	7											
Laborers (Unskilled)	8											
Service Workers	9											
TOTAL	10											
Total employment reported in previous EEO-1 report	11											

(The trainees below should also be included in the figures for the appropriate occupational categories above)

Formal On-the-job trainees	White collar 12											
	Production 13											

NOTE: Omit questions 1 and 2 on the Consolidated Report.

1. Date(s) of payroll period used:

2. Does this establishment employ apprentices?
1 ☐ Yes   2 ☐ No

Section E—ESTABLISHMENT INFORMATION (Omit on the Consolidated Report)

1. Is the location of the establishment the same as that reported last year?
1 ☐ Yes   2 ☐ No   3 ☐ No report last year

2. Is the major business activity at this establishment the same as that reported last year?
1 ☐ Yes   2 ☐ No   3 ☐ No report last year

OFFICE USE ONLY

3. What is the major activity of this establishment? (Be specific, i.e., manufacturing steel castings, retail grocer, wholesale plumbing supplies, title insurance, etc. Include the specific type of product or type of service provided, as well as the principal business or industrial activity.)

f.

Section F—REMARKS

Use this item to give any identification data appearing on last report which differs from that given above, explain major changes in composition or reporting units and other pertinent information.

Section G—CERTIFICATION (See Instructions G)

Check one
1 ☐ All reports are accurate and were prepared in accordance with the instructions (check on consolidated only)
2 ☐ This report is accurate and was prepared in accordance with the instructions.

Name of Certifying Official	Title	Signature		Date
Name of person to contact regarding this report (Type or print)	Address (Number and street)			
Title	City and State	ZIP code	Telephone Area Code	Number	Extension

All reports and information obtained from individual reports will be kept confidential as required by Section 709(e) of Title VII
WILLFULLY FALSE STATEMENTS ON THIS REPORT ARE PUNISHABLE BY LAW, U.S. CODE, TITLE 18, SECTION 1001

---

significant break from past decisions, has been essentially reversed by the *Civil Rights Act of 1991*.

✳ **DISPARATE TREATMENT.** Illegal discrimination against an individual is referred to as disparate treatment. In contrast to the cases of disparate impact, a *prima facie* case of disparate treatment exists to the extent that an individual can demonstrate the following:

- The individual belongs to a minority group.
- The individual applied for a job for which the employer was seeking applicants.
- Despite being qualified, he or she was rejected.
- After the individual's rejection, the employer kept looking for people with the applicant's qualifications.

These conditions, which basically present a case of intentional discrimination, were set forth in *McDonnell Douglas Corp. v. Green* (1973). Once a *prima facie* case of disparate treatment has been established by any one of the four ways, the employer must be given the opportunity to defend itself.[11]

DEFENDING SELECTION PRACTICES

An organization accused of illegal discrimination may be able to successfully defend its employment practices by showing one of the following:

- Job-relatedness
- Business necessity
- Bona fide occupational qualification (BFOQ)
- Bona fide seniority systems (BFSS)
- Voluntary transient affirmative action programs (AAPs)

JOB RELATEDNESS. Employee qualifications are necessary for any job. Thus employers are interested in measuring qualifications and establishing predictions on how employees who possess the qualifications will do on the job. To demonstrate **job-relatedness**, the company must show that its selection and placement procedures (predictors—tests used for selection decisions) are related to the employee success on the job (*Watson v. Fort Worth Bank and Trust*, 1988). For details, see Appendix C.

It's important to note that any test must be related to important components of the job. For example, a typing test may be an appropriate selection device for clerk-typists who spend 60 percent of their time on data entry. However, it may not be an appropriate selection device for receptionists who spend less than 5 percent of their time typing. Careful job analysis can determine this.

BUSINESS NECESSITY. Although showing the job-relatedness of a selection procedure is desirable, it may not always be possible. Some courts, recognizing this situation, have allowed companies to defend their selection procedures by showing business necessity. Whereas the job-relatedness defense often requires a demonstration of actual predictor-criterion relationships, business necessity does not. The case of *Levin v. Delta Air Lines, Inc.* (1984), where the Court decided for the plaintiff who sued because she was dismissed for being pregnant, was decided on the fact that pregnancy was not shown to affect the essence of the business (safe air travel), not on the fact that it failed to affect the ability of a flight attendant to provide service to the air travelers. In cases where business necessity clearly is high, demonstrating that a specific selection procedure is job-related is not necessary (see *Spurlock v. United Airlines*, 1972, and *Hodgson v. Greyhound Lines, Inc.*, 1974, in Appendix A).[12]

BONA FIDE OCCUPATIONAL QUALIFICATIONS. Another defense against a charge of illegal discrimination is **bona fide occupational qualifications (BFOQ)**. For example:

In disparate treatment, the qualified individual needs to show that someone else was hired instead.

Job-relatedness is evidence that a selection procedure is related to being able to do the job itself.

BFOQs are the qualifications really necessary to do the job.

. . . [T]he EEOC sued the Massachusetts State Registry of Motor Vehicles, charging that denying entry-level jobs to individuals over age 35 violated ADEA. The state argued that the 1986 ADEA amendment exempts all law enforcement officers from the scope of the act for a seven-year period, and that in any event, age is a bona fide occupational qualification for motor vehicle examiners under *Mahoney v. Trabucco*, which upheld an age-50 mandatory retirement rule for Massachusetts state troopers. EEOC countered that few motor vehicle examiners perform active law enforcement duties.

Acknowledging that the issue is a close one, the court agrees with the state that motor vehicle examiners, who are authorized to carry weapons, enforce the state's motor-vehicle laws, and perform many of the same duties as state and local police officers, are properly classified as law enforcement personnel and are therefore exempt from ADEA under the 1986 amendment (*EEOC v. Commonwealth of Massachusetts*, 1987).[13]

BONA FIDE SENIORITY SYSTEMS. Closely related to BFOQs are **bona fide seniority systems (BFSS)**. As long as a company has established and maintained a seniority system without the intent to illegally discriminate, it is considered bona fide (*International Brotherhood of Teamsters v. United States*, 1977; *United States v. Trucking Management, Inc.*, 1981; *American Tobacco v. Patterson*, 1982). Thus, promotion and job assignment decisions can be made on the basis of seniority.[14] In a major decision, the Supreme Court ruled that seniority can also be used in the determination of layoffs, even if doing so reverses effects of affirmative action hiring (*Firefighters Local Union 1784 v. Stotts*, 1984).

VOLUNTARY AFFIRMATIVE ACTION PROGRAMS. As described above, organizations may establish affirmative action programs without pressure from the EEOC and OFCCP. For them to be a defense against illegal discrimination, however, the programs need to be remedial in purpose, limited in duration, restricted in impact, flexible in implementation, and minimal in harm to innocent parties. However, there is growing ambiguity as to whether the courts will be sympathetic to these affirmative action programs despite past decisions (*Wygant v. Jackson Board of Education*, 1986; *International Association of Firefighters Local 93 v. City of Cleveland*, 1986).

CONSIDERATIONS IN THE CHOICE OF SELECTION TECHNIQUES

Several technical factors need to be considered, in choosing the right selection techniques, including which predictors and criteria to use.

PREDICTORS

Predictors are used to forecast how well a candidate is likely to perform if hired.

Selection decisions in organizations are generally made on the basis of job applicants' **predictor** scores on various tests. These tests, typically administered to the job applicants sequentially, predict how well applicants, if hired, will perform.

The selection process occurs in steps; Exhibit 8.2 shows a typical process. A wealth of techniques (background information, paper-and-pencil tests, work simulations, physical tests, interviews) can be used to predict job performance, but their usefulness depends on their reliability and validity.

Reliable and valid predictors do a better job of forecasting success on the job.

RELIABILITY. The **reliability** of a predictor is the degree to which it produces dependable or consistent results over time. Unreliable predictors produce different results at different times. Tests of physical attributions (height, weight, hear-

EXHIBIT 8.2
POSSIBLE STEPS IN THE SELECTION PROCESS

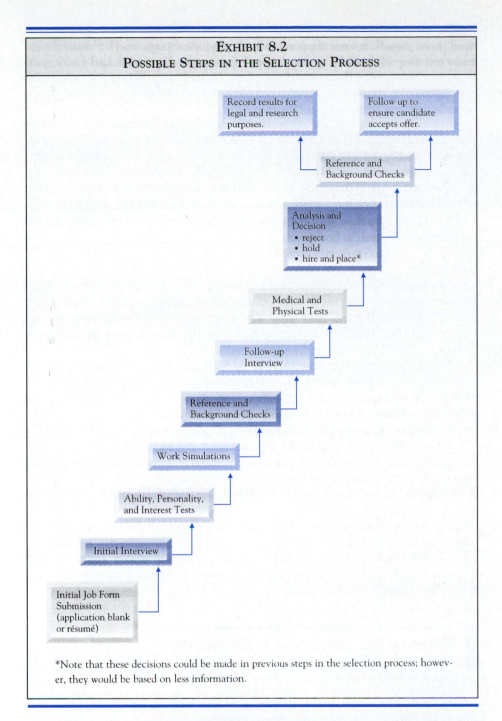

*Note that these decisions could be made in previous steps in the selection process; however, they would be based on less information.

ing) tend to be more reliable than tests of personality characteristics (neuroticism, flexible thinking, emotional stability). There are two types of reliability relevant to selection. Consider a cognitive ability test (for example, knowledge of financial principles) administered to 100 job applicants. Its reliability would be high if you retested these job applicants and received similar results the second time. This is called **test-retest reliability**. **Inter-rater reliability** focuses on how consistent the ratings of different people are. For example, in unstructured interviews, interviewers will perceive the same job applicant differently; the interviews are thus unreliable.[15]

✳**VALIDITY.** The term **validity** refers to how well a measure assesses an attribute. Validity is not absolute but is instead dependent on the situation in which the selection device is being used. For example, a test of aggression may be a valid predictor of police performance yet useless in predicting job success for machinists. Appendix C discusses the different approaches to validating selection devices in more depth.

Mathematically, validity refers to the correlation between the predictor score (selection device) and a criterion (job performance, job rating, number of absences, and so forth). Remember that in basic statistics a correlation coefficient can range from -1.00 to 1.00. The closer the correlation coefficient is to the absolute value of 1.00, the more valid the selection device. For example, work simulation tests have been shown to have average validity coefficients up to 0.47. This is substantially higher than the average validity coefficients of 0.14 for interviews.[16]

CRITERIA

Criteria are the targets that constitute job performance.

Criteria describe decisive elements of job performance. For example, in a corporate loan assistant's job, being able to document decisions accurately is probably more critical than keeping one's desk clean and organized. Establishing precise criteria and their relative importance facilitates the development of valid predictors.

Performance criteria dictate the type of information to be obtained from job applicants and, to some extent, the method used to gather the information. For example, if absenteeism is an appropriate criterion, a check of references on employment history may be helpful. If level of performance is the criterion, a written test measuring an applicant's skills, knowledge, and abilities may be useful.[17]

It is useful to compare Exhibits 6.3 and 8.3 to see the relationship between the job dimensions (criteria) and the skills, knowledge and abilities required.

As described in Chapter 6, the job analysis provides the basis for determining appropriate, relevant, and important criteria. Compare the relationship between the job dimensions of the corporate loan assistant in Exhibit 6.3 and the skills required to perform the job in Exhibit 8.3. Job incumbents identified both the skills, knowledge, and abilities and the job dimensions as discussed in Chapter 6. The dimensions were identified as the essence of the job—the job criteria. The method by which the knowledge skills are to be measured is indicated in Exhibit 8.3: they become the predictors of how well the applicant will perform the job criteria. Note that several methods are used for some knowledge skills (for example, bank services).

LEARNING OBJECTIVE 2

Describe the types of information to gather on job applicants.

TYPES OF JOB APPLICANT INFORMATION

Organizations can gather selection and placement information from job applicants related to the following categories:

- Skills, knowledge, and abilities
- Personality, interests, and preferences
- Other characteristics

SKILLS, KNOWLEDGE, AND ABILITIES

The information gathered on an applicant is generally used to match the applicants' skills, knowledge, and abilities with a suitable job. Such an endeavor is subject to legal constraints and has traditionally been of major interest to organizations because it can predict how well the individual will perform on the job.

Job-relatedness can be demonstrated by this information. However, any skills, knowledge, and abilities that can be learned in fewer than eight hours or taught on the job should not be measured or used in making selection decisions. Furthermore, if job applicants need only a specified minimum level of a skill, knowledge, or ability to perform the job, then the only information that should be obtained is whether or not the applicants meet the minimum levels. If a higher level of skill, knowledge, or ability is likely to result in better performance, then that information should be obtained so that applicants can be ranked and selected.

When making decisions in the areas of firing, demotion, layoff (where a bona fide seniority system does not exist) or discipline—all of which are selection decisions under the law—measuring task or job performance rather than skills, knowledge, and abilities is appropriate. If physical abilities are being measured, consideration must be made for job accommodation. If reasonable accommodation cannot be made for a disability that interferes with performing the essential duties of the job, the applicant can be rejected.

PERSONALITY, INTERESTS, AND PREFERENCES

Information about an individual's personality, interests, and preferences should also be gathered. If used appropriately, this information, in combination with job rewards, culture, and strategy of the firm, can increase employee satisfaction and reduce absenteeism and voluntary turnover. It can also increase job involvement and motivation.[18]

An applicant's personality, interests, and preferences can also be useful in placing the individual in a particular part or section of the organization. Should an individual climb the corporate ladder, personality, interests, and preferences will again be relevant.

OTHER CHARACTERISTICS

Employers can gather information about other characteristics such as terms and conditions of employment. These include licenses required by law; willingness to travel or work split shifts, weekends, or under adverse conditions such as confined facilities and high noise levels; uniform requirements; business-related grooming codes; tools required on the job and not provided by the employer; required training to be taken on the job; and driver's licenses. These characteristics can be required as minimum qualifications for a job. Very rarely are they used to rank applicants. Applicants either possess them, or they do not. Although these characteristics offer no indication as to how candidates will do on the job, applicants who are unwilling to comply with them can be disqualified from consideration.

OBTAINING THE INFORMATION

APPLICATION BLANK

Premised on the assumption that past behavior is a good predictor of future performance, the **application blank** is a form seeking information about the job applicant's background and present status. Usually this information is used as an initial or pre-employment screen to decide whether the candidate meets the minimum job requirements. Exhibit 8.4 shows an example of an application blank. While not prohibited per se, many traditional questions are now considered "red flags" of discrimination and should be avoided because of their potential adverse impact, for example:

- *Demographic information.* Questions related to race should be strictly avoided. Since questions regarding age, gender, religion, and national origin are difficult to prove as *bona fide occupational qualifications*, they should be avoided. Proof of age and citizenship can be required after hiring.
- *Commitment.* Questions over marital status, a spouse's job, dependents, and child-care arrangements, need to be asked of *both* men and women and given *equivalent* weight if they are asked at all. It is acceptable to ask if applicants have any social, family, or economic responsibilities that would prevent them from performing job duties.

LEARNING OBJECTIVE 3

Discuss several methods of gathering information for selection decisions.

Methods of obtaining applicant information include:

- application blanks
- interviews
- written tests
- reference verification
- drug tests
- medical and physical tests

There are many things employers can legally ask of their employees and many things they should not ask.

Exhibit 8.4
A Typical Application Blank

DATE _____
SOCIAL SECURITY
NUMBER _____
TELEPHONE NO. _____

NAME _____
LAST   FIRST   MIDDLE

ADDRESS _____
STREET   CITY   STATE   ZIP

Position Desired _____ Are You 18 or older _____ Date You Can Start _____

Are You Presently Employed? _____
If so, Where? _____

FORMER EMPLOYERS (Please list beginning with most recent)

DATE Month & Year	NAME & ADDRESS OF EMPLOYER	Telephone No. May We Call?	SALARY	POSITION	REASON FOR LEAVING

EDUCATION	NAME & LOCATION OF SCHOOL	YEARS ATTENDED	DATE GRADUATION	SUBJECT OF SPECIAL INTEREST
HIGH SCHOOL(S)				
COLLEGE(S)				
TRADE, BUSINESS OR CORRESPONDENCE SCHOOLS				

Do you have any physical defects that preclude you from performing any work for which you are being considered? _____

AVAILABILITY
Approximate Total Hours Available: ☐ 15–25   ☐ 35–45

	Weekdays	Weekends			Weekdays	Weekends			Weekdays	Weekends	
Mornings	☐	☐	Yes	Afternoons	☐	☐	Yes	Evenings	☐	☐	Yes
	☐	☐	No		☐	☐	No		☐	☐	No

Particular hours you will be unavailable to work and the reasons: _____

REFERENCES
Give below names of three persons not related to you, whom you have known at least one year.

Continued

267

EXHIBIT 8.4 (CONT.)
A TYPICAL APPLICATION BLANK

NAME	ADDRESS	OCCUPATION	YEARS KNOWN

I AUTHORIZE INVESTIGATION OF ALL STATEMENTS CONTAINED IN THIS APPLICATION. I UNDERSTAND THAT MISREPRESENTATIONS OR OMISSION OF FACTS CALLED FOR IS CAUSE FOR DISMISSAL. FURTHER, I UNDERSTAND AND AGREE THAT MY EMPLOYMENT IS FOR NO DEFINITE PERIOD AND MAY, REGARDLESS OF THE DATE OF PAYMENT OF MY WAGES AND SALARY, BE TERMINATED AT ANY TIME WITHOUT ANY PREVIOUS NOTICE.

DATE   SIGNATURE

INTERVIEWED BY   DATE

> All our tests have been revised to conform with ADA and the *Civil Rights Act of 1991.*
>
> —Dennis Hathaway, Manager, Business Development, Pinkerton National Detective Agency

- *Arrests and convictions.* Inquiries on arrest records are not permissible under any conditions. An employer can ask about convictions.
- *Disabilities.* It is acceptable to ask whether there are any disabilities that would interfere with ability to perform a specific job or whether physical accommodations are needed.
- *Physical requirements.* Height and weight measurements are acceptable for a *few* jobs. Care needs to be taken to ensure that physical requirements (height and weight) are valid since they tend to discriminate against Hispanics, Asians, and women.
- *Affiliations.* Catchall questions about organization affiliation (for example, list the organizations, country clubs, fraternal orders, lodge memberships), should be avoided. However, it is acceptable to ask about professional organizations that relate to specific jobs.[19]

The accuracy of applicant-generated information, usually through résumés, is also a concern. Verified Credentials, Inc., reports that almost 30 percent of the résumés they check for employers contain false information. Distortions vary from wrong starting date for a prior job to inflated college grades to downright lies involving education degrees, types of jobs, and former employers. The most common distortions are length of employment and previous salary.[20]

BIOGRAPHICAL INFORMATION BLANK AND BIODATA TEST. In addition to the application blank or even as a substitute for it, employers may administer a **biographical information blank**. This form generally requests more information from the applicant than does an application blank. For example, in addition to the information requested on an application blank the biographical information blank may request the applicant to indicate a degree of preference for such things as working split shifts, being transferred, working on weekends, or working alone. Exactly which items are asked should be based on the nature of the job. If the job does require working split shifts, for example, indicating preference (or lack thereof) for this may be a good predictor of turnover.[21]

Biographical information blanks ask for more information than regular application forms such as Exhibit 8.4.

A variation on preference information is information about past achievements and activities. This can be done through **biodata tests**. Biodata tests appear to be good predictors of job success and generally have less adverse impact on minorities than do many traditional tests.[22] Biodata tests ask autobiographical questions on such subjects as academic achievement, work attitudes, physical orientation, and self-perception. According to Frank Erwin, test developer and president of Richardson, Bellows, Henry & Co., biodata tests reduce by more than half the scoring differences that routinely result between applicants on traditional general abilities or intelligence tests.

Biodata tests are really records of past achievements and activities such as what you did in high school.

EDUCATION AND EXPERIENCE EVALUATIONS.   As part of the initial application process, applicants often complete a form that details their educational achievements and work experience. Validity evidence indicates that education requirements are predictive of job tenure. Like education, experience requirements may be useful in selecting for high-level, complex jobs but not for jobs that require short learning periods.

What is questionable is the *extent* of education and experience that can be required for a specific job. In order to narrow the application pool, some organizations impose inordinately high experience requirements (for example, twenty years or more for) and higher than needed levels of education. These requirements may serve as artificial barriers to those applicants who may have less opportunity to acquire education and experience.[23]

HANDWRITING ANALYSIS.   In addition to the completed application blank, an employer may request a special handwriting sample. Handwriting analysis, or graphology, is used by 85 percent of all European companies and is catching on in the United States. An estimated 2,000–2,500 U.S. employers use graphology as a selection device.[24]

Handwriting analysis is a very popular selection procedure in France.

Despite the testimonials, there is no scientific evidence that graphology can predict job performance. In one controlled study of sales success, applicants provided handwriting samples, and graphologists predicted job success. While there was limited evidence of inter-rater agreement on character traits, there was no relationship between the assessments and three measures of job performances (sales productivity and self- and supervisory performance ratings). Graphology is also costly ($50–250 per sample), considering its poor predictive ability. Therefore, it is not recommended as a selection device.

REFERENCE VERIFICATION.   Because some job applicants falsify their past and current qualifications, employers are stepping up efforts to check references. Instead of relying on unstructured reference letters (which are always positive), some organizations use outside investigators to verify credentials, others personally contact prior employers to get the information firsthand, and still others have structured the process so that the references provide only job-specific information (goals, accomplishments, degree of supervision).

References can be very predictive of performance when the information is true.

One reason for the increased rigor in reference checking is that they are quite predictive of performance if done correctly. Another reason revolves around the recent spate of negligent hiring lawsuits. Consider the following typical case:

> A woman raped by a cable television installer . . . sued the installer's employers—a cable television franchise and its independent contractor. She claimed that they gave the installer a master key to her apartment, which he used to enter her dwelling on the night of the attack. Because his employers gave him a master key to the apartments, the woman argued that they owed their cus-

tomers a special duty to ensure that he was not a violent criminal. But they had failed to check his criminal record. The employers settled out of court for $250,000.[25]

Unfortunately, it is becoming more difficult to acquire information from former employers because of the potential for defamation-of-character suits (discussed in Chapter 16). Previous employers are becoming "street-smart" and are consequently limiting the type of information they give out about former employees. However, reference checks of prior employment records are not an infringement on privacy if the information provided relates specifically to work behavior and to the reasons an applicant left a previous job. Consequently, employers still routinely verify the accuracy of information on the résumé or application blank through reference checking. Suggestions and advice regarding this process are found in the feature, "HR Advice and Application: Ask the Experts—Investigating Application Fraud."

WRITTEN TESTS

Written testing is another important procedure for gathering information about applicants. The most common types of written tests measure ability (cognitive, mechanical, and psychomotor); personality, interests and preferences; and achievement.

> Written tests can be used to measure:
> - cognitive ability
> - personality, interests and preferences
> - achievement

COGNITIVE ABILITY TESTS. Ability tests measure the potential of an individual to perform, given the opportunity. Used in the United States and Europe since the turn of the century, these devices are useful and valid. Recent studies further suggest that they are equally valid for African-American and white applicants and that their use can be generalized to different jobs in different situations. Exhibit 8.5 shows sample items for measuring seven types of cognitive abilities.

Tests have also been developed to measure special abilities. For example, sensory tests measure the acuity of a person's senses such as vision and hearing. These tests may be appropriate for such jobs as wine taster, coffee bean selector, quality control inspector, and piano tuner. Clerical tests focus primarily on perceptual speed. However, specific tests such as the Minnesota Clerical Tests measure these skills in a job-relevant context. Standard Oil developed a cognitive ability test of management reasoning and judgment, while other firms have developed programmer aptitude tests.[27]

PSYCHOMOTOR TESTS. Many jobs involve a wide range not only of cognitive abilities, but also of psychomotor skills. For example, a bank teller needs certain motor skills to operate a computer or a ten-key calculator and the finger dexterity to manipulate currency.

There are a variety of psychomotor abilities, each of which is highly specific and shows little relationship to other psychomotor abilities *or* to cognitive abilities. Control precision involves finely controlled muscular adjustments (for example, moving a lever to a precise setting), whereas finger dexterity entails skillful manipulation of small objects (assembling nuts and bolts).

Psychomotor tests, then, are useful for selecting applicants in many occupations. However, only some categories of these tests may be predictive of job performance in a specific position.

> There are many types of written tests firms use. It is the *personality test* that is often called the "psychological test."

PERSONALITY TESTS. Personality refers to the unique blend of characteristics that define an individual and determine his or her pattern of interactions with society. While most people believe personality plays an important role in job suc-

HR ADVICE AND APPLICATION

ASK THE EXPERTS—INVESTIGATING APPLICANT FRAUD

Jeffrey F. Robens, manager of government and administrative security for McDonnell Douglas Helicopter Company (Mesa, Arizona).

Q-1. What are the items most likely to be falsified on a résumé or employment application?

A-1. Education, work experience, and references. Some people claim to have degrees that they don't have, and some make claims of work experience that are fraudulent. These are just some of the reasons that more and more human resource departments are asking their company's security professionals to screen job applications and make sure that the candidates are what they say they are.

Q-2. How do applicants falsify their education credentials on a résumé or application?

A-2. What dishonest applicants exaggerate most often is the amount of their schooling. For example, applicants may indicate that they have a bachelor's or master's degree when, in fact, they don't.

Often, an investigation will reveal that the applicant was enrolled in the degree program at the college or university listed; however, the applicant never actually completed the requirements for the degree. Or applicants will claim to have graduated from an accredited technical institute, but upon investigation, the "institute" turns out to be a bus driver's school.

Q-3. What about work experience?

A-3. The "creative" applicant often counterfeits the length of time of a previous job, the responsibilities held, or the compensation received. On rare occasions, an applicant may list employment that never took place at all, perhaps with a fictitious employer.

Applicants with unsatisfactory employment records attempt to disguise the facts. Sometimes, people will say that they worked from January to December when they actually worked only from January to June and were terminated from a job.

Deceitful applicants also tend to inflate their former salaries in an attempt to make themselves look better than they are.

Q-4. What problems have you found in checking references?

A-4. Unscrupulous applicants may also list fake references to round off their other deceptions. They will list actual people who have never heard of them or fictitious people, hoping that the names and titles will give credence to their claims and that you will not bother to contact the references.

Q-5. How much information on the application or résumé should you check?

A-5. You should devise a checklist to clarify what education and experience are essential for any position that needs to be filled. By defining what is essential and what is nonessential, you will not have to verify more information than is required.

Although it is important to confirm applicants' credentials, you may not need to check everything unless you suspect that some information may be false. If a degree is not required for the position, you may not need to contact the school, provided everything else on the application appears satisfactory.

State and federal laws may limit what information is available to you or impose rules on how you should go about obtaining certain information. For instance, credit checks conducted for employment purposes must conform to the guidelines established by the federal *Fair Credit Reporting Act* and any applicable state laws.[26]

---

cess or failure, personality tests generally have not been found viable for employee selection. One reason is that personality variables have not been consistently defined. Personality tests are a diverse group of testing devices, each of which was designed to accomplish a different goal, but all of which are called **personality inventories**. The various tests are *not* equivalent in their construction, measure-

---

EXHIBIT 8.5
SAMPLES OF COGNITIVE ABILITY AND PSYCHOMOTOR TESTS

Verbal Comprehension involves understanding the meaning of words and their relationship to one another. It is measured by such test items as

Which one of the following words means most nearly the same as *dilapidated*:
(1) new   (2) injured   (3) unresponsive   (4) run-down   (5) lethargic

Word Fluency involves the ability to name or make words, such as making smaller words from the letters in a large one or playing anagrams. For example,

Using the letters in the word "measurement," write as many three-letter words as you can in the next two minutes.

_____   _____   _____

_____   _____   _____

Number Aptitude involves speed and accuracy in making simple arithmetic calculations. It is measured by such test items as

Carry out the following calculations:

$$429 \atop + 762 \qquad 7983 \atop -6479 \qquad 721 \times 52 = \text{\_\_\_\_\_} \qquad 4920 \div 6 = \text{\_\_\_\_\_}$$

Inductive Reasoning focuses on the ability to discover a rule or principle and apply it to the solution of a problem. The following is an example:

What number should come next in the sequence of five numbers?
1   3   6   10   15
(1) 22   (2) 21   (3) 25   (4) 18

Memory relates to having the ability to recall pairs of words or lists of numbers. It is measured by such test items as

You have 30 seconds to memorize the following pairs. When the examiner says stop, turn the page and write the appropriate symbols after each of the letters appearing there.

A @   C #   E Δ   G ?
B >   D *   F +   H $

Perceptual Speed is concerned with the ability to perceive visual details quickly and accurately. Usually these tests are timed and include such items as

Make a check mark in front of each pair below in which the numbers are identical. Work as fast as you can.
1. 755321 ·····················753321
2. 966441 ·····················966641
3. 334579 ·····················334579

Motor Skill—Aiming involves the ability to respond accurately and rapidly to stimuli. For example,

Place three dots in as many circles as you can in 30 seconds.
○ ○ ○ ○   ○   ○○   ○ ○

SOURCE: Modified from M. Dunnette, *Personnel Selection and Placement* (Monterey, Calif.: Brooks/Cole, 1966), 47–49.

ment goals, or underlying theoretical bases.[28] Consequently, these tests often yield different, incompatible, and even conflicting results.

Another problem is that the wrong types of personality measurements have generally been used for selection purposes. The widely used Minnesota Multiphasic Personality Inventory (MMPI) is designed to identify areas of maladjustment. While it is an appropriate selection device for high-stress jobs (for example, police, nuclear power plant employees, air traffic controllers), it is not appropriate for most jobs because the absence of psychopathology does not guarantee the presence of competence: an employee can be both well adjusted *and* hopelessly mediocre in performance.

Finally, in highly structured situations controlled by regulations, rules, and guidelines, an individual's personality is unlikely to have an effect. However, in less structured organizations in which individuality and creativity are encouraged, personality attributes are likely to make the difference between job success and job failure.[29]

While less predictive of job success than cognitive ability tests, carefully developed personality assessments can be inexpensive additions to the selection process for a few jobs. One common multidimensional test of personality that appears useful is the Ghiselli Self-Description Inventory. It includes 64 pairs of trait adjectives.[30] For each pair, a person is asked to choose the most or least descriptive adjective. Responses are then scored across thirteen personality dimensions (for example, supervisory ability, decisiveness, achievement motivation) that relate to managerial competence. The designer of this test, Edwin Ghiselli, was able to show that successful managers perceive themselves quite differently than do unsuccessful managers on these dimensions.

An important legal consideration can arise in the use of personality or "psychological" tests as they are sometimes called. The consideration is invasion of privacy. As the feature "Managing Human Resources: Psychological Testing Leads to Costly Lawsuit," describes, this consideration can be costly.

INTEREST INVENTORIES.   While applicants may be able to perform in various jobs, **interest inventories** assess their preferences for different types of work and work situations.[32] Such inventories are useful in matching people to jobs they will enjoy. Representative items from an interest inventory include the following:

> For each set, write an "M" next to the activity you most like and an "L" next to the item you least prefer.
>
> 1 _____ go to a concert   2 _____ work in the garden
> _____ play tennis   _____ go hiking
> _____ read a book   _____ paint a picture

Do your answers to those items fit your career plans and goals that you wrote in the career planning exercise in Chapter 4?

ACHIEVEMENT TESTS.   **Achievement tests** predict an individual's performance on the basis of what he or she knows. Although a test's validity is required, achievement tests may exclude applicants who have not had equal access to the opportunities to acquire the knowledge. Thus, care must be taken to ensure that the skills tested are job-related. Not all achievement tests are actual work samples of the job, and organizations need to be careful in their choice of these tests because some are less job-related than others.

Paper-and-pencil achievement tests tend to be less job-related because they measure facts and principles, not the practical use of them. For example, you could take a paper-and-pencil test measuring your knowledge of tennis and pass

AN employer that required applicants to answer intimate personal questions in a pre-employment psychological examination agrees to pay more than $2 million to settle a lawsuit over the test.

The employer, which operates a chain of retail stores in California, administered the test to about 2,500 applicants for security jobs. The test's true-or-false questions included the following:

- I have never indulged in any unusual sex practices.
- I have often wished I were a girl.
- I am very strongly attracted by members of my own sex.
- I believe my sins are unpardonable.
- I feel sure there is only one true religion.
- A minister can cure disease by praying and putting his hand on your head.

Before settling the suit, the employer argued that the test was necessary to screen out applicants who are emotionally unstable, unreliable, undependable, and not inclined to follow directions or established rules, as well as applicants with addictive or violent tendencies who might put customers or other employees at risk.

Under the settlement, the employer admits no wrongdoing, but agrees to set up a $1.3 million fund to be divided among applicants who took the test. Additionally, the employer agrees to pay $60,000 plus attorneys' fees to the four individuals who actually pursued the lawsuit, as well as the costs of notifying the 2,500 applicants.

The case "sends a strong message to other employers that they cannot trample upon the constitutionally protected privacy rights of applicants and employees," according to the applicants' attorney, Brad Seligman of Saperstein, Mayeda, Larkin & Goldstein, Oakland, California. This was the first class-action privacy case in the nation to challenge psychological testing, he adds. (*Soroka v. Dayton Hudson Corp.*, 1993).[31]

with flying colors and yet play very poorly. However, such tests continue to be used in many areas because they facilitate measuring a large number of people and because they test levels of knowledge presumed to be required. For example, applicants are admitted to the legal profession through bar exams and to the medical profession through medical boards. Paper-and-pencil tests are used in these cases because they are—or are assumed to be—related to performance in the actual job. Job-relatedness is, as with all other tests, a necessary legal defense for the use of paper-and-pencil tests.

Recognition tests, which are examples of past performance, are often used in advertising and modeling to select applicants. The applicants bring portfolios or samples of the work they have done to the job interview. However, portfolios contain no clues as to the conditions or circumstances under which they were done. Some organizations may request written samples from school work for jobs where written expression may be important.

TEST BATTERIES. It is often useful to administer a battery of tests to applicants for vocational counseling or selection. The General Aptitude Test Battery (GATB), which measures cognitive abilities—verbal, numerical, spatial, intelli-

It is often more efficient to use a battery of tests.

gence, form perceptions, clerical perceptions, motor coordination, finger and manual dexterity—is used by U.S. employment offices for counseling purposes.[33]

Alternatively, organizations may use test batteries for selection. For example, Sears has used tests of ability (American Council on Education Psychological Test), values (Allport-Vernon Study of Values), and interest (Kuder Preference Record) since the 1940s to select managers. Similarly, Exxon relied on cognitive ability (Miller Analogies, Nonverbal Reasoning, Management Judgment), personality (MMPI), and an individual background survey. Because batteries are difficult to develop, they are usually designed under the guidance of industrial psychologists.[34]

WORK SIMULATIONS

Work simulations, often referred to as **work sample tests**, require applicants to complete verbal or physical activities under structured "testing" conditions. Rather than measure what an individual knows, they assess the individual's ability to do something. Still, work sample tests are somewhat artificial because the selection process itself tends to promote anxiety and tension.[35] Exhibit 8.6 shows three sets of work sample tests and the jobs they are used for.

Work simulations or work sample tests assess how applicants can actually do parts of the job.

EXHIBIT 8.6
EXAMPLES OF WORK SAMPLE TESTS AND JOBS

JOB	PHYSICAL WORK SAMPLE TESTS
Dental assistants	Carving dexterity
Machine operators	Lathe, drill press; and tool dexterity
Meat scalers	Meat weighing
Mechanics	Belt and pulley installation; gear box repair; motor installation and alignment; sprocket reaming
Miners	Two-hand coordination
Pilots	Rudder control; direction control; complex coordination
Administrative assistants	Word processing on specific equipment; Knowledge of Word
Mental Work Sample Tests	
Magazine editors	Writing skills; page layout; headline writing
Administrators	Judgment and decision making
Engineers	Processing mathematical data
Administrative assistants	Letter composition; proofreading
Verbal Work Sample Tests	
Telephone operators	Role play of telephone contacts
Communication specialists	Oral fact-finding
Construction supervisors	Construction error recognition
Administrative assistants	Telephone screening

SOURCE: Adapted from J. J. Asher and J. A. Sciarrino, "Realistic Work Sample Tests: A Review," *Personnel Psychology* 27 (1974): 519–33.

Because they replicate the actual work, work sample tests are not easy to fake. As a result, they tend to be more valid than almost all other types of selection devices. Additionally, they do not have an adverse impact on minority applicants. Unfortunately, because simulation tests are job-specific, they are expensive to develop unless large numbers of applicants are to be examined. However, by placing work sample tests at the end of a selection process, the number of applicants tested is smaller and the price lower.

ASSESSMENT CENTER. This selection device evaluates applicants or current employees with regard to how well they might perform in a managerial or higher-level position. More than 20,000 companies now utilize this method, and its use grows each year because of its validity in predicting whether job applicants will be successful or unsuccessful.[36]

Assessment centers help identify how well someone might do in a future job.

An **assessment center** usually involves six to twelve people who have been chosen or who have chosen to attend it. It is most often conducted off the premises by the organization for one to three days. The performance of the attendees is usually rated by managers in the organization who are trained assessors. Typically, the purpose is to determine potential promotability of applicants to a first-line supervisor's job.

An in-basket exercise assesses how well a person can (1) identify what's important and (2) organize it accordingly.

At a typical assessment center, candidates undergo evaluation using a wide range of techniques. One important activity is the **in-basket exercise**, which creates a realistic situation designed to elicit typical on-the-job behaviors. Situations and problems encountered on the job are written on individual sheets of paper and set in the in-basket. The applicant is then asked to arrange the papers by priority. Occasionally, the applicant may need to write an action response. The problems or situations described to the applicant involve different groups of people—peers, subordinates, and those outside the organization. The applicant is usually given a set time limit to take the test and is often interrupted by phone calls meant to create more tension and pressure.

Leaderless group discussions and business games are often used at an assessment center.

Other tests used in managerial selection are the **leaderless group discussion (LGD)** and business games. In the LGD, a group of individuals is asked to discuss a topic for a given period of time. At IBM's assessment center, participants must make a five-minute oral presentation about the qualifications of a candidate for promotion. During the subsequent leaderless group discussion, they must defend their nomination of the candidate with five or more other participants. Participants are rated on their selling ability, oral communication skill, self-confidence, energy level, interpersonal competency, aggressiveness, and tolerance for stress. LGD ratings have been shown to be useful predictors of managerial performance in a wide array of business areas. Additionally, prior experience in LGD does not affect current LGD performance. **Business games** are "living" cases. That is, individuals must make decisions and "live" with them, much as they do in the in-basket exercise.

Because in-baskets, LGDs, and business games tend to be useful in managerial selection, they are often used together.[37] As candidates go through these exercises, their performance is observed by a trained team of observers or assessors drawn from the local management group. After the candidates have finished the program, these assessors meet to discuss the candidates and prepare performance evaluations based on their combined judgments of the candidates in such areas as organizing and planning, analyzing, making decisions, controlling oral communications, conducting interpersonal relations, influencing, and exhibiting flexibility. The composite performance on the exercises and tests is then used to determine an assessment center attendee's future promotability. It may also be used to determine the organization's training needs, as well as to make current selection and placement decisions. This rating is generally given to the attendee, who in turn can use it for his or her own personal career planning purposes.

Assessment centers have been used effectively by manufacturing companies, government, military services, utility companies, oil companies, the foreign service, and educational institutions. They appear to work because they reflect the actual work environment and measure performance in multiple dimensions. Additionally, more than one *trained* rater with a common frame of reference evaluates each participant's behavior. In terms of cost effectiveness, assessment centers are often criticized as costing too much (from $50 to over $2,000 per applicant). However, annual productivity gains realized by selecting managers via assessment centers average well above administrative costs.[38]

SELECTION AND PLACEMENT INTERVIEW

Job offers may go to applicants who *appear* most qualified because it may be difficult to determine from other available test data who really is most qualified. This reflects the fact that the job interview and the perceptions gained from it still comprise the tool most heavily used to determine who gets the job offer.[39] As shown in Exhibit 8.2, the interview is important at both the beginning and the end of the selection procedure. The reliability and usefulness of the interview depend on several factors.

DEGREE OF STRUCTURE. The unstructured interview involves little preparation. The interviewer merely prepares a list of possible topics to cover and, depending on how the conversation proceeds, asks or does not ask them. While this provides for flexibility, the digressions, discontinuity, and lack of focus may be frustrating to the interviewer and interviewee. More important, unstructured interviews result in inconsistencies in the information collected about the candidates.

> Interviews are much better predictors when they are structured.

Alternatively, in a **patterned** or **structured interview**, all the applicants are asked the same questions in the same order. While structuring the interview restricts the topics that can be covered, it ensures that the same information is collected on all candidates. As a result, managers are less likely to make snap, and possibly erroneous, judgments.

A compromise that still minimizes snap judgments is the semistructured interview. Questions are prepared in advance, and the same questions are asked of all candidates; responses are recorded. However, follow-up questions are allowed to probe specific areas in depth. This approach provides enough flexibility to develop insights, along with the structure needed to acquire comparative information.

JOB RELEVANCE. At one extreme, interviewers focus on generalities about qualifications. Such questions help interviewers form an overall impression of the candidate's competence but are not predictive of success in a specific job. A better approach is to use job analysis to generate questions about specific job skills and duties. For example, the critical incident method of job analysis (see Chapter 6) can be used to develop **situational questions**. (Exhibit 8.7 illustrates how critical incidents are then transformed into job-specific situational interview questions.)

SYSTEMATIC SCORING. Job interviews vary in the degree to which results are scored. At one extreme, an interviewer merely listens to responses, forms an impression, and makes an accept, reject, or hold decision. Alternatively, raters are given specific criteria and a scoring key to evaluate responses to each question (see Exhibit 8.7). This latter approach is more objective because it helps ensure that applicants are evaluated against the same criteria. Systematic scoring also tends to minimize **halo bias**, in which an interviewer judges an applicant's entire potential on the basis of a single characteristic such as how well the applicant dresses or talks.

NUMBER OF INTERVIEWERS. Typically, applicants are interviewed by one person at a time. Unfortunately, managers sometimes overlap in their coverage of some job-related questions and miss others entirely. An applicant may have

---

EXHIBIT 8.7
STEPS IN DEVELOPING JOB-RELATED SITUATIONAL INTERVIEW QUESTIONS

1. Generate the critical incident of good or poor behavior.

"This employee always calls in sick at the last minute for personal reasons."

2. Rewrite the incident as a situational interview question.

"Your husband and children are all sick with the 24-hour flu. Your husband urges you to stay home and take care of them. It's two hours before your shift starts. What do you do?"

3. Develop a weighted scoring key.

Managers and incumbents brainstorm possible answers to the question and then rank them in terms of their appropriateness. Assuming a weight of 5 percent for the situational question above, responses could be scored as follows:

5 "I would call the doctor and see if there is any medication I could get for them before going to work. If it's the flu, there really isn't much I can do by staying home, so I'd go to work as usual. I might call them on break to check on how they are doing."

4 "I'd call the substitution board and see if someone could fill in for me. If not, I'd go to work."

3 "I'd call my supervisor immediately, explain the situation, and stay home and take care of my family. My family comes first."

2 "I'd see if my family got any better in the next two hours. If not, I'd call my supervisor and let him know I won't be coming in due to family sickness."

1 "Because we're allowed so many sick days a year, I'd call my supervisor at the start of my shift and say I was sick."

0 "I'd stay home and take care of my family."

4. Develop similar questions and scoring keys for all important job duties.

One of the only three female employees in your group says she is being sexually harassed by some of the male workers. She says the continuous stream of lewd jokes, sexist comments, and pats on the behind are very upsetting. The other two women have not complained. How would you respond?

5. Total the scores for all questions to arrive at an overall suitability score.

SOURCE: Adapted from: G. P. Latham, L. M. Saari, E. D. Pursell, and M. A. Campion, "The Situational Interview," *Journal of Applied Psychology* 65 (1980): 422–427.

not four interviews, but one interview four times. This is a time-consuming process in which the interviewer's *and* applicant's impressions may vary, depending on what was discussed in one-on-one interviews. This problem can be overcome by using a **panel interview** in which several individuals simultaneously interview one applicant. Because all decision makers hear the same responses, panel interviews produce more consistent results. On the other hand, panel interviews are expensive because many people are involved. However, if applicants are to be interviewed by more than one person anyway, panel interviewing may be more efficient and reliable and as cost effective as individual interviews. A variation of the panel interview is the **team interview**. While several people are used, they are not used simultaneously. The benefits of using the team interview and how to prepare for it are described in the feature, "HR Advice and Application: Expert Opinion—Interviewing Skills: Using Past Performance to Predict the Future."

Team interviews improve predictions of an applicant's chances of success.

TRAINING.   Left on their own, interviewers tend to form impressions based on whatever criteria are most important or salient to them personally. For example, an applicant might be rejected by one interviewer for being "too aggressive" but accepted by another for being "assertive." Consequently, it is important to train interviewers so they interpret information consistently.[41] This can be accomplished by having potential interviewers develop items and scoring approaches such as those in Exhibit 8.7. Alternatively, an interviewer's ratings for "practice" questions can be compared to normative ratings given by other interviewers. Such training brings perceptions into closer congruence with those of the rest of the organization.

Interviews can be good predictors when structured *and* interviewers are trained.

MEDICAL, PHYSICAL, AND POLYGRAPH TESTS

Although not all organizations require medical exams or physical tests, such tests are being given in increasing numbers. One consequence is a concern about genetic screening as a part of the physical examination process.

PHYSICAL EXAMINATION.   Because of its high cost, the physical examination is often one of the final steps in the selection process. Many employers give common physical exams to all job applicants, whereas special exams are given to only a subset of all applicants.[42] For example, production-job applicants may receive back X-rays, while office-job applicants may not. According to the *Uniform Guidelines*, physical examinations should be used to screen out applicants when the results indicate that job performance would be adversely affected.

Guidelines for assessing physical abilities have been developed that detail the sensory, perceptual, cognitive, psychomotor, and physical requirements of most jobs (for example, police, firefighters, steel mill laborers, paramedics, and workers in numerous mechanical jobs). When applied carefully, these physical requirements (not physical examinations *per se*) are extremely useful in predicting job performance, worker's compensation claims, and absenteeism. However, arbitrary physical requirements can be a curse, screening out women and minorities who could do a job if given the opportunity. To accommodate workers with disabilities, organizations should also explore whether equipment can be "reasonably" adapted. Guidelines on inexpensive adaptations for most types of machinery are available from the federal government.[43] This concern is particularly relevant for employees now since the passage of the *Americans with Disabilities Act of 1990*. In fact, the ADA is giving employers an opportunity to review their entire set of policies regarding job applicants and employees with disabilities.

EXPERT OPINION—INTERVIEWING SKILLS: USING PAST PERFORMANCE TO PREDICT THE FUTURE

Glenna Sue Davis, of A. E. Staley Manufacturing (Monte Vista, Colorado)

Glenna Sue Davis is human resource and quality control manager at A.E. Staley Manufacturing's potato starch processing facility. In this position, she's responsible for recruiting and hiring engineers, supervisors, and hourly employees.

There are two things that distinguish Davis's approach to hiring: First, she makes an effort to learn what applicants did in past jobs, rather than concentrating solely on what they say they'd accomplish in the positions for which she's interviewing. Second, with hourly positions, she uses a team approach to hiring.

PAST PERFORMANCE

"You really have to be willing to dig a little if you want to get good information," Davis advises. For instance, if you ask a question and the candidate is evasive, restate the question. Davis will sometimes use this technique when she's unsure about the information she's been given.

Hypothetical questions are helpful when trying to explore applicants' backgrounds. "Particularly when I'm hiring engineers, I'll say, 'Tell me about a problem you had (in a certain area) and how you handled it,' or 'How did your past job prepare you to deal with . . . ?'" These types of questions are effective in getting candidates to discuss their experience so that Davis can get the objective information she needs to make informed hiring decisions.

There are three keys, she says, to getting helpful information about past performance and using it to predict future performance:

- *Identify your needs*. Take a good look at the job description and requirements so that you know what the position demands.
- *Identify the behaviors that will lead to successful performance on the job*. For instance, will the candidate need to be self-directed? Assertive? Independent? Cooperative?
- *Develop questions about past behaviors that will provide insights into the future*. Example: Tell me about a situation in which you had to confront an angry co-worker. How did you handle that situation, and what was the outcome?

TEAM INTERVIEWS

Davis uses the unusual approach of team interviews to fill hourly positions. "I feel it's important to get a perspective from the people who will be working directly with the new hire," she says. "Team interviewing also provides me with a more in-depth sense of what traits are needed to successfully fill a position."

Davis usually selects a supervisor, an employee from the department whose position she is filling, and a cross section of people from other departments to participate in the interview. She tries to get at least four or five people involved and makes sure there is a mix of male and female interviewers. Another benefit of the team approach to interviewing is that decisions are shared ones and are more likely to be supported by the staff.

Preparation is a critical factor in making this system work, she stresses. "We do a couple of training sessions on our wants, needs, and priorities. Then we put together the questions we'll be asking—of course, every applicant will be asked the same questions."

To make a final selection decision, Staley Manufacturing uses a rating system. "We have a numerical rating system that we use to select the three final candidates. Then the appropriate department head and I will make a final decision from among these three candidates."

Davis's advice to other interviewers is to "hone your skills. Be sure you know what you're going after, and be confident in what you're doing." An excellent way to attain this knowledge and confidence is to adapt Davis's approach to your particular circumstances. Above all, she says, "keep learning. Every time you conduct an interview, you learn something new."[40]

GENETIC SCREENING. In 1985, there were 390,000 reported cases of job-related illness and 100,000 job-related deaths. Many of these illnesses and deaths were attributable to chemical hazards. **Genetic screening** identifies individuals who are hypersensitive to harmful pollutants in the workplace. Once identified, these individuals can be screened out of chemically dangerous jobs and placed in positions in which environmental toxins do not present specific hazards.[44]

While cost-effective genetic tests have not yet been developed, 1 percent of major firms already use genetic screening, and 15 percent are considering genetic tests in the future. As scientific research on genetic screening continues, the debate over the ethics of basing employment decisions on immutable traits is likely to grow. It also seems probable that pressure will be exerted on organizations to develop engineering controls that minimize or eliminate workplace pollutants. These controls would be the preferred alternative to genetic screening, a selection criterion over which an individual has no control.[45]

DRUG AND ALCOHOL TESTING.   Alcohol and drug abuse are said to cost U.S. industry more than $100 billion annually. In a recent study conducted by the SmithKline Beecham Clinical Laboratories,

> Marijuana and cocaine continue to be the most commonly detected drugs. Of all workers and applicants screened, 56,000 (2.6 percent) tested positive for cocaine and 61,000 (3.1 percent) tested positive for marijuana. Among the individuals testing positive for drugs, 29 percent were positive for cocaine (up 4.7 percent from 1990) and 34.6 percent were positive for marijuana (up 0.8 percent from 1990).[46]

Alcohol and drug abuse persist, and their impact on individuals and society can be significant.[47] Consequently, firms will continue drug testing. Federal contractors have no choice. According to the *Drug Free Workplace Act of 1988*, firms that do business with the federal government must have written drug use policies. Regardless of what methods are used for drug testing, a key issue in adopting a drug policy is establishing a disciplinary procedure.

> If a drug policy does not state specifically that disciplinary actions will be taken when an employee tests positive for drug use, there's no reason to test. Drug testing doesn't make sense if you're not willing to take disciplinary action based on a confirmed positive test result. A policy calling for discipline in such a circumstance doesn't have to require termination. Rehabilitation can be required as an alternative.[48]

AIDS TESTING.   AIDS victims are protected by the *Rehabilitation Act of 1973* and ADA (*Chalk v. U.S. District Court for Central District of California*, 1987). Because AIDS is such a major challenge in today's workplace, organizations are establishing guidelines concerning it. Companies such as IBM, AT&T, and Johnson & Johnson have endorsed these guidelines:

- People with AIDS or who are infected with HIV, the AIDS-causing virus, are entitled to the same rights and opportunities as people with other serious illnesses.
- Employment policies should be based on the scientific evidence that people with AIDS or HIV infection do not pose a risk of transmitting the virus through ordinary workplace contact.
- Employers should provide workers with sensitive and up-to-date education about AIDS and risk reduction in their personal lives.
- Employers have the duty to protect the confidentiality of employees' medical information.
- Employers should not require HIV screening as part of general *pre-employment* or workplace physical examinations.[49]

POLYGRAPH TESTING.   With the passage of the *Employee Polygraph Protection Act of 1988*, employers are restricting their use of **polygraph tests**. In passing the law, supporters of polygraph restriction claimed the tests are accurate only two-thirds of the time and are far more likely to be inaccurate for honest employees. The new law restricts pre-employment screening and random use of the device; the law

- Permits private security firms and drug companies to continue to administer polygraph tests to job applicants and employees
- Exempts federal, state, and local government employers from the ban on polygraph testing
- Prohibits employers from disciplining, discharging, discriminating against, or denying employment or promotions to prospective or current workers solely on the basis of polygraph test results
- Provides that employers that violate any provision of the law may be assessed a civil penalty of up to $10,000

HONESTY TESTS. Partly as a response to regulatory prohibitions on employers' use of polygraphs, the use of paper-and-pencil honesty tests has increased. Paper-and-pencil **honesty tests** attempt to detect the honesty of the respondent by examining how the person responds to such items as, "Did you ever steal?" Despite endorsements from industry, honesty tests have not been subject to extensive validation and therefore caution is recommended in using them as a selection device.[50]

USING INFORMATION IN SELECTION AND PLACEMENT DECISIONS

We have discussed the primary techniques for collecting selection and placement information. Now the key question is, How can this information be used in making selection decisions? Should just one technique be used (the single-predictor approach), or should several techniques be used (the multiple-predictor approach)?

Remember, organizations want to make decisions that are correct. In other words, they want to maximize the number of true decisions and minimize the number of false decisions. **True decisions** include rejecting a candidate who would have been a bad performer or hiring a candidate who turns out good. **False decisions** include rejecting a good candidate or hiring a bad candidate. For more discussion on this subject, see Appendix C under "Base Rate Versus Predictor Rate."

Organizations want to *maximize* true positives and true negatives. Organizations want to *minimize* false positives and false negatives.

THE SINGLE-PREDICTOR APPROACH

When managers use only one piece of information or one technique for selecting an applicant, they are employing the **single-predictor approach**. Single predictors are used by many organizations to select employees, especially when the predictor can be readily validated. This occurs most frequently when a predictor encompasses the major dimension of the job, thereby making it easy to validate.

A *single predictor approach* uses just one piece of information in selecting an applicant.

> A few hiring tests are easy enough to validate, especially those in which the candidate actually performs a task he/she will have to perform on the job. It makes obvious good sense, for example, to require a candidate for a secretarial job to pass a typing test.[51]

Multiple predictors can be combined in three approaches.
- multiple hurdles
- compensatory
- combined

THE MULTIPLE-PREDICTOR APPROACH

When there is more than one selection technique being used, the information from all can be combined in one of three ways. This is the essence of the **multiple-predictor approach**.

MULTIPLE HURDLES. In the **multiple-hurdles approach**, an applicant must exceed fixed levels of proficiency on all the predictors in order to be accepted. A score lower than the cutoff score on one predictor (test) cannot be compensated for by a higher-than-necessary score on another predictor. Underlying this approach is the assumption that a specific skill or competency is so critical that inadequacy guarantees the person will be unsuccessful on the job. This assumption legitimately applies for some physical ability requirements (visual acuity for pilots) and for state-mandated licensing requirements (state licensure for nurses).

This approach can, however, create an equal employment issue as shown in the hypothetical multiple-hurdles selection case illustrated in Exhibit 8.8. While 200 African-Americans and 500 whites apply, only 52 African-Americans (41 percent) compared with 300 whites (60 percent) pass the written examination. Applying the four-fifths rule, the test has an adverse impact on African-Americans (41% <4/5ths of 60%).

Previously, organizations believed that they could construct multiple-hurdles systems and escape liability by applying what is called the **bottom-line rule**. The rule premises that an adverse impact found in one component of a selection process (written examination) can be neutralized by favorable treatment overall. In Exhibit 8.8, the final hiring rate for African-Americans (30 percent) is substantially equal to the hiring rate for whites (32 percent). Thus, the selection process "on the bottom line" does not have adverse impact. The Supreme Court, however, ruled that the bottom-line rule is no defense when adverse impact is shown for *any* component in a selection process (*Connecticut v. Teal,* 1982). For the 118 African-Americans who did not pass the written examination, the "test" classifies them in a way that deprives them of an employment opportunity. Unless the written examination can be shown to be job-related, its use is in violation of Title VII. Because of this issue, a multiple-hurdles approach is generally not recommended.

In a *multiple hurdles approach,* an applicant has to score well on all the tests.

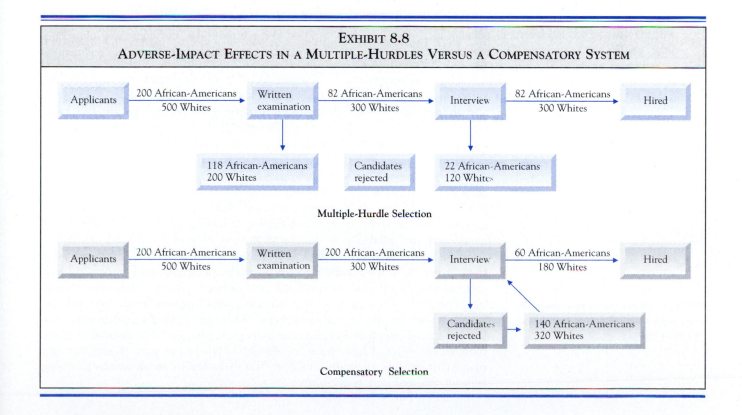

EXHIBIT 8.8
ADVERSE-IMPACT EFFECTS IN A MULTIPLE-HURDLES VERSUS A COMPENSATORY SYSTEM

| Applicants | 200 African-Americans / 500 Whites → | Written examination | 82 African-Americans / 300 Whites → | Interview | 82 African-Americans / 300 Whites → | Hired |

118 African-Americans / 200 Whites

Candidates rejected

22 African-Americans / 120 Whites

Multiple-Hurdle Selection

| Applicants | 200 African-Americans / 500 Whites → | Written examination | 200 African-Americans / 300 Whites → | Interview | 60 African-Americans / 180 Whites → | Hired |

Candidates rejected

140 African-Americans / 320 Whites

Compensatory Selection

In a *compensatory approach,* a high score on one test can compensate for a low score on another test.

A *combined approach* uses parts of the multiple hurdles approach and the compensatory approach.

Selection and placement procedures tap individuals from inside and outside the organization.

COMPENSATORY APPROACH. Since most jobs do not have truly absolute requirements, a **compensatory approach** is more realistic. This approach assumes that good performance on one predictor *can* compensate for poor performance on another (for example, a low score for a written examination can be compensated for by a high score on an interview). With a compensatory approach, no selection decisions are made until the completion of the entire process. Then, a composite index that considers performance on all predictors is developed.

Exhibit 8.8 illustrates the compensatory approach. Here, 700 applicants are interviewed, notwithstanding their scores on the written examination. Using a composite index (derived through regression analysis or by weighing criteria based on job importance), 240 candidates are hired. Unlike a multiple-hurdles approach, some of the hirees could have scored low on either the written examination or the interview—provided their overall score surpasses the hiring cutoff. The advantage of this approach is that *every* applicant, regardless of race, gets to participate in the *entire* selection process. While more time-consuming and costly than a multiple-hurdles approach, a compensatory approach is less likely to cause legal problems—provided overall hiring rates are equivalent for African-Americans and whites.

COMBINED APPROACH. Many organizations also use a **combined approach**, in which one or more specific requirements must be met. Once these hurdles are jumped, then the remaining predictor scores are combined into an overall measure of job suitability. Consider college recruiting. Many organizations only interview college students with GPAs that exceed a specific level (first hurdle). To be offered a plant visit, the candidate must first pass a campus interview (second hurdle). At corporate headquarters, the applicant may take aptitude tests, participate in an assessment center, and be interviewed. A composite index that takes into consideration performance in all three areas is used to make the final decision (compensatory).

THE DECISION ITSELF

Selection and placement decisions seek to put the right person in the right job. The right person may be from outside or inside the organization. Whether a person is "right" depends on the match between the person's skills, knowledge, and abilities and job-skill demands and between the person's personality, interests, and preferences and job and organizational characteristics. An organization may want applicants to fill newly created jobs or jobs that have become vacant as a result of retirement, transfer, or voluntary termination (turnover). Vacancies can also be created by demotions and discharges. Because demotions and discharges are an important part of managing human resources, they are discussed in Chapters 10 and 16. *Remember, however, that as far as equal employment laws are concerned, all decisions about initial hiring, transfer, promotion, demotion, layoff, termination, and admittance to training programs are regarded as selection decisions.*

The final selection and placement decision may be to hire a new person or transfer one from within the organization. The decision could be not to hire a particular applicant or set of applicants, but rather to go out and do more recruiting. The decision could be to "put on hold" some applicants who are qualified but for whom no jobs are currently open. Although generally not thought of as such, the final selection and placement decision can also be to demote or terminate an employee. These decisions should be viewed as part of selection and placement because they are subject to the same legal considerations as hiring, transfer, and promotion decisions.

Promotion Decisions

Selection decisions include bringing in candidates from the outside to fill higher-level jobs in the organization. This, however, is the exception rather than the rule, and promotion-from-within is a standard practice in most organizations because it can lower employee morale if internal candidates feel passed over.[52] Thus organizations may prefer to promote from within. Some job vacancies, particularly highly skilled jobs, however, do get filled by outside sources. This can also occur when the organization is caught by surprise and has no internal individual ready to take the job, or when the focus of the organization changes. To reduce surprises, organizations have managerial succession programs. In these programs, current managers identify employees who may one day be able to take over their jobs. While these managers are likely candidates to "fit" the organization, there are times the organization also needs to hire candidates from outside the organization. Here the concern for identifying if the candidates will "fit" can become an important issue:

> This practice of careful selection to ensure better fit between company and employee is also a critical personnel practice at Goldman Sachs. There every partner interviews every MBA job applicant to ensure that new employees "fit" the company.[53]

Organizations thus must use both internal and external sources for promotion. What may vary across firms is the importance put on one or the other. For example, the Disney organization has an HR philosophy of promotion-from-within, so it gets most of its managers from inside the company as shown in Exhibit 8.9.

TRANSFER DECISIONS.   As the 35–54 age group increases and organizations continue to reduce the number of middle management positions, transfers may become the alternative to promotions, at least in providing challenge and variety to valued employees. In addition to providing challenge and variety to employees, transfers are also likely to result in employees having a greater understanding of what employees in other parts and functional areas of the organization are doing. Many organizations are now doing this in order to promote within employees a greater understanding of the business and how their work influences the work of others and ultimately the customer. Viewed in this way, transfers are likely to be seen by organizations as vital ways to increase the organization's ability to produce high quality products/services as well as to provide the employees with interesting and challenging work assignments. As a consequence, transfer decisions are likely to become as important to organizations as promotion decisions. Thus the discussion in the next several paragraphs applies equally to transfer and promotion decisions.

TYPES OF PROMOTION AND TRANSFER.   Promotions can be selected for from a pool of people within a department, a division, or an entire organization. They occur between two nonmanagerial positions (for example, from Typist I to Typist II), between managerial positions, and between nonmanagerial and managerial positions.

Although promotions generally refer to vertical moves in the organization, promotions may occur when an employee moves to another job at the same level but with more pay or status. However, this type of promotion may violate federal wage guidelines and equal pay regulations, and should be made advisedly. Although such a move could be regarded as a transfer, a transfer generally refers to a move at the same level and at the same pay.

Advantages of internal promotion include:

- Highly qualified candidates
- Security
- Cost-efficiency
- Fairness

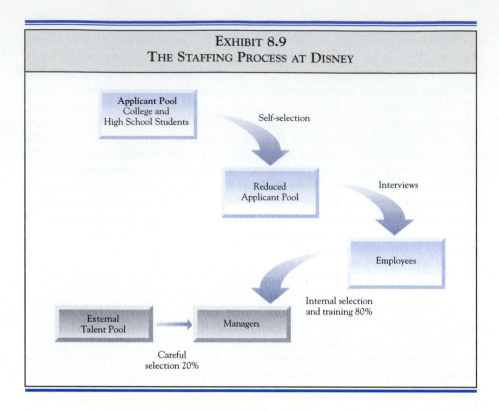

EXHIBIT 8.9
THE STAFFING PROCESS AT DISNEY

Applicant Pool
College and
High School Students

Self-selection

Reduced
Applicant Pool

Interviews

Employees

Internal selection
and training 80%

External
Talent Pool

Managers

Careful
selection 20%

During the past six years, Philadelphia Electric's culture has changed from entitlement-based to skills-based. No longer can employees move up through the company based on seniority alone; now they must prove they have management potential and demonstrate their abilities.

—William J. Kaschub, Senior Vice President, Human Resources, Philadelphia Electric

MAKING PROMOTION AND TRANSFER DECISIONS. On the one hand, immediate supervisors may have limited control in deciding who to promote or transfer. Nevertheless, when a vacancy arises, they must search for qualified candidates and assist in the choice. This process is usually carried out in close consultation with one or more higher-level supervisors who ultimately have to approve the choice.

On the other hand, immediate supervisors can sometimes have almost total control over promotion and transfer decisions. When a new job is being created, they can determine exactly who will be promoted by writing the job description to fit only one person. This is not necessarily a fair practice, but it is not uncommon. It is important to remember, however, that promotion decisions are selection decisions and, as such, must be made without illegal discrimination.

IDENTIFYING CANDIDATES FOR PROMOTION AND TRANSFER. Candidates may be identified by word of mouth, inspection of the organization's personnel records, promotion lists based on performance or managerial ratings, and formal programs for identifying potential candidates for promotion such as assessment centers. The HRIS (human resource information system) is valuable here because it can store a vast amount of information and speed the process of identifying potential candidates. It can also ensure fairness in the process by giving everyone a chance regardless of where they are currently working or for whom they are working.

COMPARING CANDIDATES. The methods that identify candidates can also be used to evaluate and compare them. Although many companies administer a battery of tests to assess mental ability, personality, and interests, one study concluded that tests are ignored more often than not as decision-making aids for internal promotions. Job experience, performance history, and assessment center results are used instead. Interviews are used as well, although more often for candidates from external sources. A powerful **sponsor** (often a manager at a higher level in the organization who "adopts" and looks out for an employee at a lower level) can see that an individual's strengths are noted by others. A final basis for comparing candidates is seniority.

MAKING THE FINAL CHOICE. Making a decision is difficult if different types of information are available for competing job applicants. Even if this is the case, however, the candidates should be evaluated and only those with obvious potential retained. Those who survive the evaluation process can then be evaluated and selected.

A *sponsor* is a powerful person in the organization who tries to help you advance.

INTERNATIONAL ASPECTS OF EMPLOYEE SELECTION

LEARNING OBJECTIVE 5

Describe how the use of expatriates, third-country nationals, and host-country nationals impacts selection and placement.

SELECTING EXPATRIATE EMPLOYEES

Although the number of American expatriate employees (Americans who work in other countries for U.S. companies) is small, their importance to companies operating in the international markets is relatively large. Without effective expatriate employees—managers and nonmanagers—U.S. companies would essentially be unable to operate successfully abroad. Nevertheless, ineffective expatriates are alarmingly commonplace. Consequently, American-based multinational companies not only need to obtain candidates for expatriate positions, but must also ensure they are effective on the job.

A key in selecting any employee is knowing what the job entails. Besides specific job assignments, expatriates are involved in a general way in six major categories of relations: (1) internal relations with their co-workers, (2) relations with their families, (3) relations with the host government, (4) relations with their home government, (5) external relations with the local culture, and (6) relations with the company's headquarters. In addition, expatriates typically work in a culture with a different language—a potential obstacle.

To be successful, then, expatriates need the skills not only to perform a specific job, but also to perform the general duties required by these six categories such as cultural empathy, flexibility, tolerance and adaptability. Using these criteria for selection, as well as for structuring a preparation process, can go a long way to increase the likelihood of success.[54]

Related to the selection of expatriate employees—also called **parent-country nationals (PCNs)**—is the more general issue of staffing operations abroad. Typically, expatriate employees fill only a few positions. Most of the employees are host-country nationals (HCNs), who are usually selected using host-country practices. The practice of using one's own human resource practices abroad is referred to as **ethnocentrism**. Allowing operations in different countries to develop and use their own human resource practices is called **polycentrism**. Developing practices that can be applied in all countries, with modest adjustments to local conditions, is called **geocentrism**.[55]

A growing but still relatively small number of positions are filled by third-country nationals (TCNs), individuals from neither the host country nor the country of the parent firm. They are often selected by the parent firm using practices similar to those used in selecting expatriates. The pros and cons of using these three types of employees are listed in Exhibit 8.10.

Expatriate employees are U.S. citizens working abroad for U.S. companies.

You could easily be an expatriate some day.

DID YOU KNOW?

10% of U.S. expatriates get yanked back home because they don't perform well.

An *ethnocentric policy* says our way is the best way!

EXHIBIT 8.10
PROS AND CONS OF PCNs, TCNs, AND HCNs

Parent-Country Nationals (PCNs)

ADVANTAGES

- Organizational control and coordination is maintained and facilitated.
- Promising managers are given international experience.
- PCNs are the best people for the job.
- There is assurance that subsidiary will comply with company objectives, policies, etc.

DISADVANTAGES

- The promotional opportunities of HCNs are limited.
- Adaptation to host country may take a long time.
- PCNs may impose an inappropriate HQ style.
- Compensation for PCNs and HCNs may differ.

Host-Country Nationals (HCNs)

ADVANTAGES

- Language and other barriers are eliminated.
- Hiring costs are reduced, and no work permit is required.
- Continuity of management improves, since HCNs stay longer in positions.
- Government policy may dictate hiring of HCNs.
- Morale among HCNs may improve as they see the career potentials.

DISADVANTAGES

- Control and coordination of headquarters may be impeded.
- HCNs have limited career opportunity outside the subsidiary.
- Hiring HCNs limits opportunities for PCNs to gain overseas experience.
- Hiring HCNs could encourage a federation of national rather than global units.

Third-Country Nationals (TCNs)

ADVANTAGES

- Salary and benefit requirements may be lower than for PCNs.
- TCNs may be better informed than PCNs about host-country environment.

DISADVANTAGES

- Transfers must consider possible national animosities (e.g., India and Pakistan).
- The host government may resent hiring of TCNs.
- TCNs may want to return to their own countries after assignment.

SOURCE: P. J. Dowling, R. S. Schuler, and D. E. Welch, *International Dimensions of Human Resources Management* 2nd ed. (Belmont, Calif.: Wadsworth, 1994): 57. Used by permission.

LEGAL CONSIDERATIONS.   In the *Civil Rights Act of 1991*, Congress affirmed its policy that American civil rights laws (specifically, *Title VII of the Civil Rights Act of 1964* and the *Americans with Disabilities Act*) apply to the employment practices of American multinationals relative to U.S. citizens employed in their foreign operations. (*The Age Discrimination Employment Act of 1967*, ADEA, was amended in 1984 to protect American workers over the age of 40 against discrimination by U.S. companies abroad.) Essentially, the action of the *Civil Rights Act of 1991* reversed the decision of the Supreme Court in *EEOC v. Arabian American Oil Company* (1991), which had concluded that Congress had *not* intended to apply *Title VII of the Civil Rights Act of 1964* to the foreign operations of American multinational firms. Furthermore, the U.S. District Court in Washington, D.C., ruled that U.S. law can even replace the laws of other nations:

> A long-standing German labor policy of mandatory retirement at age 65 does not shield an employer from the *Age Discrimination in Employment Act's* protections for American workers in Germany, a federal district court rules.
>
> The case involves a nonprofit U.S. corporation well known for two of its broadcast services—Radio Free Europe and Radio Liberty—that employs more than 300 U.S. citizens at its Munich facility. The mandatory retirement policy, contained in the employer's union contract, is found in most collective bargaining agreements in Germany. Two employees discharged because of their age filed a bias suit under ADEA. The employer conceded that the employees had been discharged because of age but argued that ADEA's "foreign laws" exemption—allowing actions taken in order to avoid violating the laws of a foreign country—applied. The "nearly ubiquitous contract terms" are considered to have "legal force" in Germany, the employer contended.
>
> Policies and practices, even when embodied in contracts, are not "laws," the court says, distinguishing a country's established "policy" from a foreign law. The former cannot deny Americans working abroad ADEA's protections against age discrimination, the court explains, ruling that "where a foreign labor union policy collides" with a law of the United States, the U.S. law "cannot be expected to bow down." (*Mahoney v. RFE/RL*, 1992).[56]

Some say that this is a rather ethnocentric policy, one that says that U.S. law is best. Conflict with the laws of other nations is bound to occur, according to the critics. What is your opinion of this ruling? Whose law should prevail in a country? Furthering this ethnocentric approach to employment law is the fact that U.S. laws are applicable to foreign firms operating in the U.S. (which currently employ about 5 million American workers):

> For many reasons having largely to do with significant cultural and managerial differences, Japanese firms have probably received the most attention regarding conflicts between their management and HR practices and those traditionally and legally followed in the United States. As many as one-third of Japanese firms with operations in the U.S. have been confronted with lawsuits for discrimination in their employment practices relative to their American employees. Part of the problem may be a lack of knowledge about U.S. employment laws. But more to the point (and one that must concern all multinational firms) is the conflict between the national culture and employment practices of the parent firm and the employment laws in the overseas locations. As is true with the multinational firms from some other countries as well, Japanese firms tend to use only parent-country (that is, Japanese) executives to run their American subsidiaries, providing few of the perquisites and no opportunities for promotion to the top management slots for their American managers. In addition, all major decision making tends to be made by the Japanese managers, often in consultation with their colleagues back in Japan, rather than in

conjunction with their American counterparts. At least three Japanese firms have settled discrimination suits for multimillion dollar figures (Honda of America, Sumitomo Corporation, and Quasar, a division of Matsushita Electric Corporation of America).

The preceding discussion notwithstanding, Japanese firms in the United States may well be protected in their staffing practices, at least at their top tiers of management. The Seventh Circuit Court of Appeals has ruled that Japanese subsidiaries operating in the United States may legally prefer Japanese citizens over U.S. citizens and that *Civil Rights Act* prohibitions against discrimination on the basis of national origin do not apply. According to the ruling in *Fortino v. Quasar Co.*, 1991, Title VII of the *Civil Rights Act of 1964* is preempted by a treaty between Japan and the United States that permits companies of either country to prefer their own citizens for executive positions in subsidiaries based in the other country. This ruling clarifies a 1982 Supreme Court decision in *Sumitomo Shoji America Inc. v. Avagliano* and, by extension, applies to both Japanese firms in the United States as well as to American firms in Japan, although U.S. multinationals are less interested in pursuing such "parent-company-executive-only" strategies.[57]

INTERNATIONAL COMPARISONS

Staffing activities in Japan present alternatives that could be used in the United States. Canada provides a useful comparison with this country in regard to equal employment and human rights legislation.

JAPAN. Japanese recruitment methods are different from those in the United States, where the emphasis is on skill or job qualifications. In Japan, the emphasis is also on the general attributes of the person being hired. All regular employees of the corporation are hired at one time of the year only (in April, immediately after the end of each academic year). They are recruited during the preceding fall from either the high school level or the college and university level. Employees not hired at this time are considered "nonregular" employees (that is, they may have been employed by other companies earlier in their careers or self-employed; in short, they are hired at times other than the beginning of their careers). In addition to regular and nonregular employees, there are temporary and part-time employees.

For the most part, company employment policies are directed toward regular employees, and a great competition takes place at the time of the April hiring, both among the companies, which seek to attract the best candidates (tests are given on academic and basic aptitudes), and among the graduates, who wish to align themselves with growth companies.

This division between regular employees (estimated to be between 30 and 50 percent of the total national work force) and the nonregular, part-time, and temporary employees makes the Japanese philosophy of lifetime commitment possible despite economic fluctuations. This, however, is changing today. In times of temporary growth or decline, additional temporary workers may be hired or laid off. Alternative solutions for dealing with down cycles that affect the retention of regular workers include shifting employees to new areas of operations or contracting employees out to other companies in more prosperous industries. The transferred employee continues to remain formally affiliated with the original employer in such cases.

In more serious circumstances, temporary layoffs may be required, though according to Japan's labor standards law, workers receive 60 percent of normal salary during this "vacation." However, because Japanese companies pay close attention to the development of long-term trends, they are generally able to predict a leveling off or decline within an industry and adjust their springtime recruitment efforts accordingly. In addition to the impact of lifetime employment on staffing, Japanese companies also have an extensive commitment to hire and accommodate disabled individuals.

Attention has recently been focused on the issue of equal opportunity for women in the Japanese work force. Traditionally, many Japanese women leave the labor force when they begin raising families. To ensure opportunities for those wishing to continue working, the Japanese legislature passed the *Equal Employment Opportunity Law*, which went into effect in 1986, however, it has relatively modest sanctions for violators.

For the long term, many Japanese companies see two major trends. One is the need to redeploy and retrain their employees for different industries. For example, Nippon steel has been shifting employees out of basic steel production and into electronics. The other trend is adjusting the management of employees under economic conditions that, in comparison to the last 20 years, will result in a period of relatively slow growth.

The traditional ways of doing business are changing, even in Japan.

Increasingly, Japanese companies are locating plants and offices in the United States. Selection is viewed by these companies as one of the most critical factors in their success here. Consequently, they put a great deal of time and effort into this activity.[58]

CANADA. Most Canadian companies use recruiting and selection techniques similar to those in the United States. At the same time, they face significantly different equal employment legislation or, more broadly, human rights legislation. Relatively comprehensive human rights legislation now exists at the federal level and in each of Canada's ten provinces. This legislation follows a common pattern but has specific deviations in each jurisdiction.

Civil rights in Canada share similar protections to those in the United States.

The typical Canadian human rights statute prohibits discrimination based on race, color, religion, ancestry, place of origin, marital status, gender, age, or physical handicap, when such discrimination involves employment or trade union membership services, accommodation that is available to the public, residential, or commercial rentals, or public notices. Some of the statutes also prohibit discrimination by occupational or professional associations, employer or business associations, and employment agencies. The statute is enforced by a human rights commission, whose staff investigates and conciliates complaints successfully, and an *ad hoc* tribunal or board of inquiry of one or more members may be appointed to hold a public hearing.

In addition to protecting basic human rights, the federal statute prohibits discrimination on the basis of criminal conviction where the person has been pardoned.[59] In the case of the physically handicapped, employment discrimination is prohibited, but other forms of discrimination are not. Employers are not compelled to renovate their premises to accommodate the handicapped. A unique feature of the federal statute in the area of sex discrimination is that employers are required to provide equal pay for work of equal value. This contrasts with the provincial legislation, which does not affect pay differentials between different jobs as long as there is no ongoing practice of denying access to these jobs because of gender.

CURRENT TRENDS

There are several trends occurring in selection and placement. One links these activities to the business and a second links them with other HR practices.

Still another is adaptive testing—that is, making tests increasingly more or less difficult depending on the individual taking the test. Because adaptive testing utilizes computer technology, it is described further in Chapter 20. The first two trends are discussed here.

LINKING SELECTION AND PLACEMENT WITH THE BUSINESS

The central tenet of this book—that organizations are increasingly realizing that people make a difference and that different types of people are required to run different types of organizations has implications for all HR activities, including selection and placement. Not only do the qualities and characteristics of the top executives matter, so do those of all the other employees.

TOP MANAGEMENT.   Reginald H. Jones, former chairman and CEO of the General Electric Company, has noted that "businesses with different missions require quite different people running them."[60] As a result, the skills, abilities, values, and perspectives of executives need to match particular types of business strategy. For example, a recently released study by the Hay Group reports that, when a business is pursuing a growth strategy, it needs top managers who are willing to abandon the status quo and adapt their strategies and goals to the marketplace. Because insiders are slow to recognize the onset of decline and tend to persevere in strategies that are no longer effective, top managers may need to be recruited from the outside. Outsiders, of course, are not always helpful. When a business is pursuing a mature strategy, what is needed is a stable group of insiders who know the intricacies of the business.[61]

GETTING THE RIGHT WORKERS.   Companies trying to enhance their competitiveness by improving quality agree that the employees on the "front line"— for example, production workers—are key to success in this endeavor. Furthermore, these same companies agree that it takes a special employee to really perform well in this situation. These companies are thus willing to devote considerable time and effort in selecting their "front-line" people—who are most likely to fill the bill of a production worker in a high-quality manufacturing environment organized around work teams. To that end, some organizations use a rather extensive set of selection methods to hire production workers, some of which are listed in Exhibit 8.11. As firms come to believe that particular HR practices are necessary for their success, they will find widespread applications for them.

LINKING SELECTION AND PLACEMENT WITH OTHER HR PRACTICES

Effective firms closely link selection and placement with other HR practices, particularly job analysis and training and development. As firms are required to validate their selection practices, they find that a systematic reliance on job analysis facilitates shaping their selection criteria and choosing methods of obtaining information. The example of the corporate loan assistant in this chapter and in Chapter 6 illustrates systematic linkage.

Firms are also linking selection and placement with training and development. Although certain firms have traditionally selected individuals and immediately put them into training programs, this has become more predominant with the advent of total quality management. Firms that pursue total quality management programs recognize that training is key to the success of their programs. Because most people have not worked in a total quality environment, employees at all job levels need some training to become familiar with these particular man-

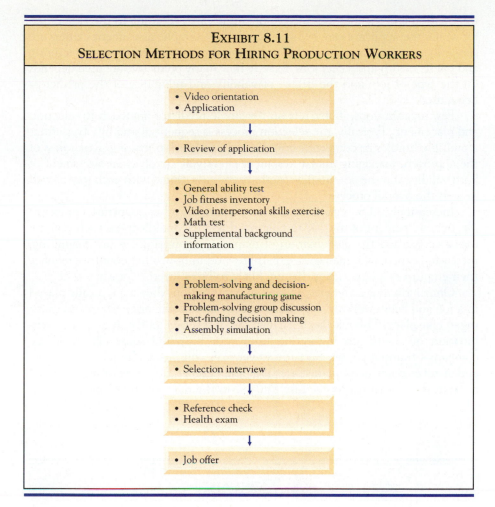

EXHIBIT 8.11
SELECTION METHODS FOR HIRING PRODUCTION WORKERS

- Video orientation
- Application

- Review of application

- General ability test
- Job fitness inventory
- Video interpersonal skills exercise
- Math test
- Supplemental background information

- Problem-solving and decision-making manufacturing game
- Problem-solving group discussion
- Fact-finding decision making
- Assembly simulation

- Selection interview

- Reference check
- Health exam

- Job offer

agement tools and techniques. These tools apply across all jobs and are equally important for all jobs; thus, training needs to be systematically linked to the selection and placement decisions of firms, particularly those pursuing total quality management.

SUMMARY

This chapter has examined selection and placement procedures, processes, methods, and decisions. To match individual skills, knowledge, and abilities to job demands and individual personalities, interests, and preferences to job and organizational characteristics, organizations need to gather information about job applicants. The three most common methods—interviewing, written testing, and application blanks—must operate within an extensive framework of legal regulations. These regulations are not intended to discourage the use of these methods but rather to ensure that the information collected, retained, and used respects the individual's right to privacy and an organization's right to select individuals on the basis of legal considerations. Consequently, the types of selection information and the methods used to obtain it vary according to the type of job for which the applicants are being selected. For example, assessment centers are generally used for managerial jobs, and physical tests are used for manufacturing and public health and safety jobs. Exactly how many predictors are used depends on the type of job, and the degree of validity and reliability of the predictors being used.

Few organizations, if any, rely on the single-predictor approach to selection and placement. Typically, the selection process is sequential and involves either a multiple hurdles or compensatory approach to decision making. Regardless of the approach, managing human resources effectively involves an assessment of both validity and the potential disparate impact associated with each step as well as with the overall process.

Increasingly, U.S. organizations are operating in other countries. For example, over 40 percent of the 500 restaurants that McDonald's opens each year are overseas. Because the globalization of many U.S. companies is just beginning, increasing expertise in managing expatriates and in how other countries manage their employees are two areas that are likely to be of interest for some time.

Once individuals are selected into an organization, they are typically placed in a job and begin working. It is usual, of course, for some orientation and training to take place. This may last for a few days or several months. It may be a combination of on-the-job instruction from your boss and some classes at the company's training center. Soon, however, you will be on the job performing, and at some point performance appraisal and compensation decisions will need to be made. Consequently, we turn to these in the next several chapters.

Key Concepts

achievement tests
adverse impact
application blank
assessment center
biodata tests
biographical information blank
bona fide occupational qualifications (BFOQ)
bona fide seniority systems (BFSS)
bottom-line rule
business games
combined approach
comparative statistics
compensatory approach
concentration statistics
criteria
demographic statistics
disparate treatment
disparate impact
ethnocentrism

executive orders
false decisions
four fifths or 80% rule
geocentrism
halo bias
honesty tests
in-basket exercise
interest inventories
inter-rater reliability
job-relatedness
leaderless group discussion (LGD)
multiple-hurdles approach
multiple-predictor approach
panel interview
parent-country nationals (PCNs)
patterned or structured interview
personality inventories
physical abilities tests

placement
polycentrism
polygraph test
predictor
psychomotor tests
recognition tests
reference verification
reliability
selection
single-predictor approach
situational questions
sponsor
team interview
test-retest reliability
Title VII
true decisions
validity
weighted application blank (WAB)
work sample tests
work simulations

REVIEW AND DISCUSSION QUESTIONS

1. A frequent diagnosis of an observed performance problem in an organization is "Joe was a selection mistake." What are the short- and long-term consequences of these so-called "selection mistakes"? Can you relate this question to your own experiences with organizations?

2. Successful selection and placement decisions are dependent on other human resource activities. Identify these activities and explain their relationships to selection and placement.

3. Given all of the weaknesses identified with the interview, why is it a popular selection device? How could you improve the interview to overcome some of these weaknesses?

4. What is genetic screening? Is this a means to assess an applicant's skills, knowledge, and abilities or personality, interests, and preferences? How might the rights of the employer conflict with the rights of the individual when genetic screening is used for selection and placement decisions? How would you resolve this conflict?

5. What factors should companies consider when selecting expatriate managers?

6. Explain the difference between single- and multiple-predictor approaches to validation of selection procedures. What approach does your instructor use in evaluating performance in your human resource management course? Is it compensatory or noncompensatory? Multiple hurdle or multiple cutoff?

7. How do organizations typically make selection, promotion, and transfer decisions?

8. Why are the best people often not the ones hired for the job?

9. Discuss the actual costs of hiring applicants as well as the potential costs that might be incurred if an incorrect selection decision is made.

10. How do the selection and recruitment strategies used in Japan and Canada differ from those used in the United States?

REVIEW: DO'S AND DON'TS IN JOB INTERVIEWS AND ON JOB APPLICATIONS

Please indicate what to do and what not to do in interviews and on job application blanks from the list of items below:

Do   Don't

1. Ask about marital status
2. Ask about the number of children
3. Ask about skills to do the job
4. Ask for a woman's maiden name
5. Ask the age of the applicant
6. Ask for driver's license
7. Ask about race, gender, religious affiliation
8. Ask about birthplace of applicant
9. Ask about club memberships
10. Ask if planning to have children
11. Ask about preferred hours of work
12. Ask about disabilities
13. Ask about other names applicant has used
14. Ask about arrest record
15. Ask about height and weight
16. Ask about nature of military discharge
17. Ask about friends or relatives with firm
18. Ask for clergy as references
19. Ask about credit questions

_____ _____ 20. Ask if the applicant is willing to travel

In most situations, it is probably fine to ask questions 3, 6 (when driving is required on the job), 11, and 20. Question 12 could be asked in this way, "Is there any condition you have that might make it impossible to perform 'essential job functions' even after some accommodation?" Even here, however, the applicant should be volunteering this information. It is probably best to ask this after a decision to hire has been made. Forget about the rest.

CAREER MANAGEMENT EXERCISE

Use your job description from the Career Management Exercise in Chapter 6 to detail a selection process. Your report should describe the following:

1. Selection procedures to be used. If you will use a cognitive ability test, identify which one. If you will use a situational interview, describe the questions that will be asked. If you will use a personality test, identify the specific test.

2. Provide a rationale for the choice of each selection device.

3. Provide the order in which the selection devices will be administered and the rationale for the ordering.

4. Specify how information will be combined (compensatory, multiple hurdles, or a combination). Detail how the selection devices will be scored. Report to the class and compare results.

CASE

THE APPRENTICE

Apex Tool Company is a small, family-owned machine shop that has been in business for 47 years. The company was founded by Herbert Shay who, until recently, was active in the shop and was also the company's president. Apex makes fine tools and precision parts for electric motors. The company has 23 full-time employees plus a number of part-timers. Promotions at Apex come slowly and have always been the result of Herb's "eye" and "feel" for the skills and abilities of the employee. All the full-time employees are men, and the majority of the part-timers are married women. All new employees begin by monitoring the machines and turning off the power switch if a problem arises. Employees who show potential are asked to become apprentices where they learn the fine skills of the tool-and-die maker.

When Herbert retired, his son Charles took over the company. Charles's first task was to hire two new employees. He placed an ad in the local newspaper. After interviewing several candidates, Charles hired Neil Burke and Shirley Weeks to monitor machines that are set up by highly skilled mechanics. Neil has had previous machine shop experience, and Charles senses that he will be a prime candidate for a tool-and-die apprenticeship.

Shirley is 41 years old, married, and the mother of two teenagers. She took the job at Apex because the work is easy and the hours of work are flexible. She plans to work part-time and to increase her hours if she likes the job.

Neil is nineteen years old and single. He hopes to demonstrate that he deserves to be an apprentice tool-and-die maker. Neil has been fooling around with machines and building things as long as he can remember. He had several shop classes in high school and excells at "working with his hands." Neil has no interest in college and believes that machine work will be a career.

It has been one year since Neil and Shirley were hired. During this time, Neil has performed many activities in addition to monitoring the machines. For example, when machines break down, Neil helps the mechanic with repairs. He has also assisted with set-ups and retooling activities. Shirley, on the other hand, has monitored the machines exclusively during the year. When her machine breaks down, Shirley waits for a mechanic to fix it. Charles has evaluated his new people in order to select a strong apprentice candidate. Neil's work performance has been excellent, and last week Charles formally offered him the opportunity to become an apprentice tool-and-die maker.

Charles did not really consider Shirley to be a viable candidate for an apprenticeship. Although her work has been good, she has not revealed any particular aptitude for more advanced work. Charles did not think twice about offering Neil the apprenticeship because Neil seemed to be an obvious choice for the position. Shirley, who up to this point has been very mild-mannered, is furious when she finds out that Neil has been offered an apprenticeship. She decides to confront Charles directly about this situation.

Shirley storms into Charles's office and demands to know why Neil was selected for an apprenticeship and she was not. She notes that she and Neil were hired at approximately the same time and that they worked together for the past year. Shirley is visibly upset and angry. She wants specific reasons why she was not given consideration for the higher-level position. Charles, who has never had to deal with a situation like this, really does not know what to say. In the intensity of the moment, he hears himself say something about Neil's range of skills, but he doesn't like the way this is going. In an attempt to bail himself out, Charles offers Shirley a raise to remain at her present job.

Shirley agrees to "think it over" for a couple of days. On Monday morning, she tells Charles point blank that his selection decision was discriminatory and illegal. Shirley told Charles that she does not want a token raise; she wants her apprenticeship. Charles is still quite perplexed as nothing like this has ever happened before at Apex. Charles informs Shirley that he *will* consider her for an apprenticeship, but he will need a little time to make a decision. When Shirley leaves his office, Charles decides that he may need some legal advice in dealing with this issue.

CASE QUESTIONS

1. Why didn't Charles consider Shirley for the apprenticeship?
2. Should Shirley expect Charles to give her the reasons he selected Neil?
3. Should Shirley accept the offer of a salary increase or hold out for an apprenticeship?
4. Could Charles change his mind and offer the apprenticeship to Shirley instead of Neil?

CASE

FALSE POSITIVE OR POSITIVE STEP?

Concerns about drug use among transportation personnel (that is, bus drivers, air traffic controllers, train engineers) have captured national headlines. In fact, the Department of Transportation (DOT) has a plan for random drug testing that affects more than half a million airline employees from pilots to mechanics. Under the drug-testing plan, employees are subject to a pre-employment test, periodic testing whenever a physical is taken, post-accident testing, and random testing as well as a test for reasonable cause. An employee is subject to an initial test on a sample of urine and a more sophisticated test if the first test shows the presence of drugs.

Tom Schultz has been a bus driver in New York City for seven years. He is married and the father of three children. His work performance has been above average, and he considers himself a conscientious and dedicated employee. Tom did not give a second thought to a management directive two months ago that stated that all bus drivers would be tested for drug use. In fact, he thought that drug tests for transportation employees was a good idea. Now, however, Tom's life has become a nightmare.

A test on a sample of Tom's urine appeared to have traces of the metabolite for cocaine. He was immediately dismissed from his job and has been unemployed for nearly two months. "I can't understand how something like this could happen," he said. "You know you're innocent, but how do you prove it? I'm guilty until proven innocent. They're out for my job." Tom is appealing his dismissal. As a public employee, he has legal recourse through his union. In the meantime, he is out of work, cannot support his family, and cannot even collect unemployment insurance.

Drug testing also affects many other types of employees in the private sector. Peter Albert was a young successful manager making a good salary in the private sector. Peter's employer tested him for drugs as part of a routine medical checkup. His urine test came back positive. Prior to the test, he had informed the nurse that he had had root canal surgery and was using codeine as prescribed by his doctor. The nurse said that this was no problem and proceeded without so much as noting the information. Peter was fired from his job, and he still does not know what drug he was supposed to have been using.

"I've lost my car. My family situation is strained. My bills are piling up. I can't find suitable work paying a suitable salary," said Peter. He has discussed his case with attorneys, but, as a private-sector employee, he does not have any legal recourse at this time.

Consider the following quotations about drug testing in light of the cases of Tom and Peter:

- "If you are not conducting the tests seriously—and I mean watching the urine pass from the body orifice—then you are just playing games."

    —Pharmacologist.
- "These tests are 100 percent accurate and we'll back that up in court."

    —Physician in charge of a drug testing laboratory.
- "The false positive rate can be 1–2 percent for the most stringent test and as high as 15–20 percent for the least expensive test."

    —Civil liberties attorney.
- "I can beat any Mickey Mouse drug test. I woke my son at 6:00 A.M. and made him urinate in the specimen jar."

    —Construction worker who uses marijuana off the job.
- "If you don't have a policy, then don't use drug testing. Testing is a tool. No employee has a right to use illegal substances on or off the job."

    —Consultant on drug testing to *Fortune* 500 companies.
- "Drug testing is the privacy issue of the decade or perhaps the century. Sifting willy-nilly through people's bodily fluids is an invasion of privacy."

    —Civil liberties attorney.
- "Drug testing is a witch hunt."

    —Peter Albert.

Drug testing has already been ruled illegal in several municipalities for police officers and fire fighters, and random drug testing has been declared unconstitutional for civilian Army employees. However, many *Fortune* 500 companies continue to include drug testing as a pre-employment hurdle for new employees. Tom Schultz and Peter Albert, however, certainly have their doubts about it.

CASE QUESTIONS

1. Should Tom and Peter consider drug testing unnecessary?
2. Do you think employers should drug-test all applicants, or only those who work in jobs involving public safety?
3. Can employers supplement their drug tests with other tests to more accurately determine whether employees are really using drugs?
4. Should only job applicants be drug-tested, or should employees be tested also?

NOTES

1. Information for the case was taken from R. Cohen, "When You Wish Upon a Deficit," *The New York Times* (July 18, 1993): Sec. 2, 1 & 18; G. E. Willigan, "The Value-Adding CFO: An Interview with Disney's Gary Wilson," *Harvard Business Review* (Jan.–Feb. 1990): 85–93; and S. Greenhouse, "Playing Disney in the Parisian Fields," *New York Times* (Feb. 17, 1991): 1 and 6; J. J. Laabs, "Disney Helps Keep Kids in School," *Personnel Journal* (Nov. 1992): 58–68; "Disney," *Personnel Journal* (Jan. 1992): 58.

2. F. L. Schmidt, D. S. Ones, and J. E. Hunter, "Personnel Selection," *Annual Review of Psychology* 43 (1992): 627–670; A. Tziner, *Organization Staffing and Work Adjustments* (Westport, Conn.: Praeger, 1990); N. Schmitt and I. Robertson, "Personnel Selection," *Annual Review of Psychology* 41 (1990): 289–319; R. D. Gatewood and H. S. Feild, *Human Resource Selection*, 2nd ed. (Hinsdale, Ill.: Dryden Press, 1990).

3. M. Miner, "Legal Concerns Facing Human Resource Managers: An Overview." In *Readings in Personnel and Human Resource Management*, eds., R. S. Schuler, S. A. Youngblood, and V. L. Huber, 3rd ed. (St. Paul, Minn.: West, 1988), 40–56; D. P. Twomey, *Equal Employment Opportunity Law*, 3rd ed. (Cincinnati, Ohio: Southwestern, 1994).

4. M. Zall, "What to Expect from the Civil Rights Act," *Personnel Journal* (March 1992): 46–50; B. Southard Murphy, W. E. Barlow, and D. D. Hatch, "Manager's Newsfront: Retroactivity of the Civil Rights Act of 1991 Unsettled," *Personnel Journal* (March 1992): 24; "EEOC Issues Policy on Retroactivity of Civil Rights Act of 1991," *FEP Guidelines* (March 1992): 1–2; "1991 Civil Rights Act Highlights," *FEP Guidelines* (Dec. 1991): 1–2.

5. B. Smith, "The Burden of Proof Grows Heavier," *HR Focus* (Feb. 1992): 1.

6. J. S. Lublin, "Graying Europeans Battle Age Bias," *The Wall Street Journal* (Aug. 14, 1990): B1; D. P. O'Meara, *Protecting the Growing Number of Older Workers: The Age Discrimination in Employment Act* (Philadelphia: The Wharton School of the University of Pennsylvania, 1989); C. S. Miller, J. A. Kaspin, and M. H. Schuster, "The Impact of Performance Appraisal Methods On Age Discrimination in Employment Act Cases," *Personnel Psychology* 43 (1990): 555–78.

7. "Americans With Disabilities Act Final Regulations," *Fair Employment Practices* (Aug. 15, 1991); B. Presley Noble, "As Seen from a Wheelchair," *The New York Times* (Jan. 26, 1992): F25; J. West, ed., *The Americans with Disabilities Act: From Policy to Practice* (New York: Milbank Memorial Fund, 1991).

8. For more on age discrimination see A. Zakarian, "Downsizing Defense," *Personnel* (Jan. 1991): 19; P. S. Greenlaw and J. P. Kohn, "Age Discrimination in Employment Guidelines," *Personnel Journal* (March 1982): 224–228; D. H. Weiss, *Fair, Square and Legal: Safe Hiring and Firing Practices to Keep You and Your Company Out of Court* (New York: AMACOM, 1991); A. M. Ryan and M. Lasek, "Negligent Hiring and Defamation: Areas of Liability Related to Pre-Employment Inquiries," *Personnel Psychology* 44 (1991): 293–319.

9. R. D. Arvey and R. H. Faley, *Fairness in Selecting Employees* (Reading, Mass.: Addison-Wesley, 1988); R. A. Baysinger, "Disparate Treatment and Disparate Impact Theories of Discrimination," in *Readings in Personnel and Human Resource Management*, 3rd ed.: 162–177; P. M. Podsakoff, M. L. Williams, and W. E. Scott, Jr., "Myths of Employee Selection Systems," in *Readings in Personnel and Human Resource Management*, 3rd ed.: 178–192.

10. "Go Ahead for AA Data Disclosure," *Fair Employment Practices* (Oct. 29, 1987): 129. Also see R. E. Biddle, "*Ward's Cove Packing v. Atonio* Redefines EEO Analyses," *Personnel Journal* (June 1990): 56, 59–62, 64–65.

11. J. Ledvinka and V. G. Scarpello, *Federal Regulations in Personnel and Human Resource Management* (Boston: PWS-Kent, 1990); R. A. Baysinger, "Disparate Treatment and Disparate Impact Theories of Discrimination," and V. L. Huber, G. B. Northcraft, and M. A. Neale, "Foibles and Fallacies in Organizational Staffing Decisions," in *Readings* (op. cit., see note 5): 162–177; 193–205.

12. For an excellent discussion of the impact and interpretation of the *Uniform Guidelines* and many other issues related to selection and testing, see the special issue of the *American Psychologist* (Oct. 1981).

13. "Age-35 Job Restriction Upheld," *Fair Employment Practices* (Jan. 7, 1988): 2.

14. T. C. McKinney, "The Management of Seniority: The Supreme Court and the California Brewers Case," *Personnel Administration* (Feb. 1984): 8–14.

15. F. N. Kerlinger, *Foundations of Behavioral Research* (New York: Holt, Rinehart and Winston, 1986).

16. For an excellent discussion about criteria for selection and placement decisions, see R. D. Arvey and R. H. Faley, *Fairness in Selecting Employees*, 2nd ed. (Reading, Mass.: Addison-Wesley, 1988).

17. For an excellent discussion about criteria for selection and placement decisions, see Schmidt, Ones, and Hunter, op. cit.; see note 2.

18. The basis for the statements and suggestions here include "Educational Requirements," *Fair Employment Practices Guidelines* 186, no. 1 (1980); "Experience Required" *Fair Employment Practices Guidelines* 190, no. 5 (1981); "The Importance of Record Keeping," *Fair Employment Practices Guidelines* 185, no. 12 (1980); "Personnel Guidelines for Managers and Supervisors," (1994); Biddle & Associates, Inc., 2100 Northrop Avenue, Sacramento, California, 95825.

19. R. S. Lowell and J. A. DeLoach, "Equal Employment Opportunity: Are You Overlooking the Application Form?" *Personnel* 59 (1982): 49–55; E. C. Miller, "An EEO Examination of Employment Applications," *Personnel Administrator* 25 (1980): 63–69.

20. D. G. Lawrence, B. L. Salsburg, J. G. Dawson, and Z. D. Fasmen, "Design and Use of Weighted Application Blanks," *Personnel Administrator* (March 1982): 57–63, 101.

21. A. Childs and R. J. Klimoski, "Successfully Predicting Career Success: An Application of the Biographical Inventory," *Journal of Applied Psychology* (Feb. 1988): 3–8.

22. C. J. Russell, J. Mattson, S. E. Devlin, and D. Atwater, "Predictive Validity of Biodata Items Generated from

Retrospective Life Experience Essays," *Journal of Applied Psychology* 75, no. 5 (1990): 569–580; H. R. Rothstein, F. L. Schmidt, F. W. Erwin, W. A. Owens, and C. P. Sparks, "Biographical Data in Employment Selection: Can Validities be made Generalizable?" *Journal of Applied Psychology* 75, no. 2 (1990): 175–184; M. A. McDaniel, "Biographical Constructs for Predicting Employee Suitability," *Journal of Applied Psychology* 74, no. 6 (1989): 964–970; A. Childs and R. J. Klimoski, "Successfully Predicting Career Success: An Application of the Biographical Inventory," *Journal of Applied Psychology* (Feb. 1988): 3–8.

23. See note 16.

24. K. K. Sackheim, *Handwriting Analysis and the Employee Selection Process* (Westport, Conn.: Quorum Books, 1990); "Handwriting Analysis," *Bulletin to Management* (May 8, 1986): 152. Reprinted by permission from *Bulletin to Management*, copyright 1986 by the Bureau of National Affairs, Inc., Washington, D.C. 20037; G. Ben-Shakar et al., "Can Graphology Predict Occupational Success? Two Empirical Studies and Some Methodological Ruminations," *Journal of Applied Psychology* (Nov. 1986): 645–853.

25. "Background Checks," FEP Guidelines, no. 266 (1987): 1; "Paper and Pencil Measures of Potential," in *Perspectives of Employee Staffing and Selection*, eds. G. Dreher and P. Sackett (Homewood, Ill.: Irwin, 1983): 349–367.

26. "Ask the Experts—Investigating Applicant Fraud," *Fair Employment Practice Guidelines* (April 10, 1993): 8. Copyrighted material. Reprinted with permission of Fair Employment Practices and Bureau of Business Practice, 24 Rope Ferry Road, Waterford, CT, 06386.

27. C. Sparks, "Paper and Pencil Measures of Potential" in *Perspectives of Employee Staffing and Selection*, eds. G. Dreher and P. Sackett, 349–367.

28. R. Hogan, B. N. Carpenter, S. R. Briggs, and R. O. Hansen, "Personality Assessment and Personnel Selection," in *Perspectives of Employee Staffing and Selection*, 21–51; "The Future of Personality Tests in Employment Settings," *Psychological Science Agenda* (Jan./Feb. 1992): 2–3.

29. M. R. Barrick and M. K. Mount, "The Big Five Personality Dimensions and Job Performance: A Meta-Analysis," *Personnel Psychology* 44 (1991): 1–26; D. V. Day and S. B. Silverman, "Personality and Job Performance: Evidence of Incremental Validity," *Personnel Psychology* 42 (1989): 25–36; T. Newton and T. Keenan, "Further Analyses of the Dispositional Argument in Organizational Behavior," *Journal of Applied Psychology* 76, no. 6 (1991): 781–787.

30. E. E. Ghiselli, *Explorations in Managerial Talent* (Pacific Palisades, Calif.: Goodyear, 1971): G. S. Taylor and T. W. Zimmer, "Viewpoint: Personality Tests for Potential Employees: More Harm than Good," *Personnel Journal* (Jan. 1988): 60.

31. "Psychological Testing Leads to Costly Lawsuit," *Bulletin to Management* (July 22, 1993): 226.

32. J. Hogan, "Interests and Competencies: A Strategy for Personnel Selection," in *Readings* 484–95.

33. Conversation with Paul Sackett, March 28, 1994; J. J. Laabs, "Legalities," Personnel Journal (Feb. 1992): 109; J. A. Hartigan and A. K. Wigdor, eds., *Fairness in Employment Testing: Validity Generalization, Minority Issues, and the General Aptitude Test Battery* (Washington, D.C.: National Academy Press, 1989).

34. R. T. von Mayrhauser, "The Mental Testing Community and Validity: A Prehistory," *American Psychologist* (Feb. 1992): 244–253; J. P. Guilford and W. S. Zimmerman, *Guilford Zimmerman Temperament Survey* (Orange, Calif.: Sheridan Psychological Services, 1976); F. L. Schmidt, J. E. Hunt, R. McKenzie, and T. Muldrow, "The Impact of Valid Selection Procedures on Workforce Productivity," *Journal of Applied Psychology* 64 (1979): 609–626.

35. For an extensive review of and guide to these tests, see L. P. Plumke, "A Short Guide to the Development of Work Sample and Performance Tests," 2nd ed. (Washington, D.C.: U.S. Office of Personnel Management, Feb. 1980). Note the interchangeability of the terms *work sample* and *performance tests*.

36. S. J. Motowidlo, M. D. Dunnette, and G. W. Carter, "An Alternative Selection Procedure: The Low-Fidelity Simulation," *Journal of Applied Psychology* 75, no. 6 (1990): 640–647; W. Arthur, Jr., G. V. Barrett, and D. Doverspike, "Validation of an Information-Processing-Based Test Battery for the Prediction of Handling Accidents Among Petroleum-Product Transport Drivers," *Journal of Applied Psychology* 75, no. 6 (1990).

37. For the LGD, see M. M. Petty, "A Multivariate Analysis of the Effects of Experience and Training upon Performance in a Leaderless Group Discussion," *Personnel Psychology* 27 (1974): 271–282. For business games, see B. M. Bass and G. V. Barnett, *People, Work, and Organizations*, 2nd ed. (Boston: Allyn & Bacon, 1981).

38. B. B. Gaugler, D. B. Rosenthal, G. C. Thornton, and C. Bentson, "Metanalysis of Assessment Center Validity," *Journal of Applied Psychology* 72 (1987): 493–511; R. Klimoski and M. Brickner, "Why Do Assessment Centers Work? The Puzzle of Assessment Center Validity," *Personnel Psychology* 40 (1987): 243–260; A. Tziner and S. Dolan, "Validity of an Assessment Center for Identifying Female Officers in the Military," *Journal of Applied Psychology* 67 (1982): 728–736; S. B. Parry, "How to Validate An Assessment Tool," *Training* (April 1993): 37–42.

39. C. L. Martin and D. H. Nagao, "Some Effects of Computerized Interviewing on Job Applicant Responses," *Journal of Applied Psychology* 74, no. 1 (1989): 72–80; W. L. Tullar, "Relational Control in the Employment Interview," *Journal of Applied Psychology* 74, no. 6 (1989): 971–977; A. Peek Phillips and R. L. Dipboye, "Correlational Tests of Predictions from a Process Model of the Interview," *Journal of Applied Psychology* 74, no. 1 (1989): 41–52; T. Hoff Macan and R. L. Dipboye, "The Relationship of Interviewers' Preinterview Impressions to Selection and Recruitment Outcomes," Personnel Psychology 43 (1990): 745–768.

40. *FEP Guidelines* (May 25, 1993): 8. Copyrighted material reprinted with permission of Fair Employment Practices and Bureau of Business Practice, 24 Rope Ferry Road, Waterford, CT, 06386.

41. H. J. Bernardin and R. W. Beatty, *Performance Appraisal: Assessing Human Behavior at Work* (Boston: Kent, 1984), 258–260; W. C. Borman, "Format and Training Effects on Rating Accuracy Using Behavior Scales," *Journal of Applied Psychology* 3 (1979): 103–115.

42. The role of the medical doctor in providing the physical exam is an important one. With it, however, is attached responsibility to the employer rather than the employee. See M. S. Novit, "Physical Examinations and Company Liability: A Legal Update," *Personnel Journal* (Jan. 1981): 47–52.

43. E. A. Fleishman, "Some New Frontiers in Personnel Selection Research," *Personnel Psychology* 41, no. 4 (1988): 679–702; E. A. Fleishman, *The Structure and Management of Physical Abilities* (Englewood Cliffs, N.J.: Prentice-Hall, 1964); D. L. Gebhardt and C. E. Crump, *Joint Mobility Evaluation Manual for Entry Level Natural Gas Industrial Jobs* (Bethesda, Md.: Advanced Research Resources Organization, 1983); D. L. Gebhardt, D. C. Meyers, and E. A. Fleishman, "Development of a Job-Related Medical Evaluation System," *San Bernardino County Medical Standard News* 1 (1984): 1–2; D. C. Meyers, M. C. Jennings, and E. A. Fleishman, *Development of Job-Related Medical Standards and Physical Tests for Court Security Officers*, ARRO Final Report #3062/r81–3 (Bethesda, Md.: Advanced Research Resources Organization, 1981).

44. Olian, "New Approaches to Employment Screening," in *Readings in Personnel and Human Resource Management*, 3d ed., 206–216.

45. R. Cropanzano and K. James, "Some Methodological Considerations for the Behavioral Genetic Analysis of Work Attitudes," *Journal of Applied Psychology* 75, no. 4 (1990): 433–439; Office of Technology and Assessment, *The Role of Genetic Testing in the Prevention of Occupational Disease* (Washington, D.C.: U.S. Government Printing Office, 1983).

46. "Employee Drug Abuse," *Bulletin to Management* (March 15, 1992): 71; J. Normand, S. D. Salyards, and J. J. Mahoney, "An Evaluation of Preemployment Drug Testing," *Journal of Applied Psychology* 75, no. 6 (1990): 629–639.

47. M. A. Konovsky and R. Cropanzano, "Perceived Fairness of Employee Drug Testing as a Predictor of Employee Attitudes and Job Performance," *Journal of Applied Psychology* 76, no. 5 (1991): 698–707; Drug Testing: Conference Policy Pointers," *Bulletin to Management* (Aug. 7, 1986); 261–262.

48. "Drug Policy Pointers," *Bulletin to Management* (Jan. 7, 1988): 8. Used by permission of *Bulletin to Management*, copyright 1988.

49. "The AIDS Epidemic and Business," *Business Week* (March 23, 1987): 122; "AIDS Focus: Employee Rights and On-Site Education," *Bulletin to Management* (March 10, 1988): 74.

50. H. J. Bernardin and D. K. Cooke, "Validity of an Honesty Test in Predicting Theft Among Convenience Store Employees," *Academy of Management Journal* 36, no. 5 (1993): 1097–1108; B. Kleinmutz, "Lie Detectors Fail the Truth Test," *Harvard Business Review* 63 (1985): 36–42; S. Labato, "Business and the Law: New Rules Limit Lie Detectors' Use," *The New York Times* (Nov. 28, 1988): 22; "Preemployment Polygraph Testing Restricted," *Bulletin to Management* (June 30, 1988): 201; L. Saxe, D. Dougherty, and T. Cross, "The Validity of Polygraph Testing," *American Psychologist* 40 (1985): 355–365.

51. M. D. Dunnette, *Personnel Selection and Placement* (Monterey, Calif.: Brooks/Cole, 1966): 174–175.

52. E. Lesly, Z. Schiller, S. Baker, and G. Smith, "CEOs with the Outside Edge," *Business Week* (Oct. 11, 1993): 60–62. M. London, "What Every Personnel Director Should Know about Management Promotion Decisions," *Personnel Journal* (Oct. 1978): 551.

53. R. S. Schuler and I. C. MacMillan, "Gaining a Competitive Advantage Through Human Resource Management Practices," *Human Resource Management* (Fall 1984): 248.

54. C. G. Howard, "Profiles of the 21st Century Expatriate Manager," *HR Magazine* (June 1992): 96; M. Jelinek and N. J. Adler, "Women: World-Class Managers for Global Competition," *Executive* (Feb. 1988): 11–20; P. Dowling and R. S. Schuler, *International Human Resource Management* (Boston: PWS-Kent, 1990); J. S. Black, M. Mendenhall, and G. Oddou, "Toward a Comprehensive Model of International Adjustment: An Integration of Multiple Theoretical Perspectives," *Academy of Management Review* 16, no. 2 (1991): 291–317; H. B. Gregersen and J. S. Black, "Antecedents to Commitment to a Parent Company and a Foreign Operation," *Academy of Management Journal* 35, no. 1 (1992): 65–90.

55. D. A. Heenan and H. V. Perlmutter, *Multinational Organization Development* (Reading, Mass.: Addison-Wesley, 1979); C. M. Solomon, "Staff Selection Impacts Global Success," *Personnel Journal* (Jan. 1994): 88–101.

56. "Age Bias in Germany," *Fair Employment Practices* (December 17, 1992): 145.

57. D. Briscoe, *International Human Resource Management* (Boston: Allyn & Bacon, 1995). This material adapted by permission of the author, Feb. 17, 1994.

58. C. A. Bartlett and H. Yoshihara, "New Challenges for Japanese Multinationals: Is Organization Adaptation Their Achilles Heel?" *Human Resource Management* (Spring 1988): 19–44.

59. This section of human rights in Canada was prepared by Robert J. Kerr, Professor of Law, University of Windsor, for use in this book.

60. C. Fombrun, "An Interview with Reginald Jones," *Organizational Dynamics* (Winter 1982): 46.

61. A. K. Gupta, "Contingency Linkages Between Strategy and General Manager Characteristics: A Conceptual Examination," *Academy of Management Review* 9 (1984): 339–412; A. K. Gupta and V. Govindarajan, "Build, Hold, Harvest: Converting Strategic Intentions into Reality," *Journal of Business Strategy* 4 (1984): 34–37. See Note 52.

EMPLOYEES want to know what they are supposed to do, what's expected of them, what the standards of performance are, how they're doing—and they want advice for doing even better the next time around. This is where performance appraisals in human resource management enter the picture. During the recruiting and selection activities, individuals get information on what job they are supposed to do. They may even begin to get information on what's expected of them and what the standards of performance are. Companies that do a great job in their staffing activities are increasingly conveying this information to potential employees early on. However, even in these companies, the newly recruited and selected applicants—and, in some cases, even the current employees—may not know exactly what's expected of them.

In contrast with the staffing activities wherein the human resource department and line management may work closely together, line managers are often on their own when it comes to employee appraisal. The HR department may contribute to the design of performance appraisal forms and attempt to impose a schedule on appraisal periods. For the most part, however, line managers convey what's expected to employees, telling them what the standards of performance are and what they can do to improve their performance. A trend that is gaining acceptance

involves everyone in the appraisal and feedback process. Thus it is likely that at some point you will be asked to appraise your own performance, that of your colleagues, and even that of your boss! Consequently, it is useful to know as much as possible about the activity of performance appraisal.

We will split the discussion of performance appraisal into two chapters. Chapter 9 covers the issues involved in gathering the

SECTION 4

APPRAISING

information used for appraisals. First, we'll discuss the importance of performance appraisal. Perhaps performance appraisal is one of the most important activities for us in our work experiences in organizations. It is certainly a critical activity for organizations if they hope to increase the performance and productivity of employees. Second, we'll look at the legal considerations in performance appraisal and describe how these considerations are related to the legal considerations we discussed under job analysis and selection. The many

processes and procedures in performance are described next. Ethical issues involved in gathering appraisal information by electronic monitoring are described because this is becoming such a significant event in many organizations. We conclude by identifying the trend of 360-degree feedback in organizations. At the end of Chapter 9 is another "Career Management Exercise" asking you to apply the material in the chapter to your future job.

Chapter 10 addresses the issues associated with using all the performance appraisal information that has been gathered by doing the things described in Chapter 9. We'll begin by discussing the inherent conflicts in performance appraisal that make the process of using the information so difficult. Then we'll discuss the processes that organizations can use to help minimize these conflicts so that the valuable process of feedback can take place. But to ensure that the right actions are taken based upon the results of the performance appraisal, we'll carefully examine the process to take in understanding why an employee is performing at a particular level. Based upon this diagnosis of performance, we'll then talk about strategies for performance improvement. To give perspective to this entire activity, some international comparisons will be offered. As with Chapter 9, you will find a "Career Management Exercise" asking you to apply the chapter material to your future job.

CHAPTER 9

PERFORMANCE APPRAISAL: GATHERING THE INFORMATION

LEARNING OBJECTIVES

When you have finished studying this chapter, you should be able to:

1. Describe the processes and procedures in performance appraisal.
2. Identify the many approaches and forms that companies use in gathering appraisal information.
3. Discuss the ethical issues in any computer monitoring of employee performance.
4. Describe the biases in appraisal and how they can be reduced.

CHAPTER OUTLINE

"Managing Human Resources at the Chrysler Corporation"

PERFORMANCE APPRAISAL

WHY IS PERFORMANCE APPRAISAL IMPORTANT?

LEGAL CONSIDERATIONS

PERFORMANCE APPRAISAL AS A SYSTEM OF PROCESSES AND PROCEDURES

"Managing Human Resources for Quality
THE BALDRIGE AWARD"

"Managing Human Resources
ETHICAL IMPLICATIONS OF COMPUTER MONITORING"

APPROACHES TO PERFORMANCE APPRAISAL

BIASES IN APPRAISAL AND APPROACHES TO APPRAISAL TRAINING

ANALYSIS OF FUTURE PERFORMANCE

CURRENT TRENDS

"HR Advice and Application
PERFORMANCE MANAGEMENT 'IN THE ROUND'"

Career Management Exercise

Case: The Pain of Performance Appraisal

Case: Improving Performance Appraisal

MANAGING HUMAN RESOURCES
at the Chrysler Corporation

IN the early 1980s, the Chrysler Corporation was about at the end of its rope, but through the coordinated efforts of Lee Iaccoca, his management team, the employees, the United Automobile Workers (UAW) union, and a little help from the federal government, Chrysler staged a rather dramatic turnaround that continues today. Today, with worldwide sales of $35 billion, making it the world's eleventh largest manufacturing organization, Chrysler is again able to call itself one of the big three U.S. automakers. As with any successful turnaround, many, many things needed to go right. The work force had to be dedicated to survival and committed to improvement. It has helped a great deal that employees at Chrysler feel that they are part of the team. Here's where performance appraisal comes in! In late 1988, Chrysler began a reverse-appraisal process. It formed a steering committee in which top management and union (UAW) leadership were represented. This was done to ensure that both parties (management and nonmanagement) were involved from the beginning—it wasn't to be seen as a "program imposed by management."

Because this program was new, Chrysler decided to initially develop and test the program in two units within just one division, the Vehicle Engineering Division. In this way, the program could be worked out, perfected, and then used in other areas. To ensure that this process of change was as objective as possible (and run as effectively as possible), Debra Dubow, management development specialist in another Chrysler division, was brought in to manage the program, which included developing the new appraisal instrument (remember, this was intended to be used by employees to appraise the performance of their bosses, not the other way around). Involved in this process was the gathering of data that would determine what criteria should be used; later on would come training in how to use the new appraisals. Here's how it got started:

Dubow first pulled together a cross section of employees from the two pilot groups, ranging from vice presidents and union management to first-line supervisors and mechanics. Through this sample of approximately 50 persons, she was able to gather valuable input from different levels of managers and employees, as well as recognize and head off resistance to the new project that might be encountered along the way.[1]

The decision resulting from these discussions was that Chrysler would develop its own performance appraisal form, not buy an existing one from another organization. The criteria that Dubow and her team initially decided to consider using were those already being used on the employees in the traditional boss-subordinate appraisal process. The final appraisal form the Chrysler team developed (after many rounds of discussions and revisions!) ended up including many criteria the employees were already familiar with. The team, of course, had to reconfigure the criteria somewhat to fit appraising the boss; examples included:

- *Teamwork:* "My supervisor promotes cooperation and teamwork within our work group."
- *Communication:* "My supervisor learns current business information and communicates it to our work group."
- *Quality:* "My supervisor demonstrates meaningful commitment to our quality efforts."
- *Leadership:* "My supervisor demonstrates consistency through both words and actions."
- *Planning:* "My supervisor provides reasonable schedules so that my commitments can be met."
- *Development of the work force:* "My supervisor delegates responsibilities and gives me the authority to carry out my job."[2]

It was determined that each of these would be evaluated on a 1 to 5 scale ("almost never" to "almost always").

By the summer of 1989, two pilot groups from top management volunteered to be the first to have their employees appraise their performance. The data were gathered on the appraisal forms, and the results read by

Continued on the next page

This feature illustrates several aspects of performance appraisal. One is that performance appraisal is important enough for all employees in the organization to be involved, from top management to the union workers in production plants. Second, creating a new performance appraisal form and process take time; it needs to be done systematically and with the involvement of all parties. Third, implementing reverse appraisals sends a strong signal to all employees: you have the right to also appraise the boss, the person who traditionally appraises your performance. This opens the process up, making appraisal more egalitarian (an we're-all-in-this-together attitude). And finally, revising an appraisal system takes time, especially in a large organization with a long history of doing things one way. Not only does change take time, but so does its impact. In this chapter, however, we will look at what types of impacts might be expected to occur.

PERFORMANCE APPRAISAL

Performance appraisal is a formal, structured way of measuring, evaluating, and influencing an employee.

Although employees may learn about how well they are performing through informal means such as favorable comments from co-workers or superiors, **performance appraisal** is defined here as *a formal, structured system of measuring, evaluating, and influencing an employee's job-related attributes, behaviors, and outcomes, as well as level of absenteeism, to discover how productive the employee is and whether he or she can perform as or more effectively in the future, so that the employee and the organization, and society all benefit.*[4]

A *performance appraisal system* involves the performance appraisal and the entire setting in which the appraisal takes place.

To account for all the factors that affect this formal, structured system of measuring and evaluating performance, the term **performance appraisal system (PAS)** is used.[5] In essence, the PAS requires the organization to:

- Conduct a job analysis to identify job duties and responsibilities for which criteria need to be developed
- Choose an appropriate and valid performance appraisal method to assess job behaviors or outcomes
- Develop a process for conveying job expectations to employees prior to the appraisal period

- Establish a feedback system relating to job performance
- Evaluate how well the PAS is doing in relation to its stated objectives and make necessary revisions

How well the system works depends on the characteristics of the organization, characteristics of the rater, the pool of employees being rated, and the individual employee. Because of the importance of this process, we devote two chapters to this topic. This chapter focuses on the *gathering* of performance information; Chapter 10 focuses on *using* appraisal information to help employees improve their performance.

WHY IS PERFORMANCE APPRAISAL IMPORTANT?

Productivity improvement concerns almost all organizations, especially during periods when the environment is highly competitive and the rates of productivity increases are relatively small. Yet, although the productivity of most organizations is a function of three areas—technology, capital, and human resources—many organizations have focused on the first two and have consequently overlooked the third one, human resources. Nevertheless, what employees do or do not do influences an organization's productivity. Fortunately, employee behavior can be measured and evaluated, particularly job performance and absenteeism. As discussed in Chapter 1, employee job performance (or simply performance) describes how well an employee performs his or her job, while absenteeism refers to whether the employee is there to do the work. Performance can be measured by an employee's job-related attributes (for example, extent of cooperation or initiative), behaviors (making a loan), and outcomes (number of cars sold).

The impact that job performance and absenteeism can have on productivity and the competitive strategy of an organization is, as we know, significant. Major quality improvement and quality of work life programs at many large corporations, such as Chrysler, General Electric, Motorola, and Xerox, have aimed at increasing productivity and achieving improved quality through reducing absenteeism and improving employee performance (discussed further in Chapter 15). While the dollar value of increased performance can be substantial, the dollar value from reduced absenteeism is enormous.

Thus, organizations are continually seeking ways to improve employee performance—and this means finding ways to improve the appraisal process as well. Organizations have recently started to focus on other behaviors that have less to do with job performance and more to do with how employees impact the operation, image, and profitability of the organization. These behaviors include employee theft, alcohol and drug use, and unethical conduct. Concern over these behaviors is generated by estimates that workplace theft and pilferage of goods cost U.S. businesses more than $40 billion a year, workplace theft of time (employees leaving early, for example) costs employers $170 billion a year, and alcohol and drug use costs employers $99 billion and $67 billion per year, respectively.[6] Although these behaviors are not typically part of performance appraisal, they certainly can significantly impact productivity and an organization's competitiveness. Consequently, organizations are as interested in changing these behaviors as they are in changing job performance and absenteeism behaviors.

An effectively designed performance appraisal form serves as a contract between the organization and the employee. This contract acts as a control and evaluation system, better enabling the appraisal process to serve many purposes.

Performance appraisal covers:

- job performance
- absenteeism
- theft
- alcohol/drug use
- unethical behavior

DID YOU KNOW?

An employee with a drug habit will miss weeks more work on average. And that drug-using employees are three times more likely to be late for work.

⚹ **Major purposes of performance appraisal are**

- evaluative
- developmental

The quality of work from motivated people is light-years ahead of what you get from people not well motivated.

—Frank Popoff, President
Dow Chemical Company

Such purposes are often condensed into two general categories: **evaluative** and **developmental**.[7] The evaluative category includes:

- *Performance measurement*, which establishes the relative value of an individual's contribution to the company and thus provides information that can be used in decisions on layoffs, terminations, and promotions.
- *Compensation*, which determines appropriate pay for performance and equitable salary and bonus incentives based on merit or results.
- *Motivation*, which is the end result of an effective evaluation.

⚹ The developmental category includes:

- *Management development*, which identifies and prepares individuals for increased responsibilities and thus provides a framework for future employee development.
- *Identification of potential*, which identifies candidates for promotion.
- *Feedback*, which informs employees of the organization's standards and how their performance measures up.
- *Human resource planning*, which audits management talent and evaluates the present supply of human resources for replacement planning.
- *Communications*, which provides a format for dialogue between superior and subordinate and improves understanding of personal goals and concerns. This can also have the effect of increasing the trust between the rater and ratee.
- *Performance improvement*, which encourages continued successful performance and strengthens individual weaknesses to make employees more effective so that organizations can successfully implement strategies such as quality enhancement.
- *Research on legal compliance*, which establishes the validity of employment decisions made on the basis of performance-based information and provides a defense for management actions such as selection, demotion, or termination.

Of the many purposes served by performance appraisal, helping an organization establish the validity (job-relatedness) of its PAS is vital in enabling an organization to be in legal compliance in other activities such as selection. There are other legal considerations as well in performance appraisal.[8]

LEGAL CONSIDERATIONS

Organizations must pay careful attention to legal considerations in the process of employee performance appraisal, as shown in Exhibit 9.1.

ESTABLISHING VALID CRITERIA AND STANDARDS

Legal considerations are associated with:

- establishing valid criteria and standards
- using valid forms

Developing appraisals that reflect important performance criteria (job components for the appraisal) is necessary if the appraisals are to be considered valid. The U.S. Circuit Court in *Brito v. Zia Company* (1973) found that Zia Company was in violation of Title VII when a disproportionate number of employees of a protected group were laid off because of low performance scores. The critical point was that the performance scores were based on the supervisor's best judgments and opinions, not on important components of doing the job. When companies make performance-based decisions on the basis of appraisals, they are using the appraisals as employment tests; thus, the appraisals must be based on identifiable job-related criteria (*Stringfellow v. Monsanto Corp.*, 1970; *U.S. v. City of Chicago*, 1978). The best way to determine whether the appraisal criteria are job-related is to do a job analysis (*Albemarle Paper Company v. Moody*, 1975).

PARTNERSHIP: WORKING TOGETHER IN PERFORMANCE APPRAISAL

LINE MANAGERS	HR PROFESSIONALS	EMPLOYEES
Work with HR professionals in developing the appraisal process.	Work with line managers in developing the appraisal process.	May appraise the work of other employees.
Complete the appraisal form on employees.	Coordinate the completion of appraisal forms.	May appraise their own performance.
Give feedback to the employees.	Train line managers in giving feedback.	Participate in the feedback process.
		May appraise the boss.

Once the appropriate performance criteria are established, levels or standards marking the degree of desirability or acceptability of each job criterion can be established. To ensure that a realistic view of job performance is captured, several criteria may be required, and, a standard established for each criterion. Having these criteria and standards is necessary, not just for legal considerations, but also for job performance reasons. Consequently, *how* they are established is important.

USING VALID PERFORMANCE APPRAISAL FORMS

Once the critical job components (criteria) are established, forms based on those components must be used. For example, if quantity of output is a criterion, appraisal forms that ask supervisors their general impressions on how personable and valuable the employees are may lead to an inappropriate appraisal, and, if used for an employment decision, such an appraisal could lead to a *prima facie* case of illegal discrimination. Appraisal forms in which the raters evaluate an employee on attributes such as leadership, attitude toward people, or loyalty are referred to as **subjective forms**. In contrast, appraisals where the evaluation involves specifically defined behaviors or outcomes—such as level of output, level of specific goal attainment, or number of days absent—are called **objective forms**.

Although the courts will allow a company to use subjective forms (*Roger v. International Paper Co.*, 1975), they generally frown on their use (*Albemarle Paper Company v. Moody*, 1975; *Oshiver v. Court of Common Pleas*, 1979; *Baxter v. Savannah Sugar Refining Corp.*, 1974; and *Rowe v. General Motors*, 1972) because they may not produce fair or accurate evaluations. Consequently, the courts have ruled that, when disparate impact is found, all performance appraisal proce-

Two types of appraisal forms are subjective and objective.

EXHIBIT 9.1
PRESCRIPTIONS FOR LEGALLY DEFENSIBLE APPRAISAL SYSTEMS

1. Job analysis to identify important duties and tasks should precede development of a performance appraisal system.
2. The performance appraisal system should be standardized and formal.
3. Specific performance standards should be communicated to employees in advance of the appraisal period.
4. Objective and uncontaminated data should be used whenever possible.
5. Ratings on traits such as dependability, drive, or attitude should be avoided.
6. Employees should be evaluated on specific work dimensions rather than on a single global or overall measure.
7. If work behaviors rather than outcomes are to be evaluated, evaluators should have ample opportunity to observe ratee performance.
8. To increase the reliability of ratings, more than one independent evaluator should be used whenever possible.
9. Behavioral documentation should be prepared for ratings.
10. Employees should be given an opportunity to review their appraisals.
11. A formal system of appeal should be available for appraisal disagreements.
12. Raters should be trained to prevent discrimination and to evaluate performance consistently.
13. Appraisals should be frequent, offered at least annually.

SOURCE: Adapted from H. J. Bernardin and W. F. Cascio, "Performance Appraisal and the Law," in *Readings in Personnel and Human Resource Management*, 3rd ed., eds. R. S. Schuler, S. A. Youngblood, and V. L. Huber (St. Paul, Minn.: West, 1988): 239.

---

dures—objective or subjective—must be shown to be job-related (*Watson v. Forth Worth Bank and Trust*, 1988).

It is also important to communicate these expectations to employees in advance of the evaluating period. In *Donaldson v. Pillsbury Company* (1977), a female employee who was dismissed was granted relief because she had never been shown her job description (which would have specified performance criteria).

LEARNING OBJECTIVE 1

Describe the processes and procedures in performance appraisal.

PERFORMANCE APPRAISAL AS A SYSTEM OF PROCESSES AND PROCEDURES

In establishing a performance appraisal system, decisions regarding what to measure should be made very early in the development of the system. Other important decisions center around the period for the appraisal and the choice of rater.

IDENTIFYING CRITERIA

A valid PAS grows out of a comprehensive job analysis that has identified important job duties and tasks. Performance criteria can then be developed. **Criteria** are evaluative dimensions against which the employee is measured. They are also performance expectations the employee strives to attain. If, for example, a bank

Criteria are targets constituting job performance.

decides that the criterion against which it will evaluate the corporate loan assistant's position described in Chapter 6 (see Exhibit 6.3) is a specific level of customer satisfaction resulting from loan transactions, then the corporate loan assistant should see this specific level as a numerical goal and concentrate on meeting this criterion.[9] At Chrysler, the criteria established included teamwork, communication, and quality. These are all central to meeting the company's goals.

OUTCOMES AND ORGANIZATIONAL EFFECTIVENESS.   Depending on the organization's strategy and its ability to measure performance, criteria that relate to *individual* or *group job behavior* or *outcomes*, or overall *organizational effectiveness* (for example, profitability, having high quality, and meeting customer service goals) can be developed. Consider the corporate loan assistant's job. Behavioral criteria for this job may include such things as "prepares follow-up documentation in a timely manner." By comparison, outcome criteria refer to the product or output produced (such as "helps generate $5 million in loans each month"). Organizational effectiveness involves an inferential leap. It entails aggregating individual and group outcomes in order to determine how well the organization is functioning. For example, an organizational effectiveness criterion for a vice president of fixed assets might relate to total profitability of the bank for a specific quarter.

A four-step hospitality checklist gives Red Lion Hotel employees a way to remember their company's customer-service goals:

1. Greet the guest.
2. Show the guest that you care.
3. Show the guest that you can help (by going out of your way to accommodate the guest's needs).
4. Appreciate the guest's business.

SINGLE OR MULTIPLE CRITERIA.   If coordinating market activities is the only job duty, then only the criteria that relate to this single duty are needed. More often, however, jobs are multidimensional, composed of numerous duties and related tasks. For the corporate loan assistant's job described in Chapter 6, the duty, "helps customers with bank problems," is accompanied by other duties such as "develops required loan documentation" or "builds rapport with customers." If job analysis identifies all of these duties as important, *all* should be measured by a performance appraisal instrument.

If the form or approach used to appraise employee performance lacks the job behaviors and the results important and relevant to the job, the form is said to be **deficient**. If the form includes appraisal of anything unimportant or irrelevant to the job, it is **contaminated**. Many performance appraisal forms actually used in organizations measure some attributes and behaviors of employees unrelated to the employee's job. These forms are contaminated and are in many cases also deficient.[10]

Deficient means the form fails to measure all behaviors or results. *Contamination* implies the inclusion of non-job-related criteria and standards.

WEIGHTING OF CRITERIA.   For jobs involving more than one duty, there is another decision to be made. How should these separate aspects of performance be combined into a composite score or criterion that will facilitate comparisons between employees? One way is to weight each criterion equally, but the most accurate approach is to weight the criteria differently based on the results of a job analysis. Criteria can also be weighted relative to their ability to *predict overall performance*. Estimates made by HR managers, line managers, and employees can be used to determine appropriate weights for each job dimension.

In addition to determining the performance criteria and deciding how they are to be weighted, **performance standards** must be identified. These standards measure how well employees are performing. With the use standards, performance criteria take on a range of values. For example, selling 100 units per month may be defined as excellent performance, and selling 80 units may be defined as average. Organizations often use historical records of how well employees have done in the past (to determine what is actually possible) to

Performance Standards tell how well the employee hits the targets.

establish standards. Time and motion studies and work samples can also be used. Whereas these methods are often used for blue-collar and other nonmanagerial jobs, different methods are used for managers. Many organizations evaluate their managers by how well goals are attained. Increasingly, managers are also evaluated by standards of profitability, revenues, costs, increases in customer satisfaction, and even national measures of excellence such as the Baldrige Award for Quality. This award is described in the insert, "Managing Human Resources for Quality: The Baldrige Award."

MATCHING THE PURPOSE TO THE PERIOD

In addition to identifying appropriate criteria, consideration should be given to the period for which performance is to be assessed. On average, most organizations require formal performance review sessions at six-month to one-year intervals. For some jobs, this may be an appropriate interval. For other jobs, performance should be evaluated more frequently. For example, a carpet layer's performance might need to be evaluated at the end of each one- or two-day job rather than annually. At least, the customers may prefer it this way because better installation would probably result.

The evaluation period can also vary depending on the purpose of the appraisal. For communication and clarity, the focus should be on *current* employee performance during a *single* performance period. For promotion and training decisions, an examination of performance across multiple appraisal periods may be more useful. If performance is steadily increasing or is consistently high, a promotion may be justified. If, however, performance remains consistently low, then performance improvement programs may be necessary.

CHOICE OF RATERS

While many different sources can be used to gather performance data, the relevance of these sources needs to be considered *prior* to the choice of rating method. Appraisal sources include supervisors, peers, subordinates, self-appraisal, customers, and computer monitoring.

Raters include:
- supervisors
- peers
- subordinates
- self
- customers
- computer monitoring

APPRAISAL BY SUPERIORS. The superior is the immediate boss of the subordinate being evaluated. The assumption is that the superior knows the subordinate's job and performance better than anyone else. But appraisal by the superior has drawbacks. First, since the superior may have reward and punishment power, the subordinate may feel threatened. Second, evaluation is often a one-way process that makes the subordinate feel defensive. Thus, little coaching takes place; justification of action prevails. Third, the superior may not have the necessary interpersonal skills to give good feedback. Fourth, the superior may have an ethical bias against "playing God." Finally, the superior, by giving punishments, may alienate the subordinate.

Because of the potential liabilities, organizations may invite other people to share the appraisal process, even giving the subordinate greater input. Allowing other people to gather performance appraisal data creates a greater openness in the appraisal process, thus helping to enhance the quality of the superior-subordinate relationship.

It is very likely that you will appraise your own job performance.

SELF-APPRAISAL. The use of self-appraisal, particularly through subordinate participation in setting goals, was made popular as an important component in management by objectives. Subordinates who participate in the evaluation process may become more involved and committed to the goals. Subordinate participation can also clarify employees' roles and reduce the uncertainty about what to do.[12]

THE 1990 Malcolm Baldrige Awards for excellence in quality management were: the Cadillac Division of General Motors; IBM of Rochester, Minnesota; Federal Express Corporation; and Wallace Company, Inc., of Houston.

The award, named for former U.S. Commerce Secretary Malcolm Baldrige, is presented once a year in three categories—large manufacturers, large service companies and small business. A maximum of two awards may be given annually in each of the categories. The sought-after award was established in 1987 and promotes high standards, recognizing total-quality management and achievement for U.S. corporations.

IBM of Rochester was named a winner in the manufacturing division. The Rochester facility employs 8,100 people and produces IBM mid-range, main-frame computers.

"Winning this award is a positive reinforcement of the things that we are doing in Rochester," said Rich Martino, director of personnel for IBM Research. "At the Rochester site, our vision is to have enabled, empowered, and excited employees. This award confirms that our efforts are working. I know the excitement level is high in Rochester, because when the news was announced there were cheers and people out in the hallways high-fiving. Our goal now is to see how we can keep on improving and continue in the right direction."

The Federal Express Corporation is the first recipient ever in the award's service category. The company employs more than 89,000 people worldwide and leads the air-express-delivery industry by handling approximately 1.3 million shipments daily.

"Federal Express is deeply honored to have been chosen as the first service company to win the award," said James A. Perkins, senior vice president of personnel for Federal Express Corporation and SHRM board member. "We believe that our people-service-profit philosophy is fundamental to the quality effort. Simply stated, it means that when our people are placed first, they will provide the highest possible service and that profits will follow. Empowering employees is essential in our quest for 100 percent customer satisfaction."

The Cadillac Division of GM is the second winner in the manufacturing category. Cadillac employs over 10,000 people at its headquarters, four manufacturing plants and at its sales and services offices.

The Wallace Company, Inc., is the winner in the small business category. The Wallace Company distributes pipe, valves, and fittings for the petrochemical industry. It employs 280 people at its headquarters and nine branch offices in Texas, Louisiana, and Alabama.

Other Baldrige winners include Milliken & Company , Xerox Business Products and Systems, The Ritz-Carlton Hotel Company, AT&T Universal Card Services, Granite Rock, Texas Instruments, Defense Systems and Electronics Group, AT&T Network Systems Group, Eastman Chemical, and Ames Rubber.[11]

At this time, self-appraisals are effective tools for programs focusing on self-development, personal growth, and goal commitment. However, self-appraisals are subject to systematic biases and distortions when used for evaluations. There is evidence that self-ratings are more lenient or higher than those obtained from supervisors. Self-ratings will correspond more closely to supervisory ratings when extensive performance feedback is given and when employees know that their performance ratings will be checked against objective criteria.[13]

According to Roger Flax, president of Motivational Systems, a New Jersey management and sales training company, self-appraisals are particularly useful in small companies:

There's a lot of assuming that in small companies employees are motivated, so there's not a lot of formal appraisal. One answer may be the employee-initiated appraisal in which employees are told they can ask for a review from their manager. The on-demand appraisal doesn't replace a conventional semi-annual review, but it promotes an attitude of self-management among workers and often makes critiques more honest.[14]

Flax suggests employees ask for as many reviews as they feel they need. Listed below are seven questions he believes employees should ask themselves and their managers in their self-initiated appraisals.

- On a scale of 1 to 10, how does my performance rate?
- What are the strongest elements of my work?
- What are the weakest elements?
- Why didn't I get a 10 (highest rating)?
- Where can I go in my job or career in the next eighteen months to four years?
- What skills, training, or education do I need to get to that point?
- What specifically can we agree on that I can do, beginning tomorrow?

Team performance and appraisal are important in organizations pursuing total quality management.

TEAM-MEMBER APPRAISAL. Team-member involvement in the appraisal process can take many different forms. Jamestown Advanced Products, Inc., a small metal fabrication firm, recently had to deal with the issue of employee tardiness. According to team members, assessment of the problem, one person's late arrival disrupted everyone else's schedule, reduced team performance, and consequently lowered financial bonuses. Traditionally, a tardy employee lost some wages but could still receive a quarterly performance bonus. Team members thought this wasn't fair. The work team was encouraged to set performance standards for themselves and to identify consequences for low performance. After the team batted around the issue of how much lateness or absenteeism employees could tolerate and how punitive they should be, the team reached agreement. Employees could be tardy—defined as one minute late—or absent without notice no more than five times a quarter. Beyond that, they would lose their entire bonus.

In addition to defining performance expectations, Jamestown team members commonly serve as evaluators; the co-worker who is at an individual's side all day has an excellent opportunity to observe that individual's behavior. Common performance dimensions on which team members have evaluation expertise include:

1. *Attendance and timeliness:* attends scheduled group meetings.
2. *Interpersonal skills:* willing to give and take on issues; not unreasonably stubborn.
3. *Group supportiveness:* offers ideas/suggestions for the group to use on the project, supports group decisions.
4. *Planning and coordination:* contributes input to assist other team members in performing their assignments.[15]

Firms such as Jamestown have learned that team members can also provide useful information for evaluating how well the team *as a whole* is functioning. Exhibit 9.2 contains questions that firms can use to assess overall team **productivity, cohesiveness**, and **motivation** (drive). Using this instrument, comparisons between groups can be made to determine the relative degree of productivity, cohesiveness, and drive. Comparisons can also be made within groups by examining group ratings at specific intervals to determine which ones

Team performance relates to:
- productivity
- cohesiveness
- motivation

EXHIBIT 9.2
REPRESENTATIVE APPRAISAL QUESTIONS TO MEASURE TEAM
OR WORK GROUP COHESIVENESS, DRIVE,
AND PRODUCTIVITY

Cohesiveness

1. People in this work group pitch in to help one another.
2. People in the work group don't get along with one another. (R)
3. People in this work group take an interest in one another.
4. There is a lot of team spirit among members of my work group.
5. The members of my work group regard each other as friends.
6. The members of my group are very cooperative with one another.
7. My group's members know that they can depend on each other.
8. Group members stand up for one another.
9. Members of my group work together as a team.

Drive

10. My group tackles a job with enthusiasm.
11. The group I work with has quit trying. (R)
12. The group is full of vim and vigor.
13. The work of my group seems to drag. (R)
14. My group works hard on any job it undertakes.
15. The group shows a lot of pep and enthusiasm.

Productivity

16. My group turns out more work than most groups in the company.
17. My group turns out as much work as our supervisor expects.
18. My group has an excellent production record.
19. My group gets a job done on time.
20. This work group has an excellent production record.

Items are scored on a 1–7 scale with "1" being strongly disagree and "7" being strongly agree. Items marked with an (R) should be reverse-scored.

SOURCE: Based on R. M. Stogdill; *Group Productivity, Drive and Cohesiveness.* (Columbus, Ohio: Bureau of Business Research, 1965).

perform effectively and which ones are dysfunctional. What are the implications of scores on these three dimensions?

UPWARD OR REVERSE APPRAISALS. While some organizations such as Johnson & Johnson and Sears have been surveying employees for their opinions of management for years, upward appraisals have recently become a hot new tool among companies seriously focusing on the new environment. Major firms, including Chrysler, Amoco, Cigna, and Du Pont, use subordinates' ratings of how their bosses manage to improve operations, to make their organizations less hierarchical, and to develop better managers.[16] While subordinates often do not have access to information about all dimensions of supervisory performance, they do have access to information about supervisor-subordinate interactions. When asked, subordinates usually complain that they do not get enough feedback. They want a pat on the back for doing well and honest criticism—even when it "hurts"—when they haven't performed well. Employees also complain that their supervisors pay only lip service to their input—that suggestions are not taken seriously and are seldom acted upon. Subordinates want their supervisor to go to bat for them more—singing their praises to others in the company—particularly when it comes to salary, promotion, or assignments. A fourth common complaint is that their supervisors don't delegate and give them enough responsibility.

One drawback is that subordinates may not always evaluate performance objectively or honestly. This is particularly likely if subordinates feel threatened (for example, "If I give my boss a low rating, she will reciprocate and give me a low rating, too"). To protect anonymity, evaluations need to be made by at least three or four subordinates and turned in to someone other than the supervisor being evaluated. Alternatively, the evaluations can be scored by a computer, as at Chrysler.

APPRAISAL BY CUSTOMERS.   Another source of appraisal information comes from customers or clients of the employee. Appraisals by customers are appropriate in situations in a variety of contexts. For example, a medical clinic in Billings, Montana, routinely has patients rate desk attendants and nursing personnel on such features as courtesy, promptness, and quality of care. Domino's Pizza hires mystery customers who order pizzas and then evaluate the performance of the telephone operator and the pizza deliveryperson. Doyle Ripley, owner of a carpeting firm in Utah, uses a customer check list to monitor the on-site performance of carpet installers.

> "When you've got the installers out on jobs everywhere, it's impossible to personally check their work. The advantage of our appraisal instrument is that it educates customers regarding what to look for in a quality installation job. Simultaneously, it provides us with inexpensive performance feedback. From the installer's perspective, the system works well because any problems can be resolved immediately without him or her being recalled back to the job."[17]

To encourage customers to return the surveys, Riley holds a monthly drawing for free carpet shampooing. Installers with the highest ratings are recognized monetarily and praised verbally.

COMPUTER MONITORING.   A more recent event in performance appraisal is the gathering of performance data by computers. Advances in computer technology make it possible for employers to continuously collect and analyze information about work performance and equipment. More and more managers are using this type of data to plan workloads, reduce costs, and find new ways to organize work. Although this method may be fast and seemingly objective, it has raised a number of critical issues in the management and use of human resources. One of the most critical is the employees' right to privacy. Nevertheless, according to the U.S. Office of Technology Assessment,

> Computer-generated statistics form the basis for the work evaluations of up to 6 million office workers, mostly in clerical occupations or jobs whose duties are largely repetitive. Similarly, some employers are using "service observations"—the practice of listening in on telephone conversations between employees and customers—to ensure that customers receive correct and courteous service.[18]

How would your performance be affected if you knew your boss was monitoring your performance with a computer? Many employees have become concerned enough with it to raise several legal and ethical questions. These include,

"Do we have a right to privacy?" and "Is it ethical to monitor employee whereabouts constantly?" This topic is discussed in more detail in the feature, "Managing Human Resources: Ethical Implications of Computer Monitoring." Now, after reading this feature, what is your position on computer monitoring?

LEARNING OBJECTIVE 3

Identify the many approaches and forms that companies use in gathering appraisal information.

APPROACHES TO PERFORMANCE APPRAISAL

At the outset of this discussion, it should be emphasized that rating forms are not to be equated with rating systems. Forms are, however, one very important part of the system. The development of a rating form comes only after systematic job analysis, the identification of criteria and appropriate raters, and decisions about the timing of appraisals. While direct output measures of performance are available for some jobs, by far the most widely used performance measurement systems are judgmental. The simplest classification of performance appraisal approaches include **norm-referenced**, **behavioral**, and **output-based**. These approaches can be supplemented by narrative essays.

NORM-REFERENCED APPRAISALS

For many types of human resource decisions, the fundamental question is often, "who is the best performer in the group," or "who should be retained, given we have to cut our work force," or "who should be assigned a specific task?" For these types of decisions, norm-referenced performance formats are appropriate. They result in a listing of employees, starting with the best.

RANKINGS.   In **straight ranking**, the superior lists the employees in order from best to worst, usually on the basis of overall performance. Employees can also be ranked by their performance of specific duties. Rankings such as this are appropriate only in small organizations. As the number of employees increases, it becomes difficult to discern differences in their performance—particularly in average performance. Alternative ranking can help. The first step in **alternative ranking** is to put the best subordinate at the head of the list and the worst subordinate at the bottom. The superior then selects the best and worst from the remaining subordinates; the best is placed second on the list, the worst next to last. The superior continues to choose the best and worst until all subordinates are ranked. The middle position on the list is the last to be filled.

PAIRED COMPARISONS.   The **paired-comparison method** involves comparing each employee to every other employee, two at a time, on a single standard to determine who is "better." A rank order is obtained by counting the number of times each individual is selected as being the better of a pair. An advantage of this approach over straight ranking is that it overcomes the problem of an "evaluation set." That is, it forces the rater to consider the performance of each employee to all other employees, one at a time.

There are several potential problems with paired comparisons. If the number to be ranked is large, the number of comparisons may be unmanageable. [There are $N(N-1)/2$ total comparisons where N is the number of individuals. Thus, for 25 incumbents, there are 300 comparisons if only overall performance is evaluated.] Multiple comparisons may also present another problem. It occurs if employee A is rated better than B, B is rated better than C, but C is rated better than A.

A problem with the methods discussed so far is that each person is assigned a unique rank. This suggests that no two subordinates perform exactly alike. Although this may be technically true, many supervisors have observed that

Approaches to performance appraisal are

- norm-referenced
- behavioral
- output-based

Rankings compare each person against the other people.

Paired comparisons and *forced distributions* also compare people against each other.

WHAT rights do you, as an employee, have to make a totally private phone call or to type a completely confidential message into the computer? Virtually none. The Fourth Amendment bars the government from unreasonable search and seizure of your scribblings at home. It does not prohibit the boss from rifling the office he's letting you use.

Consider Bonita Bourke and Rhonda Hall, who traveled the United States training car dealers, sales staff, and mechanics on how to use Nissan's electronic mail system. They also logged on for racy conversations with students and some disparaging remarks about a supervisor.

Suspicious, the supervisor overrode the women's passwords to read their E-mail and, among other things, found himself called "numbnuts." He rebuked them. A few weeks later, Bourke and Hall filed a grievance with Nissan headquarters in Los Angeles, arguing they had a reasonable expectation of privacy while using E-mail. Within days, Nissan fired them, and the women sued for reinstatement. Nissan says they were dismissed for generally poor performance, but that in any case they had no right to privacy on the E-mail network. So far, the California courts have upheld Nissan.

In 1991, two male employees of the Boston Sheraton Hotel were secretly videotaped while changing clothes in the locker room during a hunt for a drug dealer. They were not suspects, simply bystanders. Indig-nant, they sued. But don't bet on them winning in court.

Legislation that would protect employees in such situations might curtail legitimate surveillance. Companies often have good reason to monitor telephone calls of service operators and of employees who handle customer complaints.

Sometimes, though, monitoring can be excessive or pure harassment. Since 1990, Senator Paul Simon has unsuccessfully tried to pass the *Privacy for Consumers and Workers Act*. Under that act, an employer could eavesdrop on operators with fewer than 60 days on the job. Over time, employer rights would diminish, so operators with five or more years of service could be monitored only if suspected of a crime. That may sound reasonable, but how do supervisors evaluate veteran operators who might get sloppy?

The key to dealing with employee anxiety about surveillance is to inform workers in writing about policy and the reasons for it. Also, top management ought to keep a close watch on line supervisors who may abuse surveillance privileges.

Electronic snooping is so remote that it doesn't seem harmful at all—examining the patient with a CAT scan rather than cutting him open with a knife. But the practice is nonetheless invasive and sometimes addictive. Al Simon, who designs company security systems in New York, points out that you can acquire a voice stress analyzer or "truth phone" ($2,000 and up) to catch a thief but wind up cross-examining your wife. Supervisors who may hesitate to unlock employee desk drawers are less squeamish about invading electronic mailboxes. *Macworld*, a magazine for computer users, recently surveyed 301 companies from various industries and found that supervisors in 21 percent have examined employee computer files, E-mail, or telephone voice mail for the stated reasons of investigating larceny or measuring performance.

Reasonable ethics for employer spying seems simple. Says William Moroney, director of the Electronic Mail Association, a trade organization for those who create and use such systems: "Employees have the right to expect that naked pictures of them will not be passed around the office. If, however, you're running an illegal football pool, management has the right to know about it." But the line gets blurry between the poles of voyeurism and police work. Is it all right, for example, to monitor employee whereabouts constantly? Olivetti has recently developed "smart badge" an electronic ID card. Sensors around the building track the bearer as he moves and direct his phone calls to the nearest receiver. Very convenient. Unless you don't want the boss to know you're in a different division inquiring about a transfer. Before installing such devices, employers would do well to think through the ramifications.[19]

some employees perform so similarly that individual differences cannot be discerned.

FORCED-DISTRIBUTION METHOD.   The fourth method, forced distribution, was designed to overcome this complaint and to incorporate several factors or dimensions (rather than a single factor) into the rankings of subordinates. The term **forced distribution** is used because the superior must assign only a certain proportion of subordinates to each of several categories on each factor. A common forced-distribution scale is divided into five categories. A fixed percentage of all subordinates in the group fall within each of these categories. Typically, the distribution follows a normal distribution such as the following:

Number of	Lowest	Next	Middle	Next	Highest
Employees	10%	20%	40%	20%	10%
50	5	10	20	10	5

A problem with this method is that a group of subordinates may not conform to the fixed percentage. All four comparative methods assume that good and bad performers are in all groups. You may know from experience, however, of situations in which all the people in a group perform identically. If you encountered such a situation, how would you evaluate these people?[20]

CONCERNS WITH NORM-REFERENCED APPRAISALS.   Regardless of the appraisal method, they are all based on the assumption that performance is best captured or measured by one criterion: overall performance. Since this single criterion is a global measure and is not anchored in any objective index such as units sold, the results can be influenced by rater bias or favoritism. As a consequence, the rankings lack behavioral specificity and may be subject to legal challenge.[21]

Another critical problem facing the rater is that no information regarding the absolute level of performance is available. All levels of performance are relative—one employee to the other thus, managers do not know whether the best performer in a group is actually outstanding, average, or poor or whether two individuals with adjacent ranks are quite similar or quite different. Using such information for promotion decisions may also be inappropriate since an average performance could be ranked high in a low-performing group but low in comparison to high performers.

BEHAVIORAL APPRAISALS

With norm-referenced appraisals, the supervisor is forced to evaluate each employee relative to other employees. In contrast, behavioral appraisals allow supervisors to evaluate each person's performance independent of other employees but relative to behavioral criteria.

GRAPHIC RATING SCALES.   The **graphic rating** scale (form) is the most widely used performance evaluation (see Exhibit 9.3). Graphic rating forms vary in the number of performance dimensions they measure. The term *performance* is used advisedly here because many of these forms use what some call personality characteristics or traits rather than job-related attributes or actual behaviors as indicators of performance. Traits that vulnerable to legal challenge may include aggressiveness, independence, maturity, and reliability. Many rating forms, however, also use indicators of output such as quantity and quality of performance. Thus graphic forms vary in the number of traits and indicators of output they incorporate. They also vary in the range of choices (only one of which is to be

The graphic scale seems to be by far the most common.

EXHIBIT 9.3
GRAPHIC RATING FORM FOR EMPLOYEE PERFORMANCE APPRAISAL

				Date Completed
Name	Date of Birth	Date of Employment	Office Location Branch Departmental	Department
Present Job Title	Conversion Code	Years in Present Position	Soc. Sec. No.	Education

Quality of Work
General excellence of output with consideration to accuracy, thoroughness, dependability, without close supervision.

☐ Exceptionally high quality. Consistently accurate, precise, quick to detect errors in own and and others' work.

☐ Work sometimes superior but usually accurate. Negligible amount needs to be redone. Work regularly meets standards.

☐ A careful worker. A small amount of work needs to be redone. Corrections made in reasonable time. Usually meets normal standards.

☐ Work frequently below acceptable quality. Inclined to be careless. Moderate amount of work needs to be redone. Excessive time to correct.

☐ Work often almost worthless. Seldom meets normal standards. Excessive amount needs to be redone.

Quantity of Work
Consider the amount of useful work over the period of time since the last appraisal. Compare the output of work to the standard you have set for the job.

☐ Output consistently exceeds standard. Unusually fast worker. Exceptional amount of output.

☐ Maintains a high rate of production. Frequently exceeds standard. More than normal effort.

☐ Output is regular. Meets standard consistently. Works at steady average speed.

☐ Frequently turns out less than normal amount of work. A low producer.

☐ A consistent low producer. Excessively slow worker. Unacceptable output.

Cooperation
Consider the employee's attitude towards the work, fellow workers, and supervisors. Does the employee appreciate the need to understand and help solve problems of others?

☐ Always congenial and cooperative. Enthusiastic and cheerfully helpful in emergencies. Well-liked by associates.

☐ Cooperates well. Understands and complies with all rules. Usually demonstrates a good attitude. Liked by associates.

☐ Usually courteous and cooperative. Follows orders but at times needs reminding. Gets along well with associates.

☐ Does only what is specifically requested. Sometimes complains about following instructions. Reluctant to help others.

☐ Unfriendly and uncooperative. Refuses to help others.

EXHIBIT 9.3 (CONT.)
GRAPHIC RATING FORM FOR EMPLOYEE PERFORMANCE APPRAISAL

Knowledge of the job
The degree to which the employee has learned and understands the various procedures of the job and their objectives.

☐ Exceptional understanding of all phases. Demonstrates unusual desire to acquire information.

☐ Thorough knowledge in most phases. Has interest and potential toward personal growth.

☐ Adequate knowledge for normal performance. Will not voluntarily seek development.

☐ Insufficient knowledge of job. Resists criticism and instruction.

☐ No comprehension of the requirements of job.

Dependability
The reliability of the employee in performing assigned tasks accurately and within the allotted time.

☐ Exceptional. Can be left on own and will establish priorities to meet deadlines.

☐ Very reliable. Minimal supervision required to complete assignments.

☐ Dependable in most assignments. Normal supervision required. A profitable worker.

☐ Needs frequent follow-up. Excessive prodding necessary.

☐ Chronic procrastinator. Control required is out of all proportions.

Attendance and Punctuality
Consider the employee's record, reliability, and ability to conduct the job within the unit's work rules.

☐ Unusual compliance and understanding of work discipline. Routine usually exceeds normal.

☐ Excellent. Complete conformity with rules but cheerfully volunteers time during peak loads.

☐ Normally dependable. Rarely needs reminding of accepted rules.

☐ Needs close supervision in this area. Inclined to backslide without strict discipline.

☐ Unreliable. Resists normal rules. Frequently wants special privileges.

Knowledge of Company Policy and Objectives
Acceptance, understanding, and promotion of company policies and objectives in the area of the employee's job responsibilities.

☐ Thorough appreciation and implementation of all policies. Extraordinary ability to project objectively.

☐ Reflects knowledge of almost all policies related to this position.

☐ Acceptable but fairly superficial understanding of job objectives.

☐ Limited insight into job or company goals. Mentally restricted.

☐ Not enough information or understanding to permit minimum efficiency.

EXHIBIT 9.3 (CONT.)

GRAPHIC RATING FORM FOR EMPLOYEE PERFORMANCE APPRAISAL

Initiative and Judgment

The ability and interest to suggest and develop new ideas and methods; the degree to which these suggestions and normal decisions and actions are sound.

☐	☐	☐	☐	☐
Ingenious self-starter. Superior ability to think intelligently.	Very resourceful. Clear thinker—usually makes thoughtful decisions.	Fairly progressive, with normal sense. Often needs to be motivated.	Rarely makes suggestions. Decisions need to be checked before implementation.	Needs detailed instructions and close supervisors. Tendency to assume and misinterpret.

Supervisory or Technical Potential

Consider the employee's ability to teach and increase skills of others, to motivate and lead, to organize and assign work, and to communicate ideas and instructions.

☐	☐	☐	☐	☐
An accomplished leader who earns their respect and can inspire others to perform. An articulate and artful communicator, planner, and organizer.	Has the ability to teach and will lead by example rather than technique. Speaks and writes well and can organize and plan with help.	Fairly well informed on job-related subjects but has some difficulty communicating with others. Nothing distinctive about spoken or written word.	Little ability to interpret or implement. Seems uninterested in teaching or helping others. Careless speech and writing habits.	Unable to be objective or reason logically. Inarticulate and stilted in expression.

checked) for each dimension and the extent to which each dimension is described.

Graphic forms are used extensively because they are relatively easy to develop, permit quantitative results that allow comparisons across ratees and departments, and include several dimensions or criteria of performance. But because the rater has complete control in the use of the forms, they are subject to several types of error, including leniency, strictness, central tendency, and halo (discussed later in this chapter). Nevertheless, they have been shown to be as reliable and valid as more complicated forms, such as forced-distribution forms.[22]

In addition to their potential for errors, graphic forms are criticized because they cannot be used for developmental purposes. For example, they fail to tell a subordinate how to improve and are not useful for the subordinate's career development needs. Consequently, organizations often modify the form and add space for short essays so that the appraisal results can be used for developmental as well as evaluative purposes. Exhibit 9.4 shows an example of how one company modified the graphic form in Exhibit 9.3. Even when essays supplement the graphic rating form, the results are still subject to errors, and they vary in their length and detail.

This is what Chrysler did with its graphic rating scale for reverse appraisals.

322

EXHIBIT 9.4
MODIFICATION OF THE GRAPHIC RATING
FORM SHOWN IN EXHIBIT 9.3

A. Summary of Current Performance:
  1. Employee's strongest points
  2. Employee's weakest points
  3. What steps have been taken to modify weak points?
  4. Is employee properly placed in present job? Explain.

B. Employee's Potential:
  1. In what significant ways has this employee demonstrated improvement in the last twelve months?
  2. Have you made any suggestions for the employee's self-development?

      Yes ☐   No ☐

      (a) If yes, (1) What was the suggestion?
              (2) How did the employee react?
      (b) If no, what was your reasoning?
  3. In your opinion, is the employee limited to the work in the present job?

      Yes ☐   No ☐

  4. (a) If your answer to 3 is no, what have you considered as a possibility to improve the employee's position in our company?
      (b) What has been done about it?
  5. If your answer to 3 is yes, please explain.

C. Employee's Reactions:
Enter reactions or comments after you have discussed this appraisal with the employee. Are there any changes in your evaluation as a result of your interview?

| _____ | _____ |
| Supervisor's Signature | Date |

Reviewed

Department Head ☐

_____
Date

Supv. Officer ☐

_____
Date

HR Dept. ☐

_____
Date

Consequently, comparisons of ratees within a department or across departments in a company are difficult. Furthermore, the essay form provides only qualitative data. Thus these appraisals are not easily used in making zero-sum decisions (for example, salary increases, promotions, and layoffs). This also applies to several other qualitative forms of appraisal, however, including critical incidents, behavioral checklists, and forced-choice forms.

CRITICAL INCIDENTS.   Dissatisfaction with graphic rating scales has led to the development of other types of behavior rating scales. The most systematic of these approaches relies on **critical incidents** to replace ambiguous graphic scale anchors. At its most basic level, the critical incident approach requires supervisors to observe and record employee behaviors that are particularly effective or

Critical incidents are records of important job performance, good and bad.

ineffective in accomplishing their jobs.[23] These incidents generally provide descriptions of the ratee's behaviors and the situation in which those behaviors occurred. Then, the superior's feedback is based on specific behaviors rather than on personal characteristics or traits such as dependability, forcefulness, or loyalty. This feature of the critical incidents technique can increase the chances that the subordinate will improve, since he or she learns more specifically what is expected.

Drawbacks of the critical incidents technique are that (1) keeping records on each subordinate is time-consuming for the superior, (2) the technique is nonquantitative, (3) the incidents are not differentiated in their importance to job performance, and (4) comparing subordinates is difficult because the incidents recorded for each one can be quite different.

Behaviorally anchored rating scales focus appraisal on behaviors that can be changed.

BEHAVIORALLY ANCHORED RATING SCALES.   A major breakthrough in utilizing critical incidents to evaluate performance was the development of **behaviorally anchored rating scales**. These scales were developed to provide results that subordinates could use to improve performance. They were also designed to make feedback more comfortable.

The development of a behaviorally anchored rating scale generally corresponds to the first steps in the critical incidents method of job analysis (that is, collecting incidents describing competent, average, and incompetent behavior for each job category). These incidents are then placed in broad overall categories or dimensions of performance (for example, administrative ability, interpersonal skill). Each dimension serves as one criterion in evaluating subordinates. Using these categories, another group of individuals lists the critical incidents pertinent to each category. Exhibit 9.5 shows an example of one such dimension or category, transacting loans, and the critical incidents listed as pertinent to it.[24] This exhibit also shows the next step: the assignment of a numerical value (weight) to each incident in relation to its contribution to the criterion.

Armed with a set of criteria with behaviorally anchored and weighted choices, the superiors rate their subordinates with a form that is relatively unambiguous in meaning, understandable, justifiable, and relatively easy to use. Yet the form has its limitations. Since most forms use a limited number of performance criteria, many of the critical incidents generated in the job analysis stage may not be used. Thus the raters may not find appropriate categories to describe the behaviors—the critical incidents—of their subordinates.[25] Similarly, even if the relevant incidents are observed, they may not be worded in exactly the same way on the form; the rater may thus be unable to match the observed behaviors with the dimension and anchors.

Another concern with behaviorally anchored rating scales is that it is possible for an employee to simultaneously display behavior associated with high and low performance. For example, the corporate loan assistant (see job description in Exhibit 6.3) could prepare follow-up documentation in a timely manner and also receive complaints from loan applicants about rudeness and inappropriate questioning. In a situation such as this, it is difficult for the rater to determine whether the ratings should be high or low.

The trend is to develop forms based on what can make the company most successful.

STRATEGIC BEHAVIORALLY BASED RATING SCALES.   An extension of the above approach is the development of criteria that are linked with the strategy of the organization. For example, it is popular for organizations to have a market-driven, customer-oriented strategy (the terms often used for service firms seeking to improve quality). For this to be implemented successfully, all employees may

EXHIBIT 9.5
A BEHAVIORALLY ANCHORED RATING SCALE FOR
ONE DIMENSION OF THE CORPORATE LOAN ASSISTANT JOB

TRANSACTING LOANS

	10	Credit reports are always completed without error.
Prepares follow-up documentation in a timely manner.	9	
	8	Provides services desired but not asked for by customer.
Customers praise the help of the assistant.	7	
	6	Assists customers with loan applications.
Develops loan documentation accurately.	5	
	4	Prepares credit reports without having to be told.
Provides information to customers even if not asked.	3	
	2	Fails to help other banks participating in loans.
Loan applicants complain about the loan interview.	1	

need to change their performance. National Rental Car implemented such a strategy to serve their customers better and hopefully increase market share. A key to the success of the strategy was the development of strategic behaviorally based rating scales for the customer service representatives (CSR). Shown in Exhibit 9.6 is one dimension of this job, the task of customer service. You can see how much detail is provided; the customer service representative knows exactly what to do and what behaviors are aligned with the company's strategy.[26]

MIXED-STANDARD SCALES.   Mixed-standard rating scales were designed to eliminate some of the problems associated with behaviorally anchored scales. Critical incidents underscore the development of this scale. The format consists of sets of three statements that describe high, medium, and low levels of performance for a specific performance dimension. These items have been scaled using a process similar to that employed in the development of the behaviorally anchored rating scales. The three levels of performance of each dimension are arranged randomly on the rating sheet. Unlike behaviorally anchored scales, where scale values are known, no values are attached to the behavioral incidents. Instead, the rater makes one of three responses to each example.

A score on each performance dimension is calculated on the basis of the pattern of results.[27] The advantage of the mixed-standard format is that the rater is not dealing with any numbers. Consequently, some of the most common errors associated with rating are overcome. Additionally, analysis of rater response patterns can identify raters whose use of the scales is haphazard. A drawback of

Firms realize that to get quality service from employees, service has to be a part of the appraisal and compensation process.

Job Title: Office Representative Appraisal Dealing with Customers (CSR)
Task: Customer Service
(Building customer relations by the concern extended to customers, which recognizes them as individuals and makes their lives more pleasant by resolving their problems, and by making them more comfortable and at ease. It is the behavior CSRs demonstrate that influences how positive customers feel about National. It is also how we present ourselves and convey our excitement about our work, our confidence in ourselves, and co-workers in delivering the best car rental service possible.)

CSR Name: _____ Task Weight: _____ %

In the space provided below, please describe your observations of the CSR you are evaluating. Be certain that what you write are descriptions of what you have observed the employee doing during the performance period. Use words such as enters, smiles, inserts, orders, puts, etc. to describe CSR actions. Once you have documented your observations, compare your documentation to the five rating levels below and check the rating that best indicates the employees level of performance.

Documentations:
_____

_____

_____

5. WELL ABOVE STANDARD: Greets customers with a smile while making eye contact, anticipates customer's problems and provides whatever is necessary to make customers become more comfortable and co-workers more effective, asks customers what they need and tells them that we are there to serve them, checks with customers to determine if the car was satisfactory and makes notes of problems with the car to give to service, makes best presentations of self—uniform is neat, clean, and tidy, explains in detail to customers rental processing procedures, quickly communicates positive feedback to co-workers and discusses concerns in private. Keeps composure even when customers are irate with the CSR and the Company, tells customers about the organization and what makes it a good place to work.

4. ABOVE STANDARD: Acknowledges customers by using a greeting when they are standing in line behind the customer being serviced, makes eye contact with greeting, recognizes changes and/or contributions of co-workers and follows up with specific compliments, checks to be certain that customers have been heard accurately by saying "Did I understand you to say that . . . ?", makes positive comments about the organization and its employees to customers, tells people over the phone what they are going to do for them before putting them on "hold," makes certain customers understand what is expected before an activity/procedure is to begin by asking the customers if they fully understand before proceeding, makes suggestions or initiates methods to improve organizational performance, encourages the work of co-workers by letting them know when they have done a good job, works to ensure cooperative, not competitive, efforts with co-workers, makes time to help train new CSRs in rental processing.

3. STANDARD: Listens to customer's needs, apologizes for car problems, and lets them know that she/he will do the best to respond to their needs, greets customers over the phone by telling them who they are talking to and asking how they may be of help, says please and thank you when interacting with customers, grooming is well maintained, wears clean clothing, is careful with personal hygiene, meets dress code standards, gives directions by showing on the map how to get to where the customer wishes to go, explains to customer specifically what is in the rental agreement in ways the customer can understand, uses name when addressing them such as Mr., Mrs., or Ms., demonstrates respect for property and equipment by ensuring that proper care is given to equipment and appearance of public areas are clean and tidy, greets customers before customer greets them, asks customer what problems they may have had with the car, makes suggestions about ways to improve customer and service performance, tells co-workers when they have done a good job.

2. BELOW STANDARD: Does not greet others or attempt to make them feel good about our organization, does not ask how they may be of help or service to the organization, does not use customer's name when addressing them,

hair is not clean nor well groomed, does not tell others when they have done exceptional work, is not specific with customers in explaining the cost of coverages or what effect waivers have and their coverages, does not use a greeting when answering the phone, puts customers on hold without telling them that they will be on hold or why they are on hold.

1. WELL BELOW STANDARD: Does not listen to others—interrupts customers, closes the station with customers waiting, does not greet others with a smile, or make eye contact, hair and dress are not clean, uniform is soiled or does not meet the dress code, makes unfavorable comments about the organization to customers or co-workers, does not support the efforts of co-workers, does not monitor work area to ensure counter is clean and equipment is well maintained, does not explain rental procedures to customers or call them by name, discusses customers' problems in public, puts people on "hold" on the phone without telling them what is happening or hangs up on customers, complains about the organization to improve the situation, makeup is overdone, does not make positive comments when possible, discusses co-workers problems with customers, takes credit for others' work, uses abusive language with customers, criticizes co-workers for providing excellent customer service.

Rating

[ ]	[ ]	[ ]	[ ]	[ ]
Well Below	Below	Standard	Above	Well Above

SOURCE: From R. W. Beatty, "Competitive Human Resource Advantage Through the Strategic Management of Performance," *Human Resource Planning*, 3 (1989): 184–185.

mixed-standard scales is that scale values are not known. Consequently, developmental information is lost. Still, once developed, mixed-standards scales are relatively easy to use.

BEHAVIORAL OBSERVATION SCALES. Another development in behavioral scales is called the **behavioral observation scale**. Like the behavioral methods already discussed, these scales are derived from critical incidents of job behavior. Behavioral observation scales differ, however, in that job experts are *not* asked to what degree or level of performance they illustrate. Instead, job experts are asked to indicate the *frequency* with which employees engage in the behaviors. Scores are obtained for each behavior by assigning a numerical value to the frequency judgment. For example, a score of "2" may be assigned if it is almost always observed. These scores can be summed to get an overall rating. Alternatively, scale items relating to a particular performance dimension can be summed and then multiplied by an importance weight. Behavioral items are eliminated if the observed frequency is too high or too low. In either case, the item does not discriminate well between high and low performers.

Behavioral observation scales measure how frequently behaviors are observed.

Exhibit 9.7 includes examples of effective and ineffective job behaviors and the resulting behavioral observation scales. Note that the examples of ineffective performance are reverse-scored.

The advantages of this form include (1) its basis on a systematic job analysis, (2) clearly stated items and behavioral anchors, (3) employee participation in the development of the dimensions (through the identification of critical incidents in the job analysis), which facilitates understanding and acceptance, (4) its usefulness for performance feedback and improvement, since specific goals can be tied to numerical scores (ratings) on the relevant behavioral anchor (critical

EXHIBIT 9.7
BEHAVIORAL OBSERVATION SCALES FOR EFFECTIVE AND INEFFECTIVE PERFORMANCE FOR THE CORPORATE LOAN ASSISTANT JOB

Effective Performance

1. The corporate loan assistant prepares credit reports accurately.

Almost Never				Almost Always
1	2	3	4	5

2. The corporate loan assistant is friendly when interviewing loan applicants.

Almost Never				Almost Always
1	2	3	4	5

3. The corporate loan assistant is effective when interviewing job applicants.

Almost Never				Almost Always
1	2	3	4	5

Ineffective Performance

1. The corporate loan assistant fails to prepare follow-up documentation.

Almost Never				Almost Always
1	2	3	4	5

2. The corporate loan assistant does not help customers with loan applications.

Almost Never				Almost Always
1	2	3	4	5

3. The corporate loan assistant needs to be told to prepare credit reports.

Almost Never				Almost Always
1	2	3	4	5

NOTE: On an actual form, the items would neither be grouped nor identified as effective and ineffective performance.

Scales with detailed behaviors tell an employee exactly how to do things.

incident) for a performance criterion or dimension, and (5) its ability to satisfy the *Uniform Guidelines* for validity (relevance) and reliability.

The limitations of this form are connected with some of its advantages, especially the time and cost for its development as compared with forms such as conventional rating. Furthermore, several dimensions that are essentially behaviors and not duties may miss the real essence of many jobs, especially managerial where the job's essence may be the actual outputs produced regardless of the behaviors used to obtain them. When these conditions exist, some argue that a better method is one that is goal oriented or that appraises performance against output measures. Additionally, it requires more observation of performance than other types of behavior scales. If the span of control is large, this may be an impossible task for the supervisor.[28]

While the methods described above focus on job behaviors or processes, output-based appraisals focus on job products as the primary criteria. There are four variants of output-based approaches: (1) management by objectives, (2) performance standards, (3) the direct index measure, and (4) accomplishment records.

MANAGEMENT BY OBJECTIVES.   **Management by objectives**, or **MBO**, uses successful attainment of objectives to indicate quality of performance. Its application and acceptance results in part from its identity with commonly held personal values, especially the philosophy that rewarding people for what they accomplish is important. MBO can attain greater individual-organizational goals congruence and reduce the likelihood that managers are working in directions unrelated to the objectives and purposes of the organization (goal displacement).[29]

Management by objectives is premised on the assumption that an organization's objectives for a specific period should cascade down through the organization. Once goals are established, they are distributed to divisions or responsibility centers and eventually to individual employees. Central to this approach is the issue of **goal congruence**: an individual's goals must be in harmony with those of the department and organization.

In some organizations, supervisors and managers work together to establish goals; in others, supervisors establish goals for their managers. The **goals** can refer to a desired outcome, the means (activities) for achieving the outcome, or both. Goals can also relate to routine activities that comprise day-to-day duties, the identification and solution of problems that hamper individual and organizational effectiveness, or they can be innovative and have a special purpose. Regardless of their focus, the objectives are more effective if they include the following characteristics:

- *Specificity.* Objectives must identify how well the behavior must be performed or how high the output must be to be considered acceptable. Specificity reduces variability in performance and in ratings.
- *Timeliness.* The deadline for completion of the task or the attainment of the output level must be identified.
- *Conditions.* Any qualifications associated with attaining the objective (for example, if the production schedule is adhered to) need to be detailed since many factors beyond the control of the employee may hamper goal attainment.
- *Prioritization.* For behavior to be directed toward desired ends, employees need to understand which objectives are most important. Supervisors and employees can weight them, or weights can be derived from the job description.
- *Consequences.* The consequences for attaining or not attaining the specified level of performance must be spelled out.
- *Goal Congruence.* It is important for managers performing similar jobs to assign comparable goals. Individual goals must be congruent with department goals.

Although the use of goals in evaluating managers is effective in motivating their performance, capturing all the important job dimensions in terms of output is not always possible. How the job is done, (that is, job behaviors) may be as critical as the outcomes. For example, it may be detrimental to an organization if a manager meets a personal selling goal by unethical or illegal means. But even if

Output-based approaches include:

- MBO
- performance standards
- direct indices
- accomplishment records

Objectives should have these characteristics:

- specificity
- timeliness
- conditions
- prioritization
- consequences
- goal congruence

output measures accurately describe the job, establishing goals that are of equal difficulty for all managers and that are sufficiently difficult to be challenging is still a concern. Also, a rigorous effort should be made from the top down to assure a satisfactory balance between long- and short-term objectives. At Alcan, the Canadian aluminium company, management compensates for the ramifications of including longer-term objectives in an individual's annual performance evaluation by limiting attainment of objectives to 50 percent of a person's annual rating. The other half depends on how the person has carried out his or her principal duties or performed overall.[30]

Performance standards can be used quite nicely with jobs designed by the scientific method.

PERFORMANCE STANDARDS APPRAISAL. The **performance standards appraisal**, while similar to MBO, uses more direct measures of performance and is usually applied to nonmanagerial employees. Standards, like objectives, need to be specific, time-bound, conditional, prioritized, and congruent with organizational objectives. Compared to objectives, there are generally more standards, and each is more detailed. Generally, the format specifies average expected behavior as well as the level of performance that would be considered exceptional. Each standard is rated separately and multiplied by an importance weight. Scored in this manner, performance standards are compensatory in that high performance in one area can counteract deficiencies in other areas. When only one level of performance (which meets the standard) is specified, low performance cannot compensate for other areas, and the system is noncompensatory.

The major advantage of performance standards is that they provide clear, unambiguous direction to employees regarding desired job outcomes. When exceptional performance is also specified, these scales can motivate the average as well as the exceptional employee. A recent study found that, when standards were specific, extraneous factors such as the ratee's prior evaluation, the order of evaluation, and current salary level did not affect judgment. When standards were vague, these same items biased performance ratings.

The disadvantages of these work standards are that they require time, money, and cooperation to develop. As with MBO, the essence of job performance may not be captured entirely by set standards. Consequently, important job behaviors may be ignored in the evaluation process. And although set standards may provide clear direction to the employees and the goals may be motivating, they can also induce undesirable competition among employees. If this competition does not lead to undesirable consequences and if the employees want to participate in the standard- and goal-setting processes, this method can be highly motivating.[31]

DIRECT INDEX APPRAISAL. The direct index approach differs from the other approaches primarily in how performance is measured. The **direct index appraisal** measures subordinate performance by objective, impersonal criteria such as productivity, absenteeism, and turnover. For example, a manager's performance may be evaluated by the number of manager's employees who quit or by the employees' absenteeism rate. For nonmanagers, measures of productivity may be more appropriate. Measures of productivity can be broken into measures of quality and measures of quantity. Quality measures include scrap rates, customer complaints, and number of defective units or parts produced. Quantity measures include units of output per hour, new customer orders, and sales volume.

Exhibit 9.8 provides an illustration of a direct index for the director of occupational safety. This exhibit includes two direct indices (the quantitative standard for worker's compensations cost reduction and the reports produced). It also has a behavioral standard. Thus both the outcome and the behavior are impor-

---

**EXHIBIT 9.8
A DIRECT INDEX APPRAISAL WITH UNIT OUTCOME,
INDIVIDUAL OUTCOME, AND INDIVIDUAL
BEHAVIOR MEASURES**

Job Title:	Director of occupational safety
Outcome Desired:	Reduce workers' compensation cost
Quantitative standard:	Compensation cost: Present = $475,000: target = $380,000; actual $
Outcome/Task Desired:	Reviews plant facilities for violations and reports to plant manager.
Quantitative standard:	Conducts reviews and issues reports. Reports produced on time for each plant. Present = 85%; target = 92%; actual = %.
Behavioral standard:	After preparing the safety report, this director meets with each plant manager and praises reduction of possible violation incidents and warns of consequences if compliance is not met; goes over the report with each manager in detail; and returns to meet with managers and report progress every two weeks.

Overall Performance Rating:

Well below Standard	Below Standard	Meets Standard	Exceeds Standard	Well above Standard
☐	☐	☐	☐	☐

SOURCE: From R. W. Beatty and C. E. Schneier, "Strategic Performance Appraisal Issues," in *Readings in Personnel and Human Resource Management*, 4th ed., eds. R. S. Schuler, S. A. Youngblood, and V. L. Huber (St. Paul, Minn.: West, 1988): 260.

---

tant in the overall performance rating for the director's job and are combined into a single format.

ACCOMPLISHMENT RECORDS. A relatively new type of output-based appraisal is called an **accomplishment record**. It is suitable for professionals who claim "my record speaks for itself" or who claim they can't write standards for their job because every day is different. For this approach, professionals describe their achievements relative to appropriate job dimensions on an accomplishment record form. The professional's supervisor verifies the accuracy of the accomplishments. Then, a team of outside experts evaluate the accomplishments to determine their overall value. While time-consuming and potentially costly because outside evaluators are used, this approach has been shown to be predictive of job success for lawyers. It also has face validity because professionals believe it is appropriate and valid.[32]

Accomplishment records for a professional writer might include articles and books written.

WHICH APPROACH IS BEST?

Research on this question is limited. It does, however, reinforce the necessity of first identifying the purposes to be served with performance appraisal. Each approach can then be assessed in relation to the following criteria:

- *Developmental:* Motivating subordinates to do well, providing feedback, and aiding in HR planning and career development.
- *Evaluational:* Promotion, discharge, layoff, pay, and transfer decisions and, therefore, the ability to make comparisons across subordinates and departments.
- *Economical:* Cost in the development, implementation, and use.
- *Freedom from error:* Halo, leniency, and central tendency and the extent of reliability and validity (described in the following section).
- *Interpersonal:* The extent to which superiors can gather useful and valid appraisal data that facilitate the appraisal interview.
- *Practicality:* The ease with which the system can be developed or implemented.
- *User acceptance:* The degree to which users accept the appraisal format as being reliable, valid, and useful.

Typically, different types of forms are used together.

Because organizational conditions influence these criteria, it is impossible to identify which approach is really best. The human resource manager, however, should be able to evaluate any approach on these criteria in his or her organization.

LEARNING OBJECTIVE 4

Describe the biases in appraisal and how they can be reduced.

BIASES IN APPRAISAL AND APPROACHES TO APPRAISAL TRAINING

Despite the prevalence of performance appraisal systems, many people are dissatisfied with them. Their disillusionment centers on the vulnerability of these measures to intentional as well as unforeseen bias on the part of the rater and ratee.

THE RATING PROCESS

The rating process in the PAS is made more complex because it requires the condensation and analysis of large amounts of information. First, employees behavior or outcomes must be observed. This information must be aggregated and stored in the rater's short-term memory. Because of long appraisal periods, information must be condensed further and stored in long-term memory. When a judgment needs to be made, information relevant to the category to be rated must be retrieved from memory and a comparison made between observed behaviors and the rater's standards. Finally, a rating must be made based on aggregated data retrieved from memory and any additional information the rater intentionally or unintentionally chooses to include. Ratings at this point may be revised depending on the reaction of the employee or higher-level managers. Unfortunately, raters' memories are fallible. Consequently, they fall prey to a variety of rating errors or deviations between the "true" rating an employee deserves and the actual rating assigned.[33]

RATING ERRORS

When criteria are not clearly specified and there are no incentives associated with rating accuracy, a variety of errors may occur during the rating process.[34]

HALO AND HORN. Frequently, a rater will evaluate an employee similarly on all dimensions of performance. Performance on a single dimension will be so outstanding or so important that it influences the rating of other tasks. This effect is called a **halo error**. The opposite of a halo error is a **horn error** where negative performance in one dimension influences any positive performance.[35]

There are many common errors committed in performance appraisal including:

- **halo**
- **horn**
- **leniency**
- **strictness**
- **central tendency**
- **primacy**
- **recency**
- **contrast**

LENIENCY.   A second common and often intentional rating error is called **leniency error,** or the process of being too easy. In order to avoid conflict, a manager rates all employees in a particular work group higher than they should be rated. This is particularly likely when there are no organizational sanctions against high ratings, when rewards are not part of a fixed and limited pot, and when dimensional ratings are not required.

Some managers are too easy.

STRICTNESS.   At the opposite extreme of leniency is the **error of strictness** in which ratees are given unfavorable ratings regardless of performance level. Inexperienced raters who are unfamiliar with environmental constraints on performance, raters with low self-esteem, or raters who have personally received a low rating are most likely to rate strictly. Rater training, which includes reversal of supervisor subordinate roles and confidence building, will reduce this error.

Some managers are too strict.

Halo, horn, leniency, and strictness errors can be further minimized by establishing specific criteria for all performance dimensions, requiring raters to rate each performance dimension separately and then summing these ratings to attain an overall rating. Additionally, raters should receive normative information about their rating patterns.

CENTRAL TENDENCY.   Rather than using extremes in ratings, there is a tendency on the part of some raters to evaluate all ratees as average even when performance actually varies. This bias is referred to as the **error of central tendency.** Raters with large spans of control and little opportunity to observe behavior are likely to rate the majority of employees in the middle of the scale, rather than too high or too low. This is a "play-it-safe" strategy. Central tendency can also be a by-product of the rating method. The forced-distribution format requires that most employees be rated average.

Some managers tend to rate everyone as average.

PRIMACY AND RECENCY.   As noted earlier, the typical appraisal period (six months to a year) is far too long for any rater to adequately remember all performance-relevant information. As explained in Chapter 8, raters may use initial information to categorize a ratee as either a good or bad performer. Subsequently, information that supports the *initial* judgments is amassed, and disconfirming information is ignored. Thus the information initially collected is given more weight. This bias is referred to as the **primacy bias.**

Some managers pay most attention to their first impressions and some to their most recent impressions.

Conversely, a rater may not pay attention to employee performance throughout the appraisal period. As the appraisal interview draws near, the rater searches for information cues as to the value of performance. Unfortunately, recent behaviors or outputs are most salient. As a result, recent events are weighted more heavily than they should be. Called the **recency of events error,** this bias can have serious consequences for a ratee who performs well for six months or a year but then makes a serious or costly error in the last week or two before evaluations are made.

Employees and managers can minimize these two errors by keeping ongoing behavioral or critical incident files in which good and poor behaviors and outputs are recorded. Although time-consuming, they ensure that information for the entire period is incorporated into the appraisal.

CONTRAST EFFECTS.   If a criterion is not clear or a ranking system is used, **contrast effects** will occur. An average employee compared to a weak employee will appear outstanding; when evaluated against outstanding employees, the average employee will be perceived as a low performer. Again, the solution is to have specific performance criteria established prior to the evaluation period. Then, an employee with adequate performance receives an acceptable rating.

MINIMIZING BIAS

Even the most valid and reliable appraisal forms are minimally effective when too many extraneous factors impinge on the process. However, as previously noted, many of these errors can be minimized if the following steps are taken:

- Each performance dimension addresses a single job activity rather than a group of activities.
- Overall ratings are not used. Instead, ratings are made on a dimension-by-dimension basis and summed to determine the overall rating.
- The rater can on a regular basis observe on-the-job behavior.
- Terms like *average* are not used on a rating scale, since different raters have various reactions to such a term.
- The rater does not have to evaluate large groups of employees.
- Raters are trained to avoid errors such as leniency, strictness, halo and horn, central tendency, and recency of events.
- Raters are trained to share a common frame of reference.[36]

In addition to the above suggestions, rating accuracy can be improved through careful training that focuses on improving the observation skills of raters and on providing feedback and coaching. Frame-of-reference training, which was discussed in Chapter 8 as a method of increasing selection decision-making accuracy, is also useful here. A comprehensive rater training program might include the following:

A good program for rater training might include these ———→

1. Raters are given a job description and instructed to identify appropriate criteria for evaluating the job.
2. When agreement is reached, raters view a tape of an employee performing a job.
3. Independently, they evaluate the videotaped employee's performance using the organization's appraisal system.
4. The ratings of participants are compared to those of job experts and to one another.
5. With a trainer as a facilitator, the raters present the rationale for their ratings and challenge ratings and the rationale of other raters.
6. The trainer then helps raters to reach consensus regarding the value of specific job behaviors and overall performance.
7. A new videotape is shown followed by independent ratings.
8. The process continues until consensus is easily achieved.[37]

Organizations that cannot afford to develop videotapes or who use MBO performance standards can accomplish similar results using written-performance profiles instead of videotapes of behavior.

ANALYSIS OF FUTURE PERFORMANCE

The performance appraisal approaches discussed so far appraise past and current performance. Occasionally, it is useful to evaluate an employee's future potential. The **assessment center** method, discussed in Chapter 8, which is used to determine the managerial potential of employees, evaluates individuals as they take part in a large number of activities conducted in a relatively isolated environment. In a typical assessment center, an employee may spend two or

Assessment centers focus on future performance.

three days going through a series of activities, including management games, leaderless group discussions, peer evaluations, and in-basket exercises.

Advantages of the assessment center include its validity and its ability to open up the process by which an organization identifies future managers, giving more employees a chance to be recognized. Occasionally, employees find themselves placed in jobs or parts of the organization that are less visible to top management. This, combined with having a supervisor who fails to make fair evaluations of present performance, may "bury" some employees in the organization. An assessment center program that employees can volunteer to attend can reduce this potential for early "burial."

Potential limitations of the assessment center method are its cost, its focus on competition rather than cooperation, and its creation of "crown princes and princesses." The creation of a special class of employees is less likely, however, under a program where participants are either nominated by their supervisors or volunteer on their own initiative. The nature of the activities in the center, including the degree of cooperation or competitiveness, can be regulated to match the needs of the organization and its environment. The relatively high cost of the assessment center approach suggests that to justify its use of the center, the organization must clearly require its benefits such as the value derived from a better and bigger pool of potential managers.

Once performance potential is identified, organizations can establish management inventory systems to facilitate human resource planning. Using the same information, organizations can also establish career planning and training programs to eliminate any gaps between current and needed skills.

CURRENT TRENDS

Two major trends in performance appraisal are likely to affect you as you proceed in your career. Both impacted events in the performance appraisal process at the Chrysler Corporation.

THE STRATEGICALLY ALIGNED PERFORMANCE APPRAISAL

Much of what has been described in this chapter can be used in either traditional approaches or in the strategic approach. Although both are used in firms today, the strategic approach is gaining in popularity as firms see performance appraisal as an important way to achieve organizational goals. Yes, employees do tend to do what is expected (as generally defined by the performance appraisal system). Therefore, if firms incorporate such company strategies as teamwork and customer satisfaction into performance appraisal criteria, they are more likely to get teamwork and customer satisfaction from their employees as done at Chrysler. Thus firms wanting to produce total quality and/or total customer satisfaction need these criteria to be present in the performance appraisal of all employees.

Whether done traditionally or strategically, performance appraisal always involves several components. What these components are and how they get played out under the traditional and strategic approaches are illustrated in Exhibit 9.9.[38]

The example of NCR shown in Exhibit 9.6 is strategically aligned.

360-DEGREE FEEDBACK

The second major trend in performance appraisal in **360-degree feedback**. The system of reverse appraisal at Chrysler Corporation is an example of this trend. A more complete picture is developed when an individual (for example, a manager) receives performance appraisals from subordinates, peers, boss, self, and

360-degree feedback is appraisal information from all directions.

EXHIBIT 9.9
TWO APPROACHES TO PERFORMANCE APPRAISAL

	APPROACH	
COMPONENTS	TRADITIONAL	STRATEGIC
Goal	Evaluation	Achievement
Manager	Controls program	Partnership
Employee	Passive	Initiator
View	Review mirror	Prospective
Outcome	Performance Rating	Improved performance
Timing	Once a year	Ongoing
Links	None	Corporate goals
Rewards	Based on rating	Based on contribution
Theme	Control	Sharing
Criteria	Determined by manager	Suggested by and mutually determined employee
Customer	No input	Provides input
Development plan	No input	Essential element
Individual vision	Not discussed	Basis for the plan
Atmosphere	Often confrontational	Supportive

SOURCE: Adapted from "A new focus on achievement," *Personnel Journal* (Feb. 1991): 74.

---

even customers—hence the name. Firms such as Du Pont, Dow Chemical, Chrysler, and Disney use 360-degree feedback. This gives employees more information on their behaviors, thus enhancing the potential for improvement. The focus is on achievement and the fulfillment of the organization's strategy. A detailed description of 360-degree feedback is presented in "HR Advice and Application: Performance Management 'in the Round.'"

SUMMARY

Human variability is a fact of organizational life. From the point of view of HR management, it is in an organization's best interest to attempt to select and control individual variability. Chapter 8 addressed how selection and placement decisions enable organizations to staff positions for effective performance. This chapter discusses how organizations control variability in the performance appraisal system itself, and Chapter 10 will discuss how the PAS can control performance variability on the job.

Performance appraisal is not a single act or a particular format used to evaluate job behavior. Rather, it is a system or a set of processes and procedures that evolve over time. A performance appraisal system is premised on the beliefs that individuals will vary in performance over time and that individuals can exert some influence over their performance.

PERFORMANCE MANAGEMENT "IN THE ROUND"

"Employers can better manage the performance of their workers if they replace traditional employee evaluations with 360-degree feedback systems," asserts Mark R. Edwards, president of consulting firm TEAMS Inc. of Tempe, Arizona. In the next ten years, he predicts, these multiple-source assessment systems will become the most powerful human resource management tool available in motivating productive change.

A DIAGNOSTIC TOOL

In contrast to the traditional approach, where a single supervisor rates employee performance, multiple-source systems allow evaluations to be conducted by a group of colleagues and internal customers who form a circle around the employee. According to Edwards, employees are much more likely to respond constructively to a group's suggestions on how to improve their performance. As a result, the evaluation process becomes more of a diagnostic tool for employee development and less of an instrument to judge and discipline employees.

"Ten years of research at some of the largest employers in the country, including Du Pont, Dow Chemical, and Disney, provides compelling evidence that multiple-source evaluation systems are much more fair than single-source approaches," Edwards adds. "The 360-degree system has even been upheld as more reliable than single-source evaluations in several wrongful discharge lawsuits." The evaluation process produces more valid results because it involves a group of people who interact with the employee in many different ways. For the same reason, the process has proved to be less susceptible to gender and ethnicity biases than single-source evaluations.

DESIGNING AN EVALUATION SYSTEM

"As organizations become flatter and move toward team-based management structures, multiple-source evaluation systems can play an integral role in facilitating participation and enhancing productivity," Edwards notes. The essential elements of an effective 360-degree feedback system include the following:

- *Establish feedback criteria.* The first step in designing a multiple-source assessment system is selecting evaluation criteria and developing a behavior profile, so employees can be assessed relative to a model and not relative to co-workers. The process of defining evaluation criteria should be participative. For the system to work effectively, stakeholders in the organization must be given the opportunity to get involved up front.

- *Select evaluation teams.* Do not limit evaluation teams to the employee's closest colleagues. To get the most out of multiple-source assessments, the group should reflect the employee's internal customers. Teams should consist of five to eight members, including the employee being evaluated. Employees then have the opportunity to compare their self-evaluations with the group's assessments.

- *Conduct the evaluations.* Evaluation forms can be distributed in hard copy or electronically. Using an electronic mail system is one very efficient method for carrying out this process. It is important, however, to establish procedures for ensuring the anonymity of evaluators and the confidentiality of their responses.

- *Create summary reports.* After the evaluation forms are collected, summary data should be tabulated and put into a format that is easily understood by employees. Various software packages are available, including one designed by TEAMS Inc., that make it easier to generate tables and graphs from questionnaire responses.

- *Analyze results.* Along with the raw results of the evaluations, provide employees with an analysis of the data that will clarify and focus areas of strength and weakness in their performance.

- *Intervene to improve behavior.* The final step is to use evaluation results to improve employee performance. Instead of focusing only on problems, seek to identify structural constraints to improvement, and attempt to change those factors. For example, does the employee have the necessary training and tools to perform the job, and are internal procedures clearly communicated?

Continued on the next page

Thus, an effective PAS must generally serve two purposes: (1) an evaluative role to let people know where they stand and (2) a developmental role to provide specific information and direction so individuals can change (improve) their performance. Performance appraisal is therefore linked to other important human resource activities such as compensation, promotion decisions, HR planning, development and training, and validation of selection systems for legal compliance.

Appraisal data are gathered for several reasons: (1) to make the process as objective and fair as possible and (2) to comply with increasing legal considerations. In general, the more subjective the performance appraisal approach, the less likely the organization is effectively using its people and the more vulnerable the organization is to legal challenge. Although a variety of approaches to performance appraisal exist, they can be classified in three broad approaches: norm-referenced, behavioral, and output approaches. The choice of the best approach is really a function of several criteria: the purpose of the performance appraisal system (evaluation versus development), the costs of development and implementation of the system, the degree to which rater errors are minimized, and user acceptance of the system. Job analysis is an important means of developing job-related performance criteria.

Despite the best-laid plans for a performance appraisal system, HR professionals are often frustrated by the failure of line managers to apply and use the systems consistently. A number of obstacles can contribute to rater resistance: raters may not have the opportunity to observe subordinates' performance, raters may not have performance standards, raters as human judges are prone to error, or raters may view performance appraisal as a conflict-producing activity and therefore avoid it. For these reasons and others, it is important to examine not only why and how appraisal data are gathered, but also, as the next chapter explores, how they are used.

KEY CONCEPTS

accomplishment record
alternative ranking
assessment center
behaviorally anchored
    rating scale
behavioral approach
behavioral observation
    scales
cohesiveness
contaminated
contrast effects
criteria
critical incidents
deficient
developmental
direct index appraisal

error of central tendency
error of strictness
evaluative
forced-distribution
    method
goal congruence
goals
graphic rating scale
halo error
horn error
leniency error
management by
    objectives (MBO)
motivation
norm-referenced
    approach

objective forms
output-based approach
paired-comparison
    method
performance appraisal
performance appraisal
    system (PAS)
performance standards
    appraisal
primacy bias
productivity
recency of events error
self-fulfilling prophecy
straight ranking
subjective forms
360-degree feedback

REVIEW AND DISCUSSION QUESTIONS

1. Are the purposes served by a performance appraisal system the same for a superior, a subordinate, and a human resource manager? Explain.
2. Why is job analysis essential to the development of a performance appraisal system?
3. How can companies enhance the legal defensibility of their performance appraisal system?
4. Why does employee performance vary even after employees have successfully passed rigorous organizational selection and placement procedures? How can a performance appraisal system address this performance variability?
5. How is performance appraisal related to the internal and external environments? Discuss.
6. What are the three major approaches to performance appraisal? Give an example of each approach.
7. What is a behaviorally anchored rating scale? What advantages and disadvantages does each appraisal method offer?
8. Performance appraisal approaches differ according to whether behavior or results are evaluated. Can you cite organizational examples where one approach might be preferred over the other? Explain why.
9. Explain how an assessment center can be used to evaluate future performance.
10. Discuss the uses of 360-degree feedback.

FIELD PROJECT

Visit a local business and ask the store manager how workers are appraised. Try to get as much understanding as possible for how and why things are done and then report to the class.

CAREER MANAGEMENT EXERCISE: HOW SHALL WE APPRAISE YOU

Okay, you have now indicated what type of job and organization you would like to have (Chapter 4), and you have even indicated the type of job characteristics most desired (Chapter 5), and the selection procedures that should be used (Chapter 8). Let's assume you are on the job: what type of performance appraisal system would you like to have?

1. Would you like a formal performance appraisal process?

2. Please describe in as much detail as possible what you want:

a. What purposes do you want it to serve for you?
b. What form would you like your performance appraisal to take?
c. What people/groups do you want to rate your performance?
d. How frequently do you want to be appraised?

3. Whose performance would you like to appraise?

4. Do you want to have a due process system so you can appeal your appraisal if needed?

CASE

THE PAIN OF PERFORMANCE APPRAISAL

Joe Miller sat at his desk, looking over the performance appraisal form that he had just completed on Bill Cox, one of his insurance underwriters. Bill was on his way to Joe's office for their annual review session. Joe dreaded these appraisal meetings, even when he did not have to confront employees with negative feedback.

A couple of years before, Essex Insurance Company, which had experienced very rapid growth, decided to implement a formal appraisal system. All supervisors were presented with the new appraisal form, which included

five different subcategories in addition to an overall rating. They were asked to rate employees on each dimension, using a scale from 1 (unacceptable) to 5 (exceptional). They were also advised to maintain a file on each employee into which they could drop notes on specific incidents of good or poor performance during the year to use as "documentation" when completing the appraisal form. The supervisors were then told that they could only give a rating of 1 or 5 if they had "substantial" documentation to back it up.

Joe had never given ratings of 1 or 5 because he was not diligent about recording specific incidents for employee files; he believed that writing up all of the documentation necessary to justify such a rating was too time-consuming. In Joe's opinion, a couple of employees in his department deserved a 5 rating, but so far none of them had complained about his appraisals.

Bill was one of Joe's "exceptional" workers. Joe had three or four specific examples of exceptional performance in Bill's file, but in looking over the form he could not clearly identify the category in which they belonged. "Oh well," Joe said to himself, "I'll just give him 3s and 4s. I don't have to justify those, and Bill has never complained before." One of the categories was "Analyzing Work Materials." Joe had never understood what that meant or whether it was relevant to the job of insurance underwriter. He checked 3 (satisfactory) for Bill, as he did on all the evaluations he did. He understood the meaning of the other categories—Quality of Work, Quantity of Work, Improved Work Methods, and Relationships with Co-workers—although he was confused as to what a 3 or 4 indicated about each category.

Bill knocked on Joe's door and came in. Joe looked up and smiled. "Hi, Bill. Sit down. Let's get through this thing so we can get back to work, OK?"

CASE QUESTIONS

1. What problems do you see with the appraisal system Joe is using?
2. What are Bill's likely reactions to being told by Joe that he scored 3s and 4s even though he is one of Joe's exceptional workers?
3. What suggestions do you have for improving the performance appraisal system?

CASE

IMPROVING PERFORMANCE APPRAISAL

A large automobile engine plant in Saginaw, Michigan, has been having difficulty with its performance evaluation program. The organization has a program by which all operating employees and clerical employees are evaluated semiannually by their supervisors. Their evaluation form (shown in Exhibit 1) has been in use for ten years. It is scored as follows: excellent = 5, above average = 4, average = 3, below average = 2, and poor = 1. The scores for each question are entered in the right-hand column and totaled for an overall evaluation score.

The procedure used has been as follows: each supervisor rates each employee on June 1 and February 1. The supervisor discusses the rating with the employee, then sends it to the personnel department. Each rating is placed in the employee's personnel file. If promotions come up, the cumulative ratings are considered at that time. The ratings are also supposed to be used when raises are given.

The system was designed by the personnel manager who retired two years ago, Mary Bensko. She was replaced by Lillian Meyer who graduated fifteen years ago with a degree in business from the University of Michigan. Since then, she's had a variety of work experiences, mostly in the automobile industry, and she has done personnel work for about five years.

Lillian has been reviewing the evaluation system. Employees have a mixture of indifferent and negative feelings about it. An informal survey has shown that about half of the supervisors fill the forms out, give about three minutes to each form, and send them to personnel without discussing them with the employees. The rest spend more time completing the forms but communicate the results only briefly and superficially with their employees.

Lillian has found out that the forms are rarely retrieved for promotion or pay-raise analyses. Because of this, most supervisors feel the evaluation program is a useless ritual.

Lillian had seen performance evaluation in her previous employment, as a much more useful experience; it included giving positive feedback to employees, improving future employee performance, developing employee capabilities, and providing data for promotion and compensation.

Lillian has not had much experience with design of performance evaluation systems. She feels she should seek your advice on what to do.

EXHIBIT 1
PERFORMANCE EVALUATION FORM OF
AUTOMOBILE ENGINE PLANT

Performance Evaluation

SUPERVISORS: When you are asked to do so by the human resource department, please complete this form on each of your employees. The supervisor who is responsible for 75 percent or more of an employee's work should complete this form on him or her. Please evaluate each facet of the employee separately.

Quality of Work	Excellent	Above Average	Average	Below	Poor	Score
Quantity of Work	Poor	Below Average	Average	Above	Excellent	
Dependability	Excellent	Above Average	Average	Below	Poor	
Initiative at Work	Poor	Below Average	Average	Above	Excellent	
Cooperativeness	Excellent	Above Average	Average	Below	Poor	
Getting Along with Co-Workers	Poor	Below Average	Average	Above	Excellent	

Total _____

Supervisor's Signature _____

Employee Name _____

Employee Number _____

CASE QUESTIONS

1. Write a report summarizing your evaluation of the strengths and weaknesses of the present appraisal system.

2. Recommend some specific improvements or data-gathering activities to develop a better system for Meyer.

NOTES

1. J. E. Santora, "Rating the Boss at Chrysler," *Personnel Journal* (May 1992): 42.

2. *Ibid.*, 42.

3. *Ibid.*, 45. Also see A. Taylor III, "Will Success Spoil Chrysler," *Fortune* (Jan. 10, 1994): 88-92.

4. H. S. Feild and W. H. Holley, "The Relationship of Performance Appraisal System Characteristics to Verdicts in Selected Employment Discrimination Cases," *Academy of Management Journal* 25 (1982): 392–406; D. L. DeVries, A. M. Morrison, S. L. Shullman, and M. L. Gerlach, *Performance Appraisal on the Line* (Greensboro, N.C.: Center for Creative Leadership, 1986).

5. A. Mohrman, S. M. Resnick-West, and E. E. Lawler III, *Designing Performance Appraisal Systems* (San Francisco: Jossey-Bass, 1990).

6. "Alcoholism Has a High Cost," *HR Focus* (Aug. 1993): 8; S. Greengard, Theft Control Starts with HR Strategies, Personnel Journal (April 1993): 81–92.

7. M. Beer, "Performance Appraisal: Dilemmas and Possibilities," *Organizational Dynamics* (Winter 1981): 24–36; [Carroll and Schneider, *Performance Appraisal*.] See also the entire issue of *Personnel Administrator* (March 1984). For a description of how appraisals can be linked with strategy, see R. W. Beatty, "Competitive Human Resource Advantage

Through Strategic Management of Performance," *Human Resource Planning* (Summer 1989): 179–194.

8. D. I. Rosen, "Appraisals Can Make or Break Your Court Case," *Personnel Journal* (Nov. 1992): 113–118.

9. F. J. Landy and J. L. Farr, *The Measurement of Work Performance: Methods, Theory and Applications,* (New York: Academic Press, 1983), P. C. Smith, "Behaviors, results and organizational effectiveness: The problem of criteria." In *Handbook of Industrial Psychology,* M. D. Dunnette, ed. (Chicago: Rand McNally, 1976).

10. Cummings and Schwab, *Performance in Organizations;* Carroll and Schneier, *Performance Appraisal;* G. V. Barrett and M. C. Kernan, "Performance Appraisal and Terminations: A Review of Court Decisions Since *Brito v. Zia* with Implications for Personnel Practices," Personnel Journal (Autumn 1987): 489.

11. B. Leonard, "Baldrige Award Winners Empower Workers," *HR News/Society for Human Resource Management* (Nov. 1990): 13.

12. "Daily Labor Letter," *The Wall Street Journal* (May 1, 1990): A2.

13. J. L. Farh and J. Werbel, "Effects of Purpose of the Appraisal and Expectation of Validation on Self Appraisal Leniency," *Journal of Applied Psychology* 71 (1986): 527–529; R. P. Steel and N. K. Ovalle, "Self-Appraisal Based on Supervisory Feedback," *Personnel Psychology* 37 (1984): 667–685; P. R. Sackett, C. L. Z. DuBois, and A. Wiggins Noe, "Tokenism in Performance Evaluation: The Effects of Work Group Representation on Male-Female and White-Black Differences in Performance Ratings," *Journal of Applied Psychology* 76, no. 2 (1991): 263–267; D. A. Waldman and B. J. Avolio, "Race Effects in Performance Evaluations: Controlling for Ability, Education and Experience," *Journal of Applied Psychology* 76, no. 6 (1991): 897–901; P. R. Sackett and C. L. Z. DuBois, "Rater-Ratee Race Effects on Performance Evaluation: Challenging Meta-Analytic Conclusions," *Journal of Applied Psychology* 76, no. 6 (1991): 873–877:

14. "Measuring Performance: Employee Initiated Reviews," *Inc.* (July 1991): 80. Also see P. Lanza, "Team Appraisals," *Personnel Journal* (Mach 1985): 50; J. D. Coombe, "Peer Review: The Emerging Successful Application," *Employee Relations Law Journal* (Spring 1984): 659–671; J. S. Kane and E. E. Lawler III, "Methods of Peer Assessment," *Psychological Bulletin* 3 (1978): 555–586.

15. Discussions between company officials and Vandra Huber. Also see C. A. Norman and R. A. Zawacki, "Team Appraisals— Team Approach," *Personnel Journal* (Sept. 1991): 101–104; J. Fitz-Enz and J. Rodgers, "Get Quality Performance from Professional Staff," *Personnel Journal* (May 1991): 22–24; L. Thornburg, "Performance Measures that Work," *HR Magazine* (May 1991): 35–38; T. Slater, "Get it Right the First Time," *Personnel Journal* (Sept. 1991): 35–40.

16. W. Kiechel III, "When Subordinates Evaluate the Boss," *Fortune* (June 19, 1989): 201. Also see G. M. McEvoy, "Evaluating the Boss," *Personnel Administrator* (Sept. 1988): 115–120.

17. R. S. Schuler and V. L. Huber, *Personnel and Human Resource Management* (St. Paul, Minn.: West, 1990): 198–199.

18. *Bulletin to Management* (October 8, 1987): 322, 327. See also "Electronic Monitoring: Employee Rights Invaded?" *Bulletin to Management* (October 8, 1987): 322, 327; J. S. Kane, "Measure for Measure in Performance Appraisal," *Computers in Personnel* (Fall 1987): 31–39.

19. "Whose Office Is This Anyhow?" *Fortune* (August 9, 1993): 93.

20. F. J. Landy and J. L. Farr, *op. cit.,* see note 9. To be fair, all individuals performing identically should receive the same performance evaluation.

21. P. S. Eyres, "Assessment: Legally Defensible Performance Appraisal Systems," *Personnel Journal* (July 1989): 58–62.

22. L. M. King, J. E. Hunter, and F. L. Schmidt, "Halo in a Multidimensional Forced Choice Performance Evaluation Scale," *Journal of Applied Psychology* 65 (1980): 507–516; R. Jacobs and S. Kozlowski, "A Closer Look at Halo Error in Performance Ratings." *Academy of Management Journal* (March 1985): 201–212.

23. J. C. Flanagan, "The Critical Incident Technique," *Psychological Bulletin* 51 (1954): 327–358.

24. F. J. Landy and J. L. Farr, "Performance Rating," *Psychological Bulletin* (January 1980): 72–107; S. Zedeck, "Behavioral-Based Performance Appraisals," *Aging and Work* 4 (1981): 89–100; K. R. Murphy and J. I. Constans, "Behavioral Anchors as a Source of Bias in Rating," *Journal of Applied Psychology* (Nov. 1987): 573.

25. Latham and Wexley, *Improving Productivity.*

26. See R. W. Beatty, *op. cit.,* see note 7.

27. H. J. Bernardin and R. W. Beatty, *Performance Appraisal: Assessing Human Behavior at Work* (Boston, Mass.: Kent, 1984); F. J. Landy and J. L. Farr, *op. cit.,* see note 9.

28. G. Latham and K. Wexley, "Behavioral Observation Scales for Performance Appraisal Purposes," *Personnel Psychology* 30 (1977): 255–268; M. Loar, S. Mohrman, and J. R. Stock, "Development of a Behaviorally Based Performance Appraisal System," Personnel Psychology (Spring 1982): 75–88; Latham and Wexley, *Improving Productivity* (1981): 63.

29. J. S. Kane and K. A. Freeman, "MBO and Performance Appraisal: A Mixture That's Not a Solution, Part 1," *Personnel* (Dec. 1986), 26–36. J. S. Kane and K. A. Freeman, "MBO and Performance Appraisal: A Mixture That's Not a Solution, Part 2," *Personnel* (Feb. 1987): 26–32.

30. R. A. Gentles, "Alcan's Integration of Management Techniques Raises Their Effectiveness," *Management Review, AMA Forum* (April 1984), 31.

31. L. Baird, *Managing Performance* (New York: Wiley, 1986); J. J. Carlyle and T. F. Ellison, "Developing Performance Standards," in *Performance Appraisal: Assessing Human Behavior at Work*, eds. H. J. Bernardin and R. W. Beatty *op. cit.* (see note 27): 343–347.

32. L. Hugh, "Development of the Accomplishment Record Method of Selecting and Promoting Professionals," *Journal of Applied Psychology* 69 (1984): 135–146.

33. D. R. Ilgen and J. M. Feldman, "Performance Appraisal: A Process Focus," in *Research in Organizational Behavior*, eds. B. Staw and L. Cummings (Greenwich, Conn.: JAI Press, 1983): 141–197; A. DeNisi and K. J. Williams, "Cognitive Approaches to Performance Appraisal," in *Readings in Personnel and Human Resource Management*, eds. J. Ferris and K. Rowland (Greenwich, Conn.: JAI Press, 1988): 109–156.

34. H. J. Bernardin and R. W. Beatty, *op. cit.*, see note 27. F. J. Landy and J. L. Farr, *op. cit.*, see note 9.

35. M. E. Heilman and M. H. Stopeck, "Being Attractive, Advantage or Disadvantage: Performance-Based Evaluations and Recommended Personnel Actions as a Function of Appearance, Sex, and Job Type," *Organizational Behavior and Human Decision Processes* 35 (1985): 202–215; B. E. Becker and R. L. Cardy, "Influence of Halo Error on Appraisal Effectiveness: A Conceptual and Empirical Reconsideration," *Journal of Applied Psychology* (Nov. 1986): 662.

36. R. L. Dipboye, "Some Neglected Variables in Research on Discrimination in Appraisals," *Academy of Management Review* (Jan. 1985): 118–25; M. R. Edwards and J. R. Sproull, "Rating the Raters Improves Performance Appraisals," *Personnel Administrator* (Aug. 1983): 77–82; R. M. McIntyre, D. E. Smith, and C. E. Hassett, "Accuracy of Performance Ratings as Affected by Rater Training and Perceived Purpose of Rating," *Journal of Applied Psychology* (Feb. 1984): 147–156.

37. B. W. Armentrout, "Eight Keys to Effective Performance Appraisals," *HR Focus* (April 1993): 13; R. I. Henderson, *Performance Appraisal* (Reston, Va.: Reston, 1984).

38. "A New Focus on Achievement," *Personnel Journal* (Feb. 1991): 73–75.

39. "Performance Management in the Round," *Bulletin to Management* (Aug. 12, 1993): 256. Used by permission.

CHAPTER 10

UTILIZING PERFORMANCE APPRAISAL INFORMATION: IMPROVING EMPLOYEE PERFORMANCE

LEARNING OBJECTIVES

When you have finished studying this chapter, you should be able to:

1. Describe the conflicts typically involved in performance appraisal feedback.
2. Design appraisal processes for maximum results.
3. Tell why employees do not always perform well even when they have the ability.
4. Identify strategies to improve performance.

CHAPTER OUTLINE

"I HAVE seen the future and it [Chaparral Steel] works." So commented a senior executive from a large U.S. firm who listened to Gordon Forward, president of Chaparral Steel, Midlothian, Texas. In an industry with a history of high costs (requiring an average of six labor hours per ton in 1985), low performance ($70 million loss in 1985), and crushing competition from Japanese steel makers, Chaparral continues to thwart "averages." In the mid-1980s, the "mini-mill" steel company posted an 18 percent sales *gain* and produced an average of 1.7 labor hours per ton (compared to 2.3 labor hours per ton by the best equivalent steel firm in Japan). How has the firm done it?

First, the company views each employee's performance strategically as a means to help Chaparral gain competitive advantage. To accomplish this, the company links careful selection and training programs with performance expectations. In addition, Chaparral's basic philosophy of pushing decision making to the lowest level in the company has resulted in employees taking responsibility for self-management.

Self-management depends on groups of people with different perspectives solving problems. An example of Chaparral's success with this approach dates from the early 1980s when the company needed new mill stands, the equipment that flattens and shapes steel as it goes through the mill. A four-person team, including three mill workers, visited vendors worldwide, reported findings to workers and senior managers, and participated in selecting the equipment. The team then oversaw the equipment purchase (including contract negotiation) and installation. In an industry where such a major capital expenditure typically takes several years to complete, Chaparral did it in under a year.

Gordon Forward captures the basic philosophy with his comment, "It's really amazing what people can do when you let them." Supervisors have responsibility for their own hiring, training, safety programs, and deciding—with workers in their units—how to socialize and train new people. In examining performance expectations for ways that their jobs can "add more value" to the company, Chaparral's security guards have taken on new responsibilities. In addition to monitoring mills at night, security guards also do such tasks as data entry, act as paramedics, and fill up fire extinguishers.

Rather than viewing performance appraisal as a way to monitor performance, firms such as Chaparral use it to examine how to do jobs more effectively and, ultimately, how to turn them completely over to employees. The employees respond with vastly improved performance.[1]

More and more attention is being focused on improving employee performance. Firms that want to survive and remain competitive are attempting to do as much as possible to assist their employees, both managers and nonmanagers, to improve. Thus we find firms such as Chaparral training their employees in self-management skills and giving them more decision-making responsibilities. These activities are the exciting new trends, and we will return to them later in this chapter.

Giving feedback to employees based on their performance appraisal is one way to improve performance. Two key activities in this process are identifying performance deficiencies and developing strategies and plans to remove them. Unfortunately, this is easier said than done for many reasons. The conflicts inherent in performance appraisal create certain dilemmas.

Two key activities in improving performance are

- identifying deficiencies
- developing strategies to remove deficiencies

INHERENT CONFLICTS IN PERFORMANCE APPRAISAL

Performance appraisal touches on one of the most emotionally charged activities in business life—the assessment of a person's contribution and ability. The signals a person receives about this assessment have a strong impact on self-esteem and on subsequent performance. Unfortunately, the performance appraisal experience draws poor reviews from employees, employers, and experts alike. Many employees believe that their performance appraisals are often ineffective, biased, and poorly done.

Managers seem equally disgruntled with the appraisal process. In one survey, managers generally agreed that a performance appraisal should serve as a basis for determining pay increases, developing team players, and improving performance but that it often falls short of these goals. In fact, only 10 percent of all managers believe that production increases are a result of the appraisal process.[2]

In another survey, the majority of appraisers saw little or no practical value in conducting performance appraisals. Whether the feedback they gave was positive or negative, supervisors felt that at best the status quo was maintained; at worst, the perceived outcome of giving negative feedback was viewed as so aversive that managers preferred not to conduct appraisals at all. This reaction was typical since, as the study found, positive organizational consequences seldom followed accurate appraisals, and negative consequences (confrontation, "bad-mouthing," more meetings and memorandum) are assured after negative appraisals. The study concluded that managers also feared the organizational consequences of "making waves" with their subordinates.[3]

HIGH PERFORMERS ALL

One key reason that performance appraisal is viewed negatively centers on the self-evaluation of employees: the overwhelming majority believe they perform better than 75 percent of their peers. Thus, when confronted with information suggesting they performed adequately, but not outstandingly, subordinates perceive that the evaluation is unfair and that the rewards are not equivalent to their contributions. As a result, organizational commitment and job satisfaction drop and remain low for as long as a year after the evaluation.

While one would expect positive feedback to increase job satisfaction, this doesn't occur either. Because employees believe their performance is high, receiving positive feedback merely maintains their current level of satisfaction and commitment. Thus no matter what a supervisor does, the best he or she can accomplish is to maintain the status quo.

PERCEPTUAL FOCUS

Another reason that performance appraisals are problematic is that supervisors and subordinates view the process from different perspectives. For the subordinate, the perceptual focus is outward, keying in on the environmental factors (the supervisor, lack of supplies, co-workers) that impinge on his or her performance. The perceptual focus of the supervisor is on the subordinate and his or her motivation and ability. These perceptual differences are called *actor* and *observer* differences and can lead to conflict when it comes to identifying the causes of poor or good performance. This perceptual problem is accentuated by the tendency to account for performance in a self-serving manner. In order to protect one's ego, a subordinate is likely to attribute the causes of poor performance to external factors (difficult task, unclear instructions, lack of necessary

Inherent conflicts occur in performance appraisal because:

- **Most people think they are good performers.**
- **People want to maintain their self-esteem (self-image).**
- **People tend to attribute poor performance to others.**

equipment) and attribute successful performance to one's motivation and ability. Supervisors may respond similarly.

CONFLICTS IN GOALS

Goal conflict can also be the problem. Inherent in organizational and individual goals are three sets of conflict; these are the dilemmas in the appraisal process. *One* is between the organization's evaluative and developmental goals. When pursuing the evaluative goal, superiors make judgments affecting their subordinates' careers and immediate rewards. Many managers feel uncomfortable with this process because it requires them to be both judge and jury as described by Andrew Grove, chairman at Intel Corporation in the "Managing Human Resources at Intel." Communicating these judgments can lead to the creation of an adversarial, low-trust relationship between superior and subordinate. This in turn precludes the superior from performing the problem-solving, helper role that is essential if the organization wants to serve the developmental goal.

A *second* set of conflicts arises from the evaluation of various goals of the individual. On the one hand, individuals want valid feedback that gives them information about how to improve and where they stand in the organization. On the other hand, they want to verify their self-image (self-esteem) and obtain valued rewards. In essence, the goals of the individual imply a necessity to be open (that is, welcome feedback for improvement) yet protective (maintain a positive self-image and obtain rewards).

The *third* set of conflicts arises between the individual's goals and those of the organization. One conflict is between the organization's evaluation goal and the individual's goal of obtaining rewards. Another conflict is between the organization's developmental goal and the individual's goal of maintaining self-image. Exhibit 10.1 shows the nature of these conflicts.[5]

CONSEQUENCES OF INHERENT CONFLICTS

Among the several consequences of the conflicts just described are ambivalence, avoidance, defensiveness, and resistance. Some of these consequences and conflicts cannot be avoided in gathering data for and conducting performance appraisals, particularly that of the superior-subordinate relationship described in Chapter 9.

Ambivalence is a consequence for both superiors and subordinates. Superiors are ambivalent because they must act as judge and jury in telling subordinates where they stand, both because the organization demands it and because the subordinates want it. Yet, superiors are uncertain about their judgments and how subordinates will react to negative feedback. This feeling is intensified when superiors are not trained in feedback techniques. Subordinates are equally ambivalent because they want honest feedback yet want to receive rewards and maintain their self-image (that is, they really want only positive feedback). Additionally, if they are open with their superiors in identifying undeveloped potential, they risk the chance that the superiors may use this to evaluate them unfavorably.[6]

Subordinates and superiors can both be defensive in performance appraisals, particularly when feedback is negative. A classic study at General Electric made the following discoveries:

- Criticism has a negative effect on goal achievement.
- Praise has little effect one way or the other.
- The average subordinate reacts defensively to criticism during the appraisal interview.

Inherent conflicts in performance appraisal occur between:

- **organization's evaluative and developmental goals**
- **individual's protective and open goals**
- **organization and individual goals**

Consequences of inherent conflicts are

- **ambivalence**
- **avoidance**
- **defensiveness**
- **resistance**

A classic study in performance feedback found several things:

WHY are performance reviews part of the management system of most organizations? And why do we review the performance of our subordinates? Andrew Grove, founder and chairman of Intel, posed both questions to a group of middle managers and got the following responses:

- To assess the subordinate's work
- To improve performance
- To motivate
- To provide feedback to a subordinate
- To justify raises
- To reward performance
- To provide discipline
- To provide work direction
- To reinforce the company culture

Next, I (Andrew Grove) asked the group to imagine themselves to be a supervisor giving a review to a subordinate, and asked them what their feelings were. Some of the answers:

- Pride
- Anger
- Anxiety
- Discomfort
- Guilt
- Empathy/concern
- Embarrassment
- Frustration

Finally, I asked the same group to think back to some of the performance reviews they had received and asked what, if anything, was wrong with them. Their answers were quick and many:

- Review comments too general

- Mixed messages (inconsistent with rating or dollar raise)
- No indication of how to improve
- Negatives avoided
- Supervisor didn't know my work
- Only recent performance considered
- Surprises

This should tell you that giving performance reviews is a very complicated and difficult business and that we managers don't do an especially good job at it.

The fact is that giving such reviews is the single most important form of task-relevant feedback we as supervisors can provide. It is how we assess our subordinates' level of performance and how we deliver that assessment to them individually. It is also how we allocate the rewards—promotions, dollars, stock options, or whatever we may use. As we saw earlier, the review will influence a subordinate's performance—positively or negatively—for a long time, which makes the appraisal one of the manager's highest-leverage activities. In short, the review is an extremely powerful mechanism, and it is little wonder that opinions and feelings about it are strong and diverse.

But what is its fundamental purpose? Though all of the responses given to my questions are correct, there is one that is more important than any of the others: it is to improve the subordinate's performance. The review is usually dedicated to two things: first, the skill level of the subordinate, to determine what skills are missing and to find ways to remedy that lack; and second, to intensify the subordinate's motivation in order to get him or her on a higher performance curve for the same skill level.[4]

- Defensiveness resulting from critical appraisal produces inferior performance.
- The disruptive effect of repeated criticism on subsequent performance is greater among those who already have low self-esteem.[7]

Accordingly, subordinates attempt to blame others for their performance, challenge the appraisal form, and demand that their superiors justify their appraisals.

EXHIBIT 10.1
CONFLICTS IN GOALS

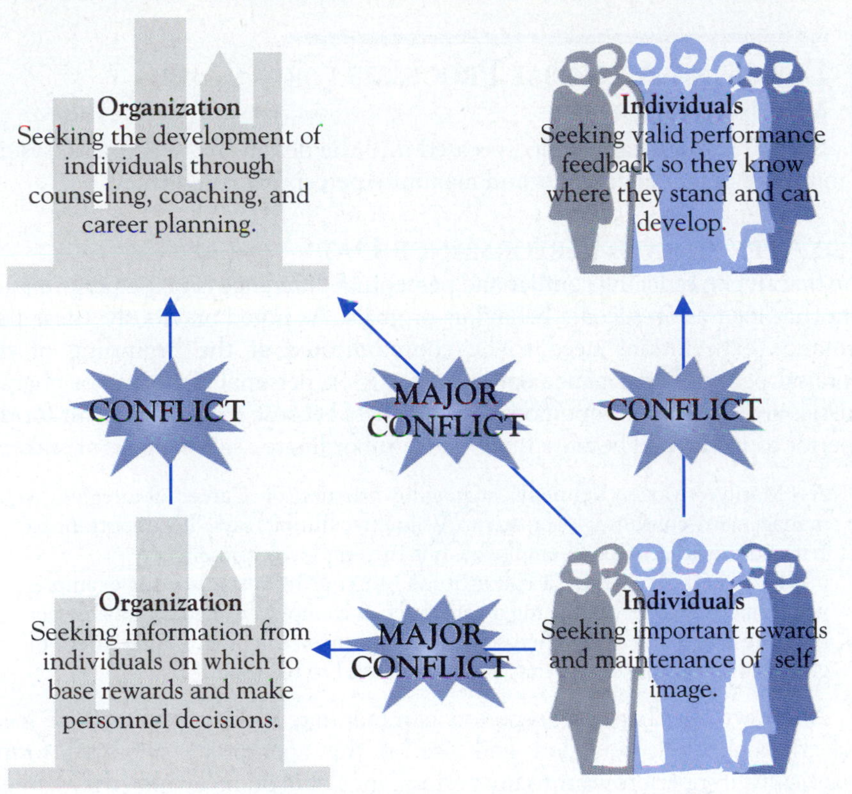

Organization
Seeking the development of
individuals through
counseling, coaching, and
career planning.

Individuals
Seeking valid performance
feedback so they know
where they stand and can
develop.

CONFLICT

MAJOR
CONFLICT

CONFLICT

Organization
Seeking information from
individuals on which to
base rewards and make
personnel decisions.

MAJOR
CONFLICT

Individuals
Seeking important rewards
and maintenance of self-
image.

SOURCE: Reprinted, by permission of the author, from "Performance Appraisal: Dilemmas
and Possibilities," by M. Beer, *Organizational Dynamics* (Winter 1981): 27 © 1981.

Initially at least, subordinates are not inclined to apologize for their behavior and seek ways to improve; in fact, they resist superiors' efforts to engage in problem solving. Consequently, superiors spend most of their time defending their appraisals and resisting subordinates' efforts to have their appraisals altered.

"It's a tough job, the equivalent of walking up to a person and saying, 'Here's what I think of your baby,'" says Robert Lefton, president of Psychological Associates, a consulting company that has provided training on how to give reviews to over 100 large companies. "It requires knowing how to handle fear and anger and a gamut of other emotions, which a lot of managers aren't comfortable with," he adds.

Increasingly, managers must do a better job of appraising employees—not only to help employees mature, but also to increase productivity and company loyalty. Comprehensive performance reviews also reduce the chances that a terminated employee who has been warned of unsatisfactory performance will sue the company.[8]

Even when good performance is involved, however, superiors still have to make evaluation decisions, and somebody may still end up looking like a poor performer. Because appraisals are uncomfortable yet necessary, seeking ways to make

**Managers would give feedback if
employees weren't so defensive.**

the process better is important. The areas of opportunity include the design of the appraisal system and modifying the characteristics of the performance appraisal interview.

LEARNING OBJECTIVE 2

Design appraisal processes for maximum results.

To reduce conflicts
- Use appropriate data
- Separate current and future appraisal
- Ensure fairness
- Empower employees
- Encourage participation
- Engage in reciprocal appraisals

DESIGNING APPRAISAL PROCESSES FOR MAXIMUM RESULTS

Several features can be incorporated into the design of the appraisal system to minimize appraisal conflicts and maximize perceptual congruence.

USE APPROPRIATE PERFORMANCE DATA

The first step in reducing conflict and perceptual difference is to use performance data that focuses on specific behaviors or goals. As noted previously, these performance expectations need to be communicated at the beginning of the appraisal period. Performance data that focus on personal attributes or characteristics are likely to prompt more defensiveness because they are difficult for the superior to justify and because more of the subordinate's self-image is at stake:

> As Marilyn Moats Kennedy, managing partner of Career Strategies, a management-consulting company in Wilmette, Illinois, says "It's important to critique the *behavior* of an employee, not the employee himself."
>
> "If you bark, 'You have a bad attitude,' to your receptionists, for example, you'll likely find yourself facing a very defensive employee. You'll probably get better results if you say, 'When someone steps up to the desk, I'd like them to get the distinct impression that you're delighted to see them.'"[9]

As shown in Chapter 9, superiors can facilitate specific performance feedback through their selection and use of the appropriate appraisal forms. Specifically, if superiors want to use performance data on behaviors, they can use a critical incident form or a behavioral observation method with specific numerical goals. Using these appraisal formats together would allow the supervisor to manage *what* subordinates are doing as well as *how* they are doing. On the other hand, if supervisors want to focus on goals, then an MBO format would be more appropriate.

SEPARATE CURRENT AND POTENTIAL PERFORMANCE APPRAISAL

Current performance may have little to do with a subordinate's performance potential, and the two should be separated in an evaluation. Supervisors, however, may unconsciously incorporate evaluations of potential into evaluations of current performance. Conversely, they may incorporate past performance into the evaluation of present performance. In either event, the appraisal of current performance is inappropriately an amalgamation of past, current, and/or potential performance.[10]

As a result, it is likely the appraisal will be unfair. Consider people with high potential. They may receive a lower and possibly unfair evaluation than equivalent performing peers because their supervisors have higher expectations of them. Conversely, adequate performers with low potential may be evaluated adversely because they don't have the ability of the high-potential people, which is unfair to employees who may have no interest in being promoted, yet perform adequately in their current job.

Part of the solution is to use **job-specific criteria** to evaluate current performance and then conduct a separate appraisal on potential. As discussed in the last chapter, the criteria for each job need to be based on job analysis.

Separating the two processes allows supervisors to avoid appraising the potential performance of employees not interested in promotion. And for those interested, *volunteering* to participate in an assessment center or other promotional process cues management that a person is interested in moving up in the organization. In fact, one study of assessment centers found that participation, rather than the evaluation rating received, was the single most important determinant of who did or did not get promoted. By separating the evaluation of current and potential performance and by allowing employees to self-nominate individual differences are recognized and incorporated in the appraisal process.[11]

ENSURE PROCEDURAL AND DISTRIBUTIVE FAIRNESS

To minimize the emotionally charged atmosphere that surrounds the performance appraisal process, managers also need to take steps to ensure that the process is perceived as fair and equitable. Performance appraisal procedures are viewed as fair to the extent that there is

- *Consistency*. Performance standards are applied consistently to all employees. Allowances are not made for workers with special problems, nor are high performers expected to carry more than their weight.
- *Familiarity*. The use of diaries to record worker outputs, frequent observation of performance, and management by "wandering around" increases a supervisor's job knowledge and consequently creates the impression that the manager and the appraisals are fair.
- *Soliciting Input*. Information regarding performance standards as well as strategies to attain them need to be solicited *prior* to evaluation. More important, this information should be *applied* at appropriate times.
- *Challenge/Rebut Evaluation*. Consistent with the problem-solving interview to be discussed in the next section, employees need to be able to challenge or rebut evaluations.

> Performance appraisals are seen as fair if they have these characteristics:

The outcome of performance appraisals is viewed as fair when outputs of the appraisal process are distributed fairly. For example, ratings need to be based on performance attained, and recommendations for salary and promotion need to be based on these ratings.[12]

EMPOWER EMPLOYEES

Part of the difficulty in managing the appraisal system is collecting and maintaining information on all employees. As the span of control increases in size, this task grows to unmanageable levels. One way to resolve this problem and simultaneously increase perceptions of fairness is to shift the responsibility for performance recordkeeping to the subordinate, as in the case of Chaparral Steel—in other words, empower the employee as described in Chapter 3. To enact this process, employees first need training in writing performance standards and in collecting and documenting performance information. In addition, the two-way communication process discussed above needs to operate effectively so employees feel free to renegotiate performance standards that have become obsolete or unattainable due to constraints.

> Organizations are empowering employees to do many things.

There are several advantages to delegating responsibility for performance planning, goal setting and recordkeeping to subordinates. First, they are no longer passive participants reacting to supervisor directives. Second, since it's their responsibility to identify performance hurdles and bring them to the attention of their manager, defensiveness is reduced. Third, the supervisor is free to manage and coach rather than police. Finally, the subordinate feels ownership over the process. The benefits to the organization are described in the opening feature on Chaparral Steel.

ENCOURAGE APPROPRIATE DEGREE OF PARTICIPATION

Recently, many companies have viewed worker participation as *the* performance elixir. It was felt, and still is, by some managers that allowing workers the opportunity to set or participate in the development of their own goals will result in higher commitment and performance. Research, however, has shown that participation, in and of itself does *not* lead to higher performance.

More important than the worker participation is the development of specific performance standards and an explanation for their existence. Participation is only useful if it helps employees identify an appropriate strategy to attain performance. That is, as long as performance standards are specific, time-bound, job relevant, and communicated, motivated employees will perform well.[13]

ENGAGE IN RECIPROCAL APPRAISALS

Reciprocal appraisals "level the playing field."

To encourage openness in the performance appraisal and to improve superior-subordinate relationships, subordinates can engage in appraisals of their superiors as well as themselves. Upward or reverse appraisals can help put into better balance, if not equalize, the power of the superior *vis-à-vis* the subordinate. Such a balance reduces the authoritarian character of the superior-subordinate relationship that contributes to defensiveness and avoidance in the appraisal.[14]

Organizations and superiors facilitate the upward appraisal process by providing forms for subordinates to use and by engaging in other human resource policies and procedures indicative of openness (for example, allowing employees to participate in decisions about their own pay increases or in analyzing their own jobs). Furthering this openness and power equalization in performance appraisal is a policy of self-appraisal. Self-appraisal is likely to result in more information for the superior, a more realistic appraisal of the subordinate's performance, and a greater acceptance of the final appraisal by subordinates and superiors.

THE PERFORMANCE APPRAISAL INTERVIEW

Choices in interview style can be made and preparations made that can enhance the effectiveness of the appraisal through the interview itself.

BEFORE THE INTERVIEW

Do before the interview:
- schedule in advance
- self-review
- gather relevant information

As emphasized throughout Chapter 9, performance appraisal is an ongoing process of which the interview is only one component. Prior to the interview, the supervisor and subordinate need to prepare.

SCHEDULE IN ADVANCE.   A week or two prior to the scheduled performance review, the supervisor should *personally* notify the ratee of the time, date, and place of the interview. Having a secretary schedule the interview increases the likelihood that the purpose and content of the session will be misunderstood. Sending a formal notice builds unneeded formality into the process and immediately shrouds the interview in ambiguity and mistrust. But most importantly, the interview will be more constructive if both parties have time to do their homework.

In setting up the interview, both parties should agree on the purpose and content of the interview. For example, will the subordinate have an opportunity to evaluate the performance of the supervisor, or will the evaluation be one-way? It is also useful, although possibly inconvenient, to select and use a neutral location for the interview. By holding the session in a neutral location, neither the supervisor nor the subordinate has a power advantage.

SELF-REVIEW.   If subordinates are empowered, advance notice will give them sufficient time to update their performance records and do a self-review. In situations where employees formally review their own performance, comparisons of self-ratings with ratings by the supervisor can actually be made by each party to the session and then used for subsequent discussion in the interview.

GATHER RELEVANT INFORMATION.   In preparing for the interview, the rater and ratee must gather all information that has any bearing on the discussions. Here, critical incident files of behavioral diaries can be reviewed. It's also important to review the employee's job description. An agenda can be developed to allow the ratee to study it and make additions or deletions.[15]

CHOOSE AN INTERVIEW STYLE

An effective interview session requires both coaching and counseling skills. Additionally, a supervisor needs to be able to listen and reflect back on what his or her subordinates are saying in regards to performance, its causes, and its outcomes.

TELL-AND-SELL.   The **tell-and-sell interview** lets subordinates know how well they are doing and sells them on the merits of setting specific goals for improvement (if needed). This interview is effective in improving performance, especially for subordinates with little desire for participation.[16] It may be most appropriate in providing evaluation; however, subordinates may become frustrated in trying to convince their superiors to listen to justifications for their performance levels.

TELL-AND-LISTEN.   This approach follows no rigid format but requires question-asking and listening skills on the rater's part. The **tell-and-listen interview** provides subordinates with the chance to participate and establish a dialogue with their superiors. Its purpose is to communicate supervisor's perceptions of subordinate's strengths and weaknesses and to let subordinates respond to those perceptions. Superiors summarize and paraphrase subordinates' responses but generally fail to establish goals for performance improvement. Consequently, the subordinates may feel better, but their performance may not change.

PROBLEM-SOLVING.   Because of the weaknesses of the approaches described above, it is often better for the rater to view the appraisal interview as a **problem-solving interview**. Here, an active and open dialogue is established between superior and subordinate. Perceptions are shared, and solutions to problems or differences are presented, discussed, and sought. Goals for improvement are also established mutually by superior and subordinate. Because this type of interview is generally more difficult for most superiors to do, training in problem solving is usually necessary and beneficial. Problem solving is also inappropriate when subordinates are performing adequately. The focus in that case should be on maintaining current performance and/or developing the employee for additional responsibilities.

MIXED INTERVIEW.   In reality, supervisors should be adaptive during the appraisal interview and the **mixed interview** allows this. Skills are needed for the tell-and-sell and problem-solving interviews, and to make the transition from one to the other. A desirable approach is to use the tell-and-sell interview for evaluation and the problem-solving interview for development. Separate interviews for each purpose, however, may not be feasible. Since corporate policies,

Types of performance appraisal interviews include

- tell-and-sell
- tell-and-listen
- problem-solving
- mixed

time, and expectations may prevent separation of purposes, a single interview must often accomplish both purposes. In this single interview, the subordinate may start out listening to the superior provide an appraisal of performance but then take a more active role in determining what and how performance improvements can be made (problem solving), concluding with agreed-upon goals for improvement.[17]

✳ EFFECTIVE FEEDBACK

Whether negative or positive, feedback is not always easy to provide. Fortunately, several characteristics of **effective feedback** have been determined.[18]

First, effective feedback is specific rather than general. Telling someone that he or she is dominating is probably not as useful as saying, "Just now you were not listening to what I said, but I felt I either had to agree with your arguments or face attack from you."

Second, effective feedback is focused on behavior rather than on the person. Referring to what a person does is more important than referring to what that person seems to be. A superior might say that a person talked more than anyone else at a meeting rather than that he or she is a loudmouth. The former allows for the possibility of change; the latter implies a fixed personality trait. Frustration only increases when people are reminded of shortcomings or physical characteristics they can do nothing about. At an extreme, workers may experience learned helplessness in which they give up trying to perform well because they know of no way to perform adequately.

Effective feedback also takes the receiver's needs into account. Feedback can be destructive when it serves only the evaluator's needs and fails to consider the needs of the person on the receiving end. It should be given to help, not to hurt.

Effective feedback is well-timed. In general, immediate feedback is most useful—depending on the person's readiness to hear it, the support available from others, and so on. Feedback is probably most effective when it is solicited rather than imposed. To get the most benefit, receivers should formulate questions for the evaluator to answer and actively seek feedback.

Sharing information rather than giving advice provides more effective feedback. In this way, receivers are free to decide for themselves on the changes to make in accordance with their own needs.

Providing only the amount of information the receiver can use rather than the amount the evaluator would like to give is also a part of effective feedback. Overloading a person with feedback reduces the possibility that he or she will use it effectively. An evaluator who gives more feedback than can be used is most likely satisfying a personal need rather than helping the other person.

Effective feedback concerns what is said or done and how—not why. Telling people what their motivations or intentions are tends to alienate them and contributes to a climate of resentment, suspicion, and distrust; it does not contribute to learning or development. Assuming knowledge of why a person says or does something is dangerous. If evaluators are uncertain of receivers' motives or intent, the uncertainty itself is feedback and should be revealed.

Finally, effective feedback is checked to ensure clear communication. One way is to have the receiver try to rephrase the feedback to see if it corresponds to what the evaluator had in mind. No matter what the intent, feedback is often threatening and thus subject to considerable distortion or misinterpretation.

Of course, the whole process of feedback is easier if you are comfortable giving feedback. Complete the following survey in Exhibit 10.2. To determine your comfort level. The lower your score, the more comfortable you are.

Effective feedback is

- specific
- behavior-focused
- sensitive to ratee
- focused on controllable factors
- solicited
- sharing information
- well-timed
- avoids information overload
- tells how, not why
- clear communication

At Federal Express, employees are told what's expected, what's rewarded, and how to do things.

How comfortable are you at giving feedback to others?

EXHIBIT 10.2
PERFORMANCE APPRAISAL DISCOMFORT SCALE

Indicate the degree of discomfort *you* would feel in the following situations. Answer as candidly as possible by indicating what is true for you. Use the following scale to write in one number in the blank to the left of each item.

5 = High discomfort
4 = Some discomfort
3 = Undecided
2 = Very little discomfort
1 = No discomfort

_____ 1. Telling an employee who is also a friend that he or she must stop coming to work late.

_____ 2. Telling an employee that his or her work is only satisfactory, when you know that he or she expects an above-satisfactory rating.

_____ 3. Talking to an employee about his or her performance on the job.

_____ 4. Conducting a formal performance appraisal interview with an ineffective employee.

_____ 5. Asking an employee if he or she has any comments about your rating of his or her performance.

_____ 6. Telling an employee who has problems in dealing with other employees that he or she should do something about it (e.g., take a course, read a book).

_____ 7. Telling a male subordinate that his performance must improve.

_____ 8. Responding to an employee who is upset over your rating of his or her performance.

_____ 9. Having to terminate someone for poor performance.

_____ 10. Letting an employee give his or her point of view regarding a problem with performance.

_____ 11. Giving a satisfactory rating to an employee who has done a satisfactory (but not exceptional) job.

_____ 12. Letting a subordinate talk during an appraisal interview.

_____ 13. Being challenged to justify an evaluation in the middle of an appraisal interview.

_____ 14. Being accused of playing favorites in the rating of your staff.

_____ 15. Recommending that an employee be discharged.

_____ 16. Telling an employee that his or her performance can be improved.

_____ 17. Telling an employee that you will not tolerate his or her taking extended coffee breaks.

_____ 18. Warning an ineffective employee that unless performance improves, he or she will be discharged.

_____ 19. Telling a female subordinate that her performance must improve.

_____ 20. Encouraging an employee to evaluate his or her own performance.

SOURCE: J. R. Abbott & H. J. Bernardin, "The Development of a Scale of Self-Efficacy," Working paper, Florida Atlantic University, 1994. Based on P. Villanova, H. J. Bernardin, S. A. Dahmus, and R. L. Sims, "Rater Leniency and Performance Appraisal Discomfort," *Educational and Psychological Measurement* 53 (1993): 789–799.

INTERVIEW FOLLOW-UP

Even with the most useful feedback, follow-up is essential to ensure that the behavioral contract negotiated during the interview is fulfilled. Because changing behavior is hard work, supervisors and subordinates both tend to put the agreement on the back burner. Consequently, a supervisor should verify that the subordinate knows what's expected, has a strategy to perform as desired, and realizes the consequences of good or bad behavior.

Additionally, immediate reinforcement for any new behavior on the job that matches desired objectives is important. If reinforcement is delayed, new behavior is less likely to become a habit. Reinforcement can be as simple as a pat on the back or a nice comment ("That was nice work, George"), or as tangible as a note placed in the employee's file indicating performance improvement.

There can be many causes of performance deficiencies: it pays to diagnose.

Performance gaps may be identified through:

• goals
• peer/departmental comparisons
• time comparisons

Symptoms of performance problems are many as shown in Exhibit 10.3.

Possible determinants of performance deficiencies are many.

Possible determinants of performance deficiencies are many.

DIAGNOSING PERFORMANCE

While the interview provides a mechanism by which performance information can be exchanged, it is only one component of an effective behavioral change process. For the appraisal to work well in the process of improving performance, the information on which the interview is based must be accurate. This means that performance gaps or deficiencies need to be identified as soon as possible and the cause of the deficiency accurately pinpointed.

IDENTIFYING GAPS IN PERFORMANCE

As discussed in Chapter 9, job performance is appraised in terms of attributes, behaviors, and outcomes and goals. These factors determine performance and identify any gaps. For example, outcomes and goals can identify deficiencies by showing how well an employee does in relation to the goals set. If an employee had a performance goal of reducing the scrap rate by 10 percent but actually reduced it by only 5 percent, a performance gap exists. The discrepancy between set goals and actual outcomes can thus be used to spot gaps. This method is valid as long as the goals are not contradictory and can be quantified in measurable terms *and* the subordinate's performance can be measured in the terms in which the goals are set.[19] Exhibit 10.3 is a checklist of symptoms associated with performance problems: more than one "yes" indicates a need to probe deeper.

In addition to comparing performance to relevant standards, the performance of employees, units, or departments can be compared with one another. For example, organizations with several divisions often measure the overall performance of each division by comparing it with all other divisions. The divisions that are ranked on the bottom become identified as problem areas (that is, they have performance gaps). Efforts to improve performance can then be expected from these divisions.

The final method by which gaps can be identified is by comparison over time. For example, a manager who sold 1,000 record albums last month but only 800 albums this month appears to have a performance gap. Although performance has declined, the supervisor needs to determine whether this gap represents a deficiency that should be or can be corrected or a normal fluctuation. The month in which 1,000 albums were sold may have been the peak of the buying season. During the second month, the employee may have had to attend an important conference vital to longer-run record sales.

Regardless of the method used to discover whether a performance deficiency exists, once detected, managers want to remove it. If they hope to improve their employees' performance, however, they must begin by examining the causes underlying any actual gaps.

IDENTIFYING THE CAUSES OF DEFICIENCIES

To uncover the reasons for performance deficiencies, a number of questions can be asked, based on a model of the determinants of employee behavior in organizations.[20] This model enables the human resource manager to diagnose deficiencies and correct them in a systematic way. In general, the model says that employees perform well if the following determinants are present:

• Ability
• Interest in doing the job
• Opportunity to grow and advance
• Clearly defined goals
• Feedback on how well they are doing

EXHIBIT 10.3
CHECKLIST FOR IDENTIFYING PERFORMANCE PROBLEMS

Read the following questions about an employee's performance. If you are thinking "yes" in response to a question, place a check mark next to that item. If not, leave it blank.

Do Peers Complain That

_____ 1. She is not treating them fairly?
_____ 2. He is not carrying his own weight?
_____ 3. She is rude?
_____ 4. He is argumentative and confrontational?
_____ 5. She is all talk and no action?

Do Customers

_____ 1. Always ask for someone else to help them?
_____ 2. Complain about her attitude?
_____ 3. Complain that he has made promises to them that he's never fulfilled?
_____ 4. Say she is bad-mouthing you, the organization, or its products?
_____ 5. Complain that he is too pushy?

Do You

_____ 1. Find it difficult to get your own work done because you spend so much time with him on his problems and mistakes?
_____ 2. Worry about what she will say to customers and clients?
_____ 3. Check his work often because you are afraid of mistakes?
_____ 4. Do work yourself that you should have delegated to her?
_____ 5. Assign work to others because they can do it faster or better than he can?
_____ 6. Hear about her mistakes from your boss or others?
_____ 7. Sometimes find out that he has lied to you or stretched the truth?
_____ 8. Seldom think of her when you're deciding who should get an important assignment?

Does He/She

_____ 1. Infrequently complete assignments on time?
_____ 2. Often show up to work late or not at all?
_____ 3. Always have an excuse for poor performance?
_____ 4. Wait to be assigned additional work rather than asking for more work when an assignment is completed?
_____ 5. Rarely complete assignments in the way you want?

- Rewards for performing well
- Punishments for performing poorly
- Power to get resources to do the job

Exhibit 10.4 shows these determinants and the specific questions to ask in locating causes. Negative responses indicate that the item is probably a cause, and based on a series of such responses, the likely causes for a performance deficiency begin to take shape. Discuss why each of these determinants is important.

EXHIBIT 10.4
DIAGNOSING PERFORMANCE DEFICIENCIES

Check which of the following factors affecting an individual's performance or behavior apply to the situation you are analyzing.

		YES	NO
I.	*Skills, Knowledge, and Abilities of the Individual*		
	A. Does the individual have the skills to do as expected?		
	B. Has the individual performed as expected before?		
II.	*Personality, Interests, and Preferences of the Individual*		
	A. Does the individual have the personality or interest to perform as expected?		
	B. Does the individual clearly perceive what's actually involved in performing as expected?		
III.	*Opportunity for the Individual*		
	A. Does the individual have a chance to grow and use valued skills and abilities?		
	B. Does the organization offer career paths to the individual?		
IV.	*Goals for the Individual*		
	A. Are there goals established?		
	B. Are the goals very specific?		
	C. Are the goals clear?		
	D. Are the goals difficult?		
V.	*Uncertainty for the Individual*		
	A. Is the individual certain about what rewards are available?		
	B. Is the individual certain about what to do?		
	C. Is the individual certain about what others expect?		
	D. Is the individual certain about job responsibilities and levels of authority?		
VI.	*Feedback to the Individual*		
	A. Does the employee get information about what is right and wrong (quality or quantity) with performance?		
	B. Does the information received tell the employee how to improve performance?		
	C. Does the employee get information frequently?		
	D. Is there a delay between the time the employee performs and receiving information on that performance?		
	E. Can the information be easily interpreted by the employee?		
VII.	*Consequences to the Individual*		
	A. Is it punishing to do as expected (immediate)?		
	B. Is it punishing to do as expected (long-term)?		
	C. Do more positive consequences result from taking alternative action (immediate)?		
	D. Do more positive consequences result from taking alternative action (long-term)?		
	E. Are there no apparent consequences for performing as desired?		
	F. Are there no positive consequences for performing as desired?		
VIII.	*Power for the Individual*		
	A. Can the individual mobilize resources to get the job done?		
	B. Can the individual influence others to get them to do what is needed?		
	C. Is the individual highly visible to others higher up in the organization?		

SOURCE: This format is based on R. F. Mager and P. Pipe, *Analyzing Performance Problems* or *"You Really Oughta Wanna"* (Belmont, Calif.: Fearon Pittman, 1970).

THE ATTRIBUTION PROCESS

The process people use to explain their behavior and the behavior of others is called an **attribution process**. Individuals attribute their and others' behavior to various causes. Understanding the attribution processes that individuals use facilitates predicting what causes and responses managers are likely to attach to the performance deficiencies they see in their subordinates.

In relation to performance, managers attribute causes of subordinates deficiencies to either the subordinates themselves, **internal attribution**, or to the subordinates' environment, **external attribution**. Internal attributions include low effort (motivation) or low ability; external attributions include task interference, back luck, lack of organizational rewards, and poor supervision. Managers are more likely to make internal attributions to the extent that the employee (1) does not perform poorly on other tasks, (2) performs poorly when other employees perform well on the same task, and (3) has performed poorly on the same task in the past. Managers are also likely to focus on motivation over ability if an employee has peformed the task adequately in the past but isn't performing adequately now.[21]

Whether the manager makes internal or external attributions influences the strategy for performance improvement likely to be selected by the manager.[22] If internal attributions are made, the manager is more likely to select strategies aimed at changing the subordinate such as retraining, termination, or reprimands. If external attributions are made, the manager will likely select strategies that modify the environment such as job redesign or rewards and punishments.

To what do you attribute your success in school?

Internal attribution is the belief that one's self is the cause.
External attribution is the belief that others are the cause.

STRATEGIES FOR IMPROVEMENT

When deficiencies are found, companies can do many things to improve employees' performance.

LEARNING OBJECTIVE 4

Identify strategies to improve performance.

POSITIVE REINFORCEMENT SYSTEM

The positive reinforcement system is based on reinforcement theory in employee motivation and performance.[23] The following is an illustration of the positive reinforcement system.[24]

Positive reinforcement system involves the use of positive rewards to increase the occurrence of the desired performance. It is based on two fundamental principles: (1) people perform in ways that they find most rewarding to them; and (2) by providing the proper rewards, it is possible to improve performance. A positive reinforcement (PR) system or program focuses on the behavior that leads to desired results rather than on the results. It uses rewards rather than punishment or the threat of punishment to influence that behavior and attempts to link specific behaviors to specific rewards. This model operates according to the **law of effect**, which states that behavior that leads to a positive result tends to be repeated while behavior that leads to a neutral or negative result tends not to be repeated. Thus an effort is made to link behavior to its consequences.

A PR system is installed by four basic steps, as shown in Exhibit 10.5: (1) conducting a performance audit, (2) establishing performance standards or goals, (3) giving feedback to employees about their performance, and (4) offering employees praise or other rewards tied directly to performance.[25]

Strategies for improving performance include:

• positive reinforcement
• positive discipline programs
• employee assistance programs
• employee counseling
• negative behavioral strategies

Positive reinforcement is the use of positive rewards to increase the occurrence of desired performance.

Here are the four basic steps in a PR system:

CONDUCTING A PERFORMANCE AUDIT. Performance audits examine how well jobs are being performed. Without audits, many managers believe that their operations are going better than they actually are. Emery Air Freight

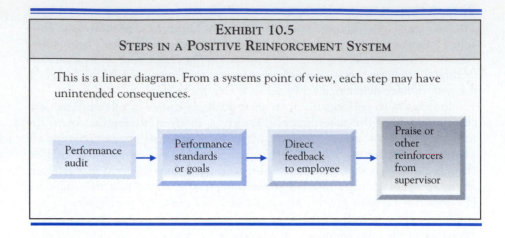

EXHIBIT 10.5
STEPS IN A POSITIVE REINFORCEMENT SYSTEM

This is a linear diagram. From a systems point of view, each step may have unintended consequences.

Performance audit → Performance standards or goals → Direct feedback to employee → Praise or other reinforcers from supervisor

Corporation conducted a performance audit on the way it was shipping packages. The cost of freight is considerably reduced if all the small packages going to a particular city are put in large containers. The managers involved in this part of the operation estimated that large containers were used in shipping about 90 percent of the time. The audit showed, however, that the actual figure was only 45 percent.[26] If possible, workers should be involved in performance audits, since they often know more about the job than anyone else.

ESTABLISHING PERFORMANCE STANDARDS OR GOALS. Standards are the minimum levels of performance accepted. They should be set after a performance audit and tied directly to the job. The goals should be measurable and attainable, and the standards should be challenging but not impossible to reach—perfection is never possible. Standards are best formed on the basis of observation and common sense, and they should be precise. "Better identification with the organization" and "increased job satisfaction" are too general to be standards.

Where possible, the workers should participate in establishing standards. At Emery Air Freight, the employees in the Chicago customer service department set and reached a standard higher than the one management would have set for giving customer answers within a specified period.[27] However, time limitations can preclude giving employees all the information they need to establish a reasonable standard.

GIVING FEEDBACK TO EMPLOYEES ABOUT THEIR PERFORMANCE. The third step in a positive reinforcement program is to give workers the basic data they need in order to keep track of their own work. The standards of performance for many jobs are not clearly stated; even when clearly stated, they are seldom available to the worker. A woman in an insurance company described her routine as follows: "I glance through the form to see if it is completely filled out. Then I separate the blue copies from the yellow copies and put them in different piles." When asked the purpose of the form, how it was used, and where the different copies went, she reported that she did not know. She had no idea if the information on the form was accurate, and she did not know the consequences for incomplete or incorrectly filled out forms. All she knew was that each line of the form had to have something on it or be returned to another department.

Performance standards are ineffective without constant measurement and feedback. The feedback should be neutral rather than evaluative or judgmental and, if possible, should come directly to the worker rather than to the supervisor.

Performance should be measured against standards, and an employee should be given direct feedback.

Prompt, direct feedback refers, of course, to knowledge of results, an important learning tool. Feedback allows the worker to know whether performance is improving, remaining the same, or getting worse.

OFFERING EMPLOYEES PRAISE OR OTHER REWARDS TIED DIRECTLY TO PERFORMANCE. As explained earlier, positive reinforcement involves the use of positive rewards to increase the occurrence of the desired performance. The fourth step in a positive reinforcement program—offering employees praise or other rewards tied to performance—is the most important one. If the reward is praise, it should be expressed in specific quantitative terms. "Keep up the good work, Chris" is too general. A better form of praise is "Chris, I liked the imagination you used in getting the product packed. You are running fairly consistently at 97 percent of standard. After watching you, I can understand why."

One of the most common rewards is money. Although money is very effective as a motivator, many organizations cannot afford to use it that way often. Other rewards can be just as effective, though. They include praise and recognition tied to the specific job behavior, the opportunity to choose activities, the opportunity to personally measure work improvement, and the opportunity to influence both co-workers and management.

Rewards for specific performance should be given as soon as possible after the behavior has taken place. Reinforcement should be more frequent at the beginning but can become less frequent and more unpredictable after the desired performance level is reached.

There are several different types of reward schedules, among them continuous reinforcement and partial reinforcement. Under **continuous reinforcement**, the employee is reinforced every time the correct performance occurs. When this schedule is used, performance improves rapidly but can regress just as rapidly when the reinforcement is removed. In addition, managers find it difficult or impossible to continuously reward performance. Therefore, managers should use **partial reinforcement**, rewarding correct behavior only part of the time. There are a number of partial reinforcement schedules, perhaps the most effective being the variable ratio schedule. Under this schedule, reinforcement is given after an average number of desired responses but not precisely at that average point; rather, the time of dispensation varies somewhere around the average point so that it cannot be predicted exactly.[28] In most organizations, pay occurs on a fixed-interval schedule such as once a week or once a month; pay increases and promotions occur on a variable-interval schedule; and praise, recognition, and similar rewards occur on a partial reinforcement schedule.

The six basic rules for using reinforcement are as follows:

1. *Do not reward everyone the same way.* Using a defined objective or standard, give more rewards to the better performers.
2. *Recognize that failure to respond also has reinforcing consequences.* Managers influence subordinates by what they don't do as well as by what they do; lack of reward can thus influence behavior. Managers frequently find the job of differentiating among workers unpleasant but necessary. One way to differentiate is to reward some and withhold rewards from others.
3. *Tell people what they must do to be rewarded.* If employees have standards against which to measure the job, they can arrange their own feedback system to let them make self-judgments about their work. They can then adjust their work patterns accordingly.
4. *Tell people what they are doing wrong.* Few people like to fail; most want to get positive rewards. A manager who witholds rewards from subordinates should give them a clear idea of why the rewards are not forthcoming.

Nobody knows better than Mary Kay Ash, Chairman Emeritus of Mary Kay Cosmetics, how to motivate a sales force. She has mastered the true power of employee praise and recognition!

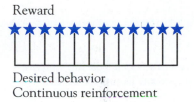

Reward

Desired behavior
Continuous reinforcement

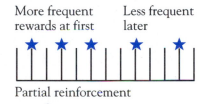

More frequent rewards at first   Less frequent later

Partial reinforcement

These six basic rules for reinforcing behavior are important to know and use:

The employees can then adjust their behavior accordingly rather than waste time trying to discover what behavior will be rewarded.

5. *Do not punish anyone in front of others*. Constructive criticism is useful in eliminating undesired behavior; so also is punishment, when necessary. However, criticizing or punishing anyone in front of others lowers the individual's self-respect and self-esteem. Furthermore, other members of the work group may sympathize with the punished employee and resent the supervisor.

6. *Be fair*. Make the consequences equal to the behavior. Do not cheat an employee out of just rewards; if someone is a good worker, say so. Some managers find it difficult to praise; others find it difficult to counsel or tell an employee about what is being done wrong. A person who is overrewarded may feel guilty, and one who is underrewarded may become angry.[29]

When the managers and employees at Emery Air Freight understood that only 45 percent of the packages were being shipped in containers, and feedback and positive reinforcement were given, the workers soon hit the standard of 95 percent. The change resulted in savings of about $65,000 per year.[30]

In summary, the manager using the positive reinforcement model should first examine the job (audit the performance) to determine standards, preferably with the assistance of the employees. Then the manager should establish methods of getting direct feedback to employees about individual or group performance. Finally, the manager should provide positive reinforcement as employees come closer to the standard, shifting perhaps from a continuous to a partial reinforcement schedule as they get very close to the standard. At the beginning, the manager might have to look carefully for even small changes in behavior in order to give positive reinforcement; otherwise, behavior might not improve.

POSITIVE DISCIPLINE PROGRAMS

Some organizations improve performance through their use of positive discipline or nonpunitive discipline.[31] The essential aspects of positive discipline programs include the following:

> When disciplinary discussions have failed to produce the desired changes, management places the individual on a one-day, "decision-making leave." The company pays the employee for the day to demonstrate the organization's desire to see him or her remain a member of the organization and to eliminate the resentment and hostility that punitive actions usually produce. But tenure with the organization is conditional on the individual's decision to solve the immediate problem and make a "total performance commitment" to good performance on the job. The employee is instructed to return on the day following the leave with a decision either to change and stay or to quit and find more satisfying work elsewhere.[32]

This program really puts the responsibility for the employee's behavior into the hands of the employee. It tells the employee, however, that the company cares and will keep the employee as long as he or she makes a commitment to do well. If the employee makes the commitment, the company has a good employee. If the employee decides to leave, he or she is not really able to blame the company. Thus far, this type of program appears to work.[33]

EMPLOYEE ASSISTANCE PROGRAMS

Employee Assistance Programs (EAPs) are specifically designed to assist employees with chronic personal problems that hinder their job performance and attendance. EAPs are often used with employees who are alcoholics or who have severe domestic problems. Since the job may be partly responsible for these problems, some employers are taking the lead in establishing EAPs to help affected workers.[34]

A company that establishes an employee assistance program generally thinks that it has a responsibility toward employees and that employees should be given a chance to correct any undesirable job behavior. Helping alcoholic employees also makes good economic sense, because the average cost to the employer in absenteeism, reduced productivity, accidents in the workplace, and use of the company medical plan is enormous—about 25 percent of the alcoholic's salary. Furthermore, about 65 to 80 percent of those who receive treatment for chemical dependency return to the work force and do what their supervisors consider a satisfactory job. Nevertheless, employees must also help themselves. If they fail to participate in an EAP or recover through other means, employers may have no choice but to dismiss them. The philosophy of most EAPs is to help individuals help themselves within a context of fairness yet firmness.

While EAPs providing assistance in alcohol and drug abuse are most common, organizations also establish EAPs for marital and family problems, mental disorders, financial problems, stress, dependent-care programs, bereavement counseling, eating disorders, weight control, smoking cessation, and AIDS support group meetings.[35]

To be successful, an employee assistance program should possess the following attributes:

- A policy statement (see the feature, "Managing Human Resources: A Drug-Free Workplace Policy")
- Top management backing
- Union or employee support
- Confidentiality
- Easy access
- Trained supervisors
- Trained union steward, if in a union setting
- Insurance
- Availability of numerous services for assistance and referral
- Skilled, professional leadership
- Systems for monitoring, assessing, and revising

> **DID YOU KNOW?**
>
> Some 20 million Americans abuse alcohol and more than 100,000 die prematurely from alcohol-related causes.

A good employee assistance program should have these characteristics:

Even though EAPs provide valuable assistance, many employees in need fail to use the programs unless faced with the alternative of being terminated. When so confronted, however, the success rate of those attending EAPs is high. The results can mean substantial gains in employee job performance and reductions in absenteeism and insurance claims. For the 67 employees receiving EAP treatment in one study, the total number of lost work days dropped 29 percent, from 476 days before treatment to 341 days following treatment. The study also found that after EAP participation:

- Combined lost work time was reduced by 18 percent—from 117 instances to 97 instances.
- The cost of health insurance claims declined 26 percent—from a total $36,472 to $27,122.
- Work suspensions dropped from five to three; written warnings decreased from eight to seven; and the number of job-related accidents went from seven to three.[37]

IT is the policy of XYZ, Inc., to create and maintain a drug-free environment in the workplace, as required by the *Drug-Free Workplace Act of 1988*. The use of controlled substances* is inconsistent with the professional and responsible behavior we expect of employees, subjects all employees and visitors to our facilities to unacceptable safety risks, and undermines XYZ's ability to operate effectively and efficiently. Therefore, the employees of XYZ are strictly prohibited from engaging in the unlawful manufacture, distribution, dispensation, possession, sale, or use of a controlled substance at the workplace or while conducting XYZ business off the company's premises. Such unlawful conduct is also prohibited during nonworking time to the extent that it (1) impairs, in the opinion of the management of XYZ, the employee's ability to perform his or her job and (2) affects the company's reputation or threatens its integrity, also in the opinion of XYZ's management.

In order to educate the employees about the dangers of drug abuse, the company has established a drug-free awareness program. Periodically, employees will be required to attend informational sessions during which the dangers of drug abuse, XYZ's policy regarding drugs, and the availability of counseling and the company's employee assistance plan will be discussed.

Employees who are convicted of offenses involving controlled substances in the workplace (including employees who plead "nolo contendere"—that is, no contest) must inform the human resources department within five days of the conviction or plea. Employees who violate any aspect of this policy are subject to disciplinary action, up to and including termination from the company. They may be required, at the company's discretion, to participate in and successfully complete a drug-abuse treatment or rehabilitation program as a condition of continued employment.[36]

*Controlled substances are identified in Schedules I through V of Section 202 of the *Federal Controlled Substances Act*. They include marijuana, cocaine, heroin and morphine, as well as barbiturates and amphetamines.

Employee assistance programs can position the organization and the employee on the same side of this difficult issue. Organizations are finding that effective EAPs can make drug testing, which has been controversial among the work force, a nonevent:

> Both Mobil and Campbell Soup strongly emphasize counseling for drug users, but insist they're not doing so in order to sell testing. Mobil is moving more vigorously to use its plan to stop and treat drug abuse. Valley Bank says its supportive get-help policy has made drug testing a nonevent with employees. American Airlines says assistance plans are more effective than testing in attempts to curb drug abuse.[38]

EMPLOYEE COUNSELING

To change the habits of chronically absent employees. McGraw Edison has devised an innovative counseling program that stresses problem-solving and goal-setting techniques. This individual approach focuses on the "5 to 10 percent of the work force" that has a history of absenteeism. Before beginning the actual counseling with individual employees, supervisors take the following steps:

- *Identify the consistently worst offenders.* Make a list of all employees who have a record of repeated absences, regardless of the "presumed legitimacy or the underlying reasons" for missing work.

- *Centralize the absenteeism data.* Records and information should be accumulated, analyzed, and maintained in one central location.
- *Collect long-term data.* Absenteeism records on individuals should be kept for a sufficiently long period to show that a clear pattern exists.

Once the decision is made to meet with the employee, supervisors then do the following:

- Examine the attendance record with the employee.
- Make sure the employee is aware of the severity of the problem, as well as the organization's attendance standards.
- Prepare a brief, accurate memo at the session's end outlining the problem, noting the reasons given by the employee, and specifying whether or not the employee responded with a desire to improve.

If the first session has not produced a significant change, a second counseling session should be scheduled. Participants in this session should include the worker's supervisor, the employee, a union representative (if applicable), and higher-management officials. An upper-level manager should be present to ensure that due process protection (Chapter 16) is provided for the employee. Results of the second counseling session should also be documented.

If the employee shows no improvement after the second session, another session can be held, which should again include an upper-level manager. At this stage, the "decision to meet the expected standard of attendance and continuity of employment" should be placed directly on the employee. To dramatize the importance and seriousness of the situation, the employee might be requested to take one-day decision-making leave to decide whether he or she wishes to resign or to commit to a long-term program of positive improvement. If no sign of improvement is shown after this step, discharging the employee may be necessary.

Helping employees improve may not always work, but it can provide support for dismissal decisions.

NEGATIVE BEHAVIORAL STRATEGIES

While most employees want to conduct themselves in a manner that is acceptable to the organization and their co-workers, problems of absenteeism, poor work performance, and rule violation do arise.

Punishment is commonly used in many organizations because of its perceived ability to correct these problems. Discipline or punishment is an effective management tool for the following reasons:

- Discipline alerts the marginal employee that his or her low performance is unacceptable and a change in behavior is warranted.
- Discipline has vicarious reinforcing power. When one person is punished, it signals other employees regarding expected performance and behavioral conduct.
- If the discipline is viewed as appropriate by other employees, it may increase their motivation, morale, and performance.[39]

A recent study in a retail store showed that managers who used the organization's disciplinary system more frequently than their peers had higher department performance ratings.[40] One reason is that individuals in a group rely on one another to learn appropriate behavior. As a result, employees model the behaviors of successful peers and impose group norms on low performers.[41]

Punishment, however, may not always be effective. Employees can resent the punishment and become angry. Their performance may get even worse. The negative effects of punishment can be reduced by incorporating several **hot-stove principles**, including the following:

- *Provide ample and clear warning.* Many organizations have clearly defined disciplinary steps. For example, the first offense might elicit an oral warning; the second offense, a written warning; the third offense, a disciplinary layoff; the fourth offense, discharge.
- *Administer the discipline as quickly as possible.* If a long time elapses between the ineffective behavior and the discipline, the employee may not know what the discipline is for.
- *Administer the same discipline for the same behavior for everyone, every time.* Discipline has to be administered fully and consistently.
- *Administer the discipline impersonally.* Discipline should be based on a specific behavior.

These are the "hot stove principles:" ➝

Because the immediate supervisor or manager plays the integral role in administering discipline, the human resource department and the organization should do the following to increase the discipline's effectiveness:

Here's how the HR department can help line managers: ➝

- Involve managers and supervisors in the selection of their employees.
- Educate managers and supervisors about the organization's disciplinary policies and train them to administer the policies.
- Set up standards that are equitable to employees and that managers and supervisors can easily and consistently implement.

Taking these steps not only reduces the likely negative effects generally associated with disciplines, but also helps ensure that employee rights are respected (discussed further in Chapter 16). This is further guaranteed with the establishment of fair work rules and policies that are consistently applied and enforced.[42]

WHEN NOTHING ELSE WORKS

Helping employees—especially the problem ones—improve their work performance is a tough job. It's easy to get frustrated and to wonder if you're not just spinning your wheels. Even when we want it to work, it sometimes doesn't work. Still, when you conclude that "nothing works," you're really saying that it's no longer worth your time and energy to help the employee improve. This conclusion should not be made in haste since the organization has already invested a great deal of time and money in the selection and training of this employee. However, there are some situations where more drastic steps may be needed.

- Performance actually gets worse.
- There's a little change but not enough.
- There is no change in the problem behavior.
- Drastic changes in behavior occur immediately but improvements don't last.

If, after repeated warnings and counseling, performance does not improve, there are four last recourses.

There are still many things to do if performance fails to improve:

- transfer
- restructure
- terminate
- neutralize

TRANSFERS.   Sometimes there is just not a good match between an employee and a job. If, however, the employee has useful skills and abilities, it may be beneficial to transfer the employee. Transferring is appropriate if the employee's skill deficiency would have little or no impact on the new position. The concern with transfers is that there must be a job available for which the problem employee is qualified.

RESTRUCTURING.   Some jobs are particularly unpleasant or onerous. For these positions, the solution may be redesigning the job, rather than replacing the employee. It may also make sense to redesign a position to take advantage of an employee's special strengths. If an employee has extraordinary technical expertise, it may be advantageous to utilize this expertise instead of having the employee perform routine tasks.

TERMINATION. While human resource policies vary across organizations and industries, termination is generally warranted for dishonesty, habitual absenteeism, substance abuse, and insubordination, including flatly refusing to do certain things requested and consistently low productivity that cannot be corrected through training. Unfortunately, termination, even for legitimate reasons, is unpleasant. In addition to the administrative hassles, documentation, and paper work involved, supervisors often feel guilty about being the "bad guy." And the thought of sitting down with an employee and delivering the bad news makes most supervisors anxious. As a result, they continue to put off the action and justify this by saying they won't be able to find a "better" replacement. Still, when one considers the consequences of job errors, drunkenness, or "being high" on the job, termination may be cost effective. Employee rights regarding termination are discussed in Chapter 16.

NEUTRALIZING. **Neutralizing** problem employee situations involves restructuring an employee's job in such a way that the areas of needed improvement have as little impact as possible. Because group morale may suffer when an ineffective employee is given special treatment, neutralizing should be avoided whenever possible.

However, it is a fact of organizational life that neutralizing may be practical when a terminating process is time-consuming and cumbersome, or when an employee is close to retiring. In neutralizing the employee, a manager shouldn't harass the employee, hoping that he or she will quit or transfer, but should assign the employee tasks that are not critical, but in which he or she can be productive.

INTERNATIONAL COMPARISONS

To understand what is distinctive about the U.S. culture, 40 international managers (all non-U.S. nationals who were familiar with the U.S. business culture) were interviewed and asked to identify cultural aspects that underlie the U.S. system of management. Of the 40 participants, 36 felt that a strong commitment to the philosophy of meritocracy is a distinctively American societal value. **Meritocracy** emphasizes fairness in evaluating people on their work-related contributions. The managers also noted the short-term orientation in America as emphasized by annual appraisals based solely on current performance.

In other cultures, meritocracy is not so firmly established as a guiding principle. In its place one finds more concern for status, family ties, and loyalty to one's supervisor or organization. In other cultures, recent performance is not always the most important criteria. Behavior over time, loyalty, and the potential for the future are emphasized much more.[43]

There is also evidence that U.S. managers believe in a "Master of Destiny" viewpoint where, if a person works hard and has the ability and motivation to perform, he or she will be able to advance in a company. A more fatalistic view predominates in many other countries. That is, people are born into a certain class, and they are not able, no matter what they do, to improve their standing. In such a culture, there may be no need for a performance management system.[44]

These are international cultural differences in performance appraisal:

Americans also have very specific ideas about performance appraisal criteria. For example, management guru Peter Drucker writes that "An employer has no business with a man's personality. Employment is a specific contract calling for specific performance and for nothing else."[45] As will be discussed in the following sections, other societies base performance judgments much more on the "whole man or woman" than on actual job performance.

THE PACIFIC RIM COUNTRIES

While actual practices vary by country, most Pacific Rim countries use informal and formal appraisal processes to develop and reward employee performance. However, there appears to be less reliance on sophisticated formalistic systems than in U.S. companies. That is, most dialogue on performance occurs informally on either a one-on-one or group basis, rather than in a formal review session.

KOREA. In Korea, performance appraisal systems are in place in almost all large and most small companies. Since promotions are based primarily on seniority, performance appraisal is conducted primarily for purposes of counseling and development. The scope of the appraisal varies with the organization, with some firms approaching the process formally, almost ritualistically, and others approaching it very informally.

Many Koreans believe the cooperative nature of work makes it impossible to differentiate performance levels among employees with any degree of accuracy. As a result, factors such as seniority, loyalty, proper attitude, and initiative are at least as important as actual job performance.

Practices at the Sunkyong Company are representative of the more formalized approach to appraisal in Korea. The appraisal process begins with an extensive self-assessment inventory that is completed by the employee. Results are discussed with the employee's immediate supervisor and later with the supervisor's supervisor. Extensive peer assessments are also used. In other companies, however, the appraisal review consists of nothing more than informal individual counseling sessions.[46]

PEOPLE'S REPUBLIC OF CHINA (PRC). Since the 1978 cultural revolution, management practices in China have undergone significant changes. Most notable is the shift from a Stalinist system of industrial management (centralization, detailed plans, standard operating procedures) to a new motivational system that emphasizes responsibility and performance. Since 1984, the imperative has been to calculate profit prior to action rather than action before calculation.

At the enterprise level, these changes have been accompanied by a move from participatory management in the *Yan'an* tradition (pluralistic decision making and tight control) to a new structure of collective leadership. According to a PRC Decision Document, "Modern enterprises must have a minute division of labor, a high degree of continuity in production, strict technological requirements, and a high degree of cooperation." This document also prescribes that enterprises must specify in explicit terms the requirements for each work post and the duties of each worker and staff.

As a result of these reforms, there is an increasing emphasis on performance in Chinese enterprises. In the past, profits reverted directly to the state. Since the cultural revolution, a portion of profits can be held out and distributed to employees. Even by western standards, performance bonuses—even for low-level workers—are high, averaging as much as one-third of one's annual salary. Still, the allocation of these rewards is based on organizational rather than individual performance.

Regarding a shift in values, a recent study found that objective performance is the most important determinant of performance ratings of both U.S. and Chinese decision makers. However, unlike Americans, Chinese are significantly influenced by employee loyalty/dependability when making performance judgments. Apparently, traditional Chinese cultural values of defining performance in broad terms still linger.[47]

Performance evaluation in China also includes one unique facet: self-criticism. The format of these meetings, called *Hsiao-tsu* sessions, are advocated by the central committee of the national government. The official objective is to create more cohesive groups through identifying insensitive and other dysfunctional behaviors. As operationalized, they appear to serve as reverse appraisal sessions in which lower-ranking employees can make perceived or real mistreatments known to management.[48]

JAPAN. On first blush, performance appraisal would seem to be an unnecessary control mechanism for the Japanese organization, which emphasizes job rotation, slow promotion, and group, rather than individual, loyalty. As William Ouchi, a cross-cultural management expert notes, "Japanese employees are controlled in a subtle, indirect manner that contrasts greatly with the explicit formal control system used in the United States."[49]

Still, an increasing number of Japanese firms are using formal appraisals to evaluate the contribution of employees and to develop them into better employees. However, the concept of performance has a different meaning in Japan than in Western countries. For example, merit ratings are based on educational attainment and job ability factors such as communication skills, cooperativeness, and sense of responsibility, rather than on work results. The Japanese concept of performance includes not only the achievement of results, but also the expenditure of a good-faith effort.[50]

CURRENT TRENDS

As mentioned earlier in this chapter, when subordinates are empowered and responsible for their own behavior, the management of performance becomes easier. Stretched to its extreme, it could even result in the disappearance of performance appraisal as we know it.

IS PERFORMANCE APPRAISAL ON THE WAY OUT?

If companies want employees to work together in teams in their pursuit of a total quality management strategy, they must adjust several human resource activities. One of the important ones is the performance appraisal system. Typically, the basis for appraisal begins to reflect team-oriented criteria rather than solely individual-oriented criteria. Longer-term criteria become included with more traditional, shorter-term criteria. Peer review is incorporated, along with the traditional supervisory review.

As is usually the case, these changes do not take place overnight; they take place gradually. People need to get comfortable with the new ways. Just as important, organizations need to experiment with what they are doing. New ways of doing things generally have to be adapted to specific conditions facing a given company. In the instance of performance appraisal, companies may continue to make the types of changes described in the above paragraph. At some point, they may ask, "Do we even need performance appraisal?"

Firms have used performance appraisal systems for a long time now. It is unlikely that they will abandon them wholesale, but some are starting to ask, "Why do we do appraisals?" As firms address these questions, they may see that

Deming said managers are the reason for most problems, so why evaluate employees and blame them for problems?

they do it more to *control* than to develop or improve employee performance—and they do it because they assume they need to. [If employee goals are different from organizational goals, then—the assumption goes—firms have to monitor and control what employees do. In some cases, firms are finding that this assumption is wrong: employees can have goals that coincide with the organization's.] W. Edwards Deming, a father in the field of quality management and statistical process control, acted on the assumption that employees will do their best when managers treat them accordingly. In fact, he argued that, in terms of performance problems, *managers*—not the employees—are largely responsible for the problems. This questioning could eventually result in the disappearance of performance appraisal as most organizations use it today, at least as a method for evaluating employees. Deming strongly maintained until his death in 1993 at the age of 93 that appraisal can be useful, but only to help an employee develop and improve.

SUMMARY

Ineffective employee performance, whether anyone wants to admit it or not, plagues all organizations at least some of the time. For a performance appraisal system to be effective, not only must it permit the gathering of performance appraisal data, it must also enable the manager to *use* this information. Organizations that have developed an effective performance appraisal system, therefore, directly influence productivity, quality of work life, legal compliance, competitive advantage, and flexibility through the gathering and use of performance appraisal data.

Because of the dual purposes of evaluation and development, conflicts are inherent and inevitable. These conflicts, if unaddressed, will cripple the effectiveness of any performance appraisal system. Recognition of their sources, however, suggests how performance feedback can be given to reduce them. From a design perspective, an effective performance appraisal system can avoid inherent conflicts by (1) separating evaluation from development, (2) focusing on behavior rather than subjective traits, (3) distinguishing evaluation of current from future performance, and (4) using multiple appraisals to improve reliability and validity.

If managers are to improve their employees' performance, they must learn how to conduct a performance appraisal interview. Feedback can be given through a tell-and-sell, tell-and-listen, problem-solving, or mixed interview. Whereas Chapter 9 emphasized the content of performance appraisal, this chapter considered the process of giving feedback. You have undoubtedly begun to realize that effective feedback requires practice. Now that you are aware of what effective feedback entails, you are encouraged to diagnose your own effectiveness in giving it.

Although numerous motivation theories exist to explain human performance in organizations, a single diagnostic model has been provided to help you, the appraiser, get at the "root cause" of the performance problem. Using this model to understand performance gaps forms a basis for choosing different strategies for improvement. From a developmental perspective, strategies that involve participation and job clarification encourage self-directed improvement.

Ultimately, problem employees may require outside assistance through counseling or employment assistance programs. Control of behavior can also be achieved by linking rewards to behavior or by using group or organizational norms (as suggested by the discussion of socialization in Chapter 7). Because all organizations experience performance problems, it is crucial that the performance appraisal system, the process of gathering and feeding back appraisal data, functions to improve individual and group performance. Performance assessment also plays a vital role in other key human resource activities, particularly compensation and training, topics explored in the chapters ahead.

KEY CONCEPTS

attribution process
continuous
    reinforcement
effective feedback
employee assistance
    programs (EAPs)
external attribution

hot-stove principles
internal attribution
job-specific criteria
law of effect
meritocracy
mixed interview
neutralizing

partial reinforcement
positive reinforcement
problem-solving
    interview
tell-and-listen interview
tell-and-sell interview

REVIEW AND DISCUSSION QUESTIONS

1. What are the inherent conflicts in a performance appraisal system? How can such conflicts be reduced?

2. Suppose you have decided that an employee is not "working out" and must be terminated. What performance appraisal approach would you use to support this decision? Why?

3. It has been argued that from a reward perspective, effective superiors should only spend appraisal time with their effective performers. What is the rationale for this strategy? Do you see any potential problems with this strategy? Explain.

4. What are typical reasons used to explain peformance deficiencies?

5. What are the characteristics of effective feedback? What factors might prevent supervisors from giving effective feedback to subordinates?

6. How can an organization recognize and reward superiors for conducting performance appraisals?

7. Using negative behavioral strategies, what steps could a superior take to discourage unwanted subordinate behavior?

8. What are possible components of a self-appraisal performance management program? (Review Chapter 9).

9. Assume that you are a professor counseling a student with a grade complaint. Describe how you would conduct this session using the (1) tell-and-sell approach, (2) tell-and-listen approach, and (3) problem-solving approach. As a professor, which approach would you feel most comfortable using? Why? As a student, which would you prefer? Why?

10. Formal performance appraisal usually takes place once or twice a year. What does this suggest about the relative use of the performance appraisal system for evaluation versus development decisions?

EXERCISES AND CASES

FIELD PROJECT

Visit some local companies, and ask them how they treat employees who have performance or attendance problems. Do they have an EAP? Compare your findings with those of the class to see how many firms have these programs.

CAREER MANAGEMENT EXERCISE: DO YOU WANT THE BAD NEWS OR THE GOOD NEWS FIRST?

In Chapter 9, you indicated the type of performance appraisal system components you would like on your job. Because a system isn't really complete without feedback, you need to describe what type of feedback you would prefer.

1. First, do you want to have regular, formal feedback on your job? _____ yes; _____ no

2. How often do you want it? _____

3. From whom do you want it? _____
_____

4. To whom do you want to give feedback? _____
_____

5. Describe the feedback characteristics you would find most useful and acceptable to you. For example, does it have to have specific behavioral examples; do you need to have more than one example to illustrate a pattern of behavior? _____
_____
_____

6. Would you want your organization to offer an EAP? (While you may not personally use one, your co-workers might, you never know.) _____ yes; _____ no

7. Do you want your organization to have a formal discipline process beginning with a warning, etc? _____ yes; _____ no

8. Are you willing to be responsible for your own performance appraisal? This includes making sure you ask for it, telling your boss and others when they should review you, and even scheduling the time they should give you the feedback. _____ yes; _____ no

ROLE PLAY: "I GOT WHAT!?"

Return to Chapter 9 and the case, "The Pain of Performance Appraisal." At the end of the case, Bill and Joe are just sitting down to discuss Bill's appraisal. Based on the information in that case, break into teams and play the roles of Bill and Joe in one of the situations listed below. Observe carefully as other pairs of students conduct the other role plays to see how different people handle these situations.

1. First, Joe decides to use the tell-and-sell interview style. Joe might not want to allow more than five minutes for this interview.

2. Second, Joe decides to use the tell-and-listen interview style. Remember, Joe is busy, so he can't let this interview go more than ten minutes.

3. Third, Joe decides to use the problem-solving interview style. Again, time is money, so Joe can't let this go more than ten to fifteen minutes.

4. Fourth, Joe uses the mixed-interview style. Again, about ten minutes.

Regardless of Joe's approach, Bill is still faced with the same concerns raised in Chapter 9, so the people playing Bill should become very familiar with the case and what's at stake. Joe's interview style changes in these role plays, but the facts remain the same.

After each role play, discuss how well each role was played and the satisfaction level of each person. Your class should get "Joe" to state the assumptions (s)he was using—for example, "getting the interview done on time was more important than making Bill satisfied." (During the role plays, someone needs to be keeping time and then giving a two-minute warning to "Joe." Flexibility may be required on the given time periods).

Class may also wish to make use of the questionnaire in Exhibit 10.2. How did the different "Joe's" feel during the role play—with both the interview style and their own feelings and value systems?

While we haven't said much about Bill's role, it can be a very exciting and dynamic one. The results will vary depending on the assumptions each "Bill" makes. For example, did Bill assume that it was important to have some participation? Conflict may have arisen if Joe was trying the tell-and-sell interview and Bill was assuming that it was important to have participation. Again, there are many possibilities to discuss, so while this looks like a relatively easy role play, it may not be quite so straightforward! However, be as systematic as possible when you discuss the results.

This role play could be done with the entire class or in small groups who then report to the rest of the class.

CASE

SO YOU WANT TO BE A MANAGER?

Wally Reibstein was beginning to get the hang of his job, having survived a grueling six months as a newly appointed division engineering manager for a large aerospace firm located on the West Coast. Wally graduated with a degree in engineering from Rensselaer Polytechnic Institute in the early 1980s. He worked first for an industrial fan manufacturer located in the Midwest, the closest job he could find related to his aeronautical engineering training. When his wife decided to pursue an advanced degree in economics at a prestigious West Coast university, Wally found employment with his current employer, and they moved.

During the first five years, Wally demonstrated considerable skill in working with others and successfully completed three different projects on time. One year ago, he was promoted to project engineering manager. Within six months, his immediate boss, a division head, was selected for promotion and recommended Wally to fill his position. Because of his past successes, he got the job, and as division manager he is in charge of a staff of over 50 professional and technical personnel. Five of these professionals are designated as project engineers responsible for specific contracts. The remaining staff of engineers and technicians are about equally distributed over five projects.

Wally has a challenging week ahead of him. He has decided that this is the week for the "rubber to meet the road" in his performance as a division manager. He's scheduled two performance appraisal interviews that promise to challenge his human relation skills. The first review is scheduled on Tuesday with Jerry Masters, a 52-year-old project engineering manager with a Ph.D. in electrical engineering and two masters degrees in computer science and business administration. In Wally's estimation, Jerry is a degree collector and a poor manager. Jerry's project has fallen far behind schedule and is headed for disaster. After reading performance reviews from Jerry's personnel folder, Wally has decided that Jerry must be reassigned. Jerry's past reviews indicate that he seldom met stated objectives despite repeated verbal counseling. Wally's former boss confided that he would have reassigned Jerry himself, but his head count was frozen and he had no one readily available to replace him. Wally has no such constraints. His overhead budget has been increased 10 percent as a result of three consecutive successful quarters of billings for his division. He has also recently interviewed a 45-year-old engineer who, in his judgment, possesses all the qualities needed to succeed where Jerry is failing.

Wally agrees with his former boss's counsel that Jerry is a valued citizen but terribly mismatched in his job; he simply cannot manage a project. Tuesday morning arrives, and Wally decides to level with Jerry and tell him that he is not working out and that he will be reassigned to another project. When Wally informs Jerry of his reassignment, he reacts by launching into a protracted emotional outburst accusing Wally of violating the trust he (Jerry) had placed in him to support his efforts. Jerry reminds Wally of his twelve years of service and the considerable influence he wields. Storming out, Jerry informs Wally that he intends to write a letter to the division president detailing the shoddy treatment he has received. Great, thought Wally, just what he needs to make an impression on the top brass.

CASE QUESTIONS

1. Is Jerry justified in his emotional outburst?
2. How should Wally have told Jerry about the reassignment?
3. Where did Wally go wrong?
4. What would you have done if you were in Jerry's shoes?

CASE

RETIRED ON THE JOB: CAREER BURNOUT OR THE NONMOTIVATED EMPLOYEE?

George Benson, the newly appointed manager of Pentarecon Corporation's Production Control and Methods Improvement Division, faces a rather perplexing personnel problem. One of the long-time employees of his division, Harry Norton, isn't performing his job properly. In questioning subordinates, Benson learned that Norton has not performed any real or substantive work for years. Furthermore, his current job actions are a source of embarassment to the entire division. "Hangover Harry" arrives at work approximately 45 minutes late each morning and proceeds to begin the work day by attempting to recover from the previous evening's outing with his "Scotch friends." Norton's method of recovery appears to involve (1) reading the paper for about an hour while smoking and drinking coffee; (2) "office hopping" with his coffee cup in order to visit, talk, and interact with his many friends who are employed within the division; (3) a two-hour, three-martini lunch break; and (4) an afternoon nap while secluded back in his office. Benson had expected the employees of his division to resent Norton's behavior and obvious poor or nonperformance. Thus he was quite surprised when he learned that Norton is almost universally liked and considered somewhat of a folk hero among nonsupervisory employees. Therefore, Benson decided to thoroughly investigate Norton's case before taking any type of personnel action.

From company records, Benson learned that Norton has been employed by Pentarecon Corporation for twelve years. He began his employment with the firm as an internal management specialist. The duties of this position involved the development of methods improvements to facilitate both management and manufacturing operations. Initially, Norton was quite successful in this position. His performance appraisals routinely cited him for both his ingenuity and complete understanding of the complex production control systems used by the firm. Norton was credited with the introduction of new work procedures that lessened both worker fatigue and industrial accidents. Additionally, several of his suggestions resulted in substantial improvements in product quality within the manufacturing department. Recognizing this performance excellence, the firm promoted Norton once and rewarded him with several cash bonuses during his first five years of employment.

During his seventh year of employment, Norton was considered for a supervisory position within the division. Everyone was surprised when Pentarecon's top management finally decided to fill this supervisory vacancy with another employee from the Research and Development Group. Norton appeared to accept this career setback with some degree of indifference. He still exhibited his friendly and engaging interpersonal style that had won him many friends within the division. Yet six months later, a project he was assigned to direct seemed to "never get off the ground" because of his failure to exhibit proper levels of leadership and enthusiasm when dealing with other project analysts. Subsequent job assignments also revealed a substantial deterioration in performance. Norton's failure to consider a variety of relevant variables in his work assignments resulted in the development of nonusable work methods and production control techniques. Norton's supervisor noted that Harry appeared to be drinking heavily during this period of time and was said to be experiencing marital difficulties. This pattern of poor performance, tardiness, and alcohol abuse continued to the point where Norton's supervisor was afraid to assign him projects of any real significance. Therefore, Harry has recently been given either small, noncritical work assignments or no work at all.

CASE QUESTIONS

1. What are the underlying causes of Norton's performance?
2. Who's responsible for the current state of Norton's performance?
3. Should a) the department management, b) Norton's supervisor, c) the company, have taken action much earlier?
4. What should Benson do now? Should Benson terminate Norton?

NOTES

1. Information taken from B. Dumaine, "Who Needs a Boss?" *Fortune* (May 7, 1990): 52–60; A. M. Kantrow, "Wide-Open Management at Chaparral Steel: Interview with Gordon E. Forward, *Harvard Business Review* (May–June 1986): 96–102; R. Karlin, "Chaparral Beats the Odds," *New Management* (Winter 1987): 15–18.

2. *The Wall Street Journal*, August 28, 1984.

3. N. Napier and G. Latham, "Outcomes Expectancies of People Who Conduct Appraisals," *Personnel Psychology* 39 (1986): 827–839.

4. A. S. Grove, *High Output Management* (New York: Random House, 1983): 181–183.

5. M. Beer, "Performance Appraisal: Dilemmas and Possibilities," *Organizational Dynamics* (Winter 1981): 26.

6. D. T. Hall, *Careers in Organizations* (Pacific Palisades, Calif.: Goodyear, 1976); D. Feldman, *Managing Careers in Organizations* (Glenview, Ill. Scott, Foresman, 1988).

7. H. H. Meyer, E. Kay, and J. R. French, Jr., "Split Roles in Performance Appraisal," *Harvard Business Review* (Jan./Feb. 1965): 125.

8. C. Hymowitz, *The Wall Street Journal* (Jan. 17, 1985): 35.

9. *Ibid*.

10. C. Carr, "The Ingredients of Good Performance," *Training* (Aug. 1993): 51–54; P. Froiland, "Reproducing Star Performers," *Training* (Sept. 1993): 33–38; W. Weitzel, "How to Improve Performance Through Successful Appraisals," *Personnel* (Oct. 1987): 18–23.

11. Separating the review of past performance and future performance is described by Beer, "Performance Appraisal;" S. J. Carroll and C. E. Schneider, *Performance Appraisal and Review Systems* (Glenview, Ill.: Scott, Foresman, 1982). For a presentation on separating development and evaluation appraisal, see E. E. Lawler, III, A. M. Mohrman, Jr., and S. M. Resnick, "Performance Appraisal Revisited," *Organizational Dynamics* (Summer 1984): 20–42.

12. J. Greenberg, "The Distributive Justice of Organizational Performance Evaluation," in *Research in Negotiations in Organizations*, eds., M. Bazerman, R. Lewicki, and B. Sheppard, (Greenwich, Conn.: JAI Press, 1986): 26–41; J. Greenberg, "Using Diaries to Promote Procedural Justice in Performance Appraisal," *Social Justice Review* (1987): 20–37.

13. G. Latham, M. Erez, and E. Locke, "Resolving Scientific Disputes by the Joint Design of Crucial Experiments by the Antagonists: Application to the Erez-Latham Dispute Regarding Participation in Goal Setting," *Journal of Applied Psychology* 73 (1988): 753–772.

14. G. P. Nicholas, "Upward Trend Continues in Appraisal Process," *HR Focus* (Sept. 1992): 17; J. S. Russel and D. L. Goode, "An Analysis of Managers' Reactions to Their Own Performance Appraisal Feedback," *Journal of Applied Psychology* (Feb. 1988): 63; F. L. Schmidt, J. E. Hunter, A. N. Outerbridge, and S. Goff, "Joint Relation of Experience and Ability with Job Performance: Test of Three Hypotheses," *Journal of Applied Psychology* (Feb. 1988): 46.

15. For a discussion of these characteristics for an effective appraisal interview, see Beer, "Performance Appraisal," 34–35 and *Bulletin to Management,* (Oct. 1984): 2, 7; P. Wylie and M. Grothe, *Problem Employees: How to Improve Their Performance* (Belmont, Calif.: Pitman Learning, Inc., 1981). Also see J. Beilinson, "Communicating Bad News," *Personnel* (Jan. 1991): 15.

16. G. P. Latham and L. M. Saari, "The Importance of Supportive Relationships in Goal Setting," *Journal of Applied Psychology*, 64 (1979): 163–168.

17. N. R. F. Maier, *The Appraisal Interview* (New York: Wiley, 1958); G. P. Latham and K. N. Wexley, *Increasing Productivity through Performance Appraisal* (Reading, Mass.: Addison-Wesley, 1981) 152–154; Carroll and Schneider, *Performance Appraisal*, 160–189.

18. D. R. Ilgen and C. F. Moore, "Types and Choices of Performance Feedbacks," *Journal of Psychology* (Aug. 1987): 401.

19. G. P. Latham, L. L. Cummings, and T. R. Mitchell, "Behavioral Strategies to Improve Productivity," *Organizational Dynamics* (Winter 1981): 4–23; S. Greengard, "Theft Control Starts with HR Strategies," *Personnel Journal* (April 1993): 81–91.

20. This section is adapted in part from R. F. Mager and P. Pipe, *Analyzing Performance Problems or "You Really Oughta Wanna"* (Belmont, Calif.: Fearon Pitman, 1970).

21. M. J. Markinko and W. L. Garner, "Learned Helplessness: An Alternative Explanation for Performance Deficits," *Academy of Management Review* 1 (1982): 195–204; M. E. and F. H. Kanfer, "The Role of Goal Acceptance on Goal Setting and Task Performance," *Academy of Management Review* (July 1983): 454–463; J. C. Naylor and D. R. Ilgen, "Goal Setting: A Theoretical Analysis in Motivation Technology," in *Research in Organizational Behavior*, eds., B. M. Shaw and L. L. Cummings, Vol. 6 (Greenwich, Conn.: JAI Press, 1984), 95–101; S. E. Jackson and R. S. Schuler, "A Meta-Analysis and Conceptual Critique of Research on Role Ambiguity and Role Conflict in Work Settings," *Organizational Behavior and Human Decision Processes* 36 (1985): 16–78; J. L. Pearce and L. W. Porter, "Employee Responses to Formal Performance Appraisal Feedback," *Journal of Applied Psychology* (May 1986): 211.

22. V. Huber, P. Podsakoff, and W. Todor, "An Investigation of Biasing Factors in the Attributions of Subordinates and Their Supervisors," *Journal of Business Research* 4 (1986): 83–97.

23. L. F. McGee, "Keeping Up the Good Work," *Personnel Administrator* (June 1988): 68–72; S. O'Neal and M. Palladino, "Revamp Ineffective Performance Management," *Personnel Journal* (Feb. 1992): 93–102; M. H. Yarborough, "Warning! Negative Influences at Work," *HR Focus* (Sept. 1993): 23.

24. Adapted from E. F. Huse, *Management*, 2nd ed. (St. Paul: West 1982): 390–391.

25. A. Bandura, *Principles of Behavior Modification* (New York: Holt, Rinehart and Winston, 1969); W. Nord, "Beyond the Teaching Machine: The Neglected Area of Operant Conditioning in the Theory and Practice of Management," *Organizational Behavior and Human Performance* 4 (Nov. 1969): 375–401; W. Hamner, "Worker Motivation Programs: Importance of Climate, Structure and Performance Consequences," in *Contemporary Problems in Personnel: Readings for the Seventies*, eds. W. C. Hamner and F. Schmidt (Chicago: St. Clair Press, 1974): 280–401.

26. E. Feeney, "At Emery Air Freight: Positive Reinforcement Boosts Performance," *Organizational Dynamics* 1 (Winter 1973); 41–50.

27. *Ibid*: 47–48.

28. W. C. Hamner, "Reinforcement Theory and Contingency Management in Organizational Settings," in *Organizational Behavior and Management: A Contingency Approach*, eds. H. Tosi and W. C. Hamner (Chicago: St. Clair Press, 1974): 86–111.

29. *Ibid*.

30. Feeney, "At Emery Air Freight," p. 42.

31. R. D. Arvey, G. A. Davis, and S. M. Nelson, "Use of Discipline in an Organization: A Field Study," *Journal of Applied Psychology* (Aug. 1984): 448–460; J. Brockner and J. Guare, "Improving the Performance of Low Self-Esteem Individuals: An Attributional Approach," *Academy of Management Journal* (Dec. 1983): 642–656; D. N. Campbell, R. L. Fleming, and R. C. Grote, "Discipline Without Punishment at Last," *Harvard Business Review* (July/Aug. 1985): 162–178; D. Cameron, "The When, Why, and How of Discipline," *Personnel Journal* (July 1984): 37–39.

32. D. A. Nadler and E. E. Lawler, "Motivation—A Diagnostic Approach," in *Perspectives on Behavior in Organizations*, eds., J. R. Hackman, E. E. Lawler, and L. W. Porter (New York: McGraw-Hill, 1977).

33. D. N. Campbell, R. L. Fleming, and R. C. Grote, "Discipline Without Punishment at Last," *Harvard Business Review* (July/August 1985): 162–178.

34. R. W. Hollman, "Beyond Contemporary Employee Assistance Programs," *Personnel Administrator* (Sept. 1981): 37–41; D. Masi and S. J. Freidland, "EAP Actions & Options," *Personnel Journal* (June 1988): 61–67.

35. S. H. Appelbaum and B. T. Shapiro, "The ABCs of EAPs," *Personnel* (July 1989): 39–46; S. J. Smits, L. A. Pace, and W. J. Perryman, "EAPs Are Big Business," *Personnel Journal* 96, (June 1989): 99–106; J. L. Goff, "Diagnose Alcoholism" *Personnel Journal* (May 1990): 107–116.

36. R. J. Nobile, "The Drug-Free Workplace: Act on It!" *Personnel* (Feb. 1990): 22.

37. "Productivity and Performance: EAP Improved," *Bulletin to Management,* (July 23, 1987): 1. For an excellent discussion of the application of discipline in organizations, see R. D. Arvey and J. M. Ivancevich, "Punishment in Organizations: A Review, Propositions, and Research Suggestions," *Academy of Management Review* 5 (1980): 123–132; W. Kiechel III, "How to Discipline in the Modern Age," *Fortune* (May 7, 1990): 179–180.

38. "Labor Letter," *The Wall Street Journal* (August 21, 1990): 1. Also see J. Beilinson, "Are EAPs the Answer?" *Personnel* (Jan. 1991): 3.

39. P. Wylie and M. Grothe, *Problem Employees: How to Improve Their Performance* (Belmont, Calif.: Pitman Learning, 1981).

40. C. O'Reilly and B. Weitz, "Managing Marginal Employees: The Use of Warnings and Dismissals," *Administrative Science Quarterly* 25 (1980): 467–484.

41. M. Bazerman, *Judgment in Managerial Decision Making* (New York: Wiley, 1986); V. Huber, "Managerial Applications of Decision Theory Concepts and Heuristics," *Organizational Behavior Teaching Review* 10 (1986): 1–24; G. Northcraft, M. Neale, and V. Huber, "The Effects of Cognitive Bias and Social Influence on Human Resource Management Decisions," in *Research in Personnel and Human Resource Management,* eds. G. Ferris and K. Rowland (Greenwich, Conn.: JAI Press, 1988).

42. H. J. Bernardin and R. W. Beatty, *Performance Appraisal: Assessing Human Behavior at Work* (Boston, Mass.: Kent, 1984); R. Henderson, *Performance Appraisal* (Reston, Va.: Reston, 1984).

43. J. Sargent, "Performance Appraisal 'American Style': Where it Came From and Its Possibilities Overseas," working paper, University of Washington, Sept. 1991; A. Nimgade, "American Management as Viewed by International Professionals," *Business Horizons* (Nov.–Dec. 1989): 98–105.

44. N. Adler, *International Dimensions of Organizational Behavior,* 2nd ed. (Boston, Mass.: PWS-Kent, 1991); W. H. Newman, "Cultural Assumptions Underlying U.S. Management Concepts," in *Management in an International Context* (New York: Harper & Row, 1972).

45. P. Drucker, *Management: Tasks, Responsibilities and Practices* (New York: Harper & Row, 1973): 424–425.

46. R. Steers, Y. K. Shin, and G. Ungson, *The Chaebol: Korea's New Industrial Might* (New York: Harper & Row, 1990): 121–122.

47. V. Huber, G. Northcraft, M. Neale, and X. Zhao, "Cognitive Similarity and Cultural Dissimilarity: Effects on Performance Appraisal and Compensation Decisions of Chinese and Americans," working paper, University of Washington, 1991.

48. S. Carroll, "Asian HRM Philosophies and Systems: Can They Meet Our Changing HRM Needs," in *Readings in Personnel and Human Resource Management,* eds., R. Schuler, S. Youngblood, and V. Huber, (St. Paul, Minn.: West, 1988): 442–455.

49. W. Ouchi, *The M-Form Society* (Reading, Mass.: Addison-Wesley, 1984).

50. T. Mroczkowski and M. Hanaoka, "Continuity and Change in Japanese Management," *California Management Review* (Winter 1989): 39–52.

51. "Out With Appraisals, In With Feedback," *Training* (Aug. 1993): 10–11.

FOR MOST PEOPLE, work is a central activity in their lives. It provides structure, meaning, and purpose. However central or important work is to people, they are unlikely to be satisfied if their employer doesn't pay them well enough, and they will strive to work for a company that pays more than other companies, all other things being equal. In some circumstances, of course, people do work for less than they can get with another company or in another occupation. For the most part, though, they work for a particular company because of the compensation they expect to receive for their contributions.

Once on the job, employees generally want to work hard and do a good job. And they want fair pay and feedback from the boss. Consequently, companies and their human resource managers usually try to ensure that their employees are paid fairly, both in terms of what others in the company are being paid and what others with similar jobs in other organizations are being paid. In the first chapter of this three-chapter section on compensating employees,

we will discuss issues associated with establishing pay plans to attract, retain, and motivate individuals.

Employees will also work more if they are paid more for their additional work; thus organizations are increasingly establishing compensation plans that tie additional compensation to additional work. Even here, employees are concerned with fairness and equity, so companies must design performance-based pay plans around performance appraisal systems that are valid and accepted by the employees. These plans can be designed

SECTION 5

COMPENSATING

for individuals, teams, or even organizational performance achievements. Because of the growing use of these plans, they are discussed extensively in Chapter 12.

Although employees certainly are concerned with getting paid regularly, and with keeping their jobs, they are also increasingly concerned with the "not so little things": health insurance coverage (a major concern of individuals, companies, and society!); disability coverage; unemployment compensation; retirement and pension benefits; vacations; wellness programs; and elder- and child-care opportunities. These programs are valuable, but costly. Consequently, organizations are trying to reduce some of their total compensation costs by cutting back on some forms of indirect compensation. These are important concerns for you and for organizations. Thus we will spend Chapter 13 discussing the aspects of indirect compensation. And you will have the opportunity to continue to expand on your future job with the "Career Management" exercises in Chapters 12 and 13.

CHAPTER 11

TOTAL COMPENSATION

LEARNING OBJECTIVES

When you have finished studying this chapter, you should be able to:

1. Identify different methods of job evaluation.
2. Describe how wage and salary levels for jobs are determined.
3. Explain issues in wage and salary administration such as employee participation, pay satisfaction, pay secrecy, and salary versus hourly pay.
4. Describe international compensation.

CHAPTER OUTLINE

"Managing Human Resources at Microsoft"

TOTAL COMPENSATION

WHY IS TOTAL COMPENSATION IMPORTANT?

LEGAL CONSIDERATIONS

"Managing Human Resources at Food Lion, Inc.

RECORD SETTLEMENT UNDER *FAIR LABOR STANDARDS ACT*"

"HR Advice and Application

ACHIEVING PAY EQUITY—NOT SIMPLE, BUT NOT SO COSTLY"

DETERMINING THE RELATIVE WORTH OF JOBS

"Managing Human Resources at Northern Telecom

SKILL-BASED PAY PROGRAM IMPROVES CUSTOMER SERVICE"

ESTABLISHING THE PAY STRUCTURE

ISSUES IN WAGE AND SALARY ADMINISTRATION

INTERNATIONAL COMPENSATION

CURRENT TRENDS

Exercise: Motivation and Pay Raise Allocation

Case: Comparable Worth Finds Rockdale

Case: Pacific Coast Electric Company

ONE of the wonder firms of the 1980s and 1990s, Microsoft Corporation, continues to dazzle customers with innovative software programs. Although the company has faced frustration in sometimes bringing a product to market before it is ready, interestingly, the firm's overall performance has not been harmed. As a former Microsoft vice president commented, "[Microsoft has] never shipped a good product in its first version … but they never give up and eventually they get it right."

"Getting it right" demands that the firm has top-notch, creative programmers. Finding such talent is difficult given the lack of programmers nationwide and given Microsoft's stringent recruiting and selection practices. The firm typically hires fewer than 1 percent of those applying for programmer slots, partly because the company's founder, Bill Gates, insists that the ranks stay lean (to hold down costs). Because Microsoft is such an attractive employer, it can have its pick of the best programmers. Contributing to its attractiveness are its compensation policies and practices.

Once the firm finds its programmers, it rewards their performance in unique ways. Rather than high salaries or perks (no company cars), the company offers generous stock options. Programmers who were on staff prior to the firm's public stock offering in 1986, for example, received options that have made them "paper millionaires."

Since then, the firm has begun a promotion and compensation plan similar to that of law firms. Programmers are evaluated yearly and placed on one of six levels. Their incentive pay and options derive from that evaluation. As a programmer reaches the top two levels, the equivalent of becoming a "partner" in a law firm, there is a big celebration, and the employee receives more stock options. Further, the firm provides multiple career paths, with comparable rewards for programmers who stay in the technical side of software development as well as those who choose to go into management. Such compensation policies and practices, coupled with an exciting work environment, have created tremendous loyalty among Microsoft employees.[1]

This feature illustrates several aspects of compensation. One is that money isn't the only thing that attracts great employees to firms and causes them to stay and perform well. Offering alternate career paths and celebrating important events can be powerful motivating forces for individuals. While money is important, the absolute level of direct compensation need not be extremely high. Bill Gates' salary is certainly low for the CEO of a very successful firm. The attractiveness, however, of stock options (especially with a successful firm) can be a substantial force in motivating individuals to join a firm, work hard, and remain committed to the firm. In turn, this helps make the firm successful. And, this is why the area of total compensation is such an important one to organizational strategy.

TOTAL COMPENSATION

Total compensation *involves the assessment of employee contributions in order to distribute fairly and equitably both direct and indirect organizational rewards in*

The pieces of total compensation include:

- Direct
- Performance-based
- Indirect

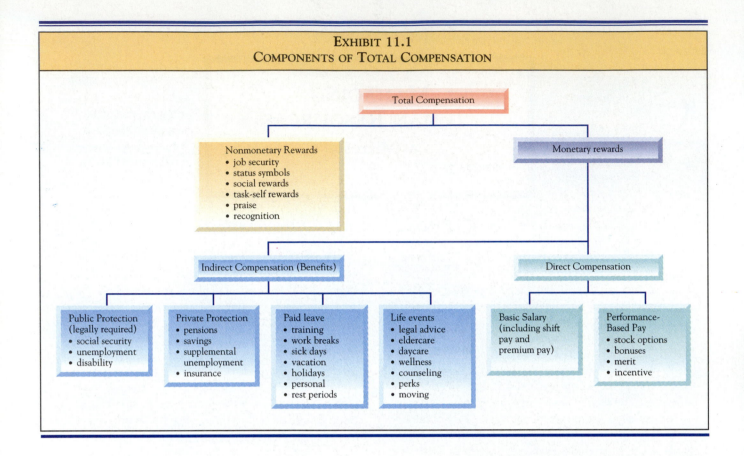

EXHIBIT 11.1
COMPONENTS OF TOTAL COMPENSATION

Total Compensation

Nonmonetary Rewards
• job security
• status symbols
• social rewards
• task-self rewards
• praise
• recognition

Monetary rewards

Indirect Compensation (Benefits)

Direct Compensation

Public Protection
(legally required)
• social security
• unemployment
• disability

Private Protection
• pensions
• savings
• supplemental
  unemployment
• insurance

Paid leave
• training
• work breaks
• sick days
• vacation
• holidays
• personal
• rest periods

Life events
• legal advice
• eldercare
• daycare
• wellness
• counseling
• perks
• moving

Basic Salary
(including shift
pay and
premium pay)

Performance-
Based Pay
• stock options
• bonuses
• merit
• incentive

There are two things people want more
than sex and money . . . recognition
and praise.

—Mary Kay Ash, Chairman Emeritus,
Mary Kay Cosmetics

exchange for those contributions. As Exhibit 11.1 shows, monetary rewards can be categorized as direct or indirect compensation. **Direct compensation** includes an employee's **base salary** and **performance-based pay**. **Indirect compensation** consists of federal- and public-mandated protection programs, private protection programs, health-care benefits, paid leave, and life-cycle benefits. Nonmonetary rewards can be very important to employees.[2] For example, job security has become important in this era of substantial and continuous layoffs by large employers.[3] Recognizing this, some employers offer job security in exchange for no increase in monetary rewards.[4] With this in mind, however, we will focus our discussion on monetary rewards.

We are about to embark on a detailed discussion of compensation. We begin with a discussion of compensation's purposes and importance, and then examine its overall role in developing and linking human resource management to the organization's strategy. Next we present various ways to attain internal and external pay equity. We examine issues associated with compensation administration (for example, resolving equity imbalances, participation, pay secrecy, and pay satisfaction). Chapter 12 continues the discussion of total compensation but focuses on individual equity, including the mix of various elements of total compensation and incentive pay. Compensation for specific groups (sales people and executives) also are delineated. In conclusion, Chapter 13 focuses on employee benefits and the role they play in fulfilling organizational objectives. Some compensation issues in other countries are also reviewed.

LINE MANAGERS	HR PROFESSIONALS	EMPLOYEES
Participate with HR professionals in job evaluation.	Perform the job evaluation with line manager input.	May participate in salary recommendations.
Top management sets policy on compensation.	Work with line managers on final salary decisions.	Indicate preferences for types of indirect compensation.
Make initial salary decisions on employees.		

WHY IS TOTAL COMPENSATION IMPORTANT?

Total compensation serves the following major purposes:

- *It attracts potential job applicants.* In conjunction with the organization's recruitment and selection efforts, the total compensation program can help assure that pay is sufficient to attract the right people at the right time for the right jobs.
- *It retains good employees.* Unless the total compensation program is perceived as internally equitable and externally competitive, good employees (those the organization wants to retain) are likely to leave.
- *It motivates employees.* Many employers seek to be productive and have a motivated work force such as Microsoft. Total compensation can help achieve this goal by tying rewards to performance—that is, by having an element of productivity incentive.
- *It administers pay within the law.* Organizations must be aware of the legal regulations relevant to total compensation and avoid violating them in their pay programs.
- *It attains human resource and strategic business plans.* An organization may want to create a rewarding and supportive climate, or it may want to be an attractive place to work so that it can attract the best applicants. Total compensation can assist these plans and also further other organizational objectives such as rapid growth, survival, or innovation.[5]
- *It gains a competitive edge.* Total compensation can be a significant cost of doing business. Depending on the industry, labor costs range from 10 to

Major purposes of total compensation are to attract applicants, retain good employees, motivate employees, administer pay legally, and attain HR/business plans.

DID YOU KNOW?

More than 2,000 Microsoft employees have become millionaires.

80 percent of total costs. To gain a competitive advantage, an organization may choose to relocate to areas where labor is cheaper or more interested in performance-based pay.

Obviously, these objectives are interrelated. When employees are motivated, the organization is more likely to achieve its strategic business objectives. When pay is based on the value of the job, the organization is more likely to attract, motivate, and retain its employees. Nonmonetary rewards, an important part of total compensation, become important in attaining the above objectives as the value of monetary rewards decreases.[6]

LEGAL CONSIDERATIONS

In general, total compensation takes place amongst a significant number of environmental conditions. For example, while organizations use wage survey results to set pay levels for jobs, organizations need to be aware that paying what the market will bear, perhaps paying women and minorities less because they are willing to accept less, is no excuse for wage discrimination. Organizations also need to be concerned over the issue of price fixing. If organizations exchange market data on their own and set pay rates based on this information, the organizations can be charged with price fixing and collusion.

DAVIS-BACON AND WALSH-HEALEY

The federal government has enacted several laws influencing the level of wages employers may pay, pay structures, and individual wage determinations. The first federal law to protect the amount of pay employees receive for their work was the *Davis-Bacon Act of 1931*; this act required organizations holding federal construction contracts to pay laborers and mechanics the prevailing wages of the majority of the employees in the locality where the work was performed. The *Walsh-Healey Public Contracts Act of 1936* extended the *Davis-Bacon Act* to include all federal contracts exceeding $10,000 and specified that pay levels conform to the industry minimum rather than the area minimum, as specified in *Davis-Bacon*. The *Walsh-Healey Act* also established overtime pay at one and one-half times the hourly rate. These wage provisions, however, did not include administrative, professional, office, custodial, or maintenance employees, or beginners, or disabled persons.

WAGE DEDUCTION LAWS

Three federal laws influence how much employers may deduct from employee paychecks. The *Copeland Act of 1934* authorized the secretary of labor to regulate wage deductions for contractors and subcontractors doing work financed in whole or in part by a federal contract. Essentially, the *Copeland Act* was aimed at illegal deductions. Protection against a more severe threat from an employer with federal contracts was provided in the *Anti-Kickback Law of 1948*. The *Federal Wage Garnishment Law of 1980* also protects employees against deductions from pay for indebtedness. It provides that only 25 percent of one's disposable weekly earnings or 30 times the minimum wage, whichever is less, can be deducted for debt repayment.

FAIR LABOR STANDARDS ACT

Partially because *Davis-Bacon* and *Walsh-Healey* were limited in their coverage to employees on construction projects, the *Fair Labor Standards Act of 1938* (or the

Legal considerations in all aspects of total compensation are very extensive.

Major compensation-related legislation includes:
- *Davis-Bacon Act of 1931*
- *Walsh-Healey Public Contracts Act of 1936*
- *Fair Labor Standards Act of 1938*
- wage deduction laws
- antidiscrimination laws

Wage and Hour Law) was enacted. This set minimum wages, maximum hours, child labor standards, and overtime pay provisions for all workers except domestic and government employees. The Supreme Court extended the coverage to include state and local government employees in 1985 (*Garcia v. San Antonio Metropolitan Transit Authority*).

1. *Minimum Wage:* The minimum wage began at 25 cents an hour and has reached $4.25. Still, subminimum wages are permitted for learners in semiskilled occupations, apprentices, handicapped persons working in sheltered workshops, and employees who receive more than $30 per month in tips (up to 40 percent of the minimum requirement may be covered by tips).[7]

2. *Child Labor:* In order to prevent abuses regarding children, the Act also prohibits minors under the age of eighteen from working in hazardous occupations. For nonhazardous positions, the minimum age ranges from fourteen to sixteen, depending on the type of work to be performed and whether the employer is a child's parent.

3. *Overtime Provisions:* The overtime provisions of the Act establishes who is to be paid overtime for work and who is not. Most employees covered must be paid time and a half for all work exceeding 40 hours per week. These are called **nonexempt employees**. Several groups of individuals are exempt from both overtime and minimum wage provisions. The **exempt employees** include employees of firms not involved in interstate commerce, employees in seasonal industries, and outside salespeople. Three other employee groups—executives, administrators, and professionals—are also exempt from overtime pay and minimum wage laws in most organizations. Trainee managers and assistant managers, however, are excluded and should thus be paid overtime.[8]

Exempt employees are not covered by overtime or minimum-wage provisions. *Nonexempt employees* are entitled to receive overtime pay.

To be exempt, professionals must spend 80 percent of their work hours in the following tasks:

- Doing work requiring knowledge acquired through specialized, prolonged training
- Exercising discretion or judgment
- Doing work that is primarily intellectual and nonroutine

The criteria for exempt status as an executive or administrator include spending at least 80 percent of work time in the following tasks:

- Undertaking management duties
- Supervising two or more employees
- Controlling or greatly influencing hiring, firing, and promotion decisions
- Exercising discretion

In both cases, a comprehensive job analysis is necessary to determine whether a job is exempt. To illustrate how alive and well the *Fair Labor Standards Act* is, read the feature, "Managing Human Resources at Food Lion, Inc.: Record Settlement Under *Fair Labor Standards Act*."

ANTIDISCRIMINATION LAWS

EQUAL PAY ACT. While not covered in the original 1938 law, the fourth provision of the *Fair Labor Standards Act* was added as an amendment in 1963. Called the *Equal Pay Act*, this extension prohibits an employer from discriminating.

... between employees on the basis of sex by paying wages to employees ... at a rate less than the rate at which he pays wages to employees of the opposite sex ... for equal work on jobs the performance of which requires equal skill, effort and responsibility, and which are performed under similar working conditions.

To establish a *prima facie* case of wage discrimination, the plaintiff needs to establish that a disparity in pay exists for men and women performing substantially equal, not necessarily identical, jobs. To determine this, the amount of skill, effort, responsibility, and working conditions required by each job must be assessed through careful job analysis. In making this judgment, job content should be examined rather than merely job title. If jobs are found to be substantially equal, wages for the lowest paid job must be raised to match those of the higher paying position. Freezing or lowering pay of the higher paid job is unacceptable.

Four exceptions can be used to legally defend unequal pay for equal work. They are the existence and use of (1) a seniority system, (2) a merit system, (3) a system that measures earnings or quality of production, or (4) any additional factor other than gender. To establish that a *prima facie* case of discrimination, the plaintiff needs to establish that a disparity in pay exists for employees on equal jobs. If the employer can show the existence of one or more of the four exceptions, however, the differential may be found to be justified.

CIVIL RIGHTS ACTS. Note that the *Equal Pay Act* provides legal coverage only for equal pay for equal work. Only when men and women are performing jobs requiring equivalent skills, effort, and responsibility are they entitled to identical pay (unless there are differences in performance, seniority, or other conditions). Title VII of the *Civil Rights Act of 1964* and the *Civil Rights Act of 1991*, however, provide broader legal coverage for pay discrimination. While these acts apply to equal pay for equal work, they also apply to compensation where the jobs, though not identical, are comparable.

COMPARABLE WORTH. An important concept in compensation is comparable worth. The heart of the **comparable worth** theory is the contention that, while the "true worth" of nonidentical jobs may be similar, some jobs (often held by women) are paid a lower rate than others (often held by men). Resulting differences in pay that are disproportionate to the differences in the "true worth" of jobs amount to wage discrimination. Consequently, according to the comparable-worth advocates, legal protection should be provided to ensure pay equity.

Several state and local governments have passed comparable-worth or pay-equity legislation. And many businesses have also taken action on pay-equity issues. Exactly what the issues are and how they can be addressed are described in the feature, "HR Advice and Application: Achieving Pay Equity—Not Simple, but Not So Costly."

Internationally, comparable worth is an idea that has been around for some time.

> The International Labor Organization (ILO), the Geneva-based agency of the United Nations and United States joined in 1934, adopted an international convention on comparable worth almost 35 years ago. And what the ILO's experience shows is that while comparable worth may have helped reduce the gap between male and female wages in some countries that have tried it, it hasn't eliminated that gap. But neither has it led to the major economic or bureaucratic headaches that its critics prophesied.[11]

Since its adoption, more than 100 governments—but not the United States—have ratified the convention. These include most of the nations of Western Europe, Canada, Australia, New Zealand, Japan, and more than 70 developing countries.[12]

DETERMINING THE RELATIVE WORTH OF JOBS

MARKET SURVEYS
As mentioned previously, market data can be used directly or indirectly to set rates of pay. Indirectly, pay rates for benchmark jobs are used to establish pay rates for all other jobs. Alternatively, a job evaluation study on existing jobs can

The legal defenses protecting unequal pay for equal work are

- seniority system
- merit system
- quality of production standards
- factors other than gender

Comparable worth means that different jobs may still have comparable value and should therefore be paid the same.

Relative job worth can be determined by market survey or job evaluation.

ACHIEVING PAY EQUITY—NOT SIMPLE, BUT NOT SO COSTLY

Pay equity is a policy that provides businesses the competitive edge to meet the challenges of the next century, declares the National Committee on Pay Equity. A consistent, fair pay policy whereby all workers are paid equally for work of equal value produces a more productive and better-motivated work force, which, in turn, promotes recruitment and retention of good workers. . . .

"Smart employers recognize that future profits depend on current investment in their most vital resource: their people," . . . says the coalition of labor, women's, and civil rights groups in its report, "Pay Equity Makes Good Business Sense."

Women and men of color are concentrated in lower-paying jobs. Additionally, when women and men of color occupy traditionally white-male-dominated positions—even after accounting for legitimate reasons for pay differences such as differing skills, work experience, and seniority—women and men of color are still paid less, contends the pay-equity committee's publication.

On the basis of every dollar paid to white men in 1988, white women were paid 65 cents, black women were paid 61 cents, and Hispanic women were paid 55 cents, the report notes. Black men were paid 75 cents, and Hispanic men were paid 65 cents for every dollar paid to white men.

Discriminatory wage practices account for between one-quarter and one-half of this disparity in wages, says the report.

WHAT IS PAY EQUITY?

Pay equity, also known in the United States, Canada, and Europe as equal pay for work of equal value, is broader than "equal pay for equal work." Pay equity is a means of eliminating race, ethnicity, and gender as wage determinants within job categories and between job categories, the report says.

Many businesses pay women and men of color less than white males. This result is often unintentional and due in part to personnel systems and wage structures that retain historical biases and inconsistencies that are, in fact, discriminatory, explains the report.

A pay-equity policy examines existing pay policies that underpay women and men of color and activates steps to correct the discrimination.

HOW TO ACHIEVE PAY EQUITY

A comprehensive audit is the first step in implementing a pay-equity policy, explains the committee's report. The audit should examine the following areas for inequities and needed changes:

- Job evaluation
- Market pricing
- Pay administration
- Recruitment

In the area of pay administration, the audit should scrutinize each individual component of a business's system including: salary-range design, salary grades, pay differentials, and the determination of hiring rates. Additional items to be examined for inequities include promotion rates, merit increases, incentive programs, and performance and seniority factors in the pay system.

PAY EQUITY IS NOT COSTLY

Following the lead of public employers, many private-sector businesses are already incorporating pay-equity analyses in their annual budget proposals. "The cost of pay equity adjustments," reports the committee, usually has been "between 2 and 5 percent of payroll."

In no cases have the wages of any workers been lowered in order to achieve pay equity, reports the committee, because the objective of pay equity is to remedy wage inequities for underpaid workers, not to penalize another group of employees.[10]

be conducted first. Then internal rates of pay are compared to existing rates. In addition to the market wage levels, other criteria for wage determinations are labor market conditions (the number of people out of work and looking for work), traditions and past history of the organization's wage structure, indexes of productivity, company profit figures or sales data, and the Consumer Price Index, which helps determine the cost-of-living increases. Through their concern for the earnings per share of stocks, investors, particularly pension fund managers buying stocks of corporations, have a significant influence on the short-term versus long-term focus of compensation.

✳ JOB EVALUATION

Job evaluation emphasizes a systematic, rational assessment of jobs to establish internal equity among different jobs in an organization. While the amount paid for a job can be based on a manager's impression of what the job is worth or on what the external market is paying, more formal methods are often used,[13] including:

- Job ranking
- Job classification
- Factor comparison
- Point rating
- Hay Method
- Skill-based evaluation

These are the many methods of job evaluation: ←

RANKING METHOD.   The least specific job evaluation method is **job ranking**. Jobs can be ranked on the basis of such factors as difficulty, criticality to organizational success, or skill required. This method is convenient when there are only a few jobs to evaluate and when one person is familiar with them all. As the number of jobs increases and the likelihood of one individual knowing all jobs declines, detailed job analysis information becomes more important, and ranking is often done by committee. Key or **benchmark jobs** are used for comparison when a large number of jobs are to be ranked. These are jobs that most employees both are familiar with and have a similar understanding of their value.

One difficulty in the job ranking method is that all jobs are forced to be different from each other. Making fine distinctions between similar jobs is often difficult, and disagreements thus arise.

The *job ranking* method involves comparing jobs in a hierarchical fashion.

Benchmark jobs are jobs against which other jobs are compared to determine relative value.

JOB CLASSIFICATION METHOD.   The **job classification method** is similar to the ranking method, except that classes or grades are established and the jobs are then placed into the classes. Jobs are usually evaluated on the basis of the whole job, often using one factor such as difficulty or an intuitive summary of factors. Again, job analysis information is useful in the classification, and benchmark jobs are frequently established for each class. Within each class or grade, there is no further ranking of the jobs.

While the point evaluation system differs from traditional job classification methods, it may produce a similar product. That is, when jobs are assigned to pay grades, jobs are essentially classified according to their worth, and similar rates of pay are issued for jobs in the same pay grade or classification.

A particular advantage of this method is that it can be applied to a large number and wide variety of jobs. As the number and variety of jobs in an organization increase, however, the classification of jobs tends to become more subjective. This is particularly true when an organization has a large number of plant or office locations, and thus jobs with the same title may differ in content. Because evaluating each job separately in such cases is difficult, the job title becomes a more important guide to job classification than job content.

A major disadvantage of the job classification method is that the basis of the job evaluation is either one factor or an intuitive summary of many factors. The problem with using one factor, such as difficulty (skill), is that it may not be important in all jobs. Some jobs require a great deal of skill, but others require a

Job classification means putting jobs into families or classes.

great deal of responsibility. Should these jobs be placed in a lower classification than jobs requiring much skill? Not necessarily. Perhaps both factors could be considered together. Thus, each factor becomes a compensable factor, one that is valued by the organization and something worth paying for. Jobs would then be evaluated and classified on the basis of both factors. However, this balancing of the compensable factors to determine the relative equality of jobs often causes misunderstandings with the employees and the labor leaders.[14] To deal with this disadvantage, many organizations use more quantified methods of evaluation.

FACTOR COMPARISON. Approximately 10 percent of employers evaluate jobs using the **factor comparison method**. This approach to job evaluation represents a significant change over ranking and classification because **compensable factors** are utilized to determine job worth. Second, the method systematically links external rates of pay with internal, work-related compensable factors.

The factor comparison method of job evaluation consists of several steps:

- *Select compensable factors.* While any number of compensable factors can be used, mental requirements, skill, and physical and working conditions are universally used.
- *Conduct job analysis.* Once the compensable factors are chosen, jobs should be evaluated in relationship to the compensable factors and job specifications that relate to each factor written.
- *Pick benchmark jobs.* Benchmark jobs serve as reference points and consequently should be chosen with care just as in the ranking method. The content of benchmark jobs should be well known and stable with consistent pay rates in the external market. Benchmark jobs should also cover the entire range of jobs being evaluated.
- *Allocate benchmark wages across factors.* Using a compensation committee, wage rates for each job are allocated to each compensable factor.
- *Slot nonbenchmark jobs.* Other jobs are then slotted into each factor scale based on the amount of pay assigned to each factor. In doing this, jobs are compared against each benchmark job to determine whether they are of greater or lesser value.

The "price" or wage rates for the benchmark jobs are determined by the market. Although this is a quick method by which to set wage rates, it has the potential to perpetuate traditional pay differentials because the wage rates for other jobs are determined against these jobs. Because the process of determining the rates of other jobs is in the hands of the wage and salary analyst, it can be subjective, furthering the potential for wage discrimination.[15] As such, it has come under attack from the job comparability advocates for claims of pay discrimination. Another concern is that the relationships among jobs may change as external rates of pay or benchmark jobs shift.

In spite of these limitations, the factor comparison method of job evaluation is a definite improvement over ranking and classification. Additionally, it has been found to be acceptable to management, unions, and rank-and-file employees. Because jobs are ranked directly in dollar value, internal and external equity is integrally linked.

POINT RATING METHOD. The most widely used method of job evaluation is the **point rating** or **point factor method**, which consists of assigning point values for previously determined compensable factors and adding them to arrive at a total. Like the factor comparison method, compensable factors play the central role in the point system. Factors are weighted relative to their importance to the firm. A job's total point value and location in the pay structure is the sum of the

In *factor comparisons,* jobs are broken down into factors in order to determine the value of the job.

These are the five steps in factor comparison job evaluation: →

Factor comparison assigns monetary value directly to benchmark jobs.

Your job will most likely be evaluated by the point rating method.

In *point rating,* factors are given points, and jobs get different point values to indicate their relative worth.

numerical values for each degree of each compensable factor that the job possesses. The point evaluation system detailed in Exhibit 11.2 has six compensable factors. Five factors are used to evaluate all jobs; supervisory jobs are evaluated on one additional dimension. As shown, problem solving is weighted heaviest (260/1,000 points) while working conditions is the least important (50/1,000 points). The factors also differ in the number and point value of degrees associated with them.

Once factors are identified and weighted, scale anchors reflecting the different degrees within each factor are developed. Exhibit 11.3 shows the degree statements developed by a broadcast company to describe problem solving. In establishing factor scales, an organization can choose to use an existing system or develop compensable factors that are specifically tailored to their needs. In either event, the factors need to be written in clear language. Once the basic system is set up, each job is rated on all compensable factors. The more points assigned to a job, the more valuable it is to the organization.

Advantages of the method are that:

- It is widely used throughout industry, permitting comparisons on a similar basis with other firms.
- It is relatively simple to understand and is the simplest of quantitative methods of job evaluation.
- A well-conceived system has considerable stability: it is applicable to a wide range of jobs over an extended period of time. The greatest assets here are consistency and uniformity and its widespread use throughout industry.
- It is a definitive approach requiring several separate and distinct judgment decisions.

The limitations of the point rating method are few, but an especially critical one is the assumption that all jobs can be described with the same factors. Many organizations avoid this limitation by developing separate factors and point rating methods for different groups of employees.

Exhibit 11.2 shows six compensable factors used by one organization to evaluate the jobs in supervisory, nonsupervisory, and clerical categories. Some factors

> These are the advantages of the point rating method: ←

EXHIBIT 11.2
SAMPLE POINT EVALUATION SYSTEM

COMPENSABLE FACTOR	FIRST DEGREE	SECOND DEGREE	THIRD DEGREE	FOURTH DEGREE	FIFTH DEGREE
1. Job knowledge	50	100	150	200	
2. Problem solving	50	100	150	205	260
3. Impact	60	120	180	240	
4. Working conditions	10	30	50		
5. Supervision needed	25	50	75	100	
6. Supervision given	30	60	90	120	150

EXHIBIT 11.3
COMPENSABLE FACTOR AND RELATED DEGREE STATEMENTS

2. Problem solving:

This factor examines the types of problems dealt with in your job. Indicate the one level that is most representative of the majority of your job responsibilities.

Degree 1: Actions are performed in a set order per written or verbal instruction. Problems are referred to supervisor.

Degree 2: Solves routine problems and makes various choices regarding the order in which the work is performed within standard practices. May obtain information from varied sources.

Degree 3: Solves varied problems that require general knowledge of company policies and procedures applicable within area of responsibility. Decisions made based on a choice from established alternatives. Expected to act within standards and established procedures.

Degree 4: Requires analytical judgment, initiative, or innovation in dealing with complex problems or situations. Evaluation not easy because there is little precedent or information may be incomplete.

Degree 5: Plans, delegates, coordinates, and/or implements complex tasks involving new or constantly changing problems or situations. Involves the origination of new technologies or policies for programs or projects. Actions limited only by company policies and budgets.

---

are more important than others, as shown by the different point values. For example, the second degree of problem solving is worth approximately three times as much as the second degree of working conditions. Each job is evaluated only on its compensable factors. The human resource department determines which degree of a factor is appropriate for the job. Then, the points assigned to each degree of each factor are totaled. Levels of compensation are determined on the basis of the point totals.

As with other job evaluation plans, the point factor method incorporates the potential subjectivity of the job analyst. As such, it can potentially be discriminatory. Bias or subjectivity can enter (1) in the selection of the factors, (2) in the relative weights (degrees) assigned to factors, (3) in the assignment of degrees to the jobs being evaluated. At stake here are equal pay and job comparability. To make sure its point factor evaluation system is free from potential bias and is implemented as objectively as possible, an organization can solicit the input of the job incumbent, the supervisor, and job evaluation experts as well as its human resource department.

These are the areas in which judgments are made: ➡️

HAY METHOD. One of the most widely used job evaluation systems in the world combines the best characteristics of point evaluation and factor comparison methods of job evaluation. Used worldwide, this method is particularly popular for evaluating executive, managerial, and professional positions but is becoming more widely used for many others, including technical, clerical, and manufacturing positions.

Operationally, the **Hay Method** or plan traditionally relies on three primary compensable factors—know-how, problem solving, and accountability (see Exhibit 11.4 for definitions). Point values are determined for each job using the

The Hay Method focuses on three factors:

- **problem solving**
- **know-how**
- **accountability**

EXHIBIT 11.4
COMPENSABLE FACTORS IN THE HAY METHOD

PROBLEM SOLVING (MENTAL ACTIVITY)

The amount of original, self-starting thought required by the job for analysis, evaluation, creation, reasoning, and arriving at conclusions.

Problem solving has two dimensions:

- The degree of freedom with which the thinking process is used to achieve job objectives without the guidance of standards, precedents, or direction from others
- The type of mental activity involved; the complexity, abstractness, or originality of thought required

Problem solving is expressed as a percentage of know-how for the obvious reason that people think with what they know. The percentage judged to be correct for a job is applied to the know-how point value; the result is the point value given to problem solving.

KNOW-HOW

The sum total of all knowledge and skills, however acquired, needed for satisfactory job performance (evaluates the job, not the person).

Know-how has three dimensions:

- The amount of practical, specialized, or technical knowledge required
- Breadth of management, or the ability to make many activities and functions work well together; the job of company president, for example, has greater breadth than that of a department supervisor
- Requirement for skill in motivating people

Using a chart, a number can be assigned to the level of know-how needed in a job. This number—or point value—indicates the relative importance of know-how in the job being evaluated.

ACCOUNTABILITY

The measured effect of the job on company goals.

Accountability has three dimensions:

- Freedom to act, or relative presence of personal or procedural control and guidance; determined by answering the question, "How much freedom has the job holder to act independently?—for example, a plant manager has more freedom than a supervisor under his or her control
- Dollar magnitude, a measure of the sales, budget, dollar value of purchases, value added, or any other significant annual dollar figure related to the job
- Impact of the job on dollar magnitude, a determination of whether the job has a primary effect on end results or has instead a sharing, contributory, or remote effect

Accountability is given a point value independent of the other two factors.

Note: The total evaluation of any job is arrived at by adding the points for problem solving, know-how, and accountability. The points are not shown here.

---

three factors and their subfactors. Additionally, jobs are compared to one another on each factor. The former approach parallels traditional point evaluation processes, and the latter parallels factor comparison methods.

According to Hay Associates (the consulting firm that installs the Hay Method), a major advantage of their system centers on the wide acceptance of the system. Because organizations worldwide use the system, Hay can provide clients with comparative pay data by industry or locale. Another advantage of the system is that it has been legally challenged and found acceptable by the courts.

Still, the Hay Method, like many standardized systems, may not reflect an organization's true needs. In response to this, Hay Associates have been modifying their traditional plan to be more consistent with the needs of companies.

SKILL-BASED EVALUATION.   Whereas the previously mentioned job evaluation plans "pay for the job," **skill-based evaluation** is based on the idea of "pay-

Skill-based evaluation pays for skills of the worker not the job.

395

Skill-based evaluation promotes multiple skills and worker flexibility.

Maturity curves determine pay levels by combining the value of the job and the employee's years of experience.

Choosing a job evaluation method depends upon these factors: ⟶

ing for the person." As such, this type of evaluation, also called "pay for knowledge," is concerned with employee skills and in developing training programs to facilitate employee skill acquisition.[16]

Skill-based evaluation plans on a starting rate given to all new employees. After coming on board, employees are advanced one pay grade for each job skill they learn. Members of each employee's team ensure that the skills are learned correctly. They decide when the employee has mastered a job. Employees reach the top pay grade in the plant after learning all skills. The positive impact of skill-based plans on organizational objectives such as customer service is described in the feature, "Managing Human Resources at Northern Telecom: Skill-Based Program Improves Customer Service."

The idea of paying for the person, or at least the person-job combination rather than just the job, is not new. Many professional organizations such as universities, law offices, and research and development labs have been doing this for a long time. Determining pay rates using **maturity curves** (that combine the job with the employees years of experience) is a method organizations sometimes use for their scientific and engineering employees. What is new, however, is paying for the person (as determined by skills possessed) in blue-collar jobs. Examples of skill-based evaluation for blue-collar jobs include some of the plants at Honeywell, Westinghouse, Steelcase, and Polaroid. Skill-based evaluation is compared with conventional job evaluation methods in Exhibit 11.5.

CHOOSING A JOB EVALUATION METHOD

Job evaluation methods differ in several respects. Some methods evaluate the whole job while others evaluate jobs using compensable factors. Job evaluation approaches also vary in regards to the type of output produced. For example, the factor comparison method evaluates jobs directly in dollar worth, while the point evaluation system requires conversion of points to dollars.

An organization's choice of method depends on several factors:

- *Legal and social background.* What job evaluation methods can be used may be limited by collective bargaining arrangements or by what is legally acceptable.
- *Organizational structure.* In small firms, simple systems such as ranking may be appropriate. However, in a multiplant enterprise, plans may be more complex.
- *Management style.* Management style can vary from autocratic to democratic. Management style will primarily affect the scope of worker participation in the design and application of a job evaluation scheme.
- *Labor-management relations.* No job evaluation scheme can succeed unless the workers accept it. Indeed, the results of many a job evaluation program have been totally rejected because of union opposition. To prevent this, organizations may choose a plan that provides for participation.
- *Cost in time and money.* Job evaluation, like other HR activities, costs time and money. There is up-front cost in developing a tailor-made plan. Canned programs (programs that can be bought off the shelf and used just as they are) may be costly in terms of purchase price and user acceptance. Usually, a job evaluation system takes between six to twelve months for firms employing more than 500 employees.[18]

SINGLE VERSUS MULTIPLE PLANS. Another decision that needs to be made is whether one or several job evaluation plans should be used. Traditionally, job evaluation plans have varied depending on the job family (for example, clerical, skilled-craft, professional). This approach is premised on the assumption that

As a supplier of products to the telecommunications industry, Northern Telecom serves a constantly changing marketplace. Customer demands are high, the pace is rapid, and the products made by the company are evolving continually. This constant change puts pressure on all Northern Telecom employees to stay abreast of new product technologies, but the product installers feel the pressure most of all.

To encourage field technicians to keep their skills current and to ensure that they're adequately compensated for their increasing skill levels, Northern Telecom established a skill-based pay program in 1991 for the 1,200 installation-department employees. This program is called *Fast Forward*.

"This is a true pay-for-skills program," explains Dennis Garfield, director of installation at the company's Technical Installation Center in Raleigh, North Carolina. "The only way our field technicians can receive an increase in their base pay is through the attainment of new skills."

All of the installation skills that Northern Telecom employees need are listed on a document called the *Skills Capability Record* (SCR). Each skill on the SCR is assigned a point value, based on the difficulty of attaining that skill as well as on how important that skill is to the installation department. Skills range in value from 2 to 40 points, with the high-point skills considered to be the most important.

These points correspond to salary zones that are divided into 100-point increments. As field technicians earn additional points, they move into higher salary zones. "Now there's no such thing as a dollar per point," Garfield emphasizes. "For field technicians to receive an increase in base salary, they must move into a new zone— into another 100-point increment. In other words, someone could go from 699 to 700 points and be eligible for a pay increase."

Employees receive these points when they demonstrate that they can perform a particular skill on a job site without supervision. When this is done, they are *certified* in that skill by a certification committee that includes:

- The district manager
- The employee's immediate supervisor
- A representative from human resources
- A peer

In Fast Forward's first eighteen months, close to 90 percent of Northern Telecom's field technicians received some sort of skill-based pay increase. What impact has this had on customer service? "We've heard many positive remarks from customers about our technician's ability to answer their questions about our products," Garfield explains. "Additionally, we have a formal survey that's completed after every job, geared specifically to the installation activity. The surveys are coming back with much higher ratings today than they did two years ago."[17]

work content of various job families is too diverse to be captured by one plan. For example, manufacturing jobs may vary in terms of working conditions and physical effort while professional jobs may not differ in terms of these compensable factors. Proponents of multiple plans contend that multiple plans are necessary to capture the unique and different job characteristics of job families.

Proponents of comparable worth and those favoring pay equity advocate a single pay plan. Their argument is premised on the assumption that there are universal compensable factors that relate to *all* jobs. Only when jobs are evalu-

EXHIBIT 11.5
COMPARISON OF SKILL-BASED PAY COMPONENTS WITH CONVENTIONAL JOB EVALUATION

COMPONENT	SKILL-BASED EVALUATION	JOB-BASED EVALUATION
1. Determination of job worth	Tied to evaluation of skill blocks	Tied to evaluation of total job
2. Pricing	Difficult because the overall pay system is tied to the market	Easier because wages are tied to benchmark jobs in the labor market
3. Pay ranges	Extremely broad; one pay range for entire cluster of skills	Variable depending on type of job and pay-grade width
4. Evaluation of performance	Competency tests	Performance appraisal ratings
5. Salary increases	Tied to skill acquisition as measured by competency testing	Tied to seniority, performance appraisal ratings, or actual output
6. Role of training	Essential to attain job flexibility and pay increases for all employees	Necessitated by need rather than desire
7. Advancement opportunities	Greater opportunities; anyone who passes competency test advances	Fewer opportunities; no advancement unless there is a job opening
8. Effect of job change	Pay remains constant unless skill proficiency increases	Pay changed immediately to level associated with new job
9. Pay administration	Difficult because many aspects of pay plan (training, certification) demand attention	Contingent upon the complexity of job evaluation and pay allocation plan

SOURCE: Adapted from G. E. Ledford, "Three Case Studies on Skill-Based Pay: An Overview," *Compensation and Benefits Review* (April 1990): 11–23; H. Tosi and L. Tosi "What Managers Need to Know about Knowledge-Based Pay," *Organizational Dynamics* (Winter, 1986).

ated using the same criteria can the relative value of *all* jobs be determined. When separate plans are used, it is much easier to discriminate against specific classes of jobs (for example, clerical versus skilled). To prevent this, universal factors need to be utilized. The Hay Method is one standardized or canned evaluation system with universal factors. It is also possible, but difficult, to develop firm-specific job evaluation systems with universal factors. Some companies such as Control Data and Hewlett-Packard use a core set of factors and another set of factors unique to particular occupation groups. However many plans are involved, the results are used to establish job classes.

✱DETERMINING JOB CLASSES

Job families involve grouping together jobs of similar value.

Before salaries are determined, job classes or families are created from the results of the job evaluation. Determining **job classes** or **job families** means grouping together all jobs that are similar in value based on job evaluation; for example, grouping all clerical or all managerial jobs together. Jobs within the same class may be quite different, but they are about equal in value to the organization according to the job evaluation. All the jobs in each class or family are assigned one salary or range of salaries. (See our discussion in Chapter 6 on job analysis.)

Job families make it easier to administer the compensation program.

Why group jobs into classes? One reason is the efficiency gained in salary administration. Also, it can be hard to justify the small differences in pay that might exist between jobs where job classes do not exist. Finally, small errors that occur in evaluating the jobs can be eliminated in the classification process. Of course, employees can also find fault with the classification results if the jobs are grouped with those they feel are less important. Sometimes the jobs grouped together are too dissimilar because there are too few classes. Using only a few classes is appropriate, however, if many of the jobs in the organization are of similar value.

✳ESTABLISHING THE PAY STRUCTURE

Once jobs are evaluated and the job classes determined, wage rates or ranges need to be established. Although job classes are determined for the purpose of developing wage rates, job classes are often based on wage rates that already exist. This practice may seem somewhat bizarre, but it is commonly done. Most organizations are already paying their employees and thus need to determine job classes only when many new jobs are introduced, or if they have never really had a sound job analysis program. In addition, if the organization has grown and incorporated many more jobs, it may need to group them into classes for purposes of salary administration. On the other hand, an organization that is just being established is most likely small and will determine the price of its jobs by surveys of what other organizations are paying. Regardless, conducting a wage survey is a critical component in establishing the pay structure.

✳WAGE AND SALARY SURVEYS

As discussed already, the market, along with other factors, can influence the wage rates established by the organization. This influence occurs whenever the organization conducts wage and salary surveys

Wage and salary surveys can be used to develop compensation levels, wage structures, and even payment plans (the amount and kind of direct and indirect compensation). Whereas job evaluation helps ensure **internal equity**, wage surveys help ensure **external equity**. Both types of equity are important if an organization is to be successful in attracting, retaining, and motivating employees.[19]

Organizations use information from and contribute information to wage surveys. Separate surveys are published for different occupational groupings; thus many larger organizations subscribe to several surveys. For example, surveys exist for clerical workers, professional workers, managers, and executives. Separate surveys are conducted not only because of wide differences in skill levels, but also because labor markets are so different. An organization surveying clerical workers may need to survey companies only within a ten-mile radius, whereas a survey of managerial salaries may cover the entire country.

✳ GRADE STRUCTURE

After deciding on the wage and salary information it wants, the organization develops a **grade structure** with pay rates for job categories. A typical grade structure is shown in Exhibit 11.6; it is based on job evaluation points associated with a point factor evaluation.

The boxes shown are associated with a range of job evaluation points (the job class) and a range of pay (the pay grade). In essence, these **pay grades** are the job families or classes. Consequently, there may be several different jobs within one box, but they are very similar in job evaluation points, if not in content. The boxes vary in shape but generally ascend from left to right. This reflects increased job worth and associated higher pay levels (shown on the vertical axis) for more valued jobs. The pay levels are established using market information (to ensure external equity).[20]

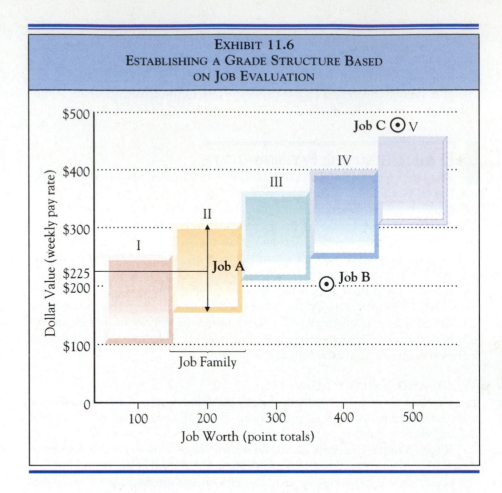

EXHIBIT 11.6
ESTABLISHING A GRADE STRUCTURE BASED
ON JOB EVALUATION

Grade structures put all jobs in pay boxes in order to organize them as shown in Exhibit 11.6.

The wage rate for each job is then determined by locating its grade and moving over to a point on the vertical axis, as done for job A in grade II. A pay limit exists for the jobs in each grade. Staying within those limits (the range) is essential to maintaining internal equity, assuming the job evaluation is valid.[21] For employees to obtain a significant salary increase, they must move into a job in the next higher grade. Generally, each job has a rate range. As shown, job A has a range from $150 per week to $300 per week. The midpoint of this range is $225. These numbers can become critical. Many organizations would like to have the average salary of employees in a job equal the midpoint. If the average is higher than the midpoint, many employees might not receive significant salary increases unless they are promoted.

Occasionally, jobs fall outside the established pay grades (jobs B and C in Exhibit 11.6). When a job falls *below* the established pay grade, it is circled, and usually a wage adjustment (sweetener) is made to bring the job within the established pay grade. Sometimes, after periods of high inflation rates, the entire salary structure has to be adjusted upward to bring jobs within established pay grades, thereby moving the midpoints up for all pay grades. This ensures external equity and that employees' salaries do not decline in real terms. Sometimes, though, a job will be overpaid (job C in pay grade V). One means of dealing with this is to circle the job, which, in this instance, means adjusting the rate downward after the incumbent leaves.

To circle a job means to highlight it so action will be taken to realign the job with its pay grade.

Employees usually start at the bottom of the range and go up. How quickly their wages rise depends on factors related to individual wage determination.

PAY GRADES FOR SKILL-BASED PAY. The establishment of external equity is more complex with skill-based pay systems than with job-based pay systems. As experienced at Northern Telecom, it was simply not possible to directly compare any particular pay levels in the firm's skilled-based pay plan with pay levels of other firms using job-based pay. While organizations using skilled-based pay rely on the market to set levels, the data is used to set minimum, maximum, and average pay levels for the *entire job family*, not to peg each particular skill step in the pay system to jobs found in the outside markets. Exhibit 11.7 depicts the salary guidelines for Northern Telecom's field technician job family. Notice there are five competency levels with an overall pay range of 270 percent. Target high rates are suggested maximum rates of pay for employees at a specific competency level.

As with job-based pay, organizations employing skill-based pay differ in their pay policies relative to the external market. According to Peter LeBlanc, director of compensation, Northern Telecom matched the market by setting the minimum of the salary range at the labor market entry rate. The maximum was established on the basis of the average rate of pay for the senior job in the firm's traditional benchmark ladder.

LABOR UNIONS
The presence of a union in a private-sector firm is estimated to increase wages by 10 to 15 percent. Union presence also adds about 20 to 30 percent to the cost of employee benefits.

Unions also have pushed for wage escalation clauses. Wage escalation clauses are designed to increase wages automatically during the life of a contract. One way unions have accomplished this is to tie wage increases to changes in the consumer price index. As discussed more in Chapter 12, **cost-of-living adjustments (COLAs)** were popular in the 1960s and 1970s; however, the number of workers covered by COLAs declined during the 1980s and 1990s—primarily because the Consumer Price Index has decelerated in recent years but also because of growing wage competition from other countries such as Taiwan, Korea, and Mexico. Exhibit 11.8 shows relative hourly compensation costs for production workers, some unionized and some not.

LABOR MARKET
The labor market influences the wage and salary structure basically through the supply of labor. Shortages in the labor market (internal or external) provide those who are qualified to fill the jobs an opportunity to negotiate better terms of employment. The juggling act between labor supply and demand has ramifications for internal as well as external pay equity. Internally, this can mean pay increases that are relatively higher than those of workers not in short supply. Externally, the firm must also pay a higher rate to attract new hires who are in short supply.

In a country as large as the United States, most organizations experience not one, but several labor markets. Workers move around. They move to where the jobs are, and they move to where they might want to live. This influences cost-of-living conditions in states throughout our country, which in turn influences pay levels. The results of this are shown in Exhibit 11.9. Such differences influence where companies set up operations and can also prompt them to move

Job-based pay describes the others we have discussed.
Skill-based pay is the newer method evaluating skills of employees.

1972 average weekly pay (today's dollars): $461.
1993 average weekly pay: $372.

Yes, the forces of supply and demand impact wages.

DID YOU KNOW?

Electricians in San Antonio, Texas, make $12.31 per hour while their counterparts in San Francisco make $25.28 per hour.

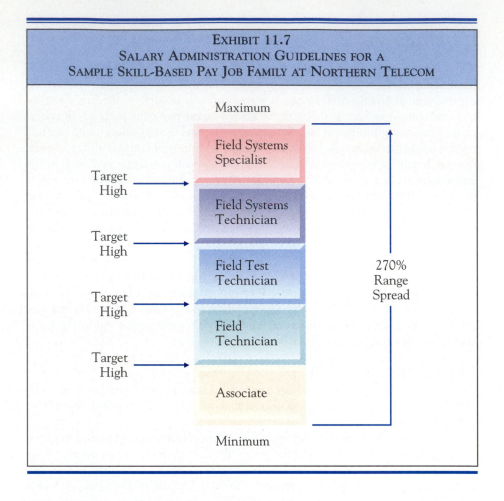

EXHIBIT 11.7
SALARY ADMINISTRATION GUIDELINES FOR A
SAMPLE SKILL-BASED PAY JOB FAMILY AT NORTHERN TELECOM

Maximum

Field Systems Specialist

Target High →

Field Systems Technician

Target High →

Field Test Technician

Target High →

Field Technician

Target High →

Associate

270% Range Spread

Minimum

operations—for example, J.C. Penney moved its headquarters from New York City to Dallas, Texas.[22]

INDIVIDUAL WAGE DETERMINATION

Once the job analysis and evaluation have been completed, the job classes established, and the wage structure determined, the question becomes how much to pay each individual. For example, consider Ann and John , both of whom work on the same job. The rate range is $3,000–4,000 per month; Ann is paid $4,000 and John $3,500. What might account for the pay differential? Although performance contribution is perhaps the logical answer, seniority, market demand, age, and experience (personal contributions) also influence individual wages.

In actuality, individual wage determinations are based on both personal contributions and performance. Thus, age and seniority as well as performance probably influence Ann and John's pay (performance-based pay is discussed in Chapter 12). Even though managers might argue that pay differences based on performance are more equitable, many Japanese companies, for example, reward seniority more than performance. This seems to result in more cooperation and teamwork from employees and a willingness to remain with the same firm for a long time.

DID YOU KNOW?

In 1971 the hourly pay (1991 dollars) for a high school dropout and a college graduate was $9.59 and $14.72, respectively. In 1991 it was $7.62 and $14.77, respectively!

Nobel prize winner Dr. Kevin Murphy at the University of Chicago proved that a major cause of rising inequality in pay has been the growing demand for sophisticated skills and training.

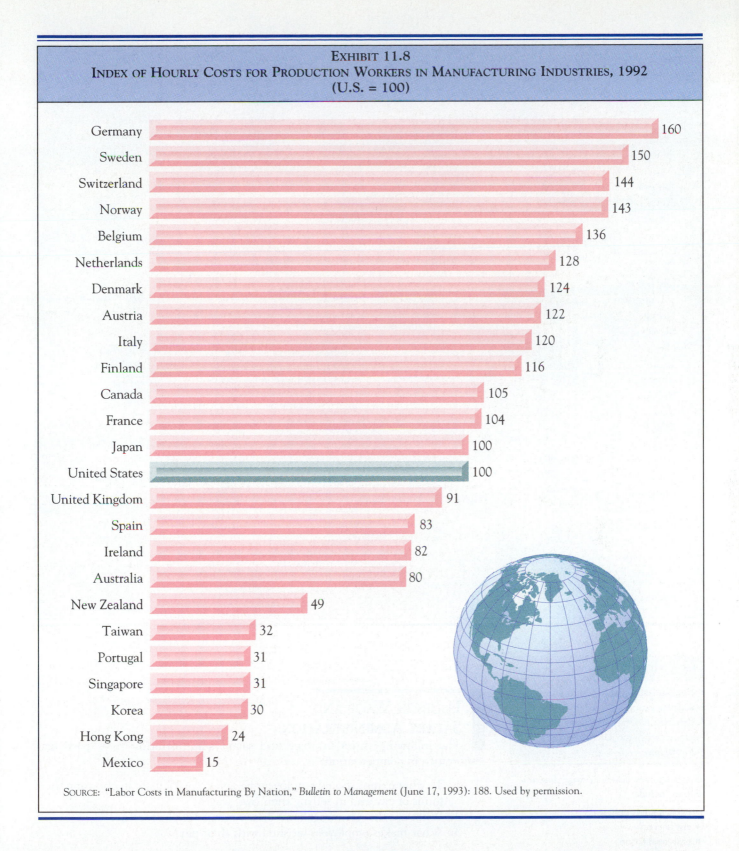

EXHIBIT 11.8
INDEX OF HOURLY COSTS FOR PRODUCTION WORKERS IN MANUFACTURING INDUSTRIES, 1992
(U.S. = 100)

Germany	160
Sweden	150
Switzerland	144
Norway	143
Belgium	136
Netherlands	128
Denmark	124
Austria	122
Italy	120
Finland	116
Canada	105
France	104
Japan	100
United States	100
United Kingdom	91
Spain	83
Ireland	82
Australia	80
New Zealand	49
Taiwan	32
Portugal	31
Singapore	31
Korea	30
Hong Kong	24
Mexico	15

SOURCE: "Labor Costs in Manufacturing By Nation," *Bulletin to Management* (June 17, 1993): 188. Used by permission.

EXHIBIT 11.9
ANNUAL PAY LEVELS AND GROWTH IN PAY BY STATE
AVERAGE ANNUAL PAY IN 1991 AND PERCENT CHANGE FROM 1990

STATE	AVERAGE ANNUAL PAY IN 1991	PERCENT CHANGE, 1990–1991	STATE	AVERAGE ANNUAL PAY IN 1991	PERCENT CHANGE, 1990–1991
Alabama	$21,287	4.0%	Montana	$18,648	4.2%
Alaska	$30,830	2.9%	Nebraska	$19,372	4.3%
Arizona	$22,207	3.6%	Nevada	$23,083	3.2%
Arkansas	$19,008	4.4%	New Hampshire	$23,600	4.4%
California	$27,499	5.0%	New Jersey	$29,992	5.4%
Colorado	$23,981	4.7%	New Mexico	$20,275	4.8%
Connecticut	$30,689	5.8%	New York	$30,011	3.9%
Delaware	$25,647	5.0%	North Carolina	$21,087	4.3%
District of			North Dakota	$18,132	2.9%
Columbia	$35,570	5.5%	Ohio	$23,603	3.3%
Florida	$21,991	4.6%	Oklahoma	$20,968	3.3%
Georgia	$23,164	4.7%	Oregon	$22,348	4.8%
Hawaii	$24,104	4.0%	Pennsylvania	$24,393	4.0%
Idaho	$19,688	3.7%	Rhode Island	$23,082	3.1%
Illinois	$26,310	3.9%	South Carolina	$20,439	3.9%
Indiana	$22,522	3.8%	South Dakota	$17,131	4.3%
Iowa	$19,810	3.0%	Tennessee	$21,541	4.5%
Kansas	$21,002	3.8%	Texas	$23,760	4.7%
Kentucky	$20,730	3.9%	Utah	$20,874	4.0%
Louisiana	$21,501	4.1%	Vermont	$21,355	4.0%
Maine	$20,870	3.6%	Virginia	$23,804	4.6%
Maryland	$25,960	5.0%	Washington	$23,942	5.7%
Massachusetts	$28,041	5.0%	West Virginia	$21,356	3.1%
Michigan	$26,125	3.0%	Wisconsin	$21,838	3.5%
Minnesota	$23,961	3.6%	Wyoming	$20,591	2.7%
Mississippi	$18,411	3.9%	UNITED STATES	$24,575	4.1%
Missouri	$22,567	3.9%			

SOURCE: Bureau of Labor Statistics

Contemporary issues in wage determination include:

- participation policies
- pay secrecy
- pay satisfaction
- salary versus hourly basis

ISSUES IN WAGE AND SALARY ADMINISTRATION

The following issues in wage and salary administration have particular importance in compensation:

1. To what extent should employees be able to participate in choosing their forms of pay and in setting their own wages?
2. What are the advantages and disadvantages of pay secrecy?
3. What makes employees satisfied with their pay?

More administration issues are addressed in the next two chapters.

EMPLOYEE PARTICIPATION

Job evaluation judgments, like other human resource decisions, can be made by a variety of raters including compensation professionals, managers, and job incumbents. An important decision is who should be involved in the development of job evaluation systems and in the determination of job worth.

Traditionally, compensation professionals and line managers had the most involvement in the design of compensation systems. Now with the theme of partnership there is an emphasis on employee involvement in job evaluation. Employees are involved in the job evaluation process to broaden their understanding of the process by which job value is established.

One of the most common ways to increase involvement is to establish a job evaluation committee composed of management, nonmanagement, and union representatives. Individuals on such a committee should be knowledgeable about a wide range of jobs. It may also be useful to co-opt antagonists. By involving representatives from all areas, communication is improved, and the likelihood that the organization's values are reflected in the job evaluation system are increased. The involvement of multiple parties does, however, increase the potential for conflict. For example, managers may try to distort job evaluation ratings of a favorite or superstar employee so pay can exceed the maximum permitted for a job of that value. Conversely, compensation professionals will want to preserve pay equity at all costs and thus try to block the efforts of managers to get special pay increases. The process of negotiation and give-and-take is usually worth it because managers and employees are less likely to accept and/or understand the results of a job evaluation study when they were not consulted.

Bonneville International, a broadcast group, has employees update their job descriptions and their supervisors sign off on the descriptions. Using the job description as a common frame of reference, supervisors and employees *independently* complete the firm's point evaluation instrument. Next, the ratings for the two groups are compared. When rating differences are found, the supervisor meets with employees to reach a consensus on the point value of the job. Because employees are personally involved, there are *no* job classification appeals, and the system is perceived as procedurally fair. These results indicate that employee participation is well worth the additional time involved.

PAY SECRECY

According to organizational etiquette, asking others their salaries is generally considered inappropriate. In a study at Du Pont, all employees were asked if the company should disclose more payroll information so that everyone would know everyone else's pay. Only 18 percent voted for an open pay system.[23] Managers also favor **pay secrecy** because it makes their lives easier. Without knowledge of pay differentials, employees are less likely to confront their supervisor about inequitable pay. Consequently, managers do not have to defend or justify their actions.

Despite these common perceptions, there are several reasons to have open communication about pay practices. First, certain research indicates that employees misperceive the pay level of other employees. They tend to overestimate the pay of those with lower-level jobs and to underestimate the pay of those with higher-level jobs. Since pay differentials are designed to motivate employees to seek promotion, this misperception may be detrimental to employee motivation. After all, why should an employee gain the experience and accept greater responsibility for only meager salary increases? A second, more practical, reason for an open pay policy is that considerable resources have been devoted to devel-

> People underestimate the pay of their bosses and overestimate the pay of those lower in the organization.

oping a fair and equitable system. For managers and employees to gain an accurate view of the system, they must be informed.

Finally, and potentially most important, pay is a powerful motivator only when its linkage to performance is explicitly stated and known to employees. For an employee to perform well, they must know what performance is desired and what the reward will be for performing well and what the consequence is for performing poorly.

Regarding what should be communicated, many employers specify the range for jobs in a typical career path. In addition to ranges, some organizations detail the typical increases associated with low, average, and top performance. A concern in communicating the latter is that the organization may not be able to maintain the same pay schedule in the future. If increases are lower in subsequent years, there is a risk that employees will become dissatisfied. Still, if it is made clear that the size of the salary increase pool is contingent on the profitability of the organization, this problem can be avoided.[24]

SATISFACTION WITH PAY

If organizations want to minimize absenteeism and turnover as well as maximize motivation through compensation, they must make sure that employees are satisfied with their pay. Since satisfaction with pay and motivation to perform are not necessarily closely related, organizations must know the determinants of pay satisfaction. With this knowledge, organizations can develop pay practices more likely to result in satisfaction with pay and motivation to perform. Three major determinants of satisfaction with pay are pay fairness, pay level, and pay administration practices.[25]

Major determinants of pay satisfaction are:

• fairness
• level
• administration practices

PAY FAIRNESS. **Pay fairness** refers to what people believe they deserve to be paid in relation to what others deserve to be paid. The tendency is for people to determine what they and others deserve to be paid by comparing what they give to the organization with what they get out of the organization. In comparing themselves with others, people may decide whether they are being paid fairly. If they regard this comparison as fair or equitable, they are more likely to be satisfied. If they see this comparison as unfair, they will likely be dissatisfied. This is referred to as **equity theory**.

People want to be paid fairly—that is, they look at themselves and others when judging the fairness of their pay. This is the essence of *equity theory*.

Fairness can be increased by giving employees a voice in compensation and also by providing due process. Thus it is important for organizations to establish formal appeals procedures. Appeals procedures vary in the degree of formality and in how independent the process is from traditional lines of authority. Union contracts often prescribe a formal system where complaints are first filed with the immediate supervisor. If a satisfactory resolution is not attained, the appeal moves forward to a higher level of management until a final decision is reached.

Professor Lawler at the University of Southern California says the best performers compare themselves with others in similar jobs with similar performance in other organizations.

PAY LEVEL. **Pay level** is an important determinant of the perceived amount of pay satisfaction. People compare actual pay with what they believe they should receive. The result of the comparison is satisfaction with pay if "should" equals "actual." Dissatisfaction results if the actual level is less than the "should" level.

Because of the media coverage, employees now know the top managers get paid a great deal.

Increasingly, pay-level satisfaction is being related to differences in pay for employees at different levels (especially in comparing nonmanagers to managers) in the organization. U.S. salary survey data show that the average hourly total compensation for all managers is about $25.00 and, for nonmanagerial service workers, it is $7.25. The average differential between the highest and lowest paid employees in large U.S. organizations is at least 20:1. In Japan, this same differ-

EXHIBIT 11.10
RELATIVE AVERAGE CEO TOTAL CASH COMPENSATION
(for firms with annual sales greater than $100 million U.S.)

Australia	42
Sweden	44
Hong Kong	45
Singapore	45
Venezuela	45
United Kingdom	48
Japan	50
Argentina	51
Netherlands	54
Mexico	55
Belgium	59
Spain	59
Brazil	60
France	60
Canada	65
Italy	67
Switzerland	73
Germany	73
United States	100

Note: Basis United States = 100%.

SOURCE: *International Compensation Report* (New York: Towers Perrin). Used by permission.

ence is about 7:1. This is caused in large part by the relatively high level of total CEO compensation. According to Exhibit 11.10, the total compensation for U.S. CEOs is substantially greater than for CEOs in 20 other countries. Of course, there are some variations within the United States. For example, Bill Gates' salary is less than $1 million a year, but the average CEO receives $1.2 million annually. However:

> Certain perquisites offered outside the United States balance the scales a bit. The United States is the only one of 20 major countries surveyed by Towers Perrin, an international HR consulting firm, where a car (often with a driver)

Companies were laying off workers, asking workers for sacrifices, while at the same time their CEOs were significantly increasing their own salaries. When there is no relationship between pay and profitability of the company, you are in an anticompetitive position.

—U.S. Senator Carl Levin

is not usually provided to the CEO of a $100-million-a-year company. And in many countries with confiscatory tax policies, companies offer tax-favored perks such as club memberships, augmented pensions, and entertainment and housing allowances. But, says Michael Emig, a principal with Wyatt Company, "the order of magnitude of these perks is nothing compared with how much wealth U.S. executives can accumulate over a period of time."

The American obsession with superstars also helps drive up the chief's pay. Says Tower Perrin's David Swinford: "In Europe and Japan they still reward longevity and loyalty by promoting from within, whereas we find a home-run hitter and pay to get him as a free agent." Adds Lance Berger of Philadelphia's Hay group: "Each time a CEO changes jobs, it cranks the whole market up a notch."[26]

Regardless of the reasons for these high levels of CEO pay, employees perceive them as too high. Especially irksome is the CEO practice of asking employees to take pay cuts, while actually increasing their own pay![27]

Pay administration issues include concern for:

- **external equity**
- **internal equity**
- **perceived performance-pay link**
- **continued relevancy**
- **trust and consistency**

PAY ADMINISTRATION PRACTICES.   What do pay fairness and pay-level issues suggest for pay administration practices? *First*, if the employer is to attract new employees and keep them satisfied with their pay, the wages and salaries offered should approximate those of other employees in comparable organizations (that is, external equity must exist).[28] *Second*, the pricing of jobs can enhance pay satisfaction when it is based on a philosophy of equal pay for jobs of comparable worth. This determination can be aided by sound job evaluations. But the worth of jobs must be evaluated according to the factors considered important by both employees and the organizations (so that internal equity exists).

Third, pay-for-performance systems must be accompanied by a method for accurately measuring the performance of employees. They must also be open enough so employees can clearly see the performance-pay relationship. This is discussed further in Chapter 12. *Fourth*, compensation rates and pay structures should be continually reviewed and revised if necessary. Over time the content of a job may change, distorting the relationship between its actual and its job-evaluated worth.

A *final* pay administration practice concerns trust and consistency. Employees need to perceive that the organization is looking out for their interests as well as for its own. They want to know that they are being trusted in the same way as the top managers of the organization. Without this knowledge and understanding, not only is the level of trust and pay satisfaction low, but pay also becomes a target for complaints regardless of the real issues. Going a long way to ensure that trust and pay satisfaction do not erode are examples set by the CEO:

> Some companies have awakened to the hidden costs of the trust gap and are experimenting with ingenious ways of sewing corporate top and bottom back together. Few CEOs have mastered the aristo-bypass, but those who have offer the following advice.
>
> Start with the obvious. Tie the financial interests of higher-ups and lower-downs closer together by making exposure to risk and to reward more equitable. When Nucor, a steel company in Charlotte, North Carolina, with $1.1 billion in sales, went through tough times, President Ken Iverson took a 60 percent cut in pay. "How often do you see that?" asks Jude Rich, president of Sibson & Co., a compensation consulting firm. "It makes a real difference if employees see that their CEO is willing to take it in the shorts along with them."[29]

INTERNATIONAL COMPENSATION

As the environment for many business firms in the United States becomes more global, international compensation becomes a more significant part of total compensation.[30]

OBJECTIVES

When developing international compensation policies, a multinational corporation (MNC) seeks to satisfy several objectives. First, the policy should be consistent and fair in its treatment of all categories of international employees. The interests of the MNC are best served if all international employees are relatively satisfied with their compensation package and perceive that they are treated equitably. Second, the policy must work to attract and retain personnel in areas of greatest need and opportunity. Third, the policy should facilitate the transfer of international employees in the most cost-effective manner. Fourth, the policy should be consistent with the firm's overall strategy and structure. Finally, compensation should serve to motivate employees. Some professional international HR managers would say that motivation is the major objective of their compensation programs.[31]

DESIGNING INTERNATIONAL COMPENSATION PACKAGES

Designing international compensation packages is more of an art than a science.

In general, the first issue facing MNCs when designing international compensation policies is whether to establish an overall policy for all employees or to distinguish between PCNs and TCNs. This differentiation may diminish in the future, but it is currently common for MNCs to distinguish between these two distinct groups.

Remember:
- PCN=parent-country national or expatriate
- TCN=third-country national
- HCN=host-country national

There is even a tendency for MNCs to differentiate among types of PCNs. Separate types of policies may be established based on the length of assignment (temporary transfer, permanent transfer, or continual relocation) or on the type of employee. Cash remuneration, special allowances, benefits, and pensions are determined in part by such classification. Short-term PCNs, for example, whose two- or three-year tours of duty abroad are interspersed with long periods at home, may be treated differently from career PCNs who spend most of their time working in various locations abroad. Both of these groups are different from TCNs, who often move from country to country in the employ of one MNC (or several) headquartered in a country other than their own (for example, a Swiss banker may be in charge of a German branch of a British bank). In effect, these are the real global employees, the ones who can weave together the far-flung parts of a MNC. As the global MNC increases in importance, it is likely that the TCNs will become more valuable and thus able to command levels of compensation equivalent to PCNs.

For PCNs, the most widely used policy emphasizes "keeping the expatriate whole" (that is, maintaining salary level relative to the PCN's colleagues plus compensating for the costs of international service).[32] The basis of this policy implies that foreign assignees should not suffer a material loss due to their transfer. This can be accomplished through the utilization of what is known as the balance-sheet approach. This approach to international compensation is a system designed to equalize the purchasing power of employees at comparable position levels living overseas and in the home country, and to provide incentives to offset qualitative differences between assignment locations.[33]

There are five major categories of outlays that cover all of the types of expenses incurred by PCNs and their families:

1. *Goods and services:* home-country outlays for items such as food, personal care, clothing, household furnishings, recreation, transportation, and medical care.
2. *Housing:* the major costs associated with the employees' principal residence.
3. *Income taxes:* payments to federal and local governments for personal income taxes.
4. *Reserve:* contributions to savings, payments for benefits, pension contributions, investments, education expenses, social security taxes, and so forth.
5. *Shipment and storage:* the major costs associated with shipping and storing personal and household effects.

Thus MNCs seek to develop international packages that are competitive in all of the following aspects of compensation:

Base Salary

- Home rate/home currency
- Local rate/local currency
- Salary adjustments or promotions—home or local standard
- Bonus—home or local currency, home or local standard
- Stock options
- Inducement payment/hardship premium—percent of salary or lump sum payment, home or local currency
- Currency protection—discretion or split basis
- Global salary and performance structure

Taxation Services

- Tax protection
- Tax equalization
- Other services

Benefits

- Home-country program
- Local program
- Social security program
- Car

Allowances

- Cost-of-living allowances
- Housing standard
- Education
- Relocation
- Perquisites
- Home leave
- Shipping and storage

International compensation packages include:

- base salary
- taxation services
- benefits
- allowances

DID YOU KNOW?

General Motors spends between $750,000 and $1 million (besides salary) on an executive and his or her family during a three-year overseas posting.

While not all these aspects of international compensation are likely to come into play for every expatriate, it is still rather expensive to have expatriates. Exhibit 11.11 shows a breakdown of just how expensive it can be. Thus firms who want to be global face rather high compensation bills if they need to staff with expatriates. Although some of these aspects of international compensation may not apply to TCNs or HCNs, all do apply to PCNs. Some of these aspects are now described in detail here, and others are described in the next chapters.

EXHIBIT 11.11
THE PRICE OF AN EXPATRIATE

An employer's typical first-year expenses of sending a U.S. executive to Britain, assuming a $100,000 salary and a family of four.

DIRECT COMPENSATION	COSTS
Base Salary	$100,000
Foreign-service premium	15,000
Goods and services differential	21,000
Housing costs in London	39,000*
TRANSFER	
Relocation allowance	5,000
Airfare to London	2,000
Moving household goods	25,000
OTHER	
Company car	15,000
Schooling (two children)	20,000
Annual home leave (tour)	4,000
UK personal income tax	56,000
Total	$302,000

Note: Additional costs often incurred aren't listed above, including language and cross-cultural training for employee and family and costs of selling home and cars in the U.S. before moving.

*Figures take into account payments by employee to company based on hypothetical U.S. income tax and housing costs.

SOURCE: *The Wall Street Journal* December 11, 1989, p. 4. Reprinted by permission.

BASE SALARY. The term **base salary** acquires a somewhat different meaning when employees go abroad. At home, base salary denotes the amount of cash compensation that serves as a benchmark for other compensation elements (for example, bonuses and benefits). For PCNs, it is the primary component of a package of allowances, many of which are directly related to base salary (foreign service premium, cost-of-living allowances, housing allowances, and tax protection, for example) as well as the basis for in-service benefits and pension contributions.

When applied to TCNs, base salary may mean the prevailing rate paid for a specific skill in the employee's home country. Typically, companies use local compensation levels as guidelines when developing HCN compensation policies. Conditions that force compensation policies to differ from those in the United States include inflation and cost of living, housing, security, school costs, and taxation. For example, it is far less costly to recruit a construction engineer from Spain or Taiwan to work in the Middle East than from the United Kingdom or the United States.

More than half of American companies now tie base salaries to the home countries of the third-country national they employ, rather than to U.S. or

International compensation is a critical and complex topic.

host-country salary structures, according to a survey of 117 international companies by Organization Resources Counselors, Inc. The number of companies doing this has risen from 38 percent to more than 52 percent in just two years, and the trend includes those with small as well as large PCN populations. The primary objective is cost saving, since base pay levels of most other countries are currently below those of the U.S.[34]

The base salary of a PCN is usually paid either in the home currency at the home rate or in the local currency at a rate equivalent to the rate paid locally for the same job. Similarly, salary adjustments and promotional practices may be fashioned according to either home-country or local standards. In some select cases, global salary and performance structures have been implemented.

STRATEGIC IMPERATIVES

To succeed in an ever-changing international environment, MNCs must look beyond next year's goals and develop clear but flexible long-term compensation strategies.

> An effective managerial reward system should be linked to long-term corporate strategy and should anticipate changes in employees' valence of different organizational rewards. On the one hand, multinational settings make the complex task of developing such a system even more difficult; on the other hand, the fact that the corporation operates in many different environments permits the establishment of unique reward programs, unavailable in more conventional environments.[35]

In addition, MNCs need to match their compensation policies with both their staffing policies and general philosophies. If, for example, as discussed in Chapter 8, an MNC has an ethnocentric staffing policy (that is, staffing with an expert chosen by headquarters), its compensation policy should be one of keeping the PCN whole. If, however, the staffing policy follows a geocentric approach (that is, staffing a position with the "best person," regardless of nationality) there may be no clear "home" for the TCN, and the MNC will need to consider establishing a system of international base pay for key managers paid in a major reserve currency such as the U.S. dollar or the Deutschmark. This system allows MNCs to deal with considerable variations in base salaries for managers such as that noted in the following report:

> In Switzerland, a department head working for a medium-sized company earns $78,000. The same executive in Germany earns only $64,000. But in the U.S., the equivalent job pays only $54,000, a figure seen as surprisingly low. However, the gap increases as U.S. executives climb the corporate ladder. At the highest levels, CEOs in the U.S. average $1.2 million while those in Switzerland average only $284,000 and in Germany only $275,000.[36]

These actual values have changed with time, but the relative values have not. Further evidence of the disparity between management compensation across countries is shown in Exhibit 11.10, which compares total cash compensation for CEOs in nineteen countries.

COMPENSATION PRACTICES IN OTHER COUNTRIES

JAPAN. The Japanese are fond of saying there are three sacred treasures of the Imperial House. The first of these is lifetime employment. The second, which stems from lifetime employment, is the traditional seniority system that determines not only wages, but also the timing of promotions. Under this system, an employee rarely works under someone with less seniority in service length, assuming both have similar educational backgrounds. This system has its roots in the traditional *Oyabun-Kobun*, or parent-child relationship, which attaches great respect to the older or senior member of the family (company). The third treasure of the Imperial House is the enterprise (or company) union.

Initially, individual companies pay almost the same starting salary for new employees hired upon graduation from either high school or college. After that, an employee's annual earnings increase according to the merit rating system. In addition, earnings will increase annually by seniority, even if an employee's job responsibilities remain unchanged, until the age of mandatory retirement, now commonly 60 years of age.

A distinguishing feature of the Japanese wage system is the provision for a semiannual bonus or wage allowance, separate from the annual incremental rate. Usually paid without exception, even in times of recession, the bonus amount is closely related to both the general economy and the profitability of the company. Generally, the equivalent of 5–6 months' salary is paid in bonuses at midsummer and at the end of the year.

In addition to basic salary, Japanese workers customarily receive compensation in the form of housing or a housing allowance, daily living support (including transportation, meals, and workers' uniforms), cultural and recreational benefits, and medical and health care.[37]

EUROPE. With the development of the European Community (or European Union), there is greater use of the common currency called the **ECU** (European Currency Unit) within business. This currency is already being used by some European firms. This will facilitate the mobility of workers across nations. Having a similar impact is the movement toward Europay. **Europay** is a practice of developing a common policy and common set of pay practices regardless of national origin and extent of location throughout Europe. This practice, primarily targeted for top management, recognizes the need to treat European operations as truly one market and their employees as truly European.

CURRENT TRENDS

Compensation is a dynamic, challenging, and exciting activity in managing human resources. It is also a valuable activity for positively influencing the bottom line of organizations as the following descriptions of two trends in compensation illustrate. Chapters 12 and 13 provide further descriptions of these trends.

LINKING TO ORGANIZATIONAL STRATEGY

A recent study by the American Compensation Association indicates that two-thirds of all firms implementing changes in their pay system do so because of a fundamental shift in the way they view and define their markets. This is, the selection of the right compensation mix is highly dependent on what a company needs from its employees to match its strategical initiatives, (for example, for entrepreneurial development, or for turnaround).[38]

General Dynamics has pursued a **turnaround strategy**. Faced with a shrinking market, the company eliminated more than 10,000 jobs through layoffs and attrition, drastically cut spending on plants and equipment, and sold several non-military subsidiaries. To retain some talent to make the turnaround, top execu-

As Japan changes, the seniority system is coming under attack as being too expensive.

Compensation is a major way to implement organizational strategy.

Organizational strategies include:
- turnaround
- entrepreneurial

tives were offered short- as well as long-term incentives linked to stock prices. However, at lower levels, wages were frozen and jobs eliminated. Participation in compensation activities was held to a minimum, perks were limited and a standard, fixed severance package with no incentives was offered.

Tandem Computers, in comparison, has successfully pursued an **entrepreneurial strategy**. To encourage employees to be innovative, to take more risks, and to be willing to assume responsibility, compensation practices are flexible, contain many perks and long-term incentives (incentive stock options or stock appreciation rights), and encourage high employee participation. Tandem's compensation philosophy is to reward people fairly but not necessarily equally. While stock options are awarded equally to most employees, cash bonuses are awarded only to top performers. A "night on the town" is given to people who make a special contribution. To further recognize employee contributions, peak performers (selected by their supervisor and peers) annually attend a special retreat at a resort. The retreat creates a place for top performers to relax, network, become acquainted, and brainstorm on key issues facing the business.[39]

LINKING TO THE ORGANIZATION'S LIFE CYCLE
The choice of a specific compensation mix is constrained by an organization's life cycle. The concept of organizational life cycle is a variation of product life cycle and relates growth in sales revenues to the age of the organization. Organizations (like products) go through different stages of development: start-up, growth, maturity, and decline

As suggested in Exhibit 11.12, growth is rapid during some stages and slow during other stages of the life cycle. During the **start-up stage**, the emphasis is on product and market development. The human resource focus is on attracting key contributors and facilitating innovation. Still, risk is high, sales growth is slow, and earnings are low. As a result, base salary and benefits are usually below the market. However, broad-based short- and long-term incentives are offered to stimulate employees to innovate. Sales growth is rapid, with moderate increases in earnings during the **growth stage**. To keep up, the organization must grow rapidly to satisfy increased demand for products and/or services. The HR focus is on rapid recruitment and training. Bonuses are offered for innovation and sales growth, and stock options are offered to encourage employees to think about the long-term growth of the company.

Because the market is saturated with the product, growth is slower and more orderly during the **mature stage**. High entry costs and exit barriers keep the number of competitors low, so organizations can focus on profitability. During this stage, the HR emphasis is on consistency and the retention of peak performers. Profit sharing, cash bonuses, and stock awards tied to short- or long-term growth may be utilized to retain key contributors. Base pay and benefits usually are competitive.

During the **decline stage**, the HR focus shifts to cutback management as market share declines. Incentives of any kind are unlikely to be awarded. Base salary and benefits are, at best, competitive and may drop below market levels as management attempts to cut back expenditures.[40]

Organizational life cycles have received wide attention as a heuristic device, but the concept has critics. More than one set of compensation policies may be appropriate for any given cycle. Additionally, organizations often have more than one product, each at a different stage of development. Due to this complexity, it may be impossible to cleanly classify a firm and its compensation mix according to its stage of development.[41]

Organizational life cycle stages include:

- start-up
- growth
- maturity
- decline

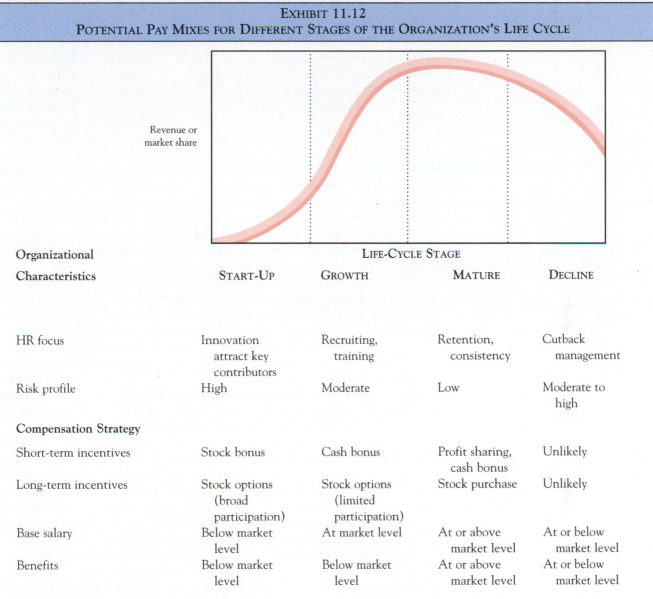

EXHIBIT 11.12
POTENTIAL PAY MIXES FOR DIFFERENT STAGES OF THE ORGANIZATION'S LIFE CYCLE

Organizational Characteristics	START-UP	GROWTH	MATURE	DECLINE
HR focus	Innovation attract key contributors	Recruiting, training	Retention, consistency	Cutback management
Risk profile	High	Moderate	Low	Moderate to high
Compensation Strategy				
Short-term incentives	Stock bonus	Cash bonus	Profit sharing, cash bonus	Unlikely
Long-term incentives	Stock options (broad participation)	Stock options (limited participation)	Stock purchase	Unlikely
Base salary	Below market level	At market level	At or above market level	At or below market level
Benefits	Below market level	Below market level	At or above market level	At or below market level

SOURCE: D. B. Balkin and L. R. Gomez-Mejia, "Compensation Systems in High Technology Companies," *New Perspectives on Compensation* (Englewood Cliffs, N.J.: Prentice-Hall, 1987), 269–277.

SUMMARY

Organizations are being forced to develop strategic compensation practices in light of a cost-conscious, competitive environment that demands high quality and a continuous flow of new products. Compensation programs must be consistent with the organization's culture and strategic objectives. In addition, compensation practices must adhere to the *Fair Labor Standards Act* and *Equal*

Pay Act. Concern over discrimination in pay also causes organizations to consider the manner in which rates of pay are determined as covered by the **Equal Pay Act** and the **Civil Rights Act**.

Job evaluation is a systematic, rational assessment of the value of jobs that is designed to establish internal equity in jobs. Ranking and job classification methods focus on evaluating the whole job. These methods are premised on intuitive judgments about job worth. Preferable methods include point evaluation and factor comparison systems, both of which evaluate jobs using compensable factors.

In conducting a job evaluation study, a decision needs to be made regarding custom designing or buying a system. While it may be expedient to buy a standardized system, such a system may not reflect organizational needs and values. To ensure systemwide equity, a single job evaluation plan is usually preferred over multiple plans. Another important decision is who should evaluate the worth of jobs. The greater the involvement of employees, the more likely they are to accept the results of the job evaluation study. Alternatively, an organization can choose a pay-for-knowledge system in which pay increases with job skill or flexibility.

Once the worth is determined, jobs must still be priced. Although job evaluation procedures are important in establishing worth, they are more relevant to establishing relative job prices than absolute job prices. To help establish absolute job prices, organizations often use market survey data, especially for those jobs that have identical or nearly identical counterparts in the marketplace. Market surveys for pricing jobs that are not found in other organizations should be done with caution. Such surveys involve subjectivity and are therefore open to potential wage discrimination charges. Organizations should be careful in using market rates to perpetuate wage differentials that are obviously discriminatory. Fair evaluations should be conducted to reduce that likelihood.

In establishing wages, organizations can rely on job evaluations and market surveys, and can use inputs from the employees themselves. Employees can responsibly set their own wages. In the few companies that have tried it, employees have set their own wages without management altering the procedures or changing decisions. The method is most successful, however, in organizations where employees and management have mutual trust and employees are provided with information to help them understand the financial status of the company.

Establishing wages and determining which job evaluation method to use, though important, are only two components of compensation. Other components include selecting the best performance-based pay plan and obtaining benefit from indirect compensation. Chapters 12 and 13 discuss these and the other important components of compensation.

KEY CONCEPTS

base salary	ECU (European Currency Unit)	grade structure
benchmark jobs		growth stage
comparable worth	entreprenurial strategy	Hay method
compensable factors	equity theory	indirect compensation
cost-of-living adjustments (COLAs)	Europay	internal equity
	exempt employees	job classses
	external equity	job classification method
decline stage	factor comparison method	job evaluation
direct compensation		job families

job ranking method
mature stage
maturity curves
nonexempt employees
pay fairness
pay grades

pay level
pay secrecy
performance-based pay
point factor method
point rating method
skill-based evaluation

start-up stage
total compensation
turnaround strategy
wage surveys

REVIEW AND DISCUSSION QUESTIONS

1. What purposes can total compensation serve?
2. What forms of pay and rewards make up total compensation?
3. What are four basic wage issues that any job evaluation system must address?
4. Describe the basic mechanics of the common job evaluation methods.
5. How do firms establish the actual pay levels for each job?
6. Describe the major issues in wage and salary administration.
7. What are the components of the typical expatriate's compensation package?
8. How do the base salaries of expatriates differ from the base salaries of employees in the United States?
9. What are the advantages of skill-based evaluation over traditional evaluation methods?
10. What is the relationship between total compensation and organizational life-cycle?

EXERCISES AND CASES

FIELD PROJECT

Interview some people, and ask them how important pay is to them and what it means to them. Ask them what things they value other than money. Report to class, and compare your findings with the results of others.

EXERCISE: MOTIVATION AND PAY RAISE ALLOCATION

STEP ONE: PRE-GROUP MEETING PREPARATION

Read the instructions to the "Employee Profile Sheet," and decide on a pay increase for each of the eight employees. Write your decisions in both dollars and percents. Be prepared to explain your decisions in class.

STEP TWO: GROUP MEETING

The group members should share the recommendations they made in Step One and explain their reasons. After all members have reported, the group should analyze and try to explain differences among everyone's recommendations. The group should then develop a set of recommendations that it can agree on. A spokesperson should be appointed to present the group's recommendations to the class.

EMPLOYEE PROFILE SHEET

You must make salary increase recommendations for eight managers whom you supervise. They have just completed their first year with the company and are now to be considered for their first annual raise. Keep in mind that you may be setting precedents that will shape future expectations and that you must stay within your salary budget. Otherwise, there are no formal company policies to restrict you as you decide how to allocate raises. Write the raise you would give each manager in the space to the left of each name. You have a total of $13,000, or about 4.91% in your budget for pay raises.

$ _____ % _____ Arnold J. Adams. Adams is not, as far as you can tell, a good performer. You have discussed your opinion with others, and they agree completely. However, you know that Adams has one of the toughest work groups to manage. Adams' subordinates have low skill levels, and the work is dirty and hard. If you lose Adams, you are not sure that you could find an adequate replacement. Current salary: $30,000.

$ _____ % _____ Bruce K. Berger. Berger is single and seems to lead the life of a carefree swinger. In general, you feel that Berger's job performance is not up to par, and some of Berger's "goofs" are well known to other employees. Current salary: $33,750.

$ _____ % _____ Carol C. Carter. You consider Carter to be one of your best subordinates. However, it is quite apparent that other people don't agree. Carter has married into wealth and, as far as you know, doesn't need any more money. Current salary: $37,000.

$ _____ % _____ Daniel Davis. You happen to know from your personal relationship that Davis badly needs more money because of certain personal problems. Davis also happens to be one of your best managers. For some reason, your enthusiasm is not shared by your other subordinates, and you have heard them make joking remarks about Davis's performance. Current salary: $34,000.

$ _____ % _____ Ellen J. Ellis. Your opinion is that Ellis just isn't cutting the mustard. Surprisingly enough, however, when you check with others to see how they feel, you find that Ellis is very highly regarded. You also know that Ellis badly needs a raise. Ellis was recently divorced and is finding it extremely difficult to support a young family of four as a single parent. Current salary: $30,750.

$ _____ % _____ Fred M. Foster. Foster has turned out to be a very pleasant surprise, has done an excellent job, and is seen by peers as one of the best people in your group of managers. This surprises you because Foster is generally frivolous and doesn't seem to care very much about money or promotions. Current salary: $32,700.

$ _____ % _____ Gloria K. Gomez. Gomez has been very successful so far. You are particularly impressed by this because Gomez's is one of the hardest jobs in your company. Gomez needs money more than many of your other subordinates and is respected for good performance. Current salary: $35,250.

$ _____ % _____

Harriet A. Hunt. You know Hunt personally. This employee seems to squander money continually. Hunt has a fairly easy job assignment, and your own view is that Hunt doesn't do it especially well. You are thus surprised to find that sev-

eral of the other new managers think that Hunt is the best of the new group. Current salary: $31,500.

Total mean $ increase	Total mean % increase

COMPARABLE WORTH FINDS ROCKDALE

Bill Starbuck was proud to be assigned to the city beat of *The Rockdale Times*. Bill, a newspaper reporter for two years now, was paying his dues at a small-town newspaper, hoping to work his way up to a larger circulation daily. The city beat would mean that Bill could draw on his background in journalism and political science at Wabash College to write news stories with substance. His prior assignment to the features section of *The Rockdale Times* was interesting but not intellectually stimulating.

Bill's first major assignment was coming up in two days with an invitation to cover a breakfast meeting with the city council. Clyde Langston, Rockdale city manager, would present the revised city budget. Bill prepared for the meeting by calling one of his contacts in the city office for some "inside" information. Bill had been dating Jill Bateman, a secretary to the personnel executive director, and he was confident he could learn something about the breakfast meeting agenda.

As Bill hung up form his call to Jill, he wondered what the rumor of a pay raise for some city employees could mean. If anything, the city was expected to trim its budget because of a slowdown in the local economy and loss of revenues due to the shutdown of two plants in the community within the past year. According to Jill, the rumor was that some of the clerical and administrative staff employees were scheduled for midyear pay adjustments. The figure working the hallways was a 3 percent pay raise, which would come as a pleasant surprise to the 95 employees in the administrative-office clerical positions.

As Bill arrived at the Wednesday morning breakfast meeting, he quickly scanned the room to identify the four city councilmen and one councilwoman. Bill wanted to interview at least three of the members for his story, which was due by 1:00 P.M. After Mayor Jim Earnie arrived, the city council, city manager, and local news reporters finished a quick and cordial breakfast.

Clyde Langston called the group to attention with a rap on his water goblet, and the cordial bantering quickly subsided. Clyde distributed a five-page report of the preliminary budget. Bill quickly scanned the report and noted that the $13.7 million total was considerably trimmed down from last year's budget of $16.4 million. Then, as Bill anticipated, Clyde pointed out a $41,000 line item increase in salaries within the pared-down budget.

Clyde proceeded to explain that the city had done an analysis of their 95 administrative-office clerical positions and their 350 technical-craft positions and decided to make some pay adjustments. All but one of the administrative-office clerks are women, while only 27 of the technical-craft workers are women. The pay range for office workers ranges from a low of $5.19 per hour to a high of $11.17 per hour, with an average of $6.30 per hour. The technical-craft jobs begin at $4.83 per hour and max out at $13.85 per hour, with an average of $9.69 per hour. The net effect of the $41,000 increase was to provide about a 3 percent increase to the administrative-office clerical workers.

Clyde pointed out that a recently conducted job evaluation study had resulted in the merger of the previously separated job families, such that all jobs were to be evaluated on a common set of attributes. Clyde elaborated further that the impetus of this change was to avoid any litigation over the comparable worth issue. After completing the budget review briefing, Clyde offered to answer questions. When the council members sat quietly, Jim Earnie thanked the council for their time and adjourned the meeting.

Bill scurried to the door to intercept the council members as they prepared to leave, hoping to get a few reactions to this surprise comparable worth initiative by the city government. Bill caught all five of the city council members and the mayor and proceeded to ask them what they thought of Clyde's proposal for the pay adjustments. Mayor Jim Earnie, along with three of the council members, indicated that they did not understand the rationale for the raises. After Bill questioned them, they even agreed that they thought that the issue deserved some further discussion.

"I did not know we were using that standard," Councilman Jim Maloney said. "If we're applying comparable worth throughout the system, it would be good to know that, and on what basis it's being done."

Councilwoman Marcie Rivera said she was in accord with the approach. "I'm inclined to agree with the way Clyde put it out," she said, "to avoid any problems in discrimination. If that's the concern here, I feel like it's a step in the right direction."

Amazing, thought Bill as he headed to his car with notes in hand. I just attended a city council breakfast meeting to review the upcoming city budget, and comparable worth is proposed by the city manager. And the mayor and city council hardly noticed until after the meeting was adjourned!

CASE QUESTIONS

1 Has Rockdale really implemented a comparable worth standard?
2. How do you think the technical-craft workers will react to the announced pay raise?
3. What other approaches are available for achieving pay equity between men and women?
4. Why have state and local governments shown more interest in comparable worth than private employers?

CASE

PACIFIC COAST ELECTRIC COMPANY

Pacific Coast Electric Company (PCEC) is a public utility company located in San Francisco. The company is so successful that it is considered a model for other utility companies. Over the past two years, however, PCEC management has become concerned with increasing payroll costs. Cost containment and a "lean and mean" structure are key ingredients in the company's success. Management wants to study this problem and, if warranted, take corrective action.

Roger Waters is a compensation specialist with PCEC. Roger has been assigned to study PCEC's compensation practices and determine whether any action is required. He decides to compile compensation data for the past five years by using the company's human resource information system (HRIS). Five years will reveal any trends, and the HRIS allows him to breakdown the data by department, length of service, gender, exempt versus nonexempt employees, and the like.

Roger has uncovered a startling situation. The data indicate that certain nonexempt employees are receiving compensation far in excess of their base pay rate. It seems that these employees are working excessive overtime because of the specific expertise they possess. Overtime rates are one-and-one-half times through 48 hours and double time after that. Employees who work overtime also receive additional compensation, including meal and travel allowances. The base salary for these employees averages $25,000 per year. With overtime, these employees make between $35,000 and $39,000 a year. This situation would be less of a concern if it involved only a few individuals, but hundreds of employees are in this situation. It should be noted that PCEC initiated the overtime policy because of the high cost of consultants—besides, the company feels that its own employees are better skilled and more capable than most consultants.

The employees in question make more than their superiors. First-line supervisors, for example, make approximately 15 percent more than the base compensation of the top craft employees. In other words, supervisors are making approximately $28,750 on the average. Supervisors can receive merit pay, but only a small number of supervisors are eligible for merit awards. Further, supervisors are not paid overtime and receive no meal allowances. Fortunately for PCEC, thinks Roger, our supervisors are not aware of the extent of the pay inequities.

Aside from the obvious problem of employees making a great deal more money than their supervisors, another problem becomes apparent. Examination of the internal labor market reveals that all of the first-line supervisors have come from outside the company. The qualified employees are not accepting "promotions" because they do not want to take a cut in pay. The longterm consequences of this situation could be very serious.

Then Roger looks at a breakdown of the data by gender for the nonexempt employees in question. Women have an average base salary of $23,500 while the average base salary for men is $25,900. Furthermore, not one of the employees receiving high salaries resulting from overtime is female. Roger is very concerned about the differences in compensation for men and women, especially because PCEC prides itself on its equal employment/affirmative action reputation. Men and women are doing essentially the same jobs.

Roger becomes lost in thought as he contemplates his findings. He knows that it will be difficult to frame a report around the compensation issues that he has uncovered. He suspects that it will be even more difficult to recommend changes that will resolve these thorny issues.

CASE QUESTIONS

1. Are there cases in which employees should be paid more than their supervisors?
2. Does Roger have a pay-equity problem?
3. What recommendations should he make?
4. How should he make compensation changes?

NOTES

1. S. Manes and P. Andrews, *Gates* (New York: Doubleday, 1993); B. Schlender, "How Bill Gates Keeps the Magic Going," *Fortune* (June 18, 1990): 82–89.

2. M. Leibman and H. P. Weinstein, "Money Isn't Everything," *HR Magazine* (Nov. 1990): 48–51; R. E. Sibson, *Compensation*, rev. ed. (New York: AMACOM, 1990); G. T. Milkovich and J. M. Newman, *Compensation*, 2nd ed. (Plano, Tex.: Business Publications, 1989); *New Perspectives on Compensation*, eds. D. B. Balkin and L. R. Gomez-Mejia (Englewood Cliffs, N.J.: Prentice-Hall, 1987). The use of divisions is practical because it is then easier to discuss compensation. This is just one way to divide up the components of compensation. For an alternative way, see R. I. Henderson, "Designing a Reward System for Today's Employee," *Business* (July–Sept. 1982): 2–12.

3. L. S. Richman, "CEOs To Workers: Help Not Wanted," *Fortune* (July 12, 1993): 42–43; R. Jacob, The Economy: Girding for Worse," *Fortune* (October 18, 1993): 10; "Employees' Views on Work," *Bulletin to Management* (Sept. 16, 1993): 289.

4. J. Fierman, "When Will You Get A Raise?" *Fortune* (July 12, 1993): 34–36.

5. See J. Kerr and J. Slocum, Jr., "Linking Reward Systems and Organizational Cultures," in *Readings in Personnel and Human Resource Management*, 3rd ed., eds. R. S. Schuler, S. A.

Youngblood, and V. L. Huber (St. Paul, Minn.: West, 1988); E. E. Lawler III, "The Strategic Design of Reward Systems" in *Readings in Personnel and Human Resources Management*, 2nd ed., eds. R. S. Schuler and S. A Youngblood (St. Paul, Minn.: West, 1984), 253–269; L. L. Cummings, "Compensation, Culture and Motivation: A Systems Perspective," *Organizational Dynamics* (Winter 1984): 33–44.

6. Leibman and Weinstein (*op. cit.*, see note 2).

7. A. Bernstein, C. Del Valle, and M. McNamee, "A Higher Minimum Wage: Minimal Damage?" *Business Week* (March 22, 1993): 92–93; S. Nasar, "Two Economists Catch Clinton's Eye by Bucking Common Wisdom," *New York Times* (August 22, 1993): 67; "Crackdown on Child Labor Violations," *FEP Guidelines* 299 (June 6, 1990); "FLSA Amendments of 1989: Higher Federal Minimum Wage, Plus New Training Wage," *Bulletin to Management* (December 28, 1989): 1–3; B. Southard Murphy, W. E. Barlow, and D. D. Hatch, "A News Report for Personnel Professionals: Subminimum Training Wages Available," *Personnel Journal* (June 1990): 19.

8. G. Ameci, "Overtime Pay: Avoiding FLSA Violations," *Personnel Administrator* (Feb. 1987): 117–118; H. Stout, "Propping Up Payments at the Bottom," *New York Times* (Jan. 24, 1988): 4.

9. "Record Settlement Under *Fair Labor Standards Act*," *Bulletin to Management* (August 12, 1993): 249.

10. "Pay Equity Makes Good Business Sense," *Fair Employment Practices* (Aug. 30, 1990): 103; A. Bernstein, "What's Dragging Productivity Down? Women's Low Wages," *Business Week* (Nov. 27, 1989): 171; "Comparable Worth Policies that Work: The Minnesota Case," *The Urban Institute/Policy and Research Report* (Summer 1990): 10–12; G. J. Meng, "All the Parts of Comparable Worth" *Personnel Journal* (Nov. 1990): 99–104.

11. T. Linesenmayer, "Comparable Worth Abroad: Mixed Evidence," *The Wall Street Journal* (May 27, 1986): 26.

12. See note 24.

13. G. Milkovich and J. Newman, *Compensation*, 2nd ed. (Plano, Tex.: Business Publications, 1989).

14. S. M. Emerson, "Job Evaluation: A Barrier to Excellence?" *Compensation and Benefits Review* (Jan.–Feb. 1991):39–51; C. L. Hughes and W. L. Wright, "Make Pay Plans Work For the People They Pay," *Personnel Journal* (May 1989): 54–63.

15. R. D. Arvey, "Sex Bias in Job Evaluation Procedures," *Personnel Psychology* 39 (1986): 315–335; D. Doverspike, B. Racicot, and C. Albertson. *The Role of Information Processing Variables in the Decision-Making Process in Job Evaluation: Results of Empirical Studies on Sex Prototypes, Person Prototypes and the Effects of Training* (Buffalo, N.Y.: First Annual Conference on HRM Decision Making, Oct. 1986); M. K. Mount and R. A. Ellis, "Investigation of Bias in Job Evaluation Rating of Comparable Worth Study Participants," *Personnel Psychology* 40 (1987): 85–96.

16. N. Gupta, G. E. Ledford, D. Jenkins, and D. Doty, "Survey-Based Prescriptions for Skilled-Based Pay," *ACA Journal* (Autumn 1992): 48–58; M. Rowland, "For Each New Skill, More Money," *New York Times* (June 13, 1993): F16.

17. S. Caudron, "The Compensation Maze," *Personnel Journal* (June 1993): 64G. Used by permission.

18. Milkovich and Newman (*op. cit.*, see note 13).

19. J. Domat-Connell, "A New Look at the Foundation of Compensation Program Design," *Compensation and Benefits Review* (Mar.-Apr. 1994): 38–46. R. J. Sokol, "Seven Rules of Salary Surveys," *Personnel Journal* (April 1990): 83–87. See Sibson (*loc. cit.*, see note 2):17–19.

20. Sibon, (*op. cit.*, see note 2).

21. For a discussion on the validity of job evaluation systems, see T. Patten, "How Do You Know If Your Job Evaluation System Is Working?" in Balkin and Gomez-Mejia (*op. cit.*, see note 2).

22. "Annual Pay Levels and Growth in Pay by State," *Bulletin to Management* (Nov. 19, 1992): 365.

23. M. Zippo, "Roundup," *Personnel* (May–June 1981): 43–50.

24. E. Lawler, *Pay and Organization Development* (Reading, Mass.: Addison-Wesley, 1981).

25. V. Scarpello, V. Huber, and R. J. Vanderberg, "Compensation Satisfaction: Its Measurement and Dimensionality," *Journal of Applied Psychology* (May 1988): 163–171.

26. "Abroad, It's Another World," *Fortune*, (June 6, 1988): 78.

27. R. Moss Kanter, "The Attack on Pay," *Harvard Business Review* (March–April 1987): 60–67; A. E. Serwer, "Payday! Payday!" *Fortune* (June 14, 1993): 102–111; "Executive Pay Doesn't Add Up," *Business Week* (April 26, 1993): 122; J. Byrne, "That Eye-Popping Executive Pay," *Business Week* (April 25, 1994): 52-58.

28. A. Farnham, "The Trust Gap," *Fortune* (Dec. 4, 1989): 56–78; G. S. Crystal and F. T. Vincent, Jr., "Take the Mystery Out of CEO Pay," *Fortune* (April 24, 1989): 217–220; "Current Issues: A Survey," *HR Reporter* (July 1990); G. S. Crystal, "Executive Compensation: Challenges in the Year Ahead," *Personnel* (Jan. 1988): 33–36; A. R. Karr, "Labor Letter," *The Wall Street Journal* (July 17, 1990): A1.

29. Farnham, (*op. cit.*, see note 28): 66.

30. The following materials are adapted from P. Dowling and R. S. Schuler, *International Dimensions of Human Resource Management* (Boston, Mass.: PWS-Kent, 1990): 117–135. Also see three excellent articles entitled, "Compensating Your Overseas Executives," Part 1 (May–June 1990); Part 2 (July–Aug. 1990); and Part 3 (Jan.–Feb. 1991). *Compensation Review*.

31. C. Reynolds, "High Motivation and Low Cost Through Innovative International Compensation," *Proceedings of ASPA's 40th National Conference* (Boston, Mass., 1989).

32. C. Reynolds, *Compensation Basics for North American Expatriates* (Scottsdale, Arizona: ACA, 1994). See B. W. Teague, "Compensating Key Personnel Overseas" (New York: The Conference Board, 1972), for a discussion of the concept of keeping the expatriate "whole."

33. This discussion of the "balance sheet" approach is based on C. Reynolds, "Compensation of Overseas Personnel," in *Handbook of Human Resources Administration*, 2nd ed., ed. J. J. Famularo (New York: McGraw-Hill, 1986).

34. *HR Reporter Update*, 3, no. 2 (Feb. 1987): 2.

35. V. Pucik, "Strategic HRM in Multinational Corporations," in *Strategic Management of Multinational Corporations*, eds. H. V. Wortzel and L. H. Wortzel (New York: Wiley, 1985), 430.

36. *HR Reporter Update*, 3, no. 1 (Jan. 1987): 5. Updated in 1994 by 30% to reflect salary increases.

37. M. S. O'Connor, *Report on Japanese Employee Relation Practices and Their Relationship to Worker Productivity*, a report prepared for the study mission to Japan, November 8–23, 1980. Her permission to reproduce this material is appreciated. Also see

Employment and Employment Policy (Tokyo, Japan: Japan Institute of Labor, 1988).

38. R. Schuler, "Managing Resource Management Choices and Organizational Strategy," in Schuler et al. (*op. cit.*, see note 5): 24–39; E. Lawler and J. A. Drexler, "The Corporate Entrepreneur," working paper, Center for Effective Organizations, University of Southern California, 1984; E. Lawler, "The Strategic Design of Reward Systems," in Schuler et al. (*op. cit.*, see note 5): 253–269.

39. D. Jamieson and J. O'Mara, *Managing Workforce 2000:*

Gaining the Diversity Advantage (San Francisco, Calif.: Jossey-Bass, 1991): 49, 59, 112, 122, and 125.

40. D. B. Balkin and L. R. Gomez-Mejia, "Entrepreneurial Compensation," in Schuler et al. (*op. cit.*, see note 5): 14–23; D. B. Balkin and L. R. Gomez-Mejia, "The Strategic Use of Short-Term and Long-Term Pay Incentives in the High Technology Industry," in Balkin and Gomez-Mejia (*op. cit.*, see note 2): 237–249.

41. G. Milkovich, "A Strategic Perspective on Compensation Management," in Schuler et al. (*op. cit.*, see note 5): 263–288.

LEARNING OBJECTIVES

When you have finished studying this chapter, you should be able to:

1. Describe the available merit pay and incentive plans that companies use to motivate employee performance.
2. Describe the incentive plans at Lincoln Electric.
3. Identify obstacles in the way of effectively implementing performance-based pay.
4. Discuss the areas where compensation can be linked to quality.

CHAPTER OUTLINE

MANAGING HUMAN RESOURCES
at Lincoln Electric

IN 1987, when Donald Hastings became president of Lincoln Electric Co., he brought with him total quality management. His goal was to build quality into the process rather than test it at the end of the production line (primarily for electric motors and arc welders). Lincoln's efforts under Donald Hastings have paid off: 25 percent fewer inspectors are needed (the employees assume the responsibility for quality) and 50 percent fewer employee-caused errors show up during testing (testing was used until management was sure that the new efforts were working effectively).

Quality is such an important part of Lincoln's strategy that they include it in their famous incentive plan. It, however, is just one piece of the incentive plan. A closer look reveals a significant number of components, and it is within one of those components, the merit-rating system, that a worker's quality is specifically evaluated and compensated. Workers receive merit ratings or "report cards" twice a year, and these determine the amount of bonus they receive at year-end. The four criteria in the merit rating include: output, quality, dependability, and personal characteristics. Incentives that go hand in hand with this are a base wage, piecework pay, profit-sharing, job security, and an employee stock-ownership plan. Do these work?

As indicated in the feature in Chapter 5 on Lincoln Electric on job design, Lincoln's productivity level is two to three times that of comparable organizations. Average employee compensation is $45,000. And Lincoln is dominant in the markets that it serves. Because the company is now a publicly traded company, its shares can be bought and sold by the public, and there is now a way to tell just *how* valuable the financial experts think the company is.[1]

This feature complements the one in Chapter 5. Together they present a broad overview of this very successful firm. Certainly, the importance of performance-based pay in achieving worker productivity and company success becomes apparent on a perusal of various human resource practices at Lincoln Electric. An array of programs are involved: it is not just one performance-based pay plan that motivates employees, but several. And some analysts say that, without job security (a no-layoff policy was adopted in 1959), the entire incentive system would be far less effective. Thus it is important to keep in mind as you think about the uses of performance-based pay, that it takes several HR practices working together to achieve highly effective employee behavior.[2] And performance-based pay is a powerful cornerstone in all of this. Thus we examine performance-based pay exclusively in this chapter.

PERFORMANCE-BASED PAY

In this chapter we discuss **performance-based pay**, *the aspect of total compensation related to motivating employees through linking pay to performance*.

Performance-based pay systems relate pay to performance in one of two ways. **Incentive pay plans** measure performance output of individuals, groups, or organizations *directly*. Incentive pay accounts for a large portion of the individual's total compensation. For example, salespersons may be assured a small base salary, but the majority of compensation is earned through commissions.[3] By

Performance-based pay motivates employees through linking pay with performance.

The two systems of performance-based pay are merit pay and incentive pay.

425

contrast, **merit pay plans** generally rely on indirect measures of performance (ratings or rankings). Because the measure of performance is indirect, merit pay plans typically affect a small percentage of an individual's total compensation.

In general, incentive pay plans appear to have substantially more motivational value, but merit pay plans remain much more frequent because they tend to be easier to set up and administer. Whereas essentially there is one type of merit plan, a wide variety of incentive plans exists. An overview of both types is shown in Exhibit 12.1.

WHY IS PERFORMANCE-BASED PAY IMPORTANT?

EMPLOYEE PERFORMANCE AND ORGANIZATIONAL COMPETITIVENESS

Money can be an extremely powerful motivator of performance. Studies of performance-based pay systems have shown that individual incentive plans can improve performance on an average of almost 30 percent over non-performance-based pay systems. Team-based incentive plans can increase performance 15 to 20 percent.[4]

As the feature on Lincoln Electric at the beginning of the chapter illustrates, pay is also important in enhancing organizational quality and competitiveness.[5] This is true even in areas where performance-based pay has traditionally not been used such as health care.[6]

Although effective in positively influencing the bottom line, performance-based pay systems have some disadvantages. One is that they take time to administer. Others include the fact that employees have to work exceptionally hard to earn large incentive bonuses, and occasionally, conflicts arise from rewarding only certain behaviors:

> A more costly example of an incentive plan gone awry made news last summer when Sears Auto Centers in California were nailed for making unnecessary repairs on customers' cars. The reward system in question based both pay and incentives on the number of parts service managers sold. The service managers allegedly pressured mechanics to install unneeded parts, and the company was

Lincoln Electric has paid out more than $500 million in year-end profit-sharing bonuses to employees since it began its bonus program in 1934.

Benefits of performance-based pay are enhanced motivation, performance, quality, and competitiveness.

EXHIBIT 12.1
PEFORMANCE-BASED PAY SYSTEMS

MERIT PAY PLANS	INCENTIVE PAY PLANS	
	INDIVIDUAL	GROUP/ORGANIZATION
• Typical merit	• Piecework plan	• Team-based incentive
• Lump-sum bonus	• Standard hour plan	• Scanlon plan
	• Measured day work	• Rucker plan
	• Sales incentive plan	• Improshare
	• Managerial incentive plan	• Profit-sharing plans
	• Suggestion systems	• Games, awards

charged with defrauding its customers by California investigators. Sears' final settlement reportedly was in the neighborhood of $15 million.[7]

Thus the advantages of performance-based pay apply only when the appropriate conditions exist for its implementation. When there are obstacles in the way of these conditions, the disadvantages far outweigh the advantages. The conditions and obstacles are critical in knowing when to use performance-based pay and are described later in this chapter under "Obstacles to Effectiveness."

RECOGNIZING EMPLOYEE CONTRIBUTIONS

The difference in performance between a peak- and low-performing employee *averages* 3 to 1 and can be as much as 20 to 1.[8] Thus, another purpose of performance-based pay is to recognize and reinforce the differential contribution of high versus low performance. Good pay and larger increases retain employees, and good performers are the ones managers most want to keep. Additionally, it has been shown that an employee who is rewarded for good performance will be more likely to continue performing well than one who is not appropriately rewarded.[9]

> The performance levels of employees on the same job can vary greatly—as much as 20 to 1!

Still, few employees—particularly middle managers—ever *see* performance really pay. While (nine out of ten managers believe) the best way to allocate scarce payroll dollars is to provide significant rewards to their top performers, only one-third of employees believe their pay is related to their performance.[10] The problem is that many plans are ill-conceived. Bonuses are not large enough nor sufficiently linked to performance to be motivational.[11] Consequently, performance-based pay plans need to be carefully conceived, implemented systematically, and clearly communicated. As we discuss later in this chapter, several obstacles also have to be removed.[12]

LEGAL CONSIDERATIONS

By definition, pay discrimination based on performance (not job status) is an inevitable and appropriate outcome of a properly administered performance-based pay system. Performance-based compensation is intended to create behaviors that lead to the accomplishment of organizational goals. Rewards that are administered contingently (that is, according to performance) cause increases in subsequent employee performance and expressions of satisfaction among high performers.[13] They encourage low performers to either perform at a higher rate or exit the organization. The legal issue, then, is not whether to discriminate in pay but how to administer performance-based pay so it does not unfairly discriminate against protected-group members.

> The tax-deductability to firms of CEO pay is limited to $1 million unless pay is performance-based.

As indicated in Chapter 11, the *Civil Rights Acts of 1964* and *1991* apply not only to selection decisions, but also to pay decisions. Under both laws, a supervisor may be charged with unlawful discrimination by an employee (in a protected group) who believes that a pay *raise was denied* on the basis of factors unrelated to performance. Raises not related to performance, however, are legal. Defensible factors (when they are equally applied to all employees) include the following:

> There are many conditions under which pay raises can be given legally.

- Position in salary range
- Time since last increase
- Size of last increase
- Pay relationships within the company or department
- Pay levels of jobs in other companies

- Salaries of newly hired employees
- Budgetary limits

What is critical for all pay plans is that the same rules are used to give raises fairly and consistently among all employees.

Merit plans are based on less direct performance measures than incentive plans.

Merit pay plans are used a lot but are not very motivating.

MERIT PAY PLANS

Although most managers would agree that the best ways to allocate scarce payroll dollars is to provide significant rewards to their top performers, most would reluctantly admit that they really do not end up paying their top performers much differently from the rest when using merit pay plans. Two principal reasons emerge:

- The typical pay system does not provide enough leeway to reward the really good performers without unfairly penalizing the satisfactory but unexceptional workers who also must be retained and kept motivated.
- Managers are not comfortable with basing large pay distinctions on the often-hazy performance information that they are able to develop.[14]

Nevertheless, the results of a survey on merit pay plans conducted by the Conference Board indicate that merit pay plans are widely used.[15] Of the companies surveyed, merit pay is granted to 96 percent of their nonexempt salaried employees, 99 percent of exempt employees, and 98 percent of top management. In contrast, only 7 percent of the unionized hourly employees receive merit pay hikes; usually they are rewarded with a general, union-negotiated increase. Non-union hourly workers are granted merit hikes by 39 percent of the companies, with 45 percent of the merit-paying firms also granting a general increase.

In merit pay plans, it is necessary to establish guidelines for determining the size of the raises, the timing of when they are given, and the relationship between the merit increments and their place in the salary range. Especially during times of high inflation rates, organizations have to address the general relationship between merit pay and cost-of-living adjustments.

MERIT PAY GUIDELINES

Because most large private organizations have some type of merit plan, it is useful to examine an example of a typical plan. As Exhibit 12.2 shows, pay increments depend not only on employee performance, but also on the employee's

EXHIBIT 12.2
TYPICAL MERIT PAY GUIDELINES

PERFORMANCE RATING	INCREASES BY EMPLOYEE'S POSITION IN SALARY RANGE			
	FIRST QUARTILE	SECOND QUARTILE	THIRD QUARTILE	FOURTH QUARTILE
Truly outstanding	13–14%	11–12%	9–10%	6–8%
Above average	11–12%	9–10%	7–8%	6% or less
Good	9–10%	7–8%	6% or less	delayed
Satisfactory	6–8%	6% or less	delayed	none
Unsatisfactory	none	none	none	none

position in the salary range.[16] This position is determined by expressing the employee's current salary as a percentage of the midpoint of the salary range for that job. The lower the position in the range (the first quartile is the lowest), the larger the percentage of the merit raise.

MERIT VERSUS COST-OF-LIVING ADJUSTMENTS

Many large organizations grant **cost-of-living adjustments (COLAs)** or general (non-performance-related) increases to their employees, especially where unions have written COLAs into their contracts. Neither COLAs nor general increases are based on performance, yet they can take the lion's share of money available for compensation increases. And where unionized workers have COLA guarantees, the pressures are great to provide the same benefits to non-union, often white-collar, employees.

Given the choice of merit pay or COLA, many organizations would prefer to eliminate their COLAs in favor of merit pay plans, primarily because COLAs have no relationship to performance yet can be expensive.[17] In addition to not relating performance to pay, COLAs often take salary control out of the hands of the organization and the compensation manager. Since most COLAs are tied to the Consumer Price Index (CPI), all the organization can do is watch salaries increase as the CPI goes up. This can leave so little for merit increases that they are ineffective. In times of high inflation, the issue may be whether to use the entire salary budget for COLAs or for merit increases rather than attempting to divide it up.

But even when the rate of inflation is low and merit raises are given, the incentive value of the raises tends to be modest. This is because of the relatively small amount that merit increases generally represent and the even smaller differences (in absolute dollars) between getting the top increase and an average one. Consequently, organizations are using a modified version of the traditional, yearly merit plan increase: the performance bonus.

PERFORMANCE BONUSES RATHER THAN MERIT RAISES

With increased emphasis on cost-effective human resource practices, firms are questioning the traditional practice of granting annual salary or merit increases.[18] Consider an employee who performs outstandingly one year and is given a 15 percent merit pay increase. The next year for whatever reason, the employee may not perform as well or even adequately. While subsequent performance may decrease, the cost of the original salary increase is a permanent cost for the organization. Merit increases administered in this way may also demotivate other employees because the employee who performed well previously may have a higher base pay rate than an employee who is currently performing well. As a result, the low performer may receive a larger increase than the better performing employee whose base pay is lower.

To rectify this situation, firms such as Timex, and Westinghouse replaced merit increases with one-time, semiannual, or quarterly **performance bonuses**. These bonuses may be distributed in one lump sum or in the traditional way (divided up into parts for each check). Bonuses are also popular in competitive high-technology firms. A recent survey showed that 7 percent of managerial, professional, and technical employees were eligible for bonuses in large high-tech firms. In smaller high-tech firms with sales less than $1 billion, almost half of all technical employees receive bonuses. These may be tied to meeting product development deadlines or to the profitability of product lines.[19]

Lump-sum bonuses, as they are also called, are also in union contracts. Common forms of bonuses in union contracts include flat amounts, a percentage

COLAs became important during the inflationary 1970s and 1980s.

My wages aren't really keeping pace. I don't feel like I'm getting ahead.

Larry Kerrigan, 31
Pipefitter, Phelps Dodge
Morenci, Arizona

Bonuses pack a bigger punch than raises.

Performance bonuses or *lump-sum bonuses* are one-time rewards of money tied to performance.

of the preceding year's pay or a specified dollar amount multiplied by the number of hours worked.

There are several advantages to bonuses instead of salary increases. First, the bonuses increase the meaning of pay. The lump-sum payment of $5,000 is more striking than a before-tax increase of $100 a week. A wise employee can leverage the value of the bonus further by investing it carefully. This is not possible when increases are spread throughout the year. Second, bonuses maximize the relationship between pay and performance. Unlike permanent salary increases, an employee must perform above average year in and year out to continue receiving bonuses.

When applied to managerial employees, these bonus plans are referred to as **variable-pay plans**. The feature, "Managing Human Resources: Variable-Pay Program Increases Taco Bell's Profits" illustrates this type of pay plan.

Performance-bonus plans for managerial employees are called *variable-pay plans*.

Occasionally, traditional merit pay and performance-bonus plans are combined. For example, reasoning that excellence is the standard, not the exception, a broadcast firm set its pay policy line at 105 percent of the external market. Pay grade minimums were also established so entry-level trainees with no experience could be paid less. Merit increases were awarded until the employee's base salary reached the pay grade midpoint. Then, annual salary increases were replaced with an annual performance bonus for all excellent or above average employees. Depending on the employee's base salary, these bonuses ranged from $1,000 to $5,000.

Whether combined or used singly, however, some organizations such as Taco Bell and Lincoln Electric think they get more out of their compensation dollars using incentive pay plans.

INCENTIVE PAY PLANS

While *individual* incentive programs are the tried-and-true form of this pay system, *group* incentive plans such as Improshare are making waves as the newest form of performance-based pay. Incentive plans can best be classified according to the level at which they are applied: individual or group.

INDIVIDUAL INCENTIVE PLANS

Individual incentive plans include:

- piecework plan
- standard hour plan
- suggestion systems

Individual incentives remain the most popular form of incentive plan: each person's output is measured, and subsequent rewards are based on the output. The utilization of these plans varies with the type of job. Very few office workers work under these plans, but textile, clothing, cigar, and steel industries rely extensively on them.

While a variety of individual incentive plans exist, they differ in terms of the method of rate determination. When the work cycle is short, units of production generally serve as the method of rate determination. For longer-cycle jobs, the standard is typically based on the time required to complete a unit. Individual incentive systems also vary in regards to the constancy with which pay is a function of production level. One option is to pay a consistent amount at all production levels (for example, 25 cents per carton). Alternatively, pay may vary as a function of production level. For example, employees may be paid 25 cents a carton up to 1,000 units a day. When this threshold is passed, the incentive rises to 27 cents a carton.

Factors enhancing the use of incentive pay plans are:

- large labor costs
- cost-competitive market
- simple technology
- independent employee output

Individual incentive plans also share a common job analysis foundation. As discussed in Chapter 6, time and motion studies are often employed to determine how wages are tied to output. The challenge is to identify a "normal" rate of production.[21]

Taco Bell Corporation's upbeat advertisements have been so successful at getting people to "make a run for the border," that the Irvine, California–based company has opened more than 350 new restaurants in the last two years. Although this is great news for hungry consumers, it was a challenge for the company's HR department to find managers for these restaurants.

"We didn't think we could find all the talent we needed to run those stores," explains Michael J. Rowe, Taco Bell's director of compensation and benefits. "So we decided to ask existing restaurant managers to start supervising two units instead of one."

Instead of increasing the managers' salaries to correlate to their added responsibilities, Taco Bell did something very interesting. The company kept the managers' base salaries the same but allowed them to earn twice as much in bonus pay through a variable-pay program.

"To continue to sell 59-cent tacos, we can't have pay programs that are inefficient," Rowe explains. "We can't afford to give $50,000 in base pay with no performance guarantees. We can, however, afford to pay $30,000 and give managers a $20,000 bonus if they drive profits to the bottom line. The way we do this is through a variable-pay program that funds incremental pay out of incremental profits."

Today the 1,600 restaurant managers are evaluated and given bonuses based on three objectives:

1. Targeted profit, which relates to bottom-line results
2. Customer service, which is evaluated by an independent marketing-research firm
3. Actual store sales

On average, managers receive a bonus worth about 30 percent of their base pay. But payments that double the base amount aren't uncommon. However, Rowe is quick to emphasize that not all managers earn a bonus all the time. "It isn't an entitlement," he says. "Between 60 percent and 70 percent of managers earn a bonus that's paid every six months. But that means 30 percent of managers don't get anything in their variable pay for six months' work. Believe me, a person who misses a $5,000 bonus payment twice a year will pay attention to the things that drive profitability: sales and customer service."

Although Taco Bell's program isn't punitive in nature, it is high risk. Under the company's previous merit pay system, about 85 percent of restaurant managers received $1,000 bonuses four times each year. "They really had to be bad not to get that money," Rowe explains, "whereas under this system, they really have to be good."

When asked how the variable-pay program fits into Taco Bell's overall corporate strategy, Rowe says that the relationship between both may be irrelevant. "A bonus program at that level should be reflective of what you want to get out of people in that job," he says. "I think it's a mistake for every bonus program in the company to have the same objectives. You have to ask yourself what kind of results you're attempting to obtain from restaurant managers. Hopefully, the answer isn't too different from what you want to get out of your president, but clearly I'm not going to expect my president to do customer service at the unit level."

Taco Bell's program has been implemented for 18 months, and it seems to be working. Food costs as a percentage of sales continue to decrease, customer service scores for 1992 were the best the company has ever had, and profit records continue to be broken.[20]

PIECEWORK PLAN. Piecework such as Lincoln Electric uses is the most common type of incentive pay plan. Under the **straight piecework plan**, employees are guaranteed a standard pay rate for each unit of production. For example, if the base pay of a job is $40 per day and the employee can produce 20 units a day at a normal rate, the piece rate may be established at $2 per unit. The incentive

431

Incentive plans can be based on productivity standards and direct indexes such as *straight piecework plans* or *differential piece rate plans*.

pay rate is based on the standard output and the base wage rate. The "normal" rate is more than what the time and motion studies indicate but is supposed to represent 100 percent efficiency. The final rate also reflects the bargaining power of the employees, economic conditions of the organization and industry, and what the competition is paying (See Exhibit 12.3 to see how Lincoln calculates the piecework).

In a **differential piece rate plan**, there is more than one rate of pay for the same job. This plan can be operationalized in different ways. Named for its developer, the Taylor Differential plan consists of a higher rate of pay for work completed in a set period. For production per unit that takes longer than the established time to complete the job, the rate of pay is lower. Merrill Lynch, one of the largest stock brokerage firms in the world, instituted a commission plan similar to Taylor's plan, but this, as applied to brokerage firms, has some potentially bad side effects, which we will discuss in the section on straight commission. Sales personnel having higher sales volume receive higher rates of commission than sales personnel with lower volume.

Also named for its developer, the Merrick's Multiple-Wage plan operates in the same way except three piece rates are established. Workers receive a 10 percent bonus when they reach 83 percent of standard and an additional 10 percent bonus when the achieve the standard.

The success of any piece rate system depends on more than merely paying individuals for more work. Its success is dependent on how employees are treated and the level of employment security provided. These two items have high priority at Lincoln Electric. But to be fair, even at Lincoln Electric there is more to their incentive system than piecework, employee treatment, and security. As shown in Exhibit 12.3, many financial incentives are offered to employees, but it is the final profit-sharing bonus figure that makes the news and makes employees wealthy. To see how this bonus is calculated, see the feature, "Managing Human Resources: How Lincoln Electric Calculates Employees' Bonuses." But even Lincoln Electric doesn't use all available incentive pay plans. There are others, as the following discussion shows.

STANDARD HOUR PLAN.   The standard hour plan is the second most common incentive plan. The **standard hour plan** is a piecework plan, except that standards are denominated in time per unit of output rather than money per unit of output. Tasks are broken down by the amount of time it takes to complete them. This can be determined by historical records, time and motion studies, or a combination of both. The time to perform each task then becomes a "standard."

Consider a standard time of two hours and a rate of pay of $12 an hour. If a worker completes six units in an eight-hour day, the worker would receive 6 × $24, or $144. This is substantially more than the standard rate of pay for eight hours of $96.

REWARDING INDIRECT LABOR.   While individual piece rate systems work well for the direct laborers, it is more difficult to reward personnel who support and make possible the productivity improvements of the direct laborers. The problem is that these workers often assist a number of direct laborers. They may sort, feed, and prepare raw materials or remove and inspect finished materials. One approach is to provide the same percent increase above normal as is earned by the *average* direct laborer.

EXHIBIT 12.3
COMPONENTS OF LINCOLN ELECTRIC'S INCENTIVE PLAN

Lincoln's incentive plan combines job security with a lucrative compensation program. Below is a summary of the plan's elements.

FEATURES	DESCRIPTION	CRITERIA
Job Security	Guaranteed 30-hour workweek.	Employees are eligible after three years of service and • Pay rates aren't guaranteed. • Job transfers may be necessary. • Overtime is required during peak demand. • Guaranteed hours may be terminated by the company with a six-month notice.
Base Wage	Standard Job Evaluation procedures are used to set the base wage. However, job evaluation and market requirements determine the actual dollar value of jobs.	Job evaluation compensable factors include skill, responsibility, mental aptitude, physical application, and working conditions.
Piecework	For every job that can be standardized, normal time-study procedures are employed to establish piece rates.	Piece rates are based on the following calculation for consistency and to eliminate constant revisions: 1934 wage rates times cost of living, which fluctuates with the index (Bureau of Labor Statistics). This product is then compared with the area average skilled hourly rate to determine the adjustments to the piece rate.
Advisory Board	Employees elect representatives to an Advisory Board. All employees, except department heads and members of the engineering and time-study departments, are eligible.	The Advisory Board analyzes suggestions that lead to organizational progress. Implemented suggestions have ranged from a savings of $2,400 to over $200,000.
Merit Ratings	Twice a year, managers appraise employee performance through a merit-rating program.	This program uses four report cards. Each card rates work performance on one of the following: output, quality, dependability, and personal characteristics, such as the ability to come up with ideas, and cooperation.
Profit Sharing	All business profits are split three ways: among the company, the shareholders, and the employees as a year-end bonus.	The company receives seed money; the shareholders receive a dividend; and the employees receive a year-end, profit-sharing bonus.
Year-End Profit-Sharing Bonus	The year-end bonus closely approximates the employees' annual earnings.	An employee's bonus is a function of his total annual earnings, biannual merit ratings, and company profits.
Employee Stock-Ownership Plan	Each employee has the opportunity to purchase a limited number of shares of company stock per year.	Employees are eligible after one year of service. On retirement or termination of employment, the company has the option to repurchase the stock.

SOURCE: C. Wiley, "Incentive Plan Pushes Production," *Personnel Journal* (August 1993): 90. Used by permission.

UNDER the Lincoln Electric Incentive Plan, employees at Cleveland-based Lincoln Electric Co. receive bonuses based on their productivity. The bonus is determined by a simple bonus-factor formula.

First, the board of directors sets the amount of the year's bonus pool, based on a recommendation by the chairman. The chairman looks at such factors as how much money the company has made, how much seed money is needed, and how much money is needed for taxes and dividends. The average bonus pool during a recent ten-year period was 10.6 percent of sales revenue.

The company then divides this bonus pool amount by the total wages paid. This quotient is the bonus factor. A bonus factor of 1.00 means that the bonus pool is the same as the total companywide wages. Typically, the bonus pool is approximately 75 percent of wages paid.

Once the bonus factor has been determined, the company calculates bonuses by multiplying the bonus factor by individual earnings and merit ratings. Here's an example. A production worker earned $35,000. His merit rating was 100 percent, or 1.00. The bonus factor is 0.75. The formula for determining his bonus would be as follows:

$$
\begin{array}{r}
\$35{,}000 \text{ (earnings)} \\
\times 1.00 \text{ (merit rating)} \\
\hline
\$35{,}000 \\
\end{array}
$$

$$
\begin{array}{r}
\$35{,}000 \\
\times .75 \text{ (bonus factor)} \\
\hline
\$26{,}250 \text{ (bonus)} \\
\end{array}
$$

This employee's full bonus would be $26,250. However, according to Paul Beddia, vice president of human resources at Lincoln, employees must pay for their own hospitalization insurance, which costs approximately $3,000. The company deducts this money from employees' year-end bonuses. Thus, this production worker would receive a bonus of $23,250 (before taxes), bringing his annual salary to $58,250.[22]

Suggestion systems can be useful when they are honestly used.

SUGGESTION SYSTEMS. **Suggestion systems** reward employees for money-saving or money-producing ideas and are used extensively. They are perhaps unique in that they attempt to increase the number of good ideas rather than output directly. Yet they are similar to other plans in that the rewards are monetary. Approximately 80 percent of the nation's 500 largest corporations have suggestion systems.[23]

Suggestion systems are also important because they can bestow substantial sums of money. Some organizations allow employees as much as 30 percent of the first year's savings. New York City–based Con Edison has a cap of $15,000 per suggestion. In 1990, more than $200,000 was awarded to employees for their suggestions. Several of those awarded received the maximum benefit of $15,000.

Suggestion systems generally do not have a favorable reputation, however, because individual awards are too small. Also, employees sometimes never learn the results of their ideas, and companies often save more than the individual receives. To resolve this problem, Con Edison publishes regular bulletins about implementing employee suggestions. They've also reduced the implementation turnaround time (three to six months versus a year).

TEAM-BASED INCENTIVES

Team incentives fall somewhere between individual-incentive and whole-organizational plans such as gain sharing and profit sharing (to be discussed next). The goals are tailored specifically to what the team needs to accomplish. Strategically, the goals of individuals are linked to those of the work group (typically ten people or fewer) to achieve financial goals.[24] According to Judy Huret, a principal with Towers Perrin in San Francisco, team incentives improve employees' "line of sight" regarding what they need to do as a group to enhance profits. For example:

> An insurance company was encountering friction between two different departments—data processing and claims. The claims people said the data processing staff never met its deadlines. The data processing people said the claims people kept changing their minds and made unreasonable demands. When the company instituted a team incentive plan, senior management facilitated a discussion between the two departments and informed them that their incentive award would be linked to how well they worked together to meet customer needs.
>
> The claims group then clearly outlined the specifications and timetable necessary to meet customer service needs and discussed them with data processing. Data processing developed a detailed project plan and shared it with claims. Now that both groups understand the ultimate objective, they can work together to achieve a common goal. The amount of their incentive award will depend on how quickly and how well the team goal is met.[25]

Given that the prerequisites listed in Exhibit 12.4 are met, team-based incentives offer four major advantages compared with individual incentive systems. First, the mere presence of team members who have some control over rewards evokes more vigorous and persistent behavior than when individuals work alone. Second, the likelihood that conflicting contingencies (peer pressure) will evoke counterproductive control over behavior is reduced. Third, the strength of the rewards is increased since they are now paired with group-administered rewards (praise, camaraderie). Research also suggests that the performance of a group is higher than that attained by individual group members (although not as high as the best person in the group). Finally, the performance of one group member (usually the high performer) can serve as a model, encouraging other members to imitate successful behavior.

In group-incentive plans, teams of employees get paid for their team's performance. Performance is typically measured by output, cost savings, and profits.

EXHIBIT 12.4
PREREQUISITES FOR THE EFFECTIVE ADMINISTRATION OF TEAM INCENTIVES

1. Everyone who's on the team, including indirect laborers and support staff members, is eligible.
2. Team-performance is measurable.
3. Performance standards are communicated to team members in advance of the performance period.
4. The incentive system is easy to understand.
5. Team members receive regular feedback on their progress towards performance targets. "War rooms," including graphs, charts, and statistical analyses, provide ongoing useful feedback.
6. Team members must believe they can affect performance outcomes.
7. Corporate culture must be congruent with team problem solving and participation.

Team-based incentives are not perfect because some members don't always pull their own weight.

The *Scanlon plan* stresses sharing and participation in company operations and profitability.

But just as Lincoln Electric's success is a sum of more than its piecework plan, meeting performance or productivity goals usually takes more than a team-based incentive plan. For example, in the case of the Aid Association to Lutherans (the AAL case in Chapter 5), a team-based incentive plan is used along with an individual incentive program, market survey data, and a skill-based pay plan. This is described in the feature, "Managing Human Resources: AAL Uses Varied Approach to Compensate Teams."

While team-based incentives are promising, administrative responsibilities are as great as those associated with individual incentive plans. Job analysis is still necessary to identify how to structure the teams and to ensure that workloads are equivalent between teams. There may also be unintended side effects, including competition between groups, that may or may not complement goal attainment. A second concern is **social loafing**, where group performance declines because team members (consciously or subconsciously) lower their inputs, believing that others in the group will pick up the slack. This is less likely to happen, however, in cases where there is broad-based employee participation and involvement such as in the Scanlon plan.

COST REDUCTION PLANS

While a variety of cost reduction programs exists, the Scanlon plan developed in the late 1930s is among the oldest. It relies on a ratio between labor costs and sales value of production as the measure for judging business performance. A newer approach, which focuses on an engineering-based productivity measurement, is called **Improshare** (IMproved PROductivity through SHARing).

SCANLON PLAN. The **Scanlon plan** is a philosophy of management that emphasizes employee-employer participation *and* sharing in operations and profitability. Used in union and non-union environments, the Scanlon plan requires good management, mutual respect, and trust on the part of management and labor. Research indicates that Scanlon plans are effective about half the time they are used and work best in small companies (500 employees or less). Productivity gains range from zero to 65 percent with an average gain of 20 percent.

At the heart of a Scanlon plan is the *ratio* between total labor costs and the sales value of production. While the ratio is affected by the factors listed in Exhibit 12.4, labor costs generally total between 35 and 45 percent of total sales. It is important to note that a small reduction in labor costs (1–2 percent) can produce a large improvement in the profitability of an organization (10–20 percent).

The size of the performance bonus is contingent on the reduction in costs below the preset level. Consider an expected monthly payroll of $1.5 million and an actual payroll of only $1.2 million. The bonus pool would be $300,000. Normally, one-fourth of the cost savings are retained in an escrow account to cover expenses when the ratio becomes too high. The remainder is shared between employees (75 percent) and the employer (25 percent).

Scanlon plans also include production and screening committees. The former operate in each organizational department. Their objective is to develop suggestions to increase productivity, improve quality, and reduce waste. The screening committee includes members of management and worker representatives and reviews suggestions and devises implementation plans.[27]

Improshare rewards employees for the savings that accrue from reaching performance targets.

IMPROSHARE. Developed in the mid-1970s by Mitchell Fein, Improshare uses easy-to-obtain past production records to establish base performance standards. Any savings arising from production of agreed-upon output in fewer than expect-

A ID Association for Lutherans (AAL), a fraternal-benefits society, leaves nothing to chance when it comes to compensating members of its insurance-service teams. The company, which is based in Appleton, Wisconsin, has devised a four-legged compensation stool, which allows the company to:

- Recognize individual achievements
- Reward team productivity
- Compensate employees for the acquisition of new skills
- Remain competitive with its salary structure

AAL has 15 service teams, organized geographically, that perform all services necessary for the company's insurance products. For example, a team, comprising 25 employees, can underwrite a policy, pay a claim, change beneficiaries, and modify coverage levels. Furthermore, team members can provide these services for any product, be it life insurance, health, or disability insurance.

Before developing the team structure in 1987, the company organized these services functionally, according to the type of product. Service requests traveled from unit to unit, increasing the amount of time needed to service a customer, and boosting the chance for errors.

"By moving to teams, we were challenging employees to see the whole job, rather than just the piece they performed individually," explains Jerry Laubenstein, vice president of insurance services. "But we also wanted them to learn additional jobs that could help the team as a whole, and we wanted the team to find ways to boost its overall performance."

To promote all of these changes, AAL revamped its compensation structure completely to include four main elements.

1. *A skill-based pay program.* The company has implemented a skill-based pay system that compensates individuals for each additional skill they acquire in an effort to help the team. As one of the first organizations to implement skill-based pay for white-collar workers, AAL developed a dictionary that describes all the services performed by team members and lists their associated dollar value. Employees are paid a base wage for the primary service they perform, and they can receive incremental pay increases for each service added to their repertoire of skills.

2. *A team incentive program.* AAL has implemented a team incentive program through which the entire team is awarded an annual bonus based on three factors:
   - Productivity
   - Customer satisfaction
   - Quality of work
   This team incentive can be worth as much as 10 percent of an employee's annual compensation.

3. *The use of market data.* The company now relies heavily on market data to ensure that employees are paid competitive wages.

4. *An individual incentive program.* AAL has added an incentive component that recognizes outstanding achievement by individual employees. This lump-sum incentive is paid once a year only to those employees who are already paid at market value. This incentive is worth as much as 6 percent of an individual's compensation.

AAL's compensation structure didn't change all at once, Laubenstein says, and there were several problems along the way. "We went to teams in 1987 and didn't put any incentives in place until 1989. Then we moved entirely to team incentives, where we didn't recognize individuals at all. This caused a lot of problems with employees who were used to being recognized individually. Finally, in 1991, we modified the program to recognize both individual and team achievements."

Is the program working? "We're on a journey, and we haven't reached the destination yet," Laubenstein cautions. "But in the five years that we've been in teams, we've increased our productivity by 40 percent. Surveys reveal that more than 90 percent of our customers are satisfied with the level of service they're receiving. I'd say things are coming along well."[26]

ed hours are shared by the firm and the employees.[28] As a percentage of pay, Scanlon plans average 5 percent payouts, whereas Improshare plans provide 10 percent.

Three controls in the Improshare plan permit changes in the measurement standards. The maximum employee gainshare is 30 percent of base wages. Gains above this amount are "banked" and added to the next payout below 30 percent. If production continues to be high, management can buy back the gain over 160 percent. Consider an employee who earns $10 an hour and worked 2,500 hours. If the gain for the year rests at 180 percent, employees receive 50 percent of the difference between 160 percent and 180 percent or $2,500 [20% (buyback) $\times$ 50% (division) $\times$ $10 (hourly rate) $\times$ 2,500 (hours worked) $2,500.] The base for future calculations would be increased by 1.8/1.6 = 1.125.[29]

PROFIT-SHARING PLANS

Profit-sharing plans enable employees to share in the profits.

Introduced first in the Gallatin glassworks factory in New Geneva, Pennsylvania, in 1794, approximately 430,000 **profit-sharing plans** now exist in American businesses. As defined by the Council of Profit Sharing, these plans include any procedure under which an employer pays or makes available to regular employees, special current or deferred sums based on the profits of business in addition to their regular pay.[30]

Profit-sharing plans fall into one of three categories. *Current distribution plans* provide for 14 to 33 percent of profits to be distributed quarterly or annually to employees. *Deferred plans* are the fastest growing type of plan due to tax advantages. Earnings are placed in an escrow fund for distribution upon retirement, termination, death, or disability. About 20 percent of firms with profit-sharing programs have *combined plans*. Here, a portion of profits is distributed immediately to employees with the remaining amount set aside in a designated account.

Profit-sharing can be used to fund retirement plans and gain employee loyalty and commitment at the same time.

Like cost reduction plans, profit-sharing plans are designed to pay out incentives when the organization is most able to afford them. They differ in that employee involvement is not an important component of the plan. The motivational potential of deferred plans is also questionable since employees are unlikely to see the relationship between their performance and profitability of the firm.[31] Examples such as Lincoln Electric, Wal-Mart, Nucor Steel, and Hallmark, however, suggest that profit sharing can be very motivational, especially when it is accompanied by employee participation and feelings of involvement.[32]

GAMES AND AWARDS

As competition increases, companies are turning to novel ways to motivate employees. Domino's Pizza spends a million dollars holding its "Distribution Olympics." Top employees from across the country are identified, flown to the national headquarters, and paid to spend three days playing job-related games. Winners of the games garner substantial cash prizes. According to a Domino's spokesperson, the games encourage employees to hone their job skills and produce a better product. They also enhance Domino's fundamental belief that the contribution of every employee matters.[33]

Other companies are using on-the-job lotteries as a way to spark high productivity. Employees with performance above a specified threshold participate in the lottery. Even bigger than games and awards for motivating employees are apartments and cars. However, smaller gifts such as a class ring can also be motivating. This and other forms of nonfinancial recognition are described in the feature "Managing Human Resources: Recognition Can Bolster Quality Efforts."

THE quality-improvement process at Appleton Papers in West Carrollton, Ohio, began in 1988. Three years into the process, the effort had created no discernible improvements in customer satisfaction, morale, safety records, or profitability.

"Quality had become more of a program than a process," explains Wayne Reveal, the organization's manager of organizational services. Why? "Because there was an obvious lack of recognition of employee behavior."

Among other things, Reveal says, quality is an attempt to create or change *behavior sets*, yet Appleton workers who performed good work went unrecognized, and employees who performed poorly escaped disciplinary action.

In an attempt to reshape and reinforce its quality effort, Appleton implemented a comprehensive worker-recognition process in 1991. Today, each line manager receives a recognition budget from which he or she can buy gifts to reward employees for good behaviors.

The company's basic rule is that recognition gifts must be personal in nature and something that the employees wouldn't buy for themselves. The organization encourages managers to use the gifts as surprise rewards for good work, as well as incentives for special achievement.

Recently, for example, a department manager wanted to offer an incentive for several of the employees on his crew to acquire their GEDs. Thinking about other important aspects of high school, he realized that he couldn't offer them the opportunity to attend the senior proms they had missed, nor could he give them an actual high-school diploma. What he could do—and did—was to give each worker who completed his or her GED successfully a class ring from the high school from which the person would have graduated.

There are no guidelines attached to the recognition process. Appleton simply encourages employees to recognize others when and where it's appropriate.

"This isn't a one-size-fits-all program," Reveal says. Instead, the company encourages managers to think about what the individual being recognized would value most. Some employees favor public recognition, for example, whereas others find such accolades embarrassing.

Managers aren't the only ones charged with the responsibility for recognizing good deeds. All employees are encouraged to give quality thank-you notes to co-workers, supervisors, and subordinates in recognition of good work. Furthermore, the organization's CEO recognizes individual and team achievement on an annual basis with lucrative, high-profile recognition items. "Employees used to think that recognition was only the job of human resources," Reveal says. "Now they realize that it's everyone's job."

In addition to recognizing good deeds, Appleton's managers must take the time to deal with inappropriate behavior as well. "We can't just reinforce positive behavior without also letting the employees know what negative behavior looks like," Reveal explains. This kind of response can range from brief verbal warnings to initiation of the progressive discipline process.

Before implementing the new recognition system, Appleton trained its managers in how both to give and to receive recognition effectively. "We didn't want an employee to recognize his or her manager for a job well done and have that manager shrug off the compliment," Reveal says. "We had to make sure that managers knew how to receive recognition gracefully as a way to reinforce the importance of it."

Is the company's quality effort more successful now because of its recognition process? Yes, according to Reveal.

Appleton has moved from an *unfavorable* to a *favorable* financial position, 75 percent less time is lost due to on-the-job accidents, and, though it's hard to measure, morale has improved. As Reveal says, "Let's just say it feels better around here."[34]

COMPENSATION FOR SPECIAL GROUPS

The performance-based systems described so far share an important characteristic: they are usually applied to employees who are covered under the *Fair Labor Standards Act (FLSA)*. There are other groups, however, for which there are special compensation concerns. This section will discuss the special compensation concerns of sales personnel, executives, and international employees.

SALES PERSONNEL

Because a large part of a salesperson's job is unsupervised, performance-based compensation programs are useful in directing sales activities. Still, only 20 percent of all sales personnel are paid by straight incentives. More than half of all sales plans use a combination of salary and individual or group incentives.[35]

STRAIGHT SALARY.   Approximately 30 percent of all sales personnel are paid a straight salary. The latter is appropriate when the major function of the sales person is providing customer service or "prospecting new accounts under low success conditions." Straight salary plans are also appropriate in jobs demanding high technical expertise but little ability to close sales. Consider the job of a product engineer for a software publishing house. Duties of this job might include developing and executing sales and product training programs, participating in trade shows, promoting new products, and meeting with distributors to encourage pushing product lines. In such jobs, a high salary to attract technically competent individuals is more critical than incentives to close the sale.

The advantages of a straight salary program are several. From the salesperson's viewpoint, it takes the ambiguity out of the salary process. It's also simpler to administer. If nonsales functions (for example, paperwork and customer support) are important, salaried sales personnel are more willing to perform these functions. The drawback is that straight salaries reduce the connection between performance and pay.

STRAIGHT COMMISSION.   In theory, a **commission** is simply a percentage of the sales price of the product. The exact percentage depends on the product being sold, industry practices, the organization's economic conditions, and special pricing during sales promotions. In establishing a sales commission program, the following questions need answering:

- What criteria will be used to measure performance?
- Are territories equivalent in sales potential?
- Will commission rates vary by product or vary depending on sales level?
- Will there be a cap on earnings?
- Will credit for a sale be given at point of sale, at delivery, or at receipt of payment?
- What will be the timing of commission payments (monthly, quarterly)?

Once these questions are answered, a program can be set up. The success of commission-only plans rests directly on the salesperson. The more sales, the greater the earnings; no sales means no income. The success also rests on whether the salespeople will even accept the incentive pay program.

The power of such incentives can be so high that it elicits unintended behaviors.[36] Churning among stockbrokers is one example. As a federal judge said recently, "As long as investment brokers are paid on straight commission, the potential exists for brokers to excessively trade accounts in an effort to gen-

Sales people can be paid by:
- straight salary
- commissions
- a combination

erate fees without regard to the customers' financial needs and investment objectives." Commission-only plans also make it difficult to direct the efforts of salespeople towards activities (paperwork) that do not have an immediate influence on obtaining additional sales.

COMBINED PLANS.   Because of these concerns, more than half of all sales compensation plans combine base salary and incentives. In setting up a combined plan, the critical question is what percentage of total compensation should be salary and what percentage should be commission. The answer to this question depends on the availability of sales criteria (sales volume, units sold, product mix, retention of accounts, number of new accounts), and the number of nonsales duties in the job. Commonly, these plans are based on an 80/20 salary to commission mix. However, organizations wishing to push sales over customer service functions may utilize different ratios (60/40 or even 50/50).

The commission portion of the sales compensation can be established in one of two ways. The simplest is to use a commission combined with a *draw*. The salesperson receives a specific salary each payday. Quarterly or monthly, the total commission due the salesperson is calculated. The amount taken as a draw is deducted with the salesperson receiving the remainder. Alternatively, bonuses can be given when sales reach a specific level.[37]

Sales plans often include contests to direct sales activities to certain products or outcomes. Vacations as well as goods such as golf clubs are commonly rewarded. These contests provide very visible rewards. Records of who is winning can be placed on the bulletin board and in company newsletters.

EXECUTIVE COMPENSATION

Annual bonuses ranging from 20 to 45 percent of base salary are the most prevalent nonsalary compensation device used by companies to reward their executives, according to a Conference Board survey of 580 large U.S. firms. Annual bonus plans are nearly universal in energy (97 percent), manufacturing (92 percent), service firms (92 percent), and banking (81 percent), but less prevalent in public utilities. Because base salaries are considerably lower in companies with bonus plans, they provide a strong incentive for executives to perform well in the short run. However, they do not work well in companies with one or more of the following characteristics: (1) tight control of stock ownership, (2) not-for-profit institutions, and (3) firms operating in regulated industries.[38]

STOCK OPTIONS.   The next most frequently used method of rewarding executives is stock options. Approximately 75 percent of energy, manufacturing, and insurance firms provide such plans. A **stock option** is an opportunity for a manager to buy the organization's stock at a later date but at a price established when the option is granted. The awarding of stock options is premised on the assumption that managers will work harder to increase their performance and the performance of the firm if they share in the firm's long-run profits. This focus on long-term incentives reflects a concern by boards of directors for long-term achievement over short-run profits. Of course, this same logic applies to firms offering stock options to their nonmanagerial workers as well. While this practice is limited, companies like Walgreen Drugstores show that it has as positive an effect on employees as it does on managers!

Following the *Economic Recovery Tax Act of 1981*, most companies with stock option plans use **incentive stock options (ISO)**. When an ISO is exercised, an executive pays only 20 percent capital gains on the first $100,000 of

Stock options are a very popular way to motivate managers to work hard to raise the value of the stock price.

Each year, 15 percent of UPS's pretax profit is used to buy company stock that is distributed to entry-level supervisors on up. "We have 25,000 owner-managers who have virtually every cent they own invested in stock of this company."

Expatriates typically get paid in dollars *and* the local currency.

Remember:
MNC = multinational corporation
PCN = parent-country nationals
TCN = third-country nationals

appreciated value. While this is far less than the previous 50 percent tax rate, these programs still require a large cash investment. Consequently, some companies are experimenting with **stock appreciation rights (SAR)**, which allow executives to realize capital gains of stock options without requiring the purchase of stocks.[39]

INTERNATIONAL EMPLOYEES

Picking up from our discussion of international employee compensation in Chapter 11,[40] if the MNC utilizes any type of incentive bonus system, a policy is usually established. Bonuses can be given according to either home- or host-country policies. Actual payments can be made in either local or foreign currency and will often be a combination of the two or at the discretion of the recipient. For example, the majority of U.S. financial services companies have an overall policy of paying PCNs according to the U.S. salary structure (this includes bonus programs and salary increase practices). Most often, this compensation is paid partly in U.S. dollars and partly in the local currency. While the local currency portion is generally pegged to pay ordinary living expenses, bonuses are typically paid in U.S. dollars. Salary practices for TCNs tend to vary more widely and may be paid according to the home structure, a U.S. structure, or the host-country structure.

Questions that MNCs generally address when planning for their incentive bonuses include:

- What techniques can be used to provide management incentives abroad?
- Incentive bonuses help many companies achieve their objectives at home, but can they be used as effectively in subsidiary operations?
- How can companies design appropriate incentive bonuses for managers in an area suffering from rapid inflation?[41]

American MNCs frequently link stock opportunities to executive performance. Recent tax changes in a number of western countries make stock ownership more feasible than in the past.[42]

Parent-country nationals often receive a salary premium as an inducement to accept a foreign assignment or to compensate for any hardship suffered due to the transfer. Under such circumstances, the definition of hardship, eligibility for the premium, and amount and timing of payment must be addressed. For cases in which hardship is determined, MNCs often refer to the U.S. Department of State's Hardship Post Differentials Guidelines to determine an appropriate level of payment. As others have noted, however, there are many problems involved with international comparisons of the cost of living.[43] It is important to note that TCNs do not receive these payments as often as PCNs. Foreign service inducements, if used, are most commonly made in the form of a percentage of salary, usually 5–40 percent of base pay. Such payments vary depending on the assignment, actual hardship, tax consequences, and length of assignment. In addition, differentials may be considered; for example, a host country's workweek may be longer than that of the home country, and a differential payment may be made in lieu of overtime, which is not normally paid to PCNs or TCNs.

Currency protection is also an issue affecting compensation. Several alternatives for this protection exist. Employees may have discretion over the currency used in payments, or a standard split basis for all PCNs may exist. A split basis may be applied on a case-by-case basis, depending on the particular assignment. With regard to local currency payments, a policy concerning exchange rate adjustments is necessary to assure that all employees are treated fairly.

ADMINISTRATIVE ISSUES

Although performance-based pay systems are capable of substantially improving productivity, many obstacles in their design and implementation may suppress their potential effectiveness. Organizations can identify these obstacles and remove them. The following discussion of the obstacles pertains equally to both merit pay and incentive pay; the second and third administrative issues apply primarily to merit pay.

OBSTACLES TO EFFECTIVENESS

Obstacles encountered in the design and implementation of performance-based pay systems can be grouped into three general categories: (1) specifying and measuring job performance, (2) identifying valued rewards (pay being just one of many rewards), and (3) linking rewards to job performance.[44]

A prerequisite to rewarding job performance is specifying what job performance is, determining the relationships between levels of job performance and rewards, and accurately measuring job performance. These steps are often difficult because of the changing nature of work, its multidimensional nature, technological developments, lack of supervisory training, and the manager's value system. These problems are detailed in Exhibit 12.5 along with their implications for management.

A second set of obstacles involves identifying rewards for desired behaviors. Rewards other than pay may have more motivational value, especially for employees whose pay increments may be largely consumed by increased taxes. Consequently, the manager must discover the rewards most valued by the employees and contingently administer those that are most reinforcing. This process is filled with potential problems. The causes and implications for a manager wishing to manage human resources effectively are shown in Exhibit 12.5.

The third category of obstacles involves the difficulties in linking rewards to job performance. The causes of these problems include inappropriate contingencies, inaccurate performance appraisal measures, and existing employee opposition. Often employee opposition is a major obstacle in successfully implementing performance-based pay, especially incentive plans. This opposition originates in employee beliefs about incentive plans, particularly the belief that management cannot be trusted.[45]

This lack of trust has immediate implications for the establishment of rates and standards that form the basis of incentive systems. Workers may play elaborate charades for the benefit of time-study engineers doing the work measurement described in Chapters 5 and 6, but these maneuvers do not entirely fool the engineers who know workers might try to be misleading. Therefore, the engineers plug in estimates of how much they are being fooled, turning scientific observation and measurement into a guessing game.[46] The result may be inaccurate or unfair rates, which reduce the incentive value of the system, the profitability of the company, or both. Even assuming these obstacles are removed, the organization still must select the pay plan that best fits the needs of the company and then audit it to make sure that it is effective.

AUDITING THE MERIT PAY SYSTEM

For any merit pay system to be successful, it must be administered accurately across employees, fairly across all units or divisions in a company, and within the pay structure for all salary grades. That is, employees have to know that their merit raise is determined in the same way throughout the company regard-

LEARNING OBJECTIVE 3

Identify obstacles in the way of effectively implementing performance-based pay.

Obstacles to effective performance-based pay include:
- specifying/measuring job performance
- identifying valued rewards
- linking rewards to performance

DID YOU KNOW?

Both UPS and Lincoln Electric believe that their success is not possible without the workers' trust in management.

Pay administration is audited by using compa-ratios and performance ratios.

EXHIBIT 12.5
OBSTACLES TO THE DESIGN OF EFFECTIVE REWARD SYSTEMS AND THEIR IMPLICATIONS FOR MANAGEMENT

OBSTACLES	CAUSES	IMPLICATIONS FOR MANAGEMENT
A. Difficulties in specifying and measuring performance	1. Changes in the nature of work • Increase in service-oriented jobs • Increase in white-collar, managerial, and professional jobs • Increases in the interdependencies and complexity of work	1. Develop techniques for specifying desirable behaviors and clarifying the objectives of the organization.
	2. Multidimensional nature of work • Single-item measures of performance are often inadequate. • In many jobs today, multiple criteria are necessary to assess performance.	2. Utilize evaluation procedures that recognize the multidimensional nature of performance.
	3. Technological developments • Technological developments often result in new and untested methods of work. • Machine-paced jobs permit little variation in performance.	3. Develop a reliable and valid performance appraisal system based on results and/or behavioral standards.
	4. Lack of supervisory training • Use of untrained, inexperienced supervisors in the evaluation process • Perceptual biases	4. Train supervisors to use the PA system appropriately and to understand potential sources of bias.
	5. The manager's value system • Lack of interest in or inability to differentiate among high and low performers • Failure to see long-range outcomes of differential rewarding	5. Clearly define long-term consequences of performance-contingent and noncontingent reward practices.
B. Problems in identifying valued rewards	1. Choice of rewards • Choosing a reward that is not reinforcing	1. Make managers aware of the effects of rewards on employee performance and satisfaction.
	2. Utilizing rewards of insufficient size or magnitude • Lack of resources • Company policy	2. Train managers to identify rewards for their subordinates.
	3. Poor timing of rewards • Size of organization: bureaucracy • Standardization/formalization of feedback mechanisms • Complexity of feedback system	3. Administer rewards of sufficient magnitude.
		4. Administer rewards as quickly after desirable responses as possible.

EXHIBIT 12.5 (CONT.) OBSTACLES TO THE DESIGN OF EFFECTIVE REWARD SYSTEMS AND THEIR IMPLICATIONS FOR MANAGEMENT		
C. Difficulties in linking rewards to performance	1. Failure to create appropriate contingencies between rewards and performance • Lack of knowledge, skill, experience • Belief system • Difficulty of administration	1. Train manager to establish appropriate contingencies between rewards and performance.
	2. Creating inappropriate contingencies • Rewarding behavior that does not increase performance • Rewarding behavior A, but hoping for B	2. Use information obtained from appraisals of employee performance as basis for reward allocation decisions.
	3. Nullifying intended contingencies • Using improper PA instrument • Improper use of PA instrument • Failure to use information obtained • Inconsistently applied	3. Administer the reward system consistently across employees.
	4. Employee opposition • Individually: mistrust, lack of fairness, inequity • Socially: restrictions due to fear of loss of work • Outside intervention: union	4. Obtain employee participation in the design and administration of the pay plan.

SOURCE: P. M. Podsakoff, C. N. Greene, and J. M. McFillen, "Obstacles to the Effective Use of Reward Systems," in *Readings in Personnel and Human Resource Management*, 3rd ed., eds. R. S. Schuler, S. A. Youngblood, and V. L. Huber, (St. Paul, Minn.: West, 1988): 284–285.

less of the supervisor and that it is based on an accurate measure of job performance. While the accuracy of performance appraisals may be ensured by using a behavioral-based appraisal method (see Chapter 9), fair and consistent administration (within the pay structure) is accomplished by means of compa-ratios and performance ratios.

Compa-ratios and performance ratios used together can highlight pay and job performance relationships by individual employee, by salary grade, by level in the organization, or by department or division in the company. The **compa-ratio** is the measure of the average salary in relation to the midpoint of the range for a given salary grade. It is determined by dividing the average salary for the grade by the midpoint for that grade and multiplying by 100. A compa-ratio of 110, for example, means that as a group, individuals are being paid 10 percent over the midpoint for the given salary grade. Assuming a normal distribution of job performance and experience levels, the average compa-ratio in any department or division should be close to 100. Ratios higher than 100 may suggest leniency (therefore inaccuracy) in pay decisions, while ratios less than 100 may mean the opposite. If allowed to exist, ratio differentials across departments or divisions can indicate inconsistent merit pay administration.

Similar conclusions can be drawn from the use of **performance ratios**. These ratios indicate where the performance rating of any employee stands relative to other employees. This is done by determining the midpoint of a performance range, dividing that into each employee's performance rating, and multiplying that figure by 100. This process can be facilitated by choosing a performance appraisal method that uses points rather than relative rankings. Most methods discussed in Chapter 9, except the ranking method, can effectively measure performance ratios.[47]

PARTICIPATION IN PERFORMANCE-BASED PAY SYSTEMS

Employee participation can occur in the design and administration stage.

Employee participation can take place at two critical points in performance-based pay systems: (1) in the design stage and (2) in the administration stage.

DESIGN STAGE. Many pay plans are designed by top management and installed in a fairly authoritative fashion. Apparently, however, employees can do the same things and even more effectively. That is, employees can be responsible for designing the pay plan, as suggested in the previous chapter. Furthermore, they understand and accept the plan more readily if they are involved. Participation in plan design can also reduce the potential resistance to change that accompanies almost any change in an organization. Consequently, employees are more motivated to increase performance.

These potential advantages of employee participation in pay plan design may not always materialize. For example, they fail to occur when management is not truly participative but rather tries to manipulate employees into participation. They also will not occur when employees prefer not to participate. These reasons also apply to employee participation in the administration of the pay plan.

ADMINISTRATION STAGE. As indicated in Chapter 11, employees can responsibly determine when and if other workers should receive pay increases. This also appears to be true for individuals determining their own pay increases. Nevertheless, employee participation may not work in all cases, nor is it necessarily appropriate under all circumstances.[48]

CURRENT TRENDS

Perhaps not surprisingly by this time, an important trend here is linking performance-based pay to the strategy of the organization. Another trend is putting pay into perspective.

LINKING TO ORGANIZATIONAL STRATEGY

Pay can be very important when getting employees to go along with a total quality management strategy.

As with total compensation, pay is or can be a powerful motivator in shaping employees' behaviors. Organizations are seizing on pay as a way to implement such programs as total-quality management. As will be described in Chapter 15 on Total Quality Management, employee behaviors are critical in getting high quality in service firms or manufacturing firms. Do you regard a smile on the face of a store clerk and a "thank you for shopping" comment from the cashier of the local store as examples of quality customer-oriented service? Many people do and are in fact willing to pay more for the goods in stores that have salespeople like these. So all stores have to do is get people who will do this. Why is this easier said than done? Well, we all know that it is easier said than done. Among other things, organizations clearly have to pay people for these behaviors. If companies want to have a strategy of total quality, they need to identify the behaviors necessary and then pay people for those behaviors. This is in fact what organizations are doing, according to a report published by the Hay Group consulting firm:

> Organizations that institute quality programs should structure their compensation practices to reward quality, concludes a report by the Hay Group. Compensation practices alone cannot make quality initiatives succeed, the report says, but they can help motivate employees to take responsibility, find innovation, and reduce costs.
>
> The shift to quality often requires fundamental organizational change, the report warns. Additionally, most organizations try several approaches to quality before they find the system that works best for them. Whatever the new quality process entails, however, the following elements must be present to ensure its success:

- Management must be committed to the quality movement and not be looking for a "quick fix."
- Management must define quality outcomes and have measurement systems to gauge progress toward those outcomes.
- Management must empower the work force and shift the focus from individual effort to teamwork.
- Management must link pay to quality-improvement goals.[49]

These are some "management musts" for a total quality management strategy:

PAY IN PERSPECTIVE

Another important trend is that both individuals and organizations are putting pay into perspective. While pay certainly remains important because it buys us goods and services and tells us how well we are doing, many people are also concluding that pay is not everything! Having good colleagues, good working conditions and opportunities for job growth are also very important! This comes at a time when organizations are faced with tremendous global competition that makes it more and more difficult to automatically pass on higher costs to the customer. This is not to say that incentive pay is likely to die on the vine because of cost pressures, but it does say that companies will likely use a combination of pay and non-pay rewards to motivate employees. And because we are now in a period of lower inflation, smaller pay increases are likely to be seen as more motivational than they were during the higher inflationary period of the early 1980s.

As the case of Lincoln Electric illustrates, companies that are using incentive pay plans are also putting pay into perspective by considering the entire needs of employees. Thus when trying to understand why Lincoln Electric employees work so hard, we must look at the human resource philosophy of the company as well as the incentive pay plans. Their human resource philosophy is built on care and concern for the employee and the employee's family as described in Chapter 5. From it come many human resource practices such as family benefits for education and health, training opportunities, and safety programs. Together, these all convey to the employee a sense of caring and belonging. They help put pay and its motivational value into perspective. In turn, they help make the incentive pay plans at Lincoln Electric successful.

SUMMARY

Performance-based pay systems continue to attract the attention of many human resource managers, and line managers continue to ask whether pay can be used as a motivator with their employees. Yet their experiences with merit pay convince them that pay does not necessarily do a good job of motivating. The success of many incentive plans, however, indicates that pay can motivate job performance, although many problems can arise because of the many obstacles associated with the implementation of incentive plans.

Which incentive pay plan is appropriate must be determined by several factors such as the level at which job performance can accurately measure performance (individual, team, or organization) for given individuals, the extent of cooperation needed between individuals, and the level of trust between management and nonmanagement. Several plans can be used together to reward different teams of employees for good job performance. However, there may be limits on a specific organization's decision to use performance-based pay; these can include management's desire to have incentive pay, management's commitment to design and implement one or several systems, the extent to which employees influence the output, the extent to which a good performance appraisal system exists, the existence of a union, and the degree of trust in the organization. Whether the organization is public or private also influences the decision. Generally, only private organizations utilize incentive systems. Both types, however, can and do use merit pay systems.

Even when organizations adopt some type of incentive plan, they still need to provide employees with indirect compensation such as pension and retirement benefits, holidays, and other benefits related only to organizational membership and not to performance. The extent, types, and costliness of such benefits are described in Chapter 13.

KEY CONCEPTS

commission
compa-ratio
cost-of-living adjustments (COLAs)
differential piece rate plan
Improshare
incentive pay plans

incentive stock options (ISO)
lump-sum bonuses
merit pay plans
performance-based pay
performance bonuses
performance ratios
profit-sharing plans
Scanlon plan

social loafing
standard hour plan
stock appreciation rights (SAR)
stock option
straight piecework plan
suggestion systems
variable-pay plans

REVIEW AND DISCUSSION QUESTIONS

1. Do you believe that an employee's behavior is always influenced by the reward expected? Is this true for your behavior in this course?
2. Suppose that people do not always do things because of the tangible rewards they can receive. Does this invalidate the theory of performance-based pay? Explain.
3. What conditions are necessary for effective performance-based pay systems?
4. What are the most common performance-based pay systems? How do you account for their popularity?
5. What obstacles arise in specifying and measuring job performance?
6. How can an organization determine whether merit pay is administered accurately across all employees or across all its units and divisions?

7. Describe a performance-based pay system that you have directly experienced. Did the system work? If not, why not?
8. Debate the following assertion: If selection and placement decisions are done effectively, individual performance should not vary a great deal; therefore, a performance-based pay system is not needed.
9. How can employees participate in both the design and administration of a performance-based pay system? In general, will employee participation have positive or negative consequences for the operation of the system?
10. Explain how a pay system can be linked to quality.

CHAPTER 12

PERFORMANCE-BASED PAY

EXERCISES AND CASES

FIELD PROJECT

Interview two or three employees (of a local company) to learn whether they are paid on the basis of their performance and, if so, on what basis. If they are not paid for performance, find out whether they would like to be and, if so, under what type—merit or incentive-based plans. Identify the type of person who prefers performance-based pay and the type who does not.

CAREER MANAGEMENT EXERCISE: SO TELL ME, "WHAT WILL IT TAKE TO GET YOU?"

Refer to your Field Project exercises in Chapters 4, 6 and 8. There you described a job you might want and developed some selection procedures for it. Now let's take this a step further: Tell me what it will take to get you to join my firm (assume I have the job you want!). That is, tell me what you want in terms of direct compensation (use any of the materials from Chapters 11 and 12; indirect compensation and materials in Chapter 13 are used in the next chapter). Let this total 100 percent. To give you as much flexibility as needed in this endeavor, there are only a few requirements:

1. First, provide some percent breakdowns of the various parts of your direct compensation package. For example:

_____% Base salary
_____% Performance-based
_____ % Merit
_____ % Incentive
_____ % Individual
_____ % Team

What is the total dollar value of your typical year's direct compensation? _____

Continue with this list as you look at the items below, making it more specific each time.

2. As you know, such things like inflation and region of the country in which you intend to work impact your exact level of pay, so pencil in some "hard" dollar numbers where is it possible in the list above.

3. To make this a bit more challenging, assume that you want to take an overseas assignment for your first three years! Now indicate percents and dollars.

4. Now, for some additional interest, refer to Chapter 4 and review the discussion of career stages. Then complete the parts in item 1 again for each career stage!

BLTC is a firm engaged in the manufacture and distribution of chemicals. Because many of the manufacturing, storage, and distribution processes of BLTC are monitored and controlled by computer technology, the firm's computer operations expenditures are substantial. Tod Jenkins, the director of the firm's computer operations division, estimated that the projected annual budget for his division would be in the neighborhood of $2,500,000. The comptroller of BLTC felt that this amount was excessive and directed Jenkins to reduce costs wherever possible. To accomplish this objective, Jenkins assigned a number of systems analysts to review the current level and type of computer services provided to the organization. These analysts were instructed to streamline operations and eliminate unnecessary or infrequently used management reports and computer equipment.

Stan Cook is one of the best and brightest systems analysts who worked for Jenkins. After weeks of intensive investigation, Cook submitted a proposal that permitted a $450,000 reduction in the computer operations budget. These budgetary reductions were accomplished by (1) consolidating the existing elements of the management/production control monitoring system, (2) eliminating redundant reporting and data collection procedures, (3) utilizing less expensive "batch" computer processing where possible, (4) eliminating unnecessary or infrequently used computer equipment, and (5) increasing utilization and coordination of existing computer resources. Thus, Cook was able to reduce operational costs without reducing the level or quality of services provided to management.

Jenkins was greatly impressed by Cook's activities and felt that he deserved some special form of recognition. Therefore, he informed Cook that he was recommending him for a special merit award (SMA). These SMAs, which are administered by the comptroller's office, constitute an important part of the firm's motivational program. Under this program, the employee's supervisor makes a recommendation as to the amount of the cash award to be received by the employee. In general, the dollar value of the SMA is a percentage of the amount of the cost savings for which the employee was responsible. Jenkins recommended that Cook receive a monetary bonus equivalent to 3 percent of the cost savings he generated, or $13,500.

Two months after Jenkins recommended Cook for the SMA, Jenkins received a letter from the comptroller indicating that Cook did not qualify for an award. The comptroller justified his decision by stating that the development of plans to reduce computer operation costs was an integral part of Cook's job and, therefore, did not warrant additional compensation. Jenkins felt that this decision was both unjustified and characteristic of an "accounting mentality." For the next several months, he and the comptroller exchanged letters and telephone calls arguing for their respective viewpoints. When Cook inquired as to the status of his SMA, Jenkins was forced to tell him of the long-running dispute with the comptroller. However, Jenkins assured Cook that the SMA would be awarded even if the firm's president had to be brought in to settle the dispute.

Approximately sixteen months after Jenkins submitted the original SMA recommendation, a compromise agreement was worked out with the comptroller. According to this agreement, Cook was to receive $250 and a printed certificate of achievement. At the awards ceremony, Cook accepted the monetary award and certificate from the comptroller. The following day, Cook informed Jenkins that he was submitting his resignation in order to accept a job offered to him by another firm.

CASE QUESTIONS

1. Was the bonus of 3 percent a fair amount?
2. What are the real problems with BLTC's suggestion system?
3. Was Cook's response justified?
4. What would you do if you were Cook?

Susan Crandall was feeling good about her new position at Western National Bank. Susan, a seven-year employee at Western, had come a long way from her starting position as a teller to her present position as human resource manager, thanks in many respects to her predecessor, Anna Bavetti.

Anna had recently resigned from the bank to take a position with a local computer software company, which was experiencing explosive growth. This company recognized they needed to systematize their staffing practices, so when Anna learned of the opportunity, she jumped. Anna was frustrated by what she considered conservative and stodgy management at the bank, so a change in scenery was a welcome relief.

Anna had begun at Western as an assistant to the then HR manager Nancy Hyer. Anna had an MBA degree from North Carolina and an undergraduate degree from Grinnell College. Anna quickly realized that her technical skills were superior to Nancy's, but she admired Nancy's street smarts and willingness to battle the CEO of the bank over new initiatives in the HR area. Nancy had put in a performance appraisal plan and an absenteeism plan before transferring to the trust department with what was touted as a promotion.

Anna, though, did not see the move as a promotion. In her estimation, Nancy had gotten too strong and was creating a lot of waves for the top brass at the bank, who were unwilling to move at the pace that Nancy had set. When the president of Western, Larry Wilson, asked Anna to assume the role of assistant vice president of personnel, Anna welcomed the opportunity to continue the initiatives begun by Nancy.

Anna decided that she was going to undertake two goals immediately. First, she was going to begin developing Susan. Nancy was too hard on Susan in Anna's estimation. Although Susan didn't have a college degree (she had had to drop out because her mother was ill), she had common sense and extremely good people skills. Over the next year, Anna progressively increased Susan's responsibilities by involving her in applicant screening and interviewing and including her on project assignments. Over time, Susan and Anna developed a teamlike approach to their work and learned to rely on each other to keep the HR management office functioning smoothly.

When Susan learned of Anna's departure, she was saddened but not surprised. Anna always seemed too liberal and progressive for upper management of the bank. Anna valued people and looked for the best in them. Anna, more than the other officers at the bank, seemed genuinely concerned about the welfare of the employees, especially the mostly nonexempt employee work force. Susan was flabbergasted, though, when Larry Wilson called her into his office and asked her to assume Anna's job. Her pay would increase by 150 percent, to say the least. Although the job would mean longer hours and more responsibilities, under Anna's tutelage, Susan felt confident that she could rise to the occasion.

Susan wanted more than anything to carry through on Anna's second goal, which was to link the performance evaluation system developed by Nancy to the annual pay increases. The bank had entered an era of competition with other banks and savings and loans, so productivity was a major concern for the bank. Besides cutting staff to the minimum, Susan believed that in the long run, linking pay to effort and performance would encourage productivity among all employees. Susan believed that Western's staff were hard working and would welcome the opportunity to see their pay linked to their performance.

Susan noticed it was almost 5 P.M. and she needed to speak with Gerry Latham, vice president for operations, regarding her proposed merit plan, which would influence his group the most. As she passed by the elevators, she noticed several employees waiting beside the time clock. It was common practice for the nonexempts to wait for a seemingly inordinate amount of time for the elevator to arrive on the fifth floor of the bank building. A common practice was to wait until the elevator bell chimed and the doors began to open before clocking out.

As several of the employees hurriedly punched the clock and dashed to the elevator, Larry Wilson appeared behind Susan. Larry called out to Susan, who was deep in thought about how to present her merit plan to Gerry Latham. "Susan, did you see that?" questioned Larry. "I'm sorry, Larry, I was lost in thought. What are you talking about?" replied Susan. As the elevator doors closed, Larry picked up his voice in obvious irritation. "I think those employees would just as soon cheat us if they are charging their wait time on the elevators. How do we know that they're not trying to cheat us in the morning when they clock in or when they return from lunch late and have a co-worker punch them in? Susan, I want you to investigate this tomorrow, first thing. This kind of fraud has got to stop immediately." Oh boy, thought Susan. How am I going to defuse this bomb? As Susan started back down the hall toward Gerry Latham's office, she began to understand the frustration that occasionally leaked through Anna's otherwise calm exterior when she occupied Susan's job.

CASE QUESTIONS

1. What strategic considerations support the concept of a performance-based pay plan in banking?
2. At a minimum, what HR activities must exist prior to implementing a performance-based pay plan in a bank or elsewhere?
3. Does the culture at Western support a performance-based pay plan?
4. How should Susan respond to Larry's directive to investigate the time clock fraud?

NOTES

1. C. Wiley, "Incentive Plan Pushes Production," *Personnel Journal* (Aug. 1993): 86–92; K. Chilton, "Lincoln Electric's Incentive System: Can It Be Transferred Overseas?" *Compensation and Benefits Review* (Nov.–Dec. 1993): 21–30.

2. A. Farnham, "Mary Kay's Lessons in Leadership," *Fortune* (Sept. 20, 1993): 68–77.

3. E. E. Lawler III, "Pay for Performance: A Motivational Analysis," in *Readings in Personnel and Human Resource Management* 2nd ed., eds. R. S. Schuler, S. A. Youngblood, and V. Huber (St. Paul, Minn.: West, 1984).

4. Wiley, "Incentive Plan Pushes Production"; J. McAdams and E. Hawk, "Capitalizing on Human Assets Through Performance-based Rewards," *ACA Journal* (Autumn 1992): 60–72.

5. "Aligning Compensation with Quality," *Bulletin to Management* (April 1, 1993): 97.

6. *The Wall Street Journal* (July 1, 1985): 1; "Compensation: Growth Bonuses," *INC.* (Feb. 1988): 100.

7. B. Filipczak, "Why No One Likes Your Incentive Program," *Training* (Aug. 1993): 21.

8. N. H. Mackworth, "High Incentives Versus Hot and Humid Atmospheres in a Physical Effort Task," *British Journal of Psychology* (1947): 90–102; P. M. Podsakoff, M. L. Williams, and W. E. Scott, Jr., "Myths of Employee Selection Systems," in R. Schuler, S. Youngblood, and V. Huber, eds., *Readings in Personnel and Human Resource Management* 3rd ed. (St. Paul, Minn.: West, 1988): 178–192.

9. L. C. Cumming, "Linking Pay to Performance: Why Is It So Difficult?" *Personnel Administrator* (May 1988): 47–52; T. Rollins, "Pay for Performance: Is it Worth the Trouble?" *Personnel Administrator* (May 1988): 42–46.

10. D. Filipowski, "Perspectives: Is Pay Linked to Performance?" *Personnel Journal* (May 1991): 39.

11. See note 7.

12. P. M. Podsakoff, C. N. Greene, and J. M. McFillen, "Obstacles to the Effective Use of Reward Systems," in *Readings in Personnel and Human Resource Management*, 275–904.

13. See note 1.

14. D. Q. Mills, *The New Competitors* (New York: Wiley, 1985); G. Milkovich and J. Newman, *Compensation* (Plano, Tex.: Business Publications, 1984); C. Cumming, "Linking Pay to Performance," *Personnel Administrator* (May 1988): 47–52; T. Rollins, "Pay for Performance: Is It Worth the Trouble?" *Personnel Administrator* (May 1988): 42–46.

15. B. P. MacLean, "Value-Added Pay Beats Traditional Merit Programs," *Personnel Journal* (Sept. 1990): 46–51; J. L. Pearce, "Why Merit Pay Doesn't Work," in *New Perspectives*; R. E. Kopelman, "The Case for Merit Rewards," *Personnel Administrator* (Oct. 1983): 60–68.

16. See note 9.

17. For a discussion of these and other aspects of merit pay administration, see E. J. Brennan, "Merit Pay: Balance the Old Rich and the New Poor," *Personnel Journal* (May 1985): 82–85.

18. R. B. Hill, "A Two-Component Approach to Compensation," *Personnel Journal* (May 1993): 154–161.

19. L. Uchitelle, "Boeing's Fight Over Bonuses," *The New York Times* (October 12, 1989): D1, D6; "Number of Lump-Sum Bonuses Escalating," *Bulletin to Management* (April 9, 1987): 113; L. Uchitelle, "Bonuses Replace Wage Raises and Workers Are the Losers," *The New York Times* (June 26, 1987): 1, 31; G. S. Crystal, "Executive Compensation: Challenges in the Year Ahead," *Personnel* (Jan. 1988): 33–36; S. L. Minken, "Does

Lump-Sum Pay Merit Attention?" *Personnel Journal* (June 1988): 77–83; A. Bernstein, "How'd You Like A Big Fat Bonus—And No Raise?" *Business Week* (November 3, 1986): 30–31; E. E. Lawler III, "Gainsharing," in *New Perspectives on Compensation*, eds. D. B. Balkin and L. R. Gomez-Mejia (Englewood Cliffs, N.J.: Prentice-Hall, 1987): 225–230.

20. S. Caudron, "Master the Compensation Maze," *Personnel Journal* (June 1993): 64I. Used by permission.

21. D. W. Belcher and T. J. Achison, *Compensation Administration* (Englewood Cliffs, N.J.: Prentice-Hall, 1977); R. I. Henderson, *Compensation Management: Rewarding Performance* (Reston, Va.: Reston, 1985); G. Milkovich and J. Newman, *Compensation*, 2nd ed. (Plano, Tex.: Business Publications, 1989).

22. Wiley, "Incentive Plan Pushes Production," 91.

23. M. A. Tather, "Turning Ideas into Gold," *Management Review* (March 1985): 4–10.

24. E. Lawler and D. Cohen, "Designing Pay Systems to Fit Teams," *ACA Journal* (Autumn 1992): 6–18.

25. J. Huret, "Paying for Team Results," *HR Magazine* (May 1991): 39–43.

26. S. Caudron, "Master the Compensation Maze," 64I.

27. R. I. Henderson, *Compensation Management: Rewarding Performance* (Reston, Va.: Reston, 1985).

28. "Gain-Sharing Plan Pointers," *Bulletin to Management* (April 16, 1987): 128; B. W. Thomas and M. Hess Olson, "Gain Sharing: The Design Guarantees Success," *Personnel Journal* (May 1988): 73–79; C. S. Miller and M. H. Schuster, "Gainsharing Plans: A Comparative Analysis," *Organizational Dynamics* (Summer 1987): 44–67; T. L. Ross, R. A. Ross, and L. Hatcher, "Communication: The Multiple Benefits of Gainsharing," *Personnel Journal* (Oct. 1986): 14–25; R. C. Scott, "Test Your Gain Sharing Potential," *Personnel Journal* (May 1988): 82–84; J.C. Horn, "Bigger Pay for Better Work," *Psychology Today* (July 1987): 54–57.

29. M. Magnus, "Vulcan Materials' Plant-Wide Bonuses Build Productivity," *Personnel Journal* (Sept. 1987): 103–104; "Productivity and Compensation: Houston Conference Highlights," *Bulletin to Management* (Nov. 20, 1986): 1.

30. R. P. McNutt, "Achievement Pays Off At DuPont," *Personnel* (June 1990): 7; J. E. Panos, "Manage Group Incentive Systems," *Personnel Journal* (Oct. 1990): 104–106; Bureau of National Affairs, "Incentive Pay Schemes Seen as a Result of Economic Employee Relation Change," *BNA Daily Report* (Oct. 9, 1984): 1; G. Milkovich and J. Newman, *Compensation* (Plano, Tex.: Business Publications, 1987).

31. G. W. Florkowski, "The Organizational Impact of Profit Sharing," *The Academy of Management Review* (Oct. 1987): 622–636.

32. L. Uchitelle, "Good Jobs in Hard Times," *The New York Times* (October 3, 1993): 1, 6; K. Matthes, "Greetings from Hallmark," *HR Focus* (Aug. 1993): 12–13; J. Labate, "Deal Those Workers In," *Fortune* (April 19, 1993): 63.

33. K. M. Evans, "On-the-Job Lotteries: A Low-Cost Incentive That Sparks Higher Productivity," *Personnel* (April 1988): 20–26; "Recognizing Reward Programs," *Personnel Journal* (Dec. 1986), 66–78; W. S. Humphrey, *Managing for Innovation: Leading Technical People* (Englewood Cliffs, N.J.: Prentice-Hall, 1987), 128–133; M. Magnus, "First Interstate Banks on Compensation Redesign to Beat Competition," *Personnel Journal* (Sept. 1987): 106–108.

34. S. Caudron, "Master the Compensation Maze," 48L.

35. C. F. Schultz, "Compensating the Sales Professional," in *New Perspectives on Compensation*, eds. D. B. Balkin and L. R. Gomez-Mejia (Englewood Cliffs, N.J.: Prentice-Hall, 1987), 250–258; J. O. Steinbrink, *Sales Force Compensation: Dartnell's 22nd Biennial Survey* (Chicago: Dartnell Corporation, 1984), 47.

36. A. Kohn, "Why Incentive Plans Cannot Work," *Harvard Business Review* (Sept.–Oct. 1993): 54–63.

37. F. Schwadel, "Chain Finds Incentives a Hard Sell," *The Wall Street Journal* (July 5, 1990): 3. Also see C. H. Deutsch, "Avon Keeps Ringing, but Wall Street Won't Answer," *The New York Times* (July 15, 1990), F7.

38. J. R. Deckop, "Top Executive Compensation and the Pay-for-Performance Issue," in *New Perspectives on Compensation*, eds. D. B. Balkin and L. R. Gomez-Mejia (Englewood Cliffs, N.J.: Prentice-Hall, 1987): 285–293.

39. P. Chingos, "Executive Compensation in the 1990s: The Challenges Ahead," *Compensation and Benefits Review* (Nov.–Dec. 1990): 20–31; M. J. Mandel, "Those Fat Bonuses Don't Seem to Boost Performance," *Business Week* (Jan. 8, 1990): 26; B. A. Stertz, "Chrysler Urges Its 100 Top Executives To Bet More of Their Pay on Firm's Fate," *The Wall Street Journal* (April 2, 1990): A4; G. S. Crystal, "Incentive Pay That Doesn't Work," *Fortune* (Aug. 28, 1989): 101, 104; G. S. Crystal, "Rendering Long-Term Incentives Less Risky For Executives," *Personnel* (Sept. 1988): 80–84; M. A. Mazer, "An End to Stock Appreciation Rights?" *Personnel Journal* (Nov. 1990): 53–57; G. S. Crystal, "Handling Underwater Stock Option Grants," *Personnel* (Feb. 1988): 12–15; M. A. Mazer, "Benefits: Are Stock Option Plans Still Viable?" *Personnel Journal* (July 1988): 48–50.

40. The following material is adapted from P. Dowling, R. S. Schuler and D. Welch, *International Dimensions of Human Resource Management* (Belmont, Calif.: Wadsworth, 1994): 154–161. A. V. Phatak, R. Chandram, and R. A. Ajayi, "International Executive Compensation," in *New Perspectives on Compensation*, eds. D. B. Balkin and L. R. Gomez-Mejia (Englewood Cliffs, N.J.: Prentice-Hall, 1987): 315–327.

41. C. Reynolds, *Compensation Basics for North American Expatriates* (Scottsdale, AZ: ACA, 1994); A. V. Phatak,

R. Chandram, and R. A. Ajayi, "International Executive Compensation," in *New Perspectives on Compensation*, eds. D. B. Balkin and L. R. Gomez-Mejia (Englewood Cliffs, N.J.: Prentice-Hall, 1987): 315–327; B. J. Springer, "1992: The Impact on Compensation and Benefits in the European Community," *Compensation and Benefits Review* (July–Aug. 1989): 20–27.

42. M. J. Bishko, "Compensating Your Overseas Executives, Part 1: Strategies for the 1990s," *Compensation and Benefits Review* (May–June 1990): 33–43; "Compensating Your Overseas Executives, Part 2: Europe 1992," *Compensation and Benefits Review* (July–Aug. 1990): 25–35.

43. H. J. Ruff and G. I. Jackson, "Methodological Problems in International Comparisons of the Cost of Living," *Journal of International Business Studies*, 5, no. 2 (1974): 57–67.

44. These have been identified by Podsakoff, Greene, and McFillen. See also R. I. Henderson, "Designing a Reward System for Today's Employee," *Business Horizons* (July–Sept. 1982): 2–12.

45. Lawler, *Pay and Organizational Effectiveness*, Lawler, *Pay and Organizational Development*; R. B. Goettinger, "Why Isn't Incentive Compensation Working?" *Personnel Journal* (June 1982): 436–442; S. R. Collins, "Incentive Programs: Pros and Cons," *Personnel Journal* (July 1981): 571–76.

46. W. F. Whyte, "Skinnerian Theory in Organizations," *Psychology Today* (April 1972): 67–68, 96, 98, 100.

47. J. D. McMillan and V. C. Williams, "The Elements of Effective Salary Administration Programs," *Personnel Journal* (Nov. 1982): 832–38; T. A. Mahoney, "Compensating for Work," in *Personnel Management*, eds. K. N. Rowland and G. R. Ferris (Boston, Mass.: Allyn-Bacon, 1982), 227–262. For a case study of merit pay assessment issues, see S. C. Freedman, "Performance-Based Pay: A Convenience Store Case Study," *Personnel Journal* (July 1985): 30–34; J. R. Terborg and G. R. Ungson, "Group Administered Bonus Pay and Retail Store Performance: A Two Year Study of Management Compensation," *Journal of Retailing* (Spring 1985): 63–77.

48. See note 5.

49. "Aligning Compensation with Quality," *Bulletin to Management* (April 1, 1993): 97.

CHAPTER 13

INDIRECT COMPENSATION

MANAGING HUMAN RESOURCES
at Steelcase

STEELCASE is a high-quality office furniture manufacturer headquartered in Grand Rapids, Michigan. With more than 20,000 employees and an ongoing concern about costs in this highly competitive business, Steelcase got serious about workers' compensation costs in the 1980s. Under the direction of Libby Child, manager of workers' compensation and medical services and with the leadership of Dan Wiljanen, director of human resources, and Jerry K. Myers, president and CEO, Steelcase developed and implemented a "return-to-work" program in 1986 that has reduced the average cost per claim by 50 percent and saved the company more than $24 million in workers' compensation costs (an average savings of $4 million per year)!

Cost reduction in this area is a crucial issue for Steelcase and most other companies because workers' comp costs are rising dramatically. Payouts in the United States have climbed from $22 billion in 1980 to $62 billion in 1990! While this is smaller than the $200 billion that employers currently pay for health-care costs, workers' comp is rising faster. State governments are concerned about the issue as well. In California, workers' comp claims has risen so high that firms are leaving the state, taking valuable jobs with them. Because worker claims and health-care costs vary by state, companies in different states pay different rates for their workers' compensation insurance.

Moving operations, however, is not always an option nor necessarily a solution to the problem. Such was the situation with Steelcase. It was decided in 1985 that a program had to be put in place to reign in workers' compensation costs. Essentially, the firm put in place two major concepts: (1) A medical review board that systematically examines the injured person and the injury situation to make the correct diagnosis of the claim: the intent here is to uncover all the facts and build an atmosphere of trust and understanding between worker and company. (2) A return-to-work component that enables workers to get back to work as soon as possible: once the injury has been diagnosed, the biggest manageable expense is the time in getting the worker back to work. By setting up therapy centers and accommodating working conditions, Steelcase reduced time away from work for most injuries by 50 percent in six years. Their average cost per claim went from $1,552 in 1983 to $1,213 in 1992. (In California, the cost per claim went from $6,000 in 1980 to $20,000 in 1992!)[1]

This feature addresses a mounting crisis in cost containment for American business. As international competition increases, U.S. firms struggle to contain their costs. For many firms, total compensation costs are a significant factor of the problem. But as many firms are discovering, these costs, although significant, are manageable. Steelcase's approach is an excellent example of what firms can do to reduce their workers' comp costs. Firms are also attempting to reduce other compensation costs by asking workers to contribute to some of the expenses—for example, to pay for some of their health care. In some cases, firms are just cutting back on what they are willing to offer employees. Because these events are likely to continue and affect you directly (at work) or indirectly (through the price of goods and services that you buy), we devote this chapter to indirect compensation.

INDIRECT COMPENSATION

Indirect compensation is an issue that is garnering much attention today—from organizations, workers, politicians, and the media. The changes occurring in our society—and the world—ensure that this will be a hot issue well into the twenty-first century. While specific elements of plans vary, employee benefits and services, **indirect compensation**, are generally defined as in-kind payments employees receive for their membership and/or participation in the organization. It includes such items as:

- Public protection programs
- Private protection programs
- Health-care benefits
- Paid leave
- Life-cycle benefits

Several of these categories are mandated by federal and state governments and must therefore be administered within the boundaries of laws and regulations. Many others are provided voluntarily by organizations and vary with the organization.

Indirect compensation provides protection against health- and accident-related problems and ensure income at the end of one's work cycle. Legally required payments include Social Security, unemployment compensation, and workers' compensation; private protection programs include health care, life insurance, and disability insurance. Retirement income is provided through pensions and savings plans. Benefits programs also include pay for time not at work (for example, vacations, holidays, sick leave and absence pay, breaks, and wash-up and clean-up time). A growing category of benefits relates to changing life-styles. These benefits enable an employee to enjoy a better life-style or to meet social or personal obligations while minimizing employment-related costs. Discounts, education assistance, and child and elder care fall into this category.

All these pieces of indirect compensation are important to all employees!

WHY IS INDIRECT COMPENSATION IMPORTANT?

Indirect compensation (also referred to as *benefits*) is provided by firms to attract and retain valued employees. Until recently, employers provided relatively generous benefits, but the tide has shifted for several reasons. First, it is a major, increasingly costly part of total compensation. In 1929, total benefits payments were 5 percent of total pay. By 1990, benefits had risen to 34 percent of wages and salaries, or roughly $6 per payroll hour or $13,126 per year per employee.[2] While these numbers are large and represent substantial dollars for employers, there are major differences across industries. Indirect compensation tends to be a bit greater on average in the manufacturing industries than in the nonmanufacturing industries, and it's greater for blue-collar workers than for white-collar and service workers.[3] Benefits are also higher in mature companies compared to start-up companies.[4]

Regardless of the type of worker or sector of the economy, the cost of benefits to organizations is enormous. While wages and salaries have increased forty-fold over the past 50 years, indirect compensation has increased even more—500 times![5]

There are several reasons why organizations pump so much money into benefits programs. They believe that benefits help by:

Indirect compensation has risen much faster than direct compensation.

- Attracting good employees
- Increasing employee morale
- Reducing turnover
- Increasing job satisfaction
- Motivating employees
- Enhancing the organization's image among employees and in the business community
- Making better use of compensation dollars

Unfortunately, there is ample research to demonstrate that these purposes are not always attained, largely because of inadequate communication. As a consequence, firms have started sending their employees more information about their benefits.[6]

Another important reason some of the purposes of indirect compensation are not attained is that employees often regard compensation benefits, not as rewards, but as conditions (rights) of employment. They also think of indirect benefits as safeguards provided by the organization as a social responsibility because they are not provided by society.[7]

Even when indirect compensation is regarded as a reward, its importance from the viewpoint of employees relative to other aspects of the organization (for example, opportunity for advancement, salary, geographic location, job responsibilities, and prestige of the job) can be low, therefore, making its motivational value less than it otherwise could be. Offering flexibility to employees in choice of indirect compensation packages tends to increase the motivational value.[8]

The perception that the benefits firms provide are very costly also increases motivational value. This perception is growing as some firms reduce or even eliminate benefits and ask workers to share the costs of providing them. This is called **cost-sharing**. In the process workers learn, not only the costs, but also the range of benefits.

Through indirect compensation, organizations seek to:

- **Attract employees**
- **Increase morale**
- **Reduce turnover**
- **Increase job satisfaction**
- **Motivate employees**
- **Enhance image**
- **Remain cost effective**

Cost-sharing affects many workers.

EXTERNAL INFLUENCES

The skyrocketing growth in the *type* and *cost* of employee benefits can be traced to several environmental trends.

- *Wage controls.* The imposition of wage controls during World War II and the Korean War forced organizations to offer more and greater benefits in lieu of wage increases to attract new employees.
- *Health-Care Costs.* Health-care costs have been increasing at an alarming rate. In 1940, U.S. health-care expenses were $4 billion, about 4 percent of GDP. In 1992, they were more than $800 billion, or 14 percent of GDP. For employers, the average health-benefit cost per employee was almost $4,000 in 1992. Regardless of the many suggested causes, the crisis health-care costs is having a major impact on indirect compensation. And as described in the opening feature, the events in workers' comp are just as severe, if not more so in some cases.[9]
- *Union bargaining.* From 1935 into the 1970s, unions were able to gain steady increases in wages and benefits for their members. As currently conceptualized, practically all benefits are mandatory bargaining items that require an employer to bargain in good faith on union proposals to add benefits.
- *Federal tax policies.* Income tax legislation has had, and continues to have, a critical influence on the design of benefits packages. Employers are interested in benefits expenses that include pretax business costs; employees want to receive benefits without the burden of increased taxation.

Health-care and disability costs have risen faster than any other area.

- *Inflation.* Benefits managers, more so than compensation managers, must anticipate the effects of inflation on medical service, education, and pension benefits. For example, double-digit inflation in the 1980s eroded the purchasing power of some retirees and resulted in adjustments in the level of benefits.
- *Competition.* Most companies label their benefit packages as "competitive." Due to increased competition, many companies are going beyond mere statements and developing innovative packages of benefits to attract and retain employees. Wellness programs, health screenings, and employee assistance programs are examples of new benefits options. Flexible benefit plans or cash options instead of benefits are new responses to external competitive pressures.
- *Social Legislation.* A variety of laws including the *Family Leave and Medical Act of 1993,* the *Americans with Disabilities Act of 1990* (ADA), the *Age Discrimination in Employment Act,* the *Health Maintenance Organization Act of 1973,* and the *Employee Retirement Income Security Act* (ERISA) have been passed that significantly affect the administration and offering of indirect compensation.
- *Expansion of Social Security.* In 1935, the *Social Security Act* covered 60 percent of all workers. Subsequently, the scope of benefits and the percentage of eligible workers has increased substantially. Now 95 percent of all workers are covered and receive disability and health benefits in addition to retirement pay.

LEARNING OBJECTIVE 2

Describe the numerous legal considerations in indirect compensation.

Early legal milestones involving indirect compensation include:

- *Social Security Act of 1935*
- *Wagner Act of 1935*
- *Inland Steel v. National Labor Relations Board,* 1948
- *W. W. Cross v. National Labor Relations Board,* 1949

More recent and significant legislation is:

- *Equal Pay Act*
- *Pregnancy Discrimination Act*
- *ADA*
- *Family and Medical Leave Act*
- *Age Discrimination in Employment Act*
- *ERISA*

LEGAL CONSIDERATIONS

Indirect compensation grew rapidly during the Great Depression of the 1930s, which produced the first major legislation involving benefits. The *Social Security Act,* passed in 1935, provided old age, disability, survivor's, and health benefits and established the basis for federal and state unemployment programs. The *Wagner Act,* or the *National Labor Relations Act of 1935 (NLRA),* ensured the growth of benefits packages by strengthening the union movement in the United States. Both the *Social Security Act* and the *Wagner Act* continue to play significant roles in the administration of benefits.

After World War II, the legal environment further stimulated indirect compensation. Two court cases expanded benefits coverage by declaring that pension and insurance provisions were bargainable issues in union and management relations. The right to bargain over pensions was established in *Inland Steel v. National Labor Relations Board* (1948), and the right to bargain over insurance was upheld in *W. W. Cross v. National Labor Relations Board* (1949). In the 1960s, Congress passed several acts that made this legal environment even more extensive.

EQUAL PAY ACT

This act, described in Chapter 12, mandates that employees on the same jobs be paid equally, except for differences in seniority, merit, or other conditions unrelated to gender. Direct as well as indirect compensation are included in the term *paid equally.* Thus, for example, women and men on the same job, other factors being equal, must receive the same level of direct and indirect compensation. Actuarial data, however, indicated that women live approximately seven years longer than men. Therefore, on the average, women will receive a greater total level of retirement benefits than men. Is this equal indirect compensation? Would it be equal if women contributed more? In *Los Angeles Department of Water v. Manhart* (1981), the court ruled against the department's policy of having female employees contribute more to their retirement than males. Furthermore, when men and women make equal contributions to their pensions, their pension benefits must be equal (*Arizona Governing Committee v. Norris*, 1983). Additional guarantees for equal pension-benefit treatment to surviving spouses, male and female, are contained in the *Retirement Equity Act of 1984*.

PREGNANCY DISCRIMINATION ACT OF 1978

A trend in recent years has been to treat pregnancy as a disability, although opponents of this trend argue that pregnancy is a voluntary condition, not an involuntary sickness, and should therefore not be covered by disability benefits. The *Pregnancy Discrimination Act of 1978*, however, states that pregnancy is a disability and qualifies a person to receive the same benefits as any other disability. Applying this statute, a state appeals court in Michigan ruled that a labor contract between General Motors and United Auto Workers that provided sickness and accident benefits of up to 52 weeks but that limited childbearing disability to 6 weeks was illegal.[10]

Another issue in this area, which is not covered by the *Pregnancy Discrimination Act*, is whether companies must offer the same pregnancy-benefit program to wives of male employees and to husbands of female employees. The Supreme Court ruled in the *Newport News Shipbuilding and Dry Dock Co. v. EEOC* (1983), that employers who provide health-care insurance to spouses of employees that includes complete coverage for all disabilities except pregnancy are violating *Title VII of the Civil Rights Act of 1964*. In essence, employers must provide equal benefit coverage for all spouses.

AMERICANS WITH DISABILITIES ACT OF 1990

The Equal Employment Opportunity Commission (EEOC) enforces the *Americans with Disabilities Act* described in Chapter 5, Job Design, and Chapter 8, Selection. Related to the selection of employees, the EEOC in 1993 issued a policy declaring that employers may not refuse to hire people with disabilities because of concern about their effect on health-care costs. In addition, disabled employees must be given "equal access" to any health insurance provided to other employees:

> The EEOC policy statement gives many examples. It suggests that an employer may not set a lower level of benefits for a specific disability like deafness, AIDS, or schizophrenia or for "a discrete group of disabilities" like cancers, kidney diseases, or various forms of muscular dystrophy.
> But under the policy, an employer could make very broad distinctions and could, for example, provide a lower level of benefits for eye care than for the treatment of other physical conditions. "Such broad distinctions, which apply to the treatment of a multitude of dissimilar conditions," do not necessarily violate the *Americans with Disabilities Act*, the policy says.[11]

Thus, especially in terms of the numbers of individuals impacted, this policy ruling on the ADA has enormous implications in terms of costs:

> Millions of people may be affected by the new policy. The Census Bureau reports that 7.7 million Americans have difficulty hearing what is said in normal conversations, while more than 13 million have impaired eyesight and 8 million have severe difficulty walking. At least 1.3 million people use wheelchairs or walkers.[12]

The ruling also impacts many businesses and health insurers (who provide health insurance to the businesses). The EEOC has recognized the impact on both sides but comes down strongly on the side of the disabled.

FAMILY AND MEDICAL LEAVE ACT OF 1993

The *Family and Medical Leave Act* requires employers with 50 or more employees to grant up to twelve weeks unpaid leave annually:

> . . . for the birth or adoption of a child, to care for a spouse or an immediate family member with a serious health condition, or when unable to work because of a serious health condition. Employers covered by the law are required to maintain any pre-existing health coverage during the leave period and, once the leave period is concluded, to reinstate the employee to the same or an equivalent job.[13]

To be eligible, employees must have worked at a company for at least twelve months and have put in at least 1,250 hours in the year before the leave. There are, however, many questions yet to be resolved:

> What's a 12-month period, for example? (Up to the company.) Calendar or fiscal year, and if it's calendar year, may employees stretch out their leave to 24 weeks by taking the last 12 weeks of one year and the first 12 weeks of the next? (Ditto.) Must they take paid sick leave before taking unpaid family leave? (Ditto.)[14]

This act is entirely consistent with what some companies have been doing for some time in their efforts to accommodate to an increasingly diverse work force and make their firms "family-friendly."

AGE DISCRIMINATION IN EMPLOYMENT ACT OF 1967

This act essentially prohibits the forced retirement of employees on the basis of age if they are working for a private business with at least 20 people on the payroll. One exception to this is top-level executives, who can be retired at age 70. These provisions are contained in a 1986 amendment to the act, which took effect on January 1, 1987. Employees can still choose to retire voluntarily at 65 and receive full benefits, however.

Some members of Congress seek to increase to 68 the age at which full Social Security benefits can start. Although this has not been done yet, Congress has attempted to reduce some of the burden on Social Security through a provision in the *Tax Equity and Fiscal Responsibility Act of 1982*. According to that act, employers with 20 or more workers must include those between the ages of 65 and 69 in their group health plans unless the employees specifically choose Medicare, funded by Social Security, as their primary coverage. Nonetheless, employers may still freeze pension contributions and plans for employees at age 65.

Amending ADEA is the *Older Workers Benefit Protection Act of 1990*. This prohibits discrimination in employee benefits. As a result of this act, Congress amended ADEA by defining the term "compensation, terms, conditions, or privileges of employment" to encompass all employee benefits, including benefits provided under a bona fide employee benefit plan.

ERISA AND PRIVATE EMPLOYERS' PENSIONS

Building on the foundation of the *Revenue Act of 1942*, the *Employees' Retirement Income Security Act (ERISA)* was enacted to protect employees covered by private pension programs. While ERISA does not require an employer to offer a pension fund, it is designed to protect the interests of workers covered by private retirement plans. Employees are eligible for private pension fund participation after one year of service or at age 25.[15]

Because of problems over ownership of pension funds, ERISA also established provisions regarding vesting. **Vesting** refers to the time when the employer's contribution belongs to the employee. There are three basic options:

1. Full vesting after 10 years of service
2. Twenty-five percent vesting after 5 years, with 5 percent additional vesting until 10 years of service, and then 10 percent vesting for years 10–15
3. Fifty percent vesting when the employee has worked 5 years and when age and service equal 45; each additional year of service increases vesting by 10 percent

Because companies in the past have used pension funds for operating expenses, ERISA also prohibits the use of unfunded pension programs that rely on the goodwill of the employer to pay retirement benefits out of current operating funds when needed. Money paid into a pension fund must be earmarked for retirees whether paid in part by the employee, as in **contributory programs**, or paid solely by the employer, as in **noncontributory programs**.

In a **defined-benefit plan**, the actual benefits received upon retirement vary by age and length of service of the employee. One concern with such plans is overfunding, or having more money in the account than is needed to meet future funding requirements. Overfunding increases the likelihood of takeover bids because an acquiring company can terminate the pension program, retrieve the excess funding, and then start a new pension fund. To resolve this problem, organizations are reducing their contributions to defined-budget plans or are switching to **defined-contribution plans**. In the latter approach, each employee has a separate account into which are added individual and/or organizational contributions. Growth of investments directly benefits the employee.[16]

Vesting means conveying full ownership of the employer's pension contributions to the employee; the ownership at vesting remains with employee even if the employee leaves the company.

In *defined-benefit plans,* employees know exactly what monthly pay they get during retirement.

Under ERISA, employers are not required to accommodate new or transferred employees who wish to deposit funds into their retirement plans. Employers can allow employees to transfer money on a voluntary basis to individual retirement accounts. When this occurs, the pension funds are said to be **portable**. Increasingly, employers are making it possible for employees to transfer their retirement funds to another firm.

In *defined-contribution plans,* employees know exactly what is put in, but they don't know what the payments will be during retirement.

Because the ERISA only covered single-employer firms, the *Multi-Employer Pension Plan Amendment Act of 1980* was passed to broaden the definition of defined-benefit plans to include multi-employer plans. If any employer withdraws from multi-employer plans, they, rather than the employees, face liability for doing so and must reimburse employees for money lost.[17] Congress also has passed several tax acts that influence the administration or level of indirect compensation programs.

ECONOMIC RECOVERY TAX ACT OF 1981

A major provision of this act is that employees can make tax-deductible contributions of up to $2,000 to an employer-sponsored pension, profit-sharing, or savings account, or to an individual retirement account. The act also made it possible for employers to provide company stock to employees and pay for it with tax credits or to establish a payroll-based stock ownership plan that facilitates employee stock ownership of organizations.[18] This is referred to as setting up an **employee stock ownership plan (ESOP)**.

Because these plans are so attractive to organizations, over 10 million employees have gained direct ownership of stock in their own companies. By the year 2000, 25 percent or more of all U.S. workers may own part or all of their companies.

ESOPs enable employees to become owners of the firm they work for.

The appeal of ownership programs goes far beyond the tax breaks available to ESOPs. At a time when competitive pressures are forcing companies to keep a lid on labor costs, many are using stock plans as a substitute for cash compensation. Stock is being used to fund bonuses, pension and savings plans, and even retiree medical benefits.

Such programs are not without risk, particularly if corporate sponsors go belly-up in future years. But they can help make companies more competitive, enhance productivity, and bolster morale when wage hikes need to be deferred. Because workers are concerned with job security, they represent a source of patient capital that is likely to value long-term performance over short-term profits.

The most intriguing aspect of this trend is the possibility that workers who own a significant share of their companies will want a voice in corporate governance, as has already happened in the case of several companies contemplating mergers. Employers who prepare for this development by setting up mechanisms for dialogue can lay the groundwork for productive cooperation between labor and management in future decision making. Those who don't may find worker ownership a mixed blessing.[19]

TAX EQUITY AND FISCAL RESPONSIBILITY ACT OF 1982

This act sharply cut the maximum benefit and contribution limits for qualified pension plans (legally covered) and set limits for loans from such plans. The maximum individual yearly retirement benefit now stands at $94,023, and the maximum employer contribution per employee per year is $30,000. As an outgrowth of the act, some organizations have established nonqualified pension plans (not legally protected) for high-income employees. Contributions to these plans are taxable, while contributions to qualified plans are not.

DEFICIT REDUCTION ACT OF 1984

Congress often passes tax acts that have important results for indirect compensation.

Along with several IRS rulings, this act makes some benefits—particularly **flexible spending plans**—taxable. In one form, employees are given the choice between several nontaxable benefits in return for reduced pay. In another, money is set aside initially and, if employees don't use the benefits, they receive the money. In still another, no money is set aside, but employees are reimbursed for some expenses.

CONSOLIDATED OMNIBUS BUDGET RECONCILIATION ACT

Passed in 1985, this act assures that terminated or laid-off employees have the option to maintain their health-care insurance by personally paying for the premiums. The option must also be extended to employees who lose their health benefits eligibility because their work hours have been reduced to the point where they no longer are eligible for coverage.

TAX REFORM ACT OF 1986

Two provisions of this act affect indirect compensation. Essentially, the act caps at $9,500 the amount of tax-exempt deferred contribution employees can make to a deferred pay plan. Effective January, 1989, the act also put into force provisions to reduce the disparity of benefits provided high- and low-income employees. Because of the difficulty of implementing this provision, it has been modified substantially.[20]

REVENUE RECONCILIATION ACT OF 1993

This act further limits the amount of money employers may contribute to qualified retirement plans. Now the percentage of salary an employer contributes is based on a maximum of $150,000 rather than $250,000.

PUBLIC PROTECTION PROGRAMS

Protection programs are designed to assist the employee and his or her family if and when the employee's income (direct compensation) is terminated and to alleviate the burden of health-care expenses. Protection programs required by federal and state government are referred to as public programs, and those voluntarily offered by organizations are called private programs. The various programs in each are listed in Exhibit 13.1.

THE SOCIAL SECURITY SYSTEM

Public protection programs are the outgrowth of the *Social Security Act of 1935*. The act initially set up systems for retirement benefits, disability, and unemployment insurance. Health insurance, particularly Medicare, was added in 1966 to provide hospital insurance to almost everyone age 65 and older.

Funding of the Social Security System is provided by equal contributions from the employer and employee under terms of the *Federal Insurance Contribution Act* (FICA). Initially, employee and employer paid 1 percent of the employee's income up to $3,000. Currently, they pay tax on the first $60,600 of the employee's income at the rate of 6.2 percent (for retirement and disability) and total of income at the rate of 1.45 percent (for hospital insurance via Medicare).

The average Social Security benefit for a single person is about $8,300; for a married couple it is about $15,000 per year, with adjustments routinely made for increases in the Consumer Price Index. The maximum benefits from Social

LEARNING OBJECTIVE 3

Describe the various public and private protection programs.

Public protection programs include:

- Social Security system
- Social Security pension benefits
- unemployment compensation benefits
- disability benefits
- workers' compensation benefits
- medical and hospital benefits

DID YOU KNOW?

Self-employed people pay at the rate of 15.3%? This is the combination of the employer's and employee's contribution.

EXHIBIT 13.1
PROTECTION PROGRAMS

COVERAGE	PRIVATE PLANS	PUBLIC PLANS
Retirement	• Defined-benefit pensions • Defined-contribution pensions • Money purchase and thrift plans (401 (k)s and ESOPs)	• Social Security old age benefits
Death	• Group term-life insurance (including accidental death and travel insurance) • Payouts from profit-sharing pension, and/or thrift plans • Dependent survivors' benefits	• Social Security survivors' benefits • Workers' compensation
Disability	• Short-term accident and sickness insurance • Long-term disability insurance	• Workers' compensation • Social Security disability benefits • State disability benefits
Unemployment	• Supplemental unemployment benefits and/or severance pay	• Unemployment benefits
Medical/dental expenses	• Hospital/surgical Insurance • Other medical insurance • Dental insurance	• Workers' compensation • Medicare

Unemployment benefits vary by state because income levels vary by state as shown in Exhibit 11.9.

Security are now around $900 a month for a person who retired in 1988. Retired people aged 65–69 can also earn about $11,000 annually without sacrificing benefits; beneficiaries under age 65 can earn about $8,000.[21]

UNEMPLOYMENT COMPENSATION BENEFITS

To control costs, the *Social Security Act* dictates that unemployment compensation programs be jointly administered through the federal and state governments. Because income levels vary from state to state, unemployment compensation also varies by state, although the federal rate is the same for all states ($133.00). Consequently, the total tax liability varies greatly across the country as shown in Exhibit 13.2.

All profit-making organizations pay a tax on the first $7,000–10,000 of wages paid to each employee. The state contribution rate for employers, however, varies according to the number of unemployed people drawing from the

---

EXHIBIT 13.2
EMPLOYERS' TAX LIABILITY* FOR UNEMPLOYMENT INSURANCE, PER EMPLOYEE, BY STATE, 1993

RANK	STATE	TOTAL TAX	RANK	STATE	TOTAL TAX
1	Rhode Island	$633.20	27	Montana	$259.00
2	Oregon	524.00	28	Missouri	251.50
3	Alaska	520.00	29	New Jersey	249.20
4	Washington	481.50	30	Kansas	248.00
5	Massachusetts	477.20	31	New Mexico	245.00
6	Michigan**	445.50	32	North Dakota	232.40
7	Pennsylvania	440.00	33	Kentucky	224.00
8	District of Columbia	416.00	34	Louisiana	217.50
9	Idaho	401.60	35	Utah	213.00
10	New York	392.00		**UNITED STATES**	**210.00**
11	Maine	322.00	36	New Hampshire	210.00
12	Minnesota	313.40	37	Mississippi	203.00
13	Arkansas	311.00	38	Colorado	196.00
14	California	308.00	38	Tennessee	196.00
15	Maryland	302.50	40	Georgia	192.00
15	Ohio	302.50	41	Alabama	184.00
17	Connecticut	297.40	42	Florida	182.00
18	West Virginia	296.00	42	South Carolina	182.00
19	Hawaii	295.00	44	North Carolina	181.00
20	Wyoming	289.10	45	Oklahoma	180.80
21	Wisconsin	287.00	46	Texas	173.00
22	Illinois	281.00	47	Arizona	161.00
23	Nevada	278.00	48	Virginia	152.00
24	Delaware	277.00	49	Indiana	140.00
25	Vermont	272.00	49	Nebraska	140.00
26	Iowa	265.60	51	South Dakota	91.00

*Total tax liability equals the sum of an employer's federal tax liability ($56.00 for each state, in 1993) and state tax liability.

State tax liabilities are based on estimates of states' average unemployment insurance tax rates.

**Total tax for Michigan includes an additional federal unemployment insurance tax of $77 per employee (total federal tax liability = $133).

Reprinted with permission from *Bulletin to Management*, p. 245 (August 5, 1993). Copyright 1993 by The Bureau of National Affairs, Inc.

fund. Consequently, during periods of high unemployment, employers make larger contributions than they do during periods of stable employment.

To be eligible for benefits, an employee must

- Have worked a specified number of weeks (set by the state)
- Be able and available to work
- Be actively looking for work
- Not be unemployed due to a labor dispute (except in Rhode Island and New York)
- Not have been terminated for gross misconduct
- Not have terminated voluntarily

The length of time an employee may receive benefits is a function of how long the employee worked prior to termination, but the standard maximum is 26 weeks. Extended benefits of up to 13 weeks are provided during periods of high unemployment or when jobs are lost due to foreign competition. The level of benefits ranges from 50 to 70 percent of base salary up to a maximum weekly amount that varies by state (around $225). With the passage of the *Tax Reform Act of 1986*, unemployment compensation became *fully taxable*, making actual benefit levels much lower.[22]

MEDICARE

When Medicare became operational in 1966, benefits managers felt this program would be a cure-all, satisfying the health-care needs of older Americans. Managers anticipated significant cost savings by coordinating private medical programs with Medicare. Unfortunately, this has not proved to be true. In the era of early retirements to reduce staffing levels, organizations have discovered that the assurance of continuing health coverage is a critical factor in an individual's decision to elect retirement. Because a majority of retirements occur before the age of 65 (the age for Medicare eligibility), there is a gap in health-care coverage that must be subsumed by organizations. Medicare has progressively shifted cost responsibility to subscribers and, as a result, retirees over age 65 are demanding supplemental health benefits from their former employers.

Because employers' liabilities for post-retirement health benefits are estimated in the *trillions* of dollars and are expected to increase, the Financial Accounting Standards Board (FASB) has specified that these liabilities be included in corporate financial statements. A partial consequence is that organizations have begun avoiding promises of specific levels of benefits for future retirees.

WORKERS' COMPENSATION AND DISABILITY

As described in the opening feature on Steelcase, Inc. workers' compensation costs are of major concern to organizations. Of the more than 6.4 million job-related injuries reported annually in the private sector, about half are serious enough for the injured worker to lose work time, experience restricted work activity, or both. Additionally, 332,000 new occupational illness cases were reported in 1990, up from 284,000 in 1989. Almost 60 percent of these illnesses were associated with repetitive motions such as vibration, repeated pressure, and carpal tunnel syndrome, and a majority require medical care and result in lost work time.[23]

When such injuries or illnesses occur as a result of on-the-job concerns, workers may be eligible for **workers' compensation insurance**. Administered at the state level and fully financed by employers, workers' compensation benefits are provided for temporary and permanent disability, disfigurement, medical expenses, and medical rehabilitation. Survival benefits are provided following fatal injuries.[24]

While specific terms and conditions vary by state, workers' compensation benefits are provided regardless of fault in an accident. Awards can consist of lump-sum monetary benefits (for example, $10,000 for the loss of an eye), the payment of medical benefits, or long-term payments tied to the worker's income level. Currently, most states award employees who are unable to work at least two-thirds of their gross, before-injury, salary. Employee contributions to the state-managed programs are contingent on their accident rates. The average premium an employer paid for an employee was more than $500 in 1991. This represents a fivefold increase in 20 years.

There are several reasons for the increase in premiums. Even though the economy has been moving from manufacturing to service, the number of claims has doubled in the past decade. In 1990, the average number of lost workdays was 78 days per incident. Some of the increase is due to real and debilitating diseases that science recently has linked to the workplace (for example, carpal tunnel syndrome, asbestosis). Increases are also due to fraud; a recent study estimates that 20 percent of all workers' comp claims are fraudulent.[25] To deal with phony claims, state-owned or state-managed workers' comp insurers are utilizing a variety of strategies ranging from case monitoring, videotaping, and media blitzes to prosecution.

Proactive workers' compensation administrators such as Gil Fry at Lincoln Electric and Libby Child at Steelcase, apply a variety of health-care cost-containment strategies to workers' comp such as:

- Developing networks of preferred provider organizations
- Specifying fees for treating workers' comp claimants
- Limiting payments to medically necessary or reasonable procedures
- Requiring precertification of hospital admissions
- Establishing concurrent review of inpatient hospital stays
- Routinely auditing hospital and health-care bills[26]

Employers also are jumping on the cost-containment bandwagon. For example, Sprague Electric Co. in Concord, New Hampshire, assembles a team consisting of the worker's supervisor, a rehabilitation counselor, and the firm's human resource manager. Using videotaped demonstrations of the employee's job and physician input, the team identifies components of the jobs the worker can still perform, as well as appropriate accommodations that need to be made.[27]

To assertively manage workers' compensation costs, Burns of Boston, a Rhode Island–based photo frame and album manufacturer, recommends four things:

1. Actively manage your workers' comp insurance carrier by using all of the services it can provide.
2. Aggressively review cases each quarter until you're satisfied that open cases are being resolved and closed appropriately.
3. Request that your carrier's loss control representative visit your office or plant location to evaluate your safety awareness program.
4. Ensure that a company representative attends every workers' comp hearing. Your presence gives incredible weight to any claims challenge and shows the hearing officer the company's concern for speedy case resolution.[28]

PRIVATE PROTECTION PROGRAMS

Private protection programs are offered by organizations but are not required by law. They include retirement income plans, capital accumulation plans, savings and thrift plans, and supplemental unemployment benefits, and guaranteed pay. Some firms also are offering work options for retirees including temporary full-time and part-time employment.

The various retirement income plans can be classified in terms of whether they will be qualified or nonqualified. A **qualified plan** means that the pension plan covers a broad, nondiscriminatory class of employees, meets Internal Revenue Code requirements, and consequently receives favorable tax treatment. For example, the employer's contributions to the plan are tax deductible for the current year, and employees pay no taxes until retirement. **Nonqualified plans** do not adhere to the strict tax regulations and cover only select groups of employees. They are often utilized to provide supplemental retirement benefits for key executives.[29]

PENSION PLANS

The largest category of private protection plans is pensions. Four out of five employees in medium and large firms are covered by some type of private pension or capital accumulation plan and rely on these plans to provide future security. A less-known fact is that the 20 largest pension funds (13 of them funds of public employees) hold one-tenth of the equity capital of America's publicly owned companies. All told, institutional investors—primarily pension funds—control close to 40 percent of the common stock of the country's largest businesses. Pension funds also hold 40 percent or more of the medium- and long-term debt of the country's bigger companies. Thus, employees via their pension funds have become one of America's largest lenders as well as business owners.[30]

DEFINED-BENEFIT PLANS. With a defined-benefit pension plan, the actual benefits received on retirement vary by age and length of service of the employee. For example, an employee may receive $50 a month for each year of company service. As described in Exhibit 13.3, defined plans are preferred by paternalistic employers and unions because they produce predictable, secure, and continuing income. Another advantage of defined-benefit plans is that they are carefully regulated by the *Employees' Retirement Income Security Act*. In addition to the reporting, disclosure, fiduciary standard, plan participation rules, and vesting standards, defined-benefit plans must adhere to specific funding-level requirements and be insured against plan termination due to economic hardship, misfunding, or corporate buyouts.

The **Pension Benefit Guaranty Corporation (PBGC)** administers the required insurance program and guarantees the payment of basic retirement benefits to participants if a plan is terminated. The PBGC can also terminate pension funds that are seriously underfunded. In July, 1991, they moved to do exactly that with Pan Am's pension fund. The airline had missed three required funding contributions over the past year. According to James Lockhart, executive director for PBGC, "We had to act immediately to keep the pension insurance safety net strong for workers and retirees and stem the rising costs for companies with well-funded pension plans."

When a plan is terminated, employees who participated in the plan are guaranteed to receive what they contributed. In the case of Pan Am, this covered 34,000 participants, including 11,000 retirees enrolled in Pan Am's

Private protection programs include:

- pension plans
- supplemental plans
- Individual Retirement Accounts
- guaranteed pay plans

Paternalistic employers are those who look out for the welfare of their employees and seek to protect them.

ASPECT	DEFINED-BENEFIT PLAN	DEFINED-CONTRIBUTION PLAN
1. Definition	Benefits vary by age and length of service according to a formula. Set amount received.	Each employee has an account to which personal, corporate or both contributions are made.
2. Source of funding	Majority funded entirely by company contributions. Some public-sector funds require employee participation.	Employer and employee both contribute to the plan. Formulas are 50-50 or higher employer to employee contribution.
3. Prevalence	20 percent of new plans. Majority of existing plans.	80 percent of new plans. Minority of existing plans.
4. Supporting culture	Paternalistic, mature, union.	Competitive, participative, start-up.
5. ERISA control	Must meet ERISA funding requirements. Must have termination insurance. Excise tax on asset reversions.	No set funding requirement. No plan termination insurance.
6. Advantages to employee	Guaranteed level of retirement income.	No set retirement income. Based on profitability of investments.
7. Disadvantages to employee	Pension may not be enough to maintain standard of living.	Contributions restricted, early withdrawals penalized, loans limited. Must contribute funds to activate.
8. Advantages to employer	Contributions are tax deductible. Rewards long-term employee.	Less costly. Less risky.
9. Disadvantages to employer	Difficult to determine how to credit employees before fund was started. May be underfunded.	Contributions increase as employees' income goes up.

SOURCE: Adapted from R. M. McCaffery, *Employee Benefit Programs: A Total Compensation Perspective* (Boston, Mass.: PWS-Kent, 1992).

Cooperative Retirement Income Plan and 750 participants in the Defined-Benefit Plan for Flight Engineers. According to Lockhart, PBGC lost more than $600 million due to the mismanagement of this plan alone. Losses like this explain why PBGC's long-term deficit now tops more than $2 billion and why retirement programs are feared to be the next "savings and loan crisis" of the 1990s.[31]

You will most likely have a defined-contribution plan.

In defined-contribution plans, usually both the employer and employee contribute.

DEFINED-CONTRIBUTION PLANS. Eighty percent of new plans are defined-contribution plans. With this type of plan, each employee has a separate account to which employee and employer contributions are added. Typically, the employee must activate the plan by agreeing to contribute a set amount of money; the employer then matches the percentage contribution to a specific level. Defined-contribution plans are more prevalent in competitive, participative organizations.

The two most common types of defined-contribution plans are money-purchase and tax-deferred profit-sharing plans. With **money-purchase plans**, the employer makes fixed, regular contributions for participants, usually a percentage of total pay, to a fund. Employees may also make voluntary contributions. The maximum amount is equal to 25 percent of earned income, up to a maximum of $30,000 for all defined-contribution plans. Monies are held in trust funds, and the employee is given several investment options that differ in terms of the degree of risk and growth potential. At retirement, accumulated funds are used to provide annuities. In some cases, lump-sum distributions are made.

One of the largest money purchase plans is the Teachers Insurance and Annuity Association–College Retirement Equity Fund (TIAA–CREF). More than 1.4 million professors and administrative staff members from nearly 4,500 colleges and universities participate in this program. Enrollees can choose to allocate contributions across four distinct CREF investment accounts (stock, money market, bond market, or a social choice). An allocation to TIAA is a premium for a contractually guaranteed amount of future lifetime annuity income.

Tax-deferred profit-sharing plans provide for employee participation in profit sharing using a predetermined formula. Monies contributed to these plans are set aside until retirement when the employees can cash in their profits. From the employer's perspective, tax-deferred profit-sharing plans are useful because they deduct up to 15 percent of participants' compensation (up to an income level of $200,000) for profit-sharing contributions. Additionally, they pass on the investment risk to the employee.[32]

SUPPLEMENTAL PLANS

In addition to Social Security and standard pension plans, large firms often offer a supplemental defined-contribution plan or savings plan. Currently, 30 percent of all employees participate in supplemental plans. Such plans serve as the third leg of the retirement income stool: they provide additional retirement income or serve as a source for accumulating funds to meet short-term needs and goals. These plans take one of two forms: savings plans that work as defined-contribution plans [called 401(k) plans], and employee stock ownership plans (ESOPs).[33]

As provided in the Internal Revenue Code, a key feature of a savings plan is that the employee must elect to participate in the program by setting aside a small percentage of pay. Other features of the plan include loan provisions and limited in-service withdrawal for hardship or for employment termination. Participants can elect to receive their entire contribution in a lump sum upon retirement or termination.

INDIVIDUAL RETIREMENT ACCOUNTS

Under current law, an employee who is not an active participant in an employer-sponsored pension plan during any part of a year may contribute up to $2,000 unconditionally to an **Individual Retirement Account (IRA)**, with an additional $250 allowed for a spousal account. The latter provision applies only if a joint tax return is filed. Employees who are involved in employer-sponsored pension plans also may participate, providing their income does not surpass limits set by the IRS.

GUARANTEED PAY PLANS

A relatively new type of income guarantee involves providing guaranteed pay to nonexempt employees who are laid off. Such plans protect employee income during periods of involuntary unemployment. In automotive, steel, and related industries, the protection project is in the form of **supplemental unemployment benefits** plans. Such plans provide income safety nets by providing corporate-financed unemployment benefits—up to 85 percent of regular take-home pay for up to three years.[34]

DID YOU KNOW?

Americans save only 5% of their income while the French, Germans, and Japanese save over 12%.

HEALTH-CARE BENEFITS

Coverage for medical expenses including hospital charges, physician charges, and other medical services is the core of a group health plan and will be discussed first. Organizations may also provide wellness programs, employee assistance programs, and short- and long-term disability insurance. Because the cost is far below what employees would pay on their own, health benefits—particularly medical insurance—represent an important, although costly, benefit. Unfortunately, most employees underestimate the cost of health benefits to the organization and view coverage as an entitlement rather than a costly benefit. In a recent study, more than 80 percent of all workers said their employers are obligated to provide health care for them, but almost half of the employees did not know what their health insurance cost their employer.[35]

In reality, health care costs more than $800 billion or 15 percent of the nation's gross domestic product (GDP). Employer-funded health-care costs, like workers' compensation, double every five years. To fund the rising health-care costs, businesses are passing the burden on to consumers. For example, Detroit automakers estimate that $500–700 is added to the retail price of each automobile to pay for employee health-care costs.[36] Exhibit 13.4 delineates what companies in five different industries had to sell to cover the cost of a simple appendectomy in 1991.

MEDICAL-CARE APPROACHES

Employers can finance and provide medical expense benefits to employees and their dependents in different ways. The most widely used source for financing group medical benefits involves insurance companies. However, a variety of other approaches are gaining in popularity as business attempts to thwart rising costs.

INSURANCE COMPANIES.   Insurance carriers offer a broad range of health-care services from which employers can select coverage. Premiums are set and adjusted depending on usage rates and increases in health-care costs. The insurance company administers the plan, handling all the paperwork, approvals, and problems. Proponents of this approach argue that insurers protect the plan sponsor against wide fluctuations in claims experience and costs and offer opportunities for participation in larger-risk pools. Insurance companies also have administrative expertise related to certification reviews, claim audits, coordination of benefits, and other cost-containment services.

EXHIBIT 13.4
WHAT COMPANIES MUST SELL TO PAY FOR AN APPENDECTOMY

COMPANY	PRODUCT
Dayton Hudson	39,000 Ninja Turtle action figures
Atlantic Richfield	192,000 gallons of gas
Southern California Edison	1 year's electricity for 330 households
Anheuser-Busch	11,627 6-packs of 12-ounce Bud
Goodyear Tire & Rubber	461 radial tires for passenger cars

SOURCE: "CEOs Seek Help on Health Costs," *Fortune* (June 3, 1991), 12. © 1991 Time, Inc. All Rights Reserved.

On the downside, the insurance company, not the employer, makes decisions regarding covered benefits. Such decisions may go against the corporation's ethics and sense of social responsibility. The Rockwell Company was advised against covering a bone-marrow transplant by the insurance company that administers its health-care plan. Because the firm was self-insured, it could ignore the advice and do what it felt was ethical. Companies who subscribe to a specific insurance plan do not have this luxury. The insurance company makes all the tough calls, and the tendency will be towards conservatism to contain their costs (not the employer's costs).

PROVIDER ORGANIZATIONS. Blue Cross/Blue Shield associations are non-profit organizations that operate within defined geographic areas. While Blue Cross plans cover hospital expenses, Blue Shield plans provide benefits for charges by physicians and other medical providers. Typically, these associations negotiate arrangements with their member hospitals and physicians to reimburse the hospital or physician at a discounted rate when a subscriber incurs a charge. As originally established, the rate represents full payment for the service, and there is no additional charge. However, recently skyrocketing costs in health care have resulted in deductibles ($50–250 per year per person) and cost-sharing (10–20 percent) on the part of employees.

All of these providers are important under a federal health-care plan.

HEALTH MAINTENANCE ORGANIZATIONS. A survey of almost 2,000 firms found that 63 percent of all organizations now offer health care through **health maintenance organizations (HMOs)**. Health-care costs with HMOs have risen only 15.7 percent a year compared to increases above 20 percent for traditional health-care plans. About one-third of all eligible employees participate in HMO plans, or about 35 million employees.[37]

The growth in HMOs was stimulated by the passage of the *Health Maintenance Organization Act of 1973 (HMO)*. This act requires that companies with at least 25 employees living in an HMO service area must offer membership in that organization to employees as an alternative to regular group health coverage, provided the HMO meets federal qualification requirements. HMO amendments of 1988 relaxed many of the federal rules governing HMOs and specifically repealed the dual-choice alternative, effective in October 1995. This shift in legislative direction is designed to make the HMO field more competitive and, as a result, employers more receptive to using HMOs.

PREFERRED-PROVIDER NETWORKS. **Preferred-Provider Organizations (PPOs)** are a relatively new option in health-care delivery. Introduced in the 1980s, these plans cover 55–60 million participants. With these programs, employers contract directly—or indirectly through an insurance company—with a provider organization to secure agreements from health-care providers (physicians, dentists, laboratories, hospitals) to deliver services to group health plan participants on a discounted basis. Because these plans are relatively unregulated with respect to rate setting and requirements, employers have a great deal of flexibility in structuring an arrangement.

Unlike HMOs, employees are not required to use PPO providers exclusively. However, there are usually incentives (lower deductibles or cost-sharing) when a PPO is utilized. For example, the employer may cover all health-care costs provided by a PPO but only 80 percent of the cost of care provided by physicians outside of the PPO network. A concern with PPOs in the 1990s is the potential for antitrust legislation since these plans involve agreeing on standard charges for health-care services.[38]

SELF-FUNDED PLANS. A growing number of companies are opting for self-insured or self-funded plans as a way to control medical plan costs and gain relief from state insurance regulations. By eliminating or reducing insurance protection, the employer saves on carrier retention charges (the amount of money not utilized to pay claims). This includes such things as state premium taxes, administrative costs, risk and contingency expenses, and reserve requirements. Typically, the employer creates a voluntary employee beneficiary association and establishes a tax-exempt trust. The trust's investment income is tax-exempt as long as it is used to provide benefits to employees and their dependents.

COST-CONTAINMENT STRATEGIES. To further control costs, firms are also employing a variety of cost-containment strategies. While no strategy can hold the line on soaring medical costs, these strategies represent employers' best efforts to date to control costs. Some of the more common strategies include:

- *Hospital utilization programs* that review the necessity and appropriateness of hospitalization prior to admission and/or during a stay
- *Coordination of benefits* with other providers to prevent duplicate payment for the same health-care service
- *Data analysis* to determine the most viable cost management approach. Simulations and experience-based utilization assumptions are used to develop models
- *Managed care* with many employers active participants in case management. Interventions include requirements for second opinions and peer reviews[39]
- *Cost-sharing with employees* by raising deductibles and contribution levels. Employers thus hold the line on overall expenses
- *Incentives* that some firms hope will change employees' behaviors so they are healthier. While this may have substantial merit, it can also have substantial risks.[40] In the worst case, companies may be in violation of the *Americans with Disabilities Act* if individuals with specific disabilities are treated differently than employees without the disability. There are also ethical dilemmas. While employees may consider it fair to give premium rebates for healthy life-styles, most would not tolerate raises in premiums for genetically linked conditions. To stimulate your own debate and discussion, the issues here are discussed further in the feature, "HR Advice and Application: Ethics and Life-Style."

WELLNESS PROGRAMS

Frustrated with efforts to manage health-care costs for employees who are already sick, a growing number of employers are taking proactive steps to prevent health-care problems. Moving beyond employee exercise classes and stress management classes, a handful of firms are implementing carefully designed wellness programs, which are producing significant savings on the bottom line.[42]

For example, the Adolph Coors Company based in Golden, Colorado, has spent the past ten years fine-tuning its wellness program. For every dollar spent on wellness, Coors sees a return of $6.15, including $1.9 million annually in decreased medical costs, reduced sick leave, and increased productivity. According to William Coors, chairman and CEO, the secret to Coor's success is really no secret. "Wellness is an integral part of the corporate culture."[43]

The commitment at Coors to wellness includes a health-risk assessment, nutritional counseling, stress management, and programs for smoking cessation, weight loss, and orthopedic rehabilitation. "When employees hear health warn-

The Camberley Hotel in Atlanta reduced health-care costs and employee turnover when it became self-insured.

It pays employers to offer incentives to employees to take care of themselves.

There are, however, ethical issues in offering incentives to employees.

Wellness programs seek to encourage employees to take care of themselves.

ETHICS AND LIFE-STYLE

Just taking in a movie with someone else's wife? Laural Allen, 23, and Sam Johnson, 20, had been working for Wal-Mart in Gloversville, New York, for several months when they began dating. Neither was a supervisor, and they were employed in different departments. Says Johnson: "One day the store manager called Laural in and fired her. Later she fired me. The reason she gave is that although Laural is legally separated from her husband, she's not divorced. They didn't tell us there's a rule like that." The couple has sued for $4 million, plus back pay and reinstatement on grounds of wrongful discharge. Wal-Mart declines to comment while the case is being litigated.

Assuming Johnson's story is true, Wal-Mart's action seems such an outrageous breach of privacy that it must be illegal. But maybe not. Employers can fire employees or reject job candidates for any reason that a contract or law doesn't specifically forbid. Federal and state laws prohibit discrimination based on race, religion, age, and gender, but Washington does not protect jobs for those who tango, motorcycle, tease pit bulls, play bridge, or otherwise amuse themselves during off hours. And only a handful of states do.

The Wal-Mart case, where morality seems the issue, is unusual. More commonly, employers try to control workers' physical well-being. Why? Cautious, healthy workers cost less. A late 1980s study of 46,000 Du Pont employees showed that each year the average smoker cost the company an additional $960 in medical claims and sick days; the overweight person, $401; the alcohol abuser, $369; a worker with elevated cholesterol, $370; one with high blood pressure, $343. Turner Broadcasting has refused to hire smokers since 1986. North Miami requires applicants to sign an affidavit that they have not used tobacco products for the previous year. Arlene Kurtz, a clerk typist denied a city job because she smokes, has sued, but Florida has no statute protecting smokers.

Twenty-eight other states, including Illinois, New Jersey, and New York, have passed laws shielding smokers from such discrimination, urged on by the strange bedfellowship of the tobacco industry and the American Civil Liberties Union. Eight of those states protect a range of activities. New York, for example, makes it illegal to fire an employee who during off-hours engages in sports, games, hobbies, exercise, reading, or watching TV or movies. Lewis Maltby, an ACLU attorney, argues that all legal activities that are not directly related to work should be protected. Says he: "We all do something dangerous, whether it's scuba diving or eating red meat."

He has a point. Firing an employee for having a couple of drinks after his shift is heavy-handed. An Indianapolis manufacturing company, Best Lock Corporation, did just that when it discharged Daniel Winn, a machine operator, several years ago. An alternative might be charging workers for bad habits that ultimately take money from colleagues' pockets. General Mills lowers workers' insurance premiums by as much as 20 percent if they live healthfully. Among the half-dozen measurements: wearing seat belts; not smoking; drinking moderately or not at all; and controlling weight and blood pressure.

Beginning next year, Butterworth Hospital of Grand Rapids, Michigan, will offer its 5,000 employees financial incentives to live healthfully—and will punish those who don't. Staffers who hew to the proper life-style will find up to $25 extra in each biweekly paycheck. Employees who do poorly on tests or who refuse to cooperate will be docked up to $25 every two weeks. Some employees consider the policy overbearing. Says one nurse, Julie Ostrander: "I resent *someone else* trying to control my behavior."

Genes determine weight and cholesterol levels as much as diet does. Should workers be penalized for their parentage? And how does the employer find out whether a worker gets tipsy on a Saturday night? Before adopting such programs, companies ought to consider the consequences thoroughly.[41]

ings and statistics on the television, the warnings are always about someone else. When they read a personalized assessment that indicates a genuine risk of heart attack based on heredity, cholesterol, and high blood pressure, the warnings take on new significance," says D. W. Edmonton, Ph.D., director of the University of Michigan Fitness Research Center.

Overweight Coors employees learn about the long-term risks associated with obesity through a health-hazard survey. They're educated about the effect of excess weight on the cardiovascular, endocrine, and musculoskeletal systems. Then an individual plan is developed. The individualized program may include individual counseling, group classes, and medical programs such as Optifast. The company even gives employees a financial incentive if they participate in the program and achieve and maintain their weight loss goal during a twelve-month period. To further encourage involvement, classes are held at the company.

Coors has been sensitive to the ADA requirements (1) that employers cannot make entry into wellness program conditioned on the passage of a medical exam and (2) that facilities be accessible to all:

> At Adolph Coors Company, in Golden, Colorado, persons with disabilities have complete access to all of the company's facilities and its wellness center, says corporate communications manager, Joe Fuentes. Part of the wellness program includes a medical questionnaire that determines employees' "health age" in relation to their "chronological age," Fuentes says. The program is totally voluntary for employees, he adds.
>
> The questionnaire asks employees whether they smoke, wear a seat belt, have high blood pressure, and exercise, and also includes questions about the employees' medical history, Fuentes says. All Coors employees are covered by their health insurance at 85 percent, he notes. Employees that pass the questionnaire are then covered at 90 percent. If employees fail the test, they can have a plan of action recommended by the community outreach person who runs the program, he explains.
>
> Test results are confidential and made available only to the community outreach person who administers the survey, Fuentes notes. In addition, employees can choose not to follow up on the test results. Thus far, he says, there have been no legal conflicts with ADA.[44]

Employee Assistance Programs

Whereas wellness programs attempt to prevent health-care problems, **employee assistance programs (EAPs)** are specifically designed to assist employees with chronic personal problems that hinder their job performance and attendance as presented in Chapter 10. EAPs are often used with employees who are alcoholics, have drug dependencies, or who have severe domestic problems that interfere with competency on the job. EAPs also assist employees in coping with mental disorders, financial problems, stress, eating disorders, and smoking cessation. They provide dependent-care programs, bereavement counseling, and AIDS support group meetings. Because the job may be partly responsible for these problems, some employers are taking the lead in establishing EAPs to help affected workers.[45] Thus EAPs serve as an important form of indirect compensation that benefits the individual and the firm.

Paid Leave

Paid leave is not as complex to administer as benefits from protection programs, but it is certainly the more costly, accounting for more than 10 percent of the total payroll. If absenteeism policies are not designed correctly, costs can escalate even further. The two major categories are time not worked *off* the job (holidays, vacations, sick days) and time not worked *on* the job (rest periods, wash-up times, lunches).

OFF-THE-JOB

The most common paid off-the-job components are vacations, sick leave, holidays, and personal days. The challenge in administering these benefits is to contain the costs of these programs while seeking better ways to package them.

VACATIONS. Vacations are granted because employees need time to recuperate away from the physical and mental demands of work. It is also believed that vacation time is an appropriate reward for service and commitment to the organization. Recently, a small number of firms have granted sabbaticals to employees (similar to those in academia), which after a stated period of service can be used for self-improvement, community work, or teaching. Tandem Computers, which has been granting six-week sabbaticals plus normal vacation time at full pay, claims that in the short term such programs have a negative impact on productivity, but in the long term they enhance productivity.

Length of vacations tend to vary by industry, locale, company size, and profession. Some firms believe that longer vacations for more senior employees help to counterbalance salary compression problems. However, there are no hard data to suggest that employees view this as a fair exchange.

In setting up vacation programs, several issues need to be addressed: (1) Will vacation pay be based on scheduled hours or on hours actually worked? (2) Under what circumstances can an employee be paid in lieu of a vacation? (3) Can vacations be deferred, or will they be lost if not taken? (4) What pay rate applies if an employee works during a vacation? The trend is toward vacation "banking," with employees able to roll over a specified period of unused vacation days into a savings investment plan.[46]

HOLIDAYS. Employees in the United States average about ten paid holidays a year. However, the actual days vary by industry and locale. For example, in some southern states, the birthdays of Jefferson Davis and Robert E. Lee are observed, in Utah there is Mormon Pioneer Day, and in Alaska there is Steward's Day.

Trends in union contract negotiations include floater holidays that meet employee preferences, as well as personal holidays in recognition of the employee's birthday. Conversely, other organizations are cutting back on the number of paid holidays because they are an investment with marginal return. Companies are also moving toward established holiday pay policies such as "In order to be eligible for holiday pay, an employee must perform work on the day before and the day after the holiday." Obviously, these policies are intended to deter absenteeism. They are also intended to reduce costs. According to the data shown in Exhibit 13.5, the employers spend about $3,465 for vacations and holidays for the average worker.

PAID ABSENCES. On any given day, 1 million American workers who are otherwise employed will *not* attend work; they will be absent. In the United States, the absenteeism rate ranges from 2 to 3 percent of total payroll. However, some organizations report absenteeism in excess of 20 percent. An estimated 400 million person days are lost each year as a result of employee absenteeism. This is almost ten times the number of person days lost to strikes over a ten-year period.[47]

Off-the-Job paid leave include:
- vacations
- holidays
- paid absences

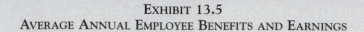

Exhibit 13.5
Average Annual Employee Benefits and Earnings

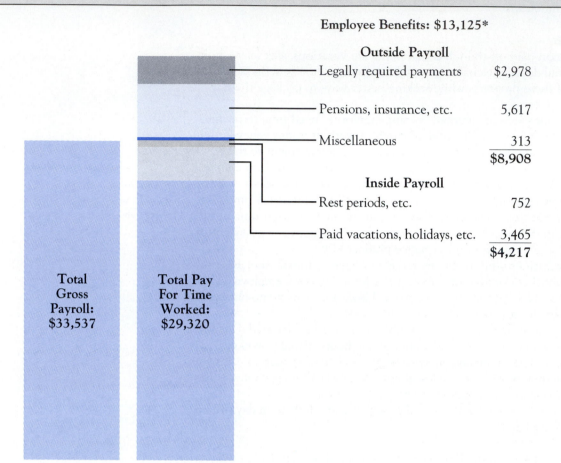

Employee Benefits: $13,125*

Outside Payroll

Legally required payments	$2,978
Pensions, insurance, etc.	5,617
Miscellaneous	313
	$8,908

Inside Payroll

Rest periods, etc.	752
Paid vacations, holidays, etc.	3,465
	$4,217

Total Gross Payroll: $33,537

Total Pay For Time Worked: $29,320

Employee Benefits as a Percentage of …

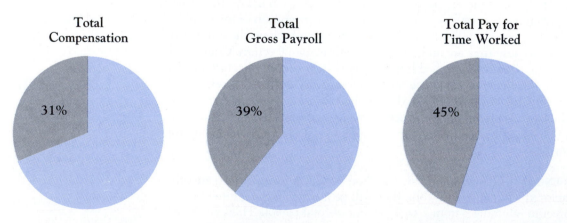

Total Compensation — 31%

Total Gross Payroll — 39%

Total Pay for Time Worked — 45%

Source: Reprinted with permission from *Bulletin to Management* (January 7, 1993): 5. Copyright 1993 by The Bureau of National Affairs.

In comparison with other countries, the United States is midrange. Japan and Switzerland have lower absenteeism rates; Italy, France, and Sweden report substantially higher rates. The problem in Italy became so severe at one point that police began arresting some of the habitual absentees, charging them with fraud.[48]

What makes absenteeism so problematic is the cost of employee replacement. It has been estimated that for every 1 percent change in the national absentee rates, the gross national product goes down by $20 billion. Absenteeism at General Motors has been estimated to cost $1 billion annually.[49]

While there are many reasons employees do not attend work (health, family problems, transportation difficulties), there is evidence that absences are proportional to the number of paid days off offered by an organization. That is, as the number of paid days off increases, the number of days of actual absence increases proportionally. As pay rates rise, absenteeism also increases, with employees potentially "buying" time off. Consequently, because of lax policies, many organizations unwittingly not only tolerate or accept absenteeism, but actually reward it. Their policies make it easier to be absent than to come to work.[50]

Negative strategies to control absenteeism include disciplinary procedures against employees who are absent weekly, once every two weeks, without a physician's excuse, before or after a holiday, after payday, without calling in, or for personal business. Absences for these reasons are subject to employee discipline ranging from oral warnings for first offenses to discharge. Unfortunately, these policies appear to be generally ineffective in controlling absenteeism among habitual offenders.

Programs that reward attendance—cash prizes, bonuses, conversion of a proportion of unused absence days to vacation days—appear more promising. To prevent unscheduled absenteeism, organizations have also moved toward a policy of paid leave for "personal days off." The logic here is that employees must notify officials in advance that they will be absent. As discussed in Chapter 10, self-management programs for habitual offenders also offer some hope to controlling excessive absenteeism.[51]

ON-THE-JOB

Paid benefits for time not worked on–the–job include rest periods, lunch periods, wash-up time and clothes-change and get-ready times. Together these benefits are the fifth most expensive indirect compensation benefit.

Another benefit that is growing in popularity is paid time for physical fitness. This is clearly pay for time not worked, but organizations often offer it because of its benefit—healthy workers.

On-the-job benefits include:

- rest periods
- lunch periods
- clothes-change time
- wash-up time
- get-ready time
- physical fitness facilities

❚ LIFE-CYCLE BENEFITS

In response to a growing number of single parents, two-earner families, employees with aging parents in need of care, and nontraditional families, employers are expanding their benefits packages to address new priorities. As shown in Exhibit 13.6, only a handful of firms currently offer these benefits. However, employers realize that a failure to address these needs in the near future will restrict their ability to compete. Three categories of life-cycle-related benefits—child care, elder care, changing life-style—will be discussed in greater detail below.

LEARNING OBJECTIVE 5

Discuss the alternative life-cycle benefits.

Life-cycle benefits include:

- child-care
- elder care
- life-style changes

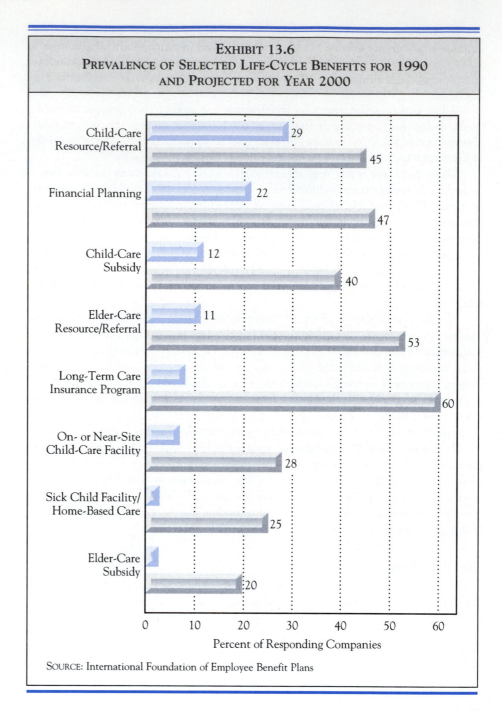

EXHIBIT 13.6
PREVALENCE OF SELECTED LIFE-CYCLE BENEFITS FOR 1990 AND PROJECTED FOR YEAR 2000

Child-Care Resource/Referral: 29, 45
Financial Planning: 22, 47
Child-Care Subsidy: 12, 40
Elder-Care Resource/Referral: 11, 53
Long-Term Care Insurance Program: 60
On- or Near-Site Child-Care Facility: 28
Sick Child Facility/Home-Based Care: 25
Elder-Care Subsidy: 20

Percent of Responding Companies

SOURCE: International Foundation of Employee Benefit Plans

Being family-friendly means the employer offers many life-cycle benefits.

CHILD-CARE SERVICES

Recognizing that child care is a shared responsibility, more and more employers are providing child-care assistance to their employees. In fact, a survey of more than 10,000 firms employing ten or more workers showed that 63 percent of all employers offer some benefits, schedule help, or services relating to child care. Employee preferences for various child-care options vary. Thus, in order to remain competitive, firms need, at a minimum, to survey their employees to find out their preferences, and they may need to offer a variety of options to meet employee needs. Exhibit 13.7 shows a possible list of options that employers can

> ### EXHIBIT 13.7
> ### FAMILY-FRIENDLY BENEFITS
>
> | | | |
> |---|---|---|
> | Summer day camp | On-site child care | Child-care referrals |
> | Scholarships | Elder care | Family-care leave |
> | Summer employment | Flexible schedules | Elder-care referrals |
> | Emergency care for adults | Family-care absence | Spouse relocation |
> | Subsidized tutoring | Relocation planning | Adoption benefits |
> | Sick-child care | Assistance plans | Reimbursement accounts |
>
> SOURCE: Adapted from B. P. Noble, "Making a Case for Family Friendly Programs," *The New York Times*, (May 2, 1993): F 25.

provide. By providing options such as these, employers such as Ben & Jerry's, develop an image of being family-friendly. The benefits of having such an image are described in "Managing Human Resources at Johnson & Johnson and Fel-Pro." While the family-friendly benefits are provided at some cost, employees can share in these costs through dependent-care reimbursement accounts.

DEPENDENT-CARE REIMBURSEMENT ACCOUNTS. Dependent-care reimbursement accounts have become the most prevalent type of child-care benefit in the 1990s. These accounts allow employees to pay for qualified expenses with pretax dollars subject to a use-it-or-lose-it rule. They benefit employees greatly, and they entail minimal administrative costs for the sponsoring organization. The maximum amount an employee can channel into one of these accounts is $5,000 a year. For an employee to participate in a reimbursement account, the child must be under the age of thirteen. Additionally, the expense must be necessary to permit an employee to work, both husband and wife to work, or a spouse to attend school full-time.

For the employee, these accounts offer potential tax advantages. Consider a single parent with a four-year-old daughter. He anticipates child-care expenses of $5,000 in the next year. His projected salary for the next year is $35,000. Listed below is the employee's disposable income without and with an employee-financed dependent-care reimbursement account.

	Without Account	With Account
Gross Salary	$35,000	$35,000
Pre-elected payroll deduction	− 0	− 5,000
	35,000	30,000
Estimated taxes (federal income tax and Social Security)	− 3,115	− 2,670
Net salary	31,885	27,330
Payment from account		+ 5,000
Available income	31,885	32,330
Payment to child-care center	− 5,000	− 5,000
Disposable income	$26,885	$27,330

As shown, the employee has $445 *more* in disposable income using a dependent-care reimbursement account.[53]

Managing Human Resources
at Johnson & Johnson and Fel-Pro

It is hard-sell gospel among advocates of "family-friendly" or "family-supportive" corporate policies that helping employees helps the bottom line. But gospel doesn't crunch as well as numbers, and the unsentimental, lynx-eyed financial types who prowl the balance sheets of corporate America in these lean times tend to be nonbelievers.

Researchers are beginning to accumulate the systematic, hard evidence that advocates need to make their case. According to two studies, companies that make it easier for employees to juggle their work and family responsibilities do reap gains in greater loyalty, increased job satisfaction and lower turnover. The benefits of the policies also seem to reverberate beyond the companies' human resources departments.

"Lavish claims for all the wonderful things work-family programs do always made us nervous because they used an untested hypothesis," said Ellen Galinsky, co-president of the Families and Work Institute, the New York research group that did one of the studies. "We knew lots of studies that showed the cost of not providing programs. Finally we have two studies that begin to address the benefits," she told an audience of human resources executives at the Conference Board's annual family and work conference last week in New York.

The studies were in essence evaluations of work-family programs at Johnson & Johnson (J & J), the consumer and pharmaceuticals giant based in New Brunswick, New Jersey, and Fel-Pro, Inc., a medium-size maker of automotive sealing products based in Skokie, Illinois.

J & J and Fel-Pro both offer an extensive menu of family programs, including on-site child care as well as dependent and elder-care resources and flexible schedules.

The Families and Work Institute found that four years after the J & J "Balancing Work and Family" program began, 38 percent of the employees who responded to the survey said they "strongly agreed" that they felt more comfortable raising personal issues at work. That was up from 18 percent in 1990, when the baseline evaluation was done. And slightly more than half the employees said they strongly agreed that supervisors—who are critical to the success of work-family programs—were responsive to their personal and family needs, up from 36 percent in 1990.

One important consequence of the changes since 1990, said Chris Kjeldsen, a J & J vice president, is that employees no longer feel they have to lie to get permission to take time off if a child is sick or for some other family emergency. "It's bringing about a positive cultural change at J & J," he said.

Nearly three-quarters of the employees who responded to the survey said the family policies were "very important" in deciding whether to stay at the company.

At Fel-Pro, researchers from the University of Chicago found that employees who took advantage of work-family programs were more likely to participate in total-quality management and other programs companies consider critical to their competitiveness. They were also more likely to be "good corporate citizens" who pitched in to help other employees, the researchers said.

Susan Lambert, the Fel-Pro study's principal investigator, said family policies are often seen primarily as a way to attract women to a company. "They have additional benefits," she said. "They can help lay the groundwork for other major cultural changes."

Neither study found evidence to support a fear common among managers that employees will exploit and abuse company programs. At J & J, Mr. Kjeldsen said, there was no increase in absenteeism or tardiness or decrease in productivity even though, because of the economy, people were working longer and had more responsibility.

In both studies, the employees who used and liked family programs most were the highest performers, the least inclined to leave the company and the least likely to have disciplinary problems. Since the J & J program began, employees seem to take their job troubles home less. Given the difficult economic times and the pressure on employees, Ms. Galinsky said, "that is an astonishing finding."[54]

RESOURCE AND REFERRAL PROGRAMS. Child-care information and referral assistance is offered by 29 percent of U.S. firms. These company-sponsored programs counsel employees about day-care options and refer them to prescreened local providers. Prescreening ensures the centers in the network meet minimum care standards and are financially responsible.

The program offered by the Eastman Kodak Company is typical. The leading manufacturer of photographic products and health-care products contracted with Work/Family Directions, Inc., a national organization that specialized in child-care resources and issues to maintain its Child-Care Resource and Referral Program. To provide Kodak employees with detailed information and referrals, Work/Family directors established contracts with community-based child-care agencies through the country. Because not all areas have sufficient child-care services, Kodak also has provided start-up costs to develop child-care programs in areas of short supply. During the program's first eighteen months, Kodak's funding resulted in the addition of 650 family day-care homes in communities where Kodak employees live.

Steelcase employs a child-care administrator whose staff evaluates day-care centers and family-care homes. An employee survey of users indicates that more than 90 percent of the employees who use the Steelcase program feel more relaxed and productive at work.[54]

> Steelcase employees feel more productive because of the company's child-care benefits.

At the 3M Company in St. Paul, Minnesota, Working Parent Resource Fairs are held biannually to give employees the chance to peruse a range of parent or child-related services. "In the spring, parents look for what to do with kids during the summer," Suzanne T. Osten, child-care administrator, noted. "We hold the fair early to give them time to plan ahead." Typically, more than 600 employees attend the four-hour fair (total cost to 3M is only $2,000), which features exhibitors from 67 organizations. Exhibits range from church social services, Parents Without Partners, the Minnesota Council for the Gifted and Talented, Minnesota Safe Kids Project, and Science Museum of Minnesota. Employers are given time off from work to attend the fair and shop for services.[55]

ON-SITE CARE FACILITIES. By 1994, there were more than 2,500 employer-sponsored on-site or near-site care centers in operation. In San Francisco, office and hotel complexes with more than 50,000 square feet must either provide an on-site facility or pay into a city child-care fund. Although the operation of such centers can be costly, a growing number of employers now accept the burden of operating and funding such centers as a social and business necessity.

Consider the comments of Dick Parker, director of administrative services for Merck & Co., at groundbreaking ceremonies for its $8 million child-care center:

> You don't provide child care just because you want to be a good guy. You do it for business reasons, Merck decided to build the center for three reasons: retention, recruitment, and productivity. Child care will become more and more of a recruitment issue in the future. If employees are worried about their child-care services, that will affect their productivity and retention.[56]

Linda Fitzpatrick, director of human resources for Gentech, a pharmaceutical company in the San Francisco area, makes a similar point noting that, "Providing a near-site center makes good business sense. Not only is the center a great recruiting tool, but we've found that employees come back to work sooner after maternity leave because they know that their child is receiving quality, nearby care." Gentech's center is open from 6:45 A.M. to 7:00 P.M. and accepts children from six weeks to six years of age. The building is maintained by Gentech, but the program is operated by an independent child-care group.

Employees pay between $390 and $490 per month (depending on age). The company offers a 50 percent scholarship to employees who earn less than $25,000.

Campbell Soup Company's child-care center is located across the street from its corporate headquarters and cares for 110 children. Contending that on-site care cuts absenteeism, reduces distractions for employees, and helps with hiring, the company picks up 40 percent of the weekly expense for each child. The Hacienda Child Development Center in Pleasanton, California, serves multiple employers (for example, Hewlett-Packard, Computerland, Prudential Insurance Company). Operating costs are funded from parent fees and business fees. Employees working in the Hacienda Business Park receive a discount on monthly rates.

ELDER CARE

Elder care will continue to grow because of the large number of baby-boomers.

Of employees over the age of 30, 28 percent currently spend an average of ten hours a week giving care to an older relative. For a significant fraction, this commitment equals a second job. Some 12 percent of workers who care for aging parents are forced to quit their jobs to do so. With the continued aging of the baby-boomers, more and more employers are considering ways to assist workers who are caring for elderly relatives. Assistance ranges from information and referral programs to specialized care insurance. As described earlier, the *Family and Medical Leave Act of 1993* supports employee time off for both child care and elder care.

INFORMATION AND REFERRAL PROGRAMS. In 1990, only 11 percent of employers offered elder-care information and referral programs to link employees with community resources that already exist; by the year 2000, the number could exceed 50 percent. Like the dependent-care programs discussed previously, company-operated elder-care referral programs are designed to assist the care giver in identifying appropriate community resources.

To address the need for elder-care assistance *and* stay within the budget, First Interstate Bank of California has entered into a public-private partnership with the County Division on Aging. The agency is a member of a nationwide elder-care resource and referral system. Linked into the system, First Interstate employees call a toll-free number and talk to a counselor about what resources they need and in what city they're needed. The counselor calls back with a list of potential resources including at-home care for the elderly, day-care centers, and support groups for the care giver.[57]

ELDER-CARE CENTERS. Recognizing that elder care is not always available, a small but growing number of firms are offering on-site or corporate-financed elder-care centers. The Stride Rite Corporation, a leading marketer of high-quality footwear for children and adults, is a leader in this venture. Stride Rite has had an on-site child-care center since 1971. In 1990, the firm opened the Stride Rite Intergenerational Day-Care Center, which houses 55 children between the ages of 15 months and 6 years and 24 elders who are over the age of 60. Group activities include reading and writing stories, cooking and eating, card games, and field trips, and routinely bring elders and children together. Employees pay a percentage of their annual household income through payroll deduction.[58]

LONG-TERM CARE INSURANCE. One of the newest and fastest growing options is long-term care insurance. While only 8 percent of firms currently offer this benefit, nearly 70 percent of companies are expected to offer this elder-care option by the year 2000. This type of insurance covers medical, social, custodial, and personal services for people who suffer from chronic physical or mental illnesses or disabling injury or disease over an extended period of time. Typically, coverage is offered to employees on an employee-pay-all basis. Premium rates are age-based, and in some plans there is a maximum age (typically 79) for participation. Benefit maximums are related to care site (nursing home versus day-care center) and include lifetime limits.[59]

CHANGING LIFE-STYLES

With demographic and value shifts, there is not a wider array of life-styles than ever before in our country. As a consequence, a rising percentage of workers—unmarried couples, divorced people, same sex domestic partners, single parents—do not fit into conventional benefits packages. Recognizing that people are assets to the organization and that the world of work can never be fully separated from the rest of one's life, cutting-edge companies are redesigning their benefits packages to address the needs of all employees.

ADOPTION BENEFITS.   In 1989, the Communications Workers of America (CWA) negotiated a benefit plan with AT&T that provides a $2,000 allowance per adoption. That agreement is expected to serve as a model for other unions to follow as part of their bargaining strategy for the 1990s. An adoption benefit plan is a company-sponsored program that financially assists or reimburses employees for the costs associated with the adoption of a child. The most frequently covered benefits include adoption agency fees, attorney fees, and court costs. Some plans also include paid or unpaid leave, and a handful cover pregnancy care expenses for the birth mother.

BENEFITS FOR SPOUSAL EQUIVALENTS.   The Lotus Development Corporation, the Cambridge, Massachusetts, software company, modified its insurance and benefits policy to offer the partners of homosexual employees the same benefits accorded heterosexual spouses. According to Russell J. Campanello, vice president for human resources, "This is fair and equal." Lotus's decision did not come easily. In 1989, three workers began petitioning Lotus for spousal benefits. Even after Lotus agreed, it took the company and the three employees two years to develop a workable policy. The insurance carrier that pays Lotus's claims above $140,000 was reluctant to take on more homosexual enrollees, largely because of potential AIDS-related bills. After researching the actual costs carefully, Lotus convinced the carrier that the cost was not a seven-digit dollar issue but about the same as treating a coronary patient, Campanello said.

Premiums for the 12 "spousal equivalents" currently enrolled in the program cost Lotus about $30,000, none of which is tax deductible because the IRS doesn't recognize unmarried partners. Participating employees pay about $1,350 in taxes a year on the premium's benefits. To be eligible, a couple must live together and share financial obligations. If they break up, the employee must wait one year before registering a new partner. In addition to health care, the plan includes life insurance, relocation expenses, bereavement leave, and a death benefit.[60]

EDUCATIONAL EXPENSE ALLOWANCES.   Faced with skill obsolescence, downsizing, and retraining demands, almost 75 percent of all medium and large firms provided some form of educational expense assistance. Most plans cover registration fees, and some assist with graduation fees, laboratory expenses, entrance examinations, professional certification, and activity fees. Typically, these programs require a relationship between the course and some phase of company operations. For example, National Healthcorp, which is headquartered in Murfreesboro, Tennessee, offers tuition assistance to any aide who wishes to become a nurse. The company will pay for up to two years of school in exchange for the aide's promise to stay on staff that long after graduation.

Educational assistance has also become a negotiated benefit for unions. During collective bargaining negotiations in 1982, the Ford Motor Company and the United Automobile Workers agreed that jointly developed and provided training and retraining programs should be made available to UAW-represented workers. Funded with five cents for every hour worked by every hourly worker, the program provides a variety of benefits. These include a tuition assistance program that provides workers with up to $2,000 per year; a skills enhancement program that focuses on basic education and English as a second language; preretirement counseling; a life/education planning program that provides career counseling to eligible employees; and the college and university options program that facilitates college entry and success.[61]

ADMINISTRATIVE ISSUES

Although organizations tend to view indirect compensation as a reward, recipients do not always see it that way. This causes organizations to become concerned with their package of indirect compensation benefits and how they are administered.

DETERMINING THE BENEFITS PACKAGE

The benefits package should be selected on the basis of what is good for the employee as well as for the employer. Often, knowing employee preferences can determine which benefits should be offered. For example, employees may have a strong preference for dental insurance over life insurance, even though dental insurance may be only one-fourth the cost to the company. As workers get older, their desire for higher pension benefits increases steadily. This is also the case for employees with rising incomes. Employees with children prefer greater hospitalization benefits than those without.[62]

Organizations are constrained, however, by their size in the feasibility of what they can offer. According to Jordan Shields, owner of a consulting firm specializing in benefits:

> Companies that have fewer than ten employees may have difficulty finding an insurance carrier, even for basic medical. Dental and vision care insurance options aren't very good. Disability plans for these small companies will be either very restrictive or very expensive.
>
> "If there are between 10 and 24 employees," says Shields, "vision, dental and disability options are OK. Medical options are a bit easier to find than for the smallest firms, but it still isn't a breeze. At that size, there's no flexibility to offer more than one medical plan." Only after a company has at least 25 employees can it begin to offer a choice of medical plans. In fact, Shields says, federal law requires that companies that have 25 employees or more may be obligated to offer more than one plan—an HMO and an indemnity plan.
>
> Companies having more than 50 employees, and certainly those with more than 100, have more options and can even participate in partial self-insurance programs. "If you self-insure, then you, as the employer, retain part of the risk for the health of the employee," says Shields. "You're acting partially as the insurance company, which means that if your employees stay fairly healthy and don't file a lot of claims, you won't pay as much in premiums."

Administrative issues in indirect compensation include:

- determining benefits package
- providing benefit flexibility
- communicating benefits package

As companies grow, they encounter fewer limitations. A firm that has 300–400 employees can choose from among many options and carriers and can establish a large plan that can be modified easily. However, a firm that grows from 10 to 150 employees within a year or two—which isn't at all unusual for these fast-growing companies—will have major changes to make. Unfortunately, like many other functions at young, fast-growing firms, benefits management tends to lag behind the more urgent line functions.[63]

PROVIDING BENEFIT FLEXIBILITY

When employees can design their own benefits package, both they and the company profit.[64] At least that is the experience at companies such as IBM, Ford Motor Company, TRW, the Educational Testing Service (ETS), and Morgan Stanley. At ETS, the company provides a core package of benefits to all employees covering basic needs such as personal medical care, dental care, disability, vacation, and retirement. In addition, each individual can choose, cafeteria-style, from optional benefits or increase those in the core package. Employees are allowed to change their packages once a year.

At Morgan Stanley, about two-thirds of its eligible employees elected their own benefit package over the standard no-choice plan. The options themselves were developed by the employees working in small group discussions. A benefits survey conducted in 1985 supports that many employees, if given the chance, would modify their benefits package.[65]

COMMUNICATING THE BENEFITS PACKAGE

Providing benefit flexibility is good not only because it gives employees what they are more likely to want, but also because it makes them aware of the benefits they are gaining and thereby not only increase their morale (because they feel well protected), but also increases their commitment to the organization.[66] Many employees are unaware of the costs of benefits and even of which benefits they are receiving. If employees have no knowledge of their benefits, there is little reason to believe the organization's benefit program objectives will be attained. Many organizations indicate that they assign a high priority to telling employees about their benefits. However, a majority spend only $10 per employee per year doing this, and the average benefits package costs over $13,000 per employee! Through communicating the benefits package and providing employees with benefit flexibility, the positive impact of indirect compensation can be increased.

INTERNATIONAL COMPARISONS

CANADA

In Canada, the sharpest contrasts with the United States concerning compensation are found in indirect compensation, particularly pensions and health care. For example, Canada has the Canada Pension Plan (CPP) and the Quebec Pension Plan in the province of Quebec, both of which are similar to the U.S. Social Security system. CPP is a mandatory plan for all employees except federal workers. Like the Social Security system, CPP pays retirement benefits, disability pensions, benefits for children of disabled contributors, orphans' benefits, and pension benefits to survivors' spouses. Canada also has private pension plans, although fewer than 40 percent of all employees are covered by these plans. The administration of these plans is governed by the *Pension Benefits Act*, which is

less extensive in its regulation of private pension plans than the *U.S. Employees' Retirement Income Security Act*.

Canada has a national health care system that covers virtually the entire population. This system is called a "single-payer" plan because the government pays for the health care costs. As a consequence of this, employers do not contribute to employee health care as they do in the U.S. This system, rather than having employers offer health care benefits directly to their employees, has employers contribute to the national health care fund. The result is that all employees are covered rather than only those employees who happen to work for employers who provide the coverage for their workers.

Because the Canadian health care system has often been seen as a possible model for the U.S., recent reports on the impact of implementing national health care were read with interest. Published by the Canadian National Bureau of Economic Research, the study indicated that since the inception of the national health care (in the late 1960s), employment levels and wages levels rose rather than fell (this was the prediction because the system required employers to pay based upon the number of employees). The explanation for the finding was that the national health care system raises labor productivity by improving employee health and by making it easier for employees to change jobs. The result is that employers are more willing to hire workers.

HOURS OF WORK

There are major differences in the hours worked by employees. These differences typically result from the variation in the number of vacation days and holidays granted to employees. And while you might think that more time off would result in less absenteeism once back on the job, this is not always the case. In Exhibit 13.8 are some numbers showing the variation in hours of work per week and absenteeism rates for several nations.

Yes, it appears that life is pretty comfortable in the four European nations, and it probably is! But with the worldwide competition, there is tremendous pressure to reduce paid vacation and holidays in these countries. Of course, this is not easy, because of social customs, the union movement and the rate of unemployment in Europe. The rate of unemployment, now above 10%, is a major social concern of the European Union, and one way to deal with this is to reduce the work week for each worker! This results in a clash between the needs of society for less unemployment and the needs of companies to reduce their labor costs by reducing paid vacations and holidays![67]

CURRENT TRENDS

The trends discussed in the previous two chapters also relate to and are likely to influence the administration of indirect compensation during the remainder of the 1990s. These trends include the linking of compensation to organizational strategy and to the organization's life cycle. But one that is uniquely related to indirect compensation is the trend to manage and reduce costs.

MANAGING AND REDUCING INDIRECT COMPENSATION COSTS

As stated earlier, the costs of indirect compensation have been rising rapidly during the past decade. Today, the average is almost $14,000 per employee, almost 50 percent of the cost of the total pay for time worked! Health-care costs alone account for almost $4,000 of this total, and they are increasing at upwards

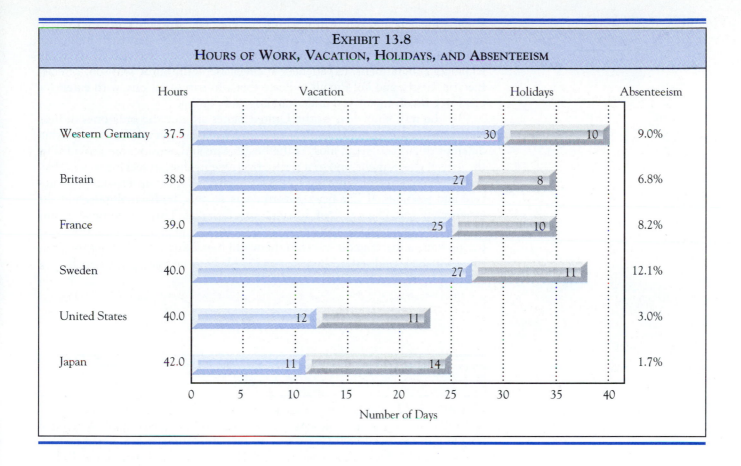

EXHIBIT 13.8
HOURS OF WORK, VACATION, HOLIDAYS, AND ABSENTEEISM

	Hours	Vacation	Holidays	Absenteeism
Western Germany	37.5	30	10	9.0%
Britain	38.8	27	8	6.8%
France	39.0	25	10	8.2%
Sweden	40.0	27	11	12.1%
United States	40.0	12	11	3.0%
Japan	42.0	11	14	1.7%

Number of Days

of 10 percent yearly. This is at the same time that global competition is increasing, particularly from nations whose direct and indirect compensation costs are one-tenth that of those in the United States.

While the role of the federal government in health care may level the playing field for competitors within the United States and is likely to provide health-care benefits to more Americans, U.S. employers will still continue to pay significantly for health care for their own workers.

Thus the trend is clear: manage and reduce benefit costs. Managing costs means having second opinions and fewer choices in health-care coverage. It means making sure that a disability is really a disability and that workers get back to work as soon as possible. It means being proactive and seeking ways to prevent sickness and injury (in this respect, the HR professionals in compensation need to work closely with those in health and safety). These all represent programs that a few companies are already doing—for example, Steelcase with disability and workers' compensation. Many more are likely to start such programs before the year 2000.

Perhaps addressed by fewer employers is the question, "By managing and reducing benefit costs, do you mean eliminating benefits?" Certainly firms are asking workers to participate in their own health care and even retirement costs. This is a big issue in the automobile industry. It is certainly consistent with employee empowerment and self-management. Workers are certainly capable of understanding business and cost conditions. By providing workers with benefit information, they may be able to assist in the cost-reduction process without eliminating benefits. Win-win situations can be created where costs are reduced and yet coverage is maintained. And when it is coverage that each individual needs, the employer is likely not only to reduce costs, but also to maintain employee commitment. Experiences at Steelcase, Johnson & Johnson, Lincoln Electric, Coors, and Fel-Pro all indicate that win-win situations, with extensive employee involvement and understanding, are possible.

By the way, employers in the United States are not the only ones dealing with benefit costs. Employers in Canada and Europe, however, face a somewhat different situation. There, most of the health care and pensions are provided by the federal government, and so it is the governments that, in seeking ways to balance their budgets, are moving to extricate themselves from providing health care and pensions. If European governments do this, both employees and the governments are likely to look to employers for relief. This is coming at a time when many European employers are already providing generous vacations and paying some of the highest wages in the world (see Exhibit 11.8). Thus the pressure to manage and reduce benefit costs is likely to be even greater in Europe than it is in the United States.

SUMMARY

Chapters 11, 12, and 13 have addressed frequently asked questions in organization orientation programs such as, "How much do I get paid?" and "When and how long is my vacation?" Organizations have traditionally responded to both questions with, "More than ever before." This has occurred despite the lack of evidence that indirect compensation attains the purposes of total compensation. Money, job challenge, and opportunities for advancement appear to serve the purposes of compensation as much as, if not more than, pension benefits, disability provisions, and services, especially for employees aspiring to managerial careers.

This is not to say, however, that employees do not desire indirect benefits; they can be motivational under the right conditions. Organizations have offered indirect benefits at such a rapid rate in part because employees desired them. The specific benefits offered by an organization have not always been valued, however, nor have employees necessarily known what benefits were offered. As a result of the existence now of the "right conditions" detailed above, some organizations are soliciting employee opinions about their preferences for compensation programs. Organizations are communicating their benefits programs more clearly today. Current evidence suggests that employees' lack of awareness of the contents and value of their benefit programs may partially explain why the programs were not perceived more favorably. Increased communication and more employee participation in the benefits packages will increase the likelihood that the organization benefits from providing indirect compensation; indirect benefits are motivational under the right conditions. And those conditions exist now: (1) The media blitz on the health-care crisis has probably made more workers aware of their coverage, or lack thereof, than all the company education programs combined. Workers are starting to say, "Wow, I've got a good deal here;" (2) Our aging population—the baby-boomers are on the brink of midlife—is about to start focusing more than ever before on pension funds and the like, especially with the coming crisis in Social Security; and (3) Now that the two-income family is the rule and not the exception, parents of young children and children of aging parents are looking to the workplace for solutions as to how to juggle these demands that often conflict with the demands of a job.

These benefits do not come without costs, although some benefits may be gained at less cost than others. To ensure that an organization is getting the most from its indirect compensation, thorough assessments must be made of what the organization is doing, what other organizations are doing, and what employees prefer to see the organization doing.

To improve the motivational value of indirect compensation, organizations should try to provide what employees want. As with direct compensation, employees, being human, will continue to want more benefits. For example, employees want greater retirement benefits, more health and insurance coverage, and more time off. Demands for dental coverage, eye care, and legal services will probably increase. Greater educational and career development opportunities are also preferred benefits. However, not all employees will want the same benefits. For example, younger employees may have a stronger preference for insurance benefits, time off, child-care assistance, and educational benefits, while older employees may have a greater interest in elder-care referrals, retirement benefits, and preretirement counseling opportunities.

In addition to providing a wide range of benefits to employees, numerous federal and state laws must be taken into account and observed. Federal laws, such as the *Family and Medical Leave Act*, the *Equal Pay Act*, and the *Americans with Disabilities Act*, have a significant influence on indirect compensation. Ignoring these federal laws and various state laws will result in fines and penalties, thus reducing the effectiveness of indirect compensation.

As more U.S. firms move into international markets, the need to understand international compensation increases in importance. As U.S. multinational corporations send more expatriates abroad, they will need to weigh the costs against the benefits. They will also need to provide training and development programs to reduce the expatriate failure rate. These and other programs are discussed in the next chapter.

KEY CONCEPTS

contributory programs
cost-sharing
defined-benefit plan
defined-contribution
    plan
employee assistance
    programs (EAPs)
employee stock
    ownership plan
    (ESOP)
flexible spending plans
health maintenance
    organizations
    (HMOs)
indirect compensation

Individual Retirement
    Account (IRA)
money purchase plans
noncontributory
    programs
nonqualified plan
Pension Benefit
    Guaranty
    Corporation
    (PBGC)
portable
Preferred Provider
    Organization
    (PPOs)

private protection
    programs
protection programs
public protection
    programs
qualified plan
supplemental
    unemployment
    benefits
tax-deferred profit-
    sharing plans
vesting
workers' compensation
    insurance

REVIEW AND DISCUSSION QUESTIONS

1. What are the purposes of indirect compensation? How can these purposes best be met?
2. In what sense is indirect compensation "indirect"?
3. What are some of the historical and legislative events that have shaped the growth of indirect compensation?
4. Describe the problems that could be encountered in administering a flexible, or cafeteria-style, indirect compensation program.
5. Distinguish between public and private protection programs, and give examples of each.
6. How would you rationalize the benefit to the organization of providing a physical fitness facility and program for the work force? How would you assess and compare benefits and costs?
7. For each broad category of indirect compensation, describe the incentives that the employer and the employee have for minimizing the cost of this benefit.
8. Explain how the hours of work vary across Japan, U.S. and Germany.
9. Describe compensation aspects of a family-friendly company.
10. Can small firms offer much indirect compensation?

EXERCISES AND CASES

REVIEW

QUESTIONS AND ANSWERS ABOUT WELLNESS PROGRAMS IN AMERICAN CORPORATIONS

Q#1. For every dollar invested in wellness programs, the average return to the company that invested it is: . . .$3.

Q#2. What is the percentage of U.S. companies with 50 or more employees that offer some form of wellness program? . . . 78%.

Q#3. By 1993, American companies paid an average of $4,000 *per employee for health care.* This figure amounts to 14% of the average company payroll.

Q#4. How many employee workdays in the United States are lost every year due to illness and injury? . . . 500 million.

Q#5. Name one of the two most common causes for the loss of workdays in the United States:

a. cold/flu; b. *back problems;* c. high blood pressure; d. alcoholism; e. *heart disease;* f. drug abuse. Back problems accounted for nearly 93 million lost workdays per year, while heart disease contributed some 26 million lost workdays to the total.

Q#6. Name one of the four cornerstones of an effective employee wellness program.

The four cornerstones of an effective employee wellness program are: **smoking policy** (smoking cessation); **alcohol policy** (alcohol abuse education); **good nutrition** (weight control); **regular exercise** (gym facilities or access to them).

Q#7. What is the most common benefit from regular exercise?

a. enhanced energy; b. weight control; c. *reduced stress*; d. improved concentration. Of the people who participate in wellness programs that include regular exercise, 90% have reported reduced stress; 60% have reported enhanced energy; 50% have reported successful weight control; 15% have reported improved concentration.

Q#8. The minimum suggested amount of cardiovascular exercise per week is . . . 20 minutes/three times a week.

Q#9. What is the most common activity in wellness programs in the United States? . . . smoking cessation— 63%.

Q#10. At the turn of the century, pneumonia and influenza were the leading causes of death in the United States. What is the top cause of death today? a. cancer; b. *heart disease*; c. work-related accidents; d. leukemia; e. spontaneous combustion.

Q#11. Which factor contributes to the most deaths?

a. human biology; b. environment; c. health care d. *lifestyle*.

Did you know?

The leading causes of death, which had been infectious diseases, have been replaced by chronic diseases associated with unhealthy behavior. Seven of the ten leading causes of death in the United States could be substantially reduced if persons at risk improve just five habits: diet, smoking, lack of exercise, alcohol abuse, and use of antihypertensive medication.

Q#12. Which of the following is the most common health risk among American workers? a. stress; b. *sedentary life-style*; c. high blood cholesterol; d. smoking.

Q#13. What percentage of American workers find their job very stressful? . . . 72%.

Q#14. What is the most common cause of stress in the workplace in the United States? a. *not doing the kind of work I want to do*; b. working too hard; c. colleagues at work; d. a difficult boss.

Q#15. What is the most current estimate for the aggregate yearly cost of stress to U.S. business? . . . 300 billion dollars.

SOURCE: Contributed by a great student group at the Stern School of Business, New York University, Spring 1993.

FIELD PROJECT

Interview a human resource manager in a local company and ask about their benefits program. How has it changed in the past several years? What methods are used to communicate the program to employees? How do they measure the effectiveness of the benefits? How do they know what the employees want, and what are the future of benefits in the company?

CAREER MANAGEMENT EXERCISE: SPEAKING OF BENEFITS

In the Career Management Exercise in Chapter 12, you provided a list of what it would take to get you to work at my firm (direct compensation). Your request there totaled 100 percent. But we now know that total compensation is composed of important indirect components, as well as the direct ones. So, in this exercise, you need to first indicate how much of your total compensation (percentage) you want (are willing) to have in direct and indirect compensation. Then you will go on and provide breakdowns for the other areas. Remember, this is what you are asking the employer to pay (give you). Indirect compensation for you in the form of legal payments (such as Social Security and worker's compensation) by the employer costs approximately 22% (Exhibit 13.5) of total compensation. These should therefore be included in your calculations. Therefore, if you want your total compensation to be 60%

direct and 40% indirect, 22% of the indirect is already taken care of with the legal payments.

1. Indicate the percentages of total compensation:
   _____ % Direct compensation (from Chapter 12)
        _____ % Base
        _____ % Performance-based
   _____ % Indirect compensation

2. This part is a bit more challenging because you must estimate what each benefit costs and calculate its percentage of indirect compensation. Use the dollar estimates of your direct compensation from item 2 in the exercise in Chapter 12. But try to make your estimates as realistic and detailed as possible by referring to Exhibit 13.5 and discussions throughout the chapter. Begin by using these general categories and expand as needed.

$ _____ ; _____ % Health and medical insurance
$ _____ ; _____ % Dental care
$ _____ ; _____ % Eye care
$ _____ ; _____ % Retirement/pension contributions
$ _____ ; _____ % Disability, short and long term
$ _____ ; _____ % Wellness, exercise programs
$ _____ ; _____ % Vacation days; holidays
     _____ # of days each: _____ / _____

$ _____ ; _____ % Family-friendly benefits
Enter choices from Exhibit 13.7.

_____

_____

_____

$ _____ ; _____ % Stock ownership plan
$ _____ ; _____ % Other? Describe and indicate percentage.

_____

_____

3. Of these items you have indicated you want the company to pay for (give you), indicate which ones you would be willing to pay for and indicate the percentage after the items:

_____ %
_____ %
_____ %
_____ %
_____ %
_____ %

4. In summary, what is the dollar value of your typical year's total compensation.

    $ _____ Direct $ _____ Total
    $ _____ Indirect

CASE

WHO'S BENEFITING?

Jack Parks is a benefits manager in the auto electronics division of USA Motors, a major manufacturer of audio systems and auto electronic ignition systems. He is very concerned after analyzing the impact of absenteeism on the division's staffing costs for the previous quarter. What troubles Jack is an agreement that the national union negotiated with USA Motors ten years ago that, in effect, paid workers for being absent. Of course, the "paid absence" agreement was not supposed to work quite that way. In theory, workers were given one week of paid absence against which they could charge their personal absences. Presumably, this system would encourage workers to notify their supervisors so that staffing arrangements could be made and production maintained.

In practice, workers discovered that by not charging off any "paid absences," they could receive a full week's pay in June when the company paid off the balance of the unused paid absences for the previous year. This cash bonus, as workers had come to think of it, often coincides with the summer vacation taken by many of the 8,000 hourly employees in June when USA Motors shuts down for inventory.

As Jack learned, employees with chronic absentee records had figured out how to charge off absences using the regular categories, which permits sick days, excused, and unexcused absences. In Jack's mind, USA Motors might just as well have negotiated a cash bonus for hourly workers or given them another 10–15 cents per hour.

After reviewing the division's absenteeism rates for controllable absences—that is, those categories of absences believed to be under the employee's own violation—Jack concludes that the company could reduce this rate from the previous year's figure of 11 percent. And then Jack has a brainstorm: what USA Motors needs to negotiate is an incentive plan for reducing absenteeism. The plan Jack has in mind entails a standard for the amount of controllable absence deemed acceptable. If a chronically absent employee exceeds the standard, then vacation, holiday, and sickness/accident pay would be cut by 10 percent during the next six months. If worker absence continues to exceed the allowable limits, then vacation, holiday, and sickness pay would be cut during the next six months by the actual percentage of absent days incurred by the chronic absentee. Hence, if a worker misses 15 percent of scheduled work days during the first six-month period, vacation pay for the next six-month period would be reduced by 10 percent. If the employee continues to be absent at the 15 percent rate, then vacation pay would be reduced by 15 percent during the next six months.

Jack immediately drafted a memorandum outlining the program and submitted it to the corporate HR manager of USA Motors for inclusion in the upcoming bargaining session. To Jack's surprise and delight, the memorandum received strong corporate support and is scheduled as a high priority bargaining topic for the fall negotiations.

CASE QUESTIONS

1. Will the incentive plan to reduce absenteeism succeed?
2. How much absenteeism is really under the employee's control?
3. Why didn't the "paid absence" plan work?
4. What plan would you suggest to USA Motors?

CASE

FLOWERS OR FIASCO?

Although secretaries, like any group of good employees, should be complimented and recognized for good work throughout the year, many organizations save their plaudits for secretaries' week. Generally, secretaries' week occurs in the spring, just at the time the doldrums of winter are leaving and the fragrances of the new season are most inviting. Thus, the secretaries of a particular university were especially delighted to be given a day off during secretaries' week last year. Like the students and faculty, they were able to enjoy a beautiful, sunny spring day. Though this fringe benefit of a day off was not planned nor formally agreed to, the secretaries were looking forward to the same thing this year. This was especially true because the winter was a severe one, and many of the secretaries had put in extra hours without pay during the year.

Consequently, the secretaries were extremely displeased, some even angry, when, on the first day of secretaries' week, the dean of the school sent them flowers. Since last year they received a day off, but no flowers, they assumed that this gesture meant they would not get a day off. And they were right! Offended and angered, they "forgot" to send the dean a note thanking him for the flowers. Several weeks passed, and the dean realized he had not received the traditional thank-you note. Puzzled, the dean related what had happened to Professor Freedman, a human relations specialist on the faculty. Professor Freedman, sensitive to the needs of both the dean and the secretaries, later that day asked the head secretary to tell him about secretaries' week. After learning the secretaries' interpretation of what had happened, Professor Freedman shared this with the dean. After the professor left, the dean muttered to himself, "It doesn't pay to try to be nice to people nowadays."

CASE QUESTIONS

1. Do you agree with the dean's final statement?
2. Where did the dean go wrong?
3. Do you think the secretaries should have been happy with the flowers? Were they ungrateful?
4. What should the dean do next year? Is there anything he should do now?

1. J. J. Laabs, "Steelcase Slashes Workers' Comp Costs," *Personnel Journal* (Feb. 1993): 72–87; "Workers' Comp Strategy Saves $4 Million Yearly," *Personnel Journal* (Jan. 1993): 55.

2. *U.S. Chamber of Commerce's 27th Survey of Employee Benefits* (U.S. Chamber of Commerce, 1615 H. St. N.W., Washington, D.C. 20062); *ERISA: The Law and the Code*, eds. D. J. Domone and D. A. Sayre (Edison, N.J.: BNA Books, 1990); "Fringe Benefits in Medium and Large Firms," *Bulletin to Management Datagraph* (Sept. 6, 1990): 284–286. Employers, however, may still provide benefits, see B. J. Coleman, *Primer on Employee Retirement Income Security Act*, 3rd ed. (Washington, D.C.: Bureau of National Affairs, 1989).

3. "Chamber's Employee Benefits Survey," *Bulletin to Management Datagraph* (Jan. 10, 1991): 4–6. Also see "Fringe Benefits in Medium and Large Firms," *Bulletin to Management* (Sept. 6, 1990): 284–286.

4. *Ibid.*

5. "Americans on Benefits: Keep Them Coming," *HR Reporter* (Feb. 1991): 4–5; M. Freudenheim, "The Price of Worker Health Care," *The New York Times* (March 2, 1993): D1; S. Caudron, "Teaming Up to Cut Health-care Costs," *Personnel Journal* (Sept. 1993): 104–118.

6. T. Chauran, "Benefits Communication," *Personnel Journal* (Jan. 1989): 70–77.

7. T. J. Bergmann and M. A. Bergmann, "How Important Are Fringe Benefits to Employees?" *Personnel* (Dec. 1987): 59–64: R. M. McCaffery, *Employee Benefit Programs: A Total Compensation Perspective* (Boston, Mass.: PWS-Kent, 1988).

8. For an excellent discussion of what attracts individuals to organizations, see D. P. Schwab, "Recruiting and Organizational Participation," in *Personnel Management,* eds. K. M. Rowland and G. R. Ferris (Boston, Mass.: Allyn and Bacon, 1982), 103–128.

9. Freudenheim (*op. cit.*, see Note 5).

10. "Permissible Pregnancy Practices," *Fair Employment Practices* (Dec., 1983): 3. *The Pregnancy Disability Amendment* also has other provisions; for a description of them, see S. R. Zacur and W. Greenwood, "The Pregnancy Disability Amendment: What the Law Provides, Part II," *Personnel Administrator* (March 1982): 55–58.

11. R. Pear, "Disabled and Chronically Ill Gain Health Coverage and Job Rights," *The New York Times* (June 9, 1991): A15.

12. *Ibid.*

13. B. P. Noble, "Interpreting the Family Leave Act," *The New York Times* (August 1, 1993): F24. Also see D. Gunsch, "The Family Leave Act: A Financial Burden?" *Personnel Journal* (Sept. 1993): 48–57.

14. *Ibid.*

15. The Bureau of National Affairs, "ERISA's Effects on Pension Plan Administration," *Bulletin to Management* (Aug. 9, 1984): 1–2; K. D. Gill, ed., *ERISA: The Law and the Code*, 1985 ed. (Washington, D.C.: Bureau of National Affairs, 1985): B. J. Coleman, *Primer on Employee Retirement Income Security Act* (Washington, D.C.: The Bureau of National Affairs, 1985).

16. R. M. McCaffery, *Employee Benefit Programs: A Total Compensation Perspective* (Boston, Mass.: PWS-Kent, 1988); Bureau of National Affairs (*loc. cit.*, see Note 15); Coleman and Gill (both *op. cit.*, see Note 15).

17. J. A. LoCicero, "How to Cope with the Multi-Employer Pension Plan Amendments Act of 1980," *Personnel Administrator* (May 1981): 51–54, 68; J. A. LoCicero, "Multi-Employer Pension Plans: A Time Bomb for Employers?" *Personnel Journal* (Nov. 1980): 922–924, 932.

18. J. Case, "ESOPs: Dead or Alive?" *INC.* (June 1988): 94–100: P. Nulty, "What a Difference Owner-Bosses Make," *Fortune* (April 25, 1988): 97–104.

19. "The Real Strengths of Employee Stock Ownership," *Business Week* (July 15, 1991): 156.

20. D. Schwartz, "The Last Word on Section 89," *Personnel Journal* (Jan. 1989): 48–57; R. E. Johnson and S. J. Velleman, "Section 89: Close the New Pandora's Box," *Personnel Journal* (Nov. 1988): 70–78; J. Ortman. "Section 89: Why You Should Act Now," *Personnel Journal* (Nov. 1988): 78–79.

21. *FEP Guidelines* (Oct. 1991): 3.

22. "1993 State Unemployment Insurance Taxable Wage Bases," *Bulletin to Management* (Nov. 26, 1992): 1, 2.

23. McCaffery, (*op. cit.*, see Note 16); B. S. Murphy, W. E. Barlow, and D. D. Hatch, "Unemployment Compensation and Religious Beliefs," *Personnel Journal* (June 1987): 36–43; L. Uchitelle, "Jobless Insurance System Aids Reduced Number of Workers," *The New York Times* (July 26, 1988): 1.

24. "Workers' Compensation: Total Disability Benefits," *Bulletin to Management Datagraph* (May 19, 1988): 156–157.

25. P. Kerr, "Fraud Pushes Worker's Comp. Near Crisis," *Seattle Times* (Dec. 29, 1991): A4.

26. *Managing Workers' Compensation Costs* (New York: William M. Mercer Company, 1991); A Tramposh, *Avoiding the Cracks: A Guide to the Workers' Compensation System* (New York: Praeger, 1991).

27. "Injured Workers: Cost-Cutting Rehabilitation Option," *Bulletin to Management* (Oct. 15, 1987): 330, 335.

28. M. W. Fitzgerald, "How to Take on Workers' Compensation and Win," *Personnel Journal* (July 1991); 31–33.

29. "Americans on Benefits: Keep Them Coming" (*op. cit.*, see Note 5): 4–5; McCaffery (*op. cit.*, see Note 16): 14–30.

30. P. F. Drucker, "Reckoning with the Pension Fund Revolution," *Harvard Business Review* (March–April 1991): 106–114.

31. B. Leonard, "Agency Protects Pan Am Pension Benefits," *HR News* (Sept. 1991): A1, 10.

32. "Pension Issues: A 50 Year History and Outlook," Newsletter 33, no. 3 (Martin E. Segal Company, New York, February 1990); T. F. Duzak, "Defined Benefit and Defined Contribution Plans: A Labor Perspective," in *Economic Survival in Retirement* (New York: Salisbury, 1990): 69; U.S. Department of Labor, Bureau of Labor Statistics, *Employee Benefits in Medium and Large Firms*, 1989 (Washington, D.C.: U.S. Government Printing Office, June 1990).

33. C. H. Farnsworth, "Experiment in Worker Ownership Shows a Profit," *The New York Times* (Aug. 14, 1993): L33 and 46; "New Developments in Global Stock Plans," *HR Focus* (Nov. 1992): 19.

34. G. A. Patterson, "Hourly Auto Workers Now on Layoff Have a Sturdy Safety Net," *The Wall Street Journal* (Jan. 29, 1991): A1, A2.

35. "Perspectives: Health Care Costs," *Personnel Journal* (July 1990): 12.

36. "CEOs Seek Help on Health Costs," *Fortune* (June 3, 1991): 12.

37. K. Matthes, "Healthcare Checkup: How to Evaluate an HMO," *HR Focus* (Sept. 1993): 3–4; "Monitoring Peformance," *Bulletin to Management* (April 8, 1993): 106; J. J. Laabs, "Deere's HMO Turns Crisis Into Profit," *Personnel Journal* (Oct. 1992): 82–89; J. J. Laabs, "How Campbell Manages Its Rural Health Care Dollars," *Personnel Journal* (May 1992): 74–81.

38. M. McNamee, J. Weber, and R. Mitchell, "Health-Care Reform: It's Already Here," *Business Week* (June 14, 1993): 114–121.

39. P. Kerr, "Betting the Farm on Managed Care," *The New York Times* (June 27, 1993): 1, 6.

40. "An Incentive a Day Can Keep Doctor Bills at Bay," *Business Week* (April 29, 1991): 22.

41. "Whose Office Is It Anyhow?" *Fortune* (August 9, 1993): 92.

42. J. E. Santora, "Sony Promotes Wellness to Stabilize Health Care Costs," *Personnel Journal* (Sept. 1992): 40–44.

43. S. Caudron, "The Wellness Pay Off," *Personnel Journal* (July 1990): 55–60; "How Healthy are Corporate Fitness Programs?" *The Physician and Sports Medicine* (March 1989). Also contact Wellness Councils of America (WELCOA), 1823 Harney St., Ste. 201, Omaha, NE 68102, (402) 444-1711.

44. "Wellness Plans and the Disabilities Act," *Bulletin to Management* (May 27, 1993): 168.

45. P. Stuart, "Investments in EAPs Pay Off," *Personnel Journal* (Feb. 1993): 43–54.

46. McCaffery (*op. cit.*, see Note 16).

47. G. Latham and N. Napier, "Practical Ways to Increase Employee Attendance," in *Absenteeism: New Approaches to Understanding, Measuring and Managing Employee Absence*, eds., P. Goodman and R. Atkins (San Francisco: Jossey-Bass, 1984); R. Steers and S. Rhodes, "Major Influences on Employee Attendance: A Process Model," *Journal of Applied Psychology* 63 (1978): 391–407.

48. D. Scott and S. Markham, "Absenteeism Control Methods: A Survey of Practices and Results," *Personnel Administrator* 27 (1982): 73–86.

49. D. R. Dalton and W. D. Todor, "Turnover, Transfer and Absenteeism: An Interdepartment Perspective," *Journal of Management* (Summer 1993): 193–220.

50. J. Chadwick-Jones, N. Nicholson, and C. Brown, *Social Psychology of Absenteeism* (New York: Praeger, 1982).

51. Scott and Markham, (*op. cit.*, see Note 48).

52. B. P. Noble, "Making a Case for Family Friendly Programs." Also read J. J. Laabs, "HR's Vital Role at Levi Strauss," *Personnel Journal* (Dec. 1992): 34–46.

53. M. B. Scott, "How Companies Help with Family Care," *Employee Benefit Plan Review* (May 1990): 12.

54. "International Foundation of Employee Benefits Plans," *Nontraditional Benefits for the Work Force of 2000: A Special Report* (Brookfield, Wis.: IFEBP, 1990).

55. S. Overman, "3M Arranges Summer Child Care," *HR Magazine* (March 1991): 46–47.

56. C. M. Loder, "Merck and Co. Breaks New Ground for Employee Child Care Centers," *The Star Ledger* (May 1990): 12; "Companies Cited for Supporting Working Mothers," *HR Focus* (Dec. 1991): 13; S. J. Goff, M. K. Mount, and R. L. Jamison, "Employer Supported Child Care, Work/Family Conflict, and Absenteeism: A Field Study," *Personnel Psychology* 43 (1990): 793–809; S. Zedeck and K. L. Mosier, "Work in the Family and Employing Organization," *American Psychologist* (Feb. 1990): 240–251.

57. E. Smith, "First Interstate Finds an Eldercare Solution," *HR Magazine* (July 1991): 152; A. E. Scharlach, B. F. Lowe, and E. L.

Schneider, *Elder Care and the Work Force* (Lexington, Mass.: Lexington Books, 1991); L. Crawford, *Dependent Care and the Employee Benefits Package* (Westport, Conn.: Quorum Books, 1990).

58. Jamieson and O'Mara (*op. cit.,* see Note 54) 150.

59. IFEBP, (*op. cit.,* see Note 54).

60. "Lotus Opens a Door for Gay Partners," *Business Week* (Nov. 4, 1991): 80–81.

61. "National Healthcorp," *Fortune* (July 29, 1991): 110; L. A. Ferman, M. Hoyman, J. Cutcher-Gershenfeld, and E. Savoie, *Joint Training Programs: A Union-Management Approach to Preparing Workers for the Future* (Ithaca, N.Y.: ILR Press, 1991).

62. K. P. Shapiro and J. A. Sherman, "Employee Attitudes Benefit Plan Designs," *Personnel Journal* (July 1987): 49–53.

63. R. Brookler, "HR in Growing Companies," *Personnel Journal* (Nov. 1992): 802.

64. B. Olmsted and S. Smith, "Flex for Success!" *Personnel* (June 1989): 50–54; M. E. Grossman and M. Magnus, "The Boom in Benefits," *Personnel Journal* (Nov. 1988): 51–55; W. Wendling, "Responses to a Changing Work Force," *Personnel Administrator* (Nov. 1988): 50–54; C. A. Baker, "Flex Your Benefits," *Personnel Journal* (May 1988): 54–60; J. E. Santora, "American Opts For Flex," *Personnel Journal* (Nov. 1990): 32–34.

65. Bureau of National Affairs, "Employees Would Change Benefits If Possible," *Bulletin to Management* (August 15, 1985): 1–2.

66. C. Murino, "What Benefit Is Communication?" *Personnel Journal* (February 1990): 64–68; Bureau of National Affairs, "Cost, Communication and Compliance Concerns," *Bulletin to Management* (March 21, 1985): 7; "Pay off," *The Wall Street Journal* (July 8, 1982): 1; R. Foltz, "Communique," *Personnel Administrator* (May 1981): 8.

67. M. J. Mandel, "Canada's Health Plan Gives Employment Figures a Rosy Glow," *Business Week* (Feb. 28, 1994): 22.

68. F. Protzman, "Rewriting the Contract for Germany's Vaunted Workers," *The New York Times* (Feb. 13, 1994): F5.

EVEN WITH the best staffing procedures, the most useful forms of performance appraisal and feedback, *and* the best methods of compensation, employees *still* may not perform at their highest levels! Such employees can be deficient in one or more skills and abilities that are really needed to do the job. This may have resulted from the employees changing jobs, from their current jobs having changed through new technologies, or simply because their deficiencies weren't picked up by the staffing procedures. Whatever the reason, these skill and ability deficiencies need to be removed.

Today, training and development programs encompass a careful discipline that melds the best current knowledge on learning principles and styles with the business and human resource needs of any given organization. Not only are the skills and abilities of the entire spectrum of workers addressed in the new training and development programs, from people on the line to people in top management, but company training programs in diversity and ethics are addressing the larger issues facing our society.

While some deficiencies can be corrected in a rather short period of time, others can take much longer. Consequently, we typically find companies offering a variety of training programs (short-term) as well as a variety of development programs (longer-term). These are the subject of our discussion in the first of two chapters of this section.

Perhaps an organization's longest-term developmental thinking has to do with staying competitive. We return to the topic of competitiveness time and again in this book because it is the driving force for business in the 1990s, and the implications for your career, for

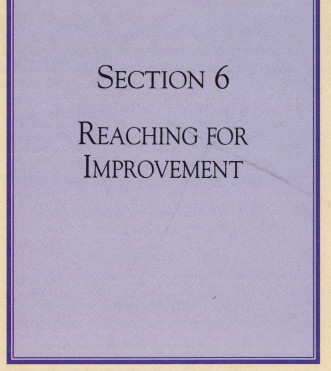

SECTION 6

REACHING FOR
IMPROVEMENT

business, and for society are enormous. One of the most promising strategies in the emerging "technology of competition" is that of total quality management, which we examine in Chapter 15.

While training and development programs can improve the skills and abilities of individuals and even of teams, to stay competitive organizations are also imple-

menting programs whose goal is to improve the entire organization. This is especially being done in companies where total quality management is being implemented. As this strategy spreads through American business, firms are finding that the success of these programs depends almost completely on whether their work force believes in the new system and on whether their workers are willing and able to change. Not a small factor in the stance of the work force is the effectiveness of the human resource management programs that have been in place prior to attempting a change as fundamental as total-quality management. Such programs involve training and development; they involve changing the processes and structure of the organization; and they involve other human resource practices such as appraisal and compensation. Conse- quently, effective human resource management is critical for organizations implementing total quality management programs. Because this new approach to management is likely to be here for a long time, and because effective human resource management is crucial to its success, we devote an entire chapter to this activity. We continue with *your* job by asking you to describe training and development programs you will want. This is at the end of Chapter 14.

CHAPTER 14

TRAINING AND DEVELOPMENT

LEARNING OBJECTIVES

When you have finished studying this chapter, you should be able to:

1. Describe the purposes and importance of training and development.
2. Determine training and development needs.
3. Answer questions about setting up training and development programs.
4. Describe the different types of training and development programs.
5. Describe how to maximize learning.
6. Indicate how to select a training program.
7. Discuss the many trends in training and development.

CHAPTER OUTLINE

THE Ritz-Carlton Hotel Company's pervasive training approach based on its culture is reminiscent of Disney's successful "Be Our Guest" motto and mission. Ritz-Carlton's rallying phrase is "We Are Ladies and Gentlemen Serving Ladies and Gentlemen."

If a Ritz-Carlton hotel can't be more truly elegant and service-oriented than the other hospitality choices in the marketplace, its very name is in trouble. So the Ritz-Carlton Hotel Company (Atlanta, Georgia), operator of 28 luxury hotels, makes a priority of its own distinctive brand of training.

Every one of the company's 14,000 employees receives not only orientation and training, but also certification in his or her position, according to Mary Anne Ollman, corporate director of training.

Certification for a maid? "Absolutely," explains Debra Phillips, training manager and quality adviser for the Ritz-Carlton New York. "'Room attendants,' as we call them, have a most important job in our organization." Phillips and her counterparts throughout the chain follow a similar procedure for each position, including office workers.

ORIENT, TRAIN, CERTIFY

"Taking a room attendant as an example, first employees must understand the overall company gold standards, allowing us to set up the employee to succeed. The new room attendant would have been selected carefully for certain basic talents and strengths. Then it's our job to train to meet Ritz-Carlton standards," Phillips says. (See the insert on their development formula that builds on employee selection.)

"For the first 60 days on the job, through orientation and training, we make certain that the employee has a thorough understanding of the technical tasks and responsibilities our guests and organization expect them to perform on the job. We repeat our gold standards to them over and over in training, even though they have heard it all in orientation. And they hear it again in the certification process."

Phillips says the training philosophy allows for individual differences in learning, so employees are allowed to choose when they take their tests for certification, as long as it's within the first 60 days of employment.

"For a room attendant, as with other positions, the test would include an inspection," says Phillips. "For example, for a duty such as the turn-down service, the second guest room service of the evening, a trainer would go back to a guest room after the new room attendant performed the service to inspect it, ensure mastery, and see that it has been done as the employee has been trained."

In other cases, according to Phillips, inspection is not possible, and observation substitutes for it. A new

RITZ-CARLTON HOTELS EMPLOYEE DEVELOPMENT FORMULA
$(T + F) \times I = G$

"One of the most critical elements in the HR process at the Ritz-Carlton Hotels is getting the correct employees in here in the first place," said Mary Anne Ollman, corporate director of training. "We've identified that the natural abilities we look for in a new employee are things like caring, empathy, high work ethic. And of course job-specific abilities such as math proficiency for an accounting function. We believe that everyone has a gift—that everyone has strengths, which, if identified and brought out, make any weaknesses irrelevant. People have an intrinsic satisfaction in their work when their strengths are used. So we have a formula for helping employees grow, taking into account people's gifts or talent, their fit with the organization, our investment in developing them."

$$(T + F) \times I = G$$

where:

T = Talent
F = Fit
I = Investment
G = Growth

Continued on the next page

501

telephone operator's work is observed until mastery is obtained and signed off by the departmental trainer.

"Certification also includes a test," Phillips adds. "It can be done in written form, or as verbal questions and answers, taking into account individual differences among employees with regard to reading, writing and languages."

What about someone like a payroll clerk, who does not connect with hotel guests? Phillips says it makes no difference. The motto, "We Are Ladies and Gentlemen Serving Ladies and Gentlemen" still applies. In these internal jobs, other employees are the customers, and all the same standards are reinforced through training.

"One thing that is unique about our training and certification standards and process is that we went to the experts to develop them—and I don't mean consultants," says Ollman, the corporate training director.

She means the employees. "In constructing our training programs, we held focus groups with employees, and our training managers worked with employees, so they would help us know how learning best takes place for our organization, as well as to understand what skills are necessary to perform in each job to near perfection," Ollman says.

QUALITY LEADERS AT EACH HOTEL

It seems clear that the training function in Ritz-Carlton Hotels has earned a healthy respect as the major force in quality improvement. While this may be partly—or even mostly—a result of being in the hospitality industry, the company still serves as an interesting model for close quality/training interface.

"In 1984, we did not have training positions in the hotels," Ollman related. "Then one of the regional vice presidents implemented a training position and presented the plan for it to the president of the company. Training has been a critical part of the organization ever since, with a training manager in each hotel."

"When we went through some organizational streamlining, there was never any thought given to eliminating training manager positions. Everyone, throughout the organization, understands that training is crucial for our business."

The Ritz-Carlton's training program has undergone changes as a result of the company's journey into quality management, according to Ollman. It was at that time that the company decided to go for the Baldrige Award for Quality.

"The Baldrige application forced us to take a look at business process design in a way that we had never really done before," she says.

"Right now we are looking at cycle time, such as how long it takes from the moment guests walk in, until they are in their rooms. We've done customer surveys and are studying eighteen cycle times throughout our systems to see where we are as an organization. Then we will be able to judge how to decrease cycle times by taking out the nonvalued elements from jobs. Using the check-in example, if we want to reduce cycle time to two minutes, we may discover we can have the desk receptionists skip an explanation of the in-room bar service, and have the bell staff do that job. Of course, then we must retrain."

Another way that the quality initiatives feed into training is through the hotels' feedback forms. Internal Defect Reports are to be completed by any employee when systems go wrong.

"For example," Ollman said, "I could be about to conduct a meeting and discover that the a/v equipment has not been delivered to the meeting room. I'd complete a report. By doing so, I could ensure this would never happen again, find the root cause and fix it forever. As another example, a desk clerk might file a report if there are no nonsmoking rooms available when a guest requests one."

"When the information is compiled and supplied to the hotel's general manager (gm) on a daily basis, it gives the manager a valuable look at what actually went on in the hotel that day. Otherwise a gm might look at the dollar and guest numbers and think, 'Well, we had a bang up day.'"

"This way, the gm can get all the information about the hotel. And the beauty of the system is that it is tracked over time. So, something like the problem of the availability of nonsmoking rooms could be pinpointed to a certain pattern. Maybe there's a shortage only on Sundays because that's when the rooms are taken out for deep cleaning."

Other times, Ollman says, a recurring problem can be traced back to training, so hotel training managers also read and act on the reports. She maintains that the system prevents pointing fingers at employees. Systems and processes get blamed instead. "We, as a company, believe that the system dictates a person's performance. It's not who, it's why," she says.

"The objective in all our work with the defect reports is to better serve guests and internal customers. The more problems we can detect, the fewer there are to be seen by guests."

Ollman won't be able to use the word "fewer" much longer with regard to defects. Another of the

Continued on the next page

This feature is representative of what many outstanding organizations are doing today with training and development.[2] Namely, these firms are using training and development to make their firms more productive and more in line with total-quality management principles. While these principles are discussed in detail in Chapter 15, Total Quality Management, it is important to first see just how important training and development is to success and competitiveness. The Ritz-Carlton feature highlights the relationship that training and development has with other HR activities, particularly selection. For training to be effective, it is necessary to understand the employee's level of ability and those personality characteristics that might influence how the person will perform in different situations. Finally, the feature indicates how important it is for companies to allow room for local differences. That is, it is important for the corporate offices of the firm not to impose a rigid and fixed program of training on all units of the organization. Individual units always have special needs to be considered, and their participation in final decisions can consider these needs and increase their feelings of participation and empowerment.

Training and development obviously serves many purposes. This chapter examines those purposes in detail. It discusses the types of needs analysis that must be conducted to determine who should receive training, what skills are necessary, and at what level they should be taught. Implementing a successful training and development program involves creating appropriate conditions for training to occur and selecting the type of program that matches needed skills and skill levels. These are described, along with techniques by which to assess training programs. International issues and comparisons in training and development conclude the chapter.

TRAINING AND DEVELOPMENT

Employee **training and development** is any attempt to improve current or future employee performance by increasing an employee's ability to perform.[3] The need for training and development can arise for many reasons. Job applicants with insufficient skills may be hired; technological changes that result in new job skills can occur; organizations can redesign jobs and also decide to develop a new product requiring technologies not used before. In some of these cases, the need for training and development can be immediate and unplanned or can be anticipated and planned for in the future.

Training and development is any attempt to improve current or future performance by increasing employee ability.

503

The purposes of training and development are to:

- remove performance deficiencies
- increase productivity
- enhance work force flexibility
- increase commitment
- lower absenteeism and turnover
- benefit the community
- support company strategy

Increasingly, employers are realizing how important it is to provide training and development if they are to stay competitive and profitable. Therefore, more organizations than ever are attempting to identify current and future training and development needs and to develop programs that enable employees to perform at the desired level.

WHY IS TRAINING AND DEVELOPMENT IMPORTANT?

A major purpose of training and development is to remove performance deficiencies, whether current or anticipated. Training to increase productivity is another important purpose. Companies find that by training employees, productivity gains more than offset the costs of training:

Motorola calculates that every $1 it spends on training delivers $30 in productivity gains within three years. Since 1987, the company has cut costs by $3.3 billion—not by the normal expedient of firing workers, but by training them to simplify processes and reduce waste. Sales per employee have doubled in the past five years, and profits have increased 47 percent.[4]

Training is important to organizations that are rapidly incorporating new technologies and consequently increasing the likelihood of employee obsolescence. Especially relevant to organizations that are rapidly incorporating new technologies, the current work force must be more flexible and adaptable—effective training and development programs are crucial to this. If an organization can increase its adaptability, it can enhance its chances for survival and profitability.

Training and development can increase employees' commitment to the organization, and it can strengthen their perceptions that the organization is a good place to work. Greater commitment results in less turnover and absenteeism, giving another boost in productivity.

Society at large benefits when individuals are productive and contributing members of organizations.[5] Expanding this idea of community involvement, United Parcel Service trains its managers by, among other things, actually requiring them to serve in the community. A description of this program is found in the feature, "Managing Human Resources at UPS: Listening to the Other America."

Finally, training is key in implementing a company's strategy. This is exactly how the people at Ritz-Carlton see their investment in training.

While training and development is important, managers sometimes view it as too costly and the payoffs too far into the future. Thus the support and commitment of the chief executive officer are often critical to the success of an organization's training and development effort:

Training and development works better when the CEO is behind it!

Grab any Wall Street analyst by the lapel and he'll tell you PepsiCo is a brilliant marketing company. Well, sure, but then ask CEO Wayne Calloway how it got that way and he'll talk, not about those slick ads starring Madonna and Michael Jackson, but about what he calls the three P's: "people, people, people." Ah, touchy-feely management? Anything but. Behind Calloway's alluringly alliterative slogan lies the country's most sophisticated and comprehensive system for turning bright young people into strong managers. Says he: "We take eagles and teach them to fly in formation."

PepsiCo takes people development more seriously than perhaps any other American corporation. Calloway spends up to two months every year personally reviewing the performance of his top 550 managers, discussing their futures with their bosses and with the personnel department. Calloway, who says he

MANAGING HUMAN RESOURCES at UPS

Listening to the Other America

IN four years as a manager at United Parcel Service (UPS), Nelson Whitlow has helped build up the company airline, talked the Federal Aviation Administration into letting UPS have its own weather information system and managed a staff of 40.

But none of that prepared him to work with Miguel DeLeon, a 17-year-old migrant worker who lives with his family in a flimsy paperboard shack in the Rio Grande Valley. When Mr. Whitlow met Miguel recently, the boy had dropped out of high school and didn't want to go back. Was he unintelligent? Unmotivated? No. He needed clothing.

"The kids in his family had nothing to wear, and that's why they had stopped going to school," said Mr. Whitlow. "So we took them to get clothing and shoes. It was a humbling experience."

Helping keep children in school is just one facet of what Mr. Whitlow did recently when UPS sent him to McAllen, Texas. Working 60-hour weeks, he and eight colleagues set up a mobile library for migrant children, laid the plans for a sewing shop to provide jobs and developed a video at a local clinic to educate indigent patients about health and nutrition.

It's all part of an unconventional training program sponsored by the $15 billion Atlanta-based freight company. Each year UPS assigns 40 middle- and upper-level supervisors to month-long community internships. The thought is that living and working in poor communities will help managers better understand employees and customers from diverse backgrounds.

Of course, seminars abound on workplace diversity, and many corporations put money into troubled communities. But what makes the UPS program unique, say training experts, is its commitment in working hours and that it has been around for 25 years.

The program was the brainchild of James E. Casey, founder and longtime president of UPS. After the passage of the *1964 Civil Rights Act*, he knew the company would have to hire more women and minorities. He began sending mobile hiring vans into poor and inner-city neighborhoods. But Mr. Casey, who died in 1983, quickly realized that bringing these people on board wouldn't work if the company's white male managers were not sensitive to their needs and background.

So he turned to Walter Hooke, a UPS senior manager, who at the time was living in a poor neighborhood in San Francisco and spending his off hours working with the Urban League. In 1968, Mr. Hooke began the companywide internships, which early on were more like extended field trips.

Since then, more than 850 UPS managers have done stints in nineteen cities. Employees today receive full salaries while spending 30 days in one of four communities. In McAllen, they assist poor Mexican-Americans and Latin American refugees. In Chicago, interns live at St. Margaret's Church of Scotland and work with young people and their families. In Chattanooga, Tennessee, managers provide aid to poor families and the disabled and severely retarded. In New York, employees work at the Henry Street Settlement helping unwed teen-age mothers find jobs, visiting mental patients and teaching poor children.

"Our founder believed you couldn't understand someone's problems unless you were in their shoes," said Dan Preble, the UPS manager who coordinates the program.

UPS employees weren't always as enthusiastic. Early on, the internships were more punitive than a sign that a manager was on the fast track. The most likely candidates were managers who had uttered racial slurs or had a bad record working with minorities. Even today, some of that apprehension lingers. Lou Bennefield, a regional manager in Atlanta, remembers how he tried to get out of going to New York in 1991. "I kept trying to figure out what I'd done wrong," he said.

Shortly after he arrived in New York, Mr. Bennefield got a firsthand view of crime in the streets, riding along with a police officer; he helped serve meals in a soup kitchen and accompanied 40 schoolchildren on the subway for a field trip.

Continued on the next page

"Before I went, I thought I knew all about the problems in the big city," he said. "But I didn't know anything at all."

The program's results are hard to measure. Mr. Preble points to an employee turnover rate under 2 percent and a solid affirmative action record, but adds that much of the change is personal. The hope is that this will translate into better management.

Kay Monroe says this happened in her case. Ms. Monroe, a regional controller with UPS in Chicago, spent her four weeks in Chattanooga in 1990 working with disabled children and disadvantaged adults.

"It helped me realize that people like this work for us," said Ms. Monroe, who, like several others, has kept up her community involvement, working at a homeless shelter.[6]

The development of our best people is the personal responsibility of management.

Roberto C. Goizueta, CEO, Coca-Cola

knows most of the 550 managers and spends anywhere from 5 to 30 minutes reviewing each one, states with conviction, "There's nothing I do that's more important." In all, he spends 40 percent of his time on people issues. He expects the people below him to do the same, so that by the end of each year every one of the company's 20,000 managers knows exactly where he or she stands.[7]

Without top management support and commitment to training, an organization is likely to concentrate on activities other than training. This is particularly true when the focus is on short-term goals and immediate results. Such a focus allows too little time for the benefits of training and development to accrue. Top management at PepsiCo began to emphasize training and development when they recognized that they had to develop their people and businesses in order to be effective.

LEGAL CONSIDERATIONS

Legal considerations are relevant to several aspects of training and development. One aspect is the determination of the training and development needs of an applicant for a job. Legally, an applicant cannot be eliminated from the selection pool just because he or she lacks a skill that can be learned in eight hours. It is thus important to determine what skills an individual needs to perform a job, what skills an applicant possesses, what training programs can remove the deficiencies, and what amount of time is necessary to complete these programs.

DISCRIMINATORY TRAINING PRACTICES

Legal considerations increasingly impact the ways in which companies go about providing training and development opportunities for current employees. Here, bans on discrimination extend to on-the-job training and one-day introductions to new jobs or equipment as well as to affirmative action and formal apprenticeship/training programs. Admission to formal training programs, however, can be limited to those under a certain age, as long as those passed over for the program are not women and minorities who have previously been denied training opportunities. Specific discriminatory training practices can often be determined by the responses to the following questions:

- Are minorities and/or women given the same training opportunities as white men? Be careful! Advertising and recruiting practices come into play here.

PARTNERSHIP: WORKING TOGETHER IN TRAINING AND DEVELOPMENT

LINE MANAGERS	HR PROFESSIONALS	EMPLOYEES
Cooperate with HR professionals in identifying training needs.	Coordinate with line managers in linking training to the needs of the business.	Identify their own training needs with HR professionals and line managers.
May participate in the delivery of training programs.	Identify training needs in cooperation with line managers.	Actively participate in training programs.
Give management commitment and support.	Develop the training programs.	

- Are requirements for entry into a training program (that is, tests, education, or experience) job-related, or are they arbitrary?
- Are nearly all machine functions or other specialized duties that require training performed by white or male workers?
- Does one class of trainees tend to get more challenging assignments or other special training opportunities?
- Do supervisors know what constitutes training? It could be almost any learning experience, from how to fit a drill bit to a two-week seminar on complex sales procedures.
- Who evaluates the results of instruction or training—only white men?
- Are all trainees given equal facilities for instruction? Are they segregated in any way?
- Do a disproportionate number of women and/or minorities fail to pass training courses? If so, find out whether it is because they are more often unqualified or because they receive inferior instruction.

There are several important questions to ask in offering training and development to employees.

DEFENSES AGAINST CHARGES OF DISCRIMINATION

Organizations can provide a reasonable defense by showing that their training programs were conceived and administered without bias. This, however, is exceedingly difficult to demonstrate unless companies have the foresight to document their training practices. Thus they should follow these guidelines:

- Register affirmative action training and apprenticeship programs with the Department of Labor. This must be done in writing. Include the goals, timetables, and criteria for selection and evaluation of trainees. Such a

Guidelines for legal training and development programs include:

- government registration
- employee records
- documented decision making
- trainee monitoring

507

record will help prove job-relatedness and that there was no intent to discriminate. It can also be valuable in proving that an organization's program was not used as a pretext to discriminate.

- Keep a record of all employees who wish to enroll in your training program. Detail how each trainee was selected. Keep application forms, tests, questionnaires, records of preliminary interviews, and anything else that bears on an employee's selection or rejection for at least two years or as long as training continues.
- Document all management decisions and actions that relate to the administration of training policies.
- Monitor each trainee's progress. Provide progress evaluations, and make sure counseling is available.
- Continue to evaluate the results even after completion of training.

Another avenue toward ensuring that training and development programs are nondiscriminatory is through federal and state government programs. Through careful use of these programs, organizations can sometimes also defray training costs and receive already trained employees. Some programs enable current employees to obtain training. Currently, support from the federal government is funneled through block grants to states and through the Office of Federal Contract Compliance Programs under provisions in the *Job Training Partnership Act of 1982*. Under this act, grants are provided to states that in turn use the money to train economically disadvantaged youths and adults as well as workers whose jobs have been eliminated.[8]

THE ROLE OF THE SUPERVISOR

Because both individual supervisors (and all managers and executives) and their employers can be sued for violations of fair and equal employment laws, training is strongly recommended as prevention. According to Lucille E. Brown, a partner at the law firm of Schatz & Schatz, Ribicoff & Kotkin:

> The Equal Employment Opportunity Commission has noted significant increases in the number of discrimination—particularly age discrimination—cases filed in the last five years. This increase seems to correspond to the increase in white-collar workers who have been laid off. "Most middle managers assumed that they would never be laid off," says Brown. "Now, employers are pushing work down to the lowest appropriate level and eliminating layers of supervisors and managers."
>
> Mid-level managers and supervisors are more likely to sue because they are often more astute, better educated, and more clued in on company policies and politics. They also have a heightened sense of what they are entitled to in the context of the employment relationship, Brown points out, partially fueled by the increased media attention on employee rights—for example, privacy.
>
> What can employers do? The best protection against liability for personnel-related actions is better training for managers and supervisors as to the consequences of their actions. Many employers promote people to supervisory levels based on their expertise and their performance as individual contributors to the company, not on their managerial abilities. Employers need to train these employees in the "science of people management," in Brown's words. "This is absolutely necessary both for the employer and for the supervisor's self-development." Employers should encourage and train supervisors and managers to
>
> - *Document personnel issues* such as performance and conduct at the time the performance or conduct becomes a problem.
> - *Assess objectively* employee performance and conduct.
> - *Review carefully* communications concerning or directed to employees.[9]

Line managers have a big role to play in training and development.

DETERMINING TRAINING AND DEVELOPMENT NEEDS

Training and development is not only important, it is also complex. Thus the success of any training and development program cannot be left to chance. It must begin with a determination of what is needed.

The three major phases of any training and development program are (1) assessment, which determines the training and development needs of the organization; (2) implementation (actual training and development), in which certain programs and learning methods are used to impart new attitudes, skills, and abilities; and (3) evaluation.[10] The relationships among these phases are shown in Exhibit 14.1.

We will focus on the assessment and implementation phases in this chapter and leave the evaluation phase for Chapter 20.

Training and development program phases include:

- assessment
- implementation
- evaluation

ORGANIZATIONAL NEEDS ANALYSIS

Organizational needs analysis begins with an examination of the short- and long-term objectives of the organization and the trends likely to affect these objectives. According to one expert, organizational objectives should be the ultimate concern of any training and development effort.[11] In addition to examining the organization's objectives, the organizational needs analysis also evaluates human resources, efficiency indexes, and the organizational climate.

Human resource analysis translates the organization's objectives into specific demands for human resources and the skills and programs for supplying them. Training and development programs play a vital role in matching the supply of human resources and skills with organizational demands.

An analysis of efficiency indexes provides information on the current efficiency of work groups and the organization. Useful indexes include costs of labor, quantity of labor, quality of output, wages, equipment use, and repairs. The organization can determine standards for these indexes and then use them to evaluate the general effectiveness of training programs and to locate training and development needs for groups within the organization.

The analysis of the **organizational climate** describes the quality of the organization, how the employees feel about it, and how effective the employees are. Like the analysis of efficiency indexes, it can help identify where training and development programs may be needed and provide criteria by which to evaluate the effectiveness of the programs that are implemented. Measures of the quality of the organizational climate include absenteeism, turnover, grievances, productivity, suggestions, attitude surveys, and accidents.

Organizational needs analysis begins with an assessment of the short- and long-term objectives of the business.

JOB NEEDS ANALYSIS

Because the organizational needs analysis is too broad to spot detailed training and development needs for specific jobs, it is also necessary to conduct a **job needs analysis**. Essentially, this analysis provides information on the tasks to be performed on each job (the basic information contained in job descriptions), the skills necessary to perform those tasks (from the job specifications or qualifications), and the minimum acceptable standards (sometimes excluded from traditional job analysis). These three pieces of information may be gathered from current employees, the human resource department, or current supervisors. They may also be gathered simultaneously by teams representing different areas of the organization.

Job needs analysis provides information on:

- tasks peformed
- skills needed
- acceptable standards

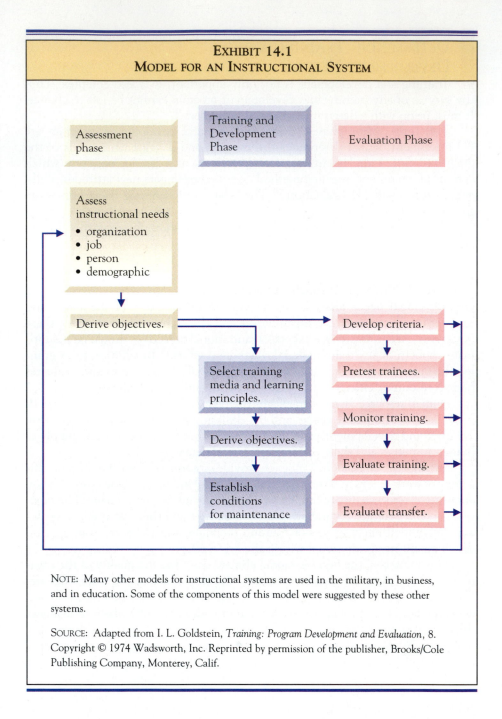

EXHIBIT 14.1
MODEL FOR AN INSTRUCTIONAL SYSTEM

NOTE: Many other models for instructional systems are used in the military, in business, and in education. Some of the components of this model were suggested by these other systems.

SOURCE: Adapted from I. L. Goldstein, *Training: Program Development and Evaluation*, 8. Copyright © 1974 Wadsworth, Inc. Reprinted by permission of the publisher, Brooks/Cole Publishing Company, Monterey, Calif.

These different approaches can be used in person needs analysis:

- output measures
- self-assessment
- attitude surveys
- competency-based assessment

PERSON NEEDS ANALYSIS

After information about the necessary skills and their importance and the minimal acceptable standards of proficiency has been collected, the analysis shifts to the individual. A **person needs analysis** can be accomplished in two different ways. Employee performance discrepancies may be identified either by comparing actual performance with the minimum acceptable standards of performance or by comparing an evaluation of employee proficiency on each required skill dimension with the proficiency level required for each skill. The first method is based on the actual, current job performance of an employee; it is therefore used to determine training needs for the current job. The second method is used to identify development needs for future jobs.[12]

Regardless of method, several different approaches can be used to identify the training needs of individuals.

OUTPUT MEASURES.   Performance data (for example, productivity, accidents, customer complaints), as well as performance appraisal ratings, can provide evidence of performance deficiencies. Person needs analysis can also consist of work sampling and job knowledge tests that measure performance capability and knowledge.[13]

SELF-ASSESSED TRAINING NEEDS.   The self-assessment of training needs is growing in popularity. A recent study of training practices in major U.S. firms showed that between 50 and 80 percent of all corporations allow managers to nominate themselves to attend short-term or company-sponsored training or education programs. Self-assessment can be as informal as posting a list of company-sponsored courses and asking who wants to attend or as formal as conducting surveys regarding training needs.[14] Exhibit 14.2 shows sample questions from a managerial self-assessment survey.

Self-assessment is premised on the assumption that employees, more than anyone else, are aware of their skill weaknesses and performance deficiencies. Therefore, they are in the best position to identify their own training needs. One drawback of self-assessment is that individuals who are fearful of revealing any weaknesses may not know or be willing to accurately report their training needs. Consequently, these individuals may not receive the education necessary to remain current in their fields. On the other hand, managers forced to attend programs that they believe they do not need or that do not meet their personal training needs can become dissatisfied with training and thus be less motivated to learn and transfer skills.

ATTITUDE SURVEYS.   Attitude surveys completed by a supervisor's subordinates and/or by customers can also provide information on training needs. For example, when one supervisor receives low scores regarding his or her fairness in treatment as compared with other supervisors in the organization, this can indicate that the supervisor needs training in that area.[15] Not only does this format provide information to management about service, but results can also be used to pinpoint employee deficiencies.

Surveys can be completed by managers' subordinates and by their bosses. For managers, such surveys can be used to identify which skills are important for managerial effectiveness. Differences in opinions can serve as a basis of discussion about what is really necessary for managerial success in today's environment. Based on the results of a recent survey, lack of differences in opinions may not be totally surprising. This survey is described in the feature, "HR Advice and Application: Managers and Supervisors Fail to Perceive Global Realities."

Generally, the results of attitude surveys contribute important information for training program design. For example, what would you recommend in the design of a training program for the managers described in the aforementioned HR Advice and Application? Which three management skills would you want to increase in importance? What training programs you would use to increase the three management skills you deem important?

COMPETENCY-BASED ASSESSMENT.   A type of needs assessment growing in popularity is competency-based assessment. This approach involves five major steps:

People instinctively want to learn. We are introducing new and improved training programs and aids to create additional opportunities to learn, so our people can use what they learn to help us grow. That's what "Delivering Our Future" to all of our constituencies—employees, customers, shareowners, and communities—is all about.

Kent C. Nelson

Chairman and Chief Executive Officer, UPS

This sort of survey is another result of self-management in organizations.

EXHIBIT 14.2
SAMPLE QUESTIONS FROM A
SELF-ADMINISTERED NEEDS SURVEY

Please indicate in the blanks the extent to which you have a training need in each specific area. Use the scale below.

To what extent do you need training in the following areas?

TO NO EXTENT				TO A VERY LARGE EXTENT
1	2	3	4	5

Basic Management Skills (organizing, planning, delegating, problem solving)

_____ 1. Setting goals and objectives

_____ 2. Developing realistic time schedules to meet work requirements

_____ 3. Identifying and weighing alternative solutions

_____ 4. Organizing work activities

Interpersonal Skills

_____ 1. Resolving interpersonal conflicts

_____ 2. Creating a development plan for employees

_____ 3. Identifying and understanding individual employee needs

_____ 4. Conducting performance appraisal reviews

_____ 5. Conducting a discipline interview

Administrative Skills

_____ 1. Maintaining equipment, tools, and safety controls

_____ 2. Understanding local agreements and shop rules

_____ 3. Preparing work flowcharts

_____ 4. Developing department budgets

Quality Control

_____ 1. Analyzing and interpreting statistical data

_____ 2. Constructing and analyzing charts, tables, and graphs

_____ 3. Using statistical software on the computer

SOURCE: Modified from J. K. Ford and R. A. Noe, "Self Assessed Training Needs: The Effects of Attitude toward Training, Managerial Level and Function," *Personnel Psychology* 40 (1987): 40–53.

Step 1: *Develop broad competency categories.* The initial step is to develop a set of broad competency areas—that is, to determine the critical skills that employees at a given level or job classification in the organization needs to be most effective.

Step 2: *Develop specific competencies.* Once broad categories are selected, the next step is to further define each and develop a list of more specific competencies.

Step 3: *Develop a resource guide and a competency rating form.* The third step involves the development of resource guides or competency manuals that will aid employers and employees in developing skills.

Step 4: *Prepare a developmental plan for each employee.* Once each employee has been evaluated, the next step would be for the boss to work with each of his or her subordinates to develop a specific improvement plan.

Step 5: *Evaluate employee progress and develop a new plan.* Periodic assessment of an employee's progress skill development is essential.[16]

MANAGERS AND SUPERVISORS FAIL TO PERCEIVE GLOBAL REALITIES

Managers and their bosses agree on the qualities that a successful manager must have, but managers generally don't live up to those expectations, according to a nationwide survey of 600 managers by Personnel Decisions, Inc. (PDI), a Minneapolis-based firm of organizational psychologists. The study also discovered that both managers and their bosses are slow to recognize some of the new demands placed on managers by the evolving business environment.

Participating managers and their supervisors were asked to list what they thought were the most critical management skills. Managers were then rated by their supervisors and peers on how well they exhibit those skills. The study also included self-assessments by each manager to produce the ratings.

The most important skill, according to an overwhelming majority of managers and their supervisors, was the ability to *act with integrity*. Other key skills were ranked in the following order: using sound judgment, providing direction, motivating others, managing execution, demonstrating adaptability, fostering teamwork, driving for results, thinking strategically, and focusing on customer needs. The study noted that managers and their supervisors ranked these attributes very similarly; however, the managers' performance in all these categories did not measure up to the importance both they and their bosses placed on each characteristic.

"In general, managers have not yet caught up with the changing demands in the business world," said Susan H. Gebelein, PDI vice president. "These changes require managers to exhibit participative—rather than autocratic—leadership, to build trust and influence others without direct challenge, and to champion change. For many, these skills are new, so they are just learning them."

Although some "new" skills have gained importance, other more traditional skills remain crucial to management such as *using sound judgment, managing execution,* and *driving for results.* Other skills rated as less important, however, actually are critical factors for success in the changing global business environment, Gebelein noted. In fact, the skill that received the lowest rating was *recognizing global implications.* Also, despite the continued support and emphasis by management experts, two other skills found their way into the bottom five: *promoting corporate citizenship* and *using financial data.*[17]

IMPORTANCE OF MANAGEMENT SKILLS

MANAGEMENT SKILL	SELF-RATED IMPORANCE (%)	SUPERVISOR-RATED IMPORTANCE (%)
Act with integrity	44.0	44.0
Use of sound judgment	38.5	39.5
Provide direction	38.5	37.5
Motivating others	38.0	37.5
Demonstrating adaptability	38.0	39.0
Fostering teamwork	37.0	36.5
Drive for results	36.5	35.5
Think strategically	33.0	32.0
Focus on customers	32.5	32.0
Use technical/ functional expertise	32.5	34.0
Prepare written communications	32.0	30.5
Use financial/qualitative data	30.0	31.5
Promote corporate citizenship	26.0	25.0
Recognize global implications	22.5	22.0

Lowest Importance = 10   Highest Importance = 50

SOURCE: *Personnel Decisions, Inc.*, Minneapolis, Minnesota.

The need for a formal assessment here appears to be very important. This allows the firm to find out what skills employees think they need. It is very possible that what managers view as needed skills are out of date and not as important as other emerging skills, given the realities of the competitive world. This is what the aforementioned HR Advice and Application seems to indicate. This being the case, top management and the HR director need to begin by checking and possibly correcting management's perceptions of what is important before embarking on any training program!

DEMOGRAPHIC NEEDS ANALYSIS

Demographic needs analysis identifies training needs by groups in the organization.

In addition to organizational, job, and person analyses, organizations need to conduct demographic studies to determine the training needs of specific populations of workers.[18] For example, Frito Lay conducted a special assessment to determine the training needs of women and minorities in its sales force. According to Dave Knibbe, Frito Lay management development director, the needs assessment was critical to find ways the organization could facilitate more rapid career advancement for these employees. This is consistent with research that indicates that different groups have different training needs. For example, first-line supervisors need more technical training (record keeping, written communications), while mid-level managers rate HR courses as most important for meeting their needs, and upper-level managers rate conceptual courses (goal setting, planning skills) as critical to their development.[19] In a study of male and female managers, male managers were found to need training in listening, verbal skills, nonverbal communication, empathy, and sensitivity; women managers, on the other hand, needed training in assertiveness, confidence building, public speaking, and dealing with male peers and subordinates.[20]

Setting up programs involves asking:

- **Who participates in training?**
- **Who conducts the training?**
- **What skills are to be acquired?**

"If you're not thinking all the time about making every person more valuable, you don't have a chance."

Jack Welch,
CEO, General Electric

SETTING UP THE PROGRAMS

Successful implementation of training and development programs depends on selecting the right programs for the right people under the right conditions.

WHO PARTICIPATES IN TRAINING?

Once a training need has been established, the deficiencies of specific groups must be determined. The decision must then be made as to which group will be the first to be trained. This is because, for most programs, only one group is in attendance, and the training program is designed to address only one topic.

Also important here is the decision as to *how many* employees are to be trained simultaneously. If only one or two employees are to be trained, then on-the-job approaches such as coaching are generally cost-effective. If large numbers of individuals need to be trained in a short period of time, then programmed instruction may be the most viable option.

WHO CONDUCTS THE TRAINING?

Many folks can be involved in conducting the training.

Training and development programs can be taught by one of several people, including:

- The supervisor
- HR staff
- A co-worker such as a lead worker or a friend
- An internal or external expert
- The employee—that is, self-paced instruction

Which of these people is selected to teach often depends on where the program is held and which skill(s) is being taught. For example, basic job skills are usually taught by the immediate job supervisor or a co-worker, whereas a basic organizational orientation is usually handled by the HR staff. Interpersonal skills and conceptual, integrative skills for management are usually taught by university professors or consultants. However, technical skills may be taught by either internal or external experts.

A concern with using immediate supervisors or co-workers as trainers is that, while they may *perform* the work tasks well, they may not be able to *instruct* anyone in the procedures. It is also possible that they will teach workers their own shortcuts rather than correct procedures. On the other hand, immediate supervisors or co-workers may be more knowledgeable than anyone else about the work procedures. If co-workers or managers are to be used as trainers, they should receive instruction in how to train and be given sufficient time on the job to work with trainees.[21]

Experts may have specific knowledge on a technical skill but may not be familiar with the culture of a specific organization. As a result, they may be respected for their expertise but mistrusted because they are not members of the work group. Still, if no one in the immediate work environment possesses the knowledge needed, or if large numbers of individuals need to be trained, the only option may be to hire experts.

Self-paced instruction is also an option. Learning at one's own pace is both an advantage and a disadvantage of self-paced instruction. Trainees benefit because they learn at a speed that maximizes retention. However, if there are no incentives for the trainee to complete the instruction in a specified period of time, the training may be placed on a back burner.

WHAT TYPES OF SKILLS ARE TO BE ACQUIRED?

In addition to using appropriate training techniques, the training program must have content congruent with the types of skills being taught. In general, skills fall into four broad areas, as discussed below.

BASIC LITERACY SKILLS. Organizations are increasingly concerned about **basic literacy skills (BLS)**. Consequently, it is estimated that training programs designed to correct basic literacy deficiencies in grammar, mathematics, safety, reading, listening, and writing will increase in the 1990s. Organizations are also learning that it pays to train customer service representatives in the art of telephone etiquette. The feature, "HR Advice and Applications: Telephone Etiquette" discusses just how important this type of training can be.[22] The feature, "Managing Human Resources at Will-Burt" in Chapter 3, is another example of just how important basic skill training can be.

As the total quality management movement spreads through U.S. industry, companies are realizing that almost all employees need a new basic skill. This basic skill is statistics, and it is fundamental to W. Edwards Deming's approach to quality, which is improvement by the numbers. In total quality management, determining causes of any lack in quality is done by **statistical process control (SPC)**. SPC is the practice of using statistical analysis to improve quality in operating processes. According to Deming, it is important to analyze the system statistically to know when a system is not producing products with acceptable reliability. At a minimum, a knowledge of means, standard deviations, and ranges is required.

Types of skills to be required:

- Basic (BLS)
- Technical (BTS)
- Interpersonal (IPS)
- Conceptual integrative (CIS)

W. Edwards Deming is one of the fathers of total quality management.

Telephone Etiquette

The following describes the option of an arbitrator who listened to the facts in this case where an employee was suspended.

"The customer was rude to me first," snapped operator Lucy Lipps. "I tried to be nice, but she was so snotty that I had to stand up to her."

"There is never a reason to be rude to a customer," argued supervisor Alex Bell. "A three-day suspension ought to convince you we're serious about customer service."

Was the suspension for just cause?

Facts: The employee worked as a telephone operator in the company's service center, answering customer questions and providing assistance. A customer contacted the employee and, feeling that she had been treated rudely, asked for the employee's name. The employee would not give her name and instead asked the customer for her name and address. The customer immediately contacted the employee's supervisor and reported the incident. When a follow-up call by the service center manager two days later corroborated the supervisor's record of the incident, the employee was suspended for three days for misconduct.

The employee protested the suspension, claiming that she had encountered a difficult customer but did her best to respond to the customer's needs. The customer was already frustrated before talking with her, she said, and therefore she should not be blamed for making the customer upset.

The company, however, contended that the employee had improperly handled the situation by not giving her name when the customer requested it and improperly asking the customer for her name and address. Further, the company argued, the customer immediately reported the incident to the supervisor on duty and also gave a consistent account of the incident two days later. Because the company's business depended on good service, it maintained, the three-day suspension was appropriate to impress upon the employee the seriousness of the offense.

Award: The suspension is upheld.

Discussion: If the customer had claimed only that the employee used a rude tone of voice and failed to give her name when asked, it might have been possible that the customer was mistaken and "was just upset already" and took her frustration out on the employee, the arbiter concedes. However, there was no explanation offered or a possible explanation as to why the customer would concoct the part of her complaint that the employee asked for her name and address, the arbiter finds. Further, the arbiter points out, even though the employee maintained that the customer was rude to her, the employee knows that rudeness on the part of the customer does not excuse rudeness on the part of a company representative.

The arbiter also notes that the employee had received counseling for similar misconduct less than two years earlier. Although the company initially issued a warning and reduced the warning to counseling, the employer may consider the incident in determining the appropriate penalty for subsequent similar offenses, the arbiter decides. While the employee has also received commendations for excellent customer service in the past, they do not excuse her rudeness, even if the customer was being difficult, the arbiter declares, upholding the three-day suspension.

Pointers: Employees who staff first-line telephone positions and toll-free lines are an organization's opportunity to make a good first impression, says Nancy Friedman, president of Telephone Doctor, a St. Louis-based consulting firm. A poorly trained employee, however, can damage a company's reputation by not knowing how to handle a telephone call.

By not training employees in proper telephone techniques, employers risk customer dissatisfaction as employees claim they are not able to help callers, as telephones ring endlessly, and as callers are put on hold or transferred to the wrong person. If a caller is already upset, Friedman recommends employees use a four-step process, including:

- *Apologize*. Callers need to hear an apology.
- *Sympathize*. Empathize with callers for the difficulties they are feeling.
- *Accept responsibility*. Take responsibility for the difficulty on behalf of the company, regardless of whether the employee had anything to do with the matter.
- *Take action*. Prepare to solve the customer's problem.[23]

BASIC TECHNICAL SKILLS. Training that expands or maintains the technical expertise of employees is a subset of **basic technical skills (BTS)** training. Due to rapid changes in technology and the implementation of automated office, industrial, and managerial systems, technological updating and skill building have become a major thrust in training to keep technical skills current.[24]

INTERPERSONAL SKILLS. Increasingly in demand are the **interpersonal skills (IPS)** in communications, human relationships, performance appraisal, leadership, and negotiations. In fact, this skill tops the list of training needs for first- and middle-level managers. The development of IPS is also important for those employees who interface with the public (for example, receptionists, sales associates).[25]

CONCEPTUAL INTEGRATIVE SKILLS. Skills in strategic and operational planning, organization design, and policy skills, called **conceptual integrative skills (CIS)**, are needed by organizational planners as well as by top management. Adapting to complex and changing environments is often a part of top-, and middle-management responsibilities, and CIS helps people enlarge their capacities in these areas. It is at the heart of today's emphasis on creativity and entrepreneurship.

WHERE IS THE TRAINING CONDUCTED, AND HOW?

A careful choice in location of training programs can enhance their success. Such decisions are constrained by the type of learning that is to occur (basic, technical, interpersonal, or conceptual), as well as by cost and time considerations. Exhibit 14.3 summarizes the various approaches to training according to the locale of the training.

ON THE JOB

A frequently used approach is to train workers on the job. **On-the-job training (OJT)** occurs when an employee is taught a new job under the direct supervision of an experienced worker or trainer. The trainee is expected to learn the job by observing the experienced employee and by working with the actual materials, personnel, and/or machinery that comprise the job. The experienced employee/trainer is expected to provide a favorable role model and to take time from regular job responsibilities to provide the instruction and guidance.

One advantage of OJT is that transfer of training is high. Because trainees learn job skills in the environment in which they will actually work, they are more apt to apply these skills on the job. Assuming the trainer works in the same area, the trainee receives immediate feedback about performance. However, such on-site training is appropriate only when a small number of individuals need to be trained and when the consequence of error is low. The quality of the training also hinges on the skill of the manager or person conducting the training.[26]

JOB INSTRUCTION TRAINING. The disadvantages of on-the-job training can be minimized by making the training program as systematic and complete as possible. **Job instruction training (JIT)** represents such a technique. It was developed as a guide for giving on-the-job training to white- and blue-collar employees.[27] Because JIT is a technique rather than a program, it can be adapted to training efforts for all employees in off-the-job and on-the-job programs.

Last year, Honda workers attended an average of about 5,000 hours of technical training every quarter; in one quarter, the down time on the assembly line allowed Honda to increase technical training to 10,000 hours.

Where and how to conduct training:
- on the job
- on site, but not on the job
- off the job

It may be rather obvious that if people spend 98–99% of their work time on the job, and only 1–2% (at most) in formal training, that most learning must occur on the job.

John Kotter,
The Leadership Factor

There are many choices in on-the-job training.

TYPE OF PROGRAM	ADVANTAGES	DISADVANTAGES
On the Job		
Job instruction training	Facilitates transfer of learning No need for separate facilities	Interferes with performance Damages equipment
Apprenticeship	No interference with real job performance Provides extensive training	Takes a long time Expensive May not be related to job
Internships or assistantships	Facilitates transfer of learning Gives exposure to real job	Not really a full job Learning is vicarious
Job rotation	Exposure to many jobs Real learning	No sense of full responsibility Too short a stay in a job
Supervisory assistance	Informal Integrated into job Inexpensive	Effectiveness rests with supervisor Not all supervisors may do it
On Site But Not On the Job		
Programmed instruction	Provides for individualized learning and feedback Faster learning	Time-consuming to develop Cost-effective only for large groups
Videotapes	Conveys consistent information to employees in diverse locations More portable than film	Costly to develop Don't provide for individual feedback
Videodisks	Stores more information than tapes Allows for fast forward Portable	Extremely costly to develop Courseware is limited
Interactive	Training draws on more senses Self-paced learning and feedback	Costly to develop and implement Requires diverse staff to develop
Telecommunications training	Provides for latest insights and knowledge Speeds up communications Standardized	Costly and difficult to set up Not feasible for small firms
Off the Job		
Formal courses	Inexpensive for many No interference with job	Require verbal skills Inhibit transfer of learning
Assessment centers	Helps learning transfer Realistic preview	Expensive to develop Takes time to administer
Simulation	Helps transfer Creates lifelike situations	Can't always duplicate real situations exactly
Role-playing	Good for interpersonal skills Gives insights into others	Can't create real situations exactly; still playing

EXHIBIT 14.3 (CONT.) **ADVANTAGES AND DISADVANTAGES OF ON-THE-JOB,** **ON-SITE, AND OFF-THE-JOB TRAINING PROGRAMS**		
Sensitivity training	Good for self-awareness Gives insights into others	May not transfer to job May not relate to job
Wilderness trips	Builds teams Builds self-esteem	Costly to administer Physically challenging

JIT consists of four steps: (1) careful selection and preparation of the trainer and the trainee for the learning experience to follow; (2) a full explanation and demonstration by the trainer of the job to be done by the trainee; (3) a trial on-the-job performance by the trainee; and (4) a thorough feedback session between the trainer and the trainee to discuss the trainee's performance and the job requirements.[28]

APPRENTICESHIP TRAINING.   Another method for minimizing the disadvantages of on-the-job training is combining it with off-the-job training. Apprenticeship training, internships, and assistantships are based on this combination. **Apprenticeship training** is mandatory for admission to many of the skilled trades such as plumbing, electronics, and carpentry. These programs are formally defined by the U.S. Department of Labor's Bureau of Apprenticeship and Training and involve a written agreement "providing for not less than 4,000 hours of reasonably continuous employment . . . and supplemented by a recommended minimum of 144 hours per year of related classroom instruction." The Equal Employment Opportunity Commission does not prevent the nation's 48,000 skilled trade (apprentice) training programs from excluding anyone aged 40 to 70 because apprenticeship programs are part of the educational system aimed at youth.[29] To be most effective, the on- and off-the-job components of the apprenticeship program must be well integrated and appropriately planned, and they must recognize individual differences.

INTERNSHIPS.   Somewhat less formalized and extensive than apprenticeship training are the internship and assistantship programs. **Internships** are often part of an agreement between schools and colleges and local organizations. As with apprenticeship training, individuals in these programs "earn while they learn," but at a rate that is less than that paid to full-time employees or master crafts workers. The internships, however, function as a source not only of training, but also of realistic exposure to job and organizational conditions. **Assistantships** involve full-time employment and expose an individual to a wide range of jobs. However, because the individual only assists other workers, the learning experience is often vicarious. This disadvantage is eliminated by programs using actual job rotation.[30]

JOB ROTATION.   **Job rotation programs** are used to train and expose employees to a variety of jobs and decision-making situations. Although job rotation does provide exposure, the extent of training and long-run benefits it provides may be overstated. This is because the employees are not in a single job for a long

The best managed firms make use of a broad array of better developmental experiences, "including adding responsibilities to jobs, creating special jobs, using inside and outside training, transferring people between functions and divisions, mentoring and coaching employees, giving those people feedback on progress, and giving them instruction in how to manage their own development."

John Kotter,
The Leadership Factor

519

enough period to learn very much and are not motivated to work hard because they know that they will move on in the near future. As a personal career planning strategy, you may want to avoid job rotation and opt instead for job assignments that are fixed and provide a greater challenge.

MENTORING.   The final and most informal program of training and development involves **supervisory assistance** and **mentoring**.[31] Assisting employees is a regular part of a supervisor's job. It includes day-to-day coaching, counseling, and monitoring workers on how to do the job and how to get along in the organization. The effectiveness of **supervisory assistance** depends in part on whether the supervisor creates a climate where mutual confidence can flourish, provides opportunities for growth, and effectively delegates tasks. **Mentoring** programs, in which an established employee guides the development of a less-experienced worker or protégé can increase an employee's skills, achievement, and understanding of the organization.

> "At NCR Corporation, protégés are usually chosen from among high-potential employees in middle or entry-level management," says James E. McElwain, vice president for personnel resources. He also notes that each executive is encouraged to select two people to mentor and must decide how to develop the relationships. Executives counsel their protégés on how to advance and network in the company and sometimes offer personal advice.[32]

ON SITE BUT NOT ON THE JOB

Another option is to conduct the training at the work site but not on the job. On-site training is appropriate for required after-hours training programs and for training programs in which contact needs to be maintained with work units but OJT would be too distracting or harmful. On-site training is also appropriate for voluntary after-hours training programs and for programs that update employees' skills while allowing them to attend to their regular duties.

For example, when a major northeastern grocery store chain switched to computerized scanners, it faced the problem of training thousands of checkers spread out across three states. The cost of training them off site was prohibitive. Yet management was also fearful about training employees on the job, lest their ineptness in learning to use the scanners would offend customers. To solve the problem, the grocery chain developed a mobile training van that included a vestibule model of the latest scanning equipment. Checkers were trained on site but off the job in the mobile unit. Once the basic skill of scanning was mastered, employees returned to the store, and the trainer remained on site as a resource person. According to one store manager, the program was effective because employees could be trained rapidly and efficiently. Yet, because the training was not conducted on the job, no customers were lost due to checker errors or slowness.

PROGRAMMED INSTRUCTION.   New technologies have rapidly increased the options available to organizations that want to provide on-site training. **Programmed instruction (PI)** is one of the oldest on-site training methods. Here, the instructional material is broken down into frames. Each frame represents a small component of the entire subject to be learned, and each frame must be learned successfully before going on to the next one.

An advantage of PI is that large numbers of employees can be trained simultaneously, with the learner free to explore the material at his or her own pace. Additionally, PI includes immediate and individualized feedback. The downside is that programming computers for PI is involved and time-consuming. It is estimated that 1 hour of programmed instruction requires 50 hours of developmen-

Mentors are the "teachers", and protégés are the "student" workers.

There are many choices in on-site but not on-the-job training.

tal work. Consequently, this approach is effective only if "canned" programs (for example, word and data-base tutorials) are used or if large numbers of employees are to be trained so that development costs for an original program can be justified.

VIDEOS.   **Videotaped presentations** can be used on site or off site and have generally replaced films as the visual medium of choice for organizational training. At its most basic level, video training includes taped instruction that can be stopped and started at any point. Because videotapes are less expensive than traditional training films, their use has increased rapidly in recent years.

An advantage of videotape instruction is that it can be standardized. When Pizza Hut faced the burden of training 10,000 employees in various locales on such matters as competing with Domino's Pizza in the home delivery market, new products, safe driving, and customer service, it turned to video. Professionally prepared video presentations were mailed out to its individual locations, and the training was then provided on site to each shift of workers. Cost savings over traditional off-site or on-site training were substantial.

VIDEODISKS.   Organizations with large budgets for training are replacing videotapes with **videodisks**. A videodisk relies on a laser beam instead of a needle to pick up images and project them on a television screen. While more expensive to produce than simple videotape programs, videodisks provide higher-quality images, quicker starts and stops, and greater durability than do tapes. Because disks are much smaller than tapes, they are also easier to transport and use. The newness of videodisk technology and the lack of standardized courseware make the cost of these systems prohibitive for small companies. Still, corporations such as Kodak are relying on videodisks for training in business, computer logic, mechanics, and new technology. Kodak uses videodisks to keep its scientists and engineers updated on technological advances.

IVT.   **Interactive video training (IVT)** combines the best features of programmed instruction with those of videotape and/or videodisk instruction. Interactive video programs present a short video and narrative presentation (via tape or disk) and then require the trainee to respond to it. Usually, the IVT is attached to a personal computer, and the learner responds to video cues by using the keyboard or by touching the screen. This sequence—packaged program, learner response, and more programmed instruction—provides for individualized learning.

Interactive video training has been used to train 400,000 General Motors workers in occupational health and safety procedures, and it has been used to train Dow Chemical employees in how to deal with petrochemical hazards. Electrical workers have learned how to solve complex writing problems by tracing patterns on touch-sensitive screens.

On the downside, development and equipment costs associated with IVT are high. Hardware alone can cost between $6,000 and $12,000 and master videodisk costs between $2,000 and $5,000. For sophisticated programs, more than 500 hours can be spent on developing one hour of interactive video training, with costs running as high as $150,000. A sizable and diverse staff is also needed to make IVT work. Instruction designers, script writers, programmers, video producers, and subject experts are all needed. Still, IVT offers fast, effective training, and, as its popularity increases, IVT's development and hardware costs should drop, making it more affordable to small organizations.

The most recent forms of training include:

- videotapes
- videodisks
- interactive video training
- telecommunications

TELECOMMUNICATIONS.   Another innovation for on-site training involves **telecommunications training** using video satellite networks. In 1987, the Public Broadcasting System (PBS) entered the field of satellite training with the establishment of the National Narrowcast System (NNS). Produced in cooperation with the American Society for Training and Development (ASTD), the network offers more than five hours of daily programming via microwave to subscribing businesses, public agencies, and colleges and universities. Contractors are free to tape programs for six months to one year, and the system has nine training tracks targeted for specific groups (for example, sales, supervision, computer literacy, effective communications).

The major advantage of telecommunications training is its potential for speeding up communications within large corporations. A cost study conducted by Kodak estimates that a new product training program beamed via satellite to three cities costs $20,000. However, Kodak also estimates that it would cost five to six times that amount to send engineers and managers on the road to do the same training. More important, six weeks of training time was saved, which is invaluable in a competitive industry.[33]

OFF THE JOB

When the consequence of error is high, it is usually more appropriate to conduct training off the job. For example, most airline passengers would readily agree that it is preferable to train pilots in flight simulators than have them apprentice in the cockpit of a plane. Similarly, it is equally useful to have a bus driver practice on an obstacle course before taking to the roads with a load of school children.

Off-the-job training is also appropriate when complex skills need to be mastered or when the focus is on specific interpersonal skills. For example, it is difficult to build a cohesive work team when members of management are constantly interrupted by telephone calls and subordinate inquiries. Team building is more likely to occur during a management retreat when there is time to focus on establishing relationships.

However, the costs of off-the-job training are high. There also is concern over transfer of knowledge to the workplace. As research has shown, the more dissimilar the training environment is from the actual work environment, the more likely it is that trainees will *not* be able to apply knowledge learned to their jobs. For example, the transfer-of-knowledge problem is minimal for vestibule training, in which trainees work in an environment that is comparable to the actual work environment. However, it may be difficult to apply teamwork skills learned during a wilderness survival program to a job because the training environment is so different from work environment.

FORMAL COURSES.   The **formal course method** of training and development can be accomplished either by oneself—using programmed instruction, computer-assisted instruction, reading, and correspondence courses—or with teachers, as in formal classroom courses and lectures. Although many training programs use the lecture method because it efficiently and simultaneously conveys large amounts of information to large groups of people, it does have several drawbacks:

- It perpetuates the authority structure of traditional organizations and hinders performance because the learning process is not self-controlled.
- Except in the area of cognitive knowledge and conceptual principles, there is probably limited transfer of the actual skills and abilities required to do the job.
- The high verbal and symbolic requirements of the lecture method may be threatening to people with low verbal or symbolic aptitude.

There are also many choices in off-the-job training.

Ameritech Corporation, putting its top 1,000 managers through intense off-site workshops, even sends executives to work for an afternoon in soup kitchens, housing projects, and AIDS clinics, all as team-building exercises.

- The lecture method does not permit individualized training based on individual differences in ability, interests, and personality.

Because of these drawbacks, the lecture method is often complemented by other training methods.

SIMULATION.   **Simulation**, a training and development technique that presents participants with situations that are similar to actual job conditions, is used for both managers and nonmanagers.[34] A common technique for nonmanagers is the **vestibule method**, which simulates the environment of the individual's actual job. Because the environment is not real, it is generally less hectic and more safe than the actual environment; as a consequence, the potential exists for adjustment difficulties in going from the simulated training environment to the actual environment. However, the arguments for using the simulated environment are compelling: it reduces the possibility of customer dissatisfaction that can result from on-the-job training; it can reduce the frustration of the trainee; and it can save the organization a great deal of money because fewer training accidents occur. Even though these arguments may seem compelling, not all organizations, even in the same industry, see the situation the same way. Some banks, for example, train their tellers on the job, whereas others train them in a simulated bank environment.

Flight simulators allow companies to train pilots for less cost and danger than actual flight training.

ASSESSMENT CENTERS.   An increasingly popular simulation technique for managers is the **assessment center method**. This is discussed in Chapter 8 as a device for selecting managers. Assessment centers are also especially useful for identifying potential training needs. Whether used for training or selection, they appear to be a valid way to make employment decisions.[35] In fact, certain aspects of the assessment center, such as the management games and in-basket exercises, are excellent for training and need not be confined to these programs.

Assessment centers can be used for selection, performance appraisal, and training.

Regardless of where they are used, **management** or **business games** almost always entail various degrees of competition between teams or trainees. In contrast, the **in-basket exercise** is more solitary. The trainee sits at a desk and works through a pile of papers found in the in-basket of a typical manager, prioritizing, recommending solutions to problems, and taking any necessary action in response to the contents.[36]

Although the in-basket exercise tends to be an enjoyable and challenging exercise, the extent to which it improves a manager's ability depends in part on what takes place after the exercise. The analysis of what happened and what should have happened in both the business games and the in-basket exercise, when done by upper-level managers in the organization, should help trainees learn how to perform like managers. The opportunity for improvement may be drastically reduced if the trainees are left to decide what to transfer from the game or exercise to the job.

Whereas the simulation exercises may be useful for developing conceptual and problem-solving skills, two types of human relations or process-oriented training are used by organizations. Role-playing and sensitivity training develop managers' interpersonal insights—awareness of self and of others—for changing attitudes and for practices in human relations skills such as leadership or interviewing.

ROLE-PLAYING.   **Role-playing** generally focuses on emotional (that is, human relations) issues rather than on factual ones. The essence of role-playing is to create a realistic situation, as in the case discussion method you have encountered at the ends of several chapters, and then have the trainees assume the parts of specific personalities in the situation. The usefulness of role-playing depends heavily on the extent to which the trainees get into the parts they are playing. If you have done any of the role-playing in this book, you know how difficult this can be and how much easier it is to simply read the part. However, when the trainee does get into the role, the result is a greater sensitivity to the feelings and insights that are presented by the role, and because of this, you will encounter more role plays in the chapters to come.

SENSITIVITY TRAINING. Another method of training and development is **sensitivity training**. Individuals in an unstructured group exchange thoughts and feelings on the "here and now" rather than the "there and then." Although the experience of being in a sensitivity group often gives individuals insight into how and why they and others feel and act the way they do, critics claim that these results may not be beneficial because they are not directly transferable to the job.[37]

WILDERNESS TRIPS. Other methods organizations use to increase employees' feelings about the here and now and their own self-esteem include programs that involve physical feats of strength, endurance, and cooperation. These can be done on wilderness trips to various destinations.

> Everyone goes overboard during strategic planning meetings of the Meridian Group. But that doesn't bother Harvey Kinzelberg, 43, chairman of the $250-million-a-year Illinois computer-leasing firm, the nation's third largest. On the contrary, he requires it. Twice a year Kinzelberg charters a boat in the Caribbean, puts his top executives aboard, and leads them in a five-day brainstorming session cum scuba-diving expedition. . . . As often as three times a day, the company's managers pause from strategizing, strap on air tanks and face masks, and go for a plunge in the briny.
>
> Kinzelberg claims the downward-bound excursions focus his executives' attention on business by eliminating the . . . distractions of the office. More important, he says, they foster team spirit . . . . "In the potentially life-threatening environment underwater," he explains, "you realize that you depend on everyone else in the company not just for your livelihood in business but for your life as well."
>
> Excursions in the deep also provide the benefits of a different perspective, says Kinzelberg. . . . After spearing and killing a large barracuda, as he did on a recent dive, Kinzelberg finds that the sharks he faces in business seem like small fries.[38]

Wilderness training is used to build team cohesiveness.

LEARNING OBJECTIVE 5

Describe how to maximize learning.

MAXIMIZING LEARNING

However appropriate and effective a training technique may be, learning will not take place if the training is not structured properly. Exhibit 14.4 details learning factors that increase the success rates of training. As shown, prior to training, the environment must be made ready for learning to occur. During training, steps need to be taken to increase self-efficacy and retention of knowledge. After training, the work environment must be monitored to ensure that what was learned is retained.

SETTING THE STAGE FOR LEARNING

Prior to launching the program, the trainer needs to consider how information will be presented. Additionally, he or she must consider the beliefs of trainees regarding task-specific competencies.

EXHIBIT 14.4
LEARNING PRINCIPLES THAT INCREASE
TRAINING EFFECTIVENESS

Setting the Stage for Learning

1. Provide clear task instructions.
2. Model appropriate behavior.

Increasing Learning During Training

1. Provide for active participation.
2. Increase self-efficacy.
3. Match training techniques to trainees' self-efficacy.
4. Provide opportunities for enactive mastery.
5. Ensure specific, timely, diagnostic, and practical feedback.
6. Provide opportunities for trainees to practice new behaviors.

Maintaining Performance After Training

1. Develop learning points to assist in knowledge retention.
2. Set specific goals.
3. Identify appropriate reinforcers.
4. Train significant others in how to reinforce behavior.
5. Teach trainees self-management skills.

CLARITY OF INSTRUCTIONS. Research has demonstrated that learning will not occur unless task instructions are clear and precise. As noted when discussing performance standards (Chapters 9 and 10), an employee must know what is expected in order to perform as desired. Giving clear instructions includes establishing appropriate behavioral expectations. As with performance standards (see Chapter 9), statements of training expectations should be specific, and conditions under which performance is or is not expected should be identified, along with the behavior to be demonstrated.

To set the stage for desired performance, it is also useful to specify up front what the reward will be for performing as desired. A trainee is more likely to be motivated if he or she knows that successful performance can lead to positive reinforcement (promotion, pay raise, recognition) or can block the administration of negative reinforcement (for example, supervisory criticism, firing).[39]

USE OF BEHAVIORAL MODELS. Even when instructions are clear, desired behavior still may not occur if the trainee does not know how to perform as desired. This problem can be overcome through behavioral modeling. **Behavioral modeling** is a visual demonstration of desired behavior. The model can be a supervisor, co-worker, or expert, and the demonstration can be live or videotaped. The important thing is to show employees what needs to be done *prior* to their attempting the behavior.[40]

Care is needed in choosing an appropriate behavioral model. If the model makes the task look too simple, trainees may lose confidence or quit the first time they encounter a difficulty. Thus, models should show not only how to achieve desired outcomes, but also how to overcome performance obstacles.

In *behavioral modeling,* a person says, "Just watch me do it" or "Here, I'll show you."

Factors to increase learning include:
- active participation
- self-efficacy
- enactive mastery
- feedback
- practice

INCREASING LEARNING DURING TRAINING

While employees should be responsible for their own learning, organizations can do much to facilitate this.

ACTIVE PARTICIPATION.   Individuals learn better when they are actively involved in the learning process. Participation may be direct (hands on) or indirect (role plays and simulations). The important point is to hook the trainee on learning. Through active participation, trainees stay more alert and are more likely to gain confidence.

SELF-EFFICACY.   Even with behavioral modeling, learning may not occur if people judge themselves low in self-efficacy. **Self-efficacy** is defined as a trainee's beliefs about a task-specific ability. If individuals dwell on their personal deficiencies relative to the task, potential difficulties may seem more formidable than they really are. On the other hand, people who have a strong sense of self-efficacy are more likely to be motivated to overcome obstacles.

The choice of an appropriate training method is critical to self-efficacy. In a recent study, a group of trainees was taught how to use computer spreadsheets. People low in self-efficacy performed better when one-on-one tutorials were conducted; individuals with high self-efficacy (they believed they could easily learn how to use spreadsheets) performed better when appropriate behavior was merely modeled. Consequently, before choosing training techniques, the level of self-efficacy for each trainee should be determined.[41]

ENACTIVE MASTERY.   Self-efficacy increases when experiences fail to validate fears and when skills acquired allow for mastery of once-threatening situations. This process is called enactive mastery. To facilitate task mastery, trainers should arrange the subject matter so that trainees experience success. While this may be easy when tasks are simple, it can be quite difficult when tasks are complex.

Solutions include segmenting the task, shaping behavior, and/or setting proximal goals. Task segmentation involves breaking a complex task into smaller or simpler components. For some jobs (for example, laboratory technician), the components (drawing blood, culturing a specimen, running a blood chemistry machine) can be taught individually and in any order. In others, segments must be taught sequentially because task B builds on task A and task C builds on task B (using mathematics, driving a car, conducting an effective interview.)[42]

Shaping includes rewarding closer and closer approximations to desired behavior. For example, in teaching managers how to conduct a selection interview, trainees can be reinforced for making eye contact and for developing situational questions.

The setting of proximal or intermediary goals also increases mastery perceptions. Consider a software developer with an overall objective of developing a new word processing package. Proximal goals might include meeting a project specifications deadline, developing algorithms for fonts by a set deadline, developing an algorithm for formatting paragraphs, and so on. These proximal goals all lead to the attainment of the distal or overall objective.[43]

PLENTY OF FEEDBACK.   In order for individuals to master new concepts and acquire new skills, they must receive accurate diagnostic feedback about their performance. When feedback is either not received or inaccurate, the wrong behaviors may be practiced. While feedback can be provided by a supervisor, co-workers, customers, computers, or the individual performing the task, it must be specific, timely, behaviorally and not personally based, and practical. If a performance discrepancy exists, the feedback should also be diagnostic and include instructions or modeling of how to perform better.[44] Of course individual differences such as the person's readiness for feedback and learning must be considered.

PRACTICE, PRACTICE, PRACTICE.   While an individual may be able to perform as desired one time, the goal of training is to ensure that desired behavior occurs consistently. This is most likely to occur when trainees are able to practice and internalize standards of performance. Practicing the wrong behaviors is detrimental. Therefore, practice must follow specific feedback.

It should be stressed that, for some jobs, tasks must be overlearned. Overlearning includes the internalization of responses so that the trainee doesn't have to consciously think about behavior before responding. For example, if a plane is losing altitude rapidly, a pilot must know how to respond immediately. There isn't time to think about what should be done! The emergency routine must be second nature and totally internalized.

MAINTAINING PERFORMANCE AFTER TRAINING

Once training is completed, the employee needs to be monitored to ensure that newly acquired behaviors will continue. Several steps can be taken to ensure this.

DEVELOPMENT OF LEARNING POINTS.   First, new skills and information are more likely to be retained when learning points are developed. Learning points summarize key behaviors—particularly those that are not obvious—and serve as cognitive cues back on the job. While learning points can be written by trainers, trainee-generated learning points—even if they are of lower quality—enhance recall and lead to better skill acquisition and retention.[45]

Maintain performance by:
- **learning points**
- **reinforcement**
- **significant others**
- **goals**
- **self-reinforcement**
- **follow-up**

REINFORCEMENT.   Learning new behaviors is difficult and threatening. To ensure that trainees continue to demonstrate the skill they have learned, behavior must be reinforced. **Reinforcement** can be positive (praise, financial rewards) or negative (if you perform as desired, I will quit screaming at you), but it must be performance contingent.[46] See Chapter 10 for a more detailed presentation of reinforcement theory.

TRAIN SIGNIFICANT OTHERS.   To ensure that reinforcers are appropriately administered, trainers must also train significant others to look for and reinforce desired changes. If a person who has been labeled a troubled employee continues to be viewed as a problem employee, there is no incentive for the person to display new behavior. If, however, a supervisor or co-worker responds positively to behavior changes, the frequency with which the new behavior will be displayed is likely to increase.

SET SPECIFIC GOALS.   It is also useful to set specific goals for subsequent performance. These goals should be challenging but not so difficult as to be perceived as impossible. Without goals, people have little basis for judging how they are doing.[47]

SELF-REINFORCEMENT.   Because it is not always possible for significant others to reinforce an individual worker, a long-term objective should be to teach employees how to set their own goals and administer their own reinforcement. When people create self-incentives for their efforts, they are capable of making self-satisfaction contingent on their own performance. Obviously, the challenge here is to ensure that personal goals are congruent with organizational goals. As noted in previous chapters, this leads to self-management.[48]

Getting someone to write it down and agree to it really gets them committed to doing it!

FOLLOW-UP.   A final principle to remember is **follow-up**. Once a participant leaves the training program, the personnel and human resource manager should provide a means of follow-up to ensure that the participant is doing what was taught. All too often, participants who want to change their current behavior get back to work and slip into the old patterns. This in turn results in a significant loss of effectiveness of the training program. One approach to preventing this from happening is the **contract plan**. Its simplicity is a key factor in its success. Each participant writes an informal agreement near the end of a training program, stating which aspects of the program he or she believes will have the most beneficial effect back on the job and then agreeing to apply those aspects. Each participant is also asked to choose another participant from the program to whom a copy of the contract is given and who agrees to check up on the participant's progress every few weeks.

Although incorporating these principles of learning is desirable, many training and development programs do not have them or are designed without considering reinforcement, feedback, goal setting and follow-up. Nevertheless, application of these principles of learning can increase the chances of successfully implementing a training and development program. Successful implementation also depends on selecting appropriate programs.

LEARNING OBJECTIVE 6

Indicate how to select a training program.

Selection of a training and development program is a result of matching needed skills with the needed level of training.

SELECTING AN APPROPRIATE PROGRAM

A knowledge of the principles of learning, the four categories of skills needed by individuals in organizations, and the methods of training and development available (including their advantages and disadvantages), form the basis for selecting the most appropriate training and development programs for a specific organization. This selection is based on the answers to the following questions:

- What skills do the employees need to learn?
- At what level do these skills need to be learned?
- What training and development programs are most appropriate for the required skills and level?

THE SKILLS NEEDED

The answers to the first two questions are determined by the results of the needs analyses. Referring to Exhibit 14.3, you can see that the question of what skills employees need to learn can be answered in part by knowing what types of employees need training. For example, if performance deficiencies exist among the supervisory and rank-and-file employees, most of the training should be aimed at increasing technical skills. On the other hand, interpersonal skills would be the primary need of middle-management employees, while top-level managers might need conceptual or managerial and administrative skills. These matches between type of employee and type of skill needed are useful guides to training employees for current and future jobs. Knowledge of this can facilitate employee career development and organizational planning for training and development programs.

THE LEVEL OF SKILLS NEEDED

But to use these matches for the benefit of the individual and the organization, it is still necessary to know the level of skill needed: increased operational proficiency, skill development, or fundamental knowledge. The results of the job and person needs analyses determine the levels required, particularly for current job training. The levels needed for future job training are determined by the organizational, job, and person needs analyses.

PROGRAM SELECTION

The final step is to determine which programs are most appropriate for the skill and level of training needed. A guide for making this choice is shown in Exhibit 14.5. For example, apprenticeship training is appropriate for those who need to increase their operational proficiency in basic literary and technical skills, whereas the case discussion method is appropriate for conceptual or managerial and administrative skill training at all three levels.

Often, organizations select not just one program but several. Training and development for almost any level or group of employees requires a combination of skills because jobs typically have several dimensions or roles. For example, for today's human resource managers to be effective, they need to perform several roles (presented in Chapter 2) that previously were not necessarily required:

- Businessperson
- Shaper of organizational change
- Consultant and partner to line managers
- Strategy formulator and implementor
- Talent manager
- Asset manager and cost controller

Activities for human resource managers that develop the skills, knowledge, and abilities to play these roles are shown in Exhibit 14.6.

EXHIBIT 14.5
SELECTING A TRAINING AND DEVELOPMENT PROGRAM

SKILLS REQUIRED

SKILL LEVEL REQUIRED	BASIC LITERACY AND TECHNICAL SKILLS	INTERPERSONAL SKILLS	CONCEPTUAL/ INTEGRATIVE SKILLS
Fundamental knowledge	Job rotation Multiple management Apprenticeship training Job instruction training	Role-playing Sensitivity training Formal courses	Job Rotation Multiple management Simulation Case discussion
Skill development	Job rotation Multiple management Simulation Supervisory assistance	Role-playing Sensitivity training Job rotation Multiple management Simulation Wilderness trips	Job rotation Multiple management Simulation Case discussion
Operational efficiency	Job rotation Multiple management Apprenticeship training Job instruction training Simulation Internship and assistantship Supervisory assistance	Role-playing Job rotation Multiple management Apprenticeship training Job instruction training Simulation	Job rotation Multiple management Simulation Case discussion

SOURCE: Adapted from T. J. Von der Embse, "Choosing a Management Development Program: A Decision Model," *Personnel Journal* (Oct. 1973): 911.

EXHIBIT 14.6
TRAINING AND DEVELOPMENT ACTIVITIES FOR HUMAN RESOURCE MANAGERS

Businessperson:

- Participates in courses on finance for nonfinancial executives as well as marketing courses
- Seeks exposure to marketing organization
- Participates in task forces, business planning teams, acquisition/divestiture teams

Shaper of change:

- Participates in team-building exercises
- Engages in formalized mentor relationships
- Researches the change process

Consultant and partner to line managers:

- Does volunteer work in professional organizations, health-care coalitions, charities, or company consortiums
- Coaches and evaluates performance
- Pairs junior with senior staffers and consults with internal staff

Strategy formulator and implementor:

- Learns content of business strategy
- Becomes knowledgeable in the strategies of all the businesses or divisions
- Describes the human resource implications of these various strategies

Talent manager:

- Talks constantly to all line managers
- Monitors what the competition is doing
- Attends conferences to develop a network

Asset manager and cost controller:

- Takes courses in finance and accounting
- Reads journal articles on utility analysis
- Confers with those in the finance and accounting departments

SOURCE: Adapted from *HR Reporter* (July 1987): 3–4. Used by permission.

Waste Management has training in ethics.

There is a growing need for many line managers to develop leadership skills. Good leaders facilitate organizational changes, employee participation, and teamwork. Facilitating teamwork is particularly important and challenging when bringing together employees who generally haven't worked together. Teambuilding exercises are critical in developing teamwork skills in managers.

Training managers in ethics is also important. Increasingly, firms need to ensure that theirs is an ethical culture and to find ways to build one if their culture is found lacking. Ethics as Waste Management envisions it is described in Chapter 3. The training they are providing to support this culture is described in the following feature, "Managing Human Resources at Waste Management."

MANAGING HUMAN RESOURCES
at Waste Management

Accotding to Jodie Bernstein vice president of environmental policy, "Waste Management is doing ethics training" in a variety of ways. One is through management training. A few years ago, we developed a pilot program with the help of consultants, Barbara Tofler and Chuck Powers of Resources for Responsible Management. Through an interview process that identified what issues were most troubling to our managers, they developed a series of case studies that were used in three-and-a-half-hour sessions with managers in our North American and Chemical Waste Management operating groups. The cases dealt with environmental and health and safety issues and also with conventional business ethics: getting and using competitive information, for example."

After some fine tuning, the program is now being incorporated into the existing corporate wide-management training program under the direction of Ron White, director of HR development. "We now offer a four-hour module that explores issues in making ethical business decisions for all levels of management," said White.

"Our top and regional managers have all been through the program, and we're now working with the mid-level managers. Next on the schedule is adapting the program to the supervisory level. Feedback on the program has been good. We can tell there's a higher level of awareness because we hear managers discussing these issues informally now, too."

"Most of the cases we're using now are not related specifically to our business, but involve situations that could occur in any business. One, for example, deals with how to handle a long-service, top-performing salesperson who lied on his resume when he was hired. There aren't any easy answers to problems like these, and people have to learn to use their best business judgment while being mindful of the ethical issues."

"If we get any complaints from the program, it's that people get frustrated by not having black-and-white answers. We've got a pragmatic bunch of people around here, and this program is really pushing them to explore options before making a decision. It's also resulting in more collaboration. People are finding that rather than making a snap decision on the spot, they are better off discussing it with others, even taking the problem to the boss if it's a big one."

"By building the module into our existing training programs, we will be able to get down into the entire organization of 60,000 employees. Right now I'm doing the management training with people on my staff who are regular trainers. But we are also training facilitators at the local level who will be able to run programs as needed in every location. We're not being naive about this. We know that one supervisory training session isn't going to make someone ethically aware forever. We have to keep working on it and reinforcing the message."[49]

Finally, the effectiveness of a training and development program must be carefully assessed. This is an important component in attaining the goal of a technologically competent and adaptable work force, and we will discuss this extensively in Chapter 20.

INTERNATIONAL COMPARISONS

In contrast to companies in the United States, Japanese companies appear to offer far more extensive training for their employees. This also appears to be the case in Germany, particularly regarding apprenticeship training and job redesign.

Japanese firms invest heavily in training.

JAPAN

According to studies of vocational training in Japan as many as 80 percent of all business enterprises conduct in-company job training. Broken down according to employee classification, job training is made available to new regular employees in 75 percent of all companies, and to nonregular employees in 52 percent of them.[50]

If classified according to the size of the firm, training increases with organizational size. Every firm with more than 5,000 employees provides its own training. Vocational training in small- to medium-sized companies depends to a greater extent on cooperative centers established through the effort of the government's employment promotion agency, aided by state, municipal, and town agencies.

The in-company form of training is looked upon as the key to each company's productivity and managerial control. Regular employees generally have academic training but few, if any, vocational skills. Training is thus the means by which an employee is shaped to the company's needs. It is not unusual, for new employees to have anywhere from one to six months of training before being integrated into the work force. Supplemental training usually continues throughout the first three years of an employee's career, with additional training provided as needed.

Descriptions of training programs generally reveal a greater emphasis on the company as a whole—its role in society (including the community, the nation, and the world), its relationship to the competition, its marketing goals and objectives. In short, training constantly seeks to develop the individual worker as a fully rounded worker who not only sees the whole picture, but is also able to respond to it. The payoffs of this philosophy are minimal levels of turnover and absenteeism.[51]

Actual job training teaches workers to apply skills to a variety of situations, thereby permitting worker rotation. All blue-collar workers are expected to be multiskilled within four or five years after joining the company. Many believe that this orientation toward skills enrichment and labor mobility is a crucial factor in the rapid growth of the Japanese economy.

The Japanese also differ substantially in the way they train today's college graduate to become tomorrow's manager. The two major aspects of this training are pre-employment education, or socialization and training given before the first day on the job, and initial managerial education. This training has the following general aims:

- To educate new graduates regarding discipline and the transition from student to company life
- To teach professionalism and the significance and meaning of work
- To provide background information about the company and to familiarize employees with distinctive management trends, rules, and etiquette
- To cultivate a spirit of harmony and teamwork among employees[52]

Pre-employment education consists of communication between the company and the future employees who are still in school. Future employees are frequently sent a directory of all new recruits, an employee handbook, a booklet on health and nutrition, and even words of encouragement from senior employees. Many companies provide an opportunity for future employees to get to know one another by holding meetings that

> . . . afford an opportunity . . . to learn the company song, to meet senior employees who are graduates of the same university, to visit the factories and

see exhibitions of the company's products, and to become familiar with the company's various departments and divisions.[53]

Initial managerial education involves starting from the ground up. For example, the current president of Matsushita Electronic Works spent his first six months carrying and shifting goods in the company's storage area. During orientation and the work experience program, new employees live together in company residences. Here they learn social rules, etiquette, human relations, and punctuality—all considered necessary for an effective manager.

An important aspect of this training and development is the evaluation of how well the new employees have done. Mitsubishi, for example, administers a quiz, which the recruits must pass, on the knowledge essential for handling the companies' products.

GERMANY

Germany's economy is based on providing high-priced, high-quality goods. German executives say a key factor in their industrial success is a sophisticated work force. "You need highly qualified people when you produce high-quality goods," says Hans-Peter Kassai, chief economist with Daimler-Benz.[54]

A relatively unique feature of training and development employees in Germany is an extensive and successful apprenticeship system. The three-and-a-half-year apprenticeship program gives employees wide expertise on many machines. The program costs about $15,000 per apprentice, and each year German companies spend about $20 billion on their programs. Apprenticeship training for almost a half million German students begins at age 15 when compulsory schooling ends. At that point, youths select one of several programs. By comparison, in the United States, many machine operators receive just a week or two of training.[55]

Germany is famous for its apprentice programs.

Even though the apprenticeship programs are costly, German firms believe it pays off because workers end up being more loyal and more willing to stay. Once the companies take on apprentices as permanent employees, they often stay for years, giving a stability and maturity to the work force that many countries lack. However, demographic shifts are impacting the future supply of skilled workers. In 1993, for the first time, the number of students entering university in Germany exceeded those entering apprentice programs. As a consequence, a number of apprentice slots went unfilled.

But Germany's programs are facing some problems.

CURRENT TRENDS

Trends in training and development are mushrooming as world competitiveness, work force diversity, and total quality management demand fundamental changes in business practices. The trends of particular importance are:

- Managing for globalization
- Linking with the needs of customers
- Training in business ethics
- Training in diversity management
- Managing the change process
- Company schools

LEARNING OBJECTIVE 7

Discuss the many trends in training and development.

MANAGING FOR GLOBALIZATION

A few things seem certain, and one is that "globalization" will continue to be an inescapable buzzword. Businesses will operate in an ever more interconnected world. With continuing advances in computers and communications, world financial markets will meld. Manufacturing prowess will appear almost suddenly in new Taiwans and South Koreas.

A shrinking world will mean an expanding clock. Managers will have to shape organizations that can respond quickly to developments abroad. As speed and agility become paramount virtues, we will see even more decentralization, with responsibility closer to the operating level.[56]

U.S. companies like Gillette are serious about developing global managers.

Organizations are having to develop a world or global structure, perspective, and strategy. Human resource policies need to mirror the necessary organizational characteristics. According to Gillette's CEO, Alfred Zeien, doing this takes a great deal of time. Gillette's approach to training for globalization is highlighted in the feature, "Managing Global Human Resources at Gillette: Building a Global Management Team."

There need to be expatriate, third/country, and host/country human resource policies to create an effective worldwide work force. The expatriate assignment increasingly needs to be made an attractive one in order to attract the best employees, and assignments anywhere have to be seen as vital components of the whole. According to Jerry Junkins, of Texas Instruments, overseas managers need to look beyond their own "fiefdoms" to consider the capabilities and needs of the company as a whole. Junkins now has all the members of the company's worldwide management group working together.[58]

Training is important for expatriates and families in order to increase their success rate.

U.S. EXPATRIATES.   The training and development of expatriates (U.S. citizens working abroad for a U.S. company) presents special challenges. Management development of expatriates should take up where selection leaves off. Although only a few companies provide expatriate training, it is critical. The basic aspects of expatriate development include the following:

- Development of expatriates before, during, and after foreign assignments
- Orientation and training of expatriate families before, during, and after foreign assignments
- Development of the headquarters staff responsible for the planning, organization, and control of overseas operations[59]

This range of training is aimed at bringing about attitudinal and behavioral changes in the expatriates, their families, and the staff (here and abroad) responsible for multinational operations.

By having such an extensive management development effort for expatriates, multinational companies can increase the effectiveness of their expatriate managers, and such a program can increase the number of domestic managers applying for expatriate positions. To really make expatriate positions attractive, however, multinational companies must also offer commensurate salaries, which makes having expatriate managers expensive. It would currently cost a company, for example, almost $200,000 a year to maintain an expatriate manager in Japan. Such a middle-level manager would earn about $60,000 at home.[60] In addition to providing an attractive salary to expatriate managers, multinationals also need to provide an attractive package of indirect compensation as described in Chapter 13, Indirect Compensation.

EFFECTIVE CROSS-CULTURAL TRAINING.   Once an employee has been selected for an expatriate position, cross-cultural training becomes the next critical step in ensuring the expatriate's effectiveness and success abroad. Depending on the assigned country, the employee and his or her family may be confronted with a culture markedly different from their own. These contrasts can extend

ROME wasn't built in a day. Neither was Gillette's international management team. According to Gillette Chairman and CEO Alfred M. Zeien, it takes at least 25 years to build an international management corps that possesses the skills, experience, and abilities to take a global organization from one level of success to the next.

Gillette, through its senior management team, has learned that developing managers through international assignments helps the business grow. The firm's International Trainee Program for new recruits is one of the company's key strategies for building its worldwide management corps. Its other key international staffing strategy is hiring and developing foreign nationals to staff its operations globally. Many of these individuals have become part of Gillette's growing international corps.

Interestingly, fewer than 15 percent of the company's international corps are expatriates—natives of the United States. At least 85 percent of Gillette's international managers come from one of the other 27 countries in which it has operations.

For the most part, Gillette hires foreign nationals to staff management positions in countries other than the United States. Often, however, the organization first identifies these individuals while they're studying at U.S. universities for their MBAs. The new hires typically work at Gillette's Boston headquarters for a year, then return to their home countries, much like trainees in the International Trainee Program.

After working in their home countries for about four years, Gillette typically moves managers on to other countries and other assignments. As Gillette managers build their international experience, they also teach and develop other potential managers within the organization.

Often these managers with international experience are prime candidates for positions that open up when the company enters into new markets or into joint ventures. Such was the case with its new joint venture last fall with a company in China. Because Gillette first started planning the joint venture in China more than four years ago, it began identifying individual managers then who would be right for assignments in that new business.

As Gillette expatriate Bob McCusker puts it, "Gillette has a lot of resources that we can apply to our new ventures." McCusker, currently on assignment in Pakistan, says that he finds it gratifying when individuals who work in a new Gillette venture in one area go on to help develop new ventures in other areas.

Gillette's policy of giving its managers international experience attracts individuals seeking international careers. Gillette managers are constantly on the lookout for individuals who show interest and promise in moving through the Gillette organization worldwide. "One of my responsibilities is to look for people who are promotable internationally," says Jorgen Wedel, president of Braun USA, a subsidiary of Gillette, and a native of Denmark. "We need people who have a global understanding of the business, and we need managers who can manage that business. I think it's one of the key responsibilities of management today."

Dieu Eng Seng agrees. Seng is the area vice president of Oral-B, another Gillette company, Asia Pacific. A native of Singapore, Seng's past service with Gillette has included assignments in Australia, Singapore, China, Hong Kong, Malaysia, and the United States. "One of my key objectives is to identify, recruit, and develop competent managers. I'm confident that from these good people will generate a flow of business growth and profits into the future."

International management teams clearly aren't built in a day. They aren't even built in a year. In Gillette's case, careful planning and constant attention to international development, however, can yield employees that support and grow a business successfully from one decade to the next.[57]

beyond the language barrier and encompass aspects of social life, political climate, and religious differences.[61]

Studies indicate that there are three areas that contribute to a smooth transition to a foreign post: cultural training, language instruction, and assistance with practical, day-to-day matters.[62] The first two phases necessarily begin prior to the international assignment. Because these phases take time, the notification of posting should be done well in advance of the departure. Business conditions, however, cannot always be planned so precisely. Recognizing this, HR specialists must nevertheless encourage line managers to plan for their global needs. The last category, practical assistance, begins once the employee arrives in the host-country.

LINKING WITH THE NEEDS OF CUSTOMERS

Organizations can use their training and development activities to link with the needs of customers. For example,

> . . . designing, manufacturing, and operating increasingly complex high-technology systems demands advanced knowledge and hands-on expertise. That's why Siemens—one of the world's leading manufacturers of high-technology equipment—conducts a variety of training programs for many of its 27,000 employees, as well as for its customers, all across America.
>
> Siemens USA courses are designed to meet the special needs of customers and their markets. For example, on-the-job training for customers ensures that all the capabilities of the company's technologically advanced systems are fully utilized, and all their benefits are fully realized. Similarly, the special classes for Siemens engineering, manufacturing, service, and administrative personnel are designed to sharpen skills, enhance professional knowledge, and improve service expertise and effectiveness.
>
> Constant, specialized training is one of the ways Siemens is fulfilling their commitment to keep customers and employees ahead of the competition in a fiercely changing, tough, and complex high-technology marketplace.[63]

TRAINING IN BUSINESS ETHICS

Although becoming increasingly important due to legal considerations, training in business ethics has been low on the priority list of much of U.S. business; witness the results of a recent survey of more than 1,000 members of the American Management Association:

> Seventy-three percent of managers surveyed said they probably would resign if their boss insisted that they carry out some action they strongly believed was unethical. This percentage is a decrease from the almost 80 percent of managers who responded the same way in 1981.
>
> Most of the recent participants agreed that corporate codes of ethics and ethics workshops were helpful to understand issues and help guide them through their daily decision making. However, more than three-quarters of these managers noted that their companies did not offer such workshops. Almost half said that their firms did not have a written code of ethics.[64]

As more companies such as Waste Management recognize the need for promoting moral excellence, however, they are beginning to provide training in ethical behavior. For example, Chemical Bank has included ethics discussions in its training programs. According to Karen Alphin, employee communications director, Chemical Bank's "Decision Making and Corporate Values" program addresses issues that are of interest not just to bankers, but also to ethical individuals. Convinced of the need for "a conversation about ethics," Polaroid Corporation set up a major internal conference that brought philosophers, ethi-

Training in ethics and diversity management is more important than ever.

cists, and business professors to the company for lectures and discussions of ethical concepts.[65]

Big Six public accounting firm, Arthur Andersen, also runs several programs on ethical behavior for its employees.[66]

TRAINING IN DIVERSITY MANAGEMENT

Organizations operating today for the foreseeable future will continue to have very diverse work forces. As indicated in Chapter 3, this diversity encompasses race, gender, religion, age, disability, language differences, and cultural differences. Human Resource and line managers are already dealing with these differences through a variety of diversity management programs (a few of which are referred to in Chapter 3). But there are also many other differences in people that are elements of work force diversity. For example, people differ on their problem-solving and decision-making styles; conflict resolution modes; preferences for different types of leadership; preferences for different degrees of empowerment and participation; and comfort with different types of job design. These are just some of the important differences among people in organizations. Knowing how to deal with these differences takes knowledge and a company position of adaptability. Jim Preston's description of what they do at Avon (Chapter 3) is worth another read.

Consequently, organizations are developing and delivering diversity programs.[67] Because each organization is unique, it is important that the firm begin with a diagnosis of the type of diversity it has. This analysis enables the firm to then match the content of its diversity program with the particular type of diversity that needs addressing. This approach also makes it easier to measure and monitor progress.

MANAGING THE CHANGE PROCESS

Programs for total quality management and for redesigning jobs represent important changes for most organizations, and their success depends on effective management. As Linda Ackerman, president of Linda S. Ackerman, Inc., in Oakland, California, says:

> Managing change is "one of the cutting-edge areas" for HR managers today. Most employees are traumatized by complex change, and managers have a responsibility to guide the changes process and minimize its effects on employees.[68]

Helping firms change is a big role for training today.

The change process, regardless of whether it is total quality management or installing automation, appears to benefit when employees communicate their needs and participate in the process and when top management supports the process and is willing to modify the corporate culture as needed. The more extensive the change—the more people and more parts of the organization significantly changing—the more likely it is that the HR practices will need to change at all levels and the more likely it is that the change will occur over time in stages.

EXECUTIVE EDUCATION.   Human resource practices change as the strategy of the organization changes, and strategical changes themselves are being orchestrated more frequently by human resources. Organizations such as Xerox, Weyerhaeuser, Northern Telecom, and General Foods implement programs of strategic change through management and executive education programs. Here the top management teams come together and identify what needs to be done to be more competitive. Executive education was crucial to the Weyerhaeuser

Company as it restructured itself in order to survive the precipitous downturn in the forest products industry in the early 1980s. Action was not only fast, it had a major impact on how the entire company was structured.

> To cope with the economic downturn and the new competitive forces, the Weyerhaeuser Company . . . made significant structural changes. Those changes included a massive reorganization. Weyerhaeuser had gone from being a highly centralized organization to a decentralized one. Decision making was pushed down to three new operating companies, of which the Weyerhaeuser Forest Products Company [FPC] was one. Essentially, the parent became a holding company, and the operating companies . . . highly autonomous.[69]

Within FPC, chief executive Charles Bingham, and his executive team, along with the director of strategic education, Horace Parker, decided that a major strategic repositioning was going to be made using executive development.

> Before that improved positioning could yield results, however, Bingham and his team realized that there would have to be a total transformation of the organization—its corporate culture, knowledge base, skills level, style of leadership, and team orientation. "We had to change the whole way we thought about the business—from being . . . primarily a raw-material manufacturing organization, which characterized us in all our 80 years of history, to being primarily a customer- and market-driven organization."[70]

Perhaps in contrast to changes many organizations have made in the past, success from organizational improvement programs is only likely to occur with everyone changing and everyone involved in the change. This requires time:

> But experience suggested the need to avoid rushing into a quick fix. [Bingham's] goal was not to "convert" a handful of top executives to the new vision of being a market-driven rather than a production-driven company. "What we needed," Bingham stresses, "was for the whole organization to 'buy into' the new strategic direction."[71]

As a result, FPC established an extensive executive development program and its own leadership institute.

> . . . To meet this need, the executive team took a risk. They decided to revitalize a complex organization. In 1986, the FPC Executive Team launched the Leadership Institute.
>
> How the organization was sold on the worth of an executive development program is an important lesson. The trump card used in closing the deal was to involve the executives at various levels of the organization in the planning stages. During those stages, they came to see, as did the executive team, that an intensive development program such as the Leadership Institute was not an expensive frill but a prerequisite for survival. The Leadership Institute, top management was convinced, would be a powerful catalyst that could accelerate the normal process of change—of everything from a corporate culture to how a salesperson deals with customers.[72]

As envisioned, the Leadership Institute has become a place where managers come to discuss the new strategy and its implications for them. The institute has expanded to offer training to managers in needed skills, knowledge, and leadership styles. Thus far, FPC appears to be on track to meet its goals for 1995. Success clearly has been due in large measure to the quality of the human resource management activities and to the skilled leadership of those at the company.[73]

In summing up the future in corporate education, some business educators speculate that advanced and specialized training will be a way of life for the foreseeable future. While some company schools will concentrate on the operational mechanics of the business they operate, others will provide more general management education, even global education. Almost without exception, the charges for training will be paid for by the home organization of the trainees, making corporate education a business within a business.

COMPANY SCHOOLS

Company schools focus on the education of employees and sometimes customers. McDonald's Hamburger University, which was begun in 1961, is among the oldest corporate universities. Started in a basement, the center now trains more than 2,500 students annually in the fine details of restaurant and franchise operations. General Electric, which has been an advocate of training and development for years, has an up-to-date facility in Croton-on-Hudson, New York, that it uses for divisional and group training. Corporate schools have also been developed by such diverse firms as AT&T, Ford Motor Company, United Airlines, Chase Manhattan, Kodak, and Digital Equipment.

Motorola dedicated its $10-million Galvin Center for Continuing Education in 1986. The facility contains 88,000 square feet of classrooms, individual instruction centers, an auditorium, lounges, dining facilities, and a fitness center. Affiliated with the National Technological Union, a consortium that teaches by satellite, Motorola offers courses leading to three master's degrees.

More recently, Motorola opened Motorola University, where it spends millions a year to teach total quality management to its own employees and to faculty from business and engineering schools.[74] Like a growing number of corporations, Motorola is committed to company-based education. Motorola is even pushing its training methods in public schools to prepare the next generation of employees.[75]

Many firms are now affiliated with the National Technological Institute of Fort Collins, Colorado, which provides training for engineers via satellite transmission. Professionals from leading universities, such as Georgia Tech, Boston University, and MIT, teach classes at 24 cooperating colleges of engineering. The companies involved provide courses both live and on tape to suit the convenience of the students. Students interact with instructors via teleconferencing and electronic mail.

What sets us apart is that we train people to be merchants. We let them see all the numbers so they know exactly how they're doing within the store and within the company; they know their cost, their markup, their overhead, and their profit. It's a big responsibility and a big opportunity.

—Sam Walton, past chairman, Wal-Mart

DID YOU KNOW?

Motorola gives employees 40 hours of training yearly. By the year 2000 it may be 160 hours.

SUMMARY

The training and development of employees is becoming an increasingly important and necessary activity of human resource management. Rapidly changing technologies make employees obsolete more quickly today than ever before. As employee training and development becomes more important, it must also be more effective. This requires careful attention to the three phases of training and development: assessment or needs analysis, program development and implementation, and evaluation. The three types of needs analysis discussed in this chapter are a careful and systematic diagnosis of the short- and long-range human resource needs of the organization; a determination of the skills and abilities necessary for specific jobs in the organization; and an analysis of the current and expected performance levels of employees in the organization compared with the performance levels desired of them. This difference between actual and desired employee performance defines a training and development need.

Effective training and development depends on a sound needs analysis and on careful selection and implementation of training programs. There is no one best way to train employees, since program effectiveness depends in part on the skills to be learned and the level at which they need to be learned. However, several learning principles can make any program better. Those qualities include providing feedback, reinforcement, follow-up, practice, goals, sufficient employee motivation, and consideration for individual differences. Making sure that these are a part of the program can help ensure changes in employee behavior.

The final question then remaining is who should be trained. In general, anyone with an important performance discrepancy should be trained. A program is then chosen that matches skills needed with the type of employee or group to be trained.

The last major phase of training and development is the evaluation phase. This phase compares data to see whether a change has occurred and to determine whether the change is due to the training and development program. This is described in detail in Chapter 20.

Training and development programs will continue to be important as the emphasis on continual education increases and as companies make radical changes in their approaches to their business. The movement to total quality management is a prime example of this, and we will examine this concept closely in Chapter 15.

KEY CONCEPTS

apprenticeship training
assessment center
    method
assistantships
behavioral modeling
basic literacy skills
    (BLS)
basic technical skills
    (BTS)
business games
conceptual integrative
    skills (CIS)
contract plan
follow-up
formal course method
in-basket exercise
interactive video
    training (IVT)

internships
interpersonal skills (IPS)
job instruction training
    (JIT)
job needs analysis
job rotation
management games
mentoring
off-the-job training
    programs (OFFJT)
on-site but not on-the-
    job
on-the-job training
    programs (OJT)
organizational climate
organizational needs
    analysis
person needs analysis

programmed instruction
    (PI)
reinforcement
role-playing
self-efficacy
sensitivity training
shaping
simulation
statistical process control
    (SPC)
supervisory assistance
telecommunications
    training
training and
    development
vestibule method
videodisks
videotaped presentations

REVIEW AND DISCUSSION QUESTIONS

1. Describe and explain the three major phases of any training and development program.
2. How do companies decide whether to invest in training? What factors would influence a company not to invest in training?

3. Reflect for a moment on your own work experience. What benefits did your former (or present) employer receive by training you? Why didn't your employer just hire someone who could perform the job without training?

4. What legal considerations influence training and development decisions? How can training and development programs avoid potential legal problems?

5. What relationship does training and development have with other activities of human resource management?

6. What are some design principles that can enhance the learning that takes place in training and development programs?

7. As a first-line supervisor, what indicators would you look for in order to decide whether a low-performing subordinate was a selection mistake or merely in need of training? Can you illustrate this dilemma with an example from your own organizational experience? (Hint: Refer to Chapter 10.)

8. Discuss the strategic involvement of training and development.

9. You have been asked to train employees to use personal computers. What factors would you consider in designing the program?

10. How can training programs in diversity management help organizations? (Hint: Refer to Chapter 3.)

EXERCISES AND CASES

FIELD PROJECT

Visit a local business, and ask the store manager to describe what training (if any) is offered to new and old employees. Report to the class and compare results.

CAREER MANAGEMENT EXERCISE: SO WHAT ARE YOUR TRAINING NEEDS AND DESIRES?

One of the trends in companies today is to empower workers, to give them the opportunity and responsibility to guide their own progress and career development. You have been doing many of these activities already regarding a hypothetical job you would like to have. This began in Chapter 4 with your indicating what type of job you would like to have after graduation. In Chapter 13, you indicated the types of indirect compensation you would like (need to have!). While not introduced in that chapter, many individuals and companies believe that the training programs organizations offer can be a really important benefit. With the rapidly changing environment and technology, skill obsolescence is occurring faster than ever before.

So let's assume that you also believe that training programs are an important part of your career, and that identifying them is, in large part, up to you to decide! As an exercise in human resource management (your own!), indicate what types of training programs you would like to have over your first five years of work. Whether you expect to change jobs and companies may have a big impact on how you answer this. Refer to Exhibit 14.3 and select those programs from those in on-the-job, on-site but not on-the-job, and off-the-job categories that you think would be most interesting and useful to you.

On-the-Job: _____

_____

_____

_____

On-Site but Not On-the-Job _____

_____

_____

_____

Off-the-Job: _____

_____

_____

_____

CASE

A Training Misdiagnosis or a Mistake

Sue Campbell, the training rep for the regional office of a large service organization, is excited about a new training program. The HR department at the headquarters office had informed her six months ago that it had purchased a speed-reading training program from a reputable firm and that statistics showed that the program had indeed proven to be very effective in other companies.

Sue knew that most individuals in the regional office were faced, on a daily basis, with a sizable amount of incoming correspondence, including internal memoranda, announcements of new and revised policies and procedures, reports of federal legislation, and letters from customers. So, a course in speed reading should certainly help most employees.

The headquarters office had flown regional training reps in for a special session on how to conduct the training, and Sue therefore began the program in her regional office with great confidence. She led five groups (30 employees each) through the program, which consisted of nine two-hour sessions. Sessions were conducted in the on-site training facilities. Altogether, 1,200 employees in the organization participated in the training, at an approximate cost to the company of $110 per participant (including training materials and time away from work). The program was well received by the participants, and

speed tests administered before and after training showed that, on average, reading speed increased 250 percent with no loss in comprehension.

A couple of months after the last session, Sue informally asked a couple of employees who went through the training whether speed reading was easing their work load. They said they were not using it at work but did use it in their off-the-job reading. Sue checked with several other participants and heard the same story. Although they were using speed-reading techniques at home and for school courses, they were not using it on the job. When Sue asked them about all the reading material that crossed their desks daily, the typical response was, "I never read those memos and policy announcements anyway!" Sue is concerned about this information but didn't know what to do with it.

Case Questions
1 Did Sue really waste valuable training funds?
2. Should Sue now start a program to get the employees to read the memos and policy announcements?
3. How could Sue have avoided the situation she now faces?
4. Should organizations provide training programs to improve skills that will not be used on the job?

SEEING THE FOREST AND THE TREES

The current face of domestic and global competition that the leaders of the Forest Products Company (FPC) and its parent, the Weyerhaeuser Corporation, saw as they surveyed an industry on its knees in the early 1980s was a far different face than the one Weyerhaeuser and its subsidiaries had successfully competed against for so long. They knew how to compete—and win—against a large-firm, commodity lumber business. But that business was in its death throes, and what was emerging from the ashes presented an entirely new set of challenges, one that would require a radical change in Weyerhaeuser's strategy. The new competitors were not the old monolithic organizations but were instead small mills, lean and mean, configured so they could tailor their products to customer demand and change their product lines rapidly, if the need arose. They were nonunion, owner-operated, and entrepreneurial and, in this configuration, were running the lowest-cost, most market-oriented operations around.

Going out of business was not an alternative anyone cared to think about, but if things didn't change it was a definite possibility. So Charley Bingham, the CEO of the Forest Products Company, knew that something had to be done—and sooner, not later. He gathered his top dozen managers, and together they decided that a massive reorganization was called for, accompanied by a radical change in strategy. According to Bingham, the change in strategy went something like this:

> Approximately 80 percent of our sales dollars in 1982 represented products sold as commodities. By 1995, we resolved that we must reverse the proportions.

The massive reorganization at FPC mirrored that occurring at its parent company. The Weyerhaeuser Corporation decided to drastically decentralize. The three operating units, of which FPC was one, were given free reign on how to do their business. Given this scenario, Bingham and his team decided they needed to cre-ate an organization capable of acting and responding just like their competitors. Thus they created 200 profit centers with each center largely responsible for its own bottom line.

This restructuring soon proved to be only a first step in the right direction. FPC's ability to implement its new strategy was being undermined by low morale, which was pervasive. In addition, many middle managers, those needed to actually carry out the change, were pessimistic about the possibility of sustained future success. Silently, they even questioned their own ability to operate the profit centers.

With insights from Horace Parker, director of executive development at FPC, the rest of the top team came to realize that there would have to be a total transformation of the organization: the corporate culture, knowledge base, skill levels, style of leadership, and team orientation would all have to change, for all employees. With 18,000 employees across the United States, Parker wasn't sure where to start. The others said they would help, but Horace had to tell them what to do. Horace, of course, is waiting to hear what you have to tell him.

CASE QUESTIONS
1. Where does Horace start? What programs does he put in place to deal with the needs of corporate culture, knowledge, skills, leadership, and team orientation?
2. How does he go about developing the programs that he needs to put in place? Does he do it by himself? Can he buy off-the-shelf programs?
3. What time frame does Horace need to implement the programs to make the change successful? If he deals only with the executive development programs, does he need to be concerned with programs for middle managers and below? How does he do this?

SOURCE: © Randall S. Schuler, New York University

ROLE PLAY: HORACE PARKER

You are Horace Parker, director of executive development at FPC. You've got 20 years with the firm, and most of the managers know and trust you. This includes the HR managers and the line managers, but you developed these relationships during the "good old days." Now times are different, and even though you are convinced that things need to be done differently, many of the middle managers are not. In large organizations, it takes time for fear of a threat or the excitement of an opportunity to increase enough to provoke action. Perhaps most of the middle managers have not had enough time to understand the new environment.

Nevertheless, you schedule a meeting with one of the most senior middle managers, John Livingston, whose understanding and support you need to make your changes. Due to the reorganization, his job function changed from being head of the entire lumber production department in FPC to being head of all of FPC's operations for the entire western region. It is well known that he is struggling to adapt to the new job. Some say that behind his outward verbal acceptance of the need for change, is a mountain of resistance and discontent.

Because many of the other managers are watching how you deal with John, it is important that you convince him, deep down, that these changes are necessary. Perhaps he needs some management development. Perhaps you need to suggest programs that he can attend or other avenues that might change his mindset.

Here comes John now. Please welcome him to your office.

ROLE PLAY: JOHN LIVINGSTON

You are John Livingston, better known as "Tree" by your close friends. You've been successful during your 25 years with FPC where, until recently, you headed the lumber production department. With the reorganization, you are now responsible for three main lines of business at FPC— lumber, real estate, and paper products for the entire western region. Of course, you're a lumberman, not a real estate or paper man. Just the thought of not smelling fresh cut logs is disgusting. In addition, you really feel inadequately prepared to deal with the needs of the other businesses. Besides you have never had real profit-center responsibility before; you have only been responsible for getting the trees to the mills and cut.

Horace Parker, director of executive development, wants to meet with you. He has known you a long time and wants to help you as much as he can. Despite your overt acceptance of the change, your behind-the-scenes complaints about the new arrangements are known to most people, and he wants to eliminate these to prevent the discontent from spreading further.

While you have only ten years to retirement, the company has been good to you and your family. However, change is hard. Perhaps you should just listen to Parker and nod your head in agreement and keep your mouth shut. Perhaps you should change, but how? What do you really need to change? Ask Horace.

NOTES

1. "Ritz-Carlton Certifies Ladies and Gentlemen," *HR Reporter* (Aug. 1993): 1–4. Reprinted from *HR Reporter* with the permission of the publisher, Buroff Publications, 1350 Connecticut Ave., N.W., Suite 1000, Washington, D.C. 20036.

2. R. Henkoff, "Companies That Train Best," *Fortune* (March 22, 1993): 62–75; R. Henkoff, "Inside Andersen's Army of Advice," *Fortune* (October 4, 1993): 78–86.

3. I. L. Goldstein, "Training in Work Organizations," *Annual Review in Psychology* 31 (1980): 229–272; G. P. Latham, "Human Resource Training and Development," *Annual Review of Psychology* 39 (1988).

4. Henkoff, "Companies That Train Best" (*op. cit.*, see Note 2).

5. T. R. Horton, "Training: A Key to Productivity Growth," *Management Review* (Sept. 1983): 2–3.

6. K. Murray, "Listening to the Other America," *The New York Times* (April 25, 1993): F25. Used by permission.

7. B. Dumaine, "Those Highflying PepsiCo Managers," *Fortune* (April 10, 1989): 78–79.

8. "The Job Training Partnership Act," *Bulletin to Management* (April 23, 1992): 124–125.

9. Personal Supervisory Liability," *Fair Employment Practice Guidelines* (May 25, 1993): 5–6.

10. I. L. Goldstein, *Training: Program Development and Evaluation*, 2nd ed. (Monterey, Calif.: Brooks/Cole, 1986).

11. "Management Training and Development: Issues and Answers," *Bulletin to Management* (March 13, 1986): 89.

12. J. W. Walker, "Training and Development," in *Human Resource Management in the 1980s*, eds. R. Schuler and S. Carroll (Washington, D.C.: Bureau of National Affairs, 1983); Goldstein (*op. cit.*, see Note 10); Wexley and Latham, *Developing and Training*.

13. L. A. Berger, "A DEW Line for Training and Development: The Needs Analysis Survey," *Personnel Administrator* (Nov. 1976): 51–55.

14. R. B. McAfee and P. J. Champagne, "Employee Development: Discovering Who Needs What," *Personnel Administrator* (Feb. 1988): 92–93.

15. Latham, "Human Resource Training and Development."

16. E. L. Bernick, R. Kindley, and K. Petit, "The Structure of Training Courses and the Effects of Hierarchy," *Public Personnel Journal* 13 (1984): 109–119.

17. *HR Focus* (March 1992): 22.

18. C. Berryman-Fink, "Male and Female Managers' View of the Communication Skills and Training Needs of Women in Management," *Public Personnel Management* 14 (1985): 307–314; Latham, (*op. cit.*, see Note 15); F. D. Tucker, "A Study of Training Needs of Older Workers: Implications for Human Resources Development Planning," *Public Personnel Management* 14 (1985): 85–95.

19. M. E. Gist, A. G. Bavetta, and C. K. Stevens, "Transfer Training Method: Its Influence on Skill Generalization, Skill Repetition, and Performance Level," *Personnel Psychology* 43 (1990): 501–523; N. Schmitt, J. R. Schneider, and S. A. Cohen, "Factors Affecting Validity of a Regionally Administered Assessment Center," *Personnel Psychology* 43 (1990): 1–12.

20. J. Main, "The Executive Yearn to Learn," *Fortune* (May 3, 1982): 234–248; M. M. Starcevich and J. A. Sykes, "Internal Advanced Management Programs for Executive Development," *Personnel Administrator* (June 1982): 27–28.

21. M. Kaeter, "Basic Self-Esteem," *Training* (Aug. 1993): 31–35; M. E. Gist, C. Schwoerer, and B. Rosen, "Effects of Alternative Training Methods on Self-Efficacy and Performance in Computer Software Training," *Journal of Applied Psychology* 74, no. 6 (1989): 884–891.

22. C. H. Deutsch, "Vocational Schools in a Comeback," *The New York Times* (July 21, 1991): F21; "Training Bosses," *Time* (June 7, 1982): 61.

23. "Telephone Etiquette," *Bulletin to Management* (June 11, 1992): 179. Reprinted with permission by the Bureau of National Affairs, (Tel. 1-800-372-1033).

24. K. H. Cowdery, "Training Inner-City Youth to Work," *Personnel Journal* (Oct. 1991): 45–48; C. Marmer Solomon, "New Partners in Business," *Personnel Journal* (April 1991): 57–67.

25. Goldstein (*op. cit.*, see Note 10).

26. B. M. Bass and J. A. Vaughan, *Training in Industry: The Management of Learning* (Belmont, Calif.: Wadsworth, 1966): 88.

27. L. A. Ferman, M. Hoyman, J. Cutcher-Gershenfeld, and E. J. Enfeld, *Worker Training: A Legacy for the 1990s* (Madison, Wis.: Industrial Relations Research Association, 1990); A. P. Carnevale, L. J. Gainer, and A. S. Meltzer, *Workplace Basics Training Manual* (San Francisco: Jossey-Bass, 1990); T. T. Baldwin, R. J. Magjuka, and B. T. Loher, "The Perils of Participation: Effects of Choice of Training on Trainee Motivation and Learning," *Personnel Psychology* 44 (1991): 51–65; A. P. Carnevale, L. J. Gainer, and E. Schulz, *Training the Technical Work Force* (San Francisco: Jossey-Bass, 1990); Goldstein (*op. cit.*, see Note 10).

28. "Planning the Training Program," *Personnel Management*, BNA Policy and Practice Series, no. 41 (Washington, D.C.: Bureau of National Affairs, 1975): 205; see also Bass and Vaughan (*op. cit.*, see Note 26): 89–90; and J. M. Geddes, "Germany Profits by Apprentice System," *The Wall Street Journal* (Sept. 15, 1981): 33.

29. S. Overman, "Apprenticeships Smooth School to Work Transitions," *HR Magazine* (Dec. 1990): 40–43; K. Matthes, "Apprenticeships Can Support the 'Forgotten Youth,'" *HR Focus* (Dec. 1991): 19; "Focus at Ford Is Education for the Sake of Education," *GED on TV* (July–Aug. 1993): 3; E. Kiester, "Germany Prepares Kids for Good Jobs; We Are Preparing Ours for Wendy's," *Smithsonian* (March 1993): 44–55.

30. M. W. McCall, Jr., M. M. Lombardo, and A. M. Morrison,

The Lessons of Experience: How Successful Executives Develop on the Job (Lexington, Mass.: Lexington Books, 1989).

31. R. F. Morrison and Adams, eds., *Contemporary Career Development Issues* (Hillsdale, N.J.: Erlbaum, 1991); A. Saltzman, *Down-Shifting: Reinventing Success—on a Slower Track* (New York: Harper Collins, 1991); S. L. Willis and S. S. Dubin, eds., *Maintaining Professional Competence: Approaches to Career Enhancement, Vitality and Success Throughout a Work Life* (San Francisco: Jossey-Bass, 1990); J. A. Schneer and F. Reitman, "Effects of Employment Gaps on the Careers of M.B.A.'s: More Damaging for Men than for Women?" *Academy of Management Journal* 33, no. 2 (1990): 391–406.

32. S. Bartlett, "Our Intrepid Reporter Wheels and Deals Currencies," *Business Week* (Feb. 1, 1988): 70–71; N. Madlin, "Computer-Based Training Comes of Age," *Personnel* (Nov. 1987): 64–65.

33. G. S. Odiorne and G. A. Rummler, *Training and Development: A Guide for Professionals* (Chicago: Commerce Clearing House, 1988).

34. G. C. Thornton III and J. N. Cleveland, "Developing Managerial Talent through Simulation," *American Psychologist* (Feb. 1990): 190–199; G. Waddell, "Simulations: Balancing the Pros and Cons," *Training and Development Journal* (Jan. 1982): 75–80.

35. For an excellent discussion of assessment centers, see G. C. Thornton III, *Assessment Centers* (Reading, Mass.: Addison-Wesley, 1992).

36. D. Gunsch, "Games Augment Diversity Training," *Personnel Journal* (June 1993): 78–83.

37. J. P. Campbell, M. D. Dunnette, E. E Lawler III, and K. E. Weick, Jr., *Managerial Behavior, Performance, and Effectiveness* (New York: McGraw-Hill, 1970); B. Mezoff, "Human Relations Training: The Tailored Approach," *Personnel* (March/April 1981): 21–27.

38. "Downward Bound," *Fortune* (Aug. 15, 1988): 83.

39. V. L. Huber, "A Comparison of Goal Setting and Pay as Learning Incentives," *Psychological Reports* 56, (1985): 223–235; V. L. Huber, "Interplay between Goal Setting and Promises of Pay-for-Performance on Individual and Group Performance: An Operant Interpretation," *Journal of Organizational Behavior Management* 7, no. 3/4 (1986): 45–64.

40. Latham (*op. cit.*, see Note 15); C. A. Frayne, *Reducing Employee Absenteeism Through Self-Management Training: A Research-Based Analysis and Guide* (Westport, Conn.: Quorum Books, 1991).

41. S. J. Ashford and A. S. Tsui, "Self-Regulation for Managerial Effectiveness: The Role of Active Feedback Seeking," *Academy of Management Journal* 34, no. 2 (1991): 251–280; S. I Tannenbaum, J. E. Mathieu, E. Salas, and J. A. Cannon-Bowers, "Meeting Trainees' Expectations: The Influence of Training Fulfillment on the Development of Commitment, Self-Efficacy and Motivation," *Journal of Applied Psychology* 76, no. 6 (1991): 759–769; M. E. Gist, "The Influence of Training Method on Self-Efficacy and Idea Generation among Managers," *Personnel Psychology* 42 (1989): 787–805.

42. Huber, "Interplay between Goal Setting and Promises of Pay-for-Performance" (*op. cit.*, see Note 39).

43. V. L. Huber, G. P. Latham, and E. A. Locke, "The management of Impressions through Goal Setting," in *Impression Management in the Organization*, eds. R. A. Giacalone and P. Rosenfield (Hillsdale, N.J.: Erlhaun, 1989).

44. P. Hogan, M. Hakel, and P. Decker, "Effects of Trainee-Generated vs. Trainer-Provided Rule Codes on Generalization in Behavioral Modeling Training," *Journal of Applied Psychology* 71 (1986): 469–473.

45. W. Honig, *Operant Behavior* (New York: Appleton-Century-Crofts, 1966); Huber, "Interplay between Goal Setting and Promises of Pay-for-Performance;" J. S. Russel, K. Wexley, and J. Hunter, "Questioning the Effectiveness of Behavior Modeling Training in an Industrial Setting," *Personnel Psychology* 34 (1984): 465–482.

46. "A Comparison of Goal Setting and Pay"; V. L. Huber, E. Locke, and G. Latham, *Goal Setting: A Motivational Technique that Works* (Englewood Cliffs, N.J.: Prentice-Hall, 1984).

47. C. Frayne and G. Latham, "The Application of Social Learning Theory to Employee Self-Management of Attendance," *Journal of Applied Psychology* 72 (1987): 387–392; Latham (*op. cit.*, see Note 15).

48. J. Fierman, "Shaking the Blue-Collar Blues," *Fortune* (April 22, 1991): 209–210, 214, 216, 218; S. R. Siegel, "Improving the Effectiveness of Management Development Programs," *Personnel Journal* (Oct. 1981): 770–773.

49. "Training at Waste Management," *HR Reporter* (April 1991): 1–3. Reprinted from *HR Reporter* with the permission of the publisher, Buroff Publications, 1350 Connecticut Ave., N.W., Washington, D.C. 20036.

50. P. J. Dowling and R. S. Schuler, *International Dimensions of Human Resource Management* (Boston, Mass.: PWS-Kent, 1990). Also see J. S. Black and M. Mendenhall, "Cross-Cultural Training Effectiveness: A Review and a Theoretical Framework for Future Research," *Academy of Management Review* 15, no. 1 (1990): 113–136.

51. "How Japan Inc. Profits from Low Wage Turnover," *Business Week* (December 7, 1987): 24; used by permission of *Business Week*, copyright 1987.

52. M. McComas, "Cutting Costs Without Killing the Business," *Fortune* (October 13, 1986): 76.

53. S. E. Prokesch, "Bean Meshes Man, Machine," *The New York Times* (December 23, 1985): 19, 21.

54. *Bulletin to Management* (July 14, 1988): 3.

55. S. Greenhouse, "An Unstoppable Export Machine," *The New York Times* (October 6, 1988): D7.

56. J. W. Walker, "Managing Human Resources in Flat, Lean and Flexible Organizations: Trends for the 1990s," *Human Resource Planning* 11, no. 2 (1988), 124–132.

57. J. J. Laabs, "How Gillette Grooms Global Talent," *Personnel Journal* (Aug. 1993): 65–76.

58. K. Labich, "The Innovators," *Fortune* (June 6, 1988) 50–64.

59. A. Rahim, "A Model for Developing Key Expatriate Executives," *Personnel Journal* (April 1983): 315.

60. P. Dowling, R. S. Schuler and D. Welch, *International Dimensions of Human Resource Management* 2nd ed. (Belmont, Calif.: Wadsworth, 1994).

61. Mendenhall and G. Oddou, "Acculturation Profiles of Expatriate Managers: Implications for Cross-Cultural Training Programs," *Columbia Journal of World Business*, (Winter 1986): 73–79; R. W. Brislin, *Cross Cultural Encounters;* and D. Landis and R. W. Brislin, *Handbook on Intercultural Training*.

62. J. S. Black and M. Mendenhall, "Cross-Cultural Training Effectiveness: A Review and a Theoretical Framework for Future Research," *Academy of Management Review*, Vol. 15, No. 1 (1990): 113–136.

63. Used by permission of Siemens, Siemens, USA, New Brunswick, New Jersey.

64. B. Z. Posner and W. H. Schmidt, "Values of American Managers: Then and Now," *HR Focus* (March 1992): 13.

65. "Ethics Exams: Focus for Too Few?" *Bulletin to Management* (Feb. 19, 1987): 64; R. W. Goodard, "Are You an Ethical Manager?" *Personnel Journal* (March 1988): 38–47; "Policy Guide," *Bulletin to Management* (Dec. 18, 1986): 420; "Values and Ethics," *HR Reporter* (March 1987): 3.

66. Arthur Andersen has an extensive set of training materials including written cases, lectures, role plays and video tapes that they use in their ethics training.

67. S. Caudron, "Training Can Damage Diversity Efforts," *Personnel Journal* (April 1993): 51–60; H. B. Karp and N. Sutton, "Where Diversity Training Goes Wrong," *Training* (July 1993): 30–34.

68. *Bulletin to Management* (July 14, 1988): 3.

69. J. Bolt, *Executive Development* (New York: Harper & Row, 1989); A. A. Vicere and K. R. Graham, "Crafting Competitiveness: Toward a New Paradigm for Executive Development," *Human Resource Planning* 13, no. 4 (1990): 281–296; J. K. Berry, "Linking Management Development to Business Strategies," *Training and Development Journal* (Aug. 1990): 20–22.

70. Bolt (*opt. cit.*, see Note 69).

71. *Ibid.*

72. *Ibid.*

73. Author's personal conversations with Bill Maki, director of human resources at Weyerhaeuser, Feb. 1994.

74. "B-School Faculty Quality Training," *Fortune* (Jan. 13, 1992): 14. Also see W. Wiggenhorn, "Motorola U: When Training Becomes an Education," *Harvard Business Review* (July–Aug. 1990): 71–83.

75. K. Kelly and P. Burrows, "Motorola: Training for the Millenium," *Business Week*, (March 28, 1994): 158-162.

CHAPTER 15

TOTAL QUALITY MANAGEMENT

LEARNING OBJECTIVES

When you have finished studying this chapter, you should be able to:

1. Describe the dimensions of quality.
2. Discuss the purposes and importance of total quality management.
3. Describe the role of people in total quality management.
4. Describe in detail the elements of TQM programs.
5. Explain the role of the HR Department in TQM.

CHAPTER OUTLINE

LEARNING AND IMPROVING QUALITY

During the 1970s and 1980s, many American firms found themselves pummeled by foreign competition. From 1982 to 1987, consumption of imported foreign goods in the United States as a share of the total market, rose from 16 percent to over 22 percent.

The 1980s for many firms meant dramatic changes in the way they conducted business. Those that were *forced* to change, or *chose* to do business differently, will likely thrive in the 1990s. Firms that recognized and repaired their problems have become the heros of the 1980s.

L.L. BEAN: WHEN LOSING REALLY MEANS WINNING

In 1987, the U.S. Department of Commerce initiated the Malcolm Baldrige National Quality Award to recognize American firms that epitomize high standards of quality. L.L. Bean, the outdoor clothing manufacturer based in Freeport, Maine, was among the few firms invited to compete for the award that first year. The company, which spent two and a half months and $80,000 developing its case, was chosen as a finalist. Managers and employees alike felt confident the company would win the award, following the three-day site visit by the Commerce Department team.

Company managers were surprised therefore when the firm did *not* receive the award; nevertheless, they turned that loss into a valuable learning experience. Feedback from the review team challenged one of the company's best known tenets: a focus on "fixing problems." In an effort to satisfy customers, L.L. Bean had long billed itself as a firm that goes to any length to "fix" whatever goes wrong. A customer can return a product years after buying it and have it repaired or replaced. In 1988, for instance, 14 percent of sales came back to the firm in returns. But the cost of fixing things really meant the cost of poor quality.

"Doing it right the first time" became the buzz phrase of a Total-Quality Initiative at L.L. Bean. The company has since clarified its key goals, sought more input from employees, implemented extensive quality training, learned to think of departments as "internal customers," and as a result, is moving toward building quality into each task, rather than inspecting for quality.

FLORIDA POWER & LIGHT: DOG BITES AND DEMING

In 1989, Florida Power & Light became the first American firm to win the prestigious Deming Prize, established in Japan many years ago as an award for quality. To reach that goal, the company made an enormous effort to change culture, mode of operation, and way of thinking among employees.

When the idea of "quality teams" began in 1981, few employees were enthusiastic. Many felt they had been told, rather than asked, to think about their jobs differently. Supervisors resented quality improvement efforts since they felt it took time away from employees doing their "normal work." Finally, many managers felt threatened since they were often not involved in the training that subordinates received when they joined quality teams. As one executive commented, "We made every mistake you could possibly make in implementing those quality programs."

By 1984, the company revised its approach. It trained managers to be "facilitators," who focused on encouraging employee quality teams to find and solve problems, taught employees to think of one another as "internal customers," and continually urged employees to see themselves as able to make a difference. Employees, who had long blamed "the bureaucracy" or "nature" of problems such as slow customer response or electrical blackouts, had to change their thinking or leave the company. Many did. Even so, senior management acknowledged that, while not all employees joined the bandwagon, the 75 percent who were committed to the new programs made the company a success.

Employees made suggestions about every aspect of their work lives that might save or make money. One team developed a way to prevent dog bites, the largest single cause of company on-the-job injuries in Miami. First, customers received a questionnaire asking if they

Continued on the next page

had a dog, if it was outside, and if it was dangerous. The data were programmed into meter readers' hand-held computers. When a meter reader goes to a house with a "BAD DOG," he or she phones the owner ahead, asking for the dog to be kept indoors.

During the nine months that Florida Power & Light employees prepared their 1,000-page application for the coveted Deming Prize, people pulled together and routinely worked twelve to sixteen hour days. Employees suggested more ideas and management listened; the firm's morale—and performance—zoomed. After learning the firm had won the prize, one employee commented, "We had proved something to ourselves—and the whole country: America's back."

NORTHERN TELECOM: HAVE IDEAS, WILL TRAVEL

Northern Telecom, a Toronto-based telecommunications firm routinely sends groups of employees on tours, hoping they will return with ideas that Northern Telecom can use to improve. The tours stem from a program begun in 1987 (by the President's council on competition) to increase employee awareness of global issues facing the firm and to stress the importance of quality in programs.

The first four tours, of about 30 employees each, have visited such firms as Tandem Computers, Inc.; Mitac (Taiwan); Fujitsu Microelectronics (Singapore), Hewlett-Packard; and IBM. Participants learned about technology and management practices that might work at Northern Telecom and gave presentations on what they learned upon their return. The company has adopted some of the ideas employees learned about on their tours, and, in addition, tour participants have gained insights about the environment that Northern Telecom faces.[1]

The Baldrige Award is named for Malcolm Baldrige, who served as Secretary of Commerce from 1981 until his tragic death in a rodeo accident in 1987. His managerial excellence contributed to long-term improvement in efficiency and effectiveness of government.

CEO Fred Smith's philosophy, active since day one of Federal Express is "People, Service, and Profit."

***Total quality management* is a systematic and coordinated effort to continuously improve the quality of the firm's products and services.**

LEARNING OBJECTIVE 1
Describe the dimensions of quality.

This feature illustrates the movement in America toward total-quality management. This is happening in firms that are service-oriented and in firms that are manufacturing-oriented. In 1990, Federal Express became the first service-oriented firm to win the Baldrige Award, the same year that Cadillac and IBM, both manufacturing-oriented firms, also won it. As the cameos in the feature indicate, firms are restructuring the way they do work and changing the way employees relate to each other. Among the changes being made are efforts to reduce layers of management and to give employees more decision-making power. Organizations are emphasizing teamwork as a key way to improve their business. With foreign competition ever keener, U.S. firms have little choice but to make improvement a way of life. And even for firms without global competition such as L.L. Bean, Florida Power & Light, Northern Telecom, and Ritz-Carlton, there are enough domestic competitors that will put constant pressure on companies to improve.

What is exciting to the people in our field is that effective HR management is central to the success of total quality management. The process of striving for total quality has generated much innovation in HR management as its importance grows and will continue to grow throughout the 1990s.

TOTAL QUALITY MANAGEMENT

In essence, **total quality management (TOM)** *is a systematic and coordinated companywide effort to continuously improve the quality of the firm's products and services*. Key here is the question, What is quality?

Quality means delivery of loyalty-producing products and services along all dimensions of quality with a single effort.[2] The eight dimensions of quality that pioneers in the field such as W. Edwards Deming, Crosby and Joseph M. Juran and line managers usually discuss are identified by Professor David Garvin of the Harvard Business School as:

1. *Performance*. A product's primary operating characteristic such as automobile acceleration, and a television set's picture clarity.
2. *Features*. Supplements to a product's basic functioning characteristics such as power windows on a car.
3. *Reliability*. A probability of not malfunctioning in a specified period.
4. *Conformance*. The degree to which a product's design and operating characteristics meet established standards.
5. *Durability*. A measure of product life.
6. *Serviceability*. The speed and ease of repair.
7. *Aesthetics*. How a product looks, feels, tastes, and smells.
8. *Perceived quality*. As seen by a customer.[3]

WHY IS TQM IMPORTANT?

American business used to view innovation as having to do only with technology, and indeed technology and innovation do go hand in hand. This partnership, however, has been enlarged to encompass the way businesses *do* their business. There is much innovation today in the way companies compete. One could say we now have a "technology of competition," and its name is total-quality management. And thus competition, domestically and internationally, will continue to grow more intense each year. The need for organizations to continually improve quality has therefore never been greater. In many cases, organizations in the 1990s have no choice but to embrace TQM: either they continually improve quality, or they go out of business (*or* get caught up in a forced merger or hostile takeover). Here's where TQM enters the picture because it

- Reduces mistakes and rework
- Improves productivity
- Increases market share
- Reduces costs
- Increases competitiveness
- Provides jobs[4]

Deming's chain reaction in Exhibit 15.1 shows how this is done.

THE CHAIN REACTION

Quality, quantity, and price have improved in unison for most successful global competitors. The world-class companies of all nations find that improved quality results in lower costs and improved productivity. David T. Kearns, former CEO of Xerox, describes their early discoveries as Xerox began to systematically focus on quality:

> Pretty early in the process, we realized the cost of noncomformance [to quality specification in manufacturing] was costing us 20 percent of revenues. The opportunity was enormous.[5]

Motorola's former CEO George M. Fisher, now head of Kodak, says, "Americans used to fall into the trap that high quality costs more. But high quality and low cost go hand in hand."[6] At Motorola, quality improvement yielded 25–30 percent reductions in costs.

Notable leaders in the worldwide quality-improvement process echo similar estimates. Juran estimates that about a third of the U.S. economy is expended on rework due to low quality. Deming suggests the cost of poor quality is in the area

Quality means delivering loyalty-producing products and services along all these dimensions of quality with a single effort:

LEARNING OBJECTIVE 2

Discuss the purposes and importance of total quality management.

"To meet the challenges of the global economy . . . our most successful companies have been eliminating unnecessary layers of management, empowering front-line workers, becoming more responsive to their customers and seeking constantly to improve the products they make, the services they provide, and the people they employ."

William J. Clinton

These are the important purposes of total quality management:

The chain reaction shows how firms can decrease costs by increasing quality.

Total customer satisfaction is fundamental to our survival.

George Fisher, CEO
Kodak

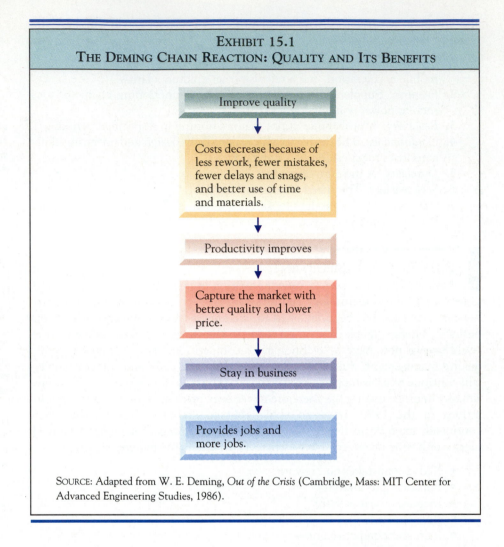

EXHIBIT 15.1
THE DEMING CHAIN REACTION: QUALITY AND ITS BENEFITS

SOURCE: Adapted from W. E. Deming, *Out of the Crisis* (Cambridge, Mass: MIT Center for Advanced Engineering Studies, 1986).

of 30 percent of current production. Some obvious costs come in the form of rework, detection (inspection and monitoring), scrap, warranty, and repairs. However, manufacturing may not be the largest source of quality problems. Richard Beutow, quality director at Motorola, guesses that 90 percent of the errors made by Motorola employees have nothing to do with manufacturing; they have to do with filling out forms correctly, acting quickly, and providing service.[7] Even within manufacturing, the costs of quality do not arise from production. Juran and other experts estimate that no more than 20 percent of defects can be traced to production; the other 80 percent come from design or purchasing policies that value low prices over higher quality.

Increasingly, product and service liability—direct and in the form of insurance costs—consume a huge portion of organizations' budgets. In businesses ranging from maternity medical services and alpine skiing to private aircraft and waste hauling, liability costs can account for over half of the consumer's price. Nevertheless, Deming contends that, for most companies, these direct costs account for a small share of the real costs to individual companies; their biggest costs come from customer dissatisfaction and defection to competitors. This leads to a lost customer base and a lost future for many companies. Those costs are significant because attracting new customers is four times more expensive than keeping them!

PARTNERSHIP: WORKING TOGETHER IN TOTAL QUALITY MANAGEMENT

LINE MANAGERS	HR PROFESSIONALS	EMPLOYEES
Support and embrace total quality management.	Develop HR activities to support total quality programs.	Learn TQM principles and concepts.
Coordinate total quality within all parts of the organization	Work with line managers to help all employees change.	Change and adapt to a continuous learning environment.
Utilize TQM principles daily	Utilize TQM principles daily	Utilize TQM principles daily

Quality improvement can reduce costs in another way, too. Because quality improvement typically involves greater employee commitment and utilization, fewer employees are needed to produce the same level of output. For example, L.L. Bean's sales have increased tenfold; the number of employees has risen only fivefold. Thanks to a quality improvement program and a cooperative work force, Toyota is producing more than 3 million vehicles a year with fewer than 25,000 production workers—the same number of workers it took to produce 1 million vehicles in 1966. Not only are Toyota workers more productive, but rejects for poor quality are fewer with an accompanying reduction in costs.

 ## LEGAL CONSIDERATIONS

NATIONAL LABOR RELATIONS ACT

Certain legal considerations must be taken into account when organizations implement programs such as TQM that involve employee input and participation. This is particularly the case when employee involvement relates to issues of wages, working conditions, grievances, and hours of employment. While employee discussions of these issues is not prohibited by law, what *is* prohibited is the domination of employee discussions by the employer. According to the *National Labor Relations Act* (NLRA), in cases where a union represents or could represent the employees, the employer must consider that almost all issues, including the establishment of programs to improve quality, may need to be negotiated with the union. In many cases, however, employers and unions can cooperatively work together on quality programs. When this occurs, the NLRA requires employers to provide information to the union, when requested, for purposes related to the quality program.

Two major pieces of legislation for TQM are

- *National Labor Relations Act*
- *Americans with Disabilities Act*

553

This concern for employer domination of employee participation efforts, even when related to TQM programs, has recently been rekindled by the *Electromation* case (1992) and the *Du Pont* case (1993). In both these cases, the National Labor Relations Board ruled that management representatives on employee committees or teams should participate only as observers or facilitators without the right to vote on proposals or suggestions. Thus employers need to be sensitive to their involvement in TQM, especially when the employees are not union members.[8]

AMERICANS WITH DISABILITIES ACT

A law more recent than the NLRA of 1935, has other important implications for employers implementing TQM. The feature, "Managing Human Resources: Implications of the *Americans with Disability Act* on TQM Programs," describes the impact that this law has on programs for total quality management.

LEARNING OBJECTIVE 3

Describe the role of people in total quality management.

Corning is one of the leaders in human resource management.

Empowering employees help TQM programs.

WHERE DO PEOPLE FIT IN TQM?

The implications of TQM for managing people are significant. The "total-quality approach" at Corning is about people, according to James Houghton, the chief executive officer, because at Corning, good ideas for product improvement often come from employees. To carry through on their ideas, Corning workers form short-lived "corrective action teams" to solve specific problems:

> Employees [also] give their supervisors written "method improvement requests," which differ from ideas tossed into the traditional suggestion box in that they get a prompt formal review so the employees aren't left wondering about their fate. In the company's Erwin Ceramics plant, a maintenance employee suggested substituting one flexible tin mold for an array of fixed molds that shape the wet ceramic product baked into catalytic converters for auto exhausts.[10]

At Corning, then, quality improvement has involved getting employees committed to these ideas. Empowering workers has been critical to accomplishing this. While policy statements emphasizing the total-quality approach are valuable, they are always followed up with specific human resource practices: feedback systems are in place; teamwork is permitted and facilitated; decision making, autonomy, and responsibility are a part of everyone's job description; and job classifications are flexible. By the way, Corning refers to giving workers more decision-making ability, autonomy, and responsibility as *empowerment*. Such employee empowerment is indigenous to the total quality movement. In fact, it is hard to find successful quality improvement or enhancement programs without it:

> Employers that mesh quality programs with empowerment efforts are twice as likely as other organizations to report significant improvements in their products and services, according to a survey of 126 employers by the Wyatt Co. and the Manufacturer's Alliance for Productivity and Innovation.
>
> For several years, the survey notes, employers have used various total-quality management methods to reduce defects and otherwise improve their products and services. Recently, many employers also are empowering employees to take more responsibility for their work. Empowerment measures include increased use of functional or cross-functional work teams, decentralization of decision making, and redesign of jobs, functions, and work groups.
>
> Employers that have best integrated quality and empowerment have achieved the most significant improvements, the survey finds. Specifically, half of employers that say they have thoroughly integrated employee involve-

MANAGING HUMAN RESOURCES

Implications of the *Americans with Disabilities Act* on TQM Programs

"As organizations move into total quality management and become more responsive to their customers and employees, ADA requirements such as reasonable accommodation can become part of the process," says Dale S. Brown, program manager for the President's Committee on Employment of People with Disabilities.

Employees and customers with disabilities should be seen as internal and external customers with valuable input concerning product design and marketing. In addition, people with disabilities are experts on their own accommodation needs and can often provide inexpensive solutions, Brown explains.

For employers who practice TQM, accommodation is the process of matching communication styles, the work environment, the expectations of the supervisor, and the production system to assure that the disability of the employee does not hamper the employee's ability to produce quality products or services. A TQM process called the Shewart cycle—including plan, do, check, and act—can be used following these steps:

- *Plan*. The individual and supervisor should define the problem and then find a way to resolve it. For example, an individual who is very small in stature is hired as a mail clerk, whose job tasks include sorting mail into individual boxes at a sorting station, delivering the sorted mail throughout the building, and returning with outgoing mail. The problem is that the individual cannot reach the highest box in the sorting station. The employee and the supervisor decide to have the employee stand on a stool.
- *Do*. The suggested accommodation is implemented. The supervisor happens to have a stool in the mail room and gives it to the employee.
- *Check*. Does the accommodation work? If the employee is able to produce well without having a negative impact on other aspects of the organization, the accommodation works. In this example, however, the supervisor real-izes that the suggested accommodation is a safety hazard.
- *Act*. If problems or questions arise, the supervisor goes through the cycle a second time, asks the employees for suggestions, and generates options. The mail room staff, which has formed a total quality team to improve operations, suggests the installation of a platform to place the boxes in easy reach of the worker. It is assumed, in this example, that the accommodation works.

"When an accommodation works, it must be institutionalized so that future supervisors will use it as well. Institutionalization is the most important aspect of the process when the accommodation involves changes in policies, procedures, and schedules," Brown says.

The foregoing steps can be applied to making reasonable accommodations in the following areas:

- *The work station*. The work station, tools, and surrounding areas, such as the lunchroom and break rooms, should be reviewed and made accessible. For example, a person with an eye disorder may require an antiglare computer screen.
- *Work distribution*. Minor duties might be reassigned to co-workers, or two workers may exchange jobs. Secretaries who are deaf may be excused from answering the telephone, for example.
- *Communication process*. The supervisor needs to know how the employee gets information best. Memoranda or written instructions might be read to a dyslexic or blind employee, while an employee with a mild hearing impairment might prefer written instructions.

"Job accommodation is part of the TQM obligation that companies have to continuously improve their product and work force," says Brown. And, she maintains that TQM ensures that people with disabilities are fully productive members of their working teams.[9]

ment and quality programs cite significant improvements in products and services. In contrast, such gains are reported by only one-quarter of employers that say their quality and empowerment programs are "not yet well-integrated" or are "becoming integrated."[11]

Deming is revered in Japan for his help in improving their quality.

These are Deming's fourteen principles: →

THE ELEMENTS OF TQM

The Ford Motor Company, who has become a leader in quality-improvement programs, is a believer in Deming's fourteen principles for total quality. As listed below, these principles guide Ford's programs:

1. Create consistency and continuity of purpose.
2. Refuse to allow commonly accepted level of delay for mistakes, defective material, defective workmanship.
3. Eliminate the need for, and dependence upon, mass inspection.
4. Reduce the number of suppliers. Buy on statistical evidence, not price.
5. Search continually for problems in the system and seek ways to improve.
6. Institute modern methods of training, using statistics.
7. Focus supervision on helping people to do a better job. Provide the tools and techniques for people to have pride of workmanship.
8. Eliminate fear. Encourage two-way communication.
9. Break down barriers between departments. Encourage problem solving through teamwork.
10. Eliminate the use of numerical goals, slogans, and posters for the work force.
11. Use statistical methods for continuing improvement of quality and productivity, and eliminate all standards prescribing numerical quotas.
12. Remove barriers to pride of workmanship.
13. Institute a vigorous program of education and training to keep people abreast of new developments in methods, materials, and technologies.
14. Clearly define management's permanent commitment to quality and productivity.[12]

Pursuing total quality management requires dedication, commitment, and employee involvement. Of course, there is not one best way or one best set of human resource practices to use in this endeavor. For most organizations, the HR component is only one of several that a company must manage effectively in improving quality as you can see when you look at the criteria used to evaluate companies competing for the **Baldrige Award**—companies such as Federal Express, Xerox, Texas Instruments and AT&T. Exhibit 15.2 shows the seven components used in scoring Baldrige Award contestants. While the fourth component is the only one directly showing HR activities, a thoughtful examination of the other criteria reveals that HR activities are integral to each.[13] This was certainly the case at Grand Union. Let's turn now to see how Bill Reffett improved the quality of service at his company through human resource practices.

The Baldrige Award is the major prize in America for TQM Achievement.

The Baldrige winners consistently communicate both good and bad news and make sure that employees find out things before the public does.

TQM THROUGH IMPROVING CUSTOMER-ORIENTED SERVICE: THE GRAND UNION CASE

While the margins on fresh pastries are more than double those on packaged donuts and cakes, the pastry business is, well, just that—another business. It's just another business, that is, from the viewpoint of running a grocery store—at least, if "grocery store" is defined as the traditional low-margin, high-volume, limited-selection, space-driven,

This case of Grand Union is an excellent illustration of the relation between people and TQM in a service company!

EXHIBIT 15.2
SCORING THE BALDRIGE AWARD

1994 EXAMINATION CATEGORIES/ITEMS	POINT VALUES
1.0 Leadership	**95**
1.1 Senior Executive Leadership 45	
1.2 Management for Quality 25	
1.3 Public Responsibility and Corporate Citizenship 25	
2.0 Information and Analysis	**75**
2.1 Scope and Management of Quality and Performance Data and Information 15	
2.2 Competitive Comparisons and Benchmarking...20	
2.3 Analysis and Uses of Company-Level Data 40	
3.0 Strategic Quality Planning......................	**60**
3.1 Strategic Quality and Company Performance Planning Process 35	
3.2 Quality and Performance Plans....................25	
4.0 Human Resource Development and Management ..	**150**
4.1 Human Resource Planning and Management20	
4.2 Employee Involvement..................................40	
4.3 Employee Education and Training................40	
4.4 Employee Performance and Recognition.......25	
4.5 Employee Well-Being and Satisfaction 25	
5.0 Management of Process Quality.............................	**140**
5.1 Design and Introduction of Quality Products and Services.................................40	
5.2 Process Management: Product and Service Production and Delivery Processes 35	
5.3 Process Management: Business and Support Service Processes 30	
5.4 Supplier Quality 20	
5.5 Quality Assessment 15	
6.0 Quality and Operational Results............................	**180**
6.1 Product and Service Quality Results 70	
6.2 Company Operational Results 50	
6.3 Business and Support Service Results...........25	
6.4 Supplier Quality Results.............................35	

Exhibit 15.2 (Cont.)
Scoring the Baldrige Award

7.0   **Customer Focus and Satisfaction**   300

    7.1   Customer Expectations: Current
         and Future 35
    7.2   Customer Relationship Management 65
    7.3   Commitment to Customers 15
    7.4   Customer Satisfaction Determination 30
    7.5   Customer Satisfaction Results 85
    7.6   Customer Satisfaction Comparison 70
    Total Points   1,000

---

discount-driven, 40,000-square-foot grocery store. However, if it is defined as a high-margin, high-volume, expanded-selection, customer-driven, service-oriented, 40,000-square-foot grocery store, can it then sell fresh pastries?

"Of course," said the top team at the Grand Union, a New Jersey–based retail grocery operation with stores up and down the East Coast, but primarily in its home state. Five years ago, the top team decided that competing with the new 100,000-square-foot stores was not a viable merchandising strategy; their competitors' volume and the size of their parking lots put Grand Union at too great a disadvantage. Competing on their terms would mean moving from all Grand Union's current, space-bound locations and uprooting relationships with all its current customers, suppliers, and communities. But even the world's greatest pâtisserie wouldn't be able to do enough volume to justify 40,000 square feet.

The top team got back to the basic questions: What business are we in? Who are our competitors? Given that we aren't moving the stores, what do our customers want?

Once they answered these questions, the team members decided to embrace a new definition of grocery store: a customer-driven, service-oriented store with an expanded selection of items. From an individual store perspective, this would mean the elimination of many of the current items to make room for more brand items and higher-margin items. The latter meant having a deli section (with the smells of barbecued chicken), an expanded fresh fruit section (more tropical fruits), a variety of small, ethnic food booths (for eating in or taking home), and, yes, a pastry shop.

All this sounded great to Bill Reffett, senior vice president of human resources for Grand Union's 20,000 employees. Asked by the others on the top team if he could "deliver the people on this one," he answered, "No problem." Bill knew the success of the store's new quality strategy depended on changing employee behaviors. He also knew that changing behaviors meant changing the store's human resource practices.[14]

The strategy is to be a customer-driven service firm.

Grand Union Strategy.   Under the guidance of Bill Reffett, Grand Union developed an HR philosophy stating that employees are a valuable, long-term source of competitive advantage and that all efforts would be made to provide exciting jobs and promotion opportunities (promotion-from-within) and continual retraining as needed. The firm described this philosophy as developmental. It was clearly recognized at this point that the role behaviors needed from all employees would change in order to match the needs of the new business.

While the physical size of the stores remained the same, employees were added because of the new sections and the need for additional staff. The new business meant it was important to keep employees longer so that they could get to know the customer and the store.[15] Consistent with the new business, the traditional command-and-control relationship across all levels was modified to accommodate a more self-directed, self-managed approach. Similarly, individual orientation was modified to be more team-oriented to better serve the customer. The *developmental HR philosophy* was carried through to this level because this was the glue that kept all the employees together.

Key issues were addressed by formalizing all the activities that were occurring to support the new business. ==Success depended on managing the business systematically, including human resources.== While there was formality in the establishment of new HR practices, there were also allowances made for local conditions. Regardless of location, however, decision-making authority was pushed down in the organization. Store managers and their staff could make more decisions in the interests of the customer and the needs of the business.

NEEDED ROLE BEHAVIORS. Grand Union directed major effort toward identifying the needed role behaviors of supervisors and the remaining staff in the stores. The HR process required the intense involvement of the employees, with guidance provided by the senior vice president of human resources. Together, they identified needed supervisory (department and store managers) and staff role behaviors based on what they saw as characterizing a customer-driven service grocery store. Then they compared these to the status quo.

> Success depends on people behaving in new ways in their roles (jobs).

SUPERVISORY ROLES. Supervisory role behaviors were identified and redistributed. What occurred here was very important. The firm decided to make a distinction between *supervisors as an employee job category* and *the responsibilities associated with the supervisory role*. This distinction made it easier to redistribute the supervisory responsibilities to enhance the level of customer service. Exhibit 15.3 lists the supervisory responsibilities that were redistributed to the employees.

STAFF ROLES. The nonsupervisory employees also addressed the question, "What does this new business orientation mean for us at the store?" Because the focus was on the customer, they first asked, "How do we currently interact with the customers?" This resulted in a before-and-after analysis of relationships with customers. The "before" analysis resulted in the following list:

- We do not know customer desires.
- We make limited use of customers.
- We are space-driven, not customer-driven.
- We have traditional departments, low margins, high quit rates.
- We feel no ownership of service.
- We lack management skills.

In contrast, the employees felt that the change would require:

> These are the before and after role behaviors:

- Having focus groups with customers
- Being customer-driven
- Including service as part of the product
- Adding high-margin departments
- Having stores coordinate efforts, exchange best practices
- Expanding management skills

EXHIBIT 15.3
REDISTRIBUTED SUPERVISORY RESPONSIBILITIES

Absence control	Personnel recordkeeping
Performance appraisal	Quality circle leadership
Staff deployment	Work planning/allocation
Discipline	Quality control
Shift rotation planning	Recruitment
Employee welfare	Team briefing
Grievance handling	Team building
Health and safety	Communicating
Induction training	

SOURCE: Adapted from R. Schuler, "Strategic Human Resource Management: Linking the People with the Strategic Needs of the Business," *Organizational Dynamics* (AMACOM: New York, Summer 1992), 26.

In addition, these employees asked, "From the broader store viewpoint, what characteristics reflect a solutions-oriented, customer-driven, service operation?" Their answers are listed in Exhibit 15.4 They used this list to analyze the needed role behaviors *vis-à-vis* the customer and concluded that substantial changes were in order. The before-and-after role behaviors for the major job categories in a store are listed in Exhibit 15.5.

NEW HUMAN RESOURCE PRACTICES. In the final stage, the employees identified HR practices that had to be formulated to match the business, based on the role behaviors needed from the employees, especially those in direct contact with customers. The analysis and formulation resulted in several significantly different HR practices; those practices most affected and how they

New role behaviors require new HR practices.

EXHIBIT 15.4
ORGANIZATIONAL CHARACTERISTICS OF A CUSTOMER-DRIVEN SERVICE ORGANIZATION

- Just-in-time inventory
- Just-in-time working commitment
- Team-oriented
- Multiskilled—technical, process, interpersonal
- Flexibility
- Trust, harmonious employee relations
- Communications
- Egalitarianism
- Distributed leadership
- Responsibility for customers
- Standard operating procedures
- Continuous improvement
- No-fault policies
- Job grade reduction
- Rewards for small improvements/suggestions
- Supplier and customer involvement
- Site visits, comparisons, benchmarks
- Customer knowledge

SOURCE: Adapted from R. Schuler, "Strategic Human Resource Management: Linking the People with the Strategic Needs of the Business," *Organizational Dynamics* (AMACOM: New York, Summer 1992): 28.

EXHIBIT 15.5
CUSTOMER-DRIVEN EMPLOYEE BEHAVIORS AT GRAND UNION

BEHAVIORS BEFORE THE CHANGE	BEHAVIORS AFTER THE CHANGE
Bag Packers	
Ignore customers	Greet customers
Lack of packing standards	Respond to customers
	Ask for customers' preferences
Cashiers	
Ignore customers	Greet customers
Lack of eye contact	Respond to customers
	Assist customers
	Speak clearly
	Call customers by name
Shelf Stockers	
Ignore customers	Respond to customers
Don't know store products/location	Help customers with correct information
	Knowledgeable about product location
Department Workers	
Ignore customers	Respond to customers
Limited knowledge	Know products
	Know store
Department Managers	
Ignore customers	Respond to customers
Ignore workers	Reward employees for responding to customers
Store Managers	
Ignore customers	Respond to customers
Stay in booth	Reward employees for service
	Appraise employees on customer service

SOURCE: Adapted from R. Schuler, "Strategic Human Resource Mangement: Linking the People with the Strategic Needs of the Business," *Organizational Dynamics* (New York: AMACOM, Summer 1992): 29.

changed are illustrated in Exhibit 15.6. While these changes in HR practices were in part driven by what the employees thought was necessary for the business, it was mostly driven by what they thought would enable them to perform as needed by the customer.

IN SUMMARY. Grand Union's involvement in TQM highlights the human resource management activities affected by the change in organizational strate-

DID YOU KNOW?

The Red Lion Hotel Company gives its employees a four-step checklist to help them remember the needed behaviors.

EXHIBIT 15.6
THE CHANGED HR PRACTICES

Human Resource Planning

Longer-term focus
Tie to the needs of the business

Staffing

More socialization
More opportunities

Performance Appraisal

Customer service measures used
Feedback provided

Compensation

Relates to performance appraisal
Awards and celebration

Training and Development

More skill training
Customer service training

SOURCE: Adapted from R. Schuler, "Strategic Human Resource Management: Linking the People with the Strategic Needs of the Business," *Organizational Dynamics* (New York: AMACOM, Summer 1992): 30.

---

gy. Making changes in these HR activities in a consistent, systematic manner was key to a smooth transition.

The fact that Grand Union involved all employees in the process of change made it more likely that they would perform the new roles well. Line employees, are often better able to identify what HR practices are needed and how to succesfully implement a strategy and because they are closer to the action they know how they will respond to alternative HR practices.

Of course, pursuing a strategy of quality improvement requires more than a set of human resource practices, but these practices are essential in achieving the necessary employee behaviors of consistency, accuracy, reliability, and concern for quality. Changes in the design of the organization—particularly in the reduction of management, layers, or decentralization—can achieve and maintain these behaviors. By decentralizing, organizations move decision making farther down the organization's hierarchy.[16] This enhances employee involvement in the company and improves productivity. Decentralization occurs in TQM as companies use teams for problem solving and quality improvement. Quality circles are thus a prime example of a decentralizing activity.

QUALITY CIRCLES

Instrumental in getting all employees involved in the quality effort have been the development, implementation, and utilization of quality circles.[17] As described by Ed Yager, President of Consulting Associates, Inc., a **quality circle** is a voluntary group of workers who have a shared area of responsibility to improve quality.[18] They meet together periodically to discuss, analyze, and propose solutions to quality problems. They are taught group communication processes, quality concepts, measurement and problem-analysis techniques, and are encouraged to draw on the resources of the company's management and technical personnel to help them solve problems. In fact, they sometimes take over the responsibility for solving certain quality problems and generate and evaluate their own feedback. In this way, they are also responsible for the quality of com-

---

Getting all the people involved in making a change is absolutely necessary for the change to be successful.

—Bill Reffett, Senior Vice-President, Human Resources, Grand Union

---

Quality circles are voluntary groups who have a shared responsibility to improve quality.

munications. ==The leader in the circle works as a group facilitator and not as a boss.==

A circle is primarily a normal work crew, ranging in size from five to ten members. If the department requires more than one circle, then a second leader is trained, and a second circle is formed. The circles then call on technical experts to assist in solving problems. Circle meetings are usually held on company time and on company premises. Where companies have unions, the union members and leaders are encouraged to take an active role in the circle, to attend leader training, and to become fully aware of circle principles.

In companies such as the Grand Union, Solectron, Motorola, Cadillac, and Xerox, employee group discussions may take on names such as problem-solving groups, leaderless team discussions, or continuous-improvement teams. ==Clearly, group discussions, group training, and group problem solving are critical components of TQM.== The topics or tasks about which teams can problem-solve and improve are numerous.[19] A sample of tasks and the frequency with which they are discussed are shown in Exhibit 5.2.

 ## The Role of the HR Department

From hiring and compensation to training and performance management, every HR system influences employee performance and thus the success or failure of a total quality initiative. Keeping HR systems aligned with quality strategies will be the challenge of the next decade.[20]

In other words, the role of the HR department in improving quality can be considerable, as was illustrated in the Grand Union example! In general, it can

- Assist in the formulation of the firm's strategic direction and needs
- Identify the human resource philosophies or culture consistent with the business needs
- Develop and implement policies and activities consistent with the culture
- Ensure that the quality improvement process is consistent with the other human resource activities

If, as in the case of the Grand Union, the strategy creates organizational change, the HR department can play a critical role in the change process by establishing an initiative—that is, a specific program that is responsible for dealing with the change. The initiative can involve

- Establishing a senior HR council and executive operating committee
- Naming a major initiative that rallies all employees to the change
- Developing a leadership program that ensures that the change clearly includes the top management (this is often called a senior management development program)

In the development of the senior management program (and other programs that facilitate the change throughout the organization), a director of executive development or strategic education, such as Horace Parker of FPC (see Chapter 14), often takes the lead. Such individuals know the top team better than any other human resource person. This being the case, they can then orchestrate the entire transition—and thus the entire HR management function.[21]

Within the HR department, there can be further division of roles and responsibilities. This often involves clarifying the relationship between the corporate-level HR department and the business unit or division-level departments. Taking a proactive stance, the corporate-level department can

DID YOU KNOW?

Motorola has its 40,000 employees compete in team quality competition each year.

Because partnerships are an important part of sustaining quality initiatives, Cadillac developed cross-functional, people-strategy teams to research, design, recommend, implement, and evaluate various human resource programs.

LEARNING OBJECTIVE 5

Explain the role of the HR Department in TQM.

The HR department can do a lot in TQM as in the case of Grand Union.

- Assist senior managers in formulating change
- Become a model of change
- Develop and guide divisional human resource departments
- Change organizational structure
- Serve as a clearinghouse
- Serve as trainer for other human resource staff
- Do benchmark analysis
- Develop HRIS capability
- Audit competencies

The corporate HR department can do these many things.

The activities of the division-level departments then reflect the activities established at the corporate level. However, division-level HR departments can also essentially perform the roles just ascribed to the corporate level. Many of these roles can be performed by line managers with or without the assistance of others. Thus it is imperative that the HR department change if it wants to be a partner in TQM programs; it too must reduce layers of management and work on quality improvement *within* the department. An excellent set of suggestions for doing this is discussed in the feature, "HR Advice and Application: Quality Within the HR Department."

The introduction of a TQM program in 1988 changed the focus of L. L. Bean's HR department from addressing traditional human resources issues to serving its customers—employees. The change has allowed the company to sustain its long-term quality efforts.

INTERNATIONAL COMPARISONS

In the United States winning the Baldrige Award, named after the late United States Secretary of Commerce, Malcolm Baldrige, is the goal of companies pursuing total quality management. In Japan winning the Deming Prize is the goal of companies pursuing total quality management. In Europe winning ISO 9000 series certification is the goal of companies pursuing total quality management. While all these share the desire and recognition of attaining superior levels of quality, there are some differences among them.

Exhibit 15.2 indicates the criteria for the Baldrige Award. These include leadership, information and analysis, strategic quality planning, human resource development and management, management of process quality, quality and operational results and customer focus and satisfaction. These criteria represent the wide number of aspects in a company that need to be given attention in order for the company to qualify for the Baldrige Award. As of 1995 organizations can compete for the Award in these categories: for-profit organizations, large and small, nonprofit organizations, and educational institutions. Organizations competing for the Award typically have their suppliers involved as well, to the point of requiring them to at least be using the Baldrige criteria in evaluating how they manage their operations.

In Japan, the award for TQM is the Deming Prize, and in Europe it is the ISO 9000 series certification.

Whereas the Baldrige Award is less than ten years old, the Deming Prize is more than 40 years old! Named after the late Dr. W. Edwards Deming, the **Deming Prize** is very highly valued among Japanese companies. Dr. Deming established his principles of total quality management in Japan during the 1950s and 1960s. The criteria of the Deming Prize are not detailed in point values like the Baldrige list in Exhibit 15.2, but they do include many of the same areas. Similar to those companies in the United States pursuing the Baldrige Award, Japanese companies pursuing the Deming Prize insist that their suppliers also practice principles of total quality. Suppliers are so important because without the quality parts and the appropriate delivery schedules, the quality of the final products is limited. Famous in Japanese quality management is the term **"Kaizen."** This is translated to mean "continuous improvement." The Japanese believe that continuous improvement is fundamental to total quality manage-

QUALITY WITHIN THE HR DEPARTMENT

Human resource professionals have two requirements to fulfill when their companies start chasing quality. They must ensure that:

1. All human resources subsystems—training, communication, and compensation—are aligned with the overall quality effort.
2. The quality function is using quality principles.

Ken Levine, who's division manager for continuous improvement for Coca-Cola USA in Atlanta, interviewed 30 companies as part of a total-quality benchmark project. In this survey, he wanted to determine the various roles that HR plays in organizationwide quality efforts. Levine was astounded to learn that none of the HR departments surveyed had implemented quality strategies within the HR function itself. "If HR wants to be a leader in the quality movement, HR professionals have to 'walk the talk.' They have to begin to pursue quality themselves," he explains.

According to Ed Lawler, who is director of the Center for Effective Organizations at the University of Southern California, the quality principles that human resources must follow are as follows.

Quality work the first time: "Scrap and rework on the shop floor," he explains, "has a counterpart in HR management." For example, if a company wants to redesign a bonus system or benefits program because employees can't understand it, this is rework. This takes time, costs money, and erodes the credibility of the department. By attempting to produce quality work the first time, HR professionals can begin living up to the standards that they're encouraging employees to meet.

Customer satisfaction: The HR department exists to serve the organization. Anytime that HR puts its own needs above the needs of line managers or other workers, it has failed to provide customer satisfaction.

A comprehensive approach to improvement: TQM may require changes in the mission, structure, and management practices of the HR function. HR professionals need to be open to changes within their own departments. For example, it may behoove HR professionals to pursue cross-training for the same reason that workers on the shop floor are being asked to learn each other's jobs. If an employee can't come to your department and get all questions answered by one person, then you aren't providing quality customer service.

Continuous improvement: One basic tenet of TQM is that continuous improvement must be ingrained as a value in the corporate culture. A company must apply it with equal emphasis in the HR department. Training programs must become more effective as time goes on, for example, and HR specialists must be willing to learn from their mistakes.

Mutual respect and teamwork: Teamwork is important everywhere in today's quality-driven companies, but it's absolutely necessary for HR professionals. As a staff function, Human Resources, by design, must gather information and respond to the needs of every department in the organization. The only way to learn these needs and respond to them effectively is by working *with* the people in those different departments.

The HR department at Milpitas, California–based Solectron Corporation embodies the quality principles exhibited elsewhere in the organization. As a 1991 winner of the Malcolm Baldrige National Quality Award, Solectron managers know what it takes to create and sustain quality. For Human Resources, this means reviewing the function's quality rating on a quarterly basis.

Every three months, according to J. William Webb, vice president of human resources, the department rates its achievements numerically in such areas as:

*   Communication
*   Staffing
*   Performance reviews
*   Overtime tracking
*   Absences

"It isn't enough for us to know how well we're doing. We must stand up in a management meeting and publicly report our results. We have to identify any problems and explain the quality process that we'll undertake to solve those problems," Webb says.

Webb says that Solectron keeps its HR department flexible so that it can respond quickly to organizational changes. "We perform a systematic review of all HR programs to make sure that they're effective, contribute to customer satisfaction, and add value to the business," he says. "If they don't, we do away with them."[22]

ment because total quality is a never-ending process. Products, suppliers, customer requirements and technology are always changing, so the definition of total quality and how it can be pursued are always changing too.[23]

ISO 9000 certification is actually a series of five quality system standards developed by the International Organization for Standardization in Geneva, Switzerland. These standards have been adopted by companies within the European Community. More technical than human resource management-oriented, the ISO 9000 criteria contain approximately one-third of the Baldrige Award criteria.[24] The criteria, however, are being much more broadly accepted by companies throughout Europe than are the Baldrige criteria in the United States. And as with the Deming Prize and the Baldrige Award, the ISO certification process insists that suppliers also be closely involved in quality. In fact, European companies are insisting that their suppliers, anywhere in the world, adopt the ISO certification standards or risk losing their supplier contracts. Thus ISO certification is becoming sought after by companies throughout the world, including firms in the United States. Consequently it appears very likely that one day you will be working in an organization pursuing total quality management.

> You can't implement quality training, revise the reward system, and change selection practices and consider your quality work done!
>
> Anne Sowles, Director, HR Operations
> L. L. Bean

CURRENT TRENDS

One important trend relates to improving the organization consistent with the theme of TQM. It is widening the influence of a company's HR practices to include its suppliers.

> With TQM, HR departments can help the suppliers and customers of the firm.

GOING BEYOND THE BORDERS

As firms seek to improve their quality, they realize that the process must be continuous. Improvements can and must always be found. And as organizations such as Xerox and the Ford Motor Company have found, a stage is reached where improvements can't be made without improving the quality of the materials coming in. That is, the organization has to work with its suppliers to improve their total quality. A larger customer firm such as Ford, can impact, especially for its smaller suppliers, a great deal of expertise in TQM. Because so much of TQM is about people—for example, setting up training programs—the HR department can be very helpful in the TQM programs in supplier firms. On occasion, a firm can help its customers improve their quality too. If a Ford dealership improves its service orientation, then it might sell more cars. The more it sells, the more Ford benefits. So why shouldn't the HR department of Ford help the dealers with their own TQM programs? AT&T's total quality approach specifically includes a partnership with their suppliers; this is shown in Exhibit 15.7.

> **DID YOU KNOW?**
>
> When Chrysler started designing its NEON subcompact in 1990, it involved 25 key suppliers.

SUMMARY

In a surprising turn in the affairs of organizations, how businesses *do* their business is becoming the key strategy of the 1990s. Total quality management is an innovation in the "technology of competition." That is enabling American business to meet the challenge of ever-increasing global and domestic competition. Domestic and international competition is so intense that anything less than a full commitment to continuous quality improvement—signals economic decline. Total quality management can achieve this commitment at every level of an organization.

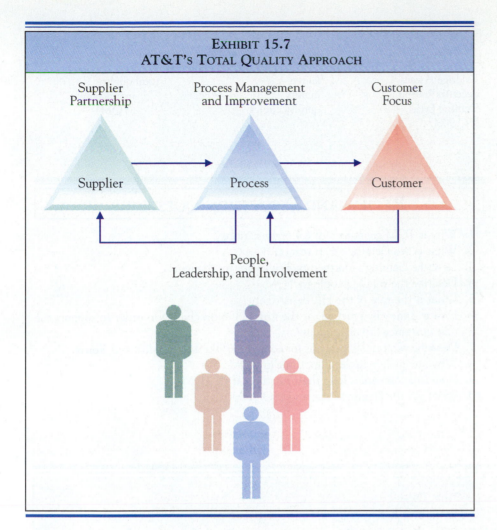

**EXHIBIT 15.7
AT&T'S TOTAL QUALITY APPROACH**

Supplier Partnership

Process Management and Improvement

Customer Focus

Supplier

Process

Customer

People, Leadership, and Involvement

More than ever, TQM depends on effective human resource management. Human resource practices must be linked to the TQM strategy. Such a linkage means redesigning jobs and creating effective teamwork structures, and it means that HR managers must know what the business is about. They must know what the products and strategies of the business are and what technologies are available in order to change HR practices if necessary.

By taking an active role in organizational improvements such as TQM, the HR manager gains more credibility as a businessperson. This in turn enables the HR manager to become a player on the management team. When the HR department is seen as a more valuable and integral part of the organization, TQM programs become more acceptable to line managers, thus making successful implementation more likely. The result of all this is organizations that are more competitive, employees that are more involved in their work, and customers who are more satisfied with the products and services of the organizations. Throughout the TQM process, however, HR professionals must work with the line managers and employees. Success only happens when there is a real partnership here. This is also true for all activities involved in establishing and maintaining effective work relationships in organizations. These activities are described in the next three chapters.

Baldrige Award
decentralization
Deming Prize
ISO 9000

kaizen
quality
quality circles

total quality
management
(TQM)

REVIEW AND DISCUSSION QUESTIONS

1. Why is TQM so important for organizations?
2. What is the Deming chain reaction?
3. Describe Deming's fourteen principles for total quality.
4. Describe the role of people in TQM.
5. What is the role of the HR department?
6. How did the HR practices at the Grand Union change in order to support the new customer-driven strategy?
7. Describe what quality means for companies like McDonald's and Xerox.
8. Why are quality circles important in TQM?
9. How can companies help their suppliers with TQM?
10. What are the Deming Prize and ISO 9000?

EXERCISES AND CASES

FIELD PROJECT

A fast-food chain has invited you in to make suggestions on improving its customer service. Top management believes improving service will mean that prices and margins can be increased. While they understand that such things as the type of food and the physical appearance of the restaurants may need to change to improve the quality of service, they want you to tell them about the implications for their employees. What are your suggestions, and what are the HR implications?

A BROADER VIEW SEIZES MORE OPPORTUNITIES

Don English, corporate vice president in charge of human resources, is now finally able to take a pause from the stream of "fire fighting" he has been engaged in since he came to Bancroft ten years ago! Like many of his colleagues in other firms, Don's knowledge of human resource management came as much from doing it as from formal education.

Because of his workload, Don tended to keep pretty narrowly focused, and he rarely read personnel journals or attended professional conferences. However, recently, things have been easing up. He has been able to recruit and train almost all the division managers in charge of human resources. Now they can do most of the fire fighting, at least that's what Don is planning on. And he has been doing more reading than ever before. Of course, Don has not been totally out of touch with the rest of the world or the growing importance of HR management planning. When he started filling the slots for division personnel managers, he made sure that it was a learning experience for him. Don always required job candidates to prepare a one-hour talk on the state of research and practice in different areas of personnel, for example, selection, appraisal, compensation, or training. He would even invite MBA candidates who had no course work in personnel and ask them to relate their field of interest to human resource management.

Don is planning to become the chief executive officer of Bancroft or some other firm of similar or larger size within the next five to seven years. He thinks he can achieve this if he remains in human resources and does an outstanding job. He will have to be outstanding by all standards, both internal and external to the firm. From his interviews during the past three years, Don knows that it is imperative to move human resources in a strategic direction while at the same time doing the best possible job with the "nuts and bolts" activities.

During a moment of reflection, Don begins to scribble some notes on his large white desk pad. In the middle is Bancroft. To its left are its suppliers and to its right are its customers. In his head are all the human resource practices he is so familiar with. He has a hunch that there must be a way to use the firm's expertise in performance appraisal and training to help Bancroft be more effective. Bancroft has been learning tremendously from its five-year drive to improve quality, but during the past year, quality gains have slowed. Bancroft must continue to improve its quality, but large internal quality gains are becoming more and more difficult as Bancroft climbs the learning curve. Don wonders, How can he help Bancroft experience the excitement of seeing large gains in quality improvement again? Don circles the list of suppliers and begins to formulate a plan that will improve his chances of becoming CEO. He now seeks your advice in exactly what to do and how to go about doing it.

(Yes, this is our case from Chapter 2. There we discussed whether Don really had a place in helping his company gain competitive advantage.)

CASE QUESTIONS

1. Let's assume that Don has gotten the approval from his boss to help Bancroft's suppliers. Should he work with them all or decide to just start with one or two and see how it goes?

2. If Don can do anything to help his suppliers with their HR management activities, what should he focus on?

3. Should Don actually go into the suppliers and do their HR work, or should he train the suppliers' HR professionals at Bancroft?

SOURCE: © Randall S. Schuler, New York University

(Before beginning, review the Grand Union materials in this chapter.)

ROLE PLAY

You are Fred Bellows, CEO of Grand Union. You are a strong supporter of the new business strategy and of Bill Reffett, the new personnel guy. You want both to succeed; however, you are not at all sure what Bill's role, or yours for that matter, will be in the transition to the new strategy. Your success in leveraged buyouts is the reason you are now CEO of Grand Union. Bill was brought to your attention by your former boss at the midwestern retail where Bill served as his personnel and labor relations man. While the two of you were not there at the same time, you knew that if he could be successful in that environment, he should be able to do well at Grand Union.

Again, you are not really sure of the HR implications of your new business strategy. You want to find out as much as possible in this first meeting with Bill and the rest of the top team. Because you have taken on a fair bit of debt, you are concerned about cash flow and expenses.

You have invited Bill in to explain what he plans to do. You have also invited Rex Donaldson, your chief financial officer, and Carla Johnson, senior vice president in charge of merchandising.

Please welcome these people to your meeting, set the agenda, and conduct your meeting.

ROLE PLAY

You are Bill Reffett. Having just spent the past two weeks deciding where to start and what to do, you enter the conference room where the rest of the top team is waiting for your report. Because this is your first meeting to discuss the HR implications of the new business strategy, you may find it most appropriate to provide only an outline of your considerations, leaving the details for subsequent meetings. This means, however, that you should at least be able to give the rest of the top team a preview of things to come.

Because of your background in the retail clothing business, you know how important it is to get people involved in the change process itself. Thus in your first meeting with others in the top team you may want to point out the importance of process in your plans for action as well as the content of those action plans.

While you have been in personnel for the past fifteen years, you have only been with Grand Union for six months.

ROLE PLAY

You are Rex Donaldson, chief financial officer for Grand Union. While you are a strong supporter of the need for a new strategy, you are not entirely sure how costly the transition will be. One thing for sure, you are not particularly interested in hearing that there will be personnel costs associated with the change. You assume, in fact, that the change in strategy will have little impact on the employees: surely the success in implementing the new strategy will not depend on the people in the stores. Whatever is necessary, the people should have no trouble carrying out what they are told to do by the store manager.

While you know that the CEO was personally responsible for hiring the new personnel guy, Bill Reffett, you have only met him in one formal meeting.

ROLE PLAY

You are Carla Johnson, senior vice president in charge of merchandising. In this role, you have responsibility for everything that goes on the store shelves, from the first decision as to whom your suppliers will be to which products get which amount of shelf space and where.

You are entering this first meeting to hear what Bill Reffett has to say about the HR implications of Grand Union's new business strategy. While you know the strategy has some significant implications for you, you are less sure what it means for personnel. Based on what you have been reading in the trade journals, however, you know that this customer-driven services marketing stuff is hot. You also know for this to succeed, you will need to get serious about such things as focus groups. Whether there are implications for your area in what Bill intends to do is unclear. You would like to find out.

While you know that merchandising is the most important function in this business, you are willing to let personnel gain in some importance if it is going to help the business.

NOTES

1. R. Jacob, "TQM: More Than a Dying Fad?" *Fortune* (October 18, 1993): 66–72. Also read C. H. Deutsch, "U.S. Industry's Unfinished Struggle," *The New York Times* (February 21, 1988): Sec. 3: 1, 6, 7; S. Caudron, "Change Keeps TQM Programs Thriving," *Personnel Journal* (Oct. 1993): 104–109; L. Dusky, "Bright Ideas: Anatomy of a Corporate Revolution," *Working Woman* (July 1990): 58–63; A. Halcrow, "Northern Telecom Employees on Tour," *Personnel Journal* (Nov. 1989): 39–41.

2. R. S. Schuler and D. L. Harris, *Managing Quality* (Reading, Mass.: Addison-Wesley, 1992): 32.

3. D. A. Garvin, "How the Baldrige Award Really Works," *Harvard Business Review* (Nov.–Dec. 1991): 80–95. Also read: W. E. Deming, *Quality, Productivity and Competitive Position* (Cambridge, Mass.: MIT Center for Advanced Engineering Study, 1982); W. E. Deming, *Out of Crisis* (Cambridge, Mass.: MIT Press, 1986): 23–24; J. M. Juran, *Juran On Quality by Design* (New York: The Free Press, 1992).

4. P. B. Dubose, *Personnel and Quality* (Milwaukee, Wis.: American Society for Quality Control, 1990).

5. "Quality at Xerox," *The New York Times* (Nov. 9, 1989): D1.

6. *Ibid*. Also see R. Henkoff, "Keeping Motorola on a Roll," *Fortune* (April 18, 1994): 67–78.

7. *Fortune* (Oct. 24, 1990): 168.

8. "Debating Employee Participation," *Bulletin to Management* (May 13, 1993): 152; B. S. Murphy, W. G. Barlow, and D. Hatch, "Du Pont's Employee Committees Ordered Disbanded," *Personnel Journal* (Aug. 1993): 24.

9. "Employers Get Advice on ADA Implementation," *Fair Employment Practices* (February 11, 1993): 15. Used by Permission.

10. R. L. Bunning, "The Dynamics of Downsizing," *Personnel Journal* (Sept. 1990): 69–74; C. Hymowitz, "When Firms Cut Out Middle Managers, Those at Top and Bottom Often Suffer," *The Wall Street Journal* (April 5, 1990): B1.

11. "Giving Quality Programs a Boost," *Bulletin to Management* (July 22, 1993): 225.

12. Deming (*op. cit. Quality*, see Note 3).

13. Garvin (*op. cit.*, see Note 3).

14. R. S. Schuler, "Strategic Human Resource Management," *Organizational Dynamics* (Summer 1992): 18–32.

15. For more detail on using human resource management in service organizations, see V. Johnston and H. Moore, "Pride Drives Wal-Mart to Service Excellence," *HR Magazine* (Oct. 1991): 79–80, 82; J. E. Santora, "Pacific Bell Primes the Quality Pump," *Personnel Journal* (Oct. 1991): 63–66; D. E. Bowen, R. B. Chase, and T. G. Cummings & Associates, *Service Management Effectiveness* (San Francisco: Jossey-Bass, 1990).

16. S. Fatis, "Xerox Rebounds with 'Empowered Workers and Customer-Driven' Focus," *Sunday Star-Ledger* (Jan. 3, 1993): Sec. 3, 7.

17. These two paragraphs adapted from Dubose (*op. cit.*, see Note 4): 4.

18. E. Yager, "Quality Circles: A Tool for the 1980's," *Training and Development Journal* (Aug. 1980): 60–62.

19. C. Bovier, "Teamwork: The Heart of an Airline," *Training* (June 1993): 53–58.

20. S. Caudron, "How HR Drives TQM," *Personnel Journal* (Aug. 1993): 48B. Used by permission.

21. J. F. Bolt, *Executive Development* (New York: Harper & Row, 1989): 140.

22. S. Caudron (*op. cit.*, see Note 20): 48F.

23. K. Ishikawa, "What is Total Quality Control? The Japanese Way," in H. Costin (ed.) *Readings in Total Quality Management* (Ft. Worth: The Dryden Press, 1994): 155–166.

24. L. Potts, *What is ISO 9000 and Why Should I Care?* (Houston: ABS Quality Evaluations, Inc., 1993).

PEOPLE want to be treated with respect and dignity, and they are actively asserting this desire in the workplace as they move to have more and more rights recognized by their employers. Numerous laws impact workplace rights, with many "rights" not covered or in "gray" areas. However, employees today think they have many rights that employers should recognize and honor, and because more employee rights are gaining legal protection, decisions such as discharges, layoffs, and demotions must be made with care and supported by evidence.

The legal qualities of American society can make failure to be in legal compliance—and the courts here often mean more than the letter of the law, they mean the spirit of the law—a costly mistake. Years of careful savings from cost-reduction programs can be blown in a single settlement—not to mention the damage to an organization's image. Hence, it is imperative that organizations have in place carefully formulated employee rights policies; that the HR department continually scan the legal environment for shifts in public and legal opinion; and that the entire work force be informed and possibly retrained in appropriate behaviors. Because this subject is so important in business today, we devote the first of the three chap-

ters in this section to employee rights and include a Career Management Exercise.

When employees feel that their rights are not being respected, that the work environment is neither safe nor healthy, and that wages and other working conditions are neither fair nor sufficient, they often seek to gather power in order to make changes, and a union or association is often a result of this process.

SECTION 7

EFFECTIVE WORK RELATIONSHIPS

Unionization is an interesting process with strong historical, cultural, and legal roots in this country. Although it is not often a careful process but is instead an emotionally charged one that even if unsuccessful can have lasting ramifications, unionization can be considerably affected by a company's human resource philosophy. First, a company must decide

whether or not unionization is in its best interests. The answer to this question is not always as predictable as it once was. Then the organization must formulate a strategy to affect the outcome of potential unionization efforts, and it must eventually deal with the outcome.

Once in place, unions represent the interests of the employees in discussions with the company. Contracts are established between the workers' union and the management of the company. These two parties negotiate and bargain over conditions of work and wages and benefits. Long adversaries with fundamentally conflicting goals, today unions and management are finding that there is no room for conflict if organizations are to remain competitive in the global economy. Thus, establishing and maintaining effective work relationships is such an important topic that it is the focus of the remaining two chapters of this section. Chapter 17 describes the history of the union movement, why unions are attractive to individuals, the structure of today's union movement and aspects associated with the formation of the unions. Chapter 18 goes on to describe the process of collective bargaining, the process by which wages and working conditions are established.

CHAPTER 16

EMPLOYEE RIGHTS

LEARNING OBJECTIVES

When you have finished studying this chapter, you should be able to:

1. Explain the purposes and importance of employee rights.
2. Describe legalities impacting employee rights.
3. Describe strategies used to preserve employee rights.
4. Discuss the trends in employee rights, especially alternative dispute resolution.

CHAPTER OUTLINE

"Managing Human Resources
TO PREVENT SEXUAL HARASSMENT"

EMPLOYEE RIGHTS

WHY ARE EMPLOYEE RIGHTS IMPORTANT?

LEGAL CONSIDERATIONS

"HR Advice and Application
AT-WILL EMPLOYEES HAVE NO 'RIGHT' TO JOBS"

"Managing Human Resources
GE WHISTLE-BLOWER IS AWARDED $13.4 MILLION"

"Managing Human Resources
STRADDLING THE LAW ON LAYOFFS"

STRATEGIES TO PRESERVE EMPLOYEE RIGHTS

INTERNATIONAL COMPARISONS

CURRENT TRENDS

Career Management Exercise

Case: The Payback

Case: Human Rights Cost Accounting

RESEARCH by Freada Klein Associates, a workplace-diversity consulting firm in Cambridge, Massachusetts, shows that 90 percent of the *Fortune* 500 companies have dealt with sexual harassment complaints. More than a third have been sued at least once, and about a quarter have been sued over and over again. Klein estimates that the problem costs the average large corporation $6.7 million a year.

Bettina Plevan, an attorney at Proskauer Rose Goetz & Mendelsohn in New York City, specializes in defending companies against sexual harassment lawsuits. She says employers spend an average of $200,000 on each complaint that is investigated in-house and found to be valid, whether or not it ever gets to court. Richard Hafets, a labor lawyer at Piper & Marbury in Baltimore, believes sexual harassment could be tomorrow's "asbestos," costing American business $1 billion in fees and damages in the next five years.

But the costs of sexual harassment go well beyond anything that can be measured on a profit-and-loss statement. Women, often still treated like interlopers in the office, say they feel vulnerable to the myriad subtle—and not so subtle—sexual power trips some men use to keep them in their place. At an Aetna Life & Casualty golfing party in September 1992, four executives vented their resentment of female managers' presence at what had traditionally been an all-male event. Their mildest offense—and the only one we're halfway willing to describe in a magazine your kids might see—was calling women executives "sluts." In response, Aetna demoted two of the men and asked the two others to resign.

Jeannine Sandstrom, a senior vice president of the executive recruiting firm Lee Hecht Harrison in Dallas, knows of instances where harassers were caught because they sent X-rated messages to their victims via voice mail or E-mail. Marvels Sandstrom: "How self-destructive do you have to be to do something like this, knowing how easy it is to trace?"

In most cases, harassment is more subtle—and far more difficult to prove. As agonizing as it may be, women have an obligation to speak up and tell someone who is hounding them to stop it. Although federal law defines sexual harassment as "unwelcome" behavior, the courts say it doesn't count as such unless the offender knows it's unwelcome. Yet a 1991 study by two professors at the University of St. Thomas in St. Paul, Minnesota, revealed that, among women in a nationwide survey who said they had been victims of sexual harassment, only 34 percent told the harasser to knock it off; just 2 percent filed a formal complaint.

With the economy in its current shaky state, many women may be too fearful of losing their jobs to speak up. Or they may be reluctant to be seen as whiners, either by their peers or by the people above them. But if a woman wants to file a grievance, it's important to be able to prove that she told the perpetrator to back off. Some experts suggest tape-recording the conversation or sending a registered letter (return receipt requested) detailing the offending behavior and declaring it not OK. This helps in any follow-up by human resources or legal staff, even in cases where witnesses or other direct proof of the harassment are available.[1]

This feature denotes the potential costliness that can occur when organizations stumble in the area of employee rights. Sexual harassment in the workplace has been a hot media issue in recent times, but it is but one of many areas where organizations must move carefully and decisively in implementing human resource policies.

Employee rights cover rights that are legally protected and some that are not.

Employee rights include job security and rights on the job.

EMPLOYEE RIGHTS

Employee rights *are those rights that employees desire regarding the security of their jobs and the treatment administered by their employers while on the job, regardless of whether or not those rights are protected by law or collective bargaining agreements.*

Employee rights cover much more than freedom from sexual harassment; there is the right to a job under almost any conditions and the right to fair, just, and respectable treatment while on the job.[2] More specific issues within these two broad areas include the right of plant closing notification; the right to refuse tests for substance abuse; the right against retaliation for whistle-blowing or filing complaints against the employer; due process treatment in discharge cases; the right to know about workplace hazards; freedom from discriminatory treatment based on sex, gender, race, religion, or national origin; the right to be assisted in correcting ineffective performance; and the right to have personal records remain confidential. Some of these rights are protected by collective bargaining agreements; however, more than 80 percent of the work force is non-unionized.[3]

As more employee rights gain legal protection, the extent of employer rights and the prerogatives management has in dealing with its work force, such as employment-at-will, diminish. Thus employee rights significantly impact human resource management.

This chapter follows the conventional distinction found in research and practice and discusses employee rights in terms of two major areas: job security and rights on the job. After we define employee rights and examine their increasing importance in managing human resources, we then review major legislation and court decisions affecting these rights. A major on-the-job issue is an employee's right to privacy, especially electronic privacy. Other significant on-the-job issues involve access to employee records; cooperative acceptance, especially in regard to sexual harassment; and notification and assistance concerning plant or office closings. Employer success in ensuring employee rights in both job security and rights on the job depends on establishing more effective communication as well as clear procedures for grievances, progressive discipline, privacy, and outplacement assistance.

LEARNING OBJECTIVE 1

Explain the purposes and importance of employee rights.

Respecting employee rights saves money and increases employee commitment to the firm.

WHY ARE EMPLOYEE RIGHTS IMPORTANT?

The discussion on recruitment and selection in Chapters 7 and 8 focused on attracting qualified people to organizations, we now direct our primary attention to establishing and maintaining relationships with the people hired and terminating those not desired by the organization. Previous chapters stressed the importance of making sure employees (new and old) are informed about what is expected of them and what opportunities are available in the organization. This, after all, is part of the basis for an equitable employer-employee relationship.[4]

Treating employees fairly and with respect once they are hired is also important. Violation of legally protected employee rights—even when what is protected is not entirely clear—can result in severe penalties and fines. A jury recently awarded an employee $1.2 million after finding that Mobil Corporation wrongfully fired him after he refused to violate environmental laws and policies. After a two-month trial in federal court in Newark, New Jersey, the jury ruled in favor of Valcar Bowman, Jr., the former manager for environmental affairs at the company's Mobil Chemical Co. unit. He claimed in his suit that he was fired in 1986 in retaliation for his refusal to remove environmental records from a Mobil plant in Bakersfield, California.

The jury award consisted of $375,000 in compensatory damages, including lost wages and pain and suffering, and $1 million in punitive damages.[5] Costs are equally as substantial in harassment cases. As described in the opening "Managing Human Resources to Prevent Sexual Harassment," costs to the average large corporation can run up to $6.7 million per year. These costs are linked to absenteeism, low productivity and turnover; they do not include the hard-to-measure costs of legal defense, time lost and tarnished public image. Anecdotal evidence suggests the costs may be even higher.[6]

Although failure to respect employee rights can be costly to organizations in terms of back-pay awards and fines, it can also be costly because a poor corporate image can make it difficult to attract and retain good employees.[7] Thus respecting employee rights is important in building and retaining a solid work force. Exhibit 16.1 lists the benefits that accrue with a good employee rights record.

DID YOU KNOW?

Companies spend an average of $200,000 on each case of sexual harassment that is investigated in the firm and found to be valid.

LEGAL CONSIDERATIONS

Because the entire activity of employee rights is laden with legal considerations, we attempt to give you a feel for the legal climate in this section by citing several court cases and regulations. The legal climate on this issue is volatile as special-interest groups and grass-root organizations find fertile grounds in our legal system to work their particular agendas. Given that ours is a very litigious society, keeping up-to-date on these issues is imperative.

LEARNING OBJECTIVE 2

Describe legalities impacting employee rights.

There are many laws that cover issues of rights to job security and rights on the job.

EMPLOYEE RIGHTS TO JOB SECURITY

Over the years, the major limit on employee rights to job security has been the employer's right to terminate employees for any reason. This right is known as

EXHIBIT 16.1
HOW A GOOD EMPLOYEE RIGHTS RECORD BENEFITS A COMPANY

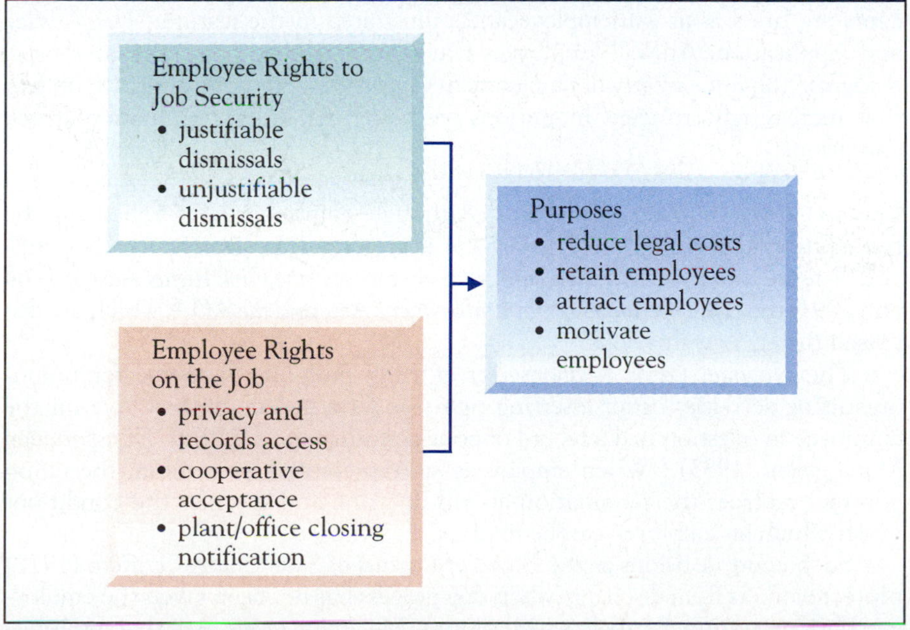
Employee Rights to Job Security
• justifiable dismissals
• unjustifiable dismissals
Employee Rights on the Job
• privacy and records access
• cooperative acceptance
• plant/office closing notification
Purposes
• reduce legal costs
• retain employees
• attract employees
• motivate employees

LINE MANAGERS	HR PROFESSIONALS	EMPLOYEES
Set policy for employee treatment.	Ensure line managers set policy in accordance with legal considerations.	Accept responsibility to respect the rights of other employees.
Are responsible for their behavior in respecting employee rights.	Develop policies and programs that respect the rights of employees.	Work with HR professionals in establishing policies and programs for employee rights.

Employment-at-will is the doctrine that says employees serve at the will of the employer.

the **termination-at-will rule** (also referred to as the **employment-at-will rule**). The termination-at-will rule, which was developed in the United States more than 100 years ago, was explained by one Tennessee court in 1884 in this way: "All may dismiss their employee(s) at will, be they many or few, for good cause, for no cause, or even for cause morally wrong without being thereby guilty of legal wrong" (*Payne v. Western & A.R.R. Co.*, 1884).

People who are hired under employment-at-will conditions are also referred to as "at-will" employees. Employers today are careful to make it clear when applicants are hired as at-will employees. As illustrated in the feature, "HR Advice and Application: At-Will Employees Have No 'Right' to Jobs," the courts still recognize the force of at-will employment conditions, but companies are finding that increasingly stringent limitations are being placed on termination-at-will conditions.

LIMITATIONS OF TERMINATION. Although employers have relied on the termination-at-will rule over the years, it is proving to be less of a legally justifiable defense today because of several recent statutes (*the Civil Rights Acts of 1964 and 1991*, the *Age Discrimination in Employment Act*, and *the ADA*, which are discussed throughout this book.

The *National Labor Relations Act of 1935* prohibits discharge for union-organizing activities or for asserting rights under a union contract, even if the employee in question had a record of poor performance (*NLRB v. Transportation Management*, 1983).[9] When employees are represented by a union, the union contract replaces the termination-at-will doctrine and specifies the conditions under which an employee can be fired.

Such court decisions as the *Board of Regents of State Colleges v. Roth* (1972) protect workers from discharge when due process has not been given the employee. Various state acts, such as Montana's *Maternity Leave Act* that prohibits

AT-WILL EMPLOYEES HAVE NO 'RIGHT' TO JOBS

A salesperson who claimed he was defrauded out of his job has no case, the U.S. Court of Appeals at Chicago rules, since he was an at-will employee and had no right to the job in the first place.

The employee had worked for 20 years at the company before it decided to eliminate 200 employees. The company offered a voluntary severance pay plan under which the employee was entitled to eleven months' pay. A week before the deadline for accepting the plan, a supervisor announced a dramatic rise in the annual sales quota and warned that a failure to meet the quota would trigger discharge. The employee reluctantly chose to resign with severance but later discovered that the quota was not stringently applied. He sued the company, claiming he had been fraudulently induced to quit his job.

Under the at-will employment doctrine, the court says, the employee could be fired by his employer at any time, with or without cause. Accordingly, it points out, the employee could not be defrauded out of a job to which he had no right (*Stromberger v. 3M Co.*, 1993).[8]

employers from terminating female employees because of pregnancy, also limits the employer's rights.

In general, discharge is *not* a legitimate action under any circumstances for the following employee actions. In fact, terminating a worker under the following conditions may result in substantial penalties, as illustrated in the feature, "Managing Human Resources: GE Whistle-Blower Is Awarded $13.4 Million."

- Whistle-blowing (for example, opposing and publicizing employer policies or practices that violate laws such as the antitrust, consumer protection, or environmental protection laws)[10]
- Garnishment for any one indebtedness
- Complaining or testifying about equal pay or wage/hour law violations
- Complaining or testifying about safety hazards and/or refusing an assignment because of the belief that the assignment is dangerous
- Engaging in union activities, provided there is no violence or unlawful behavior
- Engaging in concerted activity to protest wages, working conditions, or safety hazards
- Filing a workers' compensation claim
- Filing unfair labor practice charges with the NLRB or a state agency
- Filing discrimination charges with the Equal Employment Opportunity Commission (EEOC) or a state or municipal fair employment agency
- Cooperating in the investigation of a charge
- Reporting Occupational Safety and Health Administration (OSHA) violations[11]

These are the many illegal reasons for firing an employee:

PERMISSIBLE TERMINATION. Although termination for good cause has not been an explicitly accepted doctrine for non-union organizations, the decisions that courts are rendering suggest the safest (legal) grounds for discharge include the following:

- Incompetence in performance that does not respond to training or to accommodation

A former employee of the General Electric Company was awarded $13.4 million by a federal judge yesterday for bringing forward evidence that the company defrauded the United States in a scandal involving the sale of military jet engines to Israel.

The award was the largest to date under the federal whistle-blower statue.

The award was made to Chester L. Walsh, a former General Electric manager in Israel, for informing the Justice Department of a scheme in which GE conspired with an Israeli Air Force general to submit bills for fictitious parts and testing equipment. The bills were accepted and paid by the Pentagon.

General Electric, based in Fairfield, Connecticut, pleaded guilty in July to four federal criminal fraud charges and agreed to pay $9.5 million in fines and $59.5 million to settle a related civil case. The Israeli general, Rami Dotan, was convicted of bribery and fraud charges in Israel last year and is serving a 13-year prison sentence.

Under the *Federal False Claims Act*, whistle-blowers may receive 15–25 percent of any settlement or any financial recovery won by the government.

In his ruling yesterday, United States District Judge Carl B. Rubin in Cincinnati said the case against General Electric "would have been difficult, if not impossible, to sustain" without documents that Mr. Walsh smuggled from Israel. The judge awarded Mr. Walsh 22.5 percent of the Government's settlement, or 90 percent of the maximum award he could have received under the law.

Such a large award is a rebuff to the Justice Department and General Electric, which had argued that Mr. Walsh did not deserve such a large award because he did not bring his accusations directly to the company as corporate policy requires and that he delayed acting for several years.

A spokesman for the Justice Department in Washington declined to comment on the decision, saying that the agency was studying the matter. There are currently dozens of whistle-blower cases working their way through the courts.

In the past, the Justice Department has been ambivalent about paying multimillion-dollar awards to whistle-blowers, but recently agency officials have expressed more reservations in cases where they believe the whistle-blower might have delayed taking action in order to receive a larger settlement.

GE said in a statement yesterday that Mr. Walsh did not deserve the money and hoped the government would appeal the ruling.

John Phillips, Mr. Walsh's lawyer, said, "I think this decision is a total vindication of Mr. Walsh and the important role he played in bringing the information to light, and a clear setback for the Justice Department and General Electric, which contended that he should get less."

In a telephone interview from Orlando, Florida, Mr. Walsh said that he felt relieved by the judge's decision, which he described as "the end of a long, stressful five years."

Mr. Walsh has agreed to donate half the award to Citizens Against Fraud, a nonprofit group that represents whistle-blowers. After taxes, he will retain about $5 million, his lawyers said.

Mr. Walsh, 61 years old, said he had been "too involved in the case" to think about how he would spend the award.

Judge Rubin said in the ruling that whether Mr. Walsh should have shared his information earlier was not at issue, and he cited Mr. Walsh's argument that he feared retribution from the company and possible physical danger from General Rotan. The judge said that the Justice Department's behavior in the whistle-blower cases "has always been a mystery."

In the six years since Congress passed the updated whistle-blower law, a growing number of people have come forward to claim multimillion-dollar awards. In July, a federal judge awarded $7.5 million to a former pricing analyst for an upstate New York maker of flight simulators, CAE-Link, formerly owned by the Singer Corporation, for leading the Justice Department to a scandal in which the company was said to have over-billed the government by $77 million.[12]

- Gross or repeated insubordination
- Civil Rights violations such as harassment
- Too many unexcused absences
- Illegal behavior such as theft
- Repeated lateness
- Drug activity on the job
- Verbal abuse
- Physical violence
- Falsification of records
- Drunkenness on the job[13]

These are the many legitimate reasons for firing an employee:

Termination, even under one of these conditions, should be the last step in a progressive discipline system.[14] Furthermore, all evidence and material relevant to each step and even any decision to discharge an employee should be documented and filed.

Even though an employer may have the right to discharge an employee, the employer may be required to show evidence indicating that none of the protections against termination-at-will or for good cause was violated.[15]

EMPLOYEE RIGHTS ON THE JOB
Employee rights on the job include privacy and access to employment records, cooperative acceptance, freedom from sexual harassment, and plant/office closing notification.

RIGHTS TO PRIVACY AND ACCESS TO EMPLOYMENT RECORDS. Recently, several lawsuits have been brought against organizations for invasion of privacy rights. The *Privacy Act of 1974*, which applies only to federal agencies, pertains to the verification of references in selection and employment decisions. This act allows individuals to determine which records pertaining to them are collected, used, and maintained; to review and amend such records; to prevent unspecified use of such records; and to bring civil suit for damages against those intentionally violating the rights specified in the act.

Employee rights on the job:
- **privacy**
- **cooperative acceptance**
- **closing notice**
- **accommodation**

The second federal privacy law is the *Fair Credit and Reporting Act*, which permits job applicants to know the nature and content of the credit file on them that is obtained by the organization. The third law is the *Family Education Rights and Privacy Act*, or the *Buckley Amendment*. This allows students to inspect their educational records and prevents educational institutions from supplying information without students' consent. If students do not provide this consent, potential employers are prevented from learning of their educational record. The fourth law is the *Freedom of Information Act*, which also pertains only to federal agencies. This act allows individuals to see all the material an agency uses in its decision-making processes.

While the four laws detailed above apply primarily to federal agencies, several states (for example, California, Connecticut, Maine, Michigan, Oregon, and Pennsylvania) have enacted laws that give employees access to their personnel files and define what information employees are and are not entitled to see, as well as where, when, and under what circumstances the employees may see their files.[16]

In addition to these state and federal regulations, employees, their designated representatives, and OSHA (Occupational Safety and Health Administration) have the right to access their on-the-job medical records and records that measure employee exposure to toxic substances. These rights are provided for by the *Employee Exposure and Medical Records Regulation of 1980*.

Employee rights to privacy have recently been extended to include the right to refuse to take a polygraph test as a condition of employment (*Employment Polygraph Protection Act of 1988*) for most jobs.

Court rulings are also being applied in the area of drug testing (*O'Connor v. Ortega*, 1987). Drug testing raises several basically unresolved issues for employees and employers. On one hand, employees say they have a constitutional right to privacy and a right to have their "personal" (non-job-related) lives kept separate from their workplace lives. On the other hand, employers say they have a right to run their businesses safely and profitably, and this may require knowing whether or not their employees or job applicants are substance abusers, liars about their past, individuals who carry genetic traits making them susceptible to certain diseases, or individuals who are HIV-positive or have AIDS.[17]

While there is legal protection for individuals with HIV and AIDS and while the *Polygraph Act* protects individuals against the use of polygraph tests, courts appear to allow employers to test for drug use, particularly when public safety is an issue. An example is a program jointly developed between New York City and the Transit Authority union that allows random testing for drug and alcohol use.

> About 30,000 employees will be subject to the surprise tests, and about 10 percent of them will be tested each year, transit officials said.
>
> Workers subject to the random tests are in safety-sensitive positions and have long been tested for drugs and alcohol on hiring and after incidents like accidents or prolonged absences. But Local 100 of the Transport Workers Union had opposed random testing, saying that it could be used for harassment.
>
> The union dropped its opposition in August [1991], a day after a Lexington Avenue express train crashed near Union Square, killing five people and injuring 200. The driver, Robert E. Ray, was charged with second-degree murder after he was found to have a high level of alcohol in his blood hours after the crash.
>
> Workers will be selected for testing at random by a computer, the Transit Authority said. Tests, which will be conducted at the transit agency's medical centers, will run round the clock seven days a week.[18]

The *Americans with Disabilities Act of 1990* does not protect current drug users; however, anyone with a history of drug use who has successfully completed or is currently engaged in rehabilitation is covered. However, certain employers (for example, law enforcement and transit agencies) ". . . may also be able to impose a qualification standard that excludes individuals with a history of illegal use of drugs if it can show that the standard is job-related and consistent with business necessity." The ADA also has a stand on medical exams, indicating that they can be given only *after* a conditional job offer has been made.

RIGHT TO COOPERATIVE ACCEPTANCE. The right of employees to be treated fairly and with respect, regardless of race, gender, national origin, physical disability, age, or religion, while *on the job* (as well as in obtaining a job) is called **cooperative acceptance**.

Not only do employees have the right *not* to be discriminated against in employment practices and decisions, but also they have the right to be free of sexual harassment. The 1980 EEOC guidelines state that **sexual harassment** is a form of sex discrimination. According to the guidelines, verbal and physical conduct of a sexual nature is harassment under the following conditions:

Sexual harassment is a form of sex discrimination and is covered by civil rights laws.

- Submission to such conduct is either explicitly or implicitly made a term or condition of an individual's employment.

- Submission to, or rejection of, such conduct by an individual is used as the basis for employment decisions affecting such individuals.
- Such conduct has the purpose or effect of substantially interfering with an individual's work performance or creating an intimidating, hostile or offensive working environment.[19]

Numerous court decisions have also equated sexual harassment with sex discrimination under Title VII (*Tomkins v. Public Service Electric and Gas Company et al.*, 1977; *William v. Saxbe*, 1976; *Barnes v. Costle*, 1977; *Heelen v. Johns-Manville Corp.*, 1978; *Bellissimo v. Westinghouse*, 1984).[20]

The following Supreme Court decision illustrates why employers should be especially concerned about the issue of sexual harassment (*Meritor Savings v. Vinson*, 1986):

> A bank teller's charge that her supervisor intimidated her into engaging in a sexual liaison led to a Supreme Court ruling that demonstrates just how vulnerable employers can be to charges of sexual harassment. The bank claimed that if, in fact, she had a sexual affair with her supervisor, she submitted voluntarily to his advances, and he never conditioned employment benefits on her participation in the affair. But the Supreme Court rejected those arguments. Even if the teller wasn't forced to participate in the alleged sexual liaison, she could still make a case if she could show that those advances were "unwelcome," ruled the Court. And though there was no evidence that her supervisor conditioned tangible job benefits on her participation in the alleged liaison, she could still sue by demonstrating that his conduct created an "intimidating, hostile, or offensive working environment."[21]

In 1993, the EEOC issued a set of regulations that clarified the coverage of harassment. In doing so, they reaffirmed the standard of the "reasonable person." This standard is an expansion of the "reasonable woman" articulated in *Ellison v. Brady* (1991). There the court said that

> unsolicited love letters and unwanted attention—might appear inoffensive to the average man, but might be so offensive to the average woman as to create a hostile working environment.

The "average woman" in this case became the "reasonable woman." This was reaffirmed in *Harris v. Forklift Systems* (1993). The EEOC's 1993 regulations on harassment then explained the "reasonable person" standard and several other issues:

- Employers have a duty to maintain a working environment free of harassment based on race, color, religion, gender, national origin, age or disability.
- Conduct is harassment if it creates a hostile, intimidating, or offensive work environment; unreasonably interferes with the individual's work; or adversely affects the employee's employment opportunities. The conduct includes such things as racist epithets, raunchy jokes, and ethnic slurs and usually, though not always, has to be systematic.
- The standard for evaluating harassment is whether a reasonable person in the same or similar circumstances would find the conduct intimidating, hostile, or abusive. The perspective of the victim—his or her race, gender, age, place of origin, etc.—has an important place in the evaluation.
- Unwanted sexual conduct is not the only form of sexual harassment. "Gender-based animus" is also harassment. "It usually occurs where a woman has gone into traditionally male professions," Ms. Johnston,

The reasonable woman standard applies to any situation a reasonable or average woman would say is offensive. The reasonable person standard applies to any situation a reasonable or average person would say is offensive.

The issue of harassment today covers many groups.

EEOC assistant legal counsel, said. "Male co-workers might try to make her life miserable." However, men entering traditionally female professions can also be victims of gender-based animus.

- Employers are liable for the acts of those who work for them if they knew or should have known about the conduct and took no immediate, appropriate corrective action. Employers who fail to draw up explicit, detailed anti-harassment policies and grievance procedures may put themselves at particular risk. "Employers are not required *per se* to have policies," Ms. Johnston said, but if they do not, employees can assume "the supervisor is acting with the imprimatur of the company."[22]

RIGHTS TO PLANT/OFFICE CLOSING NOTIFICATION. The employee's **right to plant/office closing or relocation notification** is an important one. The suicide rate among displaced workers is almost 30 times the national average. The right of employers (where a union represents the workers) to move production facilities is greatly affected by federal labor law under the NLRA, Section 8(a). It has been clearly established that employers must bargain over the effects of a plant closing and relocation. The Supreme Court, however, ruled against the NLRB in one case, saying that a corporate decision to close out a particular location or even a product line is not a subject that must be negotiated in advance with the union as long as it is for solely economic reasons (*First National Maintenance v. NLRB*, 1981). However, companies must negotiate with the union before they make a decision to move if there is no basic change in the nature of the employer's operation at the new location (*NLRB v. Dubuque Packing Company*, 1991).

Several states now recognize the importance of plant or office closings and relocations and are considering legislation to control them. Maine and Wisconsin require prenotification and penalize employers who move plants without doing so. At the federal level, the *Worker Adjustment and Retraining Notification Act* (WARN) took effect in 1989. It mandates that employers give employees 60 days' notice of layoffs of 50 or more employees in situations where the number constitutes one-third of the work force. It also requires employers to give prenotification of layoffs of 500 or more workers, regardless of the total number of workers at the company. All businesses that employ 100 or more employees (excluding part-timers) are covered.[23]

Workers have a right to early warning, but not many seem to get it.

While WARN was regarded as a "ticking time bomb" when it was passed, its effects appear to be much more modest. The feature, "Managing Human Resources: Straddling the Law on Layoffs," describes them.

Workplace accommodation is a big right identified by ADA.

RIGHTS TO WORKPLACE ACCOMMODATION. As introduced in Chapter 5, the *Americans with Disabilities Act* gives individuals the right to workplace accommodation. This, however, is not without limits but is dependent on the job—for example:

A Missouri school system was justified in firing a high school interpreter for the hearing impaired who refused to "sign" profanity because of her religious beliefs, a state appeals court concludes.

In her job, the interpreter either modified language she found objectionable or informed students that the speaker had cursed or used "bad language." She interpreted the famous "Frankly, my dear, I don't give a damn" line in *Gone With the Wind* as "Frankly, I don't care," for example. After the school district adopted national Registry for Interpreters for the Deaf guidelines, which state in part that interpreters are not editors and must transmit everything that is said in exactly the same way it was intended, the employee requested a transfer to the grade school level or suggested that she discuss her non-literal inter-

WHEN Congress passed legislation in 1988 requiring companies to give 60 days' notice to workers who were about to lose their jobs, it was trying to put a tourniquet on the wounds of America's industrial heartland. Business howled, as it tends to do over measures it views as fettering its options. President Ronald Reagan, who vetoed the measure once and only reluctantly let it slip through on a second pass, used to refer to the law—known formally as the *Worker Adjustment and Retraining Act*, or WARN—as "a ticking time bomb in the back seat of any medium-sized or larger company."

In February of 1993, the General Accounting Office, the agency directed by Congress to keep tabs on the alleged time bomb, weighed in with its report. This instigated a confluence of not very coincidental events: a Congressional hearing and the release by a grass-roots labor organization of what it called a "dirty dozen" of plant closings and layoffs.

WARN requires employers with 100 or more full-time workers to give 60 days' warning of a closing or layoff to both workers and government officials when shutting down an operation affecting 50 or more full-time workers. Notification is also required for layoffs involving 50 or more full-time workers who make up at least a third of the work force or for "mass layoffs" of 500 or more workers.

On Tuesday, Linda Morra, the G.A.O. official who directed the WARN evaluation, appeared before the Senate subcommittee on labor to report her results the G.A.O., a polite and cautious institution, stopped far short of accusing companies of playing fast and loose with the exceptions to the law, but it indicated that few workers are getting the notice to which they are entitled.

The G.A.O. acknowledged that thousands of workers have received the notices due them, but it pointed out that the law excludes more than half the employers with more than 100 workers in the eleven-state sample it reviewed.

Ms. Morra was noncommitted on one topic likely to remain controversial as discussions of modifications in the law begin. Are the WARN exceptions and "thresholds"—the third-of-the-work-force threshold,

for example—really loopholes in disguise? "The law," she said, "was very much a compromise between needs of workers and local government and the needs of business." She added: "It was carefully constructed so that there were exceptions, and so that it would apply to a small number of employers."

Less sanguine was Greg Watchman, a spokesman for the labor subcommittee. "There is no question that companies are exploiting loopholes," said Mr. Watchman, whose boss is Senator Howard Metzenbaum, the Democrat of Ohio and chairman of the subcommittee. Companies can exploit hazy definitions in the law or gradually cut the work force until they fall under the legal threshold covered by WARN, Mr. Watchman said. The subcommittee has been hearing about problems with the law "not just from the G.A.O., but from people who are out there living with it," he said.

The least enthusiastic of those involved in Tuesday's meeting was surely the Federation for Industrial Retention and Renewal, a grass-roots group concerned with economic dislocation. The Chicago-based federation went to Washington to announce its third annual Plant Closing Dirty Dozen, the twelve most extreme examples, according to the group, of "irresponsible plant closings and community abandonment."

The list: Acme Boot/Farley Industries, Detroit Coke, General Motors, Haverhill Shoe, Hough Bakeries, Lewis Nut and Bolt, McDonnell Douglas, the Pittsburgh Press/Scripps Howard, the R. E. Phelon Company, Reynolds Metals/BICC Cables, Stroehmann Bakeries/Taystee, and Zenith.

The award implies that companies should be held to a higher standard than required by either the law or their collective corporate conscience. "Yes, the assumption is that they have a responsibility," said Sonia Angell, a field organizer for the federation. Workers need to gain some control over their lives and their futures. "We are looking for ways to change that are managed and planned," Ms. Angell said. "If a plant's going to close, it will close. But if we can find alternatives, a lot don't have to close."[24]

pretations with students' parents. The school district refused and discharged her, and she filed a state law religious bias claim. The state human rights commission concluded that the district failed to accommodate the employee's religious beliefs, but the circuit court found that accommodation would have imposed an undue hardship on the employer.

The employer could not have accommodated the interpreter's religious beliefs without compromising the educational entitlements of the students, the appeals court rules, adding that requiring a literal translation of classroom conversation is not an unreasonable guideline (*Sedalia Schl. Dist. v. Mo. Comm. on Human Rights*, 1992).[25]

In addition to legal considerations in employee rights on the job, "humane" considerations include outplacement assistance for employees who are no longer needed, even though they may be competent performers. Such circumstances may arise if a plant or office is moving or closing or if it must reduce its work force for economic reasons.[26] Because these conditions can be planned for, they are covered in Chapter 4, Human Resource Planning.

LEARNING OBJECTIVE 3

Describe strategies used to preserve employee rights.

STRATEGIES TO PRESERVE EMPLOYEE RIGHTS

Because of both legal and humane considerations, it is important that organizations develop and implement strategies that take into account employee rights. Effective implementation of other human resource activities is one general way to ensure that legally sanctioned employee rights are recognized. In addition, organizations can implement specific employee rights programs such as privacy policies, assistance programs, outplacement activities, and sexual harassment prevention training.

STRATEGIES FOR ENSURING JOB SECURITY RIGHTS

Strategies for Job Security Rights:

- communicate expectations
- treat equally
- due process
- progressive discipline

In addition to adhering to the laws applying to job security rights, employers can achieve fair and legal termination by communicating expectations and prohibitions, establishing grievance procedures and due process, and following progressive discipline procedures.

COMMUNICATE EXPECTATIONS AND PROHIBITIONS. Although ignorance of rules is generally no excuse in society at large, it is in the workplace. Generally, employees can be disciplined only for conduct not in accordance with what they know or reasonably understand is prohibited or required (*Patterson v. American Tobacco Co.*, 1976, 1978; *Sledge v. J. P. Stevens & Co.*, 1978; and *Donaldson v. Pillsbury Co.*, 1975). Employers must therefore ensure that performance expectations along with information about what is prohibited, are not only conveyed to employees but that employees understand the expectations and prohibitions. Employers can do this by developing and communicating written policy statements, job descriptions, and performance criteria. Written standards should also exist for promotions (*Rowe v. General Motors Corp.*, 1972; *Robinson v. Union Carbide Corp.*, 1976).

TREAT EMPLOYEES EQUALLY. Equal treatment of employees is essential in ensuring that legally protected employee rights are upheld. For example, if the employer discharges one employee for five unexcused absences, then other employees with five unexcused absences must also be discharged. (*McDonald v. Santa Fe Trail Transportation Co.*, 1976). Periodic training for supervisors can help ensure that discharge policies are communicated and administered the same way by all supervisors. Employees value fairness in treatment and may react in unproductive ways (such as stealing) if they perceive unfairness.

GRIEVANCE PROCEDURES AND DUE PROCESS. Not only do grievance procedures need to be established to ensure due process for employees, they must also be administered consistently and fairly. For example, evidence should be available to employee and employer, and both parties should have the right to call witnesses and refuse to testify against themselves.[27]

Furthermore, these grievance procedures should be clearly stated as company policy and communicated as such to employees. Increasingly, organizations are using peers to review employee grievances and appeals.

ESTABLISH PROGRESSIVE DISCIPLINE PROCEDURES. A formal grievance policy should be accompanied by a progressive discipline policy. For most violations of company rules, termination should be the last step in a carefully regulated system of escalating discipline, the progressive discipline described in Chapter 10. Possible steps in **progressive discipline** procedures include the following:

- Warning may be oral at first but should then be written, and a copy with the employee's signature kept in the personnel files. Having that information in the personnel files is important when building a case for disciplinary discharge. Unfortunately, the information needed is often missing from the file. The biggest deficiencies in employment records often surface only after an employee challenges the legality of a discharge. Valid personnel files, along with a progressive discipline policy for discharge, can be the best defense, according to several arbitration decisions regarding discharge for excessive absenteeism.
- Reprimand is official, in writing, and placed in the employee's file.
- Suspension can be for as short as part of a day or as long as several months without pay, depending on the seriousness of the employee's offense and the circumstances.
- Disciplinary transfer may take the pressure off a situation that might explode into violence, or one in which personality conflict is part of the disciplinary problem.
- Demotion can be a reasonable answer to problems of incompetence or an alternative to layoff for economic reasons.
- Discharge is the last resort, used only when all else has failed, although it might be a reasonable immediate response to violence, theft, or falsification of records. However, termination can be exceedingly painful, even though it is well organized and planned. In addition, many individuals are capable of effective performance but only in certain types of situations. Thus some organizations carefully diagnose performance deficiencies, as discussed in Chapter 10. Such a diagnosis may result in reassigning employees to different parts of the organization or trading top-level managers to other organizations.[28]

Another step in progressive discipline that may be added is the "last chance agreement." Before resorting to termination, an employer can grant an employee one more chance, but only with several stipulations. For example, instead of suspending or terminating an employee for excessive absenteeism, the employer may grant the employee one final, fixed period in which to improve. Employers may also wish to use several other positive strategies for improvement. These include positive reinforcement, employee assistance programs, and self-managed work teams. These are described in more detail in Chapter 10 as strategies to improve the performance of individuals.

Even taking all of these steps does not ensure that the problem will be solved. Termination may still be necessary. The following advice may help in performing this difficult task:

> The terminational interview should be brief. Normally, a ten- to fifteen-minute meeting is sufficient. A longer meeting increases the opportunity for the company representative (in this case, you) to make a mistake. Some mistakes can be costly.
>
> It is best to conduct the termination meeting in that person's office or in some office other than your own. If conducted in your own office, you may be trapped into a lengthy harangue by a disgruntled individual who is using you to vent . . . hostility, anger, frustration.
>
> Many individuals hear very little after they understand they have lost their job. This is understandable. They often begin to think of their future [or] the anxiety and stress of having no job, and there is strong concern about their family, especially if the individual is the chief wage earner in the family.
>
> Hence, have a written description of benefits and/or salary continuation, if applicable. Also include how the individual is to be paid.
>
> It is a good idea to role-play with someone before you actually do the termination. It is better yet if you can videotape the role play(s). Practice can help iron out the bugs and the discomfort and make it easier and less cumbersome in the actual termination meeting.[29]

Certainly a firm would not want to hurt an employee's chances of obtaining future work by defaming the person in any way. In fact, individuals can sue past employers in defamation cases. Defamation suits can occur if an employer makes a statement regarding a former employee verbally in the presence of others, over the telephone, or in a written communication that is read by others, when the statement is malicious or false (and made with knowledge of its falsity), and injures a person's character or reputation—for example:

> Firing employees and making examples out of them can prove costly for employers if such actions are not based on clear facts. This point is illustrated starkly in a Texas case, where damages in excess of $15 million were awarded a former Procter & Gamble employee who was fired after being accused of stealing a $35 telephone.
>
> The employee had worked for P&G for 41 years and, according to his attorney, had an unblemished record. He had purchased the phone with his own money and was not reimbursed because he had lost the receipt. Later, a security guard stopped the employee as he was leaving work and discovered the phone in his belongings. After an internal investigation, P&G fired the employee and announced through internal notices that he had committed a theft. The employee sued for libel, saying P&G used him as an example to prevent other thefts.
>
> Procter & Gamble committed actual malice in falsely accusing the employee of stealing the phone, the jury in the case decided. The jury awarded the employee $14 million in punitive damages and more than $1 million for actual damages to his mental and physical well-being. (*Hagler v. Procter & Gamble Manufacturing Co.*, 1993).[30]

DID YOU KNOW?

A defamation-of-character suit resulted in a fine against Procter & Gamble of $15 million.

STRATEGIES FOR PROTECTING RIGHTS ON THE JOB

Strategies in this area include developing effective policies, procedures, and programs in regard to privacy and records access, cooperative acceptance (particularly sexual harassment), and plant or office closings.

Strategies for rights on the job:

- privacy protection
- harassment training and rules
- smoke-free workplace
- layoff notice

EMPLOYEE PRIVACY RIGHTS AND RECORD ACCESS.   Since the 1960s, there has been an ongoing concern for the privacy of personnel records and employee access to personnel files.[31] As discussed previously, privacy legislation generally only covers employer-employee relationships in governmental organizations. Consequently, many companies such as General Foods and Chase Manhattan Bank have moved ahead on their own to establish policies and rules governing employee **privacy and access rights**.[32] Today a majority of the major companies have written policies regarding the privacy of personnel records. In addition, most provide employees access to records containing information about themselves.[33]

Employer concerns about employee privacy rights are also influencing pre-employment screening and the use of drug tests. Prehire practices are being examined to ensure that only job-related information is collected, because collecting nonjob information is now considered an unnecessary intrusion into the private lives of job applicants (*Americans with Disabilities Act of 1990*).[34]

At the Ciba-Geigy Corporation focus groups were formed to solicit employee opinions on drug problems. As a result, the company decided the following:

- To take an educational thrust to our program. We want supervisors and employees to recognize drug problems and know what to do about them.
- To encourage employees and their families to ask for help when they need it—before there are problems. Our Employee Assistance Program is available on a confidential basis.
- To establish a positive tone—not a punitive one. We offer a rehabilitation program through our Employee Assistance Program.
- To test when there [is] an accident or behavioral indications of alcohol or drug use.
- To take a top-down approach to training, so everyone in management would learn how to handle abuse situations—both for alcohol and for drugs.
- To provide uniform training materials for each division, so there are consistent messages throughout the company.[35]

These practices of Ciba-Geigy closely parallel those outlined in the *Drug-Free Workplace Act of 1988* and are consistent with the ADA.

EMPLOYEE RIGHTS TO COOPERATIVE ACCEPTANCE.   Although many issues are associated with employee rights to cooperative acceptance, and all forms of harassment and smoking bans have recently become prominent concerns for many employees and employers.

What was once regarded by some employees as "good-natured fun" between supervisors (or managers) and employees may today constitute sexual harassment according to 1980 EEOC guidelines. Because sexual harassment creates an offensive and hostile work environment and can result in expensive financial settlements, and because employers are ultimately responsible, they need to be particularly concerned with developing strategies to prevent sexual harassment in the workplace (*Meritor Savings v. Vinson*, 1986). The following steps constitute such a strategy.[36]

- Raise affirmatively the issue of harassment, and the fact that it exists, to the rest of the organization. The HR manager should persuade top management to make it a rule that all discharges must be reviewed by a senior corporate officer or review board.
- Set up reporting (grievance) procedures for those who have been harassed. Because the employer is liable for sexual harassment, except

where it can be shown that the organization took immediate and appropriate corrective action (when the offending individual is guilty), it pays to have an established policy and system in place.

- Establish procedures for corroborating a sexual harassment charge. That is, the HR manager should make sure that the person charged with sexual harassment has the right to respond immediately after charges are made by the alleged victim. Due process must be provided the alleged perpetrator as well as the victim.

- Specify a set of steps in a framework of progressive discipline for perpetrators of sexual harassment. These could be the same steps used by the organization in treating any violation of organization policies (see the progressive discipline procedures discussed earlier).

- Finally, make all employees aware of the company's position on sexual harassment. Provide support such as training programs for managers and supervisors.

Although implementing these steps does not guarantee elimination of sexual harassment, it establishes a clear-cut company policy in this controversial area.[37]

In addition to having a clear-cut policy, firms are also advised to offer training to prevent sexual harassment from even occurring:

> To attack the problem, many forward-thinking companies are using awareness-training programs to help employees understand the pain and indignity of harassment. Such programs, if they are comprehensive and used aggressively, can be highly effective. The cost ranges from $5,000 for a small company to $200,000 for a large one.
>
> Thus for that *Fortune* 500 company facing a $6.7 million liability, it is 34 times as costly to ignore the problem as to take steps to eradicate it. Looked at another way, a sexual harassment program can be cost-effective if it averts the loss of one key employee—or prevents one lawsuit.[38]

Under the expanded version of harassment, the EEOC in its 1993 regulations agreed that prevention is critical. And the keys to prevention of any harassment include:

- Have an explicit policy against harassment.
- Clearly and regularly communicate the policy, including sanctions for harassment, to employees.
- Develop methods to sensitize all supervisory and nonsupervisory employees on issues of harassment.
- Inform employees of their rights to raise issues of harassment and procedures for doing so.
- Provide an effective complaint procedure whereby employees can make their complaints known to appropriate officials who can act on the complaints.[39]

RIGHTS TO A SMOKE-FREE WORKPLACE. Increasingly, employers are establishing bans against smoking during breaks, lunchtime, and even when at home as well as during work. They cite the following reasons for this action:

- Each smoking employee costs employers an estimated $4,000 per year through higher absenteeism, reduced productivity due to "smoking rituals," and higher health, fire and life insurance usage.
- Smoking controls will produce productivity losses by forcing employees to leave their work to take smoking breaks.
- Employers who resist smoking controls face increasing risks of legal action

Lincoln Electric has a no-smoking policy throughout the company.

from smoke-sensitive employees who charge that employers are avoiding their legal obligation to provide a safe environment.

Some companies, however, have been hesitant to establish smoking bans. because:

- Smoking controls themselves may produce legal action.[40]

In an attempt to resolve existing conflicts, many employers have implemented one or more of the following policies: allowing smoking only during lunch or on breaks, staggering the break times of smokers and nonsmokers, segregating smokers and nonsmokers, installing more effective ventilation systems, designating certain areas for smoking or nonsmoking, instituting and encouraging participation in smoking cessation programs, and arranging for job transfers. These steps, although more expensive and administratively problematic than a total ban on smoking, involve less risk in terms of potential legal problems.[41]

LAYOFFS AND PLANT CLOSING NOTIFICATION. With the passage of the *Worker Adjustment and Retraining Act,* employers are obligated to notify employees in advance of a plant or office closing. However, layoffs that are temporary in nature or downsizings that are permanent but do not require complete shutdowns do not require advance notification. Regardless of the cause, the loss of a job can be traumatic for employees. To assuage the difficulty of this transition, organizations are pursuing several different strategies.[42]

Rather than terminating those with less seniority or poorly performing employees, some companies have initiated job-sharing programs. Job sharing involves reducing the employee's work week and pay. This helps the company cut labor costs and may actually lead to higher overall productivity because each employee is working more concentrated hours. One major disadvantage is that expenses per employee may increase because benefits are usually a function of the number of employees, not the number of hours worked or amount of pay. While few studies have investigated the payoffs of job sharing, Motorola found that job sharing, rather than layoffs, saved an average of $1,868 per employee or almost $1 million overall in one plant.[43]

While mandatory retirement at a specific age cannot be required of most employees, organizations are exploring early retirement for selected employees as a possible option to layoffs. Key to a successful early retirement program is to understand the needs of targeted employees and provide incentives that meet those needs. Incentives may include pension payments before and after age 62 when Social Security payments start, and company-paid health and life insurance. Alternatively, a company may maintain its current retirement program but lower the qualifying age to increase the pool of potential retirees.

INTERNATIONAL COMPARISONS

Particularly for U.S. multinational corporations (MNCs), the issue of employee termination needs to be handled with an awareness of international differences.

TERMINATION LIABILITIES

MNCs need to consider the strategic consequences of a decision to terminate overseas operations. Most countries have some traditional or legally required practices that come into play in the event of a plant closing or a substantial reduction of the work force.[44] In general, these practices create more extensive

Many other countries have stiff penalties for termination and plant closings.

and costlier employer obligations than do layoffs in the United States and Canada. One of the most costly obligations is the payment of cash indemnities that are in addition to the individual termination payments that may be required by law, collective bargaining agreements, or individual contracts. These indemnities can range from as high as two years' pay in Mexico to a flat amount, adjusted for increases in the cost of living, in Belgium. In some countries, these costs are spelled out in collective agreements that may stipulate termination payments greater than those required by law. In other countries, the employer may have to negotiate the amounts with employees, unions, and often the government.

In many countries, a company that wishes to close down or curtail operations must also develop a "social plan" or its equivalent, typically in concert with unions and other interested parties. The "plan" may cover continuation of pay, benefit plan coverage, retraining allowances, relocation expenses, and supplementation of statutory unemployment compensation. Frequently, a company planning a partial or total plant closing must present its case to a government agency. Authorities in the Netherlands, for example, may deny permission for a substantial work force reduction unless management is able to demonstrate that the cutback is absolutely necessary for economic reasons and that the company has an approved social plan.

MEXICO

Essentially, in Mexico, all employees work under a contract with the employer. There are two types of contracts, temporary or permanent. A temporary contract allows the company to employ workers for a determined period of time such as one month, two months or three months. As a general rule, temporary contracts would be valid for up to one year of work. Anyone who is not working on a temporary contract is working under a permanent contract. After hiring a worker under permanent contract, the employer has 28 days to evaluate the employee's work ethics. After that period, the worker is granted job security, and termination becomes difficult. This is especially true in terms of financial liability. For example, an employer who decides to fire a worker who has been with the company for six months could be charged for an additional six weeks, plus vacation pay and bonuses. Therefore, it is important to screen employees carefully. An employee is considered tenured after one year of employment. This worker may be dismissed only for causes specifically set out in the Mexican *Federal Labor Law*. These causes include falsifying employment documents and committing dishonest or violent acts during working hours. A reduction in work force necessitated by economic conditions is not considered as a justifiable cause of termination. In the event that a reduction of work force is required for the permanent contract workers, the law requires severance pay of 90 days plus 12 days of pay per year of seniority. However, this is most often negotiated with the employees, either individually or on a group basis. It is quite common, if this action is required, that the severance pay would be in the range of 30 to 60 days. As a result of specific aspects of the labor laws, it is very important to implement to practice human resource planning. In contrast, workers hired under any type of contract can be released at any time for a justifiable cause without any financial obligation.[45]

CURRENT TRENDS

Two important trends in employee rights include the use of alternative dispute resolution and the development of conflict-of-interest policies.

Alternative dispute resolution (ADR) *is a term used to describe various methods of settling legal disputes short of filing a civil lawsuit.* Although ADR is most commonly used to settle commercial disputes, a growing number of businesses are using it to resolve charges of employment discrimination or wrongful termination as well. Resolving a dispute before it reaches litigation can promote goodwill between management and employees and reduce the adverse publicity often associated with legal disputes.[46]

ADR's appeal and viability have been heightened due to recent significant legislation and court decisions. The *1991 Civil Rights Act* and the *Americans with Disabilities Act* expressly endorse ADR. Of landmark significance, the Supreme Court in *Gilmer v. Interstate/Johnson Lane Corp.* held that age discrimination claims may, in some circumstances, be subject to compulsory arbitration agreements to the exclusion of litigation.

MEDIATION. Mediation is the most popular form of ADR. This is partly because the format is more flexible than other proceedings, more informal, and therefore more relaxed. All concerned parties come before a "third-party neutral" (the mediator), who may be appointed by a judge or selected by the parties to the mediation or their attorneys. Parties to a civil dispute may be ordered into mediation by the court, or they may volunteer to submit to the process in an effort to settle the dispute without litigation.

ARBITRATION. Arbitration, which differs significantly from mediation, is also a popular method of ADR. It can be included in the employment contract, or it may be court ordered.

Here are some key ways that arbitration differs from mediation.

- Arbitration is more formal and often more expensive than mediation. Attorneys must present their cases in a formal manner.
- The third-party neutral might be an expert in the industry involved, a single arbiter, or a panel of three. Arbitrators are selected by national organizations, by a judge, or by the parties themselves.
- The arbitrator has some powers in that he or she (or the panel) can make an award after hearing both sides of the case.
- Arbitration is often specified long before any actual dispute arises. Arbitration clauses are frequently written into employment contracts or collective bargaining agreements.
- Arbitration can be binding or nonbinding. Employment or labor contracts that call for arbitration in the event of a dispute should specify whether arbitration will be binding or not. If the award is nonbinding, the process could lead to a trial. If it is binding, the arbitrator's decision is final, subject to a very limited right of appeal.

Arbitration has been used in the employment discrimination context to settle an *Age Discrimination in Employment Act* (ADEA) suit. In this case, a financial services manager was required by his employer to register as a securities representative with the New York Stock Exchange (NYSE). The NYSE registration application included an agreement to arbitrate any employment controversy.

The manager was fired at age 62 and replaced by a younger broker, age 28, whom he had trained. The manager then filed a claim with the Equal Employment Opportunity Commission (EEOC) and brought suit in federal district court alleging that he had been discharged in violation of the ADEA. The

ADR describes methods of settling disputes short of filing a lawsuit.

Mediation and arbitration are two forms of ADR.

The courts recognize the power of ADRs under the *Federal Arbitration Act*.

employer moved to compel arbitration, relying on the agreement in the manager's registration application and the *Federal Arbitration Act* (FAA). The case found its way to the Supreme Court, which held that an ADEA claim could be the subject of an arbitration agreement, enforceable under the FAA. Since the FAA reflects a liberal federal policy favoring arbitration, and since neither the text nor the legislative history of the ADEA explicitly precludes arbitration, the manager was bound by his agreement to arbitrate unless he could show an inherent conflict between arbitration and the ADEA's underlying purposes.

Mediation and arbitration are the two most common types of ADR. But grievance procedures discussed here and in Chapter 10 can be very helpful in resolving disputes without using mediation or arbitration. A common grievance procedure is a multistep system, in which aggrieved employees discuss grievances with their supervisor or department head first. If there is no resolution at this stage, employees can turn to the human resource manager and, finally, to a review panel. Such a panel could comprise equal numbers of employee and management representatives and one neutral employee (for example, a human resource officer).[47]

Because supervisors are sometimes the focus of employee grievances, employers should designate other staff members to whom employees can alternatively complain. In its *Meritor Savings Bank v. Vinson* (1986) decision, the Supreme Court noted that the employee charging sexual harassment had just one recourse—to complain to her supervisor, who happened to be the person harassing her. The Court observed that the employer's position would have been stronger if its grievance procedures were better calculated to encourage victims of harassment to come forward.

As we shall see in the next two chapters, formal grievance procedures are an important part of labor-management contracts. These procedures give employees and employers a chance to resolve disputes without costly legal procedures. This is also what ADR is intended to do. It is entirely possible that you will be asked to sign an ADR agreement on your next job.

ETHICAL BEHAVIOR AND CONFLICT-OF-INTEREST POLICIES

Another form you may be asked to sign is one that relates to a potential conflict of interest.

Conflict-of-interest policies are designed to prevent unethical behavior by employees and former employees.

> Conflict-of-interest policies are often implemented by employers to ensure ethical business conduct and high standards of integrity. Generally, such policies specify that the best interests of the company must be employees' foremost concern in all business dealings.
>
> Typical conflict-of-interest policies prohibit employees from serving, in any capacity, a competitor or a company with which the employer does business. Such policies also may require employees to:
>
> - Disqualify themselves from involvement in transactions that could lead to personal financial gain or other benefits for the employees;
> - Refuse gifts or entertainment offered by anyone who has a business relationship with the employer; and
> - Refrain from using company information for personal gain or divulging proprietary information to anyone who would use it in a manner detrimental to the employer.[48]

By developing and using these policies, the employers essentially define what is a conflict of interest and therefore what is ethical and unethical behavior. Thus what is ethical is defined not so much by the larger society, but by the specific organization. There may, however, be some overlap. For example, the company may say that a departing employee cannot take company secrets; the company may then try to enforce such action in the courts on the basis that taking company secrets and documents is stealing. Of course, the company may have unethical behavior policies other than those related to conflicts of interest. It is important for you to know what all the policies are of the firm you are joining. Only then can you decide whether you can live up to them and thereby not engage in unethical behavior.

SUMMARY

Although many employers claim that essentially all their rights in termination have been taken away, they still retain the right to terminate workers for poor performance, excessive absenteeism, unsafe conduct, and generally poor organizational citizenship. However, employers must maintain accurate records of these events for their employees and inform the employees of where they stand. To be safe, employers should also have a grievance process for employees to ensure that due process is respected. These practices are particularly useful in discharge situations that involve members of groups protected by the *Civil Rights Act of 1991*, *Americans with Disabilities Act,* and the *Age Discrimination in Employment Act.*

Today, keeping objective and orderly human resource files is more important than ever. They are critical evidence that employers have treated their employees fairly and with respect and that they have not violated any laws. Without good record keeping, organizations may be caught on the short end of a lawsuit. Although several federal laws influence record keeping, they are primarily directed at public employers. Nevertheless, many private employers have moved to give their employees the right to access their personnel files and to prohibit the file information from being given to others without employee consent. In addition, employers are discarding any non-job-related information in personnel files and also ending hiring practices that solicit that type of information.

Many employers now give their employees advance notification consistent with the *Worker Adjustment and Retraining Notification Act.* In addition to such notification, employers are implementing outplacement assistance programs. These offer employees retraining for new jobs, counseling and aid in finding new jobs or in getting transfers, severance pay, and even retention bonuses for those who stay until plant closing time. Closing a facility with notification and with outplacement assistance seems to produce positive results for the organization and to minimize the negative effects on employees.

Finally, in the area of employee rights to cooperative acceptance, employers must prevent all forms of harassment. This can be done with top management support, grievance procedures, verification procedures, training for all employees, and performance appraisal and compensation policies that reward those who practice anti-harassment behavior and punish those who do not. Where appropriate, developing policies to prevent harassment in cooperation with the union is also useful. Union cooperation should be sought on many other issues, as well. The benefits of doing so can be substantial, as we discuss in the next two chapters.

KEY CONCEPTS

alternative dispute
    resolution (ADR)
cooperative acceptance
employee rights
employment-at-will rule
privacy and access rights

progressive discipline
right to plant/office
    closing or
    relocation
    notification

sexual harassment
termination-at-will rule

REVIEW AND DISCUSSION QUESTIONS

1. What potential employee rights violations could occur with an automated HRIS (human resource information system)? What could be done to protect against these violations?
2. What do you think are the most common reasons for termination decisions?
3. What types of considerations are necessary before an employer terminates an employee?
4. Identify and discuss four federal laws that have an impact on employee rights to privacy and access to employee records.
5. What is the termination-at-will rule? Why do you suppose that courts in the late 1880s were more willing to uphold the rule than courts today?
6. What kinds of behaviors might constitute sexual harassment? How does an organization prevent those behaviors from occurring?
7. What makes a disciplinary procedure progressive? Would some types of employee behaviors warrant immediate dismissal instead of progressive discipline?
8. The industrial, occupational, and demographic composition of the work force has shifted over the past 20 years. How might these shifts coincide with heightened interest in employee rights in the 1990s?
9. What are the major issues involved in testing employees for drug use?
10. What employee rights must an employer satisfy when closing or relocating a facility?

EXERCISES AND CASES

FIELD PROJECT

Interview an individual who has experienced harassment on the job. Report to the class on the content of the interview, including such things as: (1) Where did the harassment take place? (2) Who was involved? (3) How long did it last? (4) What did the person(s) do? (5) How did the person feel? (6) What was the resolution or what is the person trying to do now to resolve the situation?

With the great job that you are looking forward to taking after graduation come responsibilities to the employer and rights to you. We have discussed some in this chapter. From the topics covered in this chapter, here are a few questions that you should think about, alone or with others.

1. Would you sign an ADR? Briefly explain: _____

_____

_____

_____

2. What would you do if your first supervisor harassed you several times in your first few months on the job?

(Alternatively, what would you advise a friend in this same situation?) _____

_____

_____

_____

3. If you saw illegal activities occurring in the company you just got your great job with, what would you do? Explain why you would or wouldn't blow the whistle.

_____

_____

_____

_____

_____

CASE

THE PAYBACK

Lucy Pascal was hired by ABC Jobbers, Inc., two months ago. ABC had wooed Lucy away from her previous employer because of her outstanding sales record. Enticed by a substantial boost in pay, commissions, and perks, Lucy was looking forward to widened professional contacts and increased income. Also, she was thrilled at having been one of the first women to be directly hired for sales work at ABC.

Lucy liked working for her new company even though she was certainly a rarity there. Virtually all of the other professionals and salespeople were male. Most were macho types, often joking and talking about their latest exploits with "a little number" met while on the road. When Lucy was around, they enjoyed teasing her to see what her reaction would be. She would change the subject pleasantly, but their conversations bothered her, and then there were all the centerfold pictures prominently displayed in a lot of the offices, which Lucy did her best to ignore. Yet, even with all this, she was still pleased she had made the job move because of its growth potential.

On one of her initial sales calls in her newly assigned district, Lucy visited Frank Grumman, a major client who was responsible for signing off on all sales contracts for his

company. Lucy gave Frank Grumman a sales pitch in her typically persuasive and professional manner. Frank responded that he was most impressed not only with the product, but also with Lucy herself. He cajoled her to go out with him so they "could get to know each other better." Lucy began feeling increasingly uncomfortable with Frank's comments. It was obvious he was more interested in her as a woman than as ABC's sales representative.

Finally, in response to his insistent urgings that they take off together for the evening, Lucy, as nicely as she could, gave him a firm no. She, with a forced smile, advised him she had to catch an early flight.

Frank, feeling rejected, testily replied that Lucy really must not want the contract very much if she wasn't going to "entertain" him. Angered, Lucy told him in no uncertain terms what he could do with the contract if "entertaining" was part of the price she had to pay in order to get it. She stormed out of Frank's office.

Upon returning to her district office, Lucy related to James Roberts, her first-line supervisor and the district sales manager, what had happened on her sales call. James reacted with laughter. He said to Lucy, "There are certain things we all have to do to keep our clients happy.

If you knew all the rounds of golf I've played with some real creeps for business purposes, then you'd realize what I was talking about." Lucy said "James, I'm not talking about playing golf. That's not the type of game he wanted me to play." James grew chilly. He told Lucy "By God, you better not lose that contract. You do, and you'll lose your district and all its fat commissions!"

Lucy had been placed in a no-win situation by both her client and her boss. As she pondered over her dilemma, the chief executive officer of ABC saw her in the hall. "Lucy," said Donald Stubbs, "what's my favorite new sales gal looking so worried about?"

"Come on into my office and tell me how things are going." The grandfatherly Mr. Stubbs gently ushered Lucy into his office. After only a few moments, Lucy blurted out her situation. Losing control, and to her great embarrassment, she broke into tears. Concerned, Mr. Stubbs placed his arms around Lucy to console her. Lucy soon calmed down enough to apologize for her behavior. Mr. Stubbs advised her he would place some phone calls and try to smooth things over. As he led her to the door, he admonished her. "You have to realize, Lucy, that men will be men. You'll just have to get used to these things in this business."

Lucy wandered down the hall wondering what was going to happen to her now. Samuel Kindel, a fellow salesperson, spotted Lucy and asked her if she'd like to have some coffee. Lucy replied she needed to talk to someone about the things that were happening to her. In the cafeteria, she told Samuel the entire story and the frustration she felt. Samuel became furious. He told her that "those guys are all no-good skunks." Lucy was relieved to have such a sympathetic ear to bend. As they continued their talk, Samuel said, "You know, I've been wanting to get to know you better ever since you got here Lucy. What do you say we take in a movie tonight and forget this place?"

Case Questions

1. What sorts of measures could ABC Jobbers take with its clients to prevent this situation?
2. Samuel Kindel asked Lucy for a date. Was she being sexually harassed by him? How do you think she should have responded?
3. Could Lucy have dealt with the situation differently?
4. What type of company policies would you recommend that ABC Jobbers, Inc., institute for its employees to forestall sexually harassing behaviors?

Notes

1. A. B. Fisher, "Sexual Harassment: What to Do?" *Fortune* (Aug. 23, 1993): 84–88. Used by permission.

2. T. Lewin, "A Case Study of Sexual Harassment and the Law," *The New York Times* (Oct. 11, 1991): A17; and "Sexual Harassment in the Workplace," *Personnel Journal* (Jan. 1992): 24; C. Marmer Solomon, "Sexual Harassment After the Thomas Hearings," *Personnel Journal* (Dec. 1991): 32–37; D. E. Terpstra and D. D. Baker, "Outcomes of Federal Court Decisions on Sexual Harassment," *Academy of Management Journal* 35, No. 1 (1992): 181–190.

3. A. M. Zack, *A Handbook for Grievance Arbitration* (New York: Free Press, 1992).

4. S. Overman, "A Delicate Balance Protects Everyone's Rights," *HR Magazine* (Nov. 1990): 36–39.

5. A. D. Marcus and S. J. Adler, "Mobile Aide Wins Wrongful Firing Case," *The Wall Street Journal* (Nov. 23, 1990): B2.

6. S. Crawford, "A Wink Here, a Leer There: It's Costly," *The New York Times* (March 28, 1993): F17.

7. J. E. Jackson and W. T. Schantz, "A New Frontier in Wrongful Discharge," *Personnel Journal* (Jan. 1991): 101–104.

8. *Bulletin to Management* (April 22, 1993): 127.

9. B. B. Durling, "Retaliation: A Misunderstood Form of Employment Discrimination," *Personnel Journal* (July 1981): 555–558.

10. "Armor for Whistle-Blowers," *Business Week* (July 6, 1981): 97–98; W. F. Westin, "Michigan's Law to Protect Whistle Blowers," *The Wall Street Journal* (April 13, 1981): 1.

11. For further description of related cases and issues, see "Another View of Employment at Will," *Bulletin to Management* (Sept. 12, 1985): 88; "Employment-at-Will Evolves," *Bulletin to Management* (April 5, 1984); B. Keller, "Of Hearth and Home and the Right to Work," *The New York Times* (Nov. 11, 1984): E8.

12. C. Sims, "GE Whistle-Blower Is Awarded $13.4 Million," *The New York Times* (Dec. 5, 1992): 35.

13. "Firing," *FEP Guidelines* no. 241(8) (1985): 3. See also "Discrimination Denied," *Bulletin to Management* (June 13, 1985): 3.

14. However, if a union-management contract exists, an arbitrator may not uphold firing if based on false application information. J. N. Drazin, "Firing Over False Applications," *Personnel Journal* (June 1981): 433. See also D. L. Beacon and A. Gomez III, "How to Prevent Wrongful Termination Lawsuits," *Personnel* (Feb. 1988): 70–72.

15. M. R. Buckley and W. Weitzel, "Employing at Will," *Personnel Administrator* (Aug. 1988): 78–82; M. Manley, "The Competitors Within," *INC.* (Sept. 1988): 137–138.

16. L. Smith, "What the Boss Knows About You," *Fortune* (August 9, 1993): 89–93.

17. *Ibid.*, and S. R. Mendelsohn and A. E. Libbin, "The Right to Privacy at the Workplace, Part 3: Employee Alcohol- and Drug-Testing Programs," *Personnel* (Sept. 1988): 65–72; A. E. Libbin and J. C. Stevens, "The Right to Privacy at the Workplace, Part 4: Employee Personal Information," *Personnel* (Oct. 1988): 56–60; A. E. Libbin, S. R. Mendelsohn, and D. P. Duffy, "The Right to Privacy at the Workplace, Part 5: Employee Medical and Honesty Testing," *Personnel* (Nov. 1988): 38–48; M. I. Finney, "The Right to be Tested," *Personnel Administrator* (March 1988): 74–75.

18. "Drug Testing to Start for Transit Workers," *The New York Times* (Nov. 9, 1991): 28.

19. B. A. Guttek, A. G. Cohen, and A. M. Konrad, "Predicting Social-Sexual Behavior at Work: A Contact Hypothesis," *Academy of Management Journal* 33, No. 3 (1990): 560–577; _____, "Reasonable Woman Standard Gains Ground," *Fair Employment Practice Guidelines* (June 25, 1993): 4.

20. B. Southard Murphy, W. E. Barlow, and D. D. Hatch, "Court Broadens Scope of Sexual Harassment Law," *Personnel Journal* (April 1990): 24–31; J. K. Frierson, "Reduce the Costs of Sexual Harassment," *Personnel Journal* (Nov. 1989): 79–85.

21. "Sexual Harassment after *Meritor Savings v. Vinson*," *FEP Guidelines* 1 (264) (1987). Used by permission.

22. B. P. Noble, "New Reminders on Harassment," *The New York Times* (August 15, 1993): F25.

23. "Employers Seldom Warn Workers About Layoffs," *Bulletin to Management* (August 26, 1993): 265.

24. B. P. Noble, "Straddling the Law on Layoffs," *The New York Times* (February 28, 1993): F37.

25. "Bad Signs," *Fair Employment Practices* (Aug. 27, 1993): 97.

26. L. S. Richman, "When Will the Layoffs End?" *Fortune* (Sept. 20, 1993): 54–56.

27. A Bernstein and Z. Schiller, "Tell It to the Arbitrator," *Business Week* (Nov. 4, 1991): 109. Also see S. A. Youngblood, L. K. Tevino, & M. Favia, (1992) Reactions to Unjust Dismissal and Third-Party Dispute Resolution: A Justice Framework. *Employee Responsibilities and Rights Journal*, 5 (4), 283–307.

28. D. N. Adams, Jr., "When Laying Off Employees, the Word is 'Out-Training,'" *Personnel Journal* (Sept. 1980): 719–721.

29. C. A. B. Osigweh, ed., *Managing Employee Rights and Responsibilities* (Westport, Conn.: Quorum Books, 1989); D. T. Brodie, *Individual Employment Disputes: Definite and Indefinite Term Contracts* (Westport, Conn.: Quorum Books, 1991).

30. "Firing Proves Costly," *Bulletin to Management* (May 13, 1993): 145; "What's New in Employment Law," *FEP Guidelines* (Jan. 25, 1994).

31. D. F. Linowes, "Update on Privacy Protection Safeguards: Is Business Giving Employees Privacy?" *Business and Society Review* (Winter 1979–80): 47–49; A. F. Westin, "What Should Be Done about Employee Privacy?" *Personnel Administrator* (March 1980): 27–30; *Employee Access to Records* (Englewood Cliffs, N.J.: Prentice-Hall/ASPA, 1984).

32. "Privacy Policy Approaches and Pointers," *Bulletin to Management* (Feb. 20, 1986): 57.

33. T. J. Wiencek, "Privacy in the Workplace: A Guide for Human Resource Professionals," *FEP Guidelines* (Dec. 10, 1993): 4–6.

34. J. A. Segal, "A Need Not To Know," *HR Magazine* (Oct. 1991): 85–86, 88, 90; "None of an Employer's Business," *The New York Times* (July 7, 1991): E10; "Is Nothing Private?" *Business Week* (Sept. 4, 1989): 74–77, 80–82.

35. "Soul-Searching at Ciba-Geigy," *HR Reporter* (May 1987): 5–6.

36. G. E. Biles, "A Program Guide for Preventing Sexual Harassment in the Workplace," *Personnel Administrator* (June 1981): 49–56; O. A. Ornati, "How to Deal with EEOC's Guidelines to Sexual Harassment," in *EEO Compliance Manual* (Englewood Cliffs, N.J.: Prentice-Hall, 1980): 377–380; R. H. Faley, "Sexual Harassment: A Critical Review of Legal Cases with General Principles and Practice Measures," *Personnel Psychology* 35 (1982): 583–600.

37. T. Segal and Z. Schiller, "Six Experts Suggest Ways to Negotiate the Minefield," *Business Week* (Oct. 28, 1991): 33.

38. Crawford (*op. cit.*, see Note 6): F17.

39. "EEOC Proposes Harassment Guidelines," *Fair Employment Practices* (July 29, 1993): 87, A. Williams, "Model Procedures for Sexual Harassment Claims," *Arbitration Journal* (Sept. 1993): 66–75.

40. "Smokers' Right: New Phenomenon," *Fair Employment Practices*, (Sept. 26, 1991): 111; J. Woo, "Employers Fume Over New Legislation Barring Discrimination Against Smokers," *The Wall Street Journal* (June 4, 1993): B1, B8.

41. "Life-style Discrimination Examined at Conference," *Fair Employment Practices* (August 12, 1993): 96; M. Janofsky, "Ban on Employees who Smoke Faces Challenge of Bias," *The New York Times* (April 28, 1994): A1, D11.

42. J. B. Treece, "Doing It Right, Till the Last Whistle," *Business Week* (April 6, 1992): 58–59; D. L. Worrell, W. N. Davidson III, and V. M. Sharma, "Layoff Announcements and Stockholder Wealth," *Academy of Management Journal* 34, no. 3 (1991): 662–678; P. D. Johnston, "Personnel Planning for a Plant Shutdown," *Personnel Journal* (Aug. 1981): 53–57.

43. T. Rendero, "Outplacement Practices," *Personnel* (July–Aug. 1980): 4–11; B. H. Millen, "Providing Assistance to Displaced Workers," *Monthly Labor Review* (May 1979): 17–22; "Outplacement Assistance," *Personnel Journal* (April 1981): 250; M. Elleinis, "Tips for Employers Shopping Around for a New Plant Site," *AMA Forum* (July 1982): 34; "Plant Closings: Problems and Panaceas," *Management Review* (July 1982): 55–57.

44. P. Dowling, R. Schuler, and D. Welch, *International Dimensions of Human Resource Management,* 2nd ed. (Belmont, Calif.: Wadsworth, 1994).

45. This material on Mexico has been adapted from "Maquiladora Program Overview," (Newport Beach, Calif.: Sarco International, 1988). Presented at ASPA-International's 11th Annual Conference, San Diego, Calif. 1988.

46. Adapted from "Alternative Ways to Resolve Disputes," *Fair Employment Practice Guidelines* (August 26, 1992): 4–5.

47. D. Phillips, J. Cooke, and A. Anderson, "A Surefire Resolution to Workplace Conflicts," *Personnel Journal* (May 1992): 111–113.

48. "A Question of Ethics," *Bulletin to Management* (July 9, 1992): 211.

CHAPTER 17

UNIONIZATION

LEARNING OBJECTIVES

When you have finished studying this chapter, you should be able to:

1. Describe the legal context of the union movement.
2. Explain the attraction the unions have for workers.
3. Explain the historical development and the current state of the union movement.
4. Describe the union organizing campaign.
5. Describe the international union movement.
6. Recommend what unions should do.

CHAPTER OUTLINE

MANAGING HUMAN RESOURCES
at Federal Express

Pilots Vote for Union

THE Air Line Pilots Association, the largest pilot union in the airline industry, won a major victory in January, 1993, when pilots at the Federal Express Corporation voted to be represented by them.

The move was a defeat for Federal Express, the nation's largest air carrier of documents, packages, and heavy air freight; the company has worked hard to keep its work force non-union; it is based in Memphis, where unions have had a difficult time winning support.

Federal Express charged that the election had been "tainted" and that the company's position had been misrepresented. It said some pilots who did not want union representation had voted for one union out of fear that another union would be elected and asked the National Mediation Board to investigate its objections.

TERMED COUP FOR UNIONS

Joseph Blasi, an expert on labor in the airline industry and a professor at Rutgers University, called the vote a major coup for unions, which have been on the defensive in the airline industry, where companies have sought concessions and have cut back employees to cope with declining passenger traffic.

"Federal Express prided itself on being a progressive non-union company whose workers did not need union representation," he said.

The breakthrough for the union was aided, he said, when Federal Express acquired Flying Tiger Line in 1989 for $880 million. Though the company gained many valuable rights to fly on international routes by buying Flying Tiger, it also inherited about 1,000 pilots who belonged to the Pilots Association.

Mr. Blasi said that there had been tension between the union and non-union pilots at Federal Express and that the union vote indicated a willingness to work together to improve compensation and benefits.

The Pilots Association was chartered by the AFL-CIO in 1931 and represents 41,000 pilots at 45 U.S. airlines. It is generally the most powerful union at any airline even though it may not be the one with the most members. A pilot strike can quickly shut down a carrier.

In the vote at Federal Express, which was monitored by the National Mediation Board, of the 2,279 pilots eligible to vote, 1,015 cast their vote for ALPA while 271 voted for the United States Pilot Association. The ballots were counted yesterday by the mediation board.

FIRST EFFORT FAILED

"Once the dust settles, I think that both Federal Express management and the pilots who didn't vote for ALPA will see that union representation for our pilots will make our company a better airline in the long run," said Captain Don Wilson, a member of the Federal Express Pilots Organizing Committee.

He said that an effort to unionize in 1989, led largely by pilots from Flying Tiger, had failed. This time, he said, a group of Federal Express pilots approached ALPA to help organize the company. "We wanted a voice on the issues that shape our careers," he said.

He said that the company had fought back with its own group of pilots opposing the union and with a literature, video, and billboard campaign.

The company has about 80,000 workers in the United States. Unions like the International Brotherhood of Teamsters and the United Automobile Workers are said to be preparing to try to organize other workers at the company.[1]

This feature highlights several points about unionization today. First, it is not necessarily dying out in the United States. While the overall percentage of Americans belonging to unions has declined over the years, there are pockets of membership gain such as with the Airline Pilots Association (ALPA) at Federal Express. ALPA, has however, been taking losses at other airlines such as United, Delta, and American as these carriers have been forced to downsize substantially. A second point is that union membership is not always built on the backs of workers in the lowest paid or least desirable jobs. For example, Don Wilson, the 20-year captain and pilot at Federal Express who was behind the organizing drive, makes more than $175,000 yearly! Another point is that union-representation elections are monitored by an outside federal organization called the National Mediation Board in the transportation industry. The Board's mission is to make elections as open and fair as possible. It is up to the Board to make the final certification of the ALPA as the bargaining agent for all the pilots of Federal Express. And a final point is that even the best managed companies cannot assume that they can maintain a non-union status forever.

Federal Express, under the leadership of Fred Smith, has been one of the outstanding companies in terms of customer satisfaction and growth. But several changes lead to the unionization drive. First, there was the merger with the Flying Tiger line and its unionized pilots. Then came the slowdown in the airline industry, the demise of Pan Am and Eastern Airlines, and the layoffs at United and American; as a result of all this, the younger pilots at Federal Express saw their chances of making captain decline dramatically. Finally, more senior pilots saw their pension benefits falling behind those at unionized carriers.

Because the conditions making unionization attractive at Federal Express can occur at almost any firm, it is important to be knowledgeable and current on unionization activities. While you may not ever become a union member, you may be influenced by others who are or have been union members. Thus it is important to know the facts behind unionization and the activity of collective bargaining, and we begin in this chapter where we examine unionization.

UNIONIZATION

Unionization is the effort by employees to act as a single unit in dealing with managements over their work.

Unionization *is the effort by employees and outside agencies (unions or associations) to act as a single unit when dealing with management over issues relating to their work.*

When recognized by the National Mediation Board or the National Labor Relations Board, a **union** has the legal authority to negotiate with the employer on behalf of employees—to improve wages, hours, and conditions of employment—and to administer the ensuing agreement.[2] The process of unionization is illustrated in Exhibit 17.1.

WHY IS UNIONIZATION IMPORTANT?

Unions have a big impact in organizations without unions.

Unionization is important for both employers and employees. To employers, the existence of a union—or even the possibility of one—can significantly influence the ability of an organization to manage its vital human resources. To employees, unions can help them get what they want (for example, high wages and job security) from their employers.

Understanding the unionizing process, its causes, and its consequences is an important part of managing human resources effectively. Unionization can result in less flexibility in hiring, job assignments, and in slowing the introduction of

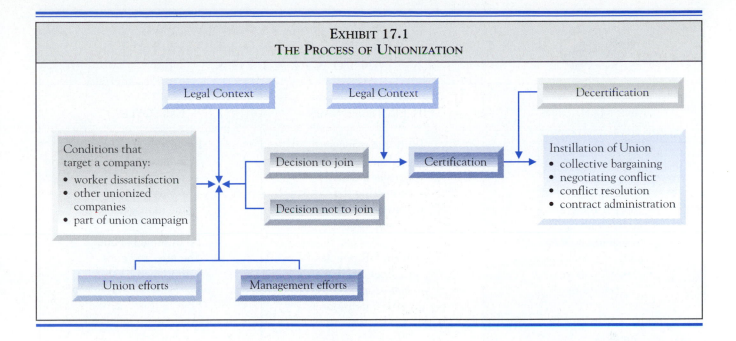

EXHIBIT 17.1
THE PROCESS OF UNIONIZATION

Legal Context

Legal Context

Decertification

Conditions that target a company:
- worker dissatisfaction
- other unionized companies
- part of union campaign

Decision to join

Decision not to join

Certification

Instillation of Union
- collective bargaining
- negotiating conflict
- conflict resolution
- contract administration

Union efforts

Management efforts

new work methods such as automation; it can also result in a loss of management control, inefficient work practices, and an inflexible job structure. As indicated in Chapter 16, unions obtain rights for their members that employees without unions do not legally have. This, of course, forces unionized companies to consider their employees' reactions to many more decisions. In some cases, however, employers who are non-union and want to remain that way give more consideration and benefits to their employees. Consequently, the claim that it is more expensive for a company to operate with unionized rather than non-unionized employees is not always true.

Unions can also assist employers through wage concessions or cooperation in joint workplace efforts, such as teamwork programs or Scanlon plans, allowing employers to survive particularly difficult times and even remain profitable and competitive during those times. This has been particularly true in the automobile and airline industries. Unions can also identify workplace hazards and improve the quality of working life for employees.

LEGAL CONSIDERATIONS

The federal government entered the labor scene in an attempt to stabilize the violent and disruptive labor situation in the 1920s and the 1930s. Court actions and efforts by employers prior to this time generally suppressed the rights of workers to act collectively to protect their interests. This was consistent with classical economic theory in which the free operation of the law of supply and demand was considered essential.

According to this theory, control of wage rates by workers artificially inflated prices, ultimately harming commerce, the community, and even workers themselves, because higher prices discouraged consumption and created unemployment. Therefore, according to many observers, the best prescription for a healthy economy was one free of either government regulation or private regulation via collective action of workers.

LEARNING OBJECTIVE 1

Describe the legal context of the union movement.

The courts have had an important impact on the union movement.

605

PARTNERSHIP: WORKING TOGETHER IN UNIONIZATION

LINE MANAGERS	HR PROFESSIONALS	EMPLOYEES
Must understand why employees might want to join a union. Support the efforts of HR professionals in making policies and programs for good working conditions. Manage employees with respect and equality.	Train line managers in the legal considerations protecting the unionization rights of employees. Develop HR policies and programs that make for good working conditions.	Present their views about working conditions to HR professionals and line managers. Be informed about the pros and cons of union membership.

Until 1935, application of these restrictive theories of law inherited from England reflected the political assumption that free competition and the sanctity of contract and property rights of individuals were fundamental values of society that must be protected.[3]

The courts protected these "fundamental values of society" by declaring that attempts by workers to band together to increase wages (that is, form a union) were conspiracies condemned by law (*Commonwealth v. Pullis, Philadelphia Cordwainers, Pennsylvania,* 1806). Later this outright condemnation was modified to include the necessity of applying a "means test" before condemning the union as an illegal conspiracy (*Commonwealth v. Hunt,* 1842). The courts then used the means test to hamper efforts at unionization.

By the 1880s, the *conspiracy doctrine* was reinforced by civil law, particularly civil injunctions. Civil injunctions maintained the status quo until the legal issues could be resolved, and they are still used for this purpose. Thus, if workers attempt to join together and strike for the purpose of attaining higher wages, an injunction can be granted by the courts forcing the workers to return to work until the legality of the strike is decided. The injunction can also be granted quickly (in order to provide an equitable remedy) without the use of juries and other time-consuming legal proceedings. The impact of injunctions on unionization was particularly evident when the Supreme Court ruled that injunctions could be used to enforce yellow-dog contracts—that is, contracts signed by employees agreeing not to join a union (*Hitchman Coal & Coke v. Mitchell,* 1917).

Further protection for the "fundamental values of society" was provided by the *Sherman Antitrust Act,* which was passed by Congress in 1890 to limit the

Yellow-dog contracts are contracts signed by employees agreeing not to join a union.

606

ability of organizations (for example, unions) to engage in acts (such as union mergers) that lessened competition. This act, as applied to unions, was upheld by the Supreme Court in *Loewe v. Lawlor* (The Danbury Hatters case), 1908. The application of the *Sherman Antitrust Act* to unions was reinforced by the *Clayton Antitrust Act of 1914* and subsequent court decisions (*Duplex Printing Co. v. Deering*, 1921; *United Mine Workers of America v. Coronado Coal Company*, 1922).

Although this supposed protection of society was largely maintained throughout the 1920s, early legislation in the railway industry (because of the industry's impact on the public welfare) suggested it was not sacrosanct. Union activities derived support from the *Arbitration Act of 1888*; the *Erdman Act of 1898*, which outlawed yellow-dog contracts in the railway industry; and *Adair v. United States* (1921), which upheld the unconstitutionality of the yellow-dog contract.

RAILWAY LABOR ACT

These events in the railway industry culminated in the *Railway Labor Act of 1926*, which brought about the demise of the "fundamental values of society" doctrine for all other industries. This act was passed by Congress in 1926 to prevent labor unrest in the railway industry from having serious economic consequences. It has since been expanded to include air carrier employees as well. It was the first act to protect "the fundamental right of workers to engage in labor organizing actively without fear of employer retaliation and discrimination."[4] Other objectives of the act were to avoid service interruption, to eliminate any restrictions in joining a union, and to provide for prompt settlement of disputes and grievances.

The act specified that employers and employees would maintain an agreement over pay, rules, working conditions, dispute settlement, representation, and grievance settlement. A board of mediation (later called the National Mediation Board) was created to settle disputes by encouraging, as necessary, negotiation, then arbitration, and finally emergency intervention by the president. A second board—the National Railway Adjustment Board—was created in 1934 to deal with grievances. This board has exclusive jurisdiction over questions relating to grievances or the interpretation of agreements concerning pay, rules, or working conditions; it makes decisions and awards binding on both parties.

NATIONAL LABOR RELATIONS ACT

The success of the *Railway Labor Act* led Congress to enact a comprehensive labor code in 1935. The purpose of the *National Labor Relations Act* (or *Wagner Act*) was to restore the equality to bargain collectively with employees and employers. Such employer refusal resulted in poor working conditions, depression of wages, and a general depression of business.

The act affirmed employees' rights to form, join, or assist labor organizations to bargain collectively, and to choose their own bargaining representative through majority rule. As stated in Section 8, the second significant portion of the act identified the following unfair labor practices on the part of the employers:

- Interference with the efforts of employees to organize
- Domination of the labor organization by the employer
- Discrimination in the hiring or tenure of employees in order to discourage union affiliation
- Discrimination for filing charges or giving testimony under the act
- Refusal to bargain collectively with a representative of the employees

Court interpretation of these unfair labor practices has made it clear that brib-

The *Railway Labor Act* sanctioned unionization in railways.

The *National Labor Relations Act* sanctioned unionization throughout industry.

Companies were prohibited from doing these things:

ing, spying, blacklisting union sympathizers, moving a business to avoid union activities, and other such employer actions are illegal.

The National Labor Relations Board (NLRB) was established to administer this act. Its major function is to decide all union-organizing efforts and unfair labor practice suits except in areas such as transportation, which are covered by the National Mediation Board. Recent rulings by the Board have focused on the second practice listed above. The rulings in the cases of *Electromation* (1992) and *E. I. Du Pont de Nemours & Co.* (1993) essentially reaffirmed that some employee committees may be unlawful because of involvement or domination by the employer. As described in Chapter 15, Total Quality Management, these decisions caution employers about their involvement or control over employee teams.[5]

Employer groups criticized the *Wagner Act* on several grounds. They argued that the act, in addition to being biased toward unions, limited the constitutional right of free speech of employers, did not consider unfair labor practices on the part of unions, and caused employers serious damage when there were jurisdictional disputes.

LABOR-MANAGEMENT RELATIONS ACT

Congress responded to these criticisms in 1947 by enacting the *Labor-Management Relations Act*, often called the *Taft-Hartley Act*. This act revised and expanded the *Wagner Act* in order to establish a balance between union and management power and to protect the public interest. It introduced the following changes:

The *Taft-Hartley Act* balances union-management power and protects the public interest.

- Employees were allowed to refrain from union activity as well as to engage in it.
- The closed shop was outlawed, and employees were required to agree in writing before union dues could be deducted from their paychecks.
- Employers were ensured of their right to free speech, and they were given the right to file charges against unfair labor practices such as coercing workers to join the unions, causing employers to discriminate against those who do not join, refusing to bargain in good faith, requiring excessive or discriminatory fees, and engaging in featherbedding activities.
- Certification elections (voting for union representation) could not be held more frequently than once a year.
- Employees were given the right to initiate decertification elections.

These provisions indicated the philosophy behind the act—as Senator Robert Taft put it—"simply to reduce the special privileges granted labor leaders."

From time to time, amendments have been added to the *Taft-Hartley Act*. For example, the 1980 amendments to the act provide for an identical accommodation for employees with religious objections to union membership or support. Thus employers and unions must respect (within reason) the religious beliefs of employees as protected by Title VII. For example, an employee may, on religious grounds, contribute to a charity in lieu of paying union dues (*Tooley v. Martin-Marietta Corp.*, 1981).

LABOR-MANAGEMENT REPORTING AND DISCLOSURE ACT

The *Landrum-Griffin Act* regulates internal union affairs.

Although the *Taft-Hartley Act* included some regulation of internal union activities, continuing abuses of power and the corruption of some union officials led to the passage of a "bill of rights" for union members in 1959. The *Labor-Management Reporting and Disclosure Act*, or the *Landrum-Griffin Act*, provided a detailed regulation of internal union affairs. Its provisions include the following:

- Equality of rights for union members in nominating and voting in elections
- Controls on increases in dues
- Controls on suspension and firing of union members
- Elections every three years for local offices and every five years for national or international offices
- Restriction of the use of trusteeships to take control of a member group's autonomy for political reasons
- Definition of the type of person who can hold union office
- Filing of yearly reports with the secretary of labor

The intention of this act was to protect employees from corruption or discriminatory labor unions. By providing standards for union conduct, the act eliminated much of the flagrant abuse of power and protected the democratic rights of employees to some degree. The United Mine Workers, for example, held their first election of international officers in 1969 as a result of the *Landrum-Griffin Act*.

COURT DECISIONS AND ACTS

One of the most significant court decisions of the 1980s is *First National Maintenance Corp. v NLRB*. In this case, the Supreme Court held that an employer is not obligated to bargain with the union about a decision to close a portion of its business. In addition, the NLRB ruled that labor law is not necessarily violated when supervisors who support union activities are fired along with workers as part of an employer plan to discourage unions. In this particular case, however, the board ruled that the employer must rehire the workers fired for union activities.

The cornerstone of labor relations, the grievance-arbitration process, was established in *Textile Workers Union v. Lincoln Mills* (1957). In that case, the Supreme Court held that the agreement to arbitrate grievances is the *quid pro quo* for an agreement not to strike through the years. This agreement, however, has led to the problem of unfair representation by the union of its members. Over the past ten years, cases filed by employees with the NLRB against their unions for unfair representation (breach of duty) have risen to several thousand annually. Although the union's obligation of fair representation is clear, the specific duties involved have been left unclear by numerous court decisions, including *Ford Motor Co. v. Huffman* (1953) and *Hines v. Anchor Motor Freight Co.* (1976).

Finally, the Supreme Court has ruled that "bona fide" seniority systems are protected under Section 703(h) of *Title VII of the Civil Rights Act of 1964*. Thus, equal employment considerations in general do not overrule seniority systems in employment decisions where a seniority system has been in existence for some time or where its intention is not discriminatory (*California Brewers Association v. Bryant*, 1980; *International Brotherhood of Teamsters v. United States*, 1977; *American Tobacco v. Patterson*, 1982). The importance given to seniority is also reflected in cases involving the *Rehabilitation Act*:

> For example, in a layoff where the employer had two workers in light-duty positions, the law would not require the employer to retain the less senior employee with a disability over the more senior workers.[6]

A similar interpretation is expected for the *Americans with Disabilities Act*.

FEDERAL EMPLOYEE REGULATIONS

These labor laws were enacted to govern labor relations in the private sector. In fact, the *Wagner Act* specifically excludes the U.S. government, government cor-

Several court decisions and acts are very relevant to the labor movement.

Federal and state employees have their own legal protections.

porations, states, and municipal corporations in its definition of employer, and for a long time, government employees lacked the legislative protection afforded private-sector workers until a series of key executive orders were put in place. Federal employee labor relations were, until recently, exclusively controlled by executive orders issued by the president.

The government's view of its employees differs from its view of private-sector employees. Several of the rights of unions in the private sector are not included in public-sector regulations, although the content of these regulations often is lifted from private-sector acts.

EXECUTIVE ORDERS. The first set of regulations for federal employee labor relations was Executive Order 10988, introduced by President John Kennedy in 1962. This order forbade federal agencies from interfering with employee organizing or unlawful union activity and provided for recognition of employee organizations. Employee organizations were denied the right to strike, however, and economic issues were not part of the bargaining process, since these are fixed by the civil service classification system. Agency heads were made the ultimate authority on grievances, and managers were excluded from the bargaining units.

Executive Order 11491, issued in 1970 and amended in 1971 (EO 11616) and 1975 (EO 11838), addressed some of the difficulties presented by the first executive order. It created the Federal Labor Relations Council to hear appeals from the decisions of agency heads, prescribed regulations and policies, and created a Federal Services Impasses Panel to act on negotiation impasses. The Council and the employee representatives could meet and discuss personnel practices and working conditions, but all agreements had to be approved by the Council head. Unfair labor practices by both agency management and labor organizations were delineated. The Council was restricted from interference, discrimination, and sponsorship of union discipline against an employee for filing a complaint and was required to recognize or deal with a qualified union. Labor organizations were also restrained from interfering, coercing management or employees, discriminating against employees, calling for or engaging in a strike, or denying membership to an employee.

These controls on employers and labor organizations are similar to those found in private-sector legislation. Yet federal employees do not have the same bargaining rights. They lack rights in four areas:

- No provision is made for bargaining on economic issues.
- Although the parties can meet and confer, there is no obligation to do so.
- The ultimate authority is the agency head rather than a neutral party.
- There is no provision for union security through the agency shop, which requires all employees to pay dues but not to join the union.

CIVIL SERVICE REFORM ACT. In 1978, the *Federal Service Labor-Management Relations Statute* was passed as *Title VII of the Civil Service Reform Act*, which has been referred to as "the most significant change in federal personnel administration since the passage of the *Civil Service Act* in 1883."[7] Several significant changes were made by the statute, prime among them, the following:

- Passage of the statute removed the president's ability to change the act through executive order and, in general, made it more difficult to change the legislation.
- It established the Federal Labor Relations Authority (FLRA), modeled after the NLRB, as an "independent, neutral, full-time, bipartisan agency"[8] created, as President Jimmy Carter said, "to remedy unfair labor

practices within the Government." Interpretation of the act is the province of the FLRA and the courts. Agency heads, including the president, cannot define the meaning of the act.

- An aggrieved person may now seek judicial review of a final order of the FLRA. The FLRA may also seek judicial enforcement of its order.
- Negotiated grievance procedures, which must be included in all agreements, must provide for arbitration as the final step.

STATE AND LOCAL EMPLOYEE REGULATIONS

Employee relations regulations at the state and local level are varied. Not all states have legislation governing their employees, but some states have legislation covering municipal employees as well. One widespread regulation can be noted: collective bargaining is permitted in most states, and it covers wages, hours, and other terms and conditions of employment. The "other terms and conditions" have caused the most difficulty in interpretation. Managerial prerogatives are usually quite strong, especially for firefighters, police, and teachers. The requirement to bargain over certain issues in the private sector is not so stringent as the state or local level. In addition, some 20 states have passed **right-to-work laws**, which prohibit union membership as a condition of employment.

Right-to-work laws prohibit union membership as a condition of employment

Although the rights and privileges of public-sector labor organizations are not as extensive as those in the private sector, the greatest growth in unionization in recent years has come in the public sector.

WHAT IS THE ATTRACTION OF UNIONIZATION?

LEARNING OBJECTIVE 2

Explain the attraction the unions have for workers.

Unions were originally formed in response to the exploitation and abuse of employees by management. To understand the union movement today, however, we need to examine what makes employees decide to join or not join unions.

THE DECISION TO JOIN

Three separate conditions that strongly influence an employee's decision to join a union are dissatisfaction, lack of power, and union instrumentality.

Employees' reasons to join a union include:

- dissatisfaction
- lack of power
- union instrumentality

DISSATISFACTION.   When an individual takes a job, certain conditions of employment (wages, hours, and type of work) are specified in the employment contract. A **psychological contract** also exists between employer and employee, consisting of the unspecified expectation of the employee about reasonable working conditions, requirements of the work itself, the level of effort that should be expended on the job, and the nature of the authority the employer should have in directing the employee's work.[9] These expectations are related to the employee's desire to satisfy certain personal preferences in the workplace. The degree to which the organization fulfills these preferences determines the employee's level of satisfaction.

Dissatisfaction can result from a broken psychological contract.

Dissatisfaction with the implicit terms and conditions of employment (the psychological contract will lead employees to attempt to improve the work situation, often through unionization. A major study found a very strong relationship between the level of satisfaction and the proportion of workers voting for a union. Almost all the workers who were satisfied voted against the union.[10]

Thus, if management wants to make unionization less attractive to employees, it must consider making work conditions more satisfying. Management and the HR department often contribute to the level of work dissatisfaction by:

- Giving unrealistic job previews that create expectations that cannot be fulfilled
- Designing jobs that fail to use the skills, knowledge, and abilities of employees and fail to satisfy their personalities, interests, and preferences
- Practicing poor day-to-day management and supervisory practices, including unfair treatment and one-way downward communication
- Failing to tell employees that management would prefer to operate without unions and that the organization is committed to treating employees with respect.[11]

Lack of power can result from low job essentiality and exclusivity.

LACK OF POWER.   Unionization is seldom the first recourse of employees who are dissatisfied with some aspect of their job. The first attempt to improve the work situation is usually made by an individual acting alone. Someone who has enough power or influence can affect the necessary changes without collaborating with others. The features of a job that determine the amount of power the job holder has in the organization are **essentiality**, or how important or critical the job is to the overall success of the organization, and **exclusivity**, or how difficult it is to replace the person. An employee with an essential task who is difficult to replace may be able to force the employer to make a change. If, however, the individual task is not critical and the employee can easily be replaced, other means, including collective action, must be considered in order to influence the organization.[12]

Essentiality asks how important the job is, and _exclusivity_ asks how difficult it is to replace the person.

In considering whether collective action is appropriate, employees are also likely to consider whether a union could obtain the aspects of the work environment not now provided by the employer and to weigh those benefits against the costs of unionization. In other words, the employees would determine union instrumentality.[13]

Instrumentality asks how likely is it that the union can help.

UNION INSTRUMENTALITY.   Just as employees can be dissatisfied with many aspects of a work environment such as pay, promotion opportunity, treatment by supervisor, the job itself, and work rules, employees can also perceive a union as being **instrumental** in removing these causes of dissatisfaction. The more that employees believe that a union can obtain positive work aspects, the more instrumental the union is for the employees. The employees then weigh the value of the benefits to be obtained through unionization against its costs such as the lengthy organizing campaign and the bad feelings among supervisors, managers, and other employees who may not want a union. Finally, the employees weigh the costs and benefits against the likelihood of a union being able to obtain the benefits: the perceived union instrumentality. When the benefits exceed the costs and union instrumentality is high, employees will be more willing to support a union.

Exhibit 17.2 summarizes the reasons for deciding to join a union. In general, the expectation that work will satisfy personal preferences induces satisfaction or dissatisfaction with work. As the level of dissatisfaction increases, individual workers seek to change their work situation. If they fail and if the positive consequences of unionization seem to outweigh the negative ones, individuals will be inclined to join the union. This, however, will not always be the case. Employees may choose not to join a union.

THE DECISION NOT TO JOIN

Deciding whether to join a union involves an assessment of the negative consequences of unionization. Employees may have misgivings about how effectively a union can improve unsatisfactory work conditions. Collective bargaining is not

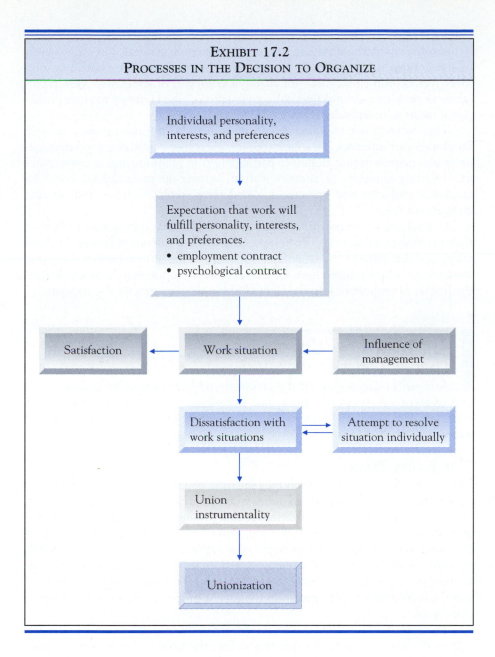

EXHIBIT 17.2
PROCESSES IN THE DECISION TO ORGANIZE

always successful; if the union is not strong, it will be unable to make an employer meet its demands. And even if an employer does respond to union demands, the workers can still be affected adversely. The employer may not be able to survive when the demands of the unions are met, and thus the company may close down, costing employees their jobs. The organization may force the union to strike, inflicting economic hardship on employees who may not be able to afford being out of work, or it may in some cases attempt reprisals against pro-union employees, although this is illegal.[14]

Beyond perceptions of unions as ineffective in the pursuit of personal goals, employees may also resist unionization because of general attitudes toward unions. Employees may identify strongly with the company and have a high level of commitment to it. They would therefore tend to view the union as an adversary, and they would be receptive to company arguments against unions.

Identification with a profession makes union membership unattractive.

Employees may also perceive the goals of the union as objectionable and likely to harm the company and the free enterprise system in general. They may object to the concept of seniority or even to the political activities of the unions. Moreover, certain employees—for example, engineers or scientists—view themselves as professionals and find collective action to be contrary to such professional ideals as independence and self-control.

The decision not to unionize can be influenced by management as well. Employers can influence the employees' decision by establishing good management practices: fostering employee participation in planning and decision making, opening channels of communication, setting up processes for handling employee problems and grievances, developing employee trust, and offering competitive wages.[15]

It should be noted that some employers perceive that they may benefit from their employees unionizing. This is especially so when the union brings some certainty and discipline to the work force. In essence, a union can help manage the work force.[16] Organizations have seldom seen unions in this way, however. In fact, the history of unionization in the United States suggests exactly the opposite.

THE HISTORICAL CONTEXT AND UNIONS TODAY

A better understanding of the attitudes and behaviors of both unions and management can be gained through a knowledge of past union-management relations. The legal considerations discussed earlier form part of this historical context.

THE EARLY DAYS

The beginning of the labor union movement in the United States can be traced back to the successful attempt of journeymen printers to win a wage increase in 1778. By the 1790s, unions of shoemakers, carpenters, and printers had appeared in Boston, Baltimore, New York, and other cities. The Federal Society of Journeymen Cordwainers, for example, was organized in Philadelphia in 1794, primarily to resist employers' attempts to reduce wages. Other issues of concern to these early unions were **union shops** (companies using only union members) and the regulation of apprenticeships to prevent the replacement of journeymen employees.

Union shops are firms using only union members.

The early unions had methods and objectives that are still in evidence today. Although there was no collective bargaining, the unions did establish a price below which members would not work. Strikes were used to enforce this rate. These strikes were relatively peaceful and for the most part successful.

One negative characteristic of early unions was their susceptibility to depressions. Until the late 1800s, most unions thrived in times of prosperity but died off during depressions. Part of this problem may have been related to the insularity of the unions. Aside from sharing information on strikebreakers or scabs, the unions operated independently of each other.

The work situation had undergone several important changes by the end of the nineteenth century. Transportation systems (canals, railroads, and turnpikes) expanded the markets for products and increased worker mobility. Increases in capital costs prevented journeymen from reaching the status of master craftworker (that is, from setting up their own businesses), thereby creating a class of skilled workers. Unionism found its start in these skilled occupations, largely because "the skilled worker . . . had mastered his craft through years of appren-

Significant labor leaders include:

• John L. Lewis, AFL-CIO
• Walter P. Reuther, UAW
• Harry Bridges, ILA

ticeship and was no longer occupationally mobile" and the alternatives were "to passively accept wage cuts, the competition of non-apprentice labor, and the harsh working conditions, or to join in collective action against such employer innovations."[17]

Unions continued to experience ups and downs that were largely tied to economic conditions. Employers took advantage of the depressions to combat unions: In "an all out frontal attack . . . they engaged in frequent lockouts, hired spies . . . summarily discharged labor 'agitators,' and [engaged] the services of strike breakers on a widespread scale."[18] These actions, and the retaliations of unions, established a tenor of violence and lent a strong adversarial nature to union-management relations, the residual effects of which are still in evidence today.

UNIONS TODAY

Today the adversarial nature of the union-management relationship has been replaced to a certain extent by a more cooperative one. This change (discussed in collective bargaining) has been dictated in part by current trends in union membership, including the shifting distribution of members.[19]

DECLINE IN MEMBERSHIP   The proportion of the labor force represented by unions has been declining steadily since the mid-1960s. In 1993, approximately 16 percent of *all* workers were represented by unions, the lowest proportion since 1945 (except for 1992) and down from 23.0 percent in 1980. In 1970, this percentage was 24.7 percent.

> Union membership increased in 1993 to 16.4 percent of all employed wage and salary workers in the United States, the Bureau of Labor Statistics (BLS) reports. This is up from 15.8 percent in 1992.
>
> In both 1990 and 1991, the proportion of American workers belonging to unions was 16.1 percent. In 1992, there were about 16.4 million wage and salary workers who were union members, down about 178,000 from 1991. BLS analysts note that union membership has declined steadily from its high of 35.5 percent of the work force in 1945.
>
> The BLS data for 1993 also show:
>
> - Workers represented by unions but not union members numbered 2.0 million in 1993. About 56 percent of these workers were employed by the government (federal, state, and local).
> - About three-fifths of union members were in private industry in 1993. Most of these (3.7 million) were in the manufacturing sector, followed by transportation and public utilities (1.9 million), services (1.5 million), wholesale and retail trade (1.4 million), and construction (900,000).
> - More working men were in unions (19 percent) than women (13 percent). Union membership also was higher among blacks (21 percent) than whites or Hispanics (both 15 percent). Black men had the highest proportion of union members (24 percent), while white and Hispanic women had the lowest (both 12 percent).
> - Industries with the highest proportion of union members were transportation and public utilities (31 percent), construction and manufacturing (both 20 percent), and mining (15 percent).
> - The median earnings for union members were $575 a week, compared to a median of $426 a week for workers not belonging to unions.[20]

Although the percentage of the work force that was unionized declined between 1970 and 1980 absolute membership in labor organizations increased because the labor force increased. Factors contributing to the percentage decline

Union membership has declined dramatically since its peak in 1945.

include the increase in public-sector employment and white-collar jobs—both of which have historically had a low proportion of union members. Other contributing factors are the decline in employment in industries that are highly unionized, the high levels of unemployment, the increased decertification of unions, union leadership, union responsiveness to membership, and management initiatives.

In the future, however, economic conditions and legislation may make unionization more feasible in white-collar and public-sector jobs. Indeed, most organizing activities today are focused on the public-sector services and health care as described in the feature, "Managing Human Resources in Hospitals."[21]

To gain more organizational ability, power, and financial strength, several unions merged. Although mergers may not automatically increase membership, they can mean more efficiency in union-organizing efforts and an end to costly jurisdictional disputes among unions. The increased organizational strength resulting from mergers may also enable unions to expand the coverage of their membership into industries and occupations previously underrepresented.

DISTRIBUTION OF MEMBERSHIP.   Historically, membership has been concentrated in a small number of large unions. In 1976, 16 unions represented 60 percent of union membership, and 85 unions represented just 2.4 percent. Similarly, the National Education Association accounted for 62 percent of all association members. Many employee associations are small because they are state organizations; their membership potential is therefore limited.

Unions today are exhibiting a substantial and increasing amount of diversification in their membership. For example, in 1958, 73 percent of the unions had at least four-fifths of their members in a single industry; this figure dropped to 55 percent in 1976. The most pronounced diversification has occurred in manufacturing. For example, of the 29 unions that represent workers in chemicals and allied products, 26 presently have less than 20 percent of their membership in a single industry.[23]

HOW AMERICAN UNIONS ARE STRUCTURED

The basic unit of labor unions in the United States is the national union (or international union), a body that organizes, charters, and controls member union locals. The national union develops the general policies and procedures by which locals operate and provides assistance to the locals in areas such as collective bargaining. National unions give the locals clout because they control a large number of employees and can influence large organizations through national strikes or slowdown activities.[24]

The AFL-CIO is the dominant organization for the union movement.

The major umbrella organization for national unions is the American Federation of Labor and Congress of Industrial Organizations (**AFL-CIO**). It represents about 85 percent of the total union membership and contains 89 national unions. The AFL-CIO is an important and powerful body with 14 million members.

Every two years the AFL-CIO holds a convention to develop policy and amend its constitution. Each national union is represented in proportion to its membership. Between conventions, an executive council (the governing body) and a general board direct the organization's affairs; a president is in charge of day-to-day operations.

The executive council's activities include evaluating legislation that affects labor and watching for corruption within the AFL-CIO. Standing committees are appointed to deal with executive, legislative, political, educational, organizing, and other activities. The department of organization and field services, for

UNION-ORGANIZ-ING activity in the health-care industry is expected to increase during the next few years, according to a report by the American Hospital Association (AHA) and BNA (Bureau of National Affairs) interviews with health-care labor relations officials. Structural changes in the industry have increased employees' job-security concerns and work-related stress levels, management and union officials note, adding that unions are expected to step up their organizing efforts in the health-care sector—proven over the past decade to be susceptible to union overtures.

AHA'S ANALYSIS

Following passage of the Taft-Hartley's 1974 health-care amendments . . . , hospital-organizing activity mushroomed. Health-care representation elections rose from 3.2 percent of the total number of elections conducted in 1974 to 11.8 percent in 1975. Since 1980, the union representation rate among health-care employees has risen some 6 percent, to an estimated 20 percent, while the overall private-sector rate has steadily declined from 23 percent of the organizable work force in 1980 to 18 percent in 1985.

The health-care industry has become an increasingly attractive target for union organizers for a number of reasons, AHA says. Widespread layoffs—the result of federal regulations and health-care cost-containment efforts—have made job security a priority issue for employees and given union-organizing drives a major boost. Moreover, while many health-care workers traditionally have viewed themselves as white-collar professionals and rejected collective bargaining, AHA says, "as professional concerns with issues such as compensation, job security, equitable policy administration, and meaningful work involvement expand, identification with unionized segments of the work force also is expanding."

CAMPAIGN CONCERNS

Employees of hospitals feel more insecure than ever before, viewing top management as less interested in them than it was several years ago, declares James Velghe, president of Management Science Associates, Kansas City, Missouri. Noting that hospitals are particularly vulnerable to unionization threats from all-professional bargaining units that include registered nurses, Velghe warns that unions are conducting more sophisticated and selective organizing campaigns.

Management's failure to respond to employees' needs accounts for the recent increase in union activity in the health-care industry, says K. Bruck Stickler, labor counsel for the American Hospital Association. As hospitals downsize, merge, and consolidate, many health-care workers feel threatened by job loss, Stickler notes, and see union representation as a way to gain clout. Employees who think they are being treated unfairly—for example, laid off without relation to seniority—are more likely to look to unions for help.[22]

instance, focuses its attention on organizing activities. Outside of headquarters, three structures exist to organize the local unions. Many of the craft unions are organized into the trade department and the industrial department, which represent them in the national union. The remaining locals are organized directly as part of the national unions. They are affiliated with headquarters but retain independence in dealing with their own union matters.

Besides the 89 national unions within the AFL-CIO, about 60 national unions, representing less than 4 million workers, operate independently. Although this separation is not considered desirable by the AFL-CIO, its impact

A *steward* serves as the union representative at the workplace.

Union activities include:

• civil rights
• community service
• economic policy
• education
• ethical practices
• housing
• international affairs
• legislation
• public relations
• research safety
• Social Security
• veterans' affairs
• publications
• special services to locals
• national politics

LEARNING OBJECTIVE 4

Describe the union organizing campaign.

has been diminished substantially since the Teamsters re-affiliated with the AFL-CIO in 1987.

At the heart of the labor movement are the 70,000 or so local unions, varying in size up to 40,000 members. The locals represent the workers at the workplace, where much of the day-to-day contact with management and the human resource department takes place. Most locals elect a president, a secretary-treasurer, and perhaps one or two other officers from the membership. In the larger locals, a business representative is hired as a full-time employee to handle grievances and contract negotiation. The other important member of the union local is the **steward**, an employee elected by his or her work unit to act as the union representative at the workplace and to respond to company actions against employees that may violate the labor agreement. The steward protects the rights of the worker by filing grievances when the employer has acted improperly.

HOW UNIONS OPERATE

Activities of union locals revolve around collective bargaining and handling grievances. In addition, locals hold general meetings, publish newsletters, and otherwise keep their members informed. Typically, however, the membership is apathetic about union activities. Unless a serious problem exists, attendance at meetings is usually low, and even the election of officers often draws votes from less than one-fourth of the membership.

At headquarters, the AFL-CIO staff and committees work on a wide range of issues, including civil rights, community service, economic policy, education, ethical practices, housing, international affairs, legislation, public relations, research, safety, Social Security, and veterans' affairs. A publications department also produces a variety of literature for the membership and outsiders. National union headquarters provide specialized services to regional and local bodies. People trained in organizing, strikes, legal matters, public relations, and negotiations are available to individual unions.

National unions and the AFL-CIO are active in the political arena. Labor maintains a strong lobbying force in Washington and is involved in political action committees and also at the state and local government level. A recent development has been the international political activities of some of the large national unions. For example, the United Auto Workers have held discussions with Japanese car manufacturers concerning levels of imports and the construction of assembly plants here. They have also lobbied Washington to restrict car imports in an attempt to bolster U.S. automakers and to increase jobs. A recent, highly publicized lobbying effort against NAFTA was unsuccessful. Thus, to help their membership, unions are expanding their activities on all levels and, in some cases, working with other organizations to attain mutual goals.

THE ORGANIZING CAMPAIGN

One of the major functions of the National Labor Relations Board (NLRB) is to conduct the election of unions to represent nongovernment employees. This is accomplished through a certification election to determine whether the majority of employees want the union. Under U.S. labor law, the union certified to represent a group of employees has sole and exclusive right to bargain for that group:

The process by which a single union is selected to represent all employees in a particular unit is crucial to the American system of collective bargaining. If a majority of those voting opt for union representation, all employees are bound by that choice and the employer is obligated to recognize and bargain with the chosen union.[25]

Because unions can acquire significant power, employers may be anxious to keep them out. Adding to this potential union-management conflict is the possibility of competition and conflict between unions if more than one union is attempting to win certification as the representative of a group of employees.

Several stages in the certification process can be identified: (1) a campaign to solicit employee support for union representation, (2) the determination of the appropriate group the union will represent, (3) the pre-election campaign by unions and employers, (4) the election itself, and (5) the certification of a union.[26] These steps are outlined in Exhibit 17.3. The next stage of the organizing process—negotiation of a collective bargaining agreement—is discussed in Chapter 18.

SOLICITING EMPLOYEE SUPPORT
In the campaign to solicit employee support, unions generally attempt to contact the employees and obtain a sufficient number of authorization cards to enable them to request an election from the NLRB.

ESTABLISHING CONTACT BETWEEN THE UNION AND EMPLOYEES.
Contact between the union and employees can be initiated by either party. National unions usually contact employees in industries or occupations in which they have an interest or are traditionally involved. The United Auto Workers, for example, would be likely to contact non-union employees in automobile plants, as they have done for the new plants that have been built in the South. Another prominent example of union initiative was the attempt of two competing unions—the United Farm Workers and the Teamsters—to organize the agricultural workers in California in the 1960s and 1970s. These unions were often aggressive, even violent, during their campaigns for worker support. One consequence of their precertification activities, which included national boycott of grapes and lettuce, was the *California Agricultural Relations Act of 1975*, which regulates union-management relations in the agriculture industry.

Unions campaign for employee support by:

- establishing contact
- obtaining authorization cards
- determining the bargaining unit
- holding a preelection campaign
- requesting an election

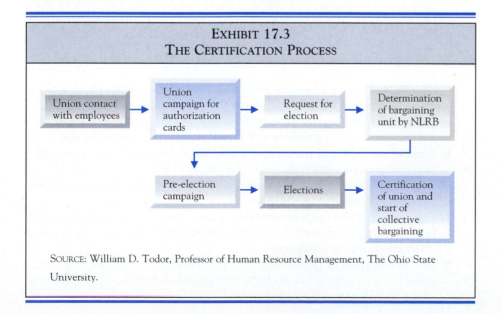

EXHIBIT 17.3
THE CERTIFICATION PROCESS

SOURCE: William D. Todor, Professor of Human Resource Management, The Ohio State University.

In many cases, the union is approached by employees interested in union representation, and the union is happy to oblige. Employees may have strong reasons for desiring this affiliation—low pay, poor working conditions, and other factors relating to dissatisfaction. Because workers generally tend to be apathetic toward unions, however, their concern must become quite serious before they will take any action. At this point, the company must be careful and avoid committing unfair labor practices. Accordingly, employers *should not*

Unfair labor practices by employers include these: ⟶

- *Misrepresent the facts:* Any information management provides about a union or its officers must be factual and truthful.
- *Threaten employees:* It is unlawful to threaten employees with loss of their jobs or transfers to less desirable positions, income reductions, or loss or reduction of benefits and privileges. Use of intimidating language to dissuade employees from joining or supporting a union also is forbidden. In addition, supervisors may not blacklist, lay off, discipline, or discharge any employee because of union activity.
- *Promise benefits or reward:* Supervisors may not promise a pay raise, additional overtime or time off, promotions, or other favorable considerations in exchange for an employee's agreement to refrain from joining a union or signing a union card, to vote against union representation, or otherwise to oppose union activity.
- *Make unscheduled changes in wages, hours, benefits, or working conditions:* Any such changes are unlawful unless the employer can prove they were initiated before union activity began.
- *Conduct surveillance activities:* Management is forbidden to spy on or request anti-union workers to spy on employees' union activities, or to make any statements that give workers the impression they are being watched. Supervisors may not attend union meetings or question employees about a union's internal affairs, nor may they ask employees for their opinions of a union or its officers.
- *Interrogate workers:* Managers may not require employees to tell them who has signed a union card, voted for union representation, attended a union meeting, or instigated an organization drive.
- *Prohibit solicitation:* Employees have the right to solicit members on company property during their nonworking hours, provided this activity does not interfere with work being performed, and to distribute union literature in nonwork areas during their free time.[27]

Employers *can*, however,

But fair labor practices by employers include these: ⟶

- Discuss the history of unions and make factual statements about strikes, violence, or the loss of jobs at plants that have unionized.
- Discuss their own experiences with unions.
- Advise workers about the costs of joining and belonging to unions.
- Remind employees of the company benefits and wages they receive without having to pay union dues.
- Explain that union representation will not protect workers against discharge for cause.
- Point out that the company prefers to deal directly with employees, and not through a third party, in settling complaints about wages, hours, and other employment conditions.
- Tell workers that in negotiating with the union, the company is not obligated to sign a contract or accept all the union's demands, especially those that aren't in its economic interests.

- Advise employees that unions often resort to work stoppages to press their demands and that such tactics can cost them money.
- Inform employees of the company's legal right to hire replacements for workers who got out on strike for economic reasons.[28]

AUTHORIZATION CARDS AND THE REQUEST FOR ELECTIONS. Once contact has been made, the union begins the campaign to collect sufficient **authorization cards**, or signatures of employees interested in having union representation. This campaign must be carried out within the constraints set by law. If the union obtains cards from 30 percent of an organization's employees, it can petition the National Labor Relations Board for an election. (Procedures in the public sector are similar.) If the NLRB determines there is indeed sufficient interest, it will schedule an election. If the union gets more than 50 percent of the employees to sign authorization cards, it may petition the employer as the bargaining representative. Usually employers refuse, whereupon the union petitions the NLRB for an election.

The employer usually resists the union's card-signing campaign. For instance, companies often prohibit solicitation on the premises. However, employers are legally constrained from interfering with an employee's freedom of choice. Union representatives have argued that employers ignore this law because the consequences are minimal—and by doing so, they can effectively discourage unionism.

During the union campaign and election process, it is important that the HR manager caution the company against engaging in unfair labor practices. Unfair labor practices, when identified, generally cause the election to be set aside. Severe violations by the employer can result in certification of the union as the bargaining representative, even if it has lost the election.

Employees interested in unionization sign *authorization cards*.

DETERMINATION OF THE BARGAINING UNIT

When the union has gathered sufficient signatures to petition for an election, the NLRB will make a determination of the **bargaining unit**, the group of employees that will be represented by the union. This is a crucial process, for it can determine the quality of labor-management relations in the future.

Employees to be represented by a union are called a *bargaining unit*.

> At the heart of labor-management relations is the bargaining unit. It is all important that the bargaining unit be truly appropriate and not contain a mix of antagonistic interests or submerge the legitimate interests of a small group of employees in the interest of a larger group.[29]

In order to assure the fullest freedom of collective bargaining, legal constraints and guidelines exist for the unit. Professional and nonprofessional groups cannot be included in the same unit, and a craft unit cannot be placed in a larger unit unless both groups agree to it. Physical location, skill levels, degree of ownership, collective bargaining history, and extent of organization of employees are also considered.

From the union's perspective, the most desirable bargaining unit is one whose members are pro-union and will help win certification. The unit must also have sufficient influence in the organization to give the union some power once it wins representation. Employers generally want a bargaining unit that is least beneficial to the union; this will help to maximize the likelihood of failure in the election and to minimize the power of the unit.[30]

PRE-ELECTION CAMPAIGN

After the bargaining unit has been determined, both union and employer embark on a **pre-election campaign**. Unions claim to provide a strong voice for employees, emphasizing improvement in wages and working conditions and the establishment of a grievance process to ensure fairness. Employers emphasize the costs of unionization—union dues, strikes, and loss of jobs.

The impact of pre-election campaigns is not clear. A study of 31 elections showed very little change in attitude and voting propensity after the campaign. People who will vote for or against a union before the election campaign generally vote the same way after. Severe violations of the legal constraints on behavior, such as using threats or coercion, are prevented by the NLRB, which watches the pre-election activity carefully.

ELECTION, CERTIFICATION, AND DECERTIFICATION

Generally, elections are associated with the process of determining whether the union will win the right to represent workers. Elections can also determine whether the union will continue to have the right to represent a group of employees.

Certification occurs when a union obtains a majority vote.

ELECTION AND CERTIFICATION.
The NLRB conducts the **certification election**. If a majority votes for union representation, the union will be certified. If the union does not get a majority, another election will not be held for at least a year. Generally, about one-third to one-half of the elections certify a union, with less union success in larger organizations. Once a union has been certified, the employer is required to bargain with that union.

Decertification removes a union from representation.

DECERTIFICATION ELECTIONS.
The NLRB also conducts **decertification elections**, which remove a union from representation. If 30 percent or more of the employees request such an election, it will be held. Decertification elections most frequently occur in the first year of a union's representation, when the union is negotiating its first contract. Union strength has not yet been established, and employees are easily discouraged about union behavior.

LEARNING OBJECTIVE 5
Describe the international movement.

Compare the U.S. with:
- Germany
- Great Britain
- Canada
- Japan
- Australia
- Mexico

Codetermination gives workers the feeling that they are represented in major decisions.

INTERNATIONAL COMPARISONS

GERMANY
The belief that workers' interests are best served if employees have a direct say in the management of the company is called codetermination. The original ideas about codetermination, called *mitbestimmung,* were conceived in Germany and are now spreading into many other European countries.

Under **codetermination**, unions are often given seats on the boards of directors of corporations. Managers are encouraged to consult with unions before making major organizational changes, whether they be mergers, investments, plant closings, or relocations. If management disagrees with the union position, management prevails. However, unions can veto subcontracts by the company, and they have access to all company records.

Under the political leadership of the Social-Democratic government in Germany, consensus was reached during the early 1980s to promote international competitiveness through technological superiority and to overcome barriers to innovation by integrating the trade unions into the process of change. The German system of labor relations, with its key features of centralization, jurisdiction, and participation, seem to be functioning well, even in the face of changed socioeconomic conditions. The efficiency and legitimacy of collective bargaining seem also to hold given the codetermination practice and similar system flexibility. Low levels of conflict and commitment to cooperation characterize the labor relations system in Germany. As German firms layoff workers in the recessionary times of the 1990s, this cooperative relationship is being tested.

Since the unions' defeat in the 1930s, the German labor movement has consisted of unions with structures that are a synthesis of traditional elements of the socialist and the Catholic labor movement. Although labor is dominated by the Social Democrats, the Catholic influence on the development of such concepts as codetermination, social partnership, or capital formation for employees has become an integral part of the German trade unions' ideology. A second principle of the trade unions in Germany is that they are organized on an industrial basis. The dominant labor organizations are the seventeen trade unions affiliated with the DGB (Confederation of Trade Unions). The DGB sets the pattern in negotiating for the majority of the workers. The other trade union federations—the DBB (Association of Civil Servants), DAG (White-Collar Association), and the CGB (Christian Trade Unions) lack significant bargaining power; hence civil servants are not allowed to strike.

In the 1980s, unionized employees who were members of DGB affiliates made up a third of the labor force. Nonetheless, their power and influence stretches significantly beyond their numbers. For example, employee support for unions far exceeds their readiness for unionization. In fact, during elections of workplace representatives, about 80 percent of all employees vote regularly for candidates who have been nominated by DGB unions. Another feature of the German unions is their centralized authority. Most of the internal decision-making takes place in the upper echelons of union bureaucracy.

German employers are also organized and centralized. There are employers' associations in several industries, often dominated by large-scale companies. The largest employers' umbrella organization is the BDA (Federation of German Employers' Association). The BDA coordinates various kinds of legally binding agreements for its members. For example, in 1978, it published a "taboo catalog" containing rules and provisions of the association designed to strengthen its bargaining power. It limited management compromise in bargaining; among its provisions was an instruction that Saturday, usually not a working day, should remain a working day in order to maximize the use of labor and machinery. Although this instruction was reversed in 1984, it illustrates the strategy of the employers' association to establish common policies. The notable efficiency of German human resource practices can be explained by the convictions of labor and management to the labor relations system and the cultural predisposition of the Germans to adhere to discipline, rules, and regulations.[31]

GREAT BRITAIN

The industrial relations system in Great Britain differs markedly from those in both the United States and other European countries. Traditionally, the framework of labor law in Britain has been noninterventionist, fostering an essentially voluntary system of industrial relations. Under this system, employers have had no general legal duty to recognize and bargain with their employees, while employees have had no legally protected rights to organize themselves in unions. Also, negotiated agreements signed between unions and employers are not enforceable as legal contracts. The collective agreements familiar to U.S. managers are more akin to "gentlemen's agreements" in Britain and are based on social rather than on legal sanctions.

As with so many aspects of life in Britain, the explanation for this state of affairs is largely historical. The development of British labor law has progressed via the granting of immunities from existing restrictive statutes—such as immunity from prosecution for criminal conspiracy—rather than through the legislation of positive rights. Unlike their U.S. counterparts, British unions have not viewed the law as a positive and protective force guaranteeing their right to existence.

In 1979, union power in Britain, measured by political influence and industrial strength as well as by membership, was undoubtedly at a postwar peak. Since the Conservative party has been in power, however, the industrial relations climate has changed dramatically. A process of step-by-step reform, including laws against secondary picketing, restrictions on the operation of the closed shop, and the establishment of secret union ballots before strikes, has effectively shifted the balance of power back toward management. High levels of unemployment have further undermined union bargaining power. Between 1979 and 1985, the percentage of the labor force in unions fell by about one-fifth from its postwar peak of about 55 percent. Despite some highly publicized disputes, which give an unduly inflated impression of Britain's overall strike proneness, strike activity has also fallen to historically low levels.

The full, long-run consequences of these changes are difficult to predict with any certainty. Managers in Britain still face a work force that is highly unionized compared with that in the United States, where less than 17 percent of the labor force is currently in unions. Managers in many parts of British industry must also negotiate with a multiplicity of unions, the representational boundaries of which often owe more to craft tradition and the accidents of history than they do to the logic of efficient production. They must also operate on a day-to-day basis without the support of legally enforceable collective agreements. Important developments at the shop-floor level do, however, offer some clues to a changed future. On the union side, both the engineering and the electricians unions have been willing to sign single-union agreements that include no-strike clauses. They have also shown a preference for cooperative over confrontational relations with management. Perhaps significantly, the key movers on the management side of these innovative agreements have often been overseas companies setting up operations in Britain. Japanese companies such as Nissan, Hitachi, and Toshiba are notable examples, but innovative agreements have also been signed with some U.S. firms. This is a useful reminder that the behavior and attitudes of both sides determine the quality of labor-management relationships.

CANADA

Approximately one-third of the Canadian labor force is unionized. About three-fourths of the union members are affiliated with the Canadian Labor Congress (CLC). As in the United States, the union local is the basic local unit. The CLC is the dominant labor group at the federal level. Its political influence may be compared with that of the AFL-CIO.

Although the labor laws in Canada are similar to those in the United States, noteworthy differences do exist. Since 1925, the majority of Canadian workers have been covered by provincial, not federal, labor laws, whereas in the United States over 90 percent of the workers are covered by the *National Labor Relations Act*. The Canadian *Industrial Relations Disputes and Investigations Act of 1973*, on the other hand, covers less than 10 percent of the labor force.

Canadian labor laws require frequent interventions by government bodies before a strike can take place. In the United States, such intervention is largely voluntary. Compulsory arbitration in Canada is governed by the *Public Service Staff Relations Act of 1967*. This law also allows nonmanagerial federal employees to join unions and bargain collectively.

This history of labor relations in Canada and the United States is similar because both nations follow British common law, except that provincial governments, rather than the federal government, have developed most of the

---

DID YOU KNOW?

The Amalgamated Engineering and Electrical Union has a single union deal with Nissan in Sunderland, England. By comparison, U.K. firms typically deal with multiple unions in one location.

Canadian labor laws. Since the decision in *Toronto Electric Commissioners v. Snider* (1925), Canadian workers have been governed primarily by provincial laws (except for employees working for the federal government and industries under federal coverage, as defined by amendments to the 1973 industrial relations act—for instance long-shoring, seafaring, provincial railroads, Crown corporations, and airlines). Many of the features of the *Taft-Hartley Act* have been incorporated into the labor laws of the Canadian provinces.

For the union movement as a whole, the trend toward concessionary bargaining to avoid layoffs and plant closings appears to be less evident than it is in the United States.[32] At the same time, Canadian labor organizations affiliated with unions dominated by labor organizations in the United States have become increasingly autonomous.

JAPAN

The third sacred treasure of the Imperial House of Japan (we discussed the first two in Chapter 13) in what is known as the enterprise union. Unlike in the United States and Europe, where unions are organized horizontally and industrywide, almost all trade unions in Japan are formed on a company-by-company, or enterprise, basis. Enterprise unions today account for nearly 90 percent of all Japanese union organizations. Four principal industrywide federations of workers serve as coordinators, formulators of unified and reliable standards, and sources of information.

Although the enterprise concept received a fair amount of attention in the United States during the 1920s and 1930s, such unions collapsed, primarily as a result of excessive management involvement and their narrow field of interest. The success of the enterprise union in Japan is attributed to two major differences. The first of these is the allocation of financial responsibility between the enterprise union and the trade or regional organizations, which reflects a difference in the organizational roles of Japanese labor unions. In Western countries, where centralized union control and authority are predominant, the national union receives union dues, decides how they are to be used, and returns a portion to the local unions for expenses. In Japan, the enterprise union controls the dues, passing on 10 percent or, at most, 20 percent to the federation.[33]

As a result of the enterprise union's role, problems in labor-management relationships can be dealt with more directly, without necessarily involving an outside body. The "mixed" union representation of all blue-collar and some white-collar workers has also proved valuable in determining more representative concerns. As a result of greater union participation by employees of a given company, some of Japan's current top management have once been active labor union leaders.

The second difference that accounts for the success of the enterprise union system in Japan is cultural: the greater company and national loyalty shown by each worker. Accordingly, workers do not look on the union solely as a negotiating body but use its structure to deal with such issues as industry and technical reforms, new plant and equipment investments, and matters of personnel and productivity development.

AUSTRALIA

It is interesting to note that the institutional framework of both U.S. and Australian industrial relations evolved from similar historical circumstances: the need to compel strong employers to meet and deal with a weak labor union movement for collective bargaining purposes.[34] The legislative solutions to this situation that were enacted in each country were, however, quite different.

DID YOU KNOW?

Harry Bridges, leader of the International Longshoremen in the 1930s, came from Melbourne, Australia.

American legislation in the 1930s carefully avoided imposing the decisions of a third party on labor and management by providing a detailed legal framework within which the parties were compelled to bargain in good faith with each other. In contrast, Australian legislation at the turn of the century provided centralized government machinery for the making and enforcement of industrial awards.[35]

In 1983, the federal government commissioned a committee of inquiry on industrial relations in Australia (generally referred to as the Hancock Committee in recognition of the chair, Professor Hancock). The Hancock Committee recommended a number of changes in the system, such as the establishment of a new labor court and the extension of grievance procedures, but it did not recommend total deregulation of the centralized system.[37]

After much debate and delay, the federal government's response to the recommendations of the Hancock Report was presented in the Industrial Relations Bill of 1988. Although the bill supports the need for increased flexibility in the industrial relations system, it presents a much diluted version of the original reforms recommended. The main elements of this bill include an updated name for the ACAC (to be known as the Industrial Relations Commission), which now has the power to hear unfair dismissal cases, and provisions for greater opportunities for enterprise-level negotiations. Despite the different approaches of labor unions and employer associations to industrial relations, both groups have advocated reforms that allow for decentralization and greater flexibility within the present system.[38]

Given the collectivist and centralist traditions of Australian labor relations, dramatic changes are unlikely, and any assumption of convergence over time to a system based solely on plant or enterprise collective bargaining, as in the United States, would be unwarranted. Foreign companies doing business in Australia still need to analyze the industrial relations implications of their business strategies in considerable detail.

MEXICO

The Mexican *Federal Labor Law* governs all labor matters, and the state labor boards oversee its enforcement. Labor relations in Mexico are somewhat different in custom and in practice than in the United States. The employee-employer relationship is somewhat closer and more in terms of a family. When a labor union declares a strike, all employees, including management, must leave the plant. If the strike is legal, the workers receive pay for the duration of the strike.

The industrial relations function of a Maquiladora company is very important in its day-to-day operation. As a group, the Maquiladora companies have done an effective job in administering the labor laws of Mexico.[39] For the most part, Maquiladoras have operated without unions. However, if a company is not operated effectively and not in accordance with good management human resource management, there is always the potential attraction of unionization.

LEARNING OBJECTIVE 6

Recommend what unions should do.

Unions are thinking seriously about this question. What do you suggest?

CURRENT TRENDS

WHAT SHOULD UNIONS DO?

The future role of the union is generating a great deal of discussion and speculation these days.[41] Some foresee a halt to the decline in union membership in the private sector. This is expected to follow from the decline in the numbers entering the work force and a subsequent tighter labor market; from more sophisticated and efficient organizing activities; from the rising appeal of unions among less skilled workers; and from their increasing ability and willingness of unions to offer a broader array of consumer benefits and new forms of membership.[42]

All this needs to be put in the perspective of the environment. The U.S. economy will continue to globalize, and firms will continue to find high-quality, low-wage workers. The decline in mass production will continue at the same time as the skill levels of the work force increase. As Ray Marshall, former Secretary of Labor, describes it "[E]conomic success will require new policies and high-performance systems more appropriate for a global, knowledge-intensive economic environment."[43] While Marshall meant this to describe the future of business, it could as easily be applied to the future of unions.[44]

A final perspective needs to be included here as well: the union movement will continue to be heterogenous. There will be differences within the movement, with some unions—such as the UAW—being more willing to enter into collaborative agreements and others less willing. Thus we are likely to see several answers to the question, What should unions do?

HIGH-PERFORMANCE WORKPLACES

Consistent with the trend more global competition in the areas of quality and cost is the desire of U.S. firms to organize themselves such that they can compete on the same terms. We saw in Chapter 15 the importance of total quality management in this endeavor and the role of employees in its success. A permutation of TQM is the high-performance workplace. Such workplaces use total quality management practices but apply them specifically to unionized situations. A description of this trend and the experiences of one employer are provided in the feature, "HR Advice and Application: High-Performance Workplaces."

The union can play a critical role in high-performance TQM workplaces. In fact, union-management cooperation seems to be essential to these workplaces.

SUMMARY

Employees are generally attracted to unionization because they are dissatisfied with work conditions and because they feel powerless to change those conditions. Some major sources of dissatisfaction are inequity in pay administration, poor communications, and poor supervisory practices. By correcting these, or not allowing them to occur in the first place, organizations can help prevent unions from being attractive. However, once a union-organizing campaign begins, a company can't legally stop it unless an unfair labor practice is committed by the union. At this point, it may be best to hire a labor attorney familiar with the NLRB and labor law to monitor the practices of the union. Should a charge be filed with the NLRB it is important to remember that it takes a long time for the charge to be heard. There are, however, other ways to delay the organizing campaign, such as challenging the bargaining unit, challenging the election procedures, and even conducting a campaign touting company-provided benefits.

Organizations can also establish initial conditions that makes unionization a less attractive alternative. For example, organizations can make sure their compensation package is in good order. Pay should be competitive, and the principles of equal pay for equal work and equal pay for comparable worth should be observed. Supervisors should be trained in effective communication styles and methods. Employee rights must be recognized and observed, both the legally pro-

HIGH-PERFORMANCE WORKPLACES

Improved relations between labor and management are essential in the transformation to high-performance workplaces, say speakers at a national conference on the future of the American workplace, held in Chicago in July of 1993. Convened by President Clinton, Labor Secretary Robert Reich, and Commerce Secretary Ronald Brown, the conference underscores the idea that workplace cooperation is a key element in boosting the United States's ability to compete in a global economy.

MAKING THE TRANSFORMATION

Cooperation is "good for business as well as for workers," Reich asserts, as it gives workers more responsibility for their company's success. To change from a traditional hierarchical organization to a high-performance workplace, he says, employers must push responsibility down to all levels, award workers a share of the profits, provide more training, and add flexibility so employees can rotate job assignments and feel a sense of ownership.

An employer's lasting competitive advantage rests in the ability of its employees to innovate and "go the extra mile," Reich contends; therefore, employers should treat employees "as assets to be developed rather than costs to be cut." A new compact is evolving, he notes, in which employees and employers recognize both the responsibility of workers to make sure the company is profitable and the responsibility of employers to increase workers' value through continuous training.

Transition to a cooperative workplace can be difficult, Reich acknowledges, particularly in organizations that must answer to investors on a quarterly basis through earnings statements. Indeed, there is a need for investors to take a longer view and see linkages to workplace policies that are aimed at long-term development.

Meanwhile, drawing from the experiences of high-performance workplaces, Reich says the following elements are needed to move organizations in the proper direction:

- Input regarding quality from all workers
- Pay linked to skills and compensation tied to company performance
- Employment security through reduction by attrition-only, no-layoff policies, or continuous learning to keep worker skills updated
- Information sharing about company markets and financial performance

- Trust between workers and management

ONE EMPLOYER'S EXPERIENCE

Through workplace cooperation, employees are being empowered to make meaningful decisions at L-S Electro-Galvanizing Co. in Cleveland, according to Cal Tinsley, plant manager, and Thomas Zidek, process technician and president of Steelworkers Local 9126. The company, commonly referred to as L-SE, was created in 1985 as a joint venture between LTV Corporation and Sumitomo Metals of Japan.

With the agreement of the union, L-SE was designed to provide a work environment in which "respect, dignity, and cooperation were to be the way of life," Zidek explains. Adversarial relationships were typical in the steel industry at the time, Zidek notes, but workers still supported the new environment. Most of the individuals hired were laid-off steelworkers who realized they wanted something new for the future.

Before startup, workers received technical training as well as extensive training in problem-solving skills and how to deal with people. Workers then chose their positions based on the skills they brought to the company. That level of involvement continues at L-SE through problem-solving teams and committees on hiring, safety, gain-sharing, skill-based pay, training, and customer concerns.

According to Tinsley, L-SE has tried to promote equality by eliminating traditional barriers between labor and mangement, whether they are physical or psychological. For example, there is no traditional personnel department at L-SE. Also, similar uniforms are worn by workers and managers, making it hard to distinguish between them, and the company has a common locker room, no assigned parking places, and no time clocks.

As part of the company's normal operations, employees hold weekly workshops that focus on quality, notes Zidek. "We are continuously improving our processes that way," he says. Moreover, he points out that employees have the power to stop production or shipments if quality is not high.

The most important innovation at L-SE, says Tinsley, is the creation of an environment where employees want to make participation work. The proof that it works is that L-SE has gained a reputation as the premium supplier of electro-galvanized material in the automotive industry.[44]

tected rights and the so-called humane rights. TQM programs and safety programs are also helpful in establishing a positive, attractive organizational climate.

Some organizations may not bother with defensive maneuvering because they may decide that unions are useful to them. Unions can bring an element of peace and stability among the workers and actually help organizations manage. At the same time, unions can also cause inflexibility and block attempts to make improvements where needed—for example, by blocking a change to total-quality management. Thus, it's also possible that an organization may prefer to help the employees get rid of an unwanted union—that is, decertify it. At this point, an organization should contact a consultant who specializes in this area. These people can ensure that an organization does not violate any labor-management laws and that its chances for success in this endeavor are reasonably high. A failure here could be costly.

Historically, unions and management have operated as adversaries because many of their goals are in conflict. But since conflict is ultimately detrimental to both management and unions, labor relations have gradually changed, thereby reducing this conflict. For instance, unions and management have begun to cooperate to achieve mutual goals. Although cooperation is not widespread, it may be the style of union-management relations in the future. Its effects are particularly apparent in collective bargaining, contract negotiation, and grievance processing, topics we will deal with in Chapter 18.

KEY CONCEPTS

AFL-CIO	essentiality	steward
authorization cards	exclusivity	union
bargaining unit	instrumental	unionization
certification election	pre-election campaign	union shops
codetermination	psychological contract	yellow-dog contracts
decertification election	right-to-work laws	

REVIEW AND DISCUSSION QUESTIONS

1. Identify and discuss the factors that make unionization attractive to employees. Are these factors different today than they were 50 years ago?
2. Briefly describe the history of the union movement.
3. What is a certification election? A decertification election? Who do you suppose wins the majority of certification elections today? Why has the rate changed over time?
4. What is the structure of unionization in the United States today?
5. What are the important legal considerations related to activities like TQM and employee participation?
6. What can a company do during a union campaign to organize the workers?
7. What is codetermination? Would it work in the United States?
8. Compare and contrast union-management conditions in the United States, Mexico, and Canada.
9. What should unions do?
10. Describe high-performance workplaces, and describe the union's role in them.

EXERCISES AND CASES

FIELD PROJECT

Interview human resource managers on their views of unions. Visit union companies and non-union companies. Interview union members, non-union members, and even union officers to learn their views on unions. Present your findings to the class.

CAREER MANAGEMENT EXERCISE

While the rate of unionization in the private sector is less than 12 percent, it is around 35 percent in the public sector (primarily local, state, and federal governmental agencies). Thus you may be in one of two situations on your new job after graduation or sometime after that in which (1) you either do or do not join a union or (2) you discourage your employees (within the guidelines of the law) from forming a union.

1. Explain why you have decided to join a union or why you have decided against it. Indicate conditions under which you would or would not join a union.

_____

_____

_____

_____

2. Now explain why you have decided to discourage your employees (your new job puts you in a managerial position right away!) from forming a union (or why you have decided not to fight unionization efforts at your company).

_____

_____

_____

_____

_____

CASE

A BAD PLACE TO WORK

Brenda C. is a nursing aide at a nursing home. She has been a diligent employee there for two and a half years, and she enjoys her work. She is considered a good worker by her supervisor. Recently, she has become increasingly concerned with the pay and the working conditions at the home.

Although the nursing aides often work extra to help a patient, and as a group are dedicated to their work, the pay scale is significantly below that of other homes in the area. In addition, the nursing aides and other hospital staff have no area where they can get away from the patients for a break; in fact, the nursing home does not provide for a coffee break at all. The nursing staff do, however, take informal breaks whenever they can get a few minutes, and Brenda has found that these help her function better in the sometimes hectic work situation. Since the staff are not allowed to eat in the cafeteria, they must provide for their lunch by eating out or bringing a bag lunch. This has also caused problems, because sometimes the staff are delayed at the restaurant when they go out for lunch.

It seems to Brenda that providing a lounge area for coffee and lunch breaks would make the job much easier for the staff and would result in better care for the patients. She approached her supervisor about the matter, but he was not receptive and suggested that she concentrate on her job. Brenda persisted and was told that the budget is too tight and space too limited.

Brenda knows that her nursing aide friends in other homes have such facilities, and she is fairly certain that those homes are financially no better off than hers. She feels she can get no further on her own, so she contacts the union that represents nursing aides in some of the other homes and arranges for a meeting after work on Friday, expecting a good turnout. She discusses the situation with her co-workers, and many of them are very interested.

On Friday afternoon, the manager of the nursing home calls her into his office and tells her that her performance has recently been inadequate (although her last review was good), that her attitude toward the patients has changed, and that he is terminating her employment as of that day. Brenda is shocked. She tells her co-workers what has happened, and they are also very surprised. Four people attend the union meeting that night. They soon leave expressing fear for their jobs.

Case Questions

1. Why is Brenda interested in getting a union involved in her situation?
2. What are the major aspects of the nursing home that you find objectionable and would prefer not to have?
3. Can unionization help Brenda and her co-workers? How?
4. What can the nursing home do to change Brenda's mind?

CASE

THAT'S HARD TO SAY

Western Manufacturing is a moderately sized (110 employees) assembly plant in the Midwest. Until recently, the employees have expressed little interest in being unionized. Their pay and fringe benefits, are competitive with comparable unionized plants in the vicinity. Moreover, Western Manufacturing has a well-defined grievance process that has been relatively successful in working employee problems.

However, several employees have suggested to their friends at the plant that a labor union might be a good idea. In fact, these employees have begun a drive to unionize. They have been campaigning rather strongly, and they intend to soon begin collecting authorization cards and then to make a formal request for election.

Management of Western Manufacturing is not pleased with these recent developments and has begun a fairly active campaign against unionizing. They have pointed out in several meetings between the shift supervisors and their employees that the wages, benefits, and working conditions are at least on a par with comparable union plants and maybe slightly better. Within six weeks, three such meetings have been called to explain the company's position to the employees.

The employees who are most active in the campaign to have union representation have complained bitterly that these meetings called by management during company time are patently unfair, a clear case of unfair labor practices. Not surprisingly, the company disagrees.

Case Questions

1. Comment on the union representatives' position with respect to the meetings.
2. Comment on the management's position with respect to the meetings.
3. Is this an unfair labor practice? Why or why not?
4. What is the fundamental, central issue involved here?

1. A. Salpukas, "Federal Express Pilots Vote for Union," *The New York Times* (Jan. 15, 1993): D4. Used by permission. Also see A. Salpukas, "Labor's Showdown at Federal Express," *The New York Times* (Feb. 7, 1993): Sec. 3, 1 and 6.

2. For a more extensive discussion of unionization and the entire union-management relationship, see H. J. Anderson, *Primer of Labor Relations,* 21st ed. (Washington, D.C.: Bureau of National Affairs, 1980); B. W. Justice, *Unions, Workers, and the Law* (Washington, D.C.: Bureau of National Affairs, 1983).

3. A good discussion of earlier contributions to labor law can be found in D. P. Twomey, *Labor Law and Legislation,* 6th ed. (Cincinnati, Ohio: Southwestern, 1990); R. C. Trussell, ed., *U.S. Labor and Employment Laws* (Washington, D.C.: Bureau of National Affairs, Cambridge University Press, 1987).

4. L. Balliet, *Survey of Labor Relations* (Washington, D.C.: Bureau of National Affairs, 1981), 44.

5. "Joint Committees Found Unlawful," *Bulletin to Management* (June 24, 1993): 200.

6. "Do Union Contracts Conflict with ADA?" *Bulletin to Management* (Dec. 9, 1991): 400.

7. H. B. Frazier III, "Labor Management Relations in the Federal Government," *Labor Law Journal* (March 1979): 131.

8. *Ibid.*

9. E. H. Schein, *Organizational Psychology* (Englewood Cliffs, N.J.: Prentice-Hall, 1965).

10. J. G. Getman, S. B. Goldberg, and J. B. Herman, *Union Representation Elections: Law and Reality* (New York: Russell Sage Foundation, 1976); "Employee Survey: Unionization and Attitude Measure," *Bulletin to Management* (April 24, 1986): 133–134.

11. "The UAW vs. Japan: Its Showdown Time in Tennessee," *Business Week* (July 24, 1989): 64–65; K. B. Noble, "Union Organizers' Task Is Uphill at Nissan Point," *The New York Times* (April 3, 1988): 18; D. P. Levin, "Nissan Workers in U.S. Test Union and Industry," *The New York Times* (Aug. 12, 1989): 8; R. Kuttner, "A Beachhead for the Beleaguered Labor Movement," *Business Week* (July 17, 1989): 14–15.

12. A. Ritter, "Are Unions Worth the Bargain?" *Personnel* (Feb. 1990): 12–14; Brett "Behavioral Research on Unions," and Brett, "Why Employees Want Unions," 47–59.

13. S. A. Youngblood, A. D. DeNisi, J. Molleston, and W. H. Mobley, "The Impact of Work Attachment, Instrumentality Beliefs, Perceived Labor Union Image, and Subjective Norms on Union Voting Intentions and Union Membership," *Academy of Management Journal* (1984): 576–590.

14. Getman et al. (*op. cit.,* see Note 10).

15. J. H. Hopkins and R. D. Binderup, "Employee Relations and Union Organizing Campaigns," *Personnel Administrator* (March 1980): 57–61.

16. Pro-union legislation in the 1920s and 1930s was favored by some pro-management groups because it was seen as a way to bring some degree of certainty and peace to union-management relationships. See Balliet (*op. cit.,* see Note 4): 13–68 and B. E. Kaufman, *Industrial Relations* (Ithaca, N.Y.: Cornell, 1993).

17. A. A. Sloane and F. Witney, *Labor Relations,* 5th ed. (Englewood Cliffs, N.J.: Prentice-Hall, Inc., 1985), 57.

18. *Ibid.*: 62.

19. For an extensive presentation of union membership data, see C. D. Gifford, ed., *Directory of U.S. Labor Organizations, 1992–93 Edition* (Washington, D.C.: BNA, 1992).

20. "Union Membership," *Bulletin to Management* (March 4, 1993): 68–69; "Union Membership," *Bulletin to Management* (March 17, 1994): 84–86.

21. "Health Care Organizing," *Bulletin to Management* (June 3, 1993): 172–173.

22. "Health Care Industry: Prime Organizing Target," *Bulletin to Management* (Feb. 12, 1987): 49. Reprinted by permission from *Bulletin to Management,* copyright 1987 by the Bureau of National Affairs, Inc., Washington, D.C. 20037.

23. Gifford, (*op. cit.,* see Note 19).

24. Balliet (*op. cit.,* see Note 4): 72–105.

25. Getman et al. (*op. cit.,* see Note 10): 1.

26. For an extensive discussion of the organizing campaign, see J. A. Fossum, "Union-Management Relations," in *Personnel Management,* eds. K. M. Rowland and G. R. Ferris (Boston, Mass.: Allyn and Bacon, 1982); W. E. Fulmer, "Step by Step Through a Union Campaign," *Harvard Business Review* (July–Aug. 1981): 94–102.

27. "Dealing with Organizing: Do's and Don'ts," *Bulletin to Management* (March 7, 1985): 8.

28. *Ibid.*

29. Twomey (*op. cit.,* see Note 3): 134.

30. Getman et al. (*op. cit.,* see Note 10): 72.

31. J. M. Markham, "German Workers Watch the Clock," *The New York Times* (May 13, 1984); P. Revzin, "Swedes Gain Leisure, Not Jobs, by Cutting Hours," *The Wall Street Journal* (Jan. 7, 1985): 10.

32. D. J. Schneider, "Canadian and U.S. Brands of Unionism Have Distinctly Different Nationalities," *Management Review* (Oct. 1983): 31–32.

33. M. S. O'Connor, *Report on Japanese Employee Relations Practices and Their Relation to Worker Productivity*, a report prepared for the Study Mission to Japan, (Nov. 1980): 8–23.

34. K. F. Walker, "The Development of Australian Industrial Relations in International Perspective," in *Perspectives on Australian Industrial Relations*, ed. W. A. Howard (Melbourne: Longman Cheshire, 1984).

35. For a comparison of laws governing union security in Australia and the United States, see B. Aaron, "Union Security in Australia and the United States," *Comparative Labor Law* 6 (1984): 415–41.

36. "Management Pressures for Change and the Industrial Relations System," Business Council of Australia submission to the Alternatives to the Present Arbitration System conference, Oct. 1984, Sydney.

37. *Report of the Committee of Review: Australia Industrial Relations Law and Systems* (Canberra: Australian Government Publishing Service, 1985).
For an analysis of these changes, see "Australia Vaults Ahead with Free Banking," *The Wall Street Journal* (Nov. 4, 1985): 10, 26.

38. P. Dowling, R. Schuler, and D. Welch, *International Dimensions of Human Resource Management* 2nd ed. (Belmont, Calif.: Wadsworth, 1994).

39. "Maquiladora Program Overview," (Newport Beach, Calif.: 1988): 10.

40. J. Hoerr, "What Should Unions Do?" *Harvard Business Review* (May–June 1991): 30–45.

41. C. McDonald, "U.S. Union Membership in Future Decades: A Trade Unionist's Perspective," *Industrial Relations* (Winter 1992): 13–30; eds. A Gladstone et al., *Labour Relations in a Changing Environment* (New York: Walter de Gruyter, 1992); M. Bognanno and M. Kleiner, "Introduction: Labor Market Institutions and the Future Role of Unions," *Industrial Relations* (Winter 1992): 1–12.

42. R. Marshall, "The Future Role of Government in Industrial Relations," *Industrial Relations* (Winter 1992): 31–49.

43. J. Reid, Jr., "Future Unions," *Industrial Relations* (Winter 1992): 122–136.

44. "High-Performance Workplaces Highlighted," *Bulletin to Management* (Aug. 5, 1993): 248. Reprinted by permission, The Bureau of National Affairs, Inc. (Tel. 1-800-372-1033).

CHAPTER 18

COLLECTIVE BARGAINING

LEARNING OBJECTIVES

When you have finished studying this chapter, you should be able to:

1. Describe the different relationships in collective bargaining.
2. Describe the process of collective bargaining.
3. Describe the elements of agreement negotiation.
4. Discuss forms of conflict resolution.
5. Explain the elements of contract administration.
6. Discuss the current trends in collective bargaining.

"IN some cases, [the union] was absolutely right," concedes Richard G. (Skip) LeFauve, President of Saturn, who adds that the protests ["refocused everyone to the urgency of the quality problems"]. Skip LeFauve is referring to the protests by the union workers at the General Motors Saturn plant in Spring Hill, Tennessee. When GM's then chairman, Robert Stempel, paid a visit to the plant in the autumn of 1991, the workers, wearing black and orange armbands, launched a work slowdown. Another one of those strikes to get higher wages? No, this was a protest against the higher production quotas GM was trying to impose on the plant. While high quality and high quantity can go hand in hand when everything is working right, it can be too much to expect in the early stages of operation. Since production at the plant was in the early stages, the workers were more concerned about quality—about the car and the customer's satisfaction with the product—than they were with quantity of output. It could be argued that the workers basically had no reason to go for quantity, since they get paid by the hour and not for the number of cars that go out the door (at least not in the short run). However, the same could be said for the workers' interest in quality.

Quality takes commitment, dedication, and training, and the United Automobile Workers (UAW) have not been known for their concerns over quality or quantity. However, the Spring Hill plant workers staged the slowdown because of concerns about quality! They believed quality was more critical than quantity for the longer term success of the company!

Why were the union workers at the Saturn plant behaving contrary to the traditional stereotype? Because management was behaving contrary to *its* stereotype. Management was giving workers more say in production and was treating workers as co-owners and as valued members of the team. Any employee who didn't want to fit into this new scheme of labor-management relationship in the auto business could collect a generous severance package ($15,000–50,000, depending on length of service), but few did. This new scheme excited the entire work force.

Reflecting upon their original agreement, GM management heard the concerns of the workers at the plant and gave them the benefit of the doubt. They knew Saturn was the real test case for whether or not GM could build cars to compete directly with the top-selling Japanese cars, and they needed the total commitment of the work force to succeed in this effort.[1]

These events at the Saturn plant highlight several important aspects of collective bargaining. One is that union workers can be as concerned about quality as anyone else. Another is that cooperation is possible between unions and management. Cooperation between UAW and GM has not only been high at the Spring Hill plant, it has also been high at GM plants in Flint, Michigan (Buick City); the NUMMI joint venture in Fremont, California; and those in the Cadillac Division, winner of the prestigious Baldrige Award for quality in 1990. The total-quality management program at Saturn shows that union-management cooperation can result in benefits both to the workers and to the company. At Saturn, these have included improved quality, lower absenteeism, increased satisfaction, more employment security and training, and increased profitability. An important aspect of **collective bargaining** relationships—and one that should never be underestimated—is that they are dynamic. New pressures at the Spring Hill plant had by early 1993 caused severe strains on its cooperative spirit; these pressures included:

- Recent hires often less committed to Saturn's employee-participation ideals
- Burnout from 50-hour-and-up workweeks
- Growing distrust of the union's close ties with Saturn's management
- Anger at lack of elections for key union posts on the shop floor
- A scaling-back of training for new workers[2]

As these conditions continue to change in the 1990s, expect the collective bargaining relationships to also change. Consequently, continually scanning the union-management environment is imperative.

COLLECTIVE BARGAINING

Collective bargaining *is a complex process in which union and management negotiators maneuver to win the most advantageous contract.* How the variety of issues involved are settled depends on the following:

- Quality of the union-management relationship
- Processes of bargaining used by labor and management
- Management's strategies
- Union's strategies
- Joint strategies

These critical determinants of the collective bargaining process are described in detail here prior to our examination of the negotiation process.

UNION-MANAGEMENT RELATIONSHIPS

To understand the union-management relationship it is critical to view it within the context of the labor relations system. This system is composed of three subunits—employees, management, and the union—with the government influencing interactions among the three. Employees may be managers or union members, and some of the union members may be part of the union management system (local union leaders). Each of the relationships is regulated by specific federal statutes: union and management by the *National Labor Relations Act*; management and employees by the *National Relations Act* and *Title VII of the Civil Rights Act of 1964*; and union and employees by the *Labor-Management Reporting and Disclosure Act* and *Title VII of the Civil Rights Act*.

Each group in the labor relations system traditionally has different goals. Workers are interested in improved working conditions, wages, and opportunities; unions are interested in their own survival, growth, and acquisition of power, all of which depends on their ability to maintain the support of the employees by providing for their needs. Management has overall organizational goals (such as profit, market share, and growth) and also seeks to preserve managerial prerogatives to direct the work force and to attain the personal goals of the managers (promotion or achievement). Government is interested in a stable and healthy economy, protection of individual rights, and safety and fairness in the workplace.

ADVERSARIAL RELATIONSHIPS. These goals are not always seen as compatible. Thus an adversarial system has emerged, with labor and management attempting to get a bigger cut of the "pie" while government oversees its own interest. In an **adversarial system** of union-management relations, the union's

---

Collective bargaining is a complex process in which union and management negotiators maneuver to win the most advantageous contract.

LEARNING OBJECTIVE 1

Describe the different relationships in collective bargaining.

Those involved in collective bargaining include:

- employees
- unions
- management
- government

Union-management relationships include:

- adversarial systems
- cooperative systems

role is to gain concessions from management during collective bargaining and to preserve those concessions through the grievance procedure. The union is thus an outsider and a critic.[3]

Historically, unions have adopted an adversarial role in their interactions with management. Their focus has been on wages, hours, and working conditions as they attempted to get "more and better" from management. This approach works well in economic boom times but encounters difficulties when the economy is not healthy. High unemployment and the threat of continued job losses have recently induced unions to expand their role, especially since many of their traditional goals—better pay, hours, and working conditions—have already been achieved. Many unions have begun to enter into new, collaborative efforts with employers. The result of this can be described as a cooperative relationship.

COOPERATIVE RELATIONSHIP. In a **cooperative system**, the union's role is that of a partner, not a critic, and the union and management are jointly responsible for reaching a cooperative solution. Thus union and management must engage in problem solving, information sharing, and integration of outcomes.[4]

Cooperative systems have not been a major component of labor relations in the United States. Other countries—Sweden and Germany, for example—have built cooperative mechanisms into their labor system. But increasingly, U.S. management and labor are evolving a cooperative relationship. Management recognizes that most organization improvement programs they undertake need the acceptance of the union to be successful, and active involvement of the union is one of the best ways to gain this acceptance.[5]

While it is not easy to switch from an adversarial to a cooperative relationship, it is not only possible, it is occurring more and more frequently. The feature, "Managing Human Resources at AT&T: More Than Labor Amity," illustrates just such a change.

As we discussed in Chapter 15, teamwork is a critical component in the efforts of firms to improve quality. Unions such as the UAW and the CWA and firms such as Ford Motor and AT&T recognize how important quality is to survival. Consequently, they are working together to ensure that teamwork programs succeed. Of course, not all unions or firms are in favor of these "workplace reforms."[7]

Regardless of whether union and management share an adversarial or cooperative relationship, they still must engage in bargaining to arrive at a union-management contract. This process is often influenced by the type of union-management relationship that exists.

PROCESSES OF BARGAINING

The most widely used description of bargaining identifies five types of processes in contract negotiations: distributive bargaining, integrative bargaining, concessionary bargaining, continuous bargaining and intraorganizational bargaining.

DISTRIBUTIVE BARGAINING. **Distributive bargaining** takes place when the parties are in conflict over the issue, and the outcome represents a gain for one party and a loss for the other. Each party tries to negotiate for the best possible outcome. This process is outlined in Exhibit 18.1.

On any particular issue, union and management negotiators each have three identifiable positions. The union has an **initial demand point**, which is generally more than it expects to get; a **target point**, which is its realistic assessment of what it may be able to get; and a **resistance point**, which is the lowest acceptable level for the issue. Management has three similar points: an **initial offer**,

---

The *adversarial system* is a competitive situation.

The *cooperative system* is a problem-solving situation.

"Today, our union is facing up to the tough task of rebuilding the nation and getting Americans back to work. Our priority is figuring out how to compete in the global economy."

"What's good for working people is good for America." We all know the middle class is the source of our country's economic strength. So we're fighting for good jobs and seeking pragmatic solutions at the bargaining tables. We're asking business and government to join us in pursuing this distinctly American strategy.

Ron Carey—President of the Teamsters Union

LEARNING OBJECTIVE 2

Describe the process of collective bargaining.

Distributive bargaining provides a win–lose resolution.

Managing Human Resources at AT&T

More Than Labor Amity

WHEN AT&T and its unions settled their differences and signed a contract in 1992, the talk afterward was of mutual interests, shared goals and cooperation in the service of the common goal—that of global competition. Conspicuously absent was the rowdy take-it-easy-but-take-it language associated in the public's imagination with collective bargaining. There was amity, but of a sort that tends to fade.

Except this year, it didn't. Last week, 1,000 members of the AT&T work force, roughly divided between management and two AT&T unions, the Communications Workers of America (CWA) and the International Brotherhood of Electrical Workers (IBEW), gathered at a conference center in the New Jersey wilderness. The object? To prepare for the "Workplace of the Future," a company-union initiative instigated by a clause in the 1992 contract calling for labor participation in business strategy decisions.

The spectacle of labor coming to the table with management, to praise mutually, not to bury, was, in the words of one longtime AT&T executive, "something not seen before in my time." Cheered on in a keynote address by Labor Secretary Robert Reich, the two ancient rivals spent the day plotting AT&T's future.

Worker participation is not entirely new at AT&T. Almost 10 years ago, the union tried to improve its members' lot with a "quality of life" proposal. The company has experimented with labor-management projects. Some of the programs continue, but some failed, victims of labor upheavals, personnel departures, or restructurings.

But the new contract calls for an unusual degree of labor-management, cooperation that only can be achieved by a huge change in culture. It is the type of change Mr. Reich and other members of Bill Clinton's policy "wonkocracy" consider critical to restoring civility to employee-employer relations and, with it, "oomph" to the American economy.

AT&T could try hauling into the next century on its current management paradigms and generally impregnable behemothness. But the suburban New Jersey-based telecommunications giant does not want to become a pregnable behemoth like its neighbor to the northeast, IBM. "It's a bread-and-butter issue," said Burke Stinson, an AT&T spokesman.

Telecommunications has not been an especially cheerful industry since 1984, when its monopoly protection went the way of the Nehru jacket. Labor strife increased. Yippy, small counterbehemoths like MCI and Sprint began circling AT&T's ankles—hence the company's interest in strategies that might smooth its return to a clear and peaceful domination of its world markets.

What's in it for the unions? Why give up the pleasure of the barricades for—gag—collaboration? In the years before 1992, the union was in a reactive mode," said Morton Bahr, CWA president. "We had no role in the decision-making process. Everything that was negotiated took place essentially after decisions were made. This contract guarantees us, in writing, to be involved in the information-sharing process that's so necessary before decisions are made."

The appropriate buzz phrase for what Mr. Bahr is talking about is "worker empowerment," which stands in for the cornier and unwieldy "giving workers dignity by giving them some control over their lives." Theoretically, at least, the contract could lead to the quality-of-worklife improvements the CWA has sought before. Theoretically, it could also institutionalize something unions have been trying to tell management, at different volumes, for years: a happy worker is a more productive worker.

In return for flexibility, the unions get a voice and a company commitment to, among other things, employment security, education, and training or retraining.

AT&T seems genuinely intent on reconfiguring its corporate culture, a task likened by one conference participant to "turning an aircraft carrier around." There is agreement between the parties that the workplace of the

Continued on the next page

future will have four components: "workplace models" as strategies for promoting change; business unit/division planning councils to improve customer satisfaction; the constructive relationship council, a remnant of the 1989 contract agreement that will review contract-related issues; and a human resources board whose scope will include external issues like health care that have an impact on AT&T employees.

Resistance to the impending change tends to come from lower- and middle-management, which probably has the most to lose by the convergence of blue-collar and white-collar interests. "There is a lot of resistance to the sharing of power," said William Ketchum, the AT&T executive responsible for the initiative. Similarly, union resistance tends to come not from the rank and file but from the local-president level, which worries about being usurped by the new model. Resistance—table-pounding as Mr. Bahr put it—may be satisfying but futile. Both the unions and AT&T seem convinced that they've seen the future, and it works.[6]

PARTNERSHIP: WORKING TOGETHER IN COLLECTIVE BARGAINING

LINE MANAGERS	HR PROFESSIONALS	EMPLOYEES
Work with HR professionals in developing an effective relationship with union representatives. Work with HR professionals and union representatives in resolving grievances.	Work with line managers in dealing effectively with union representatives. Develop mechanisms for effective grievance resolution.	Bargain in good faith through their union representatives with line managers and HR professionals.

which is usually lower than the expected settlement; a **target point**, at which it would like to reach agreement; and a **resistance point**, which is its upper acceptable limit. If, as shown in Exhibit 18.1 management's resistance point is greater than the union's, a **positive settlement range** exists where negotiations can take place. The exact agreement within this range depends on the bargaining behavior of the negotiators. If, however, management's resistance point is below the union's, there is no common ground for negotiation. In such a situation, a **negative settlement range**, or bargaining impasse, exists.[8]

In distributive bargaining, unions and management have

- initial offer or demand points
- target points
- resistance points
- settlement ranges

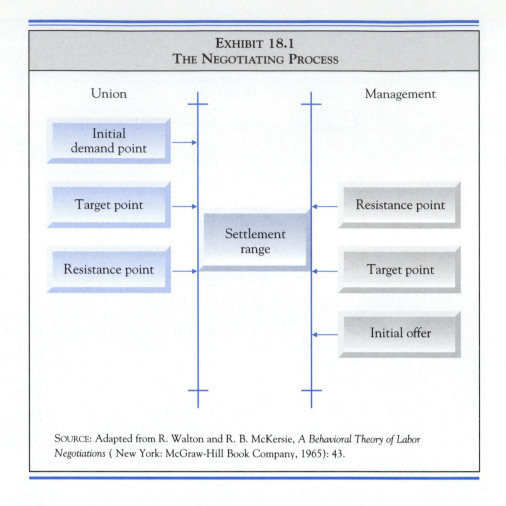

EXHIBIT 18.1
THE NEGOTIATING PROCESS

SOURCE: Adapted from R. Walton and R. B. McKersie, *A Behavioral Theory of Labor Negotiations* (New York: McGraw-Hill Book Company, 1965): 43.

Using wages as an example, the union may have a resistance point of $8.40 per hour, a target of $8.60, and an initial demand point of $8.75. Management may offer $8.20 but have a target of $8.45 and a resistance point of $8.55. The positive settlement range is between $8.40 and $8.55, and this is where the settlement will likely be. However, only the initial wage demand and offer are made public at the beginning of negotiations.

Because many issues are involved in a bargaining session, the actual process is much more complicated. Although each issue can be described by the above model, in actual negotiations, an interaction occurs among issues. Union concessions on one issue may be traded for management concessions on another. Thus the total process is dynamic.

The ritual of the distributive bargaining process is well established, and deviations are often met with suspicion. The following story illustrates this point, in which a labor lawyer tells of

> . . . a young executive who had just taken over the helm of a company. Imbued with idealism, he wanted to end the bickering he had seen take place during past negotiations with labor. To do this, he was ready to give workers as much as his company could afford. Consequently, he asked some members of his staff to study his firm's own wage structure and decide how it compared with other companies, as well as a host of other related matters. He approached the collective bargaining table with a halo of goodness surrounding him. Asking for

the floor, he proceeded to describe what he had done and with a big smile on his face made the offer.

Throughout his entire presentation, the union officials stared at him in amazement. He had offered more than they had expected to secure. But no matter, as soon as he finished, they proceeded to lambaste him, denouncing him for trying to destroy collective bargaining and for attempting to buy off labor. They announced that they would not stand for any such unethical maneuvering, and immediately asked for 5 cents more than the idealistic executive had offered.[9]

INTEGRATIVE BARGAINING. When there is more than one issue to be resolved, the potential exists to make trade-offs between the issues or to pursue integrative agreements. **Integrative bargaining** focuses on creative solutions to conflicts that reconcile (integrate) the parties' interests and yield high joint benefit. It can only occur when negotiators have an "expanding pie" perception—that is, when the two parties (union and management) value particular issues differently.[10]

Integrative bargaining focuses on creative solutions.

CONCESSIONARY BARGAINING. While distributive and integrative bargaining represent the primary approaches to bargaining, **concessionary bargaining** often occurs within these two frameworks. Concessionary bargaining may be prompted by severe economic conditions faced by employers. Seeking to survive and prosper, employers seek givebacks or concessions from the unions, giving promises of job security in return. During the past few years, this type of bargaining has been particularly prevalent, especially in the smokestack industries such as automobiles, steel, and rubber, and to some extent in the transportation industry. In these industries, concessions sought by management from the unions have included wage freezes, wage reductions, change in, or elimination of, work rules, fringe benefit reductions, delay or elimination of COLAs, and more hours of work for the same pay. Two-tier wage systems were tried in some industries, but problems of inequity and lower worker morale offset much of the savings from the lower labor costs.[11]

Concessionary bargaining means having to give back.

CONTINUOUS BARGAINING. As affirmative action, safety and health requirements, and other government regulations continue to complicate the situation for both unions and employers, and as the rate of change in the environment continues to increase, some labor and management negotiators are turning to **continuous bargaining**. A joint committee meets on a regular basis to explore issues and solve problems of common interest. These committees have appeared in the retail food, over-the-road trucking, nuclear power, and men's garment industries.[12]

Continuous bargaining means the discussions are always going on.

Several characteristics of continuous bargaining have been identified:

- Frequent meetings during the life of the contract
- Focus on external events and problem areas rather than on internal problems
- Use of outside experts in decision making
- Use of a problem-solving (integrative) approach[13]

The intention is to develop a union-management structure that is capable of adapting positively and productively to sudden changes in the environment. This continuous bargaining approach is different from, but an extension of, the emergency negotiations that unions have insisted on when inflation or other factors have substantially changed the acceptability of the existing agreement.

Intraorganizational bargaining means that the union leaders may need to confer and bargain with the membership.

Continuous bargaining is a permanent arrangement intended to avoid the crises that often occur under traditional collective bargaining systems.

INTRAORGANIZATIONAL BARGAINING. During negotiations, the bargaining teams from both sides may have to engage in **intraorganizational bargaining**—that is, conferring with their constituents over changes in bargaining positions. Management negotiators may have to convince management to change its position on an issue—for instance, to agree to a higher wage settlement. Union negotiators must eventually convince their members to accept the negotiated contract, so they must be sensitive to the demands of the membership as well as realistic. When the membership votes on the proposed package, it will be strongly influenced by the opinions of the union negotiators.

Although the selection and utilization of a bargaining strategy is important in determining the outcomes of collective bargaining, so, too, is the actual process of negotiation, or negotiating the agreement.

NEGOTIATING THE AGREEMENT

Once a union is certified as the representative of a bargaining unit, it becomes the only party that can negotiate an agreement with the employer for all members of that work unit, whether they are union members or not. Thus the union holds an important and potent position and serves as a critical link between employees and employer. The union is responsible to its members to negotiate for what they want, and it has the duty to represent all employees fairly. The quality of its bargaining is an important measure of union effectiveness.

NEGOTIATING COMMITTEES

The *negotiating committee* conducts the bargaining process.

The employer and the union select their own representatives for the **negotiating committee**. Neither party is required to consider the wishes of the other. Management negotiators, for example, cannot refuse to bargain with representatives of the union because they dislike them or do not think they are appropriate.

Union negotiating teams typically include representatives of the union local, often the president and other executive staff members. In addition, the national union may send a negotiating specialist, who is likely to be a labor lawyer, to work with the team. The negotiators selected by the union do not have to be members of the union or employees of the company. The general goal is to balance bargaining skill and experience with knowledge and information about the specific situation.

At the local level, when a single bargaining unit is negotiating a contract, the company is usually represented by the manager and members of the labor relations or human resource staff. Finance and production managers may also be involved. When the negotiations are critical, either because the size of the bargaining unit is large or because the effect on the company is great, specialists such as labor lawyers may be included on the team.

In national negotiations, top industrial relations or personnel executives frequently head a team made up of specialists from corporate headquarters and perhaps managers from critical divisions or plants within the company. Again, the goal is to have expertise along with specific knowledge about critical situations.

THE NEGOTIATING STRUCTURE

Bargaining can take place with a few or many employers.

Most contracts are negotiated by a single union and a single employer. In some situations, however, different arrangements can be agreed on. When a single union negotiates with several similar companies—for instance, firms in the construction industry or supermarkets—the employers may bargain as a group with the union. At the local level, this is called **multiemployer bargaining**, but at the national level it is referred to as **industrywide bargaining**. Industrywide bargaining occurs in the railroad, coal, wallpaper, and men's suits industries. National negotiations result in contracts that settle major issues such as compensation, whereas issues relating to working conditions are settled locally. This split bargaining style is common in Great Britain and has been used in the auto industry in the United States. When several unions bargain jointly with a single employer, they engage in **coordinated bargaining**. Although not as common as the others, coordinated bargaining appears to be increasing, especially in the public sector.

One consequence of coordinated and industrywide bargaining is often **pattern settlements**, where similar wage rates are imposed on the companies whose employees are represented by the same union within a given industry. Pattern settlements can be detrimental because they ignore differences in the employers' economic condition and ability to pay. The result can be settlements that are tolerable for some companies but cause severe economic trouble for others. As a partial consequence of this, pattern settlements have become less numerous.

Pattern settlements affect many companies at once.

A negotiating structure that exists in the contract construction industry is wide-area and multicraft bargaining. This bargaining structure has arisen in response to the need for unionized employers to be more price competitive and have fewer strikes and in response to the desire by construction trade unions to gain more control at the national level. Consequently, the bargaining is done on a regional (geographic) rather than a local basis. In addition, it covers several construction crafts simultaneously instead of one. The common contract negotiations resulting from **wide-area and multicraft bargaining** lessen the opportunity for unions to whipsaw the employer. This technique uses one contract settlement as a precedent for the next, which then forces the employer to get all contracts settled in order to have all the employees working. Under the threat of **whipsawing**, an employer frequently agrees to more favorable settlements on all contracts regardless of the conditions and merits of each one just to get all employees back to work.[14]

Wide-area and *multicraft bargaining* aims for price competitiveness and fewer strikes.

PREPARATION FOR BARGAINING

Prior to the bargaining session, management and union negotiators need to develop strategies and proposals.

MANAGEMENT STRATEGIES. In preparing for negotiations with the union, management needs to concentrate on the following areas:

1. Specific proposals for changes in contract language
2. The general size of the economic package that the company anticipates offering during the negotiations
3. Statistical displays and supportive data that the company will use during negotiations
4. A bargaining book for the use of company negotiators in which information on issues that will be discussed is compiled, giving an analysis of the effect of each clause, its use in other companies, and other facts[15]

These are the bargaining preparation activities by management:

An important part of this preparation is the calculation of the cost of various bargaining issues or demands. The relative cost of pension contributions, pay increases, health benefits, and other provisions should be determined prior to negotiations. Other costs should also be considered. For instance, what is the cost to management, in its ability to do its job, of union demands for changes in grievance and discipline procedures or transfer and promotion provisions? The goal is to be as well prepared as possible by considering the implications and ramifications of each issue and by presenting a strong argument for the management position.

UNION STRATEGIES.   Like management, unions need to prepare for negotiations by collecting information. Because collective bargaining is the major means by which a union can convince its members that it is effective and valuable, this is a critical activity.

Unions collect information in at least three areas:

> These are the bargaining preparation activities by unions: →

1. The financial situation of the company and its ability to pay
2. The attitude of management toward various issues, as reflected in past negotiations or inferred from negotiations in similar companies
3. The attitudes and desires of the employees

The first two areas give the union an idea of what demands management is likely to accept. The third area is important, but it is sometimes overlooked. The union should be aware of the preferences of its membership. For instance, is a pension increase preferred over increased vacation or holiday benefits? The preferences will vary with the characteristics of the workers. Younger workers tend to prefer more holidays, shorter workweeks, and limited overtime, whereas older workers are more interested in pension plans, benefits, and overtime. The union can determine these preferences by surveying its members.

ISSUES FOR NEGOTIATION

> Issues for negotiation:
> * mandatory
> * permissive
> * prohibited

The issues that can be discussed in collective bargaining sessions are specified by the *Labor-Management Relations Act.* This act has established three categories: (1) mandatory issues, (2) permissive issues, and (3) prohibited issues.[16]

> *Mandatory issues* include the conditions of employment.

Employers and employee representatives (unions) are obligated to meet and discuss "wages, hours, and other terms and conditions of employment." These are the **mandatory issues,** and include the issues that affect management's ability to run the company efficiently or that clash with the union's desire to protect jobs and workers' standing in their jobs. The specific topics that fall into this category have historically been the subject of considerable debate. The Supreme Court's decision in *Borg Warner Corporation v. NLRB* (1982) suggests that the distinction between mandatory and permissive bargaining issues rests on whether the topic regulates the relations between the employer and its employees. Any issue that changes the nature of the job itself or compensation for work must be discussed in collective bargaining. Mandatory issues therefore include subcontracting work, safety, changes of operations, and other actions management might take that will have an impact on employees' jobs, wages, and economic supplements. With the Supreme Court decision in the *First National Maintenance* case in 1981, management's obligation to bargain over plant closings was substantially reduced.

> *Permissive issues* are beneficial to both parties.

Permissive issues are those that are neither mandatory nor illegal. They are issues not specifically related to the nature of the job but still of concern to both parties. For example, issues of price, product design, and decisions about new jobs may be subject to bargaining if the parties agree to it. Permissive issues usually develop when both parties see that mutual discussion and agreement will be beneficial, which is more likely when a cooperative relationship exists. Management and union negotiators cannot refuse to agree on a contract if they fail to settle a permissive issue.[17]

Prohibited issues are those concerning illegal or outlawed activities such as the demand that an employer use only union-produced goods or, where it is illegal, that it employ only union members. Such issues may not be discussed in collective bargaining sessions.

Although the actual issues for negotiation can be expected to vary, they are always far more extensive than those brought out during the initial organizing campaign. In contrast to organizing, where the critical issues are grievances, economics, job security, and supervision, a multitude of mandatory issues exist for negotiation, not to mention the permissive issues. Most of the issues for negotiation are mandatory, including direct compensation.

DIRECT COMPENSATION.   Wage conflicts are the leading cause of strikes. Difficulties arise here because a wage increase is a direct cost to the employer, as is a wage decrease to the employee. As discussed in Chapters 11 and 12, rates of pay are influenced by a variety of factors, including the going rate in an industry, the employer's ability to pay, the cost of living, and productivity. All of these subjects are debated often and discussed extensively in negotiations.

INDIRECT COMPENSATION.   Because the cost of indirect compensation now runs as high as 50 percent of the total cost of wages, it is a major concern in collective bargaining. Such provisions are very difficult to remove once they are in place, so management tends to be cautious about agreeing to them. Some of the most commonly negotiated ones are as follows:

- *Pensions.* Once management has decided to provide a pension plan, the conditions of the plan must be determined (when the benefits will be available, how much will be paid, and whether they become available according to age or years of service). Finally, the organization must decide how long employees must work for the company to receive minimum benefits (vesting) and whether the organization will pay the whole cost or whether the employees or the union will be asked to contribute.
- *Paid vacation.* Most agreements provide for paid vacations. Length of vacation is usually determined by length of service, up to some maximum. The conditions that qualify an individual for a vacation in a given year are also specified. Agreements occasionally specify how the timing of vacations will be determined.
- *Paid holidays.* Most agreements provide time off with pay on Independence Day, Labor Day, Thanksgiving, Christmas, New Year's Day, and Memorial Day. Several others may also be included.
- *Sick leave.* Unpaid sick leave allows the employee to take time off for sickness without compensation. Paid sick leave is usually accumulated while working. Typically one-half to one and one-half days of paid sick leave are credited for each month of work.
- *Health and life insurance.* The employer may be required to pay some or all of the costs of health and life insurance plans.
- *Dismissal or severance pay.* Occasionally, employers agree to pay a set amount to any employee who is dismissed or laid off because of technological changes or business difficulties.
- *Supplemental unemployment benefits.* In the mid-1950s, the United Auto Workers negotiated a plan to supplement state unemployment benefits and to make up the difference when these state benefits expired. Most contracts with this provision are found in the auto and steel industries, where layoffs are common, but workers in other industries are beginning to negotiate them as well.

Prohibited issues concern illegal activities.

The frequent issues of negotiation are
- direct compensation
- indirect compensation
- hours of employment
- institutional issues
- union security
- administrative

These have been and continue to be major issues:

HOURS OF EMPLOYMENT. Finally, while organizations are required to pay overtime for work in excess of 40 hours, unions continually try to reduce the number of hours worked each week. Negotiations focus on including lunch hours in the 8-hour-day requirement. Additionally, negotiations may focus on providing overtime after any 8-hour shift, rather than after 40 hours.

INSTITUTIONAL ISSUES. Some issues are not directly related to jobs but are nevertheless important to both employees and management. **Institutional issues** that affect the security and success of both parties including the following:

Saturn Corporation chose Tennessee even though its employees are members of the UAW and it is a right-to-work state.

- *Union Security.* About 63 percent of the major labor contracts stipulate that employees must join the union after being hired into its bargaining unit. However, 20 states that have traditionally had low levels of unionization have passed right-to-work laws outlawing union membership as a condition of employment.

- *Check-off.* Unions have attempted to arrange for payment of dues through deduction from employees' paychecks. By law, employees must agree to dues check-off in writing. About 86 percent of union contracts contain this provision.

- *Strikes.* The employer may insist that the union agree not to strike during the life of the agreement, typically when a cost-of-living clause has been included. The agreement may be unconditional, allowing no strikes at all, or it may limit strikes to specific circumstances.

- *Managerial prerogatives.* Over half the agreements today stipulate that certain activities are the right of management. In addition, management in most companies argues that it has "residual rights"—that all rights not specifically limited by the agreement belong to management.

ADMINISTRATIVE ISSUES. The last category of issues is concerned with the treatment of employees at work. **Administrative issues** include the following:

- *Breaks and cleanup time.* Some contracts specify the time and length of coffee breaks and meal breaks for employees. In addition, jobs requiring cleanup may have a portion of the work period set aside for this procedure.

Job security will be a major issue throughout the 1990s!

- *Job security.* This is perhaps the issue of most concern to employees and unions. Employers are concerned with restrictions on their ability to lay off employees. Changes in technology or attempts to subcontract work are issues that impinge on job security. A typical union response to technological change was the reaction of the International Longshoremen's Association in the late 1960s to the introduction of containerized shipping. The union operated exclusive hiring halls, developed complex work rules, and negotiated a guaranteed annual income for its members. Job security continues to be a primary issue for longshoremen, telephone workers, and most other blue-collar occupations as well.

- *Seniority.* Length of service is used as a criterion for many personnel decisions in most collective agreements. Layoffs are usually determined by seniority. "Last hired, first fired" is a common situation. Seniority is also important in transfer and promotion decisions. The method of calculating seniority is usually specified to clarify the relative seniority of employees.

- *Discharge and discipline.* This is a touchy issue, and even when an agreement addresses these problems, many grievances are filed concerning the way employees are disciplined or discharged.

Unions have been major forces in safety and health.

- *Safety and health.* Although the *Occupational Safety and Health Act* specifically deals with worker safety and health, some contracts have provisions specifying that the company will provide safety equipment, first aid, physical examinations, accident investigations, and safety committees. Hazardous work may be covered by special provisions and pay rates. Often the agreement will contain a general statement that the employer is responsible for the safety of workers so the union can use the grievance process when any safety issues arise.

- *Production standards.* The level of productivity or performance of employees is a concern of both management and unions. Management is concerned with efficiency, but unions are concerned with the fairness and reasonableness of management's demands.
- *Grievance procedures.* This is a significant part of collective bargaining and is discussed in more detail later in this chapter.
- *Training.* The design and administration of training and development programs and the procedure for selecting employees for training may also be bargaining issues.
- *Duration of the agreement.* Agreements can last for one year or longer, with the most common period being three years.

FACTORS AFFECTING BARGAINING

The preceding discussion suggests that negotiations proceed in a rational manner and end in resolution when a positive contract zone—a set of outcomes that is preferred over the imposition of a strike—exists. Unfortunately, negotiators often fail to reach agreement, even when a positive contract zone exists. The question is, Why?

To fully understand the negotiation process, it is important to examine the decision processes of negotiators. If the biases of negotiators can be identified, then prescriptive approaches and training programs can be developed to improve negotiations. The following are common cognitive or mental limitations to negotiator judgments.[18]

THE MYTHICAL FIXED PIE.   All too frequently, negotiators believe that their interests automatically conflict with the other party's interests. In other words, what one side wins, the other side loses. However, most conflicts usually have more than one issue at stake, with the parties placing different values on the different issues. Consequently, the potential usually exists for integrative agreements. A fundamental task in training negotiators lies in identifying and eliminating this false "fixed pie" assumption and preparing them to look for trade-offs between issues of different value to each side.

FRAMING.   Consider the following bargaining situation. The union claims that its members need a raise to $12 an hour and that anything less will represent a loss due to inflation. Management argues that the company can't pay more than $10 an hour and that anything more would impose an unacceptable loss. If each side had the choice between settling at $11 an hour or going to binding arbitration, they are likely to take the risk and move toward arbitration rather than settlement.

Changing the frame of the situation to a positive one results in a very different outcome. If the union can view anything above $10 an hour as a gain, and if management can view anything under $12 as a gain, then a negotiated settlement is likely—at $11.

As the preceding example emphasizes, the frame (positive or negative) of negotiators can make the difference between settlement and impasse. One solu-

Negotiating may not go smoothly because of:

- **the mythical fixed pie**
- **framing**

Framing refers to how an issue is presented.

tion then to impasses is to alter the frame of references such that it is positive, rather than negative.[19]

Partly because there are so many issues over which to bargain, agreement and contract settlements are not always attained without conflict. When this occurs, forms of conflict resolution are utilized.

Conflict can be resolved by:

- strikes and lockouts
- mediation
- arbitration

Failure to reach an agreement may result in strikes or lockouts.

CONFLICT RESOLUTION

Although the desired outcome of collective bargaining is agreement, there are many occasions where negotiators are unable to reach one. In these situations, several alternatives are used to break the deadlock. The most dramatic response is the strike or lockout, but third-party interventions such as mediation and arbitration are also common.

STRIKES AND LOCKOUTS

When the union is unable to get management to agree to a demand it feels is critical, it may resort to a strike. A **strike** can be defined as the refusal of employees to work. Alternatively, management may refuse to allow employees to work, which is called a **lockout**, but this is an uncommon occurrence.[20]

To proceed with a strike, the union usually holds a strike vote to gain members' approval. Strong membership support for a strike strengthens the union negotiators' position. If the strike takes place, union members picket the employer, informing the public about the existence of a labor dispute and preferably, from the union's point of view, convincing them to avoid this company during the strike. A common practice is the refusal of union members to cross the picket line of another striking union, which adds support to the striking union.

Replacement workers enable a company to continue operations during a strike.

Employers usually attempt to continue operations while the strike is in effect. They either run the company with supervisory personnel and people not in the bargaining unit or hire replacements for the employees. Although it appears that the company can legally hire replacements, the union reacts strongly to the use of "scabs," as the **replacement workers** are called, and they can be a cause of increasingly belligerent labor relations.[21] The success of a strike depends on its ability to cause economic hardship to the employer. Severe hardship usually causes the employer to concede to the union's demands.[22] Thus, from the union's point of view, it is paramount that the cost of this lack of production be high. The union, therefore, actively tries to prevent replacement employees from working. The use of replacement workers has reached a level today where companies are keeping them even after the strike is settled (if at all). This tactic has given employers even more power in the strike situation. Thus, the union movement is seeking legislation to prevent replacement workers from becoming permanent workers.

The timing of the strike is often critical. The union attempts to hold negotiations just prior to the period when the employer has a peak demand for its product or services, when a strike will have maximum economic impact.

Strikes are in major decline.

Strikes have been on the decline (see Exhibit 18.2), but when they do occur, they are costly both to the employer, who loses revenue, and to the employees, who face loss of income. If a strike is prolonged, it is likely that the cost to employees will never fully be recovered by the benefits gained. In part because of this, employers seek to avoid strikes, and unions use them only as a last resort. Moreover, the public interest is generally not served by strikes. They are often an inconvenience and can have serious consequences for the economy as a whole.

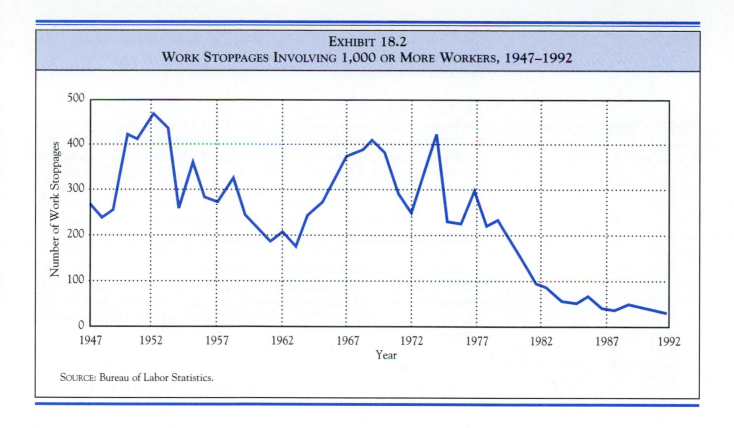

EXHIBIT 18.2
WORK STOPPAGES INVOLVING 1,000 OR MORE WORKERS, 1947–1992

SOURCE: Bureau of Labor Statistics.

SLOWDOWNS. Short of an actual strike, unions may invoke a **slowdown**. The impact of slowdowns can be more effective than an actual strike. For example,

> Until the resistance began at the Caterpillar plant here, Lance Vaughan first installed a set of small hydraulic hoses on the huge off-highway trucks that he helps to assemble, and then a big outside hose. Now he installs the big one first, and reaches awkwardly around it to attach the others, losing production time in the process.
>
> This is not sabotage. The instructions furnished by Caterpillar's engineers specify the inefficient procedure, Mr. Vaughan says. Normally, he ignores such instructions and makes a note to himself to tell the engineers to fix the mistake. Now, he no longer speaks up. Withholding initiative, he works "to the rules" furnished by the company.
>
> "I used to give the engineers ideas," said Mr. Vaughan, who is 38 and has worked at Caterpillar for nearly 20 years. "We showed them how to eliminate some hose clips and save money. And I recommended larger bolts that made assembly easier and faster, and were less likely to come loose."[23]

At Caterpillar, the slowdown was referred to as an "in-plant strategy." Regardless of the name, the impact is the same: a reduction of work output, physically and mentally.

CORPORATE CAMPAIGNS. Another indirect tactic in the form of a secondary boycott is called a **corporate campaign**. In the corporate campaign, a union may ask the public and other unions to write letters to a company asking it to change the way it bargains with the union.[24]

Third-party interventions include:

- mediation
- arbitration

Types of arbitration include:

- extension of bargaining
- final-offer
- closed-offer
- grievance
- interest

Conflict resolution that avoids work stoppages or slowdowns, which may occur regardless of the existence of no-strike clauses, may therefore be desirable from several perspectives. The major forms of this kind of conflict resolution are mediation and arbitration.

MEDIATION

Mediation is a procedure in which a neutral third party assists the union and management negotiators in reaching voluntary agreement.[25] Having no power to impose a solution, the mediator attempts to facilitate the negotiations between union and management. The mediator may make suggestions and recommendations and perhaps add objectivity to the often emotional negotiations. To have any success at all, the mediator must have the trust and respect of both parties and have sufficient expertise and neutrality to convince the union and employer that he or she will be fair and equitable.

The U.S. government operates the Federal Mediation and Conciliation Service (FMCS) to make experienced mediators available to unions and companies. A program called "Relationships by Objective" is offered by the FMCS to eliminate the causes of recurrent impasses. It uses aspects of attitudinal structuring to increase the likelihood of a cooperative relationship between union and management.

ARBITRATION

Arbitration is a procedure in which a neutral third party studies the bargaining situation, listening to both union and management and gathering information, and then makes recommendations that are binding. The arbitrator, in effect, determines the conditions of the agreement.[26] It involves the arbitrator choosing between the final offer of the union and the final offer of the employer. The arbitrator cannot alter these offers but must choose one as it stands. Since the arbitrator chooses the offer that appears most fair, and since losing the arbitration decision means settling for the other's offer, there is pressure to make as good an offer as possible. The intention of **final-offer arbitration** is to encourage the parties to make their best offer and to reach an agreement before arbitration becomes necessary. This is also true with respect to the use of **closed-offer arbitration**. Here the arbitrator receives information only on the parties' original positions without any information on the bargaining progress up to the time the arbitrator is selected.

Once the impasse is removed, union and management have a contract agreement. Abiding by it is the essence of contract administration; however, there are times when arbitration is again necessary—namely, when a grievance is filed. This type of arbitration is referred to as rights or **grievance arbitration**. In contrast, the arbitration process that deals with the contract terms and conditions (described previously) is called **interest arbitration**. Although interest arbitration is relatively infrequent in the private sector, it is more common in the public sector, where it becomes a necessary *quid pro quo* for foregoing the strike option.[27] However, only about 20 states have compulsory interest arbitration procedures.

CONTRACT ADMINISTRATION

Once signed, the collective agreement becomes "the basic legislation governing the lives of the workers."[28] That is, the daily operation and activities in the organization are subject to the conditions of the agreement. Because of the difficulty of writing an unambiguous agreement anticipating all the situations that will occur over its life, disputes will inevitably occur over its interpretation and application. The most common method of resolving these disputes is a **grievance procedure**. Virtually all agreements negotiated today provide for a grievance process to handle employee complaints.

GRIEVANCE PROCEDURES

Basically, a **grievance** is a charge that the union-management contract has been violated.[29] A grievance may be filed by the union for employees or by employers, although management rarely does so. The grievance process is designed to investigate the charges and to resolve the problem.

The following sources of grievances have been identified:

- Outright violation of the agreement
- Disagreement over facts
- Dispute over the meaning of the agreement
- Dispute over the method of applying the agreement
- Argument over the fairness or reasonableness of actions[30]

In resolving these conflicts, the grievance procedure should serve three separate groups: the employers and unions, by interpreting and adjusting the agreement as conditions require; the employees, by protecting their contractual rights and providing a channel of appeal; and society at large, by keeping industrial peace and reducing the number of disputes in the courts.

Grievance procedures typically involve several stages. The collective bargaining agreement specifies the maximum length of time that each step may take. For example, it may require the grievance be filed within five days of the incident that is the subject of dispute. The most common grievance procedure, shown in Exhibit 18.3, involves four steps:

- *Step 1.* An employee who feels that the labor contract has been violated usually contacts the union steward, and together they discuss the problem with the supervisor involved. If the problem is simple and straightforward, it is often resolved at this level. Many contracts require the grievance to be in written form at this first stage. However, cases may be resolved by informal discussion between the supervisor and the employee and, therefore, do not officially enter the grievance process.
- *Step 2.* If agreement cannot be reached at the supervisor level, or if the employee is not satisfied, the complaint can enter the second step of the grievance procedure. Typically, a company HR staff member now seeks to resolve the grievance.
- *Step 3.* If the grievance is sufficiently important or difficult to resolve, it may be taken to the third step. Although contracts vary, top-level management and union executives are usually involved at this stage. These people have the authority to make the decisions that may be required to resolve the grievance.
- *Step 4.* If a grievance cannot be resolved at the third step, most agreements require the use of an arbitrator. The arbitrator is a neutral, mutually acceptable individual who may be provided by the FMCS or some private agency. The arbitrator holds a hearing, reviews the evidence, then rules on the grievance. The decision of the arbitrator is usually binding.

Since the cost of arbitration is shared by the union and employer, some incentive exists to settle the grievance before it goes to arbitration.[31] An added incentive in some cases is the requirement that the loser pays for the arbitration.[32] The

Grievance procedures are the steps used in processing a grievance.

A grievance is a charge that the union-management contract has been violated.

These are the major sources of grievances:

DID YOU KNOW?

The American Arbitration Association has offered dispute resolution services since 1926.

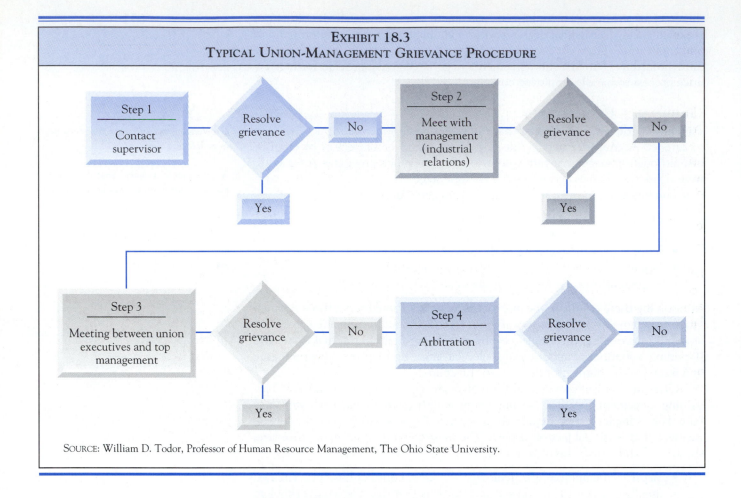

EXHIBIT 18.3
TYPICAL UNION-MANAGEMENT GRIEVANCE PROCEDURE

Step 1 — Contact supervisor → Resolve grievance — No → **Step 2** — Meet with management (industrial relations) → Resolve grievance — No
Resolve grievance — Yes
Resolve grievance — Yes

Step 3 — Meeting between union executives and top management → Resolve grievance — No → **Step 4** — Arbitration → Resolve grievance — No
Resolve grievance — Yes
Resolve grievance — Yes

SOURCE: William D. Todor, Professor of Human Resource Management, The Ohio State University.

expectation is that the parties will screen or evaluate grievances more carefully because pursuing a weak grievance to arbitration will be expensive.

Occasionally, the union will call a strike over a grievance in order to resolve it. This may happen when the issue at hand is so important that the union feels it cannot wait for the slower arbitration process.[33] This "employee rights" strike can be legal but not if the contract specifically forbids strikes during the tenure of the agreement; then it is illegal and is called a **wildcat strike**. Wildcat strikes are not common, however, because most grievances are settled through arbitration.

A strike over a grievance is a wild cat strike.

GRIEVANCE ISSUES

Grievances can be filed over any issue relating to the workplace that is subject to the collective agreement, or they can be filed over interpretation and implementation of the agreement itself. The most common type of grievance reaching the arbitration stage involves discipline and discharge, although grievances are filed over other issues as well.

Although it is accepted that absenteeism can be grounds for discharge, the critical issue is the determination that the absenteeism in question is excessive. Insubordination usually is either failure to do what the supervisor requests or the more serious problem of outright refusal to do it. If the supervisor's orders are clear and explicit and if the employee is warned of the consequences, discipline for refusal to respond is usually acceptable. The exception is when the employee feels that the work endangers health.

The most common grievance issues are
- discharge
- discipline

Because seniority usually determines who is laid off, bumped from a job to make way for someone else, or rehired, its calculation is of great concern to employees. Seniority is also used as a criterion to determine eligibility for promotions and transfers, so management must be careful to avoid complaints and grievances in this area.

Compensation for time away from work, vacations, holidays, or sick leave is also a common source of grievances. Holidays cause problems because special pay arrangements often exist for people working on those days.

Wage and work schedules can also lead to grievances. Disagreements often arise over interpretation or application of the agreement relating to such issues as overtime pay, pay for reporting, and scheduling. Grievances have been filed over the exercise of management rights—that is, its right to introduce technological changes, use subcontractors, or change jobs in other ways. This type of behavior can also be the source of charges of unfair labor practices, since these activities may require collective bargaining.

The *Taft-Hartley Act* gives unions the right to file grievances on their own behalf if they feel their rights have been violated. This act also gives unions access to the information necessary to process the grievance or to make sure the agreement is not being violated. In addition, unions may file grievances for violations of union shop or check-off provisions.

Occasionally, other activities prompt grievances. Wildcat strikes or behavior that functions as a strike (mass absences from work, for example) can result in a management grievance. The major focus of grievances, however, is in the administration of the conditions of the agreement.

MANAGEMENT PROCEDURES

Management can significantly affect the grievance rate by adopting proper procedures for taking action against an employee. One of the most important procedures involves that of discipline and discharge. The issue of just cause and fairness is central to most discipline grievances. Employers must ensure that the employee is adequately warned of the consequences, that the rule involved is related to operation of the company, that a thorough investigation is undertaken, and that the penalty is reasonable. The following activities have been identified as being useful in meeting these considerations:

- Explanation of rules to employees
- Consideration of the accusations and facts
- Regular warning procedures, including written reports
- Involvement of the union in the case
- Examination of the employee's motives and reasons
- Consideration of the employee's past record
- Familiarization of all management personnel, especially supervisors, with disciplinary procedure and company rules

These procedures can help management reduce grievance rates:

In areas outside of discipline and discharge, management can avoid grievance problems by educating supervisors and managers about labor relations and about the conditions of the collective agreement. It has been found that supervisors with labor knowledge are an important factor in the reduction of grievances.

UNION PROCEDURES

The union has an obligation to its members to provide them fair and adequate representation and to process and investigate grievances brought by its members speedily (*Vaca v. Sipes*, 1967; *Hines v. Anchor Motor Freight*, 1976; *Smith v. Hussman Refrigerator Co. & Local 13889, United Steel Workers of America*, 1980).

Unions have a duty to represent their membership fairly.

Thus it should have a grievance-handling procedure that aids in effectively processing grievances without being guilty of unfair representation.

Unfair representation, according to the NLRB, is usually related to one of four types of union behavior:

- *Improper motives of fraud.* The union cannot refuse to process a grievance because of the employee's race or gender or because of the employee's attitude toward the union.
- *Arbitrary conduct.* Unions cannot dismiss a grievance without investigating its merits.
- *Gross negligence.* The union cannot recklessly disregard the employee's interests.
- *Union conduct after filing the grievance.* The union must process the grievance to a reasonable conclusion.[34]

Because the employer can also be cited for unfair representation, management should attempt to maintain a fair grievance process. Company labor relations managers should avoid taking advantage of union errors in handling grievances so that this action does not affect fair representation.

Another important influence on the grievance process is the union steward. Since the union steward is generally the first person to hear about an employee's grievance, the steward has substantial influence on the grievance process. A steward can either encourage an employee to file a grievance, suggest that the problem is really not a grievance, or informally resolve the problem outside the grievance procedure. The personalities of stewards may, in fact, influence the number of grievances filed.[35] Because stewards are selected from the ranks of employees and may have little knowledge of labor relations, the union should train them to improve their effectiveness. The company can also be liable in a fair-representation suit and therefore should support such training.

INTERNATIONAL COMPARISONS

WITHIN NORTH AMERICA

We focus our discussion of international comparisons on Mexico, Canada and the United States. The reason is because of the increased economic activity within this region since the passage of the *North American Free Trade Agreement (NAFTA)* in 1993. Although this agreement is limited to the trading relationships among the three countries, it is likely to have major impacts on employment conditions. It is projected that as the amount of trade and economic activity increase among these three nations, conditions such as wages and benefits, health and safety will become more similar. As it is today, there are some major differences, but they are not just between Mexico and the United States and Mexico and Canada. Differences on many major employment conditions are shown in Exhibit 18.4. You might look at this exhibit carefully, however, because there are some employment conditions that exist in Mexico and Canada, for example, healthcare benefits, that do not exist in the United States. But there are also some conditions, such as unemployment insurance and workers' compensation insurance, that exist in Canada and the United States but not in Mexico.

Perhaps the biggest difference among these three nations, however, is the minimum wage. While the United States and Canada are about equal, they are much different from Mexico. This difference, combined with the relatively high

EXHIBIT 18.4
COMPARISONS OF PRIVATE-SECTOR LABOR LAW IN THE NORTH AMERICAN TRADING BLOCK*

EMPLOYMENT CONDITIONS	UNITED STATES	CANADA	MEXICO
Minimum wage (US$)	$4.25/hr	$3.51/hr	$0.46/hr. (avg.)
Maximum work week	40 hours (8 × 5)	varies with province	48 hours (8 × 6)
Pensions	optional	required contribution	optional
Social Security (old age)	required contribution	required contribution	required contribution
Social Security (disability)	required contribution	no provision	required contribution
Health-care benefits	optional	required contribution	required contribution
Unemployment insurance	required contribution	required contribution	no provision
Workers' compensation insurance	required	yes, varies with province	no provision
Pay equity/comparable worth	no provision	yes in Ontario	no provision
Plant closing notification	60 days	yes, varies with province	yes
Severance pay	optional	varies with province	90 days pay
Housing assistance	optional	optional	5% base salary
Profit sharing	optional	optional	10% net profits
Christmas bonus	optional	optional	15 days pay
Holiday leave	optional	3+ paid holidays	7 paid holidays
Vacation leave	optional	10 paid days	6+ paid days
Sick leave	required	paid by gov't. after 3 weeks	paid by gov't.
Maternity leave	required	17 weeks + 24 weeks	12 weeks
Gender discrimination	prohibited	prohibited	prohibited
Race/color discrimination	prohibited	prohibited	prohibited
Religious discrimination	prohibited	prohibited	prohibited
National origin discrimination	prohibited	prohibited	no provision
Age discrimination	prohibited	prohibited	no provision
Disability discrimination	prohibited	prohibited	no provision
Marital status discrimination	no provision	prohibited	no provision

*In all NAFTA countries, states and provinces also have jurisdiction over labor law and may set additional standards.

SOURCE: Institute for International Human Resources, Society for Human Resource Management, Briefing Paper on the North American Free Trade Agreement, January 1993.

quality of work force in Mexico, has made and continues to make Mexico attractive to employers. Over the past decade many firms, including those from Japan, the United States and Europe, have moved to Mexico to set up operations. Much of this movement can today be found along the border of the United States and Mexico. This area is often referred to as the border region. Plants and factories located there are called malquiladoras. With the passage of NAFTA it is predicted that there will be less movement of plants from the United States and Canada to Mexico, and more movement of plants from Asia and Europe into Mexico to take advantage of the employment conditions and the free trade within North America. In addition, other countries in Central and South America, for example, Chile, Brazil and Argentina, are interested in joining the NAFTA.

Thus, while the NAFTA is only a trading agreement (in contrast to the European Community (Union) which covers political, cultural and educational issues in addition to economic trading issues), it is expected to have a major impact on employment conditions within the three countries of North America.

In turn this is likely to change the living conditions and purchasing power for its more than three hundred and fifty million inhabitants.

The NAFTA is also likely to have a major impact on the union movement. In fact it has already had the impact of increasing the cooperation between the unions in the United States and Mexico:

> When the Campbell Soup Company threatened to move some operations to Mexico if Midwestern tomato pickers demanded higher wages, the Farm Labor Organizing Committee, a Midwest union, discouraged the move by helping its Mexican counterpart win a stronger contract.
>
> United States unions are also helping Mexican unions to organize, especially at American-owned factories. For instance, the United Electrical Workers—which has lost nearly one-fifth of its members to factory relocations in Mexico—has begun to subsidize organizers at Mexican plants of the General Electric Company.[36]

Such cooperation has also occurred between unions in the United States and Europe. Some observers see more of this cooperation needing to occur for the union movement to survive—as the companies whose workers they represent develop global strategies, so do the unions who want to continue to represent those workers.

LEARNING OBJECTIVE 6

Discuss the current trends in collective bargaining.

Major trends in collective bargaining:

- strategic involvement
- board membership

CURRENT TRENDS

STRATEGIC INVOLVEMENT

Management and workers alike are finding that a mutual involvement in the business strategy benefits them both. Strategic involvement is probably key in the transition from the adversarial relationship to one of mutual cooperation and partnership. Several areas stand out as prime examples of what can happen when worker and management alike are involved in business strategy.

WAGE REDUCTION EFFORTS. Labor costs are critical to the success of any business. Many companies today face possible bankruptcy because of high labor costs. Thus the wage accommodations given by unions in these vulnerable industries have been crucial in lowering costs. During the 1980s, American Airlines, Greyhound, McDonnell Douglas, Boeing, and Ingersoll-Rand negotiated two-tiered wage systems to reduce labor costs, without which these companies may not have survived. Thus a company's relationship with its union can be critical to its survival, and the better its relationship, the more likely the company is to gain a competitive advantage.[37]

QUALITY CIRCLE PROGRAMS. Ford Motor Company has engaged in a program of increased worker involvement and more cooperative labor relations with the United Auto Workers. The results have been higher product quality than its competitors and a marketing campaign centered on the slogan, "Quality is Job 1." This program has also affected efficiency in a positive way. Similar results have been obtained at Westinghouse Corporation, Saturn, AT&T, Xerox, and the Mass Transportation Authority of Flint, Michigan. In these companies, the gains have been the fruit of the increased employee commitment associated with quality circle programs. In addition to gains in quality and efficiency, these companies have experienced fewer grievances, reduced absenteeism and turnover, lower design costs, higher engineering productivity, and fewer costly changes in design cycles.

We will continue to see this strategic involvement through the year 2000 at least, and the form it will take will generally be similar to forms taken at Saturn and AT&T, the examples described in this chapter and the previous chapter. Another form of involvement is gaining momentum, however: the employee takeover (employees assume all or part of the equity ownership). In recent years, the workers at TWA acquired a 45 percent stake in the airline for granting wage concessions. Workers at Northwest Airlines and United Airlines made similar arrangements. You might watch for this trend of employees giving up wage demands for ownership in the company and the hopes of job security.

BOARD MEMBERSHIP

A second trend in collective bargaining is that of unions gaining a seat on the board of directors. Such membership is similar to the codetermination system of Germany described in Chapter 17. What is different about it is that it results from union-management bargaining rather than federal mandate. While unions now hold seats on the boards of National Steel Corporation, Wheeling-Pittsburgh Steel Corporation, and the LTV Corporation,

> Giving unions access to the board room is common in Europe, where the unions are stronger, but is still quite novel in the United States. It has generally only been entertained by troubled companies that have had to work closely with their unions to avert bankruptcy or liquidation.[38]

Only the future will tell whether this becomes a major movement where even nontroubled companies elect to make unions *bona fide* occupants of the boardroom.

SUMMARY

In the United States, collective bargaining is currently at a critical crossroads. Global competition has brought about a greater emphasis on the mutual survival of both company and union. This has resulted in a shift from the traditional adversarial relationship between union and management to one of cooperation. New bargaining strategies characterize this altered relationship. Productivity bargaining is an attempt to encourage increased effectiveness in the workplace by passing some of the savings of modernization or increased efficiency on to the employees. Another innovation is continuous bargaining, where a joint union-management committee meets on a regular basis to deal with problems.

Although obstacles exist to union-management cooperation—a history of adversarial relations, hesitancy on the part of the union to give up the traditional roles of labor, and both parties' fear of losing power—present economic conditions and the threat of an influx of foreign products are prompting many organizations to act for their mutual benefit.

The quality of the union-management relationship can have a strong influence on contract negotiations. Labor and management each select a bargaining committee to negotiate the new agreement. The negotiations may be between a single union and a single company or multiple companies, or between multiple unions and a single company. Bargaining issues are mandatory, permissive, or prohibited. Mandatory issues must be discussed, permissive issues can be discussed if both parties agree, and prohibited issues cannot be discussed. The issues can be grouped into wage issues, economic supplements issues, institutional issues, and administrative issues.

Almost all labor contracts outline grievance procedures for handling employee complaints. The most common grievance is related to discipline and discharge, although wages, promotions, seniority, vacations, holidays, and management and union rights are also sources of complaints. Management can influence the results of grievances by developing a procedure that ensures their actions are just and fair. Written records of actions taken are useful for potential arbitration. Unions have a legal responsibility to represent the employee fairly in grievances; therefore, they also need a grievance-handling procedure.

Unions also play an important role in health and safety issues. We will discuss these issues in Chapter 19.

KEY CONCEPTS

administrative issues
adversarial system
arbitration
closed-offer arbitration
collective bargaining
concessionary bargaining
continuous bargaining
cooperative system
coordinated bargaining
corporate campaign
distributive bargaining
final-offer arbitration
grievance
grievance arbitration
grievance procedure

industrywide bargaining
initial demand point
initial offer
institutional issues
integrative bargaining
interest arbitration
intraorganizational
   bargaining
lockout
mandatory issues
mediation
multiemployer
   bargaining
negative settlement
   range

negotiating committee
pattern settlements
permissive issues
positive settlement range
prohibited issues
replacement workers
resistance point
slowdown
strike
target point
unfair representation
wide-area and multicraft
   bargaining
wildcat strike
whipsawing

REVIEW AND DISCUSSION QUESTIONS

1. What is a bargaining unit? Why is its formation important?
2. Why has there been a recent trend toward cooperation between unions and management?
3. What are the steps in a typical grievance procedure? Is this process formal or informal?
4. Distinguish among mandatory, permissive, and prohibited bargaining issues.
5. Distinguish mediation from arbitration. How does a grievance procedure differ from interest arbitration?
6. How can unions assist organizations in TQM programs?
7. What is likely to be the impact of companies using replacement workers?
8. Compare and contrast wages and working conditions among the United States, Canada and Mexico.
9. Describe the strategic involvement of unions.
10. Do you expect more worker slowdowns in this decade? More strikes?

EXERCISES AND CASES

FIELD PROJECT

Interview a human resource manager in a unionized company, and discuss key bargaining issues and how the company is likely to resolve them.

CASE

THE UNION'S STRATEGIC CHOICE

Maria Dennis sat back and thoughtfully read through the list of strategies the union's committee had given her that morning. If her union is to rebuild the power it has lost over the past few years, it is time to take drastic action. If the union continues to decline as it has been, it won't be able to effectively represent its members as their exclusive bargaining agent.

Maria was elected two years before at her union's convention to be the international president of the Newspaper Workers International Union (NWIU). At the time she knew it would not be an easy job, and she had eagerly looked forward to taking on a new challenge. But she had no idea during the election just how difficult it would be to get the union back on its feet again.

The NWIU was founded in the late 1890s by newspaper typographers who were responsible for such tasks as setting type on linotype machines, creating the layout of the newspaper, proofing the articles, and printing the newspaper. Members of the union typically completed a six-year apprenticeship, learning all the different tasks involved in the printing process. Prior to 1960, the printing profession was considered to be the elite of the industrial work force. The craft demanded that typographers be literate at a time when even the middle and upper classes were not. The combination of this historical literacy with

proficiency in a highly skilled, highly paid craft gave printers elite status among manual workers.

Since the 1970s, however, the union had begun to decline. Literacy was no longer a unique characteristic, and automation had led to a deskilling of the craft. The introduction of video display terminals, optical character recognition scanners, and computerized typesetting eliminated substantial composing room work, and the demand for skilled union workers was reduced. The union experienced its peak membership of 120,000 in 1965. During the 1970s, however, membership began a substantial decline, and in 1988, the total membership was only 40,000.

The union's reduced membership has resulted in other problems for the union. First, there are fewer members to pay dues to the union, which is their main revenue-generating function. Consequently, the union is having some serious financial problems and is being forced to cut some of its services to the members.

Second, the union is experiencing a significant loss in bargaining power with newspaper management. In the past, the printers had been fairly secure in their jobs because there was a good demand in the labor market for individuals who could run the complicated printing

Continued on the next page

equipment. But the recent switch to automation has eliminated many jobs and has also made it possible for employers to easily replace union employees. Anyone can be trained in a short time to use the new printing equipment. Therefore, if union members decided to strike for better wages, hours, and working conditions, management could easily, and legally, find replacements for them. In essence, the union is increasingly unable to fulfill its main mission, which is to collectively represent those employees who have voted for it. To solve the current crisis, Maria is considering five options.

- Implement an associate member plan through which any individual can join the union for a fee of $50 a year. While these members would not be fully represented on the job, they would get an attractive package of benefits, such as low-cost home, health, and auto insurance.
- Attempt some cooperative labor-management relations programs such as trying to get member representation on newspaper boards of directors or employee participation programs in the work place.
- Put more effort into political action. For example, lobby for labor law reform or for new laws more favorable to unions. Try to initiate action that would result in harsher penalties against employers that practice illegal union-avoidance activities such as threatening to move the business if a union is voted in or firing pro-union employees.

- Appeal to community leaders to speak out in favor of the union in order to improve public relations, to recruit new members, and to encourage employers to bargain fairly when negotiating with the union.
- Search for another union with which they might merge, thus increasing their membership, strengthening their finances, increasing their bargaining power, and obtaining economies of scale.

Maria realizes each of the above options could have both positive and negative results and is unsure which strategy, if any, she should recommend for the union to pursue. In less than three hours, however, she will present the list to the council with her recommendations.

SOURCE: By Kay Stratton–Devine, University of Alberta

CASE QUESTIONS
1. What are the strengths and weaknesses of each strategy?
2. What strategies could be employed to get new bargaining units?
3. What other types of services could the union offer to its members?
4. What would your recommendation be? Justify your response.

NOTES

1. "At Saturn, What Workers Want is . . . Fewer Defects," *Business Week* (Dec. 2, 1991): 117–118. Also see D. Woodruff, "Saturn: Labor's Love Lost?" *Business Week* (Feb. 8, 1993): 122–123; D. Woodruff, J. Treece, S. W. Bhargava, and K. Miller, "Saturn," *Business Week* (Aug. 17, 1992): 87–91; J. L. Lewandowski and W. P. MacKinnon, "What We Learned at Saturn," *Personnel Journal* (Dec. 1992): 30–32; and B. P. Noble, "Toward the Factory on a Hill," *The New York Times* (Nov. 8, 1992): F25.

2. Woodruff (*op. cit.*, see Note 1).

3. J. M. Brett, "Behavioral Research on Unions and Union Management Systems," in *Research in Organization Behavior*, vol. 2, eds. B. M. Straw and L. L. Cummings (Greenwich, Conn.: JAI Press 1980), 200.

4. See J. M. Brett, "Behavioral Research on Unions," J. M. Brett, "Why Employees Want Unions," *Organizational Dynamics*

8 (1980); 45–59; W. C. Hamner and F. J. Smith, "Work Attitudes as Predictors of Unionization Activity," *Journal of Applied Psychology* 63 (1978): 415–421; "Unions Are Turning to Polls to Read the Rank and File," *Business Week* (Oct. 22, 1984): 66–67; W. Serrin, "Unions Are Shifting Gears but Not Goals," *The New York Times* (March 31, 1985): 2E.

5. D. Q. Mills, *The New Competitors* (New York: Free Press, 1985), 225–242; M. Schuster, "The Impact of Union-Management Cooperation on Productivity and Employment," *Industrial and Labor Relations Review* (April 1983): 415–430; H. C. Katz, T. A. Kochan, and K. R. Gobeille, "Industrial Relations Performance, Economic Performance, and QWL Programs: An Interplant Analysis," *Industrial and Labor Relations Review* (Oct. 1983): 3–17.

6. B. P. Noble, "More Than Labor Amity at AT&T," *The New York Times* (March 14, 1993): F25.

7. J. Hoerr, "The Strange Bedfellows Backing Workplace Reform," *Business Week* (April 20, 1990): 57. Also see R. Koenig, "Quality Circles Are Vulnerable to Union Tests," *The Wall Street Journal* (March 28, 1990): B1; L. E. Hazzard, "A Union Says Yes to Attendance," *Personnel Journal* (Nov. 1990): 47–49; B. Filipczak, "Unions: Cooperation or Capitulation in the '90s?" *Training* (May 1993): 25–34.

8. J. A. Fossum, *Labor Relations: Development, Structure, Process,* 4th ed. (Plano, Tex.: Business Publications Inc., 1988).

9. A. A. Blum, "Collective Bargaining: Ritual or Reality?" *Harvard Business Review* (Nov.–Dec. 1961): 64.

10. M. Bazerman, *Judgement in Managerial Decision Making* (New York: Wiley, 1986); M. Bazerman and J. S. Carroll, "Negotiator Cognition," in *Research in Organizational Behavior*, vol. 9, ed. L. L. Cummings and B. M. Staw (Greenwich, Conn.: JAI Press, 1987); M. H. Bazerman, T. Magliozzi, and M. A. Neale, "The Acquisition of an Integrative Response in a Competitive Market," *Organizational Behavior and Human Decision Processes* 34 (1985): 294–313.

11. K. Jennings and E. Traynman, "Two-Tier Plans," *Personnel Journal* (March 1988): 56–58.

12. A. A. Sloane and F. Whitney, *Labor Relations*, 5th ed. (Englewood Cliffs, N.J.: Prentice-Hall, 1985).

13. Fossum (*op. cit.*, see Note 8): 395–396.

14. P. T. Hartman and W. H. Franke, "The Changing Bargaining Structure in Construction: Wide-Area and Multicraft Bargaining," *Industrial and Labor Relations Review* (Jan. 1980): 170–184.

15. Sloan and Whitney (*op. cit.*, see Note 12): 59.

16. P. T. Hartman and W. H. Franke, "The Changing Bargaining Structure in Construction: Wide-Area and Multicraft Bargaining," *Industrial and Labor Relations Review* (Jan. 1980): 170–184.

17. Fossum (*op. cit.*, see Note 8).

18. M. Bazerman and M. A. Neale, "Heuristics in Negotiation: Limitations to Effective Dispute Resolution," in *Negotiating in Organizations*, eds. M. Bazerman and R. Lewick (Beverly Hills, Calif.: Sage, 1983), 51–67; M. Gordon et al., "Laboratory Research in Bargaining and Negotiations: An Evaluation, *Industrial Relations* (Spring 1984): 218–223; R. E. Walton and R. B. McKersie, *A Behavioral Theory of Labor Negotiations* (New York: McGraw-Hill, 1965).

19. M. Neale, V. Huber, and G. Northcraft, "The Framing of Negotiations: Contextual versus Task Frame," *Organizational Behavior and Human Decision Processes* 39 (1987): 228–241.

20. "Lockout and Shutdowns," *Labor Relations Reporter* (Washington, D.C.: Bureau of National Affairs, 1985), LRX 688–691, 810.

21. "Employment Law Changes Expected," *Bulletin to Management* (March 18, 1993): 88.

22. D. J. B. Mitchell, "A Note on Strike Propensities and Wage Developments," *Industrial Relations* 20 (1981): 123–127; J. Kennan, "Pareto Optimality and the Economics of Strike Duration," *Journal of Labor Research* 1 (1980): 77–94.

23. L. Uchitelle, "Labor Draws the Line in Decatur," *The New York Times* (June 13, 1993): Sec. 3, 1 and 6.

24. J. Tasini, "For the Unions, a New Weapon," *The New York Times Magazine* (June 12, 1988): 24–25, 69–71.

25. S. Briggs, "Labor/Management Conflict and the Role of the Neutral," in *Personnel and Human Resource Management*, 3rd ed., eds. R. S. Schuler, S. A. Youngblood, and V. L. Huber (St. Paul, Minn.: West, 1988).

26. D. E. Feller, "End of the Trilogy: The Declining State of Labor Arbitration," *Arbitration Journal* (Sept. 1993): 18–26; S. L. Hayford, "The Coming Third Era of Labor Arbitration," *Arbitration Journal* (Sept. 1993): 8–17, 77, 78.

27. "Judgement Day for Arbitrators," *Business Week* (April 19, 1982): 66; R. Johnson, "Interest Arbitration Examined," *Personnel Administrator* (Jan. 1983): 53–59, 73; P. Compton-Forbes, "Interest Arbitration Hasn't Worked Well in the Public Sector," *Personnel Administrator* (Feb. 1984): 99–104; "Collective Bargaining Through Diplomacy," *Bulletin to Management* (Jan. 25, 1990): 32.

28. R. L. Blevins, "Maximizing Company Rights Under the Contract," *Personnel Administrator* (June 1984): 75–82; and D. A. Hawver, "Plan Before Negotiating . . . and Increase Your Power of Persuasion," *Management Review* (Feb. 1984): 46–48; R. J. Colon, "Grievances Hinge on Poor Contract Language," *Personnel Journal* (Sept. 1990): 32–36.

29. S. H. Slichter, J. J. Healy, and E. R. Livernash, *The Impact of Collective Bargaining on Management* (Washington, D.C.: The Brookings Institution, 1960), 694.

30. *Ibid.*, 694–696.

31. J. N. Draznin, "Labor Relations," *Personnel Journal* (July 1981): 528; J. N. Draznin, "Labor Relations," *Personnel Journal* (Aug. 1980): 625; B. A. Jacobs, "Don't Take 'No' for an Answer," *Industry Week* (Jan. 26, 1981): 38–43; Kochan, *Collective Bargaining and Industrial Relations*, 385–386; I. Paster, "Collective Bargaining: Warnings for the Novice Negotiator," *Personnel Journal* (March 1981): 203–206.

32. B. R. Skeleton and P. C. Marett, "Loser Pays Arbitration," *Labor Law Journal* (May 1979): 302–309.

33. G. W. Bolander, "Fair Representation: Not Just a Union Problem," *Personnel Administrator* (March 1980): 39.

34. Memorandum 79-55, National Labor Relations Board (July 7, 1979).

35. D. R. Dalton and W. D. Todor, "Manifest Needs of Stewards: Propensity to File a Grievance," *Journal of Applied Psychology* (Dec. 1979): 654–659.

36. D. Moberg, "Like Business, Unions Must Go Global," *The New York Times* (Dec. 9, 1993): F13. Also see S. Baker, G. Smith and E. Weiner, "The Mexican Worker," *Business Week* (April 19, 1993): 84–92; and W. C. Symonds, G. Smith and S. Baker, "Border Crossings," *Business Week* (Nov. 22, 1993): 40–42.

37. T. A. Kochan, R. B. McKersie, and P. Cappelli, "Strategic Choice and Industrial Relations Theory," *Industrial Relations* (Winter 1984): 16–38; T. A. Kochan and J. Chalykoff, "Human Resource Management and Business Life Cycles: Some Preliminary Propositions," paper presented at UCLA Conference on Human Resources and Industrial Relations in High Technology Firms (June 21, 1985); D. Q. Mills, *The New Competitors*, 243–271.

38. A. L. Cowan, "Steel Pact Lets Union Name a Board Member," *The New York Times* (Aug. 1, 1993): L34.

SAFE and healthy working conditions are important to us all! Most of us would not take a job if we thought the conditions unsafe or unhealthy. Most companies would not wittingly design a job to be unsafe and unhealthy. Not only would such an action be highly illegal, it would be against the value system of the people comprising the organization. In fact, most companies find that having an outstanding record of safety and health enhances their ability to attract and retain a competent work force. Consequently, in Chapter 19, we discuss how companies can be made safe and healthy for employees if they are not already. We will also discuss just how significant a problem poor safety and health conditions are. As the nation's data-gathering capacity increases, so does the incidence of work-related diseases. What once may have gone unnoticed can become now an alarming statistical trend. High technology brings with it a potential for unforeseen side effects on health that only time and the application of more technology will reveal. This is important for you as an individual, regardless of whether you will be working at home, in a factory, in an office, or on the road because your long-term health and the quality of your life may depend on it!

In closing, we discuss in Chapter 20 the system that can facilitate the efforts of organizations in their quest to be better places to work—an organization's information system. In this chapter, we address issues surrounding data information, and assessment systems. To manage human resources effectively today requires systematic and scientific tools and techniques. Some of these tools and techniques are associated with

computer technology, automation, and human resource information and data systems. The computer has become a major tool in the repertoire of organizations as they seek to manage their human resources ever more effectively. The use of human resource information systems (HRIS) can ease and speed HR decisions such as,

SECTION 8

MONITORING AND ASSESSING THE WORK ENVIRONMENT

Who in our organization is qualified to take the job opening we have in our new office in San Francisco? How effective is our diversity program? How does our absentee rate compare to five years ago, and what might be affecting it? For the HR department to be world-class, to link more effectively with the business, and to better serve the needs of the line manager and the business, it must use the best, most up-to-date technology possible. Then it must use the most appropriate methods of assessment to evaluate the success of its chosen technologies. The increasing importance of this area has changed the role of the HRIS manager from that of a project manager to that of a strategic partner. Organizations can no longer assume that their HR activities are working or that improvements are not necessary. Continual assessment is another way HR professionals can demonstrate not only to the organization, but also to line managers and employees that what the HR department is doing is the best possible!

CHAPTER 19

OCCUPATIONAL SAFETY AND HEALTH

LEARNING OBJECTIVES

When you have finished studying this chapter, you should be able to:

1. Describe the purposes of safety and health in organizations.
2. Explain the model of occupational safety and health.
3. Discuss the legal considerations.
4. Describe the common hazards.
5. Describe what organizations are doing and can do to improve occupational safety and health.
6. Describe some safety and health issues in other countries.

CHAPTER OUTLINE

"Managing Human Resources at ACI America"

OCCUPATIONAL SAFETY AND HEALTH

WHY IS IT IMPORTANT TO IMPROVE OCCUPATIONAL SAFETY AND HEALTH?

A MODEL OF OCCUPATIONAL SAFETY AND HEALTH

LEGAL CONSIDERATIONS

"Managing Human Resources and Workplace Torts
WHO'S RESPONSIBLE?"

HAZARDS IN OCCUPATIONAL SAFETY AND HEALTH

"HR Advice and Application
THE VIOLENT EMPLOYEE—WARNING SIGNS"

STRATEGIES FOR IMPROVEMENT

"Managing Human Resources at American Building
Maintenance Industries"

"HR Advice and Application
SOLUTIONS TO WORKPLACE STRESS"

INTERNATIONAL SAFETY AND HEALTH ISSUES

CURRENT TRENDS

Case: Safety Net or Death Trap?

Case: Who's There on the Line?

Here's what William M. Minderman, vice president of human resources had to say when asked about occupational safety and health at his company, ACI America in Memphis, Tennessee. You often hear, 'Our industry is different—you can't avoid safety problems.' But you can. We are in industries noted for high accident rates—we own glass companies in the construction industry. We have seven divisions in 110 locations in about seventeen states, and we are the largest purchasers of flat glass outside General Motors. Our environments for safety are quite diverse—from retail stores to construction sites or large plants.

Our country has increased its emphasis on safety in the last ten years, and our efforts have really come together: Most states charge a percentage of payroll for workers' compensation—a percentage that's dependent on the industry. For example, for construction workers in California, the rate is $15 for every $100 of payroll. In Texas, the rate is $14 for every $100 of payroll. Typically, most employers pay those rates. We pay about 40 percent of those rates, and some of our competitors pay 120 percent of those rates. Our accident frequency is significantly lower than is typical in our industries, as shown by SIC coded data published by the National Safety Council.

PERFORMANCE COUNTS

You can't just give lip service to safety. The managers of our location have five or six key responsibilities they are accountable for on their performance appraisals—and safety is one of them. In the performance appraisal, we measure accident rates for each manager at each location and how well the manager conforms with corporate policy. Conformance with corporate policy is audited by our insurance carrier on a yearly basis, and we do our own audits as well. If the manager is having safety problems, he is given an incentive opportunity to improve his performance.

We set annual safety goals for each division, and we have good historic performance data by location.

We know our higher risk areas and seasons; for example, more construction in summer causes more injuries.

We have fairly rigid company policies for managers. For example, they must hold monthly meetings on safety (covering types of accidents, why they happen, and how to avoid them), and report accidents to both the insurance company to process the claim, and to the division HR manager. Through the insurer, we have an on-line system, and we know our daily accident rate. We get monthly and year-to-date reports, and these reports are shared with our president. The vice president and general managers of each division also get their division's performance summarized, as does each operation within each division.

We provide support at a corporate level—a safety orientation, including a videotape, and some general information applicable across the company. Our divisions do things on their own, as well.

HR's ROLE

HR managers can't do the job themselves—but they can encourage conformance to policies and procedures and reporting guidelines. Our division HR managers check reports and make sure that investigations are held and that managers have a plan on what to do.

Our HR managers help with orientations, seeing that we have company physicians and appropriate incentive programs. They provide a key focus for our safety programs.

But the most important aspect of safety is interest and commitment from the top. It doesn't take people long to separate what's said from what's meant. There have to be lots of pushes. It's critical that management keep the pressure on—day to day, year to year. Then, employees buy in because it's expected. You have to show you mean it—monitor results, and pay for performance.[1]

This feature illustrates some crucial issues about occupational safety and health. One is the increased emphasis firms are putting on safety programs. Another is the benefits associated with workplace safety: a safe work environment keeps employees healthy and productive, and it reduces the workers' compensation costs that firms pay to the state in which they do business. A third issue is the importance of making line managers responsible for safety through policies, goals, performance appraisal, and compensation. Finally, note the central role of the HR manager. While not out on the line themselves, they can still do much to assist line managers in making conditions safer and healthier. Of course, to do this effectively, HR managers need to know a lot about health and safety, and this chapter is an initiation into the issues of occupational safety and health in organizations. Workplace hazards are divided into (1) the accidents and diseases that produce physiological and physical conditions and (2) the stress and low quality of working life that result when psychological conditions are not optimal. We will briefly examine the role of the federal government in establishing and enforcing safety standards. Then we will look at strategies to improve employee safety and health, including such measures as improved record keeping, job redesign, ergonomics, and educational programs.[2]

OCCUPATIONAL SAFETY AND HEALTH

Occupational safety and health *refers to the physiological/physical and psychological conditions of an organization's work force that results from the work environment provided by the organization.*

If an organization takes effective safety and health measures, fewer of its employees have short- or long-term ill effects as a result of being employed at that organization.

Physiological/physical conditions include occupational diseases and accidents such as actual loss of life or limb; cardiovascular diseases; various forms of cancer such as lung cancer and leukemia; emphysema; and arthritis. Other conditions that are known to result from an unhealthy work environment include white lung disease, brown lung disease, black lung disease, sterility, central nervous system damage, and chronic bronchitis.

Psychological conditions refer to organizational stress and low quality of working life. These encompass dissatisfaction, apathy, withdrawal, projection, tunnel vision, forgetfulness, inner confusion about roles and duties, mistrust of others, vacillation in decision making, inattentiveness, irritability, procrastination, and a tendency to become distraught over trifles.

Two major safety and health conditions resulting from the work environment:

- physiological/physical
- psychological

LEARNING OBJECTIVE 1

Describe the purposes of safety and health in organizations.

WHY IS IT IMPORTANT TO IMPROVE OCCUPATIONAL SAFETY AND HEALTH?

Improving safety and health conditions can reduce the symptoms and costs of poor safety and health. Certain groups of employees appear to be more affected than others and perhaps should be targeted for more intensive efforts.

We've reached an accommodation with blue-collar death. Forget that a U.S. worker is five times more likely to die than a Swede. . . . Forget that a U.S. worker is three times more likely to die than a Japanese.

The sad reality is that blue-collar blood pours too easily. [Occupational Safety and Health Administration] fines amount to mere traffic tickets for those who run our companies. The small fines are simply buried in the cost of production. Blood can be cash accounted, given a number, and factored with

LINE MANAGERS	HR PROFESSIONALS	EMPLOYEES
Make safety and health a major objective of the firm.	Work with other professionals such as medical doctors and industrial engineers to develop new programs.	Participate in the development and administration of safety and health programs.
Support the HR professionals' efforts to train all employees in safety and health.	Create HR programs that train employees for safe and healthy behaviors and reward them for their success.	Perform in accordance with established safety and health guidelines.

other costs. . . .[3] This has tremendous implications for the union-management relationship, not to mention costs from poor worker morale, lower productivity and mounting litigation.

Blue-collar workers are not the only ones to suffer from workplace hazards. White-collar workers, including managers, also encounter workplace hazards:

> "Stress is the most pervasive and potent toxin in the workplace," says Leon J. Warshaw, executive director of the New York Business Group on Health, a coalition of businesses concerned about health care. In California, mental stress claims are the most rapidly increasing type of workers' compensation cases, having risen 700 percent in the last decade. And a poll earlier this year found that 25 percent of the employees surveyed at New Jersey businesses suffered from stress-induced ailments.[4]

Although the traditional ill effects on the white-collar work force have been those related to psychological conditions, there is growing concern today over physical conditions relating to the unforeseen effects of the computer terminal (eyestrain, miscarriages, carpal tunnel syndrome) and closed office buildings, where chemical components from sources such as carpeting and building construction build up and and are circulated through the ventilation system.

✴THE BENEFITS OF A SAFE AND HEALTHY WORK ENVIRONMENT

If organizations can reduce the rates and severity of their occupational accidents, diseases, and work-related stress levels and improve the quality of work life for their employees, they can only become more effective. Such an improvement

Everyone is affected by safety and health conditions.

Benefits:
- more productivity
- less absenteeism
- more efficiency
- reduced medical costs
- lower workers' compensation claims
- increased organization attractiveness
- flexibility
- profits

667

Costs:

- death
- injury
- disease
- absenteeism
- less involvement
- lower quality

Safety and health costs are caused by:

- occupational accidents
- occupational disease
- stress
- low quality of working life

can result in (1) more productivity due to fewer lost workdays, (2) increased efficiency from a more committed work force, (3) reduced medical and insurance costs, (4) lower workers' compensation rates and direct payments because fewer claims are filed, (5) greater flexibility and adaptability in the work force as a result of increased participation and an increased sense of ownership, and (6) better selection ratios because of the enhanced image of the organization.[5] Companies can thus increase their profits substantially.

THE COSTS OF AN UNSAFE AND UNHEALTHY WORK ENVIRONMENT

Back injuries are the most prevalent of all workplace injuries. Every year an estimated 10 million employees in the United States encounter back pain that impairs their job performance. Approximately 1 million employees file workers' compensation claims for back injuries. Billions of dollars are spent each year to treat back pain—$5 billion in workers' compensation payments alone.[6]

Estimates of workplace deaths range from 2,800 (Bureau of Labor Statistics) to around 10,000 yearly (National Safety Council). In either case, the numbers are significant. Nevertheless,

> Business contends that its health and safety record is much better than generally perceived and has improved over the years. Workplace-related deaths dropped from 18 per 100,000 employees in 1970 to 9 per 100,000 in 1990, according to government records.
>
> When the fact that homicide is the leading cause of workplace deaths, and nearly one-third of all occupational fatalities are the result of car and truck crashes is accounted for, the safety record gets even better.[7]

Of course, there are differences in these rates depending on job type, and sometimes even on the state. For example, the accidental rate for 100,000 workers in the United States is 7, but for the workers in Alaska's fishing industry, it is nearly 100 times this figure![8]

> Construction is one of the most dangerous jobs in America, placing workers in a constantly changing raw environment where one misstep or forgetful moment can snuff out a life or crush a limb. Pressures to finish a job quickly often push foremen and workers to take risks, industry experts say, amid a macho culture of muscle, sweat, and swagger that tends to belittle safety measures and confuse caution with timidity.
>
> The new push for safety, the experts say, is being led by large companies forced by the recession to try to save money and become more competitive by taking advantage of revised insurance industry policies that reward good safety records.
>
> "When companies understand that safety saves them money and increases productivity, they become believers," says Mr. Steven Thies, corporate safety manager for Henkels & McCoy, a 5,000-worker utility construction company based in Blue Bell, Pennsylvania.[9]

Construction, along with mining and agriculture, are typically the three most dangerous industries nationwide with deaths per 100,000 employees yearly being around 32, 43, and 40, respectively!

While it is impossible to obtain precise information, the costs of workplace deaths and injuries are estimated to be more than $50 billion. Similar cost estimates are made for the more than 100,000 workers who annually succumb to occupational diseases. In addition to the costs of the physical/physiological conditions are the enormous costs associated with the psychological conditions that include organizational stress and a low quality of working life. For example, alcoholism, often the result of attempts to cope with job pressures, costs organizations and society over $65 billion annually. Of this, $20 billion is attributed to lost productivity and the remainder to the direct costs of insurance, hospitalization, and other medical costs.[10] Perhaps more difficult to quantify, but just as symptomatic of stress and poor quality of working life, are workers' feelings of lack of meaning and involvement in their work and loss of importance as individuals.

A MODEL OF OCCUPATIONAL SAFETY AND HEALTH

The *sources* of safety and health conditions in organizations can be labeled as workplace environment hazards; these are comprised of two components: the **physical work environment** and the **sociopsychological work environment**. Together, these sources, the physical/physiological and psychological conditions, and their outcomes constitute a model of occupational health and safety in organizations (Exhibit 19.1). But before we discuss the model, we need to have an understanding of the legal context in which organizations must frame their solutions to occupational safety and health problems.

LEARNING OBJECTIVE 2

Explain the model of occupational safety and health.

Components of the model:
- sources
- conditions
- outcomes

LEGAL CONSIDERATIONS

There are four major categories into which the legal framework for occupational safety and health can be divided: the **Occupational Safety and Health Administration (OSHA)**, workers' compensation programs, the common-law doctrine of torts, and local initiatives.

LEARNING OBJECTIVE 3

Discuss the legal considerations.

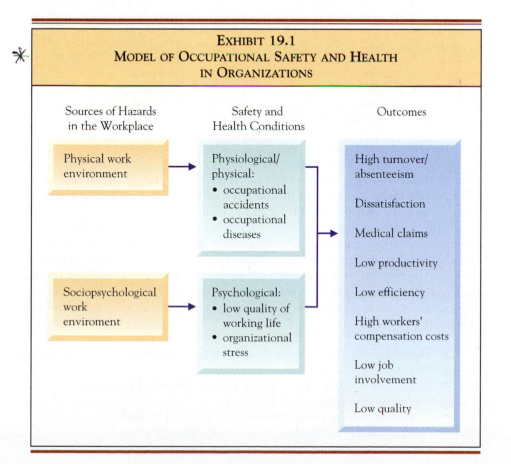

EXHIBIT 19.1
MODEL OF OCCUPATIONAL SAFETY AND HEALTH IN ORGANIZATIONS

Sources of Hazards in the Workplace	Safety and Health Conditions	Outcomes
Physical work environment	Physiological/physical: • occupational accidents • occupational diseases	High turnover/absenteeism Dissatisfaction Medical claims Low productivity Low efficiency High workers' compensation costs Low job involvement Low quality
Sociopsychological work enviroment	Psychological: • low quality of working life • organizational stress	

OSHA is the major federal agency
watching out for occupational health
and safety.

OSHA requires organizations to:
- allow inspection
- keep records
- disclose medical records

THE OCCUPATIONAL SAFETY AND HEALTH ADMINISTRATION (OSHA)

The federal government's primary response to the issue of safety and health in the workplace has been the *Occupational Safety and Health Act of 1970*, which created OSHA and which calls for safety and health inspectors of organizations regardless of size, reporting by employers, and investigations of accidents and allegations of hazards. The other two organizations are the **National Institute for Occupational Safety and Health (NIOSH)** and the Occupational Safety and Health Review Commission. The commission reviews appeals made by organizations that received citations from OSHA inspectors for alleged safety and health violations.[11] OSHA is responsible for establishing and enforcing occupational safety and health standards and for inspecting and issuing citations to organizations that violate these standards.

Regardless of whether organizations are inspected, they are required to keep safety and health records so that OSHA can compile accurate statistics on work injuries and illnesses. These include all disabling, serious, or significant injuries and illnesses, whether or not they involve loss of time from work. Excluded are minor injuries that require only first aid treatment and do not involve medical treatment, loss of consciousness, restriction of work or motion, or transfer to another job. Falsification of records or failure to keep adequate records can result in some rather substantial fines. The record keeping requirement was recently qualified, however:

> An employer may withhold injury and illness records from federal safety investigators if it has a legitimate need to keep the records private, and the Occupational Safety and Health Administration has failed to obtain a warrant granting it access to such documents, the Occupational Safety and Health Review Commission (OSHRC) rules. Rejecting the principle that OSHA compliance officers have unlimited rights to make warrantless examinations of an employer's records, the commission holds that the employer had a reasonable expectation of privacy in safeguarding the information in its injury records. Such documents, OSHRC points out, may contain proprietary information on operations and manufacturing processes that employers may want to keep confidential. (*Kings Island Division of Taft Broadcasting Co.*, 1987)[12]

Employees have a right to know about
their work environment.

In addition to keeping records, the *Access to Employee Exposure and Medical Records Regulation of 1980* requires organizations to show or give to employees, their designated representatives, and OSHA, their on-the-job medical records. This regulation also requires employers to provide access to records of measurements of employee exposure to toxic substances.

The employee's right to know has been further strengthened by the *Hazard Communication Standard* that went into effect in 1986.[13] Under this standard, employers are required to provide workers with information and training on hazardous chemicals in their work area at the time of their initial assignment and whenever a new hazard is introduced. According to OSHA, effective communication is the real key and should include information for employees on the following:

- The standard's requirements and operations in the workplace that use hazardous chemicals
- Proper procedures for determining the presence of chemicals and detecting hazardous releases
- Protective measures and equipment that should be used
- Location of the written hazard communication programs[14]

Whereas OSHA was established to provide workers protection against accidents and diseases, workers' compensation was established to provide financial aid for those unable to work because of accidents and diseases as described in Chapter 13, Indirect Compensation.[15]

WORKERS' COMPENSATION PROGRAMS

For many years, workers' compensation awards were granted only to workers unable to work because of physical injury or damage (that is, due to accidents and diseases). Since 1955, however, court decisions have either caused or enticed fifteen states to allow workers' compensation payment in job-related cases of anxiety, depression, and mental disorders.[16]

That year, the Texas Supreme Court charted this new direction in workers' compensation claims by stating that an employee who became terrified, highly anxious and unable to work because of a job-related accident had a compensable claim even though he had no physical injury (*Bailey v. American General Insurance Company*, 1955). In another court ruling (*James v. State Accident Insurance Fund*, 1980), an Oregon court ruled in favor of a worker's claim for compensation for inability to work due to job stress resulting from conflicting work assignments.[17]

THE COMMON-LAW DOCTRINE OF TORTS

Much of the legal consideration discussion we have had in this book is based upon statutory law, that is, laws passed by legislative bodies at the federal and state levels. For example, the *Civil Rights Act of 1991* and the *Americans with Disabilities Act of 1990* and *Occupational Safety and Health Act of 1970* are statutory law. But there is also the common-law doctrine of torts. This refers to decisions made in court cases regarding wrongful acts such as personal injuries committed by an employee on another employee or even customer which results in a lawsuit against the employer. Employees can obtain damage awards by suing employers. However, employees must demonstrate that the employer engaged in reckless or intentional infliction designed to degrade or humiliate. A few such cases have been successfully brought against employers, but they appear to be the exception, in part because workers' compensation programs were designed to remove workplace accidents and injury from litigation.[18] However, the cases successfully brought against employers are notable because of the costs involved. Some notable cases are detailed in the feature, "Managing Human Resources and Workplace Torts: Who's Responsible?"

A *tort* is a wrongful injury or act for which a civil action, like a lawsuit, can be brought.

LOCAL INITIATIVES

State, municipal, and city governments may pass their own safety and health laws and regulations that go beyond the coverage of OSHA. Consequently, employers need to be aware of local regulations. Sometimes these local initiatives offer a glimpse as to what other areas or even the federal government might do in the future. This seems to be the case with the law passed in San Francisco imposing safeguards on workers using video display terminals. The law requires the use of adjustable chairs and tables, angle-adjustable screens and keyboards, work time at tasks away from the computer, training of workers and supervisors, and the use of printer covers to reduce office noise. The local labor unions heralded the San Francisco law as a model for other cities and municipalities.

AMERICANS WITH DISABILITIES ACT (ADA)

As defined in Chapter 8, Selection and Placement, the ADA applies to disabled individuals; this covers applicants for jobs and treatment of current employees,

The ADA has applications here just as it does in job design, selection, training, employee rights, and compensation.

MANAGING HUMAN RESOURCES
and Workplace Torts

Who's Responsible?

EMPLOYERS may be held liable for the negligent acts of employees committed within the scope of their employment. On this basis, employers are paying huge damages claims in lawsuits for negligent hiring, retention, and supervision, say Ronald Green and Richard Rubenstein, authors of a new book on workplace torts (wrongful acts for which a civil action can be brought).

CASES IN POINT

Recent years have seen a proliferation of lawsuits against employers resulting from employees' illegal acts. Litigation is often the resort of individuals injured or damaged by incompetent, unsafe, or dangerous employees. Some employees should not have been hired initially or retained once their dangerous proclivities were discovered, the authors conclude. Cases that illustrate this point include:

- *Incompetent employees.* A retired police officer with no medical training and cataracts was hired by a hospital to coordinate its kidney transport unit. A patient was given a transplant of a cancerous kidney, causing the death of the patient. The donor's medical chart revealed that the kidney was cancerous. A $3.5 million suit was settled by the hospital for the negligent hiring of the kidney transport coordinator, who was unskilled in reading medical charts and unable to read in any event due to his cataracts. (*Kolator v. State*, 1988)
- *Unsafe employees.* An airline passenger was arguing with a boarding agent and grabbed his arm. The agent kicked the passenger in the shins and bit her hand. On request, the airline tested the agent for AIDS, and the test was positive. The passenger then charged the airline with negligent hiring, seeking $12 million in damages. The case is pending in federal court. (*Doe v. American Airlines*, 1986)
- *Dangerous employees.* A supermarket providing home delivery hired an applicant after a 20-minute job interview. While making a delivery on his fourth day of employment, he raped and robbed a customer in her home. The court ruled that when a firm provides delivery services, it has a duty to its customers to employ safe help. In this case, since the personnel director conducted "a cursory" interview and failed to check employment references, a jury could infer that the supermarket failed to exercise due care and caution. The negligent hiring suit reportedly was settled for a six-figure amount. (*Rosen-House v. Sloan's Supermarket*, 1988)
- *Violent employees.* After a customer in a car rental office argued with the rental agent, the employee struck him with a blow to the head, knocking him to the floor. As the customer lay on the floor, the employee repeatedly kicked him and pummeled him with "judo chops." In the customer's civil action for negligent retention, the evidence showed that the employee had a history of blowing up at and threatening customers. Moreover, the rental company had not disciplined the employee either before or after the incident. A jury awarded the customer $350,000 in compensatory damages and $400,000 in punitive damages. (*Greenfield v. Spectrum Inv. Group*, 1985)

PREVENTIVE MEASURES

Employers can minimize their exposure to negligent hiring claims by conducting thorough reference checks and background investigations of job applicants. For example, employers should ask applicants for explanations of gaps in employment history. Other steps employers should take include:

- Tailor investigations to the job sought.
- Have the applicant sign a release form allowing job-related information to be obtained from former employers.
- Check as many of the applicant's employment and personal records as possible. Do not make a formal job offer until all inquiries are completed.

Continued on the next page

including layoff and discharge. Here is where the relationship between the ADA and occupational health and safety kick in: employee layoffs and discharges (terminations) are constituting 50 percent of all claims filed under the ADA. And 15 percent of these are for back pain. Because victims are entitled to sue for up to $300,000, lots of employers are tempted to settle before going to trial.[20] Organizations are therefore actively seeking ways to remove hazardous conditions from the work environment.

HAZARDS IN OCCUPATIONAL SAFETY AND HEALTH

As Exhibit 19.1 shows, both the physical and the sociopsychological aspects of the workplace environment are important components of occupational safety and health. Each aspect impacts health and safety. Traditionally, hazards in the physical environment have received greater attention. Increasingly, however, both OSHA and companies themselves admit that sociopsychological conditions greatly impact health and safety, and they are doing something about it. For example, in combating stress and its symptoms:

> … at Hoffman-LaRoche Inc., the Nutley, New Jersey–based subsidiary of the Swiss pharmaceutical concern, employees receive after-hours instruction in a variety of stress management methods. They include meditation, breathing exercises, and a technique called "dot stopping." A form of biofeedback, the technique teaches employees to control their stress by recalling a wonderful moment and focusing on the feelings and sensations they had then.[21]

Today efforts to improve occupational safety and health are not complete without a strategy for reducing psychological work-related stress. Developing effective strategies begins with an understanding of the factors in the workplace environment that affect these two aspects of safety and health.

OCCUPATIONAL ACCIDENTS

Certain organizations, and certain departments within an organization, always have higher occupational accident rates than others. Several factors can explain this difference.

ORGANIZATIONAL QUALITIES. Accident rates vary substantially by industry. For example, firms in the construction and manufacturing industries have higher incidence rates than firms in services, finance, insurance, and real estate. When employees believe this, they tend to think things just can't be changed. According to Donald Brush, vice president and general manager at the Barden Corporation, Danbury, Connecticut:

Factors affecting occupational accidents are

- organizational qualities
- safety programs
- employees

673

Over the years, Barden employees assumed that, because we are a metal working shop, people were just going to get hurt. Several years ago, we created a Safety and Health Committee that meets monthly to consider our safety and health performance and to effect improvements. More recently, we created a Safety Development Committee whose members included a line superintendent as chairman, the safety engineer, the plant chemist, the occupational health nurse, and the training coordinator—a nice mix of line, staff, and human resource representation. This committee reports to the Safety and Health Committee. Its objective is to develop programs that strengthen safety awareness and performance. While it is too early to prepare a report card, early indications are that results will be favorably impressive. At about the same time, it became clear that the safety engineer was not producing the same results we wanted. After weighing the facts, we created something new and promising. We eliminated the safety engineering position as such and transferred its accountabilities to the Medical Department. The occupational health nurse had previously shown considerable knowledge about safety matters, and her aggressive investigation of accidents and near-misses prompted us to create a new position encompassing both the safety and the medical functions. The occupational health nurse has thus been promoted to a new position entitled Manager of Employee Health and Safety. We believe that this position is unique for a small company, and we are optimistic about results.[22]

Interestingly, small and large organizations (those with fewer than a hundred employees or more than a thousand) have lower incidence rates than medium-sized organizations. This may be because supervisors in small organizations are better able to detect safety hazards and prevent accidents than those in medium-size ones. And larger organizations have more resources to hire staff specialists who can devote all their efforts to safety and accident prevention.

In general, however, it is the working conditions (outdoors versus indoors), and the tools and technology available to do the job (for example, heavy machinery versus personal computers) that most impact **occupational accidents**. Next in line are the workers themselves.

THE UNSAFE EMPLOYEE? Although organizational factors certainly play an important role in occupational safety, some experts point to the employee as the pivotal cause of accidents. Accidents depend on the behavior of the person, the degree of hazard in the work environment, and pure chance. The degree to which the person contributes to the accident can be an indication of an individual's proneness to accidents. Accident proneness cannot be considered a stable set of personal traits that always contribute to accidents. Nevertheless, certain psychological and physical characteristics seem to make some people more susceptible to accidents.

For example, employees who are emotionally "low" have more accidents that those who are emotionally "high," while employees who have had fewer accidents have been found to be more optimistic, trusting, and concerned for others than those who have had more accidents. Employees under greater stress are likely to have more accidents than those with poorer vision. Older workers are likely to be hurt less than younger workers. People who are quicker at recognizing visual patterns than at making muscular manipulations are less likely to have accidents than those who are just the opposite. Many psychological conditions probably related to accident proneness—for instance, hostility and emotional immaturity—may be temporary states. Thus they are difficult to detect until at least one accident has occurred. Because none of these characteristics is related to accidents in all work environments and because they are not always present in employees, selecting and screening job applicants on the basis of accident proneness is difficult.

Sometimes accidents occur because of the employees' behaviors. Refer to "Managing Human Resources and Workplace Torts: Who's Responsible?")

THE VIOLENT EMPLOYEE?   Workplace violence is growing rapidly and employers are being held responsible, as described in the feature "Managing Human Resource and Workplace Torts: Who's Responsible?" Death by homicide is the biggest cause of death in the workplace today.[23] While it may be difficult to identify the violent employee before the fact, there are some common signs that employers are urged to be on the lookout for. These are described in the feature "HR Advice and Application: The Violent Employee—Warning Signs."

OCCUPATIONAL DISEASES

Potential sources of work-related diseases are as distressingly varied as their symptoms. Several federal agencies have systematically studied the workplace environment, and they have identified the following hazards: arsenic, asbestos, benzene, bichloromethylether, coal dust, coke-oven emissions, cotton dust, lead, radiation, and vinyl chloride. Workers likely to be exposed to those hazards include chemical and oil refinery workers, miners, textile workers, steelworkers, lead-smelters, medical technicians, painters, shoemakers, and plastics-industry workers.

The long-term consequences of these hazards have been linked to thyroid, liver, lung, brain, and kidney cancer; white, brown, and black lung disease; leukemia; bronchitis; emphysema; lymphoma; aplastic anemia; central nervous system damage; and reproductive disorders (for example, sterility, genetic damage, abortions, and birth defects). Continued research will no doubt uncover additional hazards that firms will want to diagnose and remedy for the future well-being of their work forces.[25]

CATEGORIES OF OCCUPATIONAL DISEASES.   A major category of **occupational disease** involves illnesses of the respiratory system. Chronic bronchitis and emphysema are among the fastest growing diseases in the country, doubling every five years since World War II; they account for the second highest number of disabilities under Social Security.[26] Cancer, however, tends to receive the most

> There are numerous qualities of the work environment that cause disease, both over the short term and over the long term.

HR ADVICE AND APPLICATION

THE VIOLENT EMPLOYEE— WARNING SIGNS

If any of the following warning signs are present, employers should consult resource specialists to determine whether monitoring is sufficient or whether immediate action is warranted. Possible resources include a company physician, an employee assistance provider, law enforcement officials, an attorney, or a violence-assessment specialist.

- _Verbal threats_. Individuals often talk about what they may do. An employee might say, "Bad things are going to happen to so-and-so," or "That propane tank in the back could blow up easily."

- _Physical actions_. Troubled employees may try to intimidate others, gain access to places they do not belong, or flash a concealed weapon in the workplace to test reactions.
- _Frustration._ Most cases do not involve a panicked individual who perceives the world as falling apart. A more likely scenario involves an employee who has a frustrated sense of entitlement to a promotion, for example.
- _Obsession._ An employee may hold a grudge against a co-worker or supervisor, and some cases stem from romantic interest.[24]

attention, since it is a leading cause of death in the United States (second after heart disease). Many of the known causes of cancer are physical and chemical agents in the environment. And because these agents are theoretically more controllable than human behavior, OSHA's emphasis is on eliminating them from the workplace.

OSHA's emphasis on health is not aimed solely at eliminating cancer and respiratory diseases, however. OSHA is also concerned with the following categories of occupational diseases and illnesses: (1) occupation-related skin diseases and disorders, (2) dust diseases of the lungs, (3) respiratory conditions due to toxic agents, (4) poisoning (systematic effects of toxic-materials), (5) disorders due to physical agents, (6) disorders associated with repeated trauma, and (7) all other occupational illnesses.[27] OSHA requires employers to keep records on all of these diseases.

OCCUPATIONAL GROUPS AT RISK.   Miners, construction and transportation workers, and blue-collar and lower-level supervisory personnel in manufacturing industries experience the bulk of both occupational disease and injury. The least safe occupations are mining, agriculture, and construction. In addition, large numbers of petrochemical and oil refinery workers, dye workers, dye users, textile workers, plastic-industry workers, painters, and industrial chemical workers are also particularly susceptible to some of the most dangerous health hazards. Interestingly, skin diseases are the most common of all reported occupational diseases, with leather workers being the group most affected.

Of course, occupational diseases are not exclusive to the blue-collar workers and manufacturing industries. The "cushy office job" has evolved into a veritable nightmare of physical and psychological ills for white-collar workers in the expanding service industries. Among the common ailments are varicose veins, bad backs, deteriorating eyesight, migraine headaches, hypertension, coronary heart disorders, and respiratory and digestive problems. The causes of these in an office environment include the following:

There are many hazardous conditions in the office environment.

- Too much noise
- Interior air pollutants such as cigarette smoke and chemical fumes—for example, from the copy machine
- Uncomfortable chairs
- Poor office design
- New office technology such as video display terminals[28]

In addition, dentists are routinely exposed to radiation, mercury, and anesthetics, and cosmetologists suffer from high rates of cancer and respiratory and cardiac diseases connected with their frequent use of chemicals.

WHEN THE QUALITY OF WORKING LIFE IS LOW

For many workers, a **low quality of working life** is associated with workplace conditions that fail to satisfy important preferences and interests such as a sense of responsibility, challenge, meaningfulness, self-control, recognition, achievement, fairness or justice, security, and certainty.[29] Organizational structures that contribute to a low quality of working life include:

- Jobs with low task significance, variety, identity, autonomy, feedback, and qualitative underload (Refer to these in Chapter 5)
- Minimal involvement of employees in decision making and a great deal of one-way communication with employees
- Pay systems not based on performance or based on performance not objectively measured or under employee control

- Supervisors, job descriptions, and organizational policies that fail to convey to the employee what is expected and what is rewarded
- Human resource policies and practices that are discriminatory and of low validity
- Temporary employment conditions where employees are dismissed at will (employee rights do not exist)

Many conditions in organizations are associated with a low quality of working life. The same is true of organizational stress. Remember, however, that a condition causing stress or low quality of working life for one individual may not cause it in another individual because of differences in preferences, interests, and perceptions of uncertainty in the environment.

ORGANIZATIONAL STRESS

Prevalent forms of **organizational stress** include the four S's. Other major factors include change, work pace, the physical environment, and job burnout. With these factors or sources of stress we extend the discussion of career stress in Chapter 4, where three classes of symptoms were presented: physiological, psychological, and behavioral.

THE FOUR S'S. Common stressors for many employees include the following: (1) supervisor, (2) salary, (3) security, and (4) safety.[30] Petty work rules and relentless pressure for more production are major stressors that employees associate with supervisors. Both deny worker needs to control the work situation and to be recognized and accepted.

Salary is a stressor when it is perceived as being distributed unfairly. Many blue-collar workers feel they are underpaid relative to their white-collar counterparts in the office. Teachers think they are underpaid relative to people with similar education who work in private industry.

Employees experience stress when they are not sure whether they will have their jobs next month, next week, or even the next day. For many employees, lack of job security is even more stressful than holding jobs that are generally unsafe. At least the employees know the job risks, whereas the lack of job security creates a continued state of uncertainty.

Fear of workplace accidents and the resulting injuries or death can be stressful for many workers. When pressure for production is increased, this fear over workplace safety can increase to a point that production may decrease rather than increase. This result, in turn, may lead to a vicious cycle that is counterproductive for the workers and the organization.

ORGANIZATIONAL CHANGE. Changes made by organizations are often stressful, because they usually involve something important and are accompanied by uncertainty. Many changes are made without advance warning. Although rumors often circulate that a change is coming, the exact nature of the change is left to speculation. People become concerned about whether the change will affect them, perhaps by displacing them or by causing them to be transferred. The result is that the uncertainty surrounding a change yet to come causes many employees to suffer stress symptoms.

WORK PACING. **Work pacing**, particularly who or what controls the pace of the work, is an important potential stressor in organizations. **Machine pacing** gives control over the speed of the operation and the work output to something other than the individual. **Employee pacing** gives the individual control of the operations. The effects of maching pacing are severe, because the individual is

Four sources of organizational stress are

- **supervisor**
- **salary**
- **security**
- **safety**

The ability to control one's environment is a very important one.

unable to satisfy a crucial need for control of the situation. It has been reported that workers on machine-paced jobs feel exhausted at the end of the shift and are unable to relax soon after work because of increased adrenaline secretion on the job. In a study of 23 white- and blue-collar occupations, assembly workers reported the highest level of severe stress symptoms.

PHYSICAL ENVIRONMENT. Although office automation is a way to improve productivity, it has stress-related drawbacks. One aspect of office automation with a specific stress-related drawback is the video display terminal (VDT). Currently, the findings are not complete on just how serious an effect VDT screens have on workers, although countries such as Sweden and Norway have taken more steps to deal with VDTs than has the United States. Nevertheless, NIOSH is gathering data on VDTs. Other aspects of the work environment associated with stress are crowding, lack of privacy, and lack of control over aspects of the environment that the employee would like to change (for example, moving a desk or chairs or even hanging pictures in a work area in an effort to personalize it).

THE STRESS-PRONE EMPLOYEE? Yes, there are individual differences in how people respond to the conditions just described. A classic difference used in stress work is referred to as Type A or Type B behavior. Type A people like to do things their way and are willing to exert a lot of effort to ensure that even trivial tasks are performed in the manner they prefer. They often fail to distinguish between important and unimportant situations. They are upset, for instance, when they have to wait fifteen minutes to be seated in a restaurant, since this is not in compliance with their idea of responsive service. In short, the Type A person spends much of his or her time directing energy towards the noncompliances in the environment. Still, Type A people are "movers and shakers." They enjoy acting on their environment and enjoy modifying the behavior of other people. They are primarily rewarded by compliance and punished by noncompliance. Type B people, then, are generally much more tolerant. They are not easily frustrated, easily angered, nor do they expend a lot of energy in response to noncompliance. Type B people may be excellent supervisors to work for—that is, until you need them to push upward in the organization on your behalf. They probably would permit you and other subordinates a lot of freedom but also might not provide the types of upward support necessary for effective leadership.[31]

JOB BURNOUT. A special type of organizational stress is called **job burnout**. This condition happens when people work in situations in which they have little control over the quality of their performance but feel personally responsible for their success or lack of it. People most susceptible to burnout include police officers, nurses, social workers, and teachers. When people begin to show burnout, they reveal three symptoms: (1) emotional exhaustion, (2) depersonalization, and (3) a sense of low personal accomplishment. Since this condition benefits neither the individual nor the organization, many programs have been designed to help people deal with burnout.

Symptoms of burnout include:
* emotional exhaustion
* depersonalization
* sense of low accomplishment

LEARNING OBJECTIVE 5

Describe what organizations are doing and can do to improve occupational safety and health.

STRATEGIES FOR IMPROVEMENT

Once the cause of stress is identified, strategies can be developed for eliminating or reducing it (see Exhibit 19.2). To determine whether the strategy is effective, organizations can compare the incidence, severity, and frequency of ill-

EXHIBIT 19.2
SOURCES AND STRATEGIES FOR OCCUPATIONAL SAFETY AND HEALTH

SOURCE	STRATEGY
PHYSICAL WORK ENVIRONMENT	
Occupational accidents	Record the accident
	Redesign the work environment
	Set goals and objectives
	Establish safety committees
	Provide training and financial incentives
Occupational diseases	Record the disease
	Measure the work environment
	Communicate information
	Set goals and objectives
SOCIOPSYCHOLOGICAL WORK ENVIRONMENT	
Organizational stress	Establish organizational stress programs
	Establish individual stress programs

ness and accidents before and after the intervention. There are OSHA-approved methods for establishing safety and health rates; we will describe these first, and then we will present strategies for accident control and for reducing occupational disease and improving the sociopsychological work environment.

SAFETY AND HEALTH RATES

OSHA requires organizations to maintain records of the incidence of injuries and illnesses. Some organizations also record the frequency and severity of each.

INCIDENCE RATE. The most explicit index of industrial safety is the **incidence rate**. It is calculated by the following formula:

$$\text{Incidence rate} = \frac{\text{Number of injuries and illnesses} \times 200{,}000}{\text{Number of employee hours worked}}$$

200,000 is the base for 100 full-time workers (40 hours per week, 50 weeks). Suppose an organization had 10 recorded injuries and illnesses and 500 employees. To calculate the number of yearly hours worked, multiply the number of employees by 40 hours and by 50 work weeks: $500 \times 40 \times 50 = 1$ million. The incidence rate thus would be 2 per 100 workers per year.

SEVERITY RATE. The **severity rate** reflects the hours actually lost due to injury or illness. It recognizes that not all injuries and illnesses are equal. Four categories of injuries and illnesses have been established: deaths, permanent total disabilities, permanent partial disabilities, and temporary total disabilities. An organization with the same number of injuries and illnesses as another but with more deaths would have a higher severity rate. The severity rate is calculated by this formula:

Safety and health rates are described in terms of:

- incidence
- frequency
- severity

$$\text{Severity rate} = \frac{\text{Total hours charged} \times 1 \text{ million (hours)}}{\text{Number of employee hours worked}}$$

FREQUENCY RATE. The **frequency rate** reflects the number of injuries and illnesses per million hours worked rather than per year as in the incidence rate. It is calculated thus:

$$\text{Frequency rate} = \frac{\text{Number of injuries and illnesses} \times 1 \text{ million (hours)}}{\text{Number of employees hours worked}}$$

ACCIDENT CONTROL

Designing the work environment to make accidents unlikely is perhaps the best way to prevent accidents and increase safety. Among the safety features that can be designed into the physical environment are guards on machines, handrails in stairways, safety goggles and helmets, warning lights, self-correcting mechanisms, and automatic shutoffs. The extent to which these features will actually reduce accidents depends on employee acceptance and use. For example, eye injuries will be reduced by the availability of safety goggles only if employees wear the goggles correctly.

If employees are involved in the decision to make some physical change to improve safety, they are more likely to accept the decision than if they are not part of the decision-making process. Thus the safety programs most likely to succeed are those that have the greatest support of all the employees. These programs are the ones likely to be the most thorough. An example of such a program is described in the feature "Managing Human Resources at American Building Maintenance Industries."

ERGONOMICS. Another way to improve safety is to make the job itself more comfortable and less fatiguing through ergonomics. Ergonomics considers changes in the job environment in conjunction with the physical and physiological capabilities and limitations of the employees.[33] See Chapter 5 for an extended discussion of ergonomics.

In an effort to reduce the number of back injuries, the Ford Motor Company redesigns work stations and tasks that may be causing musculoskeletal problems for workers. For instance, lifting devices are being introduced on the assembly line to reduce back strain, and walking and working surfaces are being studied to see if floor mats can reduce body fatigue. Videotapes that feature Ford employees performing their jobs both before and after ergonomic redesign are used in training.[34]

In an effort to reduce cumulative trauma disorders, Perdue Farms, a large poultry producer in Salisbury, Maryland, established an extensive ergonomics plan for several of its plants.

> Perdue Farms, Inc., paid $39,690 in penalties and instituted a comprehensive four-year program to reduce cumulative trauma disorders at its North Carolina poultry processing plants, under a settlement negotiated by the state's labor department [in 1991], Perdue, and seven worker representatives.
>
> As part of the pact, which came nearly a year-and-a-half after the state hit Perdue with precedent-setting citations for ergonomic hazards, the company agreed to issue a policy statement "demonstrating a personal concern for employee safety and health by placing a priority upon eliminating ergonomic hazards." Specifically, Perdue must investigate, study, and institute administrative controls intended to reduce exposure to ergonomic stress; implement a medical management program; and provide ergonomic awareness, training, and education. The agreement requires that a symptom survey be completed

---

Strategies for minimizing occupational accidents are

- environmental design
- ergonomics
- job redesign
- safety committees
- management by objectives
- behavior modification

MANAGING HUMAN RESOURCES
at American Building Maintenance Industries

AMERICAN Building Maintenance Industries, Inc., headquartered in San Francisco, emphasizes safety for its employees, who typically clean high-rise office buildings in downtown areas—and, to the company's credit, has shown that there's nothing more golden than the Golden Rule.

"When Texas revamped its workers' compensation law, we decided that it was time to do something—and I was given the assignment of increasing the emphasis on safety in the workplace," said Cheryl Johnstone, an HR manager at the American Building's Houston office. "It started out as just an additional responsibility, but as I've gotten involved, I've seen the value in safety. Safety is something that affects people on and off the job; it improves morale; it helps avoid injuries; it saves the company money."

Some of the safety activities that American Building Maintenance follows through on include the following:

- The company takes a constant hands-on approach toward safety.
- The company encourages a dialogue on safety all the time—being "professional without being unapproachable."
- Supervisors are required to make safety reports, and timeliness is emphasized. When an injury or problem occurs, detailed reports are required within 24 hours so that the situation can be checked out. Furthermore, supervisors know to have witnesses, pictures, and a description of what occurred. The emphasis is on fact-finding, not fault-finding.
- When a pattern of certain injuries in a particular location is revealed through report analysis (for example, back injuries may be occurring frequently at one building site), the company brings the supervisors in and reviews the safety measures they take. The company then reviews what the supervisor can do to improve safety in the area.

- The company sponsors a five-minute safety talk monthly at all locations. Posters are displayed, videos are shown and reviewed with supervisors. Emergencies are anticipated, and employees are trained to handle them (for example, in case of fire, put your nose where your belt is to breathe better air).
- Supervisors are responsible for safety, and support activities are offered the supervisors. The message is, "We're here to help you. You're important to us." Supervisors' safety records are part of their merit reviews; they are accounting for safety.
- Supervisors are responsible for training. They use training films and direct interaction to show employees the right way to do their jobs safely.
- Supervisors give employees five-minute safety talks every month, and employees must sign to show they've attended. Topics include vacation safety, lifting trash, wearing rubber gloves, handling cords, and handling hazardous materials safely. Employees are urged to read rating sheets on chemicals used, and every effort is made to see that chemicals are as safe as possible.
- Inspections are held to identify hazards. One gets so used to seeing something that it's ignored. Sometimes it takes fresh eyes to see danger. For example, extension cords or newspapers stacking up.
- Although the company wants to help employees in case of injury, it will not accept assertions blindly. Many employees do not have health insurance. Supervisors are typically in the area where the time clock is located to greet employees after the weekend and to observe the state of employees' health. This helps avoid abuse.
- When an accident happens, the company uses several clinics. One has a Spanish-speaking doctor, and since many employees are Hispanic, this has been helpful.

Continued on the next page

- The company will call doctors to question something. Vigilance is the key.
- The company sends get-well cards to injured employees, giving them information on who to call in the office if there are questions or problems.
- The company tries to get employees back to work as soon as possible. Employees are usually unskilled and working at minimum wage—their income depends on their job. Each supervisor has a list of of light-duty assignments, and supervisors share ideas on these types of jobs. Some have the employees walk floors, checking cords, for example, or checking for carpet stains.
- Although the company has not ruled out incentive programs, it has not sponsored any. Recognition is given, not material gifts, so that problems with reporting can be avoided and safety—not the prize—is the focal point.[32]

by all plant employees annually, and that Perdue hire an ergonomics expert for the life of the pact.

Additionally, the ergonomics program includes:

- An employee complaint or suggestion procedure allowing workers to express their concerns without fear of reprisal.
- A procedure for encouraging prompt and accurate reporting of signs and symptoms of cumulative trauma disorder.
- Safety and health committees, with employee members randomly selected, which will recommend corrective action.
- Ergonomic teams with the necessary skills to identify and analyze jobs for ergonomic stress and recommend solutions.[35]

SAFETY COMMITTEES. Another strategy for accident prevention is the use of **safety committees**. The HR department can serve as the coordinator of a committee composed of several employee representatives. Where unions exist, the committees should have union representation as well. Often organizations have several safety committees at the department level for implementation and administration purposes and one larger committee at the organizational level for policy formulation.

The HR department, as in ACI America, can be instrumental in accident prevention by assisting supervisors in their training efforts and by implementing safety motivation programs such as contests and in-house communications. Many organizations display signs indicating the number of days or hours worked without an accident. Many organizations display posters saying "Safety First." In safety contests, prizes or awards are given to individuals or departments with the best safety record. These programs seem to work best when employees are already safety conscious and when physical conditions of the work environment pose no extreme hazards.

BEHAVIOR MODIFICATION. Reinforcing behaviors that reduce the likelihood of accidents can be highly successful. Reinforcers can range from nonmonetary reinforcers, such as feedback, to activity reinforcers, such as time off, to material reinforcers, such as company-purchased doughnuts during the coffee break, to financial rewards for attaining desired levels of safety.

The behavioral approach relies on measuring performance before and after the intervention, specifying and communicating the desired performance to employees, monitoring performance at unannounced intervals several times a

Safety committees produce:
- good ideas
- involvement
- control
- sense of ownership

682

week, and reinforcing desired behavior several times a week with performance feedback.

A good example of an effective behavior modification program was conducted in two food processing plants. Behavior was monitored for 25 weeks—before, during, and after a safety training program. Slides were used to illustrate safe and unsafe behavior. Employees were also given data on the percentage of safe behaviors in their departments. A goal of 90 percent safe behaviors was established. Supervisors were trained to give positive reinforcement when they observed safe behavior. Following the intervention, the incidence of safe behavior increased substantially—from an average of 70 percent to more than 95 percent in the wrapping department and from 78 percent to more than 95 percent in the make-up department. One year after the program, the incidence of lost-time injuries per million hours worked was fewer than 10, a substantial decline from the preceding year's rate of 53.8.[36]

MANAGEMENT BY OBJECTIVES PROGRAMS. Behavior modification programs are often linked successfully to management by objectives programs that deal with occupational health. The seven basic steps of these programs are as follows:

1. Identify hazards and obtain information about the frequency of accidents.
2. Based on this information, evaluate the severity and risk of the hazards.
3. Formulate and implement programs to control, prevent, or reduce the possibility of accidents.
4. Set specific, difficult, but attainable goals regarding the reduction of accidents or safety problems.
5. Consistently monitor results.
6. Provide positive feedback for correct safety procedures.
7. Monitor and evaluate the program against the goals.[37]

REDUCING OCCUPATIONAL DISEASES

By far more costly and harmful overall to organizations and employees than occupational accidents are occupational diseases. Because the causal relationship between the physical environment and occupational diseases is often subtle, developing strategies to reduce their incidence is generally difficult.

RECORD KEEPING. At a minimum, OSHA requires that organizations measure the chemicals in the work environment and keep records on these measurements. Their records must also include precise information about ailments and exposures. Such information must be kept for as long a period as is associated with the incubation period of the specific disease—even as long as 40 years. If the organization is sold, the new owner must assume responsibility for storing the old records and continuing to gather the required data. If the organization goes out of business, the administrative director of OSHA must be informed of the whereabouts of the records. Guidelines for record keeping are given in Exhibit 19.3.

COMMUNICATING HEALTH AND SAFETY INFORMATION. In addition to keeping records, the *Access to Employee Exposure and Medical Records* (AEEMR) regulation of 1980 requires organizations to show or give to employees, their designated representatives, and OSHA their on-the-job medical records of measurements of employee exposure to toxic substances. The employee's right to know has been further strengthened by the *Hazard Communication Standard* that went into effect in 1986. This law requires that employees be trained prior to job

Strategies for reducing occupational diseases:

- record keeping
- communications
- monitoring
- screening

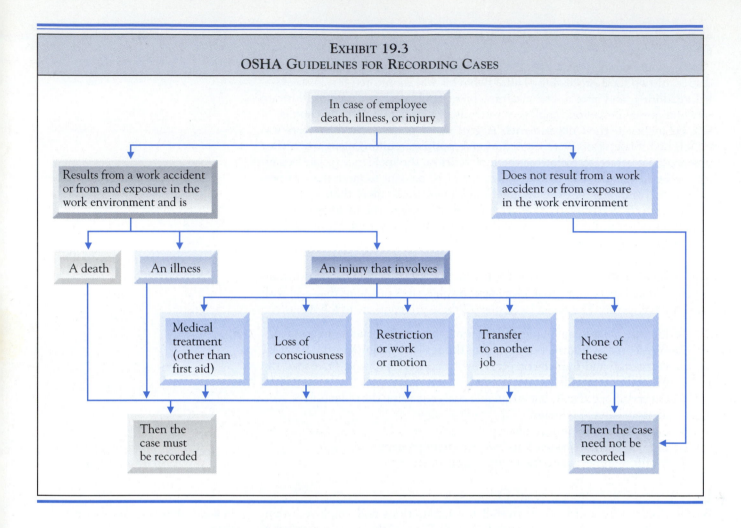

EXHIBIT 19.3
OSHA GUIDELINES FOR RECORDING CASES

In case of employee death, illness, or injury

Results from a work accident or from and exposure in the work environment and is

Does not result from a work accident or from exposure in the work environment

A death

An illness

An injury that involves

Medical treatment (other than first aid)

Loss of consciousness

Restriction or work or motion

Transfer to another job

None of these

Then the case must be recorded

Then the case need not be recorded

assignment and retrained any time a new hazard is introduced into the work environment.

MONITORING EXPOSURE. While the obvious approach to controlling occupational illnesses is to rid the workplace of chemical agents or toxins, an alternative approach is to monitor and limit exposure to hazardous substances. For example, the nuclear industry recruits hundreds of "jumpers" who fix the aging innards of the nation's nuclear generating stations. The atmosphere is so radioactive that jumpers can stay in only about ten minutes before they "burn out." Their exposure has to be closely monitored to ensure that it does not exceed more than 5,000 millirems (roughly 250 chest X-rays) annually.

Unfortunately, jumpers get rewarded for absorbing the maximum rather than a safe limit of radiation on any given job. Rather than twelve hours of pay for their ten minutes of work, jumpers get a bonus of several hundred dollars each time they "burn out" between jobs. Even with monitoring, it is estimated that 3–8 out of every 10,000 jumpers will eventually die as a result of the exposure.[38]

In addition to monitoring for radioactivity, some organizations now monitor genetic changes due to exposure to carcinogens (for example, benzene, arsenic, ether, and vinyl chloride). Samples of blood are obtained from employees at fixed intervals to determine whether the employee's chromosomes have been damaged. If damage has occurred, the employee is placed into a different job.

GENETIC SCREENING. Genetic screening is the most extreme, and consequently the most controversial, approach to controlling occupational disease. As noted in Chapter 8, the genetic makeup of individuals may make them more or less predisposed to specific occupational diseases. By genetically screening out individuals who are susceptible to certain ailments, organizations lower their vulnerability to workers' compensation claims and problems. Opponents of genetic screening contend that genetic screening measures one's predisposition to disease, not the actual presence of disease; therefore, such testing violates an individual's rights.[39]

WORK ENVIRONMENT

Increasingly, organizations are offering training programs designed to help employees deal with work-related stress. For example, J. P. Morgan offers stress management programs as part of a larger supervisory and management development curriculum. Offered to supervisors, professional staff, and officers, these courses provide supervisory and management material, specific technical supervisory/management information skills, and a developmental program designed to give experienced nonofficer managers and professionals some perspective on their roles within the bank. The emphasis here is on providing workers with concrete information to reduce the ambiguity associated with fast-paced, rapidly changing work roles.[40] Other potential remedies for workplace stress are described in the feature, "HR Advice and Application: Solutions to Workplace Stress."

Organizations can offer many activities or programs to improve physical and sociopsychological work conditions. Selecting the most appropriate activity should be based on a thorough analysis of existing safety and health hazards. It also depends on an assessment of past activities and strategies used by other organizations.

INDIVIDUAL STRESS MANAGEMENT STRATEGIES. Time management can be an effective individual strategy to deal with organizational stress. It is based in large part on an initial identification of an individual's personal goals. Other strategies that should be part of individual stress management include good diets, regular exercise, monitoring physical health, and building social support groups. Many large organizations such as Xerox encourage employees to enroll in regular exercise programs where their fitness and health are carefully monitored.[42]

Family-friendly companies help reduce stress too.

INTERNATIONAL SAFETY AND HEALTH ISSUES

LEARNING OBJECTIVE 6

Describe some safety and health issues in other countries.

As consciousness of health and well-being has risen worldwide, pressures to improve health care in work environments have increased in some countries. In other countries, however, health hazards are still ignored; by having lax safety standards, developing countries can lure large multinational firms to their shores.

CLOSER MONITORING OF FOREIGN FIRMS

Following the leakage of lethal methyl isocyanate gas at Union Carbide's pesticide plant in Bhopal, India in 1986, which killed more than 2,000 people, India formed committees in every state to identify potential hazards in factories. While foreign investments and technology are still welcome, the government now insists on knowing more about potential risks as well as identified existing risks. New regulations in India require environmental impact studies for all new plants.[43]

SOLUTIONS TO WORKPLACE STRESS

When stress invades the workplace, both employers and employees pay dearly. For employers, the costs include high turnover, stress-related health claims, and reduced productivity. For employees, stress takes its toll on health and well-being, work performance, and morale.

STRESS EFFECTS

Four in ten American workers say their jobs are "very" or "extremely" stressful, while 39 percent say they often think about quitting their job, according to a survey of 1,299 employees by Northwestern National Life Insurance Company (NWNL). Half of the surveyed employees say job stress reduces their productivity, and a third say they experience frequent stress-related illnesses. Of employees who say they have high-stress jobs, 65 percent suffer from exhaustion, and 44 percent report headaches or migraines. Also, employees in high-stress jobs are nearly three times as likely to experience anxiety, ulcers, anger, or depression, the survey concludes.

Based on the survey findings, NWNL researchers suggest the following steps to reduce tension and stress in the workplace:

- *Allow employees to talk freely with one another.* Employees thrive in an atmosphere where they can consult with colleagues about work issues. Moreover, in organizations where employees talk freely with one another, productivity and problem solving are usually enhanced.
- *Reduce personal conflicts on the job.* Employers can reduce stress by training managers and employees on how to resolve conflicts through open communication, negotiation, and respect. Managers can minimize conflicts by treating employees fairly and clearly defining job expectations.
- *Give employees adequate control over how they do their work.* Employees take greater pride in their work, are more productive, and are better able to deal with stress if they have some control over how they perform their work. Managers who let employees make decisions create an atmosphere that reduces stress and increases job satisfaction.
- *Ensure adequate staffing and expense budgets.* Staff reductions and budget cuts usually increase stress in the long run. Overburdened employees frequently suffer high stress levels that cause lower productivity, illness, turnover, and accidents.
- *Talk openly with employees.* Open communication between management and employees reduces job stress and helps employees cope with the challenges of the workplace.
- *Support employees' efforts.* When employers show their support of employees' contributions to the organization, stress levels are significantly lower. Managers can show support by regularly asking employees how their work is going, listening to them, and addressing issues that are raised.
- *Provide competitive personal leave and vacation benefits.* Workers who have time to relax and recharge after working hard are less likely to develop stress-related illnesses.
- *Maintain current levels of employee benefits.* Workers' stress levels increase when their benefits are reduced. Employers should determine whether the savings from reduced benefits are worth the risk of employee burnout.
- *Reduce the amount of red tape for employees.* When employees must deal with too much bureaucracy, they become discouraged and demoralized. Employers should ensure that employees' time is not wasted on unnecessary procedures.
- *Recognize and reward employees for their accomplishments and contributions.* A pat on the back, public praise, or a bonus or raise can result in significant increases in employee morale and productivity.[41]

By comparison, some countries have had workers' compensation programs and monitoring systems for years. For example, in 1972, New Zealand introduced a no-fault insurance program that covers job injuries. That same year, Finland passed an accident insurance act making it possible to receive workers' compensation for muscular pain and tendonitis caused by one's work. In 1977, Sweden passed a law requiring employers to modify the work environment to meet the physical and psychological makeup of workers.

The response to health hazards has been quite different in Mexico. A disaster that killed more than 500 people and wounded thousands at Pemex, a state-owned gas monopoly in Mexico, has had no noticeable effect on regulations. This is a common situation in developing countries. These countries are often so in need of economic development that they may accept any industry—even those that have the potential for significant harm. This, of course, presents serious ethical questions for firms operating in the developing nations.

CURRENT TRENDS

Companies are combating rising costs stemming from work-related injuries and disease with occupational health policies and wellness programs. Both of these trends have, however, served to open up complex ethical issues.

Three major trends are
- health policies
- wellness programs
- ethics

OCCUPATIONAL HEALTH POLICIES

As scientific knowledge accumulates and liabilities rise, more and more organizations are developing policy statements regarding occupational hazards. These policy statements grow out of concern that organizations should be proactive in dealing with this problem. For example, Dow Chemical's policy states that "No employee, male or female, will knowingly be exposed to hazardous levels of materials known to cause cancer or genetic mutations in humans."[44]

An example of the growing complexity of this problem has been the debate over whether women of child-bearing age should be allowed to hold jobs in settings that could endanger fetuses. Johnson Controls in Milwaukee, Wisconsin, which makes lead automobile batteries for such customers as Sears and Goodyear, had restricted women's access to jobs in its Bennington, Vermont, plant. Johnson's management claimed that the factory's air contained traces of lead and lead oxide. While presumably not high enough to harm adults, these toxin levels were high enough to endanger children and fetuses. Thus women were allowed to work in the plant, but only if they were unable to bear children (either because of surgery to prevent pregnancies or because they were too old to have children). According to the company, "the issue was protecting the health of unborn children."

Women's advocates and union leaders argued that the firm was guilty of sex discrimination. Specifically, they claimed that lead levels were too high for men as well, that the firm was making a decision *for* women rather than allowing women to decide whether to take the risk, that such rules invade women's privacy, and, finally, that the restrictions denied women access to high-paying jobs. A typical factory job in Bennington paid $6.35/hour verses $15.00/hour in the Johnson Controls plant.[45]

What made the situation more complex was that many workers were reluctant to leave jobs to avoid occupational exposure unless they were guaranteed that their income would not suffer. Some workers went so far as to have themselves sterilized to protect their jobs. When the Supreme Court heard this case, they ruled in favor of the workers, thus striking down the company's fetal protection policy (*United Auto Workers v. Johnson Controls*, 1991).

The policies of AT&T and Digital Equipment illustrate alternative strategies. Their policies provide income protection for pregnant production workers who might be exposed to the toxic gases and liquids used to etch microscopic circuits onto silicon wafers. Other companies are obtaining voluntary consent agreements from employees who choose to stay on hazardous jobs. While these agreements may absolve employers from punitive damages in civil court, they do not alleviate liability under workers' compensation laws and civil disability suits.

WELLNESS PROGRAMS

Corporations are increasingly focusing on keeping employees healthy rather than helping them get well. They are investing in wellness programs at record rates, and such programs appear to be paying off. A four-year study of 15,000 Control Data employees showed that employees who participate in only limited exercise spend 114 percent more on health insurance claims than co-workers who exercise more. Smokers and obese workers also had higher medical claims. Control Data, which has had its "Stay Well" program in place since the early 1980s, now markets its program to other firms such as Philip Morris and the National Basketball Association.[46]

Review Coors' wellness program in Chapter 13.

ETHICS IN SHAPING BEHAVIOR

Employers have known for a long time that a small percentage of their work force is responsible for the bulk of the health insurance claims. Originally, they tried to encourage their employees to be healthy by offering to subsidize health club memberships and building exercise facilities and jogging trails, but the results were disappointing. Now it appears that many companies are implementing incentive-based health-care programs.

Should companies be allowed to modify *your* behavior?

While no one denies that health-care costs in the United States are spiraling, some question just how far companies should be allowed to go in "encouraging" their employees to shape up. How much should employers be allowed to know about what the employees do in their spare time? This is obviously the same question we asked in an earlier chapter on employee rights. Is it possible that company policies and practices will become so financially attractive to employees that they will do things that they would not otherwise have done?

The potential for creating situations involving ethical or unethical behavior needs to be watched closely. It is too early to tell just how this situation will unfold. Doubtless, employers and employees are concerned about costs and health; perhaps creative solutions will save the day.[47] Such solutions will also have an impact not only on occupational safety and health, but also on employee rights (Chapter 16) and indirect compensation (Chapter 13).

SUMMARY

Employees' health will become increasingly important in the years ahead. Employers are becoming more aware of the cost of ill health and the benefits of having a healthy work force. The federal government, through OSHA, is also making it more necessary for employers to be concerned with employee health. The government's current concern is primarily with employee health as related to occupational accidents and diseases, both aspects of the physical environment. However, organizations can choose to become involved in programs dealing with employee health and the workers' sociopsychological environment as well. If organizations choose not be become involved with improving the sociopsychological environment, the government may prescribe mandatory regulations. Thus it pays for organizations to be concerned with both aspects of the work environment now. Effective programs for both environments can significantly improve both employee health and the effectiveness of an organization.

When the adoption of improvement programs is being considered, employee involvement is crucial. As with many quality of working life programs, employee involvement in improving safety and health is not only a good idea, but also one likely to be desired by employees. Many things can be done to make work environments better, but it is important to distinguish two types of environments: the physical and the sociopsychological. Each is different and has its own unique components. Although some improvement strategies may work well for one component of the work environment, they will not work in others. Again, a careful diagnosis is required before programs are selected and implemented.

Assuming that a careful diagnosis indicates the need for a stress management program, the challenge is in deciding which program or strategy to select from the many organizational and individual stress management strategies currently available. Programs such as time management or physical exercise could be set up so employees could help themselves cope, or the organization could alter the conditions within the organization that are associated with stress. The latter requires a diagnosis of what is happening, where, and to whom before deciding how to proceed. Because so many possible sources of stress exist, and because not all people react the same way to them, implementing individual stress management strategies may be more efficient. However, if many people are suffering similar stress symptoms in a specific part of the organization, an organizational strategy is more appropriate.

Information regarding many aspects of safety and health is insufficient—either because it does not exist (for example, knowledge of causes and effect) or because organizations are unwilling to gather or provide it. From a legal as well as a humane viewpoint, it is in the best interests of organizations to seek and provide more information so that more effective strategies for improving safety and health can be developed and implemented. Failure to do so may result in costly legal settlements against organizations or further governmental regulation of workplace safety and health. Thus the tasks of gathering and assessing data are the subject of our final chapter.

KEY CONCEPTS

employee pacing
ergonomics
frequency rate
incidence rate
job burnout
low quality of working life
machine pacing
National Institute of Occupational Safety and Health (NIOSH)

occupational accidents
occupational disease
occupational safety and health
Occupational Safety and Health Administration (OSHA)
organizational stress
physical work environment

physical/physiological conditions
safety committees
severity rate
psychological conditions
sociopsychological work environment
work pacing

REVIEW AND DISCUSSION QUESTIONS

1. How are physical hazards distinct from sociopsychological hazards? What implications does this distinction have for programs to deal with these hazards?
2. Is there such a thing as an unsafe worker? Assuming that accident-prone workers exist, how can HR managers address this problem?
3. Who is responsible for workplace safety and health? The employer? The employee? The federal government? Judges and juries?
4. What requirements does OSHA impose on the employer for promoting workplace safety?
5. Identify four sources of work stress. Why are claims relating to worker stress on the rise? How can organizations manage work stress?
6. What can employees do for themselves to manage work stress?
7. How might a company's strategy to prevent occupational accidents differ from a program to prevent occupational disease? In what ways might the programs be similar?
8. The United States prides itself on freedom, democracy, and a free market economy. If this is true, why not make the employee responsible for health and safety? In other words, employers who offer riskier employment will simply pay workers more for bearing that risk (a wage premium), and the workers, in turn, can buy more insurance to cover the additional cost.
9. In what ways can an organization prevent occupational accidents?
10. What are some ethical issues in safety and health?

EXERCISES AND CASES

FIELD PROJECT

Visit companies in the local community, and find out which jobs are most dangerous or most unhealthy (you define what this means or have the people you interview do it for you). Report to class and compare results.

SAFETY NET OR DEATH TRAP?

Appliance Park is located in Henderson, a small city in western Kentucky next to the Ohio River. Appliance Park is aptly named for the company, Appliance House, that created 800 manufacturing jobs for this small community. Appliance House manufactures washing machines, dryers, and dishwashers at its Appliance Park location. As the major employer in this small river city, employment at Appliance Park varies between 600 and 1,100 hourly employees depending on the state of the economy and the housing market. Although new housing starts slowed considerably in the past, employment at Appliance Park has stabilized and, if anything, is expected to pick up as housing starts are expected to increase now.

Two weeks ago, a tragedy occurred at Appliance Park that was felt throughout the community. Joe Kitner fell to his death at the east plant where washing machines are assembled. Joe, 24 years old, was a local football star in high school, and had worked at Appliance Park full-time since his graduation from Henderson Central High School. An investigation of the accident was conducted by representatives of the corporate safety staff and Teamster local officials who represent the nonexempt workers at Appliance Park. Although not widely reported, a curious set of factors contributed to Joe's death.

The assembly line at the washing machine division occupies two stories within a large prefab building on the east side of the park. A rope net or mesh is suspended about 30 feet above the ground-level floor to catch accessories and parts that drop from the upper conveyor system where some of the assembly of the washing machines is conducted. Periodically, when model changeovers are scheduled on the line, a changeover crew is assigned to switch the setup of the various machines throughout the assembly line. One of Joe's jobs on the changeover crew was to climb out on the net and retrieve the parts that had dropped from the previous production run. The net, though tightly strung across the ceiling, did have a tear on one side where a bracket that had fallen previously had cut part of the mesh. Although the changeover crew was responsible for inspecting and repairing the net, they often overlooked minor rips because of the production time lost in making repairs to the mesh net.

An autopsy of Joe Kitner revealed that he died of a brain hemorrhage suffered in the fall to the concrete floor below. The autopsy also revealed that Joe had a small but malignant brain tumor located near the part of the brain that controls the central nervous system. The medical examiner did not discuss whether the tumor was far enough along to affect Joe's judgment or motor abilities. But the other test result from the autopsy indicated that Joe had consumed alcohol a few hours before his death, probably at lunch. His blood alcohol level, however, was not high enough for him to have been ruled intoxicated using the state DWI standard.

The changeover crew experienced some difficulty in replacing Joe Kitner. Because the plant was unionized, his job was open to bid, but no one would bid for the job. Under these circumstances, the company used seniority to determine who would work the job among the assemblers. Luther Duncan was selected, and he really had little choice because he was low man on the totem pole with only seven years seniority at the plant. Although the changeover job involved several duties, Luther knew that inevitably he would be asked to climb out on the net.

Luther had been on the job for only eight days when his foreman ordered the assembly line shut down for a model changeover for the next production run. At first, Luther decided not to think about what he eventually would have to do. But when his time came to scale the utility ladder to the rope net, Luther balked. No amount of encouragement, cajoling, or threatening would change Luther's mind; he simply was not going up that ladder with the memory of Joe's death fresh in his mind.

Alex Stearns, the Teamster steward, pulled Luther aside and pleaded with him to obey his foreman's order to complete the job. Alex even promised to file a grievance concerning the rip on the side of the net, which still had not been repaired. Luther stood firm and adamantly refused to proceed. Despite Alex's intervention, Luther's foreman suspended him for the remainder of the day and told him to report along with Alex Stearns to the plant superintendent's office early the next morning. When Luther reported to the superintendent's office the next day, he was informed of his dismissal for insubordination.

CASE QUESTIONS

1. Do you agree with the decision to fire Luther?
2. Who was really at fault in Joe's death?
3. How could Joe's death have been prevented?
4. Why did Alex encourage Luther to obey his foreman?

CASE

WHO'S THERE ON THE LINE?

The telecommunications field is changing very rapidly. In perhaps no other field has the impact of technology had such a significant effect on the jobs of so many workers. Mitch Fields, for example, still remembers that tragic day in November 1963 when President Kennedy was assassinated while Mitch was pulling the afternoon shift as a switchman for Midwest Telephone Company (MTC). As Mitch described it, it sounded like 30 locomotives hammering their way through a large room filled with walls of mechanical switches putting phone calls through to their destination. Today that room of switches has been replaced by a microchip. Mitch himself has undergone extensive training to operate a computer console used to monitor and diagnose switching problems.

The job of operator has changed from sitting in long rows operating equipment attached to walls of jacks and cords to individual work stations that look like command centers out of a Star Trek spaceship. In addition, the competitive environment of telephone services has changed dramatically because of deregulation and competition from other phone companies offering similar services. The new thrust now is to shift operator performance from being not just fast and friendly but profitable as well, by marketing the company ("Thank you for using MTC") and selling high-profit-margin services ("Is there someone else you would like to talk to? The person-to-person rate is only additional for the first minute").

The operator's job at MTC remains unchanged in two respects: operators will talk to nearly 600 people in a typical day, some of whom are still abusive. Operator job performance is monitored by *both* supervisors and, yes, the computer. Technological innovation has enabled MTC to monitor each operator by computer to produce statistics on numbers of calls handled per shift, speed of the call, and amount of revenue generated by the calls. In addition to computer monitoring, supervisors may also listen in on operators to ensure that proper operator protocol is followed. For example, customers are never told they dialed the "wrong" number, obscene calls are routed to supervisors, and one learns to say "hold the line" or "one moment please" instead of "hang on."

Meeting performance standards based on these criteria does not typically lead to large rewards. A beginning operator usually earns about $12,000 a year working swing shifts that may begin at 8:30 A.M., noon, 2:00 P.M., 4:30 P.M., 8:30 P.M., or 2:00 A.M. Only the highest rated operators have the opportunity to be transferred, promoted, or receive educational benefits.

Steve Buckley, training and development manager for MTC, knows that to change the fast and friendly MTC operator of the past to one who is fast, friendly, and profitable as well is going to be a real challenge. Steve has not figured out yet how to get the operators to conclude each transaction by saying "thank you for using MTC." A recent clandestine supervisor survey revealed that fewer than 20 percent of the operators were using the requested reply. Steve is also being pressured by the local union leaders who represent the telephone operators to reduce the job stress brought on by the high volume of people transactions and the constant, computer-assisted surveillance. One thing is for sure, however: Steve must implement a plan for improvement.

CASE QUESTIONS

1. Can Steve really change the behavior of the operators?
2. How can Steve succeed in getting the operators to say "thank you for using MTC"?
3. Is computer monitoring the answer?
4. Should the operators really decide on the change?

1. "A Proud Record at ACI American," *HR Reporter* (Oct. 1990): 5. Reprinted from *HR Reporter* with the permission of the publisher, Buroff Publications, 1350 Connecticut Ave., N.W., Suite 1000, Washington, D.C. 20036.

2. R. S. Schuler, "Occupational Health in Organizations: A Measure of Personnel Effectiveness," in *Readings in Personnel and Human Resource Management,* 2nd ed., eds. R. S. Schuler and S. A. Youngblood (St. Paul, Minn.: West, 1984).

3. J. A. Kinney, "Why Did Paul Die?" *Newsweek* (Sept. 10, 1990): 11.

4. T. F. O'Boyle, "Fear and Stress in the Office Take Toll," *The Wall Street Journal* (Nov. 6, 1990): B1, B2.

5. K. Matthes, "A Prescription for Healthier Offices," *HR Focus* (April, 1992): 4–5; "Indoor Air Issues Confront Employers," *Bulletin to Management* (Oct. 22, 1992): 329.

6. "Back Injuries," *Bulletin to Management* (Jan. 9, 1992): 396.

7. L. Reynolds, "Labor Secretary Calls for 'Time Out' in OSHA Battle," *HR Focus* (Aug. 1993): 4.

8. B. Saporito, "The Most Dangerous Jobs in America," *Fortune* (May 31,1993): 131–140; "Occupational Injuries and Illnesses," *Bulletin to Management* (Jan. 6, 1994): 4–6.

9. J. Nordheimer, "Pressures of Costs Drive Some Contractors to Stress Worker Safety," *The New York Times* (Aug. 21, 1993): 25.

10. These estimates should be regarded as conservative because they do not include the costs due to stress and health and accident costs associated with (caused by) low quality of working life.

11. "OSHA: Reforms and Penalties," *Bulletin to Management* (Jan. 28, 1993): 25: D. Foust, "Stepping into the Middle of OSHA's Muddle," *Business Week* (Aug. 2, 1993): 53.

12. "On the Safety and Health Scene," *Bulletin to Management* (April 2, 1987): 105.

13. B. Meir, "Use of Right-To-Know Rules Is Increasing Public's Scrutiny of Chemical Companies," *The Wall Street Journal* (May 23, 1985): 10; Bureau of National Affairs, "OSHA's Final Labelling Standard," *Bulletin to Management* (Dec. 1, 1983): 1.

14. P. A. Susser, "Update on Hazard Communication," *Personnel Administrator* (Oct. 1985): 57–61; M. G. Miner, "Legal Concerns Facing Human Resource Managers: An Overview," in *Readings in Personnel and Human Resource Management,* 3rd ed., eds. R. S. Schuler, A. Youngblood, and V. Huber (St. Paul, Minn.: West, 1988). "Hazard Communication Training: Compliance Cues," *Bulletin to Management* (March 13, 1986): 81.

15. *The Wall Street Journal* (Oct. 2, 1984): 1; Bureau of National Affairs, "State Right-To-Know Laws: Toxic Substances," *Bulletin*

to Management (Nov. 22, 1984): 4–5; "Worker Right to Know," *Chemical Work* (April 18, 1984): 38–44.

16. M. Novit, "Mental Distress: Possible Implications for the Future," *Personnel Administrator* (Aug. 1982): 47–54. The *Civil Rights Act of 1871,* Section 1983, enforces the Fourteenth Amendment providing for "equal protection of the laws" and prohibits employment discrimination on the basis of race, color, national origin, religion, sex, or age.

17. Determining responsibility is sometimes difficult because determining cause-and-effect relationships is difficult, especially when reaction such as asbestosis or hypertension take so long to develop or occur only in some people working under the same conditions as others. For a discussion, see A. D. Marcus, "Fearful of Future, Plaintiffs Are Suing Firms for What Hasn't Happened Yet," *The Wall Street Journal* (July 11, 1990): B1, B8.

18. "Cutting Workers' Compensation Costs," *Bulletin to Management* (April 22, 1993): 122.

19. "Workplace Torts," *Bulletin to Management* (Oct. 1, 1992): 312. Reprinted by permission. Copyright 1992 by the Bureau of National Affairs, Inc. (800-372-1033).

20. D. Frum, "Oh My Aching . . . You Name It," *Forbes* (April 26, 1993): 53. Also see A. Farnham, "Back Ache," *Fortune* (Dec. 14, 1992): 132–140.

21. O'Boyle (*op. cit.,* see Note 4). B2.

22. From personal correspondence with Donald Brush, President, Bearings Division, Barden Corporation, March 8, 1989.

23. B. Filipczak, "Armed and Dangerous at Work," *Training* (July 1993): 39–43.

24. "Preventing Workplace Violence," *Bulletin to Management* (June 10, 1993): 177. Reprinted by permission. Copyright 1993 by The Bureau of National Affairs, Inc. (800-372-1033).

25. C. S. Weaver, "Understanding Occupational Disease," *Personnel Journal* (June 1989): 86–94.

26. *Ibid.*

27. C. L. Wang, "Occupational Skin Disease Continues to Plague Industry," *Monthly Labor Review* (Feb. 1979): 17–22.

28. K. R. Pelletier, "The Hidden Hazards of the Modern Office," *The New York Times* (Sept. 8, 1985): F3; J. Hyatt, "Hazardous Effects of VDT Legislation," *Inc.* (March 1985): 27; W. L. Weis, "No Smoking," *Personnel Journal* (Sept. 1984): 53–58; "VDT Study: Safety Charges, Design Changes," *Bulletin to Management* (July 21, 1983): 285; "Office Hazard: Factor Environment Can Boomerang," *Impact* (June 22, 1983): 1.

29. "Charges of Emotional Distress: A Growing Trend," *FEP Guidelines* (Dec. 1989): 1–4. Also see a set of references identifying and discussing each preference or interest listed here in R. S. Schuler, "Definition and Conceptualization of Stress in Organizations," *Organizational Behavior and Human Performance* 23 (1980): 184–215; R. S. Schuler, "An Integrative Transactional Process Model of Stress in Organizations," *Journal of Occupational Behavior* 3 (1982): 3–19.

30. A. B. Shostak, *Blue-Collar Stress* (Reading, Mass.: Addison-Wesley, 1980).

31. M. Friedman and R. Roseman, *Type A Behavior and Your Heart.* (New York: Alfred A. Knopf, 1974).

32. "Safety: A Quick Pay-Off, A Long-Term Commitment," *HR Reporter* (Oct. 1990): 6; also see R. Pater, "Safety Leadership Cuts Costs," *HR Magazine* (Nov. 1990): 46–47.

33. D. P. Levin, "The Graying Factory," *The New York Times* (Feb. 20, 1994): Sec 3, 1, 3; For extensive discussion of office space and physical design issues, see L. Altman, "Some Who Use VDT's Miscarried, Study Says," *The New York Times* (June 5, 1988): 22; "Reproductive Hazards—How Employers Are Responding," *Fair Employment Practices* (Oct. 29, 1987): 132; R. S. Schuler, L. R. Ritzman, and V. Davis, "Merging Prescriptive and Behavioral Approaches for Office Layout," *Production and Inventory Management Journal* 3 (1981): 131–142.

34. "National ASPA Conference Highlights," *Bulletin to Management* (July 28, 1988): 239. Also see J. R. Hollenbeck, D. R. Ilgen, and S. M. Crampton, "Lower Back Disability in Occupational Settings: A Review of the Literature from a Human Resource Management View," *Personnel Psychology* 45, no. 2(1992): 247–278.

35. "Perdue Farms Reaches Settlement," *Bulletin to Management* (Feb. 21, 1991): 50.

36. J. Komaki, K. D. Barwick, and L. Scott, "Pinpointing and Reinforcing Safe Performance in a Food Manufacturing Plant," *Journal of Applied Psychology* 63 (1978): 434–445.

37. H. M. Taylor, "Occupational Health Management-by-Objectives," *Personnel* (Jan–Feb. 1980): 58–64.

38. M. Williams, "Ten Minutes Work for 12 Hours Pay? What's the Catch?" *The Wall Street Journal* (Oct. 12, 1983): 19.

39. J. Olian, "New Approaches to Employment Screening," in *Readings in Personnel and Human Resource Management*, 3rd ed., eds. R. Schuler and S. A. Youngblood (St. Paul, Minn.: West, 1988).

40. J. C. Erfurt, A. Foote, and M. A. Heirich, "The Cost-Effectivenes of Worksite Wellness Programs for Hypertension Control, Weight Loss, Smoking Cessation and Exercise," *Personnel Psychology* 45 (1992): 5–27; D. L. Bebhardt and C. E. Crump, "Employee Fitness and Wellness Programs in the Workplace," *American Psychologist* (Feb. 1990): 262–272.

41. "Solutions to Workplace Stress," *Bulletin to Management* (Feb. 11, 1993): 48. Reprinted by permission. Copyright 1993 by The Bureau of National Affairs, Inc. (800-372-1033). For more on employee burnout see "Employee Burnout: Causes and Cures, Part 2," NWNL, P.O. Box 20, Minneapolis, Minn. 55440, (612) 342-7137; S. E. Jackson and R. S. Schuler, "Preventing Employee Burnout," *Personnel* (March–April 1983): 58–68; B. Dumaine, "Cool Cures for Burnout," *Fortune* (June 20, 1986): 78–84.

42. O'Boyle (*op. cit.*, see Note 4): B2.

43. P. R. Balgopal, C. Ramanathan, and M. Patchner, "Employee Assistance Programs: A Cross-Cultural Perspective," paper presented at the Conference on International Personnel and Human Resource Management (Dec. 1987, Singapore); "Foreign Firms Feel the Impact of Bhopal Most," *The Wall Street Journal* (Nov. 26, 1986): 24.

44. "Fetal Protection Policy Struck Down," *FEP Guidelines* (May 1991): 1–2; "Fetal Protection Ruling," *Fair Employment Practices* (March 28, 1991): 31; S. Wermiel, "Justices Bar 'Fetal Protection' Policies," *The Wall Street Journal* (March 21, 1991): B1; C. Trost, "Workplace Debate," *The Wall Street Journal* (Oct. 8, 1990): 1; B. Meier, "Companies Wrestle with Threats to Workers' Reproductive Health," *The Wall Street Journal* (Feb. 5, 1987): 25; L. Altman, "Some Who Use VDT's Miscarried, Study Says," *The New York Times* (June 5, 1988): 22; "Reproductive Hazards—How Employers Are Responding," *Fair Employment Practices* (Oct. 29, 1987): 132.

45. From S. B. Garland, "A New Chief has OSHA Growing Again," *Business Week* (Aug. 20, 1990): 57; P. T. Kilborn, "Who Decides Who Works at Jobs Imperiling Fetuses?" *The New York Times* (Sept. 2, 1990): A1, 12; R. Winslow, "Air Polluted by Carbon Monoxide Poses Risk to Heart Patients, Study Shows," *The Wall Street Journal* (Sept. 4, 1990): B4; R. Winslow, "Safety Group Cites Fatalities Linked to Work," *The Wall Street Journal* (Aug. 31, 1990): B8; and C. Trost, "Business and Women Anxiously Watch Suit on 'Fetal Protection'," *The Wall Street Journal* (Oct. 8, 1990): 1.

46. F. B. James, "Study Lays Groundwork for Tying Health Costs to Workers' Behavior," *The Wall Street Journal* (April 14, 1987): 37.

47. M. Rowland, "Matching Life-Styles to Benefits," *The New York Times* (March 1, 1992).

CHAPTER 20

HUMAN RESOURCE DATA, INFORMATION, AND ASSESSMENT SYSTEMS

LEARNING OBJECTIVES

When you have finished studying this chapter, you should be able to:

1. Describe the purposes and importance of HR data and information systems.
2. Describe computer technology, HR data and information, and their impact on HR.
3. Discuss the ethical implications of computer technology and HRIS.
4. Briefly describe how to assess each HR activity.
5. Describe the current trends in HR data, information, and assessment systems.

CHAPTER OUTLINE

"Managing Human Resources for Boardroom Impact"

HUMAN RESOURCE DATA, INFORMATION, AND
ASSESSMENT SYSTEMS

WHY ARE DATA, INFORMATION, AND
ASSESSMENT SYSTEMS IMPORTANT?

COMPUTER TECHNOLOGY, HRIS, AND HUMAN RESOURCE

ASSESSMENT SYSTEMS FOR HUMAN RESOURCE MANAGEMENT

CURRENT TRENDS

"Managing Human Resources
CHANGE AT HRIS"

Case: Computest, Inc.: The Case of Alternative Personnel
Selection Strategies

WHAT will it take to bring human resources out of the backroom and into the boardroom? In the age of information technology, a good HR department can make or break an organization. But information alone is not the answer. Creating a full partnership with line management will depend on HR's ability to provide true decision-support systems.

Decision-support systems represent the function that will redefine HR's role. To begin, you, as HR managers, must effectively weave total quality management into each aspect of every human resources function. Although TQM achieves the highest possible standards in business, the term too often is associated only with product output or end results, rather than an organization's overall approach to business. Therefore, the HR department has to break new ground by implementing TQM everywhere.

RETHINK YOUR CUSTOMERS

TQM affects all employee-related issues—from productivity, loyalty, and work ethic to overall well-being. HR provides services that greatly impact these elements, and it can directly influence a company's success or failure.

HR must be concerned not only with its own activities, but also with the organizations and vendors that the company entrusts its services to such as insurance companies, trainers and motivational speakers, and service bureaus, to name a few. Are you doing all you can to make sure these vendors have what they need to do their jobs? Insurance companies, for example, are vital to many organizations. Are you giving health-care providers timely and accurate information? Managing vendors as customers allows HR to serve its organization both in long-term strategy and in special situations.

Company departments should also be treated as customers. They rely heavily on HR to perform many functions that affect their own performance. Providing quality job candidates, filling open positions quickly, and providing timely and accurate attendance reports are just a few examples.

USE TECHNOLOGY WISELY

Weaving TQM into HR activities demands taking full advantage of today's computer technology. Automation has made it easier to be more effective and efficient. With effective HR management systems, you can provide prompt and reliable services. From timely and accurate government reports to speedy applicant screening and tracking, using technology to its fullest moves you one step closer to achieving maximum quality.

Software facilitates the accumulation of information, but it's the wise use of that information that determines HR's role in decision support. To facilitate this changing role, software companies offer integrated products that provide comprehensive information on employees, budgets, payroll, and position control. Effectively managing this information in terms of TQM brings HR into the long-term plans of an organization.

RETHINK YOUR ROLE

Information provided by integrated software systems has powerful implications for HR's role in long-term planning. Succession planning is a good example because HR is at the core of determining—and consequently planning—a succession path for both employees and positions. It's here that integrated software provides the quality information that you can incorporate into effective decision-support systems.

A solid organization needs a contingency plan for every position. Take a vice president's position, for example. Using a position-control system, you can determine the compensation, skills, education, and experience needed to fill that position. Then you can begin succession planning by grooming candidates for the inevitable vacancy (even if several years in the future). If three people are in line for that position, you can ensure that the candidates gain what they need to eventually fill the position. For instance, if one person needs an MBA degree, perhaps the successful completion of a certain number of master's degree-level classes can be tied to the individual's bonus or performance review.

Continued on the next page

This feature is particularly important for this, our final chapter, because it brings together many things. In this chapter, we tie together, among other things, total-quality management, which has been a theme throughout this book, with the growing partnership among HR professionals, line managers, and employees. This feature suggests that HR managers can extend this partnership all the way up to the boardroom. Another aspect of total quality management suggested by this feature is the treatment of line managers as customers of the HR department. Great information systems and computer technology facilitate this. Of course, these techniques aren't useful unless the data used is good, so we need to be concerned about the quality of data. Thus, with good data and today's technology, HR professionals can better serve their organizations, the line managers and the employees, and themselves! That's why we finish this book talking about them in some detail.

HUMAN RESOURCE DATA, INFORMATION, AND ASSESSMENT SYSTEMS

Human resource data and information systems are closely linked in discussion and application. Human resource information systems (HRIS), introduced in Chapter 3, generally refer to a data base used for managing human resources. For many people, **information** is something that they find useful, something they did not know or have and that can be used in the solution of a problem. **Data**, however, is more specific; it refers to facts—usually in numerical form—about people or things. In this sense, data become information when accessed by people who need it and who can use it to solve problems. And when data and information are organized, systematic, and integrated, we refer to them as **data and information systems**. An example of the type of data and information that can be stored in an HRIS is shown in Exhibit 20.1. In this chapter, we discuss these systems and their characteristics. We also discuss assessment systems.

As with data and information systems, **assessment systems** are organized approaches to measuring and evaluating the success of a human resource activity. Assessment systems enable the HR professional and others to determine whether the data and information are being used as effectively as possible.[2]

Data are numerical facts, about people, or things.

Information is data that can be used to offer insights and understanding and to solve problems.

Data and information systems are organized, systematic, and integrated.

Assessment systems are organized approaches to measuring and evaluating.

LEARNING OBJECTIVE 1

Describe the purposes and importance of HR data and information systems.

WHY ARE DATA, INFORMATION, AND ASSESSMENT SYSTEMS IMPORTANT?

Information is the true capital of business today. Without strong systems of communicating and transferring it, an organization will find itself at an overwhelming competitive disadvantage. Hence the central role of HR data, information and assessment cannot be overlooked. Together they do many things for an organization. They:

- Enable the organization to do a better job of linking HR planning with business planning

698

EXHIBIT 20.1
MAJOR TYPES OF INFORMATION STORED IN AN HRIS

BENEFITS

Tuition dollars refunded
Health plan type
Health plan coverage (family, single)
Life insurance

Accidental death and
  dismemberment
Stock option plan
Savings bonds
Company credit union

GENERAL DATA

Department code
Employee number
Social security number
Hire date
Date of birth

Status (full time, part time, ter-
  minated)
Date of status
Home address
Home telephone number

AFFIRMATIVE ACTION/EEOC

EEO code (manager, sales,
professional, etc.)
Job group code (a finer breakdown
  of EEO code)
Gender Code

Minority status (Native
  American, African-American,
  Hispanic, etc.)

COMPENSATION

Job code
Job title
Job level
Pay type (weekly, biweekly, monthly)
Salary level

Bonus payments—year to date
Incentive payments—year
  to date
Work shift
Dates associated with above

EDUCATION

Highest degree earned
Field of degree
Year degree awarded

Work specialty code
Company training courses

SOURCE: E. P. Bloom, "Creating an Employee Information System," 68. Reprinted from the
November 1982 issue of *Personnel Administrator*, copyright © 1982, Society for Human
Resource Management, 606 North Washington Street, Alexandria, VA 22314.

- Integrate HR data and information from separate parts of the organization into a central location, one that can be accessed and distributed widely
- Help line managers fulfill their HR responsibilities such as assisting their employees with career planning, performance appraisal, and training needs assessment
- Facilitate the storage of vast amounts of data and information
- Help the HR professionals fulfill their responsibilities and more closely link to the needs of the business, line managers, and employees
- Research HR activities for purposes of validation and improvement
- Enable organizations to adapt more rapidly and effectively to changes in the environment

- Enable organizations to serve the broader objectives of decentralization and employee empowerment
- Facilitate communications with employees through surveys

We will discuss each of these more extensively in the remainder of this chapter. In attaining the preceding purposes, the data and information systems make their HR department and professionals more effective and, at the same time, make the organization more competitive and successful.

While a manually operated HRIS—where records are in file cabinets and changes are made by typewriter (and white out!)—can be used, many organizations now use computer technology exclusively. And because computer costs keep dropping, computer-accessible HR data and information systems are as easily afforded by small companies as by large ones. In fact, it may even be easier for small companies to implement these systems. Regardless of size, however, as companies use the power of technology, they develop a greater capacity for success. But even as technology enlarges a company's capacity, it also brings with it a host of new issues that have to be addressed, and we will consider some of these as well.

All forms of computer and telecommunications hardware and software are making these HR systems faster and easier to use.

LEARNING OBJECTIVE 2

Describe computer technology, HR data and information, and their impact on HR.

COMPUTER TECHNOLOGY, HRIS, AND HUMAN RESOURCES

Managing human resources effectively requires a great deal of data and information. Computer technology enables organizations to combine this data and information in efficiently centralized locations (the data bases we call HRIS), and then make it available for use by others regardless of their location. The two major components of computer technology are the hardware and the software.

COMPUTER HARDWARE AND SOFTWARE

Computer hardware is the equipment, such as the computers, printers, disc drives, scanners, monitors and keyboards. Computers include mainframes, minicomputers, and microcomputers (PCs). Because the cost of computing has come down and the power of minicomputers and PCs has increased, mainframes are less prominent today (although they still operate as the "garage or attic" where a great deal of data and information can be stored). Instead, minicomputers and their ability to establish local-area networks to more easily and readily distribute data (often downloaded from the mainframe) and information are the workhorses of business. Lap-top computers and desk terminals enable more data and information to be put into the hands of more people. This is, of course, consistent with the themes of empowerment, self-management, and partnership that we have been discussing throughout this text.

Newer technologies being used today include CD-ROM technology, laser discs, and satellites.[3] These technologies and their possible uses are shown in Exhibit 20.2.

Computer software contains program instructions that indicate to the hardware what to do. There are literally hundreds of specialized programs just for HRIS. Some are specialized for benefit administration, others for succession planning, and still others for payroll administration. To stay current with what's available, it is necessary to constantly scan the PC magazines and those journals dedicated to the HR professionals.

With the power of today's hardware and software, HR professionals and their organizations find themselves able to do a great many things, very fast. To illustrate this, let us return to the purposes of HRIS that we discussed previously.

Computer hardware is the equipment:

- computers
- disc drives
- scanners
- monitors
- keyboards

Computer software is the program instructions that tell the hardware what to do.

PARTNERSHIP: WORKING TOGETHER IN HR DATA, INFORMATION, AND ASSESSMENT SYSTEMS

LINE MANAGERS	HR PROFESSIONALS	EMPLOYEES
Provide accurate and current data.	Develop user-friendly HRIS.	Use computer-based HR activities to manage own career.
Use the HRIS to solve problems.	Protect unauthorized use of HRIS.	Participate in organizational surveys.
Help assess the quality of HR activities.	Continually assess and improve HR activities.	Play an active role in assessing HR activities.
Develop policies on HR data access.	Develop policies on HR data access.	

LINKING HR PLANNING WITH BUSINESS PLANNING

Computers make it ever more feasible to relate HR planning with the planning needs of the business. At the Chevron Corporation in San Francisco, the HR group has been able to do this by decentralizing their HRIS; rather than a single centralized system, the business units each have their own HRIS. Because each unit is different in terms of business needs, planning cycles, and degree of change, decentralization allows the system to be used in a way that is comfortable for each unit. With greater comfort comes greater usage of the system.[4]

Chevron is a heavy user of decentralized HR information and data systems.

INTEGRATING DATA AND INFORMATION

The HRIS at Chevron is designed to be customer-oriented—that is, oriented to the business. It is designed to gather data from several business units. The data is gathered on the terms of the individual unit and then is made accessible again to each unit, on its terms. A key to the success of this system is an HR staff that understands each unit's business, business processes, and financial processes. In this way, the HR staff can design activities to better address the needs of each unit. This in turn encourages the units to share their good data with the central system, which makes better use of the central system.

HR data and information need to be related to the business and systematically integrated.

HELPING LINE MANAGERS AND EMPLOYEES FULFILL THEIR HR RESPONSIBILITIES

In companies where the needs of the business are understood by the HR professionals, it is likely that data and information systems exist where managers have on-line access to systems for processing pay changes, promotions, and transfers, candidate searches, staffing requests, and other transactions that traditionally

An HRIS can really help line managers in their HR responsibilities.

EXHIBIT 20.2
TECHNOLOGY AT A GLANCE

TYPE	TECHNOLOGY	COST	ADVANTAGES	DISADVANTAGES	COMMENTS
CD-ROM	Uses a laser to read up to 600 megabytes of text, graphics, audio, and video off a 4.5-inch aluminum disc. Works in conjunction with either a PC (DOS or Windows) or a Macintosh.	$300–700 per unit; approximately $4,500 for a complete station. Off-the-shelf software generally runs $75–1,500 per program; custom programs can cost $2,000–10,000 to produce.	Excellent for combining text and graphics on the same screen. Can be installed internally to save space. Thousands of off-the-shelf programs and applications available, including many reference guides.	Video quality not up to par with laser discs. Not capable of displaying video full screen.	Useful for most training situations.
Satellite Instruction	Uses a satellite to link various locations into a single classroom.	Highly variable, depending on the setup. Conventional classroom training generally ranges from $150–300 per day per student; other programs can cost $8,000–10,000 per location for a single day.	Provides an efficient way to train large numbers of people in a consistent way without investing large sums to fly them into a corporate training center. For incentive-based programs, can make learning entertaining and fun.	Requires a relatively large investment that may be suitable only for large companies. Individuals sometimes think that systems are unwieldy and inflexible.	Becoming more popular. New wrinkles offer intriguing possibilities.
CD-I	Stand-alone unit uses a laser to read up to 72 minutes of video and data from a 4.5-inch disc to a monitor.	$500–600 per unit; $400–1,200 for an accompanying monitor. Kiosk configuration can run $200–10,000.	Interactive video without a computer. Portability makes it ideal for remote training and recruiting.	Can't store data on how system is being used; can't administer tests or track scores.	More sophisticated than a VCR; less sophisticated than CD-ROM or laser disc.
Interactive-Voice Technology	Uses a program installed on a conventional PC to create an automated phone-response system.	$10,000–75,000.	Can be produced internally or purchased from outside firm. System can be updated, and new recordings added with relative ease. Frees HR staff to handle other projects; can slash printing costs for producing benefits booklets and job-opening notices.	Poorly designed or overly complicated system can create headaches for those trying to use it. System must be thoroughly tested so as not to provide inaccurate information.	Quickly growing in popularity as a way to provide information on benefits and accounts; and as a way to post job openings electronically.

EXHIBIT 20.2 (CONT.)
TECHNOLOGY AT A GLANCE

TYPE	TECHNOLOGY	COST	ADVANTAGES	DISADVANTAGES	COMMENTS
Laser Disc	Uses a laser to read one hour of video (two hours at a lower resolution) from a 10-inch disc. Picture can be displayed on a TV monitor or computer.	$300–1,000 per unit; approximately $4,500–5,000 for a complete station. Off-the-shelf software runs $1,000–15,000; custom software can run as high as $300,000.	Highest-quality video of any disc-based medium; also capable of producing digital audio. Can be used as a basic video data base with a bar-code reader or controller; or as part of a sophisticated computing system when interfaced to a PC or Macintosh.	Bulky discs; can't be used for as many applications as CD-ROM; requires a special video card (DVI) inside the computer.	Has become the media of preference for interactive training because of high-quality video and sound.

FROM: S. Greengard, "How Technology Is Advancing HR," *Personnel Journal,* (Sept. 1993): 82–83. Used by permission.

were paper driven. This really enables line managers to fulfill their HR responsibilities much more efficiently and to furnish more useful information to the HRIS.

Just as the systems can be designed so that line managers can use them, so can they be designed for employee access. Some systems provide direct computer access by employees for flexible benefit enrollments, career planning and self-assessment, job posting, and training.

RECORD KEEPING

The computerized HRIS can facilitate the easy storage of, and access to, human resource records that are vital for organizations.

To comply with federal equal employment laws, organizations must follow several HR record keeping requirements. *Title VII of the 1964 Civil Rights Act* says organizations must keep all employment records for at least six months. The *Equal Pay Act* and the *Age Discrimination in Employment Act* require records to be kept three years. Three years, however, is not always the limit. If an employee or a government agency lodges a charge against a firm (and this could be any number of years), the firm should have all of its records regarding the person making the complaint as well as records on all other employees in similar positions. The organization must also keep records on seniority, benefits, and merit and incentive plans until at least one year after the plans end.

Organizations need records to fill out the numerous reports that are required for legal compliance. Employers of 100 or more workers must annually file EEO-1 reports to comply with Equal Employment Opportunity laws. Multi-establishment employers need only file separate EEO-1 reports for each establishment employing 50 or more workers. Organizations with government contracts must fill out affirmative action reports that the Office of Federal Contract Compliance Programs (OFCCP) sends. Government contractors required to fill out Standardized Affirmative Action Formats (SAAFs) for the OFCCP can propose one SAAF to cover all its establishments as long as its HR activities are the same for each establishment.

HR data and information are required by several federal agencies.

As described in Chapter 19, Safety and Health, keeping and maintaining safety and health records is a requirement of OSHA. A good data base can also be part of a strategy to improve occupational safety and health.

HELPING HR PROFESSIONALS FULFILL THEIR RESPONSIBILITIES

Technology and sound data and information systems help HR professionals perform their responsibilities more effectively. Perhaps the areas of greatest application are in compensation and training and development.

An HRIS can also help HR professionals.

THE COMPUTERIZED HRIS IN TOTAL COMPENSATION. A computerized HRIS can be instrumental in managing total compensation and ensuring equity. The four components of total compensation are direct monetary, indirect monetary, direct nonmonetary and indirect nonmonetary rewards. In ledger format, HR specialists can maintain the value (cost) of total compensation in several configurations. For example, total compensation can be computed for each employee and the average for each position, or department. In addition, specific components of total compensation can be calculated and used for projecting and establishing salary and benefits budgets for appropriate organizational units. In conjunction with job evaluation, the HR department can determine whether compensable factors are being assigned monetary values systematically or randomly. This can serve as an initial step in minimizing inequitable compensation.

Performance appraisal information is closely related to the compensation activity. Computers can link the HR department with other departments and thereby facilitate projecting departmental salary budgets. [5]

THE COMPUTERIZED HRIS IN PERFORMANCE-BASED PAY. Much of the time spent in compensation planning is lost to pencil pushing and number crunching. The computerized HRIS can accommodate performance-based pay planning and administration in the following ways. First, establishing a merit pay plan grid on a computer system can facilitate administration because the computer can be programmed to post the appropriate percentage increases. Second, budget plans can be made simply by manipulating the percentage values on the grid, automatically changing each individual's pay, and, of course, planning strategies can be considered by department, position, or other meaningful ways. Because time is a cost to any organization, the ability to analyze this information in a minimal amount of time represents a substantial cost efficiency.[6]

A computerized HRIS facilitates the management and manipulation of the data used in projecting salary structure; compa-ratios; "compensation cost/amount of revenue generated" ratios; total cost of selected configurations of benefits packages; and the cost of compensation in the future under different rates of inflation. These calculations can be made on the basis of an individual employee, a group, or the overall organization. Selected information can be further extracted for summary reports and projections for areas other than the HR department such as a budget sheet for the comptroller or the line managers.

Computer-based training saves organizations money when it is applied to training that must be done over and over.

TRAINING AND DEVELOPMENT. Computer-based training (CBT) is now widely available. A great deal of training for airline pilots is conducted using CBT and flight simulators. While efficient, CBT is, however, not the total solution. SimuFlite Training International, a recent competitor of FlightSafety International—both offer pilot training—learned through trial and error (and customers' reactions) that CBT needs to be mixed with stand-up instructor training to be effective.[7]

At the Hudson's Bay Company, one of Canada's largest retailers, CBT is used to train new sales associates in everything from store procedures to customer-service practices. CBT has replaced the three-day intensive training program that consisted entirely of oral presentations. Because of its successes, CBT is used for training in many topics, including:

- Interviewing techniques
- Effective people management
- Retail method of inventory
- Retail marketing
- Sales promotion
- Professional selling skills
- Line-budget maintenance
- Check authorization
- Inventory systems
- Career planning
- Family budgeting[8]

Overall, the results indicate that CBT is more cost-effective than traditional training because students get to the work situation sooner and end up spending less time in the classroom.

TOTAL QUALITY MANAGEMENT.   Getting total quality and then continuously improving depends on good data, a strong HRIS, and continual assessment. While TQM data and information are not always related to human resources, a great deal of it is. So the HR department has to have the information readily available—for example: Who are the best performers? Are we selecting the best applicants regarding math skills? Are we selecting people with the greatest potential? The HR department also has to be able to train employees to understand and utilize data and information that is not directly related to personnel issues. For example, employees need to be trained in statistical process control (described in Chapter 14). So overall, the culture of TQM organizations is dependent on good data, a strong HRIS, and continual assessment. Creating this culture and making it run successfully is a role for which the HR department is especially suited.

The success of TQM depends on having HRIS.

CONDUCTING RESEARCH FOR VALIDATION AND IMPROVEMENT

On any given day, an HR department evaluates a number of candidates for a variety of positions. Deciding which predictors are relevant (valid) for a particular case and administering a multitude of predictors (tests) make this work challenging. Effective management of predictors is critical in the face of extensive laws and regulations. Doing these tasks effectively requires a great deal of information, and computer technology enhances the coordination of scheduling, administration, and evaluation of predictors by processing this information in a variety of ways.

VALIDATION STUDY.   The HR department can quickly do a validation study (described in Appendix C) by correlating the current job performance data with any of several predictors, if these data are stored in an HRIS and analyzed by computer. With a computerized HRIS, the utilization rates for affirmative action programs can also be determined quickly and easily. The results of any kind of test can be stored in an HRIS and used with job analysis data (also in the HRIS) to make better selection and placement decisions. This same information can then be used to plot career paths for employees.

INTERVIEWING. Computers are used to reduce first-impression biases inherent in the interview. Computer-aided interviewing presents a structured interview directly to an applicant, without an interviewer present. Although it does not replace the face-to-face interview, it complements it by providing a base of information about each applicant before the interviewer meets the applicant. This provides a first impression based on information that is job-relevant rather than anecdotal.

Computer interviewing is also faster. An applicant can complete a 100-question computer-aided interview in about 20 minutes. The same information would require a face-to-face interview of more than two hours. In addition to time savings, computer-aided interviewing provides an automatic record of answers that can be compared across applicants. More important, computer-aided interviews have been validated in a number of settings, including manufacturing and service industries.[9]

ENABLING ORGANIZATIONS TO ADAPT MORE QUICKLY AND EFFECTIVELY

A host of new technologies are making a difference in business today as we approach the end of the century. Information technology, office automation, factory automation, data communications, and voice communication are being implemented together faster than ever. Described in Chapter 3 as telematics technology, they are revolutionizing the ways we work and the ways we organize. Singly or together, these technologies are facilitating the following capabilities within organizations:

Telematics technologies creates these organizational capabilities.

- Networking across organizational units and countries
- Control over time and space
- Higher productivity and amplification of human cognitive functions
- New extensions of human action
- New levels of efficiency and productivity or energy and materials conserving
- New power to centralize and decentralize
- Blurring of organizational distinctions
- Promotion of monitoring, evaluation, and simulation
- Erosion of hierarchical relationships
- Shifting of power
- Shifting of authority
- Integration[10]

At Microsoft, the Redmond, Washington, software company, CEO Bill Gates uses a sophisticated electronic mail system to eliminate bureaucratic bottlenecks, where layers of people wait to get answers.

Not too far down the road, the computer will emerge as a full-fledged management aid, helping to coordinate the daily tasks of administration. The programs to do that, developed after years of studying human behavior, are called *groupware*. Action Technologies of Emeryville, California, markets a program named the Coordinator; it is based on the principle that all managerial interaction can be sorted into "offers," "counteroffers," "commitments," and "requests." The Coordinator keeps track of such transactions, minds deadlines, sends reminders, arranges meetings, and sorts electronic mail. It also enables users to organize themselves into *ad hoc* work groups. Coordination Technology, a young company in Trumbull, Connecticut, will launch its own groupware next year and uses its programs to manage the temporary groups that form to deal with specific assignments.[11]

The impact of the telematics technology revolution is also being seen in manufacturing advances.[12] The revolutions within industrial manufacturing include the emerging technologies of:

- Robotics and factory automation
- Computer aided design, manufacturing and engineering
- CAD/CAM/CAE
- Computer integrated manufacturing
- Lasers and optics
- Biotechnologies
- Polymers and alloys
- Advanced ceramics[13]

These technologies are having a big impact in manufacturing firms:

Accompanying the increased factory automation is an increase in the use of robots. Annual sales of robots are expected to be 20,000 units by the end of the century, compared with the current rate of 5,000 units. Estimates are that today robots have displaced about 5 percent of the work force. To avoid layoffs, substantial retraining will be required of many employees. The costs of this training will be offset by lower labor costs, enhanced product quality, fewer defects, and a better flow of materials.

The biggest gains in office productivity are expected to come from adapting new technologies such as work stations to the jobs of professionals and managers and making vastly greater use of technology to manage people.[14] Productivity gains are also expected to come from re-engineering programs that streamline work flow and work methods. Eventually, almost a majority of the white-collar jobs in the United States will be touched by re-engineering and the use of technology, including managers, professionals and clerical staff.

A BIG CULTURAL IMPACT. Data and information systems, whether in the factory or the office, have had, and will continue to have, an impact on organizational structuring. Because information is instantaneously available, there is little need for layers of management between the top and first-line management. Consequently, organizational culture will change significantly. Top management will, in the future, bypass middle managers on their way to first-line management—in fact, there may be few middle managers left when the transformation is complete. The chain of command will be radically different, and fast and effective communications will be the result. This is nicely illustrated by the following story of how the chairman of Mrs. Fields, Inc., Randy Fields, uses technology to manage people:

A big impact of the new technologies is the opening up of the hierarchy.

- Fields sees the computer as the most powerful tool around for managing people. For keeping the corporate staff lean. For organizing ideas. For enabling employees to communicate directly with the CEO in her Park City, Utah, headquarters. For automating most routine paperwork and decision making. Since technology is capable of doing so much, says Randy, CEOs should "understand it just like they understand operations."
- "I want to transform the workplace, what people do, and how they do it," says Fields, who identified for us the touchstones of a corporate environment in which technology is used to manage people.[15]

Some observers suggest that telematics will be used to redesign jobs à la Frederick Taylor in the name of scientific management.[16] Barbara Garson. in *The Electronic Sweatshop*, however, is concerned that the computer's ability to monitor behavior will lead to oppressive control of employees. She also suggests

There are advantages and disadvantages associated with some of the new technologies.

that what some fast-food restaurants are doing with their computer systems is creating jobs that virtually remove the need for employees to think and, therefore, to grow on the job. In essence, she sees telematics as leading to the deskilling of jobs. And while some may say this is necessary because of the evolving nature of the work force, others say that it only perpetuates the deskilling of the U.S. work force and thus the eventual decline of U.S. industry.

Although the challenges HR managers face in the telematics revolution are significant, there are other considerations. For instance, work can now go directly to the worker. The need for more day-care services can be addressed in part by allowing workers to do their work at home, linked the whole time to the company's mainframe computer or local work stations. Not only does this have implications for supervision and training, it also has legal implications. The HR department needs to monitor the legal events regarding the utilization of homework activities and the limits of liability for worker safety and health. The ability to have individuals work at home hastens the trend toward using subcontractors and contingent employees. This can lead to lower labor costs because contingent employees essentially have no benefit packages.

Thus the possibilities for organizational improvements for survival and competitiveness through automation and advanced technology are enormous. And so are the implications for our society.

COMMUNICATING WITH EMPLOYEES THROUGH SURVEYS

Communication has never been more important. Improving the avenues for communication facilitates the transmission of ideas into product improvements and organizational changes and, at the same time, enhances job involvement, participation, and one's sense of being in control.

Computer technology and an organization's HRIS can not only help organizations perform many tasks more quickly and accurately, but can also help with communications. A good illustration of this is the organizational survey.

Organizational surveys are systematic and scientific ways of gathering information for the purpose of assessing current conditions, seeking areas for improvement, and then developing the programs that will implement the improvement. While this can happen without computer technology, it is certainly much easier with it and therefore more likely to occur.

Organizational surveys are systematic and scientific ways of gathering information.

You can't give 'em what they want without asking.

—Wayne Wilson, Corporate Vice President, Human Resources, Blue Cross, Western Pennsylvania

WHAT DO WE MEASURE? In each of the uses for HR data discussed in the previous chapters, the data gathered have either been measures of job performance or predictors of job performance such as tests and background characteristics. But the HR professional often needs other types of data. For example, to develop ways to improve employee performance, the HR staff needs to measure how employees perceive their environment, including the consequences of job performance, quality of feedback, and aspects of goal setting. It is equally necessary to gather data on employees' perceptions of the quality of working life and employee stress. This is not to say, however, that the objective qualities of the job are not important. But with these two kinds of data, objective and perceptual, the HR staff can begin to make other changes for organizational improvement.

It is also important to know how employees react to the environment and job qualities. Many of these reactions, which include physical measures such as blood pressure and heart rate, are symptoms of employee stress. Because one very important criterion for all sorts of goals is employee health, systematically gathering this type of information is imperative. Thus organizational surveys generally attempt to measure the following:

- *Employee perceptions:* role awareness, role conflict, qualities of the job, and interpersonal qualities, such as those of the supervisor and group members
- *Employee reactions:* feelings, such as satisfaction, and physiological responses, such as heart rate and blood pressure
- *Behaviors:* employee performance, absenteeism, and turnover

CONDUCTING AN ORGANIZATIONAL SURVEY.   Important steps for the HR staff—or an outside consultant—to consider when conducting an organizational survey include planning, actual data collection, and ensuring employee participation.[17] These become necessary, however, only after top management has given its support for the survey.

As the first step, the following must be considered:

- Specific employee perceptions and responses that should be measured
- Methods that will be used to collect the data, including observations, questionnaires, interviews, and personnel records
- Reliability and validity of the measures to be used
- People from whom the data will be collected—all employees, managerial employees only, a sample of employees, or only certain departments within the organization
- Timing of the survey and whether to make the survey part of a longer-term effort
- Types of analyses that will be made with the data
- Specific purposes of the data—for example, to determine reasons for an organization's turnover problem

This last consideration is important, because by identifying the problem, the HR staff can determine which models or theories will be relevant to the survey. Knowing which model will be used indicates what data are needed and what statistical techniques will be necessary to analyze the data.

The next step is the actual collection of data. Three things are important here. It must be decided who will administer the questionnaire—the line manager, the HR staff, or someone from outside the organization. It must be decided where, when, and in what size groups the data will be collected. Both these considerations are influenced by the method used to gather the data. For example, if a questionnaire is used, larger groups are more feasible than if interviews are conducted. Finally, employee participation in the survey must be ensured. This can be done by gathering the data during company time and by providing feedback—for instance, by promising employees that the results of the survey will be made known to them.

The actual feedback process is the third step. As part of this process, the data are analyzed according to the purposes and problems for which they were collected. The results of the analysis can then be presented to line managers, who in turn discuss them with their employees. The feedback sessions can be used to develop solutions to any problems that are identified and to evaluate the effectiveness of programs that may already have been implemented on the basis of an earlier survey.

The extent to which employees actually participate in the development of solutions during the feedback process depends on the philosophy of top management. Organizations willing to survey their employees are also usually willing to invite their participation in deciding to make things better. It is this willingness that allows organizational surveys to be used most effectively.

ARE WE IMPORTANT?   Remember the case in Chapter 2, "Bringing the Personnel Department to the Business"? In this case, Mike Mitchell "customer-

Steps in conducting a survey:
- plan
- collect the data
- analyze the data
- feedback the data

ized" the personnel department at the Swiss Bank of North America. In order to succeed at this, he needed the help of the people in his department: they had to change their ways of behaving—they had to go out and talk with customers and develop new products for them! First Mike had to instill a new confidence in his people and show them that what they were doing was important. Here is where he relied on a short survey. The survey asked the employees in his department to indicate what impact, if any, the HR department was having in the company. In other words, he asked them to indicate if they worked in a unit that made a difference. Of course, they generally thought they did, but they hadn't really addressed this issue in very specific terms until they participated in Mike's survey, which was something like the one in Exhibit 20.3. He asked them what impact they would have if they made the HR department even better than it was—if they made it a world-class operation! He and his group discussed the results, which gave everyone an opportunity to really see just how many things in the company they did impact. This process energized the group and got them really believing in what they were doing. They were able to take this newfound confidence out into the company and show their customers all the great things the HR department could do for them!

LEARNING OBJECTIVE 3

Discuss the ethical implications of computer technology and HRIS.

There are important ethical questions with a computerized HRIS.

COMPUTER TECHNOLOGY, HRIS, AND ETHICS

With a computerized HRIS, human resource departments can quickly generate confidential personnel information in a variety of formats. Thus, many copies of confidential information may exist at any one time, increasing the likelihood that some may be misplaced or even stolen. As a result, file security is of concern. Today's HRIS systems include access protectors that limit who can read or write to a file, and they can be designed to allow a single person or a group of individuals access or no access. While these systems reduce the threat of file invasion, most designers of "secure" systems build in back door entries. If discovered by an unauthorized user, such a user can gain access to the program. Thus company computer security is of great concern and companies are doing everything to deal with it.

Today a computerized HRIS can ensure that employee policies are implemented fairly. Expert systems such as those developed by HumanTek, a San Francisco software company, guide managers with employee problems to solutions. By asking a series of questions, the computer steers the manager to organizational policies and precedents that relate to the specific performance problem. Some of the more sophisticated programs even give managers advice. According to Walter Ratcliff, HumanTek consultant, expert systems will be the best friend of tomorrow's manager. Rather than flipping through a human resource manual, a supervisor will turn on his or her computer for advice.

A computerized HRIS can be used to monitor the performance of employees, as described in Chapter 9. The Office of Technology Assessment in Washington, D.C., estimates that up to 10 million workers are regularly monitored at their computers:

> At hundreds of companies, the performance of data-entry clerks is judged by the speed of their computer-measured keystrokes. Directory-assistance operators at telephone companies are allotted 25 seconds or less to root out a number, however vague the request, and computers record their times.
>
> In supermarkets, computers measure the speed with which the checkout clerks sweep purchases over the optical scanners.
>
> In an office building in downtown St. Louis, customer-service representatives at Union Pacific Railroad offices who book shipments for companies that send their goods by rail work at the kind of pace that telephone operators and airline reservation agents do.

EXHIBIT 20.3
IMPACT CRITERIA

If an organization's HR department goes from being just average to being
excellent, what criteria are affected and to what extent?
Please check (✓) the criteria affected and circle the extent of impact.

		SMALL EXTENT	MODERATE EXTENT		GREAT EXTENT
CRITERIA		1	2	3	4	5
1. _____	Market share of firm	1	2	3	4	5
2. _____	Sales per employee	1	2	3	4	5
3. _____	Line manager satisfaction	1	2	3	4	5
4. _____	Employee satisfaction	1	2	3	4	5
5. _____	Health and safety rates	1	2	3	4	5
6. _____	Grievances filed	1	2	3	4	5
7. _____	Profitability of firm	1	2	3	4	5
8. _____	Flexibility of work force	1	2	3	4	5
9. _____	Return on assets	1	2	3	4	5
10. _____	Productivity	1	2	3	4	5
11. _____	Employee stress	1	2	3	4	5
12. _____	Absenteeism rates	1	2	3	4	5
13. _____	Turnover rates	1	2	3	4	5
14. _____	Customer satisfaction	1	2	3	4	5
15. _____	Respect from others	1	2	3	4	5
16. _____	Visits from outsiders	1	2	3	4	5
17. _____	Ease of recruitment	1	2	3	4	5
18. _____	Selection ratios	1	2	3	4	5
19. _____	Involuntary terminations	1	2	3	4	5
20. _____	Strategy implementation	1	2	3	4	5
21. _____	Role of HR in the firm	1	2	3	4	5
22. _____	Competitiveness of firm	1	2	3	4	5
23. _____	Line manager use of HR	1	2	3	4	5
24. _____	News stories about the firm	1	2	3	4	5
25. _____	HR costs	1	2	3	4	5
26. _____	Skill levels of employees	1	2	3	4	5
27. _____	Legal claims filed	1	2	3	4	5
28. _____	Quality of products/services	1	2	3	4	5
29. _____	Innovation rates	1	2	3	4	5
30. _____	Others, please describe					
_____		1	2	3	4	5
_____		1	2	3	4	5
_____		1	2	3	4	5
_____		1	2	3	4	5

© Randall S. Schuler & Susan E. Jackson, New York University.

"A customer calls in and says, 'I need two freezer cars to ship frozen french
fries from American Falls, Idaho, to a warehouse in Kentucky,'" says Tracey
Young, an official with the transportation and communication workers union.
Computers track the origin, duration, and frequency of calls, and supervisors,
secretly and at random, listen in.[18]

In such situations, employees complain of their rights to privacy being violated while companies state that they need the information to be competitive. Meanwhile, the customer may claim the right to good service, and if computer monitoring is what it takes, then companies may decide in favor of the customer. At this time, regulations on the use of computer monitoring are basically in the development stage. Needless to say, it is an important employee rights issue that is likely to gain increased attention from its increasing use.[19]

Assessment is the measurement and evaluation of HR activities and of the HR department itself!

ASSESSMENT SYSTEMS FOR HUMAN RESOURCE MANAGEMENT

Data and information systems enable the HR department and the organization to perform many functions faster and more efficiently. As we have discussed throughout this text, being able to perform the whole gamut of HR activities is important—indeed *must* be done for the HR department to be seen as an effective partner in the business. But, in addition, the HR department must also assess the effectiveness of their HRIS. Assessment systems help the HR department determine what the customer wants, how well the department is doing, and what might be done to improve products and services. As such, assessment systems are an integral part of customerization and partnership attitude. They are also consistent with a total quality management system and the philosophy of continuous, data-based improvement.

Consequently, let's begin our discussion of assessment systems for HR management by looking at the overall department operation and then at several HR activities.

We operate the HR department so that we save the company more than we cost the company.

> Paul Beddia, Vice President of
> Human Resources
> Lincoln Electric Company

STARTING WITH THE HUMAN RESOURCE DEPARTMENT

An HR department can demonstrate its contribution to the organization in many ways. As the staff seek to become partners with the rest of the organization, it is proactive of them to provide evidence of their contributions. While such contributions can be assessed against many criteria or standards, two categories put everything in perspective: doing the right things and doing things right.[20]

It is important to do the right things and do them as efficiently as possible.

DOING THE RIGHT THINGS. **Doing the right thing** means that the HR department does things that are needed by the organization to be successful. In essence, assessors ask whether the department is enabling the organization to be more successful in areas such as competitiveness, profitability, adaptability, and strategy implementation. Is it facilitating the work of line managers and the employees in their efforts to contribute to the maximum of their potential?

DOING THINGS RIGHT. **Doing things right** means that the HR department does the right things as efficiently as possible. Of course, the organization wants to hire the best people, but they want to do it at the least cost per hire possible. The HR department wants to facilitate the work of the line managers, but they want to do it in a way that maximizes the benefit and minimizes the cost.

Within each of these two categories, many more specific measures can be used. For example, "doing the right things" measures can include: knowledge of the organization's strategy; knowledge of the line managers' HR needs; development of plans that are consistent with the firm's strategy; and degree of involvement in the strategic planning process. Measures of efficiency, perhaps the more traditional way that HR departments have been assessed, are many. For example, just within the recruiting and selecting activity, measures include:

- Number of candidates interviewed per position
- Ratio of offers accepted to offers extended
- Number of good hires (tenure or performance after the first year)
- Distribution of good hires per source
- Average tenure per hire
- Percent of hires who stay for a minimum desired period of time
- Percent of hires who are outstanding second-year performers
- Cost per hire who stays three or more years

Knowing the categories for assessing HR contributions is the first step. Actually doing the assessment is the second step. As implied in the list of efficiency measures for recruiting and selecting, assessment can be made by determining the costs and benefits in dollars and cents; it can be made using measures of timeliness. In other words, assessment uses **quantitative measures**. While measures such as the "cost per hire who stays three or more years" might be regarded as a *specific* quantitative indicator, measures such as firm productivity or profitability might be regarded as *general* quantitative indicators.

Assessment also uses **qualitative measures**. For departments that want to be more customer focused, an increasingly important way to make qualitative assessments is to ask line managers their opinions of the quality of service being delivered. Of course, line managers are just one of the HR department's customers, so others may also be asked (for example, the employees).

Qualitative and *quantitative measures* can be used in assessing human resources.

While it may be easy to categorize these measures of assessment here, in reality, they are not always so clear-cut. For example, qualitative measures are subjective, and choosing categories here that are important to a specific organization and then framing the questions so that the results are useful is not a small effort. There is an art as well as a science to constructing an effective survey.

There are, on the other hand, a whole host of quantitative measures to choose from. The problem here is to make sure that they are relevant, that there are enough of them to give an accurate picture of performance, but not so many as will overwhelm the analyst and the recipients of the results with detail. This too is an art. Sometimes, simple data give a better picture of performance than the latest technical tools, and at other times, only high-tech tools will do the job. Just as there are many ways to assess the HR department, so there are many ways to assess each activity, beginning with HR planning.

HUMAN RESOURCE PLANNING

Planning can make or break an organization, especially over the long term. Without effective HR planning, an organization may find itself with a plant or an office and no people to run it. On a broad level, then, planning can be assessed on the basis of whether the organization has the people it needs—the right people at the right place, at the right time, and at the right salary.

At more specific levels, planning activities can be assessed by how effectively they, along with recruitment, attract new employees, deal with job loss, and adapt to the changing characteristics of the environment. Because an important part of planning is forecasting, HR planning can be assessed by how well its forecasts (whether of specific personnel needs or of specific environmental trends) compare with reality. Several other criteria against which planning can be assessed were presented in Chapter 4 in the section on HR planning control and evaluation.

CAREER PLANNING AND MANAGEMENT

Assessing the effectiveness of career planning and management must be done from both individual and organizational perspectives. Although the overall pur-

Career planning and management is
assessed from both individual and organizational perspectives.

pose of career management is to match individual ability to job demands and individual needs to job rewards, specific purposes relate primarily to either the individual or the organization.[21]

THE INDIVIDUAL PERSPECTIVE.   From the individual's perspective, effective career planning should result in the following beneficial outcomes:

- A more realistic awareness of skills, abilities, and weaknesses
- An awareness of needs, values, and goals
- An awareness of realistic job and career opportunities that match abilities and personalities, interests, and preferences
- A greater sense of self-esteem from doing what one wants to do
- A more satisfied and productive individual

Employees are more satisfied as a result of job placement activities that match them on personality, interests, and preferences as well as skills, knowledge, and abilities. Sometimes, however, in the initial stages of gaining self-awareness, an individual may leave an organization in search of better matches. How do organizations respond to this? If they offer career programs for their benefit as well as for that of the individual, organizations often wish the individual well because the program has identified that the optimal match lies outside the company. Or, should the program indicate that the individual is the type of employee the company wants in its pool of assets, interesting possibilities can be offered to encourage the person to stay. Flexible career paths can be a solution here.

THE ORGANIZATIONAL PERSPECTIVE.   From the organization's perspective, effective career development programs should result in the following beneficial outcomes:

- More effective use of its current work force
- Reduced absenteeism because employees are better fitted to their job situation
- Reduced turnover after employees go through career planning and find an appropriate job in the current organization
- Improved morale among employees who decide to remain
- A work force with lower potential for obsolescence and a higher level of flexibility and adaptability to changing circumstances
- More employees suitable for potential promotion
- A better image as an organization to work for and, as a result, a larger pool of job applicants to select from
- A greater likelihood of fulfilling equal opportunity employment obligations and using the skills of all employees
- And, last but not least, improved performance

Again, the evidence of how well career development programs provide these outcomes is limited. However, those organizations that do have them—for instance, Apple, Ameritrust, PepsiCo, J.C. Penney, and Procter & Gamble—indicate that they are able to identify more potential promotable employees and that they have an easier time attracting qualified candidates because they are known for offering career development opportunities. Career development is becoming a strategy that enables companies to remain competitive.

JOB ANALYSIS

A variety of standards have been proposed for analyzing the usefulness of job analysis methods. These include whether the method (1) is versatile in analyzing a variety of jobs, (2) is standardized in its procedures for data collection and analysis, (3) has user acceptability and involvement, (4) requires training for those involved in using the method, (5) is ready to use, (6) requires a lot of time to complete and obtain results, (7) is reliable and valid, and (8) has overall benefits in relation to other methods and the costs incurred in their use.[22]

Unfortunately, even leading organizations may not always employ elaborate and formalized job analysis processes. The majority of them do, however, rely on a job analysis manual and analyst training to standardize procedures with statistical analyses conducted to assess the reliability of results and user acceptance assessed through surveys. Still, even leading organizations fall short of theoretical recommendations for analyzing job analysis procedures.[23]

RECRUITMENT

The recruitment activity is supposed to attract the right people at the right time within legal limits so that people and organizations can select each other in their best short- and long-term interests. Likewise, this is how recruitment should be assessed. Exhibit 20.4 shows more specific criteria for assessing recruitment, grouped by the stage of the recruitment process in which they are most applicable.

ASSESSING COSTS AND BENEFITS.   In addition to assessing each benefit criterion of recruitment, each method or source of recruitment can be evaluated, or

---

EXHIBIT 20.4
SOME CRITERIA FOR ASSESSING RECRUITMENT

STAGE OF ENTRY	TYPE OF CRITERIA
Pre-entry	Total number of applicants
	Number of minority and female applicants
	Cost per applicant
	Time to locate job applicants
	Time to process job applicants
Offers and hires	Offers extended by source
	Total number of qualified applicants
	Number of qualified female, minority group, and disabled applicants
	Costs of acceptance versus rejection of applicants
Entry	Initial expectations of newcomers
	Choice of the organization by qualified applicants
	Cost and time of training of new employees
	Salary levels
Postentry	Attitudes toward job, pay, benefits, supervision, and co-workers
	Organizational commitment
	Job performance
	Tenure of hires
	Absenteeism
	Referrals

**Assessing recruiting can save firms
thousands of dollars!**

"costed out" on its short- and long-term benefit costs. Finally, the utility of each method can be determined by comparing the number of potentially qualified applicants hired by each method and by occupational group. The method resulting in the most qualified applicants at the lowest per-hire cost may be determined most effective in the short term.

The significant figures to review are the costs associated with hires versus costs associated with nonhires. *If an organization is spending more than two-thirds of its recruiting budget on individuals who never join the company, the recruiting program needs revamping.* Costs should include salaries of recruiters and line managers involved in interviewing and selection; all mailing, telephone, and recruiting materials; administrative support; and all recruiting advertising including receptions, videos, and programs.

PERFORMANCE APPRAISAL

Chapter 9 categorized the importance and purposes of performance appraisal into evaluation and development. Although all organizations may not desire their performance appraisal to serve both purposes, all should be concerned with the legal requirements the appraisal must meet. Assuming an organization desires to serve both purposes *and* meet the legal requirements, how can it assess how well its performance appraisal systems are doing?[24]

OVERALL ASSESSMENT.   Before evaluating specific aspects of an organization's performance appraisal system, it may be useful to perform an overall assessment to determine quickly how well the system is doing. This can direct the next level of assessment toward specific areas.[25]

A fast-start approach for an overall view is for employees, both supervisors and subordinates, to respond to a questionnaire such as the one shown in Exhibit 20.5. As indicated in the scoring instructions, three subcategories (A + B + C) are added to from an overall score. The three subcategories correspond to the major purposes of appraisal. Note that the assessment includes administrative features of appraisal—that is, whether performance appraisal records are maintained and how accessible they are. These features facilitate the developmental purpose of performance appraisal.

This questionnaire can give an organization a general picture of how well it is doing with its performance appraisal system. As a guide, scores on the subcategories of 9 or 10 suggest the purpose is being well served. Scores of 4 to 8 suggest average service, while 2 or 3 suggest it is not being served at all. Adding the scores on the three subcategories gives an overall assessment of the purposes of appraisal. Scores of 26–30 suggest the performance appraisal system is doing well, scores 21–25 suggest good, 11–20 average, and less than 11 poor. Average scores or less on the subcategories or overall total indicate room for improvement. They also suggest that specific areas should be assessed in depth to determine the cause of these scores. The HR staff can do this by asking a number of specific questions.

SPECIFIC ASSESSMENT.   The specific assessment of an organization's performance appraisal system requires an examination of the entire system.[26] The following questions can provide an assessment of its specific components:

Here are several specific questions to assess a firm's performance appraisal system: ⟶

- What purposes does the organization want its performance appraisal system to serve?
- Do the appraisal forms really get the information to serve these purposes? Are these forms compatible with the jobs for which they are being used—are they job related? That is, are the forms based on behaviors or outcomes that might be included in a critical incidents job analysis?

EXHIBIT 20.5
ORGANIZATIONAL PERFORMANCE APPRAISAL QUESTIONNAIRE EVALUATION

Respond to the following six statements by indicating the extent to which you agree (or disagree) that the statements accurately describe performance appraisal in your organization. Some statements refer to your experiences in appraising your subordinates' performance; others refer to your experiences in being appraised yourself. Try to reflect as accurately as you can the current conditions in your organization based on your experiences.

| SA = Strongly Agree | A = Agree | ? = Neither Agree nor Disagree | D = Disagree | SD = Strongly Disagree |

1. I have found my boss's appraisals to be very helpful in guiding my own career development progress.   SA A ? D SD
2. The appraisal system we have here is of no use to me in my efforts toward developing my subordinates to the fullest extent of their capabilities.   SA A ? D SD
3. Our performance appraisal system generally leaves me even more uncertain about where I stand after my appraisal than beforehand.   SA A ? D SD
4. The appraisal system we use is very useful in helping me to clearly communicate to my subordinates exactly where they stand.   SA A ? D SD
5. When higher levels of management around here are making major decisions about management positions and promotions, they have access to, and make use of, performance appraisal records.   SA A ? D SD
6. In making pay, promotion, transfer, and other administrative personnel decisions, I am not able to obtain past performance appraisal records that could help me to make good decisions.   SA A ? D SD

Scoring

Use the following grid to determine point scores for each item by transferring your responses onto the grid. Place the number in the box at the bottom of each column, then add pairs of columns as indicated.

| | Statement Number | | | | | |
Response	1	2	3	4	5	6
SA	5	1	1	5	5	1
A	4	2	2	4	4	2
?	3	3	3	3	3	3
D	2	4	4	2	2	4
SD	1	5	5	1	1	5

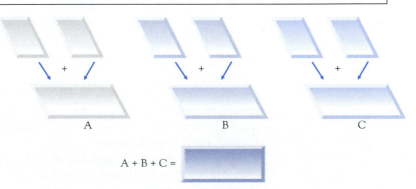

A + B + C =

- Are the appraisal formats designed to minimize errors and ensure consistency?
- Are the processes of the appraisal effective? For example, are the appraisal interviews done effectively? Are goals established? Are they developed jointly? Do superiors and subordinates accept the appraisal process?
- Are superiors rewarded for correctly evaluating and developing their employees? Are they trained in giving feedback, setting goals, and problem-solving techniques? Are they trained to spot performance deficiencies and correctly identify the causes?
- Are the evaluation and developmental components separated? Do the superiors vary their interview styles according to the purpose of the interview?
- Are superiors relatively free from task interference in doing performance appraisal?
- Are the appraisals being implemented correctly? What procedures have been set up to ensure that the appraisals are done correctly? What supporting materials are available to aid superiors in appraising their subordinates?
- Do methods exist for reviewing and evaluating the effectiveness of the total system? Do systematic procedures exist for gathering data to measure how well the goals and objectives are being met?

By addressing these questions and taking corrective action where necessary, an organization's performance appraisal system is more likely to serve its purposes and the broader organizational goals of managing human resources effectively. For an organization just beginning to implement a performance appraisal system, the implications of all these questions should be understood and taken into account in the initial performance appraisal system design.[27]

TOTAL COMPENSATION

In assessing how effectively an organization administers its compensation program, the following major purposes of total compensation must be kept in mind:

In assessment, it is important to start with the purposes being served.

- Attracting potentially qualified employees
- Motivating employees
- Retaining qualified employees
- Administering pay within legal constraints
- Attaining HR plans and strategic business objectives

If an organization hopes to achieve these purposes, employees generally need to be satisfied with their pay. This means the pay levels should be competitive, employees should perceive internal pay equity, and the compensation program should be properly administered.[28] It also means that compensation practices must adhere to the various state and federal wage and hour laws, including comparable worth considerations.

Consequently, an organization's total compensation can be assessed by comparing its pay levels with other organizations, by analyzing the validity of its job evaluation method, by measuring employee perceptions of pay equity and performance-pay linkages, and by determining individual pay levels within jobs and across jobs.

Total compensation can also be assessed by how well it helps attain strategic business objectives. Lincoln Electric is a leader in small motors and arc welders and has a compensation system tied to the company's profits. This system has resulted in the average Lincoln Electric worker making $45,000 a year or more.

In addition to having high motivation to produce, Lincoln workers rarely quit. Their turnover rate is less than 1 percent. The result of Lincoln's compensation system is a cost-efficient competitive advantage that allows it to price its products below competitors, yet maintain equal, if not better, quality. Other companies also use their compensation systems strategically. For example, TRW and Hewlett-Packard use compensation to drive their search for innovative products and services.

Hewlett-Packard stimulates entrepreneurial behavior in its project leaders by tying more rewards to their success. Successful project leaders are given banquets, stock options, and personal computers. At TRW, units or teams are given credit for sales generated in another department in return for helping that department. TRW fosters innovation by stimulating interdependence through its compensation practices. These companies get what they pay for: a steady stream of product and service improvements and enhancements that help them stand alone among their competitors, hence a strong competitive advantage.[29]

PERFORMANCE-BASED PAY SYSTEMS

Regardless of organizational conditions and considerations, performance-based pay systems can be assessed on the basis of three criteria: (1) the relationship between performance and pay—that is, the time between performance and the administration of the pay (the actual time and the time as perceived by employees); (2) how well the plan minimizes the perceived negative consequences of good performance, such as social ostracism; and (3) whether it contributes to the perception that rewards other than pay (such as cooperation and recognition) also stem from good performance. The more the plan minimizes the perceived negative consequences and the more it contributes to the perception that other good rewards are also tied to performance, the more motivating it is likely to be. Exhibit 20.6 presents an evaluation of individual and group (department and organization) plans based on these three criteria.

Exhibit 20.6 uses three objective measures to determine the level of job performance to be rewarded: sales or units made (productivity), cost effectiveness or savings below budget, and traditional superior's ratings. As discussed in Chapter 9, the more objective measures generally have higher credibility, are more valid, and are more visible and verifiable than the traditional supervisor ratings. Consequently, the objective measures (productivity and cost effectiveness) are more likely to link pay to job performance than they are to minimize negative side effects. This evaluation is based on the notion that people do what is rewarded. More objective measures tend to clarify what is rewarded and what is not. This may produce more keen competition with other workers, result in more social ostracism, and lead workers to perceive that good job performance may reduce the work available to them.[30]

INDIRECT COMPENSATION

Several purposes of indirect compensation were listed in Chapter 13. The impact of the indirect benefits in fulfilling these purposes is half of the equation for measuring the effectiveness of the benefits package. The other half involves determining the costs. Determining the effectiveness of the indirect benefit program also involves a comparison of the costs and benefits.[31]

An organization can determine the dollar value of the costs of indirect compensation in the following ways:

- Total costs of benefits annually for all employees
- Cost per employee per year divided by the number of hours worked

DID YOU KNOW?

Lincoln Electric's workers are 2½ times more productive than the industry average.

Assessing the benefits and costs of providing benefits is a major trend in the 1990s.

TYPE OF PLAN	PERFORMANCE MEASURE	TIE PAY TO PERFORMANCE	MINIMIZE NEGATIVE SIDE EFFECTS	TIE OTHER REWARDS TO PERFORMANCE
MERIT				
Individual	Productivity	+2	0	0
	Cost effectiveness	+1	0	0
	Superior's rating	+1	0	+1
Department	Productivity	+1	0	0
	Cost effectiveness	+1	0	+1
	Superior's rating	+1	0	+1
Organizationwide	Productivity	+1	0	+1
	Cost effectiveness	+1	0	+1
	Profit	0	0	+1
INCENTIVE				
Individual	Productivity	+3	−2	0
	Cost effectiveness	+2	−1	0
	Superior's rating	+2	−1	+1
Department	Productivity	+2	0	+1
	Cost effectiveness	+2	0	+1
	Superior's rating	+2	0	+1
Organizationwide	Productivity	+2	0	+1
	Cost effectiveness	+2	0	+1
	Profit	+1	0	+1

SOURCE: E. E. Lawler III, *Pay and Organizational Effectiveness*, p. 165. Copyright © 1971 by McGrw-Hill Book Company. Reprinted with permission.

- Percentage of payroll divided by annual payroll
- Cost per employee per hour divided by employee hours worked

These costs can then be compared with the benefits such as reduced turnover, less absenteeism, or an enhanced company image among employees. The dollar value of these benefits (for example, reduced absenteeism) can then be determined, enabling the organization to compare its benefits costs directly against its benefits savings.

TRAINING AND DEVELOPMENT EVALUATION METHODS AND DESIGNS

EVALUATION METHODS. Many ways of evaluating training and development programs have been proposed. Among the many options are changes in productivity, attitude survey results (covering, for example, satisfaction with supervisor, job satisfaction, stress, role conflict, and knowledge of work procedures), cost savings, benefit gains, and attitudes toward training.[32]

While different evaluation methods have been proposed through the years, most training experts agree that evaluation should depend on the criteria to be measured (the questions to be answered):

1. *Reaction to training.* Did the trainees like the program? Was the instruction clear and helpful? Do they believe that they learned the material?
2. *Learning.* Did they acquire the knowledge and skills that were taught? Can they talk about things they couldn't talk about before? Can they demonstrate appropriate behaviors in training (role play)?
3. *Behavior or performance change.* Can trainees now do things they couldn't do before (for example, negotiate, conduct an appraisal interview)? Can they demonstrate new behaviors on the job? Is performance on the job better?
4. *Produce results.* Were there tangible results in terms of productivity, cost savings, response time, quality or quantity of job performance? Did the training program have utility?

The choice of criteria influences the training evaluation method to be used. For example, a short attitude survey could be used to assess the response of trainees to the course. However, such a survey would not provide information regarding learning, behavior, and results. In fact, when learning has been stressful or difficult, the trainees' reaction may even be negative.

If the objective is to assess what was learned, then paper-and-pencil tests may be appropriate. Additionally, it is possible to analyze the content of responses to such training exercises as in-basket tests, role plays, or case analyses. While this may indicate that learning has occurred, it will not reveal whether learning has been transferred to the job.

To assess whether behavior or performance has changed, output measures, performance evaluation reports, and employee attitude surveys provide better information. For example, if employees report more positive attitudes toward supervisory communications *after* they complete an interpersonal skills program, it may be deduced (assuming other hypotheses can be ruled out) that the training resulted in behavioral change. Finally, bottom-line results might be assessed by examining work-group or unit output measures.

EVALUATION DESIGNS. Once the criteria for assessing an HR program or activity have been selected, consideration must be given to the manner by which the criteria will be evaluated. The alternatives we have are called **evaluation designs.** There are three major categories of evaluation designs—pre-experimental, quasi-experimental, and experimental—and they each offer advantages and disadvantages in accuracy of information gained, ease of use, and costs in administration.[33] Data collection techniques that can be used include surveys, interviews and organizational records.

The most rigorous evaluation design is the **experimental design.** As shown in Exhibit 20.7 there are two types of experimental designs. Both of these use the random assignment of individuals to groups to be tested (T_1 = time one and T_2 = time two) and not all groups receive a treatment (X = any program being implemented to produce change).[34] Evaluation using the experimental design allows the training manager to be more confident that:

- A change has taken place—for example, that employee productivity has increased.
- The change is caused by the program or HR activity.
- A similar change could be expected if the program were done again with other employees.

Because of many organizational constraints preventing random assignment, however, the training manager is generally not able to use the experimental design and must settle for a moderately rigorous **quasi-experimental design.**

Three important evaluation designs in training assessment are

- pre-experimental
- quasi-experimental
- experimental

EXHIBIT 20.7
**THE THREE MAJOR CLASSES OF EVALUATION DESIGNS USED
TO DETERMINE PROGRAM EFFECTIVENESS**

PRE-EXPERIMENTAL	QUASI-EXPERIMENTAL	EXPERIMENTAL
1. One-shot case study design $X \qquad T_2$	1. Time-series design $T_1 T_2 T_3 \quad X \quad T_4 T_5 T_6$	1. Pretest/post-test control group design $T_1 \quad X \quad T_2$ $T_1 \qquad\quad T_2$
2. One-group pretest/ post-test designq $T_1 \quad X \quad T_2$	2. Nonequivalent control groups $T_1 \quad X \quad T_2$ $T_1 \qquad\quad T_2$	2. Solomon four-group design $T_1 \quad X \quad T_2$ $T_1 \qquad\quad T_2$ $\qquad X \quad T_2$ $\qquad\qquad T_2$

SOURCE: Based on I. Goldstein, *Training: Program Development and Evaluation*, 2nd ed. (Monterey, Calif.: Brooks/Cole, 1986), 157–167.

In the quasi-experimental design random assignment is not done. Although using the experimental design is desirable, many organizations find it difficult to randomly assign employees to training programs. Organizations generally want all employees in a section trained, not just a few who are randomly selected. Consequently, the quasi-experimental design is the more likely evaluation that organizations use. In both classes of quasi-experimental design shown in Exhibit 20.7, however, multiple measures (T_s) are taken. In the time-series several measures are taken before the treatment and after. In the nonequivalent control groups, two groups receive multiple measurement, but only one receives a treatment. But again, though to a lesser extent than the experimental design, this design is time consuming and constrained by realities of organizations. Thus the **pre-experimental design** looks most attractive to companies.

In the pre-experimental designs shown in Exhibit 20.7, the two classes are much simpler and far less costly and far less time consuming than the other two designs. In the one-shot design, measurement is done only once and in the one-group pre-test/post-test only one group is used. But with the ease and low cost come less accuracy and confidence in measuring change that may have been the result of a training program (or any other program to produce change). These, however, are the realities of organizations and reflect the constraints and trade-offs HR professionals face daily. Similar, though unique, realities are evident in collective bargaining.

COLLECTIVE BARGAINING

Because of the unique nature of the collective bargaining process, statistical, hard-number evaluation designs may not be appropriate or easy to use. Rather, the effectiveness of the entire collective bargaining process may better be measured by the extent to which each party attains its goals, but even this approach has its difficulties. Because the two groups' goals are incompatible in many cases and can therefore lead to conflicting estimates of effectiveness, a more useful measure may be the quality of the system used to resolve conflict. Conflict is more apparent in the collective bargaining process, where failure to resolve the issues typically leads to strikes. Another measure of effectiveness is the success of the grievance process, or the ability to resolve issues developing out of the bargaining agreement.

EFFECTIVENESS OF NEGOTIATIONS.   Because the purpose of negotiations is to achieve an agreement, this agreement becomes an overall measure of bargaining effectiveness. A healthy and effective bargaining process encourages the discussion of issues and problems and their subsequent resolution at the bargaining table. In addition, the effort required to reach agreement is a measure of how well the process is working. Some indications of this effort are the duration of negotiations, the outcome of member ratification votes, the frequency and duration of strikes, the use of mediation and arbitration, the need for government intervention, and the resulting quality of union-management relations (whether conflict or cooperation exists). Certainly joint programs for productivity and quality of working life improvements could be regarded as successes in this venture.

EFFECTIVENESS OF GRIEVANCE PROCEDURES.   How successful a grievance procedure is may be assessed from different perspectives. Management may view the number of grievances filed and the number settled in management's favor as measures of effectiveness. Unions may also consider the number of grievances, but from their point of view, a larger rather than a smaller number may be considered more successful.

Although the views of management and the union may differ, an overall set of measures to gauge grievance procedure effectiveness can be related to the disagreements between managers and employees. Measures that might be included are frequency of grievances; the level in the grievance procedure at which grievances are usually settled; the frequency of strikes or slowdowns during the term of the labor agreements; the rates of absenteeism, turnover, and sabotage; and the necessity for government intervention.

The success of arbitration is often judged by the acceptability of the decisions, the satisfaction of the parties, the degree of innovation, and the absence of bias in either direction. The effectiveness of any third-party intervention rests in part on how successfully strikes are avoided because the motivation for such intervention is precisely to avert this extreme form of conflict resolution.

CURRENT TRENDS

The rapid rate of change in this area means that issues come up, get resolved, and the technology moves on, often at a mind-boggling rate. And this becomes an issue itself. Keeping up with the mind-boggling rate of change is an underlying trend that will not itself change or go away anytime soon. Another trend is securing the company's HRIS.

LEARNING OBJECTIVE 5
Describe the current trends in HR data, information, and assessment systems.

HRIS MANAGERIAL COMPETENCIES

This is a new era for the HRIS manager, the person who runs the department's data and information system. The HRIS manager is now seen not as someone concerned with how efficiently the department can store and retrieve data and information, but as someone who is a strategic partner and who manages organizational change.

Typically, when organizations first created their HRIS, they needed a specialist to manage the area; it eventually became a separate unit within the HR department with its own HRIS manager. Over the years, the role of this manager has changed from a project manager to a systems manager and now a strategic change partner. This evolution is described in the feature, "Managing Human Resources: Change at HRIS," and it parallels that of the HR manager discussed in Chapter 2. Not surprisingly, these role changes have produced the same need for new competencies in both the HR manager and the HRIS manager.

Today's HRIS manager needs a broader strategic understanding of the business. An awareness of the global environment and how the organization can be global and act local is crucial. The HRIS can enable the organization to operate as a global organization and at the same time remain sensitive to local conditions and needs. It can enable managers worldwide to tap into a data base with information on potential managers for operations in distant countries, without even knowing the candidates. A data base on career information can enable individuals to vie for an organization's jobs worldwide because they can be known to the company's managers all over the world. Thus, in the process of constructing and operating an HRIS, the manager needs to be familiar with the global needs of the business and how an HRIS can assist it in being successful.

INFORMATION SECURITY

According to Marc Tanzer, president of BCI/Information Security in Portland, "When corporate spies want confidential information, they often infiltrate HR departments first. A well-structured information-security program can keep spies from obtaining your company's secrets."[36] The names of employees, where they work, and what they do can be valuable information to other companies, especially competitors. Such information can identify employees and what company projects they are working on, and recruiting efforts can then be attempted to lure these people away. This, of course, goes on, and organizations that value openness and access to information are especially vulnerable. If companies are to empower people, they often need to have this type of openness and information accessibility. It is hard to put a limit or restriction on it without changing this culture of openness and trust. Companies such as Tandem Computers in Cupertino, California, handle this concern by:

- Creating an awareness amongst managers and employees that there is a potential problem with others gaining access to company information and data
- Tightening up telephone security so that callers need to identify themselves and the right screening questions are asked
- Weeding out bogus job candidates (that is, those who are only going through the motions to gain access to information)
- Adding more restrictions in confidentiality agreements (when individuals join the firm, they can be asked to sign agreements not to reveal company secrets to others at any time, even if they leave)
- Classifying and restricting access to information to groups of individuals on a need-to-know basis

Not only can these programs limit information leakage, they can also protect the individual employee from unauthorized people obtaining personal information—not a trivial thing today in light of rising employee violence and credit-card scams.

While some say that restricting the type and amount of information collected reduces the potential for invasion of privacy, this has to be balanced against the HR department's need for information for its various programs. Family-friendly activities such as child- and elder-care programs and employee assistance activities such as drug- and alcohol-abuse programs cannot take place without a sound data base. Nor can the numerous legal obligations that have to be met be fulfilled without an effective HRIS. Some balance must be struck, the latest security must be used, and the environment must be continually scanned for the latest computer hacking scams—the best defense here is a good offense!

SUMMARY

For organizations to succeed today, they need to be managed systematically and scientifically. That is, they need to be managed with the latest, most effective data, information, and assessment tools and techniques. In addition, a culture needs to be created to support the use of these tools and techniques, and employees' skills must be developed so that they are able to use the system. All of this falls within the responsibility of the HR department.

The success of the HR department in developing systems for collecting and utilizing information and data, however, depends on their partnership with line managers and employees. Line managers must be willing to give the data and information and then use it; employees need to be willing to learn how to use it and then be willing to change and adapt; and HR professionals must be willing to build an HRIS that will serve the needs of the organization and its people. Together, these groups can better manage the organization and accomplish their goals more effectively. The HRIS can be used to develop job-related tests so that only the applicants most likely to be successful are selected. An effective HRIS can assist in training employees to use TQM procedures so that they are better able to diagnose problems and develop effective solutions.

The HR professionals, the line managers and the employees can and must work together to effectively assess just how well the organization is managing its human resources. Through systematic approaches to assessment, these groups can carefully evaluate the organization's success in all its HR programs and activities. For example, many companies use annual, confidential surveys to assess how well they are doing regarding job satisfaction, harassment, or diversity. The results of these surveys then establish benchmarks that can assess programs for continual improvements; an HRIS is crucial to this effort.

As organizations build substantial HR data bases, the potential for misuse and abuse also increases. Consequently, the HRIS staff has a special responsibility to secure these systems; yet the goal of security must be met without limiting the organization's capacity to rapidly and correctly adapt to changing conditions. A good and successful balancing of these somewhat conflicting needs is beneficial to both the organization and the individual. Thus, as we go forward in our efforts to better manage human resources, we will see HR professionals at the forefront in the development, utilization, and protection of HR data, information, and assessment systems.

KEY CONCEPTS

assessment systems
data
data and information
    systems
computer hardware
computer software

doing the right things
doing things right
experimental design
evaluation design
information
organizational surveys

pre-experimental design
qualitative measures
quantitative measures
quasi-experimental
    design

REVIEW AND DISCUSSION QUESTIONS

1. What are the purposes of HR data, information, and assessment systems?
2. Describe how computer technology and HRIS help line managers fulfill their HR responsibilities.
3. Describe how a computerized HRIS can be used in the HR research process.
4. Should companies be limited in the amount of personal information they can keep on an HRIS?
5. What are the key steps in conducting an organizational survey?
6. How can performance appraisal systems be assessed?
7. How can performance-based pay systems be assessed?
8. How can the collective bargaining process be assessed?
9. What are the new competencies for the HRIS manager?
10. What is the relationship between TQM, computer technology, and the HR department's efforts to be more customer-oriented?

FIELD PROJECT

Interview some HR managers, and discuss the extent to which they assess the effectiveness or efficiency of their HR activities. Report to the class and compare results.

CASE

COMPUTEST, INC.: THE CASE OF ALTERNATIVE PERSONNEL SELECTION STRATEGIES

In order to answer the case questions on CompuTest, Inc., you will need to refer to the materials in Appendix C where the types of validation studies are discussed.

Fiscal 1995 was a landmark year of development and growth for CompuTest, Inc. As Jerome J. Rosner, president, indicated in a report to the stockholders, "Our company emerged to become a major force in the growing field of computerized testing." It was a year that saw the company grow from 350 to over 460 employees. Although a number of people were added to the marketing, sales, and research operations, the largest numbers were selected for clerical and administrative positions.

To date, the company has principally targeted individual mental health practitioners, psychiatric hospitals, and other medical professionals as the best markets for its products. The company expects these specialized markets to continue to represent a substantial part of their revenue base through 1998. Thereafter, CompuTest expects its sources of revenue to shift as they aggressively enter the vast industrial market. In business and industry, thousands of ability tests are administered annually. In the past, these tests were given to employees and prospective employees by traditional paper-and-pencil methods—a long, cumbersome, and expensive process. As Paul Lefebre, the company's manager of HR research states,

"CompuTest's current and future testing products have the capability of revolutionizing the area of employee screening with new technologies never before available in the HR field."

One of the newest products developed for the industrial market is a comprehensive battery of computer-administered clerical tests. The company, however, does not want to introduce these tests into the market prior to gathering evidence concerning the predictive effectiveness of the tests. Paul Lefebre is currently searching for potential sites to conduct criterion-related validity studies. One place to start is his own firm!

Recently, Lane Carpenter, the director of human resources, has brought a troubling problem to the attention of President Rosner: many complaints are being raised about the quality of clerical personnel being selected with the company's verbal ability test. She has informed President Rosner that although 170 clerical and administrative personnel have been selected with this test, the company has not conducted a criterion-related validation study to evaluate its usefulness. President Rosner has therefore called a meeting with Lane Carpenter and Paul Lefebre.

Jerome Rosner: As you both are aware, we are facing a number of complaints about the quality and quantity of clerical job performance throughout our company. I would also like to bring to your attention that we have a projected need for 50 additional clerical personnel in our current job categories by the end of 1998. This situation requires us to closely examine our current clerical selection procedures and possibly consider alternatives. I would also like us to reconsider the performance appraisal form we are currently using. Our performance appraisal system does not seem to incorporate some of the major duties or tasks that our clerical personnel are being asked to perform. Lane, you have expressed some concerns about the currently used verbal ability test for selecting clerical personnel.

Lane Carpenter: Yes, I am concerned not only with how good this test is at screening potentially successful clerical personnel, but also with how we would defend such a test if challenged in court. I assume you are aware that this test was developed and adopted only on the basis of a content-oriented validation study.

Jerome Rosner: Yes, Paul has informed me of the strategy used in developing the verbal ability test. Paul, you also mentioned in a pervious discussion that we might be able to conduct another type of validation study for this test.

Paul Lefebre: We currently have a sufficient number of clerical personnel with verbal ability test scores and performance ratings to conduct a criterion-related validation study. And, since we have just completed a comprehensive job analysis of all clerical positions and expected openings, we can now revise our clerical performance appraisal system to more accurately reflect the tasks they perform.

Jerome Rosner: Does this job analysis also indicate the abilities necessary to effectively perform these tasks?

Paul Lefebre: Yes, the job analysis clearly identifies the required abilities, and it indicates that although the major duties differ across some of our clerical jobs, the entry-level ability requirements for all of our clerical jobs are similar.

Lane Carpenter: If the ability requirements are similar, we might be able to conduct a criterion-related validation study for the verbal ability test with our current clerical employees.

Paul Lefebre: That is a definite possibility. It might also be helpful for us to consider validating our newly developed computerized clerical ability test battery. That is, we could gather some evidence for its predictive effectiveness in our own company prior to marketing it. Of course, we would have to determine which tests were appropriate or should be considered for a validation study here.

Jerome Rosner: Paul, that sounds like a good idea. If we are going to successfully market our computerized testing products, we should also be willing to use them. An important question related to your suggestion is how our computer-administered clerical test battery would compare with our currently used verbal ability test. Can we improve our predictions of who will turn out to be successful workers? If we decide to replace our current test with a battery of clerical tests, would it be cost beneficial? Paul, I would appreciate your preparing a proposal for how we might go about validating our current verbal ability test and the computer-administered clerical test battery and how we might compare these alternatives.

CASE QUESTIONS

1. What is the difference between the test being developed on the basis of a content-oriented validation study versus a criterion-related validity study?
2. Does CompuTest first have to change its performance appraisal form before doing a criterion-related validation study?
3. On what basis will Paul Lefebre go about determining the tests that would be appropriate to include in the computerized clerical test battery?
4. How should Paul Lefebre go about validating the firm's verbal ability test and the clerical test battery and comparing them?

NOTES

1. D. Harriger, "Use TQM to Reengineer Human Resources," *HR Focus* (April 1993): 17.

2. M. Kavanagh, H. G. Guental, and S. I. Tannenbaum, *Human Resource Management Information Systems* (Boston: PWS-Kent, 1990); A. J. Walker, *Handbook of Human Resource Information Systems* (New York: McGraw-Hill, 1993); and V. R. Ceriello, *Human Resource Management Systems: Strategies,* *Tactics, and Techniques* (Lexington, Mass.: Lexington Books, 1991).

3. S. Greengard, "How Technology Is Advancing HR," *Personnel Journal* (Sept. 1993): 80–90; M. Alpert, "CD-ROM: The Next PC Revolution," *Fortune* (June 29, 1992): 68–73; E. I. Schwartz, "The Power of Software," *Business Week* (June 14, 1993): 76.

4. J. F. Stright, Jr. "Strategic Goals Guide HRMS Development," *Personnel Journal* (Sept. 1993): 68–79.

5. J. J. Laabs, "OLIVER: A Twist on Communication," *Personnel Journal* (Sept. 1991): 79–82; "Compensation Advances into a New Decade: Report on 1990 ACA National Conference," *Bulletin to Management*, (Nov. 1990): 345; "Computer Use Rising in HR Departments," *Bulletin to Management* (June 15, 1989): 189; R. J. Sahl, "Get it Together! Integrating the HR Department," *Personnel* (Feb. 1989): 39–45.

6. P. Parish, "Interactive Pension Data," *Personnel Administrator* (July 1985): 10–12; E. M. Fowler, "Employees, Benefits and Computers," *The New York Times* (Feb. 16, 1988): 3; R. D. Huff, "The Impact of Cafeteria Benefits on the Human Resource Information System," *Personnel Journal* (April 1983): 282–283.

7. C. Bovier, "How a High-Tech Training System Crashed and Burned," *Training* (Aug. 1993): 26–29.

8. K. Allan, "Computer Courses Ensure Uniform Training," *Personnel Journal* (June 1993): 68. Also see "Data Base Helps Employees Learn from Experiences," *Personnel Journal* (Jan. 1993): 57; and B. C. Herniter, E. Carmel, and J. Nunamaker, Jr., "Computers Improve the Efficiency of the Negotiation Process," *Personnel Journal* (April 1993): 93–99.

9. R. S. Schuler and V. L. Huber, *Personnel and Human Resource Management*, 5th ed. (St. Paul, Minn.: West, 1993): 259–260.

10. J. F. Coates, "An Environmental Scan: Projecting Future Human Resource Trends," *Human Resource Planning* (Dec. 1987): 219–289.

11. M. J. Dreyfuss, "Catching the Computer Wave," *Fortune* (Sept. 26, 1988): 78–82; R. Tetzelli, "The Internet and Your Business," *Fortune* (March 7, 1994): 86–96.

12. J. Main, "The Winning Corporation," *Fortune* (Sept. 26, 1988): 50–56; S. Tully, "The Modular Corporation," *Fortune* (Feb. 8, 1993): 106–115.

13. Coates (*op. cit.*, see Note 10).

14. M. Mandel and C. Farrell, "The Technology Payoff," *Business Week* (June 14, 1993): 57–73; S. Sherman, "The New Computer Revolution," *Fortune* (June 14, 1993): 56–80; J. Byrne, R. Brandt and O. Port, "The Virtual Corporation," *Business Week* (Feb. 8, 1993): 98–102.

15. S. D. Solomon, "Use Technology to Manage People," *Inc.* (May 1990): 124.

16. Main (*op. cit.*, see Note 12): 82. Also see J. Byrne, "The Horizontal Corporation," *Business Week* (Dec. 20, 1993): 76–81.

17. R. B. Dunham and F. J. Smith, *Organization Surveys* (Glenview, Ill.: Scott, Foresman, 1979): 91–97. Also see, W. H. Read, "Gathering Opinion On-Line," *HR Magazine* (Jan. 1991): 51–53.

18. P. T. Kilborn, "Workers Using Computers Find a Supervisor Inside," *The New York Times* (Dec. 23, 1990): 1, 18L. Also see "Surveillance and Searches: Reducing the Risks," *Bulletin to Management* (Nov. 7, 1991): 345; *Federal Government Information Technology: Electronic Surveillance and Civil Liberties* (Washington, D.C.: Office of Technology Assessment, OTA-CIT-293, Oct. 1985); *The Electronic Supervisor: New Technology, New Tensions*, OTA-CIT-333 (Washington, D.C.: U.S. Government Printing Office, Sept. 1987).

19. *Ibid.* Also see, N. J. Beutell and A. J. Walker, "HR Information Systems," in R. S. Schuler, *Managing HR in the Information Age* (Washington, D.C.: BNA, 1991): 167–203.

20. M. E. Cashman and J. C. McElroy, "Evaluating the HR Function," *HR Magazine* (Jan. 1991): 70–73; M. Mercer, *Turning Your Human Resources Department into a Profit Center* (New York: American Management Association, 1989); B. R. Ellig, "Controlling HR Costs," *Personnel* (April 1990): 20–23; W. F. Cascio, *Costing Human Resources: The Financial Impact of Behavior in Organizations*, 3rd ed. (Boston: PWS-Kent, 1991); D. Ulrich, "Assessing Human Resource Effectiveness: Stakeholder, Utility and Relationship Approaches," *Human Resource Planning* 12:4 (1989): 301–316; L. Dyer, *Human Resource Management: Evolving Roles and Responsibilities* (Washington, D.C.: BNA Books, 1988), 187–227; J. Fitz-enz, *Human Values Management: The Value-Adding Human Resource Management Strategy for the 1990s* (San Francisco: Jossey-Bass, 1990); A. S. Tsui, "A Multiple-Constituency Model of Effectiveness: An Empirical Examination at the Human Resource Subunit Level," *Administrative Science Quarterly* 35 (1990): 458–483.

21. T. Jackson and A. Vitber, "Career Development, Part 1: Career and Entrepreneurship," *Personnel* (Feb. 1987): 12–17.

22. R. A. Ash and E. L. Levine, *Personnel* (Nov.–Dec. 1980): 53–59; E. L. Levine, R. A. Ash, and N. Bennett, "Exploratory Comparative Study of Four Job Analysis Methods," *Journal of Applied Psychology* (1980): 524–535; E. L. Levine, R. A. Ash, and F. Sistrunk, "Evaluation of Job Analysis Methods by Experienced Job Analysts," *Academy of Management Journal* (1983): 339–348.

23. F. Krystofiak, J. M. Newman, and G. Anderson, "A Quantified Approach to Measurement of Job Content: Procedures and Payoffs," *Personnel Psychology* (Summer 1979): 341–357.

24. The following assessment discussion relates to aspects of the total performance appraisal system generally. Specific parts of the performance appraisal system are discussed but not in detail. For a detailed discussion of some parts, see F. Landy and J. Far, "Performance Ratings," *Psychological Bulletin* 87 (1980): 72–107; F. Landy, J. L. Barnes-Farrel, R. J. Vance, and J. W. Steele, "Statistical Control of Halo Error in Performance Ratings," *Journal of Applied Psychology* 65 (1980): 501–506. See also Chapter 9.

25. See M. Sashkin, "Appraising Appraisal: Ten Lessons From Research for Practice," *Organizational Dynamics* (Winter 1981): 37–50.

26. M. Beer, "Performance Appraisal: Dilemmas and Possibilities," *Organizational Dynamics* (Winter 1981): 26.

27. R. I. Lazar, "Performance Appraisal: What Does the Future Hold?" *Personnel Administrator* (July 1980): 69–73; A. M. Morrison and M. E. Kranz, "The Shape of Performance Appraisal in the Coming Decade," *Personnel* (July–Aug. 1981): 12–22.

28. A "properly administered" compensation program implies several qualities of total compensation: the job evaluation process is valid; pay is administered in a nondiscriminatory way; compensation policies are communicated to be understood; the administrative costs are contained; it has sufficient motivational value; and it is supported by top management.

29. E. E. Lawler III, "The Strategic Design of Reward Systems," in *Readings in Personnel and Human Resources Management*, 2nd ed., eds. R. S. Schuler and S. A. Youngblood (St. Paul, Minn.: West, 1984), 253–269; L. L. Cummings, "Compensation, Culture and Motivation: A Systems Perspective," *Organizational Dynamics* (Winter 1984): 33–44.

30. M. Lerner, "Measuring Pay Costs in Your Organization Against Pay in Other Organizations," *Personnel* (Aug. 1988): 70–73.

31. R. B. Dunham and R. A. Formisano, "Designing and Evaluating Employee Benefit Systems," *Personnel Administrator* (April 1982): 29–36.

32. For an extensive description of training and development assessment, see M. J. Burke and R. R. Day, "A Cumulative Study of the Effectiveness of Managerial Training," *Journal of Applied Psychology* (1986): 232–245; "Cost-Effective Training Techniques," *Bulletin to Management* (Aug. 26, 1986): 284; H. E. Fisher and R. Weinberg, "Make Training Accountable: Assess Its Impact," *Personnel Journal* (Jan. 1988): 73–75; J. Fitz-enz, "Proving the Value of Training," *Personnel* (March 1988): 17–23; J. K. Ford and S. P. Wroten, "Introducing New Methods for Conducting Training Evaluation and for Linking Training Evaluation to Program Redesign," *Personnel Psychology* (Winter 1984); 651–666.

33. F. O. Hoffman, "A Responsive Training Department Cuts Costs," *Personnel Journal* (Feb. 1984): 48–53; D. L. Kirkpatrick, "Four Steps to Measuring Training Effectiveness"; H. W. Smith and C. E. George, "Evaluating Internal Advanced Management Programs"; S. B. Wehrenberg, "Evaluation of Training: Part I," *Personnel Journal* (Aug. 1983): 608–610; S. B. Wehrenberg, "Evaluation of Training: Part II," *Personnel Journal* (Sept. 1983): 698–702.

34. J. Fasqualetto, "New Competencies Define the HRIS Manager's Future Role," *Personnel Journal* (Jan. 1993): 91–99.

35. *Ibid.*, 92. Used by permission.

36. M. Tanzer, "Keep Spies Out of Your Company," *Personnel Journal* (May 1993): 45–51. Also see T. Hunter, "How Client/Server Is Reshaping the HRIS," *Personnel Journal* (July 1992): 38–46; J. J. Laabs, "Electronic Campus Captures Apple's Corporate Memory," *Personnel Journal* (Nov. 1993): 104–109.

SUMMARY CASES
FOR
MANAGING HUMAN RESOURCES

PEOPLES TRUST COMPANY

THE LINCOLN ELECTRIC COMPANY

PEOPLES TRUST COMPANY

The Peoples Trust Company first opened its doors to the public on June 1, 1875, with a total salaried staff of eight members: a treasurer; a secretary; and six assistants (three of whom held the positions of day watchman, night watchman, and messenger). Located in a large, midwestern city, the original company had occupied the basement floor of a new five-story office building with an electric-bell system, steam heat, and steam-driven elevator.

During its early years, the Trust Company had concentrated its activities on providing vault services to its customers for the safekeeping of tangible items and securities. Management had been able to develop the reputation of being a highly conservative trust company that concentrated on a relatively small and select market of wealthy individuals from the local area. In the years following, the vault service had been retained as an accommodation to its customers, but the company's emphasis had slowly shifted from vault service to a wider range of banking and trust services.

Until the early 1900s, banking services had overshadowed trust services in terms of asset volume. Following the turn of the century, trust assets had begun to grow at an increasing rate. Over the years, the company had been able to achieve an impressive record of sound and steady growth. According to a story often told in baking circles: "Peoples Trust was so conservative that they prospered even during the Depression!"

In 1963, with the appointment of a new president, a new era began for Peoples Trust Company. Between 1963 and 1978, trust assets under supervision rose by $145 million, while deposits increased by more than $20 million. The company entered 1983 with about $2 billion in trust assets and $90 million in savings deposits.

Accompanying this recent growth has been the company's desire to fashion a new image for itself. In 1979, Mr. Robert Toller assumed the presidency of Peoples Trust. In 1982, he remarked: ". . . it should be said that the old concept of a trust involving merely the regular payment of income and preservation of capital is largely obsolete." Accordingly, the Investment Division of the company had been expanded and strengthened. Similar changes had been effected in the Trust and Estate Administrative Group and other customer services. Among these were the improvement of accounting methods and procedures, the installation of electronic data processing systems, and complete renovation of the company's eight-floor building and facilities. Most recently, the company has extended its services into the field of management consulting. This had been acknowledged as a "pioneer" step for a banking institution. The president recently characterized the company as "an organization in the fiduciary business."

At the time these data were gathered, the company had a total of 602 employees. Of this number, 109 were in what is considered the "officer-group"* positions of the company. The company's relations with its employees over the years have been satisfactory, the Peoples Trust is generally recognized by city residents and those in suburban areas as a good place to work. The company hires most of its employees from the local area.

In the period before 1980 Peoples Trust had provided satisfactory advancement opportunities for its employees, and it had been possible for a young, high-school graduate who showed promise on the job to work his way up gradually to officer status. Graduates of banking institutions were also sought for employment with the company. Ordinarily individuals were considered eligible for promotion to the jobs above them after they had thoroughly mastered the details of their present positions.

Prior to 1980 the total staff of the company was small enough so that there was no need to prepare official organization charts or job descriptions. Virtually all of the employees knew each other on a first-name basis, and they were generally familiar with each other's area of job responsibility. New employees were rapidly able to learn "whom you had to go to for what."

In 1980 the company management called in an outside consultant to appraise its organizational structure and operations and to confer on the rapid expansion and diversification of banking services that the company had planned. The presence of the consultants and the subsequent preparation of organization charts and job descriptions reportedly "shook up a lot of people"—many feared loss of their jobs or, at least, substantial changes in the nature of work and assignments. However, there was little

---

*Membership in the officer group is determined by an employee's being legally empowered to represent the company in a transaction.

overt reaction among the officer-level employees in terms of turnover and/or other indices of unrest.

Over the years it had been the policy of the company to pay wages that were at least average or a little above the average paid by comparable banking organizations in the area. This, combined with favorable employee relations and the stable and prestigious nature of the work, resulted in a low turnover of personnel. The bulk of employee turnover occurred among the younger employees who filled clerical positions throughout the company's various departments.

Since 1980, the personnel picture at Peoples Trust has been shifting. Several changes have taken place in the top management of the company. By adding several new customer services, the company has altered the very nature of its business. This has resulted in a trend toward "professionalization" of many of the officer-level positions in that these positions now require individuals with higher levels of education and broader abilities. The impact of these changes on current employees has been a matter of concern to several executives in the company, particularly to Mr. John Moore, Manager of the Organization Planning and Personnel Department. Mr. Moore described his picture of the situation to the researcher as follows:

INTERVIEW WITH JOHN MOORE, V.P., ORGANIZATION PLANNING AND PERSONNEL

Our problem here is one of a changing image and along with it the changing of people. As a trust company, we had no other ties with an individual's financial needs . . . we could only talk in terms of death. We wanted to be able to talk in terms of life, so we got active in the investment-advisory business.

The old wealth around here is pretty well locked up, so we wanted to provide services to new and growing organizations and to individuals who are accumulating wealth. Our problem is one of reorientation. We used to provide one service for one customer. We now want to enter new ventures, offer new services, attract new customers. The problem has become one of how to make the change . . . do we have the talent and the people to make the change?

We have a "band" of people (see Exhibit 1) in our organization . . . in the 35–50 age group who came in under the old hiring practices and ground rules. Given the new directions in which our company is moving and the changing job requirements, it's clear that, considering their current qualifications and capabilities, these individuals have nowhere to go. Some have been able to accept this; and this acceptance includes watching others move past them. Others have difficulty accepting it . . . a few have left . . . and we haven't discouraged anyone from

leaving. For those who can't accept it, there is the problem of integrating their career strategy with ours. We've articulated our objectives clearly; now individuals need clarification of their own strategies.

As I see it, change caught up with these individuals. They had on-the-job training in their own areas, but that doesn't help them much to cope with the new demands. New functional areas are being melded on top of old ones. For example, marketing is new; so is electronic data processing. They both require qualities that our existing employee staff didn't have.

To date, we have not approached any of these people in an individual way to discuss their problems with them. Our objectives are to further develop these people, but we'll first have to get the support of the department managers who supervise them.

We want to find ways to further develop personnel of the kind represented by this group through a variety of approaches. I am thinking here not only of formal job training in management development, but also of management techniques that would help individuals identify new kinds of qualifications or possible new standards of performance they must take into consideration in planning their own personal growth.

We also have to find ways to provide more opportunities for minorities and women in the organization, particularly at the officer level. Although Peoples Trust is not a federal contractor, we would like to be seen as and be an affirmative action employer and an organization where everyone has an equal chance for employment and promotion.

We have to change the conditioning of old times throughout the company. A recently hired MBA is now an officer. Years ago that couldn't have happened so rapidly. And not everyone here is in agreement that the appointment I just mentioned *should* have happened the way it did. We have to develop support in our company for the new recruiting image.

1. We have a problem in under-utilization of resources.
2. There is a problem which is presented to the growth and development of the company in having some of the individuals I have been discussing settled into key spots.

The company really bears the responsibility for the current situation as I described it. In addition, what this all means to me is that our personnel function may change considerably over the coming year.

After this interview with Mr. Moore, the researcher talked with other company executives to learn their views of the problems outlined by Mr. Moore. The findings from these interviews are presented below.

EXHIBIT 1

EXHIBIT 1
PEOPLES TRUST COMPANY

NAME	AGE	EDUCATION	DATE OF HIRE	POSITIONS HELD
Linda Horn	37	2-year technical institute of business administration	1975	Messenger Clearance clerk Accounting clerk Unit head (working supervisor) Section head (supervisor)
Richard Gaul*	30	2-year junior college program in business administration	1977	Business machines operator Section head (supervisor) Operations officer
Fred James	35	B.A. Degree local university American Institute of Banking	1976	Loan clerk Teller Accounting unit head (working supervisor) Section head (supervisor)
Fran Wilson*	35	1 year at a local university	1981	Methods analyst Operations unit head (working supervisor) Systems Programmer Property accounting dept. head
Martin Pfieffer*	32	Prep School	1977	Messenger Accounting clerk Section head (supervisor) Department head
James Klinger	38	B.A. Degree from local university	1972	Messenger Accounting clerk Records clerk Unit head (working supervisor) Administrative specialist
Karen Kissler*	35	B.A. Degree from local university co-op program	1974	Messenger Real property specialist Assistant estate officer
Charles Ferris	42	2-year jr. college program in business administration American Institute Banking	1962	Messenger Deposit accounting section head (supervisor) Unit head (working supervisor)
William Jagger	54	High School	1949	Messenger Trust liaison clerk Accounting clerk Bookkeeping section head
Thomas Geoghigan*	42	2-year jr. college program in business administration	1969	Messenger Securities accountant Property custodian Office manager Assistant operations officer

* = Officer

INTERVIEW WITH FRED BELLOWS, HUMAN RESOURCE PLANNING

Historically we have been conservatively managed . . . you might say "ultra-conservatively." But now we want to change that image. Several years ago there was a revolution in top management. In 1979, Mr. Toller took over and brought in young people, many not from the banking field but from other types of business and consulting organizations. Our employment philosophy may be stated as follows: "We want above-average people . . . for above-average pay . . . and we want to give them a chance to learn and grow and move with the organization." This applies mainly to those in whom we see management-level potential.

They are told in their employment interview that if they don't see opportunity with us, then they should leave. This is in contrast to the old philosophy that this is a secure place to work, that you can stay here by keeping your nose clean, and that you can sit and wait for pot luck to become a trust officer.

Many people are caught in this changing philosophy. A case in the Trust Administration Division is a good example. There we have an employee in a Grade 10 job who has been with the bank eight years. We just hired a new person out of college who we put in that same Grade 10. Now they're both at the same level, but they're entirely different people in terms of education, social background, etc.

Now the Head of our Trust Division bucks this sort of thing. She argues that we don't need all "stars" in the company. Yet, the president wants young, dynamic individuals who can develop and be developed. So I'm trying to get the Trust Division to define: what does the job really require?

We have a number of people with two years of accounting training who have been with the company anywhere from six to nine years. Under our old system they'd be okay, but under the new system they're not. They're not realistic about their future. Our problem is that we're being honest, but few are getting the message.

We bring in a new individual . . . ask others to train that person . . . and then promote that person over their heads. We have people whose jobs we could get done for a lot less money. When, if ever, do we tell them to go elsewhere?

INTERVIEW WITH LARRY ANDREWS, CONTROLLER

There is no question but that there has been a complete revolution around here. In the past, we were in business to serve the community; to handle small accounts; to help the small investor who needed investment service. Our motto was "help anyone who needs help." Our employees were geared to this kind of work orientation and felt at home with it. They could easily identify themselves with this sort of approach to doing business. Most people were quite comfortable; their personal goals coincided with the company goal.

But we found that we couldn't make any money conducting this kind of business. So, we've had to extend our services to attract people who have money and can afford our service. Now the company goal has changed. For example, the Trust Department is now concerned with the management of property in general. The "dead man's bank" has become the "live people's service organization." So we've had to create a kind of snob appeal that too many of our people can't identify with or don't believe in.

Many problems have emerged from these changes. Before, individuals' knowledge of the details of their jobs was their greatest asset. They worked to develop that knowledge and protected it. Now—and I'm speaking of supervisory jobs—the important factor is to have some familiarity with the work but to be able to work with people; to get others to do the detail. Too many of our people still don't understand this. . . .

The route to the top is no longer clear. Over a five-year period this organization has changed. There have been reorganizations, new functions created, and some realignment of existing functions. Many who felt they had a clear line to something higher in the organization now find that that "something" isn't there anymore.

We've had lots of hiring-in at higher levels. Many oldtimers have been bypassed. In some cases, the new, outside hirees came into jobs that never existed before, or were hired into a job that had previously existed, but which is now a "cut" above what it was before. What used to be a top job is now a second or third spot.

What we need now are people who are "professional managers"—by that I mean a supervisor versus a technical specialist. Years ago supervision could be concentrated in a few key individuals . . . but in the past five years we've grown 20% to 30% and have a management hierarchy. A person used to be able to grow up as a technical specialist and develop managerial skills secondarily.

To a small extent it's a matter of personality too. We have a new president, and what is acceptable to him differs from what was acceptable to his predecessor. There's a new mix of personal favoritism that goes along with the new vogue. Technical specialists are "low need" as far as the company is concerned. I estimate we now have about 30 people in this category in officer-level jobs.

Interview with Tom Martin, Marketing Division Head

There have been many changes over the past six years. Mr. Toller took a look at the entire organization . . . and then hired a consultant to do an organizational study. It was sort of an outside stamp of approval.

His hope was to move some of the dead wood . . . the senior people who were past their peak and didn't represent what the company wanted anymore in its managerial and officer staff. Few of these individuals have the capacity to change and for others it may already be too late to change. Many had leveled off in their development long before these changes came about, and the changes just made it more apparent. Early retirement has been given to some of those over 60. Others remained as titular head of their departments, but in essence report to a younger person who is really running the department.

Banking used to be a soft industry . . . you were hired and never fired. If you were a poor performer, you were given a lousy job that you could stay at. No one was ever called in and told to shape up. The pay was so poor it attracted people who wanted to work in a sheltered area, and they were satisfied to try and build a career in that area. So it was a job with low pay, high prestige, and some opportunity.

Our biggest problem is to convince people that they are not technicians anymore, that they are to *supervise* their subordinates and work to develop them. Apparently, for many older individuals, and younger ones too, this is an impossible assignment. They can do the jobs themselves, but having anyone else do it in any other way runs against their grain.

If our rate of personnel growth over the next ten years is as fast as the previous ten years, I'm afraid we can only absorb about 50% of our most promising people.

Interview with Jane Farren, Trust Administration Division Head

We have several people for whom there is very little opportunity anymore. We just don't see any potential in these people. There are about fifteen of them who are in their 40s and are really not capable of making any independent decisions. We're trying to get them to see other opportunities . . . both inside and outside the company. For example, our Real Estate group was big in the 1960s and 1970s. We're trying to make it important again, and there may be some opportunities in that area.

To give you an idea of the problem we're faced with: One individual is really a personality problem. He's an attorney but he can't get along with others. He wants people to come to him; he focuses on detail too much; and he has great difficulty in telling others what to do and how to do it. He has to do the job all by himself.

Another individual: We gave him a section to supervise but he really hasn't measured up. But, he was the president's pet. I suppose we'll let him continue on . . . he's 57 . . . and then retire him early.

Interview with Mr. L. Henry, General Administration Division

The company has been undergoing basic change. In the past, if people demonstrated technical competence they were promoted, and that was fine while the company was a small, stable group, and everyone knew what the other was thinking. But then, many in the senior group began to retire. With this "changing of the guard" and the growth of the company, many of us have lost communication with our counterparts. Many of us are new in this field, new to this company, and, of course, new to each other. But we recognize this, so half the communication problem is solved. In a sense, we're not constrained by "how it was done before."

My people have reacted to all this change by sitting back and waiting, seeing which way things are going to go, then I guess deciding whether they are going to join you or not. Most of my people are relatively recent employees—as a matter of fact, of the 278 people in my division, only 11 have been with the company more than 10 years. Conversion to EDP will really create a lot of changes in my area.

SOURCE: This case was prepared by Hrach Bedrosian, New York University and is used here with his permission.

THE LINCOLN ELECTRIC COMPANY

People are our most valuable asset. They must feel secure, important, challenged, in control of their destiny, confident in their leadership, be responsive to common goals, believe they are being treated fairly, have easy access to authority and open lines of communication in all possible directions. Perhaps the most important task Lincoln employees face today is that of establishing an example for others in the Lincoln organization in other parts of the world. We need to maximize the benefits of cooperation and teamwork, fusing high technology with human talent, so that we here in the USA and all of our subsidiary and joint venture operations will be in a position to realize our full potential. *George Willis, former CEO, The Lincoln Electric Company**

The Lincoln Electric Company is the world's largest manufacturer of arc welding products and a leading producer of industrial electric motors. The firm employs 2,400 workers in 2 U.S. factories near Cleveland and an equal number in 11 factories located in other countries. This does not include the field sales force of more than 200. The company's U.S. market share (for arc-welding products) is estimated at more than 40 percent.

The Lincoln incentive management plan has been well known for many years. Many college management texts make reference to the Lincoln plan as a model for achieving higher worker productivity. Certainly, the firm has been successful according to the usual measures.

James F. Lincoln died in 1965 and there was some concern, even among employees, that the management system would fall into disarray, that profits would decline, and that year-end bonuses might be discontinued. Quite the contrary, 24 years after Lincoln's death, the company appears as strong as ever. Each year, except the recession years 1982 and 1983, has seen high profits and bonuses. Employee morale and productivity remain very good. Employee turnover is almost nonexistent except for retirements. Lincoln's market share is stable. The historically high stock dividends continue.

A HISTORICAL SKETCH

In 1895, after being "frozen out" of the depression-ravaged Elliott-Lincoln Company, a maker of Lincoln-

*Donald Hastings is the current CEO of Lincoln Electric.

designed electric motors, John C. Lincoln took out his second patent and began to manufacture his improved motor. He opened his new business, unincorporated, with $200 he had earned redesigning a motor for young Herbert Henry Dow, who later founded the Dow Chemical Company.

Started during an economic depression and cursed by a major fire after only one year in business, the company grew, but hardly prospered, through its first quarter century. In 1906, John C. Lincoln incorporated the business and moved from his one-room, fourth-floor factory to a new three-story building he erected in east Cleveland. He expanded his workforce to 30 and sales grew to over $50,000 a year. John preferred being an engineer and inventor rather than a manager, though, and it was to be left to another Lincoln to manage the company through its years of success.

In 1907, after a bout with typhoid fever forced him from Ohio State University in his senior year, James F. Lincoln, John's younger brother, joined the fledgling company. In 1914 he became active head of the firm, with the titles of General Manager and Vice President. John remained president of the company for some years but became more involved in other business ventures and in his work as an inventor.

One of James Lincoln's early actions was to ask the employees to elect representatives to a committee which would advise him on company operations. This "Advisory Board" has met with the chief executive officer every two weeks since that time. This was only the first of a series of innovative personnel policies which have, over the years, distinguished Lincoln Electric from its contemporaries.

The first year the Advisory Board was in existence, working hours were reduced from 55 per week, then standard, to 50 hours a week. In 1915, the company gave each employee a paid-up life insurance policy. A welding school, which continues today, was begun in 1917. In 1918, an employee bonus plan was attempted. It was not continued, but the idea was to resurface later.

The Lincoln Electric Employees' Association was formed in 1919 to provide health benefits and social activities. This organization continues today and has assumed several additional functions over the years. In 1923, a piecework pay system was in effect, employees got two weeks paid vacation each year, and wages were adjusted for changes in the Consumer Price Index. Approximately 30 percent of the common stock was set aside for key employees in 1914. A stock purchase plan for all employees was begun in 1925.

The Board of Directors voted to start a suggestion system in 1929. The program is still in effect, but cash awards, a part of the early program, were discontinued several years ago. Now, suggestions are rewarded by additional "points," which affect year-end bonuses.

The legendary Lincoln bonus plan was proposed by the Advisory Board and accepted on a trial basis in 1934. The first annual bonus amounted to about 25 percent of wages. There has been a bonus every year since then. The bonus plan has been a cornerstone of the Lincoln management system and recent bonuses have approximated annual wages.

By 1944, Lincoln employees enjoyed a pension plan, a policy of promotion from within, and continuous employment. Base pay rates were determined by formal job evaluation and a merit rating system was in effect.

In the prologue of James F. Lincoln's last book, Charles G. Herbruck writes regarding the foregoing personnel innovations:

> They were not to buy good behavior. They were not efforts to increase profits. They were not antidotes to labor difficulties. They did not constitute a "do-gooder" program. They were expression of mutual respect for each person's importance to the job to be done. All of them reflect the leadership of James Lincoln, under whom they were nurtured and propagated.

During World War II, Lincoln prospered as never before. By the start of the war, the company was the world's largest manufacturer of arc-welding products. Sales of about $4,000,000 in 1934 grew to $24,000,000 by 1941. Productivity per employee more than doubled during the same period. The Navy's Price Review Board challenged the high profits. And the Internal Revenue Service questioned the tax deductibility of employee bonuses, arguing they were not "ordinary and necessary" costs of doing business. But the forceful and articulate James Lincoln was able to overcome the objections.

Certainly since 1935 and probably for several years before that, Lincoln productivity has been well above the average for similar companies. The company claims levels of productivity more than twice those for other manufacturers from 1945 onward. Information available from outside sources tends to support these claims.

COMPANY PHILOSOPHY

James F. Lincoln was the son of a Congregational minister, and Christian principles were at the center of his

business philosophy. The confidence that he had in the efficacy of Christ's teachings is illustrated by the following remark taken from one of his books:

> The Christian ethic should control our acts. If it did control our acts, the savings in cost of distribution would be tremendous. Advertising would be a contact of the expert consultant with the customer, in order to give the customer the best product available when all of the customer's needs are considered. Competition then would be in improving the quality of products and increasing efficiency in producing and distributing them; not in deception, as is now too customary. Pricing would reflect efficiency of production; it would not be a selling dodge that the customer may well be sorry he accepted. It would be proper for all concerned and rewarding for the ability used in producing the product.

There is no indication that Lincoln attempted to evangelize his employees or customers—or the general public for that matter. Neither the chairman of the board and chief executive, George Willis, nor the president, Donald F. Hastings, mention the Christian gospel in their recent speeches and interviews. The company motto, "The actual is limited, the possible is immense," is prominently displayed, but there is no display of religious slogans, and there is no company chapel.

ATTITUDE TOWARD THE CUSTOMER

James Lincoln saw the customer's needs as the *raison d'etre* for every company. "When any company has achieved success so that it is attractive as an investment," he wrote, "all money usually needed for expansion is supplied by the customer in retained earnings. It is obvious that the customer's interests, not the stockholder's, should come first." In 1947 he said, "Care should be taken . . . not to rivet attention on profit. Between 'How much do I get?' and 'How do I make this better, cheaper, more useful?' the difference is fundamental and decisive." Willis, too, ranks the customer as management's most important constituency. This is reflected in Lincoln's policy to "at all times price on the basis of cost and at all times keep pressure on our cost . . ." Lincoln's goal, often stated, is "to build a better and better product at a lower and lower price." "It is obvious," James Lincoln said, "that the customer's interests should be the first goal of industry."

ATTITUDE TOWARD STOCKHOLDERS

Stockholders are given last priority at Lincoln. This is a continuation of James Lincoln's philosophy: "The last group to be considered is the stockholders who own stock because they think it will be more profitable than investing money in any other way." Concerning division of the largess produced by incentive management, he wrote, "The absentee stockholder also will get his share, even if undeserved, out of the greatly increased profit that the efficiency produces."

ATTITUDE TOWARD UNIONISM

There has never been a serious effort to organize Lincoln employees. While James Lincoln criticized the labor movement for "selfishly attempting to better its position at the expense of the people it must serve," he still had kind words for union members. He excused abuses of union power as "the natural reactions of human beings to the abuses to which management has subjected them." Lincoln's idea of the correct relationship between workers and managers is shown by this comment: "Labor and management are properly not warring camps; they are parts of one organization in which they must and should cooperate fully and happily."

BELIEFS AND ASSUMPTIONS ABOUT EMPLOYEES

If fulfilling customer needs is the desired goal of business, then employee performance and productivity are the means by which this goal can best be achieved. It is the Lincoln attitude toward employees, reflected in the following comments by James Lincoln, which is credited by many with creating the success the company has experienced:

> The greatest fear of the worker, which is the same as the greatest fear of the industrialist in operating a company, is the lack of income . . . The industrial manager is very conscious of his company's need of uninterrupted income. He is completely oblivious, evidently, of the fact that the worker has the same need.

> He is just as eager as any manager is to be part of a team that is properly organized and working for the advancement of our economy . . . He has no desire to make profits for those who do not hold up their end in production, as is true of absentee stockholders and inactive people in the company.

> If money is to be used as an incentive, the program must provide that what is paid to the worker is what he has earned. The earnings of each must be in accordance with accomplishment.

> Status is of great importance in all human relationships. The greatest incentive that money has, usually, is that it is a symbol of success . . . The resulting status is the real incentive . . . Money alone can be an incentive to the miser only.

> There must be complete honesty and understanding between the hourly worker and management if high efficiency is to be obtained.

LINCOLN'S BUSINESS

Arc-welding has been the standard joining method in shipbuilding for decades. It is the predominant way of connecting steel in the construction industry. Most industrial plants have their own welding shops for maintenance and construction. Manufacturers of tractors and all kinds of heavy equipment use arc-welding extensively in the manufacturing process. Many hobbyists have their own welding machines and use them for making metal items such as patio furniture and barbecue pits. The popularity of welded sculpture as an art form is growing.

While advances in welding technology have been frequent, arc-welding products, in the main, have hardly changed. Lincoln's Innershield process is a notable exception. This process, described later, lowers welding cost and improves quality and speed in many applications. The most widely-used Lincoln electrode, the Fleetweld 5P, has been virtually the same since the 1930s. The most popular engine-driven welder in the world, the Lincoln SA-200, has been a gray-colored assembly including a four-cylinder continental "Red Seal" engine and a 200 ampere direct-current generator with two current-control knobs for at least four decades. A 1989 model SA-200 even weighs almost the same as the 1950 model, and it certainly is little changed in appearance.

The company's share of the U.S. arc-welding products market appears to have been about 40 percent for many years. The welding products market has grown somewhat faster than the level of industry in general. The market is highly price-competitive, with variations in prices of standard items normally amounting to only a percent or two. Lincoln's products are sold directly by its engineering-oriented sales force and indirectly through its distributor organization. Advertising expenditures amount to less than three-fourths of a percent of sales. Research and development expenditures typically range from $10 million to $12 million, considerably more than competitors.

The other major welding process, flame-welding, has not been competitive with arc-welding since the 1930s. However, plasma-arc-welding, a relatively new process which uses a conducting stream of super heated gas (plasma) to confine the welding current to a small area, has made some inroads, especially in metal tubing manufacturing, in recent years. Major advances in technology which will produce an alternative superior to arc-welding within the next decade or so appear unlikely. Also, it seems likely that changes in the machines and techniques used in arc-welding will be evolutionary rather than revolutionary.

PRODUCTS

The company is primarily engaged in the manufacture and sale of arc-welding products—electric welding machines and metal electrodes. Lincoln also produces electric motors ranging from one-half horsepower to 200 horsepower. Motors constitute about 8 to 10 percent of total sales. Several million dollars has recently been invested in automated equipment that will double Lincoln's manufacturing capacity for 1/2 to 20 horsepower electric motors.

The electric welding machines, some consisting of a transformer or motor and generator arrangement powered by commercial electricity and others consisting of an internal combustion engine and generator, are designed to produce 30 to 1,500 amperes of electrical power. This electrical current is used to melt a consumable metal electrode with the molten metal being transferred in super hot spray to the metal joint being welded. Very high temperatures and hot sparks are produced, and operators usually must wear special eye and face protection and leather gloves, often along with leather aprons and sleeves.

Lincoln and its competitors now market a wide range of general purpose and specialty electrodes for welding mild steel, aluminum, cast iron, and stainless and special steels. Most of these electrodes are designed to meet the standards of the American Welding Society, a trade association. They are thus essentially the same as to size and composition from one manufacturer to another. Every electrode manufacturer has a limited number of unique products, but these typically constitute only a small percentage of total sales.

Welding electrodes are of two basic types: (1) Coated "stick" electrodes, usually 14 inches long and smaller than a pencil in diameter, which are held in a special insulated holder by the operator, who must manipulate the electrode in order to maintain a proper arc-width and pattern of deposition of the metal being transferred. Stick electrodes are packaged in 6- to 50-pound boxes. (2) Coiled wired, ranging in diameter from .035" to 0.219", which is designed to be fed continuously to the welding arc through a "gun" held by the operator or positioned by automatic positioning equipment. The wire is packaged in coils, reels, and drums weighing from 14 to 1,000 pounds and may be solid or flux-cored.

MANUFACTURING PROCESSES

The main plant is in Euclid, Ohio, a suburb on Cleveland's east side. The layout of this plant is shown in Exhibit 1. There are no warehouses. Materials flow from the half-mile long dock on the north side of the plant through the production lines to a very limited storage and loading area on the south side. Materials used on each work station are stored as close as possible to the work station. The administrative offices, near the center of the factory, are entirely functional. A corridor below the

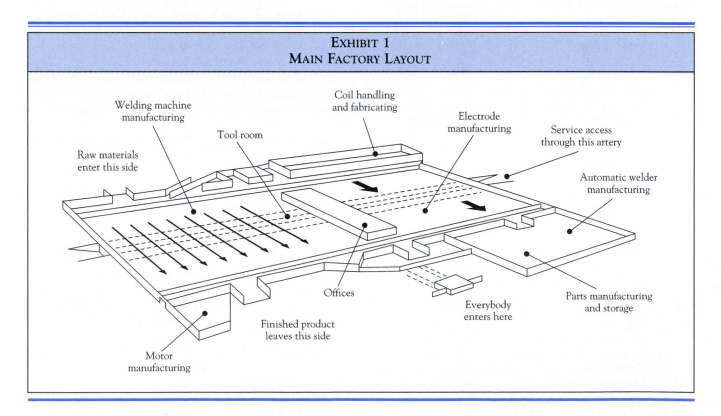

EXHIBIT 1
MAIN FACTORY LAYOUT

Welding machine manufacturing

Coil handling and fabricating

Tool room

Electrode manufacturing

Service access through this artery

Raw materials enter this side

Automatic welder manufacturing

Offices

Everybody enters here

Parts manufacturing and storage

Finished product leaves this side

Motor manufacturing

main level provides access to the factory floor from the main entrance near the center of the plan. *Fortune* magazine recently declared the Euclid facility one of America's 10 best-managed factories, and compared it with a General Electric plant also on the list:

> Stepping into GE's spanking new dishwasher plant, an awed supplier said, is like stepping "into the Hyatt Regency." By comparison, stepping into Lincoln Electric's 33-year-old, cavernous, dimly lit factory is like stumbling into a dingy big-city YMCA. It's only when one starts looking at how these factories do things that similarities become apparent. They have found ways to merge design with manufacturing, build in quality, make wise choices about automation, get close to customers, and handle their work forces.

A new Lincoln plant, in Mentor, Ohio, houses some of the electrode production operations, which were moved from the main plant.

Electrode manufacturing is highly capital intensive. Metal rods purchased from steel producers are drawn down to smaller diameters, cut to length and coated with pressed-powder "flux" for stick electrodes or plated with copper (for conductivity) and put into coils or spools for wire. Lincoln's Innershield wire is hollow and filled with a material similar to that used to coat stick electrodes. As mentioned earlier, this represented a major innovation in welding technology when it was introduced. The company is highly secretive about its electrode production processes, and outsiders are not given access to the details of those processes.

Lincoln welding machines and electric motors are made on a series of assembly lines. Gasoline and diesel engines are purchased partially assembled but practically all other components are made from basic industrial products, e.g., steel bars and sheets and bar copper conductor wire.

Individual components, such as gasoline tanks for engine-driven welders and steel shafts for motors and generators, are made by numerous small "factories within a factory." The shaft for a certain generator, for example, is made from raw steel bar by one operator who uses five large machines, all running continuously. A saw cuts the bar to length, a digital lathe machines different sections to varying diameters, a special milling machine cuts a slot for the keyway, and so forth, until a finished shaft is produced. The operator moves the shafts from machine to machine and makes necessary adjustments.

Another operator punches, shapes and paints sheet-metal cowling parts. One assembles steel laminations onto a rotor shaft, then winds, insulates and tests the rotors. Finished components are moved by crane operators to the nearby assembly lines.

WORKER PERFORMANCE AND ATTITUDES

Exceptional worker performance at Lincoln is a matter of record. The typical Lincoln employee earns about twice as much as other factory workers in the Cleveland area. Yet the company's labor cost per sales dollar in 1989, 26 cents, is well below industry averages. Worker turnover is practically nonexistent except for retirements and departures by new employees.

Sales per Lincoln factory employee currently exceed $150,000. An observer at the factory quickly sees why this figure is so high. Each worker is proceeding busily and thoughtfully about the task at hand. There is no idle chatter. Most workers take no coffee breaks. Many operate several machines and make a substantial component unaided. The supervisors are busy with planning and record keeping duties and hardly glance at the people they "supervise." The manufacturing procedures appear efficient—no unnecessary steps, no wasted motions, no wasted materials. Finished components move smoothly to subsequent work stations.

Appendix A includes summaries of interviews with employees.

ORGANIZATION STRUCTURE

Lincoln has never allowed development of a formal organization chart. The objective of this policy is to insure maximum flexibility. An open door policy is practiced throughout the company, and personnel are encouraged to take problems to the persons most capable of resolving them. Once, Harvard Business School researchers prepared an organization chart reflecting the implied relationships at Lincoln. The chart became available within the company, and present management feels that had a disruptive effect. Therefore, no organizational chart appears in this report.

Perhaps because of the quality and enthusiasm of the Lincoln workforce, routine supervision is almost nonexistent. A typical production foreman, for example, supervises as many as 100 workers, a span-of-control which does not allow more than infrequent worker-supervisor interaction.

Position titles and traditional flows of authority do imply something of an organizational structure, however. For example, the Vice-President, Sales, and the Vice-President, Electrode Division, report to the President, as do various staff assistants such as the Personnel Director and the Director of Purchasing. Using such implied relationships, it has been determined that production workers have two or, at most, three levels of supervision between themselves and the President.

PERSONNEL POLICIES

As mentioned earlier, it is Lincoln's remarkable personnel practices which are credited by many with the company's success.

RECRUITMENT AND SELECTION

Every job opening is advertised internally on company bulletin boards and any employee can apply for any job so advertised. External hiring is permitted only for entry level positions. Selection for these jobs is done on the basis of personal interviews—there is no aptitude or psychological testing. Not even a high school diploma is required—except for engineering and sales positions, which are filled by graduate engineers. A committee consisting of vice presidents and supervisors interviews candidates initially cleared by the Personnel Department. Final selection is made by the supervisor who has a job opening. Out of over 3,500 applicants interviewed by the Personnel Department during a recent period fewer than 300 were hired.

JOB SECURITY

In 1958 Lincoln formalized its guaranteed continuous employment policy, which has already been in effect for many years. There have been no layoffs since World War II. Since 1958, every worker with over two year's longevity has been guaranteed at least 30 hours per week, 49 weeks per year.

The policy has never been so severely tested as during the 1981–83 recession. As a manufacturer of capital goods, Lincoln's business is highly cyclical. In previous recessions the company was able to avoid major sales declines. However, sales plummeted 32 percent in 1982 and another 16 percent the next year. Few companies could withstand such a revenue collapse and remain profitable. Yet, Lincoln not only earned profits, but no employee was laid off and year-end incentive bonuses continued. To weather the storm, management cut most of the nonsalaried workers back to 30 hours a week for varying periods of time. Many employees were reassigned and the total workforce was slightly reduced through normal attrition and restricted hiring. Many employees grumbled at their unexpected misfortune, probably to the surprise and dismay of some Lincoln managers. However, sales and profits—and employee bonuses—soon rebounded and all was well again.

PERFORMANCE EVALUATIONS

Each supervisor formally evaluates subordinates twice a year using the cards shown in Exhibit 2. The employee

S–12

performance criteria, "quality," "dependability," "ideas and cooperation," and "output," are considered to be independent of each other. Marks on the cards are converted to numerical scores which are forced to average 100 for each evaluating supervisor. Individual merit rating scores normally range from 80 to 110. Any score over 100 requires a special letter to top management. These scores (over 100) are not considered in computing the required 100 point average for each evaluating supervisor. Suggestions for improvements often result in recommendations for exceptionally high performance scores. Supervisors discuss individual performance marks with the employees concerned. Each warranty claim is traced to the individual employee whose work caused the defect. The employee's performance score may be reduced, or the worker may be required to repay the cost of servicing the warranty claim by working without pay.

COMPENSATION

Basic wage levels for jobs at Lincoln are determined by a wage survey of similar jobs in the Cleveland area. These rates are adjusted quarterly in accordance with changes in the Cleveland area wage index. Insofar as possible, base wage rates are translated into piece rates. Practically all production workers and many others—for example, some forklift operators—are paid by piece rate. Once established, piece rates are never changed unless a substantive change in the way a job is done results from a source other than the worker doing the job.

In December of each year, a portion of annual profits is distributed to employees as bonuses. Incentive bonuses since 1934 have averaged about 90 percent of annual wages and somewhat more than after-tax profits. The average bonus for 1988 was $21,258. Even for the recession years 1982 and 1983, bonuses had averaged $13,998 and $8,557, respectively. Individual bonuses are proportional to merit-rating scores. For example, assume the amount set aside for bonuses is 80 percent of total wages paid to eligible employees. A person whose performance score is 95 will receive a bonus of 76 percent (0.80×0.95) of annual wages.

VACATIONS

The company is shut down for two weeks in August and two weeks during the Christmas season. Vacations are taken during these periods. For employees with over 25 years of service, a fifth week of vacation may be taken at a time acceptable to superiors.

WORK ASSIGNMENT

Management has authority to transfer workers and to switch between overtime and short time as required. Supervisors have undisputed authority to assign specific

Exhibit 2
Merit Rating Cards

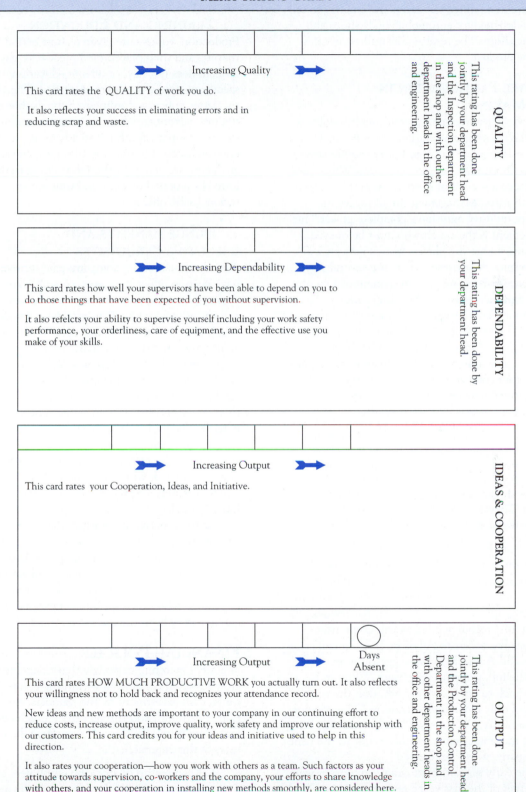

QUALITY

Increasing Quality ➤➤

This card rates the QUALITY of work you do.

It also reflects your success in eliminating errors and in reducing scrap and waste.

This rating has been done jointly by your department head and the Inspection department in the shop and with other department heads in the office and engineering.

DEPENDABILITY

Increasing Dependability ➤➤

This card rates how well your supervisors have been able to depend on you to do those things that have been expected of you without supervision.

It also refelcts your ability to supervise yourself including your work safety performance, your orderliness, care of equipment, and the effective use you make of your skills.

This rating has been done by your department head.

IDEAS & COOPERATION

Increasing Output ➤➤

This card rates your Cooperation, Ideas, and Initiative.

OUTPUT

Increasing Output ➤➤   Days Absent

This card rates HOW MUCH PRODUCTIVE WORK you actually turn out. It also reflects your willingness not to hold back and recognizes your attendance record.

New ideas and new methods are important to your company in our continuing effort to reduce costs, increase output, improve quality, work safety and improve our relationship with our customers. This card credits you for your ideas and initiative used to help in this direction.

It also rates your cooperation—how you work with others as a team. Such factors as your attitude towards supervision, co-workers and the company, your efforts to share knowledge with others, and your cooperation in installing new methods smoothly, are considered here.

This rating has been done jointly by your department head and the Production Control Department in the shop and with other department heads in the office and engineering.

parts to individual workmen, who may have their own preferences due to variations in piece rates. During the 1982–1983 recession, 50 factory workers volunteered to join sales teams and fanned out across the country to sell a new welder designed for automobile body shops and small machine shops. The result—$10 million in sales and a hot new product.

EMPLOYEE PARTICIPATION IN DECISION MAKING

Thinking of participative management usually evokes a vision of a relaxed, nonauthoritarian atmosphere. This is not the case at Lincoln. Formal authority is quite strong. "We're very authoritarian around here," says Willis. James F. Lincoln placed a good deal of stress on protecting management's authority. "Management in all successful departments of industry must have complete power," he said, "Management is the coach who must be obeyed. The men, however, are the players who alone can win the game." Despite this attitude, there are several ways in which employees participate in management at Lincoln.

Richard Sabo, Assistant to the Chief Executive Officer, relates job enlargement/enrichment to participation. He said, "The most important participative technique that we use is giving more responsibility to employees. We give a high school graduate more responsibility than other companies give their foremen." Management puts limits on the degree of participation which is allowed, however. In Sabo's words:

> When you use "participation," put quotes around it. Because we believe that each person should participate only in those decisions he is most knowledgeable about. I don't think production employees should control the decisions of the chairman. They don't know as much as he does about the decisions he is involved in.

The Advisory Board, elected by the workers, meets with the Chairman and the President every two weeks to discuss ways of improving operations. As noted earlier, this board has been in existence since 1914 and has contributed to many innovations. The incentive bonuses, for example, were first recommended by this committee. Every employee has access to Advisory Board members, and answers to all Advisory Board suggestions are promised by the following meeting. Both Willis and Hastings are quick to point out, though, that the Advisory Board only recommends actions. "They do not have direct authority," Willis says, "And when they bring up something that management thinks is not to the benefit of the company, it will be rejected."

Under the early suggestion program, employees were awarded one-half of the first year's savings attributable to

their suggestions. Now, however, the value of suggestions is reflected in performance evaluation scores, which determine individual incentive bonus amounts.

TRAINING AND EDUCATION

Production workers are given a short period of on-the-job training and then placed on a piecework pay system. Lincoln does not pay for off-site education, unless very specific company needs are identified. The idea behind this latter policy, according to Sabo, is that everyone cannot take advantage of such a program, and it is unfair to expend company funds for an advantage to which there is unequal access. Recruits for sales jobs, already college graduates, are given on-the-job training in the plant followed by a period of work and training at one of the regional sales offices.

FRINGE BENEFITS AND EXECUTIVE PERQUISITES

A medical plan and a company-paid retirement program have been in effect for many years. A plant cafeteria, operated on a break-even basis, serves meals at about 60 percent of usual costs. The Employee Association, to which the company does not contribute, provides disability insurance and social and athletic activities. The employee stock ownership program has resulted in employee ownership of about 50 percent of the common stock. Under this program, each employee with more than two years of service may purchase stock in the corporation. The price of these shares is established at book value. Stock purchased through this plan may be held by employees only. Dividends and voting rights are the same as for stock which is owned outside the plan. Approxi-mately 75 percent of the employees own Lincoln stock.

As to executive perquisites, there are none—crowded, austere offices, no executive washrooms or lunchrooms, and no reserved parking spaces. Even the top executives pay for their own meals and eat in the employee cafeteria. On one recent day, Willis arrived at work late due to a breakfast speaking engagement and had to park far away from the factory entrance.

FINANCIAL POLICIES

James F. Lincoln felt strongly that financing for company growth should come from within the company—through initial cash investment by the founders, through retention of earnings, and through stock purchases by those who work in the business. He saw the following advantages of this approach:

1. Ownership of stock by employees strengthens team spirit. "If they are mutually anxious to

make it succeed, the future of the company is bright."

2. Ownership of stock provides individual incentive because employees feel that they will benefit from company profitability.
3. "Ownership is educational." Owners-employees "will know how profits are made and lost; how success is won and lost . . . There are few socialists in the list of stockholders of the nation's industries."
4. "Capital available from within controls expansion." Unwarranted expansion would not occur, Lincoln believed, under his financing plan.
5. "The greatest advantage would be the development of the individual worker. Under the incentive of ownership, he would become a greater man."
6. "Stock ownership is one of the steps that can be taken that will make the worker feel that there is less of a gulf between him and the boss . . . Stock ownership will help the worker to recognize his responsibility in the game and the importance of victory."

Until 1980, Lincoln Electric borrowed no money. Even now, the company's liabilities consist mainly of accounts payable and short-term accruals.

The unusual pricing policy at Lincoln is succinctly stated by Willis: "At all times price on the basis of cost and at all times keep pressure on our cost." This policy resulted in the price for the most popular welding electrode then in use going from 16 cents a pound in 1929 to 4.7 cents in 1938. More recently, the SA-200 Welder, Lincoln's largest selling portable machine, decreased in price from 1958 through 1965. According to Dr. C. Jackson Grayson of the American Productivity Center in Houston, Texas, Lincoln's prices increased only one-fifth as fast as the Consumer Price Index from 1934 to about 1970. This resulted in a welding products market in which Lincoln became the undisputed price leader for the products it manufactures. Not even the major Japanese manufacturers, such as Nippon Steel for welding electrodes and Osaka Transformer for welding machines, were able to penetrate this market.

Substantial cash balances are accumulated each year preparatory to paying the year-end bonuses. The bonuses totaled $54 million for 1988. The money is invested in short-term U.S. government securities and certificates of deposit until needed. Financial statements are shown in Exhibit 3. Exhibit 4 shows how company revenue was distributed in the late 1980s.

HOW WELL DOES LINCOLN SERVE ITS STAKEHOLDERS?

Lincoln Electric differs from most other companies in the importance it assigns to each of the groups it serves. Willis identifies these groups, in the order of priority ascribed to them, as (1) customers, (2) employees, and (3) stockholders.

Certainly the firm's customers have fared well over the years. Lincoln prices for welding machines and welding electrodes are acknowledged to be the lowest in the marketplace. Quality has consistently been high. The cost of field failures for Lincoln products was recently determined to be a remarkable 0.04 percent of revenues. The "Fleetweld" electrodes and SA-200 welders have been the standard in the pipeline and refinery construction industry, where price is hardly a criterion, for decades. A Lincoln distributor in Monroe, Louisiana, says that he has sold several hundred of the popular AC-225 welders, which are warranted for one year, but has never handled a warranty claim.

Perhaps best-served of all management constituencies have been the employees. Not the least of their benefits, of course, as the year-end bonuses, which effectively double an already average compensation level. The foregoing description of the personnel program and the comments in Appendix A further illustrate the desirability of a Lincoln job.

While stockholders were relegated to an inferior status by James F. Lincoln, they have done very well indeed. Recent dividends have exceeded $11 a share and earnings per share have approached $30. In January 1980, the price of restricted stock, committed to employees, was $117 a share. By 1989, the stated value, at which the company will repurchase the stock if tendered, was $201. A check with the New York office of Merrill Lynch, Pierce, Fenner and Smith at that time revealed an estimated price on Lincoln stock of $270 a share, with none being offered for sale. Technically, this price applies only to the unrestricted stock owned by the Lincoln family, a few other major holders, and employees who have purchased it on the open market. Risk associated with Lincoln stock, a major determinant of stock value, is minimal because of the small amount of debt in the capital structure, because of an extremely stable earnings record, and because of Lincoln's practice of purchasing the restricted stock whenever employees offer it for sale.

A CONCLUDING COMMENT

It is easy to believe that the reason for Lincoln's success is the excellent attitude of the employees and their willingness to work harder, faster, and more intelligently than

EXHIBIT 3
CONDENSED COMPARATIVE FINANCIAL STATEMENTS ($000,000)*

BALANCE SHEETS

	1979	1980	1981	1982	1983	1984	1985	1986	1987
Assets									
Cash	2	1	4	1	2	4	2	1	7
Bonds & CDs	38	47	63	72	78	57	55	45	41
N/R & A/R	42	42	42	26	31	34	38	36	43
Inventories	38	36	46	38	31	37	34	26	40
Prepayments	1	3	4	5	5	5	7	8	7
Total CA	121	129	157	143	146	138	135	116	137
Other Assets**	24	24	26	30	30	29	29	33	40
Land	1	1	1	1	1	1	1	1	1
Net buildings	22	23	25	23	22	21	20	18	17
Net M&E	21	25	27	27	27	28	27	29	33
Total FA	44	49	53	51	50	50	48	48	50
Total assets	189	202	236	224	227	217	213	197	227
Claims									
A/P	17	16	15	12	16	15	13	11	20
Accrued wages	1	2	5	4	3	4	5	5	4
Accrued taxes	10	6	15	5	7	4	6	5	9
Accrued div.	6	6	7	7	7	6	7	6	7
Total CL	33	29	42	28	33	30	31	27	40
LT debt		4	5	6	8	10	11	8	8
Total debt	33	33	47	34	41	40	42	35	48
Common stock	4	3	1	2	0	0	0	0	2
Ret. earnings	152	167	189	188	186	176	171	161	177
Total SH equity	156	170	190	190	186	176	171	161	179
Total claims	189	202	236	224	227	217	213	197	227

Income Statements

	1979	1980	1981	1982	1983	1984	1985	1986	1987
Net Sales	374	387	450	311	263	322	333	318	368
Other Income	11	14	18	18	13	12	11	8	9
Income	385	401	469	329	277	334	344	326	377
CGS	244	261	293	213	180	223	221	216	239
Selling, G&A***	41	46	51	45	45	47	48	49	51
Incentive bonus	44	43	56	37	22	33	38	33	39
IBT	56	51	69	35	30	31	36	27	48
Income taxes	26	23	31	16	13	14	16	12	21
Net income	30	28	37	19	17	17	20	15	27

*Column totals may not check and amounts less than $500,000 (0.5) are shown as zero, due to rounding.

**Includes investment in foreign subsidiaries, $29 million in 1987.

***Includes pension expense and payroll taxes on incentive bonus.

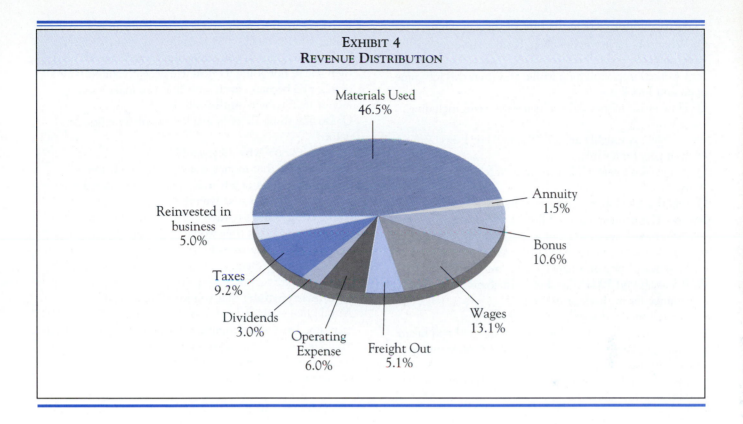

**EXHIBIT 4
REVENUE DISTRIBUTION**

Materials Used
46.5%

Annuity
1.5%

Bonus
10.6%

Wages
13.1%

Freight Out
5.1%

Operating
Expense
6.0%

Dividends
3.0%

Taxes
9.2%

Reinvested in
business
5.0%

---

other industrial workers. However, Sabo suggests that appropriate credit be given to Lincoln executives, whom he credits with carrying out the following policies:

1. Management has limited research, development, and manufacturing to a standard product line designed to meet the major needs of the welding industry.
2. New products must be reviewed by manufacturing and all producing costs verified before being approved by management.
3. Purchasing is challenged to not only procure materials at the lowest cost, but also to work closely with engineering and manufacturing to assure that the latest innovations are implemented.
4. Manufacturing supervision and all personnel are held accountable for reduction of scrap, energy conservation, and maintenance of product quality.
5. Production control, material handling, and methods engineering are closely supervised by top management.
6. Management has made cost reduction a way of life at Lincoln, and definite programs are established in many areas, including traffic and shipping, where tremendous savings can result.
7. Management has established a sales department

that is technically trained to reduce customer welding costs. This sales approach and other real customer services have eliminated nonessential frills and resulted in long-term benefits to all concerned.
8. Management has encouraged education, technical publishing, and long range programs that have resulted in industry growth, thereby assuring market potential for the Lincoln Electric Company.

Sabo writes, "It is in a very real sense a personal and group experience in faith—a belief that together we can achieve results which alone would not be possible. It is not a perfect system and it is not easy. It requires tremendous dedication and hard work. However, it does work and the results are worth the effort."

APPENDIX A: EMPLOYEE INTERVIEWS

Typical questions and answers from employee interviews are presented below. In order to maintain each employee's personal privacy, fictitious names are given to the interviewees.

INTERVIEW 1

Betty Stewart, a 52-year-old high school graduate who had been with Lincoln 13 years and who was working as a cost accounting clerk at the time of the interview.

Q: What jobs have you held here besides the one you have now?

A: I worked in payroll for a while, and then this job came open and I took it.

Q: How much money did you make last year, including your bonus?

A: I would say roughly around $25,000, but I was off for back surgery for a while.

Q: You weren't paid while you were off for back surgery?

A: No.

Q: Did the Employees Association help out?

A: Yes. The company doesn't furnish that, though. We pay $8 a month into the Employee Association. I think my check from them was $130.00 a week.

Q: How was your performance rating last year?

A: It was around 100 points, but I lost some points for attendance for my back problem.

Q: How did you get your job at Lincoln?

A: I was bored silly where I was working, and I had heard that Lincoln kept their people busy. So I applied and got the job the next day.

Q: Do you think you make more money than similar workers in Cleveland?

A: I know I do.

Q: What have you done with your money?

A: We have purchased a better home. Also, my son is going to the University of Chicago, which costs $13,000 a year. I buy the Lincoln stock which is offered each year, and I have a little bit of gold.

Q: Have you ever visited with any of the senior executives, like Mr. Willis or Mr. Hastings?

A: I have known Mr. Willis for a long time.

Q: Does he call you by name?

A: Yes. In fact he was very instrumental in my going to the doctor that I am going to with my back. He knows the director of the clinic.

Q: Do you know Mr. Hastings?

A: I know him to speak to him, and he always speaks, always. But I have known Mr. Willis for a good many years. When I did Plant Two accounting I did not understand how the plant operated. Of course you are not allowed in Plant Two, because that's the Electrode Division. I told my boss about the problem one day and the next thing I knew Mr. Willis came by and said, "Come on, Betty, we're going to Plant Two." He spent an hour and a half showing me the plant.

Q: Do you think Lincoln employees produce more than those in other companies?

A: I think with the incentive program the way that it is, if you want to work and achieve, then you will do it. If you don't want to work and achieve, you will not do it no matter where you are. Just because you are merit rated and have a bonus, if you really don't want to work hard, then you're not going to. You will accept your 90 points or 92 or 85 because, even with that you make more money than people on the outside.

Q: Do you think Lincoln employees will ever join a union?

A: I don't know why they would.

Q: So you say that money is a very major advantage?

A: Money is a major advantage, but it's not just the money. It's the fact that having the incentive, you do wish to work a little harder. I'm sure that there are a lot of men here who, if they worked some other place, would not work as hard as they do here. Not that they are overworked—I don't mean that—but I'm sure they wouldn't push.

Q: Is there anything that you would like to add?

A: I do like working here. I am better off being pushed mentally. In another company if you pushed too hard you would feel a little bit of pressure, and someone might say, "Hey, slow down; don't try so hard." But here you are encouraged, not discouraged.

INTERVIEW 2

Ed Sanderson, a 23-year-old high school graduate who had been with Lincoln four years and who was a machine operator in the Electrode Division at the time of the interview.

Q: How did you happen to get this job?

A: My wife was pregnant, and I was making three bucks an hour and one day I came here and applied. That was it. I kept calling to let them know I was still interested.

Q: Roughly what were your earnings last year including your bonus?

A: $45,000.00

Q: What have you done with your money since you have been here?

A: Well, we've lived pretty well and we bought a condominium.

Q: Have you paid for the condominium?

A: No, but I could.

Q: Have you bought your Lincoln stock this year?

A: No, I haven't bought any Lincoln stock yet.

Q: Do you get the feeling that the executives here are pretty well thought of?

A: I think they are. To get where they are today, they had to really work.

Q: Wouldn't that be true anywhere?

A: I think more so here because seniority really doesn't mean anything. If you work with a guy who has 20 years here, and you have two months and you're doing a better job, you will get advanced before he will.

Q: Are you paid on a piece rate basis?

A: My gang does. There are nine of us who make the bare electrode, and the whole group gets paid based on how much electrode we make.

Q: Do you think you work harder than workers in other factories in the Cleveland area?

A: Yes, I would say I probably work harder.

Q: Do you think it hurts anybody?

A: No, a little hard work never hurts anybody.

Q: If you could choose, do you think you would be as happy earning a little less money and being able to slow down a little?

A: No, it doesn't bother me. If it bothered me, I wouldn't do it.

Q: Why do you think Lincoln employees produce more than workers in other plants?

A: That's the way the company is set up. The more you put out, the more you're going to make.

Q: Do you think it's piece rate and bonus together?

A: I don't think people would work here if they didn't know that they would be rewarded at the end of the year.

Q: Do you think Lincoln employees will ever join a union?

A: No.

Q: What are the major advantages of working for Lincoln?

A: Money.

Q: Are there any other advantages?

A: Yes, we don't have a union shop. I don't think I could work in a union shop.

Q: Do you think you are a career man with Lincoln at this time?

A: Yes.

INTERVIEW 3

Roger Lewis, a 23-year-old Purdue graduate in mechanical engineering who had been in the Lincoln sales program for 15 months and who was working in the Cleveland sales office at the time of the interview.

Q: How did you get your job at Lincoln?

A: I saw that Lincoln was interviewing on campus at Purdue, and I went by. I later came to Cleveland for a plant tour and was offered a job.

Q: Do you know any of the senior executives? Would they know you by name?

A: Yes, I know all of them—Mr. Hastings, Mr. Willis, Mr. Sabo.

Q: Do you think Lincoln salesmen work harder than those in other companies?

A: Yes. I don't think there are many salesmen for other companies who are putting in 50 to 60-hour weeks. Everybody here works harder. You can go out in the plant, or you can go upstairs, and there's nobody sitting around.

Q: Do you see any real disadvantage of working at Lincoln?

A: I don't know if it's a disadvantage but Lincoln is a spartan company, a very thrifty company. I like that. The sales offices are functional, not fancy.

Q: Why do you think Lincoln employees have such high productivity?

A: Piecework has a lot to do with it. Lincoln is smaller than many plants, too; you can stand in one place and see the materials come in one side and the product go out the other. You feel a part of the company. The chance to get ahead is important, too. They have a strict policy of promoting from within, so you know you have a chance. I think in a lot of other places you may not get as fair a shake as you do here. The sales offices are on a smaller scale, too. I like that. I tell someone that we have two people in the Baltimore office, and they say "You've got to be kidding." It's smaller and more personal. Pay is the most important thing. I have heard that this is the highest paying factory in the world.

INTERVIEW 4

Jimmy Roberts, a 47-year-old high school graduate, who had been with Lincoln 17 years and who was working as a multiple-drill press operator at the time of the interview.

Q: What jobs have you had at Lincoln?

A: I started out cleaning the men's locker room in 1967. After about a year I got a job in the flux department, where we make the coating for welding rods. I worked there for seven or eight years and then got my present job.

Q: Do you make one particular part?

A: No, there are a variety of parts I make—at least 25.

Q: Each one has a different piece rate attached to it?

A: Yes.

Q: Are some piece rates better than others?

A: Yes.

Q: How do you determine which ones you are going to do?

A: You don't. Your supervisor assigns them.

Q: How much money did you make last year?

A: $53,000.

Q: Have you ever received any kind of award or citation?

A: No.

Q: Was your rating ever over 110?

A: Yes. For the past five years, probably, I made over 110 points.

Q: Is there any attempt to let the others know . . . ?

A: The kind of points I get? No.

Q: Do you know what they are making?

A: No. There are some who might not to be too happy with their points and they might make it known. The majority, though, do not make it a point of telling other employees.

Q: Would you be just as happy earning a little less money and working a little slower?

A: I don't think I would—not at this point. I have done piecework all these years, and the fast pace doesn't really bother me.

Q: Why do you think Lincoln productivity is so high?

A: The incentive thing—the bonus distribution. I think that would be the main reason. The pay check you get every two weeks is important too.

Q: Do you think Lincoln employees would ever join a union?

A: I don't think so. I have never heard anyone mention it.

Q: What is the most important advantage of working here?

A: Amount of money you make. I don't think I could make this type of money anywhere else, especially with only a high school education.

Q: As a black person, do you feel that Lincoln discriminates in any way against blacks?

A: No. I don't think any more so than any other job. Naturally, there is a certain amount of discrimination, regardless of where you are.

INTERVIEW 5

Joe Trahan, 58-year-old high school graduate who had been with Lincoln 39 years and who was employed as a working supervisor in the tool room at the time of the interview.

Q: Roughly what was your pay last year?

A: Over $56,000; salary, bonus, stock dividends.

Q: How much was your bonus?

A: About $26,000.

Q: Have you ever gotten a special award of any kind?

A: Not really.

Q: What have you done with your money?

A: My house is paid for—and my two cars. I also have some bonds and the Lincoln stock.

Q: What do you think of the executives at Lincoln?

A: They're really top notch.

Q: What is the major disadvantage of working at Lincoln Electric?

A: I don't know of any disadvantage at all.

Q: Do you think you produce more than most people in similar jobs with other companies?

A: I do believe that.

Q: Why is that? Why do you believe that?

A: We are on the incentive system. Everything we do, we try to improve to make a better product with a minimum of outlay. We try to improve the bonus.

Q: Would you be just as happy making a little less money and not working quite so hard?

A: I don't think so.

Q: Do you think Lincoln employees would ever join a union?

A: I don't think they would ever consider it.

Q: What is the most important advantage of working at Lincoln?

A: Compensation.

Q: Tell me something about Mr. James Lincoln, who died in 1965.

A: You are talking about Jimmy Sr. He always strolled through the shop in his shirt sleeves. Big fellow. Always looked distinguished. Gray hair. Friendly sort of guy. I was a member of the advisory board one year. He was there each time.

Q: Did he strike you as really caring?

A: I think he always cared for people.

Q: Did you get any sensation of religious nature from him?

A: No, not really.

Q: And religion is not part of the program now?

A: No.

Q: Do you think Mr. Lincoln was a very intelligent man, or was he just a nice guy?

A: I would say he was pretty well educated. A great talker—always right off the top of his head. He knew what he was talking about all the time.

Q: When were bonuses for beneficial suggestions done away with?

A: About 18 years ago.

Q: Did that hurt very much?

A: I don't think so, because suggestions are still rewarded through the merit rating system.

Q: Is there anything you would like to add?

A: It's a good place to work. The union kind of ties other places down. At other places, electricians only do electrical work, carpenters only do carpenter work. At Lincoln Electric we all pitch in and do whatever needs to be done.

Q: So a major advantage is not having a union?

A: That's right.

Written by Arthur D. Sharplin, McNeese State University. Used by permission.

Financial Highlights (In thousands of dollars, except per share data)

	1993	1992	1991
Net Sales	$845,999	$853,007	$833,892
*Net Income (Loss)	(38,068)	(45,800)	14,365
*Net Income (Loss) Per Share of Common Stock	(3.51)	(4.24)	1.33
*Cash Dividends Paid Per Share of Common Stock	.72	.72	1.15
Working Capital	149,853	172,651	203,479
Current Ratio (current assets to current liabilities)	1.9 to 1	2.2 to 1	2.3 to 1
Total Assets	$559,543	$603,347	$640,261
Shareholders' Equity	143,495	198,723	264,136
Return on Average Shareholders' Equity	-22.2%	-19.8%	5.5%

*Note: Net income (loss) and per share amounts for 1993 include the cumulative effect to January 1, 1993 of the change in method of accounting for income taxes of $2,468 and $.23 per share. Additionally, all per share amounts reported have been adjusted for the effects of the ten-for-one stock split in 1993.

The Actual is Limited — The Possible is Immense

THE LINCOLN ELECTRIC COMPANY

Cleveland, Ohio 44117-1199

Global Industrial Competitiveness

Manufacturing— America's Global Competitive Edge

Address by
Donald F. Hastings
Chairman of the Board and Chief
Executive Officer
The Lincoln Electric Company
and Chairman of the NEMA
Board of Governors

NEMA's 66th Annual Meeting
The Fairmont Hotel
Chicago, Illinois
November 16, 1992

Manufacturing— America's Global Competitive Edge

Today American quality levels not only match but exceed those of our foreign competitors.

The theme of today's meeting, Global Industrial Competitiveness, is vitally important as NEMA prepares to enter the 21st Century, now only seven years away and counting.

Many of the critics of America's industrial competitiveness, including some national political leaders, think the United States has become a "post-industrial" society. The post-industrialists say we shouldn't try to regain our competitiveness as a manufacturing nation, and they make fun of manufacturing as low-tech, "smokestack" industries.

That's wrong, dead wrong. It is, in fact, a myth.

Today, U.S. manufacturing industries directly accounts for more than a fifth of this country's gross domestic products and about half of all American economic activity depends indirectly on manufacturing.

U.S. manufacturing exports grew at a 15 percent annual rate over the five years from 1987 to 1991, twice the growth rate of foreign imports into this country.

That phenomenal growth in U.S. exports reduced the overall U.S. trade deficit from 152 billion in 1987 to 66 billion in 1991, still too high but down by 57 percent.

That was the situation as we headed into the 1980s. Now, well into the 1990s, there have been substantial improvements in both the quality and price of U.S. manufactured products. American quality levels have increased so dramatically that, in many cases, they not only match but exceed the quality standards of our foreign competitors. Ironically, that is exactly what has happened in some U.S. assembly plants operated by Japanese auto makers.

The bottom line of all this is that the myths about U.S. manufacturing are just that—myths. The reality is that manufacturing is the dynamic engine that drives our national economy. Manufacturing adds more value to raw materials, generates more real wealth and creates more good-paying jobs than any other single sector.

But if all these good things are true—and they are—why are so many of the companies in our industrial manufacturing base in apparent disarray with massive layoffs reported almost every day?

I want to focus first on some external causes. The first and perhaps most obvious cause is the erosion of U.S. manufacturing profit margins by spiralling external costs. Two extraordinary costs in particular are eating up the funds that would otherwise be available for plant and equipment modernization and employee training — both key requirements for improving our global competitiveness as a manufacturing nation.

The first and the most voracious of the external profit cannibals is skyrocketing health care costs. Completely out of control, those costs are eating many companies alive, forcing management to choose between reducing medical benefits or potential bankruptcy.

The problems of health care costs and availability were, of course, major topics of debate during the recent election campaign. I'm not sure, however, that anybody yet has a good handle on an acceptable and fair solution. Hopefully, we'll know more soon.

The second major hemorrhage of manufacturing profits is caused by the wasteful and unnecessary regulations imposed on manufacturing industries by well-meaning but over-zealous policy makers.

Pollution control costs, for example, are expected to reach a staggering 160 billion a year by 1995. But the principal improvements in almost all major pollutant categories have already been achieved. The additional improvements now being mandated by Washington are of marginal value at best and have horrendously high price tags that make them dangerous obstacles to badly needed economic growth.

Regulation quite simply has grown out of all proportion to its need or its value.

The number of people writing federal regulations has increased from 106,000 in 1989 to more than 122,000 this year. The total regulatory burden imposed by their efforts was about equal to—and by some estimates, exceeded—the total aggregate after-tax profits of all U.S. manufacturers. That can't continue without seriously damaging or even destroying our national competitiveness.

We also face major problems with our work forces. Our current employees are neither lazy nor stupid, despite what some Japanese politicians have alleged. But more and more of the young entrants into the work force lack basic education and skills, and they must be retrained at enormous cost. Like health care, education reform is not just a business problem but a national concern that our whole society must address.

So how do we overcome our problems and become more globally competitive as a manufacturing nation? It's going to be tough, but here are some of the steps I think we must take.

Global Industrial Competitiveness

The number one priority, it seems to me, has to be a major reduction in the monstrous federal budget deficit which drives up the cost of money urgently needed for private sector capital investment. NEMA should make common cause with other manufacturing industry associations, and all of our member companies should lobby individually as well, for Congress to make the tough choices that will reduce spending and increase revenues until we bring this runaway deficit under control.

And our federal government has to stop complaining about the low savings rate of Americans compared with the Japanese and pass some tax reforms that will stop the IRS from penalizing the Americans who do save. I'm thinking particularly about capital gains tax reform investment tax-credits and making IRAs available again to employees who are covered by company-funded pension plans.

We've got to let people take more control over their financial future and become less dependent on the Social Security system.

The federal government must also re-examine its regulatory policies. Nobody quarrels with cost-effective regulations that protect the health of employees as well as that of the public at large. But U.S. manufacturing companies must continue to resist aggressively the imposition of expensive regulatory burdens that are of marginal value at best.

NEMA has been extremely active in helping to defer or defeat specific legislation such as the federal lead bill and Ohio's extremely costly "right-to-know" toxic substance bill.

Our Association has also been doing an effective job in pushing for a requirement that all regulatory agencies demonstrate in advance that the benefits of proposed regulations outweigh the associated costs.

It would also be great if the Washington Beltway crowd could take some positive action on international trade policy—such as stronger and more enforceable laws against dumping by our overseas competitors, and tax incentives to encourage the growth of U.S. exports.

Like Lee Iacocca has been saying on television, you have to lead, follow or get out of the way. If our government leaders cannot do anything else to promote national competitiveness, they can at least get out of the way.

There also must be major improvements in our national educational systems to assure that we will have a constant flow of new workers who have the basic skills to hold the jobs of the future. Again, this is a task that we cannot leave to government alone. Business and business leaders must get involved to make sure our needs are met.

Now, I want to touch on what those of us in U.S. manufacturing must do to resolve some of our internal problems.

Quality is still one of those problems, although it shouldn't be. What American manufacturers have learned over the past two decades is that high quality is a given. It's the table stake you must have just to sit in as one of the players in the game of global competition.

But we can't lose sight of the equation that says quality *plus* attractive price *plus* meeting customer needs, equals marketing success for a manufactured product. It's that third element—meeting customer needs—that too often gets dropped out of the equation.

And that's exactly where our system used to fall down in the past. American manufacturers didn't have enough input on customer needs early enough in the research and development process. You can't design a product in a vacuum and then ask marketing to sell it, but that's what a lot of companies did or tried to do.

We must recognize that customers are the beginning of the marketing process, not the final step, and it is their needs that must set quality standards. Once that's accomplished, U.S. manufacturers can focus on other actions to assure consistent quality. Those include benchmarking against the best companies in the world and making all employees responsible for product quality. And that includes senior management, whose support for product quality is an absolute requirement for obtaining it.

NEMA's ISO 9000 internal auditor training sessions are helping make those good things happen at member companies. The sessions help assure compliance with the ISO 9000 standards and also aid companies in monitoring and controlling their own quality programs.

That brings me to the other major internal problem where American manufacturers still have a lot of work yet to do—people. The men and women who make up the management and production work forces of U.S. manufacturing companies are potentially our greatest strength, but they are a resource that has been sadly neglected until recently.

Our overseas competitors are perceived as doing a better job than U.S. manufacturers in enlisting the skills and talents of all their employees in the tough struggle for global market share. It's also frequently said that American manufacturers don't recognize the contributions that employees can make.

Again that is perception, not fact. A few days ago I was in Japan where a manufacturing company's senior executive told me proudly, "We got 40 suggestions from employees." I didn't tell him that over the same period at Lincoln Electric, we got about 400.

Americans do understand that nobody knows better how to improve a manufacturing process than the people on the shop floor who work with it everyday. But employees will only offer their suggestions in an environment of mutual respect, not an adversarial one where managers and workers are divided into "us" and "them" categories. And we've been busy creating that new, positive kind of environment in our companies by encouraging employee involvement.

Most managers welcome the new, less-bureaucratic structures that result from employee participation. And there simply is no longer room in U.S. manufacturing for the costly bureaucratic roadblocks caused by unnecessary layers of management. Much of Corporate America is now engaged in the painful but absolutely necessary process of stripping away those redundant layers.

That process is streamlining U.S. manufacturing organizations, leaving only a few required layers separating the CEOs from the shop floor where the money is made.

And the CEOs of U.S. manufacturing companies must demonstrate their personal commitment to quality, customer satisfaction and employee participation if the programs are to have long-term success.

In sum, to improve our global industrial competitiveness, we must focus on the truths rather than dwelling on the myths about American manufacturing.

The myth that the United States is a post-industrial society must give way to the truth that U.S. manufacturing is the prime driver of our national economy. It is the principal creator of wealth and good jobs for the American people.

To achieve the goal of a stronger, more competitive U.S. manufacturing base, we must overcome many challenges—external challenges and internal ones.

On the external front, NEMA and its member companies must make common cause with other American manufacturers to reform federal, state and local government policies that damage our ability to compete globally. And, in particular, we must resist the imposition of only marginally beneficial but extremely costly regulations that eat up profits needed for plant and equipment modernization.

Internally, we have to become the masters of change instead of being mastered by the structural changes that are transforming all of Corporate America, particularly manufacturing companies.

Specifically, we must put customers back in their rightful place at the beginning of the marketing process and let their needs set the quality standards for U.S. manufactured goods.

And we must do a better job of enlisting the skills and knowledge of all our employees in our ongoing effort to improve our products and processes.

Those are two areas in which our foreign competitors are perceived as being more effective than U.S. manufacturers. We have been making good progress toward correcting that image problem, but we have to put on a full-court press if we are to surpass them.

Competing in a truly global marketplace is the greatest challenge our industry and our nation has faced in many decades. How well we meet that challenge will determine our future success during the balance of this decade and well into the next century.

We must, we can, and we will meet that challenge successfully.

Thank you.

Mission and Values Statement

World's Leader in Welding and Cutting Products • Premier Manufacturer of Industrial Motors

The mission of The Lincoln Electric Company is to earn and retain global leadership as a total quality supplier of superior products and services.

Our Core Values

As a responsible and successful company in partnership with our customers, distributors, employees, shareholders, suppliers and our host communities, we pledge ourselves to conduct our business in accordance with these core values:

• Respond to our customers' needs and expectations with quality, integrity and value

• Recognize people as our most valuable asset

• Maintain and expand the Lincoln Incentive Management philosophy

• Practice prudent and responsible financial management

• Strive continually to be environmentally responsible

• Support communities where we operate and industries in which we participate

To Realize Our Mission and Support Our Core Values, We Have Established the Following Goals:

Respond to Our Customers' Needs and Expectations With Quality, Integrity and Value

- Assure value through innovative, functional and reliable products and services in all the markets we serve around the world.
- Exceed global standards for products and service quality.
- Provide our customers with personalized technical support that helps them achieve improvements in cost reduction, productivity and quality.
- Lead the industry in aggressive application of advanced technology to meet customer requirements.
- Invest constantly in creative research and development dedicated to maintaining our position of market leadership.
- Achieve and maintain the leading market share position in our major markets around the world.

Recognize People As Our Most Valuable Asset

- Maintain a safe, clean and healthy environment for our employees.
- Promote employee training, education and development, and broaden skills through multi-departmental and international assignments.
- Maintain an affirmative action program and provide all employees with opportunities for advancement commensurate with their abilities and performance regardless of race, religion, national origin, sex, age or disability.
- Maintain an environment that fosters ethical behavior, mutual trust, equal opportunity, open communication, personal growth and creativity.
- Demand integrity, discipline and professional conduct from our employees in every aspect of our business and conduct our operations ethically and in accordance with the law.
- Reward employees through recognition, "pay for performance," and by sharing our profits with incentive bonus compensation based on extraordinary achievement.

Maintain and Expand the Lincoln Incentive Management Philosophy

Promote dynamic teamwork and incentive as the most profitable and cost-effective way of achieving:

- A committed work ethic and positive employee attitudes throughout the Company.
- High quality, low-cost manufacturing.
- Efficient and innovative engineering.
- Customer-oriented operation and administration.
- A dedicated and knowledgeable sales and service force.
- A total organization responsive to the needs of our worldwide customers.

Practice Prudent and Responsible Financial Management

- Establish attainable goals, strategic planning and accountability for results that enhance shareholder value.
- Promote the process of employee involvement in cost reductions and quality improvements.
- Recognize profit as the resource that enables our Company to serve our customers.

Strive Continually To Be Environmentally Responsible

- Continue to pursue the most environmentally sound operating practices, processes and products to protect the global environment.
- Maintain a clean and healthy environment in our host communities.

Support Communities Where We Operate and Industries In Which We Participate

- Invest prudently in social, cultural, educational and charitable activities.
- Contribute to the industries we serve and society as a whole by continuing our leadership role in professional organizations and education.
- Encourage and support appropriate employee involvement in community activities.

LINCOLN ELECTRIC

APPENDICES

LEGISLATION, COURT, AND NRLB DECISIONS AFFECTING HUMAN RESOURCE MANAGEMENT

LEGISLATION/BASIC PROVISIONS

EMPLOYMENT LEGISLATION

ACT	JURISDICTION	BASIC PROVISIONS
Fair Labor Standards Act (1938) and subsequent amendments—FLSA	Most interstate employers, certain types of employees, are exempt from overtime provisions—executive, administrative, and professional employees and outside salespeople	Establishes a minimum wage; controls hours through premium pay for overtime; controls working hours for children
Minimum Wage Law (1977)	Small businesses	Sets graduated increases in minimum wage rates
Equal Pay Act (1963 amendment to the FLSA)	Same as FLSA except no employees are exempt	Prohibits unequal pay for males and females with equal skill, effort, and responsibility working under similar working conditions
Civil Rights Act (1964) (amended by EEOA 1972)	Employers with fifteen or more employees, employment agencies, and labor unions	Prevents discrimination on the basis of race, color, religion, sex, or national origin; establishes EEOC
Civil Rights Act of 1991	Same as the Civil Rights Act of 1964	Protects groups against discrimination (as does the 1964 act), but makes provision for jury trials and punitive compensation
Equal Employment Opportunity Act (1972)—EEOA	Adds employees of state and local government and educational institutions; reduced number of employees required to fifteen	Amends Title VII; increases enforcement powers of EEOC
Executive Order 11246 (1965) as amended by Executive Order 11375 (1966)	Federal contractors and subcontractors with contracts over $50,000 and fifty or more employees	Prevents discrimination on the basis of race, color, religion, sex, or national origin; establishes Office of Federal Contract Compliance (OFCC)
Revised Order Number 4 (1971)	Federal contractors	Defines acceptable affirmative action program
Executive Order 11478 (1969)	Federal agencies	Prevents discrimination on the basis of race, color, religion, sex or national origin
Age Discrimination in Employment Act (1967)—revised 1978; 1986	Employers with more than twenty-five employees	Prevents discrimination against persons age forty and over, and states compulsory retirement for some workers
Rehabilitation Act (1973) as amended 1980	Government contractors and federal agencies	Prevents discrimination against persons with physical and/or mental handicaps and provides for affirmative action

Americans with Disabilities Act (1990)	15 or more employees	Protects against discrimination against individuals with disabilities
Older Worker Benefit Protection Act of 1990	Same as the Age Discrimination in Employment Act as amended	Employers are prohibited from discriminating with regard to benefits on the basis of age
Immigration Act of 1990	Immigration Reform and Control Act of 1986—IRCA	Amends the employer-verification and unfair-immigration–related employment practices as defined by the IRCA
The Family and Medical Leave Act of 1993	Employers with 50 or more employees	Allows workers to take up to 12 weeks unpaid leave for pregnancy or illness of close family member
Glass Ceiling Act of 1991	Same as the 1991 Civil Rights Act	Empowers the Glass Ceiling Commission to focus greater attention on eliminating artificial barriers for advancement of women and minorities
Prevailing wage laws—1. Davis-Bacon Act (1931) and 2. Walsh-Healey Act (1935)	Employers with government contstuction projects of $2,000 (Davis-Bacon) and government contracts of $10,000 or more	Guarantees prevailing wages to employees of government contractors
Legally required fringe benefits— 1. OASDHI (1935 and amendments)	Virtually all employers	Provides income and health care to all retired employees and income to the survivors of employees who have died
2. Unemployment compensation (1935)	Virtually all employers	Provides income to employees who are laid off or fired
3. Workers' compensation (dates differ from state to state)	Virtually all employers	Provides benefits to employees who are injured on the job and to the survivors of employees who are killed on the job
Occupational Safety and Health Act (1970)—OSHA	Most interstate employers	Assures as far as possible every working man and woman in the nation safe and healthful working conditions and to preserve our human resources
Employee Retirement Income Security Act (1974)—ERISA	Most interstate employers with pension plans (no employer is required to have such a plan)	Protects employees covered by a pension plan from losses in benefits due to <ul><li>mismanagement</li><li>plant closings and bankruptcies</li><li>job changes</li></ul>
Freedom of Information Act (1966)	Federal agencies only	Allows individuals to review employers' records on them and bring civil damages
The Pregnancy Discrimination Act of 1978	Same as Civil Rights Act (1964)	Pregnancy is a disability and, furthermore, must receive the same benefits as any other disability

Privacy Act of 1974 (Public Law 93-579)	Federal agencies only	Allows individuals to review employer's records on them and bring civil damages
Uniform Guidelines on Employee Selection Procedures (1978)	Same as EEOA (1972)	Updates EEOC 1970 guidelines to more clearly define adverse impact and test validation
Guidelines on Sexual Harassment (1980)	Same as EEOA (1972)	Defines standards for what constitutes harassment
Vietnam Era Veterans Readjustment Act (1974)	Government contractors with contracts in excess of $10,000	Provides for affirmative action in the employment of Vietnam era veterans
Civil Rights Act of 1866, Section 1981	All citizens	It gives all persons, regardless of race, age, and national origin, the same contractual rights as "white citizens." Does not apply to sex-based discrimination.
Civil Rights Act of 1871, Section 1983	All citizens	As the Civil Rights Act of 1866 but does apply to sex-based discrimination
The First Amendment, U.S. Constitution	All citizens	Guarantees freedom of speech and religion
The Fifth Amendment	All citizens	No person shall be deprived of life, liberty, or property without the due process of law
The Fourteenth Amendment	All citizens	Prohibits abridgment of federally conferred privileges by actions of the state
Employee Polygraph Protection Act (1988)	Private Employers	Prohibits most employees from polygraph testing without reasonable suspicion
Drug-Free Workplace Act (1988)	Federal contractors with contracts exceeding $25,000	Requires employers to maintain drug-free workplace
Worker Adjustment and Retraining Notification Act of 1988	Employers with more than 100 employees	Requires 60 days notice of plant or office closing

LABOR RELATIONS LEGISLATION: PRIVATE SECTOR

Railway Labor Act (1926)—RLA	Railroad workers and airline employees	Provides right to organize; provides majority choice of representatives; prohibits "yellow dog" contracts; outlines dispute settlement procedures
Norris-LaGuardia Act (1932)	All employers and labor organizations	No yellow dog contracts; no injunction for nonviolent activity of unions (strikes, picketing, and boycotts); limited union liability
National Labor Relations Act (1935)—Wagner Act	Nonmanagerial employees in private industry not covered by Railway Labor Act (RLA)	Provides right to organize; provides for collective bargaining; requires employers to bargain; unions must represent all members equally

Labor Management Relations Act (1947)—Taft-Hartley	Nonmanagerial employees in private industry not covered by RLA	Prohibits unfair labor practices of unions; outlaws closed shop; prohibits strikes in national emergencies; requires both parties to bargain in good faith
Labor Management Reporting and Disclosure Act (1959)—Landrum-Griffin	Labor organizations	Outlines procedures for redressing internal union problems
Amendments to Taft-Hartley Act (1974)	Labor organizations	Specifies illegal activities within union

LABOR RELATIONS LEGISLATION: PUBLIC SECTOR

Executive Order 10988 (1962)	Federal employees	Recognizes employee's right to join unions and bargain collectively; prohibits strikes. Requires agency to meet and confer with union on policy practices and working conditions
Executive Orders 11616 (1971) and 11838 (1975)	Federal employees	Expand EO 11491 to cover labor-management relations: cover disputes of bargaining rights; order elections; consolidate units; limit scope of grievance and arbitration procedures
Civil Service Reform Act (1978)	Federal employees	Defines grievance procedure and requirements for goal-type performance appraisals; establishes Senior Executive Service (SES)

COURT AND NLRB DECISIONS/BASIC PROVISIONS

United Steelworkers of America v. Warrior & Gulf Navigation Co. (1960); *United Steelworkers of America v. American Manufacturing Co.* (1960); *and United Steelworkers of America v. Enterprise Wheel & Car Corp.* (1960)

Referred to as the "Trilogy" cases, these three cases upheld the arbitrator's authority to remedy violations of collective bargaining agreements. The court, however, could decide the question of arbitrability. If the court determines that a collectively bargained contract calls for arbitration, then the arbitrator can arbitrate it. This was further upheld in *AT&T Technologies, Inc. v. Communications Workers of America* (1986).

Stringfellow v. Monsanto Corporation (1970)
Established the precedent for giving credit to the employer for making performance appraisal-based decisions on the basis of evidence that the appraisal uses definite identifiable criteria based on the quality and quantity of an employee's work.

Phillips v. Martin Marietta Corp (1971)
Whether a BFOQ exists depends on whether it can be shown that the qualification is demonstrably more relevant to job performance for a woman than a man.

Diaz v. Pan American World Airways, Inc. (1971)
The primary function of an airline is to transport passengers safely from one point to another. Therefore, not hiring males for flight attendants is discriminatory. Business necessity is established.

Griggs v. Duke Power (1971)
Test for hiring cannot be used unless job related. Organizations must show evidence of job relatedness. Not necessary to establish intent to discriminate.

Board of Regents of State Colleges v. Roth (1972)
Protects workers from discharge when due process hasn't been given.

Richardson v. Hotel Corporation of America (1972)
Dismissal on grounds of conviction record resulted in adverse impact; but since conviction record argued (not shown) to be related to business necessity (not job performance), dismissal is okay.

Spurlock v. United Airlines (1972)
Use of college degree as a selection criterion valid because job related, even though no performance data provided.

Rowe v. General Motors Corporation (1972)
All white supervisory recommendations were based on subjective and vague standards which led to a lack of promotions for black employees. Identified five discriminatory factors.

Hodgson v. Robert Hall Clothes, Inc. (1973)
Pay differentials between salesmen and saleswomen justified on the basis of profitability of area in which employees work.

McDonnell Douglas Corporation v. Green (1973)
Employer's test device constitutes *prima facie* case of racial discrimination under four different criteria (see Chapter 7).

Brito v. Zia Company (1973)
Zia violated Title VII because they laid off a disproportionate number of a protected group on the basis of low performance scores on measures that were not validated.

Sugarman v. Dougal (1973)
The due process and equal protection clauses of the Fifth Amendment also apply to aliens in public employment.

Hodgson v. Greyhound Lines, Inc. (1974)
Could discriminate without empirical evidence on basis of age. Good faith used to show older people would make less safe drivers.

Corning Glass Works v. Brennan (1974)
The Equal Pay Act is violated by paying male inspectors on the night shift a higher base wage than female inspectors on the day shift.

Baxter v. Savannah Sugar Refining Co. (1974)
Subjective appraisal form is viewed as discriminatory.

Green v. Missouri Pacific R.R. Co. (1975)
Applying the lessons from *Griggs v. Duke Power*, the court and the EEOC have found it unlawful to refuse to hire job applicants because of their arrest record except for certain circumstances (*Richardson v. Hotel Corporation of America*).

Kirkland v. New York Department of Correctional Services (1975)
The use of quotas was rejected as a method of determining promotions except as an interim measure to be used until nondiscriminatory procedures to determine promotion are established.

Stamps (EEOC) v. Detroit Edison (1975)
Title VII does not provide for an award of punitive damages. Back pay and attorney fees are the explicit provisions of Title VII.

Rogers v. International Paper Company (1975)
Subjective criteria are not to be condemned as unlawful per se because some decisions about hiring and promotions in supervisory and managerial jobs cannot be made using objective standards alone. This opinion, however, is somewhat contrary to those in *Albemarle Paper*

Company v. Moody (1973); *Baxter v. Savannah Sugar Refining Corporation* (1974); and *Rowe v. General Motors* (1972).

Albemarle v. Moody (1975)
Need to establish evidence that test is related to content of job. Could use job analysis to do so, but not evidence from global performance ratings made by supervisors.

McDonald v. Santa Fe Trail Transportation Co. (1976)
Requires consistency in dismissal policies due to absenteeism.

Mastie v. Great Lakes Steel Corporation (1976)
As with *Stringfellow*, the court said that the objectivity of evaluation can be established by demonstrating that the company performed and relied on a thorough evaluation process intended to be used fairly and accurately.

Smith v. Mutual Benefit Life Insurance Company (1976)
Employer is not discriminating if refusing to hire male appearing to be effeminate.

Chrysler Outboard v. Dept. of Industry (1976)
Employer refuses to hire a worker who had leukemia because he was prone to infection. Court said he had to be hired because he was qualified.

Watkins v. Scott Paper Company (1976)
Performance data to validate tests that are derived from graphic scales are too vague and easily subject to discrimination.

Robinson v. Union Carbide Corporation (1976)
These two require written standards for promotion to help prevent discrimination.

Wade v. Mississippi Cooperative Extension Service (1976)
Performance scores used to decide promotions and salary issues not valid because no job analysis.

Washington v. Davis (1976)
When a test procedure is challenged under constitutional law, intent to discriminate must be established. No need to establish intent if filed under Title VII, just show effects. Could use communication test to select applicants for police force.

Castaneda v. Partida (1977)
Prima facie evidence of discrimination established when evidence of both statistical disparity and discriminatory selection procedures vis-à-vis the gross population figures.

General Foods Corp. (1977)
Corporatewide team program of employee-employer cooperation does not violate the National Labor Relations Act because program established to promote efficiency, not forestall unionization.

James v. Stockham Values and Fitting Company (1977)
An apprenticeship program was viewed as discriminatory since selections were made by supervisors who were given guidelines.

Barnes v. Costle (1977)
Sexual harassment is a form of sex discrimination under Title VII, and employer is responsible if takes no action on learning of events.

Mistretta v. Sandia Corporation (1977)
Employment decisions suspect when based on evaluations that reflect only best judgments and opinions of evaluators rather than identifiable criteria based on quality or quantity of work or specific performances that are supported by some kind of record.

Hazelwood School District v. U.S. (1977)
Labor market comparisons must be based on relevant labor market and not general labor market.

International Brotherhood of Teamsters v. United States (1977)
Bona fide seniority systems maintained without discriminatory intent are exempt from Title VII liability if established before 1964.

United Air Lines, Inc. v. McMann (1977)
Employer can force retirement before age of sixty-five if it has bona fide retirement plan.

Yukas v. Libbey-Owens-Ford (1977)
All practices against nepotism, especially close relatives and spouses, are nondiscriminatory, especially in same department and/or as in supervisor-subordinate relationship.

Flowers v. Crouch-Walter Corporation (1977)
Plaintiff established *prima facie* evidence that a discharge was discriminatory and not based on performance.

Donaldson v. Pillsbury Company (1977)
Requires clear establishment and communication of job requirements and performance standards.

James v. Stockman Values and Fittings Company (1977)
White supervisors without formal guidelines selecting applicants to apprenticeship program is discriminatory. Need more discrete performance appraisal.

Dothard v. Rawlinson (1977)
Height requirements not valid, therefore constitutes discriminatory practice.

Bakke v. Regents of the University of California (1978)
Reverse discrimination not allowed. Race, however, can be used in selection decisions. Affirmative action programs permissible when prior discrimination established.

United States v. City of Chicago (1978)
Specific promotion criteria must be used that are related to the job to which being promoted.

Detroit Police Officers Assn. v. Coleman Young (1979)
Court holds in favor of goals and quotas to reverse previous discrimination.

NLRB v. Wright Line, Inc. (1981)
In cases where an employee is fired for what may appear to be union-related activities, the employer must show (to be vindicated in the dismissal) that the discipline imposed is the same as in other cases where union activity was not an issue.

American Textile Manufacturers Institute v. Donovan (1981)
OSHA need not do cost-benefit analyses before issuing working health standards.

Tooley v. Martin-Marietta Corporation (1981)
Must be religious accommodation for employees who object to union membership or support (as long as no undue hardship on union).

Los Angeles Dept. of Water v. Manhard (1981)
Rules against department rule of having female employees contribute more to a retirement plan than men.

Clayton v. United Auto Workers (1981)
When a union member feels unfairly represented and only the employer can grant the relief requested, the employee need not exhaust internal union remedies before suing the employer.

Lehman v. Yellow Freight System (1981)
Informal affirmative action not permissible although formal voluntary one such as *Weber* is okay.

Northwest Airlines, Inc. v. Transport Workers (1981)
An employer found guilty of job discrimination cannot force an employee's union to contribute to the damages, even though the union may have negotiated the unequal terms.

County of Washington, Oregon v. Gunther (1981)
It can be illegal (under Title VII and EPA 1963) to pay women unfairly low wages even if not doing same work as men (not a comparable worth case).

First National Maintenance v. NLRB (1981)
Management does not have to negotiate with unions in advance over closing plants or dropping lines.

Texas Department of Community Affairs v. Joyce Ann Burdine (1981)
A defendant in a job discrimination case need only provide a legitimate, nondiscriminatory explanation for not hiring or promoting a woman or minority, and need not prove that the white man hired was better qualified. The burden of proving intentional discrimination rests with the plaintiff.

Fernandez v. Wynn Oil Company (1981)
Title VII does not permit employers to use stereotypic impressions of male and female roles as a BFOQ defense to sex discrimination. Employer can't use customer preferences for working with male employees as a defense of discrimination.

Connecticut v. Teal (1982)
Employers must defend each part of a selection process against adverse impact and not just the end result of the entire process (the bottom line).

Spirit v. TIAA/CREF (1982)
Retirement annuities must be equal, regardless of sex.

Borg Warner Corp. v. NLRB (1982)
Distinction between mandatory and permissible. Terms depend on whether topic regulates the employer-employee relation.

American Tobacco v. Patterson (1982)
Bona fide seniority systems without discriminating intent are exempt from Title VII liability.

Newport News Shipbuilding and Dry Dock Co. v. EEOC (1983)
If an employer supplies any level of health benefits to female workers' husbands, the employer must also supply the same level of benefits to male workers' wives, and that includes pregnancy benefits. This, in effect, reverses the Supreme Court's ruling in *General Electric v. Gilbert,* where the court said that pregnancy benefits need not be given the same treatment by employers as other health and disability programs.

Arizona Governing Committee v. Norris (1983)
Pension payouts by employers should be equal for women and men, and past unequal treatment of women must be cured by retroactive funding of pensions. This decision is in essence the other half of the issue. The first half was rendered in the Supreme Court decision of *Los Angeles Department of Water and Power v. Manhart,* where the decision was made that requiring larger contributions by females than males into pension programs is discriminatory.

NLRB v. Transportation Management (1983)
Employees are protected by the NLRA when helping organize employees. If an employee claims to be fired for trying to organize a union but the employer claims it was poor performance, the employer has the burden of proof. In cases where such "mixed" motives for employer action may exist, the employer must prove the case.

Firefighters Local Union No. 1784 v. Stotts (1984)
In this decision, the Supreme Court upheld the bona fide seniority system over an affirmative action consent decree in a situation of layoffs. Thus, the employees most recently hired could be subject to layoff even though this action could compromise the affirmative action efforts.

Otis Elevator v. NLRB (1984)
Employees need not bargain over a transfer of operation if move is based on economics, not labor cost consideration.

AFSCME v. State of Washington (1985)
State had systematically paid jobs dominated by women less than their value according to job evaluation. Court of appeals overturned this decision saying state could not be forced "to eliminate an economic inequality that it did not create."

Pattern Makers' League v. NLRB (1985)
Employees may resign from a union at any time, even during a strike or when one is imminent.

Garcia v. San Antonio Transit Authority (1985)
Extends coverage of FLSA to state and local governments.

Scott v. Sears Roebuck (1985)
Woman unsuccessful in sex harassment suit based on acts by co-workers. Woman did not complain to supervisors. Court ruled only responsible for acts of co-workers if they knew or should have known of acts and took no action.

Horn v. Duke Homes (1985)
Court endorsed principle that employers have strict liability for sexual harassment by supervisors (company claimed that it was not liable because it was not aware of the behavior). Court supported full back pay (plaintiff had been terminated).

Glasgow v. Georgia Pacific Corp. (1985)
Court accepts sexual harassment argument on basis of creating hostile work environment (no *quid pro quo*). Company was found by Court to have made sexually harassing environment a condition of employment because harassment went on for a long period of time with organization doing nothing. Court outlined four-point test for sexually harassing work environment.
1. Harassment was unwelcome
2. Harassment was because of sex
3. Harassment affected terms and conditions of employment
4. Knowledge of harassment is "imputed" to employer

Wygant v. Jackson Board of Education (1986)
The Court ruled that white teachers were illegally dismissed in order to hire minority teachers in the School Board's efforts to fulfill a voluntary affirmative action program.

Barns v. Washington Natural Gas (1986)
Employer fires an employee because he was believed to have epilepsy. Awarded two years back pay and reinstatement.

Local 28 of the Sheet Metal Workers v. Equal Employment Opportunity Commission (1986)
The Court approved a lower court order requiring a New York City sheet metal workers' local to meet a 29 percent minority membership goal by 1987. The Court also held that judges may order racial preferences in union membership and other context if necessary to rectify especially "egregious" discrimination.

Local 93 of the International Association of Firefighters v. City of Cleveland (1986)
The Court held that lower Federal courts have broad discretion to approve decrees in which employers, over the objections of white employees, settle discrimination suits by agreeing to preferential hiring or promotion of minority-group members. It upheld a decree in which Cleveland agreed to settle a job discrimination suit by African-American and Hispanic firefighters by temporarily promoting African-American and Hispanic workers ahead of whites who had more seniority and higher test scores.

Meritor Savings Bank v. Vinson (1986)
The Court held that sexual harassment is a form of sex discrimination prohibited by Title VII of the Civil Rights Act and that employers may be liable for condoning a hostile work environment. However, the Court made it clear that employers will not be automatically liable for sexual harassment by supervisors or employees.

Philbrook v. Ansonia Board of Education (1986)
An employer may choose its own method of religious accommodation over a plan suggested by the worker as long as the employer's plan is reasonable.

Johnson v. Transportation Agency, Santa Clara County (1987)
The U.S. Supreme Court ruled that the county was justified in giving a job to a woman who scored two points less on an exam than a man. The county had an affirmative action plan that was flexible, temporary, and designed to correct the imbalance of white males in the work force.

School Board of Nassau County, Fla. v. Arline (1987)
The U.S. Supreme Court ruled that contagious diseases are not automatically excluded from coverage of the handicap provisions of Section 504 of the 1973 Rehabilitation Act.

Luck v. Southern Pacific Transportation Company (1987)
The court ruled that the company wrongfully discharged Barbara Luck for refusing a drug test on the grounds that it violated her rights to privacy. Subsequently, the company stopped its random drug-testing program.

U.S. v. Paradise (1987)
The U.S. Supreme Court affirmed the affirmative action plan for the state troopers of Alabama in which promotion and hiring quotas were established in order to correct racial imbalances even though it may result in discrimination against an individual because of race or color.

Chalk v. U.S. District Court for Central District of California (1987)
Although handicapped because of AIDS, the teacher was otherwise able to perform his job within the meaning of the Rehabilitation Act of 1973 and, therefore, should be allowed to teach.

O'Connor v. Ortega (1987)
Supreme Court recognized workplace privacy for the first time.

EEOC v. Commonwealth of Massachusetts (1987)
A Massachusetts law requiring entry-level motor vehicle examiners to be aged 35 or younger does not violate Age Discrimination in Employment Act because it is a bona fide occupational qualification (BFOQ).

Watson v. Fort Worth Bank and Trust (1988)
The U.S. Supreme Court held that all selection procedures—objective or subjective, scored or unscored—should be subject to adverse impact analysis, compelling a demonstration by the employer that the procedure is job related if adverse impact is shown.

Kraszewski v. State Farm (1988)
Out of court settlement. Firm agrees to set aside half of its new sales jobs to women for ten years and to pay damages and back pay.

Arrow Automotive Industries v. NLRB (1988)
Company does not have to bargain on plant closings even if based on labor-cost considerations.

Wards' Cove Packing v. Atonio (1989)
Concentration statistics were used to prove adverse impact. Court ruled that burden of proof should not shift to employer unless it can be proved that a specific policy created the disparity.

Hopkins v. Price Waterhouse (1989)
The court upheld the award of a partnership to the female accountant who successfully claimed that sexual stereotyping prevented her promotion.

Dimaranan v. Pomona Valley Hospital (1991)
The court essentially ruled that employers can restrict the use of foreign languages only when there is a compelling business-related necessity to do so.

EEOC v. Arabian American Oil Co. (1991)
The U.S. Supreme Court decided that Title VII has no application to U.S. employers employing U.S. citizens to work abroad. ADEA and the Civil Rights Act of 1991, however, have application.

Gilmer v. Interstate/Johnson Lane Corp. (1991)
The Supreme Court ruled in favor of alternative dispute resolution (ADR) by stating that employees can be required to go to arbitration before pursuing litigation.

Electromation Inc. v. NLRB (1992)
The Board held that 'action committees' at Electromation were illegal "labor organizations" because management created and controlled the groups and used them to deal with employees on working conditions in violation of Section 8 (a) 2 of the NLRA.

Stewart v. Jackson & Nash (1992)
A truth-in-hiring lawsuit in which the appeals court declared that the law firm's misrepre-

sentations caused Stewart to join a firm in which her skills as an environmental lawyer were not used although promised to be so.

E.I. Du Pont de Nemours and Company v. NLRB (1993)
The Board concluded that Du Pont's six safety committees and fitness committee were employer-dominated labor organizations and that Du Pont dominated the formation and administration of one of them in violation of Section 8 (a) 2 of the NLRA.

St. Mary's Honor Center v. Hicks (1993)
The Supreme Court ruled in this disparate treatment case, that the suing employee has to produce evidence that the employer's true motive is not a discriminatory one. This increases the burden of proof on the employee to demonstrate that the employer intentionally discriminated.

EEOC v. AIC Security Investigations (1993)
The court ruled in favor of a director of a security firm who was discharged after he was diagnosed with terminal brain cancer and awarded the individual $572,000. The first case under ADA.

Harris v. Forklift Systems (1993)
The Supreme Court affirmed the "reasonable women" standard by sending the case back to the appeals court stating that Harris did not have to prove that she was psychologically damaged for her boss' behavior to claim sexual harassment.

*This set of court cases is meant to provide a sampling of those mentioned in the text. For descriptions of these and of other cases, see J. Ledvinka, and V. G. Scarpello *Federal Regulation of Personnel and Human Resource Management* 2nd ed. (Boston: Kent, 1991); J. Bernardin and W. Cascio, *Annotated Bibliography of Court Cases Relevant to Employment Decisions 1980–1984* (Boca Raton: Florida Atlantic University, 1984); M. D. Levin-Epstein, *Primer of Equal Opportunity*, 3d ed. (Washington, D.C.: NA, 1984); M. McCarthy, ed., *Complete Guide to Employing Persons with Disabilities* (Albertson, N.Y.: National Center on Employment of the Handicapped at Human Resources Center, 1985); M. A. Player, *Federal Law of Employment Discrimination* (St. Paul: West Publishing, 1991); D. P. Twomey, *Equal Opportunity Law* (Cincinnati: Southwestern, 1994).

INFORMATION FOR MANAGING HUMAN RESOURCES

JOURNALS, MAGAZINES AND NEWSPAPERS

Business Week, published by McGraw-Hill, 1221 Avenue of the Americas, New York, New York 10020.

Employee Relations Law Journal, published by Executive Enterprises, Inc., 33 West 60th Street, New York, New York 10023. Articles on current personnel topics with the related legal considerations are contained in each quarterly issue.

Fair Employment Practices; Bulletin to Management; the Bulletin on Training, published by the Bureau of National Affairs, 1231 25th Street N.W., Washington, D.C. 20037.

FEP Guidelines, published by the Bureau of Business Practices, 24 Rope Ferry Road, Waterford, Connecticut 06386.

Fortune, published by Time-Life, Rockefeller Center, New York, New York 10020.

Human Resource Management, published by the Graduate School of Business, University of Michigan, Ann Arbor, Michigan 48109.

Human Resource Planning, published by the Human Resources Planning Society, 41 E. 42nd Street, New York, New York 10017.

Inc., published by Inc. Business Resources, 38 Commercial Wharf, Boston, Massachusetts 02110-3883.

Industrial and Labor Relations Review, New York State School of Labor and Industrial Relations, Cornell University, Ithaca, New York. Opinions and reports of studies on labor legislation, collective bargaining, and related subjects.

Industrial Medicine and Surgery, Industrial Medicine Publishing Company, 605 North Michigan Avenue, Chicago, Illinois. Emphasizes health programs in industry, with reports on health hazards, occupational diseases, handicapped workers, medical services, and related subjects.

Industrial Relations, Institute of Industrial Relations, University of California, Berkeley and Los Angeles, California. Ideas and opinions as well as reports of research.

International Journal of Human Resource Management, published by Routledge Journals, 11 New Fetterlane, London, England. Focus is international human resource management.

Journal of the American Society of Training Directors, official publication of the American Society of Training Directors, 2020 University Avenue, Madison, Wisconsin. Broad coverage of the personnel field, with a special emphasis on training problems.

Journal of Applied Psychology, American Psychological Association, 1313 16th Street N.W., Washington, D.C. All phases of applied psychology, with numerous reports of personnel research.

Labor Law Journal, Commerce Clearing House, Inc., 214 N. Michigan Avenue, Chicago, Illinois. Generally presents nonlegalistic discussions of legal phases of industrial relations.

Management Record, The Conference Board, 247 Park Avenue, New York, New York. Numerous reports of both experience and research, surveys conducted by the National Industrial Conference Board staff, and digests of symposia.

Management Review, American Management Association, 135 W. 50th Street, New York, New York 10020. General coverage of all phases of management.

Monthly Labor Review, Bureau of Labor Statistics, U.S. Department of Labor, Washington, D.C. Summaries of staff studies on industrial relations; statistical sections include continuing series on industrial disputes, employment, payrolls, and cost of living.

HR Focus, American Management Association, 135 W. 50th Street, New York, New York 10020. Broad interest in entire field of industrial relations, with numerous reports of surveys, studies, and experience.

HR Magazine, published by the Society for Human Resource Management, 606 Washington Street, Alexandria, Virginia 22314.

Personnel Journal, published at *Personnel Journal*, 245 Fischer Ave. B-2, Costa Mesa, California 92626. Covers a broad spectrum of topics in human resource management.

Personnel Management, formerly the *Journal of the Institute of Personnel Management*, Institute of Personnel Management, Management House, 80 Fetter Lane, London, England. Theory and practice in both personnel management and labor relations.

Personnel Psychology, 745 Haskins Road, Suite A, Bowling Green, OH 43402. Emphasizes reports on research in psychological aspects of personnel.

Public Personnel Quarterly, published by the International Personnel Management Association, 1859 K Street N.W., Washington, D.C.

Studies in Personnel Policy, National Industrial Conference Board, 247 Park Avenue, New York, New York. Mainly compares experience and evaluations of programs, with frequent surveys of policy and practice.

Training, published by Lakewood Publications, 50 South Ninth St., Minneapolis, Minnesota 55402.

The Wall Street Journal, published by Dow Jones, P.O. Box 300, Princeton, New Jersey 08543-030.

Working Age, published by the AARP, 601 E. Street, N.W., Washington, D.C. 20049.

ASSOCIATIONS

AFL-CIO, 815 16th St., NW, Washington, D.C. 20006, (202) 637-5000

American Arbitration Association, 140 W. 51st St., New York, NY 10020, (212) 484-4800

American Association of Retired Persons (AARP), 601 E Street, N.W., Washington, D.C. 20042, (202) 434-2277

American Compensation Association, 14040 N. Northsight Blvd., Scottsdale, AZ 85260, (602) 951-9191

American Management Associations, 135 W. 50th St., New York, NY 10020, (212) 586-8100

American Society for Healthcare Human Resources Administration, 840 N. Lakeshore Dr., Chicago, IL 60611, (312) 280-6111

American Society for Industrial Security, 1655 N. Fort Meyer Dr., Suite 1200, Arlington, VA 22209, (703) 522-5800

American Society for Training and Development, 1630 Duke Street, Alexandria, VA 22312, (703) 683-8100

American Society of Pension Actuaries, 1700 K St., NW, Suite 404, Washington, D.C. 20006, (202) 659-3620

American Society of Safety Engineers, 1800 East Oakton, Des Plaines, IL 60018, (312) 692-4121

Bureau of Labor Statistics (BLS), Department of Labor, 3rd Street & Constitution Ave., NW, Washington, D.C. 20210

Bureau of National Affairs (BNA), 1231 25th Street, NW, Washington, D.C. 20037

Commerce Clearing House, Inc., 4025 W. Peterson Avenue, Chicago, Illinois 60646

Employee Benefit Research Institute, 2121 K St., NW, Suite 860, Washington, D.C. 20037, (202) 659-0670

Employee Relations Council, 1627 K St., NW, Washington, D.C. 20006, (202) 857-0857

Equal Employment Opportunity Commission (EEOC), 1801 L Street, N.W., Washington, D.C. 20507, 202/663-4900/1-800-699-EEOC

Human Resource Certification Institute (HRCI), 606 N. Washington, Alexandria, VA 22314, (703) 548-3440

Human Resource Planning Society, 41 E. 42nd St., Suite 1509, New York, New York 10017, (212) 490-6387

Human Resource Systems Professionals, P.O. Box 8040-A202, Walnut Creek, CA 94596, (415) 945-8428

International Labour Organization (ILO), CH-1211, Geneva, Switzerland, (212) 697-0150

Industrial Relations Research Association, 7726 Social Science Bldg., Madison, WI 53706, (608) 262-2762

International Personnel Management Association, 1617 Duke St., Alexandria, VA 22314, (703) 391-7436

Labor Management Mediation Service, 1620 I St., NW, Suite 616, Washington, D.C. 20006

National Association of Manufacturers (NAM), 1331 Pennsylvania Ave., NW, Suite 1500N, Washington, D.C. (202) 637-3000

National Association of Personnel Consultants, 3133 Mt. Vernon Ave., Alexandria, VA 22305, (703) 684-0180

National Labor Relations Board, 1099 14th St. N.W., Washington, D.C. 20570, (202) 273-1000

National Mediation Board, 1301 K Street N.W., Suite 250 E, Washington, D.C. 20572

National Safety Council, 1121 Spring Lake Drive, Itasca, IL 60143-3201, (708) 285-1121

Occupational Safety and Health Administration (OSHA), 200 Constitution Ave., NW, Washington, D.C. 20210, (202) 523-8045

Office on the Americans with Disabilities Act, Civil Rights Division, U.S. Department of Justice, P.O. Box 66118, Washington, D.C. 20035-6118, (202) 514-0301 (Voice), (202) 514-0381 (TDD), (202) 514-0383 (TDD)

Office of Federal Contract Compliance Programs (OFCCP), 200 Constitution Ave. N.W., Washington, D.C. 20210

Office of the American Workplace, Department of Labor, 200 Constitution Ave. N.W., Washington, D.C. 20210

Pension Benefit Guaranty Corporation, P.O. Box 7119, Washington, D.C. 20044

Profit Sharing Council of America, 200 N. Wacker Drive, Suite 1722, Chicago, IL 60606, (312) 372-3411

Society for Human Resource Management (SHRM), including Institute for International Human Resources, 606 N. Washington, Alexandria, VA 22314, (703) 548-3440

U.S. Chamber of Commerce, 1615 H Street, N.W., Washington, D.C. 20062

U.S. Department of Labor, 200 Constitution Ave. N.W., Washington, D.C. 20210, (202) 219-7316

The specific interpretation and application of the *Americans With Disabilities Act* is certain to be refined and modified as it is put into practice. For the most current information, contact:

The President's Committee on Employment of People with Disabilities 1331 F Street, N.W., Washington, D.C. 20004-1107, 202/376-6200 (Voice), 202/376-6205 (TDD)

For specific information on making reasonable accommodations in the workplace, contact:

National Organization on Disability, 910 16th St. NW, Washington, D.C. 20006, 202-293-1944.

Job Accommodation Network (JAN), West Virginia University, 809 Allen Hall, P.O. Box 468, Morgantown, WV 26506, 1-800-526-7734

For specific information on small business, see

The State of Small Business (1991). A Report to the President: Annual Report on Small Business and Competition. Washington, D.C.: United States Government Printing Office.

The States and Small Businesses (1993). A Directory of Programs and Activities. Washington, D.C.: United States Government Printing Office.

For specific information on unions see, C. D. Gifford, *Directory of U.S. Labor Organizations 1992–93 Edition* (Washington, D.C.: The Bureau of National Affairs, 1993).

For specific information on total quality, see The Malcolm Baldrige National Quality Award

Managed by:

United States Department of Commerce
Technology Administration
National Institute of Standards and Technology
Route 270 and Quince Orchard Road
Administration Building, Room A537
Gaithersburg, MD 20899-0001

Administered by:

American Society for Quality Control
P.O. Box 3005
Milwaukee, WI 53201-3005

THE VALIDATION PROCESS

Regardless of the method or site used to study human resource issues, HR professionals need to be concerned about the reliability and validation of measurement devices. **Reliability** refers to the consistency of measurement, whereas **validity** relates to the truth or accuracy of measurement. The concept of a correlation coefficient is important to both reliability and validity.

VALIDITY

As defined in the *Principles for the Validation and Use of Personnel Selection Procedures* (American Psychological Association), **validity** is the degree to which inferences from scores on tests or assessments are supported by evidence.[1] This definition implies that validity refers to the inferences made from use of a measure, not to the measure itself. Three primary strategies have been identified to gather evidence to support or justify the inferences made from scores on measures: criterion-related, content-oriented, and construct validation strategies.

CRITERION-RELATED STRATEGY

A **criterion-related** strategy is an assessment of how well a measure (that is, predictor) forecasts a criterion such as job performance. This tends to be the primary validation strategy used in personnel research. The major steps that make up this strategy are shown in Exhibit 1. The two types of criterion-related validation strategies are concurrent and predictive—shown in Exhibit 2.

Concurrent validation evaluates the relationship between a predictor and a job criterion score for all employees in the study at the same time. For example, this strategy could be used to determine the correlation between years of experience and job performance. Data would be collected from each person in the study about years of experience and performance scores. All persons in the study would have to be working in similar jobs, generally in the same job family or classification. Then a correlation would be computed between the predictor scores and criterion scores.

The term **correlation**, or observed **correlation coefficient** (denoted by the symbol r), is the degree to which two or more sets of measurements vary. A positive correlation exists when high values on one variable (for example, job knowledge test) are associated with high values on another variable (for example, high overall ratings of job performance). A negative correlation exists when high values on one variable are associated with low values on another variable. The correlation coefficient, which expresses the degree of linear relationship between two sets of scores, can range from positive to negative. The range is from +1 (a perfect positive correlation coefficient) to –1 (a perfect negative correlation coefficient). Illustrations of several linear relationships represented by plotting actual data of personnel selection test—job performance relationships are shown in Exhibit 3.

The steps in determining predictive validity are similar, except that the predictor is measured sometime before the criterion is measured, as shown in Exhibit 1. Thus, the **predictive validity** of a predictor could be determined by measuring an existing group of employees on a predictor and waiting to gather their criterion measures later, or by hiring a group of job applicants regardless of their scores on the predictor and measuring them on the criterion later. For either type of criterion-related validation strategy, it is important to demonstrate that the predictors and performance criteria are related to the duties of the job.

The classic example of a predictive validation study is AT&T's Management Progress Study.[2] In that study, personnel researchers at AT&T administered an assessment center, similar to the one described in Chapter 8, to 422 male employees, stored the results, and waited eight years before evaluating their predictions of how far these individuals would progress in AT&T's management hierarchy. For a group of college graduates, the predictions were highly accurate; a correlation of .71 was obtained between the assessment center predictions and level of management achieved. In addition, a twenty-year follow-up of the original predictions showed that the assessment center was still useful in predicting who would reach even higher levels in AT&T's management hierarchy.

An assessment of criterion-related validity is often important for many personnel decisions. In fact, it is the heart of most personnel decisions. The greater the validity coefficient for a test, the more efficient selection and placement decisions will be. And the more efficient these decisions, the more productive the work force will be.

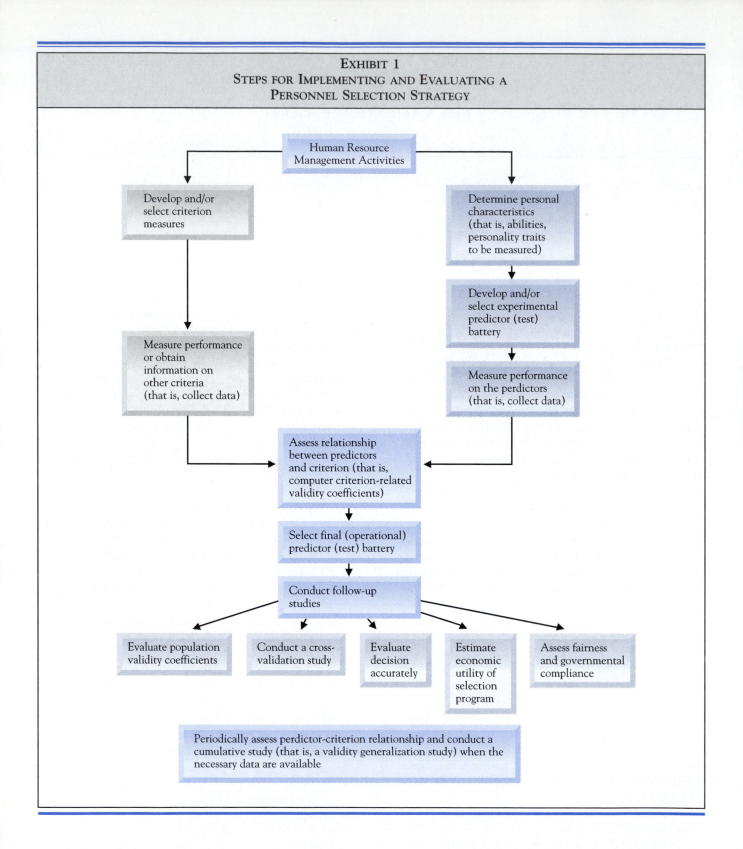

**EXHIBIT 1
STEPS FOR IMPLEMENTING AND EVALUATING A
PERSONNEL SELECTION STRATEGY**

Human Resource Management Activities

Develop and/or select criterion measures

Determine personal characteristics (that is, abilities, personality traits to be measured)

Develop and/or select experimental predictor (test) battery

Measure performance or obtain information on other criteria (that is, collect data)

Measure performance on the perdictors (that is, collect data)

Assess relationship between predictors and criterion (that is, computer criterion-related validity coefficients)

Select final (operational) predictor (test) battery

Conduct follow-up studies

Evaluate population validity coefficients

Conduct a cross-validation study

Evaluate decision accurately

Estimate economic utility of selection program

Assess fairness and governmental compliance

Periodically assess perdictor-criterion relationship and conduct a cumulative study (that is, a validity generalization study) when the necessary data are available

EXHIBIT 2
CRITERION-RELATED VALIDATION STRATEGIES

Concurrent Study

TIME 1	TIME 1	TIME 1
Test (predictor) scores are gathered	Criterion scores are gathered	Correlation between scores on predictor (x) and criterion (y), r_{xy}, is calculated

Predictive Study

TIME 1	TIME 2	TIME 2
Test (predictor) scores are gathered	Criterion scores are gathered	Correlation between scores on predictor (x) and criterion (y), r_{xy}, is calculated

Although the *Uniform Guidelines of 1978* require organizations to demonstrate the job-relatedness of a selection procedure, they do not specify the actual degree of job-relatedness. Thus, an organization can claim its selection procedures are job-related or permit valid inferences even though the correlation coefficient between the predictor and criterion is .3 rather than .6 or .7. Although the *Uniform Guidelines* do not specify the magnitude of the correlation necessary to claim job-relatedness, they do indicate that the correlation should be statistically significant.

An important aspect of criterion-related validity is the relevance or appropriateness of the criterion being correlated with the predictor. In a criterion-related validity study, the predictors should be shown to correlate with the criteria, and the criteria should be shown relevant and important to the jobs in question. Failure to establish these points was the heart of the U.S. Supreme Court's decision in the *Albemarle* case, in which the Court first looked at a validation study:

> The study in this case involved no analysis of the attributes of, or the particular skills needed in, the studied job groups. There is accordingly no basis for concluding that "no significant differences" exist among the lines of progression, or among distinct job groupings within the studied lines of progression.
>
> Albemarle's supervisors were asked to rank employees by a "standard" that was extremely vague and fatally open to divergent interpretations. . . . (T)here simply was no way to determine whether the criteria actually considered were suffi-

ciently related to the Company's legitimate interest in job-specific ability to justify a testing system with a racially discriminatory impact.

> The fact that the best of those employees working near the top of a line of progression score well on a test does not necessarily mean that that test, or some particular cutoff score on the test, is a permissible measure of the minimal qualifications of new workers entering lower level jobs.
>
> Albemarle's validation study dealt only with job-experienced white workers; but the tests themselves are given to new job applicants who are younger, largely inexperienced, and in many instances nonwhite.

On many occasions, employers are not able to obtain sufficient empirical data for a criterion-related validity study. Consequently, other methods of validation are helpful in determining the validity of measures used in personnel research.

CONTENT-ORIENTED STRATEGY

A **content-oriented validation** strategy differs from a criterion-related strategy in that it estimates or judges the relevance of a predictor as a sample of the relevant situations (for example, behaviors or tasks) that make up a job. In essence, job-relatedness here is an estimation or judgment. According to the *Uniform Guidelines of 1978*, "A selection procedure can be supported by a content validity strategy to the extent it is a representative sample of the content of the job." The administration of a typing test (actually, a work sample test if used for typists) as a selection device for hiring typists is a classic

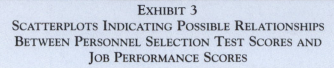

EXHIBIT 3
SCATTERPLOTS INDICATING POSSIBLE RELATIONSHIPS
BETWEEN PERSONNEL SELECTION TEST SCORES AND
JOB PERFORMANCE SCORES

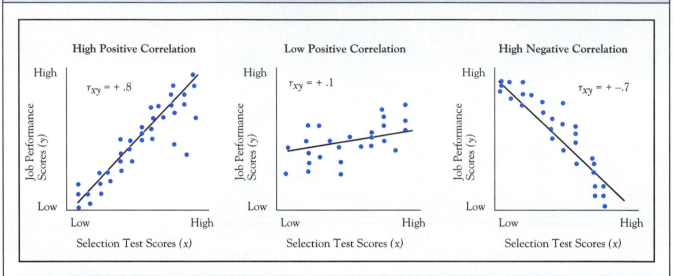

example of a predictor judged to be content valid.[3] In this case, the predictor is a skill related to a task that is actually part of the job. Thus, to employ a content validation strategy, one must know the duties of the actual job.[4] As discussed in Chapter 6, information about job tasks and duties can be obtained using one or more job analysis procedures.

Job analysis is discussed here as a critical element in content validation. It should be regarded as the starting point and the thread that ties together any basic personnel selection and validation study. It is also a critical activity in determining construct validity.

CONSTRUCT STRATEGY

Instead of showing a direct relationship between a test or other selection information (for example, education or experience levels) and job criteria, selection methods seek to measure (often by tests) the degree to which an applicant possesses abilities and characteristics (psychological traits) that are deemed necessary for successful job performance. These underlying psychological traits are called **constructs** and include, among many others, intelligence, leadership ability, verbal ability, interpersonal sensitivity, and analytical ability. Constructs deemed necessary for doing well on job criteria are inferred from job behaviors and activities (duties) indicated in the job analysis.

A **construct validation** study attempts to demonstrate that a relationship exists between a selection procedure or test (a measure of the construct) and the psychological trait (construct) it seeks to measure. For example, does a reading comprehension test reliably and accurately measure how well people can read and understand what they read? To demonstrate construct validity, one would need data showing that high scorers on the test actually read more difficult material and are better readers than low scorers on the test, and that reading ability is related to the duties shown in the job description. Other evidence that the test is measuring the relevant construct could be obtained based on its relationship to other measures that assess both similar and unrelated constructs. In essence, construct validity is not established with a single study. Rather, it is assessed based on the cumulation of a body of empirical evidence. This evidence is likely to include information gathered from both criterion-related and content-oriented validation studies.

VALIDITY GENERALIZATION

The essence of **validity generalization** is that a test or predictor predicts the same way for all individuals in similar jobs in the same or similar organizations. That is, if two similar jobs exist in two parts of an organization or in two different organizations, a given selection test should be equally valid for the two jobs. This assumes, however, that some degree of similarity in jobs and conditions can first be identified. Similarity of jobs and conditions are judged by the results of job analyses. If validity generalization can be successfully established, an organization can save a great deal of time and money in developing valid, job-related predictors. In short, if the validity of a predictor for a job has already been established, it may be utilized as a predictor in another, perhaps newly created, similar job.

BASE RATE VERSUS PREDICTOR RATE

Another big step in finding, developing, and using job-related predictors is showing how beneficial they are, if indeed they are more beneficial than using no predictors at all. In using predictors, an organization is assuming that (1) some job applicants will perform better than others; (2) they can be spotted (by using predictors) and selected; and (3) the **predictor rate**, that is, the number of true decisions relative to the total number of decisions, exceeds the **base rate**, or the proportion of applicants who would succeed on the job from those randomly selected. The more the predictor rate exceeds the base rate, the more useful the predictor.

The importance of having a higher predictor rate than the base rate can be illustrated with the concepts of **false negatives**, **false positives**, **true positives**, and **true negatives** introduced in Chapter 8. What an organization wants to do in selecting employees is to make as many *true* decisions (true positive and negative) as possible and to minimize the number of *false* decisions (false positive and negative). Using a test with a predictor rate higher than the base rate results does this. For example, if the base rate is .5 (half the applicants randomly hired turn out to be good performers) and the predictor rate is .8 (80 percent of the selection decisions are correct), then using a valid predictor will yield more correct decisions than randomly selecting applicants. This can be illustrated using two scattergrams, each with one hundred applicants hired, one showing low validity and a .5 base rate and the other showing high validity and a .8 predictor rate. A predictor (test) **cutoff score** is used to categorize those who would be hired and predicted to be good performers and those who would be rejected and predicted to be poor performers. The two scattergrams are shown in Exhibit 4.

In scattergram A there is essentially no relationship or validity between the test scores (if one had been used) and the performance scores. Note that an equal number of applicants turned out to be true positive (TP), false positive (FP), true negative (TN), and false negative (FN). (In all quadrants the number of applicants (n)=25.) Note also that the predictor rate does *not* exceed the base rate.

If the predictor with a .8 rate were used to select the applicants, the results would be substantially different. In scattergram B the number of individuals in the four categories is not equal. In fact, FP and FN are each 10, and TP and TN are each 40. Thus, 80 correct decisions were made. Hence, the predictor rate of .8 exceeds the base rate of .5. Thus, using tests with predictor rates exceeding base rates tends to improve the utility of the selection process. Final evaluation of the real utility of the selection process, however, must incorporate the assessment of several costs, including those from using the test and those resulting from false decisions.

SELECTION RATIO

An important concept in evaluating selection and placement procedures is the **selection ratio**, which is defined as the proportion of individuals actually hired among those who applied. For example, from 200 applicants, only 10 individuals are hired. This would represent a selection ratio of 10/200, or 5 percent. Generally speaking, managers prefer small selection ratios—that is, when there are many more applicants than jobs, because the organization can raise the predictor cutoff and thus be more selective.

The fewer applicants an organization has, the less sure it can be that it has the best possible applicant. With few applicants, it must be more careful in matching them to the jobs available. If an organization must hire all the applicants because there are so few, the validity of the selection and placement devices becomes irrelevant. This is especially true when there is only one type of job available.

When everyone who applies is hired, chances are slim that all will have the ability to do well. Consequently, the organization may need to establish extensive and perhaps costly training programs. The organization can also try to attract more job applicants by raising wages, but that may only lead to more trouble. For example, raising the wages of new employees may be unfair to the rest of the employees and make them unhappy (pay equity is discussed in Chapter 11). Thus, it pays an organization to attract as many potentially qualified applicants as possible and reduce its selection ratio. Without choice, the utility of selection devices is minimal; with it, their utility may be high and chances are greater the applicants chosen will do well and be satisfied.

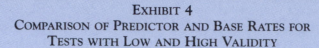

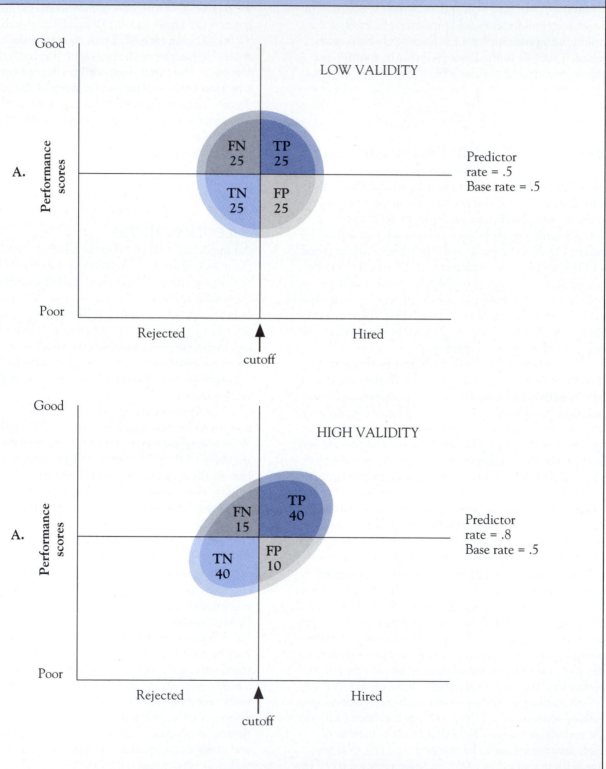

UTILITY AND COSTS

The value of selection and placement procedures can now be seen to vary as a function of the following basic criteria:

- *Magnitude of the validity (regardless of type) and reliability*. As validity and reliability increase, so does the utility of the procedures.
- *Base rate*. As the differential between the base rate and predictor rate increases (assuming the predictor rate is higher than the base rate), the utility of the selection procedures increases.
- *Selection ratio*. As selection ratios become smaller, the cost of testing increases and the utility of the selection procedures increases (assuming other factors, such as the predictor cutoff, remain constant). This is because many applicants must be tested even though only a few will be selected.[5]

The impact and utility of these three criteria may be changed significantly by the costs involved. For example, it may be more useful for an organization to use a particular selection test with a validity of .4 rather than another with a validity of .5 if the costs of developing and using the latter are twice as expensive. Against these relative costs must be compared the relative gains. The test with the higher validity may result in gains large enough to offset its greater implementation expense.

Consequently, organizations should use selection and placement procedures that maximize relative gain as opposed to cost. Generally, those procedures producing potentially greater gains are more job-related and also relatively more costly. Thus, it is necessary to measure both the benefits (of true decisions) and their costs carefully.

Actual costs incurred in hiring applicants include the following:

- Recruiting and assessment costs—salaries of personnel staff, advertising expenses, and travel expenses
- Costs of personnel testing
- Induction and orientation costs—administrative costs of adding the employees to the payroll and salaries of the new employees and those responsible for orienting them to their new jobs
- Training costs—salaries of training and development staff, salary of the new employees during training, and costs of any special materials, instruments, or facilities for training

Potential costs that might be incurred if a wrong selection decision is made include the following:

- Costs associated with hiring a person who subsequently fails—recordkeeping costs; termination costs; costs of undesirable job behavior, such as materials or equipment damaged; loss of customers, clients, or patients, loss of good will; and costs incurred in replacing a failing employee
- Costs associated with rejecting a person who would have been successful on the job—competitive disadvantage if applicant is hired by another firm (for example, loss of a top sports star to a competing team), and costs of recruiting and assessing an additional applicant to replace the rejectee[6]

In addition to comparing the costs and benefits of alternative selection and placement procedures, organizations should also compare the costs and benefits of other techniques, such as job design or supervisory training programs, that increase job performance and employee retention. The costs and benefits of alternatives to selection and placement will be influenced by the same basic criteria as well as by several other criteria.

NOTES

1. American Psychological Association, Division 14, *Principles for the Validation and Use of Personnel Selection Procedures* (Washington, D.C.: APA, 1980).

2. For a discussion of the AT&T Management Progress Study as well as an overview of assessment centers, see A. Howard, "An Assessment of Assessment Centers," *Academy of Management Journal* 17 (1974): 115–34. A twenty-year follow-up study of AT&T's original Management Progress Study predictions was reported in A. Howard, "Cool at the Top: Personality Characteristics of Successful Executives," paper presented at the Annual Convention of the American Psychological Association, Toronto, Canada, August 1984.

3. R. S. Barrett, "Is the Test Content-Valid: Or, Who Killed Cock Robin?" *Employee Relations Law Journal* 6 (4) (1981); 584–600; R. S. Barrett, "Is the Test Content-Valid: Or, Does It Really Measure Construct?" *Employee Relations Law Journal* 6 (3)(1981): 459–75.

4. For a discussion and reconceptualization of the concept of content validity, see R. M. Guion, "On Trinitarian Doctrines of Validity," *Professional Psychology* 11 (1980): 385–98.

5. R. D. Arvey, *Fairness in Selecting Employees* (Reading, Mass.: Addison-Wesley, 1979), 35–37. Arvey provides an excellent in-depth discussion of these issues. See also P. M. Podsakoff, M. E. Williams, and W. E. Scott, Jr., "Myths of Employee Selection Systems," in *Readings in Personnel and Human Resource Management*, 3d ed., eds. R. S. Schuler, S. A. Youngblood, and V. L. Huber (St. Paul: West, 1988).

6. *Ibid.*

THE RÉSUMÉ

The goal of your résumé is to effectively communicate your qualifications to prospective employers. In many cases your résumé will determine whether or not you are granted an interview. The résumé, by itself, however will not get you a job. If it gets you in the door, then it has served its purpose.

WHAT DO YOU HAVE TO OFFER?

To develop an effective résumé you must first have a thorough knowledge of the product you are selling—you! What are the talents, skills, accomplishments, and experiences that you are marketing? To adequately answer this question you may want to sit down with a counselor and have him/her assist you with the self-assessment process.

TARGETING

Once you know what skills and knowledge you have to offer, the next step is learning what qualifications are valued by employers in your field. Do different organizations in the same field look for similar or different qualifications? How much do you know about the position for which you are applying? Are any specific skills stressed in the job description? Make sure you emphasize the aspects of your experience which are most relevant to the job.

ASSIGNMENTS:

Visit your career resource center and library to research your field(s) of interest. For each occupation try to answer the following questions: What are the typical career paths for this occupation? What are the typical job responsibilities? What skills and training are required?

Talk to at least 3 knowledgeable people in your field to supplement your library research. Suggestions include Career Week speakers, internship supervisors, professors, and members of professional associations.

WHAT FORMAT SHOULD I CHOOSE?

There are basically two résumé formats—the Chronological and the Functional.

The **Chronological** résumé is by far the most popular and is generally preferred by employers. Chronological résumés are arranged in time order, with one's most recent experience listed first. They work well for students whose work experience is directly related to their professional objective.

The **Functional** résumé is organized according to specific skill categories which allow the writer to highlight particular areas of competency that may have been gained through a wide variety of experiences. This style can be beneficial for students whose experience is not directly related to the career field which they have chosen to pursue. The major drawback of the functional résumé is that certain information is taken out of context, leaving the reader with the impression that the applicant may be trying to hide something.

HOW LONG SHOULD IT BE?

A résumé is a summary of your qualifications, not a novel. The most effective résumés are concise and direct. For most fields a one page résumé is standard. Consult with a career counselor regarding your particular situation.

WHAT'S THE BEST WAY TO SAY IT?

The best résumé is clearly written, and speaks the language of the employer. Avoid repetition, wordiness, cryptic abbreviations, and jargon. Start your sentences with action verbs.

ARE LOOKS IMPORTANT?

Although your résumé's content is paramount, its appearance can determine whether or not it gets read. Your résumé must look professional. It should be printed on high quality paper of neutral color with high quality print (we recommend laser printing). Make the résumé inviting, but not flashy. Day-glo or sheepskin paper may impress your friends but will probably have an adverse effect on the employer.

WHAT SHOULD I INCLUDE?

1) **Name, Address** and **Phone Number** (day and evening)
2) **Objective** (optional)—To formulate a solid objective try to answer the following questions: What is it you really want to do? For whom? Where? At what level of responsibility?

3) **Education**—list the schools you attended (with dates, degrees, honors), classes you've taken that are relevant to your objective (you may want to describe any special projects, papers, or presentations that were a part of your course-work).

4) **Experience**—list all the positions you've ever held (include paid, volunteer, and intern positions). Put these in chronological order and for each position ask yourself:

What were my major accomplishments? (quantify, if possible)

What were my main responsibilities?

What skills did I acquire, improve, utilize?

What special knowledge did I gain?

Now decide which positions are most relevant for your résumé. You do not need to list every job you've ever held.

5) **Activities** (optional)—Were you a member of any clubs? What about other on or off-campus organizations? (e.g., fraternities, student publications, charitable groups, etc.) Were you a member of any athletic teams? Were you elected or appointed as an officer of a club organization? Describe your accomplishments in the above activities.

6) **Skills** (optional)—What hard skills do you possess (e.g., language ability, computer skills, and other technical skills)?

7) **Interests** (optional)—What do you like to do outside of work and school? Are you a weekend athlete, or a midnight Mozart? Be specific.

THE COVER LETTER

The cover letter is probably the most underrated component of the job search. If written well, it can pique the curiosity of the employer and motivate him/her to carefully read your résumé. If written poorly, the résumé may never get read.

BASIC TIPS

1) Write to a specific individual–never Dear Sir or Madam.

2) Tailor your letters—don't mass produce them.

3) Keep it brief—3 or 4 paragraphs will suffice.

4) Use stationery and print which match your résumé.

HOW DO I START?

Your introduction must answer at least the following three questions:

1) What position are you applying for?

2) How did you hear about it (e.g., through a friend, an ad, Career Services, etc.)?

3) What is/was your major?

4) When will/did you graduate?

THE BODY OF THE LETTER— YOUR SALES PITCH

This is where you need to emphasize your strengths and relate them to the requirements of the position. Tell the employer what you can do for them as opposed to what they can do for you. Stress that you possess certain skills which can help your potential employer solve certain concrete problems.

THE FINAL PARAGRAPH

Close by requesting an interview. Indicate that you will be following up by phone. Always, thank the employer for their consideration.

THE THANK YOU LETTER

This is your chance to show your appreciation to everyone who has assisted you with your job search, including those who interviewed you. The thank you letter is a nice personal touch which will create a very positive impression of you in the employer's mind. The main goal is to remind the reader of who you are, and to show them how interested you are in the opportunity being offered.

TIPS

1) Keep the letter brief—two to three paragraphs should suffice.

2) If you neglected to mention one of your strengths during the interview, here is your opportunity. Also, you may want to remind the reader of an important point that you raised during the interview.

SOURCE: This material is from the New York University 1993–94 Career Guidebook and is used here with the permission of the Office of Career Services, New York University and Future First Publishing; under the direction of Trudy Steinfeld, Director, OCS.

Glossary
for
Managing Human Resources

Ability The physical or intellectual quality or capability or capacity.

Absolute standards This approach allows superiors to evaluate each subordinate's performance independent of the other subordinates and often on several dimensions of performance.

Accommodation A human resource philosophy and practice that attempts to make workplaces and work schedules more compatible with the individual.

Accomplishment records Historical measures of performance professionals and scientists use indicating achievements.

Achievement tests Measures of an individual's performance based on what he or she knows. These may be actual work samples of the job or paper-and-pencil measures.

Administrative issues Issues concerning the treatment of employees at work such as breaks and cleanup time.

Adversarial system A view of labor and management that depicts each of the two parties in conflict over achieving incompatible goals.

Adverse impact A general expression referring to the effects of disparate treatment or disparate impact.

Affirmative action programs Programs that are designed to ensure proportional representation of employees on the basis of race, ethnic origin, sex or disability. Companies that have federal contracts exceeding $50,000 are required by the federal government to have such programs. They can also be established on a voluntary basis or as part of a consent decree.

AFL-CIO The American Federation of Labor and Congress of Industrial Organizations; a major umbrella for national unions that represents a larger majority of the union members in the United States.

Alternative dispute resolution (ADR) A term used to describe various methods of settling disputes short of filing a civil lawsuit.

Alternative procedures requirement The need to show that alternative ways or procedures may exist that result in less disparate impact than current out staffing practice. Also known as cosmic search requirement.

Alternative ranking A comparative approach in which the superior alternates between ranking the best and worst until all subordinates are ranked.

Alternative work arrangements Making available hours of work and days of work that differ from the more traditional eight to five, Monday to Friday schedule.

Application blank A form seeking information about the job applicant's background and present conditions that is used to make hiring decisions.

Apprenticeship training A training format based on learning while doing for a long time before being recognized as competent to be a full-fledged employee.

Aptitude tests Measures of an individual's potential to perform. Intelligence tests are aptitude tests.

Arbitration A procedure in which a central third party studies the bargaining situation, listening to both parties and gathering information, and then reaches a decision that is usually binding for the parties.

Assessment The process of measuring and comparing the costs and benefits to determine effectiveness or value especially as it relates to each personnel activity in a company and the entire HR department in a company.

Assessment center Used to determine managerial potential of employees; evaluates individuals as they take part in a large number of activities conducted in a relatively isolated environment. It is also useful for identifying potential training needs.

Assistantships A type of on-the-job training that involves full-time employment and exposes the individual to a wide range of jobs through assisting other workers.

Association A formal group of individuals that represents them as employees before the employer in many ways similar to a union except that the association often is involved in fewer functions than a union.

Attitudinal structuring The relationships between labor and management during collective bargaining that result in shaping of attitudes toward one another.

Attribution process The psychological condition of assigning blame or explanation to an event.

Authorization cards After initial contact between unions and employees, the union may begin to obtain signatures of employees; if 30 percent sign the card, it can petition the NLRB for a certification election.

Autonomy The freedom to make decisions in deciding how to do one's job.

Availability analysis Process of determining how many women and minorities are available to work in the relevant labor market of an organization.

Baldrige award The major award in the U.S. for TQM achievement.

Band width The maximum length of work day from which an employee can choose the hours he or she will work.

Bargaining unit The heart of the labor-management relationship. A group of employees certified by the NLRB to be able to be included in the union.

Base rate The ratio of applicants who would succeed on the job relative to the total number of applicants when the test is *not* used for selection.

Base salary The amount of pay which is stable or constant over a period of time and is received regardless of performance level.

Behaviorally anchored rating scale (BARS) A quantitative absolute form that expands upon the conventional rating form by more extensively specifying the anchors on behavioral dimensions used to evaluate the subordinate.

Behavioral approach Evaluating the performance of an employee against specific behavioral statements.

Behavioral observation scale (BOS) Similar to BARS except in development of the dimensions, scale format, and scoring.

Benchmark jobs Jobs against which the worth of other jobs are determined by an analysis of the compensable factors and their dollar values in the benchmark jobs and by extant factors existing in the other jobs.

Benchmarking A structured approach for looking outside an organization and adopting the best practices to complement internal operations with creative, new ones.

Benefit criteria Indicators used to show the positive impact of human resource activities.

Biodata Background information on a job applicant used to help make a selection decision.

Biodata test Information on a person's background, such as what he or she did in school and elsewhere before employment, that is used to predict how well the person is likely to perform on the job.

Biographical information blank A form on which an applicant may indicate information about past accomplishments, interests, and preferences that can be used to supplement an application blank.

Bona fide occupational qualification (BFOQ) A defense for disparate impact. For example, hiring only males to play male roles in theatrical productions is BFOQ.

Bona fide seniority system (BFSS) A formal system of seniority that has been and is maintained with the intent of purpose not to discriminate on the basis of Title VII.

Bottom-line rule The 80 percent rule whereby disparate impact is demonstrated if the hiring rate (after an applicant goes through all selection procedures of a minority or female applicant is less than 80 percent of the hiring rate for white males.

BSG Basic skills of grammar, math, safety, reading, listening, and writing. These represent one of the four categories of skills and abilities that can be increased by training.

BST Basic skills of a technical nature to do the specific job. These represent one of the four categories of skills and abilities that can be increased by training.

Business games A kind of work sample test used in managerial selection. Business games may be similar to in-basket exercises or simulation tests; but they are called games because there are generally rules for play and a winner.

Business neccessity Used as a basis for defending disparate impact. Business necessity suggests that the "essence" of the business operation would be undermined by hiring members of the protected group.

Candidate profiles A major component of a job matching system that contains the descriptions of the candidates available for jobs.

Career A patterned sequence of attitudes and behaviors associated with work-related experiences that span a person's life.

Career balance sheet A technique where one systematically lists the advantages and disadvantages of each job and compares them to help make a decision among more than one choice.

Career management programs Organizational programs designed to improve an employee's needs, abilities, and goals for current or future opportunities and challenges within the organization.

Career pathing Two major activities of identifying employee abilities, values, goals, strengths, and weaknesses (career planning) and providing a set of job experiences that aid the employee in satisfying those attributes (job progression).

Career planning activities Offered by the organization to help individuals identify strengths, weaknesses, specific goals, and jobs they would like to attain.

Career plateau A situation in which career progress slows and the prospects for promotion decrease dramatically.

Carpal tunnel syndrome An illness characterized by numbness, tingling, soreness, and weakness in the hands and wrists often resulting from the job.

Cash-or-deferred arrangements (CODAs) Deferred savings plans for working individuals that generally are not subject to tax.

Centralization A term applied to organizations where essential decision making and policy formulation is done at one location (for example, headquarters).

Certification election An election conducted by the NLRB to determine if a majority of the employees in a bargaining unit want the union to represent them all.

Characteristics Job design features such as skill variety, job identity, autonomy, job significance, job feedback, and cognitive and physical job elements.

CIS Behavior-based conceptual, integrative skills, such as strategic and operational planning and organizational design and policy skills. These represent one of the four categories of skills and abilities that can be increased by training.

Closed-offer arbitration A type of arbitration in which the arbitrator receives information on only the parties' original positions without any information on the bargaining process up to the time the arbitrator is selected.

Codetermination A system of governing an organization where the employees in addition to management help run the company through union representation on the board of directors.

Cognitive job elements Represent the specific parts of a job such as communicating, decision making, analyzing, and information processing.

Collective bargaining Bargaining or joint discussion over wages, hours, and conditions of employment between management and a formal representative of the employees.

Commissions Individual incentive pay plans for sales people.

Compa-ratio The measure of the average salary for a given pay grade relative to the midpoint of that pay grade.

Comparable worth Proponents of this compensation issue contend that while the "true worth" (intrinsic value) of jobs may be similar, some jobs (often held by women) are paid at a lower rate than others (often held by men). Resulting differences in pay that are disproportionate to the differences in the "true worth" of jobs amount to wage discrimination.

Comparative standards or Comparative approach In this approach to performance evaluation, subordinates are all compared against each other to determine their relative performance.

Comparative statistics Alleging disparate impact by showing that protected group members are selected at less than 4/5ths the rate of the dominant group.

Compensable factors Yardsticks or factors against which to compare or measure jobs to determine their relative worth.

Compensatory approach In a hiring process, an approach where a weak point on an applicant can be made up for (compensated) by a strong point.

Competencies A set of skills, knowledge, ability, temperments, attitudes and personality in order to perform a given role, task or job effectively in an organization.

Compressed work weeks Work weeks of fewer than the traditional five days yet equal in time to those of five days.

Computer-assisted instruction (CAI) Training that is accomplished by using computer technology, for example, software designed to teach auto mechanics.

Computer hardware The equipment that is used such as computers, printers, disc drives, scanners, monitors, keyboards, CD-ROM laser disks and satellites.

Computer software The program instructions telling the hardware what to do.

Concentration statistics Alleging disparate impact by showing that protected group members are concentrated in particular sections or jobs of a company.

Concessionary bargaining Bargaining by unions where they give up or concede issues or positions to management.

Concurrent validation Measuring the relationship between a predictor (test) and a job criterion score (job performance) whereby the predictor and criterion are collected at the same time.

Confirmation approach When a manager "loads the deck" to favor a particular candidate by selecting several candidates for final decision who have far less qualifications.

Consent decree A specific statement by an organization indicating the affirmative action steps it will take in response to an equal employment complaint.

Conspiracy doctrine A major legal tool for employers during the nineteenth century to combat and prosecute workers' organizations as illegal attempts to retrain trade.

Constructs General frames of reference that are used to encompass many specific ideas or topics.

Contaminated The degree to which a measure of performance measures or taps more dimensions of performance that are unrelated to the actual performance of an individual.

Content models Of motivation, focus on the needs and wants individuals are trying to satisfy.

Contingent rewards Extrinsic rewards given to reinforce a particular behavior. Reinforcement is an essential component of the training process.

Contingent workers Employees who work for the firm but on the provision that they may be put on lay-off or temporary suspension on short notice. Also referred to as buffer employees.

Continuous bargaining When unions and management representatives meet on a regularly scheduled basis to review contract issues of common interest.

Contract plan An informal agreement written by each participant in training specifying one aspect of the training that will be most beneficial when back on the job and agreeing to effect that aspect once back on the job. An important dimension of the contract is selecting a "buddy" to follow-up or check on the trainee's success in implementing that aspect of the training.

Contract employee Employing the services of an individual for a specific period of time and paying only the direct wages of the individual.

Contract recruiting Recruiting and hiring of individuals for a set period of time as spelled out in a contract.

Contrast effect A good person looks even better when placed next to a bad person and a good person looks not as good when placed next to a great person.

Contributory programs A type of retirement plan in which both the employee and the organization contribute for benefits to be obtained at retirement.

Conventional rating A quantitative absolute form in which a superior evaluates subordinates by checking how well they are doing on a form with several dimensions (traits) and numbers.

Cooperative acceptance Ensuring that employees have a work environment free from sexual harassment.

Cooperative system A view of labor and management that depicts each of the two parties engaging in reciprocal problem solving, information sharing, and integration of goals.

Coordinated bargaining When several unions bargain jointly with a single employer.

Core time The time in which everyone must work; there is no choice about this time.

Corporate campaign A boycott where the union appeals to the public to support its efforts against an employer.

Corporate culture The values, norms, and statements of what is important to a company and how its employees should be treated.

Cost-benefit assessment Process of measuring and comparing the costs of the benefits of doing HR activities.

Cost criteria Indicators used to show the cost of providing a human resource activity.

Cost-of-living adjustments (COLAs) Salary or compensation variation that is related to economic conditions (cost of living changes) rather than performance.

Cost-reduction strategy A method of being competitive by reducing the costs of the firm.

Cost-sharing A trend whereby firms are asking their employees to help pay for some of the costs of indirect compensation.

Criteria The measures or indicators (for example, performance appraisal results) that indicate how well an employee is doing on the job.

Critical incidents An absolute form in which the superior records the critical or important events exhibited by a subordinate on a predetermined list of critical incidents.

Critical incident technique (CIT) Method of job analysis whereby behavioral descriptions that have a critical or essential impact on the performance of a job (good, average, or bad) are recorded.

Culture Members of a group or society share a distinct way of life with common values, attitudes, and behaviors that are transmitted over time in a gradual, yet dynamic process.

Culture shock The reaction to new cultural experiences that causes psychological disorientation.

Customerization Means viewing everybody, whether internal or external to the organization, as a customer and then putting that customer first.

Cutoff scores Scores on a test or predictor below which one decision is made (not to hire) and above which another decision is made (to hire).

Data Are more basic than information and generally refer to numbers, people, or things and become information when turned into something useful for problem resolution.

Decentralization A term applied to organizations where essential decision making and policy formulation is done at several locations (for example, in the divisions or departments of the organization).

Decentralizing The process by a company of moving decision making authority to lower managerial and nonmanagerial levels.

Decertification election An election conducted by the NLRB to remove a union from representation if the employees currently represented by the union vote to do so.

Decline stage The final stage of the business when profits and sales are falling.

Deficient The degree to which a measure of performance fails to measure or tap all the essential elements in the actual performance of an individual.

Defined benefit A specific dollar benefit an individual is to receive from the pension plan upon retirement.

Defined contribution An employee pension plan to which a defined or specified contribution is made by the employer.

Delphi technique A number of experts take turns at presenting a forecast statement. As the process continues, the forecast is subject to other members' revisions until a viable forecast emerges.

Demographics Characteristics of a population (for example, ages, sex, race).

Demographic statistics Alleging disparate impact by showing that protected group members are more heavily represented in the labor market than they are in the company.

Depth interview An interview where the interviewer has only a general set of questions to ask and where the interviewee is asked to go into detail in answering.

Developmental A major purpose of performance appraisal is to spot an employee's training needs so that this person can develop.

Dictionary of Occupational Titles (DOT) Source for obtaining the job descriptions for almost 30,000 different jobs.

Differential piece rate plan An individual incentive pay plan where several rates of pay exist for the same job.

Direct compensation The basic wage and performance-based pay including merit and incentive pay.

Direct index Assessment approach that tends to be more objective because such things as actual units sold, scrap rate, absenteeism, and units produced are used to evaluate performance.

Disparate impact Illegal discrimination in employment practice in the selection of a protected group.

Disparate treatment Illegal discrimination in employment practices in the section of an individual.

Distributive bargaining A type of collective bargaining where both labor and management try to attain goals that would result in a gain for one party but a loss for the other.

Diversity management Management of heterogeneous groups, that is, groups that vary in many characteristics.

Doing the right things HR department performing activities which are the most effective for the management of human resources.

Doing things right HR department performing the activities as efficiently as possible.

Downsizing Reducing the size of a company's work force.

Duties The observable work behaviors that comprise a job are called duties. Duties form the essence of the job.

Earned time A positive behavioral control strategy to reduce absenteeism through a "no-fault" approach that provides employees potential days off they use as (if) needed.

Economic supplements A type of compensation for employees including things like pensions, vacations, paid holidays, sick leave, health insurance and supplement unemployment benefits.

ECU The new common currency unit being adopted in Europe as the nations integrate their economies (European Currency Unit).

Effective feedback Information given to employees in a performance appraisal context that enables them to use the information effectively to improve performance and accept evaluation.

Effective managers Those who have achieved high levels of quality and quantity of work performance and satisfaction.

Effectiveness An indication of contribution or value to the organization such as personnel's contribution by improving the organization's productivity, quality of work life, legal compliance, flexibility and competitive advantage.

Effectiveness indicators Measures HR departments use to demonstrate their effectiveness.

80 percent rule A selection rate for any protected group must be 80 percent of the rate for the group with the highest rate. If, for example, a company hires 50 percent of all white male applicants who apply in a particular job category, then it must hire at least 40 percent (80 percent of 50 percent) of all blacks who apply and 40 percent of all women and other protected groups.

Electronic cottage Homes of employees equipped with computers and means by which they can communicate with the main office of plant.

Employee assistance programs (EAPs) Programs specifically designed to assist employees with chronic personal problems (for example, marital dysfunctions, alcohol abuse) that hinder their job performance, attendance, and corporate citizenship.

Employee pacing Condition in which the pace or rate at which the employee works is determined by the employee and not the machine as under machine pacing.

Employee referral programs (ERPs) Essentially word of mouth advertising involving current employees recruiting (informally) potentially qualified job applicants.

Employee rights Rights desired by employees regarding the security of their jobs and the treatment administered by their employers.

Employee services and perquisites A form of indirect compensation that varies depending on employee type and organization to offset the problems of working (for example, day care) or used to symbolize a status differential (for example, company-paid memberships to country, athletic, and social clubs).

Employment-at-will A common law doctrine stating that employers may dismiss their employees for any reason. Recently, court decisions and legislation have created some exceptions to this rule.

Employment contract An agreement between the employee and the employer regarding certain conditions of employment (for example, wages, hours, and the type of work).

Employment security The offering of permanent employment status, usually in exchange for a pledge to be retrained, to be productive, and to be assigned to different jobs.

Empowering Passing on to employees the power and authority to making decisions and giving them the ability to know how to do so.

Entrepreneurial behavior Behavior for innovation characterized by risk-taking and creativity.

Entrepreneurial strategy Where the employees are encouraged to take risks and be innovative.

Environmental scanning A process of continually examining the internal and external environments.

Ergonomic approach See **Ergonomics**.

Ergonomics An approach to job design concerned with designing and shaping jobs to fit the physical abilities and characteristics of individual workers.

ERISA The Employees' Retirement Income Security Act, passed to protect employees against their company's retirement fund going bankrupt.

Error of central tendency Type of halo error where all dimensions are rated average or all individuals receive average ratings.

Error of leniency Type of halo error where all dimensions are given a favorable rating or all individuals are given a more lenient rating.

Error of strictness Type of halo error where all dimensions are given an unfavorable rating or all individuals receive a tougher rating.

ERTA The Economic Recovery Tax Act of 1981 that made it possible for employees to establish IRAs (the IRA provisions were modified by the Tax Reform Act of 1986).

Essay method A performance evaluation method in which the superior describes in writing (essay form) the performance of the subordinates.

Essentiality The amount of power a job holder (any employee) has, which is determined by how critical the job is to the organization and by exclusivity.

ESOPs Employee stockownership plans where employees can be owners of the firm's stock.

Ethics A set of guiding principles for interactions with others. Ethical behavior concerned with right and wrong.

Europay The trend to pay employees throughout Europe, especially managers, the same general amount of compensation.

Evaluation design Methods by which training programs can be evaluated to determine how effective the training programs are (that is, how much change is made).

Evaluative A major purpose of performance appraisal is to gather information that can be used to make salary and promotion decisions.

Exclusivity The difficulty in replacing a job holder.

Exempt employees Job incumbents are not paid overtime for working overtime; they are exempt from the wage-hour laws requiring overtime pay.

Expatriate employee An employee of one country who works in another country.

Expectancy The belief, expressed as a subjective estimate, that a behavior will or will not be successful.

Expectancy model Suggests that people are motivated at work to choose among different behavior if the result is rewards that are valued.

Experimental design Most rigorous form of design used to assess the impact of training programs.

Extended CIT The application of the critical incident technique to a variety of job domains identified by job incumbents.

Extension of bargaining Where the arbitrator attempts to reach a rational and equitable decision acceptable to both parties in arbitration.

External attribution Assigning the cause of an event to an outside force or person.

External environment Aspects of the external environment such as worldwide and domestic economic conditions, worldwide and domestic population characteristics, labor force educational attainment levels and values, legislative and regulatory conditions, and general economic and organizational trends that influence the nature and quality of human resource management activities.

External equity Determining the wage rates for different jobs on the basis of what other companies are paying for those jobs.

Extrinsic rewards Those given by the organization such as pay.

Factor-comparison method Similar to point rating in that it has compensable factors but in factor comparison the factors have dollar not point values.

False decisions Typically in selection of deciding not to hire someone who would have been good or hiring someone who turns out not to be good.

False negatives Incorrect predictions that applicants will perform poorly when in fact applicants will perform successfully.

False positives Incorrect predictions that applicants will perform well when in fact applicants will perform poorly.

Feasibility assessment Estimating the value of using a predictor by examining its costs and benefits and by comparing it against alternative ways.

Federal Insurance Contribution Act See **FICA**.

Federal Labor Relations Authority (FLRA) Modelled after and similar to the NLRB but intended to serve to remedy unfair labor practices in the federal government.

Federal Unemployment Tax Act See **FUTA**.

Feedback See job feedback.

FICA The Federal Insurance Contribution Act, passed to establish a way to fund the Social Security system with payments from employee and employer.

Fiduciaries Individuals entrusted with the management of money; for example, those who are responsible for the management of pension fund money as defined by ERISA.

Final-offer arbitration A type of arbitration where the arbitrator chooses between the final offers of either union or management.

Flexible compensation An approach to compensation that gives individuals a chance to choose what types of compensation they prefer as opposed to the organization just handing them a fixed compensation package.

Flexible spending plans Plans that provide some form and level of pay to employees that is nontaxable to some extent.

Flexiyear schedules A work system where employees think and schedule work time in terms of a year rather than a day or week as in the case of flextime schedules.

Flextime A work schedule that gives employees daily choice in the timing of work and nonwork activities.

Follow-up Once a person leaves a training program, it is important (in order to evaluate the effectiveness of the training program) to find out how well the person is doing once back on the job.

Forced choice form An absolute form in which the superior evaluates the subordinate by choosing which item in a pair of items better describes the subordinate.

Forced distribution method A comparative approach in which the superiors are forced to place subordinates in ranks that represent groups or percentage clusters.

Formal course method An off-the-job training program that includes self-training program and informal classrooms and lectures.

4/5 rule The bottom-rule or 80 percent rule expressing the percentage used in establishing a *prima facie* case of illegal discrimination.

401(k) plans Cash-or-deferred arrangements that enable an employee to save money; they are often tax-free and are often contributed to by the employer.

Frame of reference training Training so individuals better understand the scales or standards being used to select or appraise an individual.

Frequency rate A formula to determine amount of accidents and diseases similar to the incidence rate except that it is calculated using the number of hours worked rather than on a per annum basis.

Functional job analysis (FJA) A description of the nature of jobs, job summaries, job descriptions, and employee specifications.

Funded A characteristic of newly created pension programs (that money is earmarked for them) required by ERISA.

FUTA Federal Unemployment Tax Act that requires all profit-making organizations to pay a tax on the first $7,000 of wages paid to each employee. The purpose of unemployment compensation is to provide income to an individual who is employed but not currently working, or who is seeking a job.

Gaining competitive advantage Means using HR practices to gain a lasting advantage over the competition.

General labor market The geographical area surrounding a company from which it may or may not obtain its employees.

Genetic screening A process of selecting or not selecting people on the basis of gene tests.

Glass ceiling That invisible barrier that often prevents women and minorities from climbing the corporate ladder.

Goals Desired outcomes to be achieved that can be used to evaluate how well employees are performing, particularly in Management by Objectives.

Goals As used in Affirmative Action Programs, targets to be attained by hiring employees so as to equate availability and utilization determinations.

Goal setting People learn quickly and perform better when specific, hard, and clear objectives are set.

Golden handcuffs Extremely favorable monetary arrangements that build up over time making it more and more costly for an employee to leave an organization.

Golden parachute Extremely large sums of money made available to executives if their jobs are lost due to mergers and acquisitions.

Grade structure An arrangement showing the relationship between pay levels and the value of jobs as determined by a job evaluation method.

Graphic rating A form of performance evaluation involving dimensions of behavior against which employees are appraised.

Grievance arbitration Arbitration that takes place during the life of a contract over a grievance filed by either party.

Grievance procedure The most common method of resolving disputes between union and management over application and interpretation of the agreement or contract.

Growth stage When the profits and sales of the firm are increasing at a rapid rate.

Guidelines oriented job analysis (GOJA) A person-focused job analytic technique based on the *Uniform Guidelines*. The process involves six steps that produces information helpful for the development of performance appraisal, training, and selection procedures.

Halo error (bias) Where positive performance on one dimension overshadows performance on other dimensions.

Handicap An impairment that substantially limits one or more of a person's major life activities.

Hay Plan or Hay Method A structured procedure for analyzing jobs that is systematically tied into a job evaluation and compensation system. The Hay Plan includes information about the nature and scope of a position as well as how to reward that position.

Health maintenance organizations See **HMOs**.

Historical records Organizations often use information on how well employees have done in the past (to determine what is actually possible) to establish what is average performance or excellent performance.

HMOs Health maintenance organizations including hospitals, clinics, doctors, nurses, and technicians that came about as a result of the *Health Maintenance Organization Act* of 1973.

Honesty tests Paper and pencil tests used to measure the extent to which a job applicant is likely to be honest and not lie or cheat on the job.

Horizontal loading The adding of duties to a job that are similar to those already in the job and that require the same skills, knowledge, and abilities.

Horn error Where negative performance in one dimension supercedes any positive performance.

Host-Country-National (HCN) An individual working in the branch of a multinational corporation that is the home of the individual.

Hot stove principle A person who has once been hurt or burned severely is not likely to commit the same mistake again.

HR Mission Statements A general statement, developed by participation with everyone, describing the values, objectives and goals of the HR department.

Human resource generalist Human resource department staff member knowledgeable about many HR activities.

Human resource leader A person who heads the human resource department. See also human resource manager.

Human resource management The use of several activities to ensure that human resources are used effectively for the benefit of the individual, the organization, and society.

Human resource manager (leader) A person who heads the human resource department. See also human resource leader.

Human resource department The use of several activities to ensure that human resources are used effectively for the benefit of the individual, the organization and society.

Human resource planning The first step in any effective human resource (HR) program. It predicts or estimates future human resource needs and establishes. HR activities to enable the organization to meet the future needs.

Human resource practices Refers to all the ways in which the several HR activities can be done or practiced. For organizations these practices are choices in the ways they practice the HR activities and therefore practice managing human resources.

Human resource roles The parts that can be played by a HR department including policy formulation, innovator, monitoring, adapting and enabling.

Human resource specialist HR staff with indepth knowledge about one or two HR activities.

Human resource information system (HRIS) A method that allows more rapid and frequent data collection to back up a forecast of personnel needs.

Hygiene factors For motivation include company policy, salary, and job security.

Illegal behavior That which violates the law. See Ethics.

Illegal discrimination While selection decisions are discriminatory, the basis for some are prohibited by legal or regulatory provisions.

Improshare Improved productivity through sharing; a gain-sharing incentive pay program for employees based on improved productivity.

In-basket exercise A simulation training technique in which the solitary trainee sits at a desk and works through a pile of papers found in the in-basket of a typical manager, prioritizing, recommending solutions to problems, and taking any necessary action.

Incentive pay plan Method of monetary and non-monetary compensation related to direct indexes of performance for the individual group or organization. It generally represents a substantial proportion of an individual's direct compensation.

Incentive stock option Individual incentive plan that awards stock such as in stock option plans.

Incidence rate An explicit formula for determining the amount of accidents and diseases per year by the number of employee exposure levels. Required by OSHA.

Indirect compensation Rewards or benefits provided by the organization to employees for their memberships or participation (attendance) in the organization. Also known as fringe benefits or supplemental compensation.

Individual contemporary design Approaches to job design and redesign that enable employees to expand their skills and experience more job activities.

Industrial cottage Small manufacturing operations that are set up in the homes of individuals who then work at home.

Industrywide bargaining Where employers bargain as a group with the union at the national level.

Information For many people is something they find useful, something they did not know or have and that can be used in the solution of a problem.

Initial demand point A demand by the union for a wage settlement that is higher than what is expected to be granted.

Initial offer Made by the management to represent what wages and conditions it will grant to the union.

Innovation strategy A method to make an organization more competitive by improving its level of creativity and the number of new products and services it offers.

Institutional issues Issues not directly related to the job that affect the security and success of union and management, such as strikes and union security.

Instrumental (also instrumentality) The extent to which workers see the union as able to satisfy their demands and needs.

Integrative bargaining A type of collective bargaining where labor and management work to solve contractual problems to the benefit of both.

Interest arbitration Arbitration that deals with the terms and conditions of the contract.

Interest tests A kind of personality, interests, and preferences test of an individual's interests. These tests are not necessarily predictive of job performance, but they can predict which job will be more in line with a person's interests.

Internal attribution Assigning the cause for an event to one's self.

Internal environment Characteristics of the organization such as its culture, size, technology, structure, strategy and top management's goals and values that influence the nature of the human resource activities.

Internal equity Determining the wage rates for different jobs within one organization on the basis of the relative worth of those jobs to the organization.

Interrater reliability The consistency or agreement of two or more people (raters) on the evaluation of the same event or person.

Internships Training programs (often part of an agreement between schools, colleges, and universities and organizations) where an individual may work full-time but only for a short while.

Interpersonal competence tests Measures of social intelligence. These include aspects of intelligence related to awareness of non-verbal and social information.

Intraorganizational bargaining The process of negotiating terms influencing their constituents over changes in bargaining positions.

Intrapreneurship Entrepreneurial behavior within an existing organization rather than starting a new business outside an organization.

Intrepreneurial behavior Behavior such as risk taking. Longer-term orientation and ownership that can result in the creation of new products or services within an organization.

Intrinsic rewards Those originating from within the person such as a sense of meaningfulness.

IPS A term referring to a category of learning involved with the acquisition of interpersonal skills including communications, human relations, decision making, leadership, and labor relations.

Job analysis The process of describing or recording the purposes, task characteristics, and task duties of a job in a given organization setting to determine a match for individual skill, experience, knowledge, and needs.

Job banks Places where computerized listings of jobs and their characteristics are maintained. These banks are generally associated with public employment agencies.

Job burnout A specific set of symptoms brought on by severe or chronic stress directly related to the career rather than personal difficulties. Related symptoms are chronic fatigue, low energy, irritability, and negative attitude toward job and self.

Job classes Used interchangeably with job families.

Job classification method Similar to ranking except that classes or grades are established and then the jobs are placed into the classes.

Job description A detailed statement of the duties, purposes, and conditions under which a job is to be performed (cf. job analysis).

Job domain A category of related duties.

Job enlargement An approach to job design that leads a job horizontally, that is, that adds more of the same type of duties requiring the same skills.

Job enrichment An approach to job design that loads a job vertically, that is, that increases the number of skills needed and the sense of significance.

Job evaluation Comparison of jobs by the use of formal and systematic procedures to determine their relative worth within the organization.

Job fairs Events where many employers gather to talk with potential job applicants, often students, about job opportunities.

Job families Grouping together all jobs of nearly the same value

to the organization for the purpose of establishing a wage structure that reflects internal equity.

Job feedback The degree to which the job itself provides the worker with information about how well the job is being performed.

Job identity The degree to which a job requires completion of a "whole" and identifiable piece of work.

Job instruction training (JIT) A systematic technique for on-the-job training consisting of four steps: (1) careful selection and preparation of trainer and trainee for the learning experience to follow; (2) full explanation and demonstration by the trainer; (3) a trial on-the-job performance by the trainee; and (4) a thorough feedback session highlighting job performance and job requirements.

Job matching programs An essential function in effective recruiting that entails fitting the needs of people to the requirements of the job.

Job needs analysis An examination of the organization that provides information on the tasks to be performed on each job, the skills necessary to perform tasks, and the minimum acceptable standards of performance.

Job posting A procedure of posting within the organization a list of jobs that are available.

Job profiles A major component of a job matching system that contains the descriptions of jobs that are available.

Job progression A set of job experiences provided through a series of job assignments.

Job progression program A systematic effort by companies to tie individual career needs to the practical needs of the organization by identifying what individuals want and what organizations need and can offer.

Job ranking method A hierarchy or ladder of jobs constructed from the job analysis to reflect the relative value of jobs to the organization.

Job-relatedness Refers to selection tests and qualifications being related to an employee's being successful on the job. If a test or qualification is shown to be job-related, a disparate impact charge can be defended.

Job rotation An approach to job design that does not change the design of a job, but rather rotates the worker from job to job.

Job sex-role stereotyping The process of associating characteristics of jobs and roles with the incumbents of those jobs and roles.

Job sex-typing Classifying a job according to a male or female suffix (for example, male-foreman; female-seamstress) generally reflecting a traditional sex-role bias.

Job sharing Arrangements for two people or more to share (split) the hours of one job, for example, two people will take one job and each will work four hours daily.

Job significance The degree to which the job has a substantial impact on the lives of other people.

Job specification A detailed statement of the skills, knowledge, and abilities required of a person doing a given job (cf. job analysis).

Judgmental forecast A personnel planning forecasting technique that relies on the personal judgments of selected experts.

Kaizen The Japanese work meaning continuous improvement.

Knowledge The body of knowledge related to doing a job.

Knowledge of results An important reinforcement is the knowledge of how well a task was done or having the knowledge of results.

Labor-Management Relations Act See *Taft-Hartley Act*.

Labor-Management Reporting and Disclosure Act See *Landrum-Griffin Act*.

Labor market The number and characteristics of the persons in the work force who are either working or are looking for work.

Labor relations system A conceptual paradigm used to help elucidate the interrelationships among management, union, and employees.

Lack of control A feeling an individual has of not being able to influence what happens or what can be done to change things as they are.

Landrum-Griffin Act Passed in 1959 to regulate the internal affairs of unions; also known as the *Labor-Management Reporting and Disclosure Act*.

Laws of effect Behavior that results in positive outcomes tends to be repeated.

Leaderless group discussion A type of work sample test in managerial selection where applicants sit around and discuss a topic for a given period of time.

Leniency (error) An error of being too easy when doing performance appraisals.

Lie detector test An increasingly common part of a selection procedure used to predict employees who are likely to lie or steal; also called a polygraph exam.

Line managers Individuals who are responsible for managing employees who are involved in production and delivery of the firm's goods and services.

Liquidation/divestiture strategy Where the firm is pursuing tactics to get out of the business.

Local-country-national See host-country-national

Lockout A refusal of management to allow workers to work.

Low quality of work life A sociopsychological work environment component characterized by oneway communications, lack of respect for employee rights, poor personnel, and policies that produce unfavorable psychological conditions and outcomes.

Lump sum bonuses Salary increases in one payment rather than being divided into several smaller increases.

Machine pacing A condition under which the machine determines how fast the work must be done; therefore, the pace at which the employee works is determined by the machine.

Management by objectives (MBO) This approach evaluates the performance of managers (typically) on the basis of how well they have attained their predetermined goals or objectives.

Management position description questionnaire (MPDQ) A method of job analysis that relies upon the checklist method to analyze jobs, especially management jobs.

Manager (a.k.a., line manager) The person who directs and is responsible for other employees who are either supervisors or managers.

Managerial estimate Estimates of staffing needs made by either the top-down version or the bottom-up version.

Managerial level Human resource activities of a medium-term length to develop and implement that may involve line managers.

Mandatory issues Wages, hours, and other terms and conditions of employment over which management must bargain according to the NRLA.

Mature stage When profits and sales growth begin to slow and organizations lower costs to increase profit margins.

Maturity curves Compensation determined on the basis of years of experience in a profession such as engineering.

Measured day work An incentive pay plan where production standards are established, although not as precisely as in piecework plans, and employees are paid according to those standards.

Mediation A procedure in which a central third party assists union and management negotiations in reaching a voluntary agreement.

Merit pay plans Methods of monetary compensation (generally related to subjectively evaluated performance) that represents only a small percentage increment in an employee's direct compensation.

Meritocracy Means emphasizing fairness in evaluating people on their work related contributions.

Methods analysis The use of individual activity units to describe the way a job is to be performed and evaluated. Also known as motion study. Best application is to nonmanagerial jobs.

Midlife transition Reexamination of one's accomplishments relative to initial career goals that occurs between the ages of forty and fifty-five.

Mixed interview A performance appraisal interview in which the rater combines the tell-and-sell with the problem-solving types.

Motivation The process that energizes and directs an individual's behavior toward the fulfillment of needs and values.

Motivation factors Include a sense of accomplishment, recognition and advancement.

Motivation-hygiene model Describes factors in the workplace that dissatisfy people and factors that motivate them.

Multiemployer bargaining Where employers bargain as a group with the union at the local level.

Multilateral bargaining A type of collective negotiating where more than two parties are involved in the negotiating and there is no clear union-management dichotomy.

Multinational Corporation (MNC) A firm that operates in several countries of the world.

Multiple cutoff model A hiring process where an applicant must exceed fixed levels of proficiency (do well on all tests) but in no particular sequence.

Multiple hurdle model A hiring process where an applicant must do well on several tests or predictors and must do well in sequence.

Multiple linear regression An extension of simple linear regression where several independent variables (Xs) are used to predict or forecast future events more accurately. For example, productivity is predicted by an equation relating absenteeism (X^1), turnover (X^2) and waste (X^3) to the dependent variable productivity (Y).

Multiple management programs Training programs for managers where lower and middle-level managers get an opportunity to work with top-level managers.

Multiple predictor approach Combining several pieces of information or predictors to make a selection decision.

Narrative essay A written, open-ended statement of evaluation or appraisal of an employee.

National Institute of Occupational Safety and Health (NIOSH) A federal agency created to aid in the research, dissemination, and education of health and safety issues and provide expertise to organizations in need of such services.

National Labor Relations Act (NLRA) See **Wagner Act**.

National Labor Relations Board (NLRB) Established by the Wagner Act to administer the National Labor Relations Act.

National union A basic unit of labor unions that organizes, charters, and controls member union locals and develops general policies and procedures by which locals operate.

Need hierarchy model Describes a hierarchy of needs existing within people for motivation.

Negative settlement range When there is no overlap between union demands and management's concessions, thus resulting in no ground for settlement.

Negotiating committee Representatives from the unions and management who meet to negotiate a contract.

Network A collection of friends, acquaintances, and colleagues, both inside and outside one's workplace, that can be summoned to provide some kind of help or support.

Neutralizing The process of putting aside an employee whose performance is marginal at best, in order to prevent influencing others.

Nominal group technique A structured group process where several individuals list and identify their ideas. All ideas are considered by all members and action is decided upon after a structured evaluation is completed.

Noncompensatory approaches Hiring processes where weak points cannot be made up for by strong points.

Noncontributory programs A type of retirement plan in which the employee is the sole contributor for benefits to be obtained at retirement.

Nonexempt employees Jobs in which the incumbents are paid overtime for working overtime; they are not exempt from wage-hour laws not requiring overtime pay.

Nonqualified pension plans Pension plans that do not come under the purview of ERISA. In addition, under these plans, the employer's contribution is not tax deductible, and the employee is taxed on contributions.

Nonverbal cues Behavior that does not involve words or speech. Examples include body movement, gestures, handshake, eye contact, and physical appearance.

Norm-referenced approach (appraisal) A performance appraisal method where employees are compared to each other in terms of overall performance.

Normal time The observed time adjusted for worker performance in a time study.

No-risk standards An enforcement tool used by OSHA that would require organizations to make their work environments absolutely free of any risks from employee exposure.

Objective forms Appraisals where the evaluation is done against specifically defined behaviors or outcomes such as levels of output, level of specific goal attainment, or number of days absent.

Observed time Is simply the average of observed times in a time study.

Occupational accidents Accidents such as loss of limb, loss of hearing, or even loss of life as a consequence of the physical environment of an organization.

Occupational diseases Diseases or illnesses such as cancer and leukemia that result from aspects of the physical work environment.

Occupational safety and health Physical/physiological and psychological conditions of an organization's work force.

Occupational Safety and Health Administration (OSHA) A Federal agency vested with the power and responsibility for establishing and enforcing occupational safety and health standards and for inspecting and issuing citations to organizations in violation of such standards. Created by the *Occupational Safety and Health Act* in 1970.

Occupational Safety and Health Review Commission (OSHRC) The reviewer of appeals by organizations that have received citations from OSHA.

Off-the-job training programs (OFFJT) Training programs that are conducted outside the work organization.

On site but not on-the-job programs A set of training programs that are offered at work but not on the job of the employees.

On-the-job-training programs (OJT) A whole set of training programs that are conducted on the job or where the people are working.

Operational level Short-term human resource activities typically done by the human resource department.

Order effect Where the order or arrangement of information or job applicants influences the evaluation they receive.

Organizational culture See corporate culture.

Organizational needs analysis An examination of short- and long-term objectives of the organization, personnel resource needs, efficiency indexes, and organizational climate as they relate to the training and development needs of the organization.

Organizational strategy The nature and direction of the businesses that the firm decides in order to compete and survive.

Organizational stress A sociopsychological work environment component characterized by organizational changes, work overload, poor supervision, unfair salaries, job insecurity, and physical insecurity all producing uncertainty.

Organizational structure The number of levels of employees in an organization and the location and extent of power and decision making.

Organizational survey Gathering data from individuals in a company to determine how things are going and how workers feel.

Orientation programs Activities used by employers to help familiarize new employees with the work environment and the culture of the firm.

Output approach (Output-based appraisal) A performance appraisal approach using hard or direct measures of output, such as goals, against which to evaluate employees.

Ownership The experience employees have when feeling that they are part and parcel of an idea, service or product, with or without financial stakes.

Paired comparison method A comparative approach in which the superior compares each subordinate with every other subordinate in order to evaluate the subordinate's performance.

Panel interview An interview where there are several interviewers for just the one interviewee.

Paper-and-pencil achievement tests Measures of job-related knowledge rather than work samples of the job itself.

Parent Country National (PCN) An individual working for a multinational corporation of the same nationality. Also see expatriate employee.

Partial reinforcement Providing immediate reward or follow-up to individuals on an intermittent basis rather than continuous basis.

Patterned or structured interview An interview that has a specific set of questions in a fixed order.

Pattern settlements A settlement between a union and management that is based upon and similar to an agreement made by another company with the union.

Pay fairness Ensuring that what employees are paid is in relationship to what they and others give to the organization.

Pay for time not worked A form of indirect compensation received by an employee for time not spent working. Two categories: *off the job* (for example, vacations, sick leave, holidays, personal days, comprising the major portion of costs of indirect benefits) and *on the job* (for example, lunch and rest periods, physical fitness facilities).

Pay grades Basically families of jobs that share a similar pay range.

Pay level The absolute pay or wage that employees receive.

Pay secrecy The issue of whether employees should or should not have access to the organization's compensation schedule.

Performance appraisal A system of measuring, evaluating, and influencing an employee's job-related attributes, behaviors and outcomes, and level of absenteeism to discover at what level the employee is presently performing on the job.

Performance appraisal system (PAS) The entire system that incorporates the following: method used to gather the appraisal data; job analysis; establishment of validity and reliability of the method; characteristics of the rater and ratee that influence the process; use of the information for development and evaluation; evaluation of performance appraisal in relation to its stated objectives.

Performance-based pay Pay systems that relate pay to performance including incentive pay plans and merit pay plans.

Performance criteria Dimensions or factors used to judge an individual in performing a particular job.

Performance ratios Ratios that indicate where the performance rating of any employee stands relative to the other employees.

Performance shares Under this managerial incentive plan, managers receive shares or stocks in a company as a performance reward based upon how well the company is doing.

Performance standards Indicators or levels attached to the performance criteria to enable a judgment to be made about how well an individual is performing.

Permanent part-time Fixed arrangements for regular employees to work fewer than five days per week or forty hours per week.

Permissive issues Bargaining over these issues is not mandatory but is not specifically illegal.

Person needs analysis An examination of the deficiencies between an employee's actual performance and the desired performance or between an employer's proficiency on critical job dimensions and the desired proficiency required on the job dimensions.

Personal appraisal Identifying your abilities, values, and goals across several life dimensions that are important to you. Strengths and weaknesses are also noted.

Personal competence test A test designed to measure whether individuals know how to make appropriate and timely decisions for themselves and whether they put forth the effort to do so.

Personality inventories Tests that tap individual traits or characteristics; for example, California Psychological Inventory, Minnesota Multiphasic Personality Inventory.

Physical abilities analysis A person-focused method of job analysis that uses nine abilities to analyze the physical requirements of tasks.

Physical abilities test Tests used to measure the physical abilities of job applicants to determine whether they have the necessary strength or other physical abilities needed to do the job.

Physical job elements The specific physical properties of a job such as lifting, lighting, coloring, sound, speed, and positioning.

Physical work environment Composed of the building, chairs, equipment, machines, lights, noise, heat, chemicals, toxins, and the like that are associated with occupational accidents and diseases.

Physiological/physical conditions The conditions of the work environment that lead to occupational diseases and accidents.

Placement An activity concerned with ensuring that job demands are filled and that individual needs and preferences are met.

Point-rating or Point-factor method A job evaluation strategy that assigns point values to previously determined compensable factors and adds them to arrive at a total score used to determine wage levels.

Polygraph Test See **Lie Detector Test**.

Portable A pension that an employee can take when leaving a company.

Position analysis questionnaire (PAQ) A structured procedure used in job analysis that describes jobs in terms of worker activities; based on a person-oriented trait system that allows it to be applied across a number of jobs and organizations without modification. A salient disadvantage is its length.

Positive reinforcement system An incentive system based on the notion that behavior can be understood and modified by its consequences. The system lets employees know how well they are meeting specific goals and rewards improvements with praise and recognition. No money is involved.

Positive settlement range Overlap area between management's resistance point and the union's resistance point that facilitates an acceptable settlement.

Predictive validity Similar to concurrent validity except that the predictor variable is measured some time *before* the performance variable.

Predictor rate The proportion of correct decisions (true positive plus true negative) relative to the total number of decisions when a test is used for selection.

Predictors The tests or pieces of information used by HR departments to predict how well an applicant is likely to do if hired.

Pre-election campaign Preliminary efforts by management and labor to persuade employees to vote for or against union certification.

Pre-experimental design Least rigorous form of design used to assess the impact of training programs.

Preference tests A kind of selection test that is used to match employee preferences with job and organizational characteristics.

Preferences For expectancy motivation, indicate that some rewards are more valuable than others.

Preferred provider organization (PPO) Medical care being provided to employees that are preferred by the employer.

Preretirement counseling Counseling given to employees before retiring in order to facilitate their transition from work to nonwork. This may result in early retirement decisions but it need not always.

Prima facie As it appears or "on its face."

Primacy bias A tendency to use information gathered first in making final evaluations.

Primary effect An order effect where first information is given greater weight—the notion of a first impression.

Privacy rights An employee right on the job protected by the Privacy Act of 1974. This act applies only to federal agencies and involves the verification of references in selection and employment decisions.

Private employment agencies An external recruiting source that caters primarily to two types of job applicants: professional and managerial workers and unskilled workers. These agencies supply service for all ages of job applicants and charge a fee for setting up connections between applicants and employers.

Private Protection Programs Programs such as for insurance and retirement that are provided by the employer.

Problem-solving interview A participative performance appraisal interview in which the ratee and rater try to understand and solve performance problems.

Process Models Of motivation, focus on how managers can change the situation to better satisfy employee needs.

Productivity The outputs of an individual, group, or organization divided by the inputs needed by individual, group, or organization for the creation of outputs.

Productivity bargaining A special form of integrative bargaining where labor agrees to scrap old work habits for new and more effective ones desired by management. In exchange, management offers labor the gain of modernization and increased labor efficiency in the form of work incentives.

Profit-sharing plans An organizational-level incentive plan involving the awarding of money to employees if some level of company profit is attained.

Programmed instruction A systematic and stepwise presentation of skills and tasks broken down into "frames" where each "frame" must be successfully completed before going into the next. Feedback concerning the correctness of response for each "frame" is provided immediately and allows individuals to pace themselves.

Progressive discipline A system whereby employees are increasingly more severely disciplined or punished with the repetition of offenses.

Prohibited issues Bargaining about these issues is illegal for unions and employers.

Promotion-from-within A practice and policy of using promotions from within a company to fill vacant positions rather than hiring people from the outside.

Protection programs Indirect compensation designed to protect the employee and family if and when the employee's income (direct compensation) is terminated and to protect the employee and family against the burden of health care expenses in the event of disability.

Psychological conditions Conditions in the work place that lead to perceived stress and low quality of working life.

Psychological contract An informal and unwritten understanding between employees and employer about what it is reasonable to expect from an employee in exchange for what is in the employment contract.

Psychomotor tests Aptitude tests that combine mental and physical aspects of individual ability; for example, MacQuarrie Test for Mechanical Ability, Tweeser Dexterity Tests.

Public employment agencies An external recruiting source coordinated with the U.S. Training and Employment Service. Such agencies at the state level provide counseling, testing, and placement for everyone. These agencies also have access to a nationwide network of job information and application information.

Public Protection Programs Programs such as for insurance and retirement that are provided by the government.

Purposes The reason for the creation and existence of a job.

Pygmalion effect The self-fulfilling prophesy of telling someone they will succeed and then observing that person succeed.

Qualified pension plans Pension plans covered by and set up as defined by ERISA.

Qualitative measures Measures that are more subjective, less easy to quantify (although some attempts can be made to do so, for example, customer satisfaction is at 90%).

Quality The level of appreciation shown by the customer for the goods and services provided by an organization; or "being right the first time, every time."

Quality circles An innovative management concept that helps contribute to an organization's growth and well-being; based on the philosophy that a company's work force participation is its most valuable resource because they are often the most qualified to identify and solve work-related problems.

Quality improvement strategy A plan by which to improve the competitiveness of an organization by improving the quality of its products and services.

Quality of working life (QWL) A process by which all members of the organization, through appropriate channels of communica-

tion set up for this purpose, have some say about the design of their jobs in particular and the work environment in general to satisfy their needs.

Quantitative measures Specific, objective indicators or indicies that can be quantified.

Quasi-experimental design A design of moderate rigor to assess the impact of a training program.

Quotas Specific number or percentage goals established by an organization for minority hiring to correct underutilization or past discrimination in employment.

Railway Labor Act (RLA) Passed by Congress in 1926 to prevent serious economic consequences in the railway industry from labor unrest.

Ratee The person being appraised in an appraisal. See also **Subordinate**.

Rater The person doing the appraising in an appraisal. See also **Superior**.

Realistic job preview A recruitment technique where the potential applicant is made aware of the positive and negative aspects of the organization. An applicant is encouraged to approach current employees and the line manager and to ask questions about the appropriate fit between his or her needs and the organization's needs.

Reality shock Career disappointment from having higher expectations of jobs than the jobs can really fulfill.

Recency effect An order effect where the last or most recent information is given greater weight.

Recency-of-events error See **Recency effect**.

Recognition tests Examples of past behavior or performance that indicate the quality of an individual's work; for example, portfolios.

Recruitment The set of activities and processes used to legally obtain a sufficient number of the right people at the right place and time so that the people and the organization can select in their own best short-run and long-run interests.

Redundancy planning Developing alternative strategies for obsolete employees to acquire skills necessary for other types of work. Planning includes counseling, training, and part-time employment.

Re-engineering Taking a look at what the HR department is doing to see if it can be done better.

Reference verification A method for validating information provided by the application; for example, using school records and transcripts, calling previous employers.

Reinforcement Essentially means giving people immediate follow-up on their performance based on the premise that people will do what is rewarded and avoid doing what is punished.

Relevant labor market The geographical area from which a company obtains a large portion of its work force for a given occupational group.

Reliability The consistency of a test or test item upon repeated measurement. Also see **Test-retest reliability**.

Replacement planning Replacement charts to help plan for who will be able to replace whom in the event of a position becoming vacant.

Resistance point The lowest acceptable level that the union can take on behalf of its members or the highest acceptable level for management.

Responsibility centers A method to appraise managers by measuring how well they do in relationship to costs, profits, or revenues for a given unit or division.

Right to plant/office closing or relocation notification The right to be informed before a company closes a plant or office or before it decides to move it.

Right-to-work A Taft-Hartley provision that does not require employees to join a union to work even if a union exists.

Role awareness The degree to which an individual knows what is expected and what authority he or she has.

Role conflict The extent of conflict or incompatibility between doing what is expected and what it is possible to do.

Role playing Off-the-job training where a realistic situation is created and individuals learn by playing roles in the situation.

Rucker plan A group-based incentive pay plan that is similar to the Scanlon plan but is more complex in the determination of the size of incentives.

Safety committee A strategy for accident prevention that involves employees in safety policy formulation and implementation.

Salary compression A decrease in the range of pay between various positions (levels) in the organization.

Sandwich approach Used in performance appraisal feedback to describe the fact that negative feedback is squeezed between positive feedback.

Scanlon plan A type of companywide incentive program emphasizing management-employee relations, especially employee participation, and underscoring efficient operations through cooperation. In effect, employees share in organization profits as a result of contributing and cooperating to attain higher productivity.

Scientific approach An approach to designing jobs that minimize the skills needed by the worker to perform the job. The result is often a job that is simple and repetitive.

Selection The process of gathering information for the purposes of evaluating and deciding who should be hired, under legal guidelines, for the short- and long-term interests of the individual and the organization.

Self-assessment Evaluating one's self in the career planning process.

Self-efficacy An individual's beliefs about a task-specific ability.

Self-fulfilling prophecy Something becomes reality because of the fact it was predicted to occur.

Self-managed teams Those making many management decisions for their group.

Self-management Essentially motivating, managing and directing one's own behavior rather than having a manager do it.

Sensitivity training A method of training and development conducted in a group setting that aims to give individuals insight into how and why they and others feel and act the way they do.

Severity rate Reflects the hours actually lost due to injury or illness by differentially weighting for categories of injuries and illnesses.

Sex-role stereotyping When roles in society become defined as being or having a sex type; for example, traditionally the role of a housekeeper was defined as being female and the job of breadwinner as being male.

Sexual harassment Physical violation or verbal abuse of employees, particularly by managers and supervisors.

Shaping Rewarding closer and closer approximations to desired behaviors.

Significant risks An enforcement tool superseding the no-risk standard as a result of a court decision in *Industrial Union Department, AFLCIO v. American Petroleum Institute*, 1980. This standard implied that OSHA cannot demand compliance with the no-risk standard if the organization in question can show its existing exposure level to harmful agents is below a threshold assessment as determined by OSHA.

Simple linear regression A quantitative formula used to relate an independent variable (X) to a dependent variable (Y). For example, a forecast of future events such as sales (Y) is predicted by demand (X).

Simulation A training program that presents individuals with situations that are similar to actual job conditions and that are off the job.

Simulation tests A kind of achievement test used in the selection process. The applicant is given a task to perform, although the situation in which the task is performed is not necessarily recreated.

Single predictor approach The use of one test or piece of information to choose an applicant for the job.

Skill The demonstration of knowledge and ability evidenced in the performance of a task.

Skill-based evaluation A job evaluation strategy where the organization compensates the employee by paying the person for skills and experience relative to the organization's mission.

Skill variety The degree to which a job requires a number of different skills to be performed correctly.

Skills inventories A record or file of the skills possessed by the workforce.

Social loafing An individual in a group or team fails to contribute his/her fair share.

Social Security system A public protection program of the federal government that provides retirement benefits, disability and unemployment insurance. Funding is provided by equal contributions of employee and employer.

Social support group Individuals who provide unconditional support for the individuals in the group.

Socialization A process of bringing an individual into an organization and of transmitting norms, values and skills to that individual.

Sociopsychological work environment The non-physical parts of the work environment including such things as relationships with supervisors, company policies, structure of the organization, organizational changes, uncertainty, conflicts, and relationships with co-workers.

Standard hour plan This second most widely used incentive pay plan pays on the basis of time per unit of output rather than the quantity of output.

Standard résumé An organized chronological documentation of work and educational experience relating to one's career and qualifications. Generally prepared by an applicant for a position.

Standard time Is the normal time adjusted for normal work interruptions in a time study.

Start up stage When a company is just beginning and there is high risk.

Statistical process control (SPC) A term used to describe the concept of using the tools of statistics to assist in controlling the quality of operating processes.

Statistical projection A forecasting technique used in HR planning that, for example, uses simple linear regression to predict employment growth as a function of sales growth.

Steward An employee elected by the work unit to act as the union representative on the work site and to respond to company actions against employees that violate the labor agreement.

Stock appreciation rights Generally given to executives who can earn additional income from the gain in the value of the company's stock without buying the stock.

Stock option A managerial incentive plan where the manager is given an opportunity to buy stocks of the company at a later date, but at a price established at the time the option is given.

Straight piecework plan The most common type of incentive pay plan. Under this plan employees get a standard rate of pay for each unit of output.

Straight ranking A comparative approach in which the superior lists the subordinates from best to worst usually on the basis of overall performance.

Strategic level Human resource activities that take a longer time to implement and often are for the benefit of the entire firm.

Stress interview An interview where an applicant may be intentionally annoyed or embarrassed by the interviewer to see how the applicant reacts.

Strictness An error of being too hard when evaluating the performance of employees.

Strike A refusal of employees to work at the company.

Structured job analysis The use of a standard format for job

descriptions so that all organizations can use the same job categories.

SUB See **Supplemental Unemployment Benefits**.

Subjective forms Appraisal forms on which the raters evaluate an employee on the basis of "subjective" attributes such as leadership, attitude toward people, or loyalty.

Subordinate In Chapter 9, the term used to denote the person whose performance is being appraised.

Successful managers Those who move up the formal hierarchy quickly.

Succession planning Like replacement planning but tends to be longer term, more developmental, and offer more flexibility.

Suggestion systems A form of incentive compensation paid to employees who are responsible for money-saving or money-producing ideas for the organization.

Superior In Chapter 9, the term used to denote the person doing the appraising of another's performance.

Supervisor The person who directs and is responsible for other employees who are nonsupervisors and nonmanagers.

Supervisor Task Description Questionnaire A structured method of analyzing the jobs of supervisors.

Supervisory assistance An informal method of training, often being discussions between a supervisor and his or her employee.

Supplemental unemployment benefits (SUB) Benefits received by employees, who are on layoff, from their company until returning to work or until the benefits expire (for example, after twenty-six weeks).

Systematic approach Means determining the HR needs of the organization and then putting together HR activities and practices that send the same message to employees consistently.

Taft-Hartley Act Enacted by Congress in 1947 to restore the balance between labor and management and respond to the pro-union bias alleged to have been a part of the Wagner Act.

Tailored, or adaptive, testing Testing that is made to fit with the specific needs or environment of the company using the test.

Target point A realistic assessment of the wage and conditions of employment the union is likely to get from management.

Task inventories A method of job analysis based solely on a structured questionnaire that determines and lists the tasks for the jobs that are being analyzed.

Team contemporary A major classification of approaches to job design that focus on the group-job design interface (or relationships).

Team interviews Conducted by several people, typically not at the same time.

Teamwork Cooperation among individuals in solving problems and in performing their jobs.

Telecommuting A combination of work-at-home and work-while-traveling.

Tell-and-listen interview A performance appraisal interview in which the rater informs the ratee of the evaluation and then listens to the ratee on the evaluation.

Tell-and-sell interview A performance appraisal interview in which the rater informs the ratee of the evaluation and sells the ratee on the evaluation.

Termination-at will See **Employment-at-will**.

Termination for good cause The practice or doctrine of firing employees only for good reason or reasonable reason.

Termination for just cause The dismissal of an employee for a job performance reason such as poor performance, making the dismissal one for a just cause.

Test-retest reliability A process of determining the accuracy of a test or predictor by comparing the results from two separate uses.

Tests Any paper-and-pencil, performance measure, or other information used as a basis for making an employment decision.

Third-Country-National (TCN) An individual of one nationality working for a company of the different nationality in a branch of the company located in yet another country.

Time Study See **Work Measurement**.

Timetables Identify specific dates where affirmative action goals and quotas are to be met.

Tin handcuffs Relatively small monetary or stock inducements to entice employees to stay with the company.

Tin parachutes Relatively small amounts of monetary compensation given to employees dismissed as a consequence of a merger or acquisition.

Total compensation The activity by which organizations evaluate the contributions of employees in order to distribute direct and indirect monetary and nonmonetary rewards fairly within the organization's ability to pay and within legal regulations.

Total Quality Management An approach to improving quality that involves the entire organization.

Training and development Any attempt to improve current or future employee performance by increasing an employee's ability to perform through learning. It can be accomplished by changing the employee's attitudes or increasing his or her skills or knowledge.

True decisions Typically in selection of deciding to hire someone who performs well and rejecting someone who would have performed poorly.

True negatives Correct predictions that applicants will perform poorly, who in fact do perform poorly.

True positives Correct predictions that applicants will perform well, who in fact perform successfully.

Turnaround strategy Faced with going out of business, a firm may attempt to do things to survive, to turn it around.

Uncertainty A lack of predictability or an inability to tell what things are or will be like; a state of unpredictability.

Underutilization Employing members of minorities groups at less than the rate of their availability in the relevant labor market.

Unfair representation Breach of duty by a union to represent fairly all employees covered by the union-management contract.

Unfunded Pension programs established on the goodwill of the employer rather than on money to be used to pay pension obligations.

Union An organization with the legal authority to negotiate with the employer on behalf of the employees and to administer the ensuing agreement.

Union instrumentality The degree to which union membership can result in obtaining valued outcomes such as pay raises.

Union locals The grass-roots units of the labor organization that represents the employees who are in the same union unit at a given workplace.

Union shop A provision (in about thirty states) that says that employees must join the union (if the company has one) after a set number of days from initial employment.

Unionization or unionizing The effort by employees and outside agencies (unions and associations) to band together and act as a single unit when dealing with management over issues related to their work.

Unqualified pension plan A plan not set up under the guidelines of ERISA.

Utilization analysis Process of determining the number of women and minorities in different jobs within an organization.

Valid predictor Any test used for staffing that predicts or correlates with actual job performance.

Validity The degree to which a predictor or criterion measures what it purports to measure or demonstrates the job-relatedness of a test by showing how well an applicant will perform based on the test predictions.

Vanishing performance appraisal When the giving and receiving of performance appraisal feedback is no longer a pleasant experience, it is avoided and just vanishes.

Vertical loading Adding duties to a job that are different from those already in the job and that require different skills, knowledge, and abilities.

Vesting Pertains to qualifications required to become eligible for an organization's pension benefits.

Wage-dividend plans A special type of cash plan where the percentage of profits paid to employees is determined by the amount of dividends paid to stockholders.

Wage surveys Published reports of what several different companies are paying for different types of jobs.

Wagner Act The major comprehensive labor code enacted in 1935 with the intent by Congress to restore equality of bargaining power between labor and management. This is also known as the National Labor Relations Act.

Weighted application blank An application blank in which some information is given more importance or weight as a predictor of future success.

Weighted checklist Identical to a critical incidents format but with various points to differentiate the varying importance of different incidents.

Wellness tests Health assessments of employees that include measures of blood pressure, blood cholesterol, high density cholesterol, skin fold evaluation of diet, life-change events, smoking, drinking, and family history of chronic heart disease.

Whipsaw The process where unions use one contract settlement as a precedent for the next and force the employer to settle all contracts before work is resumed.

Wide-area and multicraft bargaining A negotiating structure that exists in the construction industry where several separate construction unions may settle with a contractor together.

Wildcat strike A strike that is not legal because the contract forbids it, yet the union strikes anyway.

Work measurement The determination of standard times for all units of work activity in any task. Includes the assessment of "actual effort" exerted and the "real effort" required to accomplish a task (cf. methods analysis).

Work pacing Refers to the rate or flow of work and who controls the rate or flow. See also **Machine Pacing**.

Work sample test A test that consists of an actual simulation of the job or critical tasks associated with the job. An example would be a typing test used to select a secretary.

Work sampling The process of taking instantaneous samples of the work activities of individuals or groups of individuals. Activities are then timed and classified according to predetermined categories. The result is a description of the activities by classification of a job and the percentage of time for each activity (cf. methods analysis).

Work standards approach A type of goal-oriented form of evaluation, similar to management by objectives, except that the predetermined goals are dictated by management and often established by work measurement.

Workers' compensation insurance A health insurance program offered by an employer to cover (compensate for) worker sickness and disability.

NAME INDEX

SUBJECT/COMPANY INDEX

OUR CHANGING WORLD

2050   12*
2000   6*
1990   .5

World Population in billions

2050   363*
2000   275*
1990   263

U.S. Population in millions

* Estimated

Profile of Employee Characteristics Firms Want

Yesterday	Today
• Individual players	• Team players
• Quantity focus	• Quality focus
• Job focused	• Company focused
• Product focused	• Customer focused
• Narrow skilled	• Multiple skilled
• Single career focus	• Multiple career focus
• Company managed	• Self-managed

Organization Characteristics

Yesterday	Today
• National	• Global
• Heirarchical	• Flat
• Functional specialists	• Cross-functional teams
• Narrow	• Diverse
• Mass production	• Total quality
• Fixed	• Flexible
• Steady	• Fast
• Internal focus	• External focus